IMPORTANT

HERE IS YOUR REGISTRATION CODE TO ACCESS MCGRAW-HILL PREMIUM CONTENT AND MCGRAW-HILL ONLINE RESOURCES

For key premium online resources you need THIS CODE to gain access. Once the code is entered, you will be able to use the web resources for the length of your course.

Access is provided only if you have purchased a new book.

If the registration code is missing from this book, please visit the registration screen on our website of within your WebCT or Blackboard course instructions are also available on how to obtain your new code. Your registration code can be used only once to establish access. It is not transferable.

To gain access to these online resources

1. **USE** your web browser to go to: **www.mhhe.com/graham7e**

2. **CLICK** on "First Time User"

3. **ENTER** the Registration Code printed on the tear-off bookmark on the right

4. After you have entered your registration code, click on "Register"

5. **FOLLOW** the instructions to setup your personal UserID and Password

6. **WRITE** your UserID and Password down for future reference. Keep it in a safe place.

If your course is using WebCT or Blackboard, you'll be able to use this code to access the McGraw-Hill content within your instructor's online course.

To gain access to the McGraw-Hill content in your instructor's WebCT or Blackboard course simply log into the course with the user ID and Password provided by your instructor. Enter the registration code exactly as it appears to the right when prompted by the system. You will only need to use this code the first time you click on McGraw-Hill content.

These instructions are specifically for student access. Instructors are not required to register via the above instructions.

The McGraw-Hill Companies

 Higher Education

Thank you, and welcome to your McGraw-Hill Online Resources.

ISBN-13: 978-0-07-304535-1
ISBN-10: 0-07-304535-7
T/A Graham: Children Moving, 7E

Children Moving

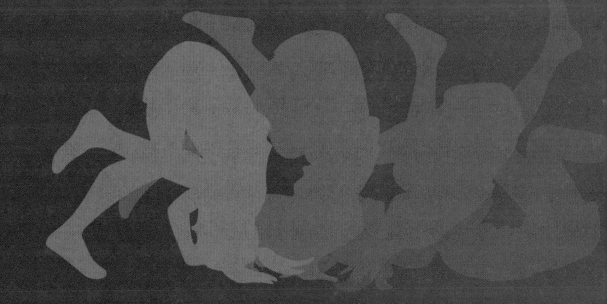

SEVENTH EDITION

Children Moving

A REFLECTIVE APPROACH TO TEACHING PHYSICAL EDUCATION

George Graham
The Pennsylvania State University

Shirley Ann Holt/Hale
Linden Elementary School, Oak Ridge, Tennessee

Melissa Parker
University of Northern Colorado

The McGraw·Hill Companies

McGraw Hill Higher Education

CHILDREN MOVING: A REFLECTIVE APPROACH TO TEACHING PHYSICAL EDUCATION
Published by McGraw-Hill, a business unit of The McGraw-Hill Companies, Inc., 1221 Avenue of the
Americas, New York, NY, 10020. Copyright © 2007, 2004, by The McGraw-Hill Companies, Inc. All
rights reserved. No part of this publication may be reproduced or distributed in any form or by any
means, or stored in a database or retrieval system, without the prior written consent of The McGraw-
Hill Companies, Inc., including, but not limited to, in any network or other electronic storage or
transmission, or broadcast for distance learning.

Some ancillaries, including electronic and print components, may not be available to customers
outside the United States.

This book is printed on acid-free paper.
Printed in China

3 4 5 6 7 8 9 0 CTP/CTP 0 9 8 7

ISBN-13: 978-0-07-304532-0
ISBN-10: 0-07-304532-2

Vice president and editor-in-chief: Emily Barrosse
Publisher: William R. Glass
Senior sponsoring editor: Christopher Johnson
Director of development: Kathleen Engelberg
Executive marketing manager: Pamela S. Cooper
Freelance development editor: Jill Eccher, Van Brien & Associates
Development editor for technology: Julia D. Ersery
Production editors: Gretchen Otto/Melissa Williams
Senior production supervisor: Rich DeVitto
Interior designer: Ellen Pettengell Design
Cover designer: Irene Morris/Kim Menning
Art editor: Gretchen Otto
Media supplement producer: Kathleen Boylan

This text was set in 9.5/12 Stone Serif by G&S Typesetters, Inc., and printed on 45#
Publisher's Matte by China Translation and Printing Services Ltd.

Library of Congress Cataloging-in-Publication Data
Graham, George, 1943–
     Children moving : a reflective approach to teaching physical education/George
     Graham, Shirley Ann Holt/Hale, Melissa Parker.—7th ed.
          p. cm.
     Includes bibliographical references and index.
     ISBN 0-07-255694-3 (hard : alk. paper)
     1. Physical education for children—Study and teaching—United States.   2. Physical
education for children—Curricula—United States.   3. Movement education—United
States.   I. Holt/Hale, Shirley Ann.   II. Parker, Melissa.   III. Title
GV443.G73.2007
372.86′044′—dc21   2005039038

www.mhhe.com

We dedicate this edition of Children Moving:

*To the teachers who guide children to a love
of physical activity*

*To undergraduate students who have chosen to invest
their professional careers in making physical education
meaningful for all children*

To children—our most valuable resource

PART FOUR

Skill Theme Development   305

CHAPTER 19

Traveling   307

CHAPTER 20

Chasing, Fleeing, and Dodging   334

CHAPTER 26

Volleying and Dribbling 503

Welcome to the seventh edition of *Children Moving!* Once again we are delighted to be able to share insights gained from our experiences teaching children, undergraduates, and teachers with you—the classroom or physical education teacher or future teacher—in this revised edition. We have blended the literature on effective teaching with research about physical activity and teacher preparation into a practical format designed to help you to understand, and successfully implement, the skill theme approach with children.

In *Children Moving* the pedagogy (teaching process) and content (what is taught) are woven together into a unified "system" that has come to be known as the skill theme approach. It is based on developmentally appropriate principles and guidelines that provide the foundation of a program that is designed for all children, not only the athletically gifted or physically fit youngsters.

When the first edition of *Children Moving* was published in 1980, the skill theme approach was new to many in our profession. Today an increasing number of teachers follow the developmentally appropriate guidelines and practices that are outlined in this book. Another thing that was different then than now was the universal lack of understanding about the importance of physical activity for children. Today, with the increasing epidemic of obesity and the associated health problems, there is little need to convince parents, administrators, and the medical community of the importance of regular physical activity for children.

Children Moving describes a process designed to ensure that the love of physical activity children are born with remains alive throughout adolescence and adulthood. As you read throughout the 34 chapters in the seventh edition, you will discover that we view the purpose of physical education as "guiding youngsters in the process of becoming physically active for a lifetime." The pages that follow describe in detail how we go about attempting to do so.

It has now been a decade since the Surgeon General's report on physical activity and the first edition of *National Standards for Physical Education* were published. Today, they have become landmark documents, and a second edition of *National Standards for Physical Education* (2004) has been published. It is clear that our task is no longer to simply understand the intent of standards, but to show how to align programs so that they meet the guidelines suggested in these documents. Physical educators can no longer justify programs that simply keep youngsters "busy, happy, and good," thereby providing classroom teachers a planning period. In this era of increased accountability and testing, state legislatures and school districts are mandating that teachers document what youngsters have and have not learned, often through high-stakes testing with highly publicized results. Now, physical education programs that do not have sound educational goals and practices guiding their instruction are more vulnerable than ever before.

This edition frequently references several national documents that have provided direction, guidance, and support for physical education in schools by translating research and consensus reports into meaningful and worthwhile experiences for children. The Surgeon General's report on physical activity and the consensus report on physical activity sponsored by the National Center for Chronic Disease Prevention and Health Promotion, both published in 1996, clearly documented the value of physical activity. They also recommended that more time be allocated for physical education programs that are designed to build the foundation for youngsters to become physically active for a lifetime. The *National Standards for Physical Education,* first published by the National Association for Sport and Physical Education (NASPE) in 1995 with a second edition in 2004, provides guidance for the content and goals of physical education programs. NASPE's *Developmentally Appropriate Guidelines for Children's Physical Education Practices for Children* (1992) and *Appropriate Practices for Elementary School Physical Education* (2000) offer counsel for the structure of quality physical education programs along with suggested content. The authors of *Children Moving* have been involved with these and other national, regional, and state projects in various ways. Our involvement is one of the key reasons for the match between *Children Moving* and the recent national and state advances substantiating the importance of physical activity. This edition includes literally hundreds of practical learning experiences and assessments for reaching the goals and objectives outlined in the combined editions of the *National Standards* and various state standards.

While we have expanded and clarified the information from the documents of the mid-1990s, much remains from previous editions, especially our goal to keep the text both informal and practical. What we wrote in the preface to the first edition remains true: "We are teachers of children first. And writers second. Individual insights gained during years of teaching experience and ideas to enhance teacher success are sprinkled throughout the text. We hope that by sharing these experiences we can help others to enrich the lives of children."

We begin the seventh edition of *Children Moving* by describing the value and purpose of physical education. Part 1, "Introduction and Content Overview," provides an overview of the skill theme approach, the name by which the program suggested in *Children Moving* has come to be known, and ties it to our beliefs and values about children's physical education. Chapter 1 highlights the benefits of physical activity for children as well as the components of a quality physical education program for children. It also links the skill theme approach to not only the School Health Index, but also Dietary Guidelines and NASPE physical activity guidelines. Chapters 2 and 3 define the skill theme approach. Chapter 2 includes an overview of motor development principles as they apply to the skill theme approach. Chapter 4 describes the importance of physical fitness for children, how it is interwoven into the skill theme approach, and appropriate fitness practices for elementary school children. It also includes examples of linking wellness into physical education lessons. Chapter 5 includes a much expanded definition of reflective teaching as well as insights into how one develops into a reflective teacher. A completely revised Chapter 6, "Teaching Diverse Learners," concludes Part 1. This chapter provides multiple strategies that allow teachers to meaningfully engage *all* children in physical education. Inclusion becomes a proactive concept, not limited to children with disabilities, but addressing the needs of every child regardless of skill, fitness, language, gender, religion, class, or physical characteristics.

Part 2, "Teaching Skills," contains Chapters 7 to 15, which focus on the process, or pedagogy, of teaching, beginning with a chapter describing our system for determining the content children are ready to learn based on their developmental needs and interests (generic levels of skill proficiency) as opposed to their age or grade level. Chapter 8 outlines planning in a four-step process with examples of how lessons can be linked to national or state standards. Taken together Chapters 9, 10, and 11 illustrate how to develop a classroom environment conducive to student learning. Chapter 9 describes the process of creating an atmosphere that is conducive to learning. It includes an expanded section on safety and legal liability. In this chapter we introduce the safety icon ⚠ as an alert for a strong

emphasis on safety in a given situation. Chapter 10 also addresses strategies for youngsters who may need extra help in learning how to function appropriately in a physical education environment. Because *Children Moving* describes a child-centered rather than a subject-centered approach to teaching, it is important that teachers constantly observe children to determine the progress they are making so that lessons can be adjusted for individual differences. Chapter 11 describes how teachers organize content into meaningful experiences by developing a logical progression of tasks (learning experiences), cues (critical elements), and challenges designed to make physical education classes a true learning experience. These ideas are presented in a user-friendly manner designed for easy understanding, and they link directly to the planning chapter. Chapter 12 provides examples of ways teachers can observe student responses to determine the potential for learning. Chapter 13, which describes a variety of instructional approaches used by teachers to heighten children's enjoyment and understanding of the lessons, includes a section on cooperative learning and provides an analysis of when each approach may be appropriate based on the needs of the students and the pedagogical skills of the teacher. Chapter 14, on assessment, describes current assessment trends. It contains a variety of assessment examples based on our teaching experiences as well as the first edition of the *National Standards*. Assessment icons are then used throughout the text to indicate performance assessments that are explained in detail in Chapter 14. In addition, the assessment tool of checks for cognitive understanding is indicated with the icon 🎥 Chapter 15 includes a variety of practical ways that teachers can assess their own teaching to determine if, and how, they are using the techniques employed by effective teachers of children's physical education.

Parts 3 and 4 of *Children Moving* focus on the content of the skill theme approach. Chapters 16 to 18 describe how the concepts of space awareness, effort, and relationships are taught in the skill theme approach. These chapters include references to both editions of the *National Standards* for both content and assessment ideas. They are followed by the skill theme chapters (19 to 28), which contain hundreds of learning experiences designed to help children learn the motor skills that are necessary for successful participation in and enjoyment of a variety of physical activities and sports. Each skill theme chapter begins with an overview of the content followed by a description of a series of tasks, the critical elements or cues necessary to succeed at these tasks, and challenges designed to maintain children's interest in learning the tasks. The tasks are organized according to the generic levels of skill proficiency in a spiral progression from beginning to advanced. Assessment options for the skill theme chapters are keyed to the assessment chapter. Part 5 includes chapters on dance, gymnastics, and games in the skill theme approach and a chapter on interdisciplinary learning. Chapters 29, 30, and 31 present ideas for the application of combined skill and movement concepts into dance, gymnastics, and games settings. Chapter 29 links the teaching of dance to the skill theme and movement concept chapters. It describes the various types of dance for children and provides information about how ethnic/folk dance can be incorporated with skill themes. Chapter 30 links the skill theme and movement concept chapters to gymnastics and provides examples of developmentally appropriate gymnastics for children. It also includes a renewed emphasis on safety and self-responsibility in children. Chapter 31, on games, provides examples of how games are used in the skill theme approach. It contains ideas for designing appropriate game and gamelike experiences for children and clarifies the competition/cooperation aspect of children's games. The final chapter in Part 5 describes how the skill theme approach can be integrated with topics typically taught in the classroom, such as mathematics and reading. It provides examples of ways classroom teachers can use movement to enhance the children's interest in subjects they are teaching in the classroom and also ways that physical education teachers and classroom teachers can work together to create interesting and relevant learning experiences for youngsters.

Chapters 33 and 34 make up the final part, "The Future," in this seventh edition of *Children Moving*. The first describes some of the changes teachers have successfully used to build support for their programs and includes references to research that can be used to support physical education programs. Chapter 34 is our favorite and includes our continued dreams for children's physical education as we enter the second half of the first decade of the new millennium.

New to This Edition

An All-New Design

The seventh edition has a completely new full-color design. This exciting new design includes aesthetic features created with the intent of making the book attractive and pleasing to the eye. The children's artwork, photographs, and other features come to new life in color. A new color scheme, new icons, redesigned

boxes, and a new presentation of the basic concept headers are just a few redesigned features.

The Wheel

This edition of *Children Moving* features a full-color, three-dimensional cardboard **Wheel** ("movement analysis framework" in the text). For many years, many of us have made wheels so that students could more fully understand the relationships between and possibility for skill themes and movement concepts. The Wheel enhances students' understanding of the book's themes and concepts; it can also be used as a handy reference tool in the classroom.

Updated Content

A key feature of this new edition is updated content, which is reflected in the text discussions and in the references and readings. Of special note is the updated information from the second edition of the *National Standards for Physical Education*. Another example is the emphasis on teaching diverse learners and the expanded concept of diversity. The idea of observing student responses (Chapter 12) is clearly linked with the notion of student learning in physical education, and the notion of analyzing our teaching (Chapter 15) is linked with those teacher practices known to facilitate student learning.

New Research

This new edition highlights many examples of the latest research in the field, such as findings that suggest a connection between ongoing physical activity and obesity, movement and learning, the use of heart-rate monitors and pedometers in learning more about movement, the creation of a learning environment and motivation in physical education, and safety and liability issues that need to be addressed.

Successful Features

Skill Theme Approach

The skill theme focus of this book guides teachers in helping children develop their motor skills with developmentally appropriate activities that are directed toward their skill level rather than their grade level. Designed for both classroom teachers and physical education teachers, the skill theme approach highlights practical ways of teaching physical education to children.

Basic Teaching Skills

This book emphasizes the foundation for teaching skills with topics such as planning, organizing, assessing, and evaluating. It offers a strong background in educationally sound theory and explains how to apply that knowledge to become an effective teacher. The focus is on reflective teaching, which involves adjusting one's teaching style to match the needs of students.

Classroom Conversations

The scripted format of the skill theme chapters offers new teachers examples of real conversations that take place in the classroom or gymnasium. In this way teachers can learn how to participate in the different dialogues that are instrumental to child-centered education.

Advocacy of Physical Education

This text focuses on physical education and its relation to physical fitness. Recognizing the value of physical education as a part of total fitness, this book incorporates the concepts of fitness and wellness throughout all chapters.

Promotion of Inclusion

The idea of inclusion is central to *Children Moving.* Examples of how all individuals can be included in high-quality physical education are found throughout this text.

Small Sided Games

Demonstrating the value of small sided games in physical education, this book offers examples of how to design such games and make them a valuable part of any physical education program. It discusses ideas about developing versatile game players who understand strategies and skills for playing well.

Pedagogical Aids

Key Concepts   Each chapter begins with a list of Key Concepts to help students focus their attention on the main topics as they begin studying the chapter. This learning tool also offers an accessible and practical method of review.

Cautions   Throughout the text discussions, the symbol ▲ indicates a safety alert for a particular situation. This tool keeps the new teacher attuned to making safety a basic element in physical education activities and helps avoid accidents.

Tasks   The skill theme and movement concept chapters feature a suggested progression of tasks, or extensions, for children. Highlighted by the symbol Ⓣ, each task is worded in a conversational style that can be used to give instructions to the children about how to perform the task.

Cues   Cues, or refinements, can be used to help the children perform a skill more efficiently. A selection of cues is presented at the beginning of each series of tasks for skill themes and movement concepts. The teacher can choose a cue that is appropriate for the children to make the task easier for them to perform.

Challenges   Challenges, or applications, are indicated by the symbol Ⓒ in the skill theme and movement concept chapters. They are designed to maintain the children's interest in a particular task. The teacher can either use the challenges listed along with the tasks or create ones that seem appropriate for the children with whom he or she is working.

Assessment Ideas   Assessment tools are designed to see what students have learned in relation to the goals set by the teacher. The symbol ☑ identifies suggested assessments that can be used as part of daily teaching rather than as a separate entity at the end of the unit. These assessment ideas include an array of options from exit (or entrance) slips that can be used to quickly assess cognitive and affective learning to teacher observation checklists and digital analysis to verify psychomotor skills.

Appendix   The appendix to this book offers four sample school-year overviews based on the material in *Children Moving.* It includes (1) a two-day-a-week program for an inexperienced class, (2) a five-day-a-week program for an inexperienced class, (3) a two-day-a-week program for an experienced class, and (4) a five-day-a-week program for an experienced class. These overviews can be followed exactly as presented or used as a model for developing individualized programs.

Summaries   The chapter summaries highlight the major topics and concepts discussed in the chapter. They can be used for clarification or for review for examinations.

Reading Comprehension Questions A set of questions appears at the end of each chapter to allow students to test their understanding of the content. This tool offers a means of reviewing and analyzing the material.

References/Suggested Readings This list at the end of each chapter includes the references that support the text discussion and additional sources for study and exploration.

Supplements

Instructor's Resource DVD

This DVD contains key teaching points for each chapter, along with learning activities for the classroom and the gym.

Computerized Test Bank

The test bank is available on the Instructor's Resource DVD as Word files and with EZ Test computerized testing software. McGraw-Hill's EZ Test is a flexible and easy-to-use electronic testing program. The program allows instructors to create tests from book-specific items. It accomodates a wide range of question types and instructors may add their own questions. Multiple versions of the test can be created and any test can be exported for use with course management systems such as WebCT, BlackBoard, or PageOut. EZ Test Online is a new service and gives you a place to easily administer your EZ Test–created exams and quizzes online. The program is available for Windows and Macintosh environments. The EZ Test CD is packaged with Quick Start Guide; once the program is installed, users have access to the complete user's manual, including multiple Flash tutorials. Additional help is available at www.mhhe.com/eztest.

On the Move: Lesson Plans to Accompany Children Moving, *Seventh Edition*, by Shirley Ann Holt/Hale

These online lesson plans are designed to offer learning experiences for children that assist them in developing a broad base of movement skills coupled with an enjoyment of physical activity that will translate into a physically active, healthy lifestyle for a lifetime. Some of the highlights are (1) instructional objectives that are attainable within a single lesson, (2) content development with a focus on skill rather than broad exploration, (3) maximum practice of the focus skill, (4) concentration on one cue at a time, (5) challenges throughout the lessons, and (6) both cognitive and performance assessments. Special features include a series of physical fitness concept lesson plans, sample lessons for integrated discipline activities, and a separate section devoted to *Children Moving* challenges written for the classroom teacher and designed for the recess or playground environment, with a focus on physical activities with minimum instruction and maximum participation for all students. Features include a discussion of curriculum mapping with a skill theme approach and a sample curriculum plan to assist teachers in the process of planning by mapping.

Classroom Performance Systems (CPS)

The Classroom Performance System is a revolutionary system that brings ultimate interactivity to the lecture hall or classroom. CPS is a wireless response system that gives you immediate feedback from every student in the class. CPS units include easy-to-use software for creating and delivering questions and assessments to your class. With CPS, you can ask subjective and objective questions. Students respond with their individual wireless response pads, providing instant results. CPS is the perfect tool for engaging students while gathering important assessment data. Benefits include:

- Better interactivity—receive instant feedback on what students have learned.
- Increased class discussion—anonymous opinion pools can be used to generate debate.
- Improved attendance by "alert" students.
- Automatically graded testing.
- Simple installation, setup, and use.
- Low cost.
- Reliable technical support.

Online Learning Center
www.mhhe.com/graham7e

The Online Learning Center to accompany this text offers a number of additional resources for both students and instructors. Visit this Web site to find useful materials such as:

For the Instructor

- Instructor's Manual
- Sample syllabus
- State curriculum guide
- The Wheel and activities
- Downloadable PowerPoint presentations

- Lesson plan websites
- Lecture outlines
- Links to professional resources

For the Student

- Self-scoring chapter quizzes
- Flash cards for learning key terms and their definitions
- *On the Move* lesson plans
- Lesson plan template
- Fitness and nutrition journal
- Videos

Classroom Performance Systems

These files are formatted for use with Classroom Performance System, a wireless response system used to increase student engagement in the classroom. The files are questions that can be used to create class quizzes, or as impromptu questions during lecture.

Course Management Systems
www.mhhe.com/solutions

Now instructors can combine their McGraw-Hill Online Learning Center with today's most popular course-management systems. Our Instructor Advantage program offers customers access to a complete online teaching website called the Knowledge Gateway, with prepaid, toll-free phone support and unlimited e-mail support directly from WebCT and Blackboard. Instructors who use 500 or more copies of a McGraw-Hill textbook can enroll in our Instructor Advantage Plus program, which provides on-campus, hands-on training from a certified platform specialist. Consult your McGraw-Hill sales representative to learn what other course management systems are easily used with McGraw-Hill online materials.

PageOut: The Course Web Site Development Center
www.pageout.net

PageOut, free to instructors who use a McGraw-Hill textbook, is an online program you can use to create your own course Web site. PageOut offers the following features:

- A course home page
- An instructor home page
- A syllabus (interactive and customizable, including quizzes, instructor notes, and links to the text's Online Learning Center)
- Web links
- Discussions (multiple discussion areas per class)

- An online gradebook
- Links to student Web pages

Contact your McGraw-Hill sales representative to obtain a password.

Primis Online
www.mhhe.com/primis/online

Primis Online is a database-driven publishing system that allows instructors to create content-rich textbooks, lab manuals, or readers for their courses directly from the Primis Web site. The customized text can be delivered in print or electronic (eBook) form. A Primis eBook is a digital version of the customized text (sold directly to students as a file downloadable to their computer or accessed online by a password).

Acknowledgments

Children Moving continues to be a work in progress. Over the past 25 years we have been fortunate to work with a number of dedicated professionals who have assisted and inspired us to continue to improve each edition. We would like to acknowledge many of the people who assisted us with this edition and previous ones. We are grateful for their efforts to work with us to continue to improve *Children Moving*.

- Christina Sinclair and Jim Stiehl, University of Northern Colorado, for expanding our understanding of the notion of teaching diverse populations and Christina for assisting with the writing of a new Chapter 6, "Teaching Diverse Learners," that incorporates those ideas.
- Laura Matney, elementary physical education teacher in Kingsport, Tennessee, for her assistance with Chapter 4, "Physical Fitness and Wellness for Children."
- Shawn Fortner, Liz Harkrader, and John Pomeroy from Roanoke, Virginia, for allowing us to take photographs of their program for the seventh edition of *Children Moving*.
- Eloise Elliott, Concord College, Athens, West Virginia, for developing Chapter 32, "Integrating the Skill Theme Approach across the Curriculum," for the sixth edition.
- Kevin Patton, of the University of Northern Colorado, for developing the PowerPoint presentation to accompany the seventh edition of *Children Moving*.
- Linda Sharp, J.D., of the University of Northern Colorado, for her ongoing expert advice related to the legal aspects of teaching physical education.

- John Pomeroy, Liz Harkrader, Shawn Fortner, Rosa Edwards, Larry Satchwell, Becky Robinson, Sharn Nicholson and so many other children's physical education teachers—for your inspiration, dedication to children, and example in serving as role models for countless other teachers and thousands of children.
- The children at St. Mary's Elementary School, Grand Forks, North Dakota; Bluff Elementary School, Bluff, Utah; and Adelante Alternative School, Greeley, Colorado, who continually added to our understanding.
- The children at Linden Elementary School in Oak Ridge, Tennessee, who create as well as follow our dreams of physical education for children.
- Lars A. Niki and Clay Thurston, for their ability to capture children's movement through photography; Mindy McLain, for her assistance with the editing and selection of photos.
- Lans Hayes of Mayfield Publishing Company, who, in 1977, took a huge risk on four unknown authors with a radical idea.
- Jill Eccher, our freelance developmental editor for this edition, for her guidance, patience, and gentle nagging.
- The entire McGraw-Hill book team who worked on this edition, Chris Johnson, Kate Engelberg, Julia Ersery, Pam Cooper, Michele Borrelli, Melissa Williams, Gretchen Otto, Rich DeVitto, Kim Menning, and Kate Boylan.
- We would like to offer special thanks to the countless teachers and students who have made so many positive and helpful comments since the first edition of *Children Moving* was published. Your support and encouragement continue to be much appreciated.

Finally, we would like to thank the reviewers for their valuable insights:

For the seventh edition

Brent Hardin
University of Alabama

Mickey Kerr
University of Mary Hardin—Baylor

Kim Duchane
Manchester College

Terri Edwards
Bacone College

Johann Murray
Peru State College

Jon Poole
Radford University

For the sixth edition

Tami Abourezk
California State University—Northridge

Nancy Colton
Montana State University—Bozeman

Anita D'Angelo-Herold
Florida Atlantic University

Rhea Gaunt
St. Francis University

Lori-J. Head
Idaho State University

Janet Holland
University of Arizona

Kathryn Kotowski
Cuyamaca College

Thomas Loughrey
University of Missouri—St. Louis

Deborah A. Smith
Clemson University

Katherine Thomas Thomas
Iowa State University

Students, are you looking for practical teaching techniques? Working hard to develop the skill theme approach with children? Trying to improve your grade? The features in *Children Moving* will help you do this and more! Take a look.

Key Concepts

Each chapter, or each part in the skills theme chapters, begins with a list of key concepts to help you focus your attention on the main topics as you begin studying each chapter. This learning tool also offers an accessible and practical method of review.

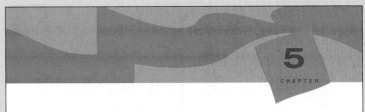

5
CHAPTER

Reflective Teaching

The good teacher must relate his teaching to the world of his students as it is, not as he would like it to be.

—HERBERT FOSTER

A search for rigid prescriptions of the right way to teach has largely been replaced with the search for propositional rules and principles to guide practice.

—JUDITH E. RINK

---

4   PART 1 Introduction and Content Overview

www.mhhe.com/graham7e

Key Concepts

- The purpose of a quality program of physical education is to guide youngsters in the process of becoming physically active for a lifetime.
- Regular physical activity helps prevent obesity, promotes motor skill development and physical fitness, and provides opportunities for goal setting, making new friends, and stress reduction.
- The health benefits associated with being physically active include a reduction in premature mortality, heart disease, colon cancer, diabetes mellitus, and drug and alcohol addiction.
- Positive, or quality, physical education programs have reasonable class sizes, a developmental and sequential curriculum, plenty of practice and movement opportunities, and adequate facilities and equipment.
- Positive physical education programs emphasize learning in all three domains: psychomotor, cognitive, and affective.

Young children are a torrent of physical activity! Unfortunately, for far too many youngsters this torrent of physical activity becomes a trickle by the time they enter adolescence. As a teacher, or future teacher, you can make a significant contribution to the lives of your students by helping to keep their love of movement and physical activity alive so that it lasts a lifetime. Over 60 percent of adults are overweight and for many of them exercise has become a negative term associated with pain, frustration, and embarrassment. Positive physical education programs emphasize enjoyable participation in physical activity and "help students develop the knowledge, attitudes, motor skills, behavioral skills, and confidence needed to adopt and maintain physically active lifestyles" (National Center for Chronic Disease Prevention and Health Promotion [NCCDPHP], 1997, p. 205). Our goal is to keep the love of movement (exercise) alive in youngsters so that they associate exercise with enjoyment and fun!

The importance of physical activity in the lives of children, and adults, is becoming more and more evident. The 2005 Dietary Guidelines for Americans recommends that "children and adolescents engage in at least 60 minutes of physical activity on most, preferably all, days of the week" (www.health.gov/dietary-guidelines/dga2005/document). In fact the 2005 revision of the food pyramid includes a figure climbing stairs to visually represent the importance of physical

MyPyramid.gov
STEPS TO A HEALTHIER YOU

activity in our lives (www.pyramid.gov). You will also find information on this Web site designed specifically for children ages 6–11 in the "for kids" section.

Physical activity and physical education are not synonymous. **Physical activity** is a behavior—for example, walking or biking to school, playing a sport, or swimming. **Physical education** is the school curriculum that leads to remaining physically active for a lifetime. Thus the goal, or purpose, of a quality physical education program is to guide youngsters in the process of becoming physically active for a lifetime. This chapter answers three questions.

1. Why do children need quality programs of physical education?
2. What health benefits are associated with a lifetime of physical activity?
3. What components of a physical education program encourage youngsters to maintain physically active lifestyles?

Why Children Need Physical Education

Why do youngsters need a quality program of physical education? The simple answer is so that they will remain physically active throughout their lifetime and reap the benefits of doing so, especially the health benefits that are detailed in the next section. Numerous other benefits have been summarized by the National Association for Sport and Physical Education (NASPE, 2002, p. 7) and are adapted here. They include:

Regular, healthful physical activity: An increasing number of youngsters are overweight and obese. Regular physical activity, as well as an appropriate diet, is the best antidote to eliminate the current obesity epidemic and also provide a positive alternative to "screen time" (both television and computers).

Skill development: In a quality program of physical education, children learn the fundamental motor

Online Learning Center Resources

Want a better grade? This address appears throughout to remind you about the study aids and other resources available at our Online Learning Center.

Children try to match their partner as they make "one-part, non-symmetrical balances."

Children try to match each other's rocking motion.

mirror, your mother putting on her makeup, or your father shaving. Practice your story until you can do it the same way three times in a row. Then we'll have the class try to guess what you're saying.

Traveling Alongside/Following

Setting: Traveling in general space with a partner

Tasks/Challenges:

Ⓣ Though we haven't really discussed it, often you were practicing another type of relationship when you followed your partner around the space: *leading and following.* So far you've always followed from behind the other person. Let's try it differently this time, with you traveling alongside or next to your partner as you follow. One person is still the leader and the other the follower, but you both move as if you were a team of horses: beside each other. Each of you should take five turns leading and then switch places. This activity is harder, so you have to watch very closely what your partner does. Start out with very easy moves.

Ⓣ Now try to speed it up a little. Watch carefully. Try to follow exactly.

The leader must be aware of the follower's capabilities so that the leader challenges the partner but doesn't frustrate the partner with movements that are too difficult.

Following with a Group

Setting: Traveling in general space with a group

Tasks/Challenges:

Ⓣ This time, you're going to try another type of following: from behind, with four or five of you in group. The first person in line is the first leader and leads the group all over the room. Then on the signal, the first person goes to the end of the line, and the second person becomes the leader; this change continues until everyone has had a chance to lead. The secret is to stay far enough apart so that you can see. The activity is just like follow the leader.

Ⓣ This time you're going to make the activity a little more challenging. I'm *not* going to give you th

---

Illustration Program

Instructional full-color illustrations and photographs throughout the book enhance learning with an exciting visual appeal.

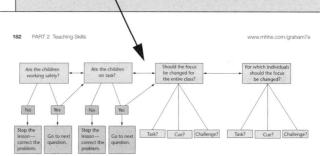

Figure 12.2 Questions reflective teachers use to guide observation.

We encourage teachers to focus initially on the entire class using the scanning technique described in the next section of this chapter. By working with individuals (intratask variation) too early, the teacher may lose focus on the entire class. We've seen this happen frequently with beginning teachers. The teacher becomes so involved helping an individual child that he or she loses focus on the entire class and may suddenly look up to find that a number of children are off task or that an unsafe condition has developed. This is not to suggest that teachers shouldn't work with children individually—we certainly should and do. But teachers must make sure that they don't become so involved with one child that they forget to concentrate on the whole class. As Locke's vignette at the beginning of the chapter suggests, doing so is a real challenge.

Recently I observed a teacher attempting to teach a child how to run and kick a stationary ball. The child was unable to adjust her run to enable her to arrive at the ball in a proper kicking position. After each unsuccessful attempt (the ball barely moved; the child appeared almost to step on the ball rather than kick it), the teacher would say to the child, "No, that's not it!" The child knew she had failed as she watched the ball erratically dribble away from her foot, and yet the teacher offered no prescription for improvement. Rather than stating results the student can readily observe, the successful instructor offers a prescription for practice, that is, a cue.

When we work with individuals, we essentially use the same process we use for the entire class. We vary the task for different children, or we provide challenges (intratask variation). If you ever have an opportunity to watch a master teacher, you'll see that this teacher is

constantly using intratask variation as he or she travels from child to child while remaining conscious of the entire class, safety, and on-task behavior. Now you can better understand why it's so important to spend time establishing a learning environment at the beginning of the year.

When presented separately, the four aspects or categories of observation—safety, on-task behavior, class movement patterns, and individual movement patterns—seem quite simple and rather easy to follow. When teaching, however, a teacher is rarely able to focus on any one aspect at a time. As Locke's vignette suggests, the teacher must concentrate simultaneously on the four aspects. To aid in your observation, Figure 12.2 provides a flow chart of the questions we use to guide our observation of classes. Note that the arrows between the questions go both ways, indicating that the observation focus isn't linear but that there's a constant interplay between the questions. And, this observation may all happen within 60 seconds!

How to Observe

Once you have decided what it is that you want and need to observe, the next step is actually observing so that you see. As we indicated earlier, observation is a learned skill and one that can improve with practice. Bird watching provides an apt analogy here. Non–bird watchers who see a bird might think, "There is a big bird." Novice bird watchers will say, "There is a big bird with a white head and dark body." Intermediate bird-watchers, with binoculars, might note a large bird with a dark body, white head, and white on the tail. An expert, with binoculars, will identify the bird as a bald eagle. It takes practice to become an expert observer, but the result is rich and detailed information about what you have seen and hence where to proceed. Three

---

Vignettes and Quotations

The authors and seasoned teachers provide real examples of experiences with students that relate to the topics discussed, for more insight into the dynamics of teaching.

Skill Theme Development Sequences

The skill theme chapters contain hundreds of learning experiences designed to help children learn. Motor skills are organized according to the generic levels of skill proficiency in a spiral progression from beginning to advanced.

Tasks/Challenges

The skill theme and movement concept chapters feature a suggested progression of tasks, or extensions, for children. Each task is worded in a conversational style that can be used to give instructions to the children about how to perform the task. Challenges are designed to maintain the children's interest in a particular task. The teacher can either use the challenges listed along with the tasks or create ones that seem appropriate for the children with whom he or she is working.

Skill Theme Development Sequence

Throwing and Catching

Proficiency Level

Throwing and catching while using simple offense and defense in a small sided invasion game
Throwing and catching with a team handball in a small sided invasion game
Throwing and catching with a football in a small sided invasion game
Throwing and catching with a Frisbee in a small sided invasion game
Throwing and catching in a small sided basketball-type game
Throwing at a stationary object while being defended
Throwing and catching in a small sided invasion game
Throwing to avoid a defender
Throwing and catching in a field, run, score gamelike situation
Throwing and catching a Frisbee in different places around the body with a partner

Utilization Level

Throwing while in the air
Catching to throw quickly to a target
Catching to throw quickly to a partner
Playing Frisbee Golf
Target backaway
Throwing for distance and accuracy
Throwing to a moving target
Throwing to make a partner move to catch
Throwing on the move
Throwing and catching while traveling
Moving to catch

Control Level

Bench Bounce Catch
Throwing and catching over a net with a partner
Throwing and catching with a partner
Throwing for distance
Throwing a ball against a wall and catching the rebound
Flying Beanbag Catch
Catching with a scoop
Throwing a Frisbee
Throwing backhand to a target
Throwing to high targets
Throwing underhand to hoops
Bowling for targets
Hit the Can
Throwing overhand at a stationary target
Catching in different places around the body
Throwing an object to different levels and catching it
Bouncing a ball to self and catching it
Overs, Unders, and Sides
Throwing sidearm
Throwing underhand
Throwing overhand

Precontrol Level

Tossing to self and catching
Drop—Catch
Catching from a skilled thrower
Catching a rolling ball
Throwing at a large target
Throwing a yarn ball against the wall

Cues

Cues can be used to help children perform a skill more efficiently. A selection of cues is presented at the beginning of each series of tasks. The teacher can choose a cue that is appropriate for a particular child to make the task easier for him or her to perform.

Assessment Ideas

Assessment tools are designed to see what students have learned in relation to the goals set by the teacher. These assessment ideas include an array of options from exit (or entrance) slips that can be used to quickly assess cognitive and affective learning to teacher observation checklists and digital analysis to verify psychomotor skills.

Tasks/Challenges:

(T) In your groups of three, you are going to take turns jumping over a swinging rope. Two of you will gently swing the rope while the third person jumps. After five jumps, trade places.

(C) Practice for 10 jumps without a mistake.

Control Level: Learning Experiences Leading to Skill Development

At the control level, we encourage children to practice both long and high jumps until their landings are balanced and controlled. We also provide opportunities for exploring variations in the flight phase of the jump and jumping in relation to different rhythms.

A note about cues: Although several cues are listed for many of the learning experiences, it's important to focus on only one cue at a time. That way, the children can really concentrate on that cue. Once you provide feedback to the children and observe that most have learned a cue, then it's time to focus on another one.

Jumping and Landing: Basic Patterns

Setting: Ropes (one per child) placed around the edge of the teaching area

Cue

Squash   (Bend your knees to absorb the force and maintain balance when you land.)

Tasks/Challenges:

(T) When we first worked on jumping, you explored different ways to jump over your rope—just for fun. Place your rope in a straight line on the floor; choose three of your favorites from those different types of jumps and practice jumping over your rope, landing each time in a balanced position without falling down. Bend your knees when you land so that your landings are very quiet.

(T) Jump over your rope, taking off on two feet and landing on two feet.

(T) Position yourself approximately 10 feet from your rope. Approach your rope with a series of running steps; jump over your rope, taking off on one foot and landing on two feet.

(T) Using a series of running steps to approach your rope, take off on one foot and land on the opposite foot on the other side of your rope. Taking off on one foot and landing on the opposite foot is called a leap.

(T) Change the shape of your rope from a straight line to a circle, rectangle, or triangle. Standing just outside the rope shape, take off on one foot and jump inside your shape, landing on the same

Running and jumping combine skill and spatial awareness.

Assessment Example

From the *National Standards* edition

Peer Observation

Students are given a task of throw at a target with a par the type and size of ball, (enough distance to produc and the height of the target by marking a score sheet fo throws. Partners change role many turns as time allows.

Criteria for Assessment

a. Chooses appropriate bal for personal competence.
b. Records partner's perfo honestly.
c. Assists partner by spea turns.
d. Assumes personal respo the activity.

NASPE (1995, p. 27)

Throwing to High Targets

Setting: Partners, with a beanbag or ball for each pair; ropes with hoops attached strung across the space

---

Arm Way across Body	be facing the target.) (Instead of bringing it to the back, bring the arm you throw with way across your body.)
Step with Same Foot	(This is one of the few

Summaries

The chapter summaries highlight the major topics and concepts discussed in the chapter. They can be used for clarification or for review for examinations.

Reading Comprehension Questions

A set of questions appears at the end of each chapter to allow you to test your understanding of the content. This tool offers a means of reviewing and analyzing the material.

References/Suggested Readings

At the end of each chapter are references that support the text discussion and additional sources for study and exploration.

Summary

An instructional approach can be defined as the way in which a teacher presents lesson content to a class. One of the myriad of questions that a teacher must answer is which instructional approach to use. The answer depends on a number of factors; the primary one is the teacher's goal for a particular lesson or series of lessons. Six instructional approaches (summarized in Table 13.1) can be used to deliver the lesson content to students.

The direct instructional approach is effective when students are to learn a specific skill technique. A task-teaching approach is helpful when having students practice a skill they have already learned. The guided discovery approaches stimulate thinking and students' involvement on a cognitive level. Peer teaching fosters cooperation and provides repeated practice and feedback for children. Cooperative learning develops group-relation skills, as well as stimulating cognitive involvement. Child-designed approaches encourage creativity and inventiveness; they involve children in creating their own learning experiences.

Each approach has its strengths, and each requires different student and teacher skills. Which strategy to select depends on the teacher's goals. One of the challenges reflective teachers face is analyzing both their students' and their own needs and skills and matching them with the goals of the lesson. Ideally, over a period of weeks, both the teacher and the children learn to work effectively, no matter which instructional strategy is selected.

Regardless of the approach used, the progression of the learning experience is always based on the students' response to the task they were given. Thus, the ability of the teacher to observe (Chapter 12) is critical.

Reading Comprehension Questions

1. What is the implication of the quote from Kate Barrett on the opening page of the chapter? How does it relate to the content of this chapter?
2. What is an instructional approach? How does it differ from teaching style? Explain the differences among the six instructional approaches presented in this chapter.
3. What criteria might the teacher use in selecting a particular instructional approach for use with a class?
4. Using the skill of punting, give examples of convergent and divergent inquiry, written in the actual form in which they would be stated.
5. Select a skill theme from one of the skill theme chapters (Chapters 19 through 28) and develop a task sheet similar to the one in Figure 13.2. Include at least six different tasks, ranging from precontrol through utilization levels.
6. Why do we say that a direct instructional approach may not be the best for children who are not developmentally ready?
7. Using the skills of throwing and catching against a defense, design a task sequence using the jigsaw cooperative learning strategy.
8. What strategies can a teacher employ to begin to use child-designed approaches for instruction? Give an example of how one strategy might be developed for a group of 11- or 12-year-olds.
9. How can different instructional approaches be used to help students meet various national standards for physical education?

References/Suggested Readings

Doolittle, S., & Girard, K. (1991). A dynamic approach to teaching games in elementary PE. *Journal of Physical Education, Recreation and Dance, 62*(4), 57–62.

Dyson, B. (2002). The implementation of cooperative learning in an elementary physical education program. *Journal of Teaching in Physical Education, 22*, 69–88.

Griffin, L., Mitchell, S., & Olson, J. (1997). *Teaching sports concepts and skills: A tactical games approach.* Champaign, IL: Human Kinetics.

Grineski, S. (1996). *Cooperative learning in physical education.* Champaign, IL: Human Kinetics.

Harrison, J., Blakemore, C., Buck, M., & Pellett, T. (1996). *Instructional strategies for secondary school physical education* (4th ed.). Dubuque, IA: Brown & Benchmark.

Kagan, S. (1990). The structural approach to cooperative learning. *Educational Leadership, 47*(4), 12–16.

Kohl, H. (1976). *On teaching.* New York: Schocken.

Two-Day-a-Week Program for an Inexperienced Class (72 Days a Year)

Week	Chapter	Day	
1	9	1	Establishing an Environment for Learning (p. 129)
	9	2	Establishing an Environment for Learning (cont.) (p. 129)
2	16	1	Exploring Self-Space (p. 254)
	16	2	Exploring General Space (p. 256)
3	16	1	Traveling in Different Directions (p. 258)
	16	2	Traveling and Freezing at Different Levels (p. 260)
4	4	1	Physical Fitness and Wellness for Children (p. 39)
	25	2	Throwing at a Large Target (p. 479)
5	25	1	Catching a Rolling Ball; Catching from a Skilled Thrower (p. 479)
	19	2	Traveling in General Space: Sliding; Galloping; Hopping; Skipping (pp. 316, 317)
6	19	1	Performing Locomotor Sequences (p. 319)
	20	2	Traveling to Flee; Fleeing from a Partner (pp. 338, 339)
7	20	1	Traveling to Dodge; Dodging the Obstacles (pp. 338, 339)
	24	2	Kicking a Stationary Ball from a Stationary Position (p. 443)
8	24	1	Approaching a Stationary Ball and Kicking; Kicking in the Air (pp. 444, 446)
	24	2	Dropping, Bouncing, and Kicking Lightweight Balls; Dropping and Punting (pp. 459, 459)
9	21	1	Jumping and Landing: Basic Patterns (p. 358)
	4	2	Physical Fitness and Wellness for Children (p. 39)
10	26	1	Striking Balloons in the Air (p. 505)
	26	2	Striking a Ball Upward (Underhand Pattern) (p. 507)
11	26	1	Bouncing a Ball Down (Dribbling) Continuously (p. 524)
	26	2	Dribbling and Walking (p. 524)
12	17	1	Exploring Time (p. 271)
	17	2	Exploring Force (p. 276)
13	17	1	Traveling and Changing Force Qualities (p. 276)
	9	2	Establishing an Environment for Learning (p. 129)
14	16	1	Exploring Pathways (p. 261)
	16	2	Exploring Extensions (p. 265)
15	19	1	Moving to Rhythms (p. 319)
	4	2	Physical Fitness and Wellness for Children (p. 39)
16	27	1	Downs; Ups (pp. 546, 547)
	27	2	Ups and Downs (p. 547)
17	21	1	Jumping over Low Obstacles: Hoops; Jumping over Low Obstacles: Hurdles (p. 360)
	21	2	Jumping a Turned Rope; Jumping a Self-Turned Rope (p. 362)
18	18	1	Identifying Body Parts; Balancing on Matching and Nonmatching Parts (pp. 285, 287)
	18	2	Traveling and Freezing in Different Body Shapes (p. 290)
19	4	1	Physical Fitness and Wellness for Children (p. 39)
	19	2	Leaping (p. 317)
20	18	1	Over, Under, Around, In Front Of, and Behind Concepts (p. 294)
	19	2	The Follow-Me Dance (p. 322)
21	23	1	The Rocking Horse; Twin Rockers (p. 419)
	23	2	Rolling Sideways; Rolling Forward (pp. 429, 421)
22		1	Special Event
	18	2	Matching; Mirroring; Matching and Mirroring (p. 299)
23	22	1	Balancing on Different Bases of Support (p. 376)
	22	2	Balancing in Different Body Shapes (p. 377)
24	23	1	Log Roll (p. 420)
	23	2	Back Rocker; Back Touch (pp. 421, 423)
25	23	1	Transferring Weight from Feet to Back (pp. 401–402)
	23	2	Transferring Weight from Feet to Hands (pp. 402, 407, 413)
26	25	1	Throwing Overhand; Throwing Underhand; Throwing Sidearm (pp. 480, 481)
	25	2	Throwing a Ball against a Wall and Catching the Rebound (p. 487)
27	22	1	Traveling on Low Gymnastics Equipment; Stationary Balances on Equipment (pp. 378, 385)
	22	2	Balancing Sequence (p. 388)

(continued)

Appendix

The appendix to this book offers four sample school-year overviews based on the material in *Children Moving*. These overviews can be followed exactly as presented or used as a model for developing individualized programs.

Introduction and Content Overview

A quality program of physical education for children is much more than simply a bunch of activities that children enjoy for 30 minutes or so several times a week. A quality program of physical education has a definite purpose, has long-term goals, and is developmentally and instructionally appropriate; in short, for children it makes a difference that lasts well beyond elementary school.

Chapter 1, "The Value and Purpose of Physical Education for Children," answers three important questions as an introduction and overview to the book. The first two answers respond to the need for, and importance of, physical education for children. The last question provides insights into the characteristics of a physical education program for children that is positive, and guides them in the process of becoming physically active for a lifetime. As you will see, these responses are based on recent publications written by some of the leading experts in physical activity for children. Together they define a clear and unified direction (outcomes) for programs of physical education while also suggesting a process (developmentally appropriate) that is consistent with contemporary approaches for teaching children.

Chapter 2, "The Skill Theme Approach," answers many of the questions that teachers often ask when they are first exposed to the skill theme approach. Because the content is organized by skills and concepts rather than by games, gymnastics, and dance, for example, some teachers initially find the approach confusing. In Chapter 2, we use a question-and-answer format to respond to these questions; then, in Chapter 3, we define the skill themes and movement concepts. Chapter 3 also includes many of the reasons that support the use of a skill theme approach in children's physical education.

Chapter 4 complements Chapter 3 in describing how physical fitness concepts are interwoven throughout our lessons. It also provides numerous examples of ways children can learn to include activities that enhance their fitness outside of organized physical education classes. It's important that children learn to do this because most programs simply don't allow enough time to help children improve both their physical abilities and their fitness.

If every school were exactly alike, we could now proceed to provide examples of activities that would "work" in every situation. As you know, however, no two schools or programs of physical education are exactly alike. "Reflective Teaching" (Chapter 5) describes how teachers adapt and adjust their programs according to the particular characteristics of their school (e.g., the number of days per week they teach physical education, the available facilities and equipment) and their children (e.g., background, experience, type of community).

The final chapter in Part 1 focuses specifically on "Teaching Diverse Learners." Chapter 6 provides an overview of some of the ways teachers can adapt both their teaching and content to include all children in physical education experiences that are beneficial, encouraging, and appropriate.

The Value and Purpose of Physical Education for Children

As the old man walked the beach at dawn, he noticed a young man ahead of him picking up starfish and flinging them into the sea. Finally catching up with the youth, he asked him why he was doing this. The answer was that the stranded starfish would die if left until the morning sun.

"But the beach goes on for miles and there are millions of starfish," countered the old man. "How can your effort make any difference?"

The young man looked at the starfish in his hand and then threw it to the safety of the waves. "It makes a difference to this one," he said.

—DONALD QUIMBY

Key Concepts

- The purpose of a quality program of physical education is to guide youngsters in the process of becoming physically active for a lifetime.

- Regular physical activity helps prevent obesity, promotes motor skill development and physical fitness, and provides opportunities for goal setting, making new friends, and stress reduction.

- The health benefits associated with being physically active include a reduction in premature mortality, heart disease, colon cancer, diabetes mellitus, and drug and alcohol addiction.

- Positive, or quality, physical education programs have reasonable class sizes, a developmental and sequential curriculum, plenty of practice and movement opportunities, and adequate facilities and equipment.

- Positive physical education programs emphasize learning in all three domains: psychomotor, cognitive, and affective.

Young children are a torrent of physical activity! Unfortunately, for far too many youngsters this torrent of physical activity becomes a trickle by the time they enter adolescence. As a teacher, or future teacher, you can make a significant contribution to the lives of your students by helping to keep their love of movement and physical activity alive so that it lasts a lifetime. Over 60 percent of adults are overweight and for many of them exercise has become a negative term associated with pain, frustration, and embarrassment. Positive physical education programs emphasize enjoyable participation in physical activity and "help students develop the knowledge, attitudes, motor skills, behavioral skills, and confidence needed to adopt and maintain physically active lifestyles" (National Center for Chronic Disease Prevention and Health Promotion [NCCDPHP], 1997, p. 205). Our goal is to keep the love of movement (exercise) alive in youngsters so that they associate exercise with enjoyment and fun!

The importance of physical activity in the lives of children, and adults, is becoming more and more evident. The 2005 Dietary Guidelines for Americans recommends that "children and adolescents engage in at least 60 minutes of physical activity on most, preferably all, days of the week" (www.health.gov/dietary-guidelines/dga2005/document). In fact the 2005 revision of the food pyramid includes a figure climbing stairs to visually represent the importance of physical activity in our lives (www.pyramid.gov). You will also find information on this Web site designed specifically for children ages 6–11 in the "for kids" section.

Physical activity and physical education are not synonymous. **Physical activity** is a behavior—for example, walking or biking to school, playing a sport, or swimming. **Physical education** is the school curriculum that leads to remaining physically active for a lifetime. Thus the goal, or purpose, of a quality physical education program is to guide youngsters in the process of becoming physically active for a lifetime.

This chapter answers three questions.

1. Why do children need quality programs of physical education?
2. What health benefits are associated with a lifetime of physical activity?
3. What components of a physical education program encourage youngsters to maintain physically active lifestyles?

Why Children Need Physical Education

Why do youngsters need a quality program of physical education? The simple answer is so that they will remain physically active throughout their lifetime and reap the benefits of doing so, especially the health benefits that are detailed in the next section. Numerous other benefits have been summarized by the National Association for Sport and Physical Education (NASPE, 2002, p. 7) and are adapted here. They include:

Regular, healthful physical activity: An increasing number of youngsters are overweight and obese. Regular physical activity, as well as an appropriate diet, is the best antidote to eliminate the current obesity epidemic and also provide a positive alternative to "screen time" (both television and computers).

Skill development: In a quality program of physical education, children learn the fundamental motor skills that enable them to develop the competence that creates confidence and leads to safe and successful participation in a wide range of sports and physical activities as adults (Chapters 16–28).

Improved physical fitness: Children are encouraged to improve their muscular and cardiovascular endurance, strength, and flexibility (Chapter 4).

Reinforcement of other subjects: Movement can be used to reinforce the understanding of many subjects taught in the classroom (e.g., mathematics and reading). Movement is also associated with enhanced brain functioning (Chapter 32).

Self-discipline: Youngsters can learn valuable lessons about accepting responsibility for their personal motor skill and fitness development (Chapter 9).

Goal setting: Physical education classes are an excellent laboratory for helping youngsters understand the process of setting and achieving goals, especially physical fitness.

Girls who do not participate in sports before the age of 10 have less than a 10 percent chance of doing so at age 25.

—Donna Lopiano, Women's Sports Foundation

Leadership and cooperation: Many physical education activities require youngsters to work in groups to solve problems or as a team. These opportunities become an excellent laboratory for developing both leadership and cooperation skills.

Enhanced self-efficacy: The motor domain is especially important to young children who have yet to fully develop their verbal communication skills. Thus, confidence in physical abilities may lead to positive feelings of self-esteem.

Stress reduction: A "good workout" helps ease stress, tension, and anxiety and may result in better attention in the classroom.

Strengthened peer relationships: Sports and physical activity are an excellent way to meet and make new friends. Confidence in one's physical abilities encourages youngsters, and later adults, to socialize more easily and "fit into" a variety of situations.

This list briefly summarizes many of the benefits that experts agree are outcomes that accrue to those who are physically active. There are also serious consequences related to not being physically active (Box 1-1). Before discussing the characteristics of a quality, or positive, physical education program thought to promote a lifetime of physical activity,

Box 1-1

The Physically Uneducated Adult

Adults who are physically uneducated often find themselves in awkward and unpleasant situations. For example, they may:

- Be overweight partly as a result of physical inactivity
- Have chronic lower back pain
- Have painful memories of being picked last when teams were chosen
- Remember being laughed at because they couldn't catch a softball or were afraid of a volleyball
- Recall being last whenever they ran laps
- Dread the memory of never being able to do even one pull-up on the physical fitness test
- Be uncomfortable starting and maintaining an exercise program
- Feel like a "klutz" and make excuses to avoid physical activity
- Believe that athletes were born that way
- Not understand that there are virtually hundreds of ways to exercise and that they would enjoy some of them

It is estimated that 65 percent of adults today are overweight or obese.

Children enjoy seeing how they can take their weight on their hands on a beautiful sunny day outside.

it is important to outline the health benefits associated with remaining physically active over a period of years.

Health Benefits Associated with a Lifetime of Physical Activity

The 1996 Surgeon General's report concludes that people of all ages, both male and female, who are physically active derive many benefits. Here are some of the observations in the report (U.S. Department of Health and Human Services [USDHHS], 1996):

- Significant health benefits can be obtained by including a moderate amount of physical activity (e.g., 30 minutes of brisk walking or raking leaves, 15 minutes of running, or 45 minutes of volleyball) on most, if not all, days of the week. Through a modest increase in daily activity, most Americans can improve their health and quality of life (p. 4).
- Additional health benefits can be gained through greater amounts of physical activity. People who can maintain a regular regimen of activity that is of longer duration or of more vigorous intensity are likely to derive greater benefit (p. 4).
- Physical activity reduces the risk of premature mortality in general, and of coronary heart disease, hypertension, colon cancer, and diabetes mellitus in particular. Physical activity also improves mental health and is important for the health of muscles, bones, and joints (p. 4).

- Consistent influences on physical activity patterns among adults and young people include confidence in one's ability to engage in regular physical activity (e.g., self-efficacy), enjoyment of physical activity, support from others, positive beliefs concerning the benefits of physical activity, and lack of perceived barriers to physical activity (p. 249).
- Physical activity appears to improve health-related quality of life by enhancing psychological well-being and by improving physical functioning in persons compromised by poor health (p. 8).

Clearly, the accumulated evidence suggests that youngsters who develop physically active lifestyles stand to gain enormous health benefits. However, this doesn't happen automatically. Programs must be carefully designed and implemented if they are to guide youngsters to become physically active for a lifetime.

As anyone who knows children will quickly acknowledge, however, fears of heart disease, stress, or back pain in later years are not major concerns for most 8- or 10-year-olds. To them, 40 seems old! Fortunately children enter school loving to move and be active. One of the early tasks of primary-grade classroom teachers is to teach children to listen and stay in their seats. Most youngsters would prefer to be up and moving. The challenge of physical educators is not so much to instill a love of movement as it is to keep alive and channel this inborn urge to move so that as individuals enter their adult years they will continue to enjoy being physically active and will derive all of the benefits—physical, emotional, and social—that come

Box 1-2

Are Youngsters Today Physically Active?

The 1996 Surgeon General's report, *Physical Activity and Health,* cites a number of alarming statistics about physical activity patterns in adolescents and also about physical education programs. For example:

- Only about one-half of U.S. young people (ages 12 to 21 years) regularly participate in vigorous physical activity. One-fourth report no vigorous physical activity.
- Approximately one-fourth of young people walk or bicycle (i.e., engage in light to moderate activity) nearly every day.
- About 14 percent of young people report no recent vigorous or light to moderate physical activity. This indicator of inactivity is higher among females than males and among black females than white females.
- Males are more likely than females to participate in vigorous physical activity, strengthening activities, and walking or bicycling.
- Participation in all types of physical activity declines strikingly as age or grade in school increases.
- Among high school students, enrollment in physical education remained unchanged during the first half of the 1990s. However, daily attendance in physical education declined from approximately 42 to 25 percent.
- The percentage of high school students who were enrolled in physical education and who reported being physically active for at least 20 minutes in physical education classes declined from approximately 81 to 70 percent during the first half of the 1990s.
- Only 19 percent of all high school students report being physically active for 20 minutes or more in daily physical education classes.

Source: Physical Activity and Health: A Report of the Surgeon General (p. 8), by U.S. Department of Health and Human Services, 1996, Atlanta, GA: Centers for Disease Control and Prevention, National Center for Chronic Disease Prevention and Health Promotion.

Children derive lifetime benefits from becoming physically active.

confidence eventually culminate in a desire to participate regularly in physical activity, because it has become an enjoyable and important part of their lives as children, as teens, and later as adults.

Characteristics of a Quality Physical Education Program

At this point in the chapter you may be asking how the program described in *Children Moving* is different from the program you had in elementary school. Hopefully most of the characteristics described below would apply to the program you experienced in elementary school. Once again we can look to the National Association for Sport and Physical Education (NASPE) for its definition of a quality physical education program (NASPE, 2002, p. 7) and also guidelines developed by the United States Department of Health and Human Services in its School Health Index (USDHHS, 2000, pp. 3–8). Some

to those who have been physically active throughout their lifetimes (Box 1-2).

Children Moving is designed to introduce you to the skill theme approach that's designed for every child, from the least skilled child in a class to the most athletic youngster. The book explains the ways you can guide all children in positive directions, enabling them to develop the competence that leads to confidence in their physical abilities. This competence and this

The Physical Activity Hourglass

Opportunities to be physically active can be depicted as an hourglass. Young children have plenty of opportunities to be physically active. Playgrounds, parks, and an increasing number of fast-food chains have equipment for children to climb on, over, around, and through. Young children also are encouraged to run and chase their friends and siblings. Many communities also have soccer, basketball, and softball or baseball leagues for young children. There are also opportunities to be on a swim team and take lessons in dance or martial arts. Unfortunately, once a youngster enters middle school many of these opportunities are reduced, unless a youngster is athletic. Too often if a middle school sponsors athletic teams, only a relatively few "make the team." The same is true at the high school level, for athletics and also intramurals. If intramurals are offered, many are limited to team sports after school. Also in many schools it is not "cool" to play intramurals or have your parents drive you to a dance lesson. After high school, however, there are once again a plethora of physical activities for adults. They include weight and fitness clubs, recreation programs, and simply walking, jogging, or biking activities that were not "cool" in secondary school but are acceptable to an adult, especially as one ages and/or puts on additional pounds.

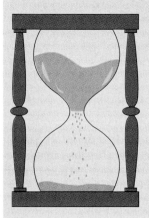

Physical Activity Hourglass

Preschool and elementary
Multitude of opportunities

Secondary school
Limited to school sports and intramurals

Adults
Multitude of opportunities

of the characteristics of a positive, or quality, program of physical education are straightforward and require little or no explanation. Others are lengthier because they are not as obvious or easily understood. The characteristics are bulleted, rather than numbered, as they are all important parts of a positive program of physical education that leads to the benefits described in the first two sections of this chapter.

- **Time:** Ideally children have physical education for at least 150 minutes each week (USDHHS, 2000). This is especially important if children are to develop the fundamental motor skills that are so necessary for

successful, and enjoyable, participation in sports and physical activities in later years. NASPE recommends 150 minutes per week in elementary school and 225 minutes for middle and high schools.

- **Class size:** The number of children in a physical education class should be the same number as in the classroom.

- **Sequential, developmental curriculum:** Teachers follow a carefully planned curriculum scope and sequence that progressively builds on past experiences and also incorporates new experiences when children are developmentally ready. (The Appendix provides examples of curricular scopes and sequences based on the content included in this book.) Lessons are not simply selected randomly with no obvious connection to past and future lessons or just as a way to keep children "busy, happy, or good" for 30 minutes.

- **Minimum of 50 percent MVPA:** Physical education is a moving experience. In quality physical education programs, teachers find ways to actively engage all children in moderate to vigorous physical activity (MVPA) for the majority of every lesson (USDHHS, 2000).

- **Plenty of practice opportunities:** In addition to being actively engaged, children also need plenty of opportunities to practice the skill or concept being taught that day. In a game of kick ball, children average fewer than two chances to throw, kick, and catch during an entire game. And girls have fewer chances than boys (Wilson, 1976)! Quality programs provide many practice opportunities for children to practice their motor skills, sometimes alone, sometimes with a partner, and sometimes in small sided games or with groups.

- **High rates of success:** In addition to copious practice opportunities, teachers also design lessons so that youngsters of all abilities have high rates of success (Chapter 12). When youngsters, especially the unskilled, experience success, they are more likely to continue practicing and working to improve than when they fail continually. This is especially important in physical education because success and failure are so readily observable. For this reason, many programs have switched from a curriculum consisting predominantly of low-organized games and team sports (e.g., kick ball, basketball, and soccer) to the skill theme approach as described in *Children Moving*. Thus, the athletic youngsters, all too often boys, are no longer allowed to dominate (Portman, 1995) and physical education is for every youngster, especially the poorly coordinated, overweight, or awkward children who stand to benefit the most from a quality program of physical education.

Developmentally and Instructionally Appropriate Experiences

In the early 1990s the National Association for Young Children published a series of articles and documents describing developmentally appropriate educational experiences for young children (Bredekamp, 1992). The ideas in these documents were extremely popular with educators and parents. Several years later the Council on Physical Education for Children (COPEC, 1992) used the same format to describe developmentally and instructionally appropriate elementary school physical education experiences for children. This position statement was also highly popular. Since 1992, similar documents have been published by NASPE for preschool, middle school, high school, and college physical education programs (COPEC, 2000; Middle and Secondary School Physical Education Council, 2001, 2004). These documents can be purchased from NASPE or downloaded from the Internet by clicking on the publications section of the NASPE Web site www.aahperd.org/naspe/.

Quality physical education is both developmentally and instructionally suitable for the specific children being served. Developmentally appropriate practices in physical education are those that recognize children's changing capacities to move and those that promote such change. A developmentally appropriate physical education program accommodates a variety of individual characteristics such as developmental status, previous movement experiences, fitness and skill levels, body size, and age. Instructionally appropriate physical education incorporates the best known practices, derived from both research and experiences teaching children, into a program that maximizes opportunities for learning and success for all children (COPEC, 1992, p. 3).

In addition to defining *developmentally and instructionally appropriate,* these documents describe in easy-to-follow, straightforward terms the tenets of the "new" physical education that has been evolving over the past three decades. They emphasize, for example, that:

- Children develop at different rates, and therefore educators should recognize these variances by designing experiences that allow for individual differences in abilities.
- For learning to occur, youngsters need lots of opportunities to practice a skill or movement at high rates of success.
- It is inappropriate to use exercise as punishment.
- The physical education curriculum should have a clear scope and sequence, with observable outcomes that can be assessed.
- Allowing captains to pick teams, overemphasizing competition, and giving fitness tests to one student at a time while the rest of the class watches are inappropriate educational practices.

These documents clearly make the point that physical education curriculums that consist solely of large-group games, often played with one ball, are both developmentally and instructionally inappropriate.

- **Positive developmental environment:** Quality physical education classes, in addition to promoting successful learning experiences, are also emotionally warm, nurturing environments in which children are encouraged to practice learning new motor skills and improve their physical fitness without feeling embarrassed or humiliated by the teacher or their peers (Chapter 9).
- **Teacher background:** The teacher has an extensive background in both the content and pedagogy of physical education for children, typically obtained as a physical education major in college. There are also classroom teachers who provide excellent movement experiences for their youngsters, despite their relatively limited background. For this reason *Children Moving* is written for both the physical education major, or specialist, and also the classroom teacher.
- **Realistic expectations:** Teachers with an extensive background in children's physical education are able

The 60-Second One-Ball Test

Typically, principals and parents do not have time to spend hours observing a physical education class to determine if it is a quality program. A rough estimate can be made in a short amount of time, however, by using the 60-second one-ball test. Here are the directions.

When you walk (or drive) by a physical education lesson, observe how many balls are in use (obviously this applies only to lessons in which balls are being used). If there is only one ball for an entire class of 20 youngsters or more, make a mental note. This typically takes less than 60 seconds, as the intent is not to observe an entire lesson. As you notice more lessons, keep track of the number of balls being used. After observing five or more lessons, you will have an idea of the amount of practice opportunities children are getting in their physical education classes. If all the lessons use only one ball, then you know the amount of practice is severely limited, just as if a reading class were using only one book for an entire class. In contrast, if every child had a ball in the lessons you observed, then you know the teacher is attempting to maximize practice opportunities for children. Although this is hardly a scientific approach, it does provide one generalized indicator about the quality of a program.

to develop realistic programs when their time is less than the recommended 150 minutes per week. The emphasis is on "developing basic motor skills that allow participation in a variety of physical activities" (NCCDPHP, 1997, p. 209).

- **Adequate equipment and facilities:** Many excellent physical education programs have substandard facilities and equipment. Ideally, however, every program has both an indoor and outdoor facility and also a wide variety of equipment so that children do not have to wait for turns to use equipment.
- **Enjoyable:** Quality physical education classes are also fun classes. Children should enjoy and look forward to coming to physical education class. The best teachers find ways to make learning fun.

Catching is a skill used in many sports and physical activities.

Box 1-3

National Standards for Physical Education

Physical activity is critical to the development and maintenance of good health. The goal of physical education is to develop physically educated individuals who have the knowledge, skills and confidence to enjoy a lifetime of physical activity.

A physically educated person:

Standard 1: Demonstrates competency in motor skills and movement patterns needed to perform a variety of physical activities.

Standard 2: Demonstrates understanding of movement concepts, principles, strategies, and tactics as they apply to the learning and performance of physical activities.

Standard 3: Participates regularly in physical activity.

Standard 4: Achieves and maintains a health-enhancing level of physical fitness.

Standard 5: Exhibits responsible personal and social behavior that respects self and others in physical activity settings.

Standard 6: Values physical activity for health, enjoyment, challenge, self-expression, and/or social interaction.

Source: Moving into the future: National standards for physical education, 2nd ed. (p. 11), by the National Association for Sport and Physical Education, 2004, Reston, VA: NASPE. With permission from the National Association for Sport and Physical Education (NASPE), 1900 Association Drive, Reston VA 20191-1599.

- **Psychomotor, cognitive, and affective domains:** Although the major emphasis in physical education is on the psychomotor domain, quality programs also take every opportunity to emphasize cognitive concepts and develop an environment that encourages positive social experiences and attitude development. Chapters 9 and 10 focus on some of the ways teachers encourage children to develop positive attitudes toward themselves and physical activity by creating safe and enjoyable learning environments. Chapter 32 focuses on interdisciplinary learning and emphasizes the role physical education can play in cognitive development. It also briefly summarizes some of the recent research related to the importance of movement and research on brain development (Jensen, 2000).

We hope this chapter has helped you to understand why a quality physical education program can be so important in a youngster's life, especially for a child who is inclined not to be a physically active adolescent or adult. This chapter also provides an overview of the components of a quality, or positive, physical education (see Box 1-3). The next two chapters describe in detail the components of the skill theme approach designed to maintain the torrent of physical activity and love of movement, which is so characteristic of young children, into the middle and high school years.

PE Central www.pecentral.org

Throughout the seventh edition of *Children Moving,* we will be referring to a variety of documents that can be accessed directly via the Internet. PE Central is the most comprehensive Web site for K–12 physical educators in the world. Virtually all the documents referred to in this edition can be located through PE Central. In addition to links to the developmentally appropriate documents, the Surgeon General's report, and the *National Standards for Physical Education* (NASPE, 2004), numerous developmentally appropriate lessons and assessment ideas are available for free on the Web site. There are also descriptions of best practices, confer-

ence and job announcements, kids' quotes, and links to many other Web sites. The Web address, or URL, for PE Central is www.pecentral.org. You will also find easy-to-use forms for sharing your lesson and assessment ideas with other physical educators.

Mark Manross currently serves as the executive editor, and Dave Hinman and Jan Bierschbach are senior editors. In addition, hundreds of other physical educators have published their ideas on PE Central and/or work on it in an editorial capacity. George Graham, a coauthor of this book, is the senior advisor for PE Central.

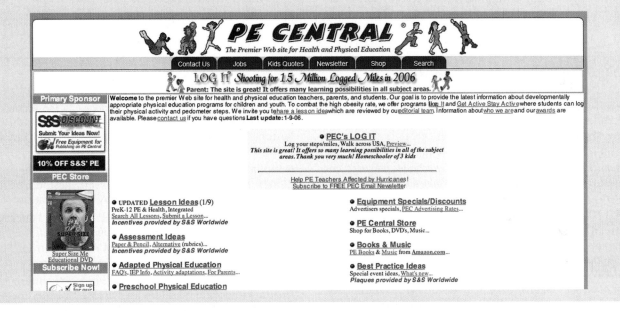

Summary

Quality physical education programs for children have never been more important than they are today. The three overarching questions in this chapter provide an introduction to the program and teaching process described in the text. The responses to the questions taken from the recent literature (1) provide reasons why children need quality physical education, (2) summarize the health benefits that may accrue to those who remain physically active for a lifetime, and (3) define a quality physical education program for children as one that is developmentally and instructionally appropriate.

Reading Comprehension Questions

1. The introduction to Chapter 1 described the purpose of a quality physical education program. Explain your reasons for agreeing or disagreeing with the purpose.

2. Chapter 1 provides a list of reasons children need quality physical education. Which of those reasons do you think are most important? Least important? Explain your reasons.

3. Categorize the reasons for a quality physical education program into two categories. The first category (column) will consist of those reasons that are predominantly the responsibility of the physical education program. In the second column, list the reasons for which other programs may also share responsibility (i.e., they are also goals for the teachers in the classroom and not specifically those of the physical education program).

4. The Physical Activity Hourglass suggests that opportunities for many youngsters are reduced once they enter secondary school. Analyze the opportunities for middle and high school youth to be physically active in your community. Contrast the opportunities with those provided for young children. Describe what your community might do to create more environmental invitations to become physically active, especially for the youngsters who are not on athletic teams.

5. Chapter 1 describes the characteristics of a quality physical education program. Make a table listing these characteristics in the left-hand column. In the second column, grade your elementary school program on each of these characteristics from A to F. In the third column, explain your reason for each grade. If you did not have an elementary school physical education program, analyze your middle or high school physical education program.

6. Assume that someone asks you why youngsters need physical education. Prepare an argument, using the information from this chapter, to convince that person that physical education is as important as many other subjects in school.

References/Suggested Readings

Bredekamp, S. (1992). What is developmentally appropriate and why is it important? *Journal of Physical Education, Recreation and Dance, 63*(6), 31–32.

Council on Physical Education for Children. (1992). *Developmentally appropriate physical education practices for children: A position statement of the Council on Physical Education for Children.* Reston, VA: National Association for Sport and Physical Education.

Council on Physical Education for Children. (2000). *Appropriate practices for elementary school physical education: A position statement of the National Association for Sport and Physical Education developed by the Council on Physical Education for Children (COPEC).* Reston, VA: National Association for Sport and Physical Education. www.aahperd .org/naspe/

Furth, H. G. (1970). *Piaget for teachers.* Englewood Cliffs, NJ: Prentice Hall.

Holt/Hale, S. (2006). *On the move: Lesson plans to accompany Children Moving* (7th ed.). New York: McGraw-Hill.

Jensen, E. (2000). Brain-based learning: A reality check. *Educational Leadership, 57*(7), 76–79.

Kirkendall, D. (1985). Effects of physical activity on intellectual development and academic performance. *Intellectual Development, 19,* 49–63.

Middle and Secondary School Physical Education Council. (2001). *Appropriate practices for middle school physical education: A position statement of the National Association for Sport and Physical Education developed by the Middle and Secondary School Physical Education Council (MASSPEC).* Reston, VA: National Association for Sport and Physical Education. www.aahperd.org/naspe/

Middle and Secondary School Physical Education Council. (2004). *Appropriate practices for high school physical education: A position statement of the National Association for Sport and Physical Education developed by the Middle and Secondary School Physical Education Council (MASSPEC).* Reston, VA: National Association for Sport and Physical Education. www.aahperd.org/naspe/

National Association for Sport and Physical Education. (2002). *2001 Shape of the nation report.* Reston, VA: National Association for Sport and Physical Education.

National Association for Sport and Physical Education. (2004). *Moving into the future: National standards for physical education.* Reston, VA: National Association for Sport and Physical Education.

National Center for Chronic Disease Prevention and Health Promotion, Centers for Disease Control and Prevention. (1997). Guidelines for school and community programs to promote lifelong physical activity among young people. *Journal of School Health, 76*(6), 202–219.

Portman, P. A. (1995). Who is having fun in physical education classes? Experiences of sixth grade students in elementary and middle schools. *Journal of Teaching in Physical Education, 14*(4), 445–453.

Quimby, D. (1988). The starfish. *TEAM, 2*(6).

Sanders, S., & Graham, G. (1995). Kindergarten children's initial experiences in physical education. The relentless persistence for play clashes with the zone of acceptable responses. *Journal of Teaching in Physical Education, 14*(4), 372–383.

Shephard, R. (1996). Habitual physical activity and academic performance. *Nutrition Reviews, 54*(4), 32–35.

Shephard, R., Volle, M., Lavallee, H., LaBarre, R., Jequier, J., & Rajic, M. (1982, November/December). Curricular time for physical education? A controlled experiment in French Canada asks how much curricular time should be spent on physical education. *Journal of Physical Education, Recreation and Dance,* 19–29.

U.S. Department of Health and Human Services. (1996). *Physical activity and health: A report of the Surgeon General.* Atlanta, GA: Centers for Disease Control and Prevention, National Center for Chronic Disease Prevention and Health Promotion.

U.S. Department of Health and Human Services. (2000). *School Health Index for Physical Activity and Healthy Eating: A self-assessment and planning guide for elementary school.* Atlanta, GA: Centers for Disease Control. Available for free download from: www.cdc.gov/nccdphp/dash.

Wilson, N. (1976). *The frequency and patterns of selected motor skills by third and fourth grade girls and boys in the game of kickball.* Unpublished master's thesis, University of Georgia, Athens.

The Skill Theme Approach

Physical fitness, movement skills, concept and affective development should be emphasized throughout the curriculum. The greatest emphasis during the preschool and early elementary grades should be upon movement skill acquisition.

—Council on Physical Education for Children, 1992

Key Concepts

- The skill theme approach describes both the content and pedagogy for physical education.

- The skill theme approach is based on developmentally appropriate principles that recognize that children have different interests, abilities, and motor skills.

- The development of fundamental motor skills and their application to a variety of sports and physical activities create the basis for the skill theme approach.

- The Curriculum Diamond suggests the content to be taught in elementary, middle school, and high school physical education programs.

- Children's abilities and interests are used to guide the selection of content in the skill theme approach, as opposed to age or grade level.

- Skill themes are initially practiced in isolation; as youngsters develop their motor skills they are practiced in sports, games, gymnastics, and dance contexts.

- Skill themes are revisited throughout the year rather than in units of several weeks.

- Cognitive, affective, and physical concepts are interwoven throughout the skill theme approach rather than taught as isolated units.

Chapter 1 provided important insights into why physical education is so important in children's lives today, followed by an overview of the characteristics of a quality, or positive, physical education program. This chapter also answers a question: What is the skill theme approach to children's physical education?

The skill theme approach describes both the *content* of children's physical education (the curriculum is detailed in Parts 3 and 4 of *Children Moving*) and also the teaching process, or *pedagogy* (described in Part 2). A question-and-answer format will help you understand the characteristics of the skill theme approach; how it differs from more traditional programs; and how dance, games, gymnastics, and physical fitness are incorporated within the skill theme approach. The chapter begins by explaining developmentally appropriate physical education.

What Is Developmentally Appropriate Physical Education?

Motor development research studies the "process of change in an individual's movement behaviors" (Barnett & Merriman, 1992, p. 5). The skill theme approach is developmentally appropriate because it reflects important motor development principles, both in curriculum design and also in the teaching process. Some of the important motor development principles upon which *Children Moving* is based are briefly explained below.

Children Develop at Different Rates

One critical premise of motor skill development is that children develop at different rates. Some kindergarten children can skip; others are not ready to skip. Some are able to track a ball in motion; others are not visually ready yet. Developmentally appropriate physical education recognizes this premise and therefore does not expect all children to be able to perform the same task identically. As you will see in subsequent chapters detailing the skill theme approach, we work hard to recognize and value the developmental differences in children's abilities, although it's not easy with 25 or more in a class.

Age Does Not Predict Motor Ability

If age were a predictor of motor ability, then all adults would be skillful athletes. Although there are certain advantages to aging (e.g., quicker reflexes, visual tracking ability), the only way individuals become skillful in motor skills is to use, or practice, them. Thus, most adults are reasonably efficient at walking. Many, however, are inefficient at catching a ball or striking an object with a racket. They are inefficient not because they do not have the potential to be skillful, but rather because they have not used the skills regularly over a period of years.

Children Develop Motor Skills Naturally through Play

Children today have fewer and fewer opportunities to develop motor skills on their own. Television viewing, computer games, the Internet, and fear of playing outside in many communities combine to mean fewer chances to be physically active. Although there is some evidence that motor skills may develop through informal play (hours and hours of basketball or soccer, for example), this possibility is becoming less and less probable in society today. The simple fact is that physical education is becoming increasingly important for children because their playtime is severely limited. This is especially true for overweight youngsters who have little or no physical activity built into their lives.

The Myth of the Natural Athlete

One sports myth is that there are natural athletes. Although some youngsters are physically (genetically) disposed to do better at some sports than others, the fact is that highly skilled children have participated in one, or many, sports from very early ages. Some children begin kindergarten with mature throwing and catching patterns, for example. They were not born this way. They played a lot of catch with parents, siblings, or friends from a young age and thus enter school more highly skilled than their peers. In time, however, their less skilled peers can catch up if they too practice and use the motor skill thousands of times as they play with friends, on teams, or with a parent.

Difference in Physical Abilities between Boys and Girls

On average, boys are more physically active than girls (U.S. Department of Health and Human Services [USDHHS], 1996). This may be one reason boys tend to be more highly skilled than girls in certain sports. Developmentally, however, girls have the potential to be equally as skillful as boys. As more and more girls play sports, and become physically active, we can expect to see a decline in any gap that exists between physical abilities. As teachers we emphasize this continually in our programs so that the girls in our classes understand that skillfulness is a result of practice, not heredity or gender.

Boys tend to be taller than girls and also have wider bones (American Academy of Orthopaedic Surgeons, 2005). As with motor skills, however, girls can dramatically improve their strength. Just as we are seeing an increasing number of girls playing sports, so too we are seeing more girls and women who have improved their strength through practice and exercise. Although a carefully designed weight-training program is appropriate for adolescents, experts recommend that children lift weights only under the careful supervision of a qualified teacher or trainer who has an extensive background in prepubescent bone ossification (Bernhardt, D.T., Gomez, J., Johnson, M.D., Martin, T.J., Rowland, T.W., Small, E., LeBlanc, C., et al., 2001). We do not recommend weight training as part of an elementary school physical education program.

In summary, developmentally appropriate physical education recognizes that youngsters develop at different rates and have different abilities, and that the environment plays a critical role in the development of motor skills. The chapter continues with a question-and-answer format that answers many questions typically asked when folks are initially introduced to the skill theme approach.

Why Don't You Describe Such Activities as Duck, Duck, Goose and Kick Ball?

We don't include many of the so-called traditional activities for three major reasons. First, activities such as these, in which children are singled out to perform solo with everyone watching them, can be both embarrassing and discouraging when the less skilled children are "on center stage." Children (or adults, for that matter) who are embarrassed or made to feel inadequate are hardly motivated to participate. One of our primary goals is to encourage children to develop positive attitudes about themselves and about physical activity so that they choose to be physically active throughout their lives. Games such as the ones named above are developmentally inappropriate in that they do not take into account the varying skill abilities of children within a class (Council on Physical Education for Children [COPEC], 1992, 2000) and thereby force some children into situations that make them unhappy and may lead them to dislike physical activity.

Games like Duck, Duck Goose are fun for a few but most of the children are inactive.

Second, these games emphasize "winning" more than learning. Another of our primary goals is to help children develop the movement competence that enables them to participate in physical activity successfully and with enjoyment. For this reason, we have organized our content, or suggested curriculum, around skill themes rather than the more complex movement forms of games, gymnastics, and dance.

Finally, many of these traditional games encourage only a few youngsters to be physically active. The less skilled, overweight, or less physically fit youngsters often find ways to avoid actively participating in games with one ball or tag games with one person who is "it."

What Are Skill Themes?

Skill themes are fundamental movements that form the foundation for success in sports and physical activities in later years. Initially they are studied in isolation (one skill at a time), and then in later grades they are combined with other skills and used in more complex settings, such as those found in dance, games, and gymnastics. The intent is to help children learn a variety of locomotor, nonmanipulative, and manipulative skills that provide the foundation to enjoyably and confidently play a sport, for example, or perform a dance consisting of an intricate set of movements.

The Curriculum Diamond (Figure 2.1), created by physical educators Dawn McCrumb and Wendy Mustain in 1995, is intended to illustrate the concept of a

motor skill foundation leading to successful participation in sports and physical activities. The model was expanded and elaborated upon by George Graham, Ken Bell, and Catherine Himberg in 1996. The intention of this model is to help physical educators think about and design curriculums that will *guide youngsters in the process of becoming physically active for a lifetime.* Grade levels are suggested in the model for illustration purposes only. Clearly, decisions about when to introduce different content will need to be based on the progress made by the students in a given program.

What Is the Curriculum Diamond?

The Curriculum Diamond suggests a curricular focus corresponding to the grade level structure of most school districts across the United States—elementary, middle, and high school. It follows the recommendations of the National Center for Chronic Disease Prevention and Health Promotion (NCCDPHP, 1997) and the *National Standards for Physical Education* (Council on Physical Education for Children, 2004) by developing a broad foundation at the elementary and middle school levels and then focusing on proficiency in a few movement forms at the high school level.

Building a Foundation (Preschool through Grade 5)

The bottom part of the diamond represents the earliest ages at which children are introduced to skill themes and movement concepts. The initial focus is on developing a functional understanding of the concepts of space awareness, effort, and relationships (Chapters 16–18). As children develop, they are introduced to skill themes designed to encourage and assist them in beginning to acquire the fundamental competencies that will become the foundation skills for many of the sports and physical activities they will pursue as adolescents and adults (Chapters 19–28). You will notice that this section of the diamond widens as each layer is laid upon the foundational layer that precedes it. This is intended to represent how skill themes and concepts are combined in the upper elementary grades.

Exploring Possibilities (Grades 6–8)

In the middle school years, the focus shifts from building a foundation to using the skills and concepts in a variety of movement forms. Skills continue to be developed and learned, but the focus is on exposing students to a broad array of content areas designed to stimulate interest in health-enhancing lifetime activi-

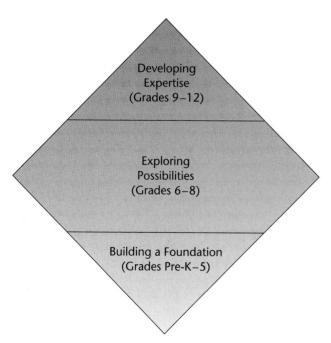

Figure 2.1 The Curriculum Diamond.

ties. Ideally this is the age when adolescents begin to discover the various sports and physical activities that are, or are not, personally appealing. Some youngsters, for example, like team sports, and others may prefer individual sports. Others will enjoy yoga, dance, martial arts, or mountain biking. The goal is to introduce youngsters to many different movement forms and then assist them to discover the types of activities that are personally enjoyable and meaningful. This is why the Curriculum Diamond is widest at the middle school level.

Developing Expertise (Grades 9–12)

Ideally the exposure to many movement options in middle school stimulates student interest in a handful of health-enhancing lifetime activities. When students enter high school, the diamond begins to narrow, suggesting that students will begin to make decisions about the activities they enjoy and desire to become proficient in. At this point students choose electives based on the possibilities they explored in middle school. As students approach the peak, the focus narrows. This is the time when students develop the expertise that enables them to participate in several activities enjoyably and with confidence, thereby allowing them to accrue the benefits that come to those who remain physically active for a lifetime. This is the time when students refine the skill themes and movement concepts they learned in the early years for use in specific sports and physical activities.

What Are the Characteristics of the Skill Theme Approach?

Four characteristics of the skill theme approach (content and pedagogy combined) clearly distinguish it from the "primary use of dance, games, and gymnastic activities . . . considered the traditional 'activity' approach" (Gabbard, LeBlanc, & Lowy, 1987, p. 3).

Characteristic 1

Competence in performing a variety of loco-motor, nonmanipulative, and manipulative motor skills is a major purpose of the skill theme approach.

The skill theme approach reflects the growing concern that children who participate in programs that emphasize game playing rather than motor skill learning don't necessarily improve their motor ability (Graham, 1987; Manross, 2000). The logical implica-

tion, of course, is that adults with inefficient motor skills tend to avoid physical activities that require them to use these poorly learned skills and as a consequence develop tendencies toward "couch potatoism." See Box 2-1 for one example of the difference in outcomes of the two approaches.

A basic assumption is that a curriculum that is "scoped and sequenced" by skill themes provides students with the requisite skills for participating in adult versions of sports, dance, and the myriad other physical activities that are available today—and those that will be invented tomorrow. As physical educators we're able to help children learn these skills more quickly and with less frustration than they would if they attempted to learn the skills on their own.

The skill themes are generic, in the sense that they are not tied to any single sport or activity. Rather, they transcend, or cut across, structured sports. Figure 2.2 illustrates this point. Introductory or beginning tasks for each skill theme start at the most basic level. The children are asked to practice the motor skill in isolation and the fundamental critical components or cues are emphasized, such as throwing a ball hard against a wall while focusing on opposition (stepping with the foot opposite the throwing hand). As children demonstrate the ability to perform the skill using the critical components, the tasks require children to combine the skill with other skills and concepts, such as throwing while running to a partner who is also running. Eventually the skill is studied within a games, gymnastics, or dance context, depending on the skill. Some skills (e.g., jumping and landing) are used in games, dance, gymnastics, track and field, and so on. Other skills are more specific to games or sports, such as dribbling.

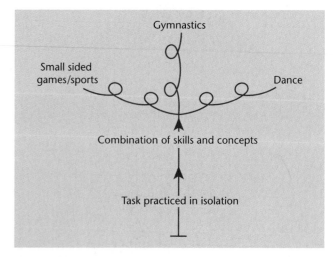

Figure 2.2 Skill themes are practiced initially in isolation, then in combination with other skills and concepts leading to their use in games, dance, and gymnastics.

Box 2-1

Critical Elements in the Skill Theme Approach

One of the sample benchmarks for second graders in the *National Standards* suggests that children be able to "identify four characteristics of a mature throw" (NASPE, 1995, p. 20). In the skill theme approach, as you will see in later chapters, we focus on children learning the critical elements. Manross (2000) interviewed 25 children who had been taught using a skill theme approach and 25 children whose curriculum consisted primarily of low-organized games. As part of his study he asked the children to identify the critical elements (cues) of the overhand throw. It was clear that the children in the skill theme approach (Pendleton Elementary School) could describe many of the critical elements of a mature overhand throw, whereas the children at the other school (Eckland) had not learned the critical elements. The table contains their responses.

Answer Stated	No. of Times
Pendleton (Skill Theme Approach)	
Turn your side to the target	17
Step with the opposite foot	15
Arm way back	10
Aim at target	9
Follow through	3
Step through with other foot	2
Let elbow lead	1
Twist body at waist	1
Bring arm straight over, not sidearm	1

Eckland (Low-Organized Games)	
Get straight in front of target	4
Hold ball with tight grip	3
Bring hand back behind shoulder	3
Follow through	2
Try your best	2
Don't know	2
Practice	2
Don't be scared of the ball	2
Take a forward step	2
Throw hard	2
Aim at target	2
Don't strain arm	2
Try to throw sidearm	1
Hold your hand straight	1
Work on stance	1
Don't throw hard	1
Pretend it is hot object	1
Don't get nervous	1
Keep mind on throwing	1
Make sure they see good	1
Have a strong arm	1
Keep eye on ball	1

Although some skill themes are typically associated with a specific sport, most are used in a variety of sports or physical activities. This is illustrated by using the skill theme of dribbling with the hands (Chapter 24). Dribbling is typically associated with the sport of basketball. The initial dribbling tasks focus on children dribbling a ball in a self-space without traveling or moving. As they gain in dribbling skill, children are challenged to dribble and travel in different pathways, at different speeds, and around stationary and eventually moving obstacles. If there is sufficient time for practice, eventually the children will be ready to dribble in complex situations that might be small sided basketball games, but children may also be challenged to create dribbling routines to music or to dribble in keep-away or tag games. In some instances the teacher designs the routine or game; in other instances the children design their routine or invent their game. Figure 2.3 illustrates how the skill theme of dribbling is developed with youngsters based on the tasks described in Chapter 24.

Some skill theme chapters include rules for games (e.g., Chapters 24, 25, and 26), but these rules are suggested as part of the skill theme progression for children at more advanced levels (e.g., utilization and proficiency levels, as described in Chapter 7). To reach the more advanced levels, the children will spend considerable time on tasks devoted to learning these skills—initially in rather static environments—before using them successfully within the dynamic setting of an organized game, for example. In this book, games are carefully selected (or designed) to enhance skill acquisition as part of a long-term progression rather than simply as a way to keep children "busy, happy, and good" for 30 minutes or so.

In addition to including a progression (sequence) of tasks for developing each skill theme from the beginning through the advanced levels (Part 4), each

Figure 2.3 The skill theme of dribbling is initially studied as an isolated skill. As the children become more skillful, it is combined with other skills and concepts. Eventually, dribbling is used in teacher- or child-designed routines, games, or small sided basketball games.

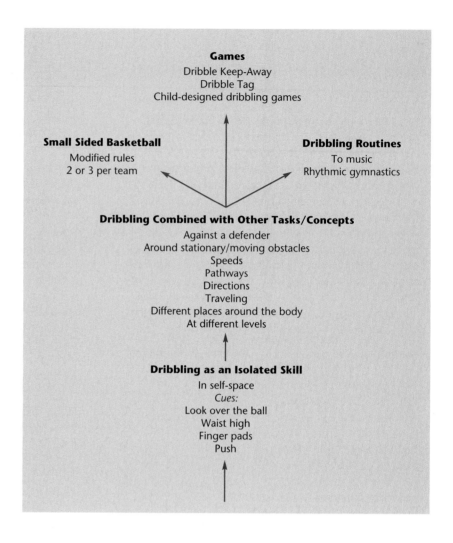

Games
Dribble Keep-Away
Dribble Tag
Child-designed dribbling games

Small Sided Basketball
Modified rules
2 or 3 per team

Dribbling Routines
To music
Rhythmic gymnastics

Dribbling Combined with Other Tasks/Concepts
Against a defender
Around stationary/moving obstacles
Speeds
Pathways
Directions
Traveling
Different places around the body
At different levels

Dribbling as an Isolated Skill
In self-space
Cues:
Look over the ball
Waist high
Finger pads
Push

chapter includes information (written descriptions, diagrams, and/or photos) to assist the teacher in the process of observing children (this process is first described in Chapter 11) to help the youngsters develop efficient and biomechanically correct motor patterns (see Chapter 12).

Characteristic 2

The skill theme approach is designed to provide experiences appropriate to a child's developmental level, as opposed to age or grade level.

One of the many challenges of teaching is to match the content of the lesson to the abilities of the students (Chapter 12). Both grade level and age are unreliable indices of ability. A second characteristic of the skill theme approach is that it uses the students' developmental level as a guide for selecting the content to be taught.

The generic levels of skill proficiency (Chapter 7) serve as guides for assessing the abilities of the children and then selecting tasks that are matched to their abilities. If the majority of children in a class, for example, were unable to hit a ball against a wall continually using a paddle so that it returned on a single bounce, we wouldn't require them to participate in a game requiring an even greater ability to strike the ball—for example, a game that required them to hit a ball to a partner (Chapter 27).

In the skill theme approach, the tasks are selected according to the children's abilities, not a predetermined calendar that implies that all children of the same grade develop at the same rate. This is especially important, for example, when the skill development of children may be limited because they have physical education classes only one or two days a week (Graham, Metzler, & Webster, 1991). In practice, this means that if three consecutive fourth-grade classes were taught by an experienced teacher using a skill theme approach, one class might be challenged with

Fitness is built into the skill theme approach as children "hop in general space."

a more difficult series of tasks than another (Graham, Hopple, Manross, & Sitzman, 1993). And within each of the three fourth-grade classes, students might be challenged individually or in groups to undertake different tasks (see Chapter 11).

We can use the skill of throwing (Chapter 25) to illustrate how a skill theme is developmentally sequenced. At the most basic level (precontrol), children are encouraged to throw a ball hard or to throw it far. These tasks lead to the development of greater trunk rotation and foot-arm opposition, for example, which combine with other critical components to form a mature (biomechanically efficient) throwing pattern. Throwing for distance, however, is only one type of throwing. As the children learn the components of an overhand throw for distance, they are challenged by tasks that involve throwing at targets, throwing to a partner, and throwing while moving. At more advanced levels (utilization and proficiency), they might be invited to participate in a game of keep-away involving throwing, such as two against two or three against one (three throwers, one defender). The teacher bases these decisions, however, on the children's readiness rather than age or grade level. Throwing efficiently and effectively then becomes a focus that is interwoven and revisited as variations of this skill theme are revisited throughout the program.

Characteristic 3

The scope and sequence of the skill themes are designed to reflect the varying needs and interests of students over a period of years.

The third characteristic of the skill theme approach can be found within the scope and sequence recom-

mendations (see Chapter 8 and the Appendix at the end of the book). Rather than focusing on the same skill theme for several weeks (in a three- or six-week unit, for example), we focus on a skill theme for brief periods and then revisit it at various times during the year. At the beginning levels (precontrol and control), we might spend only two or three days in a row on a skill theme. In fact, we might not even spend an entire class period on a single skill theme. As children gain proficiency, expanding their motor repertoire, they

Kick the ball back and forth with your partner. Try to make it go through the arch.

become more interested in spending larger amounts of time (three or four days) on the same skill theme because the tasks are more complex and involved and their success rate is higher.

Revisiting the same skill theme several times during a year also allows the teacher to teach virtually the same lesson that was taught two or three months before. This is often necessary when the skill of the children doesn't improve noticeably. A teacher who remains on the same skill theme for many days in a row, however, is tempted to make the tasks harder (in an effort to alleviate the boredom of both the children and the teacher) than the children may be ready for.

Characteristic 4

The skill theme approach emphasizes instructional alignment. Teachers decide what students can learn in a lesson (objectives) (Chapter 8); develop a series of tasks designed to assist the children to accomplish the objectives(s) for the lesson (Chapters 16–28); and then assess the objective (Chapter 14) to determine if the lesson objective(s) have been accomplished. The assessment then serves as a guide for future lessons. According to Tannehill a teacher "tells students what is important for them to know and be able to do (*the objectives*), designs appropriate tasks that allow them to practice what you taught them, and assesses them on what they have been practicing" (Tannehill, 2001, p. 19). If a teacher wants her class to learn the grapevine step she would demonstrate and explain the grapevine step, devise tasks that allow them to practice the grapevine, and then assess their ability to do the grapevine to determine if they need more practice. This process is referred to as instructional alignment and is emphasized throughout *Children Moving*.

Is It Difficult to Maintain Youngsters' Interest in a Program That Emphasizes the Fundamentals?

Ideally, children begin this program in preschool. When they do, this is really the only program they know, so their interest is high. When we introduce this program to children in the fourth and fifth grades for the first time, some initially have a difficult time adjusting, particularly the highly skilled children who enjoy playing games they dominate. In time, however, children learn to enjoy this program because they're improving. We also attempt to adjust the activities to the youngsters' skill level, and this makes the lessons more interesting. It is important to understand, how-

ever, that in the skill theme approach students do play games, albeit small sided, but only when they have the necessary skills to do so.

What Does "Adjusting the Activities" Mean?

"Adjusting the activities" is the concept of reflective teaching (Chapter 5). If a boy can't catch a ball, for example, then he isn't going to enjoy playing a game of softball in which the score is kept and winning is important. For this child we provide noncompetitive activities in which he can succeed. In the same class, however, a girl may have played softball on a team for several years and be very good. We try to provide her with gamelike activities related to softball in which she and a group of classmates may choose to keep score. For more effective learning in reading and math classes, children are grouped by ability. Although it's harder to do this in physical education, we do provide different tasks based on the youngsters' ability. This "system" for determining the skill level of the students is explained in Chapter 7. In addition, the tasks in each skill theme chapter are organized into a logical progression or sequence.

Where Is Physical Fitness in the Skill Theme Approach?

Physical fitness is an important part of the skill theme approach. As we explain in Chapter 4, it is interwoven throughout the program rather than confined to one separate unit. Our emphasis is not on *training* children so that they score well on a physical fitness test battery. Rather, we try to provide experiences that help them to understand and value the importance of physical fitness. We also try to help children enjoy physical activity so that they choose to make it a part of their daily lives for a minimum of 60 minutes a day (NASPE, 2004; www.pyramid.gov, 2005). The success of the physical fitness component within the skill theme approach is measured not by the children's scores on a physical fitness test battery but by an assessment of their understanding of, attitudes toward, and enjoyment of physical activity.

Some of our lessons are devoted primarily to helping children understand and apply the important fitness concepts. In virtually every lesson we teach, however, we try to ensure that children are moderately to vigorously active a minimum of 50 percent of the lesson (USDHHS, 2005) (Chapters 9 and 14), thereby enhanc-

"Travel under the shape made by your partner."

these important dimensions into the lessons instead of isolating them as separate units of learning.

What about Dance and Gymnastics?

Initially our focus is on helping children develop and learn the fundamental motor skills. As children learn these skills, they are placed into the contexts of dance and gymnastics (and also games) (Figure 2.2). It's important to understand that the purpose of dance, gymnastics, and games extends beyond simply skill improvement. *Dance* is a form of expression by moving to rhythm alone or with others. *Gymnastics* is a series of acrobatic skills combined into smooth, repeatable sequences performed on the floor and/or apparatus to demonstrate strength, balance, and body control. *Games* are organized activities that use manipulative skills and are played for the enjoyment and satisfaction of cooperating and competing with others.

Dance, gymnastics, and games require skills that are best learned initially *outside* these contexts. It's ineffective to always practice the skills outside these contexts, however, so the contexts of dance, gymnastics, and games are interwoven throughout the movement concept and skill theme chapters (Parts 3 and 4). The chapters on gymnastics, dance, and games (Chapters 29, 30, and 31, respectively) illustrate this technique.

An analogy with reading also illustrates this point. Most children learn to read in elementary school; as adults they choose what they'll read. In the skill theme

ing their cardiovascular benefits. We also find that running laps or doing jumping jacks, for example, seems to be a waste of time when children can obtain the same benefits while learning and enjoying physical activity—by playing tag games, learning new jump-rope tricks, or perfecting a sequence of jumping and landing and rolling.

Where Do the Cognitive and Affective Domains Fit into the Skill Theme Approach?

As with physical fitness, we try to weave cognitive and affective dimensions into our lessons rather than deal with them as separate entities. Throughout the chapters, you will find examples and suggestions that might be labeled *cognitive* or *affective*—encouraging children to cooperate with one another in designing a game, for example, or to discover the most stable type of balance they might make. In this way we blend

The fundamental motor skill of balancing has many applications.

approach we teach the fundamental motor skills that are thought to provide the foundation for a lifetime of enjoyable, hopefully regular, physical activity. The children might tell us they aren't interested in some skills now. But 20 years from now, who knows?

How Do Classroom Teachers Feel about the Skill Theme Approach?

Classroom teachers are positive about the skill theme approach because they can relate it directly to their work in the classroom—in teaching children vocabulary, for example. These teachers also appreciate the fact that the program accommodates the variation in abilities that is typical of any class of children. Many teachers also consider the program's de-emphasis of competition a welcome alternative to those programs that constantly pit one team against another in games in which the score is kept. They feel not only that this is more consistent with the approaches they use in the classroom but also that it makes their jobs easier; the children don't come angrily into their rooms after physical education class, arguing about the scores or

who cheated, for example. As detailed in Chapter 32, classroom teachers also are able to use movement to teach reading, writing, and math, for example.

How Do Middle (Junior) and High School Physical Education Teachers Feel about the Skill Theme Approach?

Clearly there are many views. Some middle school teachers are enthusiastically supportive, realizing the importance of ensuring that children maintain positive attitudes about physical activity. Their job is much harder if their students have been "turned off" to physical education. Interestingly, a number of middle school teachers have actually started emphasizing skill themes in their programs in response to their students' poor motor skill development. These teachers realize that it's extremely difficult to excite students about sports and lifetime physical activity if they have yet to acquire the basic motor skills. The skill theme approach has no age or grade limits. It can be valuable for people of any age.

Summary

The skill theme approach describes both the content (what is taught) and the pedagogy (how it is taught) that are used in a developmentally appropriate program of physical education. This approach recognizes that age or grade levels are inappropriate indicators of physical ability; therefore, lessons are designed to consider different abilities and interests. The Curriculum Diamond provides an overview of how content can be sequentially developed so that elementary, middle school, and high school programs work together to provide a solid movement foundation for youngsters to attain the competence and confidence to remain physically active throughout a lifetime.

Initially the skill theme approach emphasizes the development of fundamental motor skills (e.g., throwing, balancing, striking) in isolation. As the children progress in ability the skill themes are taught in sports, games, dance, and gymnastics contexts. Because of the rapid changes in children's development, skill themes are revisited throughout the year rather than taught in units of several weeks. Concepts related to physical fitness and the cognitive and affective domains are interwoven throughout the lessons.

Reading Comprehension Questions

1. Why aren't games such as basketball and duck, duck, goose included in this book?
2. In your own words describe the skill theme approach. Use the Curriculum Diamond (Figure 2.1) as part of your explanation.
3. Three characteristics of the skill theme approach are listed in this chapter. Which provides the most compelling reason, in your opinion, for using a skill theme approach? Why?

4. The skill theme approach can be described as developmentally appropriate. How does this concept relate to the generic levels of skill proficiency?
5. When are children ready for "organized" games? Why wouldn't it be correct to respond to this question by suggesting an age or grade level?
6. Physical fitness is an important part of the skill theme approach, yet only one chapter addresses it. How can this be explained?

7. Physical activity can be used to teach important lessons about cooperating with others. How might these lessons be taught within a skill theme approach?

8. Do you think the skill theme approach should be used in middle schools? Why, or why not?

References/Suggested Readings

American Academy of Orthopaedic Surgeons. (2005, May). Men and women not created equal in terms of predisposition to musculoskeletal problems. Retrieved November 2, 2005, from www.aaos.org/pemr/news/press_release .cfm?PRNumber=384.

Barnett, B. E., & Merriman, W. J. (1992). Misconceptions in motor development. *Strategies, 5*(3), 5–7.

Bernhardt, D. T., Gomez, J., Johnson, B. M. D., Martin, T. B., Rowland, T. W., Small, E., LeBlanc, C., et al. (2001). Strength training by children and adolescents. *Pediatrics, 107*(6): 1470–1472.

Council on Physical Education for Children. (1992). *Developmentally appropriate physical education practices for children: A position statement of the Council on Physical Education for Children.* Reston, VA: National Association for Sport and Physical Education.

Council on Physical Education for Children. (2000). *Appropriate practices for elementary school physical education.* Reston, VA: American Alliance for Health, Physical Education, Recreation and Dance.

Council on Physical Education for Children. (2004). *Physical activity for children: A statement of guidelines for children ages 5–12* (2nd ed.). Reston, VA: American Alliance for Health, Physical Education, Recreation and Dance.

Gabbard, C., LeBlanc, E., & Lowy, S. (1987). *Physical education for children.* Englewood Cliffs, NJ: Prentice Hall.

Graham, G. (1987). Motor skill acquisition—An essential goal of physical education programs. *Journal of Physical Education, Recreation and Dance, 58*(8), 44–48.

Graham, G., Hopple, C., Manross, M., & Sitzman, T. (1993). Novice and expert children's physical education teachers: Insights into their situational decision-making. *Journal of Teaching in Physical Education, 12*(2), 197–214.

Graham, G., Metzler, M., & Webster, G. (1991). Specialist and classroom teacher effectiveness in children's physical education. *Journal of Teaching in Physical Education, 10*(4), 321–426.

Manross, M. (2000). Learning to throw in physical education class: What I learned from 4th and 5th graders: Part 3. *Teaching Elementary Physical Education, 11*(3), 26–29.

National Association for Sport and Physical Education. (1995). *Moving into the future: National standards for physical education.* Reston, VA: National Association for Sport and Physical Education.

National Association for Sport and Physical Education. (2004). *Moving into the future: National standards for physical education* (2nd ed.). Reston, VA: National Association for Sport and Physical Education.

National Center for Chronic Disease Prevention and Health Promotion, Centers for Disease Control and Prevention. (1997). Guidelines for school and community programs to promote lifelong physical activity among young people. *Journal of School Health, 76*(6), 202–219.

Tannehill, D. (2001). Using the NASPE content standards. *Journal of Teaching Physical Education, Recreation and Dance, 72*(8), 19.

U.S. Department of Health and Human Services. (1996). *Physical activity and health: A report of the Surgeon General.* Atlanta, GA: Centers for Disease Control and Prevention, National Center for Chronic Disease Prevention and Health Promotion.

U.S. Department of Health and Human Services. (2005). *School health index for physical activity and healthy eating: A self-assessment and planning guide for elementary school.* Atlanta, GA: Centers for Disease Control. Available for free download from: www.cdc.gov/nccdphp/dash.

Skill Themes, Movement Concepts, and the *National Standards*

A physical education program for children which begins with an organized sport is analogous to a language arts program beginning with a Shakespearean sonnet.

—IRIS WELSH [STUDENT]

Key Concepts

- Children need to become sufficiently competent in basic motor skills if they are going to eventually enjoy playing sports or games as teens and adults.

- In the elementary school the emphasis is placed on practicing motor skills rather than learning rules or the structures of sports.

- Skill themes are analogous to verbs (i.e., they are action words). They are subdivided into three categories: locomotor, nonmanipulative, and manipulative skills.

- Movement concepts are analogous to adverbs (i.e., they describe how an action is performed). They are also subdivided into three categories: space awareness, effort, and relationships.

- In the primary grades movement concepts are taught before the skill themes.

- The movement analysis framework "wheel" is based on an analysis of human movement and describes how the skill themes and movement concepts interact with one another.

- The "spirals" outline a developmentally appropriate progression for each of the skill themes.

- *Children Moving* directly addresses national and many state physical education standards.

Our primary goal is to provide children with a degree of competence leading to the confidence that encourages them to become, and remain, physically active for a lifetime. Our intent is to help children gain enough skill and confidence for them to participate enjoyably in many activities, not just a few traditional team sports, and to avoid the abysmal failure and embarrassment that often result from a total lack of skill. By focusing on learning and practicing skills rather than on the rules or structure of a game or sport, we can dramatically increase the amount of practice the children actually receive, thereby heightening their opportunities to learn the fundamental motor skills that form the foundation for becoming a lifetime mover.

Essentially, the notion is that these elements are learned in early life through the various activities performed (such as jumping, throwing, striking, and the like), and then when a new act is to be learned in later life, the student can piece together these elements in a more efficient way to achieve the new motor goal.

The assumption is that by jumping over objects of various sizes, shapes, heights, et cetera, the student will have more effective "elements" for the performance of the next jumping tasks (e.g., the running long jump in high school).

—RICHARD SCHMIDT, "Scheme Theory: Implications for Movement Education"

Typically, children who are learning to read are taught first to recognize letters, then parts of words, then complete words, and finally sentences. Children who are studying mathematics learn to solve problems after they've grasped the basic functions of numbers and signs. Children learning to play a musical instrument typically study the scale before attempting a song. In physical education, however, all too often children have been taught games, dances, or complex gymnastic stunts before they're able to adequately perform fundamental motor skills. Too often, children know the rules for a game or the formation of a dance but don't have the motor skills needed for successful and enjoyable participation. Our way of teaching children how to participate effectively in various activities is to focus on the development of the necessary motor skills. We call this approach teaching by skill themes.

One of the easiest ways to understand skill themes is to think of a popular sport. Let's pick softball. What skills do people use when they play softball? The major ones include throwing, catching, batting, and running. Let's pick another popular sport—basketball. Throwing, catching, running, dribbling with hands, jumping and landing, and chasing and fleeing skills are used frequently in basketball. Obviously we could list a number of other sports. The point is that some of the same skills—for example, throwing, catching, and running—are used in both sports, and in many more sports that you know of. Thus, if children learn to throw and catch, for example, their chances of playing and enjoying a sport such as softball or basketball increase, because they have a reasonable chance to succeed at that sport. We have termed these skill themes because they apply to many different sports, although the way they are used (the context) differs from one sport to another. Table 3.1 lists various skill themes and indicates which sports emphasize them.

Characteristics of Themes

In music, a theme recurs in different parts of a song, sometimes in exactly the same way, at other times in a slightly different form. The *Random House Dictionary of the English Language* defines theme as "a short melodic

Table 3.1 Skill Themes Used in Sports*

Skill Themes	Aerobics	Basketball	Football	Dance	Golf	Hockey	Martial Arts	Rock Climbing	Soccer	Softball	Tennis	Track and Field	Tumbling	Ultimate Frisbee	Volleyball
Traveling	X	X	X	X	X	X	X	X	X	X	X	X	X	X	X
Chasing, Fleeing, Dodging		X	X			X	X		X	X				X	
Jumping, Landing	X	X	X	X			X	X	X	X	X	X	X	X	X
Balancing	X	X	X	X	X	X	X	X	X	X	X	X	X		X
Transferring weight	X	X	X	X	X	X	X	X	X	X	X	X	X	X	X
Rolling			X	X		X	X						X		X
Kicking	X		X	X			X		X						
Punting			X						X						
Throwing		X	X						X	X	X	X		X	X
Catching		X	X						X	X				X	
Volleying									X						X
Dribbling		X				X			X						
Striking with rackets											X				
Striking with golf clubs					X										
Striking with bats										X					
Striking with hockey sticks						X									

*This table is only intended to suggest how various skill themes are applied in sports contexts.

subject from which variations are developed." In physical education, various movements can be thought of as a theme.

By revisiting a movement—sometimes in the same context as previously and sometimes in a radically different context—we provide children with variations of a skill theme. These variations lead to proficiency as well as diversity. Jumping can be presented as jumping from an object—a box or a table—and landing softly. This movement can be revisited with a slight variation: jumping from an object and landing facing in a different direction from the takeoff position. Jumping for distance or leaping in synchronization with the leap of a partner would be radically different, yet the theme would still be jumping (Gallagher, 1984). So too would the high jump and the long jump for track and field athletes.

Some movements, such as jumping, traveling, and balancing, can be focused on in games, gymnastics, and dance contexts. Other movements, such as throwing and dribbling, are primarily used in only one of those three areas. Whenever possible, we point out to students the similarities in movements used in different contexts to enhance students' cognitive understanding of the principles that underlie successful performance of a movement. We're not certain that this influences

skill performance (transfer of learning), but it doesn't seem to have any adverse effects.

The instructor who teaches by themes can focus on helping children become skillful movers. Youngsters will have plenty of opportunities as they grow older to learn games, sports, dance, and gymnastics activities, but first they must learn the basic motor skills needed for successful participation.

> *Fundamental activities such as running, jumping, skipping, sliding, catching, kicking, and striking are the basic components of the games, sports, and dances of our society. Children who possess inadequate motor skills are often relegated to a life of exclusion from the organized and free play experiences of their peers, and subsequently, to a lifetime of inactivity because of their frustrations in early movement behavior.*
>
> —Vern Seefeldt, John Haubenstricker, Sam Reuschlein

Many adults choose not to play tennis or swim or dance. They don't enjoy these activities because they don't possess the skills needed to participate successfully. An unskilled adult attempting to learn a complex set of

Try to bat the ball without hitting the cone.

dance steps may be embarrassed and frustrated. So will the adult who is trying to learn to play tennis but cannot even hit the ball into the opponent's court.

As children become ready, they begin to combine skill themes and movement concepts into the movement forms that we typically identify as games, sports, gym-

nastics, and dance. The key word, however, is ready. We try to lead children to these experiences gradually rather than forcing them into settings prematurely; for example, we have devised a variety of ways children can practice the skill of batting (Chapter 28) without placing them in a softball game. Constantly striking out in a softball game is hardly conducive to wanting to play softball as an adult.

Skill Themes and Movement Concepts

We hope by now you understand why we have chosen to develop our curriculum using skill themes. In this section you will find two tables and two figures that are especially important to a thorough understanding of the skill theme approach. The movement concepts are listed in Table 3.2 and the skill themes in Table 3.3. If you were asked to list individual sports that could be taught in physical education, you might list golf, tennis, badminton, swimming, and archery. Tables 3.2 and 3.3 are our way of organizing the content of physical education, not by sports, but by an analysis of movements that are used in all kinds of sports and in everyday life. These tables also provide a guide to be certain that we teach all of the important movements and do not leave any out. The skill themes and movement concepts are defined and thoroughly explained in Parts 3 and 4.

The **movement analysis framework,** which has been termed "the wheel" (Figure 3.1), is intended to show how the skill themes and movement concepts interact with each other. The **spiral** (Figure 3.2) is an example of one of the developmentally appropriate progressions that we have developed for each of the skill

Table 3.2 Movement Concepts*

Space Awareness (where the body moves)		Effort (how the body moves)		Relationships
Location:	Self-space and general space	Time:	Fast/slow Sudden/sustained	Of body parts: Round (curved), narrow, wide, twisted, symmetrical/nonsymmetrical
Directions:	Up/down Forward/backward Right/left Clockwise/counterclockwise	Force: Flow:	Strong/light Bound/free	With objects and/or people: Over/under, on/off, near/far, in front/behind, along/through, meeting/parting, surrounding, around, alongside
Levels:	Low/middle/high			With people: Leading/following, mirroring/ matching, unison/contrast, alone in a mass, solo, partners, groups, between groups
Pathways:	Straight/curved Zigzag			
Extensions:	Large/small Far/near			

*This table represents many of the movement concepts taught in elementary school physical education. It is not meant to be all-inclusive but to provide examples of movement concepts.

Table 3.3 Skill Themes*

Locomotor Skills
Walking
Running
Hopping
Skipping
Galloping
Sliding
Chasing, fleeing, and dodging

Nonmanipulative Skills
Turning
Twisting
Rolling
Balancing
Transferring weight
Jumping and landing
Stretching
Curling

Manipulative Skills
Throwing
Catching and collecting
Kicking
Punting
Dribbling
Volleying
Striking with rackets
Striking with long-handled implements

*This table represents many of the skill themes taught in physical education. It is not meant to be all-inclusive but to provide examples of skill themes.

themes in Part 4. Obviously the movement content of our program consists of more than just skill themes. In fact, it's difficult to focus on a skill theme for long without introducing one or more movement concepts. The two terms, skill themes and movement concepts, differentiate the movements (skill themes) from the ideas (movement concepts) used to modify or enrich the range and effectiveness of skill employment.

The distinction between movement concepts (Table 3.2) and skill themes (Table 3.3*) can be clarified by a comparison to grammar. Skill themes are always verbs—they're movements that can be performed. Movement concepts are always modifiers—they describe how a skill is to be performed. This distinction also clarifies how movement concepts are employed to embellish, enhance, or expand the quality of a movement. A verb by itself—strike, travel, roll—is typically less interesting than one that is modified by an adverb—strike hard, travel jerkily, roll smoothly. Skills can stand by themselves. You can roll or gallop or jump, but you can't slow or high or under. Concepts modify skills.

Our initial focus with the primary-grade children is on learning and understanding the movement concept vocabulary (see Table 3.2); for this reason, the movement concepts are listed before the skill themes (see Table 3.3). We focus on movement concepts before skill themes because children in preschool and the primary grades spend a great deal of time studying vocabulary (learning new words), and many of the movement concepts are part of this vocabulary. This is also the time when children truly enjoy the challenge of learning and moving, as they demonstrate their understanding of such words as symmetrical, zigzag, and twisted.

It's important to remember, however, that although the children are focusing on learning the movement

*The major source for this explanation of skill themes and movement concepts is *Physical Education: A Movement Orientation*, 2nd ed., by Sheila Stanley, 1977, New York: McGraw-Hill.

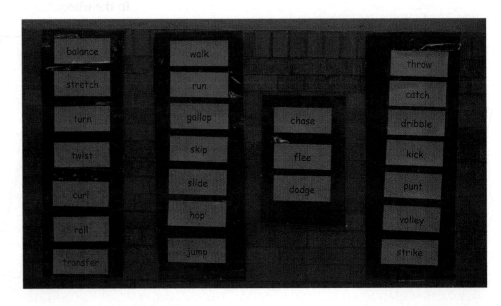

Children enjoy learning the vocabulary of the skill theme approach. This teacher has posted her skill themes on the gym wall.

The movement concept of "directions" is illustrated on the gym wall.

concepts, they are also practicing the skill themes. As soon as the children begin to move, they are practicing one or more skill themes, even though they may not be thinking about it at the time. For example, if we ask children to skip in a curved pathway, they may be thinking about the concept of curve, but they are also practicing skipping. If we ask them to land in a low level (from a jump), they are also getting jumping and landing practice. In later grades, the emphasis will shift from the low level (movement concept) to the quality of the landing—from the concept to the skill. In fact, however, this is an artificial separation, because the skill themes and movement concepts are constantly interacting.

The Wheel (Movement Analysis Framework)

The interaction between the skill themes and the movement concepts listed in Tables 3.2 and 3.3 can be represented schematically by five concentric circles (Figure 3.1). (For easy reference, we have termed the movement analysis framework "the wheel," a term our students coined.) The two inner circles represent the skill themes; the three outer circles represent the movement concepts.

The first inner circle contains the general categories of the skill themes from Table 3.3: manipulative, nonmanipulative, and locomotor skills. The next inner circle contains the breakdown of the skills in each category, such as walking and running for locomotor skills, balancing and rolling for nonmanipulative skills, and throwing and kicking for manipulative skills.

The outer circle contains the three categories of the movement concepts from Table 3.2: space awareness (where the body moves), effort (how the body moves), and relationships.* The second circle subdivides each of the three movement concept categories. For example, space awareness is subdivided to include location and directions; the subdivisions of effort include time and force; and among the relationship subdivisions are body parts and people. Finally, in the third circle, the movement concepts are subdivided even further.

In the wheel, the two inner circles representing the skill themes are stationary. The three outer circles are connected to each other but are able to rotate around the two inner circles. This rotation illustrates the idea that the same movement concept can be used to enhance the development of different skills. The concept of levels in space, for example, is useful for refining such skills as catching, striking, volleying, and balancing. The concept of fast and slow can be applied to the study of such skills as traveling, rolling, dribbling, transferring weight, and dodging. At times, some concepts blend with other concepts. For example, fast or slow may modify pathways, and forward and backward may modify over and under.

*Some movement analysis frameworks include the concept of space (direct and flexible) as a quality of movement. In our teaching, however, we use this concept so infrequently that we don't include it in our discussion of the qualities of movement.

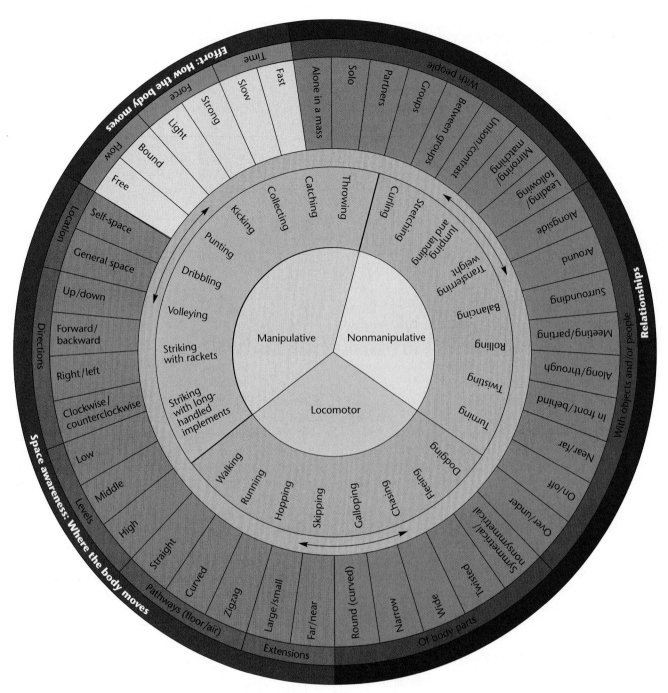

Figure 3.1 Movement analysis framework (wheel) depicting the interaction of movement concepts and skill themes. An "interactive" wheel is located inside the back cover of this book.

Context Variation

Just learning the terminology for the movement concepts (see Table 3.2) and the skill themes (see Table 3.3) is not enough to begin actually teaching them. We have developed thorough explanations for each of the movement concepts and skill themes, along with a plethora of activities, in subsequent chapters. Part 3 (Chapters 16, 17, and 18) contains the definitions and suggested activities for teaching the movement concepts. Part 4 (Chapters 19 to 28) does the same for the skill themes.

In each chapter we organize the activities from the easiest to the hardest, from less to more complex. The

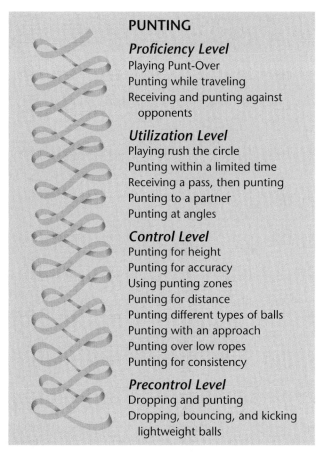

PUNTING

Proficiency Level

Playing Punt-Over
Punting while traveling
Receiving and punting against
    opponents

Utilization Level

Playing rush the circle
Punting within a limited time
Receiving a pass, then punting
Punting to a partner
Punting at angles

Control Level

Punting for height
Punting for accuracy
Using punting zones
Punting for distance
Punting different types of balls
Punting with an approach
Punting over low ropes
Punting for consistency

Precontrol Level

Dropping and punting
Dropping, bouncing, and kicking
    lightweight balls

Figure 3.2 Progression spiral illustrating the contextual variations in which skill themes can be studied.

content in each of the skill theme chapters is outlined in a figure that we call a progression spiral (Figure 3.2). The spiral is a graphic reminder that the same context (task) may be revisited and that, when appropriate, the tasks can be varied to give the learner a more difficult challenge. The spiral is intended to be read from the bottom to the top, that is, the easiest tasks are at the bottom, the hardest at the top.

The movement concept depends on the skill theme being studied. The concepts of fast and slow, for example, can be used to make a task more interesting or challenging. The skill theme of rolling or transferring weight can be made more difficult by challenging the children to move more slowly. But with a skill such as dribbling, which is easier to perform at a slower rate, the challenge "dribble faster" increases the complexity of the task. In short, there's no standard formula that can be used as a guide for varying the contexts in which all skill themes are studied. Each skill theme is different.

The spirals aren't intended to suggest the length of time to be spent studying a particular theme. In reflective teaching, the context is varied when appropriate for a particular class or child.

Finally, the spiral represents a progression from the precontrol level up to the proficiency level (see Chapter 7). When the context of a movement is varied, many children regress to a previous level. This doesn't mean that children will drop from the utilization or proficiency level to a precontrol level each time the context of a task is varied. But the teacher can expect to observe a variation in skill performance each time a task is made easier or harder. The progressions in Parts 3 and 4 are based on our knowledge of the pertinent literature and on years of teaching experience. But you may find that a different ordering of the tasks (activities) is more appropriate for a particular teaching situation. Each child, each class, each teaching environment differs from all others, and the reflective teacher adapts to these differences. See Box 3-1 for an example of one school's use of skill themes in its physical education curriculum.

The *National Standards* and the Skill Theme Approach

In this seventh edition of *Children Moving*, we attempt to show how our program fits with the content of *Moving into the Future: National Standards for Physical Education* (National Association for Sport and Physical Education [NASPE], 2004). We think this will be especially useful for those teachers who are interested in revising their programs to reflect the content suggested in the *National Standards*. Before describing how *Children Moving* might be used as a guide to developing a program designed on the *National Standards*, it seems important to provide a brief background of the process that led to the development of those standards.

Background of *National Standards* Development

In the late 1980s, the National Association for Sport and Physical Education formed a Blue Ribbon Task Force and asked its members to:

- Define a person who is "physically educated."
- Define "outcomes" and "benchmarks" that could serve as guidelines for constructing physical education program curriculums.

The Outcomes Task Force worked on the project for more than five years, and each year, at NASPE's national conference, physical educators from throughout the United States were invited to review and critique the work. The task force then revised its work based on these recommendations and presented it again the

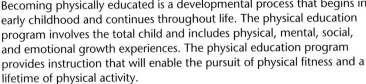

Box 3-1

Adapting the Skill Theme Approach

Since the first edition of *Children Moving* was published in 1980, a number of school districts throughout the United States have based their curriculums on skill themes. In Gwinnett County (near Atlanta, Georgia) an overview of each area of the curriculum is described on a poster that many elementary schools in the county display on their walls. The poster is prominently displayed alongside math, reading, and science posters, an arrangement conveying the message that the teachers of Gwinnett County are dedicated to educating the total child.

Physical Education
K–5 Curriculum

The fundamental objective of the physical education program is to provide opportunities for the development of motor skills and physical fitness.

Skill Themes and Fitness Concepts
Students in grades K–5 will experience a developmentally designed program of skill and fitness development, including educational games, educational dance, and educational gymnastics. The following motor skills and fitness concepts are included:

- body awareness
- balancing
- chasing, fleeing, dodging
- kicking and punting
- striking with implements (short and long handled)
- rolling
- throwing and catching
- traveling
- volleying and dribbling
- transferring weight
- jumping and landing
- cardiorespiratory endurance
- flexibility
- muscular strength and endurance
- fitness testing

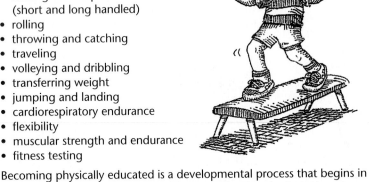

Becoming physically educated is a developmental process that begins in early childhood and continues throughout life. The physical education program involves the total child and includes physical, mental, social, and emotional growth experiences. The physical education program provides instruction that will enable the pursuit of physical fitness and a lifetime of physical activity.

Gwinnett County Public Schools

Source: Reprinted with permission of Gwinnett County Public Schools, Gwinnett County, Georgia.

following year. Over several years, the work of the task force was reviewed by hundreds of physical educators and as a result reflects the collective wisdom of much of the profession. The result of this work, published in 1992, was a document entitled *The Physically Educated Person* (NASPE, 2004, p. v), which defined a physically educated person as an individual who:

- HAS learned skills necessary to perform a variety of physical activities.
- IS physically fit.
- DOES participate regularly in physical activity.
- KNOWS the implications of and the benefits from involvement in physical activity.
- VALUES physical activity and its contributions to a healthful lifestyle.

Outcome statements were also developed for each of the five parts of the definition, along with benchmarks for kindergarten, second, fourth, sixth, eighth, tenth, and twelfth grades.

Using the same process, NASPE built upon the foundation of the "Outcomes Project" to develop national content standards for physical education, including examples for assessment. The standards were initially published in 1995 (NASPE, 1995) and revised in 2004 (NASPE, 2004). They were especially important because they paralleled work that was also being done in other disciplines, such as mathematics, science, and geography. The skill theme approach, as defined in *Children Moving*, is aligned with the *National Standards for Physical Education*.

Skill Themes and the Content Standards

Box 1-3 (in Chapter 1) lists the six content standards for physical education from the *National Standards*. *Children Moving* addresses all of the standards throughout the text, but many readers will find Parts 3 and 4 of the book especially helpful for designing, delivering, and assessing the first two content standards. The first two content standards, and part of the general description for each one, follow:

1. A physically educated person demonstrates competency in motor skills and movement patterns needed to perform a variety of physical activities.

   The intent of this standard is development of the physical skills needed to enjoy participation in physical activities. Mastering movement fundamentals establishes a foundation to facilitate continued motor skill acquisition and gives students the capacity for successful and advanced levels of performance to further the likelihood of participation on a daily basis. In the primary years, students develop maturity and versatility in the use of fundamental

motor skills (e.g., running, skipping, throwing, striking) that are further refined, combined, and varied during the middle school years. These motor skills, now having evolved into specialized skills (e.g., a specific dance step, chest pass, catching with a glove, or the use of a specific tactic), are used in increasingly complex movements . . . through the middle school years. (NASPE, 2004, p. 12).

2. A physically educated person demonstrates understanding of movement concepts, principles, strategies, and tactics as they apply to the learning and performance of physical activities.

   The intent of this standard is facilitation of learners' ability to use cognitive information to understand and enhance motor skill acquisition and performance. . . . In the lower elementary grades, emphasis is placed on establishing a movement vocabulary and applying introductory concepts. Through the upper elementary and middle school years, an emphasis is placed on applying and generalizing these concepts to real-life physical activity situations. (NASPE, 2004, p. 12).

In subsequent chapters you will find many examples of how you can teach children the skills and concepts suggested in the *National Standards*. It will also help to refer to Boxes 3-2 and 3-3, which contain sample performance outcomes from the *National Standards*, and Box 3-4, which contains guidelines for promoting lifelong physical activity from the National Center for Chronic Disease Prevention and Health Promotion. After each sample benchmark you will see one or more chapter references that indicate where you can learn more about that specific benchmark and the activities that teachers use to help children achieve the suggested goal.

In many chapters we have also quoted sample performance outcomes from the *National Standards* to assist you in understanding how the content of the *Children Moving* chapters can be developed to meet these benchmarks. When appropriate we have also included assessment examples in those chapters to assist you in determining how well your students are progressing in regard to the benchmarks.

In concluding this section on skill themes and movement concepts and how they are described in the *National Standards*, it is important to remember that the standards are not intended as a prescribed set of goals or outcomes to be achieved by all physical education programs. The *National Standards* document is not a national curriculum! As detailed in Chapter 5, "Reflective Teaching," teachers must determine the goals of their program based on the specific characteristics of the schedule, the children, and the community. The suggested grade levels, for example, are only that—suggestions. The *National Standards* can be immensely helpful,

Box 3-2

Sample Performance Indicators for National Standard 1: Movement Forms

A more detailed description of each performance indicator, along with activities to teach it, is included in the *Children Moving* chapter(s) listed below at the end of each benchmark. The critical elements (cues) of a mature form are also described in these chapters.

Grades K–2

- Skips (or hops, gallops, slides, etc.) using mature form (Chapter 19)
- Performs a simple dance step in keeping with a specific tempo (Chapter 29)
- Demonstrates clear contrasts between slow and fast movements when skipping (hopping, galloping, sliding, etc.) (Chapters 17, 19)
- Travels forward and sideways, changing directions quickly in response to a signal or obstacle using a variety of motor skills (Chapters 16, 17, 19)
- Demonstrates a smooth transition between locomotor skills in time to music (Chapters 17, 19)
- Drops a ball and catches it at the peak of the bounce (Chapter 25)
- Throws a ball underhand using mature form (Chapter 25)
- Discovers how to balance on different body parts, at different levels, becoming "like" a statue while making symmetrical and nonsymmetrical shapes (Chapters 16, 22)

Grades 3–5

- Balances with control on a variety of objects (e.g., balance board, large apparatus, skates) (Chapter 22)
- Catches a fly ball using a mature form (Chapter 25)
- Jumps vertically and lands using mature form (Chapter 21)
- Throws a ball overhand and hits a target on the wall (Chapter 25)
- Develops and refines a gymnastics sequence (or creative dance sequence) demonstrating smooth transitions. (Chapters 29, 30)
- Dribbles then passes a ball to a moving receiver (Chapter 26)
- Throws a ball to a partner 15 yards away using mature form (Chapter 25)

Grades 6–8

- Serves a volleyball underhand using a mature form (Chapter 26)
- Dribbles a ball while preventing an opponent from stealing the ball (Chapter 26)
- Places the ball away from an opponent during a tennis rally (Chapter 27)
- Designs and performs gymnastics (or dance) sequences that combine traveling, rolling, balancing, and weight transfer into smooth, flowing sequences with intentional changes in direction, speed and flow (Chapters 16, 17, 18, 19, 23)

Box 3-3

Sample Performance Indicators for National Standard 2: Movement Concepts

A more detailed description of each performance indicator, along with activities to teach it, is included in the *Children Moving* chapter(s) listed below at the end of each performance indicator.

Grades K–2

- Identifies correctly various body parts (e.g., knee, foot, arm, palm)

Grades 3–5

- Identifies four characteristics of a mature throw (Chapter 25)
- Uses concepts of space awareness and movement control to run, hop, and skip in different ways in a large group without bumping or falling (Chapters 16 and 19)

- Identifies and demonstrates the major characteristics of mature walking, running, hopping, and skipping (Chapter 19)

Grades 6–8

- Transfers weight from feet to hands at fast and slow speeds using large extensions (e.g., mule kick, handstand, cartwheel) (Chapter 23)
- Accurately recognizes the critical elements of a throw made by a fellow student and provides feedback to that student (Chapter 25)
- Consistently strikes a softly thrown ball with a bat or paddle, demonstrating an appropriate grip (Chapters 27, 28)

Box 3-4

Guidelines for Promoting Lifelong Physical Activity

Almost 30 years ago the National Center for Chronic Disease Prevention and Health Promotion (NCCDPHP) made the following recommendations for "developing students' mastery of and confidence in motor and behavioral skills for participating in physical activity." They still apply today:

- Students should become competent in many motor skills and proficient in a few to use in lifelong physical activities.
- Elementary school students should develop basic motor skills that allow participation in a variety of physical activities.
- Older students should become competent in a select number of physical activities they enjoy and succeed in.

- Students' mastery of and confidence in motor skills occur when these skills are broken down into components and the tasks are ordered from easy to hard.
- Students need opportunities to observe others performing the skills and receive encouragement, feedback, and repeated opportunities for practice during physical education class.
- Active student involvement . . . that focuses on building confidence may increase the likelihood that children and adolescents will enjoy and succeed in physical education and physical activity.

Source: NCCDPHP, 1977, p. 209.

---

however, as a well thought out document suggesting what many think ought to be included in a quality physical education curriculum that leads to physical activity for a lifetime.

It must be emphasized, however, that the *National Standards* are designed for programs that have daily physical education for grades K–12. Even then, however, the standards may represent optimistic goals. The challenge for many schools and districts that have physical education only one or two days a weeks is to carefully select the standards that they can truly accomplish in the amount of time they have allocated for their physical education programs. The standards can also provide the foundation for a strong argument for more time for physical education in the school day. It always difficult to decide which of the standards a school or district will ignore because of the lack of time allocated for physical education.

Since the *National Standards* were published in 1995, a number of states have revised or developed state standards, many of them based on the *National Standards*. If you are interested in seeing if your state has developed standards, go to PE Central (www.pecentral. org/professional/statestandards.html). It might be interesting also to see how your state standards compare to the ones developed at the national level.

Summary

Teaching by skill themes focuses on developing children's competence in a variety of motor skills and movement concepts that will eventually enable the children to acquire confidence and enjoy physical activity throughout their lifetimes. Games, sports, gymnastics, and dance typically require children to use combinations of motor skills and movement concepts that are developed only after a substantial amount of practice. Therefore, the teacher places emphasis on helping children acquire the skills and confidence necessary to participate eventually in games, gymnastics, and dance with enjoyment and confidence.

Teaching by themes also involves revisiting the same skills or concepts continually throughout the program at different times and in different contexts. In preschool and the primary grades, the focus is on learning the vocabulary associated with the movement concepts. Once this has been learned, the emphasis shifts to the skill themes. In fact, however, the skill themes and movement concepts constantly interact, as depicted in the movement analysis framework (wheel). The progression and activities for each of the skill themes are illustrated by a spiral. The spiral is a visual reminder that the child revisits each task to enhance skill acquisition and retention and that skills are best learned when they are presented in a progression from basic to advanced.

Support for the skill theme approach can be found in three national statements, the *National Standards for Physical Education* (NASPE, 1995, 2004), *Developmentally Appropriate Physical Education Practices for Children* (Council on Physical Education for Children [COPEC],

1992), and *Appropriate Practices for Elementary School Physical Education* (COPEC, 2000). Essentially, these sources recommend that physical education programs at the preschool and elementary school levels focus on helping children improve their fundamental motor skills in relatively simple environments. Physical fitness, rather than being a separate unit, is interwoven throughout the program as we help children understand and value its importance while they also learn to develop their own programs of physical fitness.

Reading Comprehension Questions

1. What do children need to learn in physical education before they're ready to play a game? Why?
2. What are movement concepts? How do they modify skill themes?
3. How can you distinguish skill themes from movement concepts?
4. What does "revisiting themes" mean?
5. What does the spiral indicate about skill development? (Use Figure 3.1, the wheel, to explain your answer.)
6. What three skill themes relate most directly to dance? To games? To gymnastics? You may not use the same skill theme twice.
7. Explain how two skill themes might be combined in a task and write three samples for a third-grade class.
8. Select a team sport. List five examples of how space awareness concepts are important for that team to succeed. You may want to refer to Chapter 16 for the more expanded explanation of skill themes.
9. Explain what the authors mean when they write that the skill themes may be used to develop a program that reflects the content suggestions in the *National Standards*.
10. Attempt to locate your state physical education standards at PE Central (www.pecentral.org/professional/statestandards.html). (If your state has not posted them, you can refer to the national standards.) Find three examples of state (national) standards for the elementary school grades that directly address the teaching of movement concepts or skill themes. Copy the standard (include the grade level and standard number) and indicate which skill theme or movement concept the standard addresses.

References/Suggested Readings

Council on Physical Education for Children. (1992). *Developmentally appropriate physical education practices for children: A position statement of the Council on Physical Education for Children.* Reston, VA: National Association for Sport and Physical Education.

Council on Physical Education for Children. (2000). *Appropriate practices for elementary school physical education: A position statement of the National Association for Sport and Physical Education.* Reston, VA: National Association for Sport and Physical Education.

Gallagher, J. (1984). Making sense of motor development: Interfacing research with lesson planning. In J. Thomas (ed.), *Motor skill development during childhood and adolescence* (pp. 123–138). Minneapolis, MN: Burgess.

Holyoak, C., & Weinberg, H. (1988). *Meeting needs and pleasing kids: A middle school physical education curriculum.* Dubuque, IA: Kendall Hunt.

National Association for Sport and Physical Education. (1992). *The physically educated person.* Reston, VA: National Association for Sport and Physical Education.

National Association for Sport and Physical Education. (2004). *Moving into the future: National standards for physical education* (2nd ed.). Reston, VA: National Association for Sport and Physical Education.

National Center for Chronic Disease Prevention and Health Promotion, Centers for Disease Control and Prevention. (1977). Guidelines for school and community programs to promote lifelong physical activity among young people. *Journal of School Health, 76*(6), 202–219.

Schmidt, R. A. (1977). Schema theory: Implications for movement education. *Motor Skills: Theory into Practice, 2,* 36–48.

Stanley, S. (1977). *Physical education: A movement orientation* (2nd ed.). New York: McGraw-Hill.

Physical Fitness and Wellness for Children

Intelligence and skill can only function at the peak of their capacity when the body is healthy and strong.

—John F. Kennedy

- The focus of fitness in elementary school physical education has shifted from strenuous exercise programs to physical activity as a preventative for disease and a formula for good health.

- Physical fitness has shifted from skills-related/athletic to health-related fitness.

- The revised formula for fitness recommends endurance-type physical activity of moderate intensity and 60 minutes of cumulative activity for most, preferably all, days of the week.

- Physical fitness for youngsters centers around understanding the health-related fitness components and concepts of fitness, and appreciating the importance of being physically active.

- The purpose of fitness assessment is to identify areas of concern and assist youngsters in establishing personal fitness goals; fitness assessment should never be used for assigning grades for children.

- Physical fitness is a product of movement that provides children with skills, confidence, and enjoyment.

- Physical fitness becomes a process, maintained through a physically active lifestyle that begins in childhood.

- Wellness encompasses emotional, mental, spiritual, social, and environmental well-being as well as fitness.

- The concepts of wellness (nutrition, personal safety, substance abuse, personal and social responsibility, and mental/emotional health) are partners with fitness and physical activity for a healthy lifestyle.

The term *physical fitness* brings to children an image of Olympic athletes, professional sports heroes, and weight lifters with bulging muscles. Physical fitness testing all too often brings moans and negative memories of unattainable goals, a self-concept that suffered on each test day, group calisthenics, and running without pleasure. Many people view physical fitness as synonymous with physical education, attainable only through a strenuous exercise program. We believe physical fitness is an integral part of physical education, a product of a quality physical education program.

The first alarm on children's physical fitness was sounded in the mid-1950s in response to a comparison of fitness levels of American and European children. The Kraus-Weber test battery had a significant impact on physical education programs in schools, resulting in increased emphasis on exercises to improve physical fitness in children and youth and fitness as the major curricular focus for physical education. The second alarm on children's fitness was sounded with the linkage of physical fitness in childhood to the prevention of cardiorespiratory and coronary disease in adults, as well as of the degenerative diseases of hypertension and diabetes. The American Academy of Pediatrics reported children as young as 8 years with risk factors of coronary disease (Olsen, 1990). The result was a curricular shift to health-related fitness and a renewed emphasis on activities to boost fitness components.

The alarm sounding today focuses on children's lack of physical activity and the increase in overweight and obese children. Childhood obesity in the United States has reached epidemic proportions!

- The children in our schools today are predicted to be the first generation *not* to outlive their parents (Katz, 2004).
- Childhood obesity has tripled in the last two decades, with disproportionately higher numbers for African American, Hispanic, and Native American children, and children from families at low socioeconomic levels (Satcher, 2003).
- Health care costs related to obesity range between $90 billion and $120 billion per year.
- Obesity is a major risk factor for the degenerative diseases of hypertension, heart disease, and type 2 diabetes.
- It is estimated that 1 in 3 children born in 2000 will develop type 2 diabetes unless the obesity epidemic is reversed (McConnaughey, 2003).
- The health risks of obesity can be largely managed through physical activity (Welk & Blair, 2000).
- Obesity is a health issue, an emotional issue, a social issue.

Inactivity is a major cause of obesity in the United States.

- Most people in the United States do not achieve the recommended minutes of physical activity daily (Centers for Disease Control and Prevention [CDC], 2003).
- Physical activity decreases with age; girls are less active than boys. Disparities exist for minority populations—children and adults.
- Children who are physically inactive tend to be less active as adults.
- Physical inactivity is a health issue, an environmental issue, an emotional issue.

The importance of physical activity as a preventative for disease and a formula for good health places the emphasis of physical fitness on a broad range of health-enhancing physical activities. Enjoyment and skill development are the two key factors given by children and adolescents as reasons to engage in and maintain programs of physical activity (Gately et al., 2000; Lohman et al., 2004).

Physical fitness is a product of movement that provides children with confidence, skills, and enjoyment. Through quality physical education, fitness becomes a process, attained and maintained through health-related physical activity.

In this chapter we provide an overview of physical fitness for elementary-school-age children. As the authors of *Children Moving*, we see physical fitness for children as health-related fitness. We discuss the components of physical fitness and, specifically, health-related fitness for children. We present physical fitness as an integral part of the elementary physical education curriculum and discuss the teaching of fitness concepts to children and ways of improving specific areas of fitness both within and beyond the school setting. Physical fitness as a process, a part of a quality program of physical education, is inherent throughout the chapter; it is the philosophy we have held since the idea of fitness for children was first introduced in the second edition of *Children Moving* (1987).

Physical . . . Fitness, Activity, Education

Healthy People 2010 (U.S. Department of Health & Human Services [USDHHS], 2000a) has as one of its two goals to increase years and quality of healthy life, with physical fitness and activity identified as a focus area. *Healthy People 2010* also identifies the 10 leading indicators that most greatly affect health for individuals and communities; physical activity is number one on that list. This focus on the importance of physical activity for health fitness is also supported in the Surgeon General's report (USDHHS, 1996) and in the *National Standards for Physical Education* (National Association for Sport and Physical Education [NASPE], 2004a).

Both the Surgeon General's report and the *National Standards for Physical Education* shift the focus from strenuous exercise as a prerequisite for health and fitness to physical activity and the development of an active lifestyle, with physical inactivity portrayed as hazardous to health.

Principles of Fitness Training

With the new guidelines for physical activity, the long-standing frequency-intensity-time/duration (FIT) formula for physical fitness now emphasizes physical

activity for a lifetime. The revised formula recommended in the Surgeon General's report for reducing health risks and improving health in adults is:

- Frequency: most, preferably all, days of the week
- Intensity: moderate
- Time/duration: 60 minutes cumulative

A frequency of at least three days per week of vigorous exercise is now *"most, preferably all, days of the week, of moderate intensity physical activity."* A minimum of 15 minutes of exercise with sufficient intensity to create overload is now *"at least 60 minutes of cumulative activity."*

Although the old frequency-intensity-duration formula is still applicable for athletic fitness, the new formula places the focus on physical activity rather than calisthenics—and on making physical activity a habit that will lead to a physically active lifestyle.

The principles of fitness training—frequency, intensity, and time—when applied to children can best be stated as *fun, intrinsic motivation,* and *two C's: competence and confidence* (Corbin, 1986). All activities in physical education, including physical fitness, should be fun. Pain is not the name of the game in fitness for children. If fitness activities are fun and if children experience success, they will be intrinsically motivated to be physically active outside the school environment. They will be motivated to improve themselves. Children who participate in physical education programs that are designed for maximum participation and that provide challenges appropriate to skill levels develop confidence in themselves as they develop competence in the skills of physical education. This combination of competence and confidence motivates children to adopt lifestyles that include moderate to vigorous activity on a regular basis. Our task as teachers of elementary physical education is to provide physical education programs that give children confidence, skills, and enjoyment and in doing so we provide (1) fitness for the present and (2) a desire to continue physical activity and as a result, fitness for the future.

Guidelines for Physical Activity

The importance of establishing physical activity habits in childhood is supported in the research. Children who are physically inactive are less likely to participate in physical activities on a regular basis as adults. Children who are active tend to be more active as adults. However, just as guidelines for children's exercise and fitness (principles of training) in the past were based on research for adults, adult physical activity guidelines for good health have been imposed on children.

Physical Fitness and the *National Standards for Physical Education*

Standard 3: Participates regularly in physical activity

Standard 4: Achieves and maintains a health-enhancing level of physical fitness

The *National Standards for Physical Education* (NASPE, 2004a) recognize the importance of physical fitness for children, with an emphasis at the elementary level on the learning of skills, knowledge, and behaviors that will enable children to be physically active now and in their adult years. The focus for children in the early elementary years is the enjoyment of activity: positive participation in physical education on the playgrounds of school and community and in active play. As children grow and mature, the focus is on an awareness of fitness concepts and their importance coupled with the development of skills and knowledge for regular participation in meaningful activity. In the *National Standards*, fitness is viewed as a product of a physically active lifestyle; a physically active lifestyle is the product of movement competency and knowledge gained through the *process* of positive participation in physical activity.

With the shift to moderate activity and cumulative time throughout the day, a Children's Lifetime Physical Activity Model (Corbin & Pangrazi, 1994) emerged, with good health and optimal functioning as a goal for all children. The Children's Physical Activity Model, emphasized the development of skills, the learning of lifetime physical activities, and fitness through activity.

The basic tenets of the Children's Physical Activity Model served as the foundation for the development of the *Physical Activity for Children Guidelines* by the Council on Physical Education for Children (NASPE, 2004b). The guidelines include the following recommendations:

- Children should accumulate at least 60 minutes, and up to several hours, of age-appropriate physical activity on all, or most, days of the week. This daily accumulation should include moderate and vigorous physical activity with the majority of the time being spent in activity that is intermittent in nature.
- Children should participate in several bouts of physical activity lasting 15 minutes or more each day.
- Children should participate each day in a variety of age-appropriate physical activities designed to achieve optimal health, wellness, fitness, and performance benefits.
- Extended periods (periods of two hours or more) of inactivity are discouraged for children, especially during the daytime hours.

Young children are active by nature; movement is their learning. Physical activity is their key to fitness. It is important then to establish guidelines for the selection of physical activity for children, physical activity that contributes positively to the child's health and well-being during the elementary school years and beyond.

The Physical Activity Pyramid from the *Physical Activity for Children* guidelines (NASPE, 2004b) outlines the physical activities appropriate for elementary-school-age children with contributions to lifetime activity and a physically active lifestyle (Figure 4.1). With a goal of 60-plus minutes of daily physical activity for all children, the pyramid depicts the types of physical activity appropriate for children, as well as the amount of activity recommended within each category.

Children should receive the largest amount of their activity at Level 1; for children ages 5 to 9 these are the activities that involve the large muscles and have very little formal organization (e.g., active play). The large-motor, natural play of children is considered to be lifestyle physical activities for children. Level 2 activities are a combination of those that have an aerobic effect (e.g., jogging, biking, and swimming) and the basic skills of physical education. Younger children are encouraged to participate in free play activities that make their hearts beat faster and make them sweat. Children ages 10–12 will begin sports involvement and more vigorous physical activities. Although sports involvement appears on the Physical Activity Pyra-

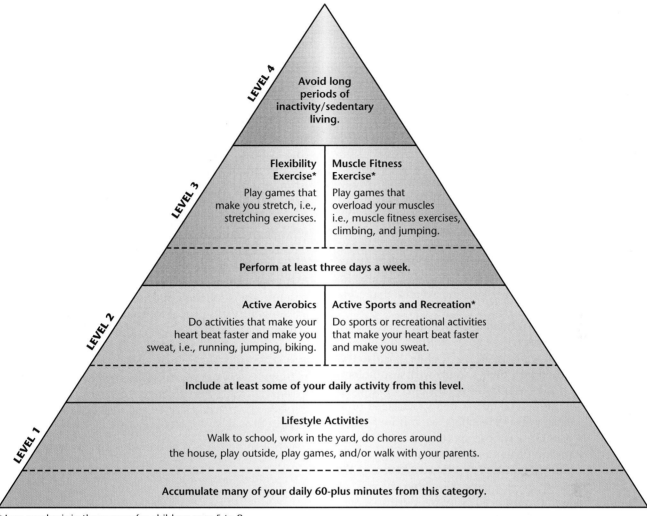

LEVEL 4

Avoid long periods of inactivity/sedentary living.

LEVEL 3

Flexibility Exercise*

Play games that make you stretch, i.e., stretching exercises.

Muscle Fitness Exercise*

Play games that overload your muscles i.e., muscle fitness exercises, climbing, and jumping.

Perform at least three days a week.

LEVEL 2

Active Aerobics

Do activities that make your heart beat faster and make you sweat, i.e., running, jumping, biking.

Active Sports and Recreation*

Do sports or recreational activities that make your heart beat faster and make you sweat.

Include at least some of your daily activity from this level.

LEVEL 1

Lifestyle Activities

Walk to school, work in the yard, do chores around the house, play outside, play games, and/or walk with your parents.

Accumulate many of your daily 60-plus minutes from this category.

* Less emphasis in these areas for children ages 5 to 9.

Figure 4.1 Physical Activity Pyramid.
Source: Physical Activity for Children: A Statement of Guidelines for Children Ages 5–12 (2nd ed.). (2004). Reston, VA: NASPE.

mid for older children at Level 2, the focus is on self-selection by the child and the match to the needs and interests of the child as the primary factor for selection. The key in Level 2 is some vigorous physical activity during the week for all children—free play, recreation, sports. Level 3 activities include a selection of developmentally appropriate physical activities to reinforce the fitness concepts of muscular strength and flexibility. Level 4 is reserved for "quiet" time set aside each day for play types other than vigorous physical activity. As the pyramid is ascended from Level 1 to Level 4, the amount of time spent at each level decreases. Thus, quiet/nonactive time, while important, receives less emphasis than active play. The Physical Activity Pyramid guidelines are based on children's needs and developmental characteristics; the guidelines focus on developmentally appropriate physical activity, skill development, and fitness through activity. The skills of physical education are the tools to maintain health and fitness (NASPE, 2004b, p. 17).

Fitness in the Physical Education Curriculum

Research has shown that children can be trained and coached in the components of fitness if (1) exercises are maintained at a rate of intensity high enough to produce the desired results, that is, Olympic-style training schedule, and (2) diversified programs of physical education are replaced with programs of just physical fitness a minimum of three times per week. Both these concepts, however, are in direct opposition to our beliefs about activity programs for children.

The use of calisthenics is unacceptable in children's physical education. Formal exercises are unrelated to child life situations and have very little, if any, carry-over value.

—Neilson & Van Hagen, 1935

Caution must be used in involving children in intensive training programs and/or distance running because short-term gains may be outweighed by long-term detriments, for example, bone growth damage and lack of interest and motivation in later years.

Programs of strenuous calisthenics for children can result in "winning the battle but losing the war." We may develop fitness in children for the period of time they're under our control, but the negative feelings associated with the forced exercise/activity often lead to negative feelings toward activity and exercise that continue into adulthood.

We try to present moderate to vigorous activity as an enjoyable experience so that children develop a positive attitude toward an active lifestyle. We also try to provide children and their parents with a sufficient knowledge of fitness and training concepts to be wise consumers of commercial fitness items, packaged programs, and health spas. As teachers, we can help children and their parents choose sports and activities to attain and maintain fitness and have fun doing so. We can also help students set realistic physical fitness goals for themselves. Fitness is a personal matter; its goal is self-improvement toward healthy living. Within our elementary physical education curriculum we can teach basic concepts of fitness, design our lessons to promote the fitness components, and help children build a repertoire of exercises for their personal use.

Heart-Rate Monitors and Pedometers

Young children enjoy learning to listen to the changes in heart rate as a result of vigorous exercise or physical activity and learning to calculate their pulse rate. Older elementary students enjoy using heart-rate monitors to assist in attaining and maintaining the level of exercise or activity needed for health benefits. Heart-rate monitors can also assist teachers in determining the amount of time spent within the physical education class with heart rates elevated for vigorous physical activity.

Pedometers can be excellent instruments for increasing children's awareness of their physical activity level. Comparing the number of "steps" taken while participating in various types of physical activity helps students categorize the intensity level—low, moderate, vigorous—of activities. Wearing pedometers dur-

ing recess and after school/at home will assist children in assessing their individual levels of activity and the amount of cumulative activity they attain in a given time period and in different environments (e.g., on the playground, in organized sports, in free play).

Children enjoy charting their steps for "A Walk Across America," matching steps with a hiker on the Appalachian Trail, calculating the miles (and steps) to various destinations within the state, or climbing Mt. Everest. Classroom teachers appreciate the reinforcements of mathematics and geography lessons. It is important to remember that 10,000 steps as a daily goal is a target number of steps set for adults. It is a goal that is too high for sedentary individuals or those with chronic diseases; it is a number that is low for many children during an average day. If pedometers are used to motivate children for increased physical activity, it is important to set personal goals after establishing baseline steps for the child, specific health goals, and sustainability of the goal for that child in a routine day (Tudor-Locke, 2002).

Thomas Jefferson introduced pedometers to America. They came into the commercial market in Japan in 1965 under the name of manpo-meter (manpo in Japanese means 10,000 steps).

—Hatano & Tudor-Locke, 2001

Physical Fitness: A Definition

Physical fitness is the capacity of the heart, blood vessels, lungs, and muscles to function at optimum efficiency. In previous years, fitness was defined as the capacity to carry out the day's activities without undue fatigue. Automation, increased leisure time, and changes in lifestyles following the Industrial Revolution meant this criterion was no longer sufficient. Optimum efficiency is the key. Physical fitness is now defined as the body's ability to function efficiently and effectively in work and leisure activities, to be healthy, to resist hypokinetic diseases, and to meet emergency situations (Corbin et al., 2001).

What is fitness?

Fitness is health in a body.

Hypokinetic diseases are those diseases or conditions associated with lack of physical activity or too little regular exercise.

—CORBIN ET AL., 2001

Physical fitness in the past focused on *skill-related* components—muscular strength, balance, power, speed, agility, and endurance—associated with athletic performance. In more recent years, fitness has centered around factors pertaining to a healthy lifestyle. The components of *health-related* fitness are muscular strength and endurance, flexibility, cardiovascular efficiency, and body composition.

Components of Health-Related Fitness

The four components of fitness discussed in this section constitute health-related physical fitness for children.

Muscular Strength and Endurance

Muscular strength is the amount of force a muscle can produce; *muscular endurance* is the muscle's ability to produce that force for a period of time. Children who are normally active and healthy possess sufficient leg strength for participation in activities. However, today there's growing concern over the upper-body strength of children and adolescents. Fewer physical chores, a decrease in safe outdoor play spaces, and an increase in sedentary activities, such as television and computers, have produced a generation of youngsters often described as excellent in the fine motor skills—using a mouse and a keyboard—but very weak in arm and shoulder strength. Lack of strength in the back and abdominal muscles is associated with poor posture and with lower back problems in later life. The vigorous physical activities that develop cardiovascular endurance also develop muscular strength and endurance in the legs. Upper-arm and shoulder strength and abdominal strength are enhanced through activities that focus on supporting weight on hands, transferring weight involving hands, gymnastics balances requiring muscular tension, stretching actions of the trunk, and challenging activities on gymnastics and playground equipment (see Chapters 22 and 23, and Appendices 4A and 4B at the end of this chapter).

Flexibility

Flexibility is the ability to use joints fully; it's the capacity of a joint to move through its potential range of motion. Very young children are extremely flexible, seemingly capable of moving their bodies in innumerable positions. With few exceptions, children remain flexible throughout their elementary school years.

Flexibility can be increased through stretching the muscles, tendons, and ligaments. Activities that emphasize extending the range of motion, such as dance and gymnastics, help children attain and maintain flexibility. Activities that promote stretching actions and extending the range of motion are incorporated into the skill themes of transferring weight, rolling, and balancing within stretching, curling, and twisting actions. See Chapters 22 and 23 for appropriate tasks.

Flexibility is specific to each joint; therefore, we carefully select activities that increase flexibility in various muscle groups, that is, the legs, lower and upper back, and shoulders. Children benefit from being taught the concept of specificity and exercises to enhance each muscle group, so they develop a cognitive understanding of the relationship between individual exercises and the specific muscle group they enhance.

Children involved in competitive athletics may experience a lack of flexibility in certain muscles as other muscles are emphasized for the particular sport. All stretching actions should emphasize a static stretch, in which the child slowly moves the joint or muscle to its stretching point and holds the position, rather than bouncing to force the body into position. As we point out in Chapter 17, slowness of movement is a difficult concept for children to grasp, yet it is a most important one.

Cardiovascular Efficiency

Cardiovascular efficiency is the body's ability to undergo vigorous exercise for a long time. Children who are physically fit have sufficient endurance to participate in vigorous activities without undue fatigue. These children can participate longer and play harder than those less fit. Cardiovascular efficiency is developed through moderate to vigorous physical activity that increases the heart rate for extended periods of time. Jumping rope, jogging, swimming, and fitness walking are examples of aerobic activities that promote cardiovascular efficiency. Within our physical education classes, we plan activities to promote cardiovascular efficiency; see Chapters 19, 20, 21, 25, and 26 and the appendices at the end of this chapter for ideas.

Body Composition

Body composition is the amount of fat cells compared with lean cells in the body mass. Lean body mass is the nonfat tissue of muscles, bones, ligaments, and tendons. Body composition is measured by skinfold thickness. Skinfold thickness remains relatively constant until age 7, after which it gradually increases until puberty. For girls, the gradual increase continues throughout adolescence; for boys, the percentage of body fat levels off or decreases.

A certain amount of body fat is essential for good health, but an extremely high or low amount of body fat is unhealthy. With the nation's emphasis on leanness, children often have misconceptions about fatness versus leanness in body composition. Children also confuse body weight and body composition. Lean muscle mass actually weighs more than the same amount of fat tissue; therefore, body weight can't be used to determine body composition.

A person's percentage of body fat is determined by heredity, nutrition, and level of activity. Increased activity can decrease body fat; however, best results are obtained through a combination of activity and diet. Body composition is a fitness component that can't be changed in a short period of time; adjustments in nutritional habits and lifestyle must be carefully planned and continued for a long time. These changes require the involvement of not just the child but also the child's family. It isn't enough to guide the child into healthy nutritional habits for school lunch and active participation during physical education and recess. To be successful, the nutrition-and-lifestyle package must be carried out at home, as well as at school. We try to be extremely sensitive to parents' perceptions, emphasizing nutrition and activity for healthy living and trying to avoid negative assessment of the family's lifestyle and eating habits. (Nutrition and activity for good health are discussed later, in the wellness section of this chapter.)

Concepts of Physical Fitness

As noted earlier, health-related fitness includes four components: abdominal and upper-body muscular strength and endurance; flexibility; cardiovascular efficiency; and body composition. Fitness concepts in elementary physical education center around children's understanding of fitness, an awareness of the linkage of fitness to good health, and a working knowledge of activities that promote a healthy level of fitness:

Physical Fitness

It is important that teachers help children understand these critical concepts about physical fitness:

- Physical fitness is important for good health.
- Physical fitness is improved with regular physical activity and exercise.

- Being physically active is fun.
- Daily physical activity or active play has positive health benefits.
- Body size does not determine fitness; physical fitness is not bulky muscles.
- Good exercise and physical activity habits begin in childhood.
- Exercise and physical activity should be a daily habit, like brushing your teeth.
- Fitness doesn't just happen; you prepare and practice.
- Athletic fitness is different from health-related fitness.
- Fitness has several components, and a truly physically fit person is healthy in each area.
- To develop a specific fitness component, for example, muscular strength, you must do exercises and activities targeted for that component.

In addition, the following are important concepts for teachers to remember:

- An emphasis on conditioning for sports is not appropriate at the elementary-school-age level.
- Overload of muscles and bones can be accomplished through activity for young children.
- Given the opportunity to be active, children will do so.
- Because physical activity participation declines as boys and girls reach adolescence, the teaching of the concepts and behaviors of fitness in the elementary school years is critically important.

Health-Related Fitness

Fitness concepts for each of the components of health-related fitness center around children's understanding of that component, its linkage to good health, and activities that promote that area of health-related fitness. Here we highlight concepts associated with each of the components of health-related fitness as they relate to elementary school children.

Muscular Strength and Endurance It is important that teachers help children understand these critical concepts about muscular strength and endurance:

- Muscular strength is the amount of force the muscles can produce, that is, how strong the muscle is; muscular endurance is how long the muscles can produce the force.
- Muscles become stronger by exercising them; the longer muscles are worked, the stronger they become.
- Muscular fitness develops from exercising longer (an increase from 5 minutes to 10 minutes of jog-

ging) and/or from exercising more (an increase from one to two reverse pull-ups).

- Muscular strength and endurance are important so that you can perform daily activities and play without getting tired quickly.
- Muscular strength is specific; different muscles require different exercises.
- Poor posture is often the result of poor muscle tone.

In addition, the following are important concepts for teachers to remember:

- Activities that require children to move and lift their body weight, as opposed to forced exercise and conditioning, are desirable at the elementary school level.
- Weight training is not appropriate for elementary students; overload of muscles and bones can be accomplished through physical activity.
- Lack of upper-body muscular strength can be very discouraging for children; therefore, focus on attainable goals and praise for progress.
- Girls may experience a decrease in upper-body muscular strength with the onset of puberty.

Flexibility These are the critical concepts children should understand about flexibility:

- Flexibility is the range of motion in a joint—the elasticity of the muscles and connective tissues.
- Stretching exercises promote range of motion and increase the length of the muscle, thus improving and maintaining flexibility.
- Flexibility is joint specific. You may be very flexible in one joint and not in another.
- You must continue to exercise to maintain flexibility.
- Stretching should be done slowly, without bouncing.
- Stretching and/or gentle activity before activity will help prevent injury in vigorous physical activity.

In addition, teachers should remember that at the upper-elementary level, boys may begin to experience a decrease in flexibility.

Cardiovascular Efficiency The important concepts about cardiovascular efficiency are:

- Cardiovascular fitness is fitness of the heart, lungs, and circulatory system.
- The heart is a muscle that benefits from exercise, as do other muscles.
- Exercising makes your heart beat harder and faster and will help keep your heart strong and healthy.
- Pulse rate is the beating of the heart as it pumps blood through the arteries.
- Jogging, swimming, and jumping rope are examples of activities that are good for cardiovascular fitness.

- Aerobic activities and exercises are whole-body activities that involve the large muscles of the body.
- Endurance running is not sprinting; pacing is important for endurance activities.
- Being on an athletic team doesn't automatically increase your cardiovascular efficiency; active participation is necessary.

In addition, teachers should remember that participation in continuous aerobic activities of long duration is not desirable for elementary-school-age children.

Body Composition The important concepts about body composition are:

- Body composition consists of the ratio of lean tissue to body fat.
- A certain amount of body fat is needed for good health.
- Too much or too little body fat contributes to a lack of good health.
- Body weight and body composition are not the same.
- A good balance of body fat and lean tissue is attained by good nutrition and physical activity.
- Body composition is affected by heredity, nutrition, and lifestyle.

In addition, teachers should remember that body fat gradually increases for girls throughout adolescence.

Fitness Testing

- The purpose of fitness assessment is to determine those areas that are below the desired range for good health.
- Fitness testing is personal; communication of results is private.
- Factors such as chronological age, maturation, and heredity influence scores on a fitness test.
- The goal of fitness assessment is a healthy level of physical fitness.

The Teaching of Fitness Concepts

Teaching the concepts of fitness involves a series of lessons, distributed throughout the year, that are designed to focus on a fitness concept or component. For example, the concept of physical fitness is chosen as the theme for a lesson in physical education. The concept is introduced with a brief discussion of children's perceptions of a physically fit person: What does a physically fit person look like? Do you know one? How do you know he or she is physically fit? Stations, various activity areas set up around the teaching space, provide active participation, targeting each of the health-related fitness components. Children working with partners discuss and answer questions regarding the activity and its contribution to fitness. Following participation at each of the stations, younger children draw a picture to illustrate a physically fit person; older youngsters write two or three sentences in their journals describing what it means to be physically fit. The lesson concludes with children's responses to a definition of physical fitness. *Lesson plans for introducing fitness components and examples of concept lessons may be found in* On the Move, *the collection of lesson plans designed to accompany* Children Moving. In addition to the focus lessons, support activities are provided for the classroom teacher, bulletin boards highlight the concept, linkage cues are given during instructional physical education, and the concept is revisited and/or expanded throughout the year.

The teaching of fitness in physical education also includes the planning of all instructional lessons to maximize active participation and reflection on the overall fitness of classes and individual children. In addition to instructional physical education, the teaching of fitness to children includes providing opportunities during and beyond the school day. Finally, the teaching of health-related fitness involves assisting those youngsters below the healthy range of fitness in the design of personal programs to meet their needs.

In-School Activities

The Surgeon General's focus on the need for physical activity and the benefits of cumulative activity throughout the day highlight the importance of physical activity beyond instructional physical education. With many school programs not affording children daily physical education, activities beyond the gymnasium are critical for meeting the guidelines for physical activity daily, as well as for establishing the pattern for a lifetime of daily participation. Jogging and jump-rope programs, and physical activity and fitness clubs, are examples of in-school physical activity beyond the instructional physical education program.

Jump-Rope Clubs

Jump-rope clubs can be organized at different skill and interest levels. Names—for example, Tigger the Tiger (basic jumps forward and backward), Dolphin Club (jumping for speed), Jiminy Cricket (tricks), Kanga and Roo (group jumping), and the Masters Club—provide motivation for children as they progress through different skills. Jump Rope for Heart, sponsored by the American Heart Association and the American Alliance for Health, Physical Education, Recreation and Dance (AAHPERD), has contributed significantly to improving cardiovascular efficiency for children. Instructional booklets and information on organizing jump-rope teams are available from local chapters of the American Heart Association. Jump-rope clubs can be organized to meet before school, after school, or during recess. Many schools award certificates for participation in the activity.

Jogging/Walking Clubs

Jogging/walking clubs can also meet before school, after school, or during recess, depending on the teacher's and students' schedules. The following guidelines are helpful for organizing the club:

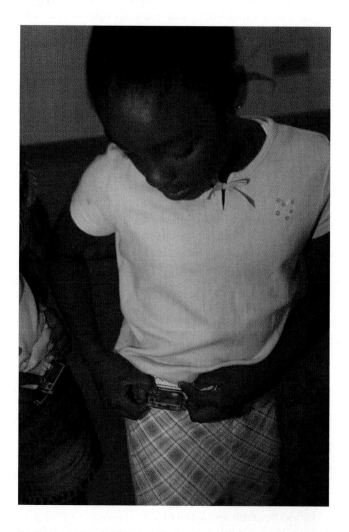

Pedometers allow children to calculate the amount of activity they receive and set goals for the future.

- Obtain written parental permission for each child's participation, including a health statement.
- Teach children the correct foot placement for jogging: feet pointing straight ahead, absorbing force when landing.
- Teach children the difference between leisure walking and power walking. Discuss the difference in heart rate with each type of walking.
- Remind children in the beginning that jogging is not running at top speed or racing with others.
- Joggers and walkers build up distance gradually; as the teacher you will need to set the upper limits.

Children enjoy selecting names for their jogging/walking clubs, such as Roadrunners, Jogging Jaguars, Snoopy and Woodstocks, and Linden Lions Jog/Walk Across America. Bulletin boards and displays portraying the theme add interest for children. For example, a Snoopy-Woodstock theme depicts Snoopy in sweatpants for his morning jog/walk, followed by individual Woodstocks. Each child in the club has a personalized Woodstock. Stick-on numbers on the cafeteria, hallway, or gymnasium wall indicate the number of miles completed. The children post their Woodstocks near the number that corresponds to the miles completed. Classroom teachers, parent volunteers, the physical education teacher, or the child can do the record keeping. Each child's monthly chart (Figure 4.2) shows the number of laps completed per day; cumulative laps/miles are recorded across the chart.

Month _November_

Previous total ___125___ laps = ___4⁵___ miles

Name _Daniel C.,_ _____ Homeroom _____

Figure 4.2 Daily jogging chart.

DAILY JOGGING IS GOOD FOR THE HEART

Membership in a jogging club provides opportunities children to improve their cardiovascular fitness.

Kid Fit and Fun

In several states, educational television or Public Broadcasting System stations provide physical activity and exercise programs for use in the schools. One such program, *Kid Fit and Fun* (Kane, 2004), is a series of minilessons on the concepts of fitness coupled with 15 minutes of physical activity for elementary-school-age children. The programs are designed for classroom use with all activities in the classroom setting. By taping the series and airing it through the school's central media center, classroom teachers are provided options for children's daily involvement in physical activity and exercise with a focus on the concepts of health-related fitness.

Outside-of-School Activities

The decrease in physical activity is recognized as an environmental issue. We are seeing a lack of play spaces, safety concerns for children at play, fewer children riding bikes or walking to school, fewer neighborhood schools, and increases in sedentary leisure activities. Increased emphasis on academics and test scores, coupled with tightening of school budgets, has resulted in decreases in instructional physical education and

These parents promote good physical fitness habits by participating with their children in a cardiovascular activity.

elimination of recess in our schools. Meeting the recommendation of 60-plus minutes of daily physical activity for children can no longer be guaranteed within the school day. Opportunities for physical activity beyond the school setting are important for the children we teach, for their parents, and for the communities that together make our nation.

Fitness clubs, physical activity clubs, and playground parcourses provide additional physical activity for youngsters and also involve their families in maintaining a healthy level of fitness. Family physical activity nights, fitness fairs, and fitness/health checks bring families together to participate in physical activity, as well as to learn the current information on fitness, physical activity, and good health. Appendix 4A at the end of this chapter contains suggested activities to promote family fitness. A brochure containing activities, along with an overview of the relationship of physical activity to good health, can be available at the family events; physical activity and wellness "tips" can also be included in the school newsletter and/or in each physical education report to parents.

Fitness clubs provide additional physical activity time within the school week, increase play activities on the playground, and foster cardiovascular fitness. Fitness clubs can provide additional skill practice for

lifetime activities and choice activities to promote responsible decision making by children and family activities outside the school setting. Such clubs become a cooperative effort among parents, the children, classroom teachers, and the physical education specialist as they all work together to promote increased physical activity and fitness. In the Super Active Kids Fitness Club (East Grand Forks, Minnesota), the physical education specialist devotes one class period per week to additional skill instruction in lifetime physical activity, classroom teachers assist children with record keeping, parents promote and assist children with at-home activity, and children gain physical skills and confidence as they assume responsibility for this portion of their health and fitness.

Students enjoy recording physical activity for a day (or longer) and coding the activity according to intensity (less vigorous, moderate, more vigorous) in relation to physical fitness. Figure 4.3 provides a sample scale for coding.

Fitness and physical activity clubs can meet before school, after school, and on weekends. Children who arrive at school early and/or stay after school in daycare can take part in fitness and physical activity

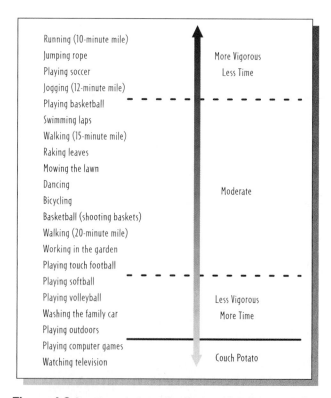

Figure 4.3 Sample scale for coding the intensity of physical activity. *Source:* Adapted from *Physical Activity and Health: A Report of the Surgeon General,* U.S. Department of Health and Human Services, Centers for Disease Control, 1996.

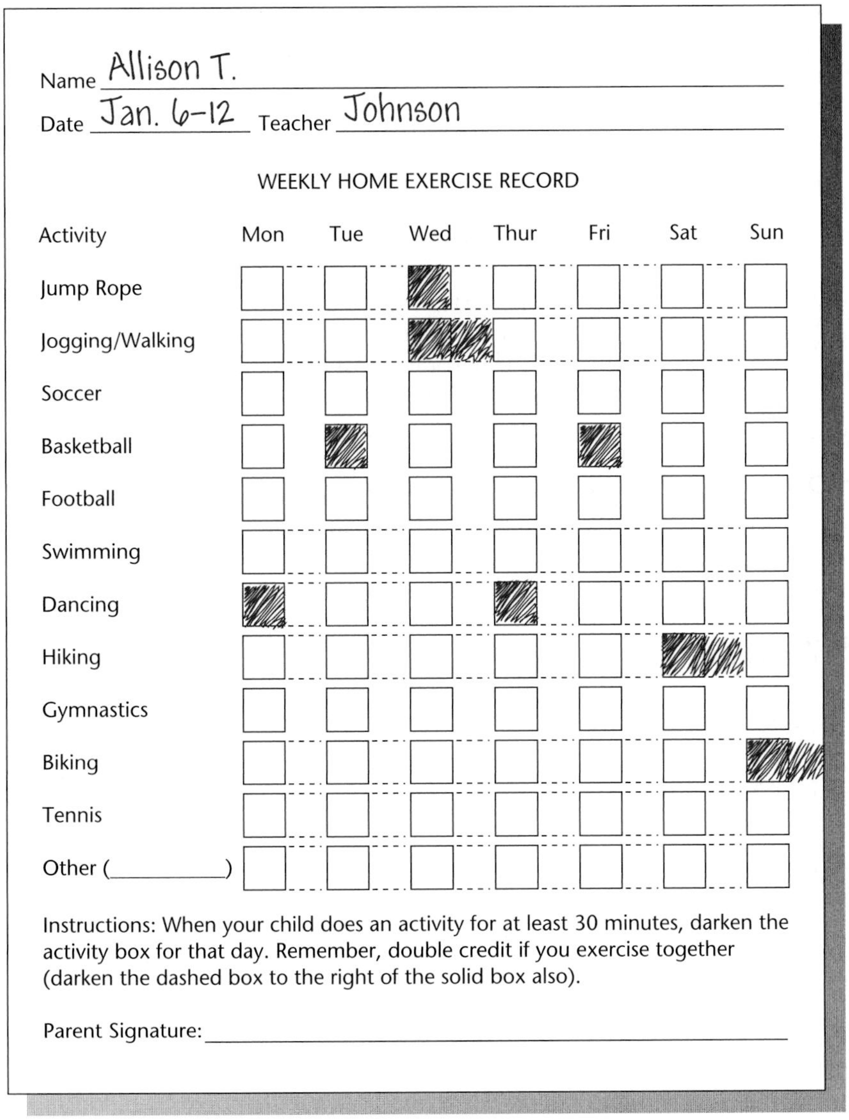

Figure 4.4 Physical activity club recording sheet.

Name Allison T.

Date Jan. 6-12 Teacher Johnson

WEEKLY HOME EXERCISE RECORD

Activity	Mon	Tue	Wed	Thur	Fri	Sat	Sun
Jump Rope			■				
Jogging/Walking			■■				
Soccer							
Basketball		■			■		
Football							
Swimming							
Dancing	■			■			
Hiking						■■	
Gymnastics							
Biking							■■
Tennis							
Other (_____)							

Instructions: When your child does an activity for at least 30 minutes, darken the activity box for that day. Remember, double credit if you exercise together (darken the dashed box to the right of the solid box also).

Parent Signature: _____

programs. Children and their parents can come to the gymnasium on a scheduled weekend time for individual and family activities.

Family fitness programs, such as a physical activity club, can provide additional activity for children outside the school setting. Family support for physical activity and parental modeling are *the* important predictors for the adoption of regular physical activity by children. When designing a physical activity club, choose activities that are readily available in the community, the majority of which require no additional expense for the family. Promote physical activities that the family can enjoy together, as well as those of special interest to children. Introduce the physical activity club to the parents with a letter of invitation and explanation; include in the letter a brief discussion of the health/fitness benefits of physical ac-

tivity, the purposes of the club, and your goals for the students.

Children can record their club participation on a chart like the one in Figure 4.4. Note that double credit is given for family participation with an older sibling or a parent.

Fitness parcourses are permanent outdoor fitness circuits. Parcourses are commercially available, or parents and teachers can build them as a PTA project. A typical parcourse includes stations for exercising various muscle groups. At each station is a large sign or laminated poster with a graphic representation of the exercise and the number of suggested repetitions for both a beginner and an experienced participant. Parcourse stations are often set up around a jogging track to promote cardiovascular activity, such as walking and jogging, as well as muscular strength and endurance and flexibility workouts. Parcourses are excellent opportunities for community and family involvement in physical fitness at the school environment after the normal school day ends, and they provide fitness opportunities for students during recess on non–physical education days.

Active Schools

Physical education teachers can be leaders in the development of the "active school concept," designed to maximize school-based opportunities for reinforcing the relevance and value of physical activity for children (Fox et al., 2004). In cooperation with classroom teachers, parents, PTA/PTO and community leaders, the following strategies can be undertaken to foster increased physical activity for all children:

- Develop "safe routes" to school for walking and biking.
- Develop (and maintain) safe neighborhood playgrounds.
- Permit access to gymnasiums and school playgrounds after school hours.
- Work with classroom teachers to incorporate "active" lessons, such as orienteering, nature walks, mapping.
- Mark outdoor paved surfaces for game play.
- Develop strong linkages with local health and fitness clubs.
- Include an article on ways to increase physical activity in each school newsletter.
- Address the issue of bullying and monitor the playground to ensure safe play for all youngsters.
- Develop a public relations policy for the school that promotes the school as being healthy, active, and safe.
- Collaborate with classroom teachers and community leaders to develop class projects that assist children in learning the environmental issues that affect physical activity, such as safe playgrounds, availability of recreational opportunities, traffic patterns, bike paths, and hiking trails. (Fox & Harris, 2003).

Incorporating Physical Fitness

Teaching physical fitness concepts is an important part of the physical education curriculum, but it doesn't happen by chance; it must be carefully planned. When planning the daily lesson, keep in mind the components of fitness and the muscle groups involved in the activities outlined for the children. Earlier in this chapter, we referred to the skill theme chapters that promote specific fitness components. We believe that through a quality program of physical education; through the promotion of additional "in school and beyond school" physically active, health-enhancing activities; and through working in cooperation with classroom teachers and parents, we can develop the skills and positive attitudes needed for active participation in physical activity, as well as assist children in attaining a healthy level of fitness.

Children who are physically active are more likely as adults to participate in physical activities on a regular basis. Physical activity programs for children are most likely to be effective when they:

- Emphasize enjoyable participation.
- Offer a range of activities that are age and developmentally appropriate.
- Give children the skills and confidence needed to be physically active.

Fitness education for children is most effective within and through quality physical education.

Assessing Physical Fitness

Physical fitness assessments can be used to culminate a unit, to motivate students, as diagnostic screening instruments, and/or as an ongoing process throughout the year. Physical fitness assessment is part of the overall fitness education for children, providing information on their levels of health-related fitness, ways to measure the components of fitness, and the linkage between physical activity and improvements in fitness. We strongly advocate using physical fitness assessments for screening purposes and as an ongoing process. If the physical fitness assessment is to be used as a diagnostic tool, administer the test in early fall. You can then use the test results to help develop yearly plans, assist youngsters in establishing personal fitness goals, and plan remedial programs for individual students. We recommend that children who have extremely low scores be given remedial fitness programs, individualized educational plans (IEPs) for their area(s) of weakness. The physical education teacher can counsel these students individually on ways to improve fitness through physical activity. Programs of activity and exercise can be designed for use at home, and parents can become active participants with their child.

Schools with available space and staffing can create a fitness/wellness lab to which children can come for physical activity and exercise designed for their areas of weakness. Working on their personal fitness

Children enjoy coming to the fitness/wellness lab for additional physical activity.

plans, under the supervision of a trained volunteer and/or the physical education teacher, children follow their prescribed programs of activity, record the activity in their fitness logs, and describe feelings via journal entries. At-home "prescriptions" can be written, for which children complete the activities along with their parents. A monthly calendar can be provided for the child to code (color, star, sticker) at the completion of the activity each day. We have found the at-home prescriptions to be an excellent introduction to family fitness as parents and children take part in the activities together. Examples of prescription activities and exercises for flexibility, muscular strength, and cardiovascular fitness can be found in Appendix 4B at the end of this chapter.

Whether the physical fitness assessment is used as a screening tool in the fall, as a culminating experience for children, or as an ongoing process, it should be an educational endeavor. Each test item should be carefully explained, emphasizing the particular component being tested. All too often, children do poorly on an assessment because they do not understand the directions. Sufficient time should be allowed for practice so that children understand the proper techniques and stretch their muscles. The purpose of the test is to motivate the children to do their personal best, not to trick them. We recommend not recording test scores of children below the fourth grade. Younger children can take the test as an educational experience, but the characteristics of young children do not promote maximum effort and extended concentration on a subject that is of more interest to the teacher than to them.

A key to successful testing is management of the time involved. Physical fitness assessment should not take an exorbitant amount of time. Carefully planning the testing and organizing the class can minimize the time necessary. Self- and peer assessments can greatly reduce the amount of teacher instructional time devoted to testing. For those times when direct teacher involvement in the testing is necessary, we've found it best to structure the study of the theme in games, gymnastics, or dance so the children can work independently while the teacher is involved in the fitness assessment. Thus, the children can continue their study of the theme, their completion of the project, and their practice and refinement of skills.

Several commercial tests are available for fitness assessment. Further information on the specifics of each test, awards systems, and so forth can be obtained by writing to the addresses in Box 4-1. When using a fitness assessment that employs different standards for achievement, we recommend that the interpretation of the test scores be divided into health standards and fitness standards—that is, that the assessor determine

Box 4-1

Physical Fitness Test Packages

Additional information concerning specific physical fitness packages, national norms, awards programs, and so on may be obtained from the following sources:

Fitnessgram

Institute for Aerobics Research
12330 Preston Road
Dallas, TX 75230
www.cooperinst.org/ftgmain.asp

Physical Best

American Alliance for Health, Physical Education, Recreation and Dance (AAHPERD)
1900 Association Drive
Reston, VA 20191
www.aahperd.org/naspe/physicalbest

President's Challenge

President's Council on Physical Fitness and Sports
200 Independence Ave., SW
Room 738H
Washington, DC 20201
www.presidentschallenge.org

what score represents a basic level of health fitness and what score is a measure of athletic fitness/skill performance. For tests with a criterion reference for health fitness, that score is the level needed for good health. Scores at a much higher level are indicative of athletic performance fitness.

Assessment of children's physical fitness should not end with the completion of the test. The recording of scores should be done in a manner that provides ownership to children, is personal and private for each individual, and assists children in setting fitness goals. Children can be active participants in the recording of their fitness scores following test completion. A simple graph can be designed listing test items (Figure 4.5). After the health fitness screening in the fall, each child

is provided his or her scores from the assessment. Using a highlighter, the child colors in the portion of the bar corresponding to the score for each test item—upper bar for fall scores. Completion of the graph provides a visual representation for the child of the areas of fitness in the health fitness range, those above, and those needing remediation. When the children have recorded their scores and reflected on the assessment results, they can write in their journals their feelings about their test results and record their personal fitness goals for the year. When the fitness assessment is repeated in the spring, each child again colors the portion of the bar corresponding to spring scores (lower bar for spring scores), using a different color highlighter. A comparison of fall and spring scores shows

Figure 4.5 Personal fitness profile.

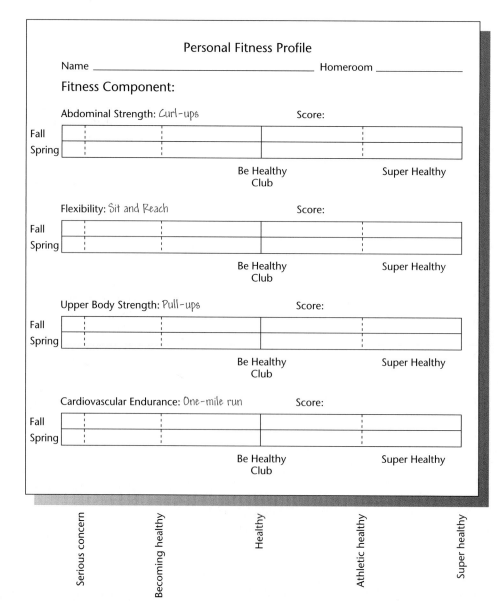

Note: Body composition should not be reported on a child's Personal Fitness Profile.

changes in fitness and progress toward personal goals established in the fall. *Note:* A simple turning of the paper reveals for each child a bar graph of the year's fitness assessments and opportunity for an integrated mathematics lesson.

Fitness comes from being physically active. Being physically active comes from enjoyment of activity, competence in skills, and confidence in self. Enjoyment, competence, and confidence come from quality physical education.

The focus of elementary physical education is the child; the focus of physical fitness should also be the child. No child should be asked to give more than his or her personal best. Scores from the assessment test are personal; they are not to be compared and not to be used for grading purposes. We recommend the following guidelines for the assessment of children's physical fitness:

- Involve students in the assessment process, not just as participants in the test but also in the recording of scores and interpretation of results. Personal involvement in the total process will facilitate acceptance of responsibility for fitness.
- Consider allowing children to select items from a test battery for each component to be assessed. For example, upper-arm strength may be tested with pull-ups, chin-ups, modified pull-ups, or push-ups. Children may make individual choices from the battery.
- Develop an assessment tool that meets your needs: times per week you see the children for physical education, entry-level fitness for children, class size, your goals for fitness.
- Assist the children in setting their personal fitness goals. Following the fall screening and graphing of scores, have the children record in their journals their personal goals for the year. Young children often need teacher assistance in setting realistic goals. All too often the school athlete is the measure of success for children. Instead, goals should be based on a reflection of assessments and increments of success.
- Praise children's accomplishments at the lower end of the spectrum, as well as those at the high-performance level. (In the fall the class cheered Molly's efforts on the mile run [21:00]; in the spring they cheered her accomplishments [16:34].)

Appropriate and inappropriate practices in regard to physical fitness and fitness testing are summarized in Box 4-2.

Jonathan, a large fourth grader, was not looking forward to the one-mile run for spring fitness testing. On the day of testing his mother appeared on the jogging track to encourage him as he began his laps. He completed his mile run in 13:35 minutes. During the last week of school, fourth graders were asked to write in their journals about their favorite activity in physical education—the favorite of all the things they had done during the year. Jonathan's favorite: the one-mile run! Enjoyment is the key to physical activity and fitness for children.

A Final Thought on Fitness

The goal of physical education for children is to enable them to develop health and activity habits that will become a lifestyle throughout adolescence and adulthood. The two most important factors in attaining this goal at the elementary school level are that the children (1) enjoy the fitness activities and (2) master the basic skills of physical education that will enable them to participate successfully in the activities that promote fitness. Only if fitness is fun will the children pursue it outside the two or three times they are with us in physical education class each week and on through middle school, high school, and beyond. The decline in physical activity is now appearing before the end of the elementary school years with adolescents becoming more vulnerable to developing sedentary lifestyles. A combination of biological, psychosocial, and environmental factors have contributed to the decline in physical activity.

Children at the elementary school level must enjoy physical activity, as well as understand and appreciate the importance of physical fitness, if they are to develop lifelong health fitness habits.

Fitness for health is not the same as conditioning for competitive sports participation. We are teachers of children in physical education, not coaches striving for the "gold" in a sports program. Therefore, we focus on the teaching and learning of skills, knowledge, and behaviors that will enable children to value physical activity and be physically active today, tomorrow, and throughout their adult lives.

Wellness

In a broader sense, fitness is wellness—optimal health and well-being. In addition to physical fitness, wellness encompasses the dimensions of emotional,

---

Box 4-2

Appropriate and Inappropriate Physical Education Practices

Component: Developing Health-Related Fitness

Appropriate Practice

Children participate in activities that are designed to help them understand the concepts of health-related fitness and to value the contributions these concepts make to a healthy lifestyle. Activity-based fitness is emphasized rather than fitness through formal exercises or calisthenics.

Fitness is presented as a positive experience in which students feel socially and emotionally comfortable, able to overcome challenges on a personal level. The joy of participation in health-enhancing activity leading to lifetime fitness is the goal of fitness development in elementary school physical education.

Inappropriate Practice

Teacher requires participation in group fitness activities but does not help students understand the reasons for fitness development. The process of fitness development is not monitored, and guidance for setting personal goals and strategies for goal attainment are not provided.

All children are required to do the same fitness activities regardless of their fitness levels.

Teachers do not teach students the difference between health-related and skill-related fitness.

Calisthenics/mass exercise is *the* only avenue for fitness development.

Component: Physical Fitness Testing

Appropriate Practice

Teachers use fitness assessment as part of the ongoing process of helping children understand, enjoy, improve, and/or maintain their physical fitness and well-being.

Test results are shared privately with children and their parents as a tool for developing personal goals and strategies for maintaining and increasing the respective fitness parameters.

As part of an ongoing program of physical education, children are physically prepared in each fitness component so they can safely complete the assessments.

Inappropriate Practice

Teachers administer physical fitness tests once or twice each year for the purpose of identifying children to receive awards or to meet a requirement of the school district or state department.

Children complete physical fitness test batteries without understanding why they are performing the tests or the relationship to their activity level and individual goals. Results are interpreted based on comparison with norms rather than in terms of how they apply to children's future health and well-being.

Individual scores are publicly posted, comparisons are made between student scores, and/or grades are based on fitness scores.

Children are required to take fitness tests without adequate conditioning.

Source: Appropriate Practices for Elementary School Physical Education: A Position Statement of the National Association for Sport and Physical Education. Developed by the Council on Physical Education for Children (COPEC), 2000, Reston, VA: National Association for Sport and Physical Education. Reprinted with permission.

---

mental, spiritual, interpersonal/social, and environmental well-being (Fahey et al., 2003). These dimensions translate for children into learning experiences in nutrition; personal safety (bicycle, auto, water, and fire); drug, alcohol, and tobacco abuse; personal and social responsibility; and mental/emotional health. Fitness in all of these areas results in optimal health and well-being—in other words, in wellness.

The Teaching of Wellness

We are teachers of physical education. Many of us see the children on less than a daily schedule. We are faced with the teaching of skills while dealing with fire drills, assemblies, and photo-day interruptions. Now the teaching of wellness has entered our gymnasium! The introduction of wellness into the physical education curriculum does not mean a reduction of time for teaching physical education. The ideas presented in this chapter are concepts for integration with the classroom teacher and for coordination with community services. We can assist in this endeavor with quotes of the week, bulletin boards, items in the newsletter to parents, teachable moments, and the conscious integration of wellness into our curriculum. We have found the inclusion of wellness to be an asset, not a disruption, to our teaching of physical education.

Technology in Fitness/Wellness Education

The world of technology relative to fitness/wellness education has exploded during recent years. Fitness technology now includes electronic portfolios and heart-rate monitors for upper elementary students, equipment for fitness/wellness labs, interactive computer programs for students, the storage and analysis of fitness data for both students and teachers, and a wealth of information via the Internet. Jogging/walking club members can now connect with other students around the world charting mileage and comparing adventures. The list of Internet resources is almost limitless in fitness, nutrition, and other areas of wellness. We encourage you as teachers of physical education to explore the use of technology in your teaching of physical education; we caution you to use technology to enhance your program of physical education, not as a substitute for quality teaching.

Wellness concepts in elementary physical education center around children's understanding of the concepts and their awareness of the linkage of the concepts to good health.

Nutrition

Children need to understand these important concepts about nutrition:

- Physical activity and good nutrition are *the* team for good health and well-being.
- The body needs food for energy; the body needs energy for activity.
- Food is the fuel that makes activity possible; too little fuel, too little energy.
- Foods are not "good" or "bad"; balance is the key.
- Some fat is essential to supply energy and to insulate and cushion vital organs.
- Carbohydrates supply energy to muscles for maximum performance. They are the main fuel source for the muscles.
- Proteins are needed to form strong bones and muscles. They are the building blocks of body tissues.
- Water makes up 50 to 70 percent of total body weight and is critical for survival. The more active you are, the more water you need.
- Good nutrition is essential for people of all ages.
- The amount of energy a person needs depends on body size, age, gender, health status, and activity.

In addition, teachers should remember to model good nutrition and fitness habits in their own lifestyles and make these evident in the environment in which they work with children.

A number of factors have contributed to the existing state of poor nutrition among school-age children in the United States. A large number of children are responsible for their own meals, especially breakfast and after-school snacks. Children do not choose fruits and vegetables as a favorite snack; neither do young children have the knowledge or skills to prepare healthy meals or snacks. For many children, the foods needed for good nutrition are not available in their homes. Thus, by choice and by circumstance, many children are the victims of poor nutrition.

Busier schedules and more fast-food meals have also contributed to a decrease in good nutrition for America's families. A positive increase in physical activity—that is, organized sports, dance, and gymnastics clubs for children—has been coupled with a decrease in family meals at home. All too often the quickest meal is one from a drive-through, one that is high in fat and low in the balance of nutrients needed for good health.

Although elementary-age children may not be interested in nutrition for good health (after all, they are immortal), we have found that they are very interested in nutrition as it relates to running, jumping, throwing, and being a better athlete. Thus, the appeal of athletics opens the door to educating children about the importance of eating fruits and vegetables, decreasing fats, attaining healthy body weight, and maintaining a balance of physical activity and nutrition as a daily pattern, a childhood pattern that becomes a lifestyle for wellness.

Children at the elementary level need an understanding of the Food Guide in MyPyramid (Figure 4.6),

Figure 4.6 USDA's food and activity guide.
Source: U.S. Department of Agriculture, Center for Nutrition Policy and Promotion, 2005; www.mypyramid.gov.

The new food and activity guide (MyPyramid) focuses on personal choice, moderation, and variety. Food groups are represented in proportionate bands, indicating in general how much food should be selected from each group. The importance of daily physical activity is symbolized by the person climbing the steps—the combination of physical activity and nutrition so essential for good health (www .MyPyramid.gov).

the contribution of the major essential nutrients to building and maintaining healthy bodies, and the necessity of balancing exercise and nutrition in maintaining good health. As children approach puberty, this balance between exercise and nutrition in maintaining proper body weight becomes very important for both boys and girls; however, for young children the emphasis on the balance is for good health.

With the obesity rate among children and adults at an all-time high, and with health problems associated with obesity continuing to emerge, teaching good nutrition is even more important. Teaching nutrition as a wellness concept, with its linkage to physical activity and performance, as well as good health, makes it an ideal concept for integrated activities with classroom teachers. For example, in physical education we discuss the relationship of nutrition to physical activity. The classroom teacher discusses the relationship of nutrition to good health. Working together, we have students record their food intake for 24 hours; categorize the foods according to the food pyramid, then compare their personal pyramid with MyPyramid. With most students finding their food pyramid "out of balance," the discussion of good nutrition becomes very relevant, very personal. *Later in the year, a similar procedure is followed for the building of a Physical Activity Pyramid* (see the Guidelines for Physical Activity section of this chapter).

Physical Activity and Nutrition

Physical activity and good nutrition are the essential ingredients for the body's *good health balance*. Envision a young child first learning to walk a balance beam; the arms are extended outward on either side of the body for good balance. If neither arm is extended or if the extension is only on one side, the child's balance is in jeopardy. In adults we speak of the match between caloric intake and daily energy expenditure, that is, energy balance. In children we call it the *good health balance*.

For reasons cited earlier in this chapter, adults in the U.S. have a tremendous mismatch between caloric intake and energy expenditure, the results of which are the obesity epidemic and the health risks associated with obesity. A combination of larger food portions, more readily available food, a lack of knowledge regarding portion sizes and number of servings within containers, and the abundance of high-fat, high-caloric food means energy expenditure, that is, physical activity, must increase. However, advances in technology and automation have created just the opposite—an environment that supports less physical activity. The same mismatch exists for children. We as teachers must take the lead in creating the *good health balance* for children—a balance of daily physical activity and good nutrition that leads to healthy, physically active lifestyles.

At Linden Elementary School, Oak Ridge, Tennessee, parents and teachers have joined together to form the Healthy Lions Club with a focus on nutrition for children. They have developed policies and brought about changes regarding school lunches, nutritious offerings for midmorning snacks at school, and nutritious birthday celebrations as well as providing parents with suggestions for economical, easy-to-prepare nutritious meals. They have supported daily recess for children, no denial of recess as punishment for incomplete classroom work, and no food fund-raising events for the PTA. Through the efforts of one school, the healthy school club has spread to other schools and their communities.

Personal Safety: Bicycle, Auto, Fire, Water

Important concepts about personal safety include:

- Seat belts save lives. Buckle up before the engine starts; unbuckle only after it stops.
- Helmets prevent head injuries (bicycle, rollerblade, skateboard . . .).
- "Stop, drop, and roll" has meaning for everyone—children and adults.

The concepts of personal safety—bicycle, auto, fire, and water—present excellent opportunities for collaborative endeavors with community agencies. Through demonstrations and hands-on activities, students learn the concepts of wellness in these important areas, leaders in community agencies gain insight into school programs just by being in the schools (with most assemblies held in the elementary school gymnasium, visually scanning bulletin boards and displays tells visitors much about the curriculum), and teachers are provided yet another opportunity for positive public relations.

Excellent resources for educational information about nutrition and the balance between nutrition and physical activity:

Dole: www.dole5aday.com

USDA Food and Nutrition Service: www.fns.usda.gov/eatsmartplayhard

Nutrition Explorations: www.nutritionexplorations.org/index.asp

American Dietetic Association: www.eatright.org

Bicycle safety actually begins as preschoolers take part in Safety City, a playground project that involves youngsters maneuvering "big wheels" and tricycles through miniature streets, learning traffic signals, and meeting police officers. From big wheels and tricycles, children advance to bicycles and bicycle safety, participating in activities that stress safe riding and consideration for others. Working together, the physical education specialist, school PTA/PTO, and the local police department can sponsor a Saturday bicycle safety program. Local police departments welcome the opportunity to teach children the concepts of bicycle safety, conduct safety inspection of bikes, and in many instances provide free helmets to children. Thus, with minimal effort and no loss of physical education instructional time, we can address this important area of wellness.

The concepts of fire safety can be addressed via a school assembly and hands-on activities conducted by the local fire department personnel. We have found fire fighters eager to come to the schools; they bring trucks and ladders for demonstrations, provide active participation in "stop, drop, and roll," as well as "stay low," and teach the basic critical emergency response, "911." Again, with minimal effort and no loss of instructional time, the critical concepts of fire safety are presented to children. For schools in the vicinity of bodies of water and recreational activities, water safety can be addressed in a manner similar to fire safety, that is, through school assemblies and hands-on activities for the children. Our experience with these cooperative endeavors has shown a positive, enthusiastic response from the adults as well as the children, an increased awareness of safety, and tremendous public relations value for the schools.

Drug, Alcohol, and Tobacco Abuse

Important concepts about substance abuse are:

- Drugs, alcohol, and tobacco can kill you.
- There is no such thing as "experimenting" with drugs.

- Physical activity is a healthy replacement for drugs, alcohol, and tobacco.

With children experimenting with drugs, alcohol, and tobacco at increasingly younger ages, it is never too early to educate children on the risks of use and dangers of substance abuse. We can no longer pretend that drug and alcohol use and abuse is limited to older adolescents and young adults. Nor can we pretend that abuse and overdose happens only somewhere else. Elementary-school-age children are experimenting with drugs and alcohol. No socioeconomic level is immune to substance abuse.

Classroom teachers and entire school systems have adopted a variety of programs to educate children on substance abuse, all with the overriding message, "Just say no." Our role as physical educators is that of supporting the classroom teachers in this endeavor, reinforcing the message, and, as with all areas of wellness, serving as a model for children to emulate (Figure 4.7). Physical educators serve a key role for children in the area of substance abuse. With daily reports of professional athletes involved in substance abuse, children receive a confusing message regarding the dangers of drugs and the consequences of use. We can provide positive role models and clear, consistent messages regarding abstinence.

Much research and thought has been given to the reasons individuals use drugs. Two of those reasons

Our coaches said drugs weren't cool
If you take them you're a fool.

If you smoke, you'll probably croak,
And if you're in a gang,
You'll lose the game.

Choose your friends,
Choose them well
'Cause if you don't, you might fail.

We learned to deal with stress.
So we don't get in a mess.
Violence isn't cool
Obey the Golden Rule.

When you do drugs and alcohol,
You'll never do anything at all.
Remember this, remember it right
Drugs do nothing for your life.

Coaches and parents say drugs aren't cool,
We agree; we're not fools!

P. Petrie (Grade 5)

Figure 4.7 A student-generated rap written for an I DARE school assembly.

are boredom and low self-esteem. A youngster actively involved in physical activity and sports is an active youngster. A youngster involved in a quality physical education program develops the skills for successful participation in a variety of sports and physical activities. A solid movement-skills base provides a positive self-image in this important area for children. Thus, physical education has the potential to contribute directly to a healthy, drug-free world for children.

Personal and Social Responsibility

Important concepts for children about personal and social responsibility include:

- I will respect myself and others.
- I will not hurt myself or others.
- I am responsible for myself, my actions, and my behavior.
- There are always choices to be made; each choice presents either positive or negative consequences.

The gymnasiums and playgrounds of our schools provide a rich environment for the development of personal and social responsibility. The physical activity setting provides a miniworld of emotional, interactive situations. Within this world of competition and cooperation, success and failure, and fast-moving action, children make a multitude of decisions on a daily basis. The development of personal and social responsibility—and its importance to the future of our society—is a reminder that we are teachers of children, not just skills, sequences, games, and dances.

The importance of personal and social responsibility is highlighted in the *National Standards for Physical Education,* in two of the six standards:

- Exhibits responsible personal and social behavior that respects self and others in physical activity settings.
- Values physical activity for health, enjoyment, challenge, self-expression, and/or social interaction (NASPE, 2004a).

Don Hellison's work on the development of personal and social responsibility through physical activity (Hellison, 2003) has served as the model for many physical education programs concerned with this critical area of wellness. Many have adopted Hellison's philosophy and adapted his model for acceptance of responsibility in physical education. Figure 4.8 shows Linda Masser's (1990) application of the Hellison model in and beyond the physical education setting.

Although we as physical educators teach in an environment rich in opportunity for the development of personal and social responsibility, it is not enough simply to let children experience decision-making situations. We guide them in the development of acceptance of responsibility through awareness talks, group

What's Your Level?

Level 4: Caring

Home: Helping take care of a pet or younger child

Playground: Asking others (not just friends) to join them in play

Classroom: Helping another student with a math problem

Physical education: Willingly working with anyone in the class

Level 3: Self-responsibility

Home: Cleaning room without being asked

Playground: Returning equipment used during recess

Classroom: Doing a science project not a part of any assignment

Physical education: Undertaking to learn a new skill through resources outside the physical education class

Level 2: Involvement

Home: Helping to clean up supper dishes

Playground: Playing with others

Classroom: Listening and doing classwork

Physical education: Trying new things without complaining and saying I can't

Level 1: Self-control

Home: Keeping self from hitting brother even though really mad at him

Playground: Standing and watching others play

Classroom: Waiting until appropriate time to talk with friends

Physical education: Practicing but not all the time

Level 0: Irresponsibility

Home: Blaming brothers or sisters for problems

Playground: Calling other students names

Classroom: Talking to friends when teacher is giving instructions

Physical education: Pushing and shoving others when selecting equipment

Figure 4.8 Levels of responsibility.

Source: From "Teaching for Affective Learning in Elementary Physical Education" by L. Masser, 1990, *Journal of Physical Education, Recreation and Dance,* 61: 18–19. Used with permission from American Association for Health, Physical Education, Recreation and Dance, and Don Hellison.

meetings, counseling, reflection, time, individual deci-sion making, and our modeling of responsible personal and social actions (Hellison, 2003). Further discussion of Hellison's model for the development of personal and social responsibility can be found in Chapter 9, "Establishing an Environment for Learning."

Responsible adults develop from responsible chil-dren who have had opportunities to make decisions, to experience success and failure, to be accepted, and to accept others. Acceptance of self and others leads to respect for self and others and to personal and social responsibility.

Mental and Emotional Health

Important concepts about mental and emotional health include:

- Accept me as I am.
- Love me.

Additionally, teachers should remember that:

- All children have the right and the need to be loved.
- Acceptance of the child, even on his or her worst days, is critical.
- What happens in elementary school affects a child throughout life.
- The most important influence in a young child's life is his or her parents; the most powerful influence at age 11 and older is the child's peers.
- Perception of self may or may not match reality; perception of self greatly affects self-esteem.

The foundation of the young child's emotional health is self-esteem—how worthy and valuable the individual considers himself or herself (Anspaugh & Ezell, 2004). Everyone needs to be accepted and loved; children are no exception. We as teachers play a critical role in how children view themselves. Our reactions to their skill or lack of skill, our reaction to their mistakes and sometimes loss of control greatly affect their view of themselves. Children's opinions of themselves are established early and are very fragile. A quick, negative response can have a lasting effect on a child. Children with a strong sense of worth and importance are free to develop their potential, better able to resolve per-sonal and interpersonal conflicts, and free to establish their independence and self-expression. R. M. Page and T. S. Page (1993) offer the following suggestions for fostering a positive classroom/gymnasium climate for emotional wellness:

- Quickly learn the names of students, call them by name, and show respect for each child.
- Be sensitive to diverse cultures, ethnicities, and races; strive to view children from their perspectives rather than your own.

- Expect no problems. Expect students to be compe-tent, capable, and eager to learn.
- When problems arise, handle them immediately and consistently.
- Avoid sarcasm, ridicule, and belittling remarks; help students to do the same.
- Avoid all suggestions of criticism, anger, or frustra-tion. Make personal corrections in private.
- Create an atmosphere in which children feel at ease.
- Arrange for a high ratio of successes to failures.
- Avoid encouraging competitiveness between stu-dents in learning activities.
- Demonstrate the characteristics of effective teach-ers: warmth, friendliness, fairness, a good sense of humor, enthusiasm, empathy, openness, spontane-ity, adaptability, and a democratic governing style.

The American Academy of Pediatrics (1996–1999) ap-proaches wellness from a positive viewpoint with a fo-cus on "solutions before problems." All adults—parents, teachers, caregivers—involved in children's lives have the responsibility to ensure that all children have:

Security—the feeling that they are safe and can trust themselves and others.

Order and organization, to help them make sense of the world around them.

Love—unconditional.

Understanding and patience that they in turn will model for others.

Truth and honesty from adults.

Identify, independence, and influence—a sense that they count.

Opportunities to explore and to expand their world freely and happily.

The teaching of wellness at the elementary school level centers around cooperative projects with classroom teach-ers and collaborative endeavors with community leaders. Two resources we have found to be of great value in the incorporating of wellness within our programs of physical education and the planning of the school's wellness program are *School Health: Findings from Evaluated Programs* by the U.S. Department of Health and Human Services (1998) and "Child Health Month" by the American Academy of Pediatrics. *School Health* is a comprehensive listing of programs target-ing the different areas of wellness, with descriptions of each of the programs and names of persons to contact for ad-ditional information. "Child Health Month" is a wellness focus that takes place each October. The American Academy of Pediatrics has educational kits with sample brochures for par-ents, activities for students, display information, and so forth.

Nurturing guidance and discipline to help them learn self-control and self-respect.

Successful life experiences that give them a sense of personal competence and pride and enhance their self-esteem.

Self-esteem—the way people think and feel about themselves and how well they do things that are important to them—is formed at an early age as young children attempt daily tasks and perceive the reaction

of nearby adults. Children's feelings about themselves continue to grow and change with reactions from parents, teachers, and peers as they progress through the elementary and middle school years. Experiences in the gymnasium and on the playground and reactions from classroom teachers (and specifically teachers of physical education) have a great impact on children's self-esteem. We are teachers of children; our interactions with them, our actions, and our language affect not just the moment, but their lives.

Summary

Physical fitness is the capacity of the heart, blood vessels, lungs, and muscles to function at optimum efficiency in work, in leisure activities, and in emergency situations. In previous years, fitness was defined as the capacity to carry out the day's activities without undue fatigue; we are now recognizing that this condition may not be sufficient for healthy hearts and lungs. Optimum efficiency is the key. That efficiency also includes resistance to hypokinetic diseases.

Physical fitness in the past focused on skill-related components—muscular strength, balance, power, speed, agility, and endurance—associated with athletic performance. In more recent years, fitness has centered around those factors pertaining to a healthy lifestyle, health-related fitness, with an emphasis at the elementary level on learning fitness concepts, as well as the skills, knowledge, and behaviors that will enable children to be physically active now and in their adult years. Fitness is a process and product of a physically active lifestyle; a physically active lifestyle is the product of movement competency and knowledge gained through the process of positive participation in physical education and physical activity.

Physical fitness for children includes a health-

related screening each fall, setting of individual goals, a cognitive understanding of the components of fitness, and moderate to vigorous activity on a regular basis. It involves the physical education specialist, the classroom teacher, the child, and the parent(s). Physical fitness can be incorporated into the theme of study, added to the lesson as a group activity, and increased through before- and after-school jogging/walking, jump-rope clubs, and fitness trails/parcourses. The focus of physical fitness for the elementary school child is the development of a positive attitude toward an active lifestyle, a knowledge of the concepts of fitness, and an understanding of how to attain and maintain personal fitness.

Wellness is optimal health and well-being. In addition to physical fitness, wellness encompasses the dimensions of emotional, mental, spiritual, interpersonal/social, and environmental well-being. For elementary school children, these dimensions translate into learning experiences relative to nutrition, substance abuse, personal safety, personal/social responsibility, and mental/emotional health. Physical education and wellness are intricately woven together in the quest for optimal health and well-being for all children.

Reading Comprehension Questions

1. Define *physical fitness*. Why can we no longer define the level of fitness as the capacity to carry out the day's activities without undue fatigue?
2. What is the difference between health-related and skill-related fitness?
3. Why do we emphasize health-related fitness in our programs?
4. What is the focus of fitness at the elementary school level?
5. Discuss the linkage of physical activity to physical fitness and health. Why is this relationship so important to children in our elementary schools?
6. Define *cardiovascular efficiency*. How is it developed? Name several activities that contribute to cardiovascular efficiency.
7. Within our physical education curriculum, what activities contribute to the development of muscular strength?
8. What does the phrase "specificity of flexibility" mean? What are the implications for physical education?
9. Explain the fitness component of body composition. What factors determine an individual's body fat?

10. What is meant by the term *good health balance?* Why is it important for children?
11. How do the *Physical Activity for Children* guidelines (COPEC) affect the physical education curriculum?
12. What is meant by the term *active schools?* Design a collaborative project for working with community leaders, the parent-teacher organization, or local agencies to increase physical activity for children.
13. Define *wellness.* What are the components of wellness for children at the elementary school level?
14. Choose one wellness component. Design a strategy for working with the classroom teacher to teach that component. Include in your action plan the integrating of the component into physical education.
15. Design a plan for community involvement in the teaching of wellness.

References/Suggested Readings

American Academy of Pediatrics. (1996–1999). *Solutions before problems.* Elk Grove Village, IL: American Academy of Pediatrics.

Anspaugh, D. J., & Ezell, G. (2004). *Teaching today's health* (7th ed.). San Francisco: Benjamin Cummings.

Bar-Or, O. (1987). A commentary to children and fitness: A public health perspective. *Research Quarterly 58*(4), 304–307.

Blair, S. N., & Meredith, M. D. (1994). The exercise-health relationship: Does it apply to children and youth? In R. R. Pate & R. C. Hohn (eds.), *Health and fitness through physical education* (pp. 11–20). Champaign, IL: Human Kinetics.

Centers for Disease Control and Prevention. (2003). Prevalence of physical activity, including lifestyle activities among adults—United States, 2000–2001. *MMWR—Morbidity & Mortality Weekly Report, 52*(32), 764–769.

Cooper, K. H. (1991). *Kid fitness.* New York: Bantam Books.

Corbin, C. B. (1986). Fitness is for children: Developing lifetime fitness. *Journal of Physical Education, Recreation and Dance, 57*(5), 82–84.

Corbin, C. B., LeMasurier, G., & Franks, B. D. (2002). Making sense of multiple physical activity recommendations. *PCPFS Research Digest 3*(19).

Corbin, C. B., Lindsey, R., Welk, G. J., & Corbin, W. R. (2001). *Fundamental concepts of fitness and wellness.* New York: McGraw-Hill.

Corbin, C. B., & Pangrazi, R. P. (1992). Are American children and youth fit? *Research Quarterly for Exercise and Sport, 63*(2), 96–106.

Corbin, C. B., & Pangrazi, R. P. (1994). Toward an understanding of appropriate physical activity levels for youth. *Physical Activity and Fitness Research Digest, 1*(8), 1–7.

Council on Physical Education for Children. (2000). *Appropriate practices for elementary school physical education: A position statement of the National Association for Sport and Physical Education.* Reston, VA: National Association for Sport and Physical Education.

Fahey, T. D., Insel, P. M., & Roth, W. T. (2003). *Fit and Well.* New York: McGraw-Hill.

Fox, K. R., Cooper, A., & McKenna, J. (2004). The school and promotion of children's health-enhancing physical activity: Perspectives from the United Kingdom. *Journal of Teaching in Physical Education 23*(4), 338–358.

Fox, K. R., & Harris, J. (2003). Promoting physical activity through schools. In J. McKenna & C. Riddoch (eds.) *Perspectives on health and exercise* (pp. 181–202). Basingstoke, UK: Palgrave Macmillan.

Gately, P. J., Cooke, C. B., Butterly, R. J., Knight, C., & Carroll, S. (2000). The acute effects of an 8-week diet, exercise and educational camp program on obese children. *Pediatric Exercise Science, 12*, 413–423.

Hatano, Y. & Tudor-Locke, C. (2001). Pedometer-assessed physical activity: Measurement and motivations. Paper presented at the American College of Sports Medicine Meeting, Baltimore, MD.

Hellison, D. (2003). *Teaching responsibility through physical activity* (2nd ed.). Champaign, IL: Human Kinetics.

Holt/Hale, S. A. (2006). *Assessing and improving fitness in elementary physical education* (2nd ed.). Reston, VA: NASPE.

Kane, M. (2004). *Kid fit & fun.* Knoxville, TN: East Tennessee Public Communications Corporation.

Katz, D. (2004). How we grew so big. *Time Magazine, 163*, 23.

Kennedy, J. F. (1960). The soft American. *Sports Illustrated, 13*, 15.

Lohman, T. G., Going, S. B., & Metcalfe, L. (2004). Seeing ourselves through the obesity epidemic. *PCPFS Research Digest 5*(3), 1–6.

Masser, L. (1990). Teaching for affective learning in elementary physical education. *Journal of Physical Education, Recreation and Dance, 61*, 18–19.

McAllister, R. (2003). Healthy lunchbox. Washington, DC, LifeLine Press.

McConnaughey, J. (2003, June 16). CDC diabetes warning for children. Associated Press.

National Association for Sport and Physical Education. (2004a). *Moving into the future: National standards for physical education* (2nd ed.). St. Louis, MO: Mosby.

National Association for Sport and Physical Education. (2004b). *Physical activity for children: A statement of guidelines* (2nd ed.). Reston, VA: National Association for Sport and Physical Education.

National Association for Sport and Physical Education. (2005). *Physical best activity guide: Elementary level* (2nd ed.). Champaign, IL: Human Kinetics.

Neilson, N. P., & Van Hagen, W. (1935). *Physical education for elementary schools*. New York: A. S. Barnes.

Olsen, E. (1990, May). 'A' is for active. *American Health*, 73–80.

Page, R. M., & Page, T. S. (1993). *Fostering emotional well-being in the classroom*. Boston, MA: Jones & Bartlett.

Rowland, T. W. (1999). Adolescence: A 'risk factor' for physical inactivity. *Research Digest, 3*(6), 1–8.

Safrit, M. J. (1995). *Complete guide to youth fitness testing*. Champaign, IL: Human Kinetics.

Sallis, J. F., & McKenzie, T. L. (1991). Physical education's role in public health. *Research Quarterly, 62*(2), 124–137.

Satcher, D. (2003, March). Address to American Alliance for Health, Physical Education, Recreation and Dance, New Orleans.

Simons-Morton, B. G., Parcel, G. S., & O'Hara, N. M. (1987). Children and fitness: A public health perspective. *Research Quarterly, 58*(4), 295–302.

Tudor-Locke, C. (2002). Taking steps toward increased physical activity: Using pedometers to measure and motivate. *PCPFS Research Digest 3*(17), 1–6.

U.S. Department of Health and Human Services. (1996). *Physical activity and health: A report of the Surgeon General*. Atlanta, GA: USDHHS, Centers for Disease Control and Prevention, National Center for Chronic Disease Prevention and Health Promotion.

U.S. Department of Health and Human Services. (1997). *Guidelines for school and community programs to promote lifelong physical activity among young people*. Atlanta, GA: USDHHS, Centers for Disease Control and Prevention.

U.S. Department of Health and Human Services Public Health Service. (1998). *School health: Findings from evaluated programs* (2nd ed.). Atlanta, GA: American School Health.

U.S. Department of Health and Human Services. (2000a). *Healthy people 2010: Understanding and improving health*. Washington, DC: Government Printing Office.

U.S. Department of Health and Human Services. (2000b). *Promoting better health for young people through physical activity and sports*. Silver Springs, MD: CDC (Healthy Youth).

Weathers, W. (1983). *Physical fitness activity program for health-related physical fitness test* (Special Projects Report). Murfreesboro: Middle Tennessee State University, Department of Physical Education.

Welk, G. J., & Blair, S. N. (2000). Physical activity protects against the health risks of obesity. *Research Digest, 3*(12), 1–8.

Appendix 4A: Family Fitness Activities

Strength and Endurance Activities

Wake-up Time

- Before getting out of bed, tighten all the muscles in your body, rest your muscles, then tighten them again—hard! Can you tighten one part of your body at a time?

Getting Ready

- While you're wringing out the washcloth, squeeze and twist it as hard as you can. What does this movement strengthen?
- After putting on your shoes, lift both your feet and legs up and down from a sitting position. How many times can you do this without stopping? Can you hold both legs in the air for 30 seconds?

Going to School

- Hold a heavy book in one hand and see how many times you can lift it up and down by bending your elbow. Try lifting the book while keeping your arm straight.

- On the bus, put your feet underneath the seat in front of you and tighten your leg muscles to make them straight and stiff.

Studying

- Hold the sides of your chair and pull as hard as you can, but don't bend your back.
- How hard can you push down on the desk with your hand and arm? Push and hold for 30 seconds.

Television Time

- Lie on your side, and lift one leg up and down in the air. Can you do each leg for a whole commercial?
- Lie on your back with knees bent, feet flat on the floor, and arms at your sides. Tighten your abdominal muscles and raise your arms, shoulders and head slightly off the floor. Hold that position for a couple of seconds.
- Lie on your back. Place a pillow between your knees and try to curl up in a ball so that your nose touches the knees. How many times can you do this during one commercial?

Flexibility Activities

Wake-up Time

- Stretch all your body in all different directions; then wiggle like Jell-O on a plate.
- Lie on your stomach, and then reach back and grab your feet with your hands. Try to make a bowl shape with your body by raising up your chest and legs and rocking on your stomach.

Going to School

- Keep one arm straight, and swing it in a big circle from the front of your body to the back. Hold on tight to your books.
- Shake your leg each time you take a step. If you're wearing long socks, try to shake them down to your ankles. The vibration of the skin and muscles will help loosen you up.

Studying

- Hold your hands together behind your chair, keeping your arms straight. Can you feel which muscles are being stretched?
- Let your head fall to one shoulder, and then roll it around to the other shoulder. Be limp, but don't fall asleep.

In the Kitchen or Den

- Stand about 3 feet from the kitchen counter or a table. Lean toward it, holding onto the edge of the counter or table. Can you keep your legs straight and your feet flat on the floor?

Television Time

- Sit on the floor and pull your feet up to your body with the bottoms of your feet together. Hold on to your feet; then use your elbows to push your knees to the floor. Next, try to touch your chest to your feet. What do you feel stretching this time?

Family Time

- Sit facing a partner with your legs spread apart and your feet touching your partner's feet. (If you're doing this exercise with your father or mother, your feet may touch only their ankles because their legs are much longer.) Hold hands; one partner leans back and slowly pulls the other partner so that he or she is stretching. Take turns stretching your partner.

Cardiovascular Activities

Wake-up Time

- Before getting out of bed, lie on your back and kick your legs up in the air. Keep kicking them as fast and as long as possible, or move them in a circular motion, as if you were riding a bicycle.

Getting Ready

- Stand in front of the mirror and pretend you're boxing with yourself. How quickly can you swing and punch? How long?

Going to School

- Walk, skip, ride a bicycle, or even jog to school or the bus stop.
- If you ride in a car pool, run to the car before mom or dad gets there, and then count the number of times you can jump up and down before she or he arrives.

Family Time

- Put on some upbeat music and dance. See who can move around the most, longest, and best.

Appendix 4B: Prescriptions for Fitness

Activities/Exercises for Abdominal Strength and Endurance

Wall Push Stand with your back against a wall, your feet only a few inches from the wall. Your knees should be slightly bent, with your arms at the sides of your body. Pull in your abdomen and press your shoulders, small of back, and buttocks against the wall. Hold the position for 5 seconds.

Untimed Sit-ups Lie flat on your back with your knees bent and your arms crossed on your chest. Gradually perform sit-ups.

Sit-up variations:

- Extend your arms forward. Shake your hands and arms as you curl up.
- Extend your arms forward. Clap your hands on the floor as you curl back to the mat.

Finger Walk Lie flat on your back with your knees bent in the sit-up position. Extend your arms at your sides. Walk your fingers forward on the mat in the direction of your feet as you tighten your stomach muscles and raise your shoulders slightly off the mat. Gently lower your shoulders to the mat and repeat.

Activities/Exercises for Upper-Body Strength and Endurance

Flexed-Arm Hang In a pull-up position, palms facing forward, chin above the bar (Figure 4.9), hold the position for 5 to 8 seconds without letting your chin touch the bar or drop below the bar. When holding for 8 seconds feels comfortable, increase the duration to 15 seconds.

⚠ The flexed-arm hang should not be held for extended periods because of the possibility of elbow injury and/or extreme muscular fatigue.

Reverse Pull-ups Hold the bar as in the flexed-arm position, chin above the bar, palms either forward or reversed. *Slowly* lower your weight to a hanging position by straightening your arms.

Walking Hands Assume a push-up position with your body fully extended and your hands on the floor behind a line or tape mark (Figure 4.10). Walk your hands forward and backward over the line as you count 1-2-3-4; aim for 60 counts. Variation: Time for 60 seconds.

Figure 4.9 Correct position for flexed-arm hang.

Figure 4.10 Weight on hands improves upper-body strength.

Figure 4.11 Correct position for pillow push-ups.

Pillow Push-ups In a push-up position (Figure 4.11), hands shoulder width apart, fingers forward, *slowly* lower your body toward the floor until your chest gently touches the pillow. Straighten your arms to raise your body back to starting position. *We have found that children have a fear of crashing to the floor when attempting*

Figure 4.12 Correct position for belly-ups.

Figure 4.13 Student performing the inner-thigh stretch on the right leg.

Figure 4.14 The lying knee-pull exercise.

a push-up. Placing the pillow under the chest eliminates this fear. You may begin with a modified push-up—knees bent—if you wish; when you are confident and ready, switch to the regular position—legs straight.

Belly-ups Sit on the floor with legs extended forward, arms at the side, hands flat on the floor, with your fingers pointing away from your body (Figure 4.12). Raise your hips, extending your body—straight like a board. Bend your elbows to slowly lower your body toward the floor; do not allow your buttocks to touch the floor. Return to the extended starting position by pushing your body upward. *Bending the elbows to lower the body is the key to building the arm muscles.*

Activities/Exercises for Shoulders, Lower Back, and Hamstring Flexibility

Trunk and Shoulder Extensions Slowly extend both your arms overhead as high as possible and hold them for 10 seconds. Gently lower arms, repeat extension.

Trunk and Shoulder Rotation With your right arm at shoulder level, look and slowly turn to your left; hold 10 seconds. Repeat the movement in the opposite direction.

Inner-Thigh Stretch Sit on the floor with your legs spread apart and extended. Slowly lean forward with one arm on each side of one leg and hold the position (Figure 4.13). Repeat the exercise on the other leg.

Lying Knee Pull Lie flat on your back with your legs extended and arms straight at your sides. Bring your left knee to your chest, grabbing under the knee with both your hands (Figure 4.14). Pull and hold your knee for 5 seconds. Repeat the exercise with your right leg. Remember to keep your extended leg straight and on the floor.

Reflective Teaching

The good teacher must relate his teaching to the world of his students as it is, not as he would like it to be.

—HERBERT FOSTER

A search for rigid prescriptions of the right way to teach has largely been replaced with the search for propositional rules and principles to guide practice.

—JUDITH E. RINK

Key Concepts

- The reflective teacher believes that students, classes, and teaching situations are different and develops lessons and the curriculum accordingly.

- The number of students in a class, frequency and length of classes, facilities, equipment, the behavior of the students, and the characteristics of the school are all factors taken into account by reflective teachers as they develop their lessons and programs.

- The personal value system of the teacher is the most important characteristic of a reflective or an invariant teacher.

- Invariant teachers rarely reflect on their effectiveness, continuing to teach the same lessons and content year after year, ignoring the progress and interest of the students.

- Reflective teachers are continually thinking about what they need to change, or do differently, to heighten their teaching and program effectiveness.

The first four chapters provided an introduction to the purpose and characteristics of a quality program of physical education, along with an overview of skill themes, and concepts of movement, physical fitness, and wellness. This short but important chapter also provides an overview—of reflective teaching, and the reasons for reflective, as opposed to invariant, teaching (Table 5.1). The actual skills of reflective teaching (planning, observing, developing the content, establishing a learning environment, and analyzing your teaching) are detailed in Part 2.

In any physical education class you'll find children who are there because they must be, not because they want to be. And you'll find some who are eager to become skillful enough to participate in varsity athletics. We're determined to foster the development and enthusiasm of all the children in our classes. We want them all to experience success and pleasure and a sense of competence that leads to their becoming physically active for a lifetime.

No two children are exactly alike. There are obvious physical differences and more subtle personality and individual differences. What is exciting to one child is boring to another. Some youngsters can accomplish a great deal on their own; other children require almost constant monitoring if they are to accomplish anything. For each child who delights in the challenge and camaraderie of a team game, another prefers the challenge and satisfaction of individual activities.

Children are different, and so are the schools they attend. Some school buildings have open designs, and others are divided into permanent classrooms. Administrators can be strict, stultifying, or supportive. Fellow teachers can be cooperative or competitive, helpful

Table 5.1 Comparison of Reflective Teaching and Invariant Teaching

Variable	The Reflective Teachers	The Invariant Teachers
Planning	Adjust lesson plans to differences between classes and children	Use the same plan for each primary grade and the same plan for each intermediate grade
Progression within and between lessons	Base progression on such factors as youngsters' (1) rate and extent of improvement; (2) physical skill needs; (3) interest in a particular topic or activity	Base progression on such factors as (1) six-week units; (2) amount of material to be covered in a semester or year; (3) a predetermined formula for progression
Methodology	Vary the methodology according to such factors as (1) characteristics of children in the class; (2) purpose of the lesson; (3) ability of the children to accept responsibility	Employ the same methodology with all classes and hope that the children will eventually fulfill the teacher's expectations
Curriculum	Design curriculum for each unique class of children after examining the children to determine their abilities and needs	Use predetermined curricular content without considering such factors as children's ability, community influences, or children's interests
Equipment and facilities	Modify activities and lessons to available equipment and facilities	Teach activities and lessons that use available equipment and facilities
Discipline	Attempt to understand management problems and then seek the causes, modifying teaching procedure accordingly	Assume that the children are misbehaving and resort to punitive measures to modify individual and class behavior
Assessment	Regularly assess the children and also seek constructive criticism about their teaching from children and colleagues	Assess sporadically and often base assessment on whether children liked the lesson, how long they remained interested, and how well they behaved

Some teachers teach most of their lessons outdoors.

or obstructive. Gymnasiums, plentiful physical education equipment, adequate field space, and small class sizes are basic necessities in some elementary schools; other schools view such facilities as frills. Parents are concerned, meddlesome, apathetic, helpful, or unavailable.

How is a teacher to succeed amid this diversity? We have no magical answers. But we are convinced that a linear approach* to teaching is not effective, and so we coined the term reflective teaching. The reflective teacher achieves success and professional satisfaction by employing a variety of teaching skills that interact effectively with the particular teaching environment.

What Is Reflective Teaching?

Reflective teaching is recognizing that children are different—and doing something about it. It could also be called "adapted" teaching because the teacher adapts the content, and his teaching, to suit the needs of individual students and classes. It is directly related to the concept of developmentally appropriate teaching, which acknowledges that students develop at different rates and stages. Invariant teaching, the opposite of reflective teaching, assumes that all children have the same abilities, interests, and level of physical fitness (Table 5.1). The concept of reflective teaching is not new. In fact, one expects that the teachers in one-

room schoolhouses were models of reflective teaching as they were required to teach children of many ages in the same classroom. Effective* (a synonym for reflective) teaching is situational rather than generic. For many teachers, the results of attempting to teach predesigned lessons without considering the unique characteristics of a class have been disastrous for both the children and themselves. As stated in a recent review of the importance of physical activity for school-age youth: "Coaching and teaching styles are particularly relevant to the self-concept in organized sport and physical education" (Strong et al., 2005).

In this book, reflective teaching doesn't refer to any particular methodology or style of teaching; it refers to the many teaching skills employed by individuals who are respected as master teachers (Graham, 2001). The reflective teacher is one who can design and implement an educational program that is congruent with the idiosyncrasies of a particular school situation. Invariant teaching, unlike reflective teaching, is characterized by the use of one approach in all teaching situations.

The Need for Reflective Teaching

If all schools, classes, and youngsters were identical, there would be no need for reflective teaching. We would simply provide you with lesson plans for each grade level and you could follow them exactly. You

---

*Dwight Allen defined linear thinking as searching for the answer to a problem by investigating a single solution without considering feasible alternatives (Allen, 1975).

*We use the terms successful teaching and effective teaching to indicate a teaching process that results in the sought-after physical, affective, and cognitive gains.

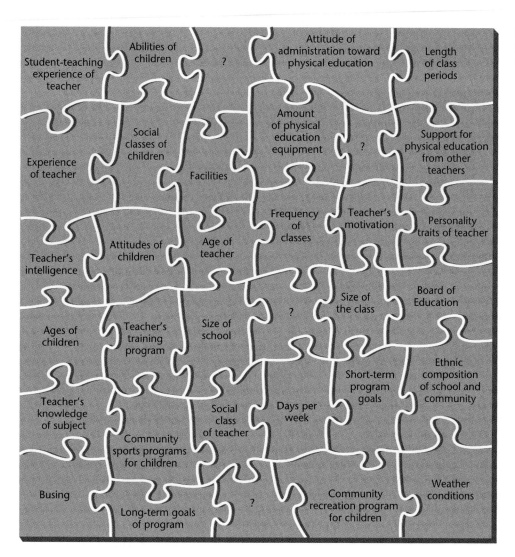

Figure 5.1 Interacting factors that contribute to the unique ecology of each school.

know, however, that schools, programs, and youngsters are different. Figure 5.1 illustrates some of the more obvious differences. It has been drawn in the shape of a puzzle to indicate that teaching is a constant challenge as we attempt to fit the pieces together into a unified, consistent program that provides youngsters with the active learning experiences they need. Reflective teachers take these differences into account and continuously modify and change their teaching and curriculum based on the needs of the students at their school. We want to focus on six of these variables that are major factors in any program necessitating reflective teaching. Although they may seem obvious, it has been our experience that far too many invariant teachers fail to account for them in their teaching. These six variables are the values of the teacher, class size, the number of class sessions per week, facilities and equipment, student behavior, and the con-

text of the school. We'll now discuss these variables in detail.

Values of the Teacher

Clearly one of the most important variables is the personal attitudes and beliefs we, as teachers, bring to our teaching situation. Some physical education teachers, for example, are more interested in coaching than teaching—and their programs reflect a lack of planning and interest in high-quality physical education. Other physical education teachers are totally dedicated to their programs and spend countless hours planning new and interesting activities, as well as volunteering time with children before and after school. Still other physical education teachers view physical education as merely a break for the children from the routine of the

Some teachers teach in gymnasiums that are used only for physical education.

classroom, so their programs consist primarily of fun activities for the children, with virtually no emphasis on learning.

In many schools, physical education is also the responsibility of the classroom teacher. Like physical education teachers, classroom teachers vary in their views of the purpose and importance of physical activity in the lives of children. Some classroom teachers, for example, find time in their hectic schedules to develop programs for children that truly enhance the development of positive attitudes and learning as suggested in Chapter 1. In contrast, other classroom teachers view physical education as a break for the children and themselves—and rely on such old standbys as kick ball, dodgeball, and duck, duck, goose to keep the children entertained during physical education class.

Ideally, every teacher, whether classroom teacher or physical education teacher, would appreciate the importance of physical education for children and develop programs that are developmentally appropriate—and effective—for children. Realistically, however, there will always be some teachers who "fall back" on the ways things were done in the past rather than working to develop innovative programs for children. In addition to the values of the teacher, a number of other variables contribute to the ease or difficulty of developing quality programs of physical education for children.

Class Size

A variable that has particular impact on what a teacher is able to accomplish in physical education is the size of the classes. Physical education classes are all too often the largest classes in a school. A person doesn't need

much teaching experience to realize that the number of students within a given class, other variables excluded, significantly dictates what a teacher can accomplish. Lessons that are possible with 25 children are difficult, if not impossible, with 100 children. This is the primary reason it is recommended that physical education classes be the same size as in the classroom (U.S. Department of Health and Human Services [USDHHS], 2000).

For teachers to do more than provide directions to a mass of children, they must have opportunities to observe and analyze and to give children feedback. The logistical problems of providing individual instruction for each child in a class of 50 children who meet for half an hour are overwhelming. The educational literature supports this viewpoint: "The more successful teachers did more tutorial teaching. They spoke to the class as a whole in order to provide structure and give general direction, but most of their actual instruction was given in small groups or to individuals" (Good et al., 1975, p. 70). Class size strongly influences the teaching approach that a given teacher can use to foster a successful educational experience.

Number of Class Sessions

In addition to the values of the teacher and the size of classes, another influential variable that must be considered is the number of class sessions per week. Children in some schools, for example, have "organized" physical education only one day a week. Children in other schools have daily physical education. Obviously, the children who have instructional physical education for 180 days a year can learn significantly more than those who have physical education only

36 days a year (National Association for Sport and Physical Education [NASPE], 2002; USDHHS, 2000). The challenge for the teacher is to make the difficult decisions about what can be learned in one or two days a week so that the children truly benefit from the program, rather than simply being exposed to a variety of activities (Graham et al., 1991). This also means that the teacher, or the district, will have to decide which state or national standards will have to be excluded because of time constraints.

In schools where children don't have daily physical education, the classroom teacher can play a vital role in reinforcing what the specialist has taught—and vice versa. When the classroom teachers and the physical education specialist work together closely, the children reap the benefits.

Facilities and Equipment

A fourth variable is the adequacy of the facilities and equipment within a particular school. Established programs of physical education often include adequate equipment and a reasonable solution to the use of indoor space during inclement weather. In contrast, fledgling programs of physical education may lack physical education equipment. In some schools, physical education classes are forced to use classrooms, cafeterias, or even hallways on rainy days.

Some teachers are masters of improvisation, but others can't function without adequate facilities and equipment. The teaching skills acquired during student teaching, when equipment and facilities were ideal, often must be adapted to less desirable conditions. You may find that there is only one ball per class instead of one ball per pupil. You may find yourself on a rainy afternoon teaching in a classroom instead of on a playground. Different environments call for different teaching skills.

At the heart of complexity in the gym is numbers. That the teacher is one and the learners are many is a fact of life which shapes every aspect of the teacher's experience. What many outsiders fail to appreciate is that an average class contains a lot of kids for one person to handle even if there were no intent to teach anything. This failure particularly is true of parents who often feel qualified as experts on child management because they deal more or less successfully with their own children in groups rarely exceeding three or four.

—LARRY LOCKE, *The Ecology of the Gymnasium: What the Tourist Never Sees*

Student Behavior

Another variable that contributes to the need for reflective teaching is generally referred to as student behavior. The ability to manage children effectively is a major concern in education today, among parents as well as teachers.

The ability to manage a class of children effectively is also one of the few teaching skills that educators agree is a prerequisite to successful teaching. A teacher must be able to create and maintain an appropriate environment if children are to learn. Some teachers are able to maintain desirable student behavior simply by glancing occasionally at certain children within a class. Other teachers spend most of their time trying to maintain order. We believe that specific teaching skills can be effectively employed to create and sustain an appropriate environment (see Chapters 9 and 10).

Unfortunately, many textbooks—and many teachers—underplay the role of discipline. These texts and teachers assume that a "good" teacher doesn't have discipline problems (Siedentop & Tannehill, 2000). Our experience suggests otherwise. During a teaching career, a teacher encounters many kinds of classes. Some will test the teacher's ability to maintain appropriate behavior; others are cooperative. Successful teachers are able to work effectively with both types of classes.

Context of the School

A sixth variable, certainly not the least important, that supports the need for reflective teaching is the context of the school. Some schools today are populated predominantly by children in transient situations, many of whom will move before the end of the school year. An increasing number of children are from homes in which both parents work outside the home and consequently are generally unavailable during the day or when the children return home after school. Rural schools continue to have children with needs different from those of children in suburban or inner-city schools. Moreover, it is typical today to have one or more children in a class who do not speak English, and it seems that more classes have mainstreamed children than ever before. Each of these situations, as well as the many variations that have not been described, presents interesting challenges to teachers—challenges that have no standard answers. The one constant in all of these situations is that children need caring, dedicated teachers, perhaps more than ever.

Some inner-city youngsters often test their teachers according to rules governing their street corner behavior rather than by their teachers' middle-class rules and expectations. This testing by street corner rules happens to teachers and administrators in inner-city schools every day. And most of the teachers and administrators neither realize nor understand what is happening. Indeed, until you actually experience this testing—when all your middle-class niceties do not count a damn and you wonder why this kid is doing that to you because you are not as prejudiced as the others and you really want to help . . . —it will be hard, if not impossible, for you to understand what I am talking about.

—HERBERT FOSTER, *Ribbin', Jivin' and Playin' the Dozens*

Reflective teachers are constantly observing their classes to determine their needs, interests, and abilities.

How Do I Become a Reflective Teacher?

The reflective teacher is able to think critically about the children and then adapt lessons, facilities, and equipment to provide a productive and worthwhile learning environment. Part 2 of the book provides thorough explanations of the techniques used by reflective teachers as they develop their programs into meaningful learning experiences for their children. The key message in this chapter is to recognize that all schools, classes, and students are not identical and that you must be willing to change your program over the years to increase its effectiveness for youngsters of all abilities, often in less than ideal teaching circumstances. The chapters in Part 2 describe the skills that you will need to become a reflective teacher. But the first step is to accept the fact that no single curriculum or program works for all teachers in every school. If you accept this premise, you are well on your way to becoming a reflective teacher.

The next step, as described in Part 2, is to continue to build your repertoire of content knowledge. The more a teacher knows the content, the more options are available to change or adapt lessons to suit the needs of individual students or different classes. When a teacher only knows one game, or one way of introducing a task, it is extremely difficult to practice reflective teaching. The reflective teacher has countless ways of presenting activities to youngsters to promote their interest and keep them learning. As with any skill, it takes years and years of practice before one can truly claim to be a reflective teacher.

Summary

Six major variables necessitate the need for reflective teaching: the values of the teacher, class size, the number of class sessions per week, facilities and equipment, student behavior, and the context of the school. The reflective teacher considers the characteristics of each class and the abilities of the individual students. A reflective teacher doesn't expect all children to respond in the same way or to achieve the same level of skill. Reflective teachers continually observe and analyze, a process that enables them to revise their expectations and adapt all the components of the program, thereby constantly improving the effectiveness of the program. The reflective approach to teaching requires that teachers constantly and accurately monitor as they attempt to design and implement a physical education program for a given school. Reflective teachers also have a wealth of content knowledge that allows them to adapt and modify tasks for individuals of varying abilities.

Reading Comprehension Questions

1. What is reflective teaching? What are its basic characteristics?
2. What does a linear approach to learning mean?
3. Provide three examples of how class size influences the way a teacher teaches a lesson.
4. What factors, typically beyond the teacher's control, contribute to the dissimilarity of teaching situations?
5. Locate the standards for your state (or use the national standards). Select a grade level and indicate which standards you would eliminate for that grade level if you were teaching in a school that had physical education only one day per week. The standards can be found at www.pecentral.org/professional/statestandards.html. Explain why you would eliminate those standards from your program.
6. Can a teacher learn to discipline classes, or is maintaining appropriate behavior an inborn ability? Explain your answer.
7. In your own words, explain the major implication of reflective teaching.

References/Suggested Readings

Allen, D. (1975). The future of education—Where do we go from here? *Journal of Teacher Education, 26,* 41–45.

Borko, H., & Livingston, C. (1989). Cognition and improvisation: Differences in mathematics instruction by expert and novice teachers. *American Educational Research Journal, 26*(4), 473–498.

Foster, H. L. (1974). *Ribbin', jivin' and playin' the dozens: The unrecognized dilemma of inner-city schools.* Cambridge, MA: Ballinger.

Good, T. L., Biddle, B. J., & Brophy, J. E. (1975). *Teachers make a difference.* New York: Holt, Rinehart & Winston.

Graham, G. (2001). *Teaching children physical education: Becoming a master teacher* (2nd ed.). Champaign, IL: Human Kinetics.

Graham, G., Hopple, C., Manross, M., & Sitzman, T. (1993). Novice and experienced children's physical education teachers: Insights into their situational decision-making. *Journal of Teaching in Physical Education, 12,* 197–217.

Graham, G., Metzler, M., & Webster, G. (1991). Specialist and classroom teacher effectiveness in children's physical education: A 3-year study [Monograph]. *Journal of Teaching in Physical Education, 4,* 321–426.

Housner, L. D., & Griffey, D. C. (1985). Teacher cognition: Differences in planning and interactive decision making between experienced and inexperienced teachers. *Research Quarterly for Exercise and Sport, 56,* 56–63.

Locke, L. F. (1975, Spring). The ecology of the gymnasium: What the tourist never sees. Southern Association for Physical Education of College Women Proceedings.

National Association for Sport and Physical Education. (2004). *Moving into the future: National standards for physical education* (2nd ed.). Reston, VA: National Association for Sport and Physical Education.

National Association for Sport and Physical Education. (2002). *2001 Shape of the nation report: Status of physical education in the USA.* Reston, VA: American Alliance for Health, Physical Education, Recreation and Dance.

Rink, J. (1996). Effective instruction in physical education. In S. J. Silverman and C. D. Ennis (eds.), *Student learning in physical education* (pp. 171–198). Champaign, IL: Human Kinetics.

Siedentop, D., & Tannehill, D. (2000). *Developing teaching skills in physical education* (4th ed.), Mountain View, CA: Mayfield Publishing Co.

Strong, W. B., Malina, R. M., Bumkie, J. R., Daniels, S. R., Dishman, R. K., Gutin, B., Hergenroeder, A. C., et al. (2005). Evidence-based physical activity for school-age youth. *Journal of Pediatrics, 146:* 732–737.

U.S. Department of Health and Human Services. (2000). *School health index for physical activity and healthy eating: A self-assessment and planning guide for elementary school.* Atlanta, GA: Centers for Disease Control. Available for free download from: www.cdc.gov/nccdphp/dash.

Teaching Diverse Learners

Movement is learning; movement is life. No matter how disabled a child, movement can make a difference in his/her life. Movement can help a child become oneself. If a child can move, he/she can become more a master of the environment rather than being controlled by it.

—JANE R. EVANS

Key Concepts

- With recent increases in the diversity of America's school children, physical education teachers must be prepared to provide a quality physical education experience to students with a wide variety of abilities, needs, and interests.

- Inclusion is the philosophy that diverse learners, including those with differences in mental and physical ability, skill level, fitness levels, gender, culture, language, religion, class, and physical characteristics can learn and develop skills in the regular physical education program.

- It is the responsibility of the physical education teacher to learn about the unique needs of each diverse learner and the implications for physical education.

- By changing basic game activity components and providing students choice among appropriate tasks, the teacher can challenge all students in ways that provide maximum opportunities for learning and development of their personal potential.

- Physical education is a direct/required service for all children with disabilities under IDEA (1990).

- The physical education teacher is a critical member of the multidisciplinary team (M-Team) and should be in attendance at all meetings that involve students he or she teaches in physical education.

- It is at the M-Team that goals are established for the child with disabilities and the environment most conducive to meeting those goals is identified.

- A top-down ecological model provides the template for successful inclusion of children with disabilities: determine critical skills, analyze existing program, design modifications.

As a group of second graders enters the gym for class on the first day of school, Mrs. Jones, the physical education teacher, notices one student rolling his wheelchair through the door and hears two other children speaking an unfamiliar language. Mrs. Jones's heart beings to beat a little faster, and even though she has several years of teaching experience, she feels a rush of self-doubt and begins to question her ability to meet the needs of *all* her students.

Although this may seem like an unusually diverse group, it is more common now than ever before to find physical education classes across the country with increasingly diverse groups of students. In addition to over 6 million special education students (Olson, 2004), currently almost 40% of the total public school population is minority students (National Center of Educational Statistics [NCES], 2000). By the year 2020, more than two-thirds of the school population will be African American, Asian, Hispanic, or Native American with Hispanic youths representing over 20% of the total 5- to 17-year-old population (Meece & Kurtz-Costes, 2001). Furthermore, physical education teachers are working with more children at low levels of fitness than in years past due to increased levels of obesity among American youths (American Obesity Association [AOA], 2002). Although finding ways to meet the needs of all students in physical education can bring both joy and challenge for everyone involved, in order to make a difference teachers must commit themselves to providing a physical education experience in which all children can be successful.

This chapter will provide strategies to help physical education teachers meet the needs of the increasingly diverse population of children entering American schools. Diversity is defined as the differences that exist among people (Chappelle & Bigman, 1998). For the purposes of this chapter, diversity includes not only differences in mental and physical ability, but also differences in skill level, fitness levels, gender, culture, language, religion, class, and physical characteristics. Our goal is for all students to experience a sense of empowerment and competence in physical education that leads to lifetime participation in physical activity. Therefore, we will first define the philosophy of inclusion and examine ways children can be different from one another. Then we shift the focus to ways children are alike and ways to include all students.

Inclusion Expanded

Traditionally in terms of physical education, inclusion means that students with disabilities are placed in regular physical education programs (Block, 2000). In order to better represent the wide variety of student abilities, needs, and interests resulting from the increased diversity of America's schoolchildren, and because teachers today are faced with more than teaching children with special needs, we expanded our philosophy of inclusion. It is time to support diverse learners, in all their variety of forms, through a broadened conceptualization of inclusion.

Inclusion is a philosophy that all children can learn, all children want to learn. It involves teachers creating a healthy learning climate in which all children feel safe, successful, motivated, and connected to others and have a sense of ownership/autonomy (Morris et al., 2006). In an inclusive environment the question is not whether children are smart but *how* they are smart. The question is not whether they can develop skills in physical education but *how* they can develop their skills. Perhaps Tomlinson (2003) put it best when she explains that it is all in how you frame the question. Rather than asking, "What labels do my students have?" instead ask, "What are their particular interests and needs?" Rather than asking, "What are my students' deficits?" instead ask, "What are their strengths?" Rather than asking, "How do I remediate students?" instead ask, "What can I do to ensure that each student works to the highest level of thought and production possible?" Instead of asking, "How can I motivate these students?" instead ask, "What releases the motivation born in all humans?" As a whole these questions capture the essence of inclusion. Discovering children's abilities and helping them learn what they are good at is critical to their success. Inclusion identifies and nurtures each student's unique abilities, recognizing that all children do better when the emphasis is on strengths (Oberti, 1993).

Physical education programs that include diverse learners have the same basic goals and objectives as any other quality program. However, strategies are used to support program goals while taking into consideration participant needs, interests, abilities, and skill and fitness levels. These strategies may include implementation of modified tasks, assistance for a child as needed, and/or support for the teacher, such as in-service training, working with a translator, or team teaching with an adapted physical education teacher. Inclusion does not mean placement of all children in the regular physical education setting with no assistance and support for the teacher. However, inclusion does mean creating conditions so the needs of children are met and program outcomes are achieved.

Inclusion begins with a teacher willing to accept all children; a teacher open and responsive to individuals and the unique needs of each; a teacher who celebrates children's strengths and adjusts, accommodates, and

In individualized physical education classes, all children can be successful.

modifies to provide maximum learning for each child. Before learning specific strategies for including diverse learners it is important to first focus on ways students may be different. The better informed you are about the diversity of your students, the better you will be

ODIE! DOGS CAN'T CLIMB TREES!

© 1982 United Feature Syndicate, Inc.

IT'S AMAZING WHAT ONE CAN ACCOMPLISH WHEN ONE DOESN'T KNOW WHAT ONE CAN'T DO

JIM DAVIS   1-19

able to teach the child using strategies we will discuss later in the chapter.

Overweight Children

As mentioned in Chapter 4, childhood obesity rates have reached epidemic proportions. In fact, obesity among children has tripled in the last two decades. Children and adolescents who are obese are more likely to be overweight or obese as adults; overweight adults are at increased risk for heart disease, high blood pressure, stroke, diabetes, some types of cancer, and gallbladder disease. Also, being overweight during childhood, and particularly adolescence, is related to increased risk of asthma, diabetes (type 2), hypertension, orthopedic complications, and sleep apnea. Additionally, negative psychosocial effects such as developing a negative body image and being subjected to weight-related teasing, jokes, and potentially hurtful comments by peers and family can have a profound effect on children (American Obesity Association [AOA], 2002).

Today's youth are considered the most inactive generation in history (AOA, 2002). Physical education teachers can help overweight children build healthy bodies and establish healthy lifestyles by teaching them ways to include physical activity in their daily lives. Physical educators can play an important role in the treatment and prevention of overweight children by giving them the skills and confidence they need to participate in physical activity for a lifetime and educating children about the importance of health-related fitness concepts as outlined in Chapter 4. In order to help children increase their physical activity levels it is important to know the factors that influence physical activity levels among children.

Factors influencing physical activity among children (National Association for Sport and Physical Education [NASPE], 2005):

Biological Factors (Include Gender, Age, Race)
- Boys are generally more active than girls.
- Physical activity declines between the ages of 6 and 18.
- Obese children prefer low-intensity activities, and obese children with obese parents view endurance activities more negatively than do lean children with lean parents.
- Only 20 percent of the variation in a person's physical activity is explained by genetics.

Psychological Factors
- If children value an activity and feel competent and satisfied while performing it, they are more likely to engage in the activity.

- For children to persist at an activity, they must feel competent and confident in their ability to reach a specific goal (self-efficacy).

Social Factors
- Parents and siblings influence physical activity behaviors of young children.
- In adolescence, peers are more likely to have a greater influence on physical activity levels.
- Enthusiastic and knowledgeable physical education teachers and coaches are more likely to influence their students' enjoyment of physical activity.

Environmental Factors
- Due to safety concerns in many neighborhoods, children engage in indoor activities such as watching television, reading, or playing video games.
- Transportation can also be a barrier to participating in group activities.

Specific implications for teaching overweight children include:

- Emphasize enjoyable participation in a variety of physical activities.
- Create a psychologically safe climate where children feel successful and have choices of activities to help them reach goals.
- Help students develop the knowledge, attitudes, and skills they need to adopt and maintain a physically active lifestyle.
- Keep all or most students active at the same time so no one feels pressure to perform alone in front of peers, because overweight children often have low skill levels and would consider this humiliating.
- Use short bouts of high-intensity activities throughout the class period. Knowing that the higher level of intensity will not last long can help motivate less fit children.
- Use heart-rate monitors with older students to help them determine when they reach their target heart-rate zone (THR). Overweight children often push themselves well beyond the THR, thinking this is what exercise feels like, when in reality they can get the full benefits of exercise by participating at a much lower and thus more comfortable intensity level.
- Modify activities so students have choices related to intensity (see Creating Conditions for Inclusion in this chapter for ways to modify activities so children have choices).
- Allow students to set individual goals related to their own skill and fitness improvement.
- Emphasize self-improvement and personal bests instead of comparing students to each other.

Cultural Differences

Culture serves as the fabric of one's being and includes language, beliefs, attitudes, and patterns of communication (Tiedt & Tiedt, 1990). The 2000 census shows that America is more ethnically, racially, culturally, and linguistically diverse than ever before. Today the national portrait is being increasingly enriched with Asian, Latino, and multiracial people (Singer, 2004). A monolingual, English-speaking physical education teacher is increasingly likely to face the challenge of teaching young children whose languages and backgrounds are completely unfamiliar. Often in this situation even the most well-meaning educators inadvertently reinforce children's conflicting feelings about their own culture and the majority culture (Cummins, 1992). To become more culturally responsive and reflective teachers (see Chapter 5) we must use the cultural knowledge, prior experiences, and learning style preferences of students from diverse cultures to make learning more appropriate and effective for them. Culturally responsive teaching is teaching to and through the strengths of these students (Gay, 2000).

The teacher plays a critical role in the success of students from diverse cultures at school. For example, Cummins (1992) points out that minority students are empowered or disabled as a direct result of their interactions with educators. The extent that each of the following characteristics is implemented in the school setting can directly affect the success of minority students:

1. Minority students' language and culture are incorporated into the school program.
2. Minority community participation is encouraged as an integral component of children's education.
3. Instruction is used to motivate students to use language actively in order to generate their own knowledge. (Cummins, 1992)

Implications for building a culturally responsive instructional approach in physical education as outlined by Sparks (1994) include:

- *Built trust.* A class climate that is perceived as trusting and accepting is important. One way you can do this is by sharing information about yourself and your own cultural background. This helps students begin to make connections with you that develop the foundation for trust. Also, learning student's names and how to pronounce them correctly in their native language indicates you are interested and want to get to know them as individuals. Physical education offers a perfect setting for breaking social barriers through cooperative and competitive as well as group and individual physical activities.

Each of these serves as a way to strengthen the bond between teacher and students.
- *Become culturally literate.* Learn about the cultural background of your students. This includes learning about traditions, communication styles, or social values of diverse cultures. Increase your cultural literacy by observing students outside of the school setting, getting to know families of students, making home visits, and allowing students to share cultural experiences in the curriculum. In addition, when students' home language is encouraged, they get a sense of acceptance of themselves and their cultural background. Challenge yourself to learn and use greetings in many languages and never hesitate to ask students how to say basic expressions. This validates the students and shows them that teachers, like the students themselves, struggle with new languages.
- *Use a variety of teaching methods.* Become aware of your students' learning styles. Some cultures use more visual cues, while others prefer tactile or auditory cues for learning. Physical education offers many opportunities for explanation and demonstration of skills. Peer teaching (see Chapter 13) allows students to assist each other in learning.
- *Promote critical thinking.* Although critical thinking and problem solving are important for all children, they can be especially helpful to children from diverse cultures. Critical thinking empowers students to make their own decisions rather than always looking to others for answers. This can help build self-esteem and confidence. Developing original routines, creating games (see Chapter 31), and using mental imagery are techniques that will challenge students to think critically in physical education.
- *Provide effective feedback.* Make all feedback concrete and specific. It is also a good idea to demonstrate what you mean when giving corrective feedback. Be sure that all students regardless of color, gender, or ethnic origin receive feedback that is positive, specific, and of equal quality. See Chapter 15 for specific information on providing student feedback.
- *Analyze instructional materials.* Be sure that all instructional materials include perspectives from different cultural groups rather than just the majority group within the class. Use materials that represent diverse cultural groups and are not discriminatory based on race, ethnicity, religion, or gender. Use the rich heritage of physical activity and sport that has evolved from cultures throughout the world to highlight unique contributions.
- *Establish positive home and community relations.* Create positive relationships with parents early in the year. This can be done through visiting the home,

making phone calls, inviting parents to come see what their child is learning, or simply sending home a letter introducing yourself to parents. Remember that many parents do not read English. For example, in the southwestern United States it is best to send home materials in English and Spanish (and required in some school districts). Seek out resources in your school district to help with translation of materials. You may also consider inviting parents to do something they are comfortable with, such as cooking or showing students how to use digital cameras.

Gender Equity

In 1972, the United States Congress passed Title IX of the Education Amendments, mandating gender equity in all educational institutions receiving federal funding. One of the intentions of Title IX was to provide equal opportunity for physical education instruction to all students. Title IX also mandated coeducational classes, which may begin the process of providing gender equity but do not ensure an equitable environment (Napper-Owen et al., 1999). For example, educational research has shown that both male and female teachers exhibit gender bias in elementary and middle school programs. In particular this research found that teachers' interactions with students favor male students (Davis, 1999). Title IX provided the foundation and motivation for change, but teachers are the key to developing these new attitudes (Davis, 2003).

Many teachers treat children differently based on gender without even realizing it. As a result students may not be getting an equitable educational experience. In order to develop gender fairness, physical education teachers must create an environment in which both sexes feel safe to explore and develop their abilities in sport and physical activity (Hutchinson, 1995).

Implications for creating a more gender-equitable environment as outlined by Napper-Owen (1994) include:

- *Grouping students.* Use categories such as their birth date, number of pets, color of clothing, or favorite foods, rather than gender.
- *Individualize instruction.* Group students for instruction by ability levels to ensure more individualized instruction.
- *Feedback.* Provide an equal amount of quality feedback to all students.
- *Student helpers.* Ask equal numbers of boys and girls to demonstrate skills, help with equipment, and answer questions in class.
- *Use first names.* Call all students by their first name.

- *Use inclusive language* such as base player, player-to-player defense, straight leg push-ups, modified push-ups (rather than boys' push-ups and girls' push-ups), and "you" rather than "you guys."
- *Activities.* Teach nontraditional activities.
- *Teaching materials* must show both boys and girls in traditional and nontraditional roles.
- *Modify activities* to maximize participation by all students.

How equitable is your teaching? A great way to increase awareness of gender equity is to videotape yourself and count how often boys and girls answer questions, participate in activity, receive feedback, and demonstrate skills. See Chapter 12 for more ways to check your gender equity awareness.

Religious Differences

The First Amendment to the U.S. Constitution granted freedom of religion to all people over 200 years ago. Today parents from diverse religious backgrounds entrust the education of their children to the teachers in public schools. Therefore it is important that schools be places where religion and religious conviction are treated with fairness and respect. Public schools uphold the First Amendment when they protect the religious liberty rights of students of all faiths or none (Haynes, 1999). Due to the confusion that has surrounded the topic of religion in public schools across the years, this is perhaps easier said than done. One of the best ways to respect the religious rights of all students is for teachers and administrators to work closely with parents and community members to apply the First Amendment fairly and justly (Haynes, 1999). Kahan (2003) provides helpful information for physical educators based on current understanding of the law:

- *Holiday lessons.* Special lessons or treats prepared for the observance of holidays occurring during the school year such as Halloween, Thanksgiving, Valentine's Day, and St. Patrick's Day have indirect roots in religious events, people, and symbols and therefore may not suit all students' religious beliefs.
- *Lesson content.* Students who object to class content on the grounds of religious beliefs should be excused without punishment.
- *Missing school.* Schools are advised but not obligated to set calendars around various religious holidays; they are required, however, to provide opportunities for students who are absent for religious reasons to make up missed work without any adverse consequences.

- *Dress and physical contact.* Students whose dress reflects their religious views or modesty should be allowed to wear such clothing in addition to their physical education uniform. For example, Muslim girls should be allowed to wear a hijab over their hair and long pants under their shorts, and Sikh boys should be allowed to wear turbans. In addition, observance of clothing customs and rules regulating physical contact and modesty may prevent some students from participating in activities such as swimming and dance.
- *Religious symbols* may be used as teaching aids (e.g., cross, crèche, menorah); however, religious symbols should not be used as seasonal decorations. Exercise restraint, plan inclusively, and consider the context of displays. For example, a bulletin board with a winter scene of snow, snowmen, presents, holly, menorahs, Christmas trees, and Kwanzaa candles may evoke general seasonal feelings and not perceptions of endorsing any single religion and would therefore be acceptable.

Overall, teaching students in one of the most religiously diverse countries in the world requires additional planning, communication, and flexibility.

Children with Special Needs

Public Law 94–142 (Education for All Handicapped Children of 1975) and the Individuals with Disabilities Education Act (IDEA) of 1990 guarantee all children with disabilities from ages 3 to 22 a free and appropriate education in the least restrictive environment. That education includes physical education as a direct service—one that must be provided for all students. IDEA defines physical education as the development of physical and motor fitness, fundamental motor skills and patterns, and skills in aquatics, dance, games, and sports. IDEA further states that to the maximum extent appropriate, children with disabilities are to be educated together with children without disabilities— that is, in their home school, in the classroom, and in the gymnasium that would be theirs if they had no disabilities.

Early interpretations of "least restrictive environment" led to the mainstreaming of children with disabilities for art, music, and physical education and to a somewhat limited exposure to the classroom environment of their peers, with the remainder of the day spent in a "special" education classroom. Parents of children with disabilities voiced concern at this separate but equal approach to education at the same time that research was questioning the benefits of the

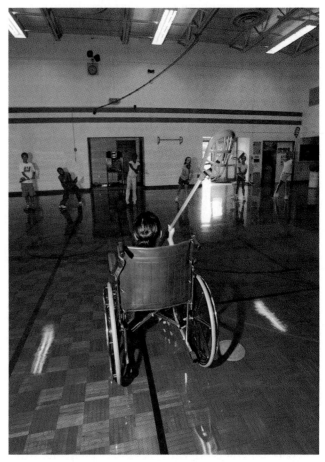

Children with disabilities can successfully participate in physical education.

approach. There was strong concern about the negative (and once affixed, everlasting) label of special education. Thus began the gradual move from mainstreaming to a philosophy of inclusion. With very few exceptions, the education of children with disabilities is done in the regular program of physical education (PL 105-17, IDEA Amendments, 1997).

Physical Activity and Fitness

Children with disabilities tend to be less physically active than children without disabilities. This is due to a number of factors: the nature of the disability itself, overprotective parents, and a lack of recreational and play facilities that are accessible for those with disabilities. Yet physical activity is extremely important for children with disabilities. Through physical activity, skills are developed for recreational use throughout life. In a physical activity environment, social skills are learned and practiced and self-confidence for

Box 6-1

Physical Fitness Test Packages for Students with Disabilities

Additional information concerning specific physical fitness packages for students with disabilities may be obtained from the following sources:

Brockport Physical Fitness Test Manual (1999), by
J. Winnick and F. Short.
Human Kinetics
P.O. Box 5076
Champaign, IL 61825-5075
www.humankinetics.com

Physical Best and Individuals with Disabilities: A Handbook for Inclusion in Fitness Programs (1995),
J. Seamon, editor.
AAHPERD
1900 Association Drive
Reston, VA 20191
www.aahperd.org/aapar

social interaction is enhanced. And through physical activity, fitness is improved. Better fitness brings increased muscle tone for those prone to being less mobile; muscle tone brings better posture, more control of manipulatives, and, thus, increased independence. A health-enhancing level of fitness is important for *all* children.

Many children with disabilities can participate in the regular fitness assessment program. However, for some boys and girls, modifications in assessment will be necessary. Box 6-1 shows sources for fitness assessment packages designed especially for students with disabilities.

Visual Impairments

The two categories of visual impairment are blindness and partial sight. Approximately 1 percent of school-age children are seriously visually impaired, with impairments ranging from blindness to blurred/distorted vision, tunnel vision, and the ability to see out of the corners of the eyes only. Children with serious visual impairments may exhibit the following characteristics:

• Self-stimulating mannerisms, for example, stamping feet, rocking, clicking fingers, and turning the

head from side to side. These mannerisms often result from boredom and lack of external stimulus.
• Awkward, clumsy total-body movements and poor motor skills from lack of experience and limited sensory information.
• Poor posture due to lack of visual modeling.
• Developmental lag of at least one year, often due to lack of stimulus and/or overprotective parents.
• Lack of fitness and tendency toward being overweight because of sedentary lifestyle.
• Difficulty dealing with abstractions and a limited conception of the "whole."
• Difficulty in conceptualizing boundaries.

The child with severe visual impairments needs auditory and tactile stimulation. As teachers, we need to encourage this child to venture beyond the known environment, to explore the gymnasium and the playground. We need to promote social interaction with peers, as well as adults, and to maximize learning through all the senses. Learning goals for children with serious visual impairments focus on attention to sensory abilities, spatial awareness, and mobility. Visually impaired children need the maximum use of their proprioceptive, auditory, haptic, and spatial perceptions.

For visually impaired children, proprioceptive perception is important for maintaining balance. Body awareness and proprioceptive perception can be increased through activities that focus on the identification of body parts and awareness of the relationship of body parts to each other and of the body part's position in space. Children can be asked to move individual body parts when the body part is named and to perform certain movements with the isolated body part, for example, swing or tap. Teachers can increase proprioceptive

Ron, a child blind since birth, was mainstreamed into a physical education class. The class was studying balance—balance on different bases of support and balance in inverted positions (Chapter 22). Ron was working independently in the space defined by the boundaries of his gymnastics mat. Suddenly he cried aloud; the entire class stopped and turned in his direction. Nothing was wrong; Ron was experiencing for the first time the change in body position and perception that accompanies being balanced in an inverted position on the hands only. Ron apologized for disturbing the class, and activity continued. During sharing time at the end of the class, Ron shared his feelings of the experience and his enthusiasm for more gymnastics.

awareness by adding small weights to body parts and then instructing children to move the parts. The gymnastics skills of balancing on different body parts and in different positions also help this development.

The senses are also used to establish spatial awareness. Children who are blind have difficulty perceiving the relationship of objects in space and the spatial relationship of themselves to objects. Lateral and directional activities, such as identification of left and right sides; movement away from self—left, right, up, down, front, back; and positioning of self in relation to equipment (for example, a table or a chair) help develop this perception in children without the visual sense. Auditory cues help these children determine distance in space. Sound-emitting devices can be placed on stationary equipment and the equipment used with a partner to help measure distance, location in space, and pathways of travel. Young children can face sounds made at different locations and thus determine near and far. Older children can follow a bike rider by the sound of cardboard on the spokes or copy the pathway of a partner by changes in intensity of the sound.

One of the greatest disabilities of visually impaired children is lack of mobility. A mobility training program in the gymnasium, as well as the outdoor play area, increases the child's independence and thus the ability and desire to participate fully. Three-dimensional models of both the indoor and outdoor physical education environments, including permanent equipment, give visually impaired children the concrete, hands-on experience to develop a conception of the whole and the ability to move within the physical education space. The mobility training should also include a peer-guided tour of the environment and time for personal exploration of the environment, including full use of tactile and auditory senses. The blind child should be free to walk, crawl, and touch the gymnasium without the embarrassment of a class of onlookers; the teacher, parent, or a trusted adult should be present to answer questions and ensure safety.

The inclusion of visually impaired children in physical education classes has implications for the teacher, the environment, and physical education equipment. Specific implications for the teacher include:

- Teach with manual guidance accompanied by verbal directions.
- Remember that the visually impaired child relies heavily on tactile perception. Manually guiding the visually impaired child can serve as the demonstration of the skill for other children, thus benefiting the group as well as the individual.
- Provide specific and immediate feedback. For profitable feedback, the teacher must thoroughly analyze movement skills and provide the verbal cues for correcting deviations.
- Use peer teaching to assist with the manual guidance and verbal feedback.
- Involve visually impaired children in small-group and partner activities rather than large-group situations.
- Avoid activities that involve throwing and catching with fast speed and travel.
- Progress from simple tasks in gymnastics and games to sequentially more difficult tasks to develop motor skill and cognitive complexity.
- Involve all children in the world of creative movement experiences and dance. Creative dance comes from the inner self; it is born of the senses. Vision is necessary only for the observer.

Adaptations in the environment include:

- Ensure that the gymnasium is well lighted to help the child with residual vision.
- Vary the texture of the boundaries for game areas—dirt/grass for the play area, sand for the surrounding area.
- Make pathways between targets or bases 3 to 4 feet wide and of a different texture.
- Keep the outdoor teaching area and the gymnasium well organized and consistent. Introduce new equipment to visually impaired children by means of three-dimensional models.
- Provide tactile markings on the floor as a reference for teaching stations, the center for teacher directions, water fountains, and so on.
- Place guide ropes across the gymnasium or playground to permit the practice of locomotor skills and freedom of travel. Tie a series of knots in the ropes to signal the approach of the boundary.

The inclusion of visually impaired children may necessitate such special equipment as:

- Brightly colored balls and objects for children with limited vision
- Sponge and foam balls for projectile activities
- Protection for the eyes; eyeglasses
- Audible beep balls for tracking and location
- Battery-powered electronic sound devices within large marker cones to serve as bases
- A large gymnastics mat to serve as "personal space" for balancing and transferring of weight activities

Contact the American Foundation for the Blind, New York, NY 10011 (www.afb.org) for catalogs of special equipment.

We expect children with visual disabilities to participate to their fullest potential in physical education, trying not to let the child use the disability as an excuse to withdraw from activity and social interaction. Game situations that involve constant contact with the participants (for example, wheelbarrow travel and parachute activity) require the least adaptation. When new activities are introduced, having children with visual disabilities play in slow motion will help their orientation to the play environment and the rules. The use of the buddy system also helps these children participate in traveling activities. Note, however, that although young children naturally hold hands with partners, they need to know the correct way to assist a visually impaired person. That is, the visually impaired person should grasp the guide's upper arm above the elbow, thus permitting the nonsighted person to maintain a sense of control rather than being led as if helpless.

Falls, scratches, and bruises are a part of physical education for children with serious visual impairments. Visually impaired children need to be permitted to recover on their own, maintain their dignity, and attain maximum independence. The teacher must discuss with all members of the class the danger of being overprotective. With the exception of ball-handling/striking activities, the visually impaired child can function quite independently in physical education classes. Following orientation and mobility training, the teacher's task is simply to help the child develop skills and a belief in self.

Hearing Impairments

The term *hearing impairment* refers to hearing loss that can range from mild to profound. The disability includes those who have trouble hearing normal speech and those who can't understand even amplified speech. Approximately 5 percent of school-age children have a hearing loss that can affect learning, but only one in 1,000 is profoundly deaf. The term *deaf* is rarely used to classify a hearing impairment; most individuals labeled deaf have some level of hearing, being able to understand speech with the help of amplification or by hearing combined with watching the speaker's lips, facial expressions, and gestures. The danger of labeling a child deaf is that it may cause peers to stop interacting with the child and may actually make the child functionally deaf as an adult.

The social domain is the greatest problem for children with serious hearing loss. The hearing-impaired young child doesn't engage in play experiences with other children; speech, if present, is garbled and communication quite limited. Hearing-impaired children don't understand their role in the play experience and often withdraw, thus denying themselves the social interaction and development of motor skills that accompany play for young children. As children's games become more complex, the hearing-impaired child is likely to be left out of the activities. Rules are developed as the game is played; instructions are shouted in the midst of play. Without special assistance, the hearing-impaired child is unable to comprehend all the intricacies of the game. Thus, the child fails to develop the social skills learned through group interaction in play. Withdrawal from activity causes a developmental lag in motor skills.

The frustration of being unable to communicate, to be understood by others, and to express emotions in socially accepted ways often leads children with serious hearing impairments to express their emotions through physical means. Aggressive behavior is often the means of expressing negative emotions. Additional characteristics of a child with a serious hearing impairment may include:

- Slow development of inner and expressive language, often leading others to mistake the child as mentally retarded
- Poor pronunciation; garbled speech
- Absence of laughter
- Difficulty in dealing with abstractions due to slowness in developing inner language
- Hyperactive appearance because of constant movement to maintain visual contact
- Lack of good balance in some hearing-impaired children caused by inner-ear damage
- Shuffling gait resulting from not hearing the sound of movement

We strongly recommend a course in sign language for teachers with hearing-impaired children in their classroom or gymnasium. Think of how much better the hearing-impaired child will feel when greeted the first day of physical education by a teacher she or he can communicate with!

Most children with hearing impairments function quite well in the regular physical education program. As a rule, adaptations in equipment or environment won't be necessary. However, the physical education teacher needs to modify certain aspects of teaching:

- Position yourself so the child with a serious hearing impairment can read your lips; be conscious of not turning your back when speaking; and be close enough for lip reading.
- Face the sun when outdoors so that the hearing-impaired child doesn't have to face the sun.
- Let the hearing-impaired child move freely in the teaching environment so that he or she can always be in the best position for hearing.

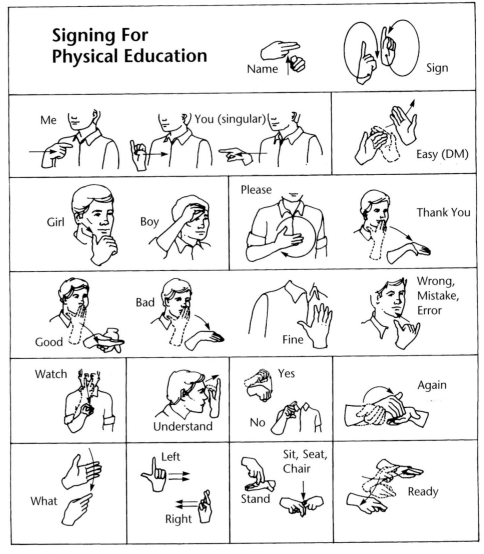

Figure 6.1 Signing for physical education.

Source: From "Signing for Physical Education," by C. B. Eichstaedt, 1978, with permission from the *Journal of Physical Education, Recreation, 49*(5): 20–21. JOPERD publication of the American Alliance for Health, Physical Education, Recreation and Dance, 1900 Association Drive, Reston, VA 20191.

- Visually and manually demonstrate skills; don't rely on verbal directions alone.
- Remember, the hearing-impaired child can't read lips or hear a whistle across the playing field or gymnasium; accompany the auditory sound with large hand signals.
- Learn the basic sign language needed for communication. Figure 6.1 provides specific signs for physical education and basic communication.

Hearing-impaired children with a developmental lag in motor skills need additional physical education to develop the motor skills and movement patterns needed for successful participation in the regular program. Those with balance problems and vertigo due to damage to the inner ear need additional work in the area of balance to develop maximum use of the visual and kinesthetic cues for balancing activities. Tumbling activities with rotation and climbing to heights on large apparatus should be done only with close adult supervision. Children who have poor motor skills and/or difficulty with balance are very conscious of how their abilities compare with those of their peers; a private place to practice can help overcome self-consciousness in attempting skills.

Like many children with disabilities, the child with a serious hearing impairment may be less skilled because of a lack of experiences. As teachers, we try to

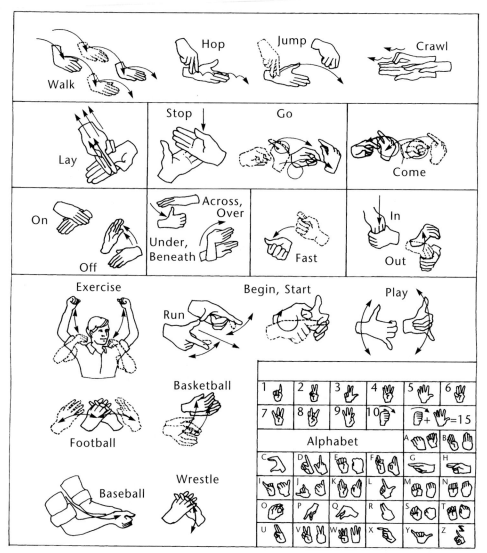

Figure 6.1 Continued.

maximize strengths rather than focusing on the weakness, the inability to hear. The child will have to experience success in activities to build the self-esteem needed for eager participation and social interaction. The directions and simple activities that the class can grasp easily may have to be carefully explained to the child with a serious hearing impairment. Encourage the other children to initiate conversation with the hearing-impaired child to help the child understand class activities, but caution them not to patronize the youngster. We need to educate all children in our classes to interact with the hearing impaired, to accept their less-than-perfect speech, and to involve them in both physical education and play activities.

The *National Standards for Adapted Physical Education* (U.S. Department of Education, 1994), is an excellent reference for further understanding of the unique attributes of learners with various disabilities and the considerations for successful inclusion of these children in our physical education programs.

Physical Disabilities

Physical disabilities include conditions resulting in orthopedic impairments, such as cerebral palsy and spina bifida, the crippling diseases of arthritis and muscular dystrophy, permanent loss of limbs, and the temporary disabilities caused by fractures. Other related health factors that can mean limited or restricted physical education for children include hemophilia, severe burns, congenital heart defects, and respiratory disorders.

Each child with a physical disability has different physical and motor capabilities, so the learning goals must be designed to meet individual needs. The child's physical education program will include two aspects: (1) the exercises and activities to meet specific needs and develop motor skills and (2) any adaptations in the regular program of physical education. The following procedure is recommended when planning the program for children with physical disabilities:

1. Identify the child's clinical condition.
2. Determine what activities would be contraindicated based on medical recommendation.
3. Determine functional motor skills needed.
4. Select activities that will develop desired motor skills.
5. Adapt the physical education environment and equipment as needed to provide the program.

It's important to remember that the program will be designed in consultation with a physician and a physical therapist. As teachers, we aren't expected to make a clinical diagnosis or to prescribe a program of individualized remedial exercises without the assistance of trained medical professionals. The professionals familiar with the child's medical history will be valuable consultants to the team developing the child's program (Box 6-2).

Cerebral Palsy Perhaps the most misunderstood of all children with disabilities are those with cerebral palsy. Because of the language and auditory dis-

---

Box 6-2

What Do I Say? What Do I Do? Tips for Times with Children Who Have Disabilities

- Act naturally. Be you. We often have a tendency to either ignore a disabled child or overattend. Like Goldilocks, pick the amount of attention that is "just right."
- Assume the child is bright. Talk as you would to any child, until you are told to do otherwise. It is better to "talk up" to someone than to talk down.
- Talk to the *child*, not to the attendant, parent, or teacher.
- Establish eye contact. This may mean sitting down, comfortably half kneeling, or moving to one side (if the child cannot look straight ahead). Avoid standing behind the wheelchair and talking. Many children rely on facial cues, gestures, and clear hearing to understand all that you are saying.
- Avoid simple yes/no questions. They make for dull, one-sided conversation—for anyone! Instead, ask about family, friends, activities. Don't ask, "Did you enjoy the circus?" but rather, "What did you see at the circus?" "Who did you go with?" and "Tell me about the elephants."
- Wait for replies . . . patiently. Repeating a question too soon may interrupt a child who is attempting to formulate an answer.
- Keep conversation about a child's wheelchair to a minimum, not because it is insulting (it isn't) but because often it is all people find to talk about (e.g., "I bet you can zoom around in that thing! I wish I had one. How fast does it go? Can I ride? How long do the batteries last?"). A little wheelchair talk is OK, but move to other topics that are more interesting to the child.
- It is fine to use phrases like "I have to run now" to a child in a wheelchair, or "I see" to a child who is blind.

- Many children cannot help drooling. Saliva won't kill you. Don't be hesitant to wipe someone's mouth (with their permission) or hold a hand that is wet.
- Yes, touching is OK. Holding hands, hugging, or a pat on the back are appropriate if they are something you would do with any child. A pat on the head is typically considered a condescending gesture. Appropriateness is the key. Keep in mind that some children are too affectionate and need to learn proper social interaction.
- Roughhousing is great—provided you get clearance (ask the parents). Being "thrown around" is part of growing up!
- Ask permission before you help a child. Ask the parents, too, if they are present—but ask the child first.
- When lifting children, first show them and then tell them where they will be set down.
- A child with a disability can misbehave just like any other child. Not to mince words: They can be snotty. Or they can be nice. Don't let yourself become so tolerant that you allow clearly unacceptable behavior.
- Don't feel as if everything you have to say needs to be funny or light. Serious topics are welcomed. Some children appreciate a break from laughing because they cannot control that response very well.

Source: Dave Taylor, *Project Active Newsletter, 12(1)*, 1991, Joe Karp, (ed.), Northshore School District, Bothell, WA. Used with permission.

One of the keys to successful inclusion of children with disabilities is to promote the acceptance of those children by their peers. Many children have never been around children with disabilities and are hesitant about beginning conversations with them or engaging in activity. The physical education teacher should coordinate efforts with the classroom teacher to orient children to the nature of the disability, its correct name, any limitations it imposes, and the potential for activity. Sensitivity training for all children can include such physical activities as:

- Forming a circle, standing with legs shoulder-width apart, and rolling a playground ball across the circle while the *eyes are closed*
- Playing a simple game with no verbal sound—no verbal clues for directions, rules, and stopping the action
- Executing simple ball-handling and racket skills with the nondominant hand

With minimal teacher assistance, this child participates successfully in the physical education program.

abilities and the lack of muscular control that often accompany cerebral palsy, the child is often labeled mentally retarded. Social acceptance and recognition of strengths are major obstacles for children with cerebral palsy. Cerebral palsy is a neurological impairment, an impairment caused by incomplete development of, or injury to, the central nervous system. Cerebral palsy may occur as a result of prenatal factors, injuries during birth, or postnatal conditions such as a serious childhood disease with a high fever or a head injury. Characteristics associated with cerebral palsy include:

- Disabilities in visual, auditory, and perceptual development and in speech
- Lack of concentration, distractability, overexcitability, and hyperactivity causing underachievement and poor behavior
- Poor coordination and lack of balance, resulting in awkward movements and frequent falls
- Difficulty in coordinating eye movements
- Tendency toward seizures

The lack of coordination associated with cerebral palsy results in a delay in motor control. The child with cerebral palsy will benefit from the breakdown of skills to basic components and sequential presentation of those components. Due to either restricted or extraneous movements, the child with cerebral palsy expends a great deal of energy when performing physical activity; a decrease in endurance may result. The physical education program for a child with cerebral palsy should concentrate on perceptual motor activities—locomotor patterns, balance, response to rhythm, development of ocular control, and form perception—as well as the development of skills for successful participation. Additional exercises may be recommended by the physical therapist to focus on the following factors:

- Muscle stretching to relieve contractures, prevent bone deformities, and permit fuller range of motion
- Muscle awareness exercises to elicit conscious control
- Relaxation techniques to help control contractures, rigidity, and spasms
- Posture alignments
- Gait training for walking patterns
- Exercises/activities to increase muscular strength

For some children with cerebral palsy, the only effect is a slight speech impairment; for others there is a total inability to control body movements. The physical education teacher will benefit from extensive reading concerning the type of cerebral palsy and from discussion with the physical therapist concerning

Teacher

I will know you.
I will touch you and hold you
And smell and taste and listen
To the noises that you make—and the words, if any.

I will know you.
Each atom of your small, lonely
Aching, raging, hurting being
Will be known to me
Before I try to teach you.
Before I try to teach
I must first reach you.

And then, when I have come to know you, intimately,
I will insist, gently, gradually, but insist
That you know me.
And later, that you trust me
And then yourself.

Now, knowing each other, we will begin to know
   the world—
The seasons, the trees, animals, food, the other children,
The printed word, books,
The knowledge of what has gone before and been
   recorded.

Then as surely as I moved toward you
I will move away.
As I once insisted on being close to you,
Demanding entrance into your half wild world
Of fear and fantasy, refusing you aloneness.

So now, I move away.
As your words come and your walk quickens,
As you laugh out loud
Or read clearly and with understanding,
I stand behind you—no longer close—
Available, but no longer vital to you.

And you—you grow!
You are! You will become!

And I, the teacher,
I turn, with pride in you,
Toward my next child.

                                      Mary MacCracken

Source: In Touch, 1(6), July 1978. Used with permission
from National Mental Health Association.

special needs and the adaptation of equipment and activities for maximum participation.

Spina Bifida   Spina bifida is a congenital condition in which the bony elements of the spine don't close properly during development in the womb. The condition may result in a cystlike formation on the spinal column that contains part of the spinal cord, a protruding sac containing covering tissue, or a malformation with no protrusion of spinal cord. In mild cases of spina bifida, the only effects may be weak muscles and deviations in posture. Because spina bifida causes paralysis in the legs and a loss of sensation in the lower limbs, children with mild spina bifida benefit from weight-bearing activities to stimulate bone growth and circulation in the lower limbs, as well as from exercises/activities to develop muscular strength in the upper body.

Children with spina bifida have normal intelligence; they have the same play and social needs as all children. Adaptations in physical education will be those needed to accommodate their mode of transportation, that is, crutches or wheelchair. In addition to the areas of need noted above, it is necessary for children with spina bifida to develop skills for participation with their peers in physical education and skills for lifetime sports and activities in which they can be successful.

Like many children with disabilities, children with spina bifida benefit from the socialization inherent in physical education, in addition to learning and developing skills. Guiding this growth is perhaps the greatest contribution we as physical educators can make in educating children with disabilities.

Muscular Dystrophy   Childhood muscular dystrophy begins between the ages of 2 and 6. It's an inherited disease; the exact nature of the inheritance isn't yet known. Muscular dystrophy is a progressive disease that affects the voluntary muscles, for example, legs and arms; involuntary muscles, such as the diaphragm, aren't affected. First affected are the muscles involved in walking and standing; the child with muscular dystrophy will begin to have difficulty maintaining posture, getting up from a chair, or walking up stairs. The degenerative nature of the disease causes the general deterioration of the muscle tissue and a replacement of muscle with fat. Thus, the young child with muscular dystrophy initially appears quite healthy as the legs and arms maintain or increase in size.

The child with muscular dystrophy has a tendency to tire easily. Fine manual dexterity is gradually lost, and the progressive weakening of the muscles causes adverse postural changes. The learning goals for the child with muscular dystrophy should concentrate on exercises to strengthen the muscles involved in the basic tasks of daily living, walking patterns, posture control, and stretching of contractures. However, these exercises must be selected in consultation with the child's physician. The child with muscular dystrophy should be kept actively involved in physical education to the extent the condition permits; inactivity only increases the atrophy of the muscles. Adaptations will be necessary as the child becomes dependent on crutches, braces, or a wheelchair.

Health-Related Impairments

Although not normally thought of as physical disabilities, several other health-related impairments can affect a child's full participation in physical education. The following disorders may require temporary adaptations in the child's environment or limitations in physical activity: juvenile arthritis, asthma, diabetes, heart defects, sickle cell anemia, severe burns, and respiratory disorders. The physical educator should review health records early in the school year, making note of any conditions that require monitoring and/or temporary adaptations. Open communication with the child's parents, rapport with the child, and an understanding of the particular disorder and its effects will result in maximum participation for the child as well as trust between you, the parents, and—most important—the child.

Asthma   Children are being affected in increasing numbers by asthma, an allergic reaction that results in wheezing, coughing, tightening of the airways, and accumulation of mucus in the bronchial tubes. An asthmatic attack can be triggered by allergens, upper respiratory infections, or even robust laughing. The most common conditions we see in physical education are reactions to changes in the weather (especially cold weather) and to strenuous exercise (e.g., the distance run for fitness assessment).

All too often in the past, physical educators treated lightly the asthmatic child who had a note, an excuse from running, or a request for adaptation in activity. Asthma is a serious health problem for millions of children. Failure to attend to the condition can result in serious and sometimes life-threatening consequences for the child.

The following suggestions will be helpful in ensuring maximum, healthy participation for children with asthma:

- Scan health records in the fall, noting children with asthma and/or serious allergies.
- Code your daily record system for individual reminders.

- Notify children with asthma or allergies and/or their parents before a day of especially vigorous activity.
- Encourage extra hydration during vigorous and/or prolonged physical activity.
- Ask the child before the activity if he or she brought an inhaler to physical education class.
- Consult with the parents of children with serious asthmatic conditions for any special safeguards or procedures.
- On days when adaptation is necessary, make needed modifications to provide maximum participation.

Diabetes   Another health impairment that necessitates our attention is type 1, insulin-dependent diabetes. Although we may experience only one or two children with diabetes in our years of teaching, the child with diabetes requires our having a thorough understanding of the disorder, an awareness of the warning signs of low blood sugar, and the knowledge to instigate immediate emergency procedures.

The goal for a child with diabetes is to make the diabetes fit into daily life as opposed to daily life fitting into the diabetes treatment plan. Children with diabetes can be expected to participate fully in physical education. If their physical education is scheduled before lunch or in the late afternoon, a snack may be advised in anticipation of the physical activity. On days of especially strenuous activity (e.g., the distance run for fitness assessment), an extra snack may be provided by the parents. Children with diabetes react emotionally as well as physically to daily insulin, ketone checks, and a routine that is different from that of their friends. Confidence in self and acceptance by peers is very important for these children. Success in movement skills extends beyond the gymnasium to aid feelings of self-worth and social acceptance.

Mental Retardation

The term *mental retardation* refers to intellectual functioning that is significantly below average, accompanied by deficits in adaptive behavior. Children with mental retardation function two or more standard deviations below average on a standardized intelligence test. They have problems of maturation, learning, and/or social adjustment, which, to different degrees, result in a degree of independence or social responsibility lower than that expected for their age. These characteristics manifest themselves during the early developmental periods of life.

The physical skills of many children with mild or moderate retardation are average and above; the difficulties center around comprehending the instructions and following through to complete the assignment. The mentally retarded youngster can more easily understand and follow directions if we remember the following:

- Keep verbal directions to a minimum; when possible use both visual and verbal instructions.
- Communicate in a direct, simple, and meaningful manner.
- Present tasks within the child's current level of physical skills.
- Structure the environment for focus on tasks and a minimum of distractions.
- Maintain a routine so that the child knows what to expect.
- Provide repetition of experiences for overlearning.
- Minimize the number of variables to which the child must attend; simplify the task.
- Present the lesson in short segments; restate the task at regular intervals.
- Reinforce strengths with frequent praise; minimize weaknesses.

Mentally retarded children can perform simple gymnastics sequences and rhythmical routines and participate in skill development activities. The teacher's attentiveness to task presentation and lesson design will result in better learning, not just for children with cognitive deficits but for all students.

Many mentally retarded children are lacking in areas of verbal expression and social interaction. Physical education classes can provide excellent opportunities for growth in both these areas. The following suggestions will help foster personal and social growth for the mentally retarded child:

- Engage the child in conversation. Ask questions; encourage a response.
- Be an attentive listener; listen when the child speaks.
- Create opportunities for cooperative activities that *actively* involve the child.
- Recognize achievements; share them with the whole class so that they can appreciate and share in the child's accomplishment.
- Encourage verbal expression of feelings.

Just as we as teachers must take an active role in interacting socially and verbally with mentally retarded children, we must also teach their fellow students to do the same. The retarded child's initial response to another child's attempts at conversation or group participation may be silence; mentally disabled children may be unsure of themselves or not understand. Remind the other children to repeat the question or to reach out with a touch to include the disabled child in the group.

Locomotor activities are just as exciting to children with disabilities as they are to those without disabilities.

For all major disabilities and health-related impairments, excellent resources for furthering our understanding and the child's maximum development are available through the national foundations/organizations for each disability. These foundations may also be readily accessed via the Internet.

Remedial Physical Education and Mental Retardation Although many children with mild or moderate mental retardation have average or above-average physical skills, others have physical skills that are far below average because of a lack of experience or as a secondary characteristic of the disabling condition. For some mentally retarded children, the small-group physical education class can provide the "extra" practice they need to succeed in the regular physical edu-

A number of children with Down syndrome have a condition called *atlantoaxial subluxation*, a maladjustment of the cervical vertebrae in the neck. Because of the possibility of serious injury, people with atlantoaxial subluxation should not participate in any activities that place stress on the head and neck muscles. Down syndrome children with atlantoaxial subluxation should not be actively involved in inverted balances, rolling activities, or other gymnastics actions that could place stress on the head and neck.

cation class. For these children, the remedial physical education class provides the environment for learning the basic skills of physical education that will enable them to participate successfully in the gymnasium and on the playground.

The content of the remedial physical education class centers around three areas of physical/motor skill development. The first area of concentration is mobility, balance, and muscular strength—hopping, jumping, and running; stepping onto a low platform or climbing the first rung of a ladder; walking a low balance beam or bench; and grasping a bar and lifting the body off the floor, taking weight on hands and feet. These areas contribute not only to success in physical education but also to greater independence throughout life.

The second area of concentration is physical fitness. Although the child's flexibility is often very good, muscular strength—both abdominal and upper body—and cardiovascular endurance may be extremely poor. See Box 4-1 in Chapter 4 and Box 6-1 in this chapter for fitness testing and educational programs for special populations.

The third content area is the basic manipulative skills of physical education—throwing, catching, dribbling, kicking, and so forth. Children who succeed in these three content areas will participate meaningfully in physical education, attain greater personal independence, and improve their recreational/leisure skills on the school playground and beyond.

Early testing of the motor skills of the children in the remedial physical education class will help the teacher develop the educational plan for each child. This plan should be based on the child's present level of functioning and include goals for the year. Although evaluation is ongoing, motor skills tests should be conducted at least by midyear and again in the spring. Records of activities and achievements can be kept in simple chart form. Remember, progress for these children is often very slow and is measured in small increments; charting their progress will help you recognize and praise achievements.

Emotional Disturbance and Behavior Disorders

In increasing numbers, children come to us with behavior disabilities: emotionally disturbed, behavior disordered, hyperactive, attention deficit disorder (ADD), attention deficit hyperactivity disorder (ADHD), distractive, aggressive, impulsive, and socially unacceptable. Children classified as emotionally disturbed or behavior disordered have deficiencies in at least one of the following: characteristics that facilitate learning, characteristics that promote interpersonal relationships, and characteristics that foster appropriate behav-

ior under normal conditions. What classifies children with these characteristics as emotionally disturbed/behavior disordered is the persistence of the behavior, its severity, and its adverse effects on educational performance.

The role of the teacher is to control the learning environment while helping the child gain control. The following guidelines have implications for teachers of physical education:

- Provide a sense of order, structure, and dependability in the learning environment.
- Teach the child that verbal responses to frustration and conflict are acceptable but that physical aggression is not.
- Make it clear to the child that he or she is accepted even when the behavior is unacceptable.
- Establish short-range, achievable goals geared to the child's current level of functioning.
- Convey your expectations through your conduct and consistent messages.
- Avoid overreacting to extreme behavior; an emotional response from the teacher is counter, productive.
- Remember that what works for one child with emotional disturbance or behavior disorders may not work for another.

Physical activity has been shown to have a positive influence on children with behavior disorders or disruptive behaviors. These children benefit from physical education programs that emphasize fitness, balance, and basic movement; many have great difficulty with competitive games and sports. Because of their behavior, these children's past experiences in physical education have included more inactivity and less skill development than other students experienced. The development of basic skills may require attention. Programs such as Hellison's responsibility model (Chapter 9) and programs with a cooperative rather than a highly competitive focus have been found to positively influence the development of personal and social responsibility for these at-risk students.

Social Interaction Disorders

Children with social interaction disorders or pervasive developmental disorders include those with autism, Asperger's syndrome, and Rett's disorder. Although each disorder has its unique characteristics and varying degrees of severity, common to all are severe impairment of communication and/or social interaction skills and the presence of repetitive behaviors. These children appear extremely shy, often withdrawn into their own world. The indoor and outdoor environments of physical education can be a nightmare with loud sounds, an abundance of visual stimuli, and constantly changing activity. Very often their recourse is to withdraw to the inner world of self-movement (stimming) and self-talk or to wander aimlessly in the midst of the physical activity/instruction/play. Motor skills are often below the level of their peers.

Children with social interaction disorders can more easily function as members of our physical education classes if we remember:

• Changes in routine and transitions in activity are very difficult for these children.
• Visual cues are much more effective than auditory.
• Motor performance tests often underrepresent ability because of the child's failure to respond to auditory directions.
• Skills should be developed in contexts (i.e., functional patterns), not as isolated skills.

Major goals for children with social interaction disorders are appropriate social behaviors and social/verbal interactions. The physical education environment is rich in opportunities for this development. For these children, such skills must be taught and consistently reinforced. Appropriate nonverbal and verbal social skills do not develop naturally, nor do the children learn them from modeling others. Close communication with the child's consultant on the multidisciplinary team will be invaluable as you work toward the short- and long-range goals of the individualized education program.

Learning Disabilities

A specific learning disability is a disorder in one or more of the basic processes involved in understanding or using language. According to the U.S. Department of Health and Human Services, the disability may manifest itself as an imperfect ability to listen, think, speak, write, spell, or do mathematical calculations. Children with learning disabilities have normal intelligence but, unlike other children, are unable to perform academically within the normal IQ range. Children with learning disabilities are typically characterized by hyperactive behavior, short attention span, impulsiveness, poor self-concept, and often a delay in play development.

The motor skills of children with learning disabilities are difficult to categorize. Some children with learning disabilities experience no motor delays; others demonstrate a number of delays. The most common difficulties include visual-motor coordination, fine motor coordination, bilateral coordination, and balance. In the past, learning goals for children with learning disabili-

Children who have mild or moderate mental retardation, learning disabilities, or emotional disturbances but whose physical appearance does not manifest the disability are sometimes the least accepted by their peers. The class has the same expectations of them as of the nondisabled, and the class can become frustrated when the disabled do not behave or respond as expected. The class response is usually due to the students' lack of awareness of the disability or knowledge of its characteristics. We as teachers must educate our students regarding specific disabilities. We must answer their questions, increase their awareness of the disability, and thus increase their understanding and acceptance of all children.

ties focused on perceptual-motor development; more recently the focus has been on sensory integration. Selection of the activities for meeting learning goals must be based on assessment of the child's deficiencies. Not all learning-disabled children have motor/perceptual delays; not all have the same deficiencies.

Children with learning disabilities can be expected to participate fully in all physical education activities. Slight teaching modifications may be needed for individual students:

• To reduce hyperactive tendencies, prepare the lesson with several short activities in mind rather than one lengthy period of concentration.
• Give clear, brief instructions; ask the child to repeat the directions before beginning the activity.
• Use small learning steps, and praise the child's efforts and accomplishments. Remember, the attitude of the learning-disabled child is, "I can't."
• Use a positive behavior modification program if needed to increase appropriate and decrease inappropriate behavior (Chapters 9 and 10).
• End the lesson with a brief relaxation period.

Teaching children with learning disabilities can be a most rewarding experience (see Box 6-2). Teachers can help the youngsters develop socialization skills, motor skills many didn't know existed, and self-confidence. We believe that children with disabilities can benefit from physical education and from integration with others.

Creating Conditions for Inclusion

The question that still remains is, How do you create an inclusive environment where all students meet program goals through maximum learning and participation? At this point the idea of meeting the needs of so many different learners may feel overwhelming. However, rather than allowing ourselves to feel overwhelmed by focusing on student differences, the purpose of this section is to provide strategies for creating five universal conditions needed to maximize student learning and participation: Students need to feel competent, to belong, to feel useful, to have a sense of ownership, and to feel optimistic (Sagor, 2002).

Kids are sacred; activities or learning tasks are not. If the learning tasks or activities you choose to teach do not align with program goals or meet these five basic needs of all learners, you have three options: (1) continue to use the activity the way it has always been done and thus not meet the needs of kids, (2) stop using the activity entirely and miss the benefits of the activity, or (3) give the activity a make-over—modify it by accentuating the positive features and minimizing or eliminating the negative or inappropriate features (Morris et al., 2006). The third option allows you to take activities and modify them in ways that meet needs specific to your own setting. Morris and coauthors point out that the three keys to making successful and effective modifications are (1) change, (2) challenge, and (3) choice.

Change

A teacher must be willing to make changes when learning tasks or activities do not meet the needs of all learners. All activities are made up of basic categories that can be changed. These categories can include **grouping** (how learners are grouped, e.g., individually, in pairs, small groups, coed), **organizational pattern** (how learners are arranged, e.g., circle, lines, scattered, in designated zones), **equipment** (any objects, materials, or props, e.g., music, hoops, task cards, ropes, balls, **movement** (e.g., crawl, walk, crab walk, strike), and **conditions** (e.g., 3 minutes, without hands, until everyone stops, four turns, with blindfold) (Morris et al., 2006). See Box 6-3. See also Chapter 31 for more categories that can be used specifically for playing games.

Simple changes across such categories can make almost any activity more inclusive. When teaching students at the precontrol level to catch by having them learn to stop a rolling ball as described in Chapter 25, simply change the equipment from a regular plastic ball to a larger, slow-moving, sound-emitting ball so visually impaired students can also learn to catch a rolling ball.

Changes can also alter the nature of student participation. For example, many students enjoy and even beg at times to play elimination games (activities that involve eliminating other students in order to win, which are not promoted or included in *Children Moving*). This creates a situation where the more skilled students are allowed to dominate the activity while less skilled students, who actually need more practice, are sitting on the side and often feeling quite discouraged. For example, modified four-square (described in Chapter 26) is traditionally played as an elimination game. Many teachers use the rule that a student who misses by not being able to return the ball to an opponent is out of the game. You can change the rule to have students count how many in a row they can hit without missing, making the game a cooperative activity. Another change could be having students earn as many individual points as they can in a given time period (2 minutes for example). These simple rule changes exemplify best practices in physical education by maximizing participation for all students.

Challenge

Changes across each of the categories in Box 6-3 also can be made to challenge all students at an appropriate level. It is important to monitor the success of students closely. They should be successful approximately 80 percent of the time; otherwise, consider modifying the task so it becomes more or less difficult. (See Chapter 11 for more on student success rates). When teaching a group of diverse learners a skill, it is not unusual for a task to challenge some at an appropriate level while others seem almost bored with the task, and still others are frustrated because the task is too difficult. In order to challenge all students at a more appropriate level the teacher needs to utilize intratask variation as described in Chapter 11. Intratask variation is a technique in which the teacher decides to modify a task for individuals or small groups within the class. As pointed out in Chapter 11, this is a private interaction between one or more students and the teacher. The following are examples of intratask variation for the activity traveling to flee (in Chapter 20). The task is for students to spread out in space and on signal flee from an imaginary chaser by walking quickly.

1. Intratask variation used to make the activity more inclusive for a visually impaired student:

   "John, I would like you to use this guide rope (place rope in the visually impaired student's hand) to practice moving away from your imaginary chaser." The guide rope extends across the gym or playground to permit the practice of locomotor skills and freedom of travel. Tie a series of knots in the ropes to signal the approach of boundaries. Other children are spread out in space and practice fleeing an imaginary chaser by walking quickly.

Box 6-3

Examples of Items and Choices in Activity Categories

Grouping	Movements	Equipment	Conditions	Organizational Pattern
Age	**Locomotor:**	Nets, walls, rackets,	One bounce, using a	Scattered, in lines, in
Coed	power walk, push wheel	bats, scarves, ropes,	wedge, four beats,	rows, with a partner, in
Mix skill levels	chair, run, skip, hop,	music, hoops, toss	lower net, all must hit,	corners, back to back,
Similar skill	gallop, grapevine	rings, discs, scoops,	three step rule, using	elbow to elbow with two
Season of birthday	**Nonmanipulative:**	sticks, skates, bicycles,	two points of balance,	people, against wall,
(fall, spring)	turn, twist, roll,	heart rate monitors,	may run to first or third	across from your group
Favorite movies	balance, stretch	spots, mats, wedges,	base, until music stops,	
Favorite fruit	**Manipulative:**	balance beams, volley	without using feet,	
Clothing colors	throw, catch, volley,	birds, climbing harness	within boundaries	
By drawing numbers	dribble, strike, kick			
or cards	**(See the wheel in**			
	Chapter 16 for more)			
	Other:			
	to music, to the beat of			
	a tambourine			

Creating Choices for Each Category

You may want to combine with another group or keep your current group.	You can throw or hit the ball over the line to start the rally with your partner. You can choose to roll, step, or jump over the rope.	You may choose a large hula hoop or a smaller one (a larger hula hoop is easier to twirl around the waist than a smaller one). You may choose to raise or lower the net height. You may also decide to hit over a line on the floor.	You may choose to let the ball bounce once per side or use a no-bounce rule. For the first four beats of music you can either do four quick single jumps side to side or do two double-count jumps, one on the right, one on the left.	You may choose to work with a partner or alone.

Source: Morris, G. S. D., & Stiehl, J. (1999). *Changing Kids' Games* (2nd ed.). Champaign, IL: Human Kinetics.

---

2. Intratask variation to make the task more inclusive for several very skilled students:

   "See if the three of you can flee an imaginary chaser while avoiding the hoops on the ground." Other children continue original task.

3. Intratask variation for a less fit student:

   "Sue, you can move away from the chaser slowly until you feel ready to walk quickly again."

Choice

When modifying activities to meet the needs of all students, choice is key (Morris et al., 2006). Offering children choice among appropriate challenges (or

tasks) not only creates a more inclusive environment but also empowers children by allowing them to make decisions about how they want to participate. When students have choices they are much more likely to participate. This becomes increasingly important as children become older, but it should also be used with elementary students. One way to offer students choice is through teaching by invitation (see Chapter 11). Unlike intratask variation, teaching by invitation allows students to decide what task they prefer to work on. The following are examples of ways to give children choices:

1. "Choose one of the objects in the hoops and keep the object from touching the ground by hitting it

up using an underhand motion." Place a variety of objects in hoops around the play area. Suggestions: Large bright items such as balloons and beach balls are slow moving and easy to see, and therefore may be appropriate for less skilled students. Medium-size, softer items such as a volleyball trainer or grocery store plastic ball may offer more challenge for others. Students may also find it motivating to use a less traditional item such as a volley bird just to try something new.

2. Station teaching or learning centers are popular instructional approaches among physical education teachers. A typical lesson may involve asking students to perform an exercise at each of several fitness stations. Jim Stiehl, a teacher of diverse learners, advises that if you want to ensure students fail, provide only one way to do something. This one-size-fits-all approach in fitness stations means requiring that everyone perform the same thing at each station. To avoid this, set up each station to represent a health-related fitness component such as muscular fitness, cardiovascular fitness, and flexibility or body composition. At each station place three color-coded plates (red, white, and blue). Tell students that red represents the most difficult task, white represents the medium-level task, and blue represents the easiest task. Then place pictures and/or descriptions of exercises under each plate. At each station students can choose to perform the red, white, or blue exercise or a combination of all three. For example, at a flexibility station the exercise under the red plate (most difficult) might be, "While sitting, touch your toes with both hands and hold for 10 seconds"; under the white plate (medium difficulty), "While sitting, see if you can touch your toes with both hands for 5 seconds"; and for the blue plate (easiest), "While sitting, see if you can touch your knees with both hands and hold for 10 seconds." Another set of plates may include red: straight-leg push-ups; white: modified push-ups (bend knees); blue: wall push-ups.

3. It is also important to break ourselves of thinking that games, dance, and gymnastic activities must be done "the way they have always been done" or even done according to their names. For example, when playing a modified striking and fielding game, a student with a disability came to bat and told the pitcher (a pre-service teacher) that he could not bat but could kick, so he wanted the pitch rolled to him. Amazingly, the idea of not participating because he was unable to bat never crossed this student's mind. Instead he quickly thought of a modification and insisted he could play as long as he had the choice to kick a larger ball rather than hitting a small ball. Less skilled students then cre-

ated their own adaptation by asking to have the larger foam ball tossed to them so they could hit it with the bat. As in this example, choice can be offered to students within the same activity by keeping an open mind about how a game or activity must be played and in this case allowing student input.

In order to create more inclusive physical activity environments, physical education teachers must make deliberate attempts to provide choices. Karl Rohnke (1989) tells us to always offer choices because a coerced player is no longer a player. Choice encourages participation, accommodates diversity, and empowers students to make responsible decisions about their own participation (Morris et al., 2006). One teacher will always struggle to meet the needs of all students. However, by structuring the environment in ways that provide choice, students can make decisions about what works best for them.

This section does not simply provide a long list of new activities; instead it provides structure for modifying learning tasks to create a more inclusive environment. Using the concepts of change, challenge, and choice as described here will enable you to create or modify any activity to better meet the needs of your own learners and achieve program goals.

Meeting the Needs of Children with Disabilities

Meeting the needs of the child with disabilities is a joint effort of school professionals, parents, and professionals from related services. The physical education teacher is a critical member of the professional staff planning for and implementing the program for a child with disabilities.

The Multidisciplinary Team

The appropriate education—both placement and curriculum—for each student with disabilities is determined by a multidisciplinary team called the *M-Team*. The M-Team is composed of all those involved in providing an appropriate education for the child: the classroom teacher, special educators, parents, and professionals from related services. Following an educational assessment by the school psychologist and other professionals as needed, the M-Team designs the educational program for the child, identifies support services needed and services to be secured from outside agencies, and establishes the educational goals to be attained within the given school year.

Because physical education is a direct service for all children with disabilities, the physical education teacher is a vital member of the multidisciplinary team. As a member of the M-Team, the physical education specialist provides information about how the identified disability will affect the child's performance in the existing program of physical education, the child's performance in physical fitness and basic motor skills and patterns of physical education, and the support services needed to facilitate maximum learning and to meet the unique needs of this child. During the M-Team meeting short- and long-term goals are written for all areas of the child's learning, and the environment most conducive to meeting those goals is identified. As the physical education professional on the M-Team, your input is needed to establish the short- and long-term goals relative to physical education and to identify the environment most conducive to meeting those goals.

Physical education options may include full inclusion, inclusion with a teacher assistant, or remedial physical education in addition to the regular program. The goal of the last is assistance in specified areas for better functioning/performance in the regular physical education program.

Individualized Education Program

Education for a child diagnosed with disabilities is formulated through the individualized education program (IEP). Generally, the IEP is limited to curricular areas of special education and related services—instruction designed to meet the unique needs of the child and the related services necessary to help the child achieve maximum success. The IEP includes:

- A statement of the present level of the child's functioning
- Annual goals
- Short-term instructional objectives with timelines
- An explanation of the extent to which the child will *not* participate in the regular educational setting (physical education program)
- Special services to be provided, including their duration and extent
- Support services needed—personnel and equipment
- Plan for evaluation of annual goals

For some students with disabilities, full participation in physical education is possible; therefore, the IEP will not address physical education. For some students, full participation is possible with support services, that is, personnel and/or equipment; these services will be identified in the IEP. For still other students, the development of skills for successful participation will require modification within the physical education curriculum, perhaps an alternative when an activity is not appropriate or is contraindicated. This alternative may be participation in another physical education class or work on a short-term physical education goal from the IEP within the class setting.

Even at the elementary level, physical education for children with disabilities should focus on the development of functional and motor skills that lead to physical activity and successful recreational participation. Short- and long-term goals for the child in physical education will center around the skills needed for meaningful participation in physical education, the remediation of deficient motor skills and fitness components, and the skills needed for successful participation in physical activities at recess and in after-school play/recreational activities.

The IEP is a projection of what professionals and the parents think the child can accomplish. If the annual goals are inappropriate, the M-Team reassesses the child's curriculum and formulates new goals better suited to the child's needs.

Least Restrictive Environment

The least restrictive environment is the educational setting that is most appropriate and most enabling for the child with disabilities. To the maximum extent appropriate, children with disabilities are to be educated with nondisabled students; thus, the philosophy of inclusion.

Legal reasons aside, there are sound educational reasons for educating children with disabilities in the least restrictive environment. Research has shown that placing these youngsters with nondisabled children yields positive benefits in behavior and life skills. Educators have long agreed on the effectiveness of peer modeling in academics and skill acquisition among children. Furthermore, the inclusive classroom and gymnasium more closely mirror the real world than does the classroom or physical education setting that consists entirely of children with disabilities. Most of the students with disabilities we see in our public schools will reside and work within our communities and participate in community activities. The least restrictive, more enabling educational environment should give students with disabilities the same opportunities to learn, to develop personal potential, and to interact and mature socially that all other students receive.

Implementing the IEP

After the IEP has been written, it's the responsibility of all teachers working with the child with disabilities to implement what is written in the program. It is the responsibility of the physical education teacher to design instruction and to modify both teaching and curriculum to meet the short- and long-term goals written for physical education within the environment deemed least restrictive by the multidisciplinary team. Implementation actually begins with the IEP itself—the long- and short-term goals for the child with disabilities. When planning for inclusion we suggest using a top-down ecological model* (Block, 2000), as follows.

Step 1: Determine the critical skills the child with disabilities will need to be successful in the present—in physical education, on the playground—and in future recreational settings. Observe the child's homeroom at recess. What activities do the children choose to participate in during this time? What skills are needed for the child with disabilities to successfully participate in activities at recess? What are the skills he or she will need to be successful in the physical education program? What are the skills needed for successful participation in recreational activities outside the school setting? These are the skills that should be contained within the goals for physical education for the child with disabilities.

Step 2: Analyze the existing physical education program to match the existing program to the long- and short-term goals of the student's IEP. Are the skills taught within the regular physical education program consistent with the needs of the child with disabilities? What existing activities within the program will benefit the child? What activities are not appropriate for this child? An analysis of the existing curriculum will reveal areas of match between goals and existing program and areas in which modifications are needed. Ask yourself the following questions: Where are modifications needed? What modifications are needed in instruction (see Chapter 13)? What modifications are needed in curriculum (see Chapter 31)?

Step 3: Design modifications in your teaching and curriculum to meet the needs of the child with disabilities. Planning for inclusion in physical education permits the child with disabilities to be physically educated along with his or her peers. Implementation of the IEP will be much easier and learning much greater

---

*A top-down ecological model implies that planning is based on the skills students need to achieve to be successful in the future. We plan for the skills they will need as they leave elementary school.

Essential Elements of Inclusion Programs

- A full continuum of placement options and services. Placement and services must be determined for each student by a team that includes all stakeholders and must be specified in the individualized education program (discussed later).
- Appropriate professional development, as part of normal work activity, for all educators and support staff associated with such programs.
- Adequate time, as part of the normal school day, to engage in coordinated and collaborative planning on behalf of all students.
- Class sizes that are responsive to student needs.
- Staff and technical assistance that are specifically appropriate to student and teacher needs.

Source: From *NEA Today* (July 1996), Washington, DC: National Education Association.

with planning for this special child and with the design of a developmentally appropriate program of physical education.

Whether the IEP specifies full inclusion, inclusion with support services, or inclusion plus a remedial program, we can no longer be content with letting the child with disabilities serve only as the scorekeeper. Neither can we accept "token" participation. Our task is to design the program to develop each child's skills in gymnastics, games, and dance, and to provide opportunities for these students to reach the goals that have been established for them.

Adaptations in tasks will permit any child to participate, to achieve, and to develop skills commensurate with personal ability. With an understanding of basic concepts, an awareness of the children's needs, and knowledge of how to adapt the environment and the curriculum, the teacher can create an enabling environment for children with special needs. Children with disabilities can function in an elementary physical education environment that allows individual response and fosters performance at the individual's skill level and that is taught by teachers who observe, reflect, and make changes in light of children's needs.

A Final Thought

As you strive to provide all students maximum opportunities to learn and to develop their personal potential, let the following student request be your inspiration.

Please, my teacher, open up your . . .
    Heart to **care** ever more deeply for us;
    mind to **think** ever more creatively about ways of
helping us learn;
    mouth to **seek** fresh ideas and feedback (including
from us!); and

classroom to **join** colleagues and parents in a
thriving community
where as teacher, parents and children together
we strive to reach our potential.
okay?
—*Ronald F. Ferguson, August 2003*

Summary

Diversity in the United States is steadily increasing. Diversity is defined as differences that exist among people. Physical education teachers must be prepared to teach all students including those with differences in mental and physical ability, skill level, fitness level, gender, culture, language, class, and physical characteristics. It is time to support diverse learners through a broadened conceptualization of inclusion that goes beyond accommodating students with special needs.

Inclusion does not mean sitting on the sidelines keeping score. Inclusion involves teachers creating a healthy learning climate where all children feel safe, successful, motivated, and connected to others and have a sense of ownership. When learning tasks or activities do not meet these basic needs of all learners, modifications must be made.

The concepts of change, challenge, and choice provide structure for making these modifications. Changes can be made to any task or activity across five categories: players, organizational pattern, equipment, movement, and rules/limits. Teachers should make changes across these categories in order to challenge all students at the appropriate level. Another strategy for meeting the needs of diverse learners is by creating conditions that allow students choice among appropriate tasks or challenges.

In addition to developing strategies for modifying learning tasks we should learn about the many ways students can be different. This includes learning about culturally responsive teaching, gender equity, religious differences, teaching overweight children, and teaching children with mental and physical disabilities. When a student with a disability or who speaks another language enters our classroom we should educate ourselves about their unique needs through extensive reading, as well as communicating with qualified professionals, parents, and community members.

When working with diverse students it is important to know that integrating children with special needs into regular educational settings is no longer a choice for teachers and administrators. The Individuals with Disabilities Education Act of 1990 guarantees each child with a disability a free and appropriate education in the least restrictive environment. The multidisciplinary team, commonly called the M-Team, determines the placement that constitutes the least restrictive environment.

The child's educational program, including annual goals, support services, and any special services, is written into the individualized education program (IEP). The IEP includes physical education as a direct service for all children with disabilities.

We need to educate all children concerning individual differences and orient them to the world of diversity. By promoting the acceptance of all individuals and presenting a curriculum that focuses on the development of skills commensurate with ability, we can promote the acceptance of all children as contributing members of physical education classes.

Reading Comprehension Questions

1. Define *diversity* and provide three specific examples of diversity in physical education.
2. Explain the term *inclusion expanded.*
3. Explain what culturally responsive teaching is. Use two specific examples of things a physical educator might do to become a more culturally responsive teacher.
4. Describe three ways a teacher can create a more gender-equitable environment.
5. Explain the purpose(s) or reasons for modifying activities.
6. Name three categories that can be used to change activities. For each category list one modification that could be made to decrease the difficulty of a task, and one modification that could be made to increase the difficulty of a task.
7. Explain how choice can be used to accommodate individual differences in physical educa-

tion. Be sure to include a specific example in your answer.

8. What is the Individuals with Disabilities Education Act? What is its impact on physical education?

9. What is a multidisciplinary team? What is its function? Who serves on the M-Team?

10. Why is the physical education teacher an important member of the multidisciplinary team?

11. What is an individualized education program? What does it include?

12. What are the three steps in planning for inclusion? Why is this planning important for inclusion of a child with disabilities in physical education?

13. Choose one physically disabling condition and explain its implications for physical education. Discuss the adaptations involved in physical education for this child—adaptations for the child, adaptations for the whole class, and adaptations for the teacher.

References/Suggested Readings

American Obesity Association. (2002). *AOA fact sheets: Obesity in youth.* Retrieved June 6, 2005, from www.obesity.org/subs/fastfacts/obesity_youth.shtml.

Auxier, D., Pyfer, J., & Huettig, C. (1997). *Principles and methods of adapted physical education and recreation.* St. Louis, MO: Times Mirror/Mosby.

Block, M. E. (2000). *A teacher's guide to including students with disabilities in regular physical education* (2nd ed.). Baltimore: Brookes.

Block, M. E., & Garcia, C. (eds.) (1995). *Including students with disabilities in physical education: A position statement.* Reston, VA: American Alliance for Health, Physical Education, Recreation and Dance.

Chappelle, S., & L. Bigman with Hillyer, F. (1998). *Diversity in action.* Hamilton, MA: Project Adventure.

Craft, D. H. (ed.). (1994). Inclusion: Physical education for all. *Journal of Physical Education, Recreation and Dance, 65*(1), 22–56.

Cummins, J. (1992). The empowerment of Indian students. In J. Reyhnor (ed.), *Teaching American Indian Students* (pp. 3–12). Norman: University of Okalahoma.

Davis, K. L. (1999). Giving women a chance to learn: Gender equity principles for HPERD classes. *Journal of Physical Education, Recreation and Dance, 70*(4), 13–15.

Davis, K. L. (2003). Teaching for gender equity in physical education: A review of the literature. *Women in Sport & Physical Activity Journal, 12*(2), 55–82.

Evans, J. R. (1980). *They have to be carefully taught: A handbook for parents and teachers of young children with handicapping conditions.* Reston, VA: American Alliance for Health, Physical Education, and Recreation and Dance.

Gay, G. (2000). *Culturally responsive teaching: Theory, research, & practice.* New York: Teachers College Press.

Haynes, C. C. (1999). *A teacher's guide to religion in the public schools.* Nashville TN: First Amendment Center. Available for free download at www.freedomforum.org/publications/first/teachersguide/teachersguide.pdf.

Houston-Wilson, C., & Lieberman, L. J. (1999). The individualized education program in physical education. *Journal of Physical Education, Recreation and Dance, 70*(3), 60–64.

Hutchinson, G. E. (1995). Gender fair teaching in physical education. *Journal of Physical Education, Recreation and Dance, 66*(1), 42–47.

Kahan, D. (2003). Religious boundaries in public school physical activity settings. (Law Review). *Journal of Physical Education, Recreation and Dance, 74*(1), 11–13.

MacCracken, M. (1978, July). Teacher. *In Touch, 1*(6).

Meece, J. L., & Kurtz-Costes, B. (2001). The schooling of ethnic minority children and youth. *Educational Psychologist, 36*(1), 1–7.

Milne, D. C., Haubenstricker, J. L., & Seefeldt, V. D. (1991). Remedial motor education. *Strategies, 4*(4), 15–18.

Morris, G. S. D., Stiehl, J., & Sinclair, C. (2006). *Change, challenge, choice: Creating strategies that include everyone.* Champaign, IL: Human Kinetics.

Napper-Owen, G. E. (1994). Equality in the elementary gymnasium. *Strategies, 8*(3), 23–26.

Napper-Owen, G. E., Kovar, S. K., Ermler, K. L., & Mehrhof, J. H. (1999). Curricula equity in required ninth-grade physical education. *Journal of Teaching in Physical Education, 19,* 2–21.

National Association for Sport and Physical Education (2005). *Physical education for lifelong fitness: The physical best teachers guide* (2nd ed.). Champaign, IL: Human Kinetics.

National Center of Educational Statistics. (2000). *The condition of education.* Washington, DC: U.S. Department of Education, Office of Educational Research and Improvement.

National Education Association. (1996, July). *NEA Today.* Washington, DC: National Education Association.

Oberti, C. (1993). Inclusion: A parent's perspective. *Exceptional Parent, 23*(7), 18–21.

Olson, L. (2004, Jan. 8). Enveloping expectations. In *Quality counts 2004: Count me in: Special education in an era of standards. Education Week on the Web.* Retrieved Sept. 14, 2005, from www.counts.edweek.org/sreports/qc04

Rohnke, K. (1989). *Cowstails and cobras II: A guide to games, initiatives, ropes courses & adventure curriculum*. Dubuque, IA: Kendall/Hunt.

Sagor, R. (2002). Lessons from skateboarders. *Educational Leadership, 60*(1), 34–37.

Seamon, J. (ed), (1995). *Physical best and individuals with disabilities: A handbook for inclusion in fitness programs*. Reston, VA: American Alliance for Health, Physical Education, Recreation and Dance.

Sherrill, C. (2004). *Adapted physical activity, recreation, and sport* (6th ed). New York: WCB McGraw-Hill.

Singer, A. (2004, December). The changing face of America. *eJournal USA: Society & Values*. Retrieved June 6, 2005, from usinfo.state.gov/journals/itsv/1204/ijse/singer.htm.

Sparks, W. G. III. (1994). Culturally responsive pedagogy: A framework for addressing multicultural issues. *Journal of Physical Education, Recreation and Dance, 65*(9), 33–36, 61.

Tiedt, P. L., & Tredt, I. M. (1990). *Multicultural teaching: A handbook of activities, information, and resources*. Boston: Allyn & Bacon. Quoted in Chepyator-Thomson, 1994.

Tomlinson, C. A. (2003). Deciding to teach them all. *Educational Leadership, 61*(2), 7–11.

U.S. Department of Education. (1994). *National standards for adapted physical education*. Washington, DC: U.S. Department of Education, Office of Special Education and Rehabilitation Services.

Winnick, J. (ed.). (1995). *Adapted physical education and sport* (2nd ed). Champaign, IL: Human Kinetics.

Winnick, J., & Short, F. (1999). *The Brockport physical fitness test manual*. Champaign, IL: Human Kinetics.

Teaching Skills

Austine-4

Part 2 describes many of the teaching skills that teachers use to help children learn and enjoy physical activity. Chapter 7, "Determining Generic Levels of Skill Proficiency," describes a system for matching class activities, or tasks, with the abilities of the children so that success rates can be high and enjoyment frequent. As we know, neither age nor grade level are accurate indicators of a child's physical abilities. Chapter 7 provides a system for observing children that can enable the teacher to match the content of the lessons (which are organized according to the generic levels) with the children's abilities.

Chapter 8, "Planning," discusses lesson planning skills. A poorly planned or inappropriately organized lesson often will fail, regardless of a teacher's ability to interact with children. Chapter 8 describes step-by-step effective planning for the year and the day and covers such important points as how to record progress, design lessons, and actually enjoy planning.

Chapters 9 to 11—"Establishing an Environment for Learning," "Maintaining Appropriate Behavior," and "Developing the Content," respectively—discuss skills used in the instructional process. Most of these skills involve direct interaction with children. Chapter 9 includes ideas for differentiating physical education class as a learning experience from recess. The chapter elaborates on various ways to establish the proper attitudes, how to foster an atmosphere conducive to learning in the gymnasium, and how to set up safety procedures.

Chapter 10 provides practical ideas on maintaining a productive environment, including approaches for working with both individual children and entire classes. Specific examples from actual teaching situations illustrate how to increase appropriate and decrease inappropriate behavior and how to maintain proper behavior. The teacher is shown how to interact positively with the children; work with them one on one; apply "punishment," such as time-outs and desists; and follow worthwhile reward systems, such as class rewards, tokens, and behavior games.

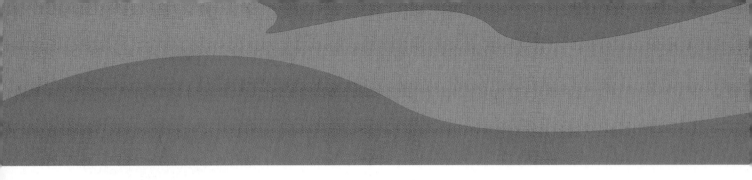

Chapter 11 outlines the process of making decisions to develop the content. Reflective teachers constantly find themselves asking such questions as these: "Which tasks are appropriate for this class of children?" "Will the children benefit from a cue (refinement), or should the task be changed to a harder or easier one?" "This task is appropriate for the children, but they seem to be getting bored—how can their interest be maintained?" These are the questions that we respond to in Chapter 11 as we explain a process for developing the content and provide practical examples. This is an especially important chapter because all of the chapters in Parts 3 and 4 are based on this approach to content development.

Chapter 12 focuses on the process of teaching physical education and includes a format for observing classes that includes safety, on-task behavior, and the movements of the entire class and individual children. Teachers are also told how to use the two observation techniques of back-to-the-wall and scanning and how to plan for observation.

Chapter 13, "Instructional Approaches," provides an overview of a few of the techniques used by physical education teachers to create active learning experiences for children. This chapter describes a number of other approaches beyond direct instruction—for example, task sheets, stations, peer teaching, cooperative learning, guided discovery, and child-designed instruction.

Each of these alternatives provides a more engaging way for children to learn as well as more fully addressing the cognitive and affective goals of our physical education classes.

The final two chapters in Part 2, "Assessing Student Learning" (Chapter 14) and "Understanding Your Teaching" (Chapter 15), both focus on attempting to determine how well lessons are going—for the children and for you as a teacher. In recent years educators have started to use alternative methods of assessing children. These techniques are ongoing (rather than a culminating experience at the end of a series of lessons) and are designed by teachers to assess specifically what they have been teaching. Some of the techniques are included in this chapter and include journals, exit slips, student drawings, and displays. Additionally, scoring rubrics are explained as a way to determine how well children learned what was taught.

Successful teachers not only assess children but also assess their own teaching. Chapter 15 describes some of the techniques teachers use to do so—by themselves or with the assistance of students and/or colleagues. This chapter concludes by discussing the importance of support groups for teachers as one way to provide encouragement and comfort in a challenging profession. As in Part 1, useful reading comprehension questions and references are provided at the end of each chapter.

Determining Generic Levels of Skill Proficiency

Where parents have a voice in physical education programs, they usually insist that the curriculum includes the dances, games, and sports skills of their culture. At the elementary level these activities are often preceded by the fundamental skills that are combined into more complex tasks as age and skill levels increase. . . . Teachers are to concentrate on the process of learning by selecting the appropriate content for whatever level of development the child demonstrates.

—VERN SEEFELDT

Key Concepts

- The generic levels of skill proficiency (GLSP) provide a relatively quick and easy way to assess the abilities of entire classes of children.

- The GLSP apply to the skill themes, not the movement concepts.

- The GLSP serve as a guide to matching the difficulty of a task (activity) to the ability of the students so they can have success, and yet still be challenged.

- Precontrol level is the beginner or novice level. At this level successful performances are typically accidents and rarely repeated.

- At the control level, tasks require intense concentration if they are to be performed successfully. Learners at this level are easily distracted.

- Learners at the utilization level are ready to combine several skills together or practice in dynamic, unpredictable contexts.

- Proficiency level is the expert or mastery level.

- It is unreasonable to expect children to advance from the precontrol to the proficiency level in a skill theme if they practice that skill only during physical education classes.

- Adults can be at the precontrol level in skill themes they have had little or no opportunity to practice.

Think about a group of your friends or maybe a class you are teaching. If they were asked to "dribble a ball with their feet through a general space" would they all be able to do it successfully? Would some, perhaps those on a soccer team, be much more proficient than others? Would some keep losing control of the ball?

You probably answered yes to the last two questions. Obviously age, or grade level, is not an accurate predictor of developmental level. If all fifth graders had identical motor skill abilities, this chapter would not be necessary. Typically, however, in a fifth-grade class there is a wide range of motor abilities—and that range only increases with age.

One challenge of reflective teaching (Chapter 5) is matching a task (activity) to the ability of a child. If a task is appropriate, not too hard and not too easy, the child will typically be successful and therefore remain interested, continue trying, and learn. If a task is too easy, however, the child will become bored and lose interest; too hard, and the child will want to do something else because of the frustration level. This is complicated drastically by the fact that we don't teach one child at a time—we typically teach 25 or more in a class. And the range of abilities within any class is typically a wide one. Some of the children may never have tried an activity, whereas others may have been playing it at home after school or on a team for several years.

In writing this book, we knew from the outset that describing and organizing activities according to the children's grade level would be inadequate. We discussed the possibility of organizing the curriculum according to the categories of beginner, intermediate, and advanced. We learned quickly, however, that even among the three of us who had been working together closely, there were different concepts of what constituted a beginning, an intermediate, and an advanced level of ability. We needed a classification system that would help us communicate with one another—and with you.

As we reviewed the literature, we came across a classification system developed by Stanley (1977), which we found to be descriptive and helpful in communicating the range of abilities related to a skill. She proposed four levels, which we have termed the *generic levels of skill proficiency (GLSP):* precontrol, control, utilization, and proficiency. As we discussed her system, we found that it was helpful to us and allowed us to describe and understand the range of motor abilities more accurately.

The term *generic* is synonymous with terms such as "universal, all-purpose, covering a broad spectrum." We thought it would be too difficult and confusing if we created a different classification system for each skill theme. Thus, we use the term *generic* to mean that the same classification system can be used to analyze youngsters' ability levels for all of the different skill themes. *Levels of skill proficiency* is the phrase we use to identify children's developmental level for each of the skill themes. We are not suggesting that the GLSP are precise, exact measures of motor ability. They are, however, immensely helpful as a way to observe a class of youngsters to quickly determine their overall ability and make an informed decision about which task is appropriate for the overall skill level of the class. The GLSP system also enables the teacher to assess individual youngsters quickly when attempting to manage an entire class.

We have organized and sequenced the content in the skill theme chapters by the GLSP. As you become familiar with these terms, we think you too will find them more descriptive and helpful than the beginner-to-advanced classifications. Before describing how we have used the GLSP throughout the text, we first need to define and describe each of the four skill levels.

Box 7-1

Observable Characteristics of the Generic Levels of Skill Proficiency

Precontrol Level

- Child is unable to repeat movements in succession; one attempt doesn't look like another attempt to perform the same movement.
- Child uses extraneous movements that are unnecessary for efficiently performing the skill.
- Child seems awkward and frequently doesn't even come close to performing the skill correctly.
- Correct performances are characterized more by surprise than by expectancy.
- When the child practices with a ball, the ball seems to control the child.

Control Level

- The child's movements appear less haphazard and seem to conform more to the child's intentions.
- Movements appear more consistent, and repetitions are somewhat alike.
- The child begins to perform the skill correctly more frequently.
- The child's attempt to combine one movement with another or perform the skill in relation to an unpredictable object or person is usually unsuccessful.
- Because the movement isn't automatic, the child needs to concentrate intensely on what he or she is doing.

Utilization Level

- The movement becomes more automatic and can be performed successfully, with concentration.
- Even when the context of the task is varied (slightly at first), the child can still perform the movement successfully.
- The child has developed control of the skill in predictable situations and is beginning to be able to move skillfully in unpredictable situations. The child can execute the skill the same way consistently.
- The child can use the skill in combination with other skills and still perform it appropriately.

Proficiency Level

- The skill has become almost automatic, and performances in a similar context appear almost identical.
- The child is able to focus on extraneous variables—an opponent, an unpredictable object, the flow of travel—and still perform the skill as intended.
- The movement often seems effortless as the child performs the skill with ease and seeming lack of attention.
- The movement can be performed successfully in a variety of planned and unplanned situations as the child appears to modify performance to meet the demands of the situation.

Identifying Levels of Skill Proficiency

Observable characteristics of each generic level of skill proficiency are discussed below and listed in Box 7-1.

Precontrol Level

The *precontrol* (beginner) level is characterized by lack of ability to either consciously control or intentionally replicate a movement. For example, a child at the precontrol level who is bouncing a ball spends more time chasing after the ball than bouncing it—the ball seems to control the child. A child who tries to do a forward roll may complete a revolution on a mat or may get stuck, not rolling at all or rolling half forward and half to the side and finishing flat on the back. A child's efforts to strike a ball with a racket are characterized by frequent misses, mishits, and an inefficient

and inconsistent striking pattern. Successful skill performances are a surprise! Most preschool and kindergarten children are at the precontrol level. By the time children are in the first grade, however, you'll observe some of them entering the control level.

Control Level

The *control* (advanced beginner) level is characterized by less haphazard movements—the body appears to respond more accurately to the child's intentions. The child's movements often involve intense concentration because the movements are far from automatic. A movement that is repeated becomes increasingly uniform and efficient. At this level, a cartwheel the child performs is identifiable as a cartwheel; the child is able to travel in a previously identified direction while briefly taking full weight on the hands. When the child tries to throw a ball at a target, the ball usually travels in the direction of the target.

Some primary-grade children are at the control level. You'll begin to observe that a few children involved in certain youth sports programs are at the next level, the utilization level. This is true only for their sport, however. For example, children involved in after-school gymnastics programs may be approaching the utilization level in the skill themes of rolling or transferring weight, but they may be at the precontrol level for throwing and catching or kicking a ball.

Utilization Level

The *utilization* (intermediate) level is characterized by increasingly automatic movements. A child at this level is able to use a movement in a variety of ways because he or she doesn't need to think as much about how to execute the movement. Dribbling a ball in a game situation is appropriate for a child at the utilization level. When children at the previous level (control) try to dribble a ball, they spend more time chasing the ball than dribbling because they're unable to focus on dribbling a ball while trying to travel away from an opponent. A cartwheel, as one in a sequence of three movements, is also an appropriate task for a child at the utilization level.

As children get older, the gap between the skill levels widens. Children in the fourth and fifth grades who are involved in youth sports programs are often at the utilization level in the skill themes used in their sport, but not necessarily in other skills. In the same class, however, it's not uncommon to have children who have remained at the precontrol level, primarily because of their lack of activity beyond formally organized physical education classes.

Proficiency Level

The fourth level, *proficiency* (advanced), is characterized by somewhat automatic movements that begin to seem effortless. At this level the child gains control of a specific movement and is challenged by the opportunities to employ that skill in changing environments that may require sudden and unpredictable movements (open skill). The challenge of repeating movements exactly and with ever increasing degrees of quality (closed skill) is also appropriate for children at this level. Rarely are elementary school children at the proficiency level in a skill. In almost every instance, their proficiency is a result of their extensive involvement in after-school youth sports programs.

One Child, More Than One Level

Now that you have an understanding of the four levels of skill proficiency, it is important to expand our use of the term *generic*. Once again, our jobs as teachers would be much easier if every child had the same ability—not only within a grade but also for every skill. If this were so, we could, for example, merely observe a child kicking a ball at the utilization level and thereby determine that the child was also at the utilization level in throwing, balancing, and jumping and landing. As you know, however, this is not the case. A child may be at the utilization level in one skill and at the precontrol level in another. It's not uncommon for children in our classes to be skillful (utilization-level) throwers and catchers and be at the precontrol level in the nonmanipulative skills of rolling, balancing, and transferring weight. By *generic*, then, we mean that the terms *precontrol, control, utilization,* and *proficiency* are used to describe a child's ability in every skill we teach—we don't use a different set of terms to describe the skill level for balancing, for example, and still another set of terms to describe the skill level for volleying. The hypothetical example in Figure 7.1 illustrates two points: (1) the GLSP apply to all of the skills we teach, and (2) children are typically at different skill levels for different skills.

Figure 7.1 also illustrates that age is not an accurate indicator of ability. If it were, all adults would be skillful

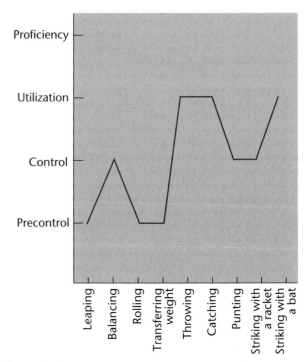

Figure 7.1 Hypothetical example representing a child's varying levels of proficiency in different skills.

at striking with a racket, for example, and we know this isn't true. We often observe fourth and fifth graders at the precontrol level when a new skill is introduced, one they have never practiced. Generally, however, because of their physical maturation and previous experiences, they move from the precontrol level more rapidly than the primary-grade children (although there are always exceptions).

Using the Generic Levels of Skill Proficiency in Teaching

The generic levels of skill proficiency provide a broad guideline for answering two important questions:

1. What is the ability level of this class?
2. Which tasks and activities work best for a class at this GLSP?

Although there will be a range of skill levels within any class, we as teachers make a judgment about the overall ability of the class. Then we modify the tasks for individuals using teaching by invitation and intratask variation, as discussed in Chapter 11.

Tasks that succeed with one class may need to be changed (made easier or harder) to meet the needs of the next class. The GLSP provide us with broad guidelines for doing so. For example, it is generally safe to assume that most of the children in school through first grade will be at the precontrol level.

In the upper grades, however, we typically find a few children who are at precontrol level, a number at control level, some at utilization level, and a few, especially in middle school, who might be at proficiency level. The higher the grade level, the greater the range of skill levels within a class.

Note that we use the generic levels of skill proficiency to describe a youngster's proficiency for each skill theme, for example, kicking, jumping and landing, striking a ball with a bat. The skill levels do *not* pertain to the movement concepts (Chapters 16 to 18), because the concepts aren't skills; they represent cognitive understanding expressed through versatile and efficient use of the skill themes. As you read further, this point will become clearer. For now, however, just remember that the four levels of skill proficiency apply to the skill themes only.

As reflective teachers we use the GLSP in two ways. First, we observe the students to determine their overall skill level. Second, we attempt to match the tasks to the skill level of the children in the class. For example, if we determine that the majority of the children in a class are at the precontrol level for the skill of kicking, we would not ask them to play a proficiency-level game such as Alley Soccer or Cone Soccer (Chapter 24). Instead, we would ask them to practice precontrol tasks, such as kicking a stationary ball from a standing position and then running to kick the ball.

Which Task?

As teachers gain experience and learn to use the GLSP, they become able to assess the overall skill level of a class rather quickly and determine which tasks will be helpful to that group (Graham et al., 1993; Housner & Griffey, 1985). For those who are new to the skill theme approach, or perhaps new to a school, it will take time and experience to learn the tasks that "work" with different grade and ability levels. Veteran teachers who have been teaching by skill themes know which tasks will work—and which will not. Beginning teachers, in contrast, will learn with practice the tasks that are most effective, and how to make them interesting and appealing to children of various grade levels. As you plan, especially when you start working with the skill theme approach, we recommend being prepared to deliver a series of tasks (10 to 15) in a lesson—not just one or two! Extensive planning will also help you learn the progression of tasks for each skill theme and movement concept. The chapters on planning and observation techniques (Chapters 8 and 12) that follow will also help you better understand how to plan for skill theme lessons—and when to use a task and when to change to a new one.

Finally, it is important to remember that there is no single, correct way to deliver the tasks in a lesson. Some teachers, for example, prefer to start at the precontrol level (for a class at the control level) and quickly progress up the spiral with a series of tasks that serve as a warm-up and review for the children. Others prefer to start with a task or activity that most closely matches that class's GLSP. If a task is too hard and children have high rates of failure and frustration, then a teacher who has planned well can move down the spiral to an easier task. That's why it is so important to plan a series of tasks rather than only one or two for a lesson.

How to Know If a Task Works

Chapter 12, "Observing Student Responses," explains in more detail how to know if a task works, but a quick overview of the process will be helpful here. A task works when youngsters are provided numerous chances to be successful—they want to keep doing the task. Tasks that are too hard or too easy lead to frustration or boredom. The GLSP will help you match tasks to the ability level of the majority of the class so that

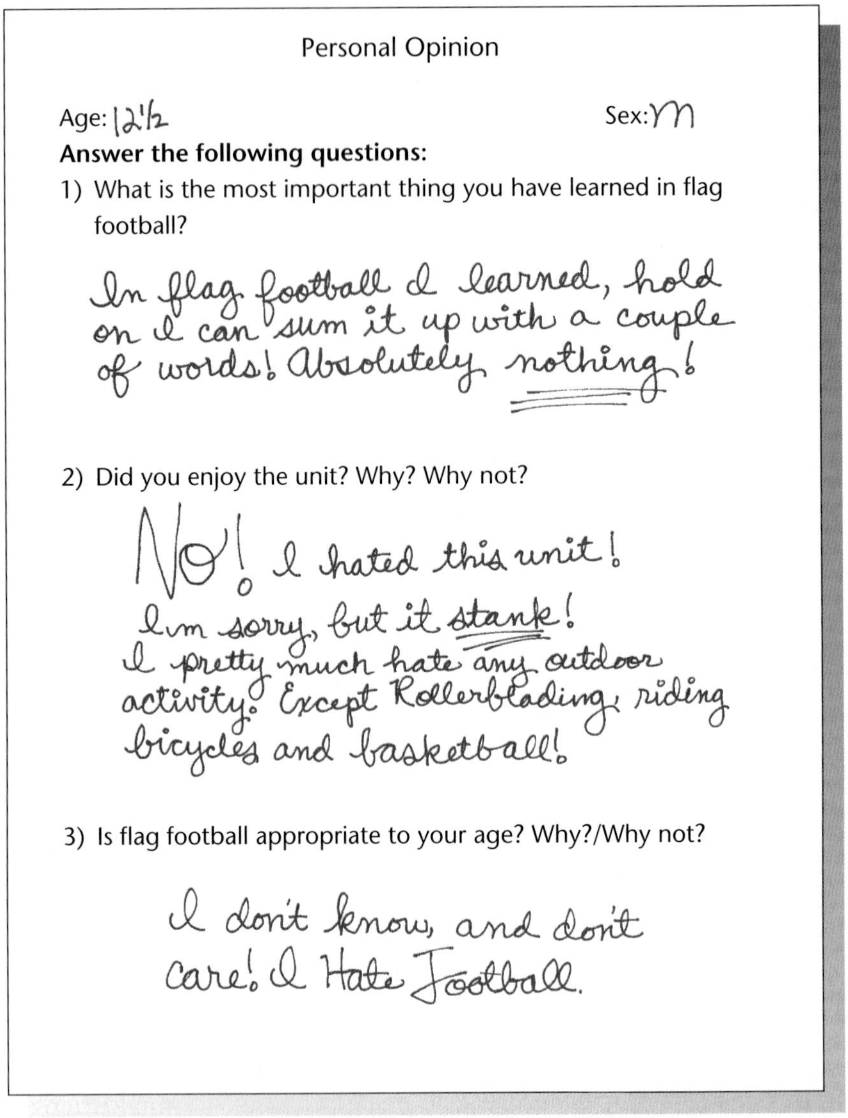

Figure 7.2 Sixth grader's evaluation of a flag football unit.

Personal Opinion

Age: 12½   Sex: M

Answer the following questions:

1) What is the most important thing you have learned in flag football?

In flag football I learned, hold on I can sum it up with a couple of words! Absolutely nothing!

2) Did you enjoy the unit? Why? Why not?

NO! I hated this unit! I'm sorry, but it stank! I pretty much hate any outdoor activity. Except Rollerblading, riding bicycles and basketball!

3) Is flag football appropriate to your age? Why?/Why not?

I don't know, and don't care! I Hate Football.

children are not frustrated or bored. This is why we did not organize the book by grade levels: There is such a wide range of variance among classes at the same grade level. As you increase your understanding of the skill theme approach, you will find that it is relatively easy to change tasks and activities with classes.

When a class is required to play a sport or participate in a predesigned game, that is, a game that has been designed with no knowledge of the class of children being taught, however, the teacher implicitly assumes that all of the youngsters have the same abilities and interests. The response of a sixth-grade boy to an opinion poll about a "flag football" unit (Figure 7.2) provides one potent example of how some children feel when they are all required to play a sport that requires proficiency-level skills. It also suggests why teaching the prerequisite skills for successful game playing, as opposed to playing games, is so important at the elementary school level—especially for those youngsters who have not reached the utilization or proficiency levels.

Insights about the Generic Levels of Skill Proficiency

Now that you're familiar with the four levels that constitute the GLSP, you need to be aware of three insights that will enhance your understanding of the levels and also help you apply them in your teaching situation.

Multiple Skill Levels in a Class

The first insight is that in the upper elementary and middle school grades, you can expect to have children in the same class at three different levels: precontrol, control, and utilization. Your challenge as a teacher is to determine the predominant skill level and then make adjustments for individuals through teaching by invitation or intratask variation (Chapter 11) and task sheets (Chapter 13), for example. In the preschool and primary grades, in contrast, many children will be at the precontrol and control levels—although there will always be an exception or two.

Control Level in Two Days a Week

The second insight we can offer is that in programs of elementary school physical education, in which children have physical education classes only once or twice a week, the children will reach the utilization level of most of the skill themes *only if they do something outside of class* (Graham et al., 1991). Unfortunately, an increasing number of children today are not physically active after school and on weekends. It is our observation that along with the decline in physical activity beginning in the middle school years (Chapter 1), children are also experiencing a decline in their skill levels from past years. The implication, of course, is that it is not uncommon for a teacher to use control-level tasks for children in the fourth and fifth grades—because the majority haven't developed their skills beyond that level. If we develop lessons using utilization- and proficiency-level tasks, we end up frustrating these children and convincing them that physical activity is not enjoyable because they are so inept.

Proficiency Level Is Rare

Our third insight is that children who are at the proficiency level in a skill are the exception. Remember that the GLSP applies to skills, not ages. Thus anyone, regardless of age, can be at the precontrol level. The standards or criteria for each of the skill levels apply across the board to all skills and all ages. Consequently,

we do not see many children at the proficiency level. In fact, it seems unlikely that many children can reach proficiency level simply by participating in a physical education program—unless that program is a quality, daily program. Typically children reach the proficiency level in a skill because they've been involved in an after-school sports program in which they practice the skill frequently or because a parent or older sister or brother is involved in a sport and the child consequently spends a lot of time practicing and receiving instruction in the backyard.

Overall, however, we do not observe children at proficiency level very often. For this reason, you will probably use the proficiency-level tasks we have listed in each of the chapters more as part of teaching by invitation and intratask variation (Chapter 11) than with entire classes of children. This does not mean, of course, that some of the children don't want to perform the proficiency-level tasks, especially the games. Children who are new to the skill theme approach, particularly those in the upper elementary and middle school grades, constantly ask the question, "When do we get to play the game?" Our standard answer is, "At recess. At home. On the weekends." In time, as the children become accustomed to the skill theme approach and we're able to individualize the program to a greater extent, they no longer ask the question—at least, not as often.

Unfortunately, some teachers succumb to the pressure from the children to "play the game." In the long run, the children end up shortchanged, just as they do when their diet consists primarily of unhealthy snacks and fast food. Although it may not be as much fun as playing games such as kick ball and dodgeball, a focus on learning and improving has the potential to help children eventually derive the benefits of regular involvement in physical activity (Malina, 2001). Failure to help children develop the prerequisite skills may mean that the children, as they age, come to feel inadequate and incompetent in physical activity. Just as it's easier for parents to let their children sit in front of the television for five or six hours a day, it's easier for teachers to let the children play kick ball and dodgeball every day. But it's not better for the children!

Summary

Organizing curriculum by grade level or age is convenient. Yet because of the range of skills found at any grade level or age, age and grade level are inadequate indicators of children's skill levels. We have adopted the concept of generic levels of skill proficiency (GLSP). Assessing children's skills in terms of these levels is a basis for planning appropriate activities. The four generic levels of motor skill proficiency are (1) precontrol, (2) control, (3) utilization, and (4) proficiency.

Children at the precontrol level are unable to consciously control or replicate a particular movement. At the control level, the child's body appears to respond more accurately to the child's intentions, and movements become increasingly similar. Movements are even more automatic and reflexive at the utilization level; children can use a movement in a variety of contexts. At the proficiency level, the child has gained control of a movement and is challenged by the goal of repeating movements exactly or using movements effectively in dynamic, unpredictable situations.

The generic levels of skill proficiency are task related—that is, a person at the utilization level in one skill may be at the control level in another skill. Age and skill level are not necessarily related.

Reading Comprehension Questions

1. What is the purpose of the GLSP? How are they used?
2. In your *own* words, explain the differences among the four levels of skill proficiency.
3. What do we mean by *generic?*
4. Why isn't age an indicator of motor skill proficiency?
5. Describe how the GLSP serve as a guide for selecting and matching tasks to the abilities of children within a class. Pick a skill theme, and describe how you would use the GLSP to help you make your decisions about which tasks to present.

6. Figure 7.1 shows a hypothetical example of a child's proficiency level at several skills. Use the following form to create your own graph. Select 10 of the skill themes that represent your range of abilities. Graph your skill levels. Which skill themes do you need to work on most? Why are you less advanced at these skills than at the others? Did you rate yourself at the proficiency level for any of these skills? If so, why do you think you attained the proficiency level for that skill? Answer the same questions if you're at the precontrol level for any of the 10 skills you selected.

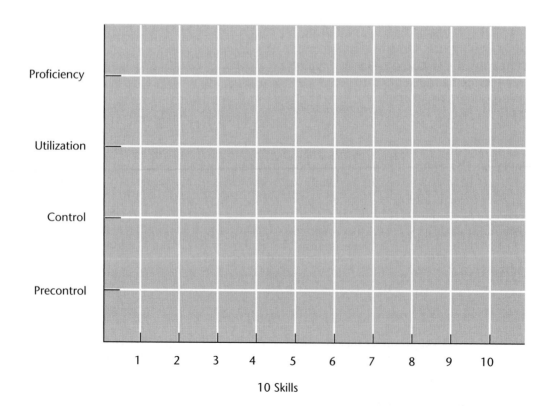

                                                    10 Skills

References/Suggested Readings

Graham, G., Hopple, C., Manross, M., & Sitzman, T. (1993). Novice and experienced children's physical education teachers: Insights into their situational decision-making. *Journal of Teaching in Physical Education, 12*(2), 197–214.

Graham, G., Metzler, M., & Webster, G. (1991). Specialist and classroom teacher effectiveness in children's physical education: A 3-year study [Monograph]. *Journal of Teaching in Physical Education, 4*, 321–426.

Housner, L. D., & Griffey, D. C. (1985). Teacher cognition: Differences in planning and interactive decision making between experienced and inexperienced teachers. *Research Quarterly for Exercise and Sport, 56*, 56–63.

Malina, R. M. (2001). Adherence to physical activity from childhood to adulthood. *Quest, 53,* 350.

Seefeldt, V. (1979). Developmental motor patterns: Implications for elementary school physical education. In C. Nadeau, W. Halliwell, K. Newell, & C. Roberts (eds.), *Psychology of motor behavior and sport.* Champaign, IL: Human Kinetics.

Stanley, S. (1977). *Physical education: A movement orientation* (2nd ed.). New York: McGraw-Hill.

Planning

"Will you please tell me which way I ought to go from here?"

"That depends a good deal on where you want to get to," said the Cat.

"I don't care much where," said Alice.

"Then it doesn't matter which way you go," said the Cat.

—Lewis Carroll

If you don't know where you are going, you will be lost when you get there.

—Yogi Berra

If you want kids to learn to skip, teach them the essential components of skipping, let them practice skipping, and then assess how well they can skip.

NASPE, 2004, p. 3

Key Concepts

- Reflective teachers plan and revise their plans over the course of a career as they continue to strive to provide the most productive and enjoyable learning experiences for children.

- Planning is divided into four parts in this chapter. The first part is the development of a curriculum scope that outlines the content to be taught for several years.

- The second planning step is to decide how many lessons will be devoted to each of the skill themes and movement and fitness concepts during a year.

- The third step is the development of benchmarks or assessments that allow the reflective teacher to determine if the children are learning what is being taught.

- The final step is the development of daily lesson plans that are interesting and beneficial to youngsters.

- Ideally lessons encourage students to be physically active during the majority of the lesson. Typically this occurs when children are able to be successful and consider the lesson fun.

- Just because a lesson is fun does not mean that it is a productive learning experience for children.

This and the next seven chapters focus on many of the techniques or skills that successful teachers use when they teach children. The first teaching skill we want to discuss is planning. Some of the material in this chapter will be new to you—and it won't be explained until later in the book. You will probably want to review this chapter again after you have read the content chapters (Parts 3 and 4), when the examples will probably make more sense to you.

We think it is important to start at the beginning. Any good program begins with a good plan. For many teachers, however, planning is one of the least enjoyable aspects of teaching. And yet it's essential, because failure to plan appropriately can lead to lessons that are disastrous. Disorganization and spending an excessive amount of time on management characterize the lessons of the teacher who hasn't planned effectively.

Inappropriate planning can also have long-term implications. One important task of physical education is to provide a variety of learning experiences that give children a broad foundation of movement abilities. Children who are skillful in only a few activities, typically games, may be the products of programs characterized by inefficient planning. Instructors who don't plan are likely to teach only what they know well and

the children enjoy, which often results in an unbalanced program over the years.

Because planning is typically done during the teacher's own time rather than during school time, there are strong temptations to avoid it. It can be much more pleasant to watch television, go to a ball game, or just go to bed early. But planning, even though you may consider it as onerous as homework, *is* necessary.

The benefits of effective planning include classes that run more smoothly with less interruption and confusion; tasks that are interesting, enjoyable, and worthwhile; and in some instances less off-task behavior. In short, well-planned classes assist children to learn the concepts and skills that are being taught.

Reflective Planning

If all schools, all children, all facilities, all teachers, all communities, and all equipment were the same, we could simply provide you with a book of lesson plans that would be successful with every class you teach, no matter the situation. As you know, however, that isn't the case. Experienced teachers are able to plan lessons—and entire programs—that consider the various unique characteristics of their teaching situation (Graham et al., 1993; Housner & Griffey, 1985).

The reflective planner considers many factors when trying to devise the best lessons possible under the circumstances. Planning can't be reduced to an exact formula, but certain factors will always influence the effectiveness of a lesson. Each factor is important, and all interact to determine the teaching environment for which the reflective teacher must plan. When planning, we consider class size, frequency of class meetings, available equipment and facilities, personal characteristics of the children, and children's skill levels and interests.

Class size often determines the amount and types of information that can be presented. For example, a class of 15 children will accomplish significantly more in a year's time than a class of 60 (Glass et al., 1979).

Frequency of class meetings is the second factor. Classes that meet once or twice a week accomplish far less than classes that meet daily because you can't present as much material in one or two days as you can in five (Kelly, 1989). And children, particularly the younger ones, tend to forget what they learned a week earlier.

To learn and understand a concept or skill, a child needs a multitude of experiences with a particular task or challenge. When the amount of *available equipment and facilities* is limited, each child has fewer opportunities to use the equipment. One result is that children learn more slowly than they would with adequate equipment that would increase learning opportunities.

Equipment also dictates which experiences can be presented. In gymnastics, for example, children who have progressed beyond the initial stages of skill development need apparatus—tables, beams—that allow them to work off the floor, because only with such equipment will they continue to be challenged. Similarly, nylon hose rackets are appropriate for children who are just beginning to learn to strike with implements. But foam paddles or actual rackets are essential if the children are to remain interested in and challenged by the skill theme of striking with implements.

Facilities also influence planning. Kicking can be studied briefly in a limited indoor space. But children can learn much more about kicking when they can practice it outdoors in a larger area. Thus, lack of adequate outdoor facilities may prevent you from devoting as much time as you'd like to a particular skill theme.

Similarly, the kind of available indoor space influences planning. Most teachers, for example, prefer to teach dance indoors. Hallways, classrooms with furniture pushed aside, school foyers—all these indoor areas can be used for teaching. But these aren't ideal settings for teaching many skill themes. It's extremely difficult, for example, to teach locomotor activities in a crowded classroom. However, you can effectively teach the movement concepts of symmetrical and nonsymmetrical shapes in a crowded, indoor area.

How responsible are the students? Children's ability to function in a variety of environments also influences planning (see Chapters 9 and 10). During the first few meetings of a class, you can gather observations about the *children's characteristics;* this information is useful when you plan lessons for a particular class. Some classes and some individual children can cooperate with others and work well in less than optimal circumstances.

The four factors just mentioned are easier to assess than *children's skill levels and interests.* You must have this information, though, to decide what tasks are appropriate and how to present those tasks. You want to challenge the students but not overwhelm them, so that they will continue to be interested and will want to learn.

If you decide that your class needs to be introduced to the concept of levels (Chapter 16), many factors, including the children's ages and abilities, will determine your plan for this lesson. Young, unskilled children often enjoy the challenge of taking different body parts into different levels—for example, "Can you move your elbow into low level?" "Can you move an ankle into high level?" Children in the intermediate grades might be bored by that task and so would probably

Effective teachers use many resources to plan successful lessons.

learn more effectively if challenged to catch or strike a ball at different levels.

When teaching children in the upper grades, it's important to consider the types of movement experiences to which they've already been exposed. You'll want to take advantage of skills learned in earlier experiences, and you'll also want to avoid repetition of material with which students are already familiar. For example, if the children are proficient in the skills used in softball, you may decide to minimize the amount of time spent on the skill theme of striking with bats.

A Four-Step Planning Process

Although there are several ways teachers plan either alone or as a group when they develop a curriculum, we suggest a four-step planning process that provides children with a progression of learning experiences over several years. At this point in the book, much of the terminology will be new to you. Our recommendation is that you continue to read with the understanding that you'll return to this chapter after reading more of the book, when the examples we provide to illustrate the four parts of the planning process will make more sense to you. Don't be frustrated, however, if you don't understand the meaning of every term we use—the definitions are in future chapters. At this point, it's important that you understand the process itself—the four steps that describe one way to develop an overall plan for a physical education program. The four steps are:

Step 1: Develop a curriculum scope and sequence for the entire five or six years of the program.

Step 2: Develop a yearly plan from the program scope and sequence, deciding approximately how many days you will devote to the various movement concepts and skill themes for each grade taught that year.

Step 3: Decide which part of each of the skill themes and movement and fitness concepts you'll focus on, with special attention to the cues or refinements (see Chapter 11) that you will be emphasizing. These are referred to as benchmarks or checkpoints.

Step 4: Write daily lesson plans.

An analogy may help explain the process. Imagine that you and a friend are going on a trip. You are planning to drive several thousand miles. You would probably ask and answer questions similar to the four steps:

1. Where do we plan to end up? What do we plan to visit along the way?
2. How many days do we plan to stay in each location?
3. What will we use as our performance indicators (or benchmarks) along the way to determine how well our plan is working?
4. How will we organize each day?

Effective teachers ask, and answer, essentially the same four questions as they plan their programs. The planning process used by teachers employing a skill theme approach—one of asking and answering these four questions—is described (with examples) in the following sections. We caution you that the process may appear complex but, just as with a long journey, taking it step by step makes it much easier.

Step 1: Developing the Scope and Sequence

The first step is deciding what you will include in your curriculum—and what you will not include. This is the *scope* of the curriculum. Teachers in Florida, for example, would probably not focus on ice skating or snow skiing, whereas teachers in Alaska and Minnesota might. Reviewing the curriculum scope tells us what is included—and what is not.

Just as in your imaginary trip with a friend, you will need to decide the *sequence* of your journey—where

Table 8.1 Sample of Movement Concept Scope and Sequence for Grades K–5 (Step 1 in Planning)

Movement Concept	K	1	2	3	4	5
Space Awareness						
Self-space	X	X				
General space	X	X	X			
Levels	X	X	X			
Directions	X	X	X			
Pathways	X	X	X			
Extensions				X	X	
Effort						
Time/speed	X	X	X	X	X	
Force				X	X	X	X
Flow				X	X	X	X
Relationships						
Body part identification	X					
Shapes	X	X	X			
Relationships with objects	X	X	X	X		
Relationships with people			X	X	X	X

Notes: This chart is intended only as an example. Reflective teachers will want to adapt this chart for their school.

X denotes that a movement concept is the major focus of lessons at a grade level. Concepts are studied at other grade levels but not as the primary focus of the lesson.

you will go first, second, and so on. The curriculum *sequence* provides an overview of the order in which the content will be taught, and at what grade levels. In the skill theme approach, the movement concepts (Table 8.1) are emphasized in grades K–2 (visited first) and the skill themes (Table 8.2) in grades 3–5. This does not mean that first graders never throw or kick in a skill theme approach, but rather that the lesson focuses not on learning to throw or kick but on using movement concepts to enhance the effectiveness of those skills. In contrast, a concept like pathways is important as fourth and fifth graders participate in small sided games in which they try to escape (flee) or catch. At the upper grades, however, the children have already learned the concept of pathways, so we do not teach them the difference between straight, curved, and zigzag the way we do with the younger children.

As we have discussed in the previous chapters, *Children Moving* focuses on youngsters learning the various skills used in a variety of sports and physical activities, but not the official, adult versions of the sports, which are more developmentally appropriate for some middle and high school youngsters (Chapters 7 and 12). Consequently, our organizing themes are not sports but skill themes and concepts (movement, fitness, and wellness). Tables 8.1 and 8.2 exemplify how we organize the content we teach—by grade levels to be consistent with the *National Standards* (National

Table 8.2 Sample Skill Theme Scope and Sequence for Grades K–5 (Step 1 in Planning)

Skill Theme	K	1	2	3	4	5
Traveling						
Walking	X	X				
Running	X	X				
Hopping	X	X	X			
Skipping	X	X	X			
Galloping	X	X	X			
Leaping	X	X	X	X		
Sliding	X	X	X	X		
Chasing, Fleeing, Dodging		X	X	X	X	X
Jumping and Landing	X	X	X	X	X	X
Balancing	X	X	X	X	X	
Transferring Weight			X	X	X	X
Rolling	X	X	X	X	X	X
Kicking			X	X	X	X
Punting					X	X
Throwing			X	X	X	X
Catching			X	X	X	X
Volleying				X	X	X
Hand Dribbling			X	X	X	X
Foot Dribbling			X	X	X	X
Striking with Rackets			X	X	X	X
Striking with Long-Handled Implements						
Bats				X	X	X
Golf clubs				X	X	X
Hockey sticks				X	X	X

Notes: This chart is intended only as an example. Reflective teachers will want to adapt this chart for their school.

X denotes that a skill theme is the major focus of lessons at a grade level. Concepts are studied at other grade levels but not as the primary focus of the lesson.

Association for Sport and Physical Fitness [NASPE], 1995, 2004). Note, though, that the grade levels merely serve as a general indicator; the decisions about what to teach and when are based on observing the actual classes of children we teach (Chapters 7 and 12). So the first two questions you will need to answer as a reflective teacher are as follows:

1. What do I want to include in my curriculum (scope)?
2. At what grade levels will I emphasize the various concepts and skills (sequence)?

Step 2: Devising a Yearly Overview

Continuing the analogy of a trip with a friend, the next step would be to decide how long you plan to spend at each destination. You will visit some places only briefly; at others you will spend several days. In curriculum development, once you have decided your scope and sequence, the next step is to develop a

Table 8.3 Sample Yearly Overview of Number of Lessons for a Two-Day-a-Week Program: Grades K, 2, and 4 (Step 2 in Planning)

Concept/Theme/Activity	K	2	4
Establishing a Learning Environment	6	4	3
Space Awareness	10	4	2
Effort	4	4	3
Relationships	6	4	3
Traveling	10	3	1
Chasing, Fleeing, Dodging	3	5	3
Jumping and Landing	4	4	3
Rolling	2	4	4
Balancing	4	4	4
Transferring Weight	2	3	4
Kicking and Punting	4	4	4
Throwing and Catching	4	6	6
Volleying	0	2	4
Dribbling	1	2	3
Striking with Rackets	2	4	4
Striking with Hockey Sticks	0	1	2
Striking with Golf Clubs	0	1	2
Striking with Bats	0	1	2
Fitness/Wellness Concepts	5	7	10
Field Day and Other Events	5	5	5
Total Days per Year	72	72	72

Note: Numbers represent days per year that a concept theme will be the *major* focus of a lesson. Numbers are intended for discussion only; the overview will differ from teacher to teacher.

yearly overview. How many days do you plan to spend teaching the movement concept "levels" to kindergarten children? How many days will you spend teaching your fourth and fifth graders to strike with paddles?

Table 8.3 exemplifies the overview of a teacher who sees children twice a week (72 days a year) for physical education. It uses the kindergarten, second-, and fourth-grade levels to be consistent with the *National Standards* and provides one example of how many days a teacher might spend on the various concepts and skills in a given year. As you review Table 8.3, two facts should strike you:

- There aren't enough days for youngsters to learn everything recommended in the curriculum guides or state or national standards.
- The primary-grade emphasis is on the movement concepts; the upper-grade emphasis is on the skill themes.

Like Tables 8.1 and 8.2, Table 8.3 is for illustrative purposes only. As a reflective teacher you will want to ask and answer this question based on your specific teaching situation: "How many days a year will I be able to allocate to teaching each concept and skill theme?"

Find Your State Standards

In the past few years many states have revised or developed state standards based on the *National Standards.* If you are interested in locating your standards, go to PE Central (www.pecentral.org). You will find the state standards listed under the "Professional Information" link on the front page.

Once you have developed a yearly overview for your program, you'll need to translate it into a yearly calendar. Essentially, this involves deciding which skill themes or concepts you'll emphasize during which days of the school year. Most school districts provide planning calendars, and preparation of the yearly calendar can be done rather easily at the beginning of the school year during planning days. Figure 8.1 shows one type of planning calendar.

Based on what we know about how children learn, it seems wise to distribute the throwing lessons over the year rather than to mass them together (Rink, 1996). If, for example, a teacher planned to teach throwing for three days of the year, two of the throwing lessons might be scheduled in September, the third in March. A teacher with a three-day-a-week program might have a total of nine throwing lessons. In such a case, the teacher might decide to devote three lessons in a row to throwing, but it's still better to spread the total number of lessons throughout the year. Continuing to revisit lessons helps the children better remember the key points; spending several days on a skill or concept and then not reviewing it for another year is much less effective. Again, it's important to emphasize that the children will actually practice throwing in more classes than just the ones that focus primarily on throwing. For example, the sessions dedicated to catching will typically offer many opportunities to throw. In these sessions, however, the teacher will focus on the way the children catch, not on the way they throw. Obviously, children don't become effective throwers in three lessons a year—it takes much more time and practice.

Week 1 M T W T F	Week 2 M T W T F	Week 3 M T W T F	Week 4 M T W T F	Week 5 M T W T F	Week 6 M T W T F
Week 7 M T W T F	Week 8 M T W T F	Week 9 M T W T F	Week 10 M T W T F	Week 11 M T W T F	Week 12 M T W T F
Week 13 M T W T F	Week 14 M T W T F	Week 15 M T W T F	Week 16 M T W T F	Week 17 M T W T F	Week 18 M T W T F
Week 19 M T W T F	Week 20 M T W T F	Week 21 M T W T F	Week 22 M T W T F	Week 23 M T W T F	Week 24 M T W T F
Week 25 M T W T F	Week 26 M T W T F	Week 27 M T W T F	Week 28 M T W T F	Week 29 M T W T F	Week 30 M T W T F
Week 31 M T W T F	Week 32 M T W T F	Week 33 M T W T F	Week 34 M T W T F	Week 35 M T W T F	Week 36 M T W T F

Figure 8.1 Yearly planning calendar.

It is possible for them to learn parts of the overhand throw, however, in three lessons a year. It is reasonable to expect, for example, that they can learn to step with the foot opposite the throwing hand or turn their nondominant side toward the target (see Chapter 11).

The beginning teacher will have to experiment with devising the lesson sequences. This process of sequencing lessons to enhance learning movement concepts or skill themes is a valuable one. With practice, you'll learn to predict, with increasing accuracy, the appropriate emphasis that you should place on a theme or concept in a given class. And experience helps you adjust the sequence of the lessons to account for individual differences within a class and among classes. Once you have outlined a sequence, you can rearrange that sequence without losing sight of the intended direction or progression of the skill theme or movement concept.

Here are helpful guidelines for developing your yearly overviews:

1. The first time you introduce a concept or theme, the children will need several lessons in a row to grasp the major ideas. Later in the year, they'll need less time. *Mass* the practice in the beginning of the year; *distribute* it later. During weeks 4 and 6, for example, you may devote four lessons to jumping and landing. For the remainder of the year, jumping and landing are the major focus of the lesson for only two days in a row. This same principle applies to any skill theme or movement concept: massed practice during initial learning, distributed practice later.

2. The older the children, the longer they're able to remain on the same skill theme. For example, children designing games or dances typically need several days in a row for this task. As the children become more skilled, you'll notice that it becomes easier to remain on a skill theme than it was initially.

3. It isn't very effective to focus on a skill once a year and then never revisit it. Three weeks of practice in February on the skill theme of rolling, for example, probably won't lead to the long-term learning that three weeks of practice, one week each in October, February, and April, will.

4. To get you started, a major task is generally appropriate for the focus of a day's lesson. If you think the children will find a single task too strenuous or uninteresting, you may want to combine a major task from two different chapters. For example, you may want to combine the ideas under the heading Jumping a Turned Rope (Chapter 21) with the major task Traveling in Different Pathways (Chapter 19). This will give the children variety. Although most of our lessons focus on one major movement

concept or skill theme, there's no reason not to focus on two themes or concepts in a single lesson.

Our experience has been that it's often difficult for beginning teachers to develop a daily calendar. In an attempt to make this process easier (and better), we have provided four sample daily calendars in the Appendix in this book. Two calendars are for classes that have physical education five times a week (180 days a year); two are for classes that meet twice a week (72 days a year). Two of the calendars are for kindergarten through grade 2, and two are for grades 3–6.

You'll want to change these calendars as you plan your year, but they're a helpful start. To the right of each activity is a page number, which indicates where in *Children Moving* you can find a thorough explanation of each task and how it can be presented to children.

Once you've written your outline, use it only as a guide and change it as often and as much as the particular situation requires. You will want to write your outlines in pencil, leaving plenty of space for changes.

Learning is not totally predictable. If the study of a particular topic is going especially well, we don't change simply because the daily outline tells us to change. If several lessons on a particular topic have proven ineffective, it's possible to change to a different focus even though the daily outline calls for teaching three more lessons on that topic.

The children's needs and interests are the guide for the lessons to be presented. No outline, however theoretically sound it may be, can unfailingly reflect the progress and the interests of all the children being taught.

Step 3: Determining Benchmarks (Performance Indicators or Checkpoints)

Now that you and your friend have decided where you want to go on your imaginary trip and how long you plan to spend at various sites along the way, your next step is to determine performance indicators (benchmarks or checkpoints) that you constantly check to be certain you are on the right road headed in the desired direction—in other words, to ensure that you don't get lost. In most cases, especially if you are not on an interstate highway, you would constantly check your map, highway signs, and anything else that would assure you that you are headed in the proper direction.

Good teachers do the same thing. They develop checkpoints to be sure the children are learning what they want them to be learning—and then constantly assess their progress along the way. These teachers don't wait until the fifth grade, for example, to assess what the children have learned (or not learned). They continually check to be sure the children are "getting it" before moving on—and revisit areas that have not been clear to the children.

The first edition of the *National Standards for Physical Education* (NASPE, 1995) included a comprehensive listing of sample *benchmarks* designed to serve as guides to what students are expected to be learning in our physical education programs. They are intended to serve as checkpoints along the way, assuring us that we are on the right course in guiding youngsters in the process of becoming physically active for a lifetime. They represent the "learnable pieces" that, when combined, result in skillful performance and the development of a positive sense of self-efficacy. Often the benchmarks are the critical elements or cues for various skills. Thus, once a teacher makes the decision to spend a certain number of days on the skill of catching, for example, she will need to decide what the students are going to learn about catching—that is, the critical elements of catching. Remember that the students will not be able to become proficiency-level catchers in one year, but they can learn one or more catching cues that year. Table 8.4 provides one example of how a teacher might define the various critical elements of catching that will be emphasized from year to year. Assume that a teacher decides to teach the four catching cues in Table 8.4. (This is one example of Content Standard 2 of the *National Standards,* which states, "Demonstrates understanding of movement concepts, principles, strategies and tactics as they apply to the learning and performance of physical activities" [NASPE, 2004, p. 11].) The teacher could then decide which cues to emphasize each year to serve as benchmarks of student progress. These four phrases would provide a checkpoint to be sure that the children were actually remembering these cues, which would assist them on their journey to becoming competent and confident catchers.

For younger children, the teacher might teach the difference between symmetrical and asymmetrical movements as described in the chapter on space awareness (Chapter 16). If the teacher wanted to adapt the assessment example from Content Standard 1 of the *National Standards*—"Demonstrates competency in motor skills and movement patterns needed to perform a variety of

Table 8.4 Sample Critical Elements (Cues) for Assessing Progress in Catching

Grade	Critical Element (Cues)
2	Eye contact (track the ball)
3	Ready position (quick feet)
4	Hand and arm position (hands up)
5	Absorption of force (give)

Table 8.5 Sample Performance Outcomes for Catching, Grades K–5

Grade Range	Performance Outcomes
K–2	Drops a ball and catches it at the peak of the bounce
3–5	Catches a fly ball using mature form (e.g., has eyes on ball, moves to position, reaches with hands, catches with hands only rather than trapping the ball, bends elbows to pull ball into chest to absorb force)

Source: NASPE, 2004, pp. 16–17

Table 8.6 Sample Performance Outcomes for Balancing, Grades K–8

Grade Range	Performance Outcome
K–2	Discovers how to balance on different body parts, at different levels, becoming "like a statue" while making symmetrical and nonsymmetrical shapes
3–5	Balances with control on a variety of objects, such as balance board, large apparatus, skates
6–8	Designs and performs gymnastic (or dance) sequences that combine traveling, rolling, balancing, and weight transfer into smooth, flowing sequences with intentional changes in direction, speed and flow

Source: NASPE, 2004, pp. 16–18

physical activities"—into a series of yearly benchmarks, they might look like the items in Table 8.5.

Again for Content Standard 1, but including older children, the teacher might want to use the criteria for assessment suggested in a gymnastics example related to balance from the *National Standards for Physical Education* (NASPE, 2004, pp. 16–18) and in Chapters 19, 22, and 23 of *Children Moving.* He might develop the performance indicators or benchmarks shown in Table 8.6.

The first three steps of the planning process involve long-range planning and some difficult decisions. Fortunately, however, you can make these decisions over a summer, for example, or over a year as you "pilot," or try out, a curriculum. Ideally, you make these decisions along with your fellow teachers as you talk about, reflect, and design a curriculum that will be successful for you in your district. The last step in the planning process, however, is one you do on your own: translating the scope and sequence completed in Step 1, the yearly outline completed in Step 2, and the benchmarks identified as part of Step 3 into a daily lesson plan.

Just as on your imaginary trip with your friend, as a reflective teacher you will need to decide on the benchmarks that fit your program. You will see that in

Parts 3 and 4 of *Children Moving*, along with the tasks and activities, we have included the cues or critical elements that we emphasize in our teaching. These cues are consistent with the *National Standards for Physical Education* and will allow you to develop your own set of benchmarks to measure the progress of your children on their journey to becoming physically active for a lifetime. Thus, the question we suggest you ask and answer for Step 3 of the planning process is this: "What are the benchmarks or checkpoints that I will use to assess the progress my students are making?" For example, if a teacher wants students to know how to

position their hands correctly to catch a ball above the waist, or below the waist, most of them should be able to demonstrate this cue correctly. If, however, most of them still cannot demonstrate the proper way to position their hands, then the teacher needs to reteach the skill so the students can eventually become successful softball or basketball players.

Step 4: Detailing Daily Lesson Plans

The final question a teacher asks as part of the planning process is, "What tasks and cues will I teach each

---

Box 8-1

Sample Lesson Plan for Skill Theme Approach

Catching

Class Name _____ Skill Level _____

Lesson Length _____

Number of Meetings per Week _____

Focus:	Catching
Subfocus:	Spatial awareness, underhand throwing
Objectives:	At the end of this lesson the children will have learned to
	1. Move their arms in front of the body (elbows flexed) in preparation for catching the ball or beanbag
	2. Extend their arms to catch the ball or beanbag
	CUES: Hands ready
	Extend
Materials/ Equipment:	Various types of large, lightweight balls (plastic, beach balls, Nerf)
	Tennis balls, whiffle, yarn, small Nerf balls for stations
	Net, 6′ × 8′ (found in decorative section of drugstore)
	Small incline surface with sides (slide from backyard jungle gym; long box with sides, ends removed)
Organization/ Management:	Children in self-space
	Children throw against a wall
Stations:	See diagram

Introduction

The skill we are working on today is actually one-half of a two-part skill—throwing and catching. We are going to focus on catching—catching the ball with hands only. The skill of catch-

ing is important in many games we play as well as in junior high and high school sports like basketball, football, and softball.

Scattered around the room are different types and sizes of balls. Some are large, some are small, but all are lightweight so they will not hurt if they hit you when you are trying to catch. Spread out in general space and begin to toss the ball to yourself and catch it.

Task Development

1.0   As I observed you warming up, I noticed several of you were having trouble tossing the ball upward. Some balls were going far from your space; others were going back over your heads. Let's review the toss for a moment.

Cue   Hold the ball slightly in front of you with both hands. Toss the ball by lifting your arms upward, stopping the lifting when your arms are at shoulder height.

T   Practice again, tossing the ball only slightly above your head.

T   The toss looks much better. Now we are ready to concentrate on the catch. See if you can catch the ball with your hands only. sometimes it helps to let it bounce one time before you catch it. (*Model.*) Toss, bounce, catch, Ready? Begin.

Cue   Remember, bend your arms as you are getting ready for the catch. Think, "hands ready."

T   Toss the ball higher this time so the bounce will go as high as your head.

day in my lessons?" On your imaginary trip with your friend, you will also need to plan each day by answering questions like these: How far do we plan to drive? Where will we stop along the way? What will we see and do there? Where will we stop for the night? And, of course, each day's plan will often not work out exactly as imagined—for many reasons.

The same is true for teachers. Although daily learning plans rarely work out exactly as designed, you will want to develop them based on the decisions you made in the first three steps of the planning process. To assist you, we have included in Box 8-1 an example

of a lesson plan for use with a skill theme approach. The plan is quite detailed because we think the detail is especially helpful to teachers planning to use a skill theme approach. In time, as you gain experience and knowledge of children's abilities and interests, you will find that you can be less detailed. In the beginning, however, detailed planning of the sort we suggest here is an excellent way to understand how to teach the skill theme content.

Short-term planning is typically done during planning periods, after school, and in the evenings. This is the step in which you take into account the specific

---

Box 8-1 (continued)

Cue   Reach for the ball. Don't wait and catch it against your body.

2.0   Stand approximately 6 to 8 feet from the wall. Remember the bubble of your self-space and your neighbors'—don't stand too close. Toss the ball to the wall and catch it after it bounces one time.

(T) Throw the ball just hard enough for it to rebound to you. Too much force will send it over your head.

(T) Practice a couple of times more as I observe your readiness.

(T) You appear to be ready to catch the ball as it rebounds from the wall without the bounce. When you feel comfortable, try this skill.

(T) Return to your self-space scattered about the room. Toss the ball upward and catch it before it bounces.

(C) See if you can catch the ball five times without a miss.

(C) I will time you for 30 seconds, Try to toss and catch in your self-space without dropping the ball. (Older students: If we are 100% successful, I will never hear a ball touch the floor.)

Children at the precontrol level of skill development need mass practice and revisitation to the theme often. Station practice as revisitation will be enjoyable and beneficial.

Stations for Practice: Four stations are set up for practice of the skill we have been learning—catching. The stations are for fun, but will give us additional practice of our catching. Even professional athletes spend lots of time practicing the skill of catching.

Station 1: (Suspend a net approximately 6 feet above the floor, with the back corner higher than the front edge so the

ball will roll off. Use 8½" plastic balls.) Toss the ball above the net. It will slowly roll down the net and drop off. Catch it before it bounces.

Station 2: (Use tennis balls, whiffle balls, yarn balls, Nerf balls.) Select a ball. Toss and catch it five times; you may let it bounce if you wish. After five catches, try another type of ball. Continue until you have used all the different types.

Station 3: (Use slide with raised edges, back against wall, slight incline; playground or plastic ball.) Toss the ball up the slide. It will come back toward you quickly. Catch it first after one bounce, then before.

Station 4: Partner toss. Face your partner. First catch after a bounce and then without the bounce. When you are successful, you may take one step back if you wish.

Use this station to note individual visual tracking of the ball, hands/arms in ready position, and reaching for the ball.

Closure

Our lesson today focused on throwing and catching. Which part were we concentrating on?
Do we catch with hands only or against the chest?
Show me the correct arm position for catching: correct, arms extended with elbows slightly bent.

Reflection

Do the children get their arms/hands in ready position in preparation for the catch?
Do they extend their arms when they catch or do they still trap the ball against the chest?

Source: Adapted from *On the Move: Lesson Plans to Accompany Children Moving.* Shirley Ann Holt/Hale. Mayfield, 2001. Mountain View, CA.

variations among individuals and classes. Long-term planning (Steps 1–3) is typically done before the school year begins, before you know the individual children you'll be teaching. Thus, it is in daily lesson planning (Step 4) that you can accommodate individual variations.

You can generate lesson ideas from a number of sources, including notes from classes, your own and others' observations, books, the Internet, workshops, conferences, articles, and discussions. Planning for lessons involves sifting through sources and then designing lessons to match the needs and characteristics of a particular class to help them learn the benchmarks developed in the previous step of the planning process. We've found few, if any, predesigned lessons that worked for us as they supposedly worked for their authors. So instead of including specific lesson plans in *Children Moving* (with the exception of Box 8-1), we provide tasks for development to encourage you to develop your own plans.

To plan effectively, you need to consider the vital information in Box 8-1, which is useful for planning lessons and for improving teaching. It is presented here only as a guide; you may want to change it or adapt it to your particular style of lesson planning. This is the format that is also used in *On the Move* (Holt/Hale, 2006). We have intentionally included more detail than a typical plan contains so that we can provide a better understanding of how we develop the content in a lesson.

The sample lesson plan in Box 8-1 has 12 parts. Each part, along with suggested modifications, is discussed in the order in which a plan is typically completed.

1. Class Name   This part isn't necessary for a classroom teacher. Physical education specialists may want to make a plan for each of their classes or, when their teaching load is particularly heavy, list the grade level (e.g., second/third grade) as a general guide. Another alternative is just to list the skill level of the class. Teachers with heavy loads, for example, 30 different classes in a week, use the same basic plan for each grade level and then make individual notes about different classes as suggested at the end of this form (part 12).

2. Skill Level   This provides a reminder of the skill level of the class. The information is based on observations and assessments.

3. Length of Lesson (Time)   This refers to the length of a class, for example, 10:00 to 10:30, or 25 minutes.

4. Number of Meetings per Week   This information is especially helpful for specialists who meet certain classes a different number of times per week from others.

5. Major Focus and Subfocus   The major focus of the lesson will be based on what you did in Step 2 of the planning process when you decided which concepts and skill themes would be taught on which days of the school year. This provides you with the focus and purpose for that lesson or lessons. The subfocus also indicates which additional concepts and skill themes will be reinforced within that lesson. In the sample lesson plan in Box 8-1, the children will spend most of their time throwing and catching, but the teacher will emphasize their catching skill. In addition, they'll need to be aware of self-space and levels (Chapter 16), although these concepts will not be the major focus of the lesson because they have already been taught in previous lessons. In this lesson, throwing (Chapter 25) will also be a subfocus.

6. Objectives   The objectives for the lesson describe what the children are to *learn* during the lesson, *rather than* what they are to do. For example, stating that the children will throw and catch a ball in self-space is not an objective—it is a task. "The children will learn to catch a ball" is an objective. Unfortunately, this objective cannot be accomplished in a 30-minute lesson; it will take many lessons, perhaps thousands of practice catches, before a child can be said to be truly able to catch a ball.

The objectives, then, are "learnable pieces" based on the benchmarks—something a child has a reasonable chance to learn in a single lesson. In the sample lesson in Box 8-1, the teacher will focus on two aspects (critical elements) of successful catching: teaching the children to (1) move their hands into a ready position before catching the ball and (2) extend their arms to avoid trapping the ball against their body. The teacher decided on these two cues after reading the chapter on catching (Chapter 25) and also the sample benchmarks in the first edition of the *National Standards for Physical Education* (NASPE, 1995, p. 20). The teacher will not simply provide chances to practice catching but will focus on teaching the children to use the hands and arms appropriately to catch a ball or an object. During the lesson she will continually pause and *remind* the children of the cue they need to work on. Sometimes she will *demonstrate* the cue. Sometimes she will *pinpoint* other youngsters as they use the critical elements in their catching (Chapter 11). As the children practice, the teacher will also move among them and provide feedback about how well they are using the cues. You will hear her constantly remind individual children to "get their hands into the 'ready' position" or to "reach for the ball." When the teacher observes individual children and then provides an analysis of how they are using a cue, the technique is called *specific, congruent feedback* (Chapter 11). Cues are extremely important;

they are what the children can actually learn during a lesson (Graham, 2001).

7. Materials/Equipment   This section of the lesson plan is simply a list of equipment and materials that will be needed for the lesson. It serves as a handy check list to make certain that everything is available before beginning the lesson. Given the hectic schedules of elementary schools, it's easy to forget a piece of equipment; the check list is designed to prevent this from occurring.

8. Organization/Management   This section of the plan provides the teacher with a place to write down the different organizations and formats that will be used during a lesson. Although this may not be necessary for experienced teachers, it's very helpful for beginning teachers; it leads them to think through the organizational formats that they might use during the lesson, thereby avoiding some of the problems that might occur, for example, when a teacher hasn't thought about how the children will move from throwing against a wall to finding a partner to throw and catch with. If not planned for carefully, these transitions can lead to wasted time, confusion, and even misbehavior.

9. Introduction   This extremely important part of the lesson sets the tone by providing the children with a cognitive scaffolding for what they'll learn—and why! Some teachers introduce the lesson as soon as the children arrive; others prefer to provide children with a chance to move for a few minutes first (instant activity) (Graham, 2001). The "why" part of the introduction is especially important for the older grades and children in middle school (Graham, 2001).

10. Task Development   The section of the lesson plan that includes the tasks and activities for the lesson is referred to as the *task development section*. However, it includes much more than simply tasks or activities. In the sample lesson plan in Box 8-1, we've provided a typical task development section that includes not only tasks (denoted by a (T) symbol), but also challenges (denoted by a (C) symbol). After you read Chapter 11, the meaning of each of these will become clearer to you as a way you can develop the tasks throughout a lesson. To provide a better feel for how teachers develop tasks, we have written the sample lesson in Box 8-1 as a teacher might actually speak it to the children. In your plan you'll want to abbreviate the format presented here. Chapter 11 provides a more concise format for planning the task development section of the lesson.

11. Closure   The closure, or conclusion, typically lasts no more than two or three minutes. The teacher calls the children together and quickly reviews the key points of the lesson that were stated in the lesson objectives and emphasized throughout the class. As the sample lesson in Box 8-1 indicates, the teacher can phrase the closure in the form of questions. This is an especially important time to remind children of what has been emphasized throughout the class. It can also provide the teacher with important insights about whether the children have attained the lesson objectives (Graham, 2001).

12. Reflection   In a perfect world, there would be time at the end of every lesson for a teacher to reflect on the lesson just completed. Did I accomplish my objectives? Which tasks worked well? Which needed to be changed? What do I need to emphasize the next time I teach catching to this class?

In the real world, however, the teacher rarely has time to reflect on the lesson that was just taught—one class follows another, often with no break. However, the teacher usually has a few minutes in the day to jot down a few notes about what the children did or didn't accomplish. We suggest guiding the reflection by asking questions related to the objectives for the lesson. Realistically, the teacher often reflects about several classes that have been taught in a row and thus makes the best guess about what the children in those classes have learned and what might be changed in future lessons.

The Kids Love It

One of the comments often heard from teachers whose goal is to keep youngsters "busy, happy and good" is that the kids "love" the game or activity. Although it is certainly desirable for youngsters to enjoy an activity, it is not our sole criterion. For example, some children would "love" to eat ice cream or doughnuts or potato chips for every meal. Obviously, however, it would not be in the best interest of these children if that was all they ate. The same is true for the classroom. There are many fun reading, math, and science games. But the successful teacher always evaluates these games or activities to be certain that if the children play them they actually lead to better reading, more effective computing, or understanding science concepts. So when we hear that youngsters "love" a game or an activity we can't help but wonder: Are the children really learning something? Is the activity truly a learning experience? Should the fact that kids love it be the sole, or major, criterion to determine the success of a lesson? Our goal is to keep youngsters "busy, happy, good"—but also learning! If they aren't learning, then what are we teaching them?

A well-developed plan can be somewhat lengthy, especially for beginning teachers. For this reason, many teachers find it helpful to write a brief outline on a 5-by-8-inch card that they carry with them during the lesson as a handy reminder.

As you review these 12 steps for the lesson plan, you may find that certain steps are unnecessary for your situation. This is to be expected. We suggest that you adapt this format to meet your needs and then make plenty of copies for the year.

Making Planning Enjoyable

Planning is hard work. It takes time and energy to plan effective lessons that are exciting and interesting to children. Teachers who fail to plan well tend to return to old standbys—kick ball, dodgeball, and four-square—that contribute minimally to children's physical education.

You'll always be able to find something to do that is more interesting than planning lessons. So it's a good idea to devise ways to make planning easier and more fun. We've found the following ideas helpful:

- Set aside some time each day specifically for planning. Then you won't be constantly trying to find time to plan. Some people find that planning at school before they leave for home is effective; others prefer to arrive at school early to plan the day.
- Try to become excited about your plans. When you're excited about trying to present an idea in a new and interesting way, planning is fun, and you communicate your enthusiasm to your students.
- Don't hesitate to experiment. The worst that can happen is that a lesson won't work as planned. When this happens, we tell the children we were trying a new idea and it didn't work. Children understand and sometimes make worthwhile suggestions about how the idea might be improved.

When you set aside appropriate amounts of time, try new ideas, and attempt to make lessons exciting, planning becomes more enjoyable. And your attitude toward teaching will be affected. Most of us experience uncertainty when beginning a lesson (or anything else) for which we're unprepared. When you've planned a lesson thoroughly, the assurance and enthusiasm you feel can be contagious.

Recording Progress

A reflective teacher will want to record the progress that a particular class, group, or individual makes during a lesson. An elementary school physical education spe-cialist may teach 8 to 12 classes a day. Each group and each student will progress to a different degree and in a different way. A reflective teacher, whose approach takes these differences into consideration, will need notes on which to base the next day's (or week's) lessons.

You can write brief comments in a standard planning book or on index cards. Some teachers use handheld computers or a tape recorder. Notes summarizing what was accomplished during a lesson help you plan the next day's lessons. Whenever possible, the day's schedule should include 5 or 10 minutes between classes; you can use this time for recording observations and, if necessary, arranging equipment for the next class. Teachers who use handheld computers to keep track of their students' progress have the advantage of easily downloading the information into a computer for ease of use and future reference. Whether you use note cards, a tape recorder, a handheld computer, or some other technique, it will certainly help you plan more efficiently. What seems clear at 9 A.M. is often opaque by 4 P.M.

Lesson Design

If children are to develop into skillful movers, they must do more than play games. Children need opportunities to practice skills in contexts that are meaningful and enjoyable to them. A successful teacher creates practice situations that are enjoyable, are appropriately designed, and allow for maximum participation. The teacher who can design interesting and exciting practice situations will rarely hear the question asked so often by highly skilled, unchallenged children, "When do we get to play a game?"

Interesting Lessons

Many children, particularly younger ones, don't understand the need to practice to become more skillful. Children typically are interested only in the present and have little concern about years later. Thus young children more easily accept and enjoy lessons with immediate meaning. For example, we wouldn't teach second graders how to turn on one foot (pivot) by having them perform a mass drill, because such an exercise would have little meaning or interest to them. We might, however, have them jog around the gym and instruct them, "Spin around on one foot when you hear the drum and then continue jogging." On the next drumbeat we might say, "Pivot on the other foot" or "Spin in the opposite direction." Later, when the children are able to travel dribbling a ball, we might say, "Spin on the drumbeat while continuing to dribble a ball." We don't teach skills as if all children really want to learn the skill because they intend to play on a varsity team in high school—they don't.

Variety in a lesson also makes the lesson more enjoyable. We try to give children a number of related practice opportunities in a single lesson, rather than having them practice the same skill the same way the entire lesson. And the only way to accomplish this goal is through extensive and thorough planning.

Appropriate Lessons

Children want to be challenged and successful at the same time. The ideal task is difficult enough so that the child can't do it as intended every time, yet easy enough so that the child is successful much of the time. If small children try to shoot a basketball through a 10-foot-high basket, their success rate may be so low that they'll quickly lose interest. If the same children are given options—for example, shooting at a basket 7 feet high or shooting through a hoop suspended from a pole—their interest will remain higher for longer periods, and their skills will therefore improve.

Maximum Participation

One of the clearest differences between more effective and less effective teachers is that the students of more effective teachers actually spend more time practicing than do the children of less effective teachers (Rink, 1996; Siedentop & Tannehill, 2000). The value of practice may seem obvious, yet practice is frequently neglected, particularly in teaching games. When a class of 30 children practices a skill such as throwing or catching and uses only three or four balls, the children's skills will improve less than the skills of children whose teacher designs the same lesson so that there is a ball for every two children in the class.

Remember, though, that not all children have learned to practice on their own. Making more equipment available doesn't guarantee increased practice time. In fact, we've observed instances in which the children in a class actually practiced more when there were only three or four balls available because most of the students in the class hadn't yet learned to work on their own.

> One study (Graham et al., 1993) that compared student teachers with experienced teachers found that veteran teachers provided children with far fewer tasks than the novice teachers. The novices believed that they had to "get through all of the tasks in their plan." In contrast, the veteran teachers were focused on the children. If a task was "right," they stayed with it for long periods of time.

Parting Thought

The planning process described above no doubt seems complex, time-consuming, and maybe even unnecessary. It's not! Think again about planning your trip. Time spent planning can heighten the enjoyment dramatically. Being lost, confused, or in the wrong place at the wrong time is no fun. Neither are poorly planned lessons that are uninteresting, dominated by a few highly skilled children (unless of course you are one of the highly skilled), or simply unproductive. If you want to become a highly successful teacher it is going to take a lot of work—and the journey starts with planning.

Summary

Planning is a crucial part of the teaching process. Successful teachers plan effectively—not only their daily lessons, but also the entire program, as well as each year of the program. Plans are guides, not cast in stone. As you learn more about the school, the children, and the context of the teaching situation, plans change!

This chapter described four steps in the planning process. Step 1 is the development of a scope and sequence for all of the grades you will be teaching. Essentially, the first step answers the questions "What will I teach?" and "In what grades?" Step 2 involves making the difficult decisions about how many days you will be able to focus on various skills and concepts—and which one's should receive more or less emphasis. Benchmarks are formulated in Step 3 as you determine when and how you will check to see what your children are learning. Step 4 is the creation of daily lesson plans. Twelve different parts of a lesson plan are described, along with examples to illustrate the process of planning daily lessons. The chapter concludes with ideas for creating lessons that are interesting and appropriate and that provide for maximum participation and success for the children.

Reading Comprehension Questions

1. What is meant by the term *reflective planning?* Think about your elementary school: Which contextual factors influenced the program and the way the teacher planned?
2. What might happen when a teacher does not bother to do Steps 1 and 2 in the planning process and only plans day to day?
3. Tables 8.1 and 8.2 present sample scope and sequences for the movement concepts and skill themes. In your own words, explain why some concepts and skills are not taught at various grade levels. Use specific concepts and skills in your explanation.
4. Using Table 8.3 as a guide select first, third, or fifth grade and do a yearly overview for that grade. Then write a brief analysis explaining what you changed from the grade before and after. So, for example, if you choose third grade, explain how your guide is different from those for second and fourth grades.
5. Use the guide for planning daily lessons (Box 8-1) to plan one of your own lessons. Use one of the movement concept or skill theme chapters as a guide, but do not use the skills of throwing and catching.
6. Veteran teachers typically spend less time planning than do beginning teachers. Why might this be the case?

References/Suggested Readings

Glass, G. V., Cahen, L., Smith, M., & Filby, N. (1979, April–May). Class size and learning. *Today's Education 68*(2), 42–44.

Graham, G. (2001). *Teaching children physical education.* Champaign, IL: Human Kinetics.

Graham, G., Hopple, C., Manross, M., & Sitzman, T. (1993). Novice and experienced children's physical education teachers: Insights into their situational decision-making. *Journal of Teaching in Physical Education, 12*(2), 197–217.

Holt/Hale, S. (2003). *On the move: Lesson plans to accompany* Children Moving. New York: McGraw-Hill.

Housner, L., & Griffey, D. (1985). Teacher cognition: Differences in planning and interactive decision making between experienced and inexperienced teachers. *Research Quarterly for Exercise and Sport, 56,* 56–63.

Kelly, L. E. (1989). Instructional time: The overlooked factor in PE curriculum development. *Journal of Physical Education, Recreation and Dance, 60,* 29–32.

National Association for Sport and Physical Education. (1995). *Moving into the future: National standards for physical education.* St. Louis, MO: Mosby.

National Association for Sport and Physical Education. (2004). *Moving into the future: National standards for physical education* (2nd ed.). Reston, VA: National Association for Sport and Physical Education.

Rink, J. E. (1996). Effective instruction in physical education. In S. Silverman & C. Ennis (eds.), *Student learning in physical education* (pp. 171–198). Champaign, IL: Human Kinetics.

Siedentop, D., & Tannehill, D. (2000). *Developing teaching skills in physical education* (4th ed.). New York: McGraw-Hill.

Establishing an Environment for Learning

A well run lesson that teaches nothing is just as useless as a chaotic lesson in which no academic work is possible.

—Walter Doyle

Key Concepts

- A learning environment is the condition created in a classroom by the teacher that supports (or hinders) learning by the students.

- A learning environment consists of two components, a managerial component and an instructional component, both of which are necessary if physical education is to reach its full learning potential.

- The managerial component establishes the structures that allow the classroom to function effortlessly.

- The instructional component refers to the subject matter activities that allow students to learn physical education content (see Chapter 11 for aspects of the instructional component).

- The development of a managerial component is a necessary, but not sufficient, condition for student learning.

- As part of the managerial component, effective teachers develop protocols including both rules and routines that ensure smooth existence in the gymnasium and on the playground.

- Rules are general expectations for behavior that cover a wide variety of situations; routines are procedures for accomplishing specific duties within a class.

- Rules and routines are most effective when they reflect a positive environment while teaching children to be responsible for their own behavior.

- The development of protocols is an integral and critical part of maintaining a safe environment.

Many would argue that this is a chapter about management—about doing things to make sure youngsters do what we want them to; about having children "behave" the way we want. Technically, it probably is, but we have a bit of a different take on management. For us, management is the creation, development, and utilization of processes resulting in a gymnasium or playground conducive to learning. You can arrive at the result, a classroom for learning, using multiple approaches, but regardless of the approach several key variables need to be addressed. As you read this chapter, decide what approaches you prefer and what kind of teacher you want to be.

To teach effectively, it's necessary to establish an environment in which learning is supported and allowed to take place. Such an environment is a necessary, although not sufficient, condition for learning. Establishing the learning environment has been called a first-base skill—you can't get to home without getting on first, but getting there is only the first step to scoring a run (Rink, 1987). Without such an environment there is little chance learning will occur; with it, learning is still not possible unless instructional activities are carried out. Establishing a learning environment involves using both managerial and instructional techniques to place students in contact with—and to keep them in contact with—the subject matter at a high success rate for as long as possible. For us, the learning environment is the simultaneous working of two parts or components: one instructional and the other managerial. Others have analogized these components to "systems" and, similar to a smoothly operating piece of machinery, both must be present for the classroom to operate (Tousignant & Siedentop, 1983). Regardless of the term used, both instructional and managerial structures must be present in order to establish an environment that has the potential for learning. One without the other is not adequate.

A component can be defined as a regular pattern of practices used to accomplish the functions of a class. The managerial component refers to the non–subject-matter activities necessary for a class to run smoothly and efficiently over a period of time. The instructional component refers to the subject-matter activities designed to see that children learn what we want them to by participating in physical education. Both components need to be developed when establishing a learning environment. All too often physical education teachers establish a managerial aspect (Mowling et al., 2004), but neglect to focus on an instructional aspect or component. This chapter and Chapter 10 are about the managerial components of the learning environment. Chapters 11, 12, and 13 are about the instructional component.

For each of these components, certain teacher practices ensure the component achieves what the teacher desires. A well-operating component, either managerial or instructional, establishes and maintains student responsibility for appropriate conduct, task involvement, and learning outcomes (see Chapter 11 and "The Instructional Component" in this chapter). The practices that accomplish this are known as accountability measures (Doyle, 1980; Siedentop & Tannehill, 2000). Whether personal or imposed, these accountability measures are so important that without them both the instructional and managerial components become lax and may not even operate (Doyle, 1980). Traditional accountability measures in physical education include tests, grades, attendance, teacher reprimands, and punishment. Those types of accountability measures are now thought to be largely inappropriate if student learning is the intended outcome of physical education. In fact, they undermine learning and communicate to the public that physical education has little to teach other than to dress and show up for class. This chapter will introduce you to a variety of other teacher practices that serve as accountability measures in establishing the managerial and instructional components necessary for a smoothly running class in which learning occurs.

Although the development of a component sounds quite rigid, sterile, and certain, the type of component developed and how it is implemented reflects what we believe not only about physical education but also about education, children, and society. It mirrors what we feel is important about our school, our gymnasium, our students, and ourselves. All components must accomplish certain things—the smooth and consistent operation of the gym—yet it is how the system is put into action that says who we are. For example, a managerial component that is solely teacher developed and directed indicates a belief that student input or helping students learn to make decisions isn't important. On the other hand, the complete lack of a managerial component could indicate an abdication by the teacher of all responsibility and a belief that it doesn't make any difference what we do (Ennis, 1995). However, components that help students learn to make decisions about managerial (noninstructional) situations and instructional (learning) situations may indicate that we have taken the responsibility not only to teach psychomotor content but also to teach the larger goals of personal and social responsibility (Parker et al., 1999; Parker & Stiehl, 2005). The *National Standards* indicate that one of the goals of physical education is to develop students who demonstrate responsible personal and social behavior in physical activity settings (National Association for Sport and Physical Education [NASPE], 2004). Although the accountability and managerial literature have largely developed from behavior management and business, where efficiency is paramount, there are models in which the development of responsibility and self-direction are important (Hellison, 2003). In these models, although initial efficiency may be slightly compromised and the teacher must be willing to relinquish some control, students gradually move toward more independent learning and responsibility.

> *Classroom management helps run an effective classroom, but doesn't solve the social problems.*
>
> —Don Hellison

It is our belief that physical education is child centered and that students should develop increasing responsibility for their own behavior, attitudes, and learning. Therefore, the prevailing philosophy of this chapter is one of components that are designed to accomplish those goals. In other words, just like fitness and motor skill development, responsibility is part of the content with which students must stay in contact.

Gymnasium Atmosphere

When the weather forecaster announces an impending low-pressure system, we know what it will feel like—heavy, humid, and often accompanied by rain or snow. Similarly, with high-pressure systems we know to expect fair weather and dry air. The atmosphere of the gym is much the same except it is created by the teacher, not weather systems. Regardless of the component—managerial or instructional—the atmosphere in the gym needs to be emotionally safe and positive. If this atmosphere is not created, then the remainder of this book is probably useless.

Of all the teacher practices involved in establishing a positive learning environment, one of the most important pieces is also one of the least tangible and most easily compromised: teacher attitude or approach to teaching and children. This is essentially the translation of beliefs into practice. The teacher's self-image and feelings about teaching, about physical education, and about children all influence atmosphere. The enthusiastic teacher conveys this attitude to the children and as a result heightens their enthusiasm for physical education. The teacher who views physical education as a time for learning and work communicates this feeling to the children in the way he or she demands that all the children adhere to certain criteria for behavior. Likewise, the teacher who believes that children are vessels to be molded and should be compliant with teacher expectations, whether they seem reasonable or not, communicates to children that they are not capable of making significant decisions.

Even though children's motivation for participation in physical education changes with age (Xiang et al., 2004), it has been said that, at any age, *in order for children to be motivated to learn they need to belong and feel competent, useful, potent, and optimistic.* When those needs are met, people commit wholeheartedly to an endeavor (Sagor, 2002). The study of physical activity settings has yielded similar findings (Galvan, 2004; Herbel & Parker, 1995; Deutsch, 1999). It has been documented that in schools or classrooms where real learning occurs there are strong feelings of membership, engagement, and commitment (Wehlage et al., 1989). It is this atmosphere that we *must* create in the gym if we want all children to be attracted to being physically active for a lifetime.

Morris, Stiehl, and Sinclair (2006) employ the practices of change, challenge, and choice as a way to ensure that the gymnasium is a place where all learners feel competent, useful, potent, optimistic, and empowered. Though slightly modified here, the premise of their work is that any aspect of an activity can (and should) be changed so that the learner is allowed to be successful at the appropriate level. For example, equipment, space, or the task itself can be modified (see Chapter 11 for intratask variation examples). The challenges listed in Chapters 19 through 28 allow tasks to be adapted so as to more appropriately challenge all children. Choice empowers and intrinsically motivates children by allowing them input that meets their needs (Mowling et al., 2004). Choice can be offered in anything from the type of equipment used to how far apart partners stand. The technique of teaching by invitation (Chapter 11) provides a mechanism for allowing choice in activities.

Besides the approach you employ as a teacher, several tried and true principles can help ensure your gymnasium is a place that attracts youngsters to physical education and doesn't turn them off (Graham, 2001; Helion, 1996).

1. *Use positive interactions.* This means that positive reinforcement and praise need to dominate interactions with children. Unfortunately, the reverse is usually true. Subtle nagging statements such as: "I am waiting for you to be quiet" and "Any time now" are more often heard than "I like the way you came in and began your warm-up" or "Thanks for listening; it makes my job easier."

2. *People are not for hurting.* Children should be psychologically safe as well as physically safe in physical education. Hurting refers to everything from physical safety to inappropriate practices such as games that pinpoint and demean (e.g., dodgeball and the like) to name-calling and making fun.

3. *Never use sarcasm.* As adults we have become used to sarcasm. Children take it literally. It has no place in the gym.

4. *There is no stupid question.* As a friend of ours puts it, "It is OK not to know, but it is not OK to continue not knowing" (Stiehl, 2002). The implication is that we need to make our gymnasiums places where children are free to ask questions.

5. *Physical education is for everyone.* Sports are for those that choose to participate in them. They are usually dominated by the highly skilled and aggressive children. Physical education is an educational activity that is designed for every child of every skill

level. This means multiple forms of equipment, multiple types of games at the same time, and inter-task variation (see Chapter 11).

6. *Walk your talk.* We chose to be teachers. We are role models.

7. *Decorate.* For many the gym is a scary place. Make your gym an attractive place to be—decorate the walls, paint with bright colors, keep the gym sparkling clean, make sure the lights are bright.

It is wise to check yourself regarding these practices on a weekly basis to make sure that you haven't slipped into an unproductive pattern.

Some educators use the terms *developing a learning environment* and *discipline* as if they were synonymous, but we don't. Creating a learning environment is proactive; discipline is reactive. Discipline is required when a child's behavior is disruptive and the teacher needs to prevent the disruption from occurring again (see Chapter 10). When establishing a learning environment, the teacher focuses on fostering acceptable behavior and creating an atmosphere appropriate for a physical education class. Some discipline may be required in a physical education class, as in any class. However, an established, consistent, positive environment in the gymnasium and appropriate tasks allow students to know exactly what is expected of them, reduce the need for discipline, and stimulate enthusiasm for learning. The remainder of this chapter deals with ways teachers have been successful in developing both managerial and instructional components to establish a productive learning environment.

The Managerial Component

The managerial component establishes structures or protocols through which the physical education class becomes predictable and operates smoothly (Rink, 2006; Siedentop & Tannehill, 2000). The managerial component essentially consists of two aspects: the creation of the learning environment (this chapter) and the maintenance of the learning environment (Chapter 10). The creation involves the development of protocols, the rules and routines that allow the gymnasium to function.

When they begin school, most children have few preconceptions about how a physical education learning environment will be structured. Within a short time they learn to function according to the teacher's expectations. The managerial component establishes the limits for behavior and the teacher's expectations for the students. Due to our belief in children developing responsibility for themselves and our dislike for constantly feeling as if it is our job to "control" students, the managerial components we develop focus not only on establishing an appropriate learning environment but also on having students take more and more responsibility for that environment. If youngsters are allowed to develop unacceptable behavior in physical education class, the teacher will find it increasingly difficult to alter their behavior. For this reason it's crucial that teachers establish an appropriate learning environment during their very first lessons with the students. How well they do this sets the tone for the remainder of the year. We've found the following techniques helpful in developing and holding students accountable for managerial components.

Developing Protocols

Research indicates that effective teachers develop gymnasium protocols that help their gyms run smoothly and minimize disruptions, thus maximizing students' learning time (Jones & Jones, 1995). These protocols consist of both rules and routines. Rules identify general expectations for behavior that cover a variety of situations. Though rules are intended to address both acceptable and unacceptable behavior, they quite often focus on inappropriate behavior. A concept that some teachers have found useful in changing to a positive focus is explaining rules as guidelines to help children examine their behavior and attitudes as they affect themselves and others (Jones & Jones, 1995). Routines are procedures for accomplishing specific duties within a class. They are different from rules in that they usually refer to specific activities and are usually aimed at accomplishing tasks rather than forbidding behavior. Evidence has shown that effective teachers spend the first few days of the year teaching protocols to their classes (Brophy & Good, 1986; Fink & Siedentop, 1989).

Protocols generally stay in effect for the school year (unless you find one that isn't working or discover that something has been neglected). It is frustrating and time-consuming to repeat the protocols for new students or for students who were absent when they were taught. Thus, we have found it valuable to videotape the lessons at the beginning of the year when protocols are presented and taught. When a new student joins the class, the videotape can be used either at school or at home to orient that student to the protocols of your gymnasium. The tape is also a useful resource to share classroom procedures with parents at parent-teacher meetings or, if needed, to document the teaching of safety procedures, rules, and routines to a class. This is also a good way to remind students of safety procedures.

Establishing Rules and Expectations That Reflect a Positive Environment

The establishment of rules does more than provide the "laws" of the gymnasium; it also sets the general atmosphere of the gym and conveys the teacher's beliefs about control and responsibility. If, for example, all the rules are developed by the teacher, are written as a series of "don'ts," and are narrow and punitive, this sends the message that the teacher is the ultimate control figure and children are merely people to be controlled. If, however, children provide input and the rules are guiding and broader, allowing children some part in the decision making, then the message is that children are people learning to be responsible; they are capable of making decisions and have self-worth. These messages may appear subtle, but they are powerful to students. Therefore, our choice in the development of rules and routines is to be broad and guiding rather than narrow and restricting. They are essentially guidelines by which our classes have agreed to operate.

Children who understand the expectations within which they are to function are less likely to test the teacher's flexibility and more likely to cooperate. A few rules stated clearly and adhered to consistently by the teacher can be helpful to everyone. One set of guidelines that we have found effective—that help children examine their behaviors and attitudes—is an adaptation of Hellison's five levels of responsibility (Hellison, 2003, see Box 9-1). These guidelines are broad enough to encompass the aspects necessary for safe group survival in the gym while guiding students well beyond simple compliance into responsibility.

Figure 9.1 shows how these guidelines can be translated into class rules. A discussion of the guidelines can cover many things that are normally included in narrower rules. For example, respect for the rights and feelings of others can include all aspects of pushing, stopping and looking when the teacher talks, sportspersonship, interrupting, use of equipment, and the like. Participation and effort is broad enough to include the whole idea of trying hard (even when you might not want to), giving 100 percent, and the like. Interestingly enough, these two guidelines alone encompass most of the rules we are accustomed to seeing in the gymnasium. The two other guidelines provide an extension that we consider important in our teaching. The third indicates that students should be able to work on their own, without the teacher's constant attention—a concept most of us relish. The fourth is one of our ultimate goals—that students care for and help each other. This can include actions as small as handing stray balls back to their owners or as broad as helping another student learn a skill. We have found that when we establish

Box 9-1

Responsibility Levels

Level 1: Respecting the Rights and Feelings of Others

Self-control
The right to be included
The right to peaceful conflict resolution

Level II: Participation and Effort

Exploring effort
Trying new things
A personal definition of success

Level III: Self-Direction

On-task independence
Personal plan
Balancing current and future needs
"Striving against external forces"

Level IV: Caring About and Helping Others

Prerequisite interpersonal skills
Compassion
Contributing member of the community and beyond
Without rewards

Level V: Going Beyond

Being responsible at home and school, with friends
Positive role model

Source: Teaching Responsibility through Physical Activity,
2nd ed. by D. Hellison, 2003, Champaign, IL: Human Kinetics.
Used with permission.

Gymnasium Rules

Be nice to classmates, the teacher,
and the equipment.

Try everything—and try hard.

Do what you are supposed to do,
even when the teacher isn't looking.

Help others.

Figure 9.1 Translation of Hellison's (2003) responsibility levels into rules.

this type of component and constantly adhere to it, students learn to manage themselves and develop the concepts of personal and social responsibility that we desire as outcomes of our programs. With such a managerial component developed and in place, we find that we are "managing" less, have more time for teaching, and have more fun teaching because we do not need to behave like police officers.

Rules are necessary for group well-being and development. Figure 9.2 shows another set of gymnasium rules that teachers have found successful in eliciting the learning environment they desire. You may wish to establish different rules; if so, the following general guidelines may help you:

- Explain why the rules are necessary. Children are far more cooperative with rules that make sense to them than with seemingly arbitrary regulations. In some cases children can help make the necessary rules.
- State rules positively. Whenever possible, avoid using the words "don't," "not," and "no." In essence, it is more productive to tell children what to do than what not to do.
- Keep the number of rules to a minimum. A good guide is to state no more than seven rules.
- Post rules in an attractive fashion so they can be seen and read easily.
- Make sure the children understand the rules. To teach rules most efficiently, first describe and demonstrate the desired behavior, then have the children rehearse the correct behavior (this usually takes more than one rehearsal), and finally provide feedback, especially the first time you ask the children to use a routine (the first days of school).
- Design, teach, post, and practice the consequences of breaking the rules.
- Especially in the beginning, prompt students toward appropriate behavior, and reinforce appropriate behavior. Let students know when they've done something correctly.

One of the obvious questions, although students don't always ask it, is, "What happens when one of the rules is broken?" No matter how well we teach, some of the children will break some of the rules, so

Physical Education Rules

1. Stop, look, & listen when you hear the signal.
   (Signal = whistle, freeze, lights out, & stop)

2. Participation = 100% every day—all day long.

3. Show good sportspersonship by playing fairly,
   following the rules, being honest, & cooperating.

4. Keep the noise level appropriate for the activity.
   Good Noise = Encouraging others.
   Bad Noise = Screeching and Screaming.

5. Treat others as you want to be treated. Work in your
   own space. Be helpful. Be courteous. Keep your
   hands to yourself.

6. Always remember SAFETY.
   Safety = wearing tennis shoes, moving
   under control, watching for others.

7. Handle equipment with care.

Figure 9.2 Gymnasium rules.
Source: Denise Horpedahl, C. B. Eielson Elementary School, Grand Forks, ND. Used with permission.

we find it helps at the outset of the year to describe the consequences for breaking a rule. These consequences are for relatively minor offenses; major offenses are discussed in Chapter 10.

The teacher needs to develop consequences appropriate to the particular teaching situation. Many teachers use a series of consequences similar to the following:

1. The first time a child violates a rule—for example, the child fails to stop and listen—give the child a verbal warning.
2. The second time a child violates a rule in the same class period, ask if the child "needs to sit out for a while." The child's response to this question is usually amazingly honest, and the question places the

responsibility on the child for his or her actions. The child can reenter class when ready without consulting the teacher.
3. The third time a child violates a rule, have the child sit out until a personal plan can be developed regarding his or her actions (see Chapter 10). This usually means the remainder of the class. Although sitting out the remainder of the class may seem a bit harsh, as teachers we need to be able to teach. A continually disruptive child takes our attention away from other children who deserve it just as much. Be aware that some lapse in following rules may be minor or a nonproblem, whereas other actions are major problems that can escalate. Be sure not to overreact to minor problems so that children do not respect the actions taken. See Chapter 10 for further discussion of maintaining the learning environment.

As much as possible, the consequences for violating a rule should be noninterruptive. We try to deliver a consequence with a word or two and avoid interfering with the learning experiences of the rest of the class. One final comment about time out: It is effective when the children find the lesson interesting. If the lesson is uninteresting, dull, or inappropriate for a child, then time out becomes a reward rather than a consequence for off-task behavior.

Establishing Gymnasium Routines

Routines are protocols designed to help the gymnasium run smoothly and efficiently. Remember, routines are specific ways to accomplish certain tasks within a lesson; they should remain consistent as much as possible. Routines also reflect what we feel is important. Here are key areas in which physical education teachers find routines to be effective: entry to and exit from the gymnasium/playground; ways to obtain, handle, and return equipment; signals for attention and starting and stopping activity; the use of space; boundaries for work spaces; and "housekeeping" items such as going to the restroom, getting drinks, and leaving the room.

Routines do much to reflect what we think of students and what we believe about them and thus send clear messages to students. By the nature of how they are implemented, routines can tell students that they are competent and capable or dependent and not to be trusted. Martinek (1988) found that teachers developed learned helplessness in students by creating low expectations for them. Conversely, Herbel (1996) found that students, when given and taught seemingly high expectations for things such as responsibility and their own learning, lived up to them. Although some of the actions may be subtle, the difference in the two scenarios appears to center around how much

Figure 9.3 Possible signals for attention.

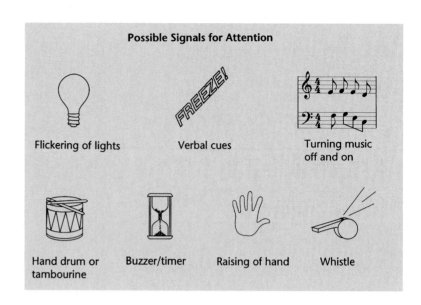

perceived control the students have over some basic decisions. Routines that rob students of basic decisions or allow no alternative seem to cause resentment and let the students transfer responsibility for their actions to the teacher. Alternatively, routines that allow students some flexibility and decision making seem to empower them. You might want to use some of the following suggestions as routines are developed for your classes.

Entering and Leaving the Gym We have found it beneficial to have a standardized way of entering and leaving the gym. It is helpful to have the classroom teacher bring students to the gym, and to have a set routine when the students get to the gym. Some teachers have children sit on the center circle or line; others post an initial activity; still others have set warm-ups to be done. Children need to have something to do when they arrive or they will make something up themselves. Exiting should be the same as entering. Most schools require that students walk quietly in lines to and from places in the school. It is helpful if teachers pick their classes up.

Stopping and Listening Skills In a successful learning environment, noise rarely exceeds a reasonable level that can be thought of as "busy noise." Hollering, shrieking, and yelling, although appropriate at recess, are not appropriate in physical education. The children shouldn't be expected to be silent, but they should be able to hear a teacher speaking in a reasonable tone, considerably below a shout.

One of the seemingly hardest routines to teach children in physical education is to stop activity quickly and listen to the teacher. When a teacher must spend time quieting the children so that the entire class can hear an explanation or comment, the amount of time left for activities is decreased. Thus, it's imperative that children learn to respond quickly and appropriately to the teacher's signal for quiet (see Figure 9.3 for examples of signals). Listening games (Box 9-2) can be used to teach children to listen as they move and to respond quickly to the teacher's signals.

You might initially assign a criterion of 5 seconds as a reasonable amount of time for the children to stop and listen after they hear the stop signal. If the entire class stops and listens in 5 seconds or less, praise them. If they don't, explain that taking more than 5 seconds is too slow and have them practice again because it's a waste of time to take that long. Gradually raise the standard as the children become more proficient. The children often view these races against the clock as fun games and delight in praise from the teacher when they perform well. They also enjoy trying to beat their own records. This approach provides far more time for activity and instruction. As the children learn the value of spending less time on management tasks, you can eliminate these races against the clock.

Teachers must be clear, concise, and to the point. As a general rule, once a class has begun, we try to keep our verbal explanations to less than one minute. Although this isn't always possible (or even appropriate), it does help to increase the children's willingness to stop and listen to us.

Equipment Getting and putting away equipment seems to be one of the biggest issues in class. We have found several things to be helpful. Have equipment

Box 9-2

Listening Games

These listening games are designed to help the children learn to stop as quickly as possible when responding appropriately to the teacher's verbal challenge. Try not to single out children who are slow, and don't use penalties as a form of discipline. Embarrassment and punishment are both counterproductive; you want children to enjoy exercise, not to think of it as unpleasant.

Stop and Go

Children travel in general space in a scattered formation. Once the children are able to (1) walk without touching others and (2) stay far away from others as they walk, you can begin to play Stop and Go. When you say "Stop," the children should stop and freeze instantly. When you say "Go," they should begin to travel again. Don't shout the signals—*speak* them, so that the children become accustomed to listening for your voice at a reasonable level.

Body Parts

This game focuses on the different body parts. Once the children have adjusted to Stop and Go, they enjoy the challenge of touching the floor with different body parts—elbow, seat, knee, wrist, waist, left hand, or right foot—as quickly as they can when you say "Stop."

Traveling

Once the children have learned to travel using different locomotor patterns, variations in these patterns are appropriate. Call out different ways of traveling—skipping, hopping, crab-walking, galloping—and challenge the children to change from one to another as rapidly as possible. You can increase the challenge of this game by combining traveling and the concept of direction—for example, gallop backward or hop to the right.

Circles

This game can be played on a painted playground surface or in a gymnasium. Before class, draw circles, triangles, squares, and so on, on the ground. The object is for the children to move as quickly as possible to the shape you name; for example, if you call out "circle," the children stand on a circle as quickly as possible. You can use colors instead of or in combination with shapes if the surface you're using is painted various colors. The terms you use will be determined by your pupils' knowledge of colors and shapes.

Numbers

In one version of this game, the children stop with the appropriate number of body parts touching the ground. For example, if you call out "three," the children should stop with three body parts touching the ground.

In a second version, the children stop in groups. The number the teacher calls determines the size of the group. This game is helpful when you want the children to form into groups of three, four, or five in a hurry.

Combinations

As children learn each variation, they find it challenging and fun to play several games at once. For example, you might call out a body part or a color or a locomotor pattern or a number. Children thrive on increasingly difficult games.

Switch and Rotate

The purpose of this game is primarily to teach listening, but it's more appropriate for older children. The object of the game is to stay so close to a partner that when the teacher says "Stop" and the players freeze, the follower can still touch the leader. When the teacher says "Switch," the partners change roles, and the follower becomes the leader.

You can make this game more difficult by increasing the size of the group to three, then four, then five. The object of the game remains the same: Each child should be able to touch the person in front as soon as you say "Stop." When you add the challenge "Rotate," the leader goes to the end of the line and becomes a follower. Children find the challenge of listening and responding instantly while trying to remain close to the children in front of them fascinating. You can make this game more challenging by varying the locomotor patterns, for example, from walking to skipping to hopping to galloping to running.

---

ready before class starts and available in various locations. For example, hula hoops create great storage areas for balls, but be sure to have multiple locations so that all children are not going to one place to get equipment. It is also important that youngsters walk to get equipment rather than running and pushing. The same is true for returning equipment at the end of activity; they need to walk and place it in its spot—not shoot from the center of the gym. Another method is to have selected groups of students—all those wearing red, for example—go to get equipment, and then other groups go. The two least effective ways to get equipment are to hand it out individually or to have it all in one place.

Once children get equipment, they need to know what to do with it. Tell them, for example, "Walk, get a paddle and ball, carry it to your space, and wait for directions," or "Walk, get a ball, carry it to your space, and begin throwing and catching by yourself." As with entering the gym, if you don't tell them what to do, children will make it up themselves and it usually is not what you had in mind.

The final aspect of equipment is what to do with it when the teacher is talking. Children, like adults, have a hard time holding onto equipment without playing with it. Many teachers will ask students to place the

ball on the floor, to hold it like a pro under one elbow, or even to hold it on their heads. Regardless of the technique, they need to have something to do with the equipment when the teacher is talking.

Partners and Groups When choosing partners or teams, the more we as teachers choose partners for children, the more we disenfranchise them. It is important to have children learn how to appropriately choose their own partners. Box 9-3 has routines for choosing partners that have worked for us.

Other Routines Other helpful routines regard getting water, responding to accidents, using the bathroom, and dressing appropriately. Table 9.1 compares gymnasium routines that enable and don't enable

Box 9-3

Forming Partners or Groups

Though the days of having a class divide into two teams and play against each other are largely over in physical education, on many occasions children need to form partners or small groups. In some classes, the act of finding a partner creates many behavior problems. Children argue over who is going to be whose partner, other children are left out, the time used in deciding partners takes longer than the task itself, and then children want to change partners. The same problems occur, even more so, when dividing children into groups. We've found the following techniques helpful in avoiding such problems as much as possible.

Getting Partners

- Put a time limit on how long children can take to choose partners, such as, "by the time I count from five to one."
- Put restrictions on who may be partners, for example, "someone you've never worked with before," "the person sitting next to you," "the person who sits next to you in class," or "someone you know you can work with in a productive manner."
- Decide ahead of class who'll be partners.
- Hand out color codes (pieces of paper, stickers, or marking-pen marks on the hand) at the beginning of class; the children who match up are partners.

Dividing into Groups

- Have children choose partners; then put one partner on one group and one on another. This works well for making groups equal.

- Assign each student a color or number (the number of colors or numbers equals the number of groups you desire) at the beginning of the year or month. When groups are to be formed, simply say, "Reds here," "Blues here," "Purples here," and "Greens here." (This is also an efficient way to take roll in your class.)
- Divide teams by certain generic characteristics, such as eye color, month of birth, number of siblings, or number of letters in first name.
- Divide groups ahead of time.
- Create a deck of cards that has the number of groups you desire. For example, if you want groups of four, configure the deck so that you use four aces, four kings, four queens, four jacks, and four 10s. Pass out the cards randomly and have the four that match become a group.

Whatever you do, don't take more than 60 seconds, and most important, don't alienate anyone. Under no circumstances should selecting partners or dividing children into groups be a popularity contest. For additional creative ways to form partners and small groups, see PECentral.org (www.pecentral.org) and look under "forming groups."

Table 9.1 Routines That Promote (and Don't Promote) Decision Making

Task	Promotes	Doesn't Promote
Getting equipment	Spread equipment and have students walk to pick it up.	Hand out equipment.
Entering the gymnasium	Post initial activity; students begin to practice as soon as they enter.	Students line up, waiting for the teacher.
Choosing partners	Students choose partners with whom they can practice productively.	Teacher assigns partners.
Dress	Students choose appropriate clothing that allows them to participate freely.	Students wear uniforms.
Getting water	Students get a drink when they need it, if no one else is at the drinking fountain.	Drinking is permitted only before or after class.

students to show responsibility. Any decisions we can help students learn to make on their own build independence, competence, self-worth, and confidence, thus reducing behavior problems. Taking away decisions students are capable of making fosters dependence and usually creates behavior problems. The key factor is first teaching students to make decisions competently. The net result of this instruction is that we as teachers are freed from trivial decisions that detract from our ability to teach—and we have a classroom that manages itself.

Getting Off to a Good Start

Typically, the first day a class meets, the teacher goes over the logistical and organizational rules and procedures she or he feels are essential for effective class

> *Students don't need to be fearful of teachers to listen to them.*
>
> —**Mark Murdock,** practicum student, after his first time teaching sixth grade

functioning. Many times we've seen this done only in the first lesson via a lecture; the rules and procedures are never taught and never reviewed again, unless something goes wrong. In recent years, it has become increasingly obvious how important the first few days of school are (Brooks, 1985; Brophy & Good, 1986; Krouscas, 1996): The first days establish the environment for the entire year. The students learn what behavior and attitude are appropriate in the gymnasium and what will be expected of them in physical

Spreading equipment out and providing equipment options are two routines that promote student responsibility.

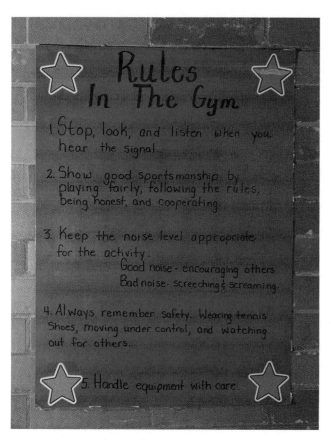

Attractively posting classroom rules is an effective way to guide children's actions.

education. It is then that they learn the class rules, both stated and unstated. When a situation arises and is consistently treated the same way, the students know the teacher means what has been said. This establishes the behavior and attitude that will typify a class for the remainder of the year. We've found the following suggestions helpful for getting off to a good start, and Figure 9.4 provides a checklist to ensure that you're ready for the beginning of the school year.

1. ***Readying the gym.*** Be certain that your gymnasium and materials are ready for the beginning of the year.
2. ***Planning protocols.*** Even if it is your plan to have students provide input into the rules and routines of the gymnasium, decide before you meet your students what general rules and routines are important and necessary for you. What is the general atmosphere you wish to create? In what ways can you guide students? Teachers who have the students decide on protocols often come prepared with generic guidelines (such as participation; treatment of others—students and teachers; safety; equipment) for operation of the gym. Students can then form

specific rules within those guidelines. If you decide to develop the rules of the gym yourself, determine what procedures students need to follow for your gymnasium to run smoothly; decide what behaviors are acceptable and unacceptable; and develop a list of rules before the students' arrival. Regardless of how the rules are established, post them.

3. ***Establishing consequences.*** As with rules, consequences need to be established for appropriate and inappropriate behavior. These, too, can be developed jointly or independently. They need to be communicated to students and followed through consistently (see the next section for more about rules and consequences).
4. ***Planning beginning-of-school activities.*** Develop activities for the first few days of physical education that will involve students at a high success rate and have a whole-group focus (see Chapter 13). This gives you an opportunity to see who follows directions and to reinforce appropriate behavior and attitudes. Don't begin independent work until you are certain that individuals know what is expected of them. Teach the rules of behavior and expected attitudes, as well as classroom routines (e.g., what to do when arriving in class; how to take out, set up, and take down equipment; what to do in a fire drill). You can most easily do this by planning what the routines will be, designing situations that allow students to practice the routines, and teaching those routines "in the gym." Spending time teaching behavior and attitudes at the beginning of the school year allows you to spend more time during the rest of the year teaching skills and much less time repeating what should already have become habit.
5. ***Communicating with parents.*** Many teachers find it valuable to communicate via a written newsletter or flier the expectations of physical education class as well what to expect in terms of learning in the gym. The newsletter can include what themes will be taught and when, a bit about special events, the safety rules of the gym and playground, and how to contact you. Some teachers leave a place for comments on the flier and request that a signed copy be returned.
6. ***Developing strategies for potential problems.*** Anticipate problems in the content or gymnasium routine, and develop ways to prevent or reduce those problems.
7. ***Monitoring.*** In the early days, routinely check with students individually to determine how they're settling in and to gain other information that may be relevant to the physical education and school setting.

CHECKLIST FOR THE BEGINNING OF SCHOOL

Item	Check When Done	Notes
Are your teaching areas and equipment ready?		
Have you decided on your class protocols?		
Are you familiar with the parts of the school that you may use (halls, cafeteria, multi-purpose room, etc.) and any procedures associated with their use?		
Do you have complete class rosters for each class you teach?		
Do you have file information on your students, including any comments from previous teachers and information on health problems?		
Do you know if you have any students with disabilities who should be accommodated for in your instruction?		
Do you have an adequate amount of equipment for your students?		
Have you established the procedure for the arrival and departure of the students from the physical education area?		
Are the children's name tags ready? Do you have some blank ones for unexpected students?		
Do you have your first day's plan of activities?		
Do you have rainy-day activities planned?		
Have you inspected all facilities for safety issues?		
Do you have a letter ready to send home to the parents with information about the school year and expectations?		
Do you know how to obtain assistance from school staff members (e.g., school nurse, office personnel, and the custodians)?		

Figure 9.4 Checklist for the beginning of school.
Source: Adapted from *Classroom Management for Elementary Teachers*, 6th ed., by C. Evertson, E. Emmer, and M. Worsham. 2003, Boston: Allyn and Bacon.

8. ***Creating accountability.*** Develop procedures that help students learn to be responsible for their work. (See Chapter 14.)

Teaching Skills for Establishing a Learning Environment

The preceding sections emphasized the importance of a managerial component, as well as the tasks necessary to create it. A number of generic teaching skills are also used by effective teachers to help create and maintain a component. Such skills include teaching the protocols, setting performance standards, and maintaining consistency.

Teaching Protocols

Rules and routines should be taught to children just as you would teach content. To teach protocols three aspects are important (Evertson et al., 2003):

1. ***Describe and demonstrate the desired behavior.*** You should use both words and actions to convey what specific behaviors are acceptable. For example, do not simply tell children you want them to display good sportspersonship, but tell them what

good means—say thank you to others, walk to get equipment, put equipment down and listen when the teacher or others are talking, walk around others to retrieve lost equipment. Second, demonstrate what each behavior looks like. Many children will have a different idea than you do about what *walking* means.

2. ***Practice the behaviors.*** Practice serves to help children learn the appropriate behavior and at the same time allows you the opportunity to see if the youngsters understand and can follow a procedure. Box 9-4 is an example of a practice activity for rules and procedures.

3. ***Provide feedback.*** Protocols, just like motor skills, are learned, and children don't often get them right the first time. After students have successfully practiced the protocol for the first time be sure to tell them they did it correctly and then praise them. If improvement is needed, tell them exactly what is needed and practice again. Even after youngsters seem to know a protocol, be prepared to prompt and give feedback if they forget.

Setting Performance Standards

Effective teachers set high but reasonable expectations for students and communicate them to the children. These expectations apply to both managerial and instructional aspects of the class. We've found that an easy way to do this is to teach with a critical demandingness (Brophy & Evertson, 1976), which means that we set standards and consistently adhere to them so that the children know exactly what is expected. For example, we've established performance standards for many of the daily management tasks, such as putting away equipment or lining up to go back to the classroom.

Performance standards are really a way for teachers to communicate exactly what they expect. When these expectations are clear, the children understand what the teacher desires. For example, children know that they're to put away the ball if the teacher has clearly stated this expectation. When the expectation isn't clear, however, several children may throw their ball from halfway across the gym, hoping that somehow the ball will land in the appropriate container or location. But the expectation is that children will place, not throw, the ball into the appropriate box (or hoop). Unfortunately, some classes need several practice episodes before the children learn that the teacher means business. The children need to learn that putting the ball away rather than throwing it isn't something the teacher hopes they do—it's something the teacher insists they do. This avoids the chaos and disruption

Box 9-4

Teaching Protocols with Group Practice: Ring the Bell

Equipment

For an average-sized class:

- Four sets of large cards, each with a protocol-practice activity written on one side (see below). Each set of cards should be a different color.
- Four medium bells.
- Any equipment necessary to practice the card activities.

Organization

After protocols have been explained and demonstrated, divide the class into four groups. Give each group a color to match the cards. All cards are spread out face down in the middle of the gym and mixed. When instructed, one member of each group retrieves a card for their group, takes it to the group, and they complete the activity. One member then returns to the middle, rings the cow bell, hands the card to the teacher, and retrieves another card. The activity continues until all cards have been completed.

Sample Card Activities

- At the regroup area, finger spell your first name.
- Go get a drink of water. One at a time, please.
- Go to the blue neighborhood and do 10 push-ups of any kind.
- Go to the Planning Area (see Chapter 10) and review the rules with each other.
- Measure the length of the gym using your bodies. Lie down on the floor head to toe.
- Go to the bathroom pass area and show your group your favorite safe balance.
- Go to the red neighborhood, get a ball, and dribble it 15 times with your right hand and 15 times with your left hand.

Assessment

This would be an opportune time to check for understanding by using student drawing or an exit slip (see Chapter 14) asking about one or two protocols.

Source: Adapted from material by Chet Bunting, Riverside Elementary School, Thornton, CO. Used with permission.

that can occur when standards for performance aren't set and adhered to.

This same idea of performance standards holds true for the instructional component as well. However, for skill development the performance standard is the use of the critical cue (see Chapter 11). To hold students accountable for using the critical cues on one day and not on another only confuses the children.

Maintaining Consistency

When establishing a classroom atmosphere, to avoid slippage (letting the children become lax as the year progresses), it's important that teachers be consistent in what they expect from one day to the next.

Students learn best when the gymnasium is a predictable place to be. Rules and routines must be followed in a habitual fashion. For example, if children are allowed to take out equipment mats by dragging them across the floor on one day but on the next day four people are required to carry each mat, what Doyle (1979) calls ambiguity exists: The students really don't know what is expected of them. These misleading practices must be eliminated, and the function of the gymnasium must follow a set routine so that procedural aspects of the class occur the same way each time.

The Instructional Component

It is not enough to create a reasonable place in which students are able to learn; we must also teach so students can learn. Learning motor skills and fitness concepts is the unique goal of physical education. It provides the focus that guides our actions as teachers and directs student attention as well as participation and attitudes. Student learning is therefore an important consideration in how we organize and maintain order in the gymnasium. Students are more likely to learn when expectations about organization, management, and learning are communicated. Although many of us are accustomed to these expectations as part of the managerial component, they also are a component of the instructional component. Simply, more learning occurs when students understand and value learning goals; when the task is appropriate and has a definite aim or focus; and when content is made personal, concrete, and familiar.

If students are to be held accountable for learning expectations that we have set, it is essential they accomplish the task as intended. Accountability in a managerial component is clear: If a student is asked to walk and instead runs, he or she is asked to start over

again and walk. Accountability also exists with motor performance, but the strategies differ. Typically we have used testing as the major accountability component for learning in physical education. Unfortunately, testing occurs infrequently and only at the end of a unit. Alternative assessment practices have helped alleviate that problem (see Chapter 14). Yet, to truly learn and understand, students need ongoing accountability components. Effective teachers utilize a variety of accountability practices to create effective instructional components that keep students on task, focused, and motivated to improve their performance. These are thoroughly developed in Chapter 11, and they are summarized here to reinforce the interrelatedness of the learning environment.

Varying the type of task builds accountability into the instructional task. The use of challenges on a regular basis gives students the opportunity to focus their work, as well as informally assess their learning between tests. Though there is no magic number or mix, we have found that a varied pattern of tasks works well. It has been our finding that appropriate, challenging content eliminates about 90 percent of the potential behavior problems in class.

Learning cues also provide students with an instructional accountability mechanism. Cues are simply short phrases or words that focus the learner on the critical elements of the skill to be practiced. Usually one cue is all that students can remember at one time. If for every task presented the last thing the teacher did was to repeat the cue(s) for the task, many students would be highly focused. Major cues are provided at the beginning of each control- through proficiency-level task in the skill theme chapters.

Providing specific congruent feedback about students' performance increases the accountability for learning. Specific congruent feedback means feedback that is directly related to the cues given with the task and nothing else. If a teacher provides such feedback, student performance is then more directed and focused.

Whatever the strategy, in order to learn, students must have a focus for the activity and be held accountable for realizing the focus. Without focus and accountability, students will lack motivation, will not learn the intended content, and will begin to behave inappropriately.

Safety

Although teaching safety procedures could logically be included within the managerial component, it is so important that we have chosen to address it separately.

We discuss it in generic terms here, but we also include specific safety aspects in each skill theme development chapter: These are coded with the safety icon ⚠.

A major responsibility of every physical education teacher is to provide students with a safe learning environment, both physically and psychologically (Siedentop & Tannehill, 2000). You as a teacher are entrusted with the safety of students in your class. The legal terminology is in loco parentis. In other words, when a child is with you, you act in place of the parent. The commonly accepted definition of this type of responsibility is that while a child is in a teacher's care, the teacher should act in a reasonable and responsible manner with respect to the child's welfare and safety. Reasonable behavior has been interpreted by the courts as what one would expect of a person with ordinary intelligence, ordinary perception, ordinary memory (Koehler, 1987), and specified academic and professional credentials. This means that teachers are held to the standard of the reasonably prudent "teacher" with all the pertinent credentials and experience that this teacher possesses (that is, if teacher X has more than the basic knowledge, certifications, and so on, teacher X is held accountable for that knowledge). Teachers are held to the standard of the reasonably prudent teacher, not that of just any adult.

Elements of Negligence

When a teacher does not act in a reasonably prudent manner, negligence can occur. Negligence has four separate elements—duty, breach of duty, proximate cause, and injury—that all must be met to prove that someone is liable.

Duty   The first element is established duty. This involves the relationship that exists between a teacher and students. By virtue of being a teacher, we have a duty to the students in our classes.

Breach of Duty   Duty requires that teachers maintain a certain standard of care regarding the students in their classes. A teacher is required to (1) anticipate foreseeable risk in any activity, (2) take reasonable steps to prevent injury, (3) provide a warning that risk is inherent in the activity, (4) provide aid to the injured student, and (5) prevent an increase in the severity of the injury. This standard of care is arrived at through expert testimony and other information that sets standards of practice. If an incident goes to court, the defendant's behavior will be compared to what the "reasonably prudent teacher" would have done in those circumstances to see if there was a breach of the standard of care. This is a critical issue because all

experts in a field may not always agree upon the accepted standard of care. For example, most would say that children should be warned and taught about the dangers of raising hockey sticks above the waist, but what about playing dodgeball as part of the physical education curriculum? Breach of duty, or of the standard of care, is the second element of negligence.

Proximate Cause   The third element of negligence is proximate cause, meaning that the teacher's behavior was the cause of the injury. An example might involve a student who has a documented medical problem that precludes participation in certain activities. The teacher requires the student to participate anyway, and the student suffers an injury directly related to the medical problem. What the teacher did was the main factor in the injury.

Injury   Injury is the final element of negligence. This element requires that the injury must have occurred because of the breach of duty. For example, if a student falls from a climbing rope that has no mats under it and no spotters and breaks a leg, an injury has occurred. If, however, a student falls under the same circumstances and no injury has incurred, then there is no case for negligence.

Areas in Which Negligence Might Occur

The four elements of negligence might occur in a variety of situations, but the three most common involve facilities and equipment, the conduct of the activity, and supervision.

Facilities and Equipment   Two major areas in which facilities and equipment are subject to negligent behavior are (1) upkeep and general safety of the equipment and (2) facilities and the appropriateness of the equipment for the child. All students have the right to participate in an environment that is safe and developmentally appropriate. Keeping facilities and equipment safe and in "good working order" is the obvious aspect of this domain. Standards for equipment and facilities are available from most school districts as well as The American Alliance for Health, Physical Education, Recreation and Dance (Council on Physical Education for Children [COPEC], 2001). Grounds should be inspected regularly for potential hazards such as sprinkler heads, holes, rocks, and ants. If a facility or equipment needs attention, it can only be attended to if reported. Make sure the right people know what needs to be repaired and follow up on it. The less obvious aspect of this domain is that equipment should be matched to the child or, in educational terms, it should be developmentally appropriate. All equipment must be of the appropriate size and weight for the child. Thus, in one class you may have multiple types of balls or rackets available to children. To ask most 6-year-olds or beginners of any age to use a regulation bat is not appropriate.

Supervision The teacher must be in the room or on the playground with the class and must be paying attention, and there must be enough supervisors for the participants present. This implies that you do not leave during class to do something else, even if it is to get equipment out of the equipment room. When present, teachers must actively observe the class (see Chapter 12) and be cognizant of what is occurring. If misbehavior, off-task behavior, or unsafe behavior exist, teachers have the obligation to respond to such behavior. Have all equipment out before class, and answer phone calls on breaks. In many schools teachers going outdoors with children now carry walkie-talkies for emergencies.

Conduct of Activities The conduct of the activity may be the least obvious negligence area. Four aspects are important here: (1) how children are taught to perform the skill, including proper progression, (2) how they are instructed to use equipment, (3) what safety precautions are taken by the teacher, and (4) whether the inherent risk is explained to the children and whether emergency medical procedures and protocols are developed. The last two aspects of safety and risk are the two that are most often the focus of teachers.

Safety precautions need to be stated as part of the general instructions to the children for every activity they undertake. These can be as simple as having students wait until everyone has thrown at a target before collecting the equipment and reminding them to walk around groups when collecting stray equipment, or more formal, as in posting specific safety rules for activities that involve hockey sticks. Children and parents also need to know the risks involved in physical education classes. This can be done by sending communications home at the beginning of the year so that parents can inform teachers of medical conditions of which they should be aware.

General safety procedures can easily be taught at the beginning of the school year by incorporating them with other gymnasium rules and routines. These safety procedures must be explained and then taught, as well as practiced.

We've found that special safety procedures, ones that deal with specialized equipment or unique situations, are most effectively taught at the time that situation arises. Again, the procedures shouldn't be glossed over; students should thoroughly understand them before you proceed. When specific safety rules are presented and taught, it is again a good time to videotape the teaching—for students who may be absent, for those who tend to forget, or in case of legal action.

It's beneficial to explain why selected behaviors are inappropriate and safety procedures necessary. Explaining the possible harmful consequences of actions helps children understand the need for stated practices. As with all ongoing gymnasium rules, the consequences of breaking safety rules must be stated; they might easily be included in the general rules for behavior. The children need to understand that safety is their responsibility as well as the teacher's when activity begins. Student safety should be the first thing the teacher observes for when the children begin a task (see Chapter 12).

The first and second areas—how children are taught to perform skills and how they are taught to use equipment—are equally critical. First, children need to be taught the appropriate use for all equipment in class. For example, jump ropes are for jumping over and using as nets, but not for slinging around heads as they are picked up.

Finally, all children are entitled to instruction that is appropriate. Proper task progressions are critically important to the safety of students. A student must possess all the prerequisite skills before beginning a new task. A teacher who skips from the precontrol level to the proficiency level when students are still at the precontrol level has not followed a proper progression. The teacher, in this case, is simply asking for safety and legal problems. Accurate records of lesson and unit plans allow teachers not only to establish proper progressions but also to document them. Directions should be clear and thorough to the point that students know exactly what they are to do and how, but not to the point of giving so much information that children are confused. Critical cues need to be provided for each task given, accompanied by an unambiguous demonstration.

Students need to behave safely in a safe environment. They also need to feel safe about what they are doing in class. Students who feel comfortable about what they are doing and are willing to participate fully by experiencing appropriate task progressions tend to behave safely, because they are challenged by the task at hand yet feel able to accomplish it.

This is a brief overview of some of the safety and legal issues teachers face. It is not intended as a compendium source. For more information, you may want to read *Sport, Physical Activity and the Law* by Neil J.

Dougherty, David Auxter, Alan S. Goldberger, and Gregg S. Heinzmann, or *Law for Recreation and Sport Managers,* 2nd ed., edited by Doyice J. Cotton, John T. Wolohan, and T. Jesse Wilde. Be sure to check with your school district regarding its safety policies and procedures.

As physical educators, we have always been conscious of safety, but in today's world of increasing legal action against teachers, we simply have to become more cautious and thorough in all that we do. To do anything less risks student injury as well as legal action.

Summary

The establishment of a learning environment is the first thing a teacher must do to have an effective physical education program. The learning environment consists of two components: the managerial component and the instructional component. The managerial component involves all those activities that are noninstructional, and the instructional component involves all activities that are designed to increase student learning. Teacher attitude and beliefs permeate both components. The types of components that are set up are a direct reflection of the teacher's atti-

tudes and beliefs about children, education, and physical education. Figure 9.5 may help you visualize the components of establishing a learning environment. Designing components that involve students in decision making, view children as capable and able, and are consistent, with clear learning expectations and appropriate tasks, usually creates an environment that is conducive to student learning and eliminates much off-task behavior. The teacher is able to teach and not have to be a police officer.

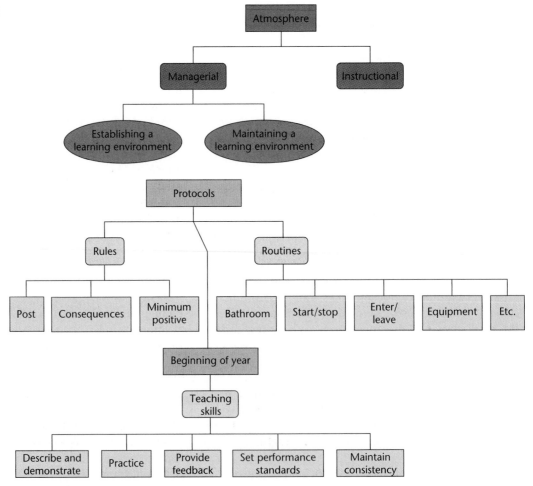

Figure 9.5 Establishing a learning environment.

Reading Comprehension Questions

1. What are the two major components in the establishment of a learning environment and how do they differ from each other?
2. What is discipline? How does discipline differ from establishing a learning environment?
3. How do teachers' beliefs about children impact the learning environment?
4. What is the role of atmosphere in the establishment of a learning environment?
5. What are protocols? What two aspects make up protocols and how do they differ?
6. What are three activities you can use to teach children to listen in a physical education environment?
7. List five guidelines for establishing rules of behavior in the gymnasium.
8. In your words, what does critical demandingness mean?
9. Why are the first lessons of the year so important? List five suggestions for those lessons.
10. Identify and describe three aspects of teaching protocols.
11. Define *accountability measures*. List three accountability measures for each of the components in physical education.
12. What are the four aspects of negligence, and in what areas of teaching are they most likely to occur?

References/Suggested Readings

Brooks, D. M. (1985). The first day of school. *Educational Leadership, 42*(8), 76–78.

Brophy, J., & Evertson, C. (1976). *Learning from teaching: A developmental perspective.* Boston: Allyn & Bacon.

Brophy, J., & Good, T. (1986). Teacher behavior and student achievement. In M. Wittrock (ed.), *Handbook of research on teaching* (pp. 328–375). New York: Holt, Rinehart & Winston.

Cotton, D. J., Wolohan, J. T., & Wilde, T. J. (2001). *Law for recreation and sport managers* (2nd ed.). Dubuque, IA: Kendall/Hunt.

Council on Physical Education for Children. (2001). *Appropriate practices in elementary physical education.* Reston, VA: National Association for Sport and Physical Education.

Deutsch, D. (1999). *The coaching club.* Master's thesis, University of North Dakota, Grand Forks.

Dougherty, N. J., Auxter, D., Goldberger, A. S., & Heinzmann, G. S. (1994). *Sport, physical activity and the law.* Champaign, IL: Human Kinetics.

Doyle, W. (1979). Making managerial decisions in classrooms. In D. L. Duke (ed.), *Classroom management: Seventy-eighth yearbook of the National Society for the Study of Education, Part 2.* Chicago: University of Chicago Press.

Doyle, W. (1980). *Student mediating responses in teaching effectiveness.* Denton: North Texas State University (ERIC Document Reproduction Service No. ED 187 698).

Doyle, W. (1986). *Classroom management and organization.* In M. Wittrock (ed.), *Handbook of research on teaching* (pp. 392–431). New York: Holt, Rinehart & Winston.

Ennis, C. (1995). Teacher's responses to noncompliant students: The realities and consequences of a negotiated curriculum. *Teaching and Teacher Education, 11*(5), 445–460.

Evertson, C., Emmer, E., & Worsham, M. (2003). *Classroom management for elementary teachers* (6th ed.). Boston: Allyn and Bacon

Fink, J., & Siedentop, D. (1989). The development of routines, rules, and expectations at the start of the school year. *Journal of Teaching in Physical Education, 8*(3), 198–221.

Galvan, C. (2004). *Investigating the impact of a service learning course on teacher candidates and underserved youth.* Unpublished doctoral dissertation. University of Northern Colorado, Greeley.

Graham, G. (2001). *Teaching children physical education: Becoming a master teacher* (2nd ed.). Champaign, IL: Human Kinetics.

Helion, J. (1996). If we build it, they will come: Creating an emotionally safe physical education environment. *Journal of Physical Education, Recreation and Dance, 67*(6), 40–44.

Hellison, D. (2003). *Teaching personal and social responsibility through physical activity.* (2nd ed.). Champaign, IL: Human Kinetics.

Herbel, K. (1996). *Youth, basketball, and responsibility: A fairy tale ending?* Unpublished master's thesis, University of North Dakota, Grand Forks.

Herbel, K., & Parker, M. (1995, October). *Same story, different setting: A case study of a program for at-risk youth.* Paper presented at the Northern Rocky Mountain Educational Research Convention, Jackson Hole, WY.

Jones, V., & Jones, L. (1995). *Comprehensive classroom management* (4th ed.). Boston: Allyn & Bacon.

Koehler, R. W. (1987). *Law, sport activity and right management.* Champaign, IL: Stipes.

Kounin, J. (1970). *Discipline and group management in the classroom.* New York: Holt, Rinehart & Winston.

Krouscas, J. (1996). No substitute for the first day of school. *Strategies, 10*(1), 5–8.

Martinek, T. (1988). Confirmation of the teacher expectancy model: Student perceptions and causal attributions of teacher behavior. *Research Quarterly for Exercise and Sport, 59,* 118–126.

Morris, G. S., Stiehl, J., & Sinclair, C. (2006). *Change, challenge, choice.* Champaign, IL: Human Kinetics.

Mowling, C., Eider, K., Brock, S., & Rudisill, M. (2004). Student motivation in physical education. *Journal of Physical Education, Recreation and Dance, 75*(6), 40–45+.

National Association for Sport and Physical Education. (2004). *Moving into the future: National standards for physical education* (2nd ed). St. Louis, MO: Mosby.

Parker, M., Kallusky, J., & Hellison, D. (1999). High impact, low risk: Ten strategies to teach responsibility in physical education. *Journal of Physical Education, Recreation and Dance, 70*(2), 26–28.

Parker, M., & Stiehl, J. (2005). Personal and social responsibility. In J. Lund, & D. Tannehill, (eds.), *Standards-based physical education curriculum.* (pp. 130–153). Sudbury, MA: Jones & Bartlett.

Rink, J. (1987). The learning game: A baseball theory of teacher effectiveness. Unpublished manuscript.

Rink, J. (2006). *Teaching physical education for learning* (5th ed.). St. Louis, MO: Mosby.

Sagor, R. (2002). Lessons from skateboarders. *Educational Leadership,* 34–38.

Siedentop, D., & Tannehill, D. (2000). *Developing teaching skills in physical education* (4th ed.). New York: McGraw-Hill.

Stiehl, J. (2002). Course outline SES 444: Teaching diverse populations. *School of Sport and Exercise Science.* Greeley, CO: University of Northern Colorado.

Tousignant, M., & Siedentop, D. (1983). The analysis of task structures in physical education. *Journal of Teaching in Physical Education, 3*(1), 45–57.

Wehlage, G. G., Rutter, R., Smith, G., Lesko, N., & Fernandez, R. (1989). *Reducing the risk: Schools as communities of support.* Philadelphia: Falmer Press.

Xiang, P., McBride, R., & Guan, J. (2004). Children's motivation in elementary physical education: A longitudinal study. *Research Quarterly for Exercise and Sport, 75*(1), 71–80.

Maintaining Appropriate Behavior

The thing that worries me is my lesson may not be good enough and students will get bored and be disruptive.

The only thing I am anxious about is if they [the students] decide to go berserk.

I am most worried that the students won't want to work as a team, that they will want to just mess around.

I am most worried that the students won't give full participation—won't listen—and I will revert back to the typical militaristic-like style.

I am anxious about discipline.

—University Students Before Teaching Sixth Grade for the First Time

Key Concepts

- The maintenance of the established learning environment is something that must be consciously cultivated.

- Appropriate behavior is not the mere absence of inappropriate behavior.

- If a learning environment is not effective, before blaming the students, assess your teaching behaviors to see if they have contributed to the nonfunctioning environment.

- Three hierarchical aspects are paramount to maintaining a learning environment: increasing appropriate behavior, decreasing inappropriate behavior, and dealing with whole-class problems.

- Both proactive and reactive strategies can be used to increase appropriate behavior.

- Proactive strategies include positive interaction with children, prompting correct responses, and eliminating differential treatment of students.

- Behavior problems can be classified as a nonproblem, minor problem, major problem, or escalating problem.

- Ignoring inappropriate behavior when it is inconsequential or a nonproblem, keen use of nonverbal interactions, and person-to-person dialogue are strategies that allow teachers to appropriately react to student behavior.

- To decrease inappropriate behavior, teachers can use desists, positive practice, time-outs, planning time, behavior contracts, letters to parents, and, as a last resort, can involve the principal.

- Entire class behavior can be maintained by developing personal and social responsibility, class rewards, and token systems.

- A variety of teaching strategies are used to maintain the class environment.

The concerns expressed by the students in the statements that introduce this chapter probably reflect what many teachers feel: Will I be able to handle my students? Will they do what is right? What will I do when they don't?

Helping children learn to be accountable for their behavior is one of the least enjoyable tasks of teaching, but it is something that all teachers must do. The notion that only poor teachers have to hold children accountable is simply not accurate. Yet holding children accountable is less likely to be a problem when effective managerial and instructional task components are in place.

Consistently maintaining the environment designed and established for the class is second only to establishing it. Some call this discipline, but the word *discipline* has so many varied, and mostly negative, connotations that we have chosen to avoid it. Discipline most often implies punishing some type of inappropriate behavior. That, for us, is the last resort. From our viewpoint, the establishment and maintenance of an environment supportive of learning is a more positive and appropriate perspective. We follow a positive approach to dealing with behavior and attitudes that are inappropriate, an approach that lets a teacher both create a positive atmosphere and teach students appropriate behavior for the gymnasium. In such a situation, the teacher's primary tasks are, first, to employ techniques that create appropriate behavior and, second, to use techniques that reduce inappropriate behavior.

We define appropriate behavior as student behavior that is consistent with the educational goals of a specific educational setting (Siedentop & Tannehill, 2000). Appropriate behavior is not the mere absence of inappropriate behavior; rather, it is itself a set of behaviors or actions. These positive behaviors or actions must replace the inappropriate behavior.

It's normal for all teachers to be concerned about how to hold students accountable for what they are "supposed" to do. Our experiences with beginning and experienced teachers, as well as our own teaching experiences, suggest that most teachers ask themselves questions about responding to student behavior. The difference between so-called good teachers and poor teachers is not their concern about holding children accountable—all teachers encounter deviant and disruptive behavior and must find ways of dealing with it. Rather, the more successful teachers are able to minimize the amount of time they devote to dealing with inappropriate behavior and do so in a largely positive manner.

Even the teacher who develops managerial and instructional components, establishes and explains rules of behavior, teaches with a critical demandingness, and sets and adheres to performance standards can't be sure that a class will perform as expected. In many classes, there will be some children who find it difficult to function in a school environment, not only in physical education but in other classes as well. Occasionally an entire class has difficulty adhering to the behavioral boundaries that have been established.

Whether it is one, several, or most of the children who are unable to abide by the rules, your first response might well be to examine your performance as a teacher. When children react in unexpected ways, you may, upon reflection, find that their reactions are justified. Children are incredibly honest. A teacher

The class proceeded through its parody of education, following a formula validated in a thousand classrooms I have visited and countless thousands I have not. The first step in the formula is an assumption, an untested hypothesis which becomes valid merely because (and as soon as) it is assumed. Children who do not easily take the imprint of their teacher's own education and values, who are not ductile enough to be drawn wire-thin so that they may slip through traditional holes in the fabric of society— these are not "promising children" and the best that can be hoped for from them is good behavior (silence) and early withdrawal (dropout). Since silence is their most positive attribute, they should be left unmolested during the class hour so long as they practice that virtue.

Perhaps worst of all the many dreadful aspects of this assumption is that the children know it. They know—and will tell you, as they told me, if they are asked—that a few of them are regarded as "good material" and the rest are nothing: "ever' time I go to her class, she make me feel like I was nothin'." Snapper, Rubbergut's half brother, said it. He said it for all the children who drown in the well of silence.

—**Daniel Fader,** *The Naked Children*

may not want to know or believe that a lesson is a dud, but the children will let the teacher know. Occasionally it's the teacher's behavior, rather than the children's, that needs to be changed. For example, when children have problems with equipment or don't understand or hear the teacher's directions, rather than ask for help, they will participate at their own level, "doing their own thing." Likewise, if a task is too boring or involves a practice situation that might provide better practice if changed (e.g., number of hits before switching roles), children will often change the task to meet their needs. Therefore, it doesn't look like the task that the teacher gave and the children will be perceived as off task.

If you determine that the lesson is appropriate and your performance as a teacher is satisfactory, you can then look for other causes for disruptive behavior. Try not to view disruptive behavior as a personal affront. A first step is to assess the behavior. Evertson and co-authors (2003) describe four possible categories of disruptive behavior: nonproblem, minor problem, major problem but limited in scope and effects, and escalating or spreading problem.

A nonproblem is a behavior that any attempt to react to it would consume too much energy and interrupt

the lesson and detract from the classroom atmosphere. Such things as brief inattention, some talk while others are talking, and short pauses while working are nonproblems.

A minor problem includes those things that run counter to classroom protocols but do not, when occurring infrequently, disrupt the class activities or seriously interfere with other students learning. An example would be excessive talking during group work. These behaviors are minor irritants as long as they are limited to a few students and are brief, and we would not give them much attention except that unattended they might persist and spread, not responding might cause an appearance of inconsistency and potentially undermine the management component, and student learning might be adversely affected.

A major problem includes activities that interfere with the learning of others. The occurrence may be limited to a single student or perhaps a few students not acting in concert. Chronically off-task behavior, constant movement around the space, or refusal to do any work would fit here. This category also includes violations of school rules or any kind of behavior that involves striking another student.

Major escalating problems constitute a threat to the learning environment. Roaming around at will, continual calling out or interference, and refusal to cooperate are examples.

Having assessed the behavior, you can deal with it in two phases: reacting appropriately in the short term and seeking to understand the cause in the long term.

Comparing a referee's or an umpire's job with the teacher's need to hold children accountable places a teacher's job in perspective. Those referees respected by players and coaches share the following characteristics: They're fair, consistent, accurate, and not emotionally involved. As teachers, we should keep these good characteristics in mind as we reflect on how to help children work within our guidelines.

Although a referee's job is less enjoyable than a player's or coach's, at least to us, it's an important aspect of organized sport. Similarly, maintaining the learning environment is an important role for a teacher. In physical education, as in sports, there will be violations and infractions.

Our goal is to help children become intrinsically motivated so that they can benefit from and enjoy physical activity. In some situations this motivation will occur naturally, and thus few of the techniques described will be necessary. In other teaching situations, however, many of the techniques will be needed. In either case, the goal is to use fewer and fewer of these techniques so that the children participate in physical education because they like it and feel it is valuable rather than because of an external reward or motivator. Our explanation of effective techniques for helping children work within our guidelines is divided into three steps: increasing appropriate behavior, decreasing inappropriate behavior, and maintaining whole-class appropriate behavior. Remember, your action as a teacher should match the magnitude of the problem. Overreacting will soon result in a negative class atmosphere and be similar to "calling wolf"—children will cease to respond. Underreacting creates an atmosphere of physical and psychological unsafety and nonlearning.

Increasing Appropriate Behavior

When behavior doesn't conform to the expectations established for the specific setting, a teacher's first strategy would likely be to increase appropriate behavior. Six techniques teachers have found useful for increasing appropriate behavior are positive interaction, eliminating differential treatment, prompting, nonverbal teacher interactions, ignoring inappropriate behavior, and person-to-person dialogue. Three of these techniques are proactive—that is, they are to be used in the absence of inappropriate behavior. The other three are reactive, to be used in response to inappropriate behavior.

Proactive Strategies

Teachers can do many things to increase the likelihood of students' behaving appropriately. And many of these things can be done proactively to increase the likelihood that appropriate behavior will prevail.

Positive Interaction As discussed in Chapter 9, one of the most powerful things a teacher can do to create an environment in which students want to be is to make the gymnasium a positive place. One of the most convincing means of creating a positive environment is to interact with students in a positive way when they behave in an appropriate manner. In essence, this approach emphasizes the positive rather than the negative. Many children who are known throughout the school as "discipline problems" have become accustomed to hearing nothing but negative comments about their behavior. Catching them in the act of doing something right and praising them for it can dramatically change their behavior (Siedentop & Tannehill, 2000).

But praise shouldn't be contrived and meaningless, offered with no genuine feeling, as is often the case.

Give praise frequently but not so profusely that it seems trivial. And give it only when a child actually displays appropriate behavior. All children are capable of receiving some type of praise—catch them being good!

This sounds like common sense, but research and our experiences have shown that this isn't the prevalent mode of operation in the gym. In 1984 Siedentop and Taggart wrote that "punitive and corrective interaction" were the most frequent forms of communication (p. 105). Almost 20 years later, it was found that although teachers espoused a positive form of classroom management, they relied almost exclusively on rewards and punishment (Kulinna et al., 2002). In other words, nothing has changed. You can stand at many gymnasium doors and hear statements like these: "I'm waiting for you!" "Ssshh!" "Ben, whenever you sit down, we'll start," and "Kari, carry the ball." Although these statements aren't openly negative, they in fact reinforce the inappropriate behavior of certain children and ignore the appropriate behavior of a large majority of students. They are what might be called nagging behaviors. The following list includes examples of positive verbal and nonverbal interactions. For an idea of how you're doing, have a student make a simple tally of your interactions or videotape a class and critique your own behavior.

Verbal Positive Statements	Nonverbal Positive Interactions
Good	High five
Terrific	Smiling
Right	Clapping
Nice job	Thumbs up
Way to go	Winking
That's it	Pat on the back
Thank you	Shaking hands
Great	Giving an OK sign
You did it this time	
Beautiful	
Excellent	
Nicely done	
OK	
All right	

Eliminating Differential Treatment Often a stranger can walk into a classroom and after a few minutes pick out the "discipline problems" or the "really good ones" in a group of children he or she has never seen before. Frequently these are the children whose names the teacher is constantly calling out: "Rico, are you listening?" "Sarah, sit down, please." or "Brady, that's great." "Abby, you're awesome." It is not uncommon to see the same children singled out repeatedly. Typically these children are masters of their craft—they know exactly how far they can go without actually being held accountable or conversely exactly what to do to gain the teacher's praise. Because they covet adult attention, these children persist in their behavior (and as long as we reinforce their behavior by acknowledging it, they become even more skilled at it). So, avoid singling out these children whenever possible.

> Every person needs recognition. It is expressed cogently by the lad who says, "Mother, let's play darts. I'll throw the darts and you say 'Wonderful.'"
>
> —DALE BAUGHMAN

One way to spot differential treatment of students in your classes is to tape-record a few lessons. Place a tape recorder in the gymnasium or attach it to a belt around your waist. (This observation and analysis technique is discussed further in Chapter 15.) After you've taped several lessons, listen to the tapes and record the number of times you call each child's name and the number of reprimands or desists as well as positive comments you issue to individual children.

A simple way to record your tally is to use a copy of the class roster that has three columns to the right of the names (Figure 10.1). The first column is a tally for each time you call a child's name; the second column is a tally for each time you reprimand or interact negatively with a specific child; and the third column is for tallying positive comments or interactions. After you complete your tallies, if you find that you single out the same few children and/or interact either positively or negatively with a select few, you know you need to take steps to change your teaching behavior.

	Name called	Reprimand	Positive Interaction
Juan	III	I	II
Sue			
Rich	II	I	I
Jesse			
Don	HHT IIII	IIII	HHT
Billie	I		I

Figure 10.1 Chart for identifying differential treatment of students.

Prompting Prompting is a teacher behavior that reminds students what is expected of them. Some teachers find themselves prompting appropriate behavior only after inappropriate behavior has occurred. This is not the most effective way to use prompts. Prompts should be used as a positive tool as often as possible rather than as a negative interaction. For example, it is more beneficial to say, "Remember to walk as you go to pick up equipment" than "I told you to *walk!*" or even "Can't you remember by now that you are supposed to walk?" Used as in the first statement, prompting is a proactive response rather than a reactive response. Initially you should prompt students quite frequently about what behavior is appropriate; later, you will probably need to prompt only when a new or different situation arises.

Reactive Approaches

Interacting positively, eliminating differential treatment, and prompting are all proactive strategies for increasing appropriate behavior. They can be used as a means of preventing inappropriate behavior. The three strategies that follow are reactive strategies designed to increase appropriate behavior. They are intended for use after the inappropriate behavior has occurred—as a means of reacting to it. Ignoring inappropriate behavior and using nonverbal interactions and person-to-person dialogue are strategies teachers can use as responses to inappropriate behavior that are designed to increase appropriate behavior, especially when the problem is a nonproblem or minor problem.

Ignoring Inappropriate Behavior The opposite of emphasizing appropriate behavior with positive interactions is ignoring inappropriate behavior. Many of us find that praising appropriate behavior is hard but that ignoring inappropriate behavior is even more difficult. Inappropriate behavior can be ignored when it can be deemed a nonproblem by meeting the following three criteria:

1. It is of short duration and is not likely to spread or persist.
2. It is a minor deviation.
3. Reacting to it would interrupt a lesson or call attention to the behavior.

Student behaviors that could be ignored in a physical education setting include occasional calling out during discussions, brief whispering, short periods of inattentiveness or nonpractice, and occasional continuation of activity after the stop signal. Thus, unless a behavior is harmful to other students, causes a safety problem, or seriously disrupts other students, reacting to it would consume too much of your energy, interrupt your lessons constantly, and detract from your classroom climate.

To be completely effective, teachers must ignore minor inappropriate behavior and simultaneously praise appropriate behavior. Yet, when we've become accustomed to saying, "Sh-h," "Hurry up!" "I'm waiting for you to get quiet," or "Tommy!!!" it's not easy to change to phrases such as, "Jody was quiet when she heard the stop signal," "Terrific, you were ready to go in 10 seconds today," and "Jimmy, you showed thoughtfulness when you helped Jay up after he fell down." Such interactions, which can create appropriate behaviors in children, imply, for many of us, that the teacher is letting Tommy or the students who aren't yet quiet get away with inappropriate behavior. For many of us this is a risky action because the perceived implication is that our control is in jeopardy. In reality, the teacher who ignores simple inappropriate behavior while praising appropriate behavior is teaching children what desired behavior is while creating an atmosphere that is warm and conducive to learning.

There's a subtle message about what merits attention in this scenario of praising appropriate and ignoring inappropriate behavior. If a teacher instead used both sets of examples described in the previous paragraph, what message would the students receive? The answer is confusion. Students would assume they could receive reinforcement and adult attention for either appropriate or inappropriate behavior.

Ignoring inappropriate behavior is for many of us an uncomfortable and awkward act. A good way to assess your skill in praising the good and ignoring the inappropriate is to tape-record your lessons and count how often you say something positive and the number of times you say something negative. Remember that even little things such as "Hurry up!" and "Sh-h" count as negative interactions. Don't be surprised at what you first discover about your behavior; look at it as an opportunity to improve.

Nonverbal Teacher Interactions   A number of simple nonverbal techniques are often sufficient to prompt appropriate student behavior when the behavior is a minor problem. Often these are called "soft" skills. Sometimes just the physical proximity of the teacher will solicit the desirable behavior from some students. For example, when giving directions or speaking to the class as a whole, the teacher merely stands near the student displaying inappropriate behavior. Another technique for increasing appropriate

behavior is to borrow the equipment the student is using for purposes of demonstration. Finally, even less obvious actions often work. For example, simple eye contact or a signal, such as nodding the head, will redirect the student.

Person-to-Person Dialogue   Another successful technique for increasing appropriate behavior with minor problems is the person-to-person dialogue. Arrange a time to meet with a child away from the class (though not immediately before or after). You might say to the child, "Robby, you don't seem to be enjoying our physical education class. I'd like you to come to my office after school today so that we can talk about it." The purpose of this meeting is to try to determine the reasons for the child's behavior in your class. This is not a time for a lecture; instead, teacher and pupil should have a dialogue. We've found that a statement such as the following enables many children to begin a discussion of their concerns: "Robby, I'd like to talk to you about physical education class. Is there something I do that bothers you?"

This statement takes the focus from the child and places it on the teacher. Many children are quite candid about what's bothering them. Remember, this is a dialogue, not a lecture. Explaining to the child something about how and why you teach is constructive and often productive. Lecturing the child about behavior or threatening the child with future punishments is coun-

Person-to-person dialogue allows a teacher to know students on an individual basis.

terproductive. This dialogue is not teacher-to-child but person-to-person. Often the temptation to lecture, accuse, or blame a child is strong, but succumbing to this temptation is the quickest way to destroy any rapport between student and teacher. If a child trusts you enough to talk candidly about personal concerns and you threaten or lecture, communication ceases. Many children—especially those who need individual attention the most—have been betrayed before, so they're likely to be sensitive and wary. Use of teacher power in this situation reinforces a child's belief that teachers are untrustworthy and that being honest only gets him or her into more trouble.

Some children never want to participate in physical education class. A person-to-person dialogue is often helpful here, as is a conference with the child's other teachers. Some children may be afraid of participating in physical activity because they've already had unsatisfactory experiences at home or on the playground. Other children may have "issues" with classmates that are easily manifested in activity-oriented settings. Still others may be unmotivated and antisocial. Regardless, if a child has a legitimate reason, we respect the child and attempt to create a satisfactory alternative. Further, if a child is unmotivated and/or antisocial, person-to-person dialogue can act as a beginning point for seeking a solution to something that may be a problem beyond physical education. Transferring the child to another physical education class or arranging a one-to-one teaching situation often leads, in time, to participation with the regular class. Forcing a child to participate in physical education classes without first understanding the reason for the reluctance may not be in the child's best interests. Once you understand why a child is reluctant to participate, you can make an informed decision about the most appropriate action.

Decreasing Inappropriate Behavior

Although our first approach in dealing with inappropriate behavior is to attempt to increase appropriate behavior, this doesn't always work. At times, with major problems or those behaviors that may lead to major problems, a teacher must decrease inappropriate behavior. When this is necessary, the teacher should have a repertoire of strategies available. Teachers in physical education have found the following techniques useful: positive practice, desists, time-outs, planning time, behavior contracts, letters to parents, and involving the principal. Note that many of the techniques fit the

psychological definition of the term *punishment*—they decrease the likelihood of an inappropriate behavior recurring by applying undesirable consequences to the behavior. These techniques should not be emotionally laden, associated with acts of anger, or said in a raised voice. Also, any action the teacher takes to decrease inappropriate behavior should be accompanied by actions to build appropriate behavior.

Nowhere in our discussion will you find strategies that advocate physical exercise as a technique to reduce inappropriate behavior. Physical activity (sit-ups, push-ups, running laps, etc.) should never be used as a technique to hold children accountable for their behavior. Besides being deemed an inappropriate practice by professional organizations (Council on Physical Education for Children [COPEC], 2000), the use of physical activity as punishment is counterproductive to what we want to happen as a result of physical education. Our goal is that children acquire the skills and desire to be physically active for a lifetime. The use of physical activity as punishment may temporarily reduce the off-task behavior that is being punished; but the long-term result is to reduce any participation in the physical activity that was used as the punishment. Instead of learning to love activity, children will hate activity because of its association with punishment. The following are all techniques that can be used to react to inappropriate behavior in an attempt to reduce and eliminate it.

The document Appropriate Practices for Elementary School Physical Education: A Position Statement of NASPE *refers to using physical exercise as punishment in this way:*

Exercise and the Use of Exercise as Punishment
Inappropriate Practice: Exercise (running or push-ups, etc.) is used as a punishment for misbehavior and/or lack of participation.

—**COPEC**, 2000

Positive Practice

Positive practice is a technique that requires the student, group, or class to practice the acceptable or desired behavior after the demonstration of an inappropriate behavior. An example would be when students are asked to walk and get equipment and they run instead. Most of us would remind them to walk or ignore the behavior. An acceptable way to have them learn to

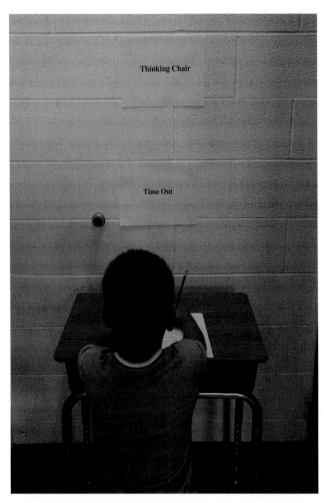

A time-out temporarily removes a child who is off task from activity.

walk is positive practice. Stop the students, and have them go back to where they started and repeat the activity of getting equipment—this time walking. You may even have them repeat it several times. Do this every time students run when you say walk and soon they will learn to walk.

Desists

Sometimes it is impossible to ignore inappropriate behavior. When that is the case, one of the most common and useful ways to react to the behavior is with a desist. A desist is a verbal statement that tells a child to stop doing something. Using desists effectively can result in behavior change. Kounin (1970) established several conditions that must be present for a desist to be effective:

1. A desist must be clear. "Ellen, stop doing that" isn't enough. The desist must contain exact information about what the student is doing wrong. For example, "Ellen, stop hitting the basketball with the tennis racket" is clear and specific. The student knows exactly what she is doing wrong.
2. A desist must be firm. Firmness is the degree to which the teacher follows through on the desist, making sure the student knows that the teacher means what was said. Brooks (1985) found that teachers who giggled or laughed after they delivered desists weren't taken seriously. Moving a bit closer to the student, looking the student momentarily in the eyes, and keeping a straight face when delivering the desist all communicate the teacher's firmness.
3. A desist must be well timed. The behavior must desist immediately, before it's allowed to spread to other students.
4. A desist must be appropriately targeted. It must be directed at the original offender, not a second or third party.
5. A desist mustn't be harsh. Kounin found that rough desists simply upset children and weren't effective. Firmness doesn't mean harshness or punitiveness; it is simply meaning what you say.

Time-outs

A time-out is like a penalty box in hockey. During a time-out, a child, either through choice or at the request of the teacher, withdraws from class for a specified amount of time or until ready to return and function according to the class rules. When ready to return to class, the child simply rejoins the activity or reports to the teacher for instructions. Teach the time-out procedure with all other procedures at the beginning of the year so you can subsequently give a time-out as a standard penalty without disrupting the rest of the class. Here are some other considerations for effective use of time-outs:

1. The student must find physical education enjoyable; if not, the time-out may be a reward instead of a punishment.
2. The time-out area should be a clearly designated place where social contact with classmates isn't possible.
3. The length of a time-out can be at the discretion of the child or the teacher. If the child determines the length, then the child must take responsibility for determining when he or she is capable of returning. Some teachers prefer to specify the length of the time-

out, for example, 3 minutes. If the time-out is to be timed, an egg timer or a clock helps children determine when the specified amount of time has passed.

Planning Time

Planning time (DeLine, 1991) is a peer-directed alternative to time-outs. It is designed for inappropriate behavior involving two students interacting with one another. When students sit alone, as in a time-out, they do not have the opportunity to discuss or resolve their problems. Planning time, by contrast, provides students who do not demonstrate appropriate behavior a chance to resolve their conflict. During planning time, students who have conflicts go to a small area of the gymnasium designated as the "planning area," where they are required to sit together and develop a resolution. To be allowed to rejoin class, they must present to the teacher a verbal plan on how to work together or how to change their behavior. In other words, No Plan, No Play!

Be aware that, as with any educational strategy, students need to be taught how to use planning time effectively. Cues and questions (Box 10-1) can be posted on the wall or on a written sheet (Figure 10.2) to prompt students toward appropriate behavior. Students can then read and review the prompts to assess the nature of their behavior and to develop an alternative. Essentially, planning time allows students who are "in trouble" to get "out of trouble." As with any new technique, learning to do it takes time, but the result is

---

Box 10-1

Possible Cues and Questions for Planning Time

The problem in my own words . . .
When and where my problem took place . . .
Strategies I used to try to avoid the problem . . .
My behavior affected others by . . .
What I will do to prevent the problem from occurring again . . .
Follow-up actions I will take now . . .
This should happen if the problem happens again . . .

---

a class that cooperates more and students who learn to resolve their differences.

Don Hellison (2003) has developed a version of planning time for individual students. In his version, the student whose behavior does not meet standards must develop a personal plan. The personal plan is actually a less formal variation of a behavior contract (see the following section) in which the student presents the teacher with a personal plan about how his or her behavior will change.

Behavior Contracts

Have you ever tried to lose weight without some "deal" with yourself or reward at the end of losing so many pounds? The same is true with some isolated children in your class. Some children need a written "deal" with the teacher to make things happen. They need it as a prompt. A behavior contract provides that. It is a written agreement between a student and the teacher regarding behavior in the physical education setting. Although it may seem like overkill, a contract can be done quietly, simply, and privately, to provide some students with the necessary focus to enjoy physical education and allow others to enjoy it.

The contract includes a statement of the desired behavior, the conditions (how much, for how long), and the rewards that will be earned if the behavior and the conditions are met (Siedentop & Tannehill, 2000). When using a behavior contract, remember that students must have a role in defining all three aspects of the contract: behavior, conditions, and rewards. After all three have been agreed upon, it is important that both parties (sometimes a third party as a witness) sign the agreement. The student should be made aware of the importance of the agreement and, just as the teacher does, view it as a formal agreement, not to be taken lightly. Figure 10.3 is an example of a behavior contract with one student.

Letters to Parents

Desists, time-outs, planning time, and behavior contracts work with some children but not with others. When a child continues to misbehave and present problems, a written report to the parents can be effective in obtaining that child's cooperation. But this technique should be used only after other approaches have proved unsuccessful.

The written report lists specific behaviors (Figure 10.4). The child is to have the report signed by a parent and then return it to you. Such a report is usually

Name: _____

Date: _____

Draw a picture of what you did.	Draw a picture of how you can change it.

Rules

1. Be safe.
2. Be honest.
3. Let others learn.
4. Let teachers teach.
5. Respect yourself and others.
6. Respect property.

1. What rule did you break?

2. How did you break this rule?

3. Who was involved?

4. What problem did this cause you?

5. What problem did this cause your classmates?

6. What problem did this cause your teacher?

7. Do you wish to discuss this problem with your teacher?

   Yes ____

   No ____

8. On the back of this paper write out a plan for yourself to help you to not break this rule again.

9. Who can help you to put your plan into action?

A

B

Figure 10.2 Cues to prompt students toward appropriate behavior. (A) is used for grades 3–5; (B) for K–3.
Source: Chet Bunting, Riverside Elementary School, Thornton, CO. Used with permission.

followed by improvements in behavior. When that occurs, you should send home another report, as soon as possible, that enumerates the improvements as clearly as the earlier report cataloged the violations. This second report congratulates the child on improved behavior and, like the first one, requires a parent's signature.

This is not to suggest that the written report to parents need be used only as a measure to decrease inappropriate behavior. The teachers of St. Andrew's Episcopal

School in Austin, Texas, found that a "good letter" (Figure 10.5) was one of the most effective strategies in their program for increasing support for the program and generating good will with parents (D. Lambdin, personal communication, July 1991). In the St. Andrew's program, a "good letter" was sent home with every deserving student during one marking period each year. The response from parents was gratifying. Many commented on how wonderful it was that teachers took time to let parents know about good behavior.

BEHAVIOR CONTRACT

Kim Thomas and Mr. Diller agree that the following plan will be in effect for the next two weeks.

Starting date _____ Ending date _____

Kim will

1. Not interrupt other students' work by trying to knock their equipment away

2. Not disturb class by talking while the teacher is talking

3. Participate in all activities and try hard to improve her skills in throwing

Mr. Diller will

1. Give Kim individual help on throwing

2. Count one point for each day that Kim meets the three points stated above

3. Let Kim help with the physical education equipment for one week if she earns five points during the two weeks of the contract

Signed _____

_____

_____

Figure 10.3 Typical behavior contract.

Involving the Principal

Sending a disruptive child to the principal may or may not be successful. When you send a child to the principal, you're acknowledging—to yourself and to the child—your inability to cope with the situation. You're also placing the child in a situation you can't control.

Some principals are positive and helpful in working with disruptive children. Others use threats or corporal punishment, techniques likely to temporarily improve the child's behavior but permanently damage the child's enthusiasm and trust.

Only when you've tried every other possible technique to deal with behavior detrimental to the child and classmates should you send a child to the principal. If you must do this, we hope yours is a principal who can help you and the child to better understand each other's needs and situations, so that you can work together more successfully.

Maintaining Appropriate Behavior in Entire Classes

The scene: May in the Southeast, a fourth-grade class with a student teacher teaching and two cooperating teachers observing. The setting: an old school, no

Figure 10.4 Behavior report for parents.

ELEMENTARY SCHOOL
PHYSICAL EDUCATION BEHAVIOR REPORT

NAME _____ DATE _____

Educational research has consistently shown that when a teacher spends class time managing discipline problems, less teaching and student learning occur. Disruptive behavior, therefore, is a primary reason for poor student achievement.

We regret to inform you that your child exhibited the following misbehavior during physical education class today:

_____ Fought with others	_____ Refused to participate
_____ Argued with others	_____ Lazy; no hustle or energy
_____ Mistreated equipment	_____ Late to class
_____ Disrupted the work of others	_____ Disruptive in hallway
_____ Discourteous to others	_____ Continually off-task; not following teacher's directions
_____ Frequently clowned, acting foolish and silly	_____ Spoke using foul language
_____ Talked while teacher was talking	_____ Did not listen to teacher

Teacher's Comments: _____

_____

_____

Please discuss today's incident with your youngster. We are concerned about the harm your child's behavior is causing himself/herself and his/her classmates. We will keep you informed of your child's behavioral progress during the coming weeks.

Thank you for your cooperation.

TEACHER _____

PARENT'S SIGNATURE _____

---

air-conditioning, all the windows open in the second-floor gym. The unit: throwing and catching. The equipment: beanbags. The task: some version of throw and catch with a partner. The result: The students thought the better task would be to throw the beanbags out the windows and see if they could hit the sidewalk below. The larger result: The teacher was befuddled, unnerved, and demoralized. (This is a true story from one of the three authors of this book!)

The moral of the story: All teachers at some time experience entire classes that test their ability to maintain the preferred learning environment. At this point two things can happen. Either you can write the class off as "bad" (it was tempting) and resign yourself to the role of a police officer trying to keep control of a group, or you can assume the role of a teacher and guide and try to find a mutually acceptable solution to the problem.

In this section we offer three approaches. The second and third, class rewards and individual rewards, are clearly "behaviorally" oriented and are designed to remedy the problem and then find out why it existed. They are for use when nothing else seems to work. The first approach, developing personal and social responsibility, is a more detailed reiteration of establishing a learning environment. We include this again here because teachers often view children as blank slates to

Figure 10.5 "Good" letter for parents.

ELEMENTARY SCHOOL
PHYSICAL EDUCATION BEHAVIOR REPORT

Name _____ Date _____

Educational research has shown that when a teacher spends class time managing discipline problems, less teaching and less learning occur. Therefore, when disruptive behavior is nonexistent in a class situation, greater student achievement is likely to result.

We are glad to inform you that _____(child's name)_____ behavior in physical education class consistently exhibits the following exemplary behaviors:

_____ Listens to the teacher   _____ Is courteous to others

_____ Is on-task, following   _____ Treats equipment with
          directions   care

_____ Is eager to participate   _____ Plays safely

Your child is doing a wonderful-terrific-dynamite job in physical education and we are proud of him/her. You are to be commended for preparing your youngster to function so well in school. We are more effective teachers because of your efforts.

Thank you for your cooperation.

TEACHER _____

be filled versus active learners that are capable of being partners in their educational experiences (Hellison, 2003; Parker & Stiehl, 2005; Stork & Sanders, 2002). The personal and social responsibility approach promotes the latter as children are viewed as competent decision makers.

Developing Personal and Social Responsibility

Because physical education largely focuses on the development of motor skills and fitness, teachers quite often ignore social and personal development—the very thing that is usually needed when an entire class seems unable to respond appropriately. Hellison (2003) states that it is usually assumed that students will be under control and that cooperation will automatically result in stability. As we know, such bliss does not occur automatically.

Personal and social responsibility involves much more. In a basic sense the concept can be defined as "personal acceptance of being answerable for our conduct concerning others, our surroundings, and ourselves" (Parker & Stiehl, 2005, p. 133). Although these attributes occur naturally to some extent, to develop fully and appropriately they must be learned, just like a motor skill. Thus they must be taught and practiced, at the developmentally appropriate time and with developmentally appropriate opportunities (Brustad & Parker, 2005). There is much debate about whether teaching responsibility is curriculum (what we teach) or instruction (how we teach); regardless, the basic premises involve including all children, inviting and making use of student input, providing choice, having students practice making choices, allowing for reflection, and being student centered (Parker & Stiehl, 2005). Don Hellison is the most widely known advocate for developing personal and social responsibility. In his book *Teaching Responsibility through Physical Activity,* he provides field-tested instructional strategies for fostering responsibility through physical activity (curriculum). In terms of instruction, he offers students guidelines for their behavior, outlines expectations, and invites greater participation in learning. Regarding curriculum, he identifies personal and social responsibility in terms of principles or goals: respect for the rights and feelings of others, participation and effort, self-direction, helping others, and leadership. These goals are then presented in a hierarchy of levels that represent an informal progression.

These ideas, the philosophy underlying the establishment of a learning environment presented in Chapter 9, are presented here specifically for use with classes that have a hard time accepting responsibility for their own actions. This approach is not a quick fix for class problems but a shift in thinking and action that permeates all activities in class. It is a philosophical approach to teaching that places the focus on creating personal and social responsibility using physical activity as the medium for all that is done. For many youngsters, this type of empowerment shifts their focus from one of fighting "the system" to actively becoming part of creating a system that works.

It is through the interaction of teaching and responsibility content that students begin to develop more responsibility for themselves and for the well-being of their classmates. The description given here is not sufficient to implement the social responsibility model. If you are interested in implementing this approach, please see Hellison's 2003 text, *Teaching Responsibility through Physical Activity,* or the Parker and Stiehl (2005) chapter "Personal and Social Responsibility" in *Standards-based Physical Education Curriculum Development.*

Reward Systems

Rewards can serve to reduce inappropriate behavior and help build a positive climate. The improvement occurs because children are attracted to the rewards and thus direct their behavior toward appropriate behavior and away from inappropriate behavior. If you decide to implement a reward system, consider the following guidelines. First, check your school and district policies to see if any rewards are prohibited. For example, parties with food are not allowed in some schools, and others restrict off-campus trips. Second, make sure the rewards are attractive to the students. Successful rewards to be earned in physical education have included public recognition (name boards, photo boards, names in school newsletter), extra physical education time, free-choice time (at the end of class or the end of the week), special privileges (helping the teacher with other classes or before school), field trips, equipment use (borrowing equipment to use at home and on weekends), and T-shirts. Regardless of what reward is established, its effectiveness is based on the children having had a part in the decision. The easiest way to do this is to ask them. Third, the rewards should target the behavior you are after. If you want children to stop activity and listen when asked, then the rewards should be for those specific behaviors. Fourth, design a reward system in which it is not too difficult to achieve the reward (which will frustrate students) or too easy (which will lose their attention). Fifth, make record keeping easy. You do not want to create a system that requires elaborate record keeping.

There is one caution regarding reward systems. Research is fairly clear (Deci & Ryan, 1985) that extrinsic rewards can reduce intrinsic motivation. That is, if students work only for the reward they will not be motivated to continue that same behavior when the reward is withdrawn. When using reward systems, be thoughtful about their use. No purpose is served by rewarding activities that are already motivating to students. With any reward system the goal is to eventually be able to withdraw the reward and have student behavior remain appropriate.

Two reward systems, one for a class and one for individuals, are described below.

Class Rewards With class rewards, the class as a whole has the opportunity to earn rewards for abiding by the class rules. The first step is to establish a reward. When an entire class does well for a day (week, month), it receives the reward. For example, if a class consistently does better than the performance standards established for management tasks over a given period of time, it receives a poster or banner to display in its room. Some teachers provide a reward for a class-of-the-week. We prefer, however, that rewards not be exclusionary. Every class should be able to earn a reward every week. Competition should be limited to the class against a standard, not the class against other classes.

Token Systems Time-out penalizes disruptive behavior; a token system rewards desirable behavior. A token system is a program with academic, organizational, or managerial outcomes accompanied by a system in which students can earn "tokens" that can be exchanged for various rewards (Siedentop & Tannehill, 2000). The intent is to reward appropriate behavior and so encourage all children to behave appropriately.

The teacher initially explains to the class that a particular rule or procedure is being violated or not being accomplished as efficiently as possible. In doing this, the teacher must clearly define the behaviors that are to be improved. After the behaviors have been defined, rewards must be developed. This is best done with the students' input by having them rank the awards the teacher has offered according to their desirability. The higher the ranking, the more the students will be motivated by the reward; the lower the ranking, the greater the probability it won't do much to encourage children to change their behavior.

Once the behavior has been specified and the rewards agreed upon, then it must be decided how many tokens it will take to earn a certain reward. For example, five minutes' free time at the end of class might cost 3 tokens, whereas a T-shirt might cost 50 tokens. Just as in a store, different merchandise costs different amounts, and if you don't have the money (tokens), you can't buy it. It is also important to specify ahead of time when the tokens can be redeemed, for example, only on Fridays.

After all aspects of the token system are in place, the project begins. For example, the teacher explains to the class that some students aren't stopping and listening as soon as they hear the signal. Beginning today, the teacher explains, he'll check off on a class list the names of the students who don't stop and listen within five seconds after the signal is given. Students who have less than five checks during class will earn one token.

As the project progresses, in an effort to get classes off the token system, the teacher gradually increases the number of tokens it takes to receive an award and/or increase the length of time between token redemptions. Once children have learned to abide by the rules that are vital for the successful functioning of a large group, the token system becomes unnecessary.

Corporal Punishment

We're unalterably opposed to corporal punishment. Besides being against the law in many states and school systems (check with yours), corporal punishment, like dodgeball, powerfully indicates that it is acceptable to hit another person. For some teachers a spanking or a paddling seems to be—inappropriately—a cathartic act that may help the teacher but is more likely to harm the child. There are times when the temptation to paddle or strike a continually misbehaving child is almost overwhelming. And yet, according to our observations, it is the same few children who receive the vast majority of the paddlings. Obviously, this shows that for many children paddling doesn't achieve the desired result. Simultaneously it proves to these children that physically striking another person is a legitimate alternative when no other course of action appears effective. Interestingly, many of the children who repeatedly receive corporal punishment are being punished for fighting or hitting others. Occasionally a first paddling achieves the desired result. But the result is only temporary and has little effect on long-term behavior; in fact, corporal punishment could become a negative reinforcer. One cannot help but wonder about the long-term impact of such an experience on a child. Use of corporal punishment is inhumane, ineffective, and an admission of failure.

Teaching Skills to Maintain a Productive Learning Environment

Near the end of the previous chapter we talked about various teaching skills that could be used to help establish a learning environment (e.g., setting performance standards and being consistent). Several other skills can be employed to help maintain the environment as well. One major reason beginning teachers struggle with classroom management is that they are so preoccupied with other things that they simply do not see the inappropriate behavior, or if they do see it they aren't quite sure how to approach it. The following strategies have been found useful in monitoring and reacting (or not) to student behavior, allowing you to be consistent in what you do.

- Keep movement patterns unpredictable. Vary the way you circulate through the class during activity. Stand in various places in the gym when you give directions or speak to the whole class.
- Scan the class frequently to "catch students being good." To scan, quickly look across the class in a predetermined direction, usually right to left, at regular intervals.
- Make sure all students can see and hear you.
- Provide clear and concise directions, and repeat them at least once for clarity; then ask for questions to check for understanding. For example, after providing the direction, "Walk, choose a ball or

beanbag to use to practice tossing and catching and carry it to your self-space. I will know you are ready when I see you standing in your space, holding the equipment" ask a student what he is supposed to do and have him repeat it back to you.

- Separate the organization aspects of directions from the content aspects (Rink, 2006). For example, explain that the task focuses on throwing and catching the ball as it is received. Then tell children how they will practice doing the task.
- Maintain the quality of appearing to have eyes in the back of your head (Kounin, 1970).
- Overlap, or attend to two tasks simultaneously (Kounin, 1970). If effectively attending to two tasks simultaneously you would be able to do such things as provide feedback to one group practicing their self-designed game while also being aware that one child had left the gym to use the restroom.
- Avoid dangles or issues left in midair (Kounin, 1970). Statements or directions left "unfinished" tend to confuse students. Not knowing what to do, they make up what they think may be an appropriate response.

- Avoid flip-flopping (terminating one activity, starting another, and returning to the first) (Kounin, 1970).
- Use targeting, or directing your interactions toward the appropriate students (Siedentop & Tannehill, 2000).
- Display the skill of timing. As a general rule, the shorter the lag time between student action and teacher behavior, the better (Siedentop & Tannehill, 2000). If, when a class is practicing balance and rolling, the teacher sees a student push another student off balance, a effective timing means reacting immediately to the incident, rather than waiting to see if it happens again.

If you practice these techniques consistently and regularly, the functioning of the gymnasium is more likely to progress in a manner that enhances learning. Inappropriate behavior problems, although they won't vanish, will be curtailed.

Summary

The key to maintaining a learning environment is the presence of appropriate behavior that supports the educational goals of the specific situation. During the time needed to establish a learning environment, behavior inappropriate for the setting may occur. When it does, the teacher should first make certain that the lesson plans are pedagogically sound. If they are, then it is appropriate to focus on the students' behavior. It's important to understand that problems with inappropriate behavior are normal; all teachers will encounter some children who are off task.

There are two phases to managing inappropriate behavior: the immediate (short-term) response to the situation and the long-term strategy. The long-term strategy involves recognizing the need to prevent the recurrence of the behavior by finding out what triggered it and developing ways of helping students learn more constructive means for dealing with inappropriate behavior. Short-term techniques give a teacher practical skills to use instantly when undesirable behavior occurs. Only after the teacher has acquired and consistently used these techniques with positive results is she or he comfortable with addressing the long-term aspects of inappropriate behavior. The techniques are simply a way of dealing with the immediate

inappropriate behavior; as a learning environment is developed and students accept the responsibility for their own behavior, such techniques should no longer be needed and can gradually be phased out.

When inappropriate behavior first occurs, the teacher should use the techniques for increasing appropriate behavior: positive interaction, eliminating differential treatment, prompting, ignoring inappropriate behavior, nonverbal teacher interactions, and person-to-person dialogue. For those times when teachers find it necessary to decrease inappropriate behavior, successful techniques include positive practice, desists, time-outs, planning time, behavior contracts, letters to parents, and involving the principal. Remember that strategies to reduce inappropriate behavior should always be accompanied by techniques to increase appropriate behavior. At no time should physical activity or hitting a child be used as a punishment. Techniques for refocusing an entire class that is off task include incorporating a system for developing student responsibility, class rewards, and token systems. Monitoring and reacting strategies can be used to help maintain an environment conducive to learning. Figure 10.6 may help visualize the interaction and relationship of the class management strategies presented in this chapter as well as Chapter 9.

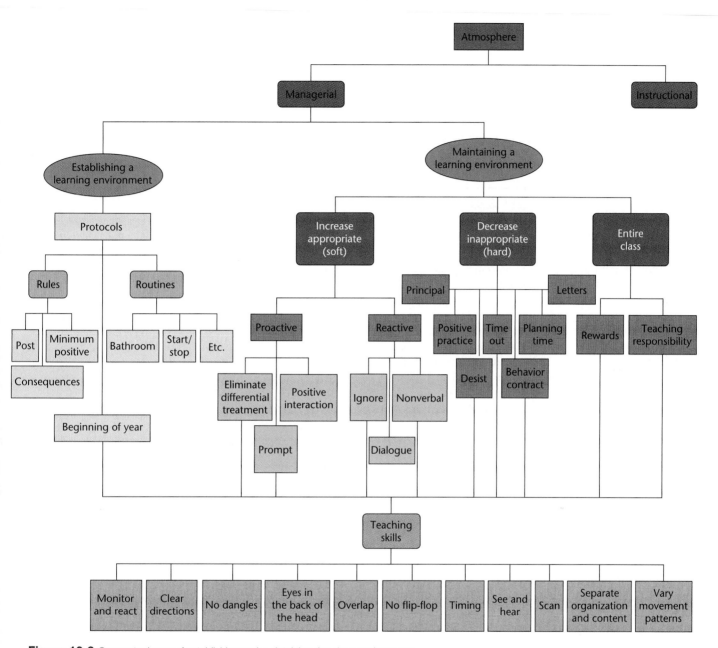

Figure 10.6 Conceptual map of establishing and maintaining the class environment.

Reading Comprehension Questions

1. What should your first step be when you find most of the students in your class misbehaving? Why?
2. Why have we chosen not to use the word *discipline*?
3. What does it mean to say that appropriate behavior is not the mere absence of inappropriate behavior?
4. What is the first strategy for maintaining an effective learning environment in the gymnasium?

What techniques can be used to accomplish this goal?
5. Why are positive interactions with students so important, especially at the beginning of the year?
6. When should you ignore inappropriate behavior?
7. What does differential treatment of children mean? How can you determine whether you are doing this?

8. What is the major point to remember in a person-to-person dialogue with a student?
9. What is the second strategy for handling inappropriate behavior in the gymnasium? What techniques can you use to accomplish this goal?
10. What are the characteristics of an effective desist?
11. What is a time-out? What points should you remember when using a time-out? When is a time-out not effective? How does planning time differ?
12. When is a letter to parents useful? What should you include in the letter?
13. What is one strategy for working with an entire class that isn't able to work productively?
14. Why should physical activity not be used as punishment?
15. Why should many of the techniques discussed in this chapter not be used as the school year progresses?

References/Suggested Readings

Brooks, D. (1985). The first day of school. *Educational Leadership, 42*(8), 76–78.

Brustad, R. & Parker, M. (2005). Enhancing positive youth development through physical activity. *Psychologica, 39,* 75–93.

Council on Physical Education for Children. (2000). *Appropriate practices for elementary school physical education: A position statement of NASPE.* Reston, VA: National Association for Sport and Physical Education/American Alliance for Health, Physical Education, Recreation and Dance.

Deci, E. L. & Ryan, R. M. (1985). *Intrinsic motivation and self-determination in human behavior.* New York: Plenum Press.

DeLine, J. (1991). Why can't they get along? Developing cooperative skills through physical education. *Journal of Physical Education, Recreation and Dance, 62*(1), 21–26.

Evertson, C., Emmer, E., & Worsham, M. (2003). *Classroom management for elementary teachers* (6th ed.). Boston: Allyn & Bacon.

Fader, D. (1971). *The naked children.* New York: Macmillan.

Hellison, D. (2003). *Teaching responsibility through physical activity* (2nd ed.). Champaign, IL: Human Kinetics.

Kounin, J. (1970). *Discipline and group management in classrooms.* New York: Holt, Rinehart & Winston.

Kulinna, P., Cothran, D., & Garrahy, D. (2002). Teacher's perspectives on classroom management. *Research Quarterly for Exercise and Sport Supplement, 73*(1), A72–73.

Parker, M., & Stiehl, J. (2005). Personal and social responsibility. In J. Lund & D. Tannehill (eds.), *Standards-based physical education curriculum* (pp. 130–153). Sudbury, MA: Jones & Bartlett.

Rink, J. (2006). *Teaching physical education for learning* (5th ed.). St. Louis, MO: Mosby.

Siedentop, D., & Taggart, A. (1984). Behavior analysis in physical education and sport. In W. Heward, T. Heron, B. Hill, & J. Trap-Porter (eds.), *Focus on behavior analysis in education.* Columbus, OH: Merrill.

Siedentop, D., & Tannehill, D. (2000). *Developing teaching skills in physical education* (4th ed.). New York: McGraw-Hill.

Stork, S., & Sanders, S. (2002). Why can't students just do as they're told?! An exploration of incorrect responses. *Journal of Teaching in Physical Education, 21*(2), 208–228.

Developing the Content

Elementary school students should develop basic motor skills that allow participation in a variety of physical activities. Students' mastery of and confidence in motor skills occurs when these skills are broken down into components and the tasks are ordered from easy to hard. In addition, students need opportunities to observe others performing the skills and to receive encouragement, feedback, and repeated opportunities for practice during physical education class.

—National Center for Chronic Disease Prevention and Health Promotion, 1997

In order to maximize the development of self-esteem, it is important to create learning opportunities that match the task difficulty with the learner's developmental capabilities. Children love to be challenged. Succeeding at a task that is too easy gives little pleasure. In contrast, causing children to work just a bit beyond their current skill can produce optimal growth. In order to do that, teachers should sequence tasks in a developmental order before presenting them to children as challenges.

—Linda Bunker

Key Concepts

- Developing the content refers to the process teachers use to provide a sequential series of learning experiences for children. It is based on effective observation.

- Developing the content has been subdivided into four parts. The first is informing children about the lesson and safety.

- The second part of content development is the careful selection of tasks (extending) that provide the most beneficial, and interesting, learning experiences for youngsters.

- Cues (critical elements) are the shortcuts to learning that are provided by expert teachers (refining) to assist youngsters in learning the skills more quickly and correctly than by trial and error.

- Reflective teachers encourage youngsters to continue practicing a task by using challenges (applications) that make the activity more interesting and appealing to the children.

- Reflective teachers adapt tasks to accommodate differences in abilities (GLSP).

- Teaching by invitation is a technique that allows the children to adapt a task to better match their skill level.

- Intratask variation is a technique used by teachers to change a task for individual students based on their observation.

How can I change this task to make it more interesting? Are the children benefiting from this task?

We have attempted to assist you with writing lesson plans and developing the content during actual lessons by organizing the movement concept chapters (Chapters 16 to 18) and the skill theme chapters (Chapters 19 to 28) in developmentally appropriate progressions based on the generic levels of skill proficiency (Chapter 7). These chapters are helpful guidelines, but as you plan you will no doubt want to add additional tasks and also modify some of the tasks to better match your particular teaching situation (Chapter 5). We don't intend that you use the progressions we have suggested in these chapters exactly as written, especially if you are an experienced teacher. We know, however, they will be extremely valuable for novice teachers and those who are new to the skill theme approach. Because you will be changing some of these tasks as you teach, as well as providing children with cues and challenges during a lesson, it is important that you understand the system we have used to develop the content in each of these chapters. In the final part of this chapter, we describe two techniques, teaching by invitation and intratask variation, that teachers use to adjust for differences in ability within the same class of children.

Overview of Content Development

In the content development process created by Rink (2006), a teacher performs four functions during a lesson to help children learn the various concepts and skills that constitute the content of the program:

1. Informing the children, that is, providing information about the concepts or skills and describing how the tasks are to be done.
2. Extending *tasks,* that is, making the activities (drills, games) that will be taught in a lesson **easier or harder,** according to the ability of the children.
3. Refining tasks, that is, providing children with *cues* or "critical elements" that will help them become more efficient in performing a skill or task.
4. Applying the task by inventing *challenges* designed to motivate the children to continue practicing or to show them how the task can be applied.

We have adapted Rink's system of content development and refer to extensions as *tasks,* refinements as *cues,* and applications as *challenges* throughout this book. In the following sections we define and give examples of each of the four aspects of content development, beginning with informing students.

One major responsibility of a teacher is to select and sequence the content of a lesson (Chapter 8). During the actual lesson, the reflective teacher determines how effectively the tasks or activities are helping the students accomplish the goals of that lesson—and makes changes accordingly. Tasks or activities that are too difficult for the children often lead to frustration, resulting in off-task behavior. Tasks that are too easy often lead to boredom, again resulting in off-task behavior (Csikszentmihalyi, 2000). One challenge for the physical education teacher during the lesson, then, is to carefully select tasks from the plan created beforehand (Chapter 8) that will allow children to feel successful—and that will result in learning and improvement.

Teaching would be much easier if lesson plans worked perfectly, exactly as designed. Reflective teaching, however, is a dynamic process—the teacher is constantly making decisions: Is this task too hard? Should I provide the children with a cue? Are they getting bored? Are the children benefiting from this task?

Informing

Effective teachers are good communicators (Graham et al., 1993; Rink, 2006). They provide clear and interesting explanations and descriptions so that the children can easily understand the information. When we provide information to children, we try to follow several guidelines: the KISS principle and the use of demonstrations and pinpointing.

The KISS Principle The KISS principle (Keep It Short and Simple) is a good guideline to follow when talking to children. The problem we face as teachers is that we have much to tell the children about a concept or skill, but the children aren't really interested in listening for long; they want to move. Although there are exceptions, we try to limit our instruction to just what the children need to know.

One trap teachers easily fall into is spending five or more minutes telling (and demonstrating) all they know about a skill or activity. There is a lot to tell the children—the problem is that the children can't possibly remember all that information when it is provided in a single minilecture. Think of a skill or exercise you know well. It would be easy for you to talk for five minutes on how to hit a ball with a bat or the correct way to do a "crunch," for example. The children won't remember all of this, however. If you don't believe it, try an experiment with one of your classes. Give them a minilecture. During the following class, use the technique Helping Murgatroid (described in Chapter 14 in the section exit [or entrance] slips) to see what they actually are able to recall from your lecture. We believe you'll find that information provided in small bits throughout a lesson is more effective than long-winded explanations that children don't remember.

Demonstrations In addition to keeping our explanations brief and to the point, we also try to demonstrate whenever possible (Graham, 2001; Rink, 2006; Sharpe et al., 1989; Southard & Higgins, 1989). This is helpful to the children who are visual, as opposed to auditory, learners, and it's necessary for the increasing number of children in our classes who do not speak English. Demonstrations of motor skills need to be done correctly, and they must emphasize the part or parts that the children need to pay attention to—the instep, the elbow, the shoulder, the hands—so that children can clearly see how that part is to be used and how it fits into the total movement. This seems obvious, yet it is amazing to see how often teachers don't provide the children with a demonstration or fail to demonstrate slowly enough or to emphasize a part, so that the demonstration is just not helpful to children. If you videotape some of your lessons, as we suggest in Chapter 15, you will be able to ascertain quickly the effectiveness of your demonstrations.

Pinpointing There are times when we choose not to demonstrate or are unable to demonstrate a skill for

This teacher can observe both the safety of the class and individual movement patterns by using the back-to-the-wall technique.

the children. In these instances, *pinpointing*—inviting several children to do the demonstration—can be an effective technique (Graham, 2001). The children are encouraged when they see that their peers can demonstrate the skill or technique. When possible we try to select two or more children to do the pinpointing; in this way we avoid placing children who are uncomfortable performing in front of other children in a solo situation.

As you will see in the movement concept and skill theme chapters (Chapters 16 to 28), each section (activity) begins by providing the children with some information about how a particular task is to be done; for example, the equipment needed, the space in which the activity will occur, the rules, and whether the children will be working alone or with others. These are considered informing tasks and for that reason are not designated as tasks, cues, or challenges. Ideally, the informing part of the lesson is both brief and clear so that the children can quickly begin practicing the starting task with few questions.

Tasks (Extensions)

Once the children have been provided with a starting task or activity, the next step in the development of the content is to observe the children to determine whether the task is too easy (the children are able to do it easily with no apparent challenge), too hard (the children are only occasionally successful, but many are unable to do the task with success), or simply unproductive (the children just aren't benefiting [learning] from doing the task). In any of these cases, the teacher will want to change the task so that more of the children can be successful. Chapter 8 outlines the process for developing a progression of developmentally appropriate tasks as part of lesson planning (Box 8-1). In addition, each of the movement concept and skill theme chapters (Chapters 16 to 28) provides a suggested progression of tasks (extensions) for children. The tasks are marked with the symbol (T).

Tasks that are "just right" allow children to succeed at the task about 80 percent of the time (Berliner, 1984; Brophy, 1983; Rosenshine, 1983; Siedentop & Tannehill, 2000). The 80 percent success rate is a rough estimate, but it provides a guideline for determining whether to make a task easier or harder. High rates of success typically motivate children to keep trying and working at the task. Tasks that are too easy or too hard prompt off-task behavior or questions like "When can we do something else?" "When do we get to play the game?"

Cues (Refinements)

Once a task is judged to be appropriate (not too easy or too hard), the teacher can provide cues (or refinements) to help the children perform the skill more efficiently. Cues are also referred to as critical elements. Providing cues is one of the most valuable roles a teacher can perform (Graham, 2001; Landin, 1994; Masser, 1987, 1993; Rink, 2006). Cues help children understand how to perform a skill. They are an important part of lesson planning (Chapter 8). In the overhand throw for distance, for example, it is important that children learn to step with the foot opposite the throwing hand. When landing from a jump, it is important that the children learn to bend, not only at the knees but also at the hips and ankles. These tips or cues (refinements) help children learn skills more efficiently than they

---

STRIKING WITH BOTH SIDES OF THE PADDLE

Setting: Each child has a paddle (foam or wood) and a ball (foam, dead tennis ball), and a carpet square or some other way to define self-space.

Cues

Flat Paddle (Place your paddle flat on the floor. Now pick it up and see if you can keep it as flat as it was on the floor—the same angle.)

Stiff Wrist (Pretend you have a cast.)

Tasks/Challenges:

(T) In tennis or racketball or badminton, players use both sides of the paddle. Let's try this. Keep hitting the ball up. Try to hit the ball with one side of the paddle, then the other.

(T) If this is easy, see if you can use both sides of the paddle and both sides of the body. Try not to always strike the ball when it is right in front of you.

(T) Can you make a rainbow with the ball—hit it on one side of your body and then the other so that the ball travels in a rainbow shape? Remember, if you miss the ball and have to chase it, go back to your self-space before you start striking again.

(C) How many rainbows can you make? Each time the ball goes over your head it counts as one. Five rainbows without a miss would be excellent.

Figure 11.1 Sample presentation of tasks, cues, and challenges for striking with rackets and paddles.

would by trial and error. The cues (critical elements) are listed at the beginning of each series of tasks for skill themes and movement concepts. (Figure 11.1, taken from Chapter 27, shows how the tasks, cues, and challenges are presented in the movement concept and skill theme development chapters.) This will help you observe the children to determine which cue or refinement will best help them improve their skill performance. In addition to helping the children learn the correct ways of performing a skill, emphasizing cues can also provide the children with a checklist of the important critical elements that they will need when they decide to play a sport on their own outside of school. Children who attend physical education class for an hour or less a week obviously don't have enough time to reach the utilization or proficiency levels. We do know, however, that they can learn the critical elements, so at least they will recall how to perform a skill appropriately (Manross, 1992).

When you begin to read and use the information in the skill theme chapters, you will notice that no cues are provided with the tasks at the precontrol level of the generic levels of skill proficiency (GLSP; Chapter 7). This is because youngsters at that level have had minimal experience with even attempting a given movement. We want them to first explore the skill until they have at least a general idea of how it feels and what is required to do it successfully. For example, if you have never attempted a movement, being told four or five cues will have little meaning, and probably won't stick with you. Obviously we must emphasize safety, but explanation and demonstration of the critical elements can begin once youngsters have a basic understanding of the movement and are at the control level. At this point in the learning curve, they are often more receptive to learning the cues because they have discovered that they are not adept at the skill and would like to know how to do it more efficiently and effectively.

You will also notice that the cues change from the control to the utilization and then the proficiency levels. This is because the movements are used differently at each of the GLSP. For example, youngsters at the proficiency level in landing from a jump do not need to be told to "bend their knees"—they learned that when they were at the control level. So just as the tasks change for each of the GLSP, so do the cues.

Each of the movement concept and skill theme development chapters provides numerous cues that the children will find helpful for enhancing the quality of their movements. The challenge for you as a teacher is to select the cue that will be most helpful for the class you are teaching. Much of this analysis is completed as part of the lesson planning when you develop the

Box 11-1

Fourth-Grade Assessment Example for Throwing

Standard 1: Movement Forms

Peer Observation

Have partners observe the preparatory phase of a designated skill in an attempt to ascertain the correct use of critical elements. For example, student A will throw a ball toward a target five times using the overhand pattern while student B observes the performance, focusing on a single critical element during the preparatory phase (e.g., opposite foot forward, side to target, arm pulled way back). The observing student gives a "thumbs-up" if the critical element is correct; if it is incorrect, the observing student tells what is needed to improve the movement.

Criteria for Assessment

a. Thrower displays the critical element that is the focus of the observation.
b. Observer makes an accurate judgment on the performance.

Source: NASPE 1995, p. 33.

progression of tasks and the appropriate cues (Chapter 8). Beware of the temptation to tell the children too much at once. As suggested in the *National Standards,* we want the children not only to hear the cues but also to remember them. Box 11-1 provides one example of how you might assess your children to determine how well they are learning the critical elements.

One Cue at a Time   Generally we try to focus on one cue at a time in our instructions. For example, to a class of second graders we might provide instruction and demonstrate the cue of stepping with the lead foot when batting (Chapter 28). We would then ask the children to continue the same task—batting off a tee against a wall or fence, for example—while we circulate and provide feedback.

If you can imagine this setting, you realize that the children may need several other cues. Some, for example, will not be swinging in a horizontal plane; some may not be swinging the bat appropriately on the backswing or following through. The problem, however, is that children at this age (and many adults for that matter) can concentrate effectively on only one cue at a time. By focusing on one cue at a time, we heighten the chances that the children will learn this cue (Graham, 2001; Rink, 2006; Rink & Werner, 1989). Once the children are actually using this cue—that is, when they are actually stepping with the lead foot as they swing, which may not happen in a single lesson—we move on to another cue. We may change the task, as suggested in the batting progression in Chapter 28, but the cue remains the same.

Congruent Feedback As the children practice a task, the teacher circulates among them, providing feedback. Again, there are many cues the teacher might provide in the form of feedback. We try, however, to provide congruent feedback, that is, feedback that is consistent with what we told the children to think about when practicing the skill (Belka et al., 1991; Graham, 2001; Rink, 2006; Rink & Werner, 1989). For example, during instruction (informing) we might ask the children to think about stepping with the lead foot as they are batting; the feedback we provide, therefore, would be about how they are (or are not) stepping with the opposite foot. We might say:

"Jackie, good step."

"Nick, don't forget to step when you swing."

"Verenda, remember to step."

"Tommy, way to step."

Interestingly, both the children and the teacher seem to benefit from this type of feedback. The children hear a consistent message—and are able to remember the cue. The teacher is able to focus quickly on a specific part of a movement while moving among the children, rather than attempting to analyze every child's batting swing. The feedback analysis checklist (Figure 15.1) is a tool to help you analyze the type of feedback you provide to the children, and the modified checklist in Figure 15.6 helps you analyze to whom you provide it.

Challenges (Applications)

In addition to informing (providing information to the children), presenting a logical progression of tasks and activities, and providing cues to the children, a teacher may also present challenges (applications) to the children to maintain their interest in a task. Even when children are doing a task and succeeding at high rates, there comes a time when they become disinterested and are ready to move on to another task. The problem is that as teachers we are not always able to

provide another task that is just a little bit harder; in some instances, a task is much harder, and if we ask the children to do this task before they are ready, many of the children will fail. Many of the challenges that will motivate the children to continue practicing are "invented" as part of the planning process (Chapter 8). The important point to remember is that the task stays the same, but the challenge is designed to motivate the children to keep practicing that task.

Let's take the example of batting. A logical progression from striking a ball from a batting tee is to strike a pitched ball (Chapter 28). Hitting a pitched ball is much more difficult for the children, especially at young ages when the throwing (pitching) skills of many children are not yet refined. The right challenge at the right time, however, will motivate the children to continue practicing batting from a tee. This will allow the teacher time to continue providing feedback about the way the children are (or aren't) stepping with the lead foot when they bat. The following are examples of batting challenges. You will note that all of the tasks still require the children to keep batting from a tee, the task they had been working on before the teacher decided to provide a challenge to the children:

"If this is easy for you, you may want to try batting a smaller ball; if it is hard for you, you may want to try batting a larger ball."

"Every time you bat the ball without hitting the tee with the bat, say a letter of your last name. Try to spell your whole name."

"See how many times in a row you can hit the ball without hitting the tee or missing the ball."

"Try to hit the fence (wall) with the ball on a fly three times in a row."

The challenges are marked in the movement concept and skill theme chapters (Chapters 16 to 28) with the symbol Ⓒ. These challenges do not substantively change the task; rather, they are designed to maintain the children's interest in that task. In gamelike settings, a challenge of keeping score, either cooperatively or competitively, would be a logical application for that task.

Some teachers find it easier to use challenges in their teaching than others. As we increase our understanding of how children at different ages think—and their sense of humor—it becomes easier to create challenges for them. Preschool children, for example, can be challenged simply by being asked to perform a task with a ball, hoop, or carpet square of a different color. Some middle-school children enjoy the challenge of competing against a friend to see who can be more successful. Others enjoy seeing if they can surpass their previous

Table 11.1 Sample Part of a Lesson Plan Using a Content Development Format

Children's objectives: Children will learn to swing their arms on the takeoff and bend their knees when they land from a jump.*

Tasks T	Cues	Challenges C
Jump over your rope, taking off and landing on two feet. See how high you can get.	Swing both arms—hard!	Make a different shape with your rope. Continue two-foot takeoff and landing jumps.
Jump using a one-foot takeoff and two-foot landing.	Bend your knees when you land.	See if you can land perfectly still—frozen on three landings in a row.
Make your rope into a circle. Let's try a hop—one foot to the same foot—into and out of the circle.	Bend your knee when you land.	How many times can you hop into and out of your rope circle without touching the other foot to the ground? (*Then try the other foot.*)
Lay your rope in a straight line. Stand next to your rope. How far away can you jump from it? (*Two-foot takeoff and landing.*)	Swing both arms—hard!	Now get a piece of masking tape from the wall. Lie on the floor. Touch your feet to the rope. Put the masking tape near your head. Can you jump your own height?
Now run and jump. Take off (*one- or two-foot*), and land on two feet. Try to take off very close to your rope.	Swing your arms as you get ready to take off. Bend your knees when you land.	Move the masking tape to where your feet first hit the floor on your landing. See if you can jump even farther next time.

*This progression is taken from Chapter 21, "Jumping and Landing."

personal records. We have provided a few examples of challenges in the subsequent chapters, but the best ones are those you create as you come to know the children you are teaching.

Assessing Your Content Development

The final chapter in Part 2, "Understanding Your Teaching" (Chapter 15), provides you with a way to determine how you are developing the content (see Figure 15.2). Ideally, you will find that your lessons include a number of cues that relate to the tasks the children are doing in that lesson. Lessons that consist entirely of tasks followed by challenges are considered undesirable sequences. Desirable task sequences consist of a more varied pattern that includes a mix of tasks, relevant cues, and challenges as needed (Belka & Short, 1991). In other words, there is not a formula that can be used for content development (task, cue, challenge). It always depends on the abilities and interests of the class being taught—as well as the amount of time and effort the teacher has spent on planning interesting, enjoyable, and worthwhile lessons.

Planning Format

Chapter 8 discussed planning and the various aspects of a lesson that teachers typically include in their plans. Now that you understand the process of content development, we want to share an alternative way to plan that some teachers have found effective (Rink,

2006; Siedentop et al., 1984). This alternative relates specifically to how a teacher writes the activities for the day. Essentially, a three-column format is used—tasks are listed in the first column; cues, in the middle column; and challenges, in the last column. For each task, the teacher writes at least one cue and one challenge in the same row; the cue(s) and challenge(s) are designed to correspond to the task the children will be practicing.

Table 11.1 provides an example of part of a lesson that was planned using this format. This format for planning is especially useful for beginning teachers and those who are new to this process of content development. Rather than carrying the entire plan with them as they teach, some teachers briefly summarize the lesson by writing a key word or two for each of the tasks, cues, and challenges on a 5-by-8-inch card, which can be easily carried in a pocket for quick reference during a lesson.

Just as we provide choices to children, we also want to provide you with planning choices. Box 8-1 and Table 11.1 provide two examples that illustrate the planning process. Ultimately you will need to decide which process is most effective for you.

Accommodating Individual Differences

We have described a process for developing the content that enables children to truly learn and benefit from physical education lessons (Rink, 2006). As you know, however, the process is made even more complicated by the fact that children in our classes have different skill levels and interests. Although we have no magical solutions, we do want to suggest two techniques that can help you to accommodate individual differences within a class—that is, to match the challenge of a task with the ability of the child (Csikszentmihalyi, 2000; Graham, 2001). We have termed these two techniques *teaching by invitation* and *intratask variation*.

Teaching by Invitation

One of the ways a teacher can adjust for individual differences is by inviting the children to decide some parameters of a given task. The teacher makes the statement to the entire class, and each child in the class then decides which task he or she wants to participate in. The following are examples of teaching by invitation:

"You may want to continue dribbling in self-space, or you may want to begin dribbling and walking in general space."

"Working alone, or with a partner, design a sequence . . ."

"You may want to continue batting from the tee, or you may want to work with a partner, taking turns pitching a ball to each other."

"You may want to continue striking a ball with your paddle, or you may want to try striking a shuttlecock."

"You decide how far away you want to be from the goal when you kick."

"In groups of two or three, make up a game . . ."

If you use this technique, you will find that most of the children make intelligent decisions about the tasks in which they choose to participate. As in every instance, there will be a few children who, in your judgment, make questionable decisions. Overall, however, we think you will find that your children will choose tasks that allow them to be successful—and yet are not too easy (Csikszentmihalyi, 2000).

Intratask Variation

Teaching by invitation allows the children to make decisions about the task they prefer to work on. Intratask variation, by contrast, is a technique in which the teacher decides to extend a task for individuals or small groups within the class (Graham, 2001). The teacher bases this decision on specific knowledge of the children's abilities and interests. Typically, intratask variation is a rather private interaction between one or more children and the teacher, who makes a task easier or harder to better match the skill level of the children. The following are examples of intratask variation:

"Morgan, why don't you try striking a balloon instead of a ball?"

"Casey, you may want to practice dribbling behind your back and between your legs." (Other children are practicing dribbling and staying in self-space.)

"Eloise and Starla, why don't you two make up a partner sequence that has rolling and transferring weight in it." (Other children are practicing rolling in backward directions.)

"I would like the four of you to move over to the next field and make up a game that has kicking and dribbling with your feet in it." (Other children are practicing dribbling with their feet; these four have been playing soccer for several years and are adroit at kicking and foot-dribbling. They move to the other field and quickly begin a 2 vs. 2 soccer game.)

Unfortunately, intratask variation is not a 100-percent-guaranteed panacea that will allow you to adjust tasks satisfactorily to meet the needs of every child in a class. As with most teaching techniques, intratask variation is effective with some children in some classes some of the time.

A teacher can heighten the potential success of intratask variation by explaining to the children, before using the technique, that sometimes during a lesson various students will be asked to do different things. Understanding why this is being done—the children are already aware that there is a wide range of skill levels within the class—will enable the children to realize that the teacher is not "playing favorites" but rather helping children benefit more from physical education class by adjusting tasks for children with differing abilities.

When using intratask variation, the teacher can also make the point that children at the higher skill levels, utilization and proficiency (Chapter 7), have most likely acquired these skills because of the activities they pursue after school and on weekends. This also provides an excellent opportunity to explain that students who are at the utilization and proficiency levels for various skill themes have practiced those skills countless times in a variety of settings. In most physical education classes, there is just not enough practice time to attain the top two levels of the GLSP. This explanation will be especially helpful to those youngsters who may be under the mistaken impression that the more skilled youngsters in a class were born that way. They weren't! They have just had more practice.

Summary

One of the truly important tasks for a physical education teacher is to develop the content in ways that allow children to learn and benefit from the activities. This chapter defines and illustrates four functions that teachers might use in developing the content. The first function is informing, or presenting information to children—ideally in brief instructional episodes accompanied by demonstration and/or pinpointing. Once an initial task has been presented, the teacher's next function is to decide whether to make the task easier or harder. The rate of success (ideally 80 percent) is one measure to use in such decisions. The third function in content development is providing cues to children that heighten their understanding and efficiency at performing a given skill or activity. Teachers should provide only one cue at a time and ensure that the feedback they provide is congruent (is about that cue). The last teacher function is providing challenges to the children to maintain their interest in a task, rather than moving on to a harder task. Teachers can use two techniques to adjust lessons for individual differences. In teaching by invitation, the teacher allows the children to make decisions, whereas in intratask variation, the teacher decides which tasks are most appropriate for children of different skill levels.

Reading Comprehension Questions

1. Can children simply play games and, as a result, learn the basic motor skills? What about children of differing abilities and interests?
2. Define *developing the content,* and explain why it is an important part of teaching physical education.
3. Pick a skill or movement concept with which you are familiar. Provide several examples of tasks designed to help children learn that skill or concept. Be sure to provide both easier and harder tasks in your progression.
4. Why is providing cues an important teaching skill for physical education teachers? What might be the result when a teacher provides no cues or does so ineffectively?
5. Refer to Table 11.1. Using the skill or concept you chose in Question 3, write at least five tasks in one column. In a second column, write alongside each task a cue that you might use when teaching that task. In a third column, write a challenge for each of the tasks in the first column. Remember that the task, the cue, and the challenge need to work together—that is, they need to complement one another.
6. As a teacher, do you think you are more likely to use teaching by invitation or intratask variation? Explain your answer.

References/Suggested Readings

Belka, D. E., Conner, K. C., & Bowyer, G. R. (1991, January). Quality and congruency of task presentations and teacher verbal feedback in preservice peer teaching episodes. Paper presented at the International Association for Physical Education in Higher Education World Congress, Atlanta, GA.

Belka, D. E., & Short, C. J. (1991, January). Implementing a content sequencing model in physical education instruction. Paper presented at the International Association for Physical Education in Higher Education World Congress, Atlanta, GA.

Berliner, D. (1984). The half-full glass: A review of research on teaching. In P. Hosford (ed.), *Using what we know about teaching.* Alexandria, VA: Association for Supervision and Curriculum Development.

Brophy, J. (1983). Classroom organization and management. *Elementary School Journal, 83*(4), 265–286.

Bunker, L. K. (1991). The role of play and motor skill development in building children's self-confidence and self-esteem. *Elementary School Journal, 91* (5), 467–471.

Csikszentmihalyi, M. (2000). *Beyond boredom and anxiety: Experiencing flow in work and play.* San Francisco: Jossey-Bass.

Graham, G. (2001). *Teaching children physical education.* Champaign, IL: Human Kinetics.

Graham, K. C., Hussey, K., Taylor, K., & Werner, P. (1993). A study of verbal presentations of three effective teachers [Abstract]. *Research Quarterly for Exercise and Sport, 64,* 87A.

Landin, D. (1994). The role of verbal cues in skill learning. *Quest, 46*(3), 299–313.

Manross, M. (1992). *What children think, feel, and know about the overhand throw.* Unpublished master's thesis, Virginia Tech.

Masser, L. (1987). The effects of refinement on student achievement in a fundamental motor skill in grades K through 6. *Journal of Teaching in Physical Education, 6*(2), 174–182.

Masser, L. (1993). Critical cues help first grade students' achievement in handstands and forward rolls. *Journal of Teaching in Physical Education, 12*(3), 301–312.

National Association for Sport and Physical Education. (1995). *Moving into the future: National standards for physical education.* St. Louis, MO: Mosby.

National Association for Sport and Physical Education (2004). *Moving into the future: National standards for physical education* (2nd ed.) Reston, VA: National Association for Sport and Physical Education.

National Center for Chronic Disease Prevention and Health Promotion. (1997). Guidelines for school and community programs to promote lifelong physical activity among young people. *Journal of School Health, 67*(6), 202–219.

Rink, J. E. (2006). *Teaching physical education for learning* (5th ed.). New York: McGraw-Hill.

Rink, J. E., & Werner, P. H. (1989). Qualitative measures of teaching performance scale (QMTPS). In P. W. Darst, D. B. Zakrasjeck, & V. H. Mancini (eds.), *Analyzing physical education and sport instruction* (2nd ed.). Champaign, IL: Human Kinetics.

Rosenshine, B. (1983). Teaching functions in instructional programs. *Elementary School Journal, 83,* 335–351.

Rosenshine, B., & Stevens, R. (1988). Teaching functions. In M. E. Wittrock (ed.), *Handbook of research on teaching* (pp. 376–391). New York: Macmillan.

Sharpe, T. L., Hawkins, A., & Wiegand, R. (1989). Model/practice versus verbal/rehearsal introductions of systems skills within an individually prescribed instructional system. *Journal of Teaching in Physical education, 9*(1), 25–38.

Siedentop, D., Herkowitz, J., & Rink, J. (1984). *Elementary physical education methods.* Englewood Cliffs, NJ: Prentice Hall.

Siedentop, D., & Tannehill, D. (2000). *Developing teaching skills in Physical education* (4th ed.). New York: McGraw-Hill.

Southard, D., & Higgins, T. (1989). Changing movement patterns: Effects of demonstration and practice. *Research Quarterly for Exercise and Sport, 58*(1), 77–80.

Werner, P., & Rink, J. E. (1989). Case studies of teacher effectiveness in second grade physical education. *Journal of Teaching in Physical Education, 8*(4), 280–297.

Observing Student Responses

It is vital for a teacher to observe children, whatever the subject or situation. It is through observation that the successful teacher assesses the moods, attributes, needs, and potential of individuals and groups.

—E. MAULDON AND J. LAYSON

Key Concepts

- Reflective teachers are effective observers.
- Accurately analyzing classes of students in a physical activity setting is a pedagogical skill that is acquired through practice and experience.
- Teachers must continually assess their classes to be certain they are, and remain, safe.

Locke (1975) provided the following description of a two-minute segment of a class of 34 fourth-grade students:

Teacher is working one-on-one with a student who has an obvious neurological deficit. She wants him to sit on a beam and lift his feet from the floor. Her verbal behaviors fall into categories of reinforcement, instruction, feedback, and encouragement. She gives hands-on manual assistance. Nearby two boys are perched on the uneven bars and are keeping a group of girls off. Teacher visually monitors the situation but continues to work on the beam. At the far end of the gym a large mat propped up so that students can roll down it from a table top is slowly slipping nearer to the edge. Teacher visually monitors this but continues work on the beam. Teacher answers three individual inquiries addressed by passing students but continues as before. She glances at a group now playing follow-the-leader over the horse (this is off-task behavior) but as she does a student enters and indicates he left his milk money the previous period. Teacher nods him to the nearby office to retrieve the money and leaves the beam to stand near the uneven bars. The boys climb down at once. Teacher calls to a student to secure the slipping mat. Notes that the intruder, milk money now in hand, has paused to interact with two girls in the class and, monitoring him, moves quickly to the horse to begin a series of provocative questions designed to reestablish task focus.

After painting this picture of the complexity of teaching, Locke aptly reminds us:

That was only 120 seconds out of the 17,000 the teacher spent that day in active instruction. A great deal of detail was unobserved or unrecorded over those two minutes, and nothing in the record reflected the invisible train of thought in the teacher's mind.

That scenario provides us with glimpses of establishing a learning environment (e.g., much student choice and independence in activities), maintaining the environment (e.g., standing near students who are off task), and developing content (e.g., providing reinforcement, instruction, feedback). It also provides us with the complexity of teaching physical education. To become a reflective (and effective) teacher who meets the needs of your students it is essential that you see and are then able to react to the responses of your students, both behavioral responses and responses to learning tasks—while you are teaching. (Locke had the luxury of sitting on the sidelines and seeing when he wrote this!) Although there are multiple reasons to observe in the gym—you could look at the Locke scenario from the perspective of teacher behavior and paint an entirely different picture, such as how much feedback the teacher provided, how time was used during the class—this chapter is dedicated to observing what students in your class are doing. Chapter 15 will deal with observations of teaching that assist you in becoming a more effective teacher.

Be gentle with yourself. Don't be disappointed initially if, in the relative tranquility after you've finished teaching, you find that you made some apparently obvious errors. Observation appears easy to the spectator, but the complexity of teaching and observing movement can be fully appreciated only when one assumes the role of the teacher. In time and with practice, you'll become increasingly satisfied with your ability to observe and analyze movement.

The ability to observe—to see with understanding—is critical for a reflective teacher. For example, you cannot provide a safe environment, offer feedback to students about their performance, or make decisions about what task to present next unless you can observe and accurately determine what students are doing. Thus, the teacher who designs and implements a successful physical education program must be able to observe perceptively, accurately, and continuously and then translate the information gained from the observation into usable material.

Coaches will easily and readily talk of observing very detailed movements of their players in both practice and game situations. When coaches and players with no formal training have been compared with physical education teachers on their ability to observe and analyze movement, the coaches and players scored significantly higher than the teachers, who had degrees in physical education (Hoffman, 1977).

Accurate observational analysis is difficult in a nonteaching or poorly managed environment. The complexity increases considerably, however, when the teacher attempts to observe the movement and behavioral characteristics of individual children and simultaneously monitor the work of an entire class during a physical education lesson (Barrett, 1977, 1979, 1983). Beginning teachers should not be dismayed by the complexity of the observation tasks; not only can the skills be learned, but they also become easier as the teacher becomes more comfortable with the content and the teaching environment.

The process of observation can be divided into two aspects: what to observe and how to observe.

- **What to observe:** This aspect includes four categories: safety, on-task behavior, class movement patterns, and individual movement patterns.
- **How to observe:** Observational techniques are generic, regardless of what is observed; they include positioning, knowing what to look for, and having an observational strategy.

The remainder of this chapter introduces you to these two aspects of observation.

What to Observe

When teaching physical education, a person is constantly bombarded by seemingly hundreds of ideas in just a few seconds, so here we've provided a procedure that we've found valuable for observing and understanding all that goes on in our classes. Because teaching is so complex, it's important that a teacher know what to look for in a particular lesson before conducting the lesson itself. This requires some planning (Chapter 8). When we don't plan, we often find it difficult to decide what to observe during a lesson, so our lessons lack focus or direction. It's almost as if we were just "doing things" with children rather than actually teaching. For this reason, when we plan, it is helpful to divide our observation into four categories: safety, on-task behavior, class movement patterns, and individual movement patterns.

Safety

The teacher's initial and constant attention must always be directed toward the children's safety. Whenever you observe an unsafe situation, remember that safety must always take priority over everything else going on in the lesson. If you have stated a task in such a way that the children are responding unsafely, stop the class, and restate the task. If equipment is unsafe or being used unwisely, stop the class to make the use of the equipment safe. Safety is the initial focus of any lesson and must be the uppermost consideration as you work with children.

We teach the children about safety as well so that they're able to understand some of the hazards they may encounter if they aren't careful. Initially, we explain the reasons for our safety procedures to enable children to better understand and make intelligent decisions about their own safety. That's not enough, however. We need to constantly be aware of unsafe conditions. The following are several of the safety precautions we constantly keep in mind as we observe the classes. Certain of these precautions are also described in Chapter 9.

1. Children are required to work independently without pushing, shoving, tripping, or otherwise interfering with other children.
2. Children are required to work in a space reasonably distant from others (the concept of self-space). When the youngsters get too close, for example, when striking with rackets, we stop the lesson and make them adjust their space.
3. Depending on the surface, our children work in tennis shoes or barefoot. We don't allow stockinged feet, especially on hardwood or linoleum floors because they're so slippery. Children enjoy sliding, but this is a definite hazard.
4. In lessons on skill themes, such as rolling, transferring weight, and balance (gymnastics context), we don't allow I Dare You and Follow the Leader games or touching and pushing.
5. Unless otherwise indicated, in lessons in which gymnastics apparatus is being used, we allow only one child on the equipment at a time. This condition changes once the learning environment has been effectively established.

Legal liability is an increasing concern of teachers, particularly those of physical education. We strongly encourage you to be certain to teach safety rules similar to those just described and to include the rules in the written lesson plan so that they're part of a permanent record in the unfortunate event you have to document safety precautions. Most of these safety rules should be taught in the first few weeks of school (Chapter 9) and then reinforced throughout the year. Again, as you observe, make sure safety is constantly the forefront of your focus.

On-Task Behavior

Once you've observed that the environment is safe, your next focus is to determine whether children are on task. Are they actually doing what you asked them to do? For example, if you asked your class to throw and catch with a partner, are they doing so? Or are they kicking the ball, running around chasing one another, or not working with a partner but in groups of four or five? If so, these are off-task behaviors, and you need to attend to them immediately. Stop the lesson!

There are three reasons why children may be off task:

1. The children are trying, but the task was stated unclearly. You must restate the task.
2. The task is too hard or too easy. If it's too easy, many children will become bored and thus off task. If it's too hard, many children will become frustrated—and thus off task. Determining the success rate of the students is one way to check the difficulty of the task. A guideline for the right success rate is 80 percent—in other words, the students you observe should be successful 80 percent of the time. Figure 12.1 provides an example of an observation sheet that can be used to assess task difficulty.
3. The children haven't yet learned to be on task. If so, you'll have to once again practice the appropriate behavior in physical education class. Although this isn't particularly enjoyable for either the children or you, it's necessary because constant off-task behavior simply can't be tolerated; it's not fair to either you or the children, especially those children who are working so hard to be on task and do what you ask.

The reality of teaching, unfortunately, is that every class always has one or two children who tend to be off task more than others. What do you do with them? After all, it's not fair to punish the entire class because of the behavior of one or two children. Refer to Chapters 9 and 10 for ideas about appropriate behavior.

Class Movement Patterns

When you've determined that the class is working safely and on task, begin observing the entire class to see how students are accomplishing the task. Constantly be on the alert, however, for unsafe and off-task situations.

As you scan the entire class to see how children are moving, observe one cue at a time. Based on that, you'll make one of three decisions according to what you observe the majority of the children doing. Your choices are to: (1) change the task, (2) provide a cue, or (3) present a challenge to the children without changing the task. Chapter 11 discussed these three content development decisions in detail. We mention them here to emphasize that these content-development decisions need to be based on what you observe, not on an arbitrary time allotment that doesn't take into account, for example, the abilities and interests of the children. As part of making the decision, you will also want to ask if the task is really helping the students learn what

they need to know (Rink, 2003). If, for example, your goal for a lesson is to guide children to reach a content standard such as "demonstrates understanding of concepts, principles, strategies, and tactics as they apply to the learning and performance of physical activities" (National Association for Sport and Physical Education [NASPE], 2004, p. 12) and the skill you have chosen is the use of "large extensions in weight transfer," then you will want to be sure that the way the children have understood and are practicing the tasks is really leading to the use and understanding of large extensions. This is easy to decide but much harder to implement with 30 children in a physical education class.

Let's take another example. Say that for this lesson you've decided that your second graders need practice throwing overhand and your goal is to begin to teach four characteristics of a mature throw. You select a series of tasks from Chapter 25. You also decide that your major focus for this lesson will be the use of opposition—that is, that the children step with the foot opposite their throwing arm. Once you've defined the task and explained the cue ("Throw the ball as hard as you can against the wall. Remember to step with the foot on the other side of your body from your throwing arm"), observe to see which children are using opposition and which ones aren't. If you observe that most of the children aren't using opposition, stop the class and remind them to use opposition (or remind children individually). You may also demonstrate the correct performance yourself or pinpoint as models several children who are using opposition. Then the children can return to their practice. Be sure to observe the responses of the children to determine whether they are performing as the cue indicates. Remember that the cue (opposition) is what you actually expect the children to learn in this lesson.

Individual Movement Patterns

After observing for safety, on-task behavior, and class movement patterns, it is time to look at the movement patterns of individuals. Observing individual movement patterns can yield two types of results—information that will assist a teacher in helping individual students and information that the teacher might record on checklists and anecdotal records for future use (see Chapter 14).

Teaching children individually is something we try to do as teachers. Obviously, however, it's not an easy job. Chapter 11 described two approaches to working with individuals: teaching by invitation and intratask variation. Use of these approaches involves the ability to observe individuals and yet maintain the focus on the entire class. This may sound easy; it isn't.

Practice Attempts Recording Sheet

Teacher: _____   Date: _____   Content: _____

Lesson Starting/Ending Time: _____ _____

Students: 1. _____   2. _____   3. _____

4. _____   5. _____

Charting Instructions: Note each task and record the number of practice attempts provided (choose two students to observe for each task and record their total practice attempts). Indicate successful (efficient) tries by circling the tally marks for that try.

Task	# of Skill Attempts	Totals (attempts/successful attempts)
1.	Student 1:	
	Student 2:	
2.	Student 1:	
	Student 2:	
3.	Student 1:	
	Student 2:	
4.	Student 1:	
	Student 2:	
5.	Student 1:	
	Student 2:	

Totals (Student 1)
   a.   # of attempts (all tasks) = _____
   b.   # of successful attempts (all tasks) = _____
   c.   % of attempts successful = _____
   d.   Rate of attempts per minute (# of attempts/# of minutes) _____

Totals (Student 2)
   e.   # of attempts (all tasks) = _____
   f.   # of successful attempts (all tasks) = _____
   g.   % of attempts successful = _____
   h.   Rate of attempts per minute (# of attempts/# of minutes) _____

Figure 12.1 Practice attempts recording sheet.

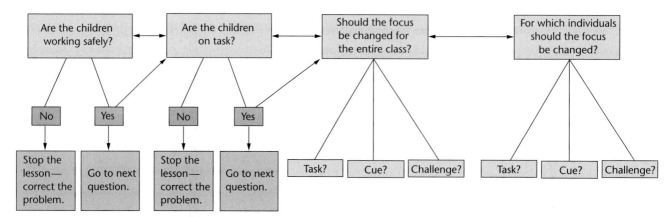

Figure 12.2 Questions reflective teachers use to guide observation.

We encourage teachers to focus initially on the entire class using the scanning technique described in the next section of this chapter. By working with individuals (intratask variation) too early, the teacher may lose focus on the entire class. We've seen this happen frequently with beginning teachers. The teacher becomes so involved helping an individual child that he or she loses focus on the entire class and may suddenly look up to find that a number of children are off task or that an unsafe condition has developed. This is not to suggest that teachers shouldn't work with children individually—we certainly should and do. But teachers must make sure that they don't become so involved with one child that they forget to concentrate on the whole class. As Locke's vignette at the beginning of the chapter suggests, doing so is a real challenge.

> *Recently I observed a teacher attempting to teach a child how to run and kick a stationary ball. The child was unable to adjust her run to enable her to arrive at the ball in a proper kicking position. After each unsuccessful attempt (the ball barely moved; the child appeared almost to step on the ball rather than kick it), the teacher would say to the child, "No, that's not it!" The child knew she had failed as she watched the ball erratically dribble away from her foot, and yet the teacher offered no prescription for improvement. Rather than stating results the student can readily observe, the successful instructor offers a prescription for practice, that is, a cue.*

When we work with individuals, we essentially use the same process we use for the entire class. We vary the task for different children, or we provide challenges (intratask variation). If you ever have an opportunity to watch a master teacher, you'll see that this teacher is constantly using intratask variation as he or she travels from child to child while remaining conscious of the entire class, safety, and on-task behavior. Now you can better understand why it's so important to spend time establishing a learning environment at the beginning of the year.

When presented separately, the four aspects or categories of observation—safety, on-task behavior, class movement patterns, and individual movement patterns—seem quite simple and rather easy to follow. When teaching, however, a teacher is rarely able to focus on any one aspect at a time. As Locke's vignette suggests, the teacher must concentrate simultaneously on the four aspects. To aid in your observation, Figure 12.2 provides a flow chart of the questions we use to guide our observation of classes. Note that the arrows between the questions go both ways, indicating that the observation focus isn't linear but that there's a constant interplay between the questions. And, this observation may all happen within 60 seconds!

How to Observe

Once you have decided what it is that you want and need to observe, the next step is actually observing so that you see. As we indicated earlier, observation is a learned skill and one that can improve with practice. Bird watching provides an apt analogy here. Non–bird watchers who see a bird might think, "There is a big bird." Novice bird watchers will say, "There is a big bird with a white head and dark body." Intermediate bird-watchers, with binoculars, might note a large bird with a dark body, white head, and white on the tail. An expert, with binoculars, will identify the bird as a bald eagle. It takes practice to become an expert observer, but the result is rich and detailed information about what you have seen and hence where to proceed. Three techniques seem helpful in learning to observe with insight (Rink, 2006):

1. Positioning
2. Knowing in advance what you are looking for
3. Having a strategy for observing

Positioning

Positioning in the gym is critical. To return to the birdwatching analogy, if you are standing behind a tree you might not be able to see the bird at all, if standing behind the bird you might only see the tail, and if standing too close you might frighten the bird. Thus, positioning is important from three perspectives: being able to see, being able to see important aspects, and affecting the performance of the learners (Rink, 2006).

First, for safety purposes, never spend long in a position where you are unable to observe all the students in your class. The back-to-the-wall technique allows the teacher to be in a position to see the whole class. Using this technique, the teacher stands outside the area in which the children are working, so that she or he can see the entire class. When the teacher enters the middle of an instructional area, he or she is unable to see part of the class (Figure 12.3) and should consequently limit the time spent in the middle. The ability to observe all that is going on, particularly with classes that are difficult to manage, is important for both effective classroom management and comprehensive observation. Once the teacher is sure that a class is capable of working without constant monitoring, he or she can reduce the use of the back-to-the-wall technique, except when using it to observe the whole class.

Second, your position must allow you to see the critical aspects of the skill on which the lesson is focused. For example, if your lesson is focused on absorbing weight through the back of the head and shoulders and keeping the body round while rolling forward, the logical observation point would be from the side of the child. If observing from the back you would not be able to see the critical characteristics for which you were looking. When teaching be sure to choose observation positions that permit you to see what you need to see.

Finally, whether we like to admit it or not, where you stand affects the performance of the children. Children tend not to work in the area immediately around where the teacher is standing. So, if you always stand in the same place to give directions or observe, some children will always manage to be in the back corner where you do not have a clear view of them. Thus, to be able to see better and increase on-task behavior you should constantly move around the space and refrain from having one position that becomes your "home base" from which you always give directions or talk to the class.

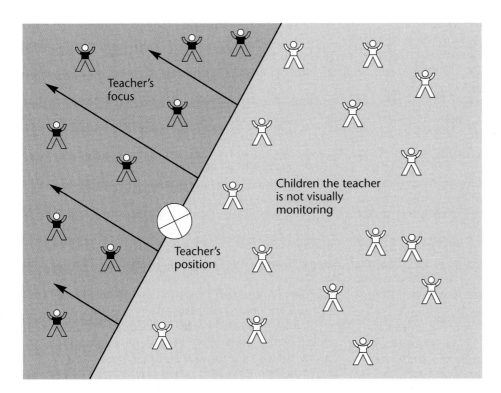

Figure 12.3 Ineffective teacher position for observation.

Knowing What to Look For

Although being in a good position to observe is a prerequisite to observation, it does not guarantee you will see what you need to. To see, you need to know what it is that you want to see. The complexity of a dynamic environment without permanent products adds to the difficulty of this task. Filtering for the critical elements of safety and skill helps to focus your observation.

Obviously, safety is the first aspect to observe, but what makes a safe environment? The elements are usually included in class protocols—not interfering with others, following directions, and so on. You must identify what that looks like. For example, what does not interfering look like if you have asked students to "throw and catch with a partner in a space that matches your abilities."? What would be the first safety aspect to observe? For us, it would be, Are the students spread out so that they do not interfere with each other? In other words, are partners not throwing across another group of partners, and do they have enough space between groups? For a different task, to "jump over a low hurdle or cane, make a wide shape in the air, land, and roll," our first observation might be that the students were actually landing before they rolled rather than diving over the hurdle. At the same time we might check the following: Is only one student on a mat at a time? Is there enough space between the mats? Are no students pushing each other?

After safety, our focus goes to on-task behavior. For the rolling task just mentioned this would again include whether students are jumping, landing, and rolling. (This is both a safety and an on-task focus because being off task here is unsafe.) Are students remaining at their own mats or traveling around the room? Are they simply rolling and forgetting to jump? Are they jumping but without wide body shapes?

Finally, our focus turns to the quality of students' skill. How do we decide what to look for in terms of skill? The obvious answer is the critical aspects of the skill being taught. But there are so many of them that it makes this task incredibly difficult. We have found that if we limit our observation to one aspect at a time, it not only focuses our observation, but the learners as well. The easiest way we have found to accomplish this focus is to list specific cues that are the focus of your lesson on the lesson plan and stick to them. One teacher who was having difficulty remaining faithful to the cues she had chosen actually wrote them on her hand or the inside of the drum she used as a stop/start signal to remind herself. This aspect of observation is compounded by your knowledge of the content you are teaching as well as the complexity of the task. For example, a forward roll on a mat from a squatting position requires the observer to know the cues for the forward roll and what they look like in practice. The task is fairly controlled, so the observation is simplified. However, a forward roll from a balanced position during a routine on a piece of equipment requires the observer to know cues that relate to making the transition from a balance to a roll and to performing a roll on a different surface and in a much more complex situation. As you plan lessons, it helps to identify specific cues (in the skill theme chapters these are identified at the beginning of every task) and focus on those cues one at a time.

Strategies

Even though a teacher is in a position to observe, has planned ahead, and knows what to observe, it doesn't mean that he or she is necessarily observing effectively. It's not unusual to become so focused on the movement or behavior of a particular individual or group that she or he becomes oblivious to other children within the class. The two strategies of scanning and limited selection are presented here to help you observe.

Scanning   The teacher who wants to observe the class as a whole can maintain an appropriate focus by scanning (Siedentop & Tannehill, 2000). Using a left-to-right sweep, the teacher can glance at an entire class in just a few seconds and accurately assess how all the children are working. For example, if you want to determine the number of children who are actively practicing a given movement, you could quickly observe the class from left to right, counting as you scan. By comparing the number practicing a particular movement with the total number of children in the class, you can rapidly (in no more than 15 seconds) assess the way the class is working. This observation technique can be used for obtaining information about the appropriateness of the movement, the behavior of an entire class, or the behavior of individuals within the class.

Limited Selection   The technique of limited selection allows you to observe only select aspects at one time. There are three ways in which we accomplish this: limiting the number of students to observe, limiting what we look at, and limiting the area in which we observe.

Limiting the number of students simply means that you observe only a few representative students. The easiest way to limit the number of students observed while getting a representative idea of what is occurring is to choose students of different skill levels to observe and have them act as your barometer for the lesson. To do this, choose three to five students of varying skill levels prior to class, and throughout that class observe those students first to "get a feel" for what is occurring. (By the way, it has been fairly well substantiated that three to five students of varying skill levels are representative of the class.) The next time the class meets, choose three to five different students. Record or mark in your records the date you observe each student until you have rotated through the entire class.

The second aspect to limit is the number of things you are looking for. Just as we suggest giving children one cue at a time on which to focus, we suggest observing one cue at a time. For example, if students are practicing the overhand throw, you might first watch for side to the target, then opposition, then rotation, and then follow-through. Trying to observe all cues at once becomes a bit overwhelming. Limiting your observational focus also makes it easier to provide specific congruent feedback to the students as described in Chapter 11.

Finally, similar to limiting the number of students observed is the idea of limiting the area in which you observe intently. The way many experienced teachers use this technique is to divide the gym into sections and only observe one section at a time, never trying to observe all during one lesson. Many teachers use this idea when they are trying to make the more specific observations that lead to written records. To limit the

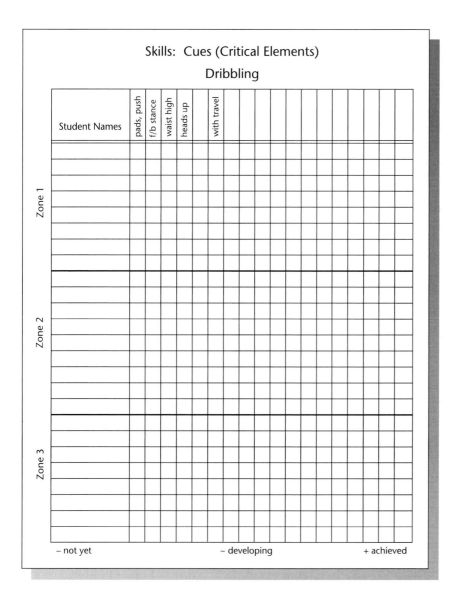

Figure 12.4 Sample of a blank checklist for observing skill.

observation area, they observe only one part of the gym, making sure the same students are always in the same section of the gym. For example, one teacher we know uses neighborhoods that are color coded; all students are assigned a neighborhood. At various times he will ask students to go to their neighborhood to practice (not always during observation). That way he knows exactly which children are in what area. Another teacher has her students in specific quadrants of the gym for the initial activity of the lesson and that is when she does her observation.

When observing for written records, first make sure your observation has a focus. To do that, make sure the students have a specific focus for their work. This is most often evident through the use of cues. If the students don't have a focus for their practice, then you will have little focus for your observation. Second, develop a checklist that contains the skill and cues listed clearly on the top of the form and the students' names listed down the left side. (See Figure 12.4 for an example of a blank checklist and Figure 14.2 for an example of a completed checklist.) Third, determine a manner of rating the skill—for example, "achieved," "developing," "not yet" (Shellhase, 1999). Fourth, observe the class. Remember to observe one cue at a time and to observe only the cues you have taught, even if you see other things; stick to your focus. Some teachers have found it helpful to reserve two or three minutes at the beginning or end of the class simply for observation.

The information gathered with checklists over a period of time lends itself to a myriad of uses. The information is useful for planning future instruction, either adding additional cues or revisiting previous ones. It also provides information as to where to begin when skill themes are revisited. Additionally, it can be used as assessment information for the student and parents (see Chapter 14).

Although limiting allows a teacher to observe with a narrowed focus, a teacher must never lose sight of the entire class. As you watch individual movement patterns, be sure to continually scan the whole class.

Summary

Observing—the ability to see with understanding—is a crucial skill for the reflective teacher. Successful observation can be learned and involves knowing what and how to observe. *What to observe* includes, first, safety, followed by on-task behavior, class movement patterns, and individual movement patterns. Although presented hierarchically, these four aspects continually interact with each other and may all be observed within a 60-second time frame. *How to observe* involves the positioning of the teacher, knowing what to look for, and observational strategies. Teacher positioning influences what a teacher is able to see, who the teacher is able to see, and how the student performs a task. The teacher's knowledge of content affects the accuracy of what he or she is able to see. Two strategies, scanning and limited selection, aid teachers as they attempt to observe the movement responses of learners.

Reading Comprehension Questions

1. In reflective teaching, what is the purpose of observation?
2. Why is observation in physical education so difficult?
3. In your own words, explain the key aspects of safety that a reflective teacher watches for.
4. What does off-task behavior look like? Give three examples.
5. Imagine you are teaching children to kick a ball to a partner. Briefly describe what you might observe that would cause you to change the task to make it easier or harder.
6. In the same imaginary situation, describe what you might observe that would cause you to provide a kicking cue rather than to change the task.
7. Again, assuming the same teaching situation, describe what you might observe that would cause you to provide a kicking challenge rather than changing the task or the cue.
8. What is the best position for observing the placement of the nonkicking foot? The use of finger pads while dribbling? The ball in striking with golf clubs or hockey sticks? Tightness of muscles in balancing?
9. How can a teacher avoid having children's performance affected by her position in class?
10. For the skill of dribbling with the feet in general space, what would you look for as a teacher?
11. If observing the cue of wide base of support while balancing, how can a teacher limit the observation?

References/Suggested Readings

Barrett, K. R. (1977). We see so much but perceive so little: Why? *Proceedings: 1977 National Conference of the National College for Physical Education for Men and the National Association for Physical Education of College Women.* Chicago: University of Illinois, Office of Publications Services.

Barrett, K. R. (1979). Observation for teaching and coaching. *Journal of Physical Education and Recreation, 50*(1), 23–25.

Barrett, K. R. (1983). A hypothetical model of observing as a teaching skill. *Journal of Teaching in Physical Education, 3*(1), 22–31.

Hoffman, S. J. (1977). Toward a pedagogical kinesiology [Monograph 28]. *Quest,* 38–48.

Kniffen, M. (1985). *The effects of individualized video tape instruction on the ability of undergraduate physical education majors to analyze selected sport skills.* Unpublished doctoral dissertation, Ohio State University, Columbus.

Locke, L. F. (1975, Spring). The ecology of the gymnasium: What the tourist never sees. *Southern Association of Physical Education for College Women Proceedings.*

Mauldon, E., & Layson, J. (1965). *Teaching gymnastics.* London: MacDonald & Evans.

National Association for Sport and Physical Education. (2004). *Moving into the future: National standards for physical education* (2nd ed.). Reston, VA: National Association for Sport and Physical Education.

Rink, J. E. (2003). Effective instruction in physical education. In S. Silverman & C. Ennis (eds.), *Student learning in physical education* (2nd ed.) (pp. 165–186). Champaign, IL: Human Kinetics.

Rink, J. E. (2006). *Teaching physical education for learning* (4th ed.). St. Louis, MO: McGraw-Hill.

Shellhase, K. (1999). *K–6 assessment system.* PE Central (www.pecentral.org).

Siedentop, D., & Tannehill, D. (2000). *Developing teaching skills in physical education* (4th ed.). New York: McGraw-Hill.

Wilkinson, S. (1986). *Effects of a visual discrimination training program on the acquisition and maintenance of physical education students' volleyball skill analytic ability.* Unpublished doctoral dissertation, Ohio State University, Columbus.

Instructional Approaches

I am convinced that specific methodologies are used because of what the teacher believes about children and the process of education, not because of what he believes about course content.

—KATE BARRETT

Key Concepts

- Instructional approaches address the issue of how content is delivered to students.

- The instructional approaches presented in this chapter are all designed to move students toward being more independent learners.

- When using the direct instructional approach, the teacher influences the responses of the students by telling them what to do, showing them how to practice, and directing their practice.

- The instructional approach of task teaching involves different students (often individually or in pairs) practicing different tasks at the same time.

- Guided discovery instructional approaches, either convergent or divergent, are designed to let students think and solve problems.

- In peer-teaching approaches, the teacher designs and communicates the task and students assume the roles of providing feedback and assessing.

- In cooperative learning approaches, group interdependence and individual responsibility are promoted without compromising the integrity of motor skill learning.

- Child-designed instruction, in the form of child-designed tasks or contracts, allows children to structure their own learning.

Instructional approaches? Organizational strategies? Teaching style? Teaching strategies? Instructional formats? What is what? When should which one be used? What are they? The choices often seem confusing—even the definitions seem confusing. Though referred to by a variety of names, instructional approaches, organizational strategies, teaching strategies, and instructional formats all refer to how content is delivered to the students—the different ways that a teacher organizes for the delivery of instruction—rather than to what is delivered (Rink, 2006; Siedentop & Tannehill, 2000). Teaching style, on the other hand, refers to the instructional and managerial atmosphere of the gymnasium (Siedentop & Tannehill, 2000). Whether the gym is warm, positive, business-like, demanding, easygoing—all are part of the teacher's style (Chapter 9). This chapter focuses on what we have chosen to call instructional approaches: various ways that the teacher can organize and deliver the content to children. We have found six instructional approaches—direct instruction, task teaching, guided discovery, peer teaching, cooperative learning, and child-designed instruction—to be most useful in our teaching of elementary school physical education. These approaches serve a dual purpose. They are designed to teach the content of physical education effectively while moving children toward becoming more responsible for their own learning and their interactions with others.

"Which instructional approach should I use when?" "Which is the best?" are both common questions. Yet the answer to the questions is, "It all depends." A number of variables affect the appropriate instructional approach to use with any given class. The teacher's beliefs about the ultimate purpose of education and the goal of a lesson should play a vital part in the instructional approach used in a class, yet both must be tempered by other aspects. The skill and preference of the teacher, the characteristics of the students, the nature of the content, and the context in which the teaching is taking place (Siedentop & Tannehill, 2000) all affect which instructional approach might be best for a certain class at a certain time (Table 13.1).

Your teaching skills, as well as your personal preferences, should be a major though not a controlling factor in the instructional approach you choose to use. Your "comfort zone" is a legitimate ingredient in how you choose to deliver content to the children. This is not to say you shouldn't ever stretch your limits, but teachers generally are more effective when they are using strategies that "fit" them. As teachers grow and develop, they acquire new ideas and see a need for new approaches to accomplish the goals they have set for their classes.

The characteristics of the children in your classes have a significant impact on the instructional approach that you choose. How much responsibility is the class ready for? How many decisions are the students capable of sharing? Will the lesson fail if the students are allowed to choose between several activities? These are some of the other considerations a teacher must take into account. For example, if the teacher believes students should be responsible for their own decisions and should direct their own learning, then direct instruction might seem to be contradictory to the teacher's goals. But for children who have never been given the responsibility to make decisions about their own learning or been taught any self-direction, a child-designed program would most likely lead to chaos. Instead, the teacher might choose to use direct instruction while giving children limited or structured choices, thus teaching them how to make responsible decisions.

Different content may lend itself to different instructional approaches. When you are trying to teach a basic skill, a direct instructional strategy may be the most effective. When the children are asked to design

Table 13.1 Characteristics of Six Instructional Approaches

Instructional Approach	Goal	Teacher Skills	Student Characteristics	Content	Context
Direct instruction	Efficient skill learning	Clarity	Control-level learners New students	Specific skills	Whole class
Task teaching	Skill learning + independence	Ability to monitor multifaceted environment	Independent working skills	Already learned skills; self-assessment; product-oriented tasks	Large spaces
Guided discovery	Skill learning + transfer problem solving	Questioning	Precontrol level learners All learners with new content	Exploration Concept-learning	Whole class
Peer teaching	Skill learning + cooperation	Active monitoring	Independent working skills	Simple, clear cues; limited performance	Large spaces Large groups
Cooperative learning	Skill learning + group interdependence; individual responsibility	Ability to design meaningful tasks	Independent working skills	Complex sequences; basic skills	Groups
Child-designed instruction	Skill learning + self-responsibility	Ability to guide and monitor	Ability to use time wisely; independent working skills	Application of learned skills	Groups

complex routines and sequences, a child-designed or guided discovery strategy may be more effective.

The environment or context in which the learning is occurring is an additional factor that influences the instructional approach used. This is especially true of facilities and equipment. If a task or lesson requires that students be spread out over a large space (such as a field), making it difficult to provide continuous feedback to and maintain verbal communication with the children, a task-teaching strategy may be appropriate. In a situation in which safety is a paramount issue, as in a first experience with large apparatus in gymnastics, direct instruction may be more appropriate.

Whatever instructional approach is chosen, it should be based on careful consideration of the goals of the lesson, the skills and preferences of the teacher, the characteristics of the children, the content, and the context. One approach is better than the other only for a particular situation.

Here is Edward Bear, coming downstairs now, bump, bump, bump, on the back of his head, behind Christopher Robin. It is, as far as he knows, the only way of coming downstairs, but sometimes he feels that there really is another way, if only he could stop bumping for a moment and think of it.

—A. A. Milne

Direct Instruction

Direct instruction is by far the most common approach used in physical education classes. It has been called by a variety of names; active instruction (Siedentop & Tannehill, 2000) and interactive teaching (Rink, 2006) are two of the best known. In direct instruction the teacher directs the responses of the students by telling them what to do, showing them how to practice, and then directing their practice. Students usually work as a whole class or in small groups. As children practice, the teacher evaluates what they are doing and provides more instruction. Each teacher decision (instruction) is based on the responses the students give to the previous task. The content is communicated by the teacher, and the pacing of the lesson is controlled by the teacher. Usually the entire class practices the same task or a variation of that task.

Direct instruction is effective when the teacher's goal is to have students learn a specific skill and perform that skill correctly in a specified manner. For example, if your goal is to teach the underhand throw, you want children to step with the foot opposite the throwing hand, extend the arm, and follow through. At this point, direct instruction would be an appropriate instructional choice—some children might learn the correct way of throwing without your assistance, but many would not. However, direct instruction is not an appropriate approach for children who are at

Using the direct instruction approach, this teacher can effectively communicate specific content to the class as a whole. Teaching the class as a whole is an effective method of organizing instruction.

the precontrol level of skill development and not developmentally ready to produce a mature skill pattern. These children need to explore a skill (see the guided discovery section that follows).

Direct instruction utilizes all the components of effective teaching, but five are particularly important:

1. Initially the teacher gives the student a clear idea of what is to be learned. The teacher or a student correctly demonstrates the skill, along with the important cues. For example, the teacher who is focusing on landing from a jump emphasizes in the demonstration that for a soft, quiet landing, the ankles, hips, and knees must be flexed before landing.

2. The second aspect is to give explanations and instructions clearly and repeat the cues often. At the end of a lesson, we often ask the children to repeat the cues so that we know whether we've been effective. The answers to the question "What are the important things to remember when you're trying to land softly and quietly from a jump?" will tell you whether the children have really remembered your teaching cues related to soft, quiet landings.

3. Next, the teacher gives specific feedback. In our example, the children now practice flexing their knees, hips, and ankles before landing; the teacher specifically tells them how well they're flexing their knees, hips, and ankles. The teacher tells the children exactly what they are (or are not) doing correctly so that they can improve. Once the children have the "big" idea—soft, quiet landings—the teacher helps them land softly and quietly by structuring

appropriate tasks and giving them information about how well they perform. The teacher proceeds in small steps, but at a brisk pace.

4. One of the most important and obvious factors in the direct approach is often overlooked. Children need considerable opportunities for practice if they're actually going to learn to land softly and quietly. For this reason we always try to structure the learning situation so that the children have plenty of practice. Most of the time we're able to arrange the environment so that children rarely, if ever, have to wait. We try to ensure that all the children are active a minimum of 60 percent of the lesson, more when possible.

5. High success rates are also important for learning, especially the basic skills. We try to provide tasks that allow children to be successful about 80 percent of the time. This motivates the children and also allows them to grasp one skill before moving on to the next level. If children can't land softly and quietly when they jump from the floor, for example, then obviously they won't be able to land effectively when they jump from a bench or a wooden box.

Each of these components is developed and explained in more detail in Chapter 11. Table 11.1 in Chapter 11 is an example of direct instruction.

Direct instruction calls for a specific response, the one the teacher is looking for and helps the children to produce. Just any response is not acceptable. For example, if you want to teach the children to use opposition when they throw overhand, you'll need to give them plenty of practice opportunities and feedback to be certain that they step with the opposite foot before moving on to another aspect of the overhand throw. If you don't require the children to practice stepping with the opposite foot until the movement is overlearned, they will quickly forget the concept of opposition once the task changes. Then you'll find yourself continually reminding children, "Step with the opposite foot when you throw." The proof of this statement can be found in any high school softball class: Watch the students play a game and see how many are inefficient throwers who've never learned the concept of opposition when they throw. They were taught the concept, but never to the point of learning it.

Direct instruction works well for beginning teachers or teachers who haven't worked with a group of students for a long while. Once the teacher has established a productive learning environment, teaching by invitation or intratask variation (Chapter 11) is helpful for changing the tasks to meet the needs of individual students within the direct instruction approach. This strategy also requires less time for organization than the other approaches, an important consideration for teachers who meet their students only once or twice a week.

Direct instruction should not be confused with a militaristic style of teaching, or what Mosston (1981) called command style teaching, in which everyone does the same thing, the same way, at the same time, and on cue. Remember, style is reflected in the atmosphere of the gym, and direct instruction is one way in which content can be delivered to the students. Direct instruction can be combined with a militaristic style, but that doesn't foster the positive atmosphere we support. We would much rather see direct instruction combined with a warm, caring, and positive style.

Task Teaching

A task-teaching instructional approach allows different students to practice different tasks at the same time. This approach is often called station teaching or learning centers. In our approach, task teaching includes both stations and task sheets. With either option, different students practice different, specified tasks, often at their own pace, throughout the lesson.

Stations provide several activity areas (or learning centers) in the teaching space, each with a different task, through which students rotate during the class. See Figure 13.1 for an example of arrangement of stations that could be used to practice a variety of skills during one lesson. The sequence for striking at high and low targets in Chapter 27 is an example of tasks that might be used at stations.

Task sheets provide another task-teaching option that allows children to practice at their own pace. Each child is given a task sheet (Figure 13.2), which contains a progression of activities. After successfully completing each task, the student records it on the task sheet with that day's date and then asks the teacher, a parent, another student, or an older child to observe the accomplishment and sign the sheet. Initially, we have

Figure 13.1 Arrangement of stations (learning centers) in the teaching space.

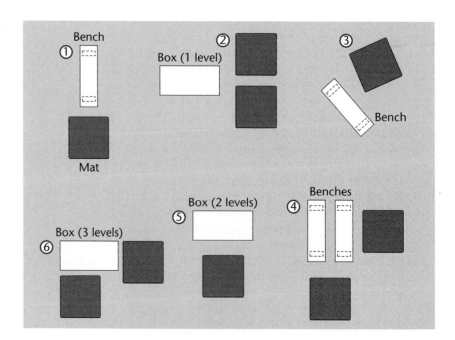

Figure 13.2 Task sheet.

Name _____ Teacher _____

BALANCE TASK SHEET

Date Accomplished	Partner Check	Challenge
		I am able to walk forward the entire length without falling off.
		I am able to walk leading with my right side the entire length without falling off.
		I am able to walk leading with my left side the entire length without falling off.
		I am able to walk backward the entire length without falling off.
		I am able to walk forward (with my hands folded on my head) the entire length without falling off.
		I am able to walk forward the entire length with an eraser balanced on my head.
		I am able to walk backward the entire length with an eraser balanced on my head.
		I am able to walk along the beam, pick up a beanbag, and walk to the other end without falling off.
		I am able to walk along the beam, balance on one knee, and walk to the other end without falling off.
		I am able to walk the entire length of the balance beam without falling off, keeping my eyes closed all the way.
		I am able to bounce a ball across the beam without a miss.
		I am able to roll a ball along a beam without either the ball or myself touching the ground.
		I am able to walk along the beam, do a complete turn on one foot only, and walk to the end without falling off.
		I am able to walk along the beam twirling a hoop on one arm, without falling off.
		I am able to walk along the beam balancing a wand in one hand without falling off.
		I am able to hop along the beam on one foot without falling off.
		I am able to throw a ball back and forth to a partner ___ times without a miss, while standing on the end of the beam.
		I am able to jump rope on a balance beam ___ times without a miss.
		I am able to do a forward roll on the beam.
		I am able to jump onto the beam from a spring board without losing my balance.
		I am able to . . . .
		I am able to . . . .
		I am able to . . . .

entire classes work on the same task sheet at the same time. As children learn to use task sheets, we let them pick from task sheets on several different skill themes.

Task teaching provides students with a structured opportunity to work on their own or with partners, but it can create management problems. Four hints seem to make task teaching more effective.

1. Explain all the stations and task sheets to the class before sending students out to practice. Tell children what they are supposed to do and, if they are to have activities verified, who is to do the verification (teacher or another student).

2. Make sure the managerial aspects are explicit. Designate the areas in which activities are to occur or where specific stations are located. Design, explain, and teach a rotation system between stations or areas. With stations, we initially have children change stations on a signal. Once children are able to function using this strategy, they can be allowed to choose the stations at which they'd like to work (though we usually limit the number of students at any one area or station). Eventually students can rotate from one station to another at their own discretion. Post the necessary cues and directions at each station or practice area. This technique substantially

reduces the time spent in providing additional instruction.

3. Check with students frequently to see how they are doing; move around the room.
4. Start slowly, with only a few (maybe three) stations or a small task sheet (maybe five items) at the end of the lesson. It has been our experience that children enjoy working on task sheets and in stations, especially as a culminating activity, but they need guidance if this approach is going to succeed for them and you.

With task teaching, children won't all be involved in the same activity simultaneously; they and the teacher need to be ready to have more than one activity happening at the same time. Efficient task teaching demands complex organizational and managerial skills on the part of the teacher. To benefit from the task-teaching approach, students need to have good independent working skills and to be able to function without close teacher supervision. Stopping when asked, rotating systematically, and not interfering with others are skills that students need to practice before they can use stations effectively.

A task instructional approach works well when students are practicing skills that have already been taught, doing self-assessment, or performing product-oriented tasks. The approach is not very effective for introducing new or complex skills. Task teaching works best with simple tasks that can be clearly and completely described and that have a clear goal—for example, make 10 throws that hit the target and then take a step back.

One advantage of the task-teaching approach is that it allows you to set up areas that don't require students to wait in line for turns, thus making up for limitations in space and equipment. If, for example, in a balance unit you have a limited number of balance boards and balance beams, you can design tasks for each piece of equipment and have students rotate among the stations. Task-teaching instructional approaches also work well when children have to be spread out over a large space and verbal communication is difficult.

Guided Discovery

Guided discovery, an approach some call teaching through questions (Siedentop & Tannehill, 2000), a cognitive strategy (Rink, 2006), inquiry learning (Harrison et al., 1996), or problem solving, is designed to let children think and solve problems rather than copy the teacher's or another student's correct performance. In this approach, the teacher typically gives the task by asking questions. The teacher most often describes

how the task will be practiced and some way to measure success, but exactly how to perform the task is left to the child to explore and interpret. For example, the teacher may say, "From your spot on the floor, try to kick the ball to the wall both in the air and on the ground." The child knows how to practice (from the spot on the floor, kick) and a little about success (to the wall, in the air, and on the ground), but the rest is left up to the child.

We use two versions of guided discovery, convergent and divergent. One asks children to find multiple answers to a task, whereas the other encourages children to find a single answer.

I recently walked into a large multipurpose room full of 30 second graders. As I sat to watch, I noticed that six very diverse activities were taking place: striking with hockey sticks in a game situation, doing pull-ups, jumping rope, shooting at targets, wall-climbing, and jumping and landing using a vaulting horse. The teacher was walking around from group to group talking to the children, offering feedback and encouragement but no instructions or managerial directions. At this point, I started to look more closely. All the children were active and on task. The noise level was productive; there was no screaming or yelling. Children were moving from activity to activity as they saw fit. Some were recording scores on wall charts. The teacher was never asked to make the decisions of a referee in the game. Children calmly retrieved stray equipment without interfering with other activities or sending the mob to chase a stray ball. These were 7-year-olds. I then asked the teacher how this situation came to be. His response: "I taught them at the beginning of the year the rules for Fridays (the designated day for choice activities), and we practiced."

Convergent Inquiry

Convergent inquiry encourages children to discover the same answer(s) to a series of questions the teacher asks. The teacher guides the children toward one or more correct answers. Several educators (Doolittle & Girard, 1991; Thorpe & Bunker, 1989; Werner & Almond, 1990) have successfully adapted this approach to teaching game skills and strategies. It is the fundamental principle underlying teaching games for understanding or the tactical approach to teaching games (Griffin et al., 1997). Mosston (1981) suggested that children can discover ideas, similarities, dissimilarities, principles (governing rules), order or system, a particular

Writing directions on poster boards and posting them at task-teaching stations can increase time spent in activity.

physical activity or movement, how, why, limits (the dimensions of "how much," "how fast"), and other elements. When we want children to learn one of these elements, we often use the discovery approach to increase their involvement.

The following sequence illustrating Mosston's (1981) classic slanty rope technique is a very good example of convergent inquiry encouraging children to find ways to avoid eliminating others from activity. This excerpt is from page 166 of his work.

Step 1: Ask two children to hold a rope for high jumping. Invariably they will hold the rope horizontally at a given height (for example, at hip level).

Step 2: Ask the group to jump over. Before they do so, you might want to ask the rope holders to decrease the height so that everybody can be successful.

Step 3: After everyone has cleared the height, you ask, "What shall we do now?" "Raise it!" "Raise it!" is the answer—always! (The success of the first jump motivates all to continue.)

Step 4: Ask the rope holders to raise the rope just a bit. The jumping is resumed.

Step 5: "Now what?" "Raise it!" the children will respond.

Step 6: Raising the rope two or three more times will create a new situation, a new reality. Some children will not be able to clear the height. In traditional situations these children will be eliminated from the jumping, and only some will continue; there will be a constantly diminishing number of active participants. The realization of individual differences becomes real; the design for opportunity for all has not yet come about.

Step 7: Stop the jumping and ask the group, "What can we do with the rope so that nobody will be eliminated?" Usually one or two of the following solutions are proposed by the children: (a) Hold the rope higher at the two ends and let the rope dip in the center. (b) Slant the rope! Hold the rope high at one end and low at the other.

The effectiveness of convergent inquiry is largely dependent upon the questions asked by the teacher. We can offer three suggestions for making the questions work successfully.

1. Formulate in advance the questions to be asked so that you can determine the correct sequence of questions that will lead children to the answer you desire.
2. Ask questions in relatively small steps, rather than spanning too large a gap.
3. Wait for an answer (even 10 to 15 seconds; count to yourself), rather than becoming impatient and giving the answer.

The Throwing to a Moving Target sequence (page 492) in Chapter 25 is an example of convergent inquiry used to teach the concepts of throwing to an open space and leading a receiver.

Divergent Inquiry

In divergent inquiry, the teacher outlines a problem and then challenges the children to find many answers. This technique encourages children to find movement alternatives. A typical divergent question is, "Find at least three different ways to travel under the hoop (supported on cones) and at least three different ways to travel over the hoop."

In the divergent inquiry approach, the teacher must be careful not to impose personal values on the children's responses. The emphasis is on obtaining a variety of responses, not a single answer. For this reason, Mosston (1981) warned of two verbal behavior patterns that we try to avoid when using divergent inquiry. "You can do better than that" in response to a child's movement indicates that the teacher doesn't really value the response or that the teacher has a particular response in mind. Another counterproductive verbal behavior is a statement such as "Stop. Everyone watch Penny." After Penny finishes her movement, the teacher says, "Terrific, Penny." This behavior by the teacher, although perhaps innocent in nature, suggests to students that there's a right answer and therefore encourages the children to attempt to find a correct answer (convergent) rather than searching for a variety of alternatives, the goal of divergent inquiry.

In contrast, two productive verbal behaviors might include such statements as these:

"Now that you have found two ways, try to make the third one quite different."

"Stop. Everyone watch this half of the class. Good! Now, let's watch the other half. Great."

These two statements allow the teacher to provide feedback while encouraging creativity and diversity of responses.

We have found the following points helpful in our use of divergent inquiry.

1. Provide feedback that encourages exploration and problem solving rather than a single right answer (see the Mosston examples in the preceding paragraphs).
2. Structure questions (tasks) that challenge children in small, sequential steps. These questions are based on a detailed knowledge of the content and knowing what should come next.
3. Become a master at providing children with prompts—encouraging them to keep practicing by trying different ways or looking for different solutions.

The Jumping to Form a Body Shape During Flight sequence (page 364) in Chapter 21 is an example of divergent inquiry.

We've found guided discovery especially helpful for encouraging children to think on their own to discover new and different approaches to performing skills and to solve questions related to teamwork and strategy. Guided discovery is also important for those children who aren't developmentally ready to learn a mature version of a skill, and simply need opportunities to explore the movement. It is often the strategy we use at the precontrol level when students are exploring a new skill. It provides children a chance "to try things out" without a specific focus or direction.

Teachers have to learn how to provide transitions for their pupils. It is not possible for most young people to make choices after five or six years of being told what to do every minute they are in school. It is equally hard for them to share resources, help other students, or decide what they want to learn after years of being expected to hoard, compete, and conform. Transitional situations often have to be provided. Some students need workbooks for a while; others want to memorize times tables or have weekly spelling tests. Young people are no different from adults. When faced with new possibilities they want something old and predictable to hold onto while risking new freedom. Inexperienced teachers often make the mistake of tearing down the traditional attitudes their students have been conditioned to depend upon before the students have time to develop alternative ways of learning and dealing with school. In their impatience they become cruel to students who do not change fast enough or who resist change altogether. One just cannot legislate compassion or freedom. Teaching as a craft involves understanding how people learn; as an art it involves a sensitive balance between presenting and advocating things you believe and stepping away and encouraging your students to make their own sense of your passion and commitment.

—Herbert Kohl, *On Teaching*

Peer Teaching

Peer teaching provides an experience that meets multiple educational goals: It provides an effective medium for children to learn a skill—they receive multiple practice opportunities, plentiful feedback, and a chance to cognitively analyze skill—and at the same time children learn to work with each other. This instructional approach uses peers teamed in pairs or small groups to actively teach one another. In peer teaching the teacher plans the tasks and communicates them to the children; the children assume the roles of providing feedback and assessing. Demonstration of the task is shared between the children and the teacher. Often the teacher will demonstrate initially and the children, as peer teachers, will repeat the demonstration as necessary. A simple example of peer teaching would be using peers to help teach the overhand throw. After initial instructions and practice, children divide into pairs. Their task is to "coach" their partner to see if the partner brings the arm way back, steps forward on the opposite foot, and follows through. If the partner does, then he or she gets a "thumbs up"; if the partner doesn't, the peer teacher tells the partner what to correct next time. The peer assessment card for cuts and pivots while dribbling (Figure 14.9) in Chapter 14 provides an example of peer teaching.

For peer teaching to be an effective instructional approach, several key points should be followed.

1. The skill should be simple, the cues for observation very clear, and the performance easily measured.
2. Post the cues either on the wall or on individual cue cards so that the "peer" teachers can remember them.
3. Start small. You might consider including one peer-teaching task in a lesson and then expand.

Children must be able to work cooperatively and independently for peer teaching to be a success. They must be responsible enough to take seriously the task of teaching another student. Children are asked to provide feedback as well as analyze performance; therefore, they must know the cues and what the skill looks like. The teacher, besides having to design the task, must be able to provide feedback to the peer teachers to assist them in their teaching.

Peer teaching can work with any content, but it works best when the skills are simple, there are clear criteria for observation, and the performance is limited and easily measured. For example, peer teaching works well with basic skills but is much more difficult with dynamic and strategic skills.

Children thoroughly enjoy being the teacher, but for the strategy to be successful they must be able to both analyze skill and provide feedback—something the teacher can help them learn through her or his presentation of the task.

> *Teaching was easy. All you did was tell them and they did it.*
>
> —Fourth grader after teaching a self-designed game to another group

Cooperative Learning

Cooperative learning is an instructional approach designed to promote group interdependence and individual responsibility while teaching content. There are three common cooperative learning formats: pairs-check, jigsaw, and co-op (Kagan, 1990).

In pairs-check, children are in groups of four with two partner-pairs in each group. Each pair practices a task, teaching each other as in peer teaching. The two pairs then get together to assess each other to see if they are achieving the same outcomes, to provide further feedback, and to practice. For example, the pairs-check strategy could be used to teach dribbling with the hands. After the initial task is given, pairs would work with each other, focusing on using the finger pads, having the knees bent, and keeping the hand on top of the ball. Then, when the members of each pair thought they had mastered the task, they would come together to check the other pair. In this sense, pairs-check is much like peer teaching.

In the jigsaw format, children are usually in "home" groups of three or four. Each child becomes an "expert" on one aspect of a skill or task by working with the children who are experts from other groups. Children then return to their home group and teach their group their piece of the skill. The jigsaw format can be used quite effectively to teach activities with multiple parts and simultaneously develop interdependence.

For example, the jigsaw approach could be used when learning offensive and defensive strategies. The class would be divided into home groups of four. At the beginning of class, four stations would be set up—one on moving to an open space, one on leading the receiver, one on pressuring the ball, and one on hustling back. One person from each home group would go to each station and learn about the strategy there. Each child would then return to his or her home group as an expert on the strategy and teach it to the group.

Co-op is a cooperative learning format in which small groups are used to create a project with many components (Grineski, 1996). Each small group is responsible for one component of the larger project. The co-op format can be used to have children create a dance sequence in which several elements are to be portrayed. For example, in the dance depicting African American heritage described in Chapter 29, one group might develop the concept of slavery, another the concept of freedom, another the concept of strength as a people, another dispersal, another gathering, and another respect. Each group would then bring its piece to the full dance.

Cooperative learning works equally well with children who have highly developed responsibility skills or with children who need to learn to work together. Research suggests that cooperative learning has affective as well as cognitive benefits (Slavin, 1990). Teachers must be skilled in designing tasks that are meaningful to children.

Cooperative learning strategies provide a chance for skill learning and teach responsibility. However, a word of caution must be issued here. The goal of skill learning should not be sacrificed when using cooperative learning activities. The primary purpose of many cooperative learning activities is group development and problem solving. These activities have their place and are often fun; however, they do not teach the primary content of physical education. For cooperative learning to be a viable part of physical education, it needs to integrate psychomotor, cognitive, and personal-social responsibility goals. It must provide what Rink (2006) calls a rich learning experience. The cooperative learning activity must teach a psychomotor goal while addressing the other goals.

Dyson (2002) has suggested the following ideas for teachers who want to successfully use cooperative learning approaches. First, make sure that as a teacher you communicate clearly both the academic and social goals for the activity. Second, teach the children the roles they will need in the group. For example, if students need to provide feedback to others, teach them what feedback to provide. Third, an assessment or accountability system (see Chapter 14) should be designed so that the children are responsible for the end result or product as well as the process. Fourth, students need to learn how to communicate with each other. In other words, it is not enough to be able to provide feedback; they must learn how to deliver it so it is heard by others and not hurtful. Finally, cooperative learning takes time. Like any instructional format that calls for problem solving and student input, allow ample time for the children to work through the process of the task.

A variety of content, from basic skills to complex sequences, can be adapted for use with cooperative-learning strategies. To find out more about cooperative learning in physical education, read Steve Grineski's book, *Cooperative Learning in Physical Education.* (1996).

Child-Designed Instruction

Child-designed instructional approaches allow the child to be the center of the learning activities. In these strategies the teacher serves as a guide or mentor.

Child-designed instructional approaches allow children to actively take the major responsibility for their learning. When used with careful planning and patience, these approaches empower children. Children

Child-designed activities allow children to develop tasks appropriate to their own needs and interests.

become engaged and most often design activities that are appropriate to their level of development. Although it is not always easy and often messy, we are committed to children designing their own experiences. There are several child-designed strategies; child-designed tasks and contracts are the two we use most often. We have found that, with guidance and direction, older elementary students are fully capable of designing personal contracts and the use of child-designed games and routines can begin with 8-year-olds. Child-designed games or routines ask students to create their own "game" or "routine" within certain parameters. The game, dance, or gymnastic routine is based on the skill theme being studied and allows students to apply what they have learned in a setting that matches their interests and abilities. See the volleying game on page 515 in Chapter 26 for an example of a child-designed game.

See Chapters 29, 30, and 31 for explicit details about how to develop child-designed activities in dance, games, and gymnastic contexts.

As children become accustomed to working on their own, the teacher can use independent contracting to make instruction more personal. A teacher who uses independent contracting is saying to the students, "I trust you to make intelligent and responsible decisions about what you need to practice."

We've used the written contract illustrated in Figure 13.3. Each child writes down the skill or activity she or he will be practicing or playing, the goal to be achieved, the time to be spent practicing each activity, and (when appropriate) the name of a practice partner. Recognizing the dynamic nature of a physical education class, we let the children change their contracts during class, provided that they write down all changes. We encourage the children to save time by coming to physical education class with their contracts already completed for that day. In the final few minutes of a class, we ask the children to evaluate their accomplishments for that day.

Contracts can be used in physical education classes in a variety of ways. When you first use independent contracting, it is wise to restrict each child to a single skill theme or even a certain aspect of the skill theme

Figure 13.3 Individual contract.

Name _____

Contract for _____ 20 _____
(date)

Time Allowed	Activity	Goal	Partner for the Day

COMMENTS:

1) How do you know you accomplished your goal? Or didn't accomplish it?

2) What do you need to work on during the next class?

3) Do you want to tell me about the class?

or unit. For example, some teachers have used contracts as a culminating activity to let students decide how they want to complete their learning on a specific topic. The sequence on throwing for distance and accuracy on page 493 in Chapter 25 is an example of a modified contract.

For teachers who want to try to incorporate child-designed approaches in their teaching, but aren't sure where to begin, we found the following suggestions helpful.

1. Employ moderation and structure as the keys to success. Give specific directions. The results can be disastrous if you simply say, "Make up your own game; it has to include throwing and catching," or "Write a contract about what to do in physical education." We know from experience. Try to give children more specific instructions for designing activities that include the exact focus of the activity and what the final product is to be, such as:

"Design beginning and ending movements for the balance, roll, balance sequence you've been practicing."

"You've been practicing five movements: leaping, spinning, sinking, exploding, and freezing. Use them in a sequence that flows together smoothly."

"We have been practicing dribbling for the past few lessons and will continue to do so for another week. Design a contract that tells what you will do each day for the first five minutes of class to practice your dribbling skills."

2. Provide the managerial aspects of the task, such as how large the space can be and where; when the task should be completed; how long before they should be practicing; the maximum and minimum number of people in the group; and the equipment available.
3. Check with groups often to see how they are doing (especially those who seem to be having a difficult time getting started). Move around the area. Ask questions about their activity. Prompt.
4. Provide feedback while resisting telling children how to practice. At times suggestions help, but much of the benefit of the activity is learning to make something work. Teacher responses to child-designed activities need to encourage children to stay on task while at the same time provide reinforcement for the decisions the students are making.
5. Allow enough time. Designing instruction takes time. We usually find that it takes the majority of a lesson (and sometimes two lessons) for children to design and implement self-designed activities.

Instructional Approaches Cited in the National Standards for Physical Education

The instructional strategy of peer teaching is referred to in the *National Standards for Physical Education* (National Association for Sport and Physical Education, 2004) as a sample performance outcome for grades K–2 under Standard 5: Exhibits responsible personal and social behavior that respects self and others in physical activity settings. The sample performance outcome states: "Assists partner by sharing observations about skill performance during practice" (p. 40). The approach is also cited as a grade 3–5 sample performance outcome under Standard 2: Demonstrates understanding of movement concepts, principles, strategies, and tactics as they apply to the learning and performance of physical activities. That sample performance outcome states: "Accurately recognizes the critical elements of a catch made by a fellow student and provides feedback to that student" (p. 23).

The use of child-designed instructional strategies is identified as a grade 6–8 sample performance outcome under Standard 1: Demonstrates competency in motor skills and movement patterns needed to perform a variety of physical activities. The sample performance outcome states: "Designs and performs gymnastics (or dance) sequences that combine traveling, rolling, balancing, and weight transfer into smooth, flowing sequences with intentional changes in direction, speed, and flow" (p. 18).

---

6. Find ways for children to be accountable for what they are doing. Reflection time allows children to spend time thinking about what they accomplished for the day and what they want to accomplish during the next class. It also lets children think about how much effort they put into accomplishing their independent tasks. You can set aside a few minutes at the beginning or end of class to have students reflect. Reflection is enhanced if children put their thoughts in writing. (See Chapter 14 for use of student journals.) Student sharing at the end of a lesson lets children offer their opinions about what they did or share their accomplishments with others. Teaching others what they have developed or learned also provides a strong accountability mechanism.

To function productively with a child-designed approach, children need to be highly motivated, be self-directed, and have the skills to work independently. They need to be knowledgeable about using the time and materials available to them. The teacher must be skilled in designing the initial task—and then must let the students work on their own, making their own

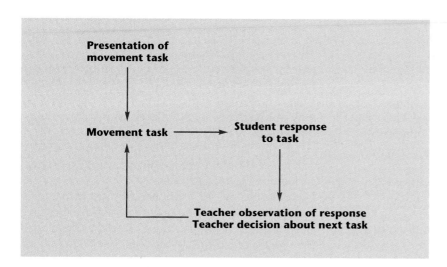

Figure 13.4 Instructional cycle.

decisions and their own mistakes. This is very hard for many of us to do. Child-designed strategies work well after the basic skill has been learned. They are especially useful with dynamic situations, when children are at different skill levels, and as culminating activities.

A Final Thought

Regardless of the instructional approach used, it is important to carefully observe the children's responses to the task and make your next decision as a teacher based on what you observed. For example, suppose that while using the direct approach you have the children focus on dribbling using their finger pads, and observe they are not doing that. The next step is to stop and redirect the task to the use of finger pads. However, if you're using a peer-teaching approach to teach the same skill and the children are not using their finger pads, you would refocus the peer teachers on what to look for. In any case, how you progress is based on the children's response to the task given. Figure 13.4 provides an overview of this instructional cycle.

Summary

An instructional approach can be defined as the way in which a teacher presents lesson content to a class. One of the myriad of questions that a teacher must answer is which instructional approach to use. The answer depends on a number of factors; the primary one is the teacher's goal for a particular lesson or series of lessons. Six instructional approaches (summarized in Table 13.1) can be used to deliver the lesson content to students.

The direct instructional approach is effective when students are to learn a specific skill technique. A task-teaching approach is helpful when having students practice a skill they have already learned. The guided discovery approaches stimulate thinking and students' involvement on a cognitive level. Peer teaching fosters cooperation and provides repeated practice and feedback for children. Cooperative learning develops group-relation skills, as well as stimulating cognitive involvement. Child-designed approaches encourage creativity and inventiveness; they involve children in creating their own learning experiences.

Each approach has its strengths, and each requires different student and teacher skills. Which strategy to select depends on the teacher's goals. One of the challenges reflective teachers face is analyzing both their students' and their own needs and skills and matching them with the goals of the lesson. Ideally, over a period of weeks, both the teacher and the children learn to work effectively, no matter which instructional strategy is selected.

Regardless of the approach used, the progression of the learning experience is always based on the students' response to the task they were given. Thus, the ability of the teacher to observe (Chapter 12) is critical.

Reading Comprehension Questions

1. What is the implication of the quote from Kate Barrett on the opening page of the chapter? How does it relate to the content of this chapter?
2. What is an instructional approach? How does it differ from teaching style? Explain the differences among the six instructional approaches presented in this chapter.
3. What criteria might the teacher use in selecting a particular instructional approach for use with a class?
4. Using the skill of punting, give examples of convergent and divergent inquiry, written in the actual form in which they would be stated.
5. Select a skill theme from one of the skill theme chapters (Chapters 19 through 28) and develop a task sheet similar to the one in Figure 13.2. Include at least six different tasks, ranging from precontrol through utilization levels.
6. Why do we say that a direct instructional approach may not be the best for children who are not developmentally ready?
7. Using the skills of throwing and catching against a defense, design a task sequence using the jigsaw cooperative learning strategy.
8. What strategies can a teacher employ to begin to use child-designed approaches for instruction? Give an example of how one strategy might be developed for a group of 11- or 12-year-olds.
9. How can different instructional approaches be used to help students meet various national standards for physical education?

References/Suggested Readings

Doolittle, S., & Girard, K. (1991). A dynamic approach to teaching games in elementary PE. *Journal of Physical Education, Recreation and Dance, 62*(4), 57–62.

Dyson, B. (2002). The implementation of cooperative learning in an elementary physical education program. *Journal of Teaching in Physical Education, 22,* 69–88.

Griffin, L., Mitchell, S., & Olson, J. (1997). *Teaching sports concepts and skills: A tactical games approach.* Champaign, IL: Human Kinetics.

Grineski, S. (1996). *Cooperative learning in physical education.* Champaign, IL: Human Kinetics.

Harrison, J., Blakemore, C., Buck, M., & Pellett, T. (1996). *Instructional strategies for secondary school physical education* (4th ed.). Dubuque, IA: Brown & Benchmark.

Kagan, S. (1990). The structural approach to cooperative learning. *Educational Leadership, 47*(4), 12–16.

Kohl, H. (1976). *On teaching.* New York: Schocken.

Milne, A. A. (1926). *Winnie the Pooh.* New York: Dutton.

Mosston, M. (1981). *Teaching physical education* (2nd ed.). Columbus, OH: Merrill.

National Association for Sport and Physical Education. (2004). *Moving into the future: National standards for physical education* (2nd ed.). Reston, VA: National Association for Sport and Physical Education.

Rink, J. (2006). *Teaching physical education for learning* (5th ed.). St. Louis, MO: Mosby.

Siedentop, D., & Tannehill, D. (2000). *Developing teaching skills in physical education* (4th ed.). New York: McGraw-Hill.

Slavin, R. (1990). Research on cooperative learning: Consensus and controversy. *Educational Leadership, 47*(4), 52–55.

Thorpe, R., & Bunker, D. (1989). A changing focus in games teaching. In L. Almond (ed.), *The place of physical education in the schools.* London: Kogan Page.

Werner, P., & Almond, L. (1990). Models of games education. *Journal of Physical Education, Recreation and Dance, 61*(4), 23–27.

14

CHAPTER

Assessing Student Learning

The primary goal of assessment should be seen as the enhancement of learning, rather than simply the documentation of learning.

—NATIONAL ASSOCIATION FOR SPORT AND PHYSICAL EDUCATION [NASPE], 2004

Key Concepts

- Assessment asks and answers two questions: What was learned and how well was it learned?

- To determine what was learned, there must be some type of performance to assess.

- The performance that is to be assessed should occur in a real-life setting, not a contrived "skills test" setting.

- Assessment that is meaningful, that occurs in a real setting, is called alternative assessment.

- Alternative assessment shares the following characteristics: It is linked directly to instruction, it views the student as the primary client, it is meaningful, it happens as part of instruction, and students know what it is they are supposed to learn ahead of time.

- Teacher observation, exit slips, student journals, homework, peer observation, self-assessment, event tasks, videotape and digital analysis, student drawings and displays, and portfolios are all viable alternative assessment items in physical education classes.

- Holistic or analytic rubrics are used to distribute assessment criteria to students and subsequently evaluate student performance.

- Assessment should occur in cognitive, affective, and psychomotor domains of learning.

- When student achievement is reported to parents, they should be made aware of what students have learned in physical education and where students are with respect to essential learning.

It has been said, "That which is not assessed will be lost." In the current educational world of high stakes testing and public accountability for educational outcomes, we agree. Some would say that we have always assessed. Many of us can vividly remember fitness tests in the fall and spring with a few cognitive tests on rules and history thrown in during the year. But are isolated fitness scores and rules and history what we want students to really learn from our classes? Are the "age-old" ways of measuring that knowledge really the best way? Two basic questions emerge: "What do we want to know?" and "How do we test what it is that we want to know?"

Assessment has changed from the scenario above and from what most of us remember. This "new" assessment is more teacher and student friendly. The purpose of this new assessment is to "determine if and to what extent a student can demonstrate, in context, his/her understanding and ability relative to identified standards of learning" (Lambert, 1999, p. 6). This definition contains several key pieces that are critical to overall understanding of the assessment process. These pieces are: What was learned, how well it was learned, and in what context the demonstration of learning took place.

Understanding Assessment

Let's explore these ideas a bit further. The idea of demonstrating what was learned implies that the student completes some type of *performance* that can be evaluated by others. How well something is learned implies that the performance of the student is evaluated against preset criteria that are known ahead of time. This performance with its evaluation criteria should take place in an authentic or *real setting* as far as possible. Finally, the performance, the criteria, and the setting should directly reflect a *previously identified standard* (goal) to be achieved.

An example may help. One of the grades 3–5 sample performance outcomes under Standard 1 (NASPE, 2004) is to dribble and pass a basketball to a moving receiver. This is a potential indication of learning for Standard 1 at these grade levels. A possible demonstration of the ability to dribble and pass might be to have students receive and throw a basketball pass to a partner on the move. The preset criteria for determining how well it was learned might be these: The student receives and passes in one motion; the student passes ahead of the moving players (so that the receiver does not have to stop to receive the pass); and the receiving student cuts into the space to receive the pass. Students would be considered "proficient" if they could do all three; "almost there" if two were accomplished; and "still working on it" if they could accomplish only one of the criteria. To use a "real" context, the whole class might perform the task while the teacher walks around with a checklist evaluating the criteria. This assessment might occur over several days.

In the current vernacular, the assessment technique just described is called, variously, *alternative assessment, performance assessment, outcome assessment,* or *authentic assessment.* Though each of those terms has a slightly different meaning, we have chosen to use *alternative assessment* to represent them all. This may shortchange some of the subtleties involved in each, but it makes our discussion much simpler. What are the characteristics that separate alternative assessment from previous types of assessment (skill tests, knowledge tests, and the like)?

Authentic assessment strikes me as being quite interesting. The reason for this involves my current experiences as an eighth-grade basketball coach. When choosing players for the team during tryouts, I evaluated players mostly on drills. However, I have realized that while they do quite well during drills, many of them do not utilize these skills in a game situation. Next time, I believe I will use much scrimmage time to evaluate my players.

—ANDY BARRY, sophomore physical education major and first-year basketball coach

Although alternative assessment has many distinctions that separate it from traditional assessment, we have elected to focus on five:

1. Assessment and instruction are linked.
2. The student is the primary client of assessment, not the teacher.
3. Assessment is an ongoing part of teaching, not an end or an afterthought.
4. Assessment comprises meaningful tasks performed in context.
5. The criteria for evaluation are distributed to the students ahead of time.

These ideas for alternative assessment are supported by the *Appropriate Practices* document (Council on Physical Education for Children [COPEC], 2000; see Box 14-1).

Linking of Assessment and Instruction

Alternative assessment is based on the idea that assessment is just another part of effective teaching and that the two are inextricably tied to each other. In fact, neither one is very good without the other. Assessment is part of the whole learning process. It allows children and teachers not only to see that something has been learned but also to actually demonstrate it. This aspect is becoming critical to education. This new idea is beginning to change the relationship between teachers and students, as well as student outcomes. It addresses how we teach, as well as student achievement. It is said that if assessment and teaching are done well, the student should not know the difference between the two. It may be like the Friday night basketball game: Is the game an assessment of what was learned in practice during the week, or is it just another activity in which to participate?

Student as Primary Client

How many times have you been told that the purpose of a midterm exam was to help you as a student? It is much like being told that a punishment hurts your

Box 14-1

Appropriate Practices for Assessment

Appropriate Practice

Teacher decisions are based primarily on ongoing individual assessments of children's performance as they participate in physical education classes. This information is used to individualize instruction, plan yearly curriculum and weekly lessons, communicate with parents, identify children with special needs, and evaluate the program's effectiveness.

Individual children's evaluations are obtained through a variety of assessment techniques that assess children's cognitive and affective learning as well as their physical performance. Many different forms of assessment, including check lists, self- and peer assessment, portfolios, and student journals, are incorporated into the process.

Inappropriate Practice

Assessment addresses primarily compliance with classroom rules and procedures. Dress, attendance, and effort are counted as the affective portion of the grade.

Assessment is not multifaceted but addresses only a single performance score on fitness tests, rules tests, and/or motor skills tests. Assessment only occurs in the context of grading; for example, children receive a grade in physical education based on their scores on a standardized fitness test or the number of times they can continually jump rope.

Assessment items focus on isolated skills in an artificial context (e.g., dribbling between cones for time as compared to dribbling in a game situation).

Source: Appropriate Practices for Elementary Physical Education: A Position Statement of the National Association for Sport and Physical Education by the Council on Physical Education for Children, 2000, Reston, VA: NASPE/AAHPERD. Reprinted with permission.

parents more than it hurts you. It may be true in your parents' or teachers' minds, but it is rarely true for you. Alternative assessment strives to view the child or student as the person who benefits most from the assessment (remember that assessment is supposed to be a learning experience). First and foremost, assessments should provide feedback to the student—feedback they can use and make sense of. (Failing a midterm, without feedback, simply tells us that we failed—either we didn't guess well, or the teacher didn't ask the questions we knew, or others did better than we did—it doesn't tell us how well we know something.) What would happen if a teacher provided many little checks before a test that let you know how you were doing but that weren't recorded as part of your final grade? Alternative assessment is laden with those little checks. What this also means is that *assessment* is not *grading*. The primary purpose of assessment is to give information to the students that they can use to enhance learning. The secondary use of assessment is for reporting or grading purposes. This idea requires us to change the view of assessment that has been ingrained in our thoughts for our entire educational career, but it is the "new" view of assessment.

> *Because the student is the primary client of all assessment, assessment should be designed to improve performance, not just monitor it.*
>
> —GRANT WIGGINS

Ongoing Process

How many of you have been in a class, physical education or otherwise, in which assessment (testing) was done at the end? Sometimes this was at the end of a unit and other times at the end of the course. Does this type of information provide you, as a student, useful information that you are able to use in your learning or improving your skill or knowledge? More than likely not. Alternative assessment is an ongoing and continuous process, not an afterthought. Alternative assessment is a means to an end, not an end in itself. This aspect makes alternative assessment largely formative (or ongoing)—not used for grading but brimming with feedback. Summative assessment (that done at the end) is part of alternative assessment, but it is done only after an immense amount of formative feedback. Alternative assessment is not a collection of pieces to give to students. It is part of the ongoing route to student learning. It is not just a test or a task. It should provide meaningful feedback to the learner on an ongoing basis.

Meaningful Tasks

I once had a student who was a Division I varsity soccer player. The university at which I taught allowed students to "test out" of activity courses if they showed a proficiency level of skill. Proficiency was always demonstrated by a series of skills tests. One of the skills tests for soccer involved kicking a ball to a wall from a certain distance a certain number of times in an allotted amount of time. The soccer player failed the skills test twice. On the third and final attempt, he failed again. As he left, he turned and said, "I can play soccer,

but this has nothing to do with soccer." Today he is a professional soccer player.

That scenario is telling. The current assessment movement calls for assessment to be more meaningful and worthwhile. Assessment should provide students with information that will fuel their interests (Questioning, 1996). A good assessment model supports students' desire to learn. Such an assessment model calls for us as teachers to relinquish some of the control we have held over assessment and give it to the students.

Alternative assessment employs tasks that make sense, that are in context, that are real. Alternative assessment does not ask children to demonstrate skills in situations that don't relate to what they are supposed to be learning. These real contexts may be either contrived or natural, but they are as close to the actual situation in which the skill is used as possible. In other words, no more wall volleying in volleyball (since when do you get to use the wall in a volleyball game?).

Distribution of Criteria

How would you feel if you knew ahead of time what material you were going to be assessed on? If you didn't have to guess what you were supposed to learn? Alternative assessment does that: It provides children with the assessment criteria (called *scoring rubrics*) before they actually start the learning or assessment. This is especially true with summative assessment options that are used for reporting.

We realize all this sounds wonderful (especially if you are a college student and can get your instructors to accept it). Yet the larger question remains, How do we do this type of assessment? This is where a map analogy from Chapter 8 really helps. We have adapted the work of Leslie Lambert (1999) and expanded to eight the number of planning steps listed in Chapter 8 of *Children Moving* to assist you in making alternative assessment not only happen but also work the way it should (as part of learning). The steps are:

1. Decide on the standard or learning goal. This comes from the standard (or goal) you have set for what you want students to learn. Although many of us are tempted to skip this stage, by doing so we often find ourselves on a trip to nowhere or anywhere. Judy Rink (2006) uses the analogy of a car without a driver to describe programs that do not have defined goals. Prusak and Vincent (2005) make the point that we always encourage students to set goals and work toward achieving them. These goals serve as a starting point, a point of reference, and a place to return when things get complicated. If this is sound

advice for students, it must certainly be good for teachers as well.

2. Decide on the content that will be learned and applied toward attaining the goal. This content should realistically reflect your teaching situation and what you are able to accomplish. It may be influenced by geography, weather, facilities, equipment available, or even your comfort zone.

3. Establish performance outcomes at various points to determine if your students are achieving the goal. Although we label these as performance outcomes, you will also see them referred to in the literature as benchmarks (NASPE, 1995), checkpoints, and performance indicators. Again, as with the names of the "new" assessment, there are subtle differences between each of the terms, but for simplicity and usefulness we have decided to use performance outcomes. These performance outcomes are in fact intermediate progress points on the way to the final goal. Figure 14.1 is an example of one school district's grade level performance indicators for the skill theme of jumping and landing.

4. Select and develop assessment methods, strategies, and criteria for use in judging student learning regarding the standard.

5. Select rich, developmentally appropriate instructional progressions aimed at student learning of the goal.

6. Teach the progressions with lots of student practice and feedback.

7. Use the assessment strategies developed in Step 4.

8. Use the assessment results to help students correct themselves, to evaluate student learning, to improve instruction, and to refine the learning goal.

If you use the *National Standards for Physical Education* (NASPE, 2004) to outline essential learning of standards or goals for all students in physical education, Step 1 is accomplished. The skill theme chapters in *Children Moving* provide possible content selections for meeting those standards. Your task will be to choose which content to teach and how to order it—this is your scope and sequence. Step 3 is accomplished once you have developed yearly plans as discussed in Chapter 8. Our next task is Step 4, choosing the types of assessment items we want to use.

Assessment is just like instruction. It needs a plan to guide the process and to give direction and focus to the various assessment pieces. If we pursue the trip analogy from Chapter 8, Steps 1 and 2 require us to choose both a destination and a means of travel. In Steps 3 and 4 we determine if we are really on the route and how we are progressing in getting there. For example, if we want to travel across country to Denver by

flying (destination and method) to see a Denver Broncos game, as we travel we need to check to be sure we are really on our way to Denver by plane. At the airport the ticket agent will check us in and reaffirm that we are going to Denver. When we get to the gate, the sign reads "Denver." The gate agent takes our ticket for the Denver flight, and on the plane the pilot announces that this is the flight to Denver. In reality, we have just experienced four assessments to make sure we are on the right route. So how will you figure out if your students are on the right route to their goal?

A variety of options exist. Although the topics of deciding on the goal and content as well as developing and teaching instructional progressions are dealt with elsewhere in this text, they are mentioned here to reinforce how assessment is linked to instruction. The remainder of this chapter provides options for selecting and developing assessment tools (the "how to assess" piece) and strategies (the "in what context to assess" piece). Additionally, criteria for use in judging the student performance (the "how well" piece) will be included. Suggestions will also be provided about what to do with the results.

What Has Been Learned? Selecting Assessment Options

Our task, at this point, is to design and select assessment options that match our student learning goals. For convenience and clarity, we present assessment options separately from material on instruction, but keep in mind that they are nearly inseparable from instructional tasks.

Many instructional tasks are in reality informal assessments. For example, throughout the skill theme chapters, challenge tasks are presented as part of the progression of tasks. Although these tasks are designed primarily to maintain interest and focus, they also serve as a "minicheck" on how well a child is progressing toward a goal. The challenge task of "see how many times in a row you can hit the ball without hitting the tee or missing the ball" provides children, as well as the teacher, with feedback. If most of the class can hit the ball only once or twice, the teacher knows he or she needs to provide more practice before moving on. Likewise, if an individual student can hit it only once or twice, the teacher knows he or she needs to work with that student. Students can also measure their ability to hit in the same manner.

Alternatively, the Checks for Understanding distributed throughout the skill theme chapters are informal mini cognitive assessments. Checks for

---

SAMPLE PERFORMANCE INDICATORS JUMPING AND LANDING

By the end of *sixth* grade students should be able to:

- Design a repeatable rope-jumping routine using a variety of relationships with a partner or group (behind, beside, mirroring, matching).
- Perform a rope-jumping routine using a variety of relationships with a partner or group.
- Demonstrate an approach, a takeoff, flight, and controlled landing (with running long jump, spring board jump).

By the end of *fifth* grade students should be able to:

- Demonstrate an approach, a takeoff, flight, and controlled landing (with running long jump, spring board jump).
- Jump (smooth and rhythmical) a self-turned rope *using **more** than five* different foot patterns.
- Design a repeatable rope-jumping routine with a partner or a small group using various jumping skills (with or without music).
- Perform a repeatable rope-jumping routine with a partner or small group using various jumping skills (with or without music).

By the end of *fourth* grade students should be able to:

- Jump for distance (controlled bent-knee landing).
- Jump for height (controlled bent-knee landing).
- Jump on and off low equipment; land on feet with control.
- Jump (smooth and rhythmical) a self-turned rope *using **at least** five* different foot patterns (single bounce).

By the end of *third* grade students should be able to:

- Jump and land (controlled, bent-knee) from a low or medium level.
- Demonstrate correct rope turning using a self-turned rope.
- Demonstrate correct rope turning using a long rope (for group jumping).
- Jump a self-turned rope (smooth, rhythmical jumping) and perform the following:
  Single bounce forward and backward.
  Double bounce forward and backward.
- Jump a self-turned rope (smooth, rhythmical jumping) *using **at least** three* different foot patterns (e.g., side to side, straddle, hop).

By the end of *second* grade students should be able to:

- Jump off the ground or low level equipment (with different body shapes; (e.g., "T," "knee-slapper") and land in a controlled bent knee position.
- Jump a self-turned rope and perform the following with yielding landings:
  Single bounce forward and backward or double bounce forward and backward.
- Jump an overhead turning long rope with a double bounce and yielding landing.

By the end of *first* grade students should be able to:

- Jump and land using a variety of takeoffs and landings (in, out, over) in relation to various equipment (e.g., hoops, low hurdles, rope shapes).
- Jump (single or double bounce) a swinging rope (long or short) with yielding landings.
- While jumping, demonstrate correct rope-turning (self-turned).

By the end of *kindergarten* students should be able to:

- Jump and land using a variety of takeoff and landing patterns (two feet to two feet, one foot to two feet).
- Jump over a line or rope using two feet to two feet pattern (double or single bounce).

Figure 14.1 Sample performance indicators: jumping and landing.
Source: Austin Independent School District, Austin, TX. Used with permission.

understanding ask children to show their understanding of a particular aspect of the lesson that has been taught (Graham, 2001). For example, the check for understanding of locomotor actions provided on page 401 of Chapter 23 would allow the teacher to informally ascertain whether children understood the differences between skipping, jumping, and hopping regardless of whether they were actually able to skip, hop, and jump. Checks for understanding can be in the form of quick questions to the entire class at the end of a lesson and may call for verbal or physical answers or just a showing of hands or a simple thumbs up or thumbs down.

The assessment options that follow are more formal assessments. Our purpose in these assessments is to see what students have learned: Are they on the road to their goal, or have they achieved their goal? Of the multitude of assessment options available, we outline 11 here that are designed to provide feedback to the teacher, as well as the student. These are broader than the challenges and The Checks for Understanding, often assessing the cognitive domain (knowledge base) and affective domain (values and feelings), as well as the psychomotor domain. And, with the exception of the student journal, these assessment options could provide either formative assessment to students or a summative product that can be scored for reporting. In the skill theme chapters we include suggestions (identified with the assessment icon 🗊) as to when these assessments might be used. The examples show how we make assessment part of our daily teaching, not a separate entity at the end of a unit. Although we focus on a limited number of assessment options here, many more are available. We hope that these suggestions will allow you to develop other options that are specific to your situation. When you find an assessment option that really works, we invite you to share it with us.

There are two key points to remember as you are choosing or designing any assessment option: (1) *You cannot assess it if you didn't teach it,* and (2) *You can't assess without a goal.* The first point, to teach before assessing, is largely self-explanatory—you have to have taught precisely what it is that you want to assess, or the assessment won't yield information that promotes student learning. The second point, to assess with a goal, is related to the first but slightly different. For example, a goal for throwing and catching at the precontrol or control levels might be to demonstrate the mature form of the skill in an isolated situation. When performance moves toward combining skills and skill performance in dynamic situations (utilization/proficiency), the skill will be performed in an environment more

closely resembling the actual environment in which the skill will be used. A goal might be to throw and catch with a partner while on the move. Assessment should be done in a context appropriate to the skill. Skill themes develop from the simple to the complex, or from the mastery of basic skills, then combinations of skills, then the use of skills in a more complex and dynamic environment. Assessment should follow the same guidelines. Assessments at the early control level should assess the elements critical to the mature pattern in an isolated situation. As children progress to later control and early utilization levels, assessment will focus on the use of the skill in a variety of contexts and combinations. Later, utilization- and proficiency-level assessments will focus on the use of the skill in changing environments. Additionally, at each level of skill development, cognitive understanding needs to be assessed, as does the affective dimension of our work.

Teacher Observation

Teacher observation is the most common form of assessment utilized in physical education classes. It is generally employed to assess psychomotor performance but can be applied to the affective domain as well. It is highly appropriate for assessing the acquisition of critical elements of skill that together form a mature motor pattern. Figure 14.2 shows a teacher checklist used to assess the critical elements of dribbling. Suggestions for designing and using such checklists are included in Chapter 12, "Observing Student Responses." The key factors involved in designing checklists that yield the information you want are identifying the critical elements (or goals, at this point) and designing the checklist so that it is usable. A final hint for using checklists is to observe one cue or element at a time. Just as we teach children by using one cue at a time, we should observe one element at a time.

Exit (or Entrance) Slips

Exit slips are short written pieces that are designed to assess cognitive and affective (personal-social) goals. They are developed to assess learning outcomes specific to the lesson just taught. The slips quite often contain two or three questions or ask the student to write in some form about specific learning cues or affective goals for the lesson (Figure 14.3).

Helping Murgatroid provides another format for exit slips. This is how we use Helping Murgatroid; modify the instructions to fit your situation:

The assessment strategies of journals, event tasks, homework, peer observation, videotaping, student drawing, student displays, teacher observation, self-assessment, and portfolios are all referenced in the National Standards for Physical Education (NASPE, 1995). Examples of these techniques from the National Standards can be found throughout the skill theme chapters.

Figure 14.2 Teacher observation checklist. Source: *Assessing Motor Skills in Elementary Physical Education,* by S. Holt/Hale, 1999, Reston, VA; American Alliance for Health, Physical Education, Recreation, and Dance.

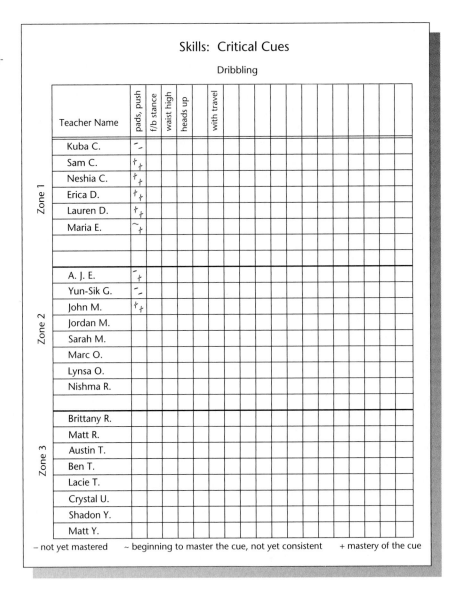

The lesson is being taught in a multipurpose room that becomes a cafeteria from 11:30 A.M. to 1:00 P.M. On one side of the room, lunch tables are permanently set up. Before beginning the lesson, the teacher places pencils and pieces of paper on the lunch tables, enough for each child in the upcoming class. The lesson begins as normal. At some point, the teacher stops the lesson and says to the children, "Remember several weeks ago we were practicing throwing? What I want you to do now is sit at one of the lunch tables so that you each have a piece of paper and a pencil. Then I want you to write a note to your friend Murgatroid. Murgatroid is not a very good thrower. List five cues that might help Murgatroid become a better thrower. As soon as you are finished, you can return to the other side of the 'gym' and continue working on your jumping-and-landing sequence."

The entire Helping Murgatroid process takes less than five minutes, but it can be enormously helpful in assessing what the children remember from past lessons. Figure 14.4 provides three examples of Helping Murgatroid cues written by children. Which set of responses would you be satisfied with?

Student Journals

Student journals are like diaries. They are written records of participation, results, responses, feelings, perceptions, or reflections about actual happenings or outcomes (NASPE, 1995). Student journals provide a wonderful opportunity to assess the affective domain of our teaching (Cutforth & Parker, 1996). Students can simply be asked to write down their feelings, or

Jordan

Draw the pathway beside the word.

Straight ————————

Curved ⌒   *Great*

Zig Zag ∿∿∿∿∿∿

How did you work in physical education today?

great   (good)   not-so-good   bad

Practice Plan — Throwing Game

To be done as a team.

1. Think back about how your team played today.

2. What did you do well?

3. What do you need more practice doing?

4. For the first 10 minutes of our next class you will have a chance to practice with your team what you need to improve upon. Your job now is to design a task (or 2) that you can use to help your team get better. The task(s) must focus on the cues we used. You have 10 minutes for practice, so design your task to fit into that amount of time.

Figure 14.3 Exit slips.

Name _Destanie_   Date _9/2/2004_

Throwing and Catching

1. Using stick figures show what a student would look like performing the four steps of throwing.

2. Circle the student that is using correct form when performing the three steps of catching.
   a. Should the student catch with their hands or trap the ball with their body?

   b. Should the student reach for the ball or wait for it to get to their body?

   c. Should the student keep their eyes on the ball or take their eyes off the ball?

3. In each situation, circle the spot where the thrower should throw the ball if the other student was on the run.
(The player with the arrow is the catcher.)

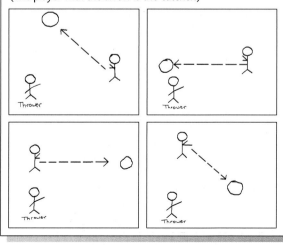

1. use both hands

2. try throwing over your head

3. move your feet apart a little

4.

5.

1. hold the ball in one hand and when you throw step with the oposite foot.

2. follow through

3. keep your ey on the target

4. put your side to the target

5. throw hard enough to get it to the target but dont throw to hard

1. watch my friends first.

2. then you try.

3. then well help you throw strat.

4. then you would try.

5. then you would get it right

Figure 14.4 Sample responses to the question, "What cues would you suggest to help Murgatroid become a better overhand thrower?"

they can be asked to respond to structured questions to assess more specific goals (Figure 14.5).

Remember, the purpose of journals is for students to reflect on their feelings, growth, frustrations, joys, and successes regarding physical activity and physical education (Figures 14.6 and 14.7). Students have to feel safe in doing that. One sure way to stifle the honesty and reflectivity of the students is to grade journals. This is one assessment piece that is used almost solely as a formative assessment. The purpose of journals is to give students a venue for writing honestly and freely.

The use of journals and exit slips appears time-consuming. (See Box 14-2 for suggestions as to how to manage them.) It has been our experience that although they may take some time, they yield invaluable information about what students are understanding in class and how they feel about being in physical education class.

Homework

In most schools today the time allocated to physical education does not allow for the learning we would like to help students achieve. Homework can be used to

Teacher Question: How do you feel about today's tournament compared to the others, when you were playing with smaller teams?

Brenda: I liked the two-on-two game better than the tournament.

Justin: Bad, it's harder to win.

Dustin: It was the best tournament I played in.

Casey: It was funner than others because you [could] play the whole thing.

Beau: It sucked. Because too many people and the teams sucked and I got in a fight.

Figure 14.5 Sample journal question with student responses. *Source:* Steve Sorenson and Brad Rempel, as quoted in "Promoting Affective Development in Physical Education: The Value of Journal Writing," by N. Cutforth and M. Parker, 1996, *The Journal of Physical Education, Recreation, and Dance* 67(7), p. 22. Used with permission from American Alliance for Health, Physical Education, Recreation, and Dance.

Box 14-2

Managing Journals and Exit Slips

From the teacher's perspective, the management of journals and exit slips is the key to their success (or lack of it). Four guidelines may help:

- *Determine the major purpose of the journal or exit slip.* Limit the scope initially. Focus on learning cues, on behavior, or on students' thoughts about the lesson—choose one. Expand the scope when you feel comfortable.

- *Decide on a format for writing.* Because students are not accustomed to writing in physical education, their writing may initially be shallow and unfocused. Therefore, we have found it useful to provide students with a question to answer. As students become accustomed to writing, the level of the question may be increased to ask for more open-ended responses.

- *Organize writing procedures.* To effectively respond to journals, many teachers use journals with only two or three classes at a time and then switch to another group of classes at the end of a marking period. We have found it most effective to keep the journals in containers in the gym (or sometimes with classroom teachers) organized by class. This way you can read them when you get the chance and don't have to hunt them down. One of the best ways to encourage children to keep a journal is to let them personalize it (Figure 14.6). We have used everything from college blue books to manila folders to laminated construction paper. Usually we have students write for about three minutes at the end of class (Figure 14.7). Some teachers prefer the beginning of class if they want students to reflect on their previous journal entry before class.

- *Read and respond.* One key aspect of journals and exit slips is providing feedback to students. Teachers need to respond to student writing. Responses can be short, snappy phrases (e.g., "Good job!") or longer, probing questions. Generally, it takes less than a minute to respond to each student's entry, but the minutes add up. To manage the time, some teachers have students do journals or exit slips only once a week; others have the children do them for every lesson but review them only once a week; still others use them with selected classes only.

Figure 14.6 Personalized journal cover.

Figure 14.7 Child's class journal.

Sept. 13
Today in class we were working outside with balls and we were throwing over handed and under handed. Erin was my partner today. I had fun. but it was not. Sometimes I would catch the ball sometimes and sometimes I would not. I throw the ball ok I guess, That is what I did today.

Sept. 14
Today in class I was working on not too much. But handsprings Everybody was with me I had fun. I also worked on round off.

Sept. 15
Today in class we were working with Mats it was fun. we had to roll font and back.rolls we had to land on our feet and not fall down. I tried and I did it. Then we ran and landed in a almost falling over way, I think it was fun.

Nov. 2
Today in class we were doing all diffrent kinds of shapes. it was fun. My partner was Erin D. We worked all diffrent shapes together.

Nov. 3
Today in class we worked with beanbags. My partner was Machiel. She was not a very good worker. My other partner was going to be Corntnay, but Miss parker put me with Machiele. It was fun (I guess).

Nov. 21
Today in class we worked on balls of anything that we wanted to do. It was fun. My partner was Corntnay.

Figure 14.8 Homework assignment: fitness.
Source: Super Active Kids Program Instructor's Manual (unpublished manuscript) by B. Entzion et al., 1991, Grand Forks: University of North Dakota, Department of Health, Physical Education, and Recreation. Used with permission.

After School/Weekend Exercise Records

After School/Weekends	Activity	After School/Weekends
□□□□□	Jump Rope	□□□□□
□□□□□	Jogging/Walking	□□□□□
□□□□□	Soccer	□□□□□
□□□□□	Basketball	□□□□□
□□□□□	Football	□□□□□
□□□□□	Swimming	□□□□□
□□□□□	Dancing	□□□□□
□□□□□	Hiking	□□□□□
□□□□□	Gymnastics	□□□□□
□□□□□	Biking	□□□□□
□□□□□	Tennis	□□□□□
□□□□□	Other (_____)	□□□□□
⸬⸬⸬⸬⸬	Did Nothing	⸬⸬⸬⸬⸬

cut

Parent Signature

Date: ___/___/___

Parent Signature

Date: ___/___/___

Instructions:

1. When your child does an activity for at least 20 minutes, draw around the box to highlight it (more than 20 minutes still only counts as one activity credit).

2. Write which day the activity was done in the box. Use the letters M, T, W, R, F, or S.

3. Sign and date the record, and cut it out for your child to bring to school.

supplement in school physical education. Essentially, homework is work a student completes outside of the physical education class. Other classes use homework to enhance cognitive understanding; we can use active homework (Smith & Claxton, 2003) to enhance psychomotor learning and physical activity. This homework can be "fun" and personalized in that it allows children to choose their own activities. Furthermore, it can produce records of student progress, process, and participation.

Figure 14.8 illustrates a homework assignment that documents regular participation in physical activity. We often ask parents to verify the work. Physical education homework is similar to reports of reading done at home, and we have found homework quite useful, especially in terms of fitness or activity participation.

Peer Observation

Peer observation of students by other students can be used to assess competence in performance of skills and demonstration of selected critical elements. Peer observation is easily built into tasks by asking students to work as partners and to provide each other with selected feedback regarding performance. For example, while working on dribbling with the hands, one student can be asked to watch the other and see if the partner uses the finger pads, bends the knees, and has a staggered stance. To more fully tie assessment to instruction and learning, the partner can provide feedback to the performer to help him or her improve. On a more formal basis, students can record their observations for later use by the teacher.

Children enjoy peer observations (and peer teaching), but a few key points help in making the task more successful. First, the teacher must define the cues clearly enough so that the partner can observe and comment. Second, structure the task so that children observe only one cue at a time. Remember, doing peer observation requires practice and independent learning skills (see Chapter 13). Start small and simply. Figure 14.9 provides examples of peer assessments of balancing and dribbling used with fourth-grade students.

Self-Assessment

Self-assessments can be used to assess psychomotor, cognitive, and affective aspects of children's work. Although peer and teacher observations are a useful tool for assessment of the critical cues for skills, self-assessments provide a unique opportunity to evaluate larger components of a skill or the beginning use of a skill (Holt/Hale, 1999). For example, in the case of learning to dribble, we might ask children if they could dribble and pivot using the preferred hand, the nonpreferred hand, while walking, while traveling at a jog, without a defensive player, and with a defensive player. Figure 14.10 provides an example of a self-assessment designed to ask questions like these. Self-assessments may be used at the end of a unit to have students assess their achievement. Alternatively, the self-assessment may be used throughout a unit as each of the components is introduced and practiced. In this case, each individual assessment would be dated and would provide a record of the child's achievement of the various components. Regardless of when self-assessment is used, children need to have ample opportunity to practice the various components before completing it. If it is used at the end, children should have a chance for a brief practice period before completing the assessment.

Another version of self-assessment that can be used with older children is a self-rating scale (Figure 14.11). The self-rating scale contains the same skill categories as the self-assessment, but the rating scale provides students an opportunity to assess themselves on a numerical scale. The key to this is providing descriptors for the numbers so children are able to anchor their self-assessments on clear criteria. Self-rating scales can be appropriately used for assessment before teaching as well as after.

Peers can provide meaningful and relevant feedback to each other.

Self-assessments can also provide a glimpse into children's feelings and attitudes. Some children's ratings may be significantly higher or lower than the teacher's observations. At this point, the self-assessment becomes an opportune place to begin discussions with individual children. Another option is to ask children directly on self-observations how they feel about performing certain skills.

Some teachers often voice concerns about the honesty of children when doing self- and peer assessments. We have found that children are incredibly honest when assessing their own skills and those of others (they take the assessment of others very seriously). Some children may initially inflate scores, but if self-assessments are a regular part of instruction and children become aware of their role in the evaluation process and of the purposes of assessment, this is short-lived (Holt/Hale, 1999).

Figure 14.9 (A) Peer assessment observation card. (B) Fourth grade balancing check sheet.
Source: Figure 14.9B developed by Charles Cuny as a class project for PE 341, University of Northern Colorado. Used with permission.

Physical Education—Dribbling Coach's Check

Coach: _Danny_   Player: _Yidam_

Cut:

Ball in same hand as planted foot	yes	no	(sometimes)
Ball changes hands	(yes)	no	sometimes
Player goes the other way	(yes)	no	sometimes

Pivot:

Ball in other hand than pivot foot	(yes)	no	sometimes
Turn to back	(yes)	no	sometimes
Ball changes hands	yes	no	(sometimes)

A

Fourth Grade Balancing Check Sheet

Name: _Krystle S._   Name: _Hilary H._

Directions: Each set of partners will rate the stillness of the body parts which they used as a base of support in different balances.

Head	held still	(wiggle)	wobble
Knees	held still	wiggle	(wobble)
Stomach	(held still)	wiggle	wobble
Hip	(held still)	wiggle	wobble
Shoulders	held still	(wiggle)	wobble
Hands	(held still)	wiggle	wobble
Elbows	(held still)	wiggle	wobble
Back	(held still)	wiggle	wobble
Feet	(held still)	wiggle	wobble

What could your group do to improve on their balancing skill?

Key:	still = 4 seconds still
	wiggle = 2 seconds still
	wobble = can't hold still

B

Event Tasks

Event tasks are performance tasks that can be completed in one class period or a portion of it. The task is designed broadly enough so that there are multiple solutions. The task might be entirely psychomotor, or it may include cognitive aspects as well. Event tasks that we use frequently are self-designed games (see Chapter 31) or developing gymnastics routines (see Figure 14.12). Other tasks might include such things as designing a presentation for a parent-teacher conference on the skills they have been learning or preparing to make a presentation to younger students on the critical pieces of a skill. The success of event tasks depends on the attractiveness of the task (whether it captures children's

Dribbling and Pivots

Name: _____ Homeroom: _____ Date: _____

Self-Evaluation of Dribbling and Pivots

	I still need to practice at this skill.	I'm good at this skill.	I would like my teacher to see this skill.
1. Dribbling and pivoting with preferred hand			
2. Dribbling and pivoting with other hand			
3. Dribbling and pivoting while walking			
4. Dribbling and pivoting while jogging			
5. Dribbling and pivoting at full speed			
6. Dribbling and pivoting against a defense			

Test for Understanding

1. The critical cues for dribbling are _____ , _____ ,

   _____ , _____ .

Teacher Comments:

Figure 14.10 Example of a student self-rating scale.

attention) and the structure the teacher provides. Event tasks require independent and group working skills. See Chapter 13 for ways to determine when children and teachers might be ready use those skills.

Videotape/Digital Pictures

Though not accessible in all schools, videotape or digital pictures can provide a final, permanent product for gymnastics sequences, dances, or self-designed games. It can also let students display their knowledge and skill with respect to critical aspects of a skill. One possible task is to have students videotape or take pictures of each other performing a certain skill and then analyze the critical cues for that skill. Likewise, students can videotape each other and provide "color commentary" regarding the performance. Another videotape assessment might require students to develop an infomercial about a certain skill or fitness activity.

For video/digital analysis to be successful, the criteria for the task must be made explicit and a sufficient amount of time must be allotted. When they know what they are looking for, children love to watch themselves on tape. It is initially helpful to provide children with checklists (see Figure 14.2) or observation cards (see Figure 14.9) to guide their observations. Children may

Figure 14.11 Example of a student self-assessment.

Dribbling and Pivoting Self-Rating

Name: _____ Homeroom: _____ Date: _____

1	2	3	4	5	6	7	8	9	10

1 – 3 I still need to practice this skill.
4 – 6 I am pretty good at this skill.
7 – 8 I am very good at this skill.
9 – 10 This is my best skill.
* This is my favorite skill.

	Rating	Comments
1. Dribbling and pivoting with preferred hand		
2. Dribbling and pivoting with other hand		
3. Dribbling and pivoting while walking		
4. Dribbling and pivoting while jogging		
5. Dribbling and pivoting at full speed		
6. Dribbling and pivoting against a cone		
7. Dribbling and pivoting against a passive defense		
8. Dribbling and pivoting against an active defense		
9. Dribbling and pivoting without breaking stride		
10. Dribbling and pivoting while keeping head up		
11. Dibbling and pivoting in a game situation		

You may add comments if you wish.

Teacher Comments:

also combine video analysis with homework, thereby eliminating the need for multiple playback units.

Student Drawings

Children love to draw, and we have found drawing one of the most rewarding assessment tools. The options for student drawing are endless. Children can be asked to draw about themselves, what a sequence looks like, what a skill looks like, what they liked best. Figure 14.13 shows a student drawing used as an assessment piece.

Student Displays

Student displays are public displays of student work that communicate what the children have learned. These can take a variety of forms, from posters on which students have drawn a person displaying a skill and labeled the cues, to photographs, to bulletin boards.

Portfolios

Some researchers have said that to be truly effective, assessments must not only measure current achievement but also monitor and report students' achievement over

Gymnastics Sequence

Student Name _Shannon M._ Grade _4_ Date _2-20-03_

Task: Design a gymnastics sequence that includes a balance, a roll, and a traveling action on your mat.

Using a stick figure draw your beginning shape. _____

Describe in sequence the rest of your routine:

1. _Forward roll._
2. _Balance into a v seat—legs straddled._
3. _Sideways pencil roll to a front support._
4. _Tuckjump to a stand._
5.
6.

Using a stick figure draw your ending shape. _____

Check for:

Definite beginning and ending position	(Yes)	No
At least one roll	Yes	No
At least one balance	Yes	No
At least one traveling action	Yes	No
Smooth transitions	Yes	No
Appropriate for my skill level	Yes	No

Figure 14.12 Gymnastics sequence.

Figure 14.13 Second grader's drawing assessing the cue of using the shoelaces to kick.

They are powerful because they help students learn about their learning (Davies, 2000). Portfolios provide an opportunity for students to share the responsibility for collecting proof of their learning. Additionally, they provide a rich resource for reporting to both teachers and parents.

> Whenever a value is set forth which can only be attained by a few, the conditions are ripe for widespread feelings of personal inadequacy. An outstanding example in American society is the fierce competitiveness of the school system. No educational system in the world has so many examinations, or so emphasizes grades, as the American school system. Children are constantly being ranked and evaluated. The superior achievement of one child tends to debase the achievement of another.
>
> —MORRIS ROSENBERG, *Society and the Adolescent Self-Image*

time (Wolf & White, 2000). Portfolios do this. Portfolios are collections of student work over a single unit, an entire school year, or students' whole elementary careers. Some have likened a portfolio to a trophy case of a child's accomplishments (Wilson & Roof, 1999).

The first consideration with a portfolio is its purpose. It is quite difficult to select items without a sense of purpose. Common purposes include keeping track of progress, providing students a way to assess their own accomplishments, and determining the extent to which learning objectives have been achieved. For example, if one of the purposes of your physical education class is helping students practice a healthy lifestyle, their portfolios might include various pieces that attest to their knowledge of fitness, activities they do to stay fit, and indications of how they value fitness. Many of the products of the assessment options discussed in this chapter could be included in a portfolio. For example, a fitness portfolio might include some of the following artifacts: results of a health-related fitness test given at the beginning of the school year, goals set as a result of that test, activities in which the student participated to achieve the goals set, weekly homework sheets that document physical activity, a written fitness report, results of a fitness test later in the year, an indication of how well personal goals were met, and finally, goals for the summer. The teacher may specify some items in the portfolio, but because the portfolio is a personal record, the student should be allowed and encouraged to decide which items will most strongly "make the case."

A portfolio communicates more when the reader knows why pieces have been chosen for inclusion. When children are including certain pieces, they might use categories such as "my best work," "the hardest skill I can do now," and "my most improved skill." By having criteria regarding the inclusion of items, students understand better what they are to learn and how to talk about it. Thus, portfolios serve as a powerful link from instruction and assessment to learning.

The development and use of portfolios seems intimidating. Davies (2000) has the following suggestions for beginning portfolio work with children:

1. Maintain a clear purpose.
2. Keep the portfolio process simple. Start small.
3. Remember that there is no one best way to do portfolios. Decide what is right for you and your situation.
4. Include more than written work. Video or digital analysis is helpful here.
5. Ask children to explain and record why they chose each piece of work.
6. Ensure that children have involvement and ownership. Portfolios document their learning.

Hoerr (2000) has suggested having "portfolio days" on which students share their portfolios with parents in lieu of the traditional parent-teacher conference.

One concern that has been voiced by many physical education teachers is that these alternative assessment options take time (and we have little time as it is in physical education). That is true, but remember that alternative assessment links instruction and assessment by providing meaningful learning tasks. Well-designed assessment tasks thus enhance learning.

The development of assessment items and tasks that are meaningful also takes time. To simplify that process we encourage you to use examples that you find here and modify examples you find elsewhere. PE Central (www.pecentral.org) is a wonderful source of possible assessment items.

Assessing How Well Something Was Learned

Not all assessment items will (or need to) be scored. Any of the assessment options listed previously could be done with students and simply used to provide feedback to the students. For example, the peer coach's check in Figure 14.9 could be given to the student by the coach or the teacher with some feedback that the child needs to practice this aspect more. But some items do need to be scored in order for children and teachers to know to what extent the goal has been achieved. To return to our travel analogy, did we get to the Broncos game or just to Denver? Or to the Denver airport? Or did we ever get on the plane? Remember, though, that what is assessed must match the task, what was taught, and what was expected to be learned.

Rubrics describe varying levels of quality or achievement for a specific task. Their purpose is to give students informative feedback about their work and to give detailed assessment of the final product. The development of rubrics takes time, but the results make learning expectations clear, provide feedback, and support learning and the development of skills and understanding (Andrade, 2000).

There are three components to a rubric: the criteria, or essential components to be assessed; the steps of quality, or the rating scale; and the descriptors that illustrate how each of the steps is related to the criteria. The criteria match those asked for in a task. They are the essential elements determined necessary to achieve the specified goal. It is not necessary or feasible to include every possible element, so select ones that are appropriate for the level of development. For example, at the control level, the essential elements might be the critical cues of the mature motor pattern; at the proficiency level, essential elements would be the use of a variety of skills in a game situation. For students, this can often be translated into "what counts."

The steps of quality, or the rating scale, identify various levels of the standard that might be achieved or various levels of competence. These can be thought of as steps or stops along the way to the final goal. These steps can be called by a variety of names: 1, 2, 3, 4; "excellent," "above average," "needs improvement," "incomplete;" Junior Olympian, Bronze Medal, Silver

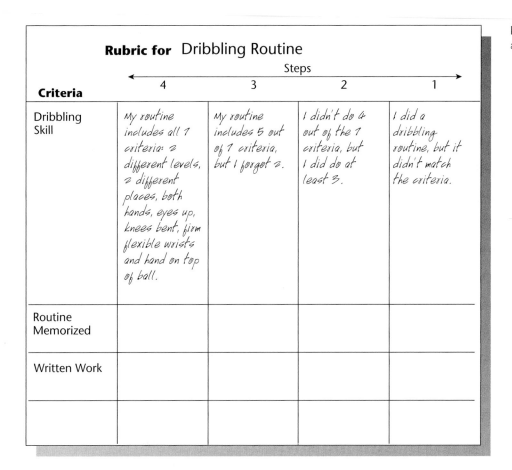

Figure 14.14 Example of an analytic rubric.

Medal, Gold Medal; Little League, Minor League, Major League, Coach; and so forth. Regardless of the scale used, it must distinguish one level of achievement from another.

The last aspect of a rubric, descriptors illustrate or describe what the scale looks like at each level for each criterion. This is the aspect that lets children know specifically what is expected. One author (Andrade, 2000) proposed the following scale: 4 = *yes* (I did all the aspects of the criterion); 3 = *yes, but* (I did X and Y criteria but didn't do Z); 2 = *No, but* (I didn't do X and Y criteria but did do Z); and 1 = *no* (I didn't do X, Y, or Z criteria). Using our travel analogy, one criterion might be getting on the right plane. The possible scale or steps might be the following: 4 = checking in at the ticket counter, going to the right gate, giving the ticket to the gate agent, and getting on the right plane; 3 = going to the right gate, giving the ticket to the agent, getting on the right plane, but not checking in at the ticket counter; 2 = giving the ticket to the gate agent and getting on the right plane, but forgetting to check in at the ticket counter and going to the wrong gate first; 1 = getting on the right plane, but not checking in, going to the wrong gate, and giving the wrong ticket to the agent; and 0 = not getting on the right

plane. Figure 14.14 illustrates a rubric written for the skill aspect of the dribbling routine using the same format. These rubrics are called *analytic rubrics*. They are time-consuming but provide invaluable information for the teacher and the student (Schiemer, 2000).

Rubrics can also be holistic. Holistic rubrics assess children's performance as a whole. They combine a variety of essential performance elements in order to determine an overall level of achievement. The result is then reflected in a single score. Holistic rubrics are easier to use and are effective in assessing large numbers of students. They use the same set of components as analytic rubrics, but all descriptors for a certain level are listed together; to achieve that level, the student must accomplish all aspects of the criteria at the level indicated. A holistic rubric for the Denver trip might be: 4 = getting on the right plane, getting off the plane in Denver, getting downtown, acquiring tickets for a Broncos game, and attending the game; 3 = getting on the right plane, getting off in Denver, and getting downtown, but being unable to get tickets to a Broncos game; 2 = getting on the right plane and getting off in Denver, but being unable to figure out how to get downtown or to a Broncos game; 1 = getting on the right plane, but getting off at the wrong destination; and

0 = not getting on the right plane or any plane. As you can see, this assessment looks at the whole process of getting to the Broncos game, not just the one aspect of getting on the right plane. Figure 14.15 illustrates a holistic rubric for a dribbling routine.

Regardless of the type of rubric chosen, here are strategies to make designing them easier:

1. Look at models of well-written rubrics.
2. Initially develop rubrics for content areas in which you have the most expertise.
3. List the criteria, then relist and relist them until they don't overlap and they indicate the learning you want to see achieved.
4. Have a friend review your rubric.
5. Revise the draft. Be ready to write and rewrite. Creating good rubrics takes time.
6. Try out the rubric with one class.
7. Revise again.

Rubrics take time (and patience), but the end result clarifies student learning and your teaching. The time is well spent.

A technique that we find helps immensely with the evaluation of complex assignments that contain a variety of components such as event tasks and portfolios is to create an assessment checklist that designates each of the components. The teacher develops this checklist in advance, showing all components of the assessment, with space for recording student data and comments. For written work like portfolios, the assessment checklist can be stapled to the student item. This way, a teacher can simply fill out slips when projects are successful. The teacher assessment checklist in and of itself is not an assessment, but it allows you to organize and manage large assessment projects. Figure 14.16 shows an assessment slip for the dribbling routine.

Figure 14.15 Holistic rubric for dribbling/ball-handling skills.
Source: Assessing Motor Skills in Elementary Physical Education, by S. Holt/Hale, 1999, Reston, VA; American Alliance for Health, Physical Education, Recreation, and Dance.

Rubric for Dribbling/Ball-Handling Skills

4 Written work completed
Routine memorized
A minimum of 7 dribbling/ball-handling skills
Combination of traveling and dribbling
A touch of creativity
Positive contribution to group effort

3 Written work completed
Routine memorized
5 dribbling/ball-handling skills
Some traveling
Positive contribution to group effort

2 Written work completed
Routine "almost" memorized
5 dribbling/ball-handling skills
Minimal contribution to group effort

1 Written work—minimum completion
Memorization—reminders necessary
Fewer than 5 dribbling/ball-handling skills
No contribution to group effort

0 Written work incomplete
No sequence of events, unable to repeat routine
No contribution to group effort

Figure 14.16 Teacher assessment slip to be used with assessing dribbling/ball-handling skills in Figure 14.15.
Source: Assessing Motor Skills in Elementary Physical Education, by S. Holt/Hale, 1999, Reston, VA; AAHPERD.

Ball-Handling Routine Assessment Slip

Date: _____   Comments:

Written work completed: _____

Focus on dribbling: _____

Routine memorized: _____

Number of skills: _____

Travel and/or combination skills: _____

_____

Touch of creativity: _____

Assessing All Three Domains

We do not teach only motor skills and fitness. For us, there are clear affective and cognitive goals in our programs. Therefore, we must also assess those goals. The examples provided in the previous section include assessment ideas in all three domains. Assessments for motor skills and fitness include homework and peer observation. Assessment of the affective domain can occur in the form of student journals. (For more information on assessment in the affective domain, see O'Sullivan & Henninger [2000] and Gibbons et al. [2002].) The cognitive domain can be assessed through exit slips (e.g., Helping Murgatroid) or simply by checking for understanding with questions during class, identified in skill themes chapters by the Check for Understanding icon ♚. The move to more authentic assessment has provided teachers with noninvasive, instructional ways to assess all three domains.

Also, in recent years it has become increasingly obvious to us that physical education programs that are limited to one or two days a week have less impact on children than daily programs of physical education (Graham et al., 1991). Although it may not be possible for children to reach utilization or proficiency level in a skill such as throwing in the limited time allotted to physical education, it is realistic to expect that children can at least learn the key cues for the points that we emphasize in our programs. Although that is not totally satisfactory, it does represent progress. It is encouraging to realize that even though all of the children in our program are not throwing at the utilization level, they do know how to throw correctly if, and when, they choose to throw on their own.

Fitness Assessments

In Chapter 4 we discuss in depth the use of fitness assessments in physical education. We encourage you to refer to that chapter when conducting fitness assessments. The assessment of fitness should follow the same guidelines as all other learning in physical education. The potential downfall of fitness scores is that although they are easy to collect and report, often they are not an indication of learning in physical education. As with other types of assessment, we must have taught the content of fitness with clear goals throughout the physical education program, used multiple formative assessments along the way, and provided much activity and practice. Otherwise, fitness reporting does not provide an indication of achievement in physical education. Readers sometimes think we are antifitness due to the stand we take on formal exercises/calisthenics and fitness testing for children. We believe very strongly in personal health-related fitness for children; we also believe in fitness as a process and as a product of quality physical education programs.

A Word about Assessing Movement Concepts

As you might have noticed, our discussion of assessment has largely focused on skill themes. Some might ask, "What about assessing movement concepts?" You will find some assessment options in the movement concept chapters, but they are largely cognitive. Cognitive understanding of the concepts precedes application of the concepts in children's movement. Early assessment of the concepts, therefore, centers on cognitive understanding; for example, checking the class for understanding, asking for partner-to-partner recall (two students sharing key points of the lesson with each other), or using exit slips. As movement skills develop, concepts and skills are used in combination, for example, striking to send a ball to the right or left, using easy force for the drop shot, or free-flow rolling in gymnastics. At this point, it is hard to separate the understanding of concept from the ability to do the skill. Understanding and application of the concepts at this point are assessed in performance situations; for example, sequences, student projects, and game playing.

Assessment of Students with Disabilities

Alternative assessment offers a unique opportunity for the teacher of the child with disabilities to provide feedback and guidance to that child. Experts (Block et al., 1998) have strongly suggested the use of alternative assessment for children with disabilities to counteract the pitfalls of traditional assessment with these children. They contend that traditional assessment is misused for determining IEPs because it has no functional relevance, doesn't help determine instructional techniques, may be inaccurate, and doesn't communicate much to parents. They claim that alternative assessment in adapted physical education allows a direct link between assessment, programming, and instruction and promotes measurement of performance in a variety of settings, including real-life functional settings. They suggest using rubrics with certain modifications to accommodate children with disabilities. First, the rubric should be extended to accommodate more levels of development. Second, rubrics within rubrics (or analytic rubrics) should be designed to accommodate specific goals included on the IEP, such as social behavior. For example, if a child is in a gymnastics unit, items can be added that include social behavior as part of the gymnastics rubric. Third, individual rubrics may

Annual Goals	Specific Educational Services Needed	Present Level of Performance	Person Delivering Service
Goal 1. Trevor will improve abdominal strength.	Special physical education consultant services.	Performs eight bent-leg sit-ups with assistance.	Morgan Stewart, special physical educator
Goal 2. Trevor will improve throwing skills.	Special physical education consultant services.	With a tennis ball, Trevor hits a 2'x2' target five feet away on 2 of 10 trials.	Morgan Stewart, special physical educator

Short-Term Objectives	Date Completed	Special Instructional Methods and/or Materials	Grade
Goal 1. Objectives			
1. In the gym, with assistance, Trevor will perform 10 bent-leg sit-ups.	10-21-01	mat; social praise; a performance graph	C
2. In the gym, without assistance, Trevor will perform eight bent-leg sit-ups.	11-7-01	same	B
3. In the gym, without assistance, Trevor will perform 25 bent-leg sit-ups.	Progressing; can do 21	same	A
Goal 2. Objectives			
1. With a tennis ball, Trevor will hit a 2'x2' target 5 feet away on 6 of 10 trials.	11-14-01	tennis ball and target	C
2. With a tennis ball, Trevor will hit a 2'x2' target 10 feet away on 6 of 10 trials.	11-21-01	same	B
3. With a tennis ball, Trevor will hit a 2'x2' target 20 feet away on 8 of 10 trials.	12-10-01	same	A

SIGNATURES AND TITLES OF APPROPRIATE TEAM MEMBERS: (Signatures indicate approval of this IEP)

_____   _____   _____
(Parent)   (Teacher)   (Administrator/Supervisor)

Figure 14.17 Sample grading contract.
Source: H. Henderson, R. French, and L. Kinnison (2001). Reporting grades for students with disabilities in general physical education. *Journal of Physical Education, Recreation and Dance, 72*(6), 50–55.

be needed for children with more severe problems. Alternative assessment, especially with the use of appropriate rubrics, may well help teachers more fully and appropriately include children with disabilities in their classes. For further information, see Block and coauthors (1998).

A second option for assessing students with disabilities is to develop a grading contract based on the student's IEP (Henderson et al., 2001). The grading contract lists the goals and objectives that the child is to achieve in physical education. The student is evaluated based on the extent to which these goals are achieved. The objectives should be graduated so that they lead to the desired goal. See Figure 14.17 for an example of a grading contract.

What to Do with the Results of Assessment, or Summarizing and Reporting Progress

At some point teachers are required to summarize and report children's progress to parents and others. This summative evaluation provides parents and children with an indication of what the child has learned and where he or she is with respect to the essential learning in physical education. It also provides teachers with information about their program—what has been accomplished and what needs to be worked on. For physical education teachers, reporting has always been nothing short of a nightmare due to the sheer numbers of children we teach. The three systems discussed here have made reporting practical and formative, and provide an ongoing record over time.

Three Practical Systems

Austin Independent School District The reporting form (Figure 14.18) used in this district is grade level specific and emanates directly from the district standards and the performance outcomes for each grade. It allows for one year of reporting on one form and explains the exact nature of the performance required to meet the standard. Figure 14.19 is the teacher observation sheet containing the critical performance cues used to collect the information reported on the Assessment Report. Notice that this report corresponds to the third-grade level of the jumping and landing performance outcomes in Figure 14.1.

Linden Elementary The system used at Linden Elementary School in Oak Ridge, Tennessee, is similar to the Texas system except that the report cards are individually designed for each class or grade level based on their units of study (Figure 14.20). This allows you to adapt the report to the various performance outcomes taught at each grade level while providing a bit more detail.

Lambdin System Dolly Lambdin's system (Figure 14.21), a form sent home at the time of each report period, lists the objectives or benchmarks (performance outcomes) for the report period under the broader standard that is a goal of her physical education program. Students then evaluate themselves on a "beginning," "learning," "mastered," "I have problems" scale (actually control, utilization proficiency, and precontrol levels, put into kids' language). If the child's rating differs from hers, Lambdin marks hers in a different color ink. At the end of the year the report-period sheets are summarized on one sheet for the permanent record.

Similarities All three of these reporting systems involve multiple assessments—at least two and sometimes more—for each theme studied. Most often the assessments include at least one teacher observation of critical elements of the skill, one event task, and one self-assessment. Often the reliability of self-assessments is questioned. The teachers using these systems found that student self-assessment was not only accurate and honest but also increased student learning while integrating instruction and assessment. The assumptions of these systems are that when children think about their own learning, they attend more carefully to that learning. All teachers found that students are good and

honest at assessing their own abilities. Additionally, the approach helped these teachers—even though they kept lots of records—find the time, energy, and ability to assess each child more accurately. Note that none of these systems reported student learning as "grades" per se: All the teachers found that grading did not communicate much to the parents or the students. Both the Lambdin and Linden systems, in fact, led to the study and possible redesign of the school report card.

Grading

We have often been asked about "grading." To many, assessment and grading are synonymous. In reality, there are subtle but significant differences. Assessment essentially involves how teachers find out what students know and can do in relation to the standards or learning goal. Grading, on the other hand, involves procedures for compiling data so that an evaluation can be made for reporting to parents (Franklin, 2002). All the report systems that we have shown report progress and achievement linking the content to standards and reporting student progress toward achieving the standard. We think that grades without an indication of what the standard is do not communicate meaningful information to parents or others. After all, what does an A say about what a child can do or has learned? We would much rather provide information that can be used as feedback and guidance. However, we realize that some school districts require you to grade. If that is the case, we first recommend specifying as clearly as possible what each grade means in relation to the standard (as on rubrics). Then assess exactly the same thing as specified. Translate your scales from the rubrics into grades and report to parents (either the Lambdin or Linden system could be used here). For example, Lambdin's ratings—"beginning," "learning," "mastered," "problems"—could be translated into 2, 3, 4, 1 or C, B, A, D. Remember, though, as with all assessment, there should be many assessment opportunities and options. Grades should be a result of all of these. If at all possible, we suggest reporting progress and achievement in ways that are the most meaningful. Grades rarely indicate such.

Finding the Time for Assessment

Time has always been an issue in physical education. Some would argue that even authentic assessment takes time away from activity. In some sense that may be true, but the information gathered from and provided by the assessment options is critical to children's learning, to instructional decisions that meet the needs of the child, and to the design of the program. The

AUSTIN INDEPENDENT SCHOOL DISTRICT
Physical Education Assessment Report
THIRD GRADE

Listed below are the AISD Physical Education Content Standards and Benchmarks developed by the *National Association for Sport & Physical Education, Texas Essential Knowledge & Skills*, and the AISD Physical Education Curriculum Framework. These standards cover a wide range of movement, skill themes, social and health concepts, as well as motor skills that are <u>developmentally appropriate</u> for each grade level. (Please note that spaces on the assessment report will remain blank until that standard has been formally assessed. There are two spaces beside each content standard: 1) initial assessment, 2) demonstrates improvement when appropriate.)

The content standards have been assessed using the following rubric:

---

4 = **(Excellent)** Student is performing the skill using <u>all</u> the cues taught and demonstrating <u>all</u> the cues correctly <u>without reminders</u>.
3 = **(Accomplished)** Student is performing the skill demonstrating <u>most</u> of the cues taught with <u>occasional reminders</u> of a particular cue.
2 = **(Developing)** Student is performing the skill demonstrating <u>some</u> of the cues taught with <u>reminders of several cues</u>.
1 = **(Just Beginning)** Student is showing the beginning stages of learning the skill with <u>constant</u> reminders of <u>all</u> cues.

BASIC SOCIAL AND HEALTH PROMOTION SKILL & CONCEPTS
__/__1. Develop positive self-management and social skills needed to work independently and with others.
__/__2. Identify and develop personal goals.
__/__3. Show evidence of developing strength, endurance and flexibility.
__/__4. List the effects of smoking on physical activity and health.

CHASING, FLEEING AND DODGING
__/__1. Move in a variety of ways that focus on accelerating and decelerating speed.
__/__2. While moving within a boundaried area dodge stationary opponents and/or objects.

JUMPING AND LANDING
__/__1. Jump and land (controlled, bent-knee) from a medium level.
__/__2. Jump a self-turned rope using <u>at least three</u> different foot patterns. (e.g., side to side, straddle, hop)
__/__3. Jump a self-turned rope forward and backward using double <u>and</u> single bounce landings (smooth, rhythmical jumping).
__/__4. Demonstrate correct rope turning using a self-turned <u>and</u> long rope.

BODY ROLLING, WEIGHT TRANSFER AND BALANCE
__/__1. Perform a forward roll and finish in a tucked or standing position.
__/__2. Transfer weight across the mat (upright and inverted) in a variety of ways with large extensions.
__/__3. Transfer weight (hands-on, feet-over) over low equipment or apparatus. (e.g., beam, bench, box, mat)
__/__4. Design and perform gymnastic sequences involving changes in directions, levels, pathways and extensions.

EDUCATIONAL DANCE/RHYTHMS
__/__1. Travel and smoothly change directions or movements in a 3 or 4 beat pattern.
__/__2. Move in various ways using definite contrasts of bound and free-flowing movements.
__/__3. Use "matching or mirroring" and "meeting or parting" to design and perform dance sequences with a partner or small group.

BASIC EYE-HAND COORDINATION
Throwing and Catching
__/__1. Throw a ball <u>overhand</u> using varied amounts of force and speed.
__/__2. Catch a ball tossed by a partner at different levels (high, medium, low).

__/__3. Manipulate various pieces of equipment. (e.g., hoops, wands, sticks)
Dribbling with the Hands
__/__1. Dribble a ball and change <u>direction</u> on cue.
__/__2. Dribble a ball and change <u>speed</u> (slow, medium, fast) on cue.

EYE-HAND COORDINATION WITH EXTENSIONS
Volleying
__/__Strike a lightweight ball (tossed by a partner) using a <u>forearm pass</u> (bump) to return the ball to partner.

BASIC EYE-FOOT COORDINATION
Kicking, Dribbling and Trapping
__/__1. Run and kick an incoming rolled ball.
__/__2. Use the inside and/or outside of each foot to dribble the ball.
__/__3. Dribble a ball safely while changing pathways and directions (straight, curved, zigzag, forward, sideways).
__/__4. Dribble and trap a ball in a boundaried area without losing control of the ball or colloiding with others.

STRIKING WITH AN IMPLEMENT
Striking with Short-Handled Implements
__/__1. Using a <u>forehand</u> motion, continuously strike a rebounding ball with a lightweight paddle or racket.

Striking with Long-Handled Implements
__/__1. Strike a ball off a tee with a bat.
__/__2. Travel slowly in different directions and dribble a variety of objects using a variety of long-handled implements.
__/__3. Strike a ball or puck along the ground to a stationary partner using a hockey stick.

CONDUCT AND EFFORT
(4 = Consistently, 3 = Frequently, 2 = Occasionally, 1 = Rarely)

Willingly participates; shows consideration of self, others, and equipment; listens and follows directions; stays on task.

NINE-WEEK AVERAGE

1st 9 wks.   2nd 9 wks.   3rd 9 wks.   4th 9 wks.

Student's Name _____

Classroom Teacher _____

Physical Education Teacher _____

School Year _____

Figure 14.18 Sample report card.

Source: Austin Independent School District, Austin, TX. Used with permission.

TEACHER OBSERVATION

Third Grade: Jumping and Landing

Student Names:	Jump and land from a medium level.	Jump a self-turned rope using at least three different foot. patterns.	Jump a self-turned rope forward and backward using double and single bounce landings.	Demonstrate correct rope turning using a self-turned and long rope.	
	Date:	Date:	Date:	Date:	Date:
	4 3 2 1	4 3 2 1	4 3 2 1	4 3 2 1	4 3 2 1
	4 3 2 1	4 3 2 1	4 3 2 1	4 3 2 1	4 3 2 1
	4 3 2 1	4 3 2 1	4 3 2 1	4 3 2 1	4 3 2 1
	4 3 2 1	4 3 2 1	4 3 2 1	4 3 2 1	4 3 2 1
	4 3 2 1	4 3 2 1	4 3 2 1	4 3 2 1	4 3 2 1
	4 3 2 1	4 3 2 1	4 3 2 1	4 3 2 1	4 3 2 1
	4 3 2 1	4 3 2 1	4 3 2 1	4 3 2 1	4 3 2 1
	4 3 2 1	4 3 2 1	4 3 2 1	4 3 2 1	4 3 2 1
	4 3 2 1	4 3 2 1	4 3 2 1	4 3 2 1	4 3 2 1
	4 3 2 1	4 3 2 1	4 3 2 1	4 3 2 1	4 3 2 1
	4 3 2 1	4 3 2 1	4 3 2 1	4 3 2 1	4 3 2 1
	4 3 2 1	4 3 2 1	4 3 2 1	4 3 2 1	4 3 2 1
	4 3 2 1	4 3 2 1	4 3 2 1	4 3 2 1	4 3 2 1
	4 3 2 1	4 3 2 1	4 3 2 1	4 3 2 1	4 3 2 1
	4 3 2 1	4 3 2 1	4 3 2 1	4 3 2 1	4 3 2 1
	4 3 2 1	4 3 2 1	4 3 2 1	4 3 2 1	4 3 2 1
	4 3 2 1	4 3 2 1	4 3 2 1	4 3 2 1	4 3 2 1
	4 3 2 1	4 3 2 1	4 3 2 1	4 3 2 1	4 3 2 1
	4 3 2 1	4 3 2 1	4 3 2 1	4 3 2 1	4 3 2 1
	4 3 2 1	4 3 2 1	4 3 2 1	4 3 2 1	4 3 2 1
	4 3 2 1	4 3 2 1	4 3 2 1	4 3 2 1	4 3 2 1
	4 3 2 1	4 3 2 1	4 3 2 1	4 3 2 1	4 3 2 1
	4 3 2 1	4 3 2 1	4 3 2 1	4 3 2 1	4 3 2 1
	4 3 2 1	4 3 2 1	4 3 2 1	4 3 2 1	4 3 2 1
	4 3 2 1	4 3 2 1	4 3 2 1	4 3 2 1	4 3 2 1
	4 3 2 1	4 3 2 1	4 3 2 1	4 3 2 1	4 3 2 1
	4 3 2 1	4 3 2 1	4 3 2 1	4 3 2 1	4 3 2 1
	4 3 2 1	4 3 2 1	4 3 2 1	4 3 2 1	4 3 2 1
	4 3 2 1	4 3 2 1	4 3 2 1	4 3 2 1	4 3 2 1
	CUES Controlled, bent knee Land on balls of feet	**CUES** Side to side, straddle, hop, skip, step, fast, running skip step, forward, backward	**CUES** Smooth, rhythmical jumping Keep elbows close to body Make small jumps Swing rope backward forward	**CUES** Elbows close to body Smooth turns Rhythmical (turn rope with large, smooth, swings)	**CUES**

Figure 14.19 Sample of a teacher observation.

Source: Austin Independent School District, Austin, TX. Used with permission.

**Physical Education
Grade Three
End-of-Year Report**

Child's Name _____ Homeroom _____

Listed below are the major themes of study for this semester. The following codes have been used in evaluating your child's progress in skill development:

(SP) Still Practicing–Children have been introduced to the skill. They cannot consistently demonstrate the skill or show very little understanding of the concept.
(S) Satisfactory–Children are making satisfactory progress in the development of the skill appropriate for third grade. Some errors still occur, but teacher correction is at a minimum.
(M) Mastery–Children demonstrate mastery of the skill or concept at the third grade level. They can apply the skill correctly and independently.

	SP	S	M
Skill: Jumping and Landing (Preparation for Gymnastics)			
Lands safely (knees bent, no crash landings)			
Combines jumps with turns and shapes in the air			
Jumps and lands safely off gymnastics apparatus			
Combines jumps with balances and/or rolls in a gymnastics sequence (see attached)			
Skill: Gymnastics			
Balances on different bases of support			
Maintains stillness in balances			
Works safely on gymnastics apparatus			
Creates a gymnastics sequence on chosen apparatus with an approach, balances, and dismounts from the apparatus (final project)			
Skill: Dance and Rhythms			
Demonstrates designated dance steps and movement patterns			
Performs dances representative of different cultures			
Skill: Dribbling and Shooting Baskets			
Dribbles and travels at moderate speed with control of ball and body			
Combines dribbling with traveling and shooting baskets for lay-ups			
Shooting set-shots as in basketball (self-evaluation attached)			
Skill: Striking with Rackets (Mini-Tennis)			
Skill: Jump Rope (see attached checklist)			

		SP	S	M
Overall Health-Related Fitness: (see attached report)	Serious Concern			
Overall Motor Skill Development:	Serious Concern	Satisfactory		Excellent

	Serious Concern	Needs Improvement	Satisfactory	Excellent
Daily Work Habits				
Listening				
Independent Task Completion				
Cooperative Work with Others				

Figure 14.20 Report card based on units of study. *Source:* From Shirley Holt/Hale. Used with permission.

Figure 14.21 Lambdin reporting system. Used with permission.

SAMPLE REPORT CARD

Essential for Good Health—A Physically Active Lifestyle

Child's Name _____   Class_____

I CAN   Physical Education Report
4th 6 week period 1993–94
Grade 4

Your child has rated his/her ability level in the space next to each skill. If my rating is different from your child's rating you will see my rating in GREEN. Please ask your child "What do these letters you wrote mean?" Hopefully you will get a thoughtful answer like, "I put L for learning because I can do that some of the time, but not all the time." If my rating is different you may also want to ask why s/he thinks they are different. There may be a very good reason. Encourage your child to think about what s/he needs to work on and celebrate new skills. Thanks, Dolly Lambdin

> B = Beginning—I can do it once in a while.
> L = Learning—I can do it most of the time—but I have to really think about it.
> M = Mastered—I can always do it—It is easy for me.
> P = Problems—I have problems with this.

In physical education we learn to move our bodies and objects with skill and confidence.

Short Rope Jumping Skills
____ Forward single bounce	____ Forward double bounce
____ Backward single bounce	____ Backward double bounce
____ Cross arms	____ Front to back
____ Skier	____ Jump, side swing, jump

Long Rope Jumping Skills   **Dance**
____ Jump	____ Belle Kawe
____ Run in and jump	

Body Management (Gymnastics)
____ Backward shoulder roll
____ Forward shoulder roll
____ Weight on hands and land lightly
____ Jump off bench and land lightly, bending knees
____ Perform a movement sequence

We encourage and support each other and make class a good place to learn.
____ I listen during instructions.	____ I move safely.
____ I follow the directions.	____ I am kind to others.
____ I do quality work.	____ I like to move.

- -

Thanks for reading this 4th report card. Have your child return this slip for a "playdough" treat.
Child's Name_____   Parent's Signature_____
Walk, jog, bike, EXERCISE with your children!!! Enjoy a healthy lifestyle.

---

assessment movement has meshed evaluation with instruction. The two are no longer separate entities but pieces of the same puzzle. Assessment is an ongoing process that occurs in every lesson, simply by the nature of the tasks students do. Assessment is instruction. Assessment is simply teaching well.

No instructor who teaches several hundred children each week—as many physical education instructors do—has time to use all the assessment techniques described in this chapter. But a reflective teacher is aware of these techniques and uses them with different classes for different purposes. Perhaps you'll have one class at a time keeping logs. And you may be able to send only one written report a year to parents.

Select from the various assessment techniques those that are most appropriate; each technique provides a different type of information. For example, journals provide fascinating insights into how children are progressing in designing their own games or dances, but a checklist would be far less appropriate for that purpose. In contrast, a checklist is useful for assessing children's individual abilities in a new situation—for example, for a class of kindergarten children or during a teacher's first year in a new school.

Even when you narrow the assessment options to be used with your classes, time can still be an issue. For example, it's counterproductive to assess one child while the others stand in line waiting their turn. There are at least four ways to minimize the waiting time for children during assessment:

1. Set up stations or learning centers (Chapter 13). Stay at one of the stations, and use that as the assessment station. If you plan to do this, be certain the children are familiar with the other stations so that you can devote most of your time to helping with the assessments rather than explaining procedures at the other stations.
2. Ask the classroom teacher (or another teacher, paraprofessional, parent, or high school student) to assist with the class. The assistant can either help some children while you work with the other children or supervise most of the class while you work with a few children at a time.
3. Videotape the children so that you can make your judgments about skill levels and progress during your planning time or after school.
4. Use a tape recorder as you teach, and use the class list as a guide for observing each child; then make comments about the child's ability level and improvement.

The recent surge of handheld computer assessment programs that you can use to download results into desktop computers makes assessment much less time-consuming. Many programs allow you to record "on the spot" children's scores and the results of assessment tasks and then enter them automatically into various record-keeping programs. These programs and computers have become much more affordable, accessible, and user-friendly. This information changes on almost a daily basis, but we suggest you check Bonnie Mohnsen's book, *Using Technology in Physical Education* (2001), or your district's technology department for more information on these programs.

Handheld computers could easily revolutionize assessment practices due to the reduction of paperwork and increased efficiency they provide. However, as indicated in the Chapter 4 box Technology in Fitness/Wellness Education, although we encourage the use of technology to enhance your physical education program, do not confuse the increased use of technology with effective teaching.

Summary

Assessment can be defined as determining if and to what extent a student can demonstrate, in context, his or her understanding and ability relative to identified standards of learning. This definition alludes to three critical elements: It includes a *performance* of learning in a *real setting* against *previously set standards.*

Assessment also provides a direct measure of teaching effectiveness. No longer is assessment an "end-of-the-unit thing"; now it is an ongoing process that happens on a daily basis in physical education classes. This type of assessment is known as *alternative assessment.* Alternative assessment is directly linked with instruction, not separated from it. In this way, instruction and assessment inform the whole learning process.

Many alternative assessment options exist. The ones we have chosen to focus on include journals, exit slips, homework, peer observation, event tasks, video/digital analysis, student drawings, student displays, teacher observation, self-assessment, and portfolios. These assessment options can be used to assess student learning, report progress to parents, and discover individual children's needs and interests. Progress reports to children's parents are the preferred mode of reporting student progress whenever feasible.

Reading Comprehension Questions

1. What is alternative assessment? How does it differ from traditional assessment modes?
2. What are the purposes of assessment in physical education?
3. What does it mean to tie assessment to instruction and the whole learning process?
4. What are five options available for alternative assessment?
5. What is the purpose of having children keep a journal? How does the journal differ from the other assessment options?
6. What are scoring rubrics? How do they work?

7. What is the difference between assessment and grading?

8. Select one of the reporting systems and provide an argument for using that system as opposed to the others. Imagine you are actually teaching as you write your answer.

9. Explain why assessment is necessary in children's physical education.

References/Suggested Readings

Andrade, H. (2000). Using rubrics to promote thinking and learning. *Educational Leadership, 57*(5), 13–19.

Block, M., Lieberman, L., & Connor-Kuntz, F. (1998). Authentic assessment in adapted physical education. *Journal of Physical Education, Recreation and Dance, 69*(3), 48–55.

Council on Physical Education for Children. (2000). *Appropriate practices for elementary physical education: A position statement of the National Association for Sport and Physical Education.* Reston, VA: National Association for Sport and Physical Education.

Cutforth, N., & Parker, M. (1996). Promoting affective development in physical education: The value of journal writing. *Journal of Physical Education, Recreation and Dance, 67*(7), 19–23.

Davies, A. (2000). Seeing the results for yourself: A portfolio primer. *Classroom Leadership, 3*(5), 4–5.

Entzion, B., Fairchild, M., Parker, M., Pemberton, C., Steen, T., Taylor, D., & Whitehead, J. (1991). *Super active kids program instructor's manual.* Unpublished manuscript, University of North Dakota at Grand Forks, Department of Health, Physical Education and Recreation.

Franklin, J. (2002, Spring). *Assessing assessment: Are alternative methods making the grade? Curriculum Update.* Alexandria, VA: Association for Supervision and Curriculum Development.

Gibbons, S., Robinson, B., Bruce, P., Bremen, K., Lundeen, L., Mouritzen, J., Perkins, J., Stogre, T., & Wejr, C. (2002). Using rubrics to support assessment and evaluation. *Strategies, 15*(4), 28–33.

Graham, G. (2001). *Teaching children physical education* (2nd ed.). Champaign, IL: Human Kinetics.

Graham, G., Metzler, M., & Webster, G. (1991). Specialist and classroom teacher effectiveness in children's physical education. *Journal of Teaching in Physical Education, 10*(4), 321–326.

Henderson, H., French, R., & Kinnison, L. (2001). Reporting grades for students with disabilities in general physical education. *Journal of Physical Education, Recreation and Dance, 72*(6), 50–55.

Hoerr, T. (2000). Reporting what we respect. *Classroom Leadership, 3*(5), 2–3.

Holt/Hale, S. (1999). *Assessing motor skills in elementary physical education.* Reston, VA: American Alliance for Health, Physical Education, Recreation and Dance.

Lambert, L. (1999). *Standards based assessment of student learning: A comprehensive approach.* Reston, VA: American Alliance for Health, Physical Education, Recreation and Dance.

Melograno, V. J. (1994). Portfolio assessment: Documenting authentic student learning. *Journal of Physical Education, Recreation and Dance, 65*(8), 50–61.

Mohnsen, B. (2001). *Using technology in physical education* (3rd ed.). Champaign, IL: Human Kinetics.

National Association for Sport and Physical Education. (1995). *Moving into the future: National standards for physical education.* St. Louis, MO: Mosby.

National Association for Sport and Physical Education. (2004). *Moving into the future: National standards for physical education* (2nd ed.). Reston, VA: National Association for Sport and Physical Education.

O'Sullivan, M., & Henninger, M. (2000). Assessing student responsibility and teamwork. *Journal of Physical Education, Recreation and Dance, 76*(6), 25–28.

Prusak, K., & Vincent, S. (2005). Is your class about something? Guiding principles for physical education teachers. *Journal of Physical Education, Recreation and Dance, 76*(6), 25–28.

Questioning our motives. (1996). *Education Update, Association for Supervision and Curriculum Development, 38*(4), 5.

Rink, J. (2006). *Teaching physical education for learning* (4th ed.). St. Louis, MO: McGraw-Hill.

Schiemer, S. (2000). *Assessment strategies for elementary physical education.* Champaign, IL: Human Kinetics.

Smith, M. A., & Claxton, D. B. (2003). Using active homework in physical education. *Journal of Physical Education, Recreation and Dance, 75*(5), 28–32.

Werner, P. (1997). Using PE Central and the National Standards to develop practical assessment instruments. *Teaching Elementary Physical Education, 8*(3), 12–14, 19.

Wiggins, G. (1993). *Assessing student performance.* San Francisco: Jossey-Bass.

Wilson, S., & Roof, K. (1999). Establishing a portfolio process for K–8 learners. *Teaching Elementary Physical Education, 10*(5), 10–14.

Wolf, D., & White, A. (2000). Charting the course of student growth. *Educational Leadership, 57*(5), 6–12.

Understanding Your Teaching

Of all the things teachers undertake, the most important, it seems to me, is doing the thinking of teaching or the reflecting about the complexities of their work . . . learning is continuous as reflective teachers engage in the work of thinking and doing . . . in this way, learning is central to teaching.

—Anna Richert

Key Concepts

- Reflection on teaching is an essential aspect of effective teaching.

- Regular and thoughtful strategies for reflection on teaching allow teachers to become more effective.

- Systematic observation is one way that teachers can reflect on their own teaching.

- Systematic observation allows a teacher to obtain clear and detailed information about various aspects of teaching.

- Unless there is a reflective purpose to systematic observation, it is useless.

- Systematic observation techniques include unassisted techniques, student-assisted techniques, and peer-assisted techniques.

- Collecting information on feedback and lesson content development are unassisted techniques.

- Student-assisted techniques that provide more observable information include such things as data on the pathways a teacher follows in class, interaction patterns with students, and the quantity of practice opportunities the students have.

- Peer-assisted techniques allow for still a higher level of detail and include the quality and quantity of practice opportunities and feedback, and the use of time in class.

- Observation techniques should be combined and designed to answer the questions that teachers generate based on their own reflection.

One implication of Chapter 5 is that teaching is an incredibly complex activity. As teachers we have to attend to a variety of influences including our experience as a teacher, the facilities in which we work, frequency of our class meetings, the number of students in our classes, attitudes of children toward physical education, our beliefs as a teacher, and the like. Beyond attending to these influences, the tasks that we perform are diverse. We have to choose content to teach, determine how to deliver it in the most meaningful way, deliver it to meet the needs of all learners, and assess the results. We have to interact with children, administrators, parents, custodians, and other teachers. We have to observe students, read student journals and portfolios, and assess their work. We have to comfort the fearful child and assure concerned parents. Additionally, we cultivate hope, coax curiosity, and celebrate success. This list of "jobs"

could go on and on, and as Locke (1975) indicates, it represents only a portion of what is necessary to do the work of good teaching. Yet, our job doesn't end here. Equally important as doing or attending to all these obligations is the thinking that is associated with doing them (Richert, 1995).

Some have asked us why we even include this chapter in *Children Moving*. It is precisely because this continuing to wonder, worry, and reflect on what is happening in their gymnasiums and classrooms and on their playgrounds is what separates effective from ineffective teachers. These teachers learn by inquiring into their practice. They think about their experiences in order to make sense of them. When faced with a situation for which there is no easy or certain answer, they engage in reflective inquiry. They gather as much information as possible about the situation that puzzles them, then scrutinize the information to determine how they will act in the future. Most often this process is informal—we all engage in it to some extent to answer the millions of questions we encounter in our work on a daily basis. Occasionally the process is more formal. Either way, it is this constant and ongoing process of reflection that provides the basis for learning in teaching. It is this process of learning in teaching that makes good teaching responsive to the uncertainties of the rapidly changing world of which it is a part (Richert, 1995).

Reflective teachers work to improve their teaching and the learning of their students throughout their teaching careers. Unfortunately, reflection and inquiry into teaching are left largely to the individual teacher. Historically, a number of informal (and in many cases inaccurate) approaches to obtaining information about teaching have been used. For example, an assessment based on how much the students like a teacher doesn't provide much useful information about that teacher's performance, nor does a principal's evaluation based on a five-minute, once-a-year visit to the gymnasium. Some student teachers receive feedback from their supervisors that is both helpful and accurate. Few teachers, however, continue to receive throughout their teaching careers the amount and type of feedback vital to improving teaching performance.

The notion that, upon certification, a teacher knows all there is to know about how and what to teach and requires little, if any, assistance is quickly being discredited (Stroot, 2001). In its place is growing acceptance of the belief that teachers, if they are to progress in their teaching, can benefit from reflection, guidance, and assistance. Although some school districts provide mentors for beginning teachers, few arrange for ongoing assistance and development opportunities throughout the teaching years. This chapter provides some strategies and techniques for reflecting on your teaching to make it congruent with your beliefs about school, children, physical education, and learning. Chapter 12 provided you with techniques to allow you to "see" your students; this chapter will allow you to "see" yourself. We will provide you with systematic observation and written tools you can use by yourself, tools children can help you with, and then tools that require the assistance of other adults. All of these can and should be adapted to your own needs and situation to allow you to reflect on your own teaching.

> *Elementary school physical education teachers have been observed who clocked as little as three and a half minutes of significant face-to-face contact with other adults between the hours of 7:30 A.M. and 4:30 P.M. The teacher can be psychologically alone in a densely populated world. The physical (architectural) isolation of the gym located away from the political heartland of the school and the social isolation of the physical educator role, which may make the teacher peripheral to the real business of the school, both seem to sustain and intensify the feelings of isolation. Teaching physical education in some schools is a lonely job, awash in an endless sea of children.*
>
> —LARRY LOCKE, "The Ecology of the Gymnasium: What the Tourist Never Sees"

Self-Reflection

Housner (1996) suggests that ongoing reflection regarding one's knowledge, beliefs, instructional practices, and teaching effectiveness is essential to ongoing professional growth. Self-reflection allows a teacher to contemplate and act upon the struggles and successes encountered in teaching (Stroot & Whipple, 2003). Self-reflection can be accomplished through a journal or an audiotaped log—or some other method of maintaining a record of thoughts and reflections. Regardless of how self-reflection is accomplished, there are two keys to its success. First, be consistent with it. Set a time frame for self-reflection. It might be daily, biweekly, or weekly. But regardless of the time period you choose, do it consistently. Second, whether your reflection is written or verbal, review it periodically. These reflections often lead teachers to identify concerns and begin to think about how to reduce problems and enhance the learning environment. When specific concerns are identified or interests arise, systematic observation can be employed to obtain more formal and reliable information.

Systematic Observation

Consistent self-reflection allows us to determine points of exploration about our teaching; systematic observation allow us to obtain more objective information about those points. Again, in view of the usual lack of assistance teachers receive, many of the techniques we include in this chapter can be carried out on your own or with the assistance of another teacher, a videotape, or an "untrained" observer.

Getting Started

Regardless of who is collecting the information about your teaching, the most important aspect is deciding what teaching action to look at or target. Although it may seem as if we are stating the obvious, we have seen more than one teacher collect information about their teaching without having a clear purpose. These "targets" may stem directly from your self-reflection or from the variables that have been shown to be related to effective teaching (Silverman & Ennis, 2003). Box 15-1 enumerates some of the actions, gleaned from research on teaching, of effective teachers. Earlier we

Box 15-1

Actions of Effective Teachers

Research has shown that effective teachers—whether classroom or physical education teachers—share similar behaviors. Effective teachers:

- Give students time to learn by devoting a high percentage of time to the academic subject.
- Communicate high, yet realistic, expectations for students.
- Establish routines and organizational structures that lead to a positive classroom management climate.
- Present meaningful and challenging tasks in which students are highly successful.
- Move the class forward with determined direction.
- Communicate the content clearly and hold students accountable for completing tasks.
- Assess students' skill progress closely and change practice to fit students' needs.
- Communicate warmth through clear, enthusiastic presentations.

Source: "Improving Your Teaching through Self-Evaluation" by B. Cusimano, P. Darst, & H. van der Mars, 1993, October, *Strategies*, p. 28. Used with permission.

Box 15-2

Determining What to Observe

If you're having problems with inappropriate behavior, select one or more of the following:

1. Look at your plans for potential breakdowns.
2. Transcribe all your instructions to the class, and check for clarity. Did you know what was supposed to happen? Did you mix the organizational and content portions of your instruction?
3. Videotape a lesson to analyze your time. Was there an extreme amount of management time? Waiting time?
4. Record your feedback. Did you handle inappropriate behavior promptly and consistently, or did you nag often?

To check the atmosphere of your class, do one or more of the following:

1. Tally your feedback. Was there a large percentage of negative feedback?
2. Check student interaction patterns. Did you favor one group over another?

To assess the instructional environment, select from the following:

1. Check your task development. Did you disperse challenges throughout the lesson or only at the end?
2. Assess each student's practice opportunities. Did children have lots of practice chances?
3. Check the general use of class time.
4. Tally feedback with specific attention to skill feedback.

Ways to analyze your answers to these questions and obtain some helpful insights are discussed in the remainder of the chapter.

stated that establishing a learning environment is a necessary but not sufficient condition for student learning and that the class environment indicates what you believed about children and physical education. Therefore, if nothing else seems to fit, determining whether you have set up a learning environment and what that environment is like may be a good place to start. The checklists in Box 15-2 can help you decide what to look for, based on your questions about teaching.

Unassisted Techniques

You can learn much about your teaching without relying on others for observation, interpretation, or analysis. You can learn, for example, the amount of time you spend actually talking to the entire class or to individuals within a class. You can discover which children receive most of your attention and whether you spend more time discussing their movement or their behavior. How do children react to your teaching performance? How, and how often, do you use positive or negative comments? How much time do the children spend getting out or putting away equipment? You can answer these and other key questions with self-assessment techniques.

Tape-Recording for Self-Analysis   One simple technique for analyzing your teaching performance is to tape-record your verbal interactions and instruction. You can strap or tape a microcassette recorder to your arm while teaching, or belt a recorder around your waist. These methods allow you to record both interactions with individual children and instructions to the whole class. The children quickly become accustomed to seeing the tape recorder, and before long they forget about it. By taping different classes, you can obtain answers to such important questions as these:

- What percentage of a lesson did I spend talking to the entire class? To groups? To individuals?
- Are my verbal comments clear? Do I repeat myself frequently?
- What percentage of my comments to the children are positive? Negative? Neutral? Do I nag children?
- Do I interact with many children in a class? Or do I focus on just a few, constantly calling their names?
- How do I develop the lesson content?

These and many other questions can be answered by making tape recordings. Finding the answers involves defining what you want to assess, listening to the tape, tallying the number of times each behavior occurs or recording the length of time something occurs, and then determining percentages.

Feedback Analysis   Feedback, the information the teacher provides to individual or small groups of children about the quality of their movement or behavior, based on observation, is one aspect of teaching that can be analyzed from an audiotape. (An analysis can be made from a videotape only if you have a cordless microphone that permits you to hear your individual interactions with children. The microphone on most videocameras is unable to pick up teacher–child interactions in the relatively noisy environment of a playground or gym.)

The teacher feedback form (Figure 15.1) allows you to analyze your feedback by tallying each comment you make to children. Depending on the lesson and your interest, you may simply want to total the amount

Teacher Feedback

Teacher: _____ Date: _____
Grade/Activity: _____ # of Pupils: _____
Start time: _____ End time: _____ Elapsed time: _____

FEEDBACK	BEHAVIOR FEEDBACK		SKILL FEEDBACK				
	Praise	Scold	Positive	Corrective	Negative	Congruent	Incongruent
Specific							
General							
Total							
Rate/Minute							

Rate/Minute _____ _____ _____ _____ _____ _____ _____
COMMENTS:

Figure 15.1 Teacher feedback form.

and type of feedback you give to children. You may also want to determine which children receive your feedback—and what type of feedback they receive. If you want to analyze total feedback, simply tally each statement, placing it in one of the categories defined below. (If you want to analyze feedback to individual children, see the discussion of Figure 15.6 later.)

There are several categories on the teacher feedback form (Figure 15.1). You may want to use all of them or just one or two. Your first choice is specific versus general feedback.

Specific feedback has to do either with the child's skill or with the child's behavior. If, however, there is no way for the child to tell (based just on the statement) whether the comment is about skill or behavior, the feedback is general. "Good" is probably the most common general feedback statement heard in physical education lessons, followed closely by "OK." If the feedback is specific, the next step is to deter-

mine whether it is about skill (movement) or behavior. Then, ask yourself whether the child to whom the comments were provided would perceive them as positive, corrective, or negative. In addition, you may want to determine whether the feedback was congruent or incongruent with the cues of the lesson—specifically, with what you asked the children to think about when you last gave instruction. Congruent feedback relates directly to what you said immediately before the children began their activity. Incongruent feedback, in contrast, might be about something the children were never told or hadn't been reminded of for several weeks. (Note that if you code congruent/incongruent feedback, it will be a "double tally" in a row. One for positive, corrective, or negative and one for congruent/incongruent.) This sounds complicated, but as the process is broken down it will become easier. A number of examples are provided to show you how the checklist works.

Assume the children are practicing striking with paddles (Chapter 27) and the teacher is focusing on teaching them to turn their sides to the target so that they can swing more efficiently. The following are examples of feedback and the way each statement would be coded on the teacher feedback form:

- "Marilyn, that swing was great! You really turned your side to the target." (Specific, Skill, Positive, Congruent)
- "Terrific." (General, Positive)
- "Mark, remember to keep your eye on the ball." (Specific, Skill, Corrective, Incongruent)
- "Christine, stay in your own space." (Specific, Behavior, Scold)
- "Kakki, way to keep your side to the target." (Specific, Skill, Positive, Congruent)
- "Good side, Rosie." (Specific, Skill, Positive, Congruent)
- "Austin, that's wrong." (General, Negative)
- "Side, Steve." (Specific, Skill, Corrective, Congruent)
- "Juan, you are facing the target; don't do that." (Specific, Skill, Negative, Congruent)

When you tally your various feedback statements, you will have a profile that lets you know what type of feedback you tend to give. Additionally, you can determine a feedback rate per minute by dividing the total number of statements into the elapsed time to find out how much feedback you give. Don't worry if your pattern doesn't initially appear as you would like it to be—after all, anything we do takes practice. The good news is that adjusting feedback is relatively easy (van der Mars, 1987).

Lesson Content Another useful type of information you can collect from audio- or videotape is how you develop the content of the lesson when you teach. As described in Chapter 11, there are three categories of information you may wish to collect regarding your lessons: the tasks you give the children, the cues you provide, and the challenges you offer. The tasks are the activities you actually ask the students to do. Examples might be asking the children to bounce a ball in self-space or to bounce a ball while traveling in general space. Cues, or critical elements, are the hints you provide the children to help them perform the task more effectively or correctly. Examples would be "finger pads" and "bend your knees." Cues always seek to improve the quality of the student performance and are listed at the beginning of each task segment in the skill theme chapters. Challenges shift the focus to using the skill in a more demanding or testing situation. These are most often self-testing or competitive situations.

Figure 15.2 is a graph for determining how content is developed in a lesson. Before using it, listen to your tape and write down, in order, every task, cue, and challenge presented during the class session. Then categorize each as a task, cue, or challenge. (For this project, record only tasks, cues, or challenges that are given to the entire class, not feedback or suggestions that are given to individual students.)

After you have labeled the tasks, cues, and challenges, plot them on the graph in the order in which they occurred. Once you have finished, you will have a picture of how your lesson progressed. Although there is no "perfect" pattern of content development, a good rule of thumb is that the graph should reflect a zigzag pattern and not steps. The use of tasks, cues, and challenges should be mixed across the lesson rather than practice, practice, practice, game. This mix allows children to progressively develop their skills while staying motivated and focused.

Student-Assisted Techniques

Mature, responsible students can occasionally help you assess your teaching performance by using techniques they can learn in just a few minutes. These methods can provide information that cannot be obtained by the unassisted techniques.

Teacher Pathway Give the student a sketch of the teaching area—the gym or playground (Figure 15.3). Have the student trace the pathways that you make during the lesson. This is especially helpful when you're learning to increase your effectiveness as an observer (Chapter 12). You can also teach the student to make a mark on the pathway each time you interact individually with a child.

Interaction Patterns It's important to interact, verbally or nonverbally, with each child during each lesson. You can use an interaction checklist (Figure 15.4) to obtain information about your patterns of interaction with an entire class.

Select a student who knows the names of all the children in the class. Give that student a checklist on which you've listed the names of the entire class. The student can then make a tally, in the appropriate column, across from the name of each child you talk to, touch, or smile at during one class period. At the conclusion of the lesson, you can use the completed checklist to analyze your teaching pattern.

If you analyze data on a larger level, you may be able to determine whether there's a disparity in your interactions with different groups of children. Are you

CONTENT DEVELOPMENT

TEACHER: _____ DATE: _____ GRADE: _____ NO. OF STUDENTS: _____

Directions: Write down, in order, the statements made to the entire class about motor skills. At times you may need to leave out a few words, but try to get down the intent of the statement. After the lesson is over, classify each statement as a task, cue, or challenge, and then graph the statements in the order they occurred. Use the back of the sheet if necessary.

1.

2.

3.

4.

5.

6.

7.

8.

9.

10.

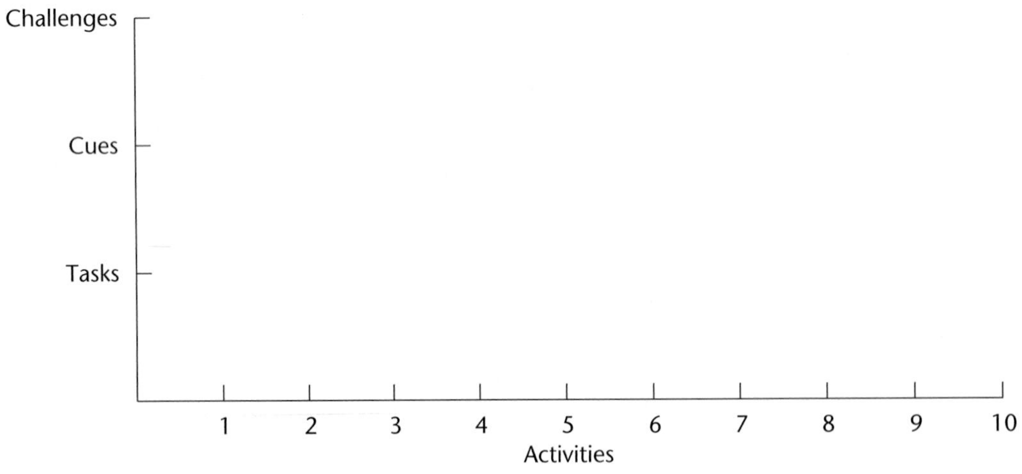

Challenges ⊢

Cues ⊢

Tasks ⊢

            1   2   3   4   5   6   7   8   9   10

                          Activities

Definitions:

    Tasks: Activities that present the skill to be practiced

    Cues: Words that focus on the critical elements of the skill

    Challenges: Self-testing or competitive experiences

Analysis: Number of tasks, cues, or challenges/Total number of activities = %

_____ % tasks

_____ % cues

_____ % challenges

Figure 15.2 Content development graph.

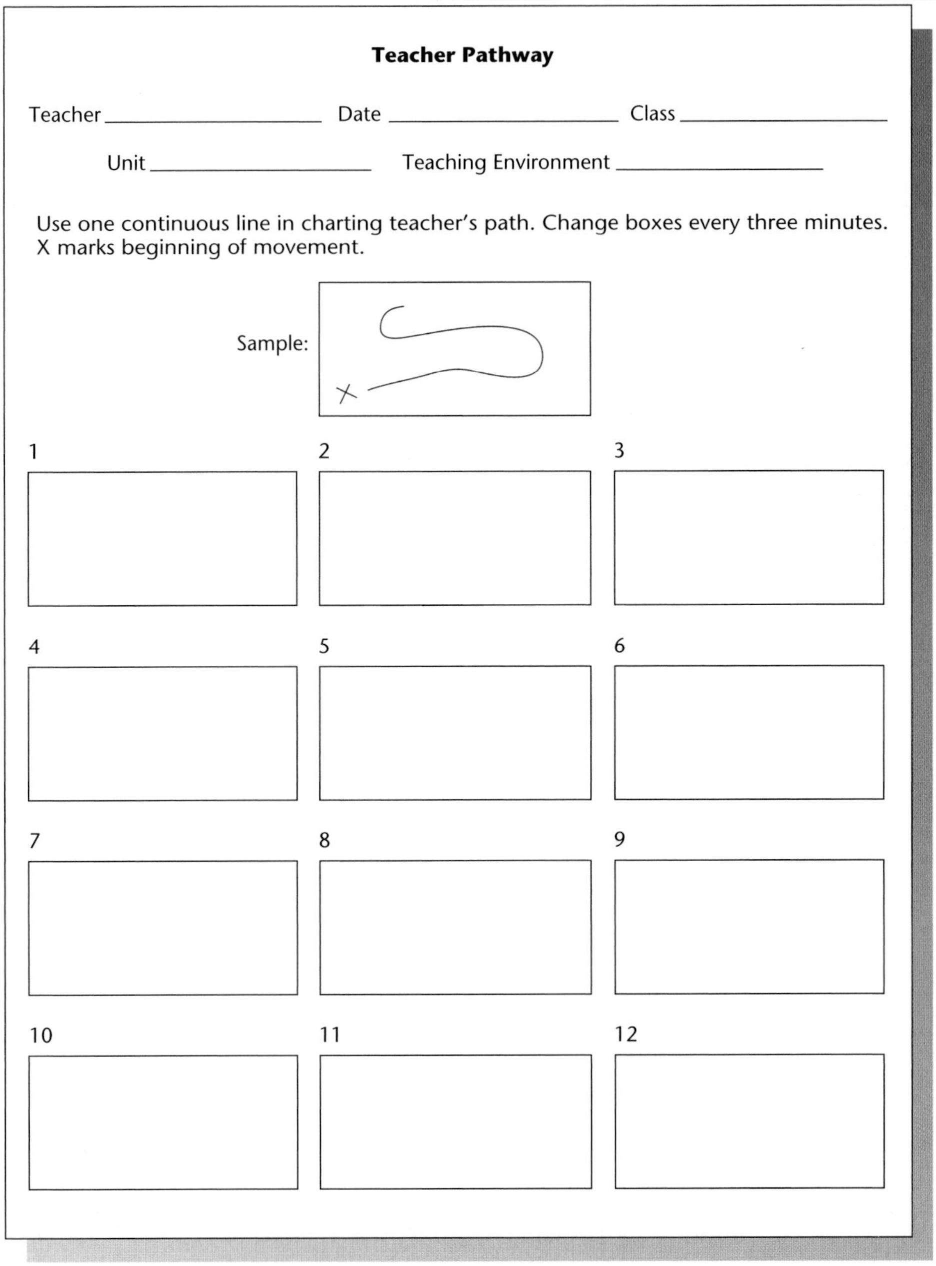

Teacher Pathway

Teacher _____   Date _____   Class _____

Unit _____   Teaching Environment _____

Use one continuous line in charting teacher's path. Change boxes every three minutes. X marks beginning of movement.

Sample:

1

2

3

4

5

6

7

8

9

10

11

12

Figure 15.3 Teacher pathway observation.

interacting more with the most-skilled children than with the least-skilled ones? Are you interacting with boys more than girls? Are you interacting with one race more than the others? Or do the interaction patterns indicate some other distribution of attention? Again, you can use the information on an interaction checklist that a student has filled in. For example, identify a most-skilled and a least-skilled group—each group should include about 25 percent of the class. From an analysis of the interactions with each group and a comparison of these two interaction patterns, you determine the group to which you are devoting more time.

Practice Opportunities Effective teachers give children plenty of practice opportunities. One way to indirectly assess the number of practice opportunities students are getting in a class is to teach a student helper to observe and record the number of practices for selected students (Figure 15.5). You may want to select the children to be observed, or the student helper can select two or more children to observe. This

Figure 15.4 Interaction checklist.

INTERACTION CHECKLIST

Teacher Observed: _____ Date: _____
Start Time: _____ End Time: _____

Student's Name	Types of Interaction			
	Talked To	Smiled At	Touched	Total
Nick	||		|	3
Tom	|||	|		4
Carlos	||			2
Melinda		|		1
Abbey	|||||		||	7
Total Interactions	12	2	3	17

COMMENTS:

technique works best when the lesson focuses on discrete skills, such as rolls, catches, or kicks, that can be written on the form before the lesson.

Peer-Assisted Techniques

Some children could learn to use the data-gathering systems described below, but it's more realistic to seek the assistance of a colleague who's willing to help you assess your teaching performance. Such an arrangement can be mutually beneficial, because the systems described in this section can be easily adapted for use in a classroom setting. Thus, if there's only one physical education specialist in the school, a classroom teacher could work as peer assistant with the specialist.

Practice Opportunities and Feedback Checklist This system goes a bit further than the practice opportunities checklist (Figure 15.5) and the teacher feedback form (Figure 15.1) described in the previous sections. Using the form shown in Figure 15.6, a colleague selects several children without your knowledge and records their practice opportunities. By circling successful attempts, quality can be determined. She also codes feedback statements you make to the students being observed. Each statement is coded as related to the child's movement or behavior, and each statement is coded as positive or negative when possible. Neutral statements are not recorded under the behavior heading.

The statement "Nice catch, Carmelita" would be

Date _____

Teacher _____ Observer _____
Theme of Lesson _____

OBSERVATIONAL DATA

Practice Opportunities

Name of Child	ROLL	CATCH	KICK	THROW

Figure 15.5 Practice opportunities checklist.

coded on the checklist as Movement, Positive. The statement "Jeff, you never listen!" would be coded as Behavior, Negative. This observation system is relatively simple to learn and can be used reliably after just a few minutes of practice.

Duration Recording System Duration recording allows you to see how you use time within your physical education class. It provides a look at what students are actually doing and for how long. This system, which is a bit more difficult to use than the teacher feedback form, divides the use of time in class into four categories: (1) instruction time, (2) management time, (3) activity time, and (4) waiting time. The total amount of time, in minutes and seconds, is determined for each of the

four categories, allowing the teacher to see how the class spent its time. Minutes and seconds can be converted into percentages, so that you can compare one lesson with another.

The duration recording form (Figure 15.7) contains five time bars, each representing seven minutes, tick-marked in 15-second increments. The form defines the codes the peer assistant should use to report what is happening: A for activity, I for instruction, M for management, and W for waiting. The peer assistant records the exact time the lesson begins—the time at which the children enter the gym or playground. (Alternatively, you can analyze a videotaped lesson.) From that moment until the end of the lesson, the peer assistant, using a watch that allows for the

Figure 15.6 Practice opportunities and teacher feedback checklist.

Teacher _WANDA_ Observer _JUDY_ Date _FEBRUARY 12_

Theme of Lesson _KICKING AND CATCHING_

OBSERVATIONAL DATA

Name of Child	Practice Opportunities			Teacher Feedback			
				MOVEMENT		BEHAVIOR	
	KICKS	CATCHES		POSITIVE	NEGATIVE	POSITIVE	NEGATIVE
MARK	ЖЖ ЖЖ IIII	ЖЖ IIII		II	I	II	
CARMELITA	ЖЖ II	III		IIII		II	
TODD	ЖЖ ЖЖ ЖЖ ЖЖ	ЖЖ ЖЖ ЖЖ III		III		I	I
JEFF	I ЖЖ ЖЖ	ЖЖ ЖЖ			ЖЖ	I	III
SUSIE	ЖЖ ЖЖ ЖЖ III	ЖЖ ЖЖ II		III	I	II	I

determination of seconds, marks the time bars to reflect what is happening in the class. When there is a change in student behavior, the assistant indicates the change by writing the appropriate letter in the next space on the bar. At the end of the lesson, the time is recorded. The peer assistant uses the definitions and examples in Table 15.1 as guides to accurate coding. It is important to remember to code what 51 percent (or more than half) of the students are doing and to code what is happening for the majority of the segment. So, if only 10 of 25 students are active or if 15 students are active but only for 5 seconds of the 15-second segment, a W would be recorded (if the students are waiting for a turn).

After the lesson, the teacher uses the information on the duration recording form to calculate what percentage of class time was spent in each category. The following procedure should be used: Add up the seconds for each of the four categories. Divide each category total by the total lesson time in seconds, and then multiply each by 100. The calculations at the bottom of Figure 15.7 illustrate how the percentages for that sample lesson were determined.

In the beginning, the peer assistant may be uncertain about how to code a particular event. This is not uncommon when one is learning to use any type of analysis system. The assistant should make a decision and then code other such events the

Table 15.1 Coding Guide for the Duration Recording System

Category	Definition	Examples
Activity Practice	Time when most students (51 percent or more) are involved in physical movement consistent with the specific goals of the particular lesson.	Performing exercises; designing a game, dance, or gymnastic sequence; participating in a group or individual game; providing assistance for a partner
Instruction	Time when students have an opportunity to learn. They may be receiving verbal or nonverbal information. Most students (51 percent or more) are *not* engaged in physical activity.	Listening to a lecture, watching the teacher or another student demonstrate a skill, participating in a class discussion, answering teacher's questions
Management	Time when the opportunity to learn is *not* present. Most students (51 percent or more) are involved in activities only indirectly related to class learning activity. There is no instruction, demonstration, or practice.	Changing activities, numbering off for an activity, listening for roll call, getting out or putting away equipment, getting into line
Waiting	Time not defined by the other three categories.	Waiting for class to begin, or waiting for instruction to resume when it has been interrupted by another teacher, student messenger, parent, principal, or public address system; waiting in line for a turn

Figure 15.7 Duration recording form.

LEARNING TIME ANALYSIS

Teacher: _____ Grade/Activity: _____
Coder: _____ Date: _____ # of Students: _____

TIMELINE

Codes: Activity = A   Instruction = I   Management = M   Waiting = W

Time Analysis: No. of intervals × 15 seconds = 56 × 15 = 840 (total lesson time in seconds)

Total Lesson Time

M = 8 × 15 = 120/840 = 14%   A = 33 × 15 = 495/840 = 59%

I = 12 × 15 = 180/840 = 21%   W = 3 × 15 = 45/840 = 5%

Note: Percentages don't equal 100 due to rounding.

COMMENTS:

During instructional time, the opportunity to learn is present, but the students aren't active.

same way. That will enable you to compare a succession of lessons to determine what progress you're making.

Combining and Adapting Techniques

Many observation systems have been developed to analyze the teaching performance of physical education teachers (Darst et al., 1989; Rink, 2006; Siedentop & Tannehill, 2000). The preceding examples have all been about "standard" effective teaching constructs. They may or may not fit your needs, as presented. You need to make the technique yours. You can do this in a number of ways. First, you can combine instruments and begin to code teacher and student behavior simultaneously—for example, how many students are off task at a particular moment or how many positive and negative feedback statements you make.

Second, you can develop your own coding instrument based on your environment and particular needs. For most of the questions you want to ask about your teaching, you can develop similar, uncomplicated systems that will give you the specific information you want to know. The secret to developing such systems is to define the behavior (what you want to observe or listen to) very precisely so that you can tell when it does and doesn't happen. It doesn't help very much to say, "I want to find out if I was clear or not when I talked to students"; you need to define what "clear" means to you. It could mean that students didn't have to ask you questions about how to do a task after you gave the task; it could mean that you didn't mumble and slur your words when you gave a task;

or it could mean that you didn't have to turn the tape recorder up to 9 to be able to hear yourself. Whatever it is, define it, and then try to assess it by listening to your tape.

Once you've obtained baseline data about your teaching performance, you can measure improvement over a period of weeks or months. You may find it challenging to set teaching goals for yourself: "During this class I want to interact at least once with every child in the class," or "During this class I want to make at least 80 percent of my comments positive." When you listen to a tape after a class, you'll learn whether you've achieved your goal. Remember that what is measured or how it is measured is less important than the continuing effort to systematically assess and improve your teaching performance. Relying on your subjective judgment ("I think I'm getting better") or that of a colleague ("That lesson looked good") is not nearly as effective as collecting and analyzing relatively objective data that you can refer back to in a few days, months, or even years.

Being Observed

Because many of us are reluctant to be observed while we teach, it may be less threatening to begin your assessment process with the unassisted or student-assisted techniques. When you've progressed to the point where you want more complex data and can no longer use students to help obtain data, be thoughtful about whom you ask to observe you. We've found it easier and more comfortable to use a colleague who is a friend and nonjudgmental, someone you're will-

Waiting time can include the minutes when students are waiting in line for their turn with an activity.

During activity time, the children are involved in movement that is consistent with the teacher's goals.

ing to expose both your good points and weaknesses to. For most of us, it takes a while to build up to this point—take it slowly.

Always remember that you're obtaining this information to help improve your teaching. The information is yours to do with as you wish; no one else needs to see it unless you want them to. When viewed this way, assessing your teaching performance can be interesting and challenging, not threatening (Hellison & Templin, 1991).

Written Instruments

A written instrument, completed by the children, can provide information about how students perceive your teaching. The children can circle appropriate faces (Figure 15.8) to indicate their responses. You can hand out the answer sheets and then read the questions to the whole class. When you read the questions to the entire class, you minimize reliance on children's ability to read.

DIRECTIONS: Circle the face that best describes your teacher for each statement.

My teacher gives me good directions.

My teacher will repeat his or her directions if someone misunderstands them.

My teacher gives me a second chance to learn what I need to learn if I didn't the first time.

My teacher talks to me politely and wants me to do the same to him or her and my classmates.

My teacher makes me behave.

My teacher calls on me or my classmates by name.

My teacher keeps me working during the entire class.

Figure 15.8 Form for assessing student reaction to teaching performance.

Be careful in interpreting the results of such an instrument, and remember that it is only one of many techniques that can be used to obtain information about your teaching performance. Judiciously employed, however, such an instrument can provide valuable insights about the children's reaction to your teaching.

Linking and Finding Out More

Equally as important as collecting data is knowing what you want to collect data about. The data about your teaching should link directly to what you want to know about teaching, and the ability to collect such data comes from reflection on your teaching situation and goals. It is useless to collect data just for the sake of collecting data.

The observation and reflection techniques just discussed are based to a large degree on information from research on teaching—the things that have been found to affect student learning of skills. Many teachers may want to find out more—they may desire to know if their teaching is successfully accomplishing the student learning they desire. To find this out, you will want to use the alternative assessment options discussed in Chapter 14 and found throughout the skill theme chapters. If you consistently find that students do not learn what you intend them to, then you may

The time taken to retrieve equipment is considered management.

want to use some of the techniques outlined in this chapter to try to discover if some of the basic constructs of effective teaching are not aligned in your teaching the way you want them to be.

Additionally, many of the techniques discussed in this chapter deal largely with student learning of psychomotor and cognitive goals (e.g., activity time relates directly to the learning of psychomotor goals). If you have affective and cognitive goals in your lesson, you may want to revise these instruments or devise others that allow you to discover how much time you are spending with these goals. Again, a number of teachers have found that keeping a teacher journal, much like a diary, allows them to look back on their own teaching over time and provides revealing insights into the nature of their work. The important point to remember is to reflect on your own teaching in an effort to continually find ways to enhance student learning. Employing systematic observation without the purpose of improving teaching to improve learning is a fruitless, time-consuming undertaking that often produces only defensive behavior.

Support Groups

The techniques described for analyzing one's teaching are effective approaches to improving performance. But successful teaching is more than using specific teaching behaviors in predetermined ways. Teaching can never be totally reduced to specific formulas of behavior that guarantee success for all teachers with all classes (Hellison & Templin, 1991; Schon, 1987). However, systematic observation can help answer some questions

and provide information that can influence a teacher's success. Other questions require careful thought and analysis, and cannot be answered solely by systematic observation. Sometimes we need to sit down with colleagues who'll listen carefully and help us understand (analyze) a particular situation. This is what a support group does. Teachers form support groups to build helping relationships between two or more individuals who've learned to trust one another. These individuals share their concerns, questions, dreams, and hopes about themselves as teachers.

If you're not careful, teaching can be a lonely and difficult profession. As a poster depicting an exhausted teacher at the end of an obviously difficult day reminds us: "No one ever said teaching was going to be easy." When your teaching isn't going well, or when you've had a spectacular day, a support group can provide comfort and encouragement or share your excitement. It's reassuring to have a stable group of colleagues who'll listen carefully, verbally applaud your successes, and help you analyze your concerns.

Most teachers occasionally complain about teaching conditions, parents, administrators, or fellow teachers. We all have our down days. Within a support group, however, complaining is inappropriate because it's often toxic and tends to contaminate the thinking of others. A support group is designed to make people feel better about their teaching, not worse.

Teaching will never be an exact, predictable science. There will always be some art to teaching effectively. Self-reflection, systematic observation techniques, and support groups are three approaches to improving both teaching performance and one's personal satisfaction and enthusiasm for teaching.

Summary

Teaching is a developmental process. Because effective teaching involves learning, it is a continuous, lifelong process. Teachers who want to become more effective can use various techniques to reflect on their teaching. These techniques, which include self-reflection and systematic observation, are classified into three categories: (1) unassisted, (2) student-assisted, and (3) peer-assisted.

When no one is available to help, teachers can use written instruments and videotape or audiotape to obtain information about teaching performance. A teacher's pathways, interaction patterns, and the number of practice opportunities given to children can be documented with student assistance. A peer can provide even more technical information by using a feedback and practice opportunities checklist or a duration recording system.

A very different but equally valuable aid is the support group. Such a group, made up of fellow teachers, can provide comfort and encouragement for all participants. When a group of peers actively listens to each other's questions and helps clarify each other's thoughts, the teaching attitude of all the members is improved.

Reading Comprehension Questions

1. Why is this chapter included in *Children Moving?* What is the value of self-reflection?
2. Identify two reflective techniques you can use by yourself. What information can you obtain from each technique?
3. When would you want to use written instruments?
4. What is the use of knowing the pathway you traveled during class?
5. What kind of analysis can you make from student–teacher interactions?
6. How does the combined feedback and practice opportunities checklist (Figure 15.6) work?
7. What is duration recording? What categories does it contain? How is each category defined? How does a duration recording system work?
8. Why is the use of systematic observation without a clear purpose of improving teaching to improve student learning counterproductive?
9. What are support groups? What is their value?

References/Suggested Readings

Cusimano, B., Darst, P., & van der Mars, H. (1993, October). Improving your teaching through self-evaluation. *Strategies,* 26–29.

Darst, P. W., Zakrajsek, D. B., & Mancini, V. H. (eds.). (1989). *Analyzing physical education and sport instruction.* Champaign, IL: Human Kinetics.

Hellison, D., & Templin, T. (1991). *A reflective approach to teaching physical education.* Champaign, IL: Human Kinetics.

Housner, L. (1996). Innovation and change in physical education. In S. Silverman & C. Ennis (eds.), *Student learning in physical education: Applying research to enhance instruction* (pp. 367–389). Champaign, IL: Human Kinetics.

Locke, L. F. (1975, Spring). The ecology of the gymnasium: What the tourist never sees. *Southern Association of Physical Education for College Women Proceedings,* 38–50.

Richert, A. (1995). Introduction. In T. Russell & F. Korthagen (eds.), *Teachers who teach teachers: Reflections on teacher education* (pp. 1–7). London: Falmer Press.

Rink, J. (2006). *Teaching physical education for learning* (5th ed.). St. Louis, MO: Mosby.

Schon, D. A. (1987). *Educating the reflective practitioner.* San Francisco: Jossey-Bass.

Siedentop, D., & Tannehill, D. (2000). *Developing teaching skills in physical education* (4th ed.). New York: McGraw-Hill.

Silverman, S., & Ennis, C. (2003). *Student learning in physical education: Applying research to enhance instruction* (2nd ed.). Champaign, IL: Human Kinetics.

Stroot, S. (2001, March). Once I graduate, am I an expert? *Teaching Elementary Physical Education, 12*(2), 18–20.

Stroot, S. & Whipple, C. (2003). Organizational socialization: Factors impacting beginning teachers. In S. Silverman & C. Ennis (eds.), *Student learning in physical education: Applying research to enhance instruction* (2nd ed.) (pp. 311–328). Champaign, IL: Human Kinetics.

van der Mars, H. (1987). Effects of audiocueing of teacher verbal praise on students' managerial and transitional task performance. *Journal of Teaching in Physical Education, 66*(1), 48–59.

Lauren Cunningham

Movement Concepts Defined

The three chapters in Part 3 explain the concepts of space awareness (Chapter 16), effort (Chapter 17), and relationships (Chapter 18) and present ideas for teaching them to children. Because these are concepts rather than actual skills, levels of skill proficiency are not discussed. As children study space awareness, effort, and relationships, they learn to demonstrate, through movement, their understanding of the meaning of each concept. You will find many activities for each of the concepts. As a reflective teacher, you will want to make decisions about which tasks will best meet the needs of your students and assist them in gaining a functional understanding of the concepts. The range of activities suggested provides a breadth of experiences related to each concept. Once children have acquired this functional understanding, the concept is used primarily as a subfocus—or an adverb—to enhance the range and quality of skill development that result from the study of the various skill themes (Part 4).

Suggested tasks are designated with the symbol **T**; challenges are designated with the symbol **C**; tasks and challenges were described in Chapter 11. In addition, you will also find suggested assessments (Chapter 14) to help you determine how well the children are understanding the concepts.

When teaching the concepts it's easy to forget that the purpose is to have the children actually *know* what each concept means. Imagine that one of us is going to teach a class of your second graders. Before teaching, we might ask whether your children know the space awareness concepts. If you say yes, we'd assume that the children can show movement of body parts and total body in self- and, or general space when asked to do so. Or we'd assume the children can travel in straight, curved, and zigzag pathways and that they can move body parts at high, medium, and low levels. "Knowing" doesn't mean that the concepts were taught; knowing means that the children are able to show their understanding through their movement. In other words, the children have *functional understanding*.

If one of us were going to teach a second-grade art class, we might ask the teacher whether the children know their colors. If the teacher says yes, we'd assume that the children know the difference among red, brown, black, orange, and so forth. We'd further expect that they can readily use these colors in the lesson we would teach. If the teacher says the children don't know their colors, however, we'd design our lesson to help them learn their colors. *Functional understanding* means the children know and can use the concepts in their movement.

Space Awareness

All movement occurs in space. Because children who develop a keen space sense will be better able to move safely as they travel through physical education environments, it's beneficial to focus on the concept of space awareness at the beginning of the physical education program.

Children can be made aware of the different aspects of space and then challenged to think about spatial considerations as they engage in game, gymnastics, and dance experiences. As children move their bodies in different ways through varying spatial conditions, they begin to feel and understand space in new ways. As relationships between the body and space become clear, adeptness at controlling movements in functional or expressive physical education activities is enhanced. For example, children learn to maneuver across a large span of climbing equipment, traveling around, over, and under other youngsters without bumping any of them or losing control of their own movements. See Box 16-1 for information on space awareness from the *National Standards for Physical Education*.

Box 16-1

Space Awareness in the *National Standards for Physical Education*

The movement concept of space awareness is referenced in the *National Standards for Physical Education* (National Association for Sport and Physical Education [NASPE], 2004) under Standard 2: Demonstrates understanding of movement concepts, principles, strategies, and tactics as they apply to the learning and performance of physical activities. The intent of the standard is facilitation of learners' ability to use cognitive information to understand and enhance motor skill acquisition and performance. At the lower elementary level, emphasis is placed on establishing a movement vocabulary and applying introductory concepts. At the upper elementary level, emphasis is placed on applying and generalizing the concepts to physical activity situations.

Sample performance outcomes from the *National Standards* include:

- Travels forward and sideways, changing directions quickly in response *to a signal or* obstacle using a variety of locomotor skills. (K–2)*
- Designs and performs gymnastics (or dance) sequences that combine traveling, rolling, balancing, and weight transfer into smooth, flowing sequences with intentional changes in direction, speed, and flow (6–8)*

*Grade-level guidelines for expected student learning.

Recall from earlier chapters that the movement analysis framework consists of both movement concepts and skill themes. Space awareness—where the body moves—is one of the three categories of movement concepts (Chapter 3, Table 3.2). The space awareness categories are shaded in the movement analysis framework wheel (Figure 16.1). The position of space awareness on the wheel indicates that it is a movement modifier or concept. In other words, it describes *how* a skill is to be performed as opposed to stating *what* skill is to be performed.

The space awareness section is subdivided into five categories that delineate various aspects of space: location, directions, levels, pathways, and extensions. In turn, each of these categories is further subdivided into specific components that are the working or teachable aspects of space awareness. For example, the location category is subdivided into general space and self-space. Study Figure 16.1 to determine all the subdivisions for each of the separate aspects of space. It helps to think of the three outermost portions of the wheel as three levels of the same idea. The first level, or outside ring, describes the idea, the second ring gives the categories that make up the idea, and the third ring defines what is found in each category.

Activities in this section are planned as beginning tasks not only to introduce but also to teach children the five categories of space indicated in the second ring of the wheel. Children *must* understand these concepts before they attempt to apply them in conjunction with skill themes.

We usually begin by acquainting children with the two basic orientations of *location:* self-space and general space. These two ideas are crucial to all future learning; they're the foundation upon which everything else is built. *Self-space* is all the space that the body or its parts can reach without traveling away from a starting location. *General space* is all the space within a room, an outdoor teaching space, or a boundary that the body can penetrate by means of locomotion. At the precontrol level, space awareness denotes the ability to move throughout the work/play area without bumping others. At the utilization and proficiency levels, the ability to see open spaces, to move to open spaces, and to throw/kick to open spaces is a key element in successful games play.

The remaining four categories of space describe the relationships of the body to the space aspects of directions, levels, pathways, and extensions. *Directions* in space are the dimensional possibilities into which the body or its parts move or aim to move—up and down, forward and backward, right and left, clockwise and counterclockwise. *Levels* in space are divided into low, middle, and high. Low level is the space below the

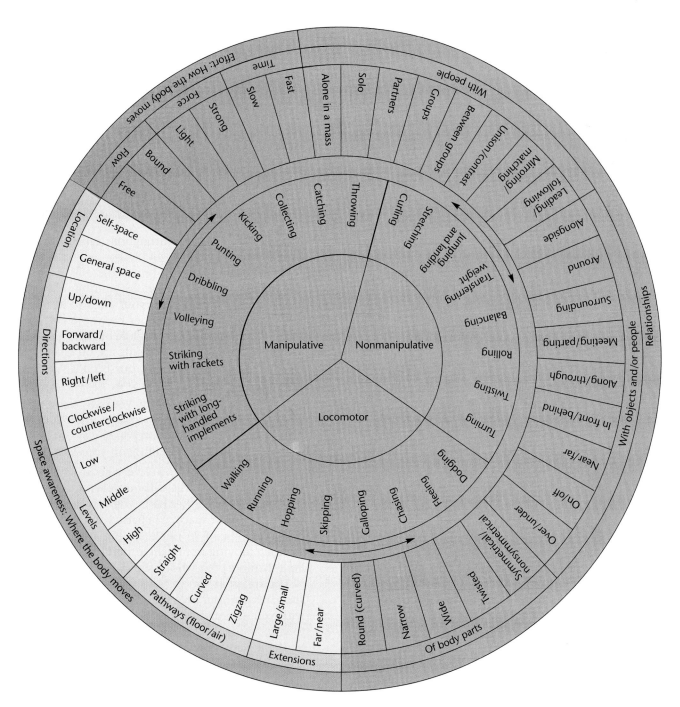

Figure 16.1 Movement analysis framework: space awareness concepts.

knees. Medium level is the space between the knees and the shoulders when the child is in a standing position. High level is the space above the shoulders. *Pathways* in space are the floor patterns (straight, curved, and zigzag) the body can create by traveling through space. The term *pathways* also denotes the possible floor or air patterns of a thrown or struck object—for example, the arched flight of a basketball set shot or the curved path of a pitcher's curveball.

The category *extensions* includes the size of movements of the body or its parts in space (for example, small arm circles or large arm circles) and the distances from the center of the body that the parts reach to carry out a movement. The tennis serve a skilled player performs is a far extension, whereas the tennis serve a beginner executes is often much closer to the body.

The ideas for developing each space concept are stated in direct terms. Remember, though, that the

This young girl, appropriately challenged, is enthralled with the process of exploring space.

method used to study each concept can be varied according to your purposes and the characteristics of the children in your class (see Chapter 13).

Developing the Concept of Self-Space

We've found that the best way to teach the concept of *location* is to focus on its two components—self-space and general space—separately. We first teach self-space and then proceed to general space. You should repeat all the activities involved in teaching self-space and general space until it's clear that the students understand the distinction between the two concepts as well as the need to use space effectively.

⚠️ An understanding of self-space and general space plus starting and stopping on signal are crucial for students' safety.

If children understand the concept of self-space, their awareness of movement possibilities in the space immediately surrounding their bodies increases. Without a keen sense of the relationship of self-space to surrounding space, children's range of potential movements is restricted. When young children are introduced to a wide repertoire of movement skills in self-space, they begin to build a foundation of nonlocomotor skills (such as twisting and turning) that can be used to enhance the development of concepts and of other skills.

Teaching the Concept of Self-Space

To teach the self-space concept, we give the children learning experiences they can accomplish in one location, without traveling. The absence of locomotion enhances kinesthetic awareness of stretching, curling, twisting, and swinging (nonlocomotor) movements, as well as builds the children's movement vocabularies.

Learning Experiences Leading to Movement Concept Understanding

Exploring Self-Space

Setting: Children scattered throughout general space

Tasks/Challenges:

Ⓣ While standing in a place all by yourself, not traveling anywhere else, move your arms in as many places as possible around your body. Pretend that you're on an island in the middle of shark-infested waters and that all your friends are on islands of their own. You can't reach your friends on their islands, and they can't reach you. You're stranded.

Ⓣ This time, while in a place by yourself, move your legs all around you. Try places that you think are difficult to get to, like behind you or way out to the side; come very close to falling off your island.

Ⓣ Once you think that you're very good with moving your arms and legs without leaving the space you're in, choose other parts you can move without leaving your space. Use parts you think would be really difficult to move around in your space without moving your whole body from your island. Explore your whole island.

The area that you've just explored is called *self-space*; it's like your own island or armor that travels with you wherever you go. Your self-space belongs to you, and no one else is allowed in it unless you let them. Remember too that you're not allowed in anyone else's self-space unless they invite you.

Even with the best analogies in the world, it's sometimes difficult for children, both young and old, to understand the concept of self-space. When this happens, we've used hoops, carpet squares, ropes shaped into circles, and X's marked on the floor to help children differentiate and remember what their self-space really looks like. As soon as children properly understand what self-space is and are able to consistently remain in self-space, you can remove these prompts.

Each individual is surrounded by a self-space as he or she travels—the possible movements into space immediately surrounding the body will be the same regardless of location. But children will understand this

Spatial awareness is critical to working safely in group situations.

concept most easily if they learn it while remaining stationary. Staying in one location will clarify for the children the difference between the movements possible in the space immediately surrounding the body and the movements possible when the body travels through general space.

Curling, Stretching, and Twisting in Self-Space

Setting: Children scattered throughout general space

Tasks/Challenges:

T While staying in self-space, where you can't touch anyone else, curl your body up very tightly so that you look like a little ball. Now that you're curled up, begin to stretch, ever so slowly, until you're stretched as tall and wide as possible. As you stretch, remember that you can't leave your own space. You're in your own birdcage. Slowly stretch just one arm, then the other arm. Slowly stretch only one leg, then the other leg. Don't forget to stretch your fingers and toes while you are in self-space.

T Pretend that you're trying to reach the cookie jar that is on a shelf at the very top of your cage. Stretch as tall as you can to get it. Now, just as you have two cookies in your hand, your mother walks in. Sink very quickly back to the floor and make yourself very small to hide.

T This time, a big spider is on the floor of the cage, near your feet. Stretch tall; you're trying to reach the top rungs of your cage to pull yourself up out of the spider's way. Now the spider climbs to the top; shrink slowly to get away from the spider.

T Now that you've practiced your stretching and curling actions, you're going to add twisting actions to them. You want to twist your *whole* body, not just one part. To start, make believe the cookie jar is on the very back of the shelf, behind two boxes; as you stretch, twist your body so you can get to the cookie jar.

T Stretch toward the top of the birdcage (as you did to get away from the spider). Now pretend that suddenly you have an itch in the middle of your back. Hold on to the top of the cage with one hand and try to scratch your back with your other hand.

T Pretend that you have an itch in the middle of your back that is impossible to reach. Twist your body in different directions as you attempt to reach the itch. Stretch, curl, and twist body parts in self-space to scratch the itch.

C See how many body parts you can stretch in self-space. How many different ways can you curl without moving from your self-space? Isolate different body parts for twisting in self-space.

Moving the Whole Body in Self-Space

Setting: Children scattered throughout general space

Tasks/Challenges:

T So far, all you've done in self-space is to curl, stretch, and twist; you haven't really moved your whole body using any kind of specific movement. This time, let's practice walking in place in self-space. Remember that you can't go anywhere off your island or out of your birdcage—that's all the area you have.

Other actions to practice in self-space: skipping, hopping, jumping, and turning slowly like a music box dancer.

These youngsters are just beginning to understand the concept of extensions.

Developing the Concept of General Space

General space is all the space within a room or boundary into which an individual can move by traveling away from the original starting location (self-space).

We help the children learn different ways of traveling safely through general space by providing appropriate movement tasks. Once the children are able to travel safely (without bumping or losing control) in general space, they're ready to experience more complex tasks that include several concepts in combination, such as speed, pathways, and directions. Manipulating balls as one travels through general space is an even more difficult challenge.

Teaching the Concept of General Space

The learning experiences in this section are designed to help children learn to travel safely and efficiently through general space. You can increase the complexity of the activities by focusing on the concepts of speed, pathways, and directions and on the manipulation of objects through general space. Traveling in general space is an excellent warm-up or limbering activity that you can use each day; it also provides additional opportunities for practice of the various locomotor skills.

Learning Experiences Leading to Movement Concept Understanding

Exploring General Space

Setting: Children scattered throughout general space

Tasks/Challenges:

T Find a space by yourself within the boundaries of our work area. I'll know you're ready when I see you standing very still in a space where you can't touch anyone else. When I say "Go," begin to walk around the room, trying not to come near anyone else and at the same time not leaving any empty spaces in the room. On signal *(verbal signal or drumbeat),* stop very quickly right where you are. When you stop, you shouldn't be able to touch anyone else.

This area that you just moved in is called *general space;* it's all the space available for you to move in. As you move in general space, your self-space goes with you, like a bubble that surrounds you, so that you're protected.

T Let's try the same activity again, but this time move a little faster through general space. Remember that as you move and when you stop, you shouldn't be able to touch anyone else.

A Increase the speed only when you observe that the children are able to travel without bumping into one another; for some classes this will take several days. Always start slowly.

T This time, instead of walking through general space, you're going to jog *(or skip, leap, hop, gallop, etc.)* through general space. Remember to always stay as far away from other people as you can. Think about visiting different places in the area, such as the corners and the middle of the area.

After you give the stop signal, you can further enhance concept development by giving the children feedback, for example:

1. *Praise youngsters who stop in isolated areas.*
2. *Praise youngsters who stop quickly and safely.*
3. *Point out congested or vacant spaces.*
4. *Praise youngsters who've avoided collisions by traveling defensively.*

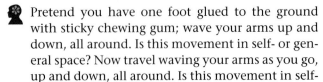 Pretend you have one foot glued to the ground with sticky chewing gum; wave your arms up and down, all around. Is this movement in self- or general space? Now travel waving your arms as you go, up and down, all around. Is this movement in self- or general space?

Open Spaces

Setting: Children scattered throughout general space

Tasks/Challenges:

T Travel throughout general space, constantly moving to an open space. When you arrive at that open space, quickly move to another one when someone invades your open space or you see a second or a third open space.

T Travel throughout general space looking for an open space. When you see an open space, pretend you are throwing a ball to that space, then quickly travel to that space to "catch" the ball. Look for another open space, "throw," and travel again.

T Travel throughout general space looking for an open space. Each time you travel to an open space, claim that space as your own by calling "yes." Then quickly move to a new open space.

Reducing the Size of the General Space

Setting: Children scattered throughout general space facing the teacher, who is positioned at the edge of the general space. *(All the children will be moving within the boundaries. When you want the space to become smaller, take a step or two toward the center of the general space—the idea is an entire wall moving forward at one time.)*

Tasks/Challenges:

T Spread out and find a space by yourself. On the signal, begin to travel on your feet in general space, not touching anyone else. The difficult part this time will be that I'm going to keep making your space smaller as you move. For me to do that, you must always stay in front of me; I'll keep moving forward until your general space is very small.

City Streets, Crowded Spaces

Setting: Children divided into two groups in a reduced amount of general space as in the previous activity

Tasks/Challenges:

T Let's move within this reduced amount of space as if we were in a crowded city. We will begin walking at a moderate speed to avoid bumping others on the crowded streets. On signal, increase the speed of your walking as if you were in rush-hour traffic. Remember, no collisions.

T Now move very slowly, because the area is congested. Increase your speed again.

T Group 1, stand very still in your self-space. You are the tall buildings in the city; you may be tall and wide or just tall. Group 2, walk throughout the general space without bumping other walkers or the buildings. Listen for the signal to increase or decrease your speed. *(Switch the groups after 30 seconds.)*

Dodging in General Space

Setting: Children divided into two groups: half the children on one side of the work area, half on the other side

Tasks/Challenges:

T Let's practice our moving in general space in a game. The object of the game is for both groups to get to the other side of the area without touching anyone else. The difficult part is that both groups will be moving at the same time. Remember, all of you in both groups are trying to switch sides without touching anyone else. I'll watch very carefully to see if I can find anyone touching.

T Now, instead of walking, you're going to gallop *(or skip, hop, jump, etc.)* to the other side.

⚠ Permit children to travel at fast speeds, such as running, only after they have mastered stopping on signal and moving with no collisions.

Traveling Over, Under, and Around Obstacles in General Space

Setting: Small obstacles (hoops and ropes on the floor, milk crates, and low benches) spread out in various places around the area

Tasks/Challenges:

T Travel around the space without touching any piece of equipment or any other person. You may go over, under, or around any of the obstacles, but don't touch anyone or anything. Remember, if someone else is at a piece of equipment, go on to another one; don't wait in line.

Assessment Example

From the *National Standards for Physical Education*

Teacher Observation

The teacher uses a check list to assess the degree to which a class or individual students can identify a "good personal space," work in "personal space," and move in "general space" during a manipulative lesson.

Criteria for Assessment

a. Finds a personal space within general space that provides maximum room to work.

b. Stays in or returns to personal space during lesson.

c. Moves with an awareness of others as well as of space available within general space.

NASPE (1995, p. 7)

Obstacle Course

Setting: Jump ropes, wands, hoops, yardsticks, crates, and similar small equipment placed around the edge of the work area

Tasks/Challenges:

Ⓣ Today you are going to design an obstacle course for our traveling in general space. What is an obstacle course? Right, an area to travel through without bumping into things or going outside the boundaries. Select two or three pieces of the small equipment, and place them on the floor; you may wish to place them so they are touching or so that they connect with the equipment of the person working next to you. *(Allow two to three minutes for the children to construct the obstacle course.)*

Walk throughout general space, avoiding the obstacles placed on the floor; travel without touching the equipment or any other person.

Ⓣ Travel in a way other than walking.

Developing the Concept of Directions

Directions in space are the dimensional possibilities into which the body or its parts move or aim to move—up and down, right and left, forward and backward, clockwise and counterclockwise. There is no universally correct direction; direction is a function of the body's orientation in space. Forward and backward, for example, depend on the way a person is facing rather than a location in a room. Left and right refer to the respective sides of the body, not a certain wall or location in a gymnasium. Because the concepts of right and left (sideways) and clockwise and counterclockwise require cognitive as well as physical maturation for correct execution, it's not uncommon to find that children learn the directions forward and backward and up and down before they learn the directions right and left and clockwise and counterclockwise.

Teaching the Concept of Directions

The learning experiences in this section provide ideas for helping children understand the concepts of forward and backward, up and down, sideways, clockwise and counterclockwise, and right and left. As the children become more capable, the complexity of the tasks is increased—the children are challenged to combine two or more direction concepts and to move in different directions in relation to objects or people.

Learning Experiences Leading to Movement Concept Understanding

Traveling in Different Directions

Setting: Children scattered throughout general space

Tasks/Challenges:

Ⓣ On the signal, walk as you usually walk, with the front of your body going first. This direction is called *forward.*

Ⓣ This time, walk with your back going first. This direction is called *backward.* Sometimes going backward is hard because you have to look over your shoulder to see where you're going.

Ⓣ Now walk with one side of your body going first. This direction is called *sideways.* You can move to either your right or left side. Let's practice both ways. First move with your right side going first. When you hear the beat of the drum *(if you don't have a drum, use a tin can, a baby rattle, or a New Year's noisemaker),* change so that your left side goes first.

Ⓣ Skip forward, walk slowly backward, slide from side to side like an ice skater, and jump up and down as though you were on a pogo stick.

Moving Clockwise and Counterclockwise

Setting: Children scattered throughout general space

Tasks/Challenges:

Rotation describes movement in a clockwise or a counterclockwise direction. When we want children to turn, spin, or pivot, using the terms right *and* left *is inaccurate. Instead, the terms* clockwise *and* counterclockwise *indicate the appropriate direction in which to move.*

Ⓣ Look down at the floor. Imagine that there's a clock on the floor in front of you. Slowly turn around, turning in the direction the hands on the clock move. This direction is called *clockwise.* Now turn in the other direction. This direction is called *counterclockwise.*

T Now practice the different directions some more. See if you can spin clockwise on one foot. Now change and spin counterclockwise on the same foot.

T Swing your arms in the direction you want to spin and see if you can spin all the way around before you stop. Swinging your arms will help you spin farther. Remember to swing in the direction you want to go.

✿ Is it easier to spin in a clockwise or a counterclockwise direction? Why do you think so? Find a partner. One of you spin or jump and turn while the other watches. See if your partner can tell you whether you were spinning (turning) in a clockwise or a counterclockwise direction. Now watch as your partner spins (turns).

T This time try jumping. Stay in your self-space, and jump and turn all the way around so that you land facing the same direction you were facing when you started. Bend your knees to land in a balanced position.

T Practice turning clockwise and counterclockwise when you jump. Can you turn farther in one direction than the other?

T Now you're going to try something different. Travel in general space. When you hear one drumbeat, spin in a clockwise direction and keep traveling. When you hear two drumbeats, spin in a counterclockwise direction and keep traveling. If you hear three drumbeats, change the way you're traveling, for example, from a skip to a slide. Do you think you can remember all this? Let's see!

You can also teach and reinforce the concepts of clockwise and counterclockwise when working with several of the skill themes by having the children dribble in a clockwise or counterclockwise direction, for example, or push a puck with a hockey stick in both directions.

Exploring Directions

Setting: Children scattered throughout general space

Tasks/Challenges:

T In your self-space, point with the body part named in the direction that I call out. (*You can continue the list with any body part.*)

With your foot, point forward.
With your elbow, point backward.

With your hip, point to the left.
With your left foot, point forward.

As you point, make sure the direction you're pointing to is very clear—so I could easily tell which way to go if you were pointing out a direction to me.

Changing Directions on Signal

Setting: Children scattered throughout general space

Tasks/Challenges:

T Now that you know the directions, move a little faster when you practice them, and mix them all up. On the signal, begin to travel in general space in a forward direction. After that, each time you hear the signal, change the direction you're moving in. For example, if you start out moving in a forward direction, the first time you hear the signal change to a sideways direction; the next time you hear the signal change to a backward direction; and the next time change back to a sideways direction. Remember to make your directions very clear.

While the children are waiting for the signal, have them think about how they're going to change direction.

T This time, change not only the direction of your travel, but also the locomotor movement you use, for example, gallop forward, walk backward, or slide to the right.

T This time the changes of direction are going to be a bit more difficult. They'll be in code. One beat of the drum means forward. Two beats of the drum mean sideways. Three beats of the drum mean backward. Spread out in general space in a space by yourself. When you hear the beat of the drum, begin to travel in the direction indicated by the code. When you hear the next beat of the drum, change and travel in the direction that it indicates. Listen very carefully to the drumbeats because I might try to trick you.

Turning While Moving in Different Directions

Setting: Children positioned around the perimeters of the gymnasium, facing the walls

Tasks/Challenges:

T Spread out around the outside of the room and face the wall. When you hear the drumbeat, begin to travel around the space by using a sliding pattern. As the drum beats again, turn, without stopping, to face the inside of the room—keep sliding. Each time the drum beats, change the way you're facing, and continue moving sideways. When you do this, I'm looking for turns that are smooth and slides that don't stop as you turn.

Developing the Concept of Levels

Levels are the horizontal layers in space where the body or its parts are positioned or can move. *Low level* is the space below the knees, close to the floor. A stamp or twist of the foot is an action at a low level. Crawling, creeping, or rolling are locomotor actions performed at a low level.

Medium level is the space between low level and high level—the area between the knees and shoulders. Catching a thrown ball, for example, typically occurs in middle level.

High level is the space above the shoulders, toward the ceiling. Although one can't move the whole body into high level, actions such as stretching the arms up high or standing on the balls of the feet bring body parts into a high level. A jump can take much of the upper body into a high level, while part of the body remains at a medium or low level because of the pull of gravity.

Teaching the Concept of Levels

The learning experiences in this section give children movement challenges that help them learn to move the body, body parts, and objects into different levels in space.

Learning Experiences Leading to Movement Concept Understanding

Traveling and Freezing at Different Levels

Setting: Children scattered throughout general space

Tasks/Challenges:

Ⓣ Spread out and find a space by yourself. On signal, begin to travel in general space. When you hear the drumbeat, stop where you are, with your whole body at a low level.

Ⓣ This time, travel, and on the signal stop with your body at a low level and a body part at a high level. Make it very clear which part is at a high level.

Ⓣ This time, when you stop, stop with your body at a medium level. Remember that a low level means below your knees, a medium level is from about your knees to your shoulders, and a high level is above your shoulders.

Traveling with Body Parts at Different Levels

Setting: Children scattered throughout general space

Tasks/Challenges:

Ⓣ Travel around general space with as many of your body parts as possible at a low level. Remember that your body parts should always be at a low level when you're traveling, not just when you freeze.

Ⓣ As you travel this time, try to have as many body parts as possible at a medium level. Remember that it isn't possible to have all body parts at a medium

Spatial awareness becomes very important when manipulating objects in general space.

level as you travel because your feet always have to be on the floor, but have as many parts as possible at a medium level and none at a high level.

T This time as you travel, have as many parts as possible at a high level. This activity is harder than the other two, so be very careful that all possible body parts are at a high level.

✽ Show me hands at high level, medium level, low level.

Young children enjoy exploring body parts at different levels in self-space (e.g., feet, elbows, nose, as well as combinations of levels, such as one foot low, one foot high).

Rising and Sinking to Create Different Levels

Setting: Children scattered throughout general space

Tasks/Challenges:

T Find a space by yourself, and get into a low position that you like. I'm going to beat the drum very slowly eight times. As I beat the drum, rise very slowly to the eight beats until you attain a position of stillness with as many body parts as possible at a high level. Remember to rise slowly. But also remember that you have only eight beats in which to get to a high level, so judge your movement so you get there in time. After you've reached your high position, on the next eight beats slowly sink back to your low position. The sequence then goes like this: a low position, eight beats to get to a high still position, eight beats to return to your low position. Let's try it.

Traveling While Rising and Sinking

Setting: Children scattered throughout general space

Tasks/Challenges:

T As you travel around the space this time, I'll give you drumbeats to guide your actions. The drumbeats will be in counts of four, with the accent on the first beat. Start by traveling at a low level. On the accented first beat, quickly jump and stretch into a high level and then immediately return to a low level of travel until the next accented beat. Your movement should look like this: travel low, jump high, travel low, jump high, travel low, and so on. Make your jump very clear and as high as possible and your travel at a low level very clear. I should be able to easily tell the difference between the two levels.

Developing the Concept of Pathways

A pathway is an imaginary design that the body or its parts when moving through space create along the floor or through the air. A pathway is also the trail of an object (a ball or hockey puck) as it travels from one player to another or toward a goal.

At first, young children may have difficulty understanding the concept of pathways in space. However, a class of young children can become enthralled with the process of discovering and experimenting with the many pathways the body can travel. A teacher can plan experiences that enable youngsters to recognize pathways and to effectively use knowledge of pathways to improve control of travel. For instance, even very young children can come to understand that a curved or angular pathway is effective for avoiding collisions when traveling through a crowd.

Teaching the Concept of Pathways

Children learn to travel in straight, zigzag, and curved pathways, and in combinations of these pathways, by experiencing the activities in this section. More difficult learning experiences involve manipulating various objects in pathways and traveling in relation to others along various pathways.

Learning Experiences Leading to Movement Concept Understanding

Exploring Pathways

Setting: Tape markings on the floor similar to those shown in Figure 16.2; children scattered throughout general space

Tasks/Challenges:

T Today you're going to learn about pathways. A line that doesn't turn or twist and is always straight is called a *straight pathway.* A line that circles around is called a *curved pathway.* A semicircle is a curved pathway. A line that looks like a lot of Z's put together is a *zigzag pathway.* Now find a space on one of the pathways marked on the floor. Travel along that pathway on your feet; be able to tell me what kind of pathway it is when I ask you.

T This time as you travel, change your direction, sometimes going forward along your pathway, sometimes sideways, and sometimes backward. Try out all directions on your pathway.

T Now change the way that you travel along your pathway. Sometimes you may want to hop, sometimes leap, sometimes run. Find at least four

Figure 16.2 Pathways taped on the floor.

different ways that you can travel along your pathway.

During the activity, have the children regularly change places so that they're on a different pathway.

Using Pathway Maps

Setting: A card, similar to the ones shown in Figure 16.3, for each child

Tasks/Challenges:

🅣 Take a card and find a space by yourself. Travel on your feet and follow the pathway indicated on your card. Pretend that your card is a map showing the route to take to get to a new place. Keep practicing your pathway until you're very sure it's just like the one on the card and you can do it the best you can. Be able to tell me the name of the pathway you're following whenever I ask you.

Figure 16.3 Pathway cards.

🅣 Now trade cards with someone else and practice that pathway until you think it's perfect.

Designing Pathways

Setting: Children scattered throughout general space

Tasks/Challenges:

🅣 Pick a spot on the wall across the room from you. Remember where your spot is, and in your mind plan a pathway that will take you from where you are now to that spot. Think about it a long time so you can remember it when you start to move. When I give the signal, travel along your made-up pathway until you get to the spot you've picked out. Stop when you get there. On the next signal, travel back to the place you started from, following the same pathway you took coming over. This is similar to following a path through the woods: You can't go off the path or you'll get lost.

🅣 Now I am *not* going to give you the signal any more. Practice your pathway on your own until you have memorized and can repeat it exactly every time.

✅ *Student Drawing.* Asking children to draw the various pathways and label them would be an easy way to assess their understanding.

Creating Follow-the-Leader Pathways

Setting: Sets of partners scattered throughout general space

Tasks/Challenges:

🅣 Find a partner and stand in a space together. I'll know that you're ready when I see each of you standing quietly in your space. Decide which of you is going to be the leader. On the signal, the leader travels a pathway to somewhere else in the room. On the second signal, the leader stops, and the follower moves along the same pathway the

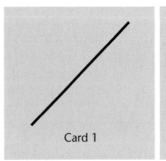

Card 1

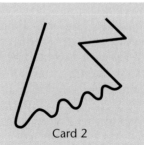

Card 2

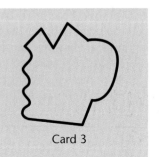

Card 3

leader took until the follower catches up with the leader. After doing this three times, the leader and follower switch places. The secret is for the follower to watch the leader very closely. In the beginning, the leader should not make up difficult pathways. Followers, remember to copy the leaders' pathways exactly.

Traveling Pathways and Obstacles

Setting: Half the class positioned throughout general space; the other half, around the perimeter of the space

Tasks/Challenges:

T Now you're going to travel in pathways that go around, over, and under obstacles in your way. Always remember that your classmates are the obstacles, so you have to be very careful of them. You can't touch anyone else. People who are obstacles must remember to stay very still so as to not interfere with anyone who's moving. Obstacles, go find a position in a space by yourself that you can hold still. It can be any position that you like—a bridge, a statue, or a balance. Those of you on the side of the space, pick a point on the other side of the room and plan a pathway to get there. Remember that your pathway can go over, under, or around any of the obstacles. Think about it and really make it different from anything you've done before.

Give the children a few seconds to plan their pathway and the obstacles time to select their position.

On the signal, follow your pathway to the point you picked on the other side of the room. Stop when you get to the point you picked. On the next signal, try to retrace your pathway until you get back to your starting position.

C Now, on your own, practice your pathway four times. Remember to avoid running into other travelers as you cross the space. Always have a clear beginning and end to your pathway.

When all have completed their pathways, have the students switch places and perform the activity. You can enhance activities such as these by asking children who are doing the activities correctly to demonstrate for the rest of the class.

Following-the-Dots Pathways

Setting: A pencil plus a card with dots randomly plotted on it for each child; carpet squares on the floor in a pattern similar to that of the dots on the card

Mr. Jenning's Kindergarten Class Discovers Pathways

Teacher: Hey gang! How did we get to the physical education space today?

Children: We walked!

Teacher: Yes! And what parts of our bodies did we use?

Children: Our feet . . . our legs.

Teacher: You got it! Tell me, did we leave a trail behind us? Any footprints on the floor?

Children: No! (*Loud and laughing*)

Teacher: I don't see any either. But what if your shoes were muddy. Would we have left a trail?

Children: Yeah! But Mrs. Farmer (*the principal*) sure would be mad!

Teacher: I think she would be, too! But if we did leave muddy footprints from your classroom all the way to the physical education space, what would our path look like?

Children: Long . . . Messy . . . we go by the library.

Teacher: I think you're all right. I have an idea . . . Let's look at the chalkboard. Here's your room way over here and this is where the physical education space is. Look at our pathway. Although we didn't leave any real footprints, we did follow a path. We follow this same pathway each time we come to the physical education space. Tell me, is our path just one straight line or did we make any turns?

Children: We turned when we came out of the room. At the library.

Teacher: You people are sharp today. Hey! Can you think of any other pathways you follow each day?

Children: We go to lunch . . . Walk to school . . . Down to the playground.

Teacher: We follow a lot of pathways each day. Let's see if we can have some fun with pathways today. Pick a spot somewhere on the outside edge of the room (for example, a brick, a picture) and when I say "Go," you stand up and walk in a straight line to your spot and freeze. Here we go!

Tasks/Challenges:

T Connect the dots on your card to form any design you like. After you've finished connecting the dots, follow the path that you drew from one carpet square to the other. Make sure you know the type of pathway you've designed because I might ask you.

T Now trade maps with someone else. Follow that person's map. Figure out if that pathway is different from yours.

Figure 16.4 Task sheet for pathways, levels, and directions.

Name _____ Teacher _____

Pathways, Levels, and Directions Task Sheet

Date	Who Watched	Challenge
		I can walk forward in a straight pathway.
		I can walk backward in a straight pathway.
		I can walk sideways in a straight pathway.
		I can walk forward in a curved pathway.
		I can walk backward in a curved pathway.
		I can walk forward, low, and curved.
		I can walk backward, high, and zigzag.
		I can run sideways, medium, and curved.
		I can slide backward, medium, and zigzag.
		I can
		I can
		I can
		(Make up three things you can do on your own using pathways, levels, and directions.)

Combining Pathways, Levels, and Directions

Setting: A task sheet, similar to that in Figure 16.4, for each child

Tasks/Challenges:

This activity lets you combine pathways, levels, and directions. It's also a good way to test yourself. Once you think you're able to perform a challenge, have a friend watch you and sign the line on the task sheet beside the challenge. When you're finished, I'll come and check you out. You may use a friend to help you if you want extra help.

Younger children can use a smile face instead of having someone else initial the sheet.

Peer Observation. The above task sheet would make a perfect peer observation.

Developing the Concept of Extensions in Space

Extensions in space are best understood as two separate possibilities. First, extensions are spatial relationships of body parts to the entire body. Body extremities can be held in close to the body, as in a curl, or they can be opened up, as in a stretch. Extensions are also the size of movements in space. Movements with extremities held close to the body are *small movements,* such as putting a golf ball; those with the extremities extended or opened up are *large movements,* such as driving a golf ball.

Teaching the Concept of Extensions in Space

The concept of extensions is taught through learning experiences that give children an operational understanding of the differences between large and small, as well as near and far extensions (movements).

Learning Experiences Leading to Movement Concept Understanding

Exploring Extensions

Setting: Children scattered throughout general space

Tasks/Challenges:

(T) Find a space by yourself. With your hands, explore all the space close to your body. Remember to not reach very far from your body; this is an extension near your body. We call it a *near* extension.

(T) Now, without leaving your self-space, explore all the space that is far away from your body. Try to reach as far as you can without leaving your space. Remember to explore above and behind as well as in front of you. This is called an extension that is far away from your body. We call it a *far* extension.

Traveling and Extensions

Setting: Children scattered throughout general space

Tasks/Challenges:

(T) Travel around the room. When you hear the beat of the drum, stop in a position where your body reaches as far into space as possible. Be very sure that all possible body parts are as far away from the center of your body as you can get them.

(T) This time as you travel, when you hear the drumbeat, stop with all body parts as close to your body as possible. Remember to keep all your body parts as close to yourself as you can.

(T) Now try traveling with change. When you hear the sound of the drum, jump high into the air, extending your arms and legs as far away from your body as possible. When you land, hold a position very still, with all body parts very close to the center of your body. Really try to make a clear difference between the far and near extensions.

Changing from One Extension to Another

Setting: Children scattered throughout general space

Tasks/Challenges:

(T) Find a space by yourself, and get into a tight position you like. I'll beat the drum six times, in slow beats. On the first six beats, gradually extend all body parts far away from your body. On the next six beats, slowly move to your tight curled position. The movement then goes like this: first a tight, curled position; on six beats, slowly move to a spread-out position; on the next six counts, slowly move back to a near extension. Try to make the extensions you use very clear. We'll practice this activity a number of times so you can work on doing your best possible.

Using Extensions and Imagery

Setting: Children scattered throughout general space

Tasks/Challenges:

(T) As you travel around general space, pretend you're carrying an object you don't want anyone to see

To respond to the challenge of catching while traveling, this child must have a functional understanding of the concept of space.

or that you're trying to hide or protect something, such as a baby bird, a million-dollar jewel, or a lot of money. As you walk, think very carefully about how you'd actually carry the object you've chosen.

T Now, instead of having an object you want to hide, you have one you're proud of and want to show off—maybe a trophy that you just won. How would you carry it? Go!

✿ In which activity did you use a near or small extension? In which activity did you use a large or far extension?

Applying the Concept of Space Awareness

Self-space and general space are often appropriate beginning concepts for children who have had little experience in formal physical education classes. One of the important skills that children need to develop early is the ability to occupy an area or to travel in an area while maintaining awareness of others. Self-space and general space are helpful concepts to use when teaching these skills.

The concepts of directions, levels, and pathways are usually introduced after children have developed the ability to differentiate self-space from general space. Until the children actually acquire a functional understanding of directions, levels, and pathways (high, medium, low levels; forward, sideways, backward directions; straight, zigzag, and curved pathways), the observational focus is primarily on the concept rather than on correct performance of a particular skill. For example, if you ask the children to throw so that the ball starts off at a high level, you're less interested in the actual mechanics of throwing than in the child's ability to release the ball at a high level. Once you're confident that the children are able to apply the concepts, you can focus more on appropriate skill technique.

Most children take a longer time to grasp the concepts of right and left, air pathways, and extensions. Thus, it's wise to introduce the other concepts to children before focusing on these three ideas.

The ability to understand the concept of right and left is related to cognitive maturation. Some children will need more time and more practice opportunities than others to master left and right. Many children easily acquire cognitive understanding of the concepts of extensions and air pathways for objects, but most require a certain degree of skill before they can express these ideas in movements. Children with immature throwing and kicking patterns, for example, have difficulty propelling objects so that they travel in different (but intended) air pathways. Children with immature striking or catching patterns are unable to consistently catch or strike an object far from or near to the body.

If you wait until children have developed the skills that are related to these concepts, you'll find that the pupils grasp the concepts more easily than if you try to teach the concepts and then the skills. There's no universally successful sequence for the introduction of these concepts. The reflective teacher uses all available information and makes judgments about the most appropriate time, sequence, and duration for introducing and studying the concepts of space awareness and the application of the concepts to specific skill-practice situations. *Sample lesson plans for teaching the movement concepts can be found in* On the Move, *a collection of lesson plans designed to accompany* Children Moving.

Reading Comprehension Questions

1. What is the primary reason for focusing on the concept of space at the beginning of a physical education program?
2. What does the term *space awareness* mean? What are the characteristics of someone who is "aware of space"?
3. Why is space awareness such an important concept for children at the precontrol level?
4. Why is the concept of open spaces important for proficiency and utilization movers?
5. What directions in space are studied in this program? Why do children find some directions more difficult than others to understand?

6. Distinguish the three levels of space from one another.
7. List the three types of pathways an individual might travel. Explain the difference between a floor pathway and an air pathway.
8. Give two examples each of a far extension and of a near extension.
9. Why do we have children study self-space while stationary rather than traveling?
10. What does it look like when children are able to travel safely in general space?
11. Using the movement analysis wheel, manipulate the wheel to show space awareness in relation

to locomotor, manipulative, and nonmanipulative skills. Identify two skills for each category that

space awareness can modify and write a sample task for each.

References/Suggested Readings

Holt/Hale, S. (2006). *On the move: Lesson plans to accompany* Children Moving. New York: McGraw-Hill.

National Association for Sport and Physical Education. (1995). *Moving into the future: National standards for physical education.* St. Louis, MO: Mosby.

National Association for Sport and Physical Education. (2004). *Moving into the future: National standards for physical education.* (2nd ed.) Reston, VA: National Association for Sport and Physical Education.

Effort

This chapter provides an explanation of and multiple learning experiences for the effort concept. (See Table 3.2 in Chapter 3 for a full listing of the movement concepts taught in elementary school physical education.) Remember, we first provide experiences for children to attain a functional understanding of the concepts. When children have a functional understanding of the movement concepts, the concepts are then used to enhance the skill themes—adverbs to enrich action verbs.

Too often teachers make no conscious, planned attempt to help children understand the effort concepts of time, force, and flow and the application of these concepts to specific skills.* Many teachers don't feel comfortable teaching these concepts, which are vague and abstract. It is not like teaching a child to strike a ball with a paddle, in which the objective of striking is obvious and the result easily perceived. Despite the hesitancy of many teachers to undertake the teaching of effort concepts, there is agreement that an applied understanding of these concepts is essential in skill development, from beginning through advanced levels. See Box 17-1 for information on effort from the *National Standards for Physical Education*.

The concept of effort defines how the body moves. The concept is divided into three components: time, force, and flow, which are defined by observable characteristics that can be taught to children. Figure 17.1 conceptualizes this idea and puts it into perspective with the other movement concepts and skill themes. The effort category is in the shaded portion of the framework. The outside ring defines the concept, the second ring states the components of the concept, and the third ring defines the three components.

Highly skilled (proficiency level) movers have developed an internalized, almost reflexive knowledge of the proper amount and degree of time, force, and flow. They're able to adjust the quality of movements in relation to the demands of a situation—harder or softer, faster or slower, bound or free.

We begin to teach effort concepts to children by providing experiences to help them understand the contrasts of fast-slow, strong-light, and bound-free. Once the children have grasped the differences between the extremes, we focus on the concepts as they apply to specific skills (such as throwing, striking, and transferring weight) and in different situations (for example, to assist in the expression of an idea or to accomplish

---

*Some movement analysis frameworks include the concept of space (direct and flexible) as a quality of movement. In our teaching, however, we use this concept so infrequently that we've chosen not to include it in the discussion of the qualities of movement.

Box 17-1

Effort in the *National Standards for Physical Education*

The movement concept of effort is referenced in the *National Standards for Physical Education* (National Association for Sport and Physical Education [NASPE], 2004) under Standard 2: Demonstrates understanding of movement concepts, principles, strategies, and tactics as they apply to the learning and performance of physical activities. The intent of the standard is facilitation of learners' ability to use cognitive information to understand and enhance motor skill acquisition and performance. At the lower elementary level, emphasis is placed on establishing a movement vocabulary and applying introductory concepts. At the upper elementary level, emphasis is placed on applying and generalizing the concepts to physical activity situations.

Sample performance outcomes from the *National Standards* include:

- Demonstrates clear contrasts between slow and fast movement when skipping (or hopping, galloping, sliding, etc.) (K–2)*
- Develops and refines a gymnastics sequence (or creative dance sequence) demonstrating smooth transitions (3–5)*
- Designs and performs gymnastics (or dance) sequences that combine traveling, rolling, balancing, and weight transfer into smooth, flowing sequences with intentional changes in direction, speed, and flow (6–8)*

*Grade-level guidelines for expected student learning.

---

a particular strategy). As children become more skillful, we focus on the gradations among the extremes. To illustrate, initially we might ask children to travel rapidly and to travel slowly. As children develop the ability to differentiate between the extremes, we focus more on the movement possibilities that occur between the extremes—faster, slower, accelerating, decelerating, sudden changes of speed.

Many of the activities in this chapter use imagery to help children distinguish among different effort concepts. It's important to keep in mind that the focus is on the movement qualities of the various images rather than on the images themselves. For example, when we say "Move like a hippo," we're not asking the children to pretend to be hippos; we're using this task to help the children envision a slow, lumbering movement. Box 17-2 and Chapter 29 contain additional

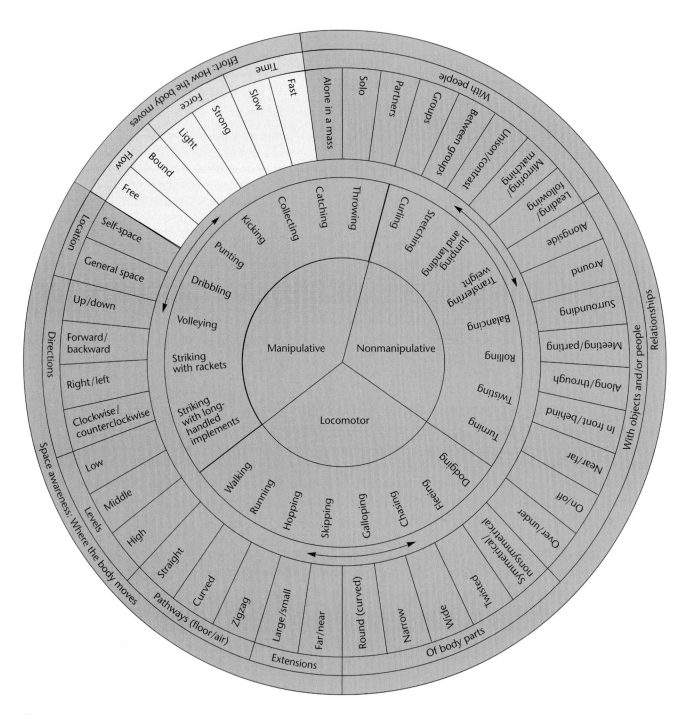

Figure 17.1 Movement analysis framework: effort concepts.

information about the appropriate use of imagery in teaching movement.

Developing the Concept of Time

Time to a young child is the ticktock of a grandfather clock, the cuckoo clock on the wall, or the numbers racing by on a digital timepiece. When spoken of

in relation to movement, time is fast—being able to run like the wind; being the fastest in the class; zip, dash, zoom.

In physical education speed is often the measure of success; therefore, children often have difficulty comprehending slowness and seeing the importance of this rate of movement in their activities. Yet the performer executing a walkover on the balance beam grasps the concept of slowness, as does the leaping dancer who

Box 17-2

Imagery and Movement

Much has been said about imagery and movement, specifically related to dance. We've all had the experience of asking children to "show a flower growing," only to discover that instead of exploring the movement possibilities available, the children were pretending to be flowers. Herein lies the pitfall of imagery: Concept development isn't pretending; it's understanding.

To be beneficial, the teaching of movement concepts and ultimately dance must begin with children learning a movement vocabulary and then relating it to other ideas (much like the development of movement skills before relating them to game play). This notion implies that we must talk about movement first and use images to lead to an understanding or enhancement of that movement. It precludes moving or dancing "about" something (anger, fear, excitement, horses, etc.) or pretending to be something (a piece of fruit, a cowboy, a flower, an airplane, etc.).

Mary Joyce (1994) developed three useful phases regarding dance and imagery that can be easily applied to any creative movement:

1. Images that lead to movement: "Make your back curved like a banana."
2. Images that arise from movement: "You're in a curved shape. What else do you know that is curved?"
3. Images as a basis for movement: "What kind of movement might a banana do?"

Always remember to talk about the movement first and the image second.

---

seems to remain suspended in the air while the hands and arms express a certain feeling or emotion.

Changes in the timing of a movement usually occur without forethought as children adapt to different situations—speeding up or slowing down to maintain possession, to avoid being tagged, to get in open space and receive a pass. Many movements and specific skills dictate the rate of movement. A handspring is done quickly, but a back walkover is performed slowly. In some activities, the child is free to assess a situation and then perform a skill at the best rate. For example, a movement executed quickly in dance or gymnastics elicits feelings of power and speed; the same movement executed slowly expresses the ultimate in control.

We begin teaching the concept of time to young children by contrasting extremes. Gradually we advance to work that focuses on degrees of speed along a continuum—the ability to execute movements at

varying speeds for the purpose of adapting, changing, or creating a situation.

Teaching the Concept of Time

The learning experiences that follow are designed to help children develop a functional understanding of time by contrasting fast and slow actions of the total body and body parts, as well as by focusing on acceleration-deceleration. *When the children are traveling fast, try to keep the activity period short to avoid undue fatigue.*

Learning Experiences Leading to Movement Concept Understanding

Exploring Time

Setting: Children scattered throughout general space

Tasks/Challenges:

T Find a space by yourself. Without leaving your space, move with the beat of the drum. The beat will be very loud and quick to begin with, so you'll want your movements to be very sharp and quick. The trick to having very quick actions is to make them very short; something that's really quick can't go on for very long. This action is called a *sudden* movement.

T This time the beat of the drum will be slower and longer. Try to move your whole body as slowly as the drumbeats, much like a balloon floating through the air or a feather being dropped from a high building. Think about moving every part of your body slowly, not just your arms but your head, shoulders, back, stomach, legs, everything. This action is called a *sustained* movement.

Using Different Speeds in Self-Space

Setting: Children scattered throughout general space

Tasks/Challenges:

T In a space by yourself, bring your hands together very slowly, as if to catch an insect that might try to fly away. At the very last moment before your hands are going to touch, quickly separate them as if you're surprised to find out that the insect is a bee. When you do your slow movements, remember to make them very slow but to always keep your hands moving; make your quick movements so quick that they're like flashes of lightning.

C Let's try those movements five more times. You can bring your hands together any way you want as long

These young children are enjoying the sensation of running—a fast movement.

Slowness is necessary for travel at a low level.

as you do so slowly, and then quickly take them away any way you want. Remember to make your slow and quick movements as clear as they can be. Five times. Go.

🅣 Now, on your own, find other body parts that you can bring together slowly and then quickly pull apart. Try to find at least three combinations. Practice each movement so that the difference between fast and slow is very clear.

This activity is more difficult than it sounds because it asks for extremes of a movement. You can have children practice this activity over and over; always ask for faster and slower actions than the children previously exhibited.

Moving at Different Speeds

Setting: Children scattered throughout general space

Tasks/Challenges:

🅣 On the signal, move as fast as you can, but remain in self-space; on the next signal, freeze in a balanced position that you can hold very still. Remember to try to go as fast as you can, but you must be able to stop on the signal without falling over.

🅣 Now, on the start signal, move as slowly as you can in self-space. Try to move very slowly, but always keep moving. On the stop signal, freeze in a balanced position. Remember to stay in your self-space.

Your first movement was at a fast speed; your second, at a slow speed. Could you tell the difference? Again, you're going to practice both fast and slow speeds. Try to make the movements very clear so I can really tell the difference between them. As you move, I'll call out "Fast" or "Slow," and you change your speed accordingly. So if I call out "slow," move very slowly, and if I call out "fast," move fast. Listen very carefully because I might try to trick you. Make your fast really fast and your slow really slow.

Once the children demonstrate an understanding of speed in self-space, you can transfer these same tasks to traveling in general space.

Traveling and Freezing by Using Changes in Time

Setting: Children scattered throughout general space

Tasks/Challenges:

This time, begin your traveling with a quick explosion of speed, and keep going at a fast speed; then freeze very quickly in a balanced position. The movement should be like this: Begin really fast as if you've been shot out of a cannon, then move fast as if you're running from someone, then freeze quickly as if someone has surprised you and you can't move. Make each segment of your traveling very clear so that I can tell when you change from one part to the other. I'll give you the start signal, then you're on your own.

Now that you've practiced sudden starts, traveling fast, and then freezing, you're going to make up a sequence using those speeds. Choose one sudden-start, fast-travel, and freeze position that you really like, and practice it until you can do it smoothly and with control. Each of the three parts should be very clear and very different from one another. After you think the sequence is really good, practice it three more times. Remember to start and end in the same place each time. Your three movements should look the same every time, as if they'd been videotaped.

Now begin very slowly, as a car does on a cold morning. As you warm up, gradually increase your speed until you're moving fast. Then, freeze suddenly. The sequence should look like this: a slow start, a gradual increase to fast speed, then a freeze. This is different from your last traveling action, so make that difference very clear.

Now make up a sequence that includes a slow start that gradually increases to a fast speed and suddenly

Box 17-3

Designing Sequences

Helping children learn how to design movement sequences is much like helping them learn how to design their own games (see Chapter 31). Following are several tips we've found helpful when beginning to have children design sequences.

1. It takes time.
2. Structure the sequence into a simple form that is easily remembered, for example, a starting shape, a middle moving phase based on a specific aspect of movement, an ending shape.
3. Practice the starting and ending shapes separately before adding the middle movement.
4. Initially, provide a beginning signal, some time to practice (20 to 25 seconds), and then an ending signal.
5. During the first stages, prompt the children during the movement aspect about exactly what movements need to be included (change of level, speed, etc.).
6. Have children repeat their sequence several times. The middle movement aspect may vary slightly each time, but the beginning and end should remain constant.
7. In some way hold the children accountable for what they've created, for example, divide the class in half and have them present their sequence, present their sequence to another person, or write it down.

As the children's ability to design sequences increases, you can gradually relax some of these guidelines, but we've found these steps useful for both the students and the teacher when children first begin to create movement sequences.

Source: Adapted from *First Steps in Teaching Creative Dance to Children*, 3rd ed., by Mary Joyce, 1994, Palo Alto, CA: Mayfield.

freezes. Practice the sequence until you're ready to show someone else, who, after seeing it, should be able to tell you what the three parts were.

Children often equate slowness with heavy, jerky, stiff actions rather than with graceful movement. Examples of slow-moving animals can be useful here. Box 17-3 also contains hints for helping children learn to design movement sequences.

Combining Imagery and Time

Setting: Children scattered throughout general space

Tasks/Challenges:

This time you're going to practice traveling the way different things that move fast or slow do.

Remember that you aren't really trying to act like the things you're pretending to be; you're just trying to move at the speed they move. Let's practice one movement. On the signal, move as a turtle would move. Think carefully about it—a turtle moves very slowly. Now try moving as fast as a rabbit. Go really quickly.

T How does a well-tuned race car move? Let's try to go as fast as a race car can. There's only one thing different about this race car: It goes so fast that it can't make any noise. So go as fast as a silent race car. Change your race car to an old jalopy trying to go uphill; the car is really tired and old, so remember that it goes very slowly.

Some classes enjoy and can accept the responsibility for making the sounds of race cars and jalopies. You'll have to use your judgment about whether to encourage the sounds, which can be either productive or detrimental, depending on the circumstances.

T Now pretend that the carnival is in town and you're going to go with your friends tonight to ride all the rides and eat all your favorite foods. How excited are you? Really let your excitement show as you go home from school. Try it. Now, instead of going to the carnival, you're going home, and you know you'll be in trouble because your mom told you not to take any more cookies from the cookie jar, and you got caught taking the last two.

T You're the fastest sprinter in the Olympics and are in the starting blocks waiting for the gun to go off. Go. Now you're a distance runner just about to start a 10-mile race; you have a long way to go, and you don't want to wear yourself out.

T You're a mouse running from a cat. Now you're a hippopotamus with a full stomach trying to run.

☸ Show me fast movement with your fingers.
Show me slow movement with your fingers.
Show me slow jogging, fast running.

Differentiating among Time Words

Setting: Children scattered throughout general space

Tasks/Challenges:

T Show me the difference among the words "dash," "waddle," "dart," and "crawl." First, dash. Go. Now, waddle. Go. Now, dart. Go. Next, crawl. Remember to change speeds with each word so the speeds are very clear.

T Let's try them again. Listen very carefully because I'm going to start calling them out faster, and you'll have to change quickly from one to the other.

Other pairs of words can be used to elicit changes in time: creep/explode, pop/sneak, gallop/totter, slither/stride. See Box 17-4 for other action words that can be used in teaching the various effort concepts.

Combining Sport Skills and Time

Setting: Children scattered throughout general space

Tasks/Challenges:

T Before beginning, I want you to think of your favorite sports person. Be sure you can tell me who it is when I ask, because this is important. After you decide who your favorite person is, choose one action she or he performs that you really like. For example, if you choose a famous football quarterback as your favorite person, you might pick "throwing the bomb" as your favorite action. Think carefully to pick your person and action.

T Now, on the signal you'll perform the action you chose as if it were on video set at a fast speed—in a fast motion instead of slow motion. Repeat your fast-motion action four times, each time making the motion faster.

T Now do the same action as if it were in slow motion, just like instant replays. Make sure there's a clear difference between your fast and slow motions. I should be able to tell just from watching which motions are fast and which ones are slow.

Continually Changing in Time While Traveling

Setting: Children scattered throughout general space

Tasks/Challenges:

T As you're standing in your self-space, pick a point across the room you want to focus on. All the traveling you do will be directed toward that point. On the signal, slowly begin to travel around the point you've chosen, much like a lion stalking its prey. Gradually increase your speed so you're traveling at your maximum speed. Just before you reach the spot you've chosen, slow down, slowly circle, then suddenly pounce. The differences in the speeds at which you travel should be very clear. Thus, your sequence should go like this: Pick a point to focus on, start slowly circling toward that point, gradually pick up speed until you're going really fast, then gradually slow down and suddenly pounce toward your spot.

C Now that you have the idea, pick a new spot and practice your circling routine five times so that it's

Box 17-4

Action Words

When you're teaching the effort concepts, action words help elicit many of the responses desired. For the exercise to be productive as well as exciting, students need to have more than a few common words repeated over and over. Here are some possibilities.

Single Action Words

Traveling Actions			Nontraveling Actions				Stopping Actions	
Run	Hop	Creep	Flick	Squeeze	Contract	Dangle	Pause	Collapse
Dash	Skate	Sneak	Jerk	Compress	Fold	Jab	Stop	Slide
Dart	Jump	Slither	Twitch	Explode	Splatter	Slash	Freeze	Flop
Skip	Bounce	Crawl	Writhe	Spread	Punch	Chop	Anchor	Crumble
Gallop	Slide	Step	Stab	Tense	Pull	Saw		
Stamp	Kick	Stride	Grip	Relax	Press	Drip		
Whirl	Spin	Shuffle	Release	Push	Lower	Drag		
Waddle	Totter							

Sinking Actions			Rising Actions			Vibratory Actions	
Melt	Spin	Screw	Evaporate	Spin	Swell	Shake	Wriggle
Flop	Turn	Hammer	Float	Pop	Inflate	Rattle	Squirm
Drop	Slink	Spread	Rise	Grow	Lift	Vibrate	Snake
Collapse	Squash	Deflate	Turn	Blossom		Gyrate	Whisk
Pounce	Shrink	Crumple				Tumble	

Sentences of Action Words

Run—freeze—skip	Slither—inflate—explode	Rise (turn)—twitch—skip
Dart—collapse—pop	Squeeze—jump—release	Gallop—stamp—screw
Grow—spin—deflate	Creep—pounce—explode	Jump—freeze—jab
Writhe—jerk—pop	Skip—pause—flop	Chop—whirl—slash

Descriptive Words (for use with action words)

Droopy	Excited	Light	Springy	Spikey	Square
Tired	Heavy	Tense	Carefree	Sharp	Angular
Happy	Strong	Floppy	Carefully	Rounded	Curvy
Greedy	Loving	Gentle	Fierce	Soft	Hard
Prickly	Spongy	Big	Small	Enormous	Tiny
Bubbling	Nervous	Unsure	Confident	Bold	Afraid

Nonsense Words

Snickersnack	Spelunk	Krinkle	Blump
Gallumph	Brip	Siczac	Crickcrock
Cavort	Bruttle-brattle	Swoosh	Snap-crackle
Flip-flop	Achoo	Kerumph	Wheezey
Grunch	Hic-up	Squizzog	

Source: Education through the Dance Experience by David Docherty, 1975, Bellingham, WA: Educational Designs and Consultants. Used with permission from the author.

very good. Try to make it the best that you can because we're going to show some of them to the class. Slow should be really slow, fast really fast, and the pounce as quick as lightning.

To help clarify this activity, choose three or four children who are successfully completing it to demonstrate (they can all demonstrate at the same time). Reinforce the notions of gradually increasing speed and the sudden contrast of the pounce.

Developing the Concept of Force

Force is the contrast of muscular tensions. The extremes are *strong* and *light,* but there are obvious gradations between the extremes. Just as *speed* to a young child is "as fast as you can go," *force* often means trying to bat a ball as hard as possible, whether the situation calls for a bunt or an outfield placement. A preschooler is likely to use the same degree of force to throw a ball 3 feet as to throw it 10 yards.

We usually introduce the concept of force by combining it with a skill that has been developed to the control level, preferably to the utilization level. For example, think of the child at a precontrol level who is learning to strike a moving ball. The youngster is so fully concentrating attention on making contact with the ball that the concept of force is an unnecessary and probably confusing thought. Hard and easy hits can come later, once the child is able to hit a ball consistently.

A dancer exemplifies the qualities of strong and light movement while expressing aggression, strength, and power; the gymnast exemplifies the qualities in floor and apparatus routines while combining firm and fine actions and balancing in a demonstration of muscular control and strength.

Teaching the Concept of Force

This section provides suggestions for helping children to understand the concept of force. The learning experiences presented help youngsters develop a functional understanding of the strong (firm) and light (fine) actions of body parts and of the entire body. *Actions of concentrated movement and muscular tensions are very tiring; keep the activity periods short.*

Learning Experiences Leading to Movement Concept Understanding

Exploring Force

Setting: Children scattered throughout general space

Tasks/Challenges:

🅣 In your own space, with your whole body, make a statue that shows how strong you are. (A strong force is also called "heavy" or "firm.") Now practice the activity again, but think about making *every* muscle in your body strong, even your head, neck, stomach, back, hands, and feet.

🅣 Now make a statue that is very light, such as a ghost would be. Your statue should be so light that it would blow away if a strong wind came along. This is what is called a light force. Try a light shape again, such as a leaf floating through the wind.

🅣 When I beat the drum, change from a strong to a light statue and then back.

Traveling and Changing Force Qualities

Setting: Children scattered throughout general space

Tasks/Challenges:

🅣 This time you're going to travel around the whole space. But as you travel, try to be as strong as you can be. You're an indestructible and all-powerful force; make all your body parts strong.

🅣 Now, as you travel, make yourself as light as can be, just as if you were floating away. All your muscles should be loose, not tight at all; make your entire body light.

Using Imagery and Force

Setting: Children scattered throughout general space

Tasks/Challenges:

🅣 This time you're going to use different images you know to help understand the force qualities. On the signal, think of yourself as a pat of butter left out on a hot day. All day long you sit in the hot sun, all weak and melted. Then suddenly someone puts you in the refrigerator, and in a little while you feel strong and solid again. Remember to make it clear with your whole body what it's like to be weak, and then make it clear with your whole body when you're strong again.

The imagery sequences you design provide experiences in extreme contrasts. Focus on the degrees along the continuum (the subtle changes) in conjunction with the actual skill, such as jumping and landing or balancing. For tips on observing children during activity, see Box 17-5.

✅ *Exit Slip.* This would be an appropriate time to use an exit slip to check students' understanding of the force concepts.

Young children's attempts at strong shapes show a beginning under-standing of the concept.

Showing Contrasts of Force

Setting: Children scattered throughout general space

Tasks/Challenges:

Ⓣ Now you're going to show the force differences in your movements. On the signal I'll call out an idea; you show me what the idea looks like by moving either strong or light. Make it very clear which you are: strong or light.

Young children often equate the concept of strong force with the concept of size. Be careful to not pair all imagery examples as such—for example, big-firm or small-fine.

Ideas:

1. **Frosty the Snowman.** You're going to show the life of Frosty the Snowman. First you're a single

Observing during Activity

When concentrating on developing tasks, it's quite easy to forget to really look at the students and the responses they're making. Here's a practical way to observe them: After you give a task and before saying anything to the class, move to the outside of the area, and observe for 10 to 15 seconds. You should quickly assess these three questions:

1. Are the children working safely without interfering with others?
2. If any equipment or apparatus is involved, is it being used within the context of the lesson?
3. Is the assigned task appropriate for the developmental level of the class and of interest to the class?

When you can answer yes to all three questions, look at the aspects you've determined to be important for the specific skill being practiced, and extend or refine the task as appropriate.

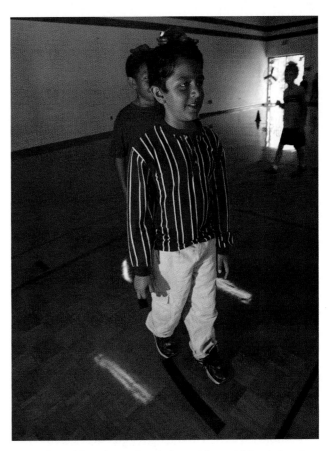

To elicit bound flow, the teacher challenged these children to travel while balancing beanbags on their heads.

snowflake falling through the air; then you're several snowflakes that are beginning to stick together to make a shape; now you're the solid, sturdy snowman that can't be knocked over; and finally you're the snowman melting slowly as the sun comes out.

2. *Punch/flick.* Now we're going to use words to help us tell the difference between strong and light movements. The first two words are "punch" and "flick." I'll give you a story and you make the movements that go with it. One movement should be strong, the other light. Make each movement very clear. Pretending that you're a boxer, punch your opponent as hard as you can. Now, just flick a fly off your mother's freshly baked chocolate cake.

3. *Creep/pounce.* The words "creep" and "pounce" can help us learn strong and light movements. Let's try it. You're playing hide-and-seek; creep very quietly from your hiding place so no one will see or hear you. Now, you're creeping up to catch your runaway kitten. You've found her and are ready to pounce and grab her before she runs away again. Ready, pounce. Oops, you missed.

 Which movement was strong and which was light?

4. *Sneak/scare.* This time you're going to show light and strong actions when I use the words "sneak" and "scare." Let's pretend your brother has a letter from his girlfriend. You want to know what it says, so you sneak up behind him to find out. You can't read over his shoulder, so you figure if you scare him, he'll drop the letter and run. Go. You need to sneak, then scare.

5. *Float/collapse.* Have you ever seen a hang glider? It's like a big kite that floats through the air, but a person is floating with it, just as if he or she were attached to a kite. You're now a hang glider, sailing over the mountains. Go. Oh, no—all the wind suddenly died; your hang glider is crashing to the ground. You just collapse as you hit the ground.

6. *Glide/stomp.* You're a very good skater, and today you go roller-blading. You're at the local roller-blading rink, gliding along, having a grand time. Now something sticks to your skate; you don't fall, but you have to stomp your skate really hard to try to get the object off. Clearly show the difference between your light and strong movements.

7. *Raindrop/thunderstorm.* You're a raindrop in a gentle spring rain, a rain that makes all the flowers bloom and the grass turn its greenest green. Now you're a raindrop in a bad summer thunderstorm—you know, a storm where the wind blows so hard you think the trees will fall down and the sky turns very dark. Remember to make it very clear which raindrop is strong and which one is light.

8. *Friends/foes.* Now you're going to show strong and light as you greet your friend and then as you meet an enemy. Pretend you're walking down the street and see an old friend. How would you greet her? Now play as if you've just seen the biggest bully in the school. How would you greet him?

 Which force was light? Which one was strong?

9. *Ant/rock.* Imagine what an ant trying to lift a rock feels like. Try hard; you're the only hope of the rock getting off the ground. Now you're a strong person trying to lift the same rock that the ant lifted. How are your actions different?

10. *Olympic weight lifter.* You're an Olympic weight lifter going for the gold medal; this is the heaviest weight you've ever lifted. As you pretend, remember to keep your entire body strong. Even show in your face that you're strong. Now you're lifting a five-pound bag of flour. How easy is it for you? Make your whole body light as you show this action. All your muscles should be loose, as if they're hardly being used at all.

Developing the Concept of Flow

Watch a very young child running down a hill. The actions are unstoppable, almost out of control, until the child reaches the bottom. A batter's swing at a baseball, the smash a tennis player executes, a gymnast's giant swing on the high bar—all these are examples of *free flow* in movement. It seems that the performer is lost in the movement; the movement, not the performer, seems to control the situation.

Bound actions are stoppable, cautious, and restrained. The performer is in control at all times. Pushing a heavy object, traveling an angular pathway while trying to stay within boundaries, executing a slow cartwheel with a pause for a handstand before traveling on are all examples of *bound flow.*

Teaching the Concept of Flow

This section provides learning experiences designed to help children understand and demonstrate the difference between free flow and bound flow. The activities encompass a variety of movements that are important for both skill performance and safety. *Music can greatly enhance the feel of bound and free flow.*

Learning Experiences Leading to Movement Concept Understanding

Traveling and Flow

Setting: Children scattered throughout general space

Tasks/Challenges:

T On the signal, travel around the room and pause the instant you hear the stop signal. I'm really looking for stops that happen suddenly, without you taking any extra steps. Freeze in your tracks. This kind of movement—jerky and with lots of stops—is said to have *bound* flow. In other words, it doesn't flow very smoothly.

Children tend to anticipate the teacher's signals. Make stop signals close together and frequent so this activity will be successful.

T This time as you travel around the space, pretend you're completely free, like an eagle soaring high, or a really happy person who has no cares in the world. Make your traveling seem as if it has no end; it could just keep going and going. This type of movement is said to have *free* flow; it doesn't stop, much like a balloon or cloud floating in the air.

Eliciting Flow Qualities

Setting: Children scattered throughout general space

Tasks/Challenges:

T This time I'm going to give you some actions to help you practice bound flow. Pretend to do each action that I tell you, always showing the bound flow of what you're doing. Remember, bound flow can be stopped and is generally slow and sometimes jerky.

1. Press the floor with your hands and feet as you move. Make sure you keep a bound flow throughout the whole motion.
2. Pretend you're pushing a heavy box.
3. Now carry a glass of milk that is too full without spilling any of it.
4. Play as if you're pulling from the bottom of a well a full bucket of water on a pulley.

T Now I'll give you some actions that require free flow. Free flow can be more difficult than bound flow, so really concentrate on making your movements seem as if they could go on forever. Make it very clear that these are free movements and unstoppable.

1. Pretend to flick away a fly.
2. This time you're really mad at your brother. Slash your arms through the air to show how really mad you are.
3. You're cooking bacon on the stove, and the grease starts to spatter; jerk your head and arms away so you won't get burned.

T This next action will combine free and bound flow. Raise your arm high above your head with bound flow, stoppable at any moment. Let your arm fall freely downward in an unstoppable action.

✱ Which movement is unstoppable—bound or free? Which movement is stoppable at any time—bound or free?

✓ *Student Display.* Flow is a difficult concept for students to understand. Having children bring in magazine pictures that illustrate the various qualities in action and then creating a student display labeling the qualities is a useful assessment.

Following Flow Sentences

Setting: Children scattered throughout general space

Tasks/Challenges:

T On the board are a number of sentences. The first one says "Walk, run, jump." On the signal, begin to travel, using the sentence as your guide. The words are clear; the commas mean to pause or hesitate, and the periods mean to stop. Make it very clear where your pauses are and when you stop. Repeat the action of the sentence three times.

Other possible sentences: "Walk, sneak, pounce." "Leap, stamp, twist." "Creep, hop, flop."

T What you just did was an example of bound flow. Now you're going to turn the same thing into free flow. This time, on the signal, you're going to follow the same sentences but without the punctuation marks—in other words, no commas and no periods or no pauses or stops. So you'll start at the beginning of the sentence and keep going all the way through; no one should know when you're going to change to the next action. Your action should just flow smoothly, one action leading to the next. When you get to the end of a sentence, just start over again. On the signal, let's start with the first sentence.

Children enjoy using interpretations of different punctuation marks, such as the comma, exclamation point, and question mark, as different ending shapes.

C Now that you're so good at the sentences, you're going to make up one of your own. On the board is a list of words. (Such words as walk, shrink, gallop, skip, explode, jump, roll, and hop are good to use.) Choose three of the words, and make your sentence. Put punctuation in, because punctuation is the key to when you stop or pause. Practice your sentence five times with the punctuation in it; then practice it five times without punctuation. Practice it very carefully, because we'll show some of the sentences to the class. It should be obvious when the punctuation is and isn't in the sentence.

Practicing Flow Sequences

Setting: Children scattered throughout general space

Tasks/Challenges:

🅣 This time, there are two columns of words on the board, but no punctuation. You're going to join the words together to make a sequence. The first column of words reads *melt, inflate, slither, shrink*. On the signal, practice the words in the order you see them. It is your choice when to change from one word to the next. Go.

Now, do the second column of words: *jump, spin, stride, pop*.

🅐 Which sequence gave you a bound feeling? Which one a free feeling?

🅒 Now go back and practice each sequence three times, making it very clear each time which one is bound and which one is free.

Using Flow Conversations

Setting: Children with partners, scattered throughout general space

Tasks/Challenges:

Children beginning sequence work often need guidance in restricting the length of the sequence; generally two or three actions are appropriate for the initial sequence.

🅣 Now you're going to work with a partner and talk to your partner. The only catch is that neither of you can use your voice to talk. You're going to talk with your body. One of you needs to be bound flow and the other one free flow; go ahead and decide that now. Ready? This is how you'll talk: The partner who is bound flow will talk about being imprisoned and not being allowed to go out to see the world; the partner who is free flow will talk about

how wonderful it is to roam and explore and run up and down the hills; in other words, what it's like to be free. Now, one of you start; with your body talk about your aspect. Keep your sentence very short. As you move, your partner listens or watches. After you make your statement, stop; your partner then answers with a statement, and you listen. When your partner finishes, you again provide an answer. The whole conversation should go back and forth until each of you has moved five times.

🅒 After you've completed the conversation once, go back and practice it twice more so that it's very clear who's free flow and who's bound flow. I know this is a bit hard to understand, so let me go over it one more time. You and your partner are going to talk about bound and free flow with your body actions, not your voices. Just as in any conversation, it's a give and take. One of you will make a short body action sentence and then the other one will answer. Each of you gets to talk five times and then it ends. After you've finished once, go back and practice two more times. Remember that two people can't talk at once, so listen when your partner is talking. "Still" is the word.

It really helps to find at least one twosome (ideally more) doing the activity correctly and have them demonstrate. Be patient; the task will take time if the children are to really develop their conversations. Children should switch roles after sufficient time to practice the other aspect of flow.

Combining Time, Force, and Flow

Setting: Children scattered throughout general space

Tasks/Challenges:

🅣 The task sheet (Figure 17.2) for today will allow you to practice combining the concepts of time, force, and flow. After you practice each challenge so that you feel it's as clear as you can make it, find a friend to watch you. If the friend feels you've done the challenge correctly, she or he signs her or his name in the blank; if not, you'll have to go back and practice some more. I'll walk around the class, and at any time I can ask you to show me any challenge you've marked off. If you have any questions, ask me.

✔ *Self-Assessment.* The above task sheet could easily serve as a self-assessment of the effort concepts by changing "who watched" to "I still need practice" or "I'm good" or "I need help." *(See Chapter 14 for more information on developing student self-assessments.)*

Figure 17.2 Task sheet for time, force, and flow.

Name _____ Teacher _____

Time, Force, and Flow Task Sheet

Date	Who Watched	Challenge
		Find three body parts that you can move at a slow speed.
		Find three body parts (different from the ones in the first challenge) that you can move at a fast speed.
		Find four ways to move while showing free and light qualities.
		Find two movements that you can first make strong and slow and then make light and fast.
		Find any movement you want that combines two aspects of the effort concept (**time:** fast-slow, **force:** strong-light, **flow:** bound-free). After you finish, write down your movements and the concepts they included. Movement Concept _____ _____ _____ _____ _____ _____ _____ _____

Applying the Effort Concepts

We focus on concepts until the children have learned the basic terminology related to the effort qualities of movement. When the children are able to accurately demonstrate the differences between the extremes of each concept, we no longer focus on the concept. Instead, we focus on how the concept relates to the performance of a particular skill: fast dribble, fluid roll, or light gallop. We want the children to learn the effort concepts so that they can apply the concepts to actual skill-learning situations.

The ability to use gradations of movement qualities distinguishes the inept performer from the skilled one, the sloppy movement from the polished one. An individual can learn to execute the basic requirements of a cartwheel, for example, so that it can be recognized as a cartwheel. But when that cartwheel is executed in a ragged, uneven, uncontrolled manner, it is clearly and easily distinguishable from a cartwheel performed by an experienced, trained gymnast. We teach children to apply the qualities of movement to their skill performances to help them become skillful movers.

Generally, the concept of time (fast-slow) is easier for children to grasp than either the concept of force (strong-light) or the concept of flow (bound-free). For this reason, you may need to focus more on force and flow than on time. Time can be studied as an applied concept—fast and slow skips, rolling fast and rolling slowly, accelerated and decelerated change of levels—before force or flow. The difference is that in teaching a concept, our observational focus is primarily on the children's ability to understand and apply the effort concept. In contrast, when we use a concept as a subfocus, we know that the children already understand the concept from previous lessons, and therefore our teaching focus is primarily on the skill and how it can be executed by using varying movements.

Reading Comprehension Questions

1. How is a movement performed fast different from the same movement performed slowly?
2. How is a movement executed with strong force different from the same movement performed with light force?
3. How is a movement performed with bound flow different from the same movement performed with free flow?
4. Initially, the extremes, rather than the gradations, of the effort concepts are emphasized. Why?
5. When is slowness an important concept? List several movements.
6. What does the term *acceleration-deceleration* mean? Answer by using examples from the text or from your own experiences.
7. What does focusing on the movement quality of an image rather than on the image itself mean?

This statement will help you: "Imagine that the floor is covered with peanut butter six inches deep." Why is this focus important?

8. When do you change from focusing on the effort concept to focusing on how the concept relates to the performance of a particular skill?
9. What is the purpose of teaching children to apply the qualities of movement to their skill performances?
10. Using the movement analysis wheel, manipulate the wheel to show the movement concept of effort in relation to locomotor, manipulative, and nonmanipulative skills. Identify two skills for each category that an effort concept can modify and write a sample task for each.

References/Suggested Readings

Joyce, M. (1994). *First steps in teaching creative dance to children* (3rd ed.). Palo Alto, CA: Mayfield.

National Association for Sport and Physical Education. (2004). *Moving into the future: National standards for physical education* (2nd ed). New York: McGraw-Hill.

Relationships

Our lives are made up of relationships—to people and to objects—that occur not only in physical education classes but also in everyday life. Driving to and from work in an automobile, maneuvering through a crowded aisle in a supermarket, or dodging around an icy spot on a sidewalk—all these activities involve complex, dynamic relationships.

And each relationship involves several contextual variables (bodies, body parts, and objects) in simultaneous interaction.

The movement concept of relationship defines with whom or with what the body moves; it gives meaning to the interaction between individuals and their environment. The concept is divided into three major

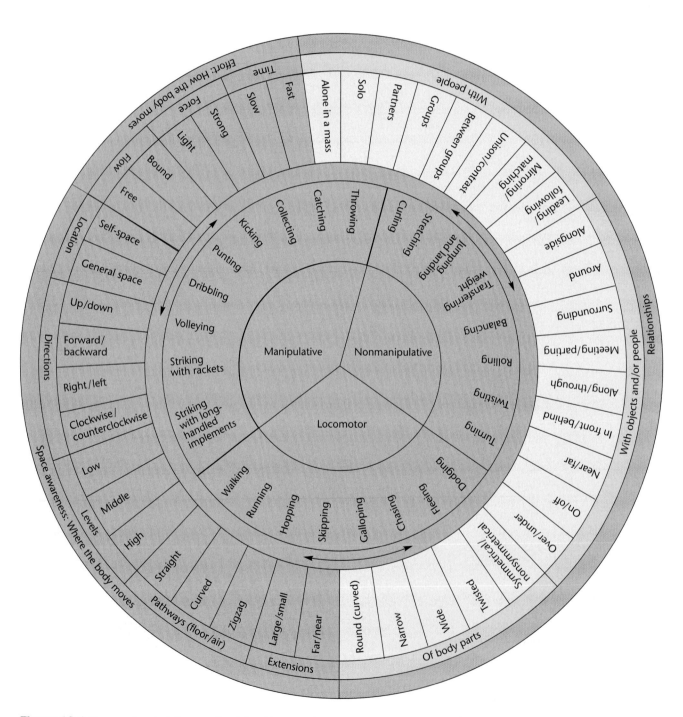

Figure 18.1 Movement analysis framework: relationship concepts.

components: relationships of body parts, relationships with objects and/or people, and relationships with people, as first introduced in Chapter 3 (Table 3.2). In turn, each of these constructs is defined by observable characteristics that can be taught to children. Figure 18.1 conceptualizes this idea, putting it in perspective with the other movement concepts and skill themes. The relationship category is in the right-hand side of the movement framework. The outermost ring defines the concept, the second ring presents the three components of the concept, and the third ring defines the aspects of the three components.

When teaching the relationship concepts, we typically begin with the simplest relationships for children to understand—the self relationships. Because so many young children are still at the "I" stage, the initial lesson focus is simply identifying body parts and their relationship to one another, followed by body part shapes. As the children develop a functional understanding of the relationships among body parts, we shift the emphasis to moving in relation to different objects and also to one another. In preschool settings, many of the relationship concepts will be new to children. In the primary grades, however, some of these concepts will simply be a review for the children, and therefore the lessons can progress rather rapidly. The third category of concepts, relationships with others, is typically combined with the study of other concepts and skill themes. Initially the focus is on working with partners, and when the children develop the social and physical maturity needed to collaborate with three or four others, we're able to include tasks that require them to work in groups.

When teaching the relationship concepts it's easy to forget that the purpose is to have the children actually *know* what each relationship concept means. Imagine that one of us is going to teach a class of your second graders. Before teaching, we might ask whether your children know the relationship concepts. If you say yes, we'd assume that the children can make a symmetrical shape or a nonsymmetrical shape when asked to do so. Or we'd assume that the youngsters know the difference between mirroring and matching, over and under, and so forth. "Knowing" doesn't mean that the concepts were taught; knowing means that the children are able to show their understanding through their movement. In other words, the children have *functional understanding.*

If one of us were going to teach a second-grade art class, we might ask the teacher whether the children know their colors. If the teacher says yes, we'd assume that the children know the difference among red, brown, black, orange, and so forth. We'd further expect that they can readily use these colors in the lesson we would

teach. If the teacher says the children don't know their colors, however, we'd design our lesson to help them learn their colors.

Developing the Concept of the Relationships of Body Parts

Before children can focus on the relationships among body parts, they need to be able to identify specific body parts. Thus, it's essential that each child acquire a functional vocabulary of body part names. Examples of tasks that can be used in teaching this vocabulary include:

1. Pointing to the ceiling with the elbow (knee, nose)
2. Touching the floor with the wrist (waist, stomach)
3. Traveling around the room and on the signal stopping and touching heels (shoulders, heads) with another person

Once the children have learned the names of the body parts, lessons focus on making shapes (round, narrow, wide, twisted, symmetrical, and nonsymmetrical) and using body parts in relation to one another. For example, we might ask children to:

1. Travel and stop in a twisted shape.
2. Change from a symmetrical to a nonsymmetrical shape.
3. Make a wide shape during flight.
4. Move their feet so that the feet are higher than their head.

Teaching the Concept of the Relationships of Body Parts

This section provides suggestions for teaching children to identify and use different body parts and to develop an understanding of how different body parts can relate to one another. Suggestions for teaching the concepts of various body shapes and body part shapes also are presented. You can use any body parts for the activities given here, but with the tasks that require balancing, be careful not to use parts that will elicit balances that may be too complex for some students. For example, when using parts such as the head and hands, make it clear that other parts can be used in conjunction with them.

Learning Experiences Leading to Movement Concept Understanding

Identifying Body Parts

Setting: Children in self-space (on a carpet square; on an X on the floor)

Tasks/Challenges:

T I'm going to call out different body parts. Touch the body parts I call out as quickly as possible when you hear them. Remember to pay close attention to what I'm saying, because I may start to go faster or try to trick you. Ready? Remember, touch each body part as I call it out.

Body parts can include nose, arm, chin, ankle, ear, foot, elbow, temple, wrist, neck, shoulder, eyebrow, eye, teeth, cheek, leg, forehead, knee, thumb, mouth, side, hip, lip, earlobe.

T This time, instead of just touching a body part as I name it, you'll have to touch whatever hand I call out to the different body parts I call out. This activity will be harder, because you'll have to remember which is your right and which is your left. For example, if I say "Right hand to left knee," touch your right hand to your left knee. Try to do this as quickly as possible, but be careful in deciding what body parts to use. Just to help you out, let's review right and left. Raise your right hand. *(Check to see that they're correct.)* Ready? Let's try it.

Body parts used can include left hand to right knee, right hand to left elbow, left hand to left shoulder, right hand to left knee, left hand to left foot. Thick rubber bands worn on a wrist or ankle can assist children to learn their right from their left.

T This time you're going to play a game with finding body parts, similar to Simon Says, except you don't have to sit out if you miss. Here's how to play. I'll call out "Simon says to touch your toes," and you'll touch your toes. But if I don't say "Simon says," then you aren't supposed to do it. So if I just say "Touch

your toes," you aren't supposed to touch your toes, because Simon didn't say to do it. Pay attention, because the game will start to go very quickly. Remember I'm watching to see if you touch the right parts and how quickly you can do it.

T This time, instead of touching your hands to different body parts, you're going to touch two different body parts together. For example, I'll call out "Knee to elbow," and you'll touch your knee to your elbow. You'll have to think hard on this one. Ready? I'm looking to see if you can get the correct different parts together.

Possible body part combinations include knee to elbow, hands to waist, head to knees, foot to shoulder, knee to foot, elbow to wrist, back of wrist to back of knee.

Balancing While Using Different Body Parts

Setting: Each child on a carpet square

Tasks/Challenges:

T Find a carpet square for yourself, and sit on the square. I'll know that you're all ready when I see everyone seated on a carpet square. This time when I call out a body part, you should put that body part on the carpet square and make a shape with the rest of your body, leaving the one part that I called out on the carpet. So if I call out "Elbow," put your elbow on the carpet, and then make a shape with the rest of your body. When you make your shape, be sure to hold it very still so I can see what part is on the carpet and what your shape looks like. Ready? Let's try it.

T Shapes that you hold very still are called *balances,* almost like statues. Let's try this activity again; make your balances and shapes very clear and still.

T Now you're going to balance on different numbers of body parts. I'll call out a number of parts; you balance by touching that number to the floor. Count your parts touching the floor very carefully because I'll be coming around and asking you how many parts are on the floor and which parts they are.

Four parts
Three parts
More than four parts
Two parts
One part

For each number, offer suggestions or hints, or have several students demonstrate the possible combination of parts. Also mix up the order in which the parts are called out.

Can you travel through the hoop without touching it?

Freezing on Different Body Parts

Setting: Children scattered in general space

Tasks/Challenges:

🅣 You're going to travel around the space on your feet. When you hear the stop signal, touch the body part I call out to the floor. So if I call out "Elbow" as you stop, touch your elbow to the floor. As you move, be very careful to stay in a space by yourself, so you don't touch anyone when you're trying to touch different body parts to the floor. This activity will start to go very fast, so touch the parts to the floor as quickly as possible, and make it very clear which part is touching the floor.

Body parts can include arm, ankle, foot, leg, side, hip.

🅣 When you travel this time, instead of touching body parts to the floor, touch the body parts I call out to the same parts of another person. So if I call out "Heels," stop, touch your heels to the heels of one other person, and then freeze. As you do this, make the touching parts very clear; don't just stand beside the other person. To be safe, make sure as you touch that you stop first and then touch easily so no one gets hurt. The idea is to quickly and easily touch and then be ready to go again. Ready?

Body parts can include wrist, shoulder, forehead, knee, thumb, arm, ankle, foot, elbow, leg, side, hip.

Traveling on Different Body Parts

Setting: Children scattered in general space

Tasks/Challenges:

🅣 This time, instead of balancing on different body parts, you're going to travel on different body parts. What body parts do we usually travel on? Let's start with the feet, just to get warmed up. Make sure to travel in all the space and to stay on your feet. Let's start by walking.

🅣 Now try something a little different: the hands and feet. Remember to travel with your hands and feet both touching the floor at some time. Ready? Make sure you actually go someplace, and be careful of others.

🅣 This time you're going to make up your own way of traveling using different body parts. As you do this, make sure that I can tell from just looking at you what body parts you're using for traveling; you should be using two different body parts to move around the room. Be very careful to watch where you're going and not touch anyone else.

Balancing on Matching and Nonmatching Parts

Setting: Each child in a personal space

"Touch ears with hands." These young children, who are at the "I" stage, benefit from tasks designed to clarify the relationships among body parts.

Tasks/Challenges:

T This time, instead of balancing on a certain number of parts, you're going to balance on parts that are alike and parts that are different. Parts that are alike are called matching parts. What parts do you have that are matching or alike? *(Children respond "Hands," "Feet," etc.)* Good; let's try to balance on some of those parts. First let's try an easy one: the feet. Now, how about the knees? Think up one of your own. Make sure that the parts you use are matching parts.

T Now pick one set of matching parts and make up a balance that you like and practice it until you can hold it very still. Be sure you know the name of the matching parts you're balancing on because I'll come around and ask some of you, just to make sure.

T This time you're going to balance on different parts. *Different* parts are parts that don't match each other; they aren't alike. What are some possible combinations of different parts? *(Children respond "Knee and elbow," "Back and hands," etc.)* Let's try some. First, try the seat and the feet. Now try the shoulders and the elbows. What about the knees and the elbows? Now, make up one combination on your own.

T Now pick one set of different parts and make up your own balance. Practice your balance until you can hold it very still. See if you can hold it perfectly still until I count to three alligators. *(Children enjoy fun ways to challenge themselves—you can make up your own terms to challenge the children to hold their balances for several seconds.)* Be sure the different parts you're using are very clear, because I might ask you what they are.

Round, Narrow, Wide, and Twisted Body Shapes

Setting: Each child in personal space

Tasks/Challenges:

T Today you're going to learn about different shapes you can make with your bodies. Everyone find a self-space so that you can't touch anyone else. The first shape you're going to make is a pretzel. All of you try to make a pretzel out of your body; hold very still. This shape is called a twisted shape.

T Now, try a twisted shape on your own. As you do so, make sure your whole body is twisted, not just your arms and legs. Try to twist your stomach, too.

T The next shape is a circle. Try to make your whole body look like a circle. This is called a round shape.

T Now try to make up a different round shape by yourself. Make sure that your whole body is making

"Freeze in a low wide shape." This task requires children like this girl to consider relationships among body parts.

the round shape and that it is very round. Remember, round things have no bumps in them.

T This time you're going to make a skinny shape. Try to make your body as skinny as possible, so skinny that if you turned sideways, no one would be able to see you. This is called a narrow shape.

T Find another narrow shape by yourself. Make it as skinny as possible, as if you were trying to hide.

T What do you think the opposite of narrow is? *Wide,* right. Make your body as wide as possible.

T Try another wide shape by yourself. Remember to get as wide as possible, as if you were trying to stop someone from getting around you.

C This time pick your favorite kind of shape, and make it, holding it very still. I'm going to come around and guess which type of shape it is, so make your shape as clear as possible. Your shape should be wide, narrow, round, or twisted.

T Things are going to be a little harder this time. Still staying in your own space, you're going to make a wide shape. Then, when I give the signal, change your wide shape to a narrow shape, and hold it very still. The difference between the wide and narrow shape should be very clear. Make a wide shape, and hold it. Now change that wide shape to a narrow shape.

T Try it again—another wide shape; change to a narrow.

T Now, a third.

© This time pick the shape you liked the most, and practice it until it changes very easily from wide to narrow. Work on it until it's your best and both shapes are very clear.

T You thought the last activity was hard? This one is even harder! Think you can do it? You're going to change from a twisted shape to a round shape. So find your twisted shape. Got it? On the signal, change that twisted shape to a round shape.

T Now, let's try a different twisted to round shape. Go.

T And a third twisted to round shape. Make sure that your twisted shape is really twisted and your round shape is very round. I should be able to easily tell the difference between the two shapes.

© Now, pick your favorite round and twisted shape. Practice your favorite one so that your move from twisted to round is smooth (not jerky) and that your shapes are so clear the principal could easily tell the difference if he or she walked in.

Changing from One Body Shape to Another

Setting: Children in self-space moving to a drumbeat

Tasks/Challenges:

T You'll really need to be in a good self-space for this activity, so make sure you're as far away from everyone else as you can be. Again you're going to change from one shape to another, but I'm going to give you drumbeats to help. You're going to move from a round shape to a wide shape, but instead of just doing it on your own, you'll have six beats of the drum to get from the round shape to the wide shape and then six beats to get back to your round shape. Listen now while I give you the beats of the drum. Does everyone understand? You'll start in a round shape and on the six beats of the drum open to a wide shape. You'll hold your wide shape very still, and then on the next six beats of the drum you'll return to your round shape. Let's try it. Find your round shape.

T Let's try it again; this time find different round and wide shapes.

T Now, let's do a third set of shapes.

© You're now going to practice one set of shapes four more times, so you can make it really good. Pick your favorite shapes. Remember as you move to make each shape very clear, and make sure that the movement goes with the beats of the drum.

Pinpoint two or three children who are succeeding with the activity, and ask them if they'd like to show it to the class.

T You're going to make the shapes a little different this time. Instead of opening up on six beats and closing on six, you're going to open up on one quick beat and then close slowly on six. So the sequence will now go like this: Start in a round shape; on the beat, quickly open up to a wide shape, and hold it still; then on the next six beats of the drum, slowly return to your round shape. Remember to open from the round to the wide shape very, very quickly, as if you were a flash of lightning.

Pinpoint several children to show the activity to the rest of the class.

© Now practice your favorite shapes four times. Remember not only to make the quick shape sudden and the slow shape sustained but also to make your round and wide shapes very clear. To look really good, remember to hold the beginning and the end very still so that we all know when you started and when you finished.

For the distinction between the movement concepts of body shapes and the skills needed to achieve those shapes, see Box 18-1.

Box 18-1

Stretching, Curling, Twisting, and Turning

There is a subtle, yet important, distinction between the *movement concepts* of round, narrow, wide, and twisted (body shapes) and the *skills* of stretching, curling, twisting, and turning. When the children are in the process of actually moving—the "ing" part—it is technically a skill; once they have arrived, it is technically a concept. For example, when a child has finished making a twisted shape, it is considered a concept. When the child is in the process of twisting, however, it is technically a skill (i.e., an actual movement). For this reason, you will find the movements of stretching, curling, twisting, and turning listed under the nonmanipulative category of the skill themes (Chapter 2) and the tasks for helping children achieve quality stretches, twists, turns, and curls described primarily in Chapters 21, 22, and 23. The tasks for helping children learn the difference among the movement concepts of round, narrow, wide, and twisted are described in this chapter. In actuality, this distinction is important only from a theoretical standpoint—the children don't necessarily need to understand this distinction. They just need plenty of opportunities to understand the meaning of the concepts (which we describe in this section) and truly develop their abilities to stretch, curl, twist, and turn.

Traveling and Freezing in Different Body Shapes

Setting: Children traveling in general space

Tasks/Challenges:

T Instead of making shapes in your self-space, this time you're going to travel around the space and on the signal stop and quickly make the shape I call out. For example, if you're traveling and I call out "Twisted," on the signal, make a twisted shape. As you make your shapes, be sure they're very clear so that I can easily tell what they are. If I can't tell what they are, I'll have to ask you. As you travel, be careful of your classmates.

T Now, as you stop to make your shape, try to do it as quickly as possible, almost as if you just froze in that shape when you stopped. Remember, frozen shapes don't fall over.

Making Symmetrical and Nonsymmetrical Shapes

Setting: Children in self-space

Tasks/Challenges:

T You've already learned about wide, narrow, round, and twisted shapes. This time you're going to learn about two different kinds of shapes. The words describing these shapes are hard, so listen carefully. First, find a body shape that looks exactly alike on both sides of your body; in other words, if you were divided in half, both sides of you would look alike. This is called a symmetrical shape.

T Try making a symmetrical shape. Remember, both sides of your body must look exactly alike.

T Now find a shape in which the two sides of your body don't look alike. In other words, if you were cut in half, each side would have a different shape. We call this a nonsymmetrical shape.

T Make another nonsymmetrical shape. Remember, both sides must be different.

T Since you now know the difference between symmetrical and nonsymmetrical, let's find three more balances of each shape. First do symmetrical; remember, both sides are alike. Try to make each of your balances very clear so I can tell without thinking what kind of shape it is.

T Now do nonsymmetrical shapes. Find three more nonsymmetrical shapes. Try to make the sides of your body as different as possible so no one could possibly confuse your shape with a symmetrical one.

C Once you've found three more nonsymmetrical shapes, practice your favorite one five extra times so you can show it to the whole class. *(Half the class demonstrates their favorite nonsymmetrical shape, and then the other half shows their favorite nonsymmetrical shape.)*

✓ *Event Task.* This would be an appropriate time to use an event task to determine if students are able to make different body shapes. A possible task might be the following.

You and a partner are going to make up a routine. It will consist of three shapes. In each of the shapes you and your partner should match—you should look exactly alike. Here are three shapes:

1. Symmetrical, narrow shape
2. Twisted shape
3. Nonsymmetrical wide shape

Start with the first shape and hold it for three seconds (crocodiles, elephants, hamburgers, your city or state). When I say change (or beat the drum), change to the second shape. Hold it for 3 seconds, and then change to the third shape and hold that one for 3 seconds.

Creating Postcard Sculptures

Setting: Museum postcards of statues, one postcard for every child. (Photos laminated from magazines can also be used for this task.) Children love to play the roles of statues and sculptors but tend to get silly during this activity. Remind them that they need to respect their partners. Also caution them to place others only in shapes they can hold without too much difficulty, so no one gets hurt.

Tasks/Challenges:

T You're going to pretend that you're sculptors who are creating great statues. To do this you'll need a partner. When I say "Go," find a partner, and sit beside your partner. I'll know you're ready when I see everyone seated beside a partner. Each set of partners has two postcards (photos) of statues; you're going to form each other into these statues. Decide which partner will be the sculptor first; the sculptor then decides which statue to make the partner into. First, make the statue just as it is on the card, as close as possible to what you see. Then, if the statue is symmetrical, change it to nonsymmetrical; if it's nonsymmetrical, make it symmetrical. Mold each statue very carefully, and be sure you can tell me which statue is symmetrical and which is nonsymmetrical. After you make your statue, trade places with your partner.

(T) This time you're going to design your own statues. You'll still need your partner. Go ahead and decide which of you is to be the sculptor first. Make your first statue symmetrical. The statue stays "frozen" until the signal. At the signal, move to someone's else's statue and redesign it to suit yourself. On the next signal, move to another new statue and redesign it. Keep doing this until you're told to change. When you hear the change signal, change places with whatever statue you're with.

Let's practice once. Form your partner into a symmetrical statue. *(Allow at least one minute.)* Now, move to another statue and remake it, still into a symmetrical shape. Do you have the hang of it? *(Select several children for demonstration.)* Go to the next statue.

(T) Now trade places with the statue you've just made. The activity changes a little this time; you're going to create nonsymmetrical statues. Ready? Without moving to a new place, form a nonsymmetrical statue out of your partner.

(T) Change to a new statue, and then change this statue to a nonsymmetrical shape. Remember: *Nonsymmetrical* means that both sides of the body are very different from each other.

(T) Change one more time. Make this your best statue yet.

If you have access to a digital camera, the postcard sculptures are excellent photo opportunities. They also can be used in a bulletin board with actual sculpture photographs next to them. This project can be especially interesting in combination with the study of European countries.

Creating Body Shapes in the Air

Setting: Boxes, benches, low beams, and milk crates set up around the space. Figure 18.2 shows a typical equipment setup.

Tasks/Challenges:

(T) Now you're going to combine all the different kinds of body shapes that you've practiced so far. What you're going to do may be hard, but it'll be fun. Remember that as you work, all the rules for gymnastics apply. *(See Chapters 9 and 30 for establishing an environment for learning and for the rules of a gymnastics environment.)* Three or four of you will be at a piece of equipment at once. One at a time, you'll each jump off the equipment and make a shape in the air. Each time you jump, try to make

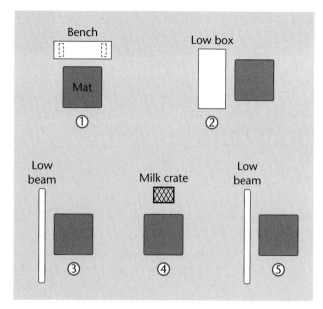

Figure 18.2 Equipment setup.

that shape in the air. Let's start with a wide shape. Make sure that you land on your feet after the jump, and don't crash to the ground. See if you can hold your landing as still as a statue.

After a while, change to narrow, twisted, round, symmetrical, and nonsymmetrical shapes.

(T) Now that you've been through all the shapes separately, you may practice them in any order you wish. Make the shapes so clear that I don't have to ask you what they are. Remember to land on your feet.

Developing the Concept of the Relationships with Objects

Some concepts are studied in relation to objects; others have more meaning when they're practiced in relation to people. The concepts of *on* and *off, along, through, over, under, around,* and *surrounding* apply primarily to relationships with objects. The concepts of *near* and *far, in front, behind,* and *alongside* are generally studied as person-to-person relationships. Because objects are more predictable (less dynamic) than children, however, we first focus on the concept of relationships with objects and then relationships with people.

Children frequently identify a lesson by the object they related to rather than by the concept they studied. For example, after a lesson in which hoops were used to study the concepts of traveling over, under, and through, children might say, "Hey, that was fun! Are we going to play with hoops again tomorrow?" In time, however, children begin to understand and use the terminology that we use. For instance, a child might say, "It's easier to go over and under the hoop than to go through the hoop."

Within the context of a game or a dance lesson, specific terms are classified as objects. In dance, for example, wands, streamers, newspapers, or scarves are considered objects. Goals, boundaries, nets, and targets are objects with which the child learns relationship concepts within a game context. See Box 18-2 for information from the *National Standards* on relationships.

Teaching the Concept of the Relationships with Objects

The activities in this section will enhance the children's awareness and ability to function effectively in relation to the objects that exist in various physical activity contexts.

Learning Experiences Leading to Movement Concept Understanding

Traveling Over, Close To, Far Away, Inside

Setting: A hoop or a rope for each child (Figures 18.3 and 18.4)

Tasks/Challenges:

- **T** To warm up, travel *over* your piece of equipment in any way you want to. As you travel, make sure that you actually go over the equipment, not around it.

- **T** This time as you travel over your equipment, try to stay as *close to* the equipment as possible. Try to keep as much of your body as possible close to the equipment, not just one body part.

- **T** Now, instead of being close to the equipment, try to have as many body parts as possible as *far away* from the equipment as possible. Only the parts

---

Box 18-2

Relationships in the *National Standards for Physical Education*

The movement concept of relationships is referenced in the *National Standards for Physical Education* (National Association for Sport and Physical Education [NASPE], 1995) as a sample kindergarten benchmark under Standard 2: Applies movement concepts and principles to the learning and development of motor skills. The sample benchmark states that a child "identifies and uses a variety of relationships with objects, e.g., over/under, behind, alongside, through" (p. 8).

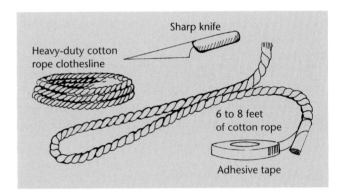

Figure 18.4 Construction of a rope. Use 1/2-inch cotton rope. The cotton will eventually loosen up and give, so different shapes can be made. Single ropes should be from 6 to 8 feet long. After you cut the ends of the rope, tape them to prevent fraying. You can use tape of different colors to quickly identify the length of the rope (e.g., green for a 6-foot rope, red for a 7-foot rope, and yellow for an 8-foot rope).

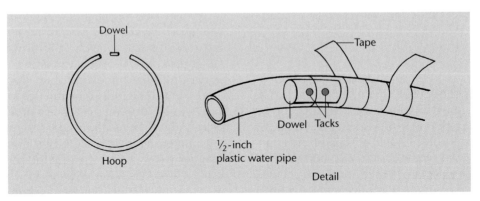

Figure 18.3 Construction of a hoop. Cut hoops form 1/2-inch plastic air-conditioner or water pipe. Make the connection with a dowel rod held in place with staples or tacks. You can also use special pipe connectors or fuse with heat to close the gap. For a 30-inch-diameter hoop, you'll need 95 inches of pipe; for a 36-inch hoop, you'll need 113 inches of pipe; and for a 42-inch hoop, you'll need 132 inches of pipe.

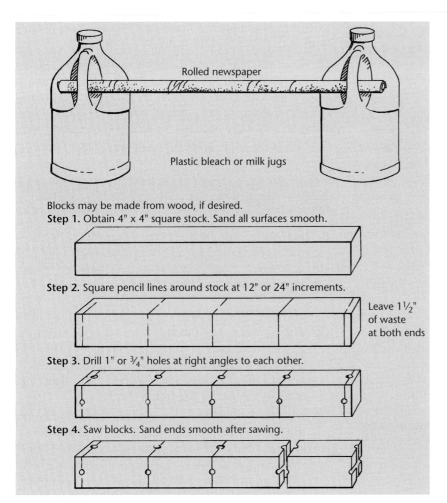

Rolled newspaper

Plastic bleach or milk jugs

Blocks may be made from wood, if desired.
Step 1. Obtain 4" x 4" square stock. Sand all surfaces smooth.

Step 2. Square pencil lines around stock at 12" or 24" increments.

Leave 1½" of waste at both ends

Step 3. Drill 1" or ¾" holes at right angles to each other.

Step 4. Saw blocks. Sand ends smooth after sawing.

Figure 18.5 Construction of hurdles. Hurdles can made from plastic bleach or milk jugs and rolled newspaper held together with masking tape. A more permanent type of hurdle can be made from wood and dowel rods.

that are really used to support your body should be near the equipment. Make sure that your whole body is as far away as possible, not just the upper parts of your body.

T The activity is a little harder now. Start on the *outside* of your equipment, put your weight down on your hands *inside* the hoop *(or a circle made with a rope),* and then continue to travel over the equipment. Make sure that you shift your weight to your hands inside the hoop *(rope)* at some point.

T These are all relationships that your body can have to equipment or other people. We can go over things, we can be close to things, we can be far away from things, or we can go inside things. Practice all four of these relationships on your own: over, close to, far away, and inside. See if you can find three ways to do each relationship. Be sure you know which ones you're practicing, because I'll come around and ask you.

If you say you're going to come around and ask the children questions or see their work, do it! Otherwise, the children may soon stop believing you.

Traveling Over, Under, Close To, and Far Away From Equipment

Setting: A hurdle or other object that the children can travel over and under (Figure 18.5) for each child in the class, scattered throughout the space

Tasks/Challenges:

T To begin, travel *over* the hurdle any way that you can; you can jump, use your hands and feet, or use only your hands. Whatever you do, make sure that you can land on your feet on the other side without falling down. This is called going over an object. Sometimes when we try to go over an object, we cheat and actually go around the side of it. Make very, very sure that you really do go over and not around.

T Now, instead of going over the hurdle, you're going to go *under* it. This will be hard because the hurdle isn't very far off the ground. You'll really have to scrunch up. Try to do it without upsetting the hurdle.

Now, let's try going under in different ways. Sometimes go under feet first, sometimes head first, sometimes on your back, and sometimes on your stomach. Be careful; always know where your body is, even those parts that you can't see.

One more activity. This time you're going to put part of your weight on your hands and bring your feet down in different places around the hurdle. To begin, bring your feet down very *close to* the hurdle. You may take your feet across the hurdle or simply leave them on one side; whatever you do, be sure your feet come down close to the hurdle.

Now try bringing your feet down *far away from* the hurdle. Make sure that every time your feet touch the floor, they're far away from the hurdle.

Now, as you work, your feet can be close to the hurdle or far away, but sometimes have your feet land close to each other, sometimes spread far apart from each other. Be able to tell me if your feet are close together or far apart when I ask you. Remember, *close together* means almost so close that nothing could get between, and *far apart* means spread out so much that a person could crawl through.

Onto/Off Concepts

Setting: A low box or a milk crate for each student, scattered throughout the space

Tasks/Challenges:

You're now going to learn two more types of relationships: *onto* and *off*. I think you probably already know what these two ideas mean, but let's practice them just to make sure. Find at least three ways to get onto and off your piece of equipment. I'm really looking for very different ways to get onto and off the equipment.

After you find three ways, practice the way you like best four extra times, so that you can show it to the class. Make it really special.

I'm going to make the activity a little harder this time by combining different types of relationships. When I say "Go," each of you get a hoop and place it on the floor beside your box. Travel *into* the hoop before you travel *onto* and *off* the box. So your sequence will involve three different relationships: into, on, and off. Find three different ways to do this. Make them very different from each other. Go.

Pinpoint several children who are doing the activity correctly or have found very creative ways to accomplish the activity to demonstrate their actions for the rest of the class. Be sure to use a variety of students so that the rest of the

class has a number of different creative ideas to base their work on.

Now you're going to make up a sequence of the relationships you practiced with the box and hoop. You must include the concepts of *off, onto,* and *into* in your sequence. Once you find a sequence that you really like, practice it until you can do it from memory and it looks the same each time.

Over, Under, Around, In Front Of, and Behind Concepts

Setting: A streamer, such as one used in rhythmic gymnastics, for each child; paper and pencils (You can make streamers from 2-inch-wide crepe paper or from surveyors' tape cut into 4- to 10-foot lengths.)

Tasks/Challenges:

Just to warm up, practice moving your streamer anywhere around your body. Remember to always try to keep the streamer in the air. To do this, you'll have to keep the streamer moving all the time; you can't let it stop, or it'll touch the floor.

Now that you know how to keep the streamer in the air, try to make it go *over, under, around, in front of,* and *behind* different body parts, such as your head, legs, and trunk. As you do this, think about what relationship each position has to each body part. Remember, you must keep the streamer moving at all times.

Now you're going to pretend you're Olympic gymnasts. Make up a sequence in which your streamer goes over, under, around, in front of, and behind two different body parts. After you make up a sequence that you like, practice it until it looks the same each time and you can do it from memory. It's very important that you remember exactly what you did, because we're going to do something really special with it.

Do you remember your sequence? Now you're going to write it down on a piece of paper and exchange the paper with a friend. Your friend will try to do your sequence, and you will try to do your friend's sequence just by reading the directions on the paper, so make it very clear which parts you went over, under, around, in front of, and behind.

Now practice your friend's sequence until you think you've learned it perfectly. When you think you're ready, ask your friend to watch you do the sequence. In a few minutes I'll ask for volunteers to show routines that clearly have all five of these concepts.

This series of activities is also very good for developing the concept of free flow. It is best to gradually combine the concepts, for example, over, then under, then over and under together, and so on.

Traveling Along Equipment

Setting: Low balance beams, benches, or ropes on the floor set up around the room

Tasks/Challenges:

T So far we've practiced the relationships of *on, off, over, in front of, under, around,* and *behind.* Now we're going to learn the relationship of *along.* At your piece of equipment, each of you, one at a time, should travel along the beam or bench by walking. Make sure that you travel from one end of the beam or bench to the other. This relationship of *along* means being on a piece of equipment and traveling from one part of it to another.

If it's easy for you to walk on the beam, try some other ways. Try a slide. If you need help keeping your balance, spread your arms out to either side.

As children progress with learning how to travel on or along equipment, you can increase the complexity of the activities by changing the locomotor pattern required for traveling. Patterns can include hopping, skipping, running, or fun movements like waddling. Before you change the pattern, be sure the children are able to advance safely to the next pattern. In other words, don't have them run on the balance beam before they can keep their balance at a fast walk.

T This time, we're going to be funny by combining two different relationships while you travel along the bench. Have some of your weight on the bench and some on the floor. For example, have one hand and foot on the bench and one hand and foot on the floor, or have both your feet on the bench and both your hands on the floor. The idea is to place part of your weight on the equipment and part on the floor. Make sure that I can tell where your weight really is.

C Make up one way you like to travel with part of your weight on the floor and part on the bench, and practice it so that you can show the class. Try to give your movement a name.

Traveling Through Obstacles

Setting: Hoops on foam supports

Tasks/Challenges:

T So far we have practiced traveling over, under, around, in front of, behind, and along. Now we are going to practice traveling *through* obstacles. Look around the area. You will see hoops standing up straight on foam supports. See if you can travel through the hoops without touching the sides. Start going through at a slow speed. If that is easy, gradually go through at a faster speed.

T If you can travel through the obstacle without knocking it down or touching it at a fast speed, then try going through it in a backward direction—slowly at first and then faster and faster.

C See if you can go through the hoop three times without touching it in a forward direction at a fast speed. See if you can travel through three times in a backward direction without touching the obstacle.

T This game is called rolling hoops. You may work alone or with a partner. The object is to travel through a rolling hoop without touching it so that the hoop keeps rolling after you travel through it. If you work with a partner, ask your partner to roll the hoop slowly or to make it spin by throwing it so that the hoop spins back to the thrower. Try to go through the hoop when it changes direction and starts back to the thrower.

✓ *Teacher Observation.* The following task might be used with a teacher observation to assess children's ability to use the concepts of *over, into, out of, around,* and *along.*

I am going to ask you to travel in relationship to a hoop and do five things.

1. Travel *over* the hoop. (It's OK if you just travel over part of the hoop.)
2. Travel *into* the hoop.
3. Travel *out of* the hoop.
4. Travel *around* the hoop.
5. Travel *along* the hoop. (Don't worry if you fall off sometimes; just keep trying.)

I will call out each relationship. Don't start the next one until I ask you to change. Sometimes you will keep moving. Sometimes you will stop after the movement is done.

Remember that cognitive understanding precedes the ability to perform. If children are having difficulty "doing" the concepts, you may want to assess their cognitive understanding.

Going Over and Under the Obstacle Course

Setting: An obstacle course made by placing elastic or regular ropes at various heights around the room. Chairs, volleyball standards, and benches can be used to anchor the ropes.

Moving in relationship to a rolling hoop is a fascinating challenge for the skilled child.

Tasks/Challenges:

T You can see that the whole room is now a giant maze. Your task is to go through the maze by going over or under the ropes. Everyone can move at once, but be sure to not touch anyone else as you find your way through the maze.

T Now that you've gone through the maze at least once, I'm going to make the activity harder. This time, try to go over some of the high ropes that you went under and to go under some of the low ropes that you went over. Be very careful to not touch anyone else, and try not to touch the ropes.

C This will take a lot of concentration—pretend the ropes are electric fences that will shock you if you touch them.

This is a good initial activity because you can set it up before class and then have the children help you take it down if you don't want to use it for the entire class. Children really enjoy this activity.

Using Partners as Obstacles

Setting: Partners in a self-space

Throughout this series of tasks emphasize that the children move in relationship to their partners without touching them. Sometimes a partner will need to create a nonsymmetrical shape, with some body parts at a low level to allow a partner to travel over her.

Tasks/Challenges:

T Things are going to change a little this time. Instead of using equipment as obstacles, you're going to use partners. To warm up, partner 1 freezes in any shape he or she likes and can hold still. Partner 2 tries to find as many ways as possible to go over, under, around, and through the shape, without touching partner 1. When partner 2 has found two ways to do each of the four movements, he or she changes places with the partner.

T Now, partner 1 makes a shape and holds it while partner 2 finds three ways to go over that shape without touching it. Make sure you're actually going over the shape, not around it. After you've found three ways to go over the shape, trade places with your partner.

T To make things a bit harder, this time as you cross the low-level shape, try to match it. So if your partner is in a small round shape, you want to be in a small round shape in the air as you cross over your partner. Your partner on the floor makes three different shapes and then switches. I'll be watching to see how closely the two shapes match each other.

T This time, instead of matching, you're going to try to look the opposite as you cross. So if your partner is in a round, curled shape, you want to be in a wide, spread-out shape. After you do this three times, trade places.

T Let's make the activity even more difficult. Partner 1 forms a shape, and partner 2 crosses the shape. Partner 2 now makes a shape for partner 1. Partners keep taking turns making shapes and crossing them. Every time you cross a shape, you immediately stop and form a shape for your partner to cross. Let's try it. Each partner should make three shapes and then stop. Remember not to touch your partner.

T Let's work on making the movement smoother so it flows together well. This time, cross the shape, and smoothly and immediately go into your shape, as if you just flowed into it. The person getting up should begin movement as soon as her or his shape has been crossed. Partners should perform as if they can read each other's mind and are continually changing places.

It may help to plan your shapes ahead of time. Talk about your shapes first, so you know exactly what you're going to do. Remember, you must go over your partner, not around.

T This will be the hardest activity yet. Each set of partners should mark off their own space. No one else can travel in this space, and the partners can't travel out of it. This is very important, so do it now. You must be able to show me the boundaries to your space when I ask. You may use ropes, cones, lines, or benches to mark your space.

Now that you have your space, here's what you'll be doing. Both of you will be traveling on your feet in your space. Suddenly, one of you will stop and make a low-level shape; when this happens, the other person quickly travels over the shape, and then both of you continue traveling. Do this again, with the other partner making the shape. The whole movement is split-second and unpredictable. No one knows when a shape will be made, and it is barely made before it's crossed. The action goes like this: Both of you travel, one of you stops and makes a low-level shape, the other one crosses the shape, and you keep moving. The object is to perform this movement three times without breaking the flow of the movement or touching each other. Let's give it a try.

The secret to this task is to react as soon as you see your partner beginning to make a shape. You have to anticipate, somewhat like making an interception in football. Try again and see if you can move more smoothly, with fewer breaks and jerks.

Developing the Concept of the Relationships with People

When children understand the concept of relationships with people, they have increased awareness of the interplay that occurs—in games, dance, and gymnastics—among the persons involved in the movement. Such interplay occurs, for example, when dancers converge and move around, between, and beside each other, and when soccer players work as a unit to advance a ball downfield.

Children often think of relationships to others simply as children working with other children. The term *relationships*, as we use it in physical education, is generally unknown to children. When teaching youngsters about relationships with people, we focus on these: alone in a mass, solo, partners, groups, and between groups. These relationships can occur in a variety of ways: Each child dribbles a ball in general space (alone in a mass); one child demonstrates a sequence before an entire class (solo); a child mirrors or matches the movement of a partner or partners; children meet or part in a dance with a group to express an idea (groups); and individuals work with others as a team to accomplish a task against another team (between groups).

Alone in a Mass

This relationship occurs when all children move simultaneously, with no intent of observing one another. It's frequently seen in lessons that use a problem-solving or guided discovery approach (Chapter 13). The children are indirectly relating to one another as they move throughout general space. In contrast to a solo relationship, the children say they feel they're truly on their own, even though they're surrounded by classmates. A child is alone in a mass when dribbling his or her own ball through general space. So too is each child when an entire class is running simultaneously to a predetermined location.

Solo

A solo relationship exists between an individual and the audience the person is performing before and who is observing the person. Examples are the pitcher on a baseball team, a featured performer in a ballet, and a gymnast. Because some children experience unpleasant pressure or tension when they're the center of attention, we make solo performances voluntary rather than mandatory. This is particularly important for the poorly skilled child, who often feels increased tension and pressure when asked to perform in front of an

Working with a partner increases the fun of a physical activity.

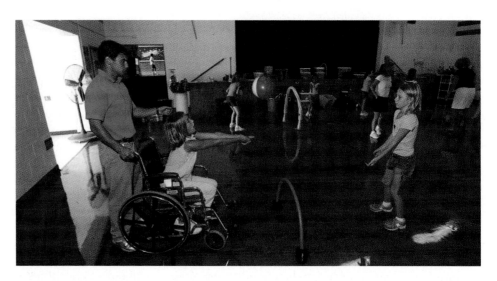

audience. For this reason, we always try to pinpoint two or more children (Chapter 11). Some children, however, enjoy the challenge of solo performances and actually seem to do better when watched by a group. The feeling experienced when moving and being observed by others is an interesting phenomenon and one that we want children to explore, but in a safe, nonthreatening environment. In all classes we discourage the children from laughing at or criticizing the performances of other children.

Partners

Partners are two individuals relating to each other through their movements. Most primary-grade children will be able to work cooperatively with a partner to explore different relationships. In every class, however, there may be a few children who are not yet developmentally ready to cooperate with a partner. Examples of partner relationships include two dancers moving in synchronization to express harmony or peace, two people paddling a canoe, and two synchronized swimmers performing a routine together. Relationship concepts introduced as children work with partners (or groups) include:

1. Meeting and parting—traveling toward or away from a partner.
2. Unison and contrast—both partners intentionally do the same thing (unison), or they intentionally do the same thing in different ways (contrast)
3. Leading and following—one partner leads, the other follows
4. Matching—partners are side by side and attempt to duplicate one another's movements instantaneously (to make the same movement at the same time)
5. Mirroring—partners face one another and form the reverse reproduction of the partner's movements, as if looking in a mirror

Groups

Group cooperative relationships occur when more than two children work together for a common purpose. These relationships include children working together to express an emotion in dance, to design a game or a sequence, or as a team trying to keep a ball from touching the floor, but without catching it.

As the size of the group increases, so too does the complexity of the relationship. A partner relationship involves being aware of one other child; a successful group relationship necessitates an awareness of two or more children. The difficulty of decision making also increases proportionately with the size of the group. The concepts of meeting and parting, unison and contrast, and leading and following all become increasingly challenging as the size of a group increases.

We typically assign specific tasks to children in groups. This enables the children to develop the skills of moving in relationship to others before they try group tasks that require them to make decisions—such as those required when children make up a game or invent a sequence. Asking children who have had little opportunity to work in groups to make group decisions about their work has proved counterproductive. Once children become proficient at group relationships, however, they are challenged by the adventure and creative opportunities of group decision making.

Between Groups

A between-group relationship occurs when two or more children relate to two or more children. It's the most complex of relationships because it involves not only being aware of one's own group but having a responsibility to relate to another group. This relationship is extremely challenging, as demonstrated by the wide appeal of sports that match one team against another.

We keep intergroup relationships small (two to three on a side) and try to allow choices about whether to participate in an intergroup relationship.

Between-group relationships can be competitive (working with a group to outmaneuver another group) or collaborative (two groups striving for a common goal). We usually begin with collaborative relationships and provide children the opportunity to choose competitive activities.

Teaching the Concept of the Relationships with People

The following activities are designed to improve children's ability to function successfully with other individuals and groups in a variety of situations.

Learning Experiences Leading to Movement Concept Understanding

Matching

Setting: Partners in a self-space

Tasks/Challenges:

Ⓣ Stand alongside a partner. Partner 1 should make a shape, and partner 2 should try to copy it exactly. Try to make the shapes so alike that you look like twins. After five shapes, partners should change places, with partner 2 now making the shapes while partner 1 copies them. Work hard to make the shapes exactly alike.

Ⓣ These types of shapes are said to *match;* they look alike as much as possible. Now you're going to make matching balances a little harder by playing follow the leader. On the signal, partner 1 leads by traveling; partner 2 follows. On the stop signal, you both stop, and the follower, partner 2, matches the balance the leader, partner 1, makes. As you make your shapes, try to match exactly what your partner does. Your whole body should do this, not just your trunk. After four turns, switch places. Be sure that when you're the leader you make a shape that your partner can actually do—not one that's too hard.

Traveling and Matching

Setting: Partners traveling in general space

Tasks/Challenges:

Ⓣ Now you'll perform matching actions while traveling instead of being still. With your partner, make up five ways that you can travel and then perform

the movements side by side at the exact same time, as if you're both part of a marching band that does everything alike. Practice doing the movements together so you do them at exactly the same time. It may help to count to yourselves as you move.

Mirroring

Setting: Partners in a self-space

Tasks/Challenges:

Ⓣ This time you're going to try something a little different. Face your partner; partner 1 will be the leader and partner 2 the follower. The leader will make a balance, and the follower will then make the same balance, only opposite. For example, if partner 1 uses her right arm to do something, partner 2 uses his left arm. Make five statues, and then trade places. Hold each statue for two elephants (seconds) before moving to the next statue. Work very hard to make every part of the statue the exact opposite of what you see. These types of actions are called *mirroring* actions because the effect is that of looking in a mirror.

Matching and Mirroring

Setting: Partners in a self-space

Tasks/Challenges:

Ⓣ This activity tests how well you understand the difference between mirroring and matching. With your partner, make a matching balance. On the signal, change that balance so that you mirror each other.

It helps to have a group that is doing the activity correctly demonstrate it for the class.

Ⓣ With your partner, now try to find five more balances that you can change from matching to mirroring. I'm going to come around as you practice and ask to see at least one of your combinations, so be sure you know the difference. If you have questions, ask now.

Ⓣ This time, the activity will be harder. Instead of copying a still statue your partner makes, you're going to mirror your partner's movements. Remember that this is still in your own space and that there's no traveling. So if your partner moves his or her left arm down, you move your right arm down. Make four moves and change places. This is hard. Think about it.

Ⓣ This time, try to tell a story with your mirroring actions, such as a baby first seeing herself in the

Children try to match their partner as they make "one-part, non-symmetrical balances."

Children try to match each other's rocking motion.

mirror, your mother putting on her makeup, or your father shaving. Practice your story until you can do it the same way three times in a row. Then we'll have the class try to guess what you're saying.

Traveling Alongside/Following

Setting: Traveling in general space with a partner

Tasks/Challenges:

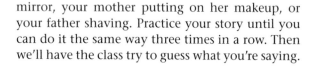 Though we haven't really discussed it, often you were practicing another type of relationship when you followed your partner around the space: *leading and following*. So far you've always followed from behind the other person. Let's try it differently this time, with you traveling alongside or next to your partner as you follow. One person is still the leader and the other the follower, but you both move as if you were a team of horses: beside each other. Each of you should take five turns leading and then switch places. This activity is harder, so you have to watch very closely what your partner does. Start out with very easy moves.

(T) Now try to speed it up a little. Watch carefully. Try to follow exactly.

The leader must be aware of the follower's capabilities so that the leader challenges the partner but doesn't frustrate the partner with movements that are too difficult.

Following with a Group

Setting: Traveling in general space with a group

Tasks/Challenges:

(T) This time, you're going to try another type of following: from behind, with four or five of you in a group. The first person in line is the first leader and leads the group all over the room. Then on the signal, the first person goes to the end of the line, and the second person becomes the leader; this change continues until everyone has had a chance to lead. The secret is to stay far enough apart so that you can see. The activity is just like follow the leader.

(T) This time you're going to make the activity a little more challenging. I'm *not* going to give you the signal to change anymore. Your group will have to make up its own change signal, such as a hand clap. You'll start as you did before, with the first person leading. Then at some time the second person in line will give the change signal and at the same time start traveling a new way. When this happens, the whole line starts to follow the new leader, and the old leader goes to the back of the line. The hard part is that you're going to do this without stopping the movement; the line must always keep moving. The same process continues until everyone has had a chance to be the leader. Remember, it's always the second person in line who gives the change signal.

Meeting/Parting

Setting: Partners working in self- and general space

Tasks/Challenges:

🅣 Now you're going to work with partners again. First you and your partner are going to work only with your hands while seated in your self-space. Very slowly, try to bring your hands as close to your partner's as you can without touching them. As soon as your hands are close, pull them as far away as you can without moving your body.

🅣 This relationship is called *meeting and parting*. To make it a little easier, I'm going to give you a drumbeat to go by. On the six slow counts of the drum, bring your hands as close as possible without touching them, and freeze. Then, on a sudden loud beat, quickly pull your hands as far away as possible, as if you don't want them to touch poison.

🅣 Now try meeting and parting with your whole body. In a small space, use the six slow drumbeats to bring your bodies as close together as possible without touching, and then freeze. On the sudden beat, quickly pull away. The secret is to pull away quickly, as if you were a flash of lightning, and then freeze very still.

> *When children begin to work with others in collaborative and competitive situations involving a manipulative skill, the skill level tends to deteriorate briefly if they're concentrating on the relationship. This should be expected and explained. The children, though, do need to have a certain level (control level) of manipulative ability before beginning these situations, or the activity will become very frustrating to them.*

🅣 The activity will be harder this time. You'll still have the same partner, but you will be separated. You're all going to travel around the room, and on the beat of the drum quickly come toward your partner and freeze very close to each other, just for a few seconds, and then begin your traveling again. Do this every time you hear the signal. The secret is to always know where your partner is. Maintain eye contact.

🅣 This time, as you and your partner meet on the sound of the signal, come together as if you're greeting a friend you haven't seen in a long time; then, as you get right up to each other, you realize that you really don't know the person. It could be really funny.

Forming Cooperative and Collaborative Relationships

Setting: Groups of four traveling, throwing, and catching in a large space

Tasks/Challenges:

🅣 So far, all our relationships with people involved how we moved with those people. You're now going to work on a few different types of relationships that involve not only how you move with people but also how you think. In your group of three, you're going to travel in a line spread out across the field toward the goal. As you travel, throw the ball back and forth to each other, always trying to stay the same distance apart. Imagine a marching band moving across the field but throwing a ball as they move. The secret is that the receivers move slightly ahead of but not toward the passers, and the passers throw the ball ahead of the receivers so that they don't have to come back to catch it. This type of relationship is called a *cooperative* relationship, because everybody has to work together to make it work.

This idea works well if a lined field (such as a football field) is available and the children can follow the lines as guides.

🅣 Now you're going to change the cooperative relationship a little. You're still going to work with your group to move the ball across the field while staying the same distance apart, but one person is going to try to steal the ball while it is in the air coming toward you. It will be really hard to resist the temptation to go close to your own players to try to help them, but remember you have two goals: to stay away from your teammates and to not let the other person steal the ball. It really does help to stay away from the other people on your team.

This is called a *collaborative* relationship, because you have to work with the people on your team to keep the other person from getting the ball. Let me give you a few more hints on how to make such a relationship work really well. First, when it's your turn to receive the ball, move slightly in front of the passer so the passer can easily throw the ball to you. Second, pass before the defender gets close to you; when you're free to pass, don't wait until the defender is so close that you're forced to pass.

As the children become more proficient with these activities, you may want to try manipulative skills other than throwing, such as kicking, passing, or striking.

Meeting and Parting in a Cooperative Group

Setting: Groups in general space

Tasks/Challenges:

Ⓣ This time, instead of meeting and parting with a partner, you're going to meet and part with a small group. Your group forms a group shape—remember: close, but not touching. Then on the signal, suddenly leave, as if you're in a hurry, but take only a few steps and by yourself freeze into a shape you like. On the next signal, slowly come back to your group and form the same group shape with which you started. To repeat, start with a group shape, on the signal quickly leave and form a shape of your own, and on the next signal return to the first group shape—almost as if someone were playing a movie forward, backward, forward, backward.

Ⓒ Let's work on this activity with one series that you really like. Practice it so it works out the same each time. This will involve hard thinking. It may help to count your steps so you know exactly how far to move. It also helps not to laugh too much. Who knows, you could be stars!

Performing Solo

Setting: Groups of six, each group with a foam ball and cones to define their area; pencil and paper for each child

Tasks/Challenges:

Ⓣ You're going to play a bunch of small tag games— only six people in a group. Start with two people as taggers. When you get tagged, do *not* sit out, but

become a tagger, so in the end there will be many taggers and one person in the middle. When you finish one game, just start another one. The last two players left in the middle are the first taggers in the next game. Remember to think about what it's like to be left in the middle.

After the youngsters have played the game, you have an excellent opportunity to briefly discuss the feelings of being in a solo relationship when each child is the center of attention. Point out that some people (probably the highly skilled) like being solo, but others (probably the less skilled) prefer to not be solo.

☑ It is important to determine children's understanding of relationships. Either of the following ideas will allow you to do that rather quickly.

1. ***Exit slip.*** Ask children to draw a symmetrical shape and a nonsymmetrical shape.
2. ***Homework.*** Ask children to find an example of a shape (e.g., wide, narrow, round, or twisted) in a magazine or newspaper. Ask them to label the shape.

Applying the Concept of Relationships

The concept of relationships with objects and people is a beginning theme in the gymnastics and dance areas as the children are taught the concepts of over, under, inside, outside, along, and onto. There the focus is on whether the child understands the concept rather than on whether she or he can accomplish the skill involved. For example, you'd observe whether a child was actually jumping symmetrically over a hurdle rather than whether she was crossing without knocking it over. Once you're sure that the child understands the concept, begin to focus on the skill. Once a particular concept has been learned, it can also be used for expressive purposes in dance.

We don't introduce the concept of relationships with objects in the games area until children have reached at least the control level (Chapter 7). Children must learn to manipulate objects with some consistency before they can reasonably be expected to manipulate them in relation to objects or people. If children are given tasks involving manipulative skills and relationships too early, they become frustrated and bored.

The concept of relationships with others is the last concept we introduce. Socially, children enjoy working near other children at a very young age, but often physically and cognitively they aren't able to function effectively in relationship to others. For example, children at the precontrol level don't possess enough skill to be able to consistently work with a partner—when such children are asked to throw an object back and forth to partners, only one out of three throws is likely to reach the partner. Therefore, it's best not to deal with relationships with others as a *concept* until the children's skills are adequate and they've matured enough socially so that their abilities are enhanced when they work with other children. There are no magical ages or times for introducing the different relationship concepts. Each teacher must reflect on information about the environment, the children, the skill, and personal ability as a teacher to determine the best time for introducing the concept of relationships.

Competition

We were not sure where to discuss competition within the skill theme approach, so we chose to place it at the end of the relationship chapter because most competitive situations involve relationships, between individuals, partners, or groups. The Council on Physical Education for Children (1992, 2000) suggests that requiring students to compete in games in which there are "winners and losers" is an inappropriate practice for elementary school physical education, especially when there are rewards for winning and losing in class games (COPEC, 2000, p. 17). Traditionally, however, physical education classes consisted of a plethora of team sports, especially at the secondary level.

We are not opposed to competition! We are opposed, however, to requiring youngsters to compete in games against their will. When youngsters, or adults for that matter, choose not to compete it is often because they do not have the prerequisite skills (are at the precontrol or control level), or prefer not to be placed in situations that are potentially humiliating or embarrassing. This is hard for many to understand, especially physical education majors, many of whom were varsity athletes and thrive on competitive situations. An emphasis on winning creates an intense emotional involvement that can produce disturbing feelings in some children.

In the skill theme approach, if competition is involved it is often de-emphasized by the teacher and you will not find games pitting one half of a class against another. You will, however, find many ideas for small sided games and opportunities for youngsters to design their own games (Chapter 31). When youngsters play small sided games they have a choice to keep score or not. (We often find that they intend to keep score, but have forgotten to do so after a few minutes into the game.) In the skill theme approach we try to help youngsters to understand that it's acceptable to choose not to keep score.

Finally, we need to realize that there are many opportunities for youngsters to participate in competitive situations outside of physical education. By the time youngsters are in third grade, many have already been on softball, basketball, soccer, or swim teams, or participated in other types of competitive situations. Thus, competition is not new for most youngsters. When teachers can help youngsters place competition in perspective, and understand the strong feelings associated with winning and losing, they need to do so. The major purpose of the skill theme approach, however, is to encourage youngsters to develop motor skill proficiency and positive attitudes toward physical activity. Although some youngsters thrive in competitive situations, others do not. For this reason, in the skill theme approach we present competition as a choice, not as a requirement.

Reading Comprehension Questions

1. List three examples each of relationships of body parts, relationships with objects, and relationships with people (total of nine examples).
2. What does the term *functional understanding* mean?
3. Define symmetrical and nonsymmetrical by listing examples of each concept.
4. We recommend that you teach the concept of relationships with objects before teaching relationships with people. Why?
5. What does the term *alone in a mass* mean? What does *solo* mean?
6. We recommend that solo performances and intergroup experiences be voluntary, not required. Why?
7. Explain the difference between mirroring and matching.
8. What factors should you consider when making decisions about the most appropriate times to introduce the various relationships?

References/Suggested Readings

Council on Physical Education for Children. (1992). *Developmentally appropriate physical education practices for children: A position statement of the Council on Physical Education for Children.* Reston, VA: National Association for Sport and Physical Education.

Council on Physical Education for Children. (2000). *Appropriate practices for elementary school physical education: A position statement of the National Association for Sport and Physical Education.* Reston, VA: National Association for Sport and Physical Education.

National Association for Sport and Physical Education. (1995). *Moving into the future: National standards for physical education.* St. Louis, MO: Mosby.

Skill Theme Development

Kelsey
E-4

Chapters 19 to 28 discuss the content of the skill themes we focus on in our physical education programs. Each chapter begins with an introduction to the skill theme; the introduction includes a discussion of the skill theme's characteristics and how the theme can be applied to teaching children. It's tempting to skip the introduction and get to the actual lesson ideas, but we recommend that you carefully read the introduction so that you'll be able to adapt the skill theme to your particular needs. Obviously you'll change some of the ideas; an understanding of the skill as taught to children will help you make these adaptations.

Each skill theme chapter is arranged in a logical progression, from precontrol through proficiency levels, as explained in Chapter 7. This progression is accompanied by what we call a *progression spiral,* which outlines the content of each skill theme. Each line in the spiral corresponds to a section in the chapter that explains how to develop that idea. The progressions are presented as a series of tasks (not lessons) that you will be able to develop based on the skill level and abilities of the classes you teach.

Each series of tasks begins by describing the space and equipment you will need. At the precontrol level, children are exploring a movement and therefore cues are not provided. At the next three generic skill levels, however, cues are provided before the actual task(s). You are reminded that it is probably most effective to focus on only one of these cues at a time. The reason we provide several at the beginning of the series of tasks is to allow you to observe your children to determine which cue will be the most appropriate for them. At times when it was not logical or safe to omit a cue from a task, we have included some cues within the tasks. When this occurs the cue is in bold print. Following the cues are one or more suggested tasks (which are designated with the symbol **T**) and also challenges (which are designated with the symbol **C**). As you recall, tasks, cues, and challenges were described in Chapter 11. In addition you will find suggested assessments

(Chapter 14) to help you determine how well the children are understanding the concepts and skills you are teaching.

Finally, we encourage you to adapt the suggested progressions and implied methodologies to suit your students' needs and your teaching goals. Our suggestions are certainly not prescriptions. Reflect on your situation, your students, and design the curriculum for your children.

Finally, we encourage you to change the suggested progressions and implied methodology to suit your students' needs and your teaching goals. Our suggestions are certainly not prescriptions. The chapters in Part 4 are ordered in the progression we'd use to organize our yearly plan (discussed in Chapter 8), but you should reflect on your situation and design the curriculum for *your* children.

Key Concepts

- Skill themes are fundamental movements that are modified into more specialized patterns in which activities of increasing complexity are built.

- Skill themes include: manipulative (kicking and punting, throwing and catching, volleying and dribbling, striking with rackets, paddles, and long-handled implements), nonmanipulative (rolling, balancing, transferring weight, jumping, and landing), and locomotor skills (traveling, chasing, fleeing, and dodging).

- Learning experiences in the skill theme chapters are designed to assist children in moving from precontrol to control to utilization to proficiency levels of skill proficiency.

- Children need multiple and recurring experiences with each skill to become competent movers.

- When skill themes are introduced, the initial tasks allow children to explore the skill (precontrol). Tasks then focus on helping children produce the correct skill in nonchanging environments (control). This is followed by combining skills in dynamic situations (utilization) and finally the use of skills in a variety of changing environments (proficiency).

- It is only after the skill can be produced in a consistent manner that it is made more complex with the addition of movement concepts.

- As children gain increasing competency with skills, the skills are applied in games, dance, and gymnastics environments.

Traveling

Children are first capable of changing the location of their bodies at about three months of age, when they turn over from their backs onto their stomachs. Unless seriously handicapped, they'll soon begin to crawl, then creep. At about one year, they'll take their first step. And by the time they enter school, they'll exhibit relatively mature walking and running patterns. Unlike other skills—such as throwing, catching, and striking—the basic locomotor patterns develop naturally in most children.

Most school-age youngsters, therefore, are beyond the precontrol level in walking and running. Nevertheless, the teacher's first task is to evaluate traveling performance to ensure that any youngsters who exhibit severely immature or inefficient patterns will receive remedial assistance. Most children attain a mature walking pattern through experience. Verbal cues

from the teacher, plus the modeling of the correct pattern, will help children with inefficiencies. Continued deviations (e.g., toes turned out or in) signal the need for a thorough physical examination by a pediatrician.

Similarly, it's important to ascertain how many students can perform the fundamental locomotor skills that emerge from the walk-run pattern: hopping, leaping, sliding, galloping, and skipping. Young children need much practice of each skill when the skills are introduced, and they also need distributed practice of the locomotor skills throughout the primary grades. Young children inexperienced in different locomotor skills may not be able to give the correct locomotor response to a verbal command because they often lack cognitive understanding rather than motor performance. We've found that modeling is the best way for young children to learn these skills; the children follow the example of the teacher and other children who've mastered the skill. It's also important to name the locomotor skill each time you or others demonstrate it to the children.

By approximately age 8, we expect children to be able to execute the locomotor skills of hopping, leaping, sliding, galloping, and skipping in response to a verbal command. This expectation implies that children recognize the word and the action it represents and that they've mastered the skill. Consequently, most of the activities in this chapter are geared to the precontrol and control levels. At the utilization and proficiency levels, traveling most often occurs as combinations of skill themes, such as traveling while dribbling, or in a game, dance, or gymnastics context, for example, traveling to run bases. See Box 19-1 for information on traveling from the *National Standards*.

Box 19-1

The Skill of Traveling in the *National Standards for Physical Education*

The movement skill of traveling is referenced in the *National Standards for Physical Education* (National Association for Sport and Physical Education [NASPE], 2004) under Standard 1: Demonstrates competency in motor skills and movement patterns needed to perform a variety of physical activities. The intent of the standard is developing the physical skills needed to enjoy participation in physical activities, with the mastery of movement fundamentals as the foundation for continued skill acquisition. At the lower elementary level, students achieve mature forms of the basic locomotor skills and vary the manner in which these skills are performed in relation to changing conditions and expectations. At the upper elementary level, students demonstrate locomotor skills for performance outcomes, using locomotor skills in dynamic and complex environments, and in combinations.

Sample performance outcomes from the *National Standards* include:

- Skips (or hops, gallops, slides, etc.) using mature form (K–2)*
- Performs a basic tinikling step (3–5)*
- Performs a variety of simple folk and square dances (6–8)*
- Designs and performs gymnastics (or dance) sequences that combine traveling, rolling, balancing, and weight transfer into smooth, flowing sequences with intentional changes in direction, speed, and flow (6–8)*

*Grade-level guidelines for expected student learning.

Fundamental Locomotor Skills

Walking

Walking is a process of alternately losing balance and recovering it while moving forward in an upright position. While moving forward, the body should display little up and down or side to side movement. The arms and legs move in opposition. A mature walking pattern looks smooth and is accomplished in an easy manner.

When assessing the walking pattern of young children, look for the following inefficiencies:

1. Bouncy walk—too much vertical push
2. Excessive swing of the arms away from the sides
3. Failure to swing the arms at the shoulders
4. Feet held too close together so that the entire body looks jerky as the child walks
5. Feet held too far apart—duck walk

6. Toes turned out
7. Toes turned in—pigeon-toed
8. Head too far forward—body leaning forward before the lead foot touches the ground

Running

During the earliest stage of running (at about 24 months), a child's new speed produces precarious balance. The child makes exaggerated leg movements. In particular, the knee of the recovery leg swings outward and then around and forward in preparation for the support phase. This knee action is accompanied by the foot of the recovery leg toeing out. These exaggerated movements gradually disappear as the legs become longer and stronger.

Most school-age youngsters are able to run at a relatively fast speed and are fairly successful at changing direction while running. In a mature running pattern (observed when the children are attempting to run at maximum velocity), each leg goes through a support phase and a recovery phase, and the full sequence produces two periods of nonsupport. The essentials of the mature running pattern are as follows (Wickstrom, 1977, pp. 37–57):

1. The trunk maintains a slight forward lean throughout the stride pattern.
2. Both arms swing through a large arc and in synchronized opposition to the leg action.
3. The support foot contacts the ground approximately flat and nearly under the center of gravity.
4. The knee of the support leg bends slightly after the foot has made contact with the ground.
5. Extension of the support leg at the hip, knee, and ankle propels the body forward and upward into the nonsupport phase.
6. The recovery knee swings forward quickly to a high knee raise, and simultaneously the lower leg flexes, bringing the heel close to the buttock.

Use the key observation points in Box 19-2 to assess running patterns. The illustrations of "correct" and "incorrect" patterns help you answer the questions you should ask yourself as you evaluate a youngster's performance.

Hopping

A hop is a springing action from one foot, in any direction, to a landing on the same foot (Figure 19.1). The knee seldom straightens fully; the work of the ankle joint is primarily what accomplishes the push into the air and the absorption of the landing shock.

Leaping

A leap is an extension of a run—greater force is used to produce a higher dimension than a run (Figure 19.2). A one-foot takeoff propels the body upward to a landing on the opposite foot. Arm opposition is the same as for the run. There's an emphasis on body extension for height or for distance. Upon touching the floor, the landing leg bends to absorb the force of the body.

Sliding

A slide is a combination of a step and a run. The lead step is quickly followed by the free foot closing to replace the supporting foot (Figure 19.3). The lead foot quickly springs from the floor into a direction of intended travel. The weight is primarily on the balls of the feet. The sequence is repeated for the desired distance. The same foot always leads in a slide, producing an uneven rhythm: step-close, step-close, step-close.

Galloping

A gallop is an exaggerated slide in a forward direction. The lead leg lifts and bends and then thrusts forward to support the weight. The rear foot quickly closes to

Figure 19.1 Hopping pattern.

Box 19-2

Key Observation Points: Running

NO   YES

Leg Action

Does the knee of the child's recovery leg swing forward and backward rather than outward, around, and then forward?

NO   YES

Arm Action

Do the child's arms move forward and backward in opposition to the legs without crossing the midline?

Do the child's arms stay close to the body throughout the action?

NO   YES   NO   YES

Trunk Position

Does the child's trunk lean slightly forward?

NO   YES

Box 19-2 (continued)

Foot Placement

Is the child's support foot approximately flat when it contacts the ground?

NO   YES

Mature Stage

When children are at the mature stage of running, do their runs look similar to the following sequence?

Figure 19.2 Leaping pattern.

Figure 19.3 Sliding pattern.

replace the supporting leg as the lead leg springs up into its lifted and bent position. The rhythm is uneven, the same as that of a slide.

Skipping

A skip is a combination of a step and a hop, first on one foot and then on the other foot (Figure 19.4). The pattern has the alternation and opposition of the walk plus the same-sided one-foot hop. The skip has an uneven rhythm.

Levels of Skill Proficiency

In many schools, usually in communities in which parents provide their preschoolers with an abundance of movement experiences, most 5- and 6-year-old children will already have mastered the traveling skills, and their classmates will be quick to catch on. However, we have observed some situations in which a number of the students were unable to perform many locomotor skills beyond walking and running. Such children

need basic precontrol-level travel experiences so they will learn to:

1. Crawl along the floor.
2. Creep on hands and knees.
3. Walk along a line on the floor.
4. Crawl underneath a low bar without touching it.
5. Step over a low obstacle without touching it.

Precontrol-level experiences provide a multitude of exploration experiences in travel: traveling in different ways, exploring various locomotor patterns, the world of imagery and travel, and traveling just for the sheer enjoyment of moving. Once youngsters can identify and perform the basic modes of travel relatively easily, they are ready for control-level challenges.

Control-level challenges include mastery of the different locomotor patterns. Following mastery of the basic skills, the children can attempt variations of those skills by combining a skill with other skills and concepts: walking at a low level, skipping backward, galloping, changing direction on signal, and running in a crowded room without touching anyone. Next,

Figure 19.4 Skipping pattern.

the youngsters can try traveling rhythmically or expressively: skipping to the uneven beat of the teacher's drum, running and leaping on the accented beat, walking as if on hot sand, and walking mechanically, like a robot.

Once children are easily able to perform a variety of locomotor skills and can use their travel abilities to carry out a primary objective, they're ready for utilization-level activities. At this point, an involvement in challenging situations can refine and expand the youngsters' repertoires of travel skills.

The children can combine two or more travel operations into a short sequence, such as run-jump-roll, or run–leap–turn-in-air–run. They can try to perform another skill while traveling: keeping a long ribbon from touching the ground by traveling swiftly, or striking a balloon and traveling to keep it up.

Children can improvise or plan in detail expressive travel for short dance phrases, focusing on:

1. The purpose, idea, or theme of the phrase—harmony, a battle, autumn
2. The most appropriate pathway of travel—straight, angular (zigzag), or curved
3. The specific travel skills to be incorporated—running, leaping, collapsing
4. The travel qualities to be exhibited—smooth-flowing, jagged-jerky

The youngsters can use effective travel skills and strategic pathways in dynamic game situations:

1. React quickly to a batted ball by charging forward, to the left or right, to collect a ground ball and throw accurately to a teammate
2. Run a planned pass pattern, using fakes and quick changes of direction to lose an opponent and receive a ball a teammate throws

When students consistently use a variety of travel skills and pathways effectively in game, dance, and gymnastics settings, they're ready to put all the elements together through participation in proficiency-level experiences.

- **Games:** Youngsters play teacher- and/or student-designed games that demand alert and accurate performance of travel skills and strategic use of travel pathways while performing another skill, for example, dribbling.
- **Dance:** Students and teacher work together to design dance studies. Specific travel pathways and locomotor skills are decided upon, practiced, revised, and refined. This process ends in a completed dance that clearly reflects the theme or idea that stimulated the study.
- **Gymnastics:** Students and teacher cooperatively design travel patterns and select specific locomotor skills (as well as positions of stillness, i.e., balances) for individual or group gymnastics routines.

Our progression spiral on page 314 shows the sequence for developing the skill theme of traveling at the precontrol, control, utilization, and proficiency levels.

Precontrol Level: Activities for Exploration

The activities that follow are designed to introduce children to the fundamental locomotor patterns and to help them explore the skill of traveling.

Traveling in General Space

Setting: Children scattered throughout general space

Skill Theme Development Sequence

Traveling

Proficiency Level

Traveling in gymnastics
Traveling in games and sports
Performing rhythmical patterns: tinikling
Traveling to show tradition versus change
Depicting primitive tribes through travel

Utilization Level

Traveling to Tom Foolery rhymes
Traveling in bound and free flow
Traveling to express age: The Fountain of Youth Dance
Performing rhythmical patterns
Meeting and parting while traveling with a partner
Shadowing
Traveling with a partner: changing speed and direction
The Copy Cat Dance
Traveling with a partner: matching pathways

Control Level

Combination locomotors
Slow-Motion Replay: The Sports Dance
A Dance of Water, Steam, and Ice
Changing speeds to music
Traveling using different directions, levels, pathways, and
    locations
Traveling at different speeds
The Follow-Me Dance
The Locomotors Dance
Traveling in different pathways
Slidestepping
Traveling in different directions
Traveling an obstacle course
Traveling with music
Traveling in confined spaces
Moving to rhythms
Performing locomotor sequences
Traveling to open spaces
Traveling with different locomotor patterns
Running
Leaping
Skipping
Hopping
Galloping
Sliding

Precontrol Level

Traveling among the large and tall
Traveling through rope pathways
Traveling with imagery
Traveling in different ways
Traveling with different locomotor movements
Traveling in general space

Tasks/Challenges:

(T) On the signal, travel any way you wish in general space. Avoid colliding with others, and stop without falling when you hear the drum.

(T) Change to a different way to travel ... Some of you are hopping; some are galloping; most are running. Travel throughout general space any way except running. Watch out for others as you travel.

(T) See how many different ways you can travel on your feet, sometimes traveling on one foot, sometimes on two feet, sometimes on one foot and then the other.

(C) Show me three different ways you can travel on your feet.

Traveling with Different Locomotor Movements

Setting: Children scattered throughout general space

Tasks/Challenges:

(T) When we explored different ways to travel, some of you were hopping, some were walking, some were galloping. Let's explore the different locomotor skills as we travel in general space. Travel throughout general space with your favorite locomotor movement; I will name the ones I see: walking, running, galloping ...

(T) Travel throughout general space with a *hop,* staying on one foot. Switch to the other foot after several hops so you will not become tired and lose your balance.

(T) Travel throughout general space with a *jump,* two feet to two feet. Make some of your jumps small and low, some of them long, some of them high in the air.

(T) Travel throughout general space with a *gallop,* one foot always staying in front of the other. Can you gallop backward?

(T) Travel throughout general space with a *run,* always looking for the open spaces. Remember to stop on the signal, without falling down.

(C) Thus far, you have traveled by hopping, jumping, galloping, and running; you were already very good at walking. Of those five locomotor actions, choose your favorite three and practice them as if you were going to teach them to someone who does not know how to do them—perfection!

Traveling in Different Ways

Setting: Children scattered throughout general space

This child explores pathways in self-space.

Tasks/Challenges:

T Travel throughout general space on two feet. On the signal, change the way you are traveling, yet remain on your feet.

C How many different ways can you travel on your feet?

T Travel throughout general space on two feet and two hands; travel forward, backward, sideways on your feet and hands.

T Travel throughout general space on body parts other than your feet. How many different combinations of body parts can you use for travel?

Traveling with Imagery

Setting: Children scattered throughout general space

Tasks/Challenges:

T Travel throughout general space like a rabbit, jumping from two feet to two feet; travel like a frog, jumping from pad to pad.

T Travel throughout general space, walking as if in sticky mud or a sea of peanut butter.

T Walk like a robot. March like a soldier.

T Travel throughout general space like a large elephant. Will your steps be heavy or light?

T Travel like a tall giraffe, with your head above the clouds.

T Run quietly, like deer through the forest.

T Slither like a snake. Crawl like an inchworm, then like a snail.

The imagery of animals for movement is almost endless. Always remind children of the movement with a simple lead question, such as "How does a giraffe move?"

Traveling Through Rope Pathways

Setting: An obstacle course of marker cones and ropes on the floor to form varying pathways of different widths for travel (Figure 19.5)

Tasks/Challenges:

T On the signal, travel around the cones and between the rope boundaries without touching them. I will time you for 30 seconds. Try to finish with a perfect score—no touches.

C Challenge yourself to travel throughout the obstacle course three times with no collisions with others or the items in the course.

Figure 19.5 Rope pathways as an obstacle course.

These children are enjoying traveling at a low level.

Traveling Among the Large and Tall

Setting: Children with partners, scattered throughout general space

Tasks/Challenges:

Ⓣ Stand in your self-space, stretching in all directions to be sure you have a clear self-space; it is not important that you be near your partner. Partners A, stand in your self-space, extending your arms to make a very large, wide shape. Partners B, travel throughout general space with any locomotor pattern you wish; avoid touching anyone traveling or a stationary wide shape. *Have partners switch travel and stationary activities after one or two minutes of travel.*

Ⓣ Partners B, stand in your self-space with a tall, narrow shape. Partners A, run throughout general space with no collisions; always look for open spaces as you travel. *Switch activities after one or two minutes.*

Control Level: Learning Experiences Leading to Skill Development

Control-level experiences are designed to help children master the basic locomotor skills and to expand their traveling abilities. The learning experiences challenge youngsters to use different traveling patterns with other concepts, such as speed and direction.

A note about cues: Although several cues are listed for many of the learning experiences, it's important to focus on only one cue at a time. That way, the children can really concentrate on that cue. Once you provide feedback to the children and observe that most have learned a cue, then it's time to focus on another one.

Traveling with Different Locomotor Patterns

Setting: Children scattered throughout general space

Cues	
Heads Up	(Keep your head up for good balance and to avoid collisions with others.)
Balanced Stops	(Spread your feet apart and lower your hips slightly to maintain your balance when you stop.)

Tasks/Challenges:

Ⓣ On signal, travel any way you wish in general space. Avoid colliding with others, and stop without falling when you hear the drum.

Sliding

Cue	
Buoyant Landings	(Make light, "springy" actions as you travel.)

Ⓣ Raise your right arm and point toward the far side of the blacktop (gymnasium). On the signal, use a slidestep to travel across the area. When your left foot almost touches your right foot, step again quickly to the side with your right foot.

Ⓣ Slide across the area like a dancer, arms extended to the side and your body stretched upward as you "leap."

Ⓣ Slide like a basketball player with your knees bent, hips lowered, and arms extended in front.

Galloping

Cue	
Same Foot Forward	(Keep the same foot in front as you gallop.)

(T) On the signal, gallop in general space, keeping the same foot in front throughout the action.

(T) Now lead with the other foot as you gallop.

Hopping

Cue

Up, Up, Light, Light (Make light, quick actions as you hop.)

(T) Hop on one foot five times, and then hop on your other foot five times. Continue to alternate hopping on your right foot and then your left foot until you hear the signal to stop.

Skipping

Cue

Lift Your Knees (Lift your knees, swing your arms . . . step, hop.)

(T) Now that you can hop and gallop, try skipping. Skip throughout general space until you hear the signal to stop.

Developmentally, children progress from a gallop to a skip only on the dominant side, then to a mature skipping pattern.

Leaping

Cue

Arms Up . . . Stretch (Lift your arms; stretch your arms and legs as you leap.)

(T) We did leaping when we worked on jumping and landing. Who can remember what a leap is? Right, it's taking off on one foot and landing on the other, with the body airborne between the takeoff and landing. Travel in general space by running. After running three steps, leap high in the air, and when you land, continue to run. Your travel will be this: Run, run, run, run, leap; run, run, run, leap . . . **Remember to land softly by bending your knee.**

(T) I'm going to number you off in 1s and 2s. The 1s will be spread throughout general space, standing with your arms stretched high over your heads. On signal the 2s will run throughout general space, leaping high in the air each time you pass a 1 standing with arms stretched high. Try to leap so high in the air that you are higher than the stretched arms of the 1s. On signal, the 2s will stand with arms stretched high and the 1s will run and leap.

Keep the activity short in duration with a focus on leaping. Repeat several times for endurance.

(A) When children are running and leaping, a reminder for sufficient space and awareness of others is important to avoid airborne and landing collisions.

Running

Cue

Light on Your Feet (Make light, buoyant landings for quick steps.)

(T) Now that you can move without bumping others and stop on signal, try running throughout general space. Cover as much area as you can. Be sure your entire foot contacts the floor, not just your toes.

Assessment Example

From the *National Standards for Physical Education*

Teacher Observation

The student will be asked to travel through general space with a steady run and, upon a designated signal, perform the next locomotor action announced by the teacher (e.g., walk, hop, gallop). Upon observing the student's performance, the teacher marks on a check list mastery of the various critical elements (e.g., arm swing, balance, foot placement).

Criteria for Assessment

a. Demonstrates selected critical elements of locomotor skills.

b. Responds with correct locomotor skill as named by teacher.

NASPE (1995, p. 6)

Traveling in general space lets children practice finding open space.

Traveling while manipulating an object is used in a game setting.

Assessment Example

From the *National Standards of Physical Education*

Event Task

Students will perform a "Dance of Locomotors" in which they travel in different ways through general space. Upon hearing a designated signal from the teacher, students will change to the locomotor pattern named by the teacher. Repeat the dance, but this time upon the signal to change locomotor pattern the students will respond by selecting any locomotor pattern they desire. The teacher should encourage creative modes of travel.

Criteria for Assessment

a. Demonstrates a variety of locomotor skills.
b. Identifies and models locomotor movements shown by the teacher.
c. Exhibits correct locomotor skill when the skill is named by the teacher.

NASPE (1995, p. 7)

Traveling to Open Spaces

Setting: Children scattered throughout general space

Cues	
Heads Up	(Keep your head up for good balance and to avoid collisions with others.)
Balanced Stops	(Spread your feet apart and lower your hips slightly to maintain your balance when you stop.)

Tasks/Challenges:

(T) In your self-space, look around the work space. Do you see open spaces that no one has taken as their space? On the signal, run to that open space. When you arrive, stop and look for another open space; run to that space.

(T) Travel throughout general space, always looking for the open spaces. This time you will only pause at an open space long enough to see your next open space.

(C) I will time you for 60 seconds of travel. Your task is to travel throughout general space always looking for and moving to open spaces with no collisions.

Performing Locomotor Sequences

Setting: On index cards (or slips of paper placed inside film cylinders), write a sequence of locomotor movements—for example, "Walk, hop, gallop"—one sequence card per child.

Cues

Heads Up (Keep your head up for good balance and to avoid collisions with others.)

Pause and Go (Pause momentarily; then continue your locomotor movement.)

Balanced Stops (Spread your feet apart and lower your hips slightly to maintain your balance when you stop.)

Tasks/Challenges:

(T) Think of your favorite locomotor movement that you've practiced. On signal, use that movement to travel in general space. I should be able to identify the locomotor movement by watching you travel.

(T) There are cards spread around the wall. When I say "Go," get a card and bring it back to your space. Go. Read your card. Each card contains a movement sentence: three locomotor movements separated by commas. What does a comma mean in your reading? Right—pause. After each locomotor movement you'll pause. Your sequence will be travel, pause; travel, pause; travel, stop. Practice your movement sentence until you can do it the same way three times.

Children whose reading level reflects ways to end a sentence enjoy stopping with an image of a period, an exclamation, or a question mark.

From the *National Standards of Physical Education*

Event Task

Students are asked to design and practice a movement sequence of three different locomotor skills. Following the practice period, students demonstrate their movement sequence for the class.

Criteria for Assessment

a. Demonstrates three different locomotor movements.

b. Demonstrates mature pattern of each locomotor skill.

c. Demonstrates smooth transitions between locomotor patterns.

NASPE (1995, p. 19)

Moving to Rhythms

Setting: Children scattered throughout general space

Cues

Heads Up (Keep your head up for good balance and to avoid collisions with others.)

Pause and Go (Pause momentarily; then continue your locomotor movement.)

Tasks/Challenges:

(T) Listen to the drumbeat. I'll beat a cadence of one, two, three, four, and then you'll clap the same. Listen. *(Beat drum four times in even rhythm.)* Now clap. Walking and running are both even rhythms. Let's try again. Listen, then clap.

(T) Let's walk the rhythm of the beat. Listen to the speed. *(Beat four times in even rhythm, slowly.)* Ready? Walk as I beat the drum. Clap as you walk.

(T) You'll need to walk more quickly or slowly now, depending on the beat of the drum. I'll pause between each segment so you can hear the change in tempo.

(T) Now run to the beat of the drum. It's an even rhythm but a faster speed. Be sure you listen for the beat. Ready, go.

Traveling in Confined Spaces

Setting: Large marker cones designating general space for travel; children scattered throughout this space

Cues

Heads Up	(Keep your head up for good balance and to avoid collisions with others.)
Open Spaces	(Look for open spaces as you travel.)
Speed Check	(Slow your speed slightly to avoid others.)

Tasks/Challenges:

🅣 For today's class, the area inside the cones is your city, and you cannot go out of the city until class is over. Travel throughout the city in any locomotor pattern you wish.

🅣 This time, the city has begun to shrink and will keep doing so—so watch the cones. *Begin to move the cones closer in as the children become more adept at moving without bumping into each other or falling down.*

Traveling with Music

Setting: Children scattered throughout general space; music with appropriate even and uneven beats for different locomotor movements; hoops, one per child, at the edge of the space

Cues

| Heads Up | (Keep your head up for good balance and to avoid collisions with others.) |
| Balanced Stops | (Spread your feet apart and lower your hips slightly to maintain your balance when you stop.) |

Tasks/Challenges:

🅣 Walk, skip, gallop, or hop throughout general space without touching anyone else. Remember, you may have to move to the right or left to avoid bumping into someone else. When I give the signal, stop quickly with both your feet on the floor.

🅣 I've selected music for each of our locomotor movements. The first is for skipping. Listen to the beat. Is it an even or uneven rhythm? Right, skipping is an uneven rhythm. Begin skipping when you hear the music. Stop when the music stops.

🅣 Now listen to the music for the gallop; it's also uneven *(Pause, play music.)* Ready? Gallop.

🅣 The music for hopping is short and quick. Clap the rhythm. Is it even or uneven? Hop on one foot to the music.

🅣 I've saved your favorite locomotor movement until last. What is it? Running. Run quietly so you'll hear the music stop.

Children tend to practice only their favorite locomotor skill when the task is open. We find it helps to specify each skill in addition to "your choice" or "your favorite."

🅣 This is a game like musical chairs, except that you are never out. When the music begins, travel throughout the whole space using the traveling action that I call out. When the music stops find a space inside a hoop as quickly as possible. Each time I will remove some of the hoops. The trick is that someone must be in every hoop, but any number of people can be inside the hoops when there are not enough left.

Traveling an Obstacle Course

Setting: An obstacle course of hoops, bamboo poles, low beams, and other items (Figure 19.6)

Cues

| Heads Up | (Keep your head up for good balance and to avoid collisions with others.) |
| Pause, Look, Go | (Pause momentarily to avoid others who are also moving.) |

Tasks/Challenges:

🅣 You've worked on various locomotor skills and on moving with control. Using a combination of a hop, skip, gallop, leap, walk, and slide, move through the obstacle course without touching other people, the hoops, or the bamboo poles.

Traveling in Different Directions

Setting: Children scattered throughout general space

Cues

| Heads Up | (Keep your head up for good balance and to avoid collisions with others.) |
| Hips over Feet | (Keep your body centered over your feet for good balance and quick changes of direction.) |

Tasks/Challenges:

🅣 You have learned six directions. Let's name them together: forward, backward, right, left, up, and

Figure 19.6 An obstacle course.

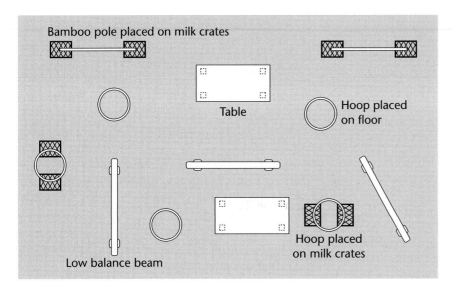

Bamboo pole placed on milk crates

Table

Hoop placed on floor

Low balance beam

Hoop placed on milk crates

down. This time as you walk, run, or hop, change directions as you travel.

T Begin walking forward. On the signal, change directions and walk backward. Exaggerate your movements so you look like a toy soldier or robot.

T On the signal, run in a forward direction. When you hear the drum, slow your speed, and run to the side or backward. Take only a few steps; then continue running forward.

T Pretend you're going to draw a square with one foot. Hop forward, backward, to the right, and to the left to draw your square.

C This time, we will really see how well you can travel in different directions. I will call out a traveling action and a number. If the number is even, travel forward; if it is odd, travel backward.

Remember to do this task only with students who know the difference between odd and even numbers. It can be quite embarrassing for students not to know how to travel because of their math skills.

Tasks/Challenges:

T Use a sliding action (a slidestep) to travel toward the far end of the field. On the signal, change the direction of your slidestep.

T Using the slidestep, travel eight steps to the right, then eight steps to the left. Stop and balance on one foot. Repeat eight steps to the left, eight steps to the right. Stop and balance in a wide shape. This combination of travel and balances is the ingredients of the folk dance "Seven Jumps." Many folk dances use this slidestep.

C In a small group of four, six, or eight persons, use a combination of slidesteps and balances to create your own version of "Seven Jumps." Practice with your group until you are ready to show the dance to the class. We will then videotape the dances for your portfolios.

✓ *Videotape/Digital Analysis.* With the establishment of criteria, videotape is an excellent means for assessing children's work. Refer to Chapter 14 for details on checklists for use in observing critical cues.

Slidestepping

Setting: Children scattered throughout general space

Cues	
Heads Up	(Keep your head up for good balance and to avoid collisions with others.)
Hips over Feet	(Keep your body centered over your feet for good balance and quick changes of direction.)

Traveling in Different Pathways

Setting: Children scattered in general space

Cues	
Heads Up	(Keep your head up for good balance and to avoid collisions with others.)
Hips over Feet	(Keep your body centered over your feet for good balance with changes in direction and/or pathways.)

Tasks/Challenges:

🅣 A while ago you learned three different pathways. Who remembers what they were? That's right: straight, curved, and zigzag. This time, change your pathway as you travel. Begin by walking in a straight pathway. On the signal, change to a curved pathway. **Exaggerate your movements so that the pathway is really quite curved.**

🅣 This time, practice traveling in a zigzag pathway. **Remember, zigzag looks like the letter Z; make really sharp angles.**

🅣 On the signal, begin traveling in a straight path. You may use any form of traveling that you wish. When you hear the drum, change to another pathway. The next time you hear the drum, change your pathway again.

🅣 This will be a test of how well you can travel using the different pathways. The game is like follow the leader. When I say "Go," find a partner whose skill in traveling is about the same as yours. Go. Now, the shorter one of you will be the first leader. You are to travel using any traveling action you like and as many different pathways as possible. The follower will try to copy your every move. But don't make it so hard that your follower can't possibly keep up with you. Make it a fun game. When you hear the signal, you must be able to stop without falling over or touching each other. After three times as a leader, switch positions.

The Locomotors Dance

Setting: Class divided into groups of five to eight persons; paper and pencil for each group

Cues	
Heads Up	(Keep your head up for good balance and to avoid collisions with others.)
Hips over Feet	(Keep your body centered over your feet for good balance with changes in direction and/or pathways.)

Tasks/Challenges:

🅣 You have practiced hopping, skipping, galloping, sliding, leaping, and running. You have traveled in different directions and pathways. In your group, combine the locomotors with directions and path-

ways to create a dance of locomotors. You will need to decide:

• The amount of space you'll need

• A leader or changes in leaders

• Which locomotors and what directions and pathways

When you have created your dance, record it on paper, and practice it several times; then we will watch them. The criteria for observation will be correct execution of the locomotors, cooperative work with your group, and creative ideas in the dance.

✓ *Event Tasks.* Children's dance projects can serve as events tasks and provide excellent assessments of student learning. *See Chapter 14 for establishing criteria and designing rubric guidelines.*

The Follow-Me Dance

Setting: Instrumental music with a strong beat (e.g., hoedown or country music); children scattered throughout general space, facing the teacher

Cues	
Heads Up	(Keep your head up for good balance and to avoid collisions with others.)
Hips over Feet	(Keep your body centered over your feet for good balance and quick changes of direction.)
Balanced Stops	(Spread your feet apart and lower your hips slightly to maintain your balance when you stop.)

Tasks/Challenges:

🅣 We're going to practice our locomotor skills today; we'll combine the skills with rhythm and keeping the beat in self-space. This is called Follow Me, country-western style. Spread throughout general space, facing me. I'll move to the right, the left, forward, and backward. You'll mirror my direction. So if I go left, you go right; if I go forward, you go backward. I'll hop, jump, gallop, slide, walk, and move in other ways. After each locomotor phrase, you'll stop in self-space and do such things as touch your hands to your heels, nod your head forward and backward, cross your knees as in a Charleston, and so on. You only need to watch and follow me.

Keep all activities in a count of eight—for example, eight slides to the left, eight slides to the right, stop, touch hands to heels in time with the music; one, two, three, four, five, six, seven, eight; gallop forward eight steps, gallop backward eight steps, stop, clap hands in time with the music: one, two, three, four, five, six, seven, eight.

Traveling at Different Speeds

Setting: Sheets of newspapers stacked at the edge of the gymnasium; children scattered throughout general space

Cues

Heads Up	(Keep your head up for good balance and to avoid collisions with others.)
Pause and Go	(Check your speed slightly to avoid others.)

Tasks/Challenges:

T Each of you will need one sheet of newspaper. After you get your sheet, unfold it and place it against your chest, holding it at your shoulders. At the signal, begin running; you'll no longer have to hold your newspaper. What will happen to the newspaper when you stop running? Ready, go.

T Try running at different speeds, sometimes very fast, sometimes very slowly, to see if the paper will stay up.

Traveling Using Different Directions, Levels, Pathways, and Locations

Setting: Several sets of task cards: one set that names single locomotor actions (e.g., walk, run, or hop); a second set that names different directions; a third set that names different levels; a fourth set that names different locations (general and self-space); and a final set that names different pathways. *It is helpful to color-code the different sets.*

Cues

Heads Up	(Keep your head up for good balance and to avoid collisions with others.)
Hips over Feet	(Keep your body centered over your feet for good balance with changes in direction and/or pathways.)

Tasks/Challenges:

T Choose a card from each color (stack), and return to your self-space. You are going to travel using the directions on the cards you have. For example, if your cards say "Walk," "Backward," "Low," and

"General Space," you walk backward at a low level in general space.

T This time, change one card of the same color with the person next to you. Now move according to the new directions.

The combinations here are endless. You could trade as many cards as you like until the children have practiced a multitude of combinations.

C With the last set of cards that you have, practice the action until you think it is so clear that anyone could figure it out just by watching you. *(Give children time to practice.)* Now, when I say "Go," choose a partner whom you can work with well. Go. Show your partner your sequence, and see whether he or she can guess what your cards said. Now, switch: Watch your partner's sequence, and you guess.

Changing Speeds to Music

Setting: Recordings of music at 78, 33, and 16 rpm or variable speed control; children scattered throughout general space

Cues

Heads Up	(Keep your head up for good balance and to avoid collisions with others.)
Speed Check	(Slow your speed slightly to avoid others.)
Balanced Stops	(Spread your feet apart and lower your hips slightly to maintain your balance when you stop.)

Tasks/Challenges:

T Listen to the music; it will start slowly and gradually increase in speed to a faster tempo. Do you think you can run with a gradual increase and decrease in your speed? Match your running speed with the music. Begin slowly, and gradually increase to your fastest speed; as the music begins to slow, decrease your speed to a jogging pace.

A Dance of Water, Steam, and Ice

Setting: Children scattered throughout general space

Cues

Pause and Go	(Pause between actions to emphasize changes.)
Exaggerate	(Exaggerate movements and shapes for emphasis.)

Tasks/Challenges:

🅣 Let's think about how water changes form as the temperature changes. At normal temperature, water is a liquid whose molecules are moving at a medium speed. As the temperature increases, the water molecules move faster and faster until the water is transformed into steam. As the temperature decreases, the molecules move more and more slowly until they finally freeze, forming ice. Let's put this story into a creative dance. As I tell the story, you'll travel with changes in speed as the molecules increase their speed, decrease their speed, and freeze.

Slow-Motion Replay: The Sports Dance

Setting: Children scattered throughout general space

Cues	
Pause and Go	(Pause between actions to emphasize changes.)
Exaggerate	(Exaggerate movements and shapes for emphasis.)

Tasks/Challenges:

🅣 Think about how the players move when a film is shown in slow motion or when the sports announcer replays a special segment from a game.

I want each of you to think of your favorite moment in a sport. Is it when the quarterback breaks away to run for a touchdown, or was it when you scored the winning soccer goal? Perhaps it was the throw of the javelin at the Olympics or the relay team running at the track meet. Decide what kind of locomotor movement would portray your favorite moment. Combine your movements as in a slow-motion replay. How would you begin—in what position? How will the replay end? Practice the segment until you can do it three times the same way, just like a replay. Remember, it's slow motion. We'll look at the movements when you're ready.

Other ideas for creative dance and travel include walking through a thick jungle, walking through a completely dark and haunted house, walking on the ledge of an 80-story building, traveling across a high wire on a windy day, traveling during an earthquake.

Combination Locomotors

Line dances, as well as traditional folk and square dances, are combinations of locomotor skills and nonlocomotor body actions. Although there are excellent resources available for the teaching of such dances (see Chapter 29, Box 29-3), we encourage our students—and you as teachers—to create new line, square, and folk dances. See Boxes 19-3 and 19-4.

Box 19-3

The Grapevine Step

The grapevine step is used in many line dances, as well as in intermediate folk dances; it may be done to the right or to the left. Children enjoy combining it with forward and backward steps and turns to create new dances.

Cue: Front, side, Back, Side

Count 1: Cross right foot over in front of left foot.
Count 2: Step to left on left foot.
Count 3: Cross right foot behind left foot.
Count 4: Step to left on left foot

The Grapevine Step

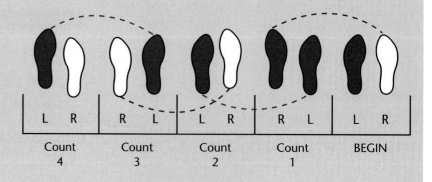

Count 4	Count 3	Count 2	Count 1	BEGIN
L R	R L	L R	R L	L R

Box 19-4

The Margie Dance

Description

This line dance was choreographed as attribute to Margie Hanson for her contributions to children's dance and physical education.

Music

"I'd Like to Teach the World to Sing," Metromedia KMD1051.

Formation

Lines

Counts and Steps

1–2—Introduction, sway with body or hands.

3–4—Hands in air and sway to the right, left, right, and left.

5–8—Walk to right and give a high-five greeting on step 8.

1–4—Walk to left and give a high-five greeting on step 4.

5–8—Hands in air and sway to the right, left, right, and left.

1–4—Join and raise hands.

5–8—Lower hands.

1–4—"Thank you" in sign language (see illustration below), two times.

5–8—"I love you" in sign language (hold two middle fingers down and keep pinky, index finger, and thumb up) and raise hands.

Repeat dance three more times. At the end, hug your neighbors in this world and give them some N and G's, which means tell them some nice and good things.

"Thank you" in sign language

Source: Rhythmic Activities and Dance (pp. 87–88) by J. P. Bennett and P. C. Riemer, 1995, Champaign, IL: Human Kinetics. With permission from John P. Bennett.

Utilization Level: Learning Experiences Leading to Skill Development

The learning experiences in this section challenge children to travel in increasingly complex ways. Tasks are designed to develop the travel skills used in many dance, game, and gymnastics sequences.

A note about cues: Although several cues are listed for many of the learning experiences, it's important to focus on only one cue at a time. That way, the children can really concentrate on that cue. Once you provide feedback to the children and observe that most have learned a cue, then it's time to focus on another one.

Traveling with a Partner: Matching Pathways

Setting: Sets of partners scattered throughout general space

Cue

Heads Up (Keep your head up for good balance and to avoid collisions with others.)

Tasks/Challenges:

🅣 Stand back to back with a partner. When I say "Go," each partner travels in the direction he or she is facing. That is, each of you travels away from your partner. When you hear the drum, stop, turn around, and return to your partner with the exact pattern and locomotor movements you used before *(Figure 19.7)*. Return at the same speed you used to travel away from your partner.

🅣 Earlier you learned that there are three pathways. *(See "Space Awareness," Chapter 16.)* What are they? *(Ask for answers.)* All patterns are made up of those pathways or combinations of those pathways. This time as you travel away from your partner,

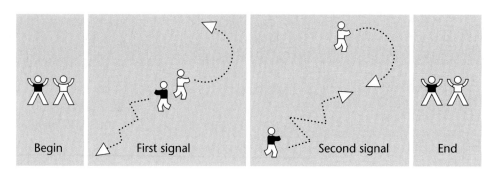

Figure 19.7 Traveling in pathways away from and toward a partner.

Box 19-5

Designing Floor Patterns for Dance

The floor patterns created in dance experiences and the locomotor movements used are important components of creative dance. The patterns created as the dancer moves can tell a story, set a mood, or portray an idea. The various ways of travel used in dance and the patterns created aren't accidental; they're planned and carefully designed. When designing the travel pattern of a dance, teacher and children can focus upon the following concerns:

1. What idea stimulated the dance? Was it a music selection? A bullfight? A wiggly snake?
2. What qualities are inherent in the theme of the dance or the music selection? Is the tempo slow, moderate, or fast? Is the rhythm even or uneven? Is the music harmonious? Vibrant? Mellow?
3. What pathway best expresses the feelings or emotions you sense? Advancing, attacking? Retreating? Collapsing? Gathering? Departing? Wavy? Angular Jagged?

It's a good idea to have the children keep notes and diagram their pathways as they design them, for several reasons. First, they will clearly visualize what the floor pattern looks like and be better able to evaluate its suitability for the dance. Second, children usually use several classes to put together a completed dance and often fail to remember ideas they had in earlier classes. Third, when children finish a dance, they take with them a written record of their accomplishments.

It's often beneficial to post several examples of pathways around the room on the walls, to give children an idea of what's expected. Another effective teaching aid is to post drawings of locomotor skills and positions of stillness that the children have experienced. Rather than trying to diagram a sequence from memory, youngsters can look at these posters and select movements to incorporate along their floor patterns.

Even those of us with no artistic abilities can trace beautiful diagrams using an opaque projector!

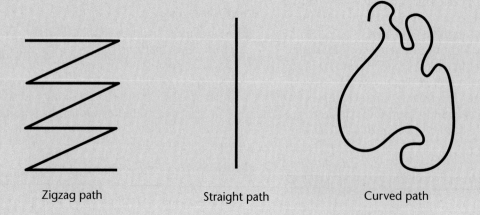

Zigzag path   Straight path   Curved path

be aware of the pathways you use. On your return, copy the same pathways.

(T) Stand beside your partner. This time as you travel, use a slidestep to move away from your partner. Remember to return using the same pathway.

(T) Select a partner, and decide who's to be the first leader. When the follower says "Go," the leader travels across the field with a combination of straight, curved, and zigzag pathways. When the leader stops, the follower then travels the same pattern. The other partner then designs the pattern. *(For tips on helping children learn to design floor patterns for dance, see Box 19-5.)*

The Copy Cat Dance

Setting: Music, such as "Dueling Banjos," that features copy phrases; sets of partners scattered throughout general space

> **Cue**
>
> **Heads Up** (Keep your head up for good balance and to avoid collisions with others.)

Tasks/Challenges:

(T) Earlier this year you practiced traveling with a partner, copying pathways. This time you will copy not only pathways with your partner but also locomotors and directions. For your beginning, you may choose to stand beside or behind your partner. Partner A will travel away from partner B as the first phrase of music plays; partner B will then travel with the exact pattern and locomotor. The dance continues as one partner leads and the other copies. Listen to the phrases of the music to time the length of your travel.

(✓) *Event Task.* Creative dance projects provide event tasks that are excellent assessments of children's work. The above task could easily be made into an event task by having students write out their dance and perform it, for someone else. *See Chapter 14 for the development of rubrics to accompany event tasks.*

Traveling with a Partner: Changing Speed and Direction

Setting: Sets of partners scattered throughout general space

> **Cues**
>
> **Heads Up** (Keep your head up for good balance and to avoid collisions with others.)
>
> **On Your Toes** (Keep your weight on the balls of your feet for quickness.)

Tasks/Challenges:

(T) Stand facing a partner approximately 3 feet apart: One of you is the leader; the other, the follower. The leader slides to the right or left, changing directions quickly. The follower tries to stay directly across from the leader at all times. I'll give the signal every 60 seconds for you both to switch positions. Note that by adding dribbling a ball and defensive arm position to this pattern, we form an offensive-defensive drill in basketball.

Shadowing

Setting: Sets of partners scattered throughout general space

> **Cues**
>
> **Heads Up** (Keep your head up for good balance and to avoid collisions with others.)
>
> **On Your Toes** (Keep your weight on the balls of your feet for quickness.)

Tasks/Challenges:

(T) Choose a partner whose speed and ability to change directions are very similar to yours. Partner 1 stands approximately 2 feet behind partner 2. When I say "Go," partner 2 travels quickly, changing directions with sharp turns to the right and to the left; partner 1 attempts to stay within an arm's distance at all times. When you hear the drum hit, stop without colliding or losing your balance. Partner 1 now stands in front, ready to be the new leader. Keep your eyes on your partner's waist when you're the follower.

Meeting and Parting While Traveling with a Partner

Setting: Sets of partners scattered throughout general space

> **Cue**
>
> **Heads Up** (Keep your head up for good balance and to avoid collisions with others.)

Tasks/Challenges:

T This task is called Leapin' Lizards. On the signal, you are to travel throughout the general space. On the cue "Leapin' Lizards," find a partner as quickly as possible, travel side by side for a few steps, then leap in unison and split up to continue traveling using the new pattern I call out. The next time you hear the signal, find a new partner, travel and do two leaps, then split to travel in a new way. We will continue until the number of leaps gets to five.

T This time, instead of partners find a group of three whenever you hear the cue. Make sure all of you leap at the same time. With a larger group it is harder to coordinate your leaps. It might help if one person calls out "One, two, three, leap."

Performing Rhythmical Patterns

Setting: Hoops, one per child, scattered throughout general space

Cues

Heads Up	(Keep your head up for good balance.)
Soft Landings	(Bend your knees for a soft landing.)

Tasks/Challenges:

T Jump in and out of your hoop with a four-four rhythm: two jumps in, two jumps out, or three jumps in, one jump out. Maintain an even tempo by clapping the four counts as you jump.

I'll clap the rhythm I want you to use for your jumps: one, two, three, four. Let's all clap the rhythm together before we begin our jumps. *(Group practices with teacher as leader.)*

C Practice until you can match the rhythm three times with no mistakes.

T Try your jumping pattern in and out of the hoop with the music. Remember, you may choose a three-one or a two-two pattern in and out.

Traveling to Express Age: The Fountain of Youth Dance

Setting: Children scattered throughout general space

Cue

Exaggerate	(Exaggerate your actions and gestures for expression.)

Tasks/Challenges:

T Using combinations of locomotor movements, body language, and gestures, tell the story of an old, old person who discovers the Fountain of Youth. Let me set the stage for you. An old, old person is walking down the street. The person feels weary, tired, without enough energy to hold his or her head high. While walking down the street, the oldster sees a bottle in a gutter. An examination of the bottle reveals the words *Fountain of Youth Juice*. Puzzled, hesitant, yet desperate, the oldster takes a drink and then a few more. The transformation begins . . . The old person is changed into an ecstatic youth who dances merrily down the street. Think of the following as you prepare your dance:

Folk/cultural dances are combinations of locomotors—combinations into specific steps, changes in directions, and partner/group formations. See Chapter 29, "Skill Themes in Dance," for the teaching of folk/cultural dance in elementary physical education.

What type of movements would the old person use? Jerky or smooth? Slow or fast?

What body posture and what hand gestures would the old person assume?

How would the oldster approach the bottle?

Will the transformation occur quickly or be rather slowly executed?

How would you contrast the oldster's movements with those of the ecstatic youth: type of travel, speed, level, gestures?

Traveling in Bound and Free Flow

Setting: Children scattered throughout general space

Cues

Exaggerate	(Exaggerate your actions and gestures for expression.)
Free Flow	(Unstoppable from beginning to end.)
Bound Flow	(Jerky; stoppable at any moment.)

Tasks/Challenges:

T Here are two additional ideas for short dance phrases based on imaginary situations. First, a rag doll comes to life for a brief time. One interpretation is that the rag doll slowly comes to life with jerky, uncoordinated (bound) movements, falls over, and has trouble gaining control and balance; the doll gradually improves and is then running and leaping, turning in the air (free), and enjoying life. Then the doll suddenly stops, slowly walks back to the starting location, sits and sighs, freezes, and is a doll once again.

T Second, a balloon filled with helium escapes from the hands of its owner, floats across the sky, leaks, and falls back to earth.

These types of dance experiences are often short, culminating the practice of travel patterns. Discuss with the children the travel qualities and movement concepts (space awareness, effort) appropriate for each activity. Each dance should have a clear beginning, rise to a climax, and then wind down to a conclusion.

Traveling to Tom Foolery Rhymes

Setting: Children divided into groups of four; Tom Foolery rhymes written on cards and placed around the room, enough cards for one per group. *Some children may be able to write their own rhymes.*

Cues	
Exaggerate	(Exaggerate your actions and gestures for expression.)
Free Flow	(Unstoppable from beginning to end.)
Bound Flow	(Jerky; stoppable at any moment.)

Tasks/Challenges:

T In your group, make up a humorous sequence to the rhythmic pattern of the Tom Foolery rhyme written on your card. You decide the rhythm of the chant and the locomotor patterns you'll use to accompany the rhyme. Travel around the room with your chosen locomotor patterns, chanting the rhyme as you go.

Here are the Tom Foolery rhymes:

Soft feet, gentle, quick run:
   Pit-a-pat, pit-a-pat, pit-a-pat, jump back!

Swaying, rocking steps:
   See-Saw Mar-ger-y Daw,
   Jack shall have a new mas-ter.
   He shall have but a pen-ny a day,
   Be-cause he won't work an-y fast-er.

Skipping:
   Here's a word to the wise:
   Don't get soap in your eyes!

   I hope the dope who thought up soap
   Has to eat it—I repeat it, Eat It!

Bouncy Jumps:
   Boinggg, boinggg, boingg, boingg, boingg, bammmm!

Proficiency Level: Learning Experiences Leading to Skill Development

The following learning experiences encourage youngsters to use their travel skills and knowledge of travel patterns in combination with other skills to design and perform dances, gymnastics routines, and strategic game maneuvers.

A note about cues: Tasks are more complex at the proficiency level, typically requiring children to coordinate several movements simultaneously in a dynamic context. A list of cues is provided to assist the children in being more successful in the learning experience. The challenge for the teacher is in determining which cue will be most beneficial for each child . . . and when. Thus, careful observation and critical reflection are important as you watch the children move and then decide which cue will be the most helpful to move each learner to a higher skill level.

Depicting Primitive Tribes through Travel

Setting: Class divided into two groups

Tasks/Challenges:

T Dance can be a story without words. You're going to tell the story of primitive tribes through shapes and actions. *(Show children cave drawings of tribal dances.)* Use your imagination as you look at the drawings. How do you think these people lived? What was their work? What was home like for them—did they have a home? Now let's put your ideas into movement terms. At what level would the people move? Would their movements be flowing or sustained, jerky or smooth?

Your dance will tell the story of two primitive tribes. Part 1 of your dance will show how the people live as a group. Show through your movements and gestures the life of a person in a primitive tribe. Part 2 of your dance will portray the two tribes discovering each other, their fear of the unknown, and their battle to defend their territory. In Part 2, each group begins with the movements portraying preparation for battle. The battle will consist of approach, attack *(with no contact)*, and a retreat.

The following questions will help you design your movements for this dance story:

1. Will your travel be fast or slow when preparing for battle, approaching the enemy, retreating from the battle?
2. How can your gestures best represent the punching, jabbing, kicking, slashing actions of battle?
3. Will your travel be low, with angular actions, or high and smooth?
4. As you retreat from battle, how will your travel show caution, fear, injury?

Traveling to Show Tradition Versus Change

Setting: Class divided into two groups

Tasks/Challenges:

 Dance doesn't always tell a story. Sometimes dance is a study in form—the shapes we can make with our bodies, the spatial patterns we create as a group. Group 1 will represent tradition. Use your body shapes and group travel to show the characteristics of tradition; for example, a firm, solid shape, such as a square group; formed by the identical and simultaneous group movements; use of a small amount of space; and firm, sustained quality—control at all times.

Group 2 will represent the forces of change. The characteristics of change include individualized shapes, travel in different directions, use of a large amount of space, and a variety of movements. Working together as a group, design a dance that combines at least five shapes and three locomotor patterns to portray the characteristics of your group.

When we look at the tradition group, we should see oneness, sturdiness, caution; the shapes and actions of the change group should portray individuality, risk taking, and freedom.

Dance that tells a story can easily become only pantomime. Children will need guidance in avoiding exactly replicating gestures and using more total body movement and space.

✓ *Videotape.* Videotaping dances for future analysis, accompanied by a written description with established criteria and rubric, would be an excellent summative assessment.

Performing Rhythmical Patterns: Tinikling

Setting: Sets of tinikling poles, approximately 12 feet in length, either made from bamboo poles or purchased commercially. Each set of poles will accommodate four children—two for tapping the poles and two for jumping (Figure 19.8). *In its traditional form, tinikling is performed with a three-four rhythm, with the poles tapping "out, out, in" and the dancers performing "in, in, out." We have found a four-four rhythm to be much easier for children first learning the activity.*

Cues	
Weight Balanced over Poles	(Keep your shoulders and hips over the poles.)
Feet In, In, Out, Out	(Your feet go inside, inside the poles, then outside, outside the poles.)

Figure 19.8 Basic tinikling setup.

Tasks/Challenges:

T Tinikling is a rhythmical activity that involves co-ordinated stepping, hopping, jumping actions with the tapping of long bamboo poles. In the beginning position, the bamboo poles are approximately 2 feet apart; they're tapped down on the floor twice: tap, tap. The poles are then brought together for two counts: tap, tap. This pattern is repeated: apart, apart, together, together. This opening and closing position is maintained while dancers step or jump in and out without touching the poles. Let's do the action of the poles with our hands; clap the rhythm with me: out, out, in, in. *(Demonstrate with your hands apart, apart, together, together.)* This is the action of the bamboo poles for all our tinikling skills: out, out, in, in.

T Divide into groups of four. Two people clap the four-four rhythm; the other two people practice the tapping action with the poles.

We find it helps to tape the ends of the poles where the children grip them to prevent the bamboo poles from cracking and pinching the children's fingers.

T You now know how to clap the four-four rhythm and to tap the bamboo poles to that rhythm. Now you'll learn the basic single-step pattern.

Stand on your left foot; hop two times on your left foot. Step on your right foot between the lines; transfer your weight to your left foot between the lines. Hop on your right foot two times outside the lines. Repeat the action to the left. Clap the four-four beat as you hop.

Figure 19.9 shows the single-step pattern. Have the children stand outside the parallel tape lines on the floor. Their right sides should be toward the tape lines.

C Practice until you can perform the pattern four times with no mistakes. You'll then be ready to practice the single-step pattern with two people tapping the poles. Remember, your feet go in, in, out, out while the poles go out, out, in, in.

T After you feel comfortable with the single-step pattern, try the double-step or the hopping pattern *(Figures 19.10 and 19.11)*. When you're really good, you can create a new pattern with a four-four or three-four beat.

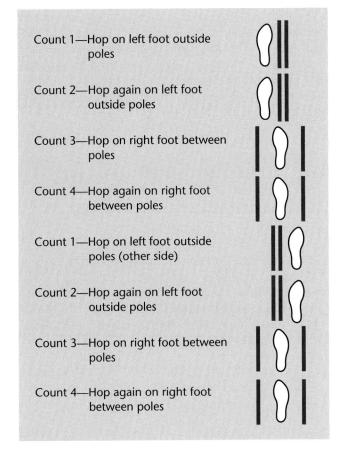

Count 1—Hop on left foot outside poles

Count 2—Hop again on left foot outside poles

Count 3—Hop on right foot between poles

Count 4—Hop again on right foot between poles

Count 1—Hop on left foot outside poles (other side)

Count 2—Hop again on left foot outside poles

Count 3—Hop on right foot between poles

Count 4—Hop again on right foot between poles

Figure 19.9 Tinikling: single-step pattern.

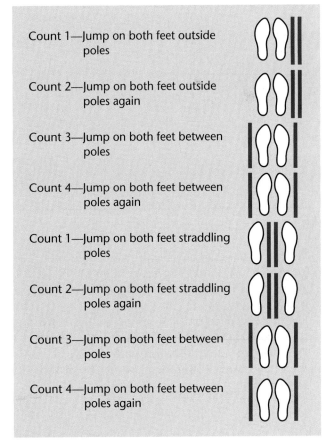

Count 1—Jump on both feet outside poles

Count 2—Jump on both feet outside poles again

Count 3—Jump on both feet between poles

Count 4—Jump on both feet between poles again

Count 1—Jump on both feet straddling poles

Count 2—Jump on both feet straddling poles again

Count 3—Jump on both feet between poles

Count 4—Jump on both feet between poles again

Figure 19.10 Tinikling: double-step pattern.

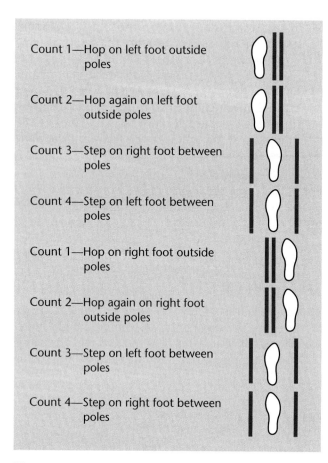

Count 1—Hop on left foot outside poles

Count 2—Hop again on left foot outside poles

Count 3—Step on right foot between poles

Count 4—Step on left foot between poles

Count 1—Hop on right foot outside poles

Count 2—Hop again on right foot outside poles

Count 3—Step on left foot between poles

Count 4—Step on right foot between poles

Figure 19.11 Tinikling: hopping.

Students with advanced tinikling skills enjoy the action with four poles—two poles crossed over two poles—and the combination of basic tinikling actions with gymnastics stunts, for example, cartwheels and walkovers between the poles as they move apart.

Traveling in Games and Sports

The ability to travel in games is often what separates the skilled player from the average player. Many children can throw and catch accurately and with control while they're stationary, but they regress to a precontrol level when travel is added. Thus, traveling is an important part of the utilization and proficiency sections of the games skills chapters. Games-related tasks that incorporate traveling are discussed in Chapter 20, "Chasing, Fleeing, and Dodging," and in Chapter 24 through 28: "Kicking and Punting," "Throwing and Catching," "Volleying and Dribbling," "Striking with Rackets and Paddles," and "Striking with Long-Handled Implements," respectively.

Traveling in Gymnastics

Traveling in gymnastics supplies the buildup of force necessary for step and spring takeoffs when transferring weight on mats and onto equipment, as well as for many Olympic stunts (Figure 19.12). The floor patterns the travel creates form an important component of gymnastics routines. Travel in relation to gymnastics is discussed in Chapters 21, 22, and 23: "Jumping and Landing," "Balancing," and "Transferring Weight and Rolling," respectively.

Reading Comprehension Questions

1. What components of traveling are taught in a program of physical education for children?
2. What does "naturally developing skill" mean? List two examples.
3. List the fundamental locomotor skills. Why are these skills important for children?
4. Describe a mature running pattern. Do all children have mature running patterns? Do all adults? Explain.
5. What are the differences among a hop, a leap, a slide, and a gallop?
6. Describe how travel is studied at the proficiency level in games, gymnastics, and dance.
7. How can you use a Tom Foolery rhyme to stimulate different ways of traveling?
8. What is tinikling?

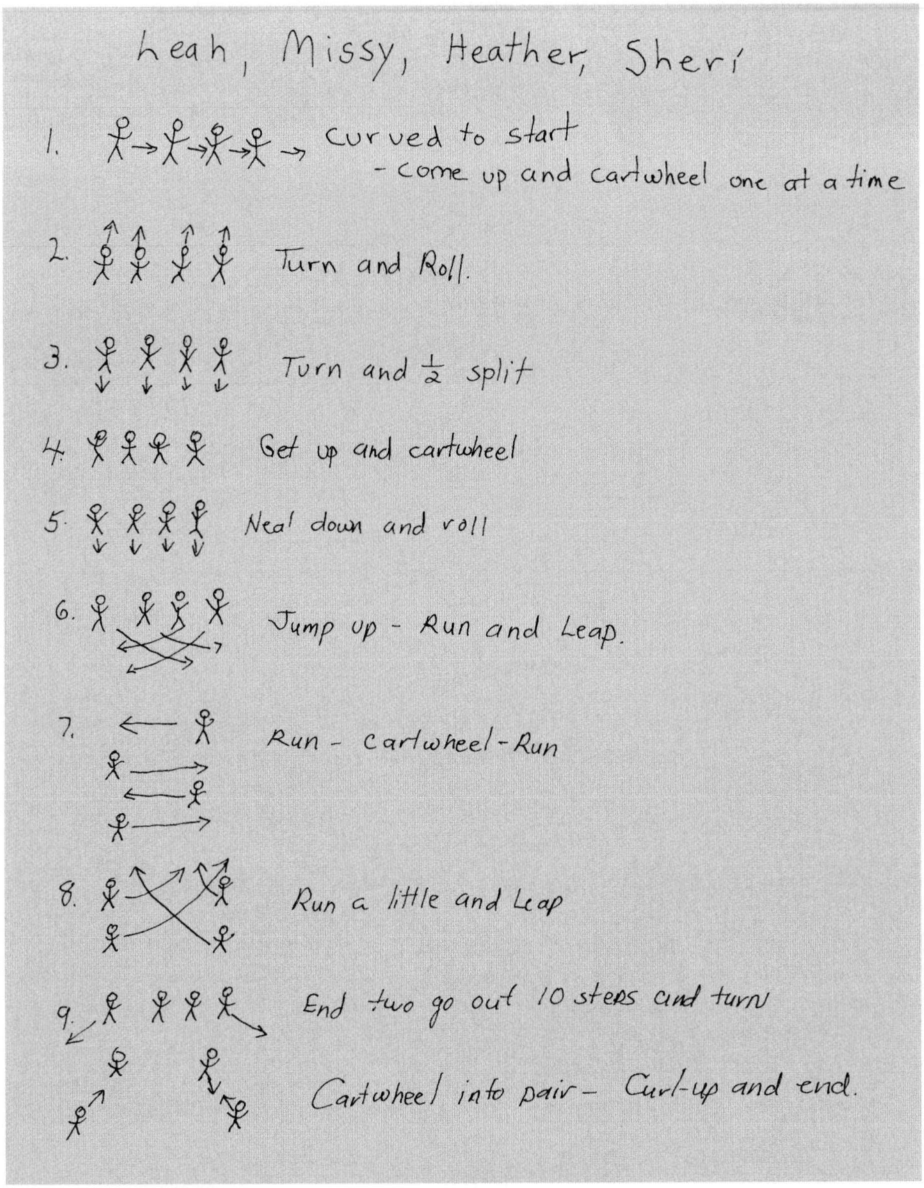

Figure 19.12 Children's travel patterns in gymnastics.

Leah, Missy, Heather, Sheri

1. curved to start
   - come up and cartwheel one at a time

2. Turn and Roll.

3. Turn and ½ split

4. Get up and cartwheel

5. Neal down and roll

6. Jump up - Run and Leap.

7. Run - cartwheel - Run

8. Run a little and Leap

9. End two go out 10 steps and turn

   Cartwheel into pair - Curl-up and end.

References/Suggested Readings

Bennett, J. P., & Riemer, P. C. (1995). *Rhythmic activities and dance*. Champaign, IL: Human Kinetics.

National Association for Sport and Physical Education. (1995). *Moving into the future: National standards for physical education*. St. Louis, MO: Mosby.

National Association for Sport and Physical Education. (2004). *Moving into the future: National standards for physical education*. (2nd ed.) Reston, VA: National Association for Sport and Physical Education.

Wickstrom, R. L. (1997). *Fundamental motor patterns* (2nd ed.). Philadelphia: Lea & Febiger.

Chasing, Fleeing, and Dodging

Since ancient times children have delighted in countless chasing, fleeing, and dodging games. These games all challenge children to evade a chasing player through dodging and fleeing. Such sports as basketball, hockey, soccer, and football are simply more elaborate forms of these games using the same elements. Physical education programs can build on the innate pleasure that children experience from playing these games. By providing a variety of challenging tasks and game situations, a teacher can help youngsters develop chasing, fleeing, and dodging skills (see our progression spiral, page 336).

Experience suggests that it's best to focus on chasing, fleeing, and dodging skills after children have developed a working understanding of space awareness concepts and have mastered fundamental traveling skills. Many consider chasing, fleeing, and dodging to be the utilization and proficiency levels of traveling. Although they do require traveling skills of a higher level, chasing, fleeing, and dodging also involve the use of some tactical skills in combination with other skill themes. Therefore, we have chosen to address these skills in a separate chapter.

Chasing, fleeing, and dodging tasks and games using these skills are best played outdoors in large, grassy areas. Box 20-1 notes what the *National Standards for Physical Education* say about chasing, fleeing, and dodging.

Chasing

Chasing is traveling quickly to overtake or tag a fleeing person. In many game situations, the fleeing player is given a head start and allowed time to run away before the chaser can begin traveling. The fleeing player tries to avoid being caught or tagged. Thus, the chaser needs to be able to run at full speed and to react quickly to changes in the direction of the fleeing player's travel.

Fleeing

Fleeing is traveling quickly away from a pursuing person or object. In most game situations, the fleeing person tries to keep as much distance as possible between him and the chaser. However, when the pursuer does close in, the fleeing player uses any maneuver possible to avoid being tagged—the fleeing person dodges, changes direction quickly, or runs full speed. This continual demand on the fleeing player, to react quickly to emerging, threatening situations, is what makes tag games such thrilling activities for children.

Dodging

Dodging is the skill of quickly moving the body in a direction other than the original line of movement. This includes any maneuver a person undertakes to avoid being touched by a chasing person. Dodging may occur while a person is fleeing or stationary. Effective dodging actions include quick fakes, twisting, and stretching.

Levels of Skill Proficiency

We've found that most school-age children are familiar with a variety of tag and dodging games. But some youngsters whose chasing, fleeing, and dodging skills are at the precontrol or control level of proficiency have limited success in playing these games; that is, although many children can chase, flee, and dodge, they can't perform these skills effectively in dynamic game situations. In a game of tag, for instance, the child doing the chasing is often unable to overtake or tag any of the fleeing players and quickly tires of playing the game. In their classic study of children's games, Iona Opie and Peter Opie (1969) noted that chasing games were often plagued with arguments and ended prematurely in heated disputes.

A teacher's initial task, therefore, is to help youngsters develop those skills prerequisite to becoming a capable chaser, fleer, or dodger in various game situations. In school situations in which preschool youngsters' opportunities to play with other children are limited, a teacher may need to provide precontrol-level chasing, fleeing, and dodging activities—for example:

1. Running as fast as possible from one location to another

Box 20-1

Chasing, Fleeing, and Dodging in the *National Standards for Physical Education*

The skill theme of chasing, fleeing, and dodging is referenced in the *National Standards for Physical Education* (National Association for Sport and Physical Education [NASPE], 2004) under Standard 3: Participates regularly in physical activity. The standard addresses the child's ability to use chasing, fleeing, and dodging activities to participate in physical activity.

The standard states:

- Participates in chasing and fleeing activities outside of school (K–2)*

*Grade-level guidelines for expected student learning

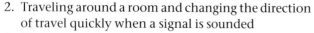

Skill Theme Development Sequence

Chasing, Fleeing, Dodging

Proficiency Level

Dodging while manipulating an object in an invasion gamelike situation
Using team strategy for chasing, fleeing, and dodging invasion gamelike situation
Dodging in a target gamelike situation
Dodging in an invasion gamelike situation
Chasing and dodging simultaneously
Chasing and fleeing in an invasion gamelike situation
Dodging while maintaining possession of an object
Continual fleeing and chasing with a large group

Utilization Level

Dodging while manipulating an object
Dodging in a dynamic situation
Dodging and chasing one person in a mass
Dodging semistationary obstacles
Dodging and faking moves to avoid a chaser
Dodging stationary obstacles

Control Level

Fleeing a chaser
Overtaking a fleeing person
Dodging with quick changes of direction
Dodging the obstacles
Fleeing from a partner
Dodging in response to a signal

Precontrol Level

Make-Believe Chase
Traveling to dodge
Traveling to flee
Moving obstacles

2. Traveling around a room and changing the direction of travel quickly when a signal is sounded
3. When a signal is given, quickly performing a designated dodging maneuver
4. Running as fast as possible away from a partner; on the signal, running quickly toward a partner

Children who can competently perform a variety of quick, dodging maneuvers while running fast are at the control level. A teacher can provide challenging tasks designed to have these children keep their eyes focused on a target child and react quickly to the movements of that child by chasing, fleeing from, or dodging the target child. Such tasks include:

1. Staying as close as possible to a fleeing, dodging partner
2. Chasing after a person who has been given a slight head start and is fleeing
3. Trying to run across a field while dodging one or more chasers

When children can effectively dodge a chasing person and can react quickly and accurately to others' swift, darting movements, they're ready for utilization-level activities. Now the youngsters' chasing, fleeing, and dodging skills enable them to enjoy testing their abilities in ever-changing and complex game environments. Challenging activities include the following:

1. The players of one group flee and/or dodge the players of an opposing group while controlling an object (such as a football, Frisbee, or basketball).
2. One team chases the members of an opposing group but, instead of fleeing their chasers, tries to run past and dodge them without being touched.

Many utilization- and proficiency-level activities incorporate dynamic and often gamelike tasks in the development of chasing, fleeing, and dodging skills. Due to the nature of the skills themselves, the use of dynamic gamelike activities may be more prevalent here than with other skill themes, and the tasks may initially look and sound more like "traditional" games. Look closely beyond the name. All the tasks involve small sided groups in reduced spaces and are designed to help children develop and subsequently apply the skills of chasing, fleeing, and dodging. The tasks should be used as an integral part of the lesson, after the prerequisite skills are developed; not just as an activity to do. As noted, many of these experiences involve the use of groups. The groups recommended here are of small sizes and can usually be designed by having children form their own groups. See Box 9-3 (in Chapter 9) for tips on partner and group formation.

At the proficiency level, children are able to use chasing, fleeing, and dodging skills effectively in a wide variety of game contexts. Both the chasers and the fleeing, dodging players are skilled. At times the chaser gets the target; at other times the fleeing, dodging player escapes. Advanced chasing, fleeing, and dodging skills are evident in situations such as the following:

1. A runner in a football-type game darts quickly past the defense, dodging around the players who are chasing the runner.

2. A soccer player dribbles a ball past a defense player by faking one way and then traveling quickly in the opposite direction.
3. A defense player in a football-type game runs 20 to 30 yards to overtake an offensive runner heading for a score.
4. A basketball player races down court to score a lay-up even though a defense player is chasing right behind.

In elementary school settings, children at the proficiency level enjoy playing teacher- and student-designed games in which chasing, fleeing, and dodging are the primary movements.

Children are inherently attracted to chasing, fleeing, and dodging activities, and it is easy for us and the children to get caught up in the excitement and lose sight of the quality of the movement. Children can't continue these intense activities for long periods without tiring, which is almost always accompanied by a deterioration in quality. It is best to pursue these skills for short periods.

A note about dodgeball, which was included in the first edition of *Children Moving:* Over the past 30 years our knowledge of child growth and development has expanded and practices have changed. Thus, we have eliminated all dodgeball activities from the development of dodging skills. A number of things have influenced this decision. From a psychological perspective, we believe that throwing an object at another person, with the intent of hitting the person, subtly supports violence and goes against all that we know and believe about appropriate practice (Council on Physical Education for Children [COPEC], 2000; Williams, 1992; see Box 20-2). From a safety standpoint, the risk of detached retinas, as well as other serious head injuries, is extreme in dodgeball (regardless of the type of ball used). From a transfer perspective, we know of no sport that utilizes the skill of throwing at a human being. From a legal perspective, many states have already banned dodgeball from schools (check yours).

If you are a physical education major reading this book, you are probably thinking, "I loved dodgeball" and that it was "really fun." For you it was, because you were the skilled player. If you are an elementary education major reading this, you are probably joyous that it has been eliminated. It is important to remember that physical education is for all students, not just the skilled. There are aspects of dodgeball that we all like— the intrigue, the fast pace, the challenge—and we encourage you to redesign activities to keep these aspects while removing the aspects that are counterproductive. For more information about redesigned games, see

Box 20-2

Dodgeball in *Appropriate Practices for Elementary Physical Education*

Appropriate Practices for Elementary Physical Education says that dodgeball-type activities "are physically and/or psychologically unsafe for many children (e.g., dodgeball, in any form, promotes the use of fellow students as targets . . .)."

Source: Council on Physical Education for Children (2000). *Appropriate Practices for Elementary Physical Education: A Position Statement of the National Association for Sport and Physical Education.* Reston, VA: National Association for Sport and Physical Education, and American Alliance for Health, Physical Education, Recreation and Dance.

Chapter 31 or Don Morris and Jim Stiehl's book, *Changing Kids' Games* (1998).

Precontrol Level: Activities for Exploration

Activities at the precontrol level are designed to help children explore the skills of chasing, fleeing, and dodging in simple situations. Before beginning any practice with this theme, children should be at the control level of traveling and have had ample practice with space awareness.

⚠ When working with chasing, fleeing, and dodging activities that involve a finish line, make sure that the line is far away from any obstructions. This precaution allows the children to run through the finish line at full speed safely.

Moving Obstacles

Setting: Children scattered in general space

Tasks/Challenges:

Ⓣ At the signal, travel in general space. Make sure that you look up so that you can avoid collisions with others.

Ⓣ This time make your travel faster but still avoid others.

Have half the children move to one side of the room and half to the other.

(T) On the signal, both lines will try to walk to the opposite side of the room without touching anyone else.

(T) This time travel with three body parts touching the floor. Still no touching.

(T) Now you will cross the space using different levels. Everyone who has blue eyes will travel with his or her body parts high in the air; those with brown eyes should travel at a low level, and those with green or gray eyes, at a medium level.

(T) This time you can choose any way you wish to travel, but go at a medium speed.

(T) Try jogging or running, if you feel ready.

(C) You have 10 points to start; subtract 1 point for every collision. Try to end with all 10 points.

Begin slowly. Have children walk. Gradually increase speed as you observe the children traveling competently and without collisions.

(⚠) Because of the exciting nature of chasing, fleeing, and dodging activities, children's speed tends to increase, sometimes to unsafe levels. Monitor the speed of activities, always reminding children that they must be able to stop and change directions without falling. They should be able to tag someone without pushing.

Traveling to Flee

Setting: All children spread out in a space (an outside grassy space is best) about 20 yards by 20 yards

Tasks/Challenges:

(T) You've all played games in which you had to run away from someone who was chasing you. This time you are going to have an imaginary chaser. On the signal, practice fleeing from your chaser by walking very quickly. On the next signal, stop. Remember, everyone is moving, so look up.

(T) This time, practice fleeing your chaser by running.

(T) How fast can you move to get away from your chaser?

Traveling to Dodge

Setting: Carpet squares, hoops, milk jugs, or ropes spread out on the floor as obstacles

Tasks/Challenges:

(T) On the signal, travel around the general space without touching anyone else or any of the objects on the floor. Be sure to keep your head up so you can avoid collisions.

(T) How many different ways can you find to avoid the obstacles?

(T) This time try to go as fast as you can with no collisions and avoiding all the objects.

Make-Believe Chase

Setting: Children spread out in general space

Tasks/Challenges:

(T) On the signal, try to catch your make-believe partner. Your partner is very quick, so you will really have to work hard to catch him or her. Remember, everyone is chasing, so look up to avoid collisions.

(T) This time, you will chase your dog, who got off the leash. You want to catch your dog before it gets to the street.

(🔑) What are the differences among chasing, fleeing, and dodging?

Control Level: Learning Experiences Leading to Skill Development

Learning experiences at the control level are designed to allow children to practice chasing, fleeing, and dodging in relatively static situations. Often chasing, fleeing, and dodging are combined with only a single other variable.

A note about cues: Although several cues are listed for many of the learning experiences, it's important to focus on only one cue at a time. That way, the children can concentrate on that cue. Once you provide feedback to the children and observe that most have learned a cue, then it's time to focus on another one.

Dodging in Response to a Signal

Setting: Children scattered in general space

Cues	
Fake	(Step/lean one way; go the other.)
Split Second	(Make your moves quicker than light.)

Tasks/Challenges:

(T) Now you're going to become really sneaky. As you travel throughout the general space, when you hear the signal, pretend that you are going in one direction and then quickly change and go in a different direction.

🅣 This time, whenever you hear the signal, try not to let anyone know which direction you'll travel; try to fake them out.

🅣 Now, instead of me giving you the signal, you'll fake on your own. Whenever you come to another person, pretend that you're going to go one way, but go another. Really try to confuse the other person so he or she doesn't know where you'll be going. **Make your move quickly once you decide which way you're going.**

🅒 See if you can travel and dodge for 20 seconds without colliding with anyone.

Fleeing from a Partner

Setting: Partners about 10 feet apart

> **Cue**
>
> **Split Second** (Make your moves quicker than light.)

Tasks/Challenges:

🅣 Face your partner. On the signal, walk slowly toward each other until you are as close as you can be without touching. Then, quickly jump back, as if you're scared, and walk backward to your starting position, keeping a close watch on your partner.

🅣 This time, you're going to do the activity a little differently because you seldom would move slowly to get away from someone. Try to move a little quicker and faster as you flee or go away from your partner. Just remember to not go so fast that you fall down.

🅣 Now, instead of walking away from your partner, try jogging.

Dodging the Obstacles

Setting: Low- and medium-height objects placed around the room as obstacles

> **Cues**
>
> **Split Second** (Make your moves quicker than light.)
> **Change Speed** (Use changes of speed to avoid the obstacles.)
> **Change Direction** (Use changes of direction to avoid the obstacles.)

Tasks/Challenges:

🅣 On the signal, travel around the general space without touching anyone else or any of the obstacles on the floor. Everything is poison. Be sure to watch for other people as well as the objects.

🅣 This time try to move through the area a little faster.

🅒 I will time you for 30 seconds. See if you can travel for that long with no touches.

Children never seem to tire of this task, regardless of their skill level. As the children's skill levels increase, decrease the space between obstacles or use more obstacles to increase the complexity of the task.

Dodging with Quick Changes of Direction

Setting: Children scattered in general space

> **Cues**
>
> **Fake** (Step/lean one way; go the other.)
> **Split Second** (Make your moves quicker than light.)

Tasks/Challenges:

🅣 This is very similar to what you practiced before. Travel around in the general space. When you come close to someone, get as close as possible, and then quickly dodge away and look for another person to approach. There should be a clear burst of speed as you dodge away from the person—as if you're trying to escape. Remember, watch out for others.

🅣 Dodging with speed as you did is called darting. This time practice getting as close to the person you approach as you can before quickly darting away. Make the dart very clear.

🅒 Practice until you can make five darts in a row without having to stop.

Overtaking a Fleeing Person

Setting: Partners scattered in general space

> **Cues**
>
> *Runner* Split Second (Make your moves quicker than light.)
> Fake (Step/lean one way; go the other.)
> Change Direction (Use changes of direction to avoid the chaser.)
> *Chaser* Watch the Hips (Watch the hips of the runner to tell his or her next move.)

Tasks/Challenges:

T In this task you are going to try and catch your partner, who has a head start. On the first signal, the front partner darts away from the back partner. After 3 seconds, another signal is sounded, and the second partner, who has remained still, chases after the first partner, trying to tag him or her before I blow the stop whistle in 20 seconds. For the next round, switch places. You must always stay inside the boundaries. So the activity goes like this: Stand together. On the first signal, partner 1 takes off running. On the second signal, partner 2 takes off and tries to catch partner 1 before I blow the whistle in 20 seconds.

T Let's go again. Remember never to give up, even if the runner keeps getting away. See if you can use all the moves you know.

This task is appropriate when the children have learned to travel in general space without bumping into one another. Initially, children can perform this task more easily (and safely) in large areas, because they're able to focus more on their partners and less on avoiding other children.

✓ *Exit Slip.* This is an appropriate time to use an exit slip (Chapter 14) to assess whether the children know the difference between chasing, fleeing, and dodging and the cues associated with each.

Fleeing a Chaser

Setting: Six people in a group. See Figure 20.1 for setup.

Chasing, fleeing, and dodging situations are favorites of youngsters.

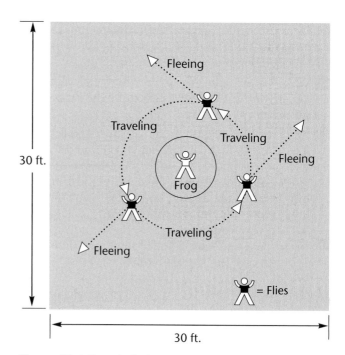

Figure 20.1 Setup for fleeing a chaser.

Cues

Runner Split Second (Make your moves quicker than light.)
Fake (Step/lean one way; go the other.)
Change Direction (Use changes of direction to avoid the chaser.)

Chaser Watch the Hips (Watch the hips of the runner to tell his or her next move.)

Tasks/Challenges:

T This task is designed to let you practice fleeing from a chaser. We'll call it Frogs and Flies. The chaser is the frog, and the runners are the flies. There will be six people in a group—one frog and five flies. The frog, who is in the middle circle, tells the flies how to travel. The flies then travel in a circle around the frog. When the frog gets to his or her feet, all the flies run toward the outside of the square, trying not to get tagged. A fly that is tagged helps the frog the next time. When all the flies are caught, the last fly caught becomes the new frog. Frogs, be sure to change the traveling action each time.

Several games can go on at once, but be sure there is ample space between games so that the fleeing children do not disrupt another game. Mark the boundaries clearly.

✓ *Teacher Observation.* Each of the preceding tasks is an opportune place for teacher observation of the use of critical cues for skills of chasing, fleeing, and dodging before moving on to more dynamic settings. See Chapters 12 and 14 for the development of assessment items and observation checklists.

Utilization Level: Learning Experiences Leading to Skill Development

Children at the utilization level are ready to test their skills in increasingly complex and gamelike situations. In these experiences, children will have to fake and dodge quickly in reaction to the deceptive movements of others.

A note about cues: Although several cues are listed for many of the learning experiences, it's important to focus on only one cue at a time. That way, the children can really concentrate on that cue. Once you provide feedback to the children and observe that most have learned a cue, then it's time to focus on another one.

Dodging Stationary Obstacles

Setting: Groups of six: three taggers, three runners, each group with a space about 10 feet by 20 feet, carpet squares or Xs on the floor to indicate where the taggers are to stand.

Cues

Split Second	(Make your moves quicker than light.)
Fake	(Step/lean one way; go the other.)
Change Direction	(Use changes of direction to avoid the obstacles.)

Tasks/Challenges:

🅣 This task will give you a chance to practice your dodging skills. Three people in each group are taggers and the others are dodgers. Taggers stand on the Xs (or carpet squares) marked on the floor. Both feet must always be on the X (or carpet square). The dodgers start on one side of the room and try to get to the other side of the room without being tagged. After five runs, switch places. If you get tagged, try to figure out how to avoid being tagged the next time.

🅣 Now the activity gets a little harder. If you're tagged, you must freeze right where you're tagged and become a tagger. Dodgers, this will get really hard at the end, so be on your toes.

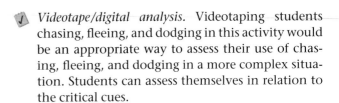 *Videotape/digital analysis.* Videotaping students chasing, fleeing, and dodging in this activity would be an appropriate way to assess their use of chasing, fleeing, and dodging in a more complex situation. Students can assess themselves in relation to the critical cues.

Dodging and Faking Moves to Avoid a Chaser

Setting: Groups of six, each with a space about the size of a quarter of a basketball court

Cues

Dodgers Split Second (Make your moves quicker than light.)
Fake (Step/lean one way; go the other.)
Change Direction/Change Speed (Use changes of direction and speed to avoid the chaser.)

Chasers Watch the Hips (Watch the hips of the runner to tell his or her next move.)
Teamwork (Decide your plan for catching together.)

Tasks/Challenges:

🅣 This chasing and fleeing task will really make you work hard. You can't be slow; if you are, you'll be caught. Make sure you know where your boundaries are. Two people will start out as chasers—you decide who they'll be. The other four players are runners. On the signal, the chasers have one minute to try to catch all the runners. If tagged, a runner has to freeze and then count to 10 out loud before starting to run again. The object is for the taggers to catch all the runners at the same time. After the first minute, change taggers and play again. Remember, the taggers have to try to catch everyone, and no one can go outside the boundaries.

🅐 When children tag one another, they can be quite rough, sometimes knocking others over. Here are two rules which have helped us: (1) A tag is only a touch, not a slap or hit, and (2) all tags must be on the shoulders or below.

Dodging Semistationary Obstacles

Setting: Class divided into two groups; tape or chalk marks on the floor approximately an arm's length apart to designate where the members of one group must place their feet (Figure 20.2)

Figure 20.2 Setup for dodging semistationary objects.

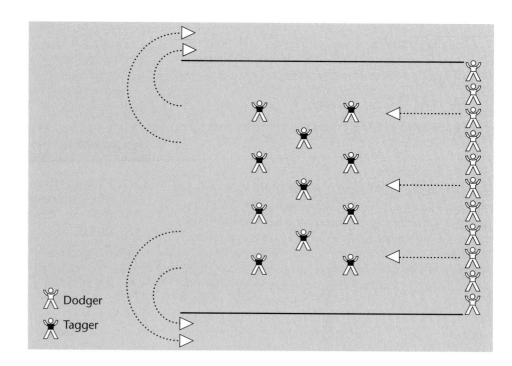

Cues

Split Second (Make your moves quicker than light.)

Fake (Step/lean one way; go the other.)

Change Direction (Use changes of direction to avoid the obstacles.)

Tasks/Challenges:

T To play this game, half of you will be taggers, and you must stand on the marks on the floor. You can't move either of your feet from your mark. The other half of you are dodgers. You'll begin at this end of the room and try to travel through the taggers without being touched. After the dodgers make it to the other side of the room, return around the outside of the room, and keep trying to get through the taggers until you hear the stop signal. On the stop signal, switch places.

T This time things are going to be a little harder for the taggers. Instead of just tagging the dodgers, the taggers have to tag the left knees of the dodgers with their right hands.

You can change these directions to several combinations of body parts—for example, right hand–right knee, left hand–right knee, left hand–right elbow.

T This time, let's make it harder for the dodgers. Taggers can now move one foot to tag. The other foot has to be on the mark.

Dodging and Chasing One Person in a Mass

Setting: Partners spread apart on a field

Cues

Dodgers Split Second (Make your moves quicker than light.)
Fake (Step/lean one way; go the other.)
Change Direction/Change Speed (Use changes of direction and speed to avoid the chaser.)

Chasers Watch the Hips (Watch the hips of the runner to tell his or her next move.)

Tasks/Challenges:

T For this task, you and your partner are on opposite teams. One of you is a tagger; the other one is a dodger. On the signal, the taggers will spread out inside the boundaries, and the dodgers will line up on this side of the field. On the next signal, the dodgers will try to get to the other side of the field without being touched by their partners, the taggers. The trick is that each dodger can be tagged only by his or her partner. When the dodgers get to the other side, they return to the starting line by going around the outside of the field and continue to travel across the space until they hear the stop signal. On the stop signal, trade places with your partners.

T This time I'm going to decrease the space to half the size it was. Ready? Go again.

C Can you stay untagged until the signal sounds?

✓ *Peer Observation.* This would be an appropriate opportunity for a peer observation assessment. Two sets of partners could be paired. One set would participate and the other set would observe. The observers would have an index card with the critical cues listed and a space for names and would assess whether the participants used the cues. After five tries the observers and participants would switch places. See Chapter 14 for the development of peer observation checklists and scoring rubrics.

In some school yards we've observed classes of children playing a game popularly called Bombardment, Killer, or Murder Ball. As these names imply, the game can be dangerous. Typically, a class is divided into two teams, with a middle line separating each team. Each team throws a hard ball in an attempt to strike players on the opposing team; the teams often throw from close range and toward an unsuspecting child. We don't support this activity. There are many other dodge-type experiences you can plan that are safer, allow more children to participate, and are more apt to result in skill development.

Dodging in a Dynamic Situation

Setting: Groups of 10: eight runners and two chasers

Cues

Dodgers Split Second (Make your moves quicker than light.)
Fake (Step/lean one way; go the other.)
Change Direction/Change Speed (Use changes of direction and speed to avoid the chaser.)

Chasers Watch the Hips (Watch the hips of the runner to tell his or her next move.)
Teamwork (Decide your plan for catching together.)

Tasks/Challenges:

T This activity could be called body-part tag. The object, if you are a tagger, is to tag the runners on the named body part or, if you're a runner, to avoid being tagged on the named body part. Chasers, try to touch the runners on the body part I call out. Any runners you tag must freeze. The tagged runners can be unfrozen if they're tagged by a free runner on a body part other than the tagged part. The taggers will have one minute to try to catch all the runners. At the end of one minute, start again with two new taggers. You must stay inside your boundaries. "Shoulders"—Go.

Dodging While Manipulating an Object

Setting: Areas about the size of a basketball key circle, marked off on the floor or the pavement; two or three children occupying each circle

Children should be at the utilization level in dribbling before attempting this task.

Cues

Dodgers Protect the Ball (Keep your body between the ball and the other players.)
Fake (Step/lean one way; go the other.)
Change Direction/Change Speed (Use changes of direction and speed to avoid the chaser.)

Taggers Watch the Hips (Watch the hips of the runner to tell his or her next move.)

Tasks/Challenges:

T The object of this game is to dribble a ball and at the same time try to take a ball away from someone else. Here's how it works. Each of you in your circle will be dribbling a ball. As you dribble the ball, you'll be trying to knock the other players' balls out of the area while keeping your ball from being knocked away. If your ball gets knocked out, just go get it and start again.

Proficiency Level: Learning Experiences Leading to Skill Development

Children at the proficiency level are ready to use their skillful chasing, fleeing, and dodging abilities in a variety of complex and ever-changing, gamelike situations. In the experiences provided here, two groups of players are required to chase, flee, and dodge one another. Although some activities are included here, when children are at the proficiency level of chasing, fleeing, and dodging they are in actuality using those skills in combination with manipulative skills. Thus, appropriate activities would be gamelike proficiency-

These children practice overtaking a fleeing person.

level manipulative activities in which chasing, fleeing, and dodging skills lend the strategic dynamics to the game. See proficiency-level tasks in the manipulative skill theme chapters (Chapters 24 through 28).

Note about cues at the proficiency level: At the proficiency level, tasks are more complex, typically requiring children to coordinate several movements simultaneously in a dynamic context. A list of cues is provided to assist the children in being more successful in the learning experience. The challenge for the teacher is in determining which cue will be most beneficial for each child . . . and when. Thus, careful observation and critical reflection become very important as you watch the children move and then decide which cue will be the most helpful to move each learner to a higher skill level.

Continual Fleeing and Chasing with a Large Group

Setting: Children scattered throughout the space: three taggers (with blue armbands); the rest, dodgers

Cues
Dodgers Split Second (Make your moves quicker than light.) Fake (Step/lean one way; go the other.) Change Direction/Change Speed (Use changes of direction and speed to avoid the chaser.)

Chasers Watch the Hips (Watch the hips of the runner to tell his or her next move.) Teamwork (Decide your plan for catching together.)

Tasks/Challenges:

🅣 This task is very much like freeze tag, except that when you are tagged, you must freeze with your legs wide apart and your hands clasped to your head. You can then be "freed" by any free player crawling through your legs. There will be three taggers, each with a blue armband.

Note: It is virtually impossible for the taggers to catch all the dodgers, so set a time for play (e.g., 3 to 5 minutes) and switch taggers.

✺ How did you use teamwork to catch the runners?

Dodging While Maintaining Possession of an Object

Setting: For each child, a rumble rhumba (Figure 20.3) and a beanbag

Tasks/Challenges:

🅣 For this task, you will need a rumble rhumba tied around your waist with one beanbag in it *(Figure 20.4).* When I say "Go," you will try to snatch the beanbags from other people's rumbles without having yours snatched. If you snatch a beanbag, it

Figure 20.3 To make a rumble rhumba, you'll need a one-gallon plastic jug (e.g., an empty milk or water container) and one yard of clothesline cord. Cut the bottom inch form the jug, and make two holes on either side of the handle. Then run a length of clothesline through the holes, and tie the jug (open end up) around the waist.

goes in your rumble. The other rules are (1) you can take a beanbag only from a rumble, not someone's hands; (2) you can't protect your rumble with your hands; and (3) you can't touch anyone.

T How many points can you get? Score one point for each beanbag you snatch; subtract five points if yours is taken.

In many primitive tribal games, the tribes believed that the chaser was evil, magic, or diseased and that the chaser's touch was contagious. Although today's games are a far cry from fleeing possible death, one has a hard time believing otherwise when observing the intensity and all-out effort children display when fleeing a chaser!

Chasing and Fleeing in an Invasion Gamelike Situation

Setting: Groups of six, each with a ball; enough flag belts (of two colors) for all the youngsters; a space about 20 yards by 10 yards

Cues	
Offense	Toward Goal (Always move toward your goal.)
	Fake (Step/lean one way; go the other.)
	Change Direction/Change Speed (Use changes of direction and speed to avoid the chaser.)
Defense	Watch the Hips (Watch the hips of the runner to tell his or her next move.)
	Teamwork (Decide your plan for catching together.)

Figure 20.4 Rumble rhumba in position around the waist.

Tasks/Challenges:

T Each group of six should divide into two teams, each with a different-colored flag belt. One team will start with the ball. On the signal, a player on the team with the ball (team 1) tries to pass or run the ball from its goal line to the other team's goal line without the ball touching the ground or team 2 grabbing the flag of the player with the ball. If a flag is grabbed, the ball touches the ground, or the goal line is crossed, the other team gets the ball.

✓ *Videotape/Digital Analysis.* The above task, with established criteria and a rubric, would provide a wonderful opportunity for video analysis of the use of the critical cues in a dynamic situation. Each team could do its own analysis.

Chasing and Dodging Simultaneously

Setting: Start with groups of about six children; as the children become more proficient, you can increase the size of the groups.

Cues	
Dodgers	Split Second (Make your moves quicker than light.)
	Fake (Step/lean one way; go the other.)
	Change Direction/Change Speed (Use changes of direction and speed to avoid the chaser.)
Chasers	Watch the Hips (Watch the hips of the runner to tell his or her next move.)

Tasks/Challenges:

T This task pits each player against every other player. The object is to snatch the flag from another player's belt without losing your own flag and while staying within the designated boundaries.

If your flag is pulled off, another player can put it back on and you can keep on playing. You can't put your own flag back on. You've really got to watch all the other players and move to stay out of their way. Remember all the turning, twisting, and jumping dodges.

Ⓒ How many points can you accumulate? Score one point for every flag you take; subtract three points for every time your flag is taken.

Dodging in a Gamelike Situation

Setting: A large marked-off area, containing hoops as safety bases (Figure 20.5); teams of no more than five

Cues

Dodgers Split Second (Make your moves quicker than light.)
Fake (Step/lean one way; go the other.)
Change Direction/Change Speed (Use changes of direction and speed to avoid the chaser.)

Chasers Watch the Hips (Watch the hips of the runner to tell his or her next move.)
Teamwork (Decide your plan for catching together.)

Tasks/Challenges:

This task is called Safety Bases. The object is for one group of runners, group 1, to cross the space without being touched by a group of taggers, group 2. Group 1 begins at one end of the field; the taggers on group 2 begin at the other end. On the signal, the runners try to cross the field without being tagged; the taggers try to stop any runners from getting across the field. The runners are safe—can't be tagged—when they're in any of the hoops. The runners have about one minute to cross the field. After two turns, you'll switch places. The safety bases will help, but use them wisely—only as a last resort when you're about to be tagged. Don't just stand in them the whole time.

You have used teamwork before to catch runners. How does the teamwork in this game differ? What teamwork strategies did you use here?

Dodging in a Target Gamelike Situation

Setting: A marked-off square playing area with a hoop in its center and a beanbag inside the hoop (Figure 20.6); groups of five

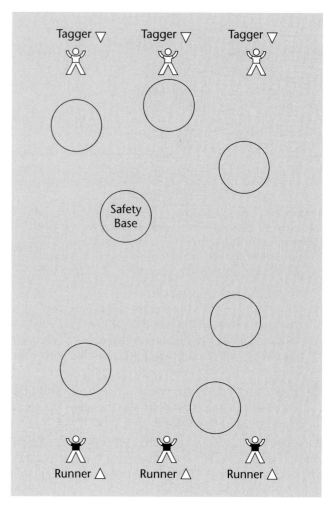

Figure 20.5 Setup for dodging in a gamelike situation.

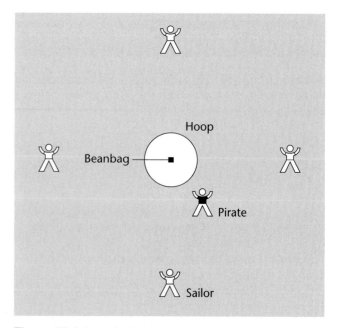

Figure 20.6 Setup for dodging in a target gamelike situation.

Cues

Offense   Split Second (Make your moves quicker
(sailors)   than light.)
         Fake (Step/lean one way; go the other.)
         Change Direction/Change Speed (Use
         changes of direction and speed to avoid
         the chaser.)
         Heads and Shoulders Up (As you bend
         to retrieve an object be sure to keep
         your head and shoulders up and bend at
         the knees.)
Defense   Watch the Hips (Watch the hips of the
(pirate)   runner to tell his or her next move.)

Tasks/Challenges:

T We will call this chasing, fleeing, and dodging task Pirate's Treasure. The object is for the free players to try to steal the treasure, which is in the bean-bag, from the middle of the space and return it to the outside of the space without being tagged by the pirate, who is protecting the treasure. There are five players in each group: one pirate and four sailors trying to get the treasure. The pirate's job is to protect the treasure from the sailors. On the signal, the sailors have 2 minutes in which to steal the treasure from inside the hoop and get it to the outside of the square without being touched by the pirate. If the sailors get the treasure to the outside or the 2-minute limit is reached, play starts over again, and a new pirate tries to protect the treasure. The pirate cannot go inside the hoop.

⚠ This is a task that children love, but much attention needs to be paid to children keeping their heads and shoulders up as they try to steal the treasure. If children are dodging with their heads down there is an increased likelihood that heads will collide.

☑ *Event Task.* A likely assessment option would be to have each team write out the strategy the members plan to use in the game. After the game is over, they can analyze how well it worked and what they will need to practice next time in order to be more effective. This plan can then serve as the initial activity in the next lesson.

Using Team Strategy for Chasing, Fleeing, and Dodging in an Invasion Gamelike Situation

Setting: A flag belt with two flags on it for each team member; each opposing team member has a different-colored flag. Groups of eight: four players in each group.

Cues

Dodgers   Split Second (Make your moves quicker
         than light.)
         Fake (Step/lean one way; go the other.)
         Change Direction/Change Speed (Use
         changes of direction and speed to
         avoid the chaser.)
Chasers   Watch the Hips (Watch the hips of the
         runner to tell his or her next move.)
         Teamwork (Decide your plan for
         catching together.)

Tasks/Challenges:

T The object of this task is to see how many of the other team's flags you can get without losing your own. One team begins at each end of the space. On the signal, both teams move into the playing area, and each team tries to snatch as many flags as possible from the other team's belts while preventing the other team from stealing their own flags. On the next signal, all play stops, and the teams return to their sidelines and count how many flags they were able to steal.

☑ *Journal.* For a journal entry at this point, you might ask children how they feel about their chasing, fleeing, and dodging abilities.

Practicing dodging moves with a partner would be an appropriate control level task.

Dodging While Manipulating an Object in an Invasion Gamelike Situation

Setting: This activity requires utilization-level skills in the manipulative activity you choose to use. It can be done with virtually any manipulative skill; the most common are dribbling and passing with the hands or feet, throwing and catching, or striking with a hockey stick. Whatever skill you choose, you will need one ball per group and appropriate other equipment. Groups of 10: five on a team.

Cues

Offense Split Second (Make your moves quicker than light.)
Fake (Step/lean one way; go the other.)
Change Direction/Change Speed (Use changes of direction and speed to avoid the chaser.)

Defense Watch the Hips (Watch the hips of the runner to tell his or her next move.)
Teamwork (Decide your plan for catching together.)
Play the Ball (Force the pass by playing the ball first.)

Tasks/Challenges:

T This task is like keep-away. There will be five on each team. You must clearly mark your boundaries, which can be no larger than half a basketball court. The object is for your team to keep the ball away from the other team. Here are the rules:

1. A ball can be stolen only on a pass; it cannot be taken when someone else has control of it.
2. No one can hold onto the ball longer than 5 seconds before passing it.

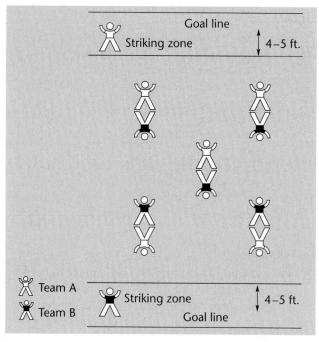

Figure 20.7 Goal line for manipulative activity keep away.

3. There can be no direct hand-offs; the ball must be passed.
4. If the ball goes out of bounds, it belongs to the other team.

T We are going to change the game a little this time. You will keep your same teams, but each team will be trying to score by getting the ball across a goal line. All you have to do is get the ball across the line; the trick is that you cannot throw or hit it across until you are in the striking zone marked on the floor *(Figure 20.7)*. The difference between this game and the last one is that now you should be moving in one direction, not all over.

Reading Comprehension Questions

1. List the differences among chasing, fleeing, and dodging.
2. Describe three effective dodging movements.
3. What are the characteristics of each of the four levels of skill proficiency for chasing, fleeing, and dodging?
4. Rank the following tasks by placing the number 1 in front of the easiest (most basic), the number 2 in front of the next, more difficult level, and so on.
   ( ) A defensive player in a football-type game pursues an offensive runner.

( ) You travel around the room. On a signal, you change directions as quickly as possible.
( ) You stay as close as you can to your partner, who'll try to get away from you.
( ) One team chases the members of an opposing team.
5. What is a fake? Give several examples of when a fake might be used.
6. Why do you use large areas when introducing the chasing, fleeing, and dodging skills?

7. Why have we eliminated dodgeball activities from the development of dodging skills?

8. What are some important cues to give when you're teaching fleeing? List at least three.

9. When a child is tagged during a tag game, what is one alternative to eliminating the child until a new game begins?

10. Killer (also called Bombardment) is a game that has been played for years in elementary schools. What is our reason for not recommending it?

11. What are two strategies for offense and two for defense that apply when chasing, fleeing, and dodging while manipulating an object?

References/Suggested Readings

Council on Physical Education for Children. (2000). *Appropriate practices for elementary school physical education: A position statement of NASPE.* Reston, VA: National Association for Sport and Physical Education.

Morris, G. S., & Stiehl, J. (1998). *Changing kids' games.* Champaign, IL: Human Kinetics.

National Association for Sport and Physical Education. (2004). *Moving into the future: National standards for physical education* (2nd ed.). Reston, VA: National Association for Sport and Physical Education.

Opie, I., & Opie, P. (1969). *Children's games in street and playground.* New York: Oxford University Press.

Williams, N. (1992). The physical education hall of shame. *Journal of Physical Education, Recreation and Dance, 63*(6), 57–60.

Jumping and Landing

Jumping is a locomotor pattern in which the body propels itself off the floor or apparatus into a momentary period of flight. As an isolated maneuver or in combination with other basic patterns, jumping—particularly the flight phase when the body is unsupported in the air—is a fascinating body action.

A jump is performed for one of two reasons: (1) to raise the body vertically (straight up) for height or (2) to raise the body with a forward momentum to travel over a distance. Children who learn to jump effectively for height and distance are prepared for a multitude of game, dance, and gymnastics activities in which the performer needs to be a skilled jumper. See Box 21-1 for information on jumping and landing from the *National Standards for Physical Education.*

Fundamental Jumping Patterns

Wickstrom (1977, p. 63) suggested that children are developmentally capable of performing a jumping action when they're approximately 24 months old. He described the types of jumps preschool children achieve in terms of progressive difficulty:

Jump down from one foot to the other.

Jump up from two feet to two feet.

Jump down from two feet to two feet.

Run and jump from one foot to the other.

Jump forward from two feet to two feet.

Jump down from one foot to two feet.

Run and jump forward from one foot to two feet.

Box 21-1

The Skill of Jumping and Landing in the *National Standards for Physical Education*

The movement skill of jumping and landing is referenced in the *National Standards for Physical Education* (National Association for Sport and Physical Education [NASPE], 2004) as a sample performance outcome, across the 3–5 grade-range, under Standard 1: Demonstrates competency in motor skills and movement patterns needed to perform a variety of physical activities. The standard speaks of children developing mature forms in the basic skills and performing those skills in changing conditions and in combinations. The sample performance outcome states that a child "jumps vertically to a height of 9 inches and lands using mature form" (p. 17).

Jump over object from two feet to two feet.

Jump from one foot to same foot rhythmically.

It's safe to assume that, within an average class of young children, some will be incapable of performing one or more of these jumping tasks. Initial observations will probably reveal a wide range of jumping abilities. Typically, kindergarten students are at the precontrol level. Their jumps usually achieve little height or distance, and they jump on two feet to ensure that they maintain their balance. Children at this level seem to be jumping merely to enjoy the sensation of momentarily losing contact with the ground and the challenge of maintaining balance upon landing. A teacher can build on this natural fascination by providing learning activities that progressively lead children toward the mature performance of jumping and landing in different dance, game, and gymnastics situations. (See our progression spiral on page 357.)

The fundamental jumping pattern consists of the following five basic variations:

1. Two-foot takeoff to a one-foot landing
2. Two-foot takeoff to a two-foot landing
3. One-foot takeoff to a landing on the same foot (hop)
4. One-foot takeoff to a landing on the other foot (leap)
5. One-foot takeoff to a two-foot landing

However, the specific actions of the body in performing a jump vary according to the purpose or intention—for example, jumping to catch or jumping to dismount from apparatus.

Levels of Skill Proficiency

When we begin to focus on jumping, we have children think of the skill as three successive phases:

1. **Takeoff:** Actions of the body as it's propelled off the ground
2. **Flight:** Actions of the body while it's off the ground and in the air
3. **Landing:** Actions of the body as it reestablishes contact with the ground

Our key observation points illustrate the correct and incorrect forms for the takeoff, flight, and landing phases as well as illustrating the mature stage. Box 21-2 contains key observation points for jumping for height and landing; Box 21-3 shows the key observation points for jumping for distance.

Following the initial exploration of jumping "just for fun," we explore jumping for height and distance,

Box 21-2

Key Observation Points: Jumping for Height and Landing

Takeoff

Do the child's hips, knees, and ankles flex in a crouch as the child prepares to jump?

Do the child's arms extend vigorously forward and then upward upon takeoff, reaching full extension above the head at liftoff?

Flight

Does the child's body extend fully in the air during the jump, especially the arms?

Box 21-2 (continued)

Landing

Do the child's ankles extend in preparation for landing?
Do the child's hips, knees, and ankles flex to absorb the shock of landing?

Mature Stage

When children are at the mature stage of jumping for height, do their jumps look similar to the following sequence? The hips, knees, and ankles flex in a preparatory crouch. The jump begins with a vigorous forward and upward lift by the arms. The thrust is continued by forceful extension at the hips, knees, and ankles. The body remains in extension until the feet are ready to retouch, and then the ankles, knees, and hips flex to absorb the shock of landing.

Source: Fundamental Motor Patterns (2nd ed.) by R. L. Wickstrom, 1977, Philadelphia: Lea & Febiger.

Box 21-3

Key Observation Points: Jumping for Distance

Takeoff

Do the child's arms extend vigorously forward and then upward upon takeoff, reaching full extension above the head at liftoff?

Are the child's hips, knees, and ankles fully extended at takeoff? Is the takeoff angle at 45 degrees or less?

Flight

Does the child bring the legs forward and the arms downward in preparation for landing?

Box 21-3 (continued)

Landing

Do the child's heels contact the ground first?
Are the child's knees flexed and the arms thrust forward at the moment of contact?

NO   YES

Mature Stage

When children are at the mature stage of jumping for distance, do their jumps look similar to the following sequence? The hips, knees, and ankles flex in a preparatory crouch. The arms extend backward, then vigorously swing forward and then upward upon takeoff, reaching full extension above the head at liftoff. The hips and knees are extended fully, with the takeoff angle at 45 degrees or less. In preparation for landing, the arms are brought downward and the legs thrust forward until the thighs are parallel to the surface. The center of gravity of the body is far behind the base of support (feet) upon contact, but at the moment of contact, the knees are flexed and the arms are thrust forward to maintain the momentum to carry the center of gravity beyond the feet.

Source: Fundamental Motor Patterns (2nd ed.). by R. L. Wickstrom, 1977, Philadelphia: Lea & Febiger.

Young children are challenged by the task of propelling the body off the ground for a momentary period of being airborne.

jumping a rope, and different patterns of jumping and landing. As they experiment with different takeoff and landing combinations, children begin to sense which takeoff procedures result in the highest jumps as opposed to which result in the longest jumps. They find that actions of the legs, arms, torso, and head during the flight phase influence the trajectory of the jump. They come to recognize the unique giving action of the ankles, knees, and hips in absorbing the shock of landing.

During the control level phase of our work on jumping and landing, children begin to accurately perform the basic jumping variations using vigorous takeoffs and balanced, controlled landings. At this point, we also emphasize the flight phase of children's jumps.

For example, we encourage them to begin to explore bodily actions in flight, such as the following:

Jumping and making body shapes in the air

Jumping and gesturing with an arm (for example, punching)

Jumping and twisting the trunk

Jumping and turning

Low apparatus are used to create new jumping situations, such as:

Jumping over hurdles and hoops

Jumping onto and off low equipment

Once children can repeatedly jump to fulfill a variety of objectives and their jumps continually exhibit a mature pattern, utilization-level tasks are appropriate:

Jumping on an accented beat

Performing a series of light, gentle leaps

Jumping to catch a ball

Jumping to mount or dismount apparatus

Performers at the proficiency level are able to jump high enough to carry out complex maneuvers in the air and to use a variety of jumping actions to express a feeling, idea, or attitude. Examples of proficiency-level performances include:

Jumping and throwing a ball to a target

Hurdling

The one-foot takeoff to a two-foot landing of a jump-stop in basketball and volleyball, the split-step in tennis

Leaping reception of a football against an opponent

The extended flight phase, the midair suspension, in basketball before releasing the ball to the basket

Standard patterns of jumping (for example, long jump, high jump)

Precontrol Level: Activities for Exploration

The following activities are designed for exploration of jumping. Through these activities children will begin to discover different types of jumps as well as jumps that take them high and jumps that take them far.

Jumping and Landing: Different Patterns

Setting: Ropes (one per child) placed around the edge of the teaching area

Skill Theme Development Sequence

Jumping and Landing

Proficiency Level

Hurdling jumps
Jumping, dancing, and imagery
Jumping as part of a dance creation
Jumping with a springboard
Jumping with a partner to match actions
Jumping with a partner to mirror actions

Utilization Level

Jumping to an accented beat
Throwing and catching while jumping
Jumping on a bench
Jumping to throw
Jumping to catch

Control Level

Jumping and landing task sheet
Jump, Squash, TaDa
Jumping on and off equipment using buoyant and yielding
   landings
Jumping over equipment using buoyant landings
Performing jumping sequences and making body shapes
Traveling, jumping, and body shapes
Jumping to form a body shape during flight
Jumping using buoyant and yielding landings
Jumping a self-turned rope
Jumping a turned rope
Jumping in rhythmical sequences
Jumping rhythmically
Jumping over low obstacles: hurdles
Jumping over low obstacles: hoops
Jumping for height
Standing long jump
Jumping and landing: basic patterns

Precontrol Level

Jumping over a swinging rope
Jumping for height
Jumping for distance
Jumping and landing: different patterns

Tasks/Challenges:

🅣 At the edge of our working space are ropes. Select a rope and place it in a straight line in your self-space. Jump over the rope and land on the other side without falling down.

🅣 Explore different ways to jump over your rope, sometimes taking off on one foot and landing on two, sometimes taking off on two feet and landing on two.

🅣 Jump high in the air as you travel over your rope.

🅣 Stand at one end of your rope with a foot on either side of it. See if you can jump the distance of your rope.

🅐 It is important to stress from the beginning that children land on their feet when jumping, not fall to the floor when they land.

🅣 Arrange your rope in a shape different from a straight line—for example, a circle or a rectangle. Jump into the shape and out the other side. Jump across your new rope shape.

Jumping for Distance

Setting: Ropes (one per child) placed around the edge of the teaching area; strips of masking tape (one per child) on the wall

Tasks/Challenges:

🅣 Place your rope on the floor away from others. Jump over your rope, landing as far from your rope as possible.

🅣 Place your piece of masking tape on the floor. Lie down with your feet touching the tape, and place the rope by the top of your head. If you have trouble, ask a friend to help. The distance from the rope to the tape is how tall you are. Standing behind your rope, try to jump your height.

🅐 **Remember, land on your feet.**

🅒 Can you jump even farther than your height?

Jumping for Height

Setting: Streamers hung at various heights from a rope stretched along the work area

Tasks/Challenges:

🅣 Jump to see if you can touch the streamers hanging from the rope.

🅣 Run and jump to touch the streamers.

Jumping over a Swinging Rope

Setting: Class divided into groups of threes, each group with a "long" rope

Tasks/Challenges:

(T) In your groups of three, you are going to take turns jumping over a swinging rope. Two of you will gently swing the rope while the third person jumps. After five jumps, trade places.

(C) Practice for 10 jumps without a mistake.

Control Level: Learning Experiences Leading to Skill Development

At the control level, we encourage children to practice both long and high jumps until their landings are balanced and controlled. We also provide opportunities for exploring variations in the flight phase of the jump and jumping in relation to different rhythms.

A note about cues: Although several cues are listed for many of the learning experiences, it's important to focus on only one cue at a time. That way, the children can really concentrate on that cue. Once you provide feedback to the children and observe that most have learned a cue, then it's time to focus on another one.

Jumping and Landing: Basic Patterns

Setting: Ropes (one per child) placed around the edge of the teaching area

> **Cue**
>
> **Squash** (Bend your knees to absorb the force and maintain balance when you land.)

Tasks/Challenges:

(T) When we first worked on jumping, you explored different ways to jump over your rope—just for fun. Place your rope in a straight line on the floor; choose three of your favorites from those different types of jumps and practice jumping over your rope, landing each time in a balanced position without falling down. Bend your knees when you land so that your landings are very quiet.

(T) Jump over your rope, taking off on two feet and landing on two feet.

(T) Position yourself approximately 10 feet from your rope. Approach your rope with a series of running steps; jump over your rope, taking off on one foot and landing on two feet.

(T) Using a series of running steps to approach your rope, take off on one foot and land on the opposite foot on the other side of your rope. Taking off on one foot and landing on the opposite foot is called a leap.

(T) Change the shape of your rope from a straight line to a circle, rectangle, or triangle. Standing just outside the rope shape, take off on one foot and jump inside your shape, landing on the same

Running and jumping combine skill and spatial awareness.

foot. What locomotor action did you just do with this jump? A hop. Hop into and out of your rope.

Peer Observation. Peer observation of the different jumping patterns would be beneficial at this point. *Review Chapter 14 for specific examples of assessments.*

Standing Long Jump

Setting: Ropes (one per child) placed around the edge of the work area; large color/panel gymnastics mats; strips of masking tape (one per child) on the wall

Cues	
Squash	(Bend your knees to absorb the force and maintain balance when you land.)
Swing Forward	(Swing your arms forcefully forward for maximum distance.)

Tasks/Challenges:

T Stand at one end of your rope with the rope between your feet. Bend your knees and swing your arms in preparation for the jump. Taking off on two feet and landing on two, jump forward as far as you can, trying to jump the full length of your rope.

T Remember when you practiced jumping your height by placing a piece of masking tape on the floor at the place of your feet and your rope on the floor the distance from your feet to your head. Try that jump again, taking off on two feet and landing on two feet. If you jump farther than your height, move the tape to where your heels first land.

T Standing at one end of the mat, jump as far as you can toward the other end of the mat. Count your score by the number of panels you jumped over. **Remember to bend your knees and swing your arms in preparation for the jump, then swing your arms forward for a really far jump.** Keeping your arms stretched forward will also keep you from falling backward when you land!

The three tasks just described work well in station format for practice of the two-foot to two-foot standing jump.

Jumping for Height

Setting: Balloons suspended at various heights from a stretched rope; milk crates or low boxes (packed with newspaper) at large gymnastics mats

Cues	
Squash	(Bend your knees to absorb the force and maintain balance when you land.)
Swing Upward	(Swing your arms upward for good height.)

Tasks/Challenges:

T Scatter throughout general space and jump high in the air, returning to the floor in your same self-space. Take off on two feet and land on two feet.

T Jump high in the air, taking off on two feet and landing on two feet. Swing your arms upward; this will help you jump higher.

At the control level, youngsters enjoy running and jumping over low obstacles.

Positioned around the work area are milk crates and boxes stuffed with newspaper on large gymnastics mats. Standing on the box or crate, jump high in the air and land on two feet on the mat in front of the box or crate. **Remember to swing your arms upward, reaching for the sky, to gain maximum height on your jump.**

Travel throughout general space; on the signal, jump high in the air by taking off on one foot and landing on the opposite foot. This is the leap we practiced earlier; swing your arms upward as you jump to stay airborne as long as possible.

Positioned around the work area are balloons suspended from stretched ropes. Using a two-foot takeoff and a two-foot landing, jump to touch the balloons like a basketball player trying to tap the ball on the jump.

Approach the balloon with a series of running steps using a one-foot takeoff and a two-foot landing to jump for the balloon. Which type of jump gives you more height: A two-foot takeoff or a one-foot takeoff? A standing jump or a running approach to the jump?

Assessment Example

From the *National Standards for Physical Education*

Teacher Observation

Students are requested to demonstrate the skills introduced in class as the teacher observes their performance and records the satisfactory use of the critical elements of the skills on a check list.

Criteria for Assessment

a. Demonstrates critical elements of the selected skills (jumping and landing) over several trials.

NASPE (1995, pp. 18–19)

Jumping over Low Obstacles: Hoops

Setting: Hoops (one per child) scattered throughout the teaching area

Cues	
Squash	(Bend your knees to absorb the force and maintain balance when you land.)
Swing Upward	(Swing your arms upward for good height.)
Swing Forward	(Swing your arms forcefully forward for maximum distance.)

Tasks/Challenges:

Jump over your hoop. As your feet touch the ground, freeze your body perfectly still; this means you must bend your ankles, knees, and hips as you land. **Think of your feet sinking into the floor as if the floor were a sponge.**

Practice jumping over your hoop with two-foot takeoffs and landings until you can land without falling three times in a row. Can you then do the same three perfect landings with a one-foot takeoff and a two-foot landing?

Travel throughout general space, leaping over hoops. **Remember to extend your arms up for good height as you leap.**

Jumping over Low Obstacles: Hurdles

Setting: One hurdle (cones and rolled newspaper or rope) per child

Cues	
Squash	(Bend your knees to absorb the force and maintain balance when you land.)
Swing Upward	(Swing your arms upward for good height.)

Tasks/Challenges:

Standing just behind your hurdle, jump over it, using a two-foot takeoff and a two-foot landing. Try to be really high when you cross the top—**push with your toes; reach for the sky.**

Now as you jump over the hurdle, try to use the different types of jumps you have learned. Try the easiest ones first and then the most difficult ones.

Practice each jump until you can do it three times with a soft landing and without touching the crosspiece.

Stand approximately 6 feet behind your hurdle. Approach the hurdle with quick, running steps. Jump over your hurdle using a one-foot takeoff and a two-foot landing.

When you can clear the hurdle without touching the crossbar and land without falling down, approach the bar with quick, running steps. Jump over the bar using a one-foot takeoff and then land on the opposite foot; continue with a few quick, running steps before you stop. Wow! You look ready for the Olympics.

Jumping Rhythmically

Setting: Carpet squares scattered throughout general space; a recording of the sounds of tools and machines; a recording of "Pop Goes the Weasel"

Cues	
Spring, Spring	(Quick, springy landings for the fast beat.)
High Jumps, Full Squash	(Full squash following the high jumps.)
Heads Up	(Keep your head and shoulders up for good balance.)

Tasks/Challenges:

Ⓣ Standing on your carpet square, jump while keeping beat with the drum. You'll have to listen carefully, because the drumbeat will change at different times. **To do this without losing the beat, take little jumps so that your feet barely leave the floor.** In other words, you'll be almost bouncing on your toes.

For the next task, play music with the sounds of tools and machines. (Children enjoy electronic/synthesizer music.)

Ⓣ This time, instead of a drumbeat you'll hear the sounds of different machines and tools that you're familiar with. Staying on your carpet square, take little jumps, keeping time with the tool and machine sounds you hear. The sounds will change often, so be alert, and take little bouncy jumps on your toes.

Ⓣ Again, the drumbeat will guide your jumps. As you hear the slow beat, take big, high jumps. When you hear the quick beat, take small jumps. This maneuver involves careful listening, so be prepared to change at any time. Make sure that your jumps are clearly big on the slow beats and really little on the fast beats; adjust the height of your jump for fast (low) and slow (high).

Place the carpet squares in a circle with approximately 6 to 8 inches between each carpet.

Ⓣ Let's combine our jumping and rhythmic response to "Pop Goes the Weasel." Select a carpet square, and stand on it without moving it from the circle. We will stay on our carpet squares, our self-space, during the verse of the song. Follow the leader (me) during that portion as we do self-space actions—stretching, twisting, clapping, tapping, jogging in place, and so forth. When we come to the "Pop" in the song, jump from your carpet square to the next one—clockwise around the circle. Be ready

for new nonlocomotor actions in self-space when you land.

Choose a new leader for the self-space actions after each jump. Younger students enjoy singing "Pop Goes the Weasel" along with or instead of the recording.

The folk dance "Jump Jim Joe" is an excellent activity for the practice of rhythmical jumping. Young children enjoy the repetitive nature of the jumping in the dance.

Jumping in Rhythmical Sequences

Setting: Children scattered throughout general space

Cues	
Spring, Squash	(Springy landings to continue travel; full squash to stop.)
Heads Up	(Keep your head and shoulders up for good balance.)
Swing Upward	(Swing your arms upward for good height.)

Tasks/Challenges:

Ⓣ This time, you're going to travel and then jump and travel again, always keeping the same rhythm. To begin, you'll all practice the same travel jump pattern, which will go like this: Run, run, leap/ run, run, leap. As you move, all of you will say together "Run, run, leap" so you can stay together. Let's practice saying that and keeping the same tempo before beginning to move. *(Practice saying the phrase in tempo.)* As you jump and run this time, remember to stay with the voices; everyone should be jumping at the same time if you're all together.

Ⓣ Now instead of saying the phrase, you're going to clap it as you go. You'll have to remember what to do on your own.

Ⓣ Now that you can follow the phrase that I designed for you, you're going to make up your own and follow it. Your phrase should contain two traveling actions followed by one jumping pattern. You should repeat the sequence three times before coming to a stop. Practice the whole thing until you think that it's the best you can do. As you begin, it helps to say to yourself what you're supposed to be doing, just as you did in the previous activity. When you think you know it, try clapping instead of saying it. When you're really good, practice doing it with no noise at all. Remember: two traveling actions followed by one jumping action, repeated three times. Keep the same rhythm throughout each part of the sequence. *(Pinpoint several children who've created an interesting sequence—they don't have to be the most skilled children in the class.)*

Jumping a Turned Rope

Setting: Class divided into groups of two or three, each group with one long rope. *If the children are in groups of two, attach one end of the rope to a fence post, pole, or chair.* Mark a box on the floor at the center of the rope for the jumper and an X on the floor where the turner or turners stand.

> **Cues**
>
> ***Jumpers*** Heads Up (Keep your head and shoulders up for good balance.)
> Jump, Jump (Small, springy jumps with very little height.)
> ***Turners*** One, Two, Three (Swing the rope back and forth before the first swing over the head, counting "One, two, three"; this will help the jumper be ready.)
> Smooth Turns (Turn the rope with large, smooth swings.)

Tasks/Challenges:

T At your ropes, two people will turn and one person will try to jump. Jumpers should try to stay in the box marked on the floors as you jump. After 10 jumps, trade positions.

T When you can successfully jump the rope by starting in the middle, try to start from the outside: run in and jump. Turners: Turn the rope so it turns toward the jumper—the front-door approach. Jumpers: Start your run as soon as the rope touches the floor.

C Create a new rhyme as you jump the long rope. *Record the children's rhymes in a booklet of "Jump Rope Rhymes."*

Jumping a Self-Turned Rope

Setting: Ropes of different lengths so that each child has a personal rope of the proper length

> **Cues**
>
> **Heads Up** (Keep your head and shoulders up for good balance.)
> **Jump, Jump** (Small, springy jumps with very little height.)

Tasks/Challenges:

T Practice jumping your rope by turning it over your head. Some of you will find that jumping forward is easier; others will find that jumping the rope as it turns backward is easier. Be sure you try jumping both ways.

T If you're having trouble, bring the rope over your head, and stop it on the floor in front of your feet, and then jump over the rope. As you become successful, go a little faster, and don't let the rope stop so much. As you practice, you will find yourself stopping the rope less.

T When you become successful at jumping in one direction (forward or backward) without missing, try jumping in the other direction.

C Set a goal for yourself of the number of jumps you want to make without a mistake.

T Try jumping with the different types of jumps we have learned—two feet to two feet, one foot to the other foot, two feet to one foot, and so forth.

Jumping Using Buoyant and Yielding Landings

Setting: Children scattered throughout general space; paper and pencil available outside work area

> **Cues**
>
> **Yielding Landings** (Bend your knees to absorb the force when you land, as if sinking into the floor.)
> **Buoyant Landings** (Bend your knees as you land, then spring up quickly.)
> **Swing Upward** (Swing your arms upward for good height.)
> **Heads Up** (Keep your head and shoulders up for good balance.)

Tasks/Challenges:

T Jump three times in a row on two feet, pausing between each jump. This is called a yielding landing.

T This time, jump three times in a row using a two-foot takeoff and a two-foot landing without pausing between each jump. This is a buoyant landing. **Spring up quickly after each jump.**

T Now, jump twice in a row, the first time with a buoyant landing and the second time with a yielding landing. Make sure that your landings are clearly different so that I can tell which one you're doing simply by watching.

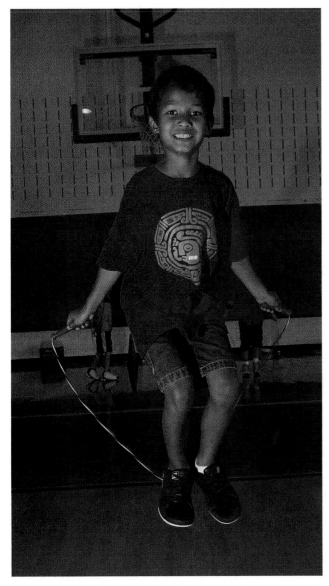

Jumping rope is a favorite pastime of children.

Children learn to jump off apparatus and land safely.

T This time on the signal, jump high, turn in the air, land balanced, and freeze. Again, use yielding landings.

T Now, jump high, turn in the air, and upon landing collapse to the floor, curl, and freeze. **Remember to use your arms to help you turn in the air.**

T Try this one: Jump high, turn in the air, and upon landing collapse to the floor, curl, and freeze for an instant—and then quickly resume traveling. Make your moves very smooth so that they really go together and you know exactly what you're doing and what comes next. Use your arms to help you get up in the air. Strive for a yielding landing.

C So far I've made up all your jumping and traveling patterns. On your piece of paper *(pass out paper to the youngsters),* write down a jumping/traveling pattern that you'd like to do yourself. After you've written it down, practice it until it goes smoothly and you know it by heart. Make sure that you always begin and end in the same place, which is one way you know you're doing the same thing each time. I should be able to tell what you're doing and the type of landing by watching you. If I can't, I'll ask you.

Jumping to Form a Body Shape During Flight

Setting: Children scattered throughout general space, each with a hurdle or a rope in a shape on the floor

Cues

Yielding Landings (Bend your knees to absorb the force when you land, as if sinking into the floor.)

| Swing Upward | (Swing your arms upward for good height.) |
| Heads Up | (Keep your head and shoulders up for good balance.) |

Tasks/Challenges:

🅣 Jump over your equipment, and form a narrow body shape while you're in the air. A narrow body shape is very skinny. **Remember to make all the parts of your body skinny, not just one part.** Practice your shape until it's as narrow as it can be.

🅒 Now think of five more narrow body shapes that you can make while you're in the air. Practice all the shapes until they're the best you can do. I'll come and ask each of you to show me your best shape, so be ready. **Remember not to fall over on your landings; your feet should stick as if you had glue on them. What kind of landings will you need?**

🅣 This time you're going to jump using wide body shapes in the air. A wide shape is very big and spread out, like a wall. **Remember as you jump to make your whole body wide in the air, by stretching your arms and legs outward from your body.** Practice your shape until it's as wide as it can be.

🅒 Now that you know what a wide shape is, think of five more wide shapes you can make when you jump. Let them be really different, even weird. Practice all the shapes until they're the best you can do. I'm going to ask some of you to show your wide shapes, so work hard.

Pinpoint several children who are using wide shapes.

🅣 This time, you're going to learn some new names for body shapes. First, you're going to make symmetrical shapes in the air. A *symmetrical* shape looks exactly alike on both sides. For example, if I were to cut you in half from head to toe, you'd look the same on both sides. At your equipment, practice making a symmetrical shape in the air. Be sure that both sides of your body look exactly alike.

🅒 Create five more symmetrical shapes with your jumps.

🅣 This time you're going to do nonsymmetrical jumps. In a *nonsymmetrical* jump, both sides of your body look really different. So if I were to cut you in half, one arm might be up in the air and the other one out to the side, or one leg might be going forward and the other one backward. In other words, one side shouldn't look like the other one. In your space, create a nonsymmetrical jump. **Remember to absorb force when you land by bending your knees.**

🅒 Create five nonsymmetrical jumps you can do in the air.

🅣 Try to do wide symmetrical jumps. Find three that you really like, and practice them.

🅣 Now try to find three narrow symmetrical jumps. After you do that, find three wide nonsymmetrical jumps and three narrow nonsymmetrical jumps. I'm going to ask some of you to show your jumps to the class, so make them the best that they can be.

🅣 Approach your hurdle or rope shape with a series of running steps. Jump in the air, making a wide shape. **Land in a balanced position without falling down.**

🅣 Try your other shapes in the air combined with your short running approach.

⚠ Students should attempt running, jumping, and making shapes while airborne only after they have demonstrated safe landings in self-space—absorbing the force by bending the knees and landing in a balanced position without falling forward.

Traveling, Jumping, and Body Shapes

Setting: Children scattered throughout general space

Cues	
Buoyant Landings	(Bend your knees as you land, then spring up quickly.)
Swing Upward	(Swing your arms upward for good height.)
Heads Up	(Keep your head and shoulders up for good balance.)

Tasks/Challenges:

🅣 As you travel around the room, make the kind of jump that I've called out each time you hear the drumbeat. The jump may simply be wide, or it may be narrow and nonsymmetrical. You'll have to be alert to what I'm saying as well as watching out for others. We'll use buoyant landings so that we can be ready to travel again. Remember to make your shapes as clear as you possibly can.

Performing Jumping Sequences and Making Body Shapes

Setting: Note cards with various body-shape sequences written on them, each sequence containing at least four different body shapes (e.g., wide; wide symmetrical; narrow nonsymmetrical; narrow); children scattered throughout general space, each with a sequence card.

Cues

Buoyant Landings	(Bend your knees as you land, then spring up quickly.)
Yielding Landings	(Bend your knees to absorb the force when you land, as if sinking into the floor.)
Swing Upward	(Swing your arms upward for good height.)
Heads Up	(Keep your head and shoulders up for good balance.)

Tasks/Challenges:

🅣 On your card are listed four body shapes. You're going to make up a sequence of jumps that shows those body shapes in the air. To do this, you'll first travel a bit and then jump, showing the first body shape; then you'll travel again and jump and show the second body shape listed; you'll travel again and jump using the third body shape; you'll travel one more time and jump showing the last body shape. So your sequence should be like this: Travel, jump; travel, jump; travel, jump; travel, jump, freeze. Repeat the sequence enough times so that you can do it the same way each time. Memorize it. When it's memorized, show the sequence to a friend. **Remember, use buoyant landings between jumps and a yielding landing after your last jump.**

Jumping over Equipment Using Buoyant Landings

Setting: Pairs of hurdles around the room, spaced so that children can jump the first and then the second hurdle

Cues

Buoyant Landings	(Bend your knees as you land, then spring up quickly.)
Yielding Landings	(Bend your knees to absorb the force when you land, as if sinking into the floor.)
Heads Up	(Keep your head and shoulders up for good balance.)

Tasks/Challenges:

🅣 Earlier in our work, you practiced taking off on one foot and landing on the opposite foot, as in a leap. This is the action you use to clear a hurdle. Approach the first hurdle with quick, running steps; jump over the first hurdle with the one-foot to one-foot action; use a buoyant landing to continue your travel and jump over the second hurdle.

🅒 Practice this activity until you seem to just pop over the first and then the second hurdle.

Jumping On and Off Equipment Using Buoyant and Yielding Landings

Setting: Boxes, low benches, milk crates, and other low equipment around the room

Cues

Buoyant Landings	(Bend your knees as you land, then spring up quickly.)
Yielding Landings	(Bend your knees to absorb the force when you land, as if sinking into the floor.)
Heads Up	(Keep your head and shoulders up for good balance.)

Tasks/Challenges:

🅣 Jump onto a piece of equipment, and use a buoyant landing to quickly spring off with another jump to the floor. **You should barely touch the equipment before you are off again and back to the floor, almost as if you were on a springboard—no stopping between jumps.**

🅣 This time, jump onto the piece of equipment using a yielding landing, hold still on top of the equipment a couple of seconds, then jump to the floor with another yielding landing. **Remember, on this jump, your knees should really bend and you should be able to hold still when you finish.**

🅣 Try jumping onto the equipment with the different jumps we have learned—two feet to two feet, one foot to two feet, and so on. Sometimes use a buoyant landing on the equipment so that you can quickly jump off; sometimes use a yielding landing on the equipment, pausing before you jump off. Always use a yielding landing on two feet when you jump off the equipment to the floor.

🅔 Which landing is used for a quick, springy action to continue movement? Which landing is used for landing and holding still?

Assessment Example

From the *National Standards for Physical Education*

Videotape

Students are asked to skip, gallop, and jump off a low box. A camera is set up in one corner of the gym to record their performance. Each student is asked to go in front of the camera and perform the specified movement patterns. The teacher uses a check list to assess the extent to which mature and skilled patterns have been attained.

Criteria for Assessment

a. Exhibits mature form for each of the movement patterns.

b. Demonstrates consistent and smooth performance.

NASPE (1995, P. 19)

Jump, Squash, TaDa

Setting: Low benches, low balance beam, folded mats positioned throughout general space; children divided into groups for stations

Cues	
Squash	(Bend your knees to absorb the force and maintain balance when you land.)
Swing Upward	(Swing your arms upward for good height.)
Heads Up	(Keep your head and shoulders up for good balance.)

Tasks/Challenges:

🅣 Have you ever watched gymnasts perform a stunt and then extend their arms high above their heads? Why do you think they do this movement? They do it to regain balance and proper body alignment after the gymnastics action. In the cartoon "Calvin and Hobbes," Calvin called this recovery the "TaDa" of gymnastics, the recovery to a balanced position no matter what has happened during the movement. Let's add that action to our jumping and landing work today. Jump from your mat (bench, beam) with a two-foot takeoff and a two-foot landing. Jump for maximum height, squash into a balanced position, then stretch your body upward, extending your arms to the sky as you say "TaDa."

🅣 Jump off your mat (bench, beam) with a quarter turn in the air. Land in a balanced position; recover with a full extension. **Don't forget the TaDa!**

🅣 When a friend gives you a thumbs-up for a good landing on your quarter turn, you may want to try a one-half turn. Practice turning your body clockwise and counterclockwise.

🅣 Jump off the mat (bench, beam), make a shape in the air, land in a balanced position, and recover with a full gymnastics extension.

🅣 Combine jumping off the low equipment, landing, and rolling in a gymnastics sequence; finish your sequence by returning to a standing TaDa.

⚠ Use the previous task only if children have mastered rolling from Chapter 23 or in combination with work from that chapter.

(See Chapter 23 for additional combination tasks, as well as for transferring off low apparatus.)

Jumping and Landing Task Sheet

Setting: A jumping and landing task sheet (similar to the example in Figure 21.1) for each child

Cues	
Buoyant Landings	(Bend your knees as you land, then spring up quickly.)
Yielding Landings	(Bend your knees to absorb the force when you land, as if sinking into the floor.)
Heads Up	(Keep your head and shoulders up for good balance.)
Swing Upward	(Swing your arms upward for good height on the jump.)
Swing Forward	(Swing your arms forcefully forward for maximum distance.)

Select cues appropriate to the tasks on the sheet (e.g., jumping forward, jumping upward, jumping and continuing action, jumping/landing with a stop of movement).

Tasks/Challenges:

🅒 This task sheet lets you test the jumping skills you've practiced so far. Whenever you've practiced a challenge and think you can do it correctly, ask a friend to watch you. If your friend thinks you've done the challenge well, the friend signs her or his name on the sheet next to the challenge.

Utilization Level: Learning Experiences Leading to Skill Development

At the utilization level, we provide contexts that help children use jumping and landing in combination with other movements, with complicated rhythms, and as a means for expression. We make the manipulative learning experiences more difficult by selecting different objects for the children to throw. We start with beanbags; then, as the children improve, we switch to whiffle balls, foam footballs, and, for the highly skilled, tennis balls.

Figure 21.1 Task sheet for jumping and landing.

Name _____ Teacher _____

Jumping Task Sheet

Verification	Challenge
	I can jump starting on two feet and landing on two feet.
	I can jump from two feet to one foot.
	I can jump from one foot to the other foot.
	I can hop from one foot to the same foot.
	I can jump from one foot to two feet.
	I can jump, turn in the air, and land without falling.
	I can jump off a box and land without falling.
	I can jump off a box, turn in the air, and land without falling.
	I can run and jump over a hurdle and land without falling.
	I can turn a jump rope myself and jump 15 times without missing.
	I can
	I can
	I can

A note about cues: Although several cues are listed for many of the learning experiences, it's important to focus on only one cue at a time. That way, the children can really concentrate on that cue. Once you provide feedback to the children and observe that most have learned a cue, then it's time to focus on another one.

Jumping to Catch

Setting: Low benches, chairs, or milk crates scattered throughout general space; sets of partners with beanbags, plastic balls, foam footballs, tennis balls

Cues

Yielding Landings (Bend your knees to absorb the force when you land, as if sinking into the floor.)

Swing Upward (Swing your arms upward for a full extension and added height on the jump.)

Tasks/Challenges:

T One partner stands on the low bench (chair, milk crate) and then jumps from the bench to catch the ball the other partner tosses. Catch the ball

Catching at a high level combines jumping and stretching.

while in the air. After three jumps, switch catcher–thrower positions with your partner. Hint for the thrower: Stand close and begin the toss as soon as your partner begins to jump.

For the next task, clear the general space of benches, crates, and other obstacles.

Ⓣ Pairs, scatter throughout general space. See how many times you can jump and catch without a mistake; count your score only if you catch the ball before you land. After three trials, switch thrower/catcher as you did earlier.

Ⓣ When the activity becomes easy for you and your partner, try throwing the ball so your partner has to reach to the left or to the right to make the catch.

Ⓣ Throw the ball so your partner is forced off the ground to catch it; this means that you have to throw the ball to a point above where the catch will actually be made. This is a high-level catch—feet off the floor, arms extended above the head. Throwers: It helps to pick a spot on the wall (tree, telephone pole) to aim at.

Ⓣ Try both one- and two-foot takeoffs.

Ⓣ Switch with your partner after five throws. You are now the catcher; your partner will throw the

ball above your head, so you must jump for the catch.

Ⓣ When you are confident throwing and catching while jumping, you and your partner can add a new element—traveling. Practice running, jumping, and catching in the air. For the two of you to do this task well, your partner will need to make a good throw. At first, run and jump from right to left; then, run and jump from left to right.

Ⓣ When you are able to make at least three catches in a row, run away from the thrower—that is, start close to and run away from your partner, as you might in a football game.

Jumping to Throw

Setting: Low benches, chairs, or milk crates throughout general space; sets of partners with whiffle balls, tennis balls, footballs

Cues	
Yielding Landings	(Bend your knees to absorb the force when you land, as if sinking into the floor.)
Vertical Jumps	(Jump upward, not outward, to throw.)

Tasks/Challenges:

Ⓣ Stand 10 to 12 feet from your partner. Jump from the bench (chair, crate) and throw the ball to your partner before you land. Try to throw the ball so your partner can catch it easily. Switch with your partner after four jumps/throws.

Clear the general space of benches, crates, and other obstacles.

Ⓣ Pick a target, such as a target on the wall (or a basketball backstop, a hoop, or a stationary partner). Jump and throw the ball to the target.

Ⓣ When you hit the target five times in a row, move farther away from the target. It counts as a successful throw only if you hit the target and make your throw while in the air.

Ⓣ As this activity gets easier, try running, jumping, and throwing to the target.

Jumping on a Bench

Setting: Low benches scattered throughout the work area

The skill of jumping is important to success in games, dance, and gymnastics.

Cues

Squash　　　　(Bend your knees to absorb the force and maintain balance when you land.)

Arms Extended (Extend your arms outward for good balance.)

Tasks/Challenges:

T You will work one at a time on the bench. Travel to the middle of the bench; jump upward, taking off and landing on two feet on the bench. **Focus your eyes on the end of the bench.**

T When you're able to do this activity several times without falling off, practice landing on only one foot. Hold your balance on the bench before your other foot comes down on the bench. Try to hold your balance for two or three seconds.

C Design a sequence along the bench that includes at least two different jumps. For example, hop on one foot along the bench, jump and turn so that you land facing the opposite direction, and travel back to the start using small leaps. At first, your jumps won't be very high, but as you get better, you'll want to make them higher. Practice your sequence until you can do it three times in a row without falling off.

When you observe that children are competent and comfortable with different types of jumps on the bench, they may progress to low and medium balance beams. This is an excellent opportunity for intratask variation.

Throwing and Catching While Jumping

Setting: A court, its boundaries marked with a rope or a net (size of court is determined by space available; the larger the court, the more difficult the game)

Cues

Buoyant Landings (Bend your knees as you land, then spring up quickly—to throw or travel.)

Yielding Landings (Bend your knees to absorb the force, and sink into a balanced position.)

Tasks/Challenges:

T The game you're going to play will give you a chance to practice throwing and catching while jumping. The object is to have the ball touch the floor on the opposite side of the net. Here are the rules:

1. There are three players on a team.
2. There is one team on each side of the rope (or net).
3. A player must be off the floor when the ball is thrown or caught.
4. At least two players on your team must touch the ball before it is thrown back over the rope (net).

5. Points are scored when the ball lands out of bounds, the ball hits the floor inbounds, or a player throws or catches the ball while that player's feet are touching the ground.

This game can also be played cooperatively: Both teams work together to see how many times the ball can cross the rope or net without breaking any of the rules. A point is scored each time the ball crosses the net. A good score to aim for is 10 throws in a row over the net without breaking a rule.

Jumping to an Accented Beat

Setting: Children scattered throughout general space, each with a hoop

Cues

Buoyant Landings (Bend your knees, then spring up quickly to travel.)

Tasks/Challenges:

Ⓣ When I beat the drum, jump into and out of your hoop every time you hear the drumbeat.

Ⓣ Now take off on two feet, and land on two feet. As the drumbeat gets faster, be ready to jump by having your knees bent and your arms flexed. Try to land on only the balls of your feet, which means that your heels won't touch the ground.

Ⓣ Take off on one foot, and land on the same foot.

Ⓣ Try to keep up with the beat—it's going to get faster and faster. When one leg gets tired, change to the other leg.

Ⓣ Listen as I beat the drum. The first beat is louder than the others. This is called an *accented* beat. Use one- or two-foot takeoffs and landings, but jump on only the accented beat. The first beat will be accented; the next three beats will be unaccented.

Proficiency Level: Learning Experiences Leading to Skill Development

At the proficiency level, dynamic dance, game, and gymnastics experiences are designed to help youngsters use, refine, and enjoy their jumping abilities. Children almost always jump in relation to objects or other people (or both) and use jumping for both expressive and functional purposes.

A note about cues: At the proficiency level, tasks are more complex, typically requiring children to coordinate several movements simultaneously in a dynamic

context. A list of cues is provided to assist the children in being more successful in the learning experience. The challenge for the teacher is in determining which cue will be most beneficial for each child . . . and when. Thus, careful observation and critical reflection become very important as you watch the children move and then decide which cue will be the most helpful to move each learner to a higher skill level.

Jumping with a Partner to Mirror Actions

Setting: Two pieces of equipment (benches, tables, or vaulting boxes) about 15 feet apart, with a large mat on the floor between; children with partners

Cues

Yielding Landings (Bend your knees to absorb the force, and sink into a balanced position.)

Buoyant Landings (Bend your knees as you land, then spring up quickly.)

Heads Up (Keep your head and shoulders up for good balance.)

Tasks/Challenges:

Ⓣ You and your partner are going to mirror each other's jumps. *Mirroring* means that you face each other and copy the other's movements, as if you were looking in a mirror. Therefore, if your partner uses the left arm, you'll use your right arm. To start, decide which of you will be the first leader. The leader makes up the first jump and shows it to the partner. Then you both face each other and do that jump at the same time, mirroring each other exactly. This activity will be hard at first, because you'll have to take off at the same time, jump the same height, and do everything exactly together. Start with some easy jumps and then go to harder ones. Each person takes three turns as leader and then switches. Again, make your jumps look like a reflection of your partner's. **Don't forget: Yielding and buoyant landings will be part of the mirror action.**

Pinpoint several pairs who are mirroring jumps accurately.

Ⓣ As you get better at mirroring your partner, you may want to include such actions as gesturing in the air, turning in the air, or rolling after landing. **This will really take a lot of work; you may want to count out everything before you do it.**

Jumping with a Partner to Match Actions

Setting: Two pieces of equipment (benches, tables, or vaulting boxes) about 15 feet apart, with a large mat on the floor between; children with partners

Cues	
Travel, Jumps, & Landings	(Everything must match your partner—travel, jumps, and landings.)
Heads Up	(Keep your head and shoulders up for good balance.)

Tasks/Challenges:

T Now that you've become very good at mirroring a partner's actions and jumps, you're going to try matching jumps. *Matching* means that you do the same thing at the same time; thus, if you're facing your partner, your actions look the opposite of your partner's. If you use your right leg, then your partner must also use the right leg. Again, decide which of you will be the first leader. The leader makes a jump and faces the partner; the two of you then match jumps. Take three turns as leader, and then switch. Start with easy jumps. **Counting will help you match starting each jump.**

T Once you've become quite good at matching jumps with your partner while facing each other and standing still, try this: Travel a short distance together, and then, at a set point, do matching jumps in the air. This activity will be hard. You must pick a starting point, count exactly how many steps you'll travel before you jump, and then jump and land. First, by yourself practice the traveling by itself and then the jump by itself; then, combine the traveling and jumping. Finally, try to do the task with your partner. The sequence is this; Travel, jump, land, freeze—all movements exactly matching those of your partner. You two should look like twins.

T To the sequence you just made up, add a second traveling action and a second jump.

Jumping with a Springboard

Setting: Springboards positioned throughout the work space with sufficient large mats for safe landings

Cues	
Push	(Push hard with your feet and legs as you contact the board.)
Swing Upward	(Swing your arms upward for good height.)
Squash	(Bend your knees and spread your feet for a stable, soft landing.)

Tasks/Challenges:

T Using the nearest springboard, run and jump, using a two-foot landing/takeoff on the board; spring up high and land on two feet on the mat.

T As you become good at going off the springboard and landing without falling over, add a turn in the air as you jump so that you end up facing the place where you started. **Remember to bend your knees and spread your feet apart when you land.**

T When you're able to do this activity, try a complete 360-degree turn in the air before you land. To get all the way around, you'll have to throw your arms up and around in the direction that you want to turn.

Jumping as Part of a Dance Creation

Setting: Children divided into small groups, no more than four per group

Cues	
Individual cues as needed	

Tasks/Challenges:

T Now you're going to use jumps to make up a dance. The main actions of the dance will all use different jumps. First think of a theme for your dance, such as a fight. If you use that idea, your jumps will contain such gestures as punching, slashing, jabbing, protecting, and retreating.

As a group, think of what you want your dance to say. Once you've decided the theme, try to put together a series of jumps that express that idea. You'll be using your jumps and other movements to tell a story. It may be that you all move at the same time, or that two of you move and then the other two move. Your dance needs to have a definite beginning and a definite end, with at least six different jumps in the middle. Try to make the dance look really professional. This will take a while to do; I'll be available to help each group as you work. Toward the end of class, we'll show the dances to the rest of the class.

Jumping, Dancing, and Imagery

Setting: Children divided into small groups, no more than four per group.

Cues

Individual cues as needed

Tasks/Challenges:

T Jumps can be used to create a dance about the things around you (the flight of a bird, leaves in the wind, etc.). This time, you're going to create a dance that uses one of these things as its main idea. Jumps will communicate that idea to your audience. You must decide in your group what natural thing you'd like to communicate in a dance using jumps.

After you've decided, begin to develop your dance, keeping the following ideas in mind:

1. The actions you're demonstrating should clearly portray your theme.
2. The starting location of each person should be clear.
3. The dance should rise to a climax and then wind down to a conclusion.
4. The jumps and gestures you're using to communicate your ideas should be the most effective ones you can create.
5. The pathways used in the dance should be clear.

At the end of class, we'll show all the dances you want to the class.

Hurdling Jumps

Setting: A series of hurdles set up throughout the work area, with sufficient space between for children to run between, jumping over each; stopwatches at starting line (optional)

Cues

Foot to Foot	(Opposite: one foot to the other foot.)
Extend	(Front leg upward and forward.)
Heads Up	(Keep your head and shoulders up for good balance.)

Tasks/Challenges:

T In this activity you'll be *hurdling*, which is sprinting over barriers, called hurdles, placed along the way. Begin behind the first hurdle, and run to the end of the line of hurdles. Each time you come to a hurdle, jump it and keep going. Run to the end of the line, come back to the first hurdle, and start again. Start your jump *before* you reach the hurdle by extending your front leg upward and forward. Try to get over the hurdles by barely clearing them rather than jumping really high over them. You need a horizontal rather than a high vertical jump for hurdles.

Use low barriers at first so that youngsters can focus on proper technique without worrying about clearing the obstacles. Once children begin to exhibit quality hurdling actions, you can gradually increase the height of the barriers. Milk crates spread apart with bamboo poles supported between them are satisfactory barriers.

C As you feel you're getting better at hurdling, time yourself and see if you can improve each time. You can use one of the stopwatches available at the starting line of each row of hurdles.

For transferring weight over apparatus (vaulting box), see Chapter 23.

Reading Comprehension Questions

1. Name the two basic reasons for performing jumps.
2. What are the three phases of a jump?
3. List in order of difficulty the different takeoff and landing patterns for jumping.
4. What does a precontrol jump look like?

5. What are the characteristics of jumping and landing at each of the four skill levels? For example, what does a utilization-level jump look like?
6. What is the focus of the jumping and landing activities for the control and proficiency levels?

(The introductory text to each section will get you started.)

7. Describe a low obstacle that children can safely practice jumping over.

8. What is the difference between a buoyant landing and a yielding landing?

9. Describe a sequence for teaching young children to jump rope.

10. Describe how jumping is used in (1) gymnastics, (2) games/sports, (3) dance. Give a specific example of jumping in each of these content areas.

References/Suggested Readings

National Association for Sport and Physical Education. (1995). *Moving into the future: National standards for physical education.* St. Louis, MO: Mosby.

National Association for Sport and Physical Education. (2004). *Moving into the future: National standards for physical education.* (2nd ed.). Reston, VA: National Association for Sport and Physical Education.

Wickstrom, R. L. (1977). *Fundamental motor patterns* (2nd ed.). Philadelphia: Lea & Febiger.

Balancing

Jim nasctics KATLYN E·5

erriam Webster's Collegiate Dictionary, Eleventh Edition, defines *balance* as "stability produced by even distribution of weight on each side of the vertical axis" and also as "an aesthetically pleasing integration of elements." There's no extraneous motion, no flagrant waving of arms to maintain position, no near topple or wobble from side to side. The center of gravity is clearly over the base of support.

The elementary school child attempting to do a headstand, walk a beam, ride a skateboard, or use in-line skates encounters different types of static and dynamic balance challenges. Among the key teaching concepts in providing balance experiences are these:

1. It's easier to balance over a wide base of support than a narrow base.
2. The center of gravity should be aligned over the base of support for stationary balance (Figure 22.1).
3. Extensions to one side of the body beyond the base of support necessitate extensions in the opposite direction for counterbalance.

Static balance involves maintaining a desired shape in a stationary position; gymnastics balances, headstands, and handstands are examples. *Dynamic* balance involves maintaining an on-balance position while moving, starting, or stopping. Dynamic balance occurs in weight transference, jumping, throwing, catching, and all forms of travel. Balance as a concept is discussed in Chapters 19, 21, 23, and 25 as it applies to learning specific skills. See Box 22-1 for information on balancing from the *National Standards for Physical Education*.

Box 22-1

The Skill of Balancing in the *National Standards for Physical Education*

The movement skill of balancing is referenced in the *National Standards for Physical Education* (National Association for Sport and Physical Education, 2004) under Standard 1: Demonstrates competency in motor skills and movement patterns needed to perform a variety of physical activities. The standard speaks of children demonstrating control in traveling, weight bearing, and balance activities on a variety of body parts, and being able to participate with skill in gymnastics.

Sample performance outcomes from the *National Standards* include:

- Discovers how to balance on different body parts, at different levels, becoming "like" a statue while making symmetrical and nonsymmetrical shapes (K–2)*
- Balances with control on a variety of objects (e.g., balance board, large apparatus, skates) (3–5)*
- Develops and refines a gymnastics sequence demonstrating smooth transitions (3–5)*
- Designs and performs gymnastics sequences that combine traveling, rolling, balancing, and weight transfer into smooth, flowing sequences with intentional changes in direction, speed, and flow (6–8)*

*Grade-level guidelines for expected student learning.

Figure 22.1 Center of gravity over base of support.

Levels of Skill Proficiency

At the precontrol level, children sporadically achieve balance; it's often more coincidental than intentional. Activities at this level are designed to introduce weight bearing and stillness as prerequisites to balance. Appropriate tasks include:

1. Exploring the use of different body parts as bases of support
2. Using wide bases to balance
3. Stopping in balanced positions

The child at the control level is ready to focus on holding stationary supports for several seconds, balancing on smaller bases, and maintaining inverted balances. Appropriate tasks include:

1. Supporting weight on combinations of body parts (for example, head and hands)
2. Momentarily supporting weight on hands alone
3. Balancing on more narrow bases and in inverted positions
4. Holding stationary balances on various types of large apparatus

The child at the utilization level is ready to study balancing on equipment and in dynamic situations, combining balance with locomotion and weight transference. Appropriate tasks include:

1. Combining stationary balances with actions on benches, tables, and beams
2. Moving from an on-balance to an off-balance position
3. Moving into and out of balances with stretching, curling, and twisting actions

Proficiency-level balance tasks focus on maintaining balance on inverted and narrow bases. Children practice moving into and out of stationary balances with changes in time, dynamic balances on narrow equipment, and combining/contrasting balance-time factors in sequences on the floor and on apparatus. Appropriate tasks include:

1. Extensions away from the body when balanced on a narrow base
2. Partner and group balances
3. Rapid turns and twists into balanced positions
4. Dismounts (from apparatus) that conclude with landings in balanced, stationary positions

The sequence for developing the skill theme of balancing at the precontrol, control, utilization, and proficiency levels is shown in our progression spiral on page 377.

Precontrol Level: Activities for Exploration

Activities at the precontrol level are designed to provide exploration of the concept of balance, supporting weight on different body parts as bases of support and in different shapes. As children explore the concept of balance, they begin to maintain simple stationary balances and to stop in balanced positions while traveling.

Balancing on Different Bases of Support

Setting: Carpet squares or small mats placed throughout general space, with sufficient room between for children to work without bumping others

Tasks/Challenges:

🅣 Balance on different bases of support on your mat. Your base of support is the body parts that are holding you in the balance. See how many body parts can be bases of support. Hold each balance as you count to yourself 3 seconds: "one thousand one, one thousand two . . ."

🅣 Try different combinations of body parts as you create your balances.

🅣 Let's list all the body parts you've used as bases of support for your balances. *(List on board or flip chart as students give responses.)* Do you see some body parts listed as bases of support that you didn't try? Take a few minutes to try all the combinations.

⚠ Some children will watch others in class, often the more skilled students, and attempt to copy their balances. This can result in injury to the less skilled. A reminder to the group and/or to the less confident students of what the teacher is looking for eliminates this potential problem.

🅣 Now I'll name the body parts that I want to be the bases of support. First, hand(s) and feet. Be creative in your balance. Although you're all using the same base of support, the gymnastics balances may be very different.

Additional exploration: feet and head, knees and elbows, stomach, base of spine, and shoulders in combination with other body parts.

⚠ Sometimes children attempt to balance on body parts that aren't appropriate for supporting weight.

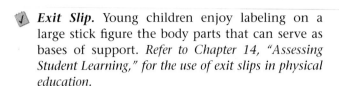

Balancing

Skill Theme Development Sequence

Proficiency Level

Performing apparatus sequences that combine stationary balances and traveling with movement concepts
Transferring off equipment with weight on hands
Balancing on hanging ropes
Balancing while supporting the weight of a partner

Utilization Level

Performing sequences that combine stationary balances and traveling on mats
Performing inverted balances on equipment
Traveling into and out of balances by rolling
Moving out of and into balances by stretching, curling, and twisting
Balancing on crates

Control Level

Balance boards
Balancing on stilts
Balancing sequence
Traveling while balanced
Traveling on large apparatus
Stationary balances on equipment
Traveling and stopping in balanced positions
Doing kickups
Alignment of body parts
Performing inverted balances
The Gymnastics Dance
Balancing in different body shapes
Balancing symmetrically and nonsymmetrically
Counterbalance
Tightening the gymnastics muscles
Balancing on different bases of support

Precontrol Level

Balancing on boards
Traveling on low gymnastics equipment
Traveling and stopping in balanced positions
Balancing in different body shapes
Balancing on a wide base of support
Balancing on different bases of support

Don't let youngsters balance in unsafe positions that could result in stress or injury.

C Balance on your favorite bases of support, holding the balance very still. Let's pretend I am going to take a photo of the balance—no wiggles, no wobbles.

✓ *Exit Slip.* Young children enjoy labeling on a large stick figure the body parts that can serve as bases of support. *Refer to Chapter 14, "Assessing Student Learning," for the use of exit slips in physical education.*

Balancing on a Wide Base of Support

Setting: Carpet squares or small mats placed throughout general space with sufficient room between for children to work without bumping others

Tasks/Challenges:

T On the mat (ground, create a four-part balance on your hands and lower legs; have your hands under your shoulders and your legs approximately the same distance apart as the width of your hips. This wide base of support creates a very stable balance.

T Move your hands toward each other and your legs toward each other until they touch. Do you feel stable now? Could I push you over?

T Explore the concept of wide to narrow balances with different bases of support: hands and feet, knees and elbows.

Balancing in Different Body Shapes

Setting: Carpet squares or small mats placed throughout general space, with sufficient room between for children to work without bumping others

Tasks/Challenges:

T Create a gymnastics balance on a wide base of support. Create a wide body shape by extending free body parts outward from your trunk (free body parts are those you're not using as bases of support).

T Create a narrow-shape gymnastics balance on the base of your spine—long and thin like a piece of spaghetti. Keep all free body parts close to your trunk.

T Create a curled-shape gymnastics balance on your chosen base of support. Free body parts can be tucked close to the body, or they may be added to the curled shape by bending them in the curve.

T Create a twisted-shape gymnastics balance. Use your two feet as your base of support and twist your body like a pretzel.

Figure 22.2 Equipment arrangement for traveling.

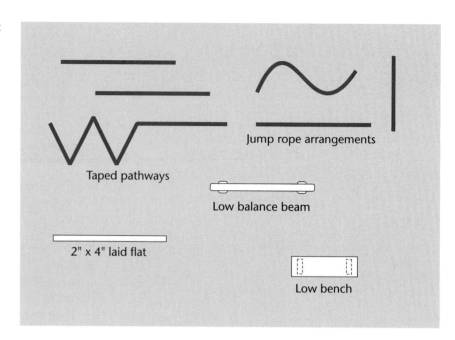

Taped pathways

Jump rope arrangements

Low balance beam

2" x 4" laid flat

Low bench

Traveling and Stopping in Balanced Positions

Setting: Children scattered throughout general space

Tasks/Challenges:

T Travel through general space any way you choose. On the signal, stop and create a gymnastics balance with two feet and two hands touching the floor.

Additional exploration: two feet and one hand, base of spine, two knees and one hand . . .

T Travel again, but this time balance on three body parts when you hear the signal. Think which three parts you're going to use before traveling. Ready? Go.

Additional exploration: four body parts, five body parts, two body parts.

Traveling on Low Gymnastics Equipment

Setting: Jump ropes; low balance beams; 2- by 4-inch planks; low, narrow benches; and tape pathways arranged on the floor (Figure 22.2)

Tasks/Challenges:

T Travel on the different pieces of equipment without losing your balance and falling off.

Additional exploration: travel backward; travel with your arms above your head; walk with a beanbag on your head.

Balancing on Boards

Setting: Square, rectangle, and circular balance boards arranged as a station for the study of balance (Figure 22.3)

Tasks/Challenges:

T Balance on a balance board without falling off or letting the edges of the board touch the ground. You may want a partner to stand in front of the balance board to help when you first step up; place your hands on the partner's shoulders for support.

T Explore standing with your feet shoulder-width apart and with your feet close together. Which gives you better balance on the board?

Control Level: Learning Experiences Leading to Skill Development

Learning experiences at the control level focus on maintaining the stillness and control of a balance. Children balance on increasingly smaller bases of support, while holding the body in inverted positions, and in stationary balances on apparatus. These experiences begin to provide the ingredients for a movement repertoire of balances that may be included in sequences involving traveling and other balances. *Several of the tasks explored at the precontrol level will be repeated at the control level, with the focus on refinement cues.*

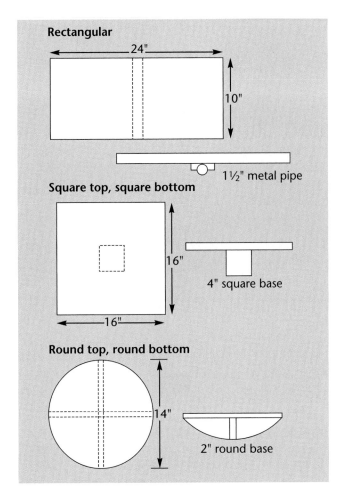

Figure 22.3 Construction of balance boards of various shapes.

A note about cues: Although several cues are listed for many of the learning experiences, it's important to focus on only one cue at a time. That way, the children can really concentrate on that cue. Once you provide feedback to the children and observe that most have learned a cue, then it's time to focus on another one.

Balancing on Different Bases of Support

Setting: Carpet squares or small mats scattered throughout general space with sufficient room between for children to work without bumping others

Cues

Stillness (No wiggles, no wobbles—hold perfectly still for 3 seconds.)

Tasks/Challenges:

T Earlier in the year we explored balancing on different bases of support. Balance on different bases

of support on your mat or carpet square. See if you can remember which body parts can serve as good bases for gymnastic balances.

T Listed on the board (flip chart) are the body parts that serve as bases of support. I will call out the combination of body parts; you create the balance with that base—for example, feet and hands. What other body parts can you use with your feet to create a good base for gymnastic balances?

T Create balances using the following combination of bases: head and hands, head and knees, head and feet; elbows and knees; elbows, feet, and head; stomach only; base of spine only; shoulders, upper arms/elbows, and head.

T Create balances by adding your chosen base or bases to the following:

feet and _____
head and _____
elbows and _____

C From all the balances you have practiced, choose three of your favorites, each showing a different combination of body parts as bases of support. Practice until you can hold each balance 3 seconds without moving or losing your balance. When you are ready, show your balances to a partner, who will give you a "thumbs up" if you hold the balance stationary for 3 seconds.

Tightening the Gymnastics Muscles

Setting: Carpet squares and/or small mats scattered throughout general space, with sufficient room for children to work without collisions

Cues

Stillness (No wiggles, no wobbles—hold perfectly still for 3 seconds.)

Tight Muscles (Muscular tension is the key to holding the balance.)

Tasks/Challenges:

T Balance on your favorite base of support, holding the balance very still. Tighten the muscles of the body parts supporting your balance to maintain stillness.

T Balance on a different base of support. Tighten the muscles of the free body parts to hold a stretched or curled shape very still.

T Assume your favorite balance position. See if you can tighten the muscles without changing the appearance of your balance. You should look the same but feel the tightening inside.

C Continue to practice your balances with a focus on tightening the muscles without changing the appearance of the balance. As I walk by you, I should feel the tightness in the extended arm or leg if I touch you.

This tightening of the muscles is a key factor in holding the balance very still without extraneous movement and in maintaining the position.

Counterbalance

Setting: Carpet squares or small mats scattered throughout general space, with sufficient room between mats for children to work safely

Cues	
Stillness	(No wiggles, no wobbles for 3 seconds.)
Tight Muscles	(Muscular tension is the key to holding the balance.)
Extensions	(Extend free body parts for stability in your balance.)

Tasks/Challenges:

T Balance on one foot. Extend your arms and free leg, holding the balance very stationary. Repeat the balance, extending the arms but not the leg. Which balance is easier to maintain? Right, the one with arms and free leg extended in opposite directions. This is the concept of counterbalance. Extensions to one side of the body necessitate extensions in the opposite direction.

T Balance on the base of your spine. Extend free body parts to one side only; repeat with the extension in the opposite direction.

T Explore balances on different bases of support, extending your body parts in different directions from your body for counterbalance.

Balancing Symmetrically and Nonsymmetrically

Setting: Carpet squares and/or small mats scattered throughout general space, with sufficient room for children to work safely

Cues	
Tight Muscles	(Muscular tension is the key to holding the balance.)

These youngsters maintain stillness in symmetrical and nonsymmetrical balances.

Extensions	(Extend free body parts for stability in your balance.)
Smooth Transitions	(Move slowly from one balance to the next for a smooth transition.)

Tasks/Challenges:

- Balance on the base of your spine, with your arms and legs extended outward. Create exactly the same shape on both sides of your body. This is called a symmetrical shape; both sides of the body look the same.

- Keeping the same base of support, change your free body parts, still creating a symmetrical shape.

- Balance on your chosen base of support. Create a symmetrical shape. Now change to a nonsymmetrical shape—the sides look different—while balanced on that same base.

- Balance on your shoulders, back of head, and arms. Create a symmetrical shape with your legs. Change to a nonsymmetrical shape and then back to a symmetrical one.

- Repeat this three-part symmetrical, nonsymmetrical, symmetrical sequence; slowly change your legs into the different shapes. This smoothness in transition is an important component of gymnastics.

Assessment Example

From the *National Standards for Physical Education*

Peer Observation

Students are asked to work on balancing on different bases of support (e.g., two hands and one foot, hands and knees, headstand). Students should balance in four different positions, two using symmetrical shapes and two using asymmetrical shapes. Students are asked to draw their favorite symmetrical and asymmetrical balances on paper, labeling "S" and "A," respectively. Students now select a partner who will observe their balances and then indicate on the paper: (1) if the drawn figures were labeled correctly and (2) if the balances were held still for 3 seconds.

Criteria for Assessment

a. Completes four balances—two symmetrical and two asymmetrical.
b. Correctly labels balances "S" and "A."
c. Maintains stillness in balance for 3 seconds.
d. Observer correctly assesses the appropriateness of the labels and the extent to which the performer was still.

NASPE (1995, p. 19)

Balancing in Different Body Shapes

Setting: Small mats and/or carpet squares scattered throughout general space, with sufficient room for children to work safely

Cues

Tight Muscles	(Muscular tension is the key to holding the balance.)
Extensions	(Extend free body parts for stability in your balance.)
Smooth Transitions	(Move slowly from one balance to the next for a smooth transition.)

Tasks/Challenges:

- Remember when we explored basic body shapes for physical education. Who can name the four shapes? Wide, curled, twisted, narrow, that's right. Let's create balances that show each of those shapes. Now that you have learned to balance on different bases of support, try to have a different base of support for each of your balances.

- Let's focus on wide-shape balances. Create wide-shape balances with different bases of support. Remember, extensions of arms and legs away from the body create wide shapes.

- I'm going to put on some background music for a few minutes. Create three balances that show wide shapes; each balance is to have a different base of support. Challenge yourself with a level of difficulty that tests your skills. When the music stops, we will look at the balances.

- Now let's create gymnastics balances that show narrow shapes. Remember, we create narrow-shape balances by holding body parts close to each other. How many different narrow balances can you create?

- Create a narrow balance on the base of your spine. **Stretch your legs and arms to counterbalance.**

- Create two new narrow balances, one at a low level, the other at medium level.

- You can create a curled (round) shape by curling your spine forward or arching your spine backward. Free body parts may be tucked close to the body, or they may be added to the curled image by bending in the curve. Create a curled gymnastics balance on your chosen base of support.

- Create a curled-shape gymnastics balance in which the spine curls forward; slowly change into a curled-shape balance with your spine arched backward.

- Stand in a balanced position, with both feet as bases of support for your weight. Create a twisted shape by turning your body to the right or the left without moving your feet. Now balance, using your left foot and the lower portion of your right leg as bases of support. Create a twisted shape from this base.

T Create twisted shapes by rotating your trunk, arms, legs, neck, ankles, and wrists while balanced on different bases of support.

T Balance on three body parts. Create a twisted shape by rotating free body parts, for example, arms, legs, trunk, neck. Create two more twisted-shape balances on various bases of support.

C Think of all the balances you have created today. They represent four shapes: wide, narrow, curled, twisted. Review the balances you did; choose your favorite balance for each shape. On each signal, show me your favorite wide, narrow, curled, and twisted shape balance. **Concentrate on holding each perfectly still and moving smoothly from balance to balance.**

☑ *Peer Observation.* Peer observation of body shapes and balances would be appropriate here. A possible task would be to have students, using stick figures, draw each of the four balances, one representing each of the four shapes. Have them label the body shape of each figure, then exchange papers with a neighbor, who will be the "gymnastics judge" (Figure 22.4). *Refer to Chapter 14, "Assessing Student Learning," for the use of peer observation as assessment.*

Figure 22.4 Student balance drawings and peer assessment results.

C Working in groups of four, create a balance statue in which each person partially supports another. Each person should represent one of the four basic shapes; wide, narrow, curled, and twisted. After you make the body-shape statue, convert it to a movable monster by moving as a unit in either self-space or general space.

The Gymnastics Dance

Setting: Children scattered throughout general space

Cues	
Tight Muscles	(Muscular tension is the key to holding the balance.)
Extensions	(Extend free body parts for stability in your balance.)
Smooth Transitions	(Move slowly from one balance to the next for a smooth transition.)

Tasks/Challenges:

T Let's create a gymnastics dance that focuses on body shapes and balance. I will select one person to form a statue by holding a gymnastics balance with a wide base of support. Hold your wide balance as others come and go.

T Each person in the group will slowly add to the statue by making a wide, narrow, curled, or twisted shape and touching the first statue with *one* body part.

T That looks really good; the shapes are clear and the balances are stationary. After everyone in the group has added to the statue by making a balance and touching the first person, begin to move slowly from the original wide-shape balance that was the first one created without disturbing others in the group. I will touch you as a signal for you to move from the main statue. Use a locomotor movement or a turning action to move from the group.

T On the signal, move slowly back into the large balance statue, with clear shapes and stillness. Move away again, forming an individual statue by yourself with a different base of support and different shape from the one you used before.

Performing Inverted Balances

Setting: Small mats and/or carpet squares scattered throughout general space, with sufficient room between mats for children to work without bumping others

Cues	
Tight Muscles	(Tighten your abdominal muscles to hold the inverted balance— stretch toward the sky!)
Equal Weight	(Take weight equally on all body parts that are bases of support.)

Tasks/Challenges:

T Balance with your head and two feet as your base of support.

A When performing an inverted balance involving the head, it's important to distribute the body weight equally among all body parts serving as the base of support.

T Balance on your head and hands, with your knees resting on your elbows (Figure 22.5).

T When performing these inverted balances, concentrate on taking your weight equally on the following bases:

1. Head and knees
2. Head, hands, one foot
3. Back of head, shoulders, arm

T Explore other inverted balances that you can safely hold for 3 seconds (Figure 22.6).

Alignment of Body Parts

Setting: Small mats and/or carpet squares scattered throughout general space, with sufficient room for children to work safely

Cues	
Tight Muscles	(Tighten your abdominal muscles to hold the inverted balance— stretch toward the sky!)
Alignment	(Toes over knees, over hips, over shoulders to form a straight line.)

Figure 22.5 Inverted balance on head and hands.

Figure 22.6 Other inverted balances.

Tasks/Challenges:

Ⓣ Repeat your balance on head and hands with knees resting on elbows. **Concentrate on tightening your abdominal muscles to align your hips over your shoulders.**

Ⓣ Balance on your head and hands, with your trunk and legs extended toward the ceiling. Form a triangular base with your weight equally distributed on your head and hands. **Stretch your body like a straight line, aligning hips over shoulders, feet over hips. Pretend your toes are attached by a string to the ceiling . . . stretch.**

⚠ Teach children to roll safely out of an off-balance head and hands position by pushing with the hands, tucking the chin, and curling the back.

Doing Kickups

Setting: Large gymnastics mats and/or small mats that will not slip scattered throughout general space, with sufficient room for children to work safely

Cues	
Tight Muscles	(Tighten your abdominal muscles to hold the inverted balance—stretch toward the sky!)
Alignment	(Toes over knees, over hips, over shoulders to form a straight line.)

Spotting

The question of spotting—physically assisting a child with a skill—often arises with gymnastics. Spotting is seldom used in educational gymnastics as it often encourages or forces children to attempt a skill before they are ready. See Chapter 30 for a more complete discussion on the use of spotting.

Tasks/Challenges:

Ⓣ Place one foot in front of the other (front-back stance); lean forward, and place your hands on the floor shoulder-width apart, fingers pointing forward. Using your back leg as a lever, kick your leg upward so that your weight is supported on your hands only.

Ⓒ Practice counting seconds as you balance on your hands.

With practice, the success rate for balancing on hands is very high, but practice must be massed and distributed.

⚠ Teach the children to come safely out of an off-balance weight-on-hands position by twisting the trunk slightly to bring the feet down in a new place.

Traveling and Stopping in Balanced Positions

Setting: Children scattered throughout general space

Cues

Stillness	(Hold your balance perfectly still—no wiggles, no wobbles.)
Tight Muscles	(Muscular tension is the key to holding the balance.)
Extensions	(Extend free body parts for stability in your balance.)

Tasks/Challenges:

T We worked earlier on traveling through general space and creating a gymnastics balance when we stopped. Let's review those skills: Travel through general space any way you choose. On the signal, stop and create a gymnastics balance with two hands and one foot touching the floor.

T This time, change your way of traveling. If you ran before, skip or gallop through general space. On the signal, stop and create a balance with four body parts as bases of support. Think of the four parts you will choose before traveling.

T Repeat the travel, stop, balance sequence with different combinations of body parts as bases of support and different ways to travel.

C Remember the balance you created with four bases of support? Think of the balance you created with two bases. Now you are going to make a sequence of two travels and two stationary balances. Your sequence will be this: Travel, stop and balance on four bases; travel, stop and balance on two bases of support. I'll give the signal for travel each time. You will decide the ways you are going to travel; use the balances you just practiced. We will practice several times so you can repeat the travel, balance sequence exactly the same way each time.

C After you have completed your two-part sequence and feel good about your travel and balances, create a larger sequence by adding other ways to travel and additional balances—for example, three bases, five bases. How about going from five bases of support to one base, with travel between the balances? Remember, there are ways to travel other than on your feet.

Stationary Balances on Equipment

Setting: Various pieces of gymnastics apparatus arranged throughout general space: low tables, boxes, benches, climbing frames, low balance beams, and sawhorses. (See Figures 22.7, 22.8 and 22.9 for plans for constructing balance beams, sawhorses, and balance benches, respectively.)

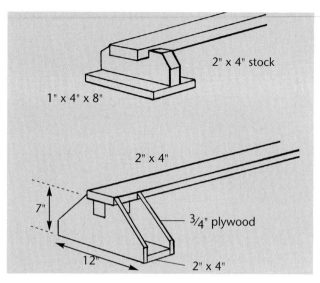

Figure 22.7 Construction of a balance beam.

Cues

Stillness	(Hold your balance perfectly still—no wiggles, no wobbles.)
Tight Muscles	(Muscular tension is the key to holding the balance.)
Extensions	(Extend free body parts for stability in your balance.)

Tasks/Challenges:

T Earlier in the year we explored traveling safely on gymnastics equipment. Select the piece of apparatus you want to begin working on; spend a few minutes exploring the apparatus until you are comfortable on this new surface and height. Travel forward and backward on the apparatus. Try some of the balances you did on the floor/mat surface on the apparatus.

T Perform your balances at different places on the apparatus: on the top, near one end, in the middle, on a low rung, underneath. Try some balances with a combination of bases on the floor and on the apparatus.

T Balance on your hands only on the low bench, low beam, or crate. The chart on the wall (Figure 22.10) will provide examples of balances that do not require you to be inverted when you balance on hands only on the equipment.

T Create a balance on the apparatus, then move slowly to another part of the apparatus for your second balance. Can you create a combination of travel and three different balances?

Figure 22.8 Construction of a wooden sawhorse.

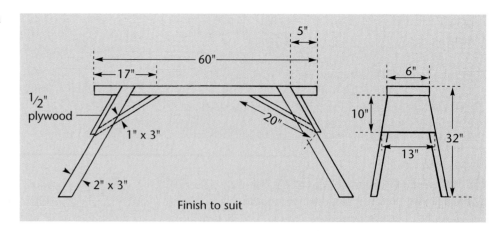

Finish to suit

Figure 22.9 Construction of a balance bench.

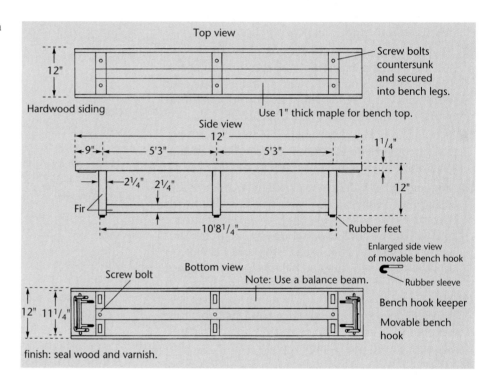

After you create three balances on the first piece of apparatus, move to another piece of gymnastics apparatus and create balances on that one. You may be able to repeat balances from before, or you may need to create balances on different bases of support to suit the different apparatus. Continue rotating to the various pieces of apparatus until you've created three balances on each piece of apparatus.

When children first begin this type of gymnastics, they may not be able to move independently from apparatus to apparatus. We have found it best in the beginning to assign the children to groups and rotate the stations.

Create combinations of balances and travel on each of the pieces of apparatus.

Choose your favorite piece of apparatus for a sequence. Create a sequence of four balances and four different ways to travel on that apparatus. Select different combinations of body parts as your bases of support, and be creative in your ways to travel on the apparatus. Don't forget different levels and directions as you create your sequence.

Portfolio. Sequences provide a good opportunity for portfolio use. Have students record their sequences on paper using stick-figure drawings and writing; place the sequences in their portfolios. Make sure you let students know that you will return to this work later in the year, possibly when you work on approaches and dismounts from apparatus.

These children transfer floor skills to apparatus by practicing nonsymmetrical balances on equipment.

Figure 22.10 Noninverted, hands-only balances on apparatus.

Maintaining stillness while balancing on different body parts is important before balancing on equipment.

⚠️ Permit the children to attempt balances on apparatus only after they can safely hold the balances for 3 to 5 seconds on the floor or mats.

Traveling on Large Apparatus

Setting: Large apparatus—benches, tables, beams, commercial gymnastics equipment—arranged in open space

Cues	
Eyes Forward	(Focus on a spot on the wall or the end of the beam, keeping your head up for good balance.)
Extensions	(Extend your arms for good balance as you travel.)

Tasks/Challenges:

T Travel forward and backward on the large apparatus. **Focus your eyes on something stationary to help maintain your balance as you travel.**

T Sometimes travel with your center of gravity close to the apparatus—that is, lower your hips. Sometimes travel with your center of gravity high—for example, walk on your tiptoes with your body stretched toward the ceiling.

T Walk forward the length of the beam or bench; make a half turn and walk forward again. The secret to the turn is to take your weight on the balls of your feet and then pivot and quickly drop your heels so they make contact with the beam.

T Practice turning both clockwise and counterclockwise while traveling forward and backward.

T Walk to the center of the apparatus, and lower your hips into a squat position. Execute your turn in this low-level position.

Traveling While Balanced

Setting: Large apparatus—benches, tables, beams, commercial gymnastics equipment—arranged in open space

Cues	
Eyes Forward	(Remember to focus your eyes on something stationary when you travel.)
Extensions	(Extend your arms for good balance when doing your locomotors.)

Tasks/Challenges:

T Travel on the apparatus using a series of gallops, hops, or skipping steps. You'll probably want very little height when you perform these skills on the apparatus.

T Travel across the apparatus on four body parts.

T If you are comfortable doing forward rolls on the mats, try rolling slowly forward across the apparatus. **Pretend you are executing the skill in slow motion; tighten your abdominal muscles for control.**

⚠ Students should perform rolling on apparatus only after demonstrating mastery of the rolls on the floor or mats.

C Perform the tasks on each piece of apparatus.

T Add changes in directions and levels to your locomotors on the apparatus.

Balancing Sequence

Setting: Large apparatus—benches, tables, beams, commercial gymnastics equipment—arranged in open space

Cues	
Eyes Forward	(Remember to focus your eyes on something stationary when you travel.)
Smooth Transitions	(Move smoothly between balances and travels.)

Note: Individuals, sometimes classes, may need reminders of earlier cues, for example, Stillness, Extensions, Tight Muscles.

Tasks/Challenges:

T Remember those balances you created on apparatus earlier in the year. You recorded them on paper and placed them in your portfolios. We are now going to revisit that lesson to create a sequence of traveling and balancing on your favorite piece of apparatus. Your task will be to design a sequence of traveling and balancing on one piece of equipment. You will choose either sequence A or sequence B.

Sequence A: Create a sequence of traveling combined with balancing on different bases of support. Your sequence must contain three balances with different bases and at least two travels.

Sequence B: Create a sequence of traveling combined with balancing in the basic body shapes. Your sequence must contain the four basic shapes—wide, narrow, curled, twisted—and at least three travels.

Practice your sequence on the floor and then on the apparatus. When you have the sequence memorized, let a friend watch it to see if:

1. The bases of support are clear.
2. The balances are stationary.
3. The travels are smooth.

T You have refined your sequence nicely, with a friend giving pointers. Now we need to add the beginning shape and the ending of the sequence. Begin your sequence on the apparatus positioned in what you wish to be your starting shape. The beginning shape you choose will be determined by your first action: travel or balance. Think of the level you need, and the direction, as well as the shape.

T Now that you have a beginning shape, let's focus on the ending of your sequence. Earlier in the year we studied jumping and landing—jumping for height and landing safely. We will review those skills and then you can select the type of jump/land action with which you want to end your sequence. *Review jumping off apparatus (Chapter 21) with the children, emphasizing safe landings and body shapes in the air.*

C On the assignment table you will find the forms for sequence A or B. The paper is divided into four parts: beginning shape, travel and balances, dismount, and ending shape. Using stick figures to represent your balances, write/draw your sequence, remembering the number of balances needed for the sequence. When you can repeat the sequence without referring to your paper, ask a friend to watch it. After the friend watches your "dress rehearsal," come to me for your final assessment.

✓ *Event Task.* The above task can easily become an event task assessment of children's work. *Specifics for development of criteria and rubrics can be found in Chapter 14, "Assessing Student Learning."*

Balancing on Stilts

Setting: Several stations in general space at which children can experience/practice dynamic balance; tin-can stilts (see Figure 22.11 for instructions for making them) at some of the stations; wooden stilts (see Figure 22.12) at others; marker cones placed around the general space

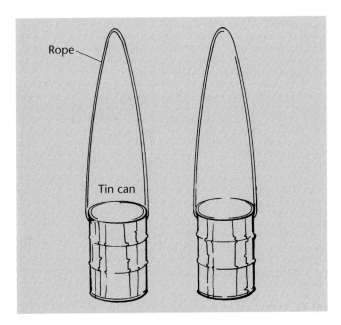

Figure 22.11 Construction of tin-can stilts from discarded rope and large cans from the school cafeteria. To create, (1) Cut two holes in the top sides of the cans and (2) string rope through the holes and tie it together inside each can. To use the stilts, children put each foot on a can and pull on the rope with their hands.

Cue

Heads Up (Eyes focused forward, shoulders erect.)

Children first experiencing this type of dynamic balance can develop confidence on tin-can stilts before progressing to regular stilts.

T Walk forward on the tin-can stilts. You'll have to take smaller steps than you would when walking normally.

T Walk backward.

T Walk around the marker cones.

T After you've mastered walking on the tin-can stilts, you're ready for the higher wooden stilts. It's easier to mount the stilts from an elevated position, such as from a step or chair.

T Walk forward, backward, and sideways.

T Walk around the marker cones.

T Shift your weight to one stilt; lift your other leg, and swing it around.

Balance Boards

Setting: Balance boards set up as one of several stations at which children can experience static and dynamic balance

Cues

Heads Up (Eyes focused forward, shoulders erect.)

Extensions (Extend arms to the sides for good balance.)

Tasks/Challenges:

T Remember when we did balances on boards earlier in the year? You practiced balancing on the different boards and learned that a wide base of support—feet shoulder-width apart—created a more stable balance on the boards, as in all balances. Practice your balance skills on the boards. Try to maintain your balance, without partner support, for several seconds.

T When you can stand on the board for 5 seconds without the support of your partner and without losing your balance, you're ready to try the tasks written on the chart:

1. Slowly move your arms above your head. What happens to your center of gravity? *(Right—it moves upward.)*

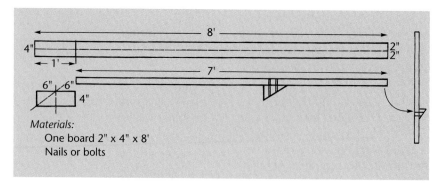

Figure 22.12 Construction of wooden stilts. (Each board makes one set of stilts.)

Directions:

1. Cut 12 inches from one end of the board.
2. Cut the 12-inch board in half.
3. Cut the 6-inch board diagonally in half for the steps.
4. Cut the remaining 7-foot board lengthwise to make two 2-inch by 7-foot poles.
5. Nail or bolt the steps to the poles.

Figure 22.13 Task sheet for balance board activities. Younger children enjoy drawing the smile face for completed tasks; older children can record the date of successful completion.

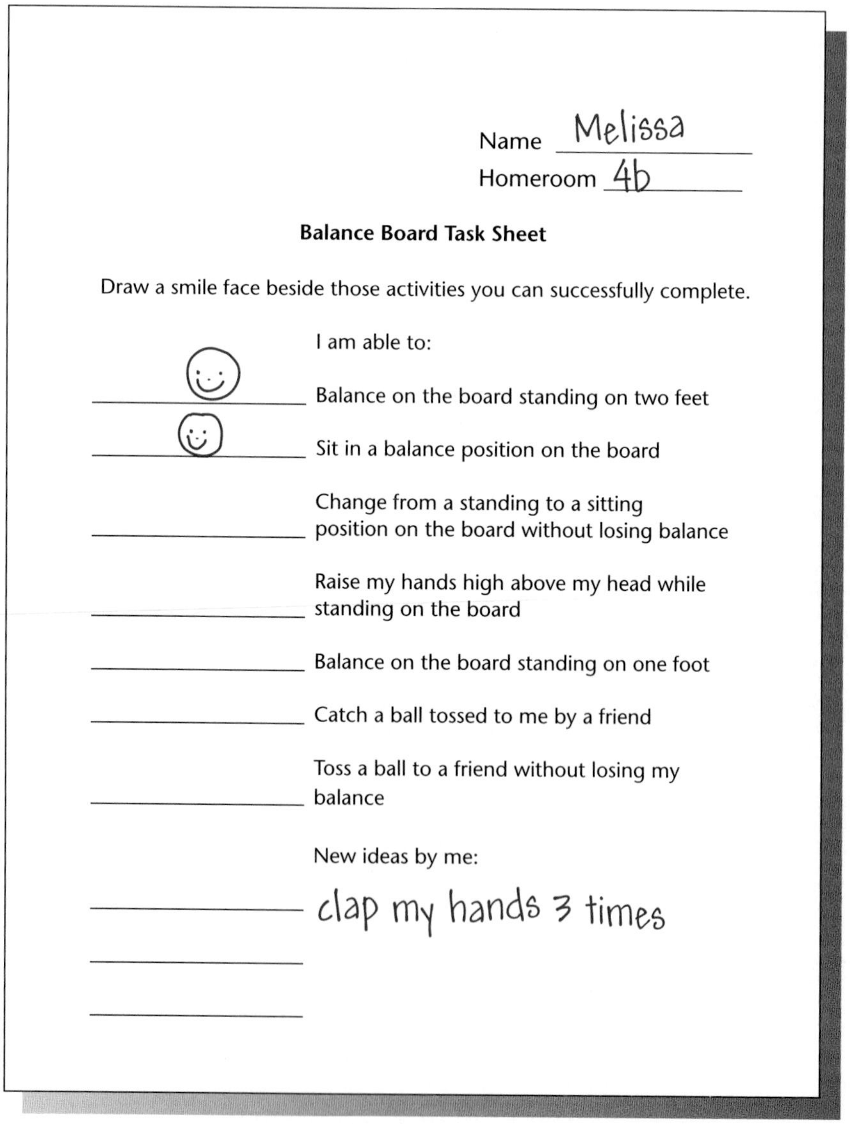

Name Melissa

Homeroom 4b

Balance Board Task Sheet

Draw a smile face beside those activities you can successfully complete.

I am able to:

☺ _____ Balance on the board standing on two feet

☺ _____ Sit in a balance position on the board

_____ Change from a standing to a sitting position on the board without losing balance

_____ Raise my hands high above my head while standing on the board

_____ Balance on the board standing on one foot

_____ Catch a ball tossed to me by a friend

_____ Toss a ball to a friend without losing my balance

New ideas by me:

_____ clap my hands 3 times

_____

_____

2. Slowly move from a standing to a squat or low curl position. Which is more stable? Why is the low position more stable? *(When working on large apparatus, remember that we're better balanced when the center of gravity is low.)*

3. Catch a ball thrown by your partner; toss the ball to your partner.

Write additional tasks on flip charts or task cards near the balance board. Balance board activities can also be recorded on a task sheet (see Figure 22.13).

Utilization Level: Learning Experiences Leading to Skill Development

Learning experiences at the utilization level combine balancing and transferring weight for a contrast in stillness and action. Experiences include balancing in dynamic environments and transferring weight into stationary, still balances on various bases of support, as well as approaches to and dismounts from apparatus. Tasks that involve sequences of movement, on the floor and on apparatus, are particularly important and valuable. Children make decisions about the combination of movements and select and invent ways for one balance or action to move smoothly into another.

A note about cues: Although several cues are listed for many of the learning experiences, it's important to focus on only one cue at a time. That way, the children can really concentrate on that cue. Once you provide feedback to the children and observe that most have learned a cue, then it's time to focus on another one.

Balancing on Crates

Setting: Milk crates and boxes (stuffed with newspaper or computer packing materials and taped closed so they will support a child's weight) positioned throughout general space, with sufficient room between for children to work safely

Cues	
Tight Muscles	(Muscular tension is the key to holding the balance.)
Extensions	(Extend free body parts for balance/counterbalance.)
Alignment	(Position yourself over your base of support or extend free body parts for counterbalance.)

Tasks/Challenges:

🅣 In our previous work on balance, you explored balancing on different bases of support and in different shapes. You practiced holding balances stationary while performing them on mats, on low equipment, and on large apparatus. Review your balances on different bases of support on the crate or box. Many of the balances that were easy for you to perform on the mat or the low equipment will be more difficult on the crate or box because of the added height and the size of the surface.

🅣 Create a series of balances without ever leaving the surface of the crate or box. Transferring from one balance to the next will now be a major part of the sequence.

🅣 Create a sequence of balances on your crate or box that includes an approach to the crate, a transfer onto the crate, a series of balances on the crate, and a dismount from the crate. You may choose to focus on either bases of support or different shapes.

Select tasks from Chapter 23, "Transferring Weight and Rolling," for a review of approaches to and dismounts from low equipment.

🅣 Select a partner to work with for a sequence on the crates. Explore matching symmetrical and non-symmetrical balances on the crates or boxes. You may choose to work side by side matching shapes or face to face to mirror shapes.

🅒 Design a partner sequence of symmetrical and non-symmetrical balances on the crate or box. Your sequence must contain the following:

1. Three symmetrical and two nonsymmetrical balances.
2. A minimum of three different bases of support.
3. An approach to the crates or boxes and a dismount.

Your sequence should represent a double image. Not only will your balances match those of your partner, but also the transitions between will be the same action and the same speed.

🅥 *Videotape.* The children's sequences provide an excellent means of assessing their gymnastics skills. A possible idea is to have partners videotape their completed sequence. Both partners can then evaluate the sequence using the guidelines discussed in class. After the initial evaluation, children may make changes in the sequence. *Refer to Chapter 14, "Assessing Student Learning," for examples of videotape analysis and assessment.*

These youngsters are challenged to create matching nonsymmetrical balances.

Extensions provide aesthetic appeal as well as good balances.

Moving out of and into Balances by Stretching, Curling, and Twisting

Setting: Sufficient mats for children to work safely without bumping others as they practice

Cues	
Line of Gravity	(Extending beyond your line of gravity will make you lose your balance unless you have an extension for counterbalance.)
Smooth Transitions	(Move smoothly through the transition from balance to balance.)

Tasks/Challenges:

Ⓣ Balance on a very narrow base of support. Stretch your free body parts in one direction away from the base. When you begin to lose your balance, you have moved just beyond the "line of gravity." At the moment of moving beyond the line of gravity—of moving off balance—transfer your weight to a new base of support.

Ⓣ Balance on one foot. Stretch forward until you are off balance; transfer your weight to your hands and feet in a new balance.

Ⓣ Balance on favorite bases of support. Extend free body parts with a stretching action to move into a new balance.

Ⓣ Balance on your head and hands with knees on elbows as in a three-point stand or tripod. Push with your hands, tuck your head, and curl your back to roll out of the balance. Make a new stationary balance after the rolling action.

Ⓣ Explore curling your spine to roll out of different balances until you find three balances that you can use the curling action to get out of and into a new balance.

Ⓣ Balance on the base of your spine only, as in a V-seat. After you have held the balance very still, twist your trunk until the action moves you off balance and into a new balance with a different base of support.

Ⓣ Balance on two hands and one foot, with the free leg extended. Twist your trunk and the free leg until you transfer to a new balance on hands and feet.

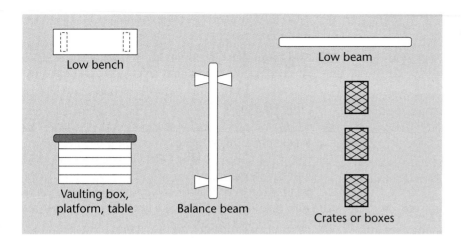

Figure 22.14 Low equipment for inverted balances.

Low bench

Low beam

Vaulting box, platform, table

Balance beam

Crates or boxes

(C) Practice balances with different bases of support and moving out of the balance by either stretching, curling, or twisting. When you are comfortable with one of each, put them together in a sequence as follows: balance, stretching action into new balance, curling action into new balance, twisting action into new balance. Your sequence will include four stationary balances and three transitions.

Additional balances with stretching, curling, and twisting actions can be found in Chapter 23, "Transferring Weight and Rolling."

Traveling into and out of Balances by Rolling

Setting: Sufficient mats for children to balance and roll without bumping into others as they practice

Cues	
Stillness and Action	(Remember to hold your balance perfectly still for 3 seconds, then move smoothly through the rolling action.)
Rounded Body	(Keep your back round and your chin tucked for a good roll.)

Tasks/Challenges:

(T) Rock backward into a shoulder stand; hold the balance for 3 seconds, and then roll either forward or backward.

Children functioning at the utilization level in balancing should also have mastered rolling forward and backward.

(T) Balance in a headstand for 3 seconds; then, press with your hands, and roll forward.

(T) Balance with your weight on your hands, slowly lower yourself to the mat, and roll forward. **Remember to tuck your chin and curl your back.**

(T) Transfer your weight from your feet to your hands; pause in the handstand; then make a quarter turn, and transfer your weight back to your feet.

Performing Inverted Balances on Equipment

Setting: Boxes or crates, benches, and/or low tables arranged for balancing, with sufficient mats around them for children to work safely

Cues	
Tight Muscles	(Remember to tighten the abdominal muscles plus free body parts for stillness in your balances.)
Alignment	(Position yourself over your base of support or extend free body parts for counterbalance.)

Tasks/Challenges:

(T) Balancing in an inverted position on a piece of apparatus is quite different from balancing on the mats or the floor. The position of your hands is often quite different, and the surface is much smaller. Perform the balances until you are quite comfortable and skilled with them on the low equipment before you attempt them on the higher, more narrow apparatus (Figure 22.14).

(T) Balance on your shoulders, back of your head, and arms. Stretch your legs upward.

(T) Balance on your head and hands in a tripod position.

T Balance on your head and hands with your legs extended toward the ceiling.

T Balance on your hands only in an inverted balance.

T While balanced on your hands only, turn slightly, bringing your feet down to the floor beside the beam, bench, or crate. This is the safety skill you will need when you become overbalanced.

T Perform your inverted balance on the larger pieces of apparatus—vaulting box, balance beam, climbing frames.

⚠ 1. Inverted balances on apparatus should be attempted only after children show mastery of the balances on the floor or mats. Always have a mat area available for children to use to practice before performing their balances on apparatus.

2. Position yourself at the station where children are doing inverted balances; be sure you maintain a visual scan of the entire class.

Performing Sequences That Combine Stationary Balances and Traveling on Mats

Setting: A floor gymnastics area designed using available mats

Cues	
Stillness in Balances	(Tighten the muscles to hold the balance very still.)
Smooth Transitions	(Make transitions between balances very smooth, whether they're fast or slow.)
Extensions	(Extend free body parts for aesthetic appeal as well as good balance.)
Alignment	(Position yourself over your base of support or extend free body parts for counterbalance.)

Tasks/Challenges:

T Create a sequence that combines stationary balances and travel. As with an Olympic-style gymnastics routine, design your sequence to cover the length of the mat, as well as each corner. Your sequence must include the following:

1. A minimum of six balances, each with a different base of support
2. A minimum of three travels, with a change in direction and level

3. At least two inverted balances
4. A beginning and an ending shape

T Add contracts in time of actions—some fast, some slow—and changes in force—some powerful movements, some delicate—to add interest to your sequence.

C Tomorrow we're going to practice the routines to music. If you like, bring a recording of music from home, or you may select from those we have. You will then practice your routine with the music until you can repeat it three times exactly the same way. *(See Figure 22.15 for an example of a routine.)*

✓ Gymnastics routines are excellent projects for assessment of children's gymnastic skills and their understanding of the critical cues. *Refer to Chapter 14, "Assessing Student Learning," for guidelines for developing criteria and rubrics.*

Proficiency Level: Learning Experiences Leading to Skill Development

At the proficiency level, balance is studied on the floor and on various pieces of apparatus in combination with movement concepts to express contrast in power, stillness, and excitement in sequences. Children are encouraged to perfect the flow of their movements from one position to another and to develop their use of focus and full extension.

Although often not readily available, such activities as unicycling, skating, skiing, and surfing are challenging dynamic balancing experiences for children at the proficiency level. Sometimes these experiences can be provided during field trips or after-school programs.

A note about cues: At the proficiency level, tasks are more complex, typically requiring children to coordinate several movements simultaneously in a dynamic context. A list of cues is provided to assist the children in being more successful in the learning experience. The challenge for the teacher is in determining which cue will be most beneficial for each child . . . and when. Thus, careful observation and critical reflection become very important as you watch the children move and then decide which cue will be the most helpful to move each learner to a higher skill level.

Balancing While Supporting the Weight of a Partner

Setting: Sufficient mats for children to work safely without bumping others

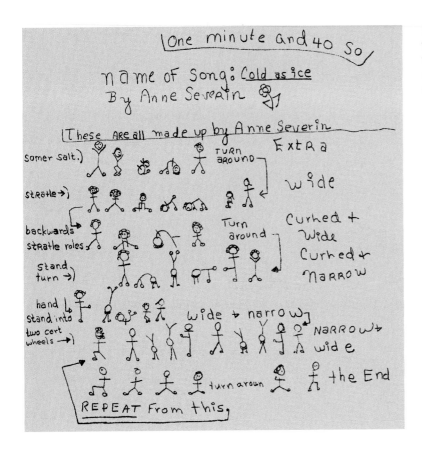

Figure 22.15 Child's sequence to music, showing use of rolling; weight transfer; balance; and concepts of narrow, wide, curled, and directions.

Cues

Wide Base (A wide base of support provides greater stability.)

Extensions (Extensions beyond the line of gravity require extensions in the opposite direction for counterbalance.)

Tasks/Challenges:

T Working with your partner, create a balance that shows one wide and one narrow shape. You and your partner must be helping each other by partially supporting the other's weight.

T Create different balances with your partner in which you are partially supporting each other's weight. If you are not the same weight, which of you will be the supporting partner?

T Create a balance in which the base partner is supporting the weight of the top partner, who is in an inverted position.

⚠ *Base partner.* Your bases of support—for example, your arms and legs—should be no farther apart than the width of your hips and shoulders. *Top partner:* Make sure you put your weight over your

partner's arms and hips, never in the middle of the back, which is unsupported.

C Create two new balances supporting your partner's weight (Figure 22.16). You will need to make decisions based on the weight of both partners: Will you partially support each other, or will one of you totally support the other? Draw your two balances on a sheet of paper and post them at the partner balance center.

The combination of partner/group balancing, tumbling, and dance has evolved into an activity called Acrosport. Groups perform routines of supportive dynamic and static balances connected by tension balance positions.

Balancing on Hanging Ropes

Setting: Hanging ropes with sufficient mats below for children to work safely

Cue

Tight Muscles (Tighten your muscles to support body weight and maintain balance on ropes.)

Figure 22.16 Student-created balances supporting a partner.

Tasks/Challenges:

- On a hanging rope, support your weight with both hands, then your hands and your legs, and finally one hand. Create each of the basic shapes—wide, narrow, curled, twisted—with your free body parts (Figure 22.17). Perform your balances on the hanging ropes with your head upward.

- Create a series of symmetrical and nonsymmetrical shapes while supporting your weight on the rope.

- ⚠ Permit inverted balances on the hanging ropes at low height and only for children with sufficient upper arm/shoulder strength.

Transferring off Equipment with Weight on Hands

Setting: Gymnastics apparatus positioned throughout general space, with sufficient mats for children to work safely

Cues	
Alignment	(Feet over hips, over shoulders, over hands for a straight-line weight on hands.)
Tight Muscles	(Muscular tension is the key to holding the balance.)

Tasks/Challenges:

- Balance momentarily on your hands on the apparatus, make a quarter turn, and transfer your weight from your hands to your feet on the mat. **Remember the cues for safety as you land.**

- Practice this skill on the floor and on the low apparatus to be sure you can turn to the right or to the left.

- ⚠ Be sure students have mastered this skill on the floor or mats and on low apparatus before they attempt it on higher, narrower apparatus.

Performing Apparatus Sequences That Combine Stationary Balances and Traveling with Movement Concepts

Setting: Gymnastics apparatus positioned throughout general space, with sufficient mats and spacing for children to work safely

Cues	
Individual cues as needed	

Figure 22.17 Head-up balances on hanging ropes.

This student creates a symmetrical balance on a hanging rope.

Tasks/Challenges:

T Select a piece of equipment that will be your choice for your final gymnastics project. Your assignment will be the design of a sequence combining stationary balances and travel in relation to that piece of apparatus. The sequence must include the following:

1. An approach to the apparatus and a mount onto the apparatus
2. A series of stationary balances and travels on the apparatus
3. A dismount from the apparatus

You can add excitement and interest to your sequence with:

1. Contrasts in fast and slow actions
2. Turning, twisting, curling actions
3. Changes in levels and directions
4. Combinations of slow, controlled movements and quick, sharp movements
5. Inverted balances and actions

Practice your sequence as if you were preparing for the Olympics. When you have completed and timed it with your music, show it to a friend and then to me. We will videotape the sequence for inclusion in your portfolio.

Ⓣ Select a grouping of three to four pieces of gymnastics apparatus for your final project. Design a sequence that combines stationary balances and travel in relation to each piece of apparatus, as well as travel between the pieces of apparatus. The sequence must include the following:

1. An approach to the first pieces of apparatus and a mount onto the apparatus
2. A series of stationary balances and travels on the apparatus
3. A dismount from the apparatus
4. Travel to the next piece of apparatus
5. A series of balances and travels on that apparatus
6. A repeat of steps 4 and 5 until you have visited each of the three (or four) pieces of apparatus in the grouping
7. A dismount and ending shape

Remember, excitement and interest are added to your sequence with changes and contrasts in movement concepts. *(See listing above.)* Also, grouping the apparatus and traveling between them frees the inner spirit for creativity, as dance and gymnastics are combined for your final project.

Ⓙ ***Portfolio.*** *It is good to provide portfolio opportunities as an option for students. As an example, you might tell students the following:* Practice your sequence as if you were preparing for a gymnastics competition or a recital. When you have completed and timed it with your music, show it to a friend and then to me. If you wish, we will then videotape the sequence for inclusion in your portfolio as your self-expression in gymnastics. *Refer to Chapter 14, "Assessing Student Learning," for the use of portfolios for assessment in physical education.*

Reading Comprehension Questions

1. In your own words, define *balancing*. Be sure to include the meanings of *base of support* and *center of gravity*.
2. Draw or diagram (stick figures are best) the three key teaching concepts that are emphasized in providing balance experiences.
3. What is the difference between a static balance and a dynamic balance?
4. What are the characteristics of balancing for each of the skill levels? For example, what does a precontrol-level balance look like?
5. List three concepts or skills typically used as subthemes with balance.
6. Why are muscular tension, counterbalance, and alignment of body parts important in the teaching of gymnastics for children?
7. List five different pieces of equipment that children can use to practice balancing. Include a task you might use with each piece of equipment.
8. Educational gymnastics does not require Olympic-style apparatus. List or diagram four pieces of non-Olympic gymnastics equipment that can be used for balancing. List three tasks for your balance study on the equipment.
9. What does *inverted balance* mean?
10. Why are jumping and landing studied in conjunction with balances on apparatus?
11. How is transfer of weight typically combined with balancing to present challenging tasks to children at the utilization and proficiency levels?

References

National Association for Sport and Physical Education. (1995). *Moving into the future: National standards for physical education.* St. Louis, MO: Mosby.

National Association for Sport and Physical Education. (2004). *Moving into the future: National standards for physical education.* (2nd ed.). Reston, VA: National Association for Sport and Physical Education.

Transferring Weight and Rolling

To travel—walking, running, leaping, rolling, stepping, springing, sliding—is to transfer weight on hands, on feet, on different body parts. The infant creeping on trunk and elbows is transferring weight, as is the toddler shifting weight from side to side during the beginning phase of walking unassisted, the gymnast performing a walkover, the Russian dancer executing a series of rapid mule kicks, the athlete poised to shift her weight to fake an opponent, and the dancer collapsing to the floor in an expression of grace and control. Locomotion is transfer of weight.

Probably the most common form of weight transfer is from foot to foot. In its simplest form, this is walking. At an advanced level—and when combined with the stretching, curling, and twisting actions of layouts and with full body twists—it demands extraordinary kinesthetic awareness, muscular strength, and control. See Box 23-1 for information on weight transfer from the *National Standards for Physical Education.*

Levels of Skill Proficiency in Transferring Weight

Children at the precontrol level are still trying to achieve control of their bodies when they transfer weight to different body parts. They enjoy traveling on body parts other than their feet, and they enjoy exploring apparatus. Activities at the precontrol level include:

1. Traveling on specific body parts (such as feet and seat or hands and feet)
2. Transferring weight by sliding, slithering, or creeping

Children at the control level are ready to transfer their weight onto specific body parts, such as the back for rolling actions and the hands for inverted balances and travel. Activities at the control level focus on:

1. Stretching, curling, and twisting into transfers
2. Transferring weight following step-and-spring takeoffs
3. Transferring weight onto and off equipment using different body parts
4. Transferring weight from feet to hands

Children at the utilization level are ready to transfer their weight onto their hands for travel and balances, for spring takeoffs, and for walkovers. At this level, weight is also transferred by rolling. At the utilization level, the child tries movements that combine the transfers onto specific body parts with stretching and twisting. Challenging activities include:

1. Vaulting over apparatus
2. Mounting apparatus by using inverted positions
3. Traveling on apparatus with curling actions

Children proficient in transferring weight enjoy the transfer from feet to feet with aerial actions between the contacts. They combine stretching, curling, and twisting with flight onto, off, and over apparatus. Proficiency-level weight transference includes many Olympic-style stunts and specific gymnastics apparatus. These tasks are best taught by trained coaches in club gymnastics.

The progression in gymnastics is from mats on the floor to low apparatus with a large surface to higher apparatus with a narrow surface. Our progression spiral (page 401) presents the full spectrum of weight transfer, from the precontrol level to the proficiency level. Alternative ways of further developing the ideas are discussed in Chapter 13.

Box 23-1

The Skill of Transferring Weight in the *National Standards for Physical Education*

The movement skill of transferring weight is referenced in the *National Standards for Physical Education* in (National Association for Sport and Physical Education, 2004) under Standard 1: Demonstrates competency in motor skills and movement patterns needed to perform a variety of physical activities.

Sample performance outcomes from the *National Standards* include:

- Develops and refines a gymnastics sequence demonstrating smooth transitions (3–5)*
- Designs and performs gymnastics sequences that combine traveling, rolling, balancing, and weight transfer into smooth, flowing sequences with intentional changes in direction, speed, and flow (6–8)*

*Grade-level guidelines for expected student learning.

Precontrol Level: Activities for Exploration of Weight Transfer

Tasks at the precontrol level are designed for the exploration of transferring weight to different body parts. Through this exploration children will begin to develop an awareness of the body parts best suited for weight transfer.

Locomotor Actions

Setting: Children scattered throughout general space

Tasks/Challenges:

ⓣ All locomotor movements are actions of transferring weight. When you walk, hop, skip, or gallop, you transfer your weight from foot to foot. Let's review some of the locomotor movements. Travel throughout general space with a skip or gallop.

ⓣ Travel with a jump—two feet to two feet.

ⓣ Hop on one foot. Do you transfer weight to different body parts when you hop? No, you move on one foot only.

Additional exploration:

ⓣ Travel and jump high in the air like a basketball player.

ⓣ Travel and jump over a brook; a large, flat rock; a puddle. This jump is sometimes called a leap—taking off on one foot and landing on the other.

ⓣ Explore other ways to travel throughout general space, transferring weight from foot to foot; twirl, spin, slide . . .

ⓣ Explore traveling on body parts other than your feet: slither, crawl, walk like a crab . . .

ⓜ When you skip, you transfer weight from what body part to what body part? When you jump, you transfer from what to what? What is the difference between a jump and a hop?

Transferring Weight from Feet to Back

Setting: Individual mats and/or carpet squares throughout general space, with sufficient room between for children to work safely

Tasks/Challenges:

ⓣ Squat on your feet with your back rounded like an egg. Transfer your weight from your feet to your back with a rocking action.

ⓣ Transfer your weight from your feet to your rounded back, and return to your feet with the rocking action.

ⓣ Give the rocking action a little extra effort, transferring your weight from feet to rounded back, to feet, and then returning to a standing position.

Transferring Weight from Feet to Hands

Setting: Large gymnastics mats and/or small mats that will not slide as children transfer weight, scattered throughout general space

Tasks/Challenges:

(T) Transfer your weight from your feet to your hands to your feet, momentarily taking your weight on your hands only.

Wedge mats or folded or rolled mats may be easier for children just beginning to take weight on their hands and/or for those uncomfortable with transfer from standing position to mat on floor.

Transferring Weight onto and off Equipment

Setting: Low gymnastics equipment—benches, tables, balance beams, and so on—scattered throughout general space

Tasks/Challenges:

The focus for exploration of equipment at the precontrol level is safety—getting on and off equipment with personal safety and without creating an unsafe situation for others.

Control Level: Learning Experiences Leading to Skill Development in Weight Transfer

Tasks at the control level are designed to help children transfer their weight to specific body parts—feet to back, to hands, to head and hands—as they travel and/or balance. For children to maintain control of their bodies during weight transfer is the goal at this level.

A note about cues: Although several cues are listed for many of the learning experiences, it's important to focus on only one cue at a time. That way, the children can really concentrate on that cue. Once you provide feedback to the children and observe that most have learned a cue, then it's time to focus on another one.

Transferring Weight to Hands Across Mats

Setting: Small mats (carpet squares or ropes stretched on the floor) scattered throughout general space with sufficient room between for children to work safely

Cues	
Strong Muscles	(Strong arms and shoulders—no collapse.)
Stretch Your Legs	(Extend your legs upward—stretch to the sky.)

Tasks/Challenges:

(T) When we were exploring transferring weight, you practiced taking your weight on your hands and bringing your feet to the floor at the same place. Practice taking your weight on your hands and bringing your feet down safely at a new place—to the right or the left of their original place.

(T) Now you are going to transfer your weight from your feet to your hands to travel across your mat or rope. Begin at one end of your mat (carpet square or rope), transfer your weight to your hands, and bring your feet down on the other side. You will travel across your mat by transferring your weight to your hands and back to your feet.

You may want to begin in a squat position with your feet on the floor and your hands on the other side of the rope or carpet square, or relatively close to your feet on the mat. Transfer your weight to your hands and bring your feet down a short distance away—just over the rope or carpet square.

(C) When you are comfortable taking your weight on your hands a longer time and you are landing safely, kick your legs higher in the air to remain on your hands even longer. **Stretch your legs as you kick them higher.**

(T) Stand at the side of your mat (square, rope) in a front-back stance. Extend your arms upward. Step forward with your lead foot, and transfer your weight to your hands. Bring your feet to the floor on the opposite side of your mat (square, rope). If you stretch your trunk and legs as you transfer your weight to one hand and then the other, you will begin to do a cartwheel.

Transferring Weight from Feet to Back

Setting: Small mats and/or carpet squares scattered throughout general space

Cues	
Rounded Back	(Keep your back rounded, body curled for a good roll.)
Push with Your Hands	(Remember to push with your hands so your head does not get stuck when you roll.)

Tasks/Challenges:

T Remember when you did the rocking action by transferring your weight from your feet to your rounded back? We are going to use that action now for a roll. Transfer your weight from your feet to your rounded back. As you rock back to your shoulders, push with your hands to roll backward across the mat. Remember to push hard with your hands so your neck doesn't get stuck.

If this is the children's first experience with rolling, follow the teaching progression for rolling in the second half of this chapter. If this is a revisitation, review the progression carefully with the children.

✿ Rolling backward is a weight-transfer skill. What body part do you transfer *to* in a backward roll? Feet to what?

T Think of the forward roll. When you do a forward roll, you transfer your weight from your feet to what? What is *the* critical cue for rolling? Now travel across your mat, transferring your weight, as in a forward roll.

✓ *Peer Observation.* After successfully completing transfers of weight with a forward or a backward roll, maintaining a rounded back, a friend could then observe the roll. That person should then record the date and initial the roll on a gymnastics check list in children's portfolios. *Refer to Chapter 14, "Assessing Student Learning," for more on the use of peer observation for assessment in physical education.*

⚠ Forward and backward rolls should always be optional for children; insisting that students perform specific rolls can result in serious neck injuries.

Transferring Weight from Feet to Combinations of Body Parts

Setting: Small mats and/or carpet squares scattered throughout general space, with sufficient room between for children to safely transfer weight

Cues	
Strong Muscles	(Strong arms and shoulders for the transfer to hands—no collapse.)
Rounded Back	(Curl your back and body for all rolling skills.)

Stretch Your Legs (Extend your legs upward, as if there is a string attached pulling your legs to the sky.)

Tasks/Challenges:

T Transfer your weight from your feet to other combinations of body parts as you travel across your mat or carpet square. Always return to your feet *(Figure 23.1).*

Stretching, Curling, and Twisting into Transfers

Setting: Small mats and/or carpet squares scattered throughout general space

Cues	
Smooth Transitions	(Move smoothly through the transition from balance to off balance to balance.)
Tight Muscles	(Tighten your abdominal muscles as you transfer weight, for control of the action.)

Tasks/Challenges:

T Balance on one foot. Bend at the waist, extending your arms forward and your free leg backward. Stretch your arms forward until you are off balance; then transfer your weight to your hands and next to your curled back to roll forward out of the balance.

⚠ Children should demonstrate a mastery of rolling forward with a rounded back before they attempt this task.

T Balance on your knees and one hand. Extend your free arm under your body, twisting your trunk until your weight transfers to your shoulder and new bases of support. Twist gently into the new balance.

T Balance in a shoulder stand with your weight on your shoulders, upper arms, and head, stretching your legs toward the ceiling. Twist your legs and trunk, bringing your feet to the mat behind you in a new balance.

T Balance on your chosen base of support. Twist until you are momentarily off balance; transfer your weight onto a new base of support.

Figure 23.1 Transfer of weight from feet to other body parts.

🅣 Balance on your chosen base again. Use different stretching, curling, and twisting actions to transfer onto new bases of support.

Performing Spring/Step Takeoffs

Before practicing spring and step takeoffs in weight transfer, children should be at the control level of jumping and landing (Chapter 21).

Setting: Large gymnastics mats throughout general space

Cues	
Heads Up	(Keep your head and shoulders erect for a balanced landing.)
Soft Landings	(Bend your knees on landing to absorb the force.)

Tasks/Challenges:

🅣 Approach your gymnastics mat from a distance of 10 to 12 feet. Just before you reach the mat, use a two-foot takeoff to spring high in the air; land softly in the center of the mat. The *spring takeoff* in gymnastics is very similar to the approach on the diving board.

The spring takeoff is used for gymnastics skills requiring power—e.g., mounts onto beams and parallel bars, handsprings, and vaulting. It is a jump for height; that is why the arms are extended upward. It is also the takeoff used for a basketball jump ball or rebound.

🅣 Approach the mat, spring off your two feet, make a quarter turn, and land in a balanced position. Now try the turn in the opposite direction.

🅣 When you are comfortable with the quarter turn, try a half turn. Remember to practice both clockwise and counterclockwise turns.

(T) Approach the mat from the distance of 10 to 12 feet. Using a *step takeoff,* land on your two feet in the center of the mat.

The step takeoff is the takeoff used for gymnastics skills requiring slow control. Who can give some examples of those? Right, walkovers and cartwheels. It is also the take-off needed for a layup in basketball.

Performing Spring/Step Takeoffs onto Crates and/or Benches

Setting: Milk crates positioned against large gymnastics mats

(A) Place the crates against mats to prevent them from sliding.

> **Cues**
>
> **Heads Up** (Keep your head and shoulders erect for a balanced landing.)
> **Easy On** (Slowly absorb weight on crate—with control.)

Tasks/Challenges:

(T) Approach the crate or bench from a distance of 10 to 15 feet. Using either a spring or a step takeoff, land in a balanced position on the crate.

(C) Practice each takeoff until you can transfer your weight onto the crate or bench in a balanced position three times.

(T) Approach the crate or bench, use a spring takeoff, and transfer your weight to your feet and hands on the crate or bench. **Remember to take your weight momentarily on your hands and then softly lower your body to the crate or bench.**

(T) Approach the crate or bench, use a step takeoff, and transfer your weight momentarily to your hands only on the crate or bench. **Remember, strong arms for weight on hands.**

Transferring Off Low Apparatus (Bench, Crate, or Low Table)

Setting: Benches, crates, and/or low tables surrounded by mats and positioned throughout general space

> **Cues**
>
> **Rounded Back** (Keep your back rounded, body curled with chin tucked for a good roll.)
> **Soft Landings** (Bend your knees on landing to absorb the force.)

Tasks/Challenges:

(T) Transfer your weight off the bench or crate by assuming a kneeling position, placing your hands on the mat, slowly lowering your weight to the mat, and rolling forward.

(A) Transferring off apparatus by rolling should be introduced only after children have mastered rolling on the floor or mats.

(T) Transfer your weight off the bench or low table with a jump. Make a wide body shape by extending your arms and legs while in the air. Land in a balanced position on two feet on the mat. **Remember to keep your head and shoulders erect as you jump.**

(T) Transfer off the bench or low table with a jump, making curled, narrow, and twisted shapes while in the air, and then each time land in your balanced position.

(T) Transfer off the bench or low table with a jump, turning in the air so that you land facing in a different direction. Remember to twist your shoulders in the direction you wish to turn.

(T) When you are comfortable with a quarter turn, try to execute a half turn in the air so you land facing in a different direction.

Revisit/review "Jumping to Form a Body Shape During Flight," in Chapter 21, for additional tasks. Although specific tasks for transferring weight with large apparatus aren't listed until the utilization level, children at the pre-control and control levels need exploration time on large apparatus to become familiar with the equipment and to gain confidence moving on it.

Making Spring/Step Takeoffs with Sequences

Setting: Benches, crates, and/or low tables surrounded by mats

> **Cues**
>
> **Soft Landings** (Absorb the force; land softly *on* and *off* the equipment.)
> **Smooth Transitions** (Move with control from balance, to transfer, to balance . . .)
> **Rounded Back** (Remember, a curled body with chin tucked for all rolls.)

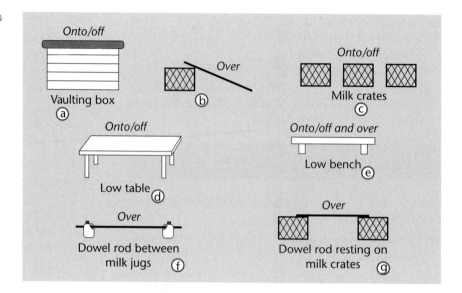

Figure 23.2 Equipment setups for transfer of weight when traveling over low apparatus.

Children should be able to tell you the critical cues for the skills and demonstrate the individual skills before combining skills in sequences.

Tasks/Challenges:

T Approach the bench (crate, table), and use either a step or a spring takeoff to transfer onto it. Decide what body parts are going to serve as your first bases of support before you begin; this will determine whether you use a step or a spring takeoff.

T Create a series of four balances by transferring your weight to different body parts on the bench (crate, table).

Review "Balancing on Different Bases of Support," "Balancing in Different Body Shapes," and "Balancing Symmetrically and Nonsymmetrically" in Chapter 22.

T Transfer off the bench (crate, table) in one of the following ways: (1) jumping and turning, (2) jumping and making a shape while in the air, (3) rolling, or (4) using a transfer that you have created.

A Have the student tell you if the transfer off the low apparatus includes inversion or weight on hands; if so, be sure the student demonstrates mastery on the floor or mats before attempting a transfer off the low apparatus.

Traveling Over Low Apparatus

Setting: Milk crates, benches, low tables, hurdles, and milk-jug/rolled-newspaper or dowel-rod "hurdles" throughout general space (Figure 23.2)

Cues

Strong Muscles (Strong arms and shoulders— no collapse.)

Stretch Your Legs (Extend your legs upward— stretch to the sky.)

Tasks/Challenges:

T Travel over the various pieces of low equipment by transferring your weight from your feet to your hands to your feet. At the hurdles and the newspaper or dowel rods, place your hands on the mat on the other side of the hurdle or rod, and then transfer your weight over, landing on your feet. At the benches and milk crates, place your hands on the equipment, take your weight on your hands only, and land on your feet on the opposite side of the equipment.

T As you become comfortable taking your weight on your hands, kick higher toward the ceiling, stretching your legs and trunk.

Transferring Onto Low Apparatus

Setting: Benches, crates, and/or low tables surrounded by mats in general space

Cues

Strong Muscles (Strong arms and shoulders for transfer onto hands.)

Soft Landings (Absorb the force on feet and/or hands and lower body gently onto apparatus.)

Traveling over, under, and through apparatus builds youngsters' skills transferring weight to a variety of body parts, as well as their comfort with the equipment.

Cues

Strong Muscles (Strong arms and shoulders to take weight on hands.)
Stretch to the Sky (Stretch your trunk and legs upward.)
Alignment (Feet over hips, over shoulders, over hands—in a straight line.)

Tasks/Challenges:

🅣 Transfer your weight from your feet to your hands to your feet, momentarily taking your weight on your hands only. Reach downward, not forward, with your hands. **Stretch your legs toward the ceiling and tighten your stomach muscles to maintain your balance.**

You may want to begin in a squat position with your hands and feet touching the floor. Transfer your weight to your hands by kicking your feet in the air.

Use a step action to transfer your weight to your hands; try to have your shoulders directly over your hands when you kick your legs up.

🅣 When you are comfortable with your feet being just a few inches off the floor, begin to kick your feet higher in the air.

🅒 Practice until you can balance for 3 seconds on your hands. Transfer your weight back to your feet in their original position each time.

🅐 Teach children in the practice stages of taking weight on hands to twist the trunk, doing a quarter turn and bringing feet down to the floor safely, if they begin to overbalance. This prevents falling on the back in the event of an overbalance.

🅙 *Journal.* This is an opportune time to have children record in their journals the date on which they successfully took their weight on their hands for 3 seconds. Have them describe the feeling of "weight on hands." *Refer to Chapter 14, "Assessing Student Learning," for the use of journals in physical education.*

Transferring Weight to Hands by Stepping: Cartwheels

Setting: Large gymnastics mats throughout general space, with sufficient room for children to work safely

Cues

Strong Muscles (Strong arms and shoulders to take weight on hands.)

Tasks/Challenges:

🅣 Use the benches (crates, low tables) to practice transferring your weight onto equipment. Transfer your weight from your feet to your hands on the equipment by springing off your two feet and landing on your hands and feet. Take your weight momentarily on your hands, then softly lower to your feet; don't jump onto the equipment.

🅣 Using your spring takeoff, transfer your weight to your hands and knees on the apparatus. Yes, you still take your weight momentarily on your hands only.

🅣 Use a front-back stance and step into the transfer, momentarily taking your weight on your hands only on the equipment, then lowering your total body onto additional body parts. Be sure your hands are firmly planted on the equipment so you won't slip when you transfer to hands only.

Transferring Weight from Feet to Hands

Setting: Large gymnastics mats scattered throughout general space, with sufficient room between for children to work safely

This child is discovering one of the ways to transfer weight across large apparatus.

| **Stretch** | (Stretch your trunk and legs toward the sky—legs straight.) |

Tasks/Challenges:

🅣 Using a step action, alternate transferring your weight to your feet and to your hands, returning to your feet in a step action, as in a cartwheel. Your weight transfers momentarily from one foot to the other foot, to one hand, to the other hand, to the foot, to the other foot.

🅣 Experiment with beginning the cartwheel by facing the mat or by standing sideways with one shoulder toward the mat. You may choose either starting position.

🅣 As you feel comfortable with the foot-foot-hand-hand-foot-foot transfer, try to make a straight pathway with your feet and hands along the mat.

🅣 Practice leading first with your right and then with your left side so you can do a cartwheel in either direction.

🅒 Practice until you can perform your cartwheel in a straight line three times.

✅ ***Portfolio.*** Achievements in weight transference are exciting for children. When they can perform a cartwheel in a straight line, with legs fully stretched in the air, have a partner assess the skill. Have them record the date on a gymnastics check list in their portfolios. *Refer to Chapter 14, "Assessing Student Learning," for guidelines on assessment.*

🅣 Transfer your weight to your hands, as in the cartwheel. While you are balanced in the inverted position, bring your feet together, twist a half turn, and bring your feet down quickly to face in the opposite direction; this is a roundoff.

Children won't master gymnastics tasks in only one or two 30-minute lessons. A station format plus revisitation (see Chapter 13) provides opportunities for distributed practice of skills.

Utilization Level: Learning Experiences Leading to Skill Development in Weight Transfer

Children at the utilization level of transferring weight learn to transfer their weight to their hands for longer periods of time and in combinations with stretching, curling, and twisting actions. Tasks are designed to teach children to transfer weight onto, over, and off large apparatus. The tasks also emphasize the development of more complex sequences involving weight transference.

A note about cues: Although several cues are listed for many of the learning experiences, it's important to focus on only one cue at a time. That way, the children can really concentrate on that cue. Once you provide feedback to the children and observe that most have learned a cue, then it's time to focus on another one.

Transferring Weight to Hands: Walking

Setting: Large gymnastics mats throughout general space, with sufficient room for children to work safely on transfers

Cues	
Strong Muscles	(Strong arms and shoulders for weight on hands.)
Stretch	(Stretch your trunk and legs toward the sky—legs straight.)
Alignment	(Feet over hips, over shoulders, over hands—in a straight line.)

Tasks/Challenges:

(T) When you are confident and comfortable balancing on your hands for three seconds, try walking on your hands.

(A) Children should attempt walking on their hands only if they have sufficient upper body strength to support weight in the inverted position for several seconds and can move into and out of a balance on their hands only with control.

Transferring Weight to Hands and Twisting

Setting: Large gymnastics mats throughout general space, with sufficient room for children to work safely on transfers

Cues

Strong Muscles (Strong arms and shoulders for weight on hands.)
Stretch (Stretch your trunk and legs toward the sky—legs straight.)
Alignment (Feet over hips, over shoulders, over hands—in a straight line.)

Tasks/Challenges:

(T) Transfer your weight to your hands, twist your body a half turn, and bring your feet to the floor so that you are facing in the opposite direction.

(T) While balanced on your hands, slowly walk on your hands a half turn to face in the opposite direction.

Transferring Weight to Hands and Forming a Bridge

Setting: Large gymnastics mats throughout general space

Cues

Strong Muscles (Strong arms and shoulders for supporting weight on hands.)
Tight Muscles (Tighten the abdominals for control.)
Extend (Stretch from your fingertips to your toes as you transfer from feet to hands to feet.)

Tasks/Challenges:

(T) Using a step action, transfer your weight to your hands with sufficient force to continue the forward motion. Your feet should remain in the steplike stance as they move upward over your hands. Just before your feet contact the floor, bring them

together, and bend your knees slightly. You will then balance in a "bridge" with your feet and hands supporting your weight. Keep your legs in the steplike stance throughout the transfer.

(T) As your feet contact the surface, push with your hands to continue your transfer to a standing position. This transfer without a pause is a walkover.

Transferring Weight onto Large Apparatus

Setting: Large apparatus—benches, tables, vaulting boxes, balance beams, parallel bars, large climbing frames—placed around the gym (*Many transfers at the utilization and proficiency levels of transferring weight are specific to particular pieces of apparatus; the name of the apparatus appears in parentheses following the task title.*)

Cues

Heads Up (Keep your head and shoulders erect as you approach the apparatus.)
Soft Landings (Absorb the force on your feet and/or hands and lower your body slowly to the apparatus.)

Tasks/Challenges:

(T) Transferring weight onto large apparatus in gymnastics usually includes an approach to build momentum, a spring or step takeoff, and the transfer onto the apparatus. Approach the apparatus from about 15 feet. Using a spring takeoff, transfer your weight from your feet on the floor to your feet and hands on the apparatus (box, beam, table). **Remember, you will need a spring takeoff for power and/or height; a step takeoff is a slower way to transfer weight.**

(T) Transfer your weight to your feet and hands with your body curled in a tuck position. (Model.)

(T) Transfer your weight to your feet and hands with legs extended in a straddle position. (Model.)

(T) Transfer your weight to your feet and hands in a "wolf" position: one knee bent, one leg straight (*Figure 23.3*). (Model.)

(T) Approach the apparatus from the sides as well as the front. Practice both spring and step takeoffs to transfer your weight to various body parts on the apparatus. **Remember, you will need a spring takeoff for power and/or height; a step takeoff is a slower way to transfer weight.**

Many of the control-level tasks for transferring weight onto and off low apparatus can be repeated for large apparatus. This is good practice because it enables children to adjust

Figure 23.3 Tuck, wolf, and straddle positions on large apparatus following spring takeoffs.

comfortably to the increased height and narrower surface of large apparatus.

Transferring Weight to Head and Hands on Apparatus (Box, Beam, Table)

Setting: Large apparatus placed throughout general space, with sufficient mats for children to work safely

Cues	
Heads Up	(Keep your head and shoulders erect as you approach the apparatus.)
Strong Muscles	(Strong arm and shoulder muscles to support weight on the apparatus.)
Soft Landings	(Absorb the force on your feet and/or hands and lower your body slowly to the apparatus.)

Tasks/Challenges:

T Approach the apparatus, and use a spring takeoff to transfer your weight to your hands and head on the apparatus. Push hard with your legs on the takeoff for sufficient height and time for the transfer, taking your weight first on your hands only and then gently, with control, on your head and hands.

⚠ Have the children approach the box, beam, or table from the end rather than the side for this transfer to head and hands. This allows sufficient space for rolling across the apparatus if they overbalance.

⚠ Teach the children to roll slowly across the apparatus if they overbalance on the head-and-hands transfer; teach them to transfer weight back to their feet on the floor if they do not have sufficient push to move into the inverted position on the apparatus.

Transferring Weight onto Bars (Parallel Bars, Climbing Frame)

Setting: Large apparatus placed throughout general space, with sufficient mats surrounding for safety

Cues	
Heads Up	(Keep your head and shoulders erect as you approach the apparatus.)
Strong Muscles	(Strong arm and shoulder muscles to support weight on the apparatus.)

Soft Landings	(Absorb the force on your feet and/or hands and lower your body slowly to the apparatus.)

Tasks/Challenges:

Ⓣ Standing under the apparatus, use a spring takeoff to transfer your weight to your hands on a high bar. Hanging on the bar, pull up with your arms as you swing your legs over a lower bar and balance in a sitting position.

Ⓣ Approach the apparatus with a series of steps. Using a spring takeoff, grasp the bar with your hands and jump up. Push really hard with your arms to lift your body above the bar; balance with your hands and upper thighs on the bar. Swing a leg over the bar so you can straddle the bar.

Ⓣ Approach the apparatus with a series of steps. As you step under the bar, grasp the bar with your hands, and kick your rear leg forcefully upward to bring your hips to the bar. Keeping your arms bent and pulling your body close to the bar, assume a pike position by bending at the hips. The momentum of the leg kick will cause your body to circle the bar. Balance on your hands and upper thighs on the bar.

Ⓒ You have now practiced jumping into a hip mount and doing a hip circle with the body in a pike position. Practice these skills until you master them. Then add them to your gymnastics check list in your portfolio.

Ⓣ Approach the apparatus from the back, front, and side; practice both spring and step takeoffs to transfer your weight to various body parts on the apparatus.

Transferring Weight Over Apparatus (Vaulting Box)

Setting: Vaulting boxes, with sufficient mats for safety, in general space

Cues

Heads Up	(Keep your head and shoulders erect as you approach the apparatus.)
Strong Muscles	(Strong arm and shoulder muscles to support weight on the apparatus.)
Soft Landings	(Bend your knees for a controlled landing.)

The ability to transfer weight to travel along low equipment is a prerequisite for transferring weight on large apparatus.

Tasks/Challenges:

Ⓣ Approach the vaulting box with light running steps, keeping your weight on the balls of your feet. Using a spring takeoff, plant your hands firmly on the box, shoulder-width apart. Travel over the vaulting box, landing on your two feet on the mat.

⚠ Position yourself at the vaulting station when children are transferring weight over the apparatus. As a spotter, you should not help the children perform the skill, but you can help prevent serious injury from a fall. Because spotting techniques differ for each skill, you should consult a gymnastics text or certified gymnastics coach before attempting to spot students in specific gymnastics tasks.

Ⓣ Now transfer over the box by placing your hands shoulder-width apart on the apparatus, bringing your legs up between your arms in a tuck or curled position. Pause momentarily on the box in this curled shape; then jump forward to the mat.

(T) Push harder with your hands this time to bring your body into a curled position, and push yourself over the box without pausing in the tuck position on top of the box.

(A) Children should attempt vaulting over the box with a curled, straddle, or wolf vault only after they have mastered transferring onto the apparatus with these techniques.

(T) Transfer over the vaulting box by bringing your feet and legs together, stretched to one side, as you cross over the box. Place your hands shoulder-width apart on the box, and shift your weight to one hand as you swing your legs over the box. Push off from the vaulting box with the supporting hand, landing on two feet with your back to the vaulting box. This is called a flank vault. That spring takeoff we practiced earlier becomes increasingly important as you work on mounts onto and transfers over large apparatus.

(T) Transfer your weight onto the vaulting box in a wide shape by placing your hands shoulder-width apart and stretching your legs to either side of the box, supporting your weight momentarily on your feet and hands. From a standing position on the vaulting box, transfer your weight to your feet by jumping to the mat. You will need a really strong takeoff to gain the height for this transfer.

(T) Transfer your weight over the vaulting box by taking your weight on your hands, shoulder-width apart, and bringing your feet over the box in the stretched, wide shape. Keep your head and shoulders erect to prevent losing your balance. This is called a straddle vault. Do not attempt this vault without the spotter (teacher or qualified adult) at the station.

(A) Always have the children tell you which vault they are attempting and whether they are stopping on top or transferring over before they begin their approach. This allows you to be ready for the proper spotting of that skill.

Transferring Weight Along Apparatus

Setting: Stationary bar, tables and benches of various heights, vaulting boxes, balance beam, a stage

Many of the gymnastics skills learned on the floor and on low equipment can also be performed on large apparatus. Before children try them on a large apparatus, they should review the skills on the floor or mats, then on the low equipment, concentrating on the skill and its critical cues.

This student practices transferring off an apparatus, taking weight on hands.

Transferring Weight by Rolling (Bench, Box, or Table)

Setting: Benches, vaulting boxes, and/or tables of various heights, surrounded by sufficient mats for children to work safely

Cues	
Rounded Back	(Keep your back curled, chin tucked for a good roll.)
Control	(Tight muscles, slow-motion action for control throughout the roll.)

Tasks/Challenges:

(A) Remind children to position themselves at one end of the bench, box, or table to start the roll so that they will have enough surface to complete the rolling action.

(T) Transfer your weight to your feet and hands on the bench, box, or table, with your back curled. Place your thumbs and the sides of your palms on top of the bench or box, with your hands and fingers on the sides of the apparatus. (Although this position is quite different from that used for rolling on mats, it provides a steady grip and constant awareness of the width of the surface.) Tuck your head, and slowly roll forward across the apparatus.

T Transfer your weight to your feet and hands with a curled back. Slowly transfer to your curled back and hands for rolling backward across the bench, box, or table. Extend your hands above your head to hold onto the sides of the box or bench; place your head to one side, and roll backward over one shoulder.

T Roll backward on the apparatus by transferring your weight from your curled back to one bent knee with one leg extended. This backward transfer is often easier when balancing on the small surface.

A Permit students to transfer weight by rolling across the apparatus only after they have demonstrated sustained control of the rolling action on the low apparatus. They should be able to stop the movement at any point in the rolling action.

Transferring Weight from Feet to Hands

Setting: Tape lines on the gym floor, with sufficient space between for children to work safely; low benches surrounded by mats

Cues	
Strong Muscles	(Strong arms and shoulders to take weight on hands.)
Stretch	(Stretch your trunk and legs toward the sky—legs straight.)
Muscular Tension	(Maintain tension through arms, trunk, and legs for full extension—stretched for cartwheels, arched for walkovers.)

Tasks/Challenges:

T Practice a cartwheel on a tape line on the floor until you can do it perfectly three times. Now transfer your weight from your feet to your hands in a cartwheel on the low bench.

Teaching by invitation or intratask variation is very effective when working with transferring weight on apparatus. Permit only those children who are clearly ready to do so to practice inverted weight transference along apparatus.

T Transfer your weight from your feet to your hands, as in a walkover, on the bench.

T Transfer your weight from your feet to your hands, slowly execute a half turn, and bring your feet down on the apparatus surface facing the opposite direction.

A Teach children to push with their hands to move the body away from the bench and to transfer weight to their feet on the floor if they feel off balance or unable to complete the transfer after inverting.

C Create three ways to transfer your weight while moving along the apparatus. Consider changes in levels and directions of travel. Diagram and/or describe your transfers on paper. Show your three transfers to a friend; ask the friend to give you pointers to make your transfers even better.

✓ *Peer Observation.* Children working together, as in the preceding task, can be an excellent type of assessment. *Refer to Chapter 14, "Assessing Student Learning," for more information on peer assessment.*

Transferring Weight on Bars

Setting Parallel bars and/or large climbing frame, with sufficient mats surrounding

Cues	
Strong Grip	(Maintain a strong grip on the bars to work safely.)
Strong Muscles	(Strong arm and shoulder muscles to maintain control on the bars.)

Tasks/Challenges:

T Transfer your weight to different body parts as you move from bar to bar on the parallels or other climbing apparatus. Make some of your transfers very slowly; others, quickly.

T Circle the bar with your body curled, in a pike position.

T Use twisting actions to move your body off balance and into the transfer.

Combining Skills on Mats

Setting: Large gymnastics mats in general space, with sufficient room between for children to work safely

Cues
Individual cues as needed

Tasks/Challenges:

T Travel the length of your mat, transferring your weight from your feet to other body parts, in various combinations to create a sequence. For example:

- Perform slow movements and then very quick movements for contrast.
- Do movements that show strength and then movements that demonstrate slowness and smooth control.
- Perform twisting, turning actions—for example, a roundoff, weight on your hands, a 360-degree turn on your hands.
- Travel the length of your mat, combining a balance, a jump, a roll, and a hands/feet action.
- Travel the length of your mat, transferring your weight from your feet to your hands, followed by a roll and an ending balance.

Combining Weight Transfer and Balances into Sequences on Mats and Apparatus

Setting: Large and small gymnastics apparatus, the large apparatus positioned in general space

Cues
Individual cues as needed

Tasks/Challenges:

Gymnastics routines on mats and apparatus are combinations of weight transfers and balance. Children at the utilization and proficiency levels of balance and weight transfer are ready for sequences involving combinations of skills and travel. Figure 23.4 gives an example of an assignment, plus guidelines for completing it.

Assessment Example

From the *National Standards for Physical Education*

Event Task

As the final project in gymnastics, students are to design a 90-second routine for either mats or apparatus. They may choose to work alone or with a partner; the partner relationship may be mirror or side by side. The routine must include an approach, development, and ending shape or dismount. The development portion of the routine must include the following: a minimum of four balances of different shapes and bases of support, a minimum of three locomotor and/or nonlocomotor actions, weight transfer, and at least two in-

versions. The selection of music for the routine is a student decision. The routine is to be diagrammed or written on paper and practiced until the sequence is memorized in its entirety. The routine will be videotaped for inclusion in student portfolios.

Criteria for Assessment

a. Routine includes all necessary components: approach, balances, weight transfers, inversion, dismount (ending shape).
b. Routine matches music in length.
c. Demonstrates changes in tempo in routine.
d. Selects balances and weight transfers that can be correctly performed (i.e., skills matched to personal gymnastic ability).
e. Maintains stillness in balances.
f. Displays creativity in routine design.
g. Transitions between movement are smooth.

NASPE (1995, pp. 47–48)

Proficiency Level: Learning Experiences Leading to Skill Development in Weight Transfer

Tasks at the proficiency level focus on increasing the horizontal and/or vertical distance of the weight transfer, as well as the intricate maneuvers (twisting and curling actions) that the body and its parts perform as weight is transferred from and received by different body parts. Examples include hands-only vaulting; performing stretching and twisting actions while airborne; and dismounting from apparatus by transferring weight from hands to feet combined with aerial twists, turns, and curls.

Activities at this level use specific gymnastics equipment and more closely resemble Olympic-style stunts. These skills are most often learned through club gymnastics. We do not teach them to the total class because very few children attain this level of performance. For those children who are ready to learn these skills or already proficient in these tasks, we provide individual teaching or coaching (see Chapter 30).

Levels of Skill Proficiency in Rolling

Children find the sensations of rolling—dizziness, loss of perception, and not knowing where they are or how they'll finish a roll—fascinating. The feeling of not knowing where you are or where you will end up, which is characteristic of a child's first attempts at roll-

Name _____

Final Project: Gymnastics

Grade 6: (a) mat sequence, (b) equipment sequence

Alone; with a partner: mirror, side by side

1. Beginning
   A. Approach:
      distance, starting point, pathway
      <u>walk</u>, run, leap, roll, walkover, cartwheel
      other _____
   B. Takeoff:
      spring, <u>step</u>
2. Development of sequence: Mix <u>in any order</u> for interest.
   A. Balances:
      minimum of four body shapes/four different bases of support
   B. Actions:
      minimum of three
      stretch curl; twist turn
   C. Transfers:
      movement
      feet to hand, back, head/hands
      (headstands, cartwheels, rolls, etc.)
   D. Inversion:
      minimum of two
3. Ending shape or dismount
   A. Music selection: ninety seconds
   B. On back side of page, list the progression of section 2; illustrate it if you wish.

Figure 23.4 Sample assignment for utilization- or proficiency-level weight-transfer and balance sequence.

ing, is both intriguing and perplexing. So children love to roll. As they become adept at rolling, the fascination of traveling upside down is augmented by the pleasure of being able to roll in different directions and at various speeds. Rolling is the act of transferring weight to adjacent body parts around a central axis. In physical education classes, rolling is generally dealt with in a gymnastics context, as a transference of weight. In gymnastics, safety through rolling is a skill introduced early to help children avoid crashing to the floor when they lose their balance. In dance and games, rolling is dealt with briefly to increase the children's range of movement and to enhance expressive abilities (see the progression spiral on page 416).

The precontrol level of rolling is characterized by exploration of various ways in which the body is able to be round. This exploration includes rocking actions from the head to feet on the back and stomach. At this level, children are challenged when asked to perform actions such as rocking back and forth like a rocking chair or rolling in a stretched position like a log. Rocking in a ball-like position, in preparation for rolling, is also explored at this level. When a child first begins to roll, the arms and hands are of little use. The child may

Skill Theme Development Sequence

Rolling

Proficiency Level

Club gymnastics

Utilization Level

Catching, throwing, and rolling
Striking and rolling
Rolling to meet and part
Balancing and rolling on equipment
Rolling onto low equipment
Throwing, catching, and rolling
Rolling to express an idea
Rolling, balancing, and rolling
Traveling and rolling between pieces of equipment
Rolling off low equipment
Rolling on low equipment
Rolling over low hurdles
Touch-and-go rolls
Busy Mat

Control Level

Traveling, jumping, landing, and rolling
Rolling, levels, directions, and jumping
Jumping over equipment, landing, and rolling
Jumping from different heights and rolling
Jumping for height, landing, and rolling
Jumping off equipment, landing, and rolling
Rolling using different directions and speeds
Linking rolls
Rolling from different directions and positions
Rolling in different directions
Rolling backward
Handclasp backward
Back shoulder
Rolling at different speeds
Rolling from different positions
Back touch
Rolling forward
Through the legs
Back rocker
Shoulders sideways
Egg roll
Log roll
Twin Rockers

Precontrol Level

The Ball
Rolling sideways
The Rocking Horse
Rounds

"get over," but the whole body usually uncurls in the middle of the roll, and the child lands sitting down.

At the control level, children become capable of controlling their bodies while rolling. They are able to roll in different directions, using their arms and hands to push while the body stays curled. The emphasis at this level is on control and the ability to roll in various situations. Rolls are performed as floor activities, and rolling is developed as a safety skill. Tasks such as the following can be presented to children:

1. Changing the direction of the rolls—backward, sideways, forward
2. Changing the speed of the rolls—fast or slow
3. Rolling from different positions—starting from low or standing positions and different balances (on one foot, two feet, or three body parts)
4. Combining jumping, landing, and rolling
5. Traveling and rolling

At the utilization level, children no longer have to "think about" staying round and are able to use the roll in combination with other skills and on equipment and large apparatus. Additionally, they can use rolling as an expressive form and in combination with manipulative skills. Activities such as the following challenge children at this level:

1. Rolling with something in their hands
2. Rolling after catching an object
3. Rolling on or over low equipment
4. Combining rolling with other locomotor forms as an expressive movement.

Children proficient in rolling enjoy rolling over high equipment and aerial rolls. They also combine rolling as a means of weight transfer between various forms of balance and other forms of weight transference. At this level, children are capable of difficult and sophisticated rolls, but because of safety considerations, the teacher's skills, equipment requirements, and the student-teacher ratio of physical education classes, we do not teach them. Such rolls as dive rolls; rolls along high, narrow equipment; and rolls from aerial positions are better left to club gymnastics.

Children who master the skill of rolling are able to participate comfortably and safely in activities that involve the risk of being off balance and falling, because they possess sufficient recovery techniques. This skill also gives children a fluid way to connect different balancing actions and to change direction and/or speed in a dynamic, unpredictable situation.

When introducing the skill of rolling, we prefer to have one mat for each child. When we don't have a

Rolling is a skill that fascinates children.

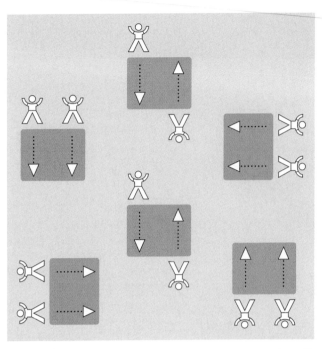

Figure 23.5 Mat positions that minimize the likelihood children will rock or roll into each other.

mat for each child, we use as many mats as possible. We've found that a good ground rule for any rolling situation is to have only one child at a time on the mat. This does *not* mean that the other children must stand in line and wait; they can stand around the mat and roll, in turn, as soon as the mat is empty. (See Figure 23.5 for a class set-up that maximizes rolling opportunities for each child.) Sometimes we set up learning centers to prevent long waits in line. Grassy areas or carpeting can also serve as appropriate areas for practicing rolling. When children roll on or over equipment, we make sure that the surrounding area is covered with mats. When teaching rolling it is especially important to employ the back-to-the-wall observational technique discussed in Chapter 12.

The key observation points in Box 23-2 show the correct and incorrect forms for rolling. Observe children carefully to help them overcome any problems with rolling.

As with any weight-bearing activity, it is critical to give careful consideration to the physical maturity and skill of each child. Before they're ready to attempt "traditional" forward and backward rolls, children *must be able to support their body weight with their arms.* We believe that children should not be forced to do any specific forward or backward roll. We are especially concerned about asking children to do "traditional" backward and forward rolls when they haven't yet developed the strength they need to protect themselves from back and neck injuries. Thus, we have provided illustrations of the hand and body positions for a variety of rolls.

Finally, while children love the sensation of rolling, it is an activity that cannot be done for extended periods. In an effort to maintain the quality of the skill and to prevent off-task behavior because children are "too dizzy," we have often found it more productive to focus on rolling for only part of a lesson. Thus, especially in the early stages of rolling, children are able to "recover" between practices of rolling.

Precontrol Level: Activities for Exploration of Rolling

At the precontrol level, children explore arching or rounding their bodies as a prerequisite to rolling. Once they are able to curve their bodies, they explore rocking and rolling actions that can be used for traveling and transferring weight.

Box 23-2

Key Observation Points: Rolling

1. Do the child's hands and arms receive the body weight evenly at the beginning of the roll without the body collapsing to one side?

2. Does the child's head slide through as the weight goes from the hands to the upper back and leave the mat as soon as the shoulders touch?

3. Do the child's arms come off the mat as soon as the shoulders touch?

4. Does the child's body stay curled and does the roll end on the feet?

5. When children are at the mature stage of rolling, do their rolls look similar to the following sequence?

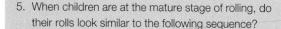

Rounds

Setting: A mat, space on a mat, or a carpet square in a grassy area for each child; children positioned so that they will not rock into each other (Figure 23.5)

Tasks/Challenges:

T On your mat try to find as many ways as possible to curl your body so that it is round. Three different ways would be good.

The Rocking Horse

Setting: A mat, space on a mat, or a carpet square in a grassy area for each child; children positioned so that they will not rock into each other

Tasks/Challenges:

T In self-space, you're going to pretend to be a rocking horse. But this rocking horse can do special things. First, you want to find out what it is like to rock on your back. To rock on your back, you must make your back round, because flat things can't rock.

T Now your special rocking horse is going to try to rock on its stomach. Remember to make your stomach round so you can rock smoothly.

T Now you are going to try to do what no rocking horse has ever done: You are going to try to rock on your side. Can you make your side round? Try it.

T Your rocking horse is just getting warmed up, so let's see if it can go faster. See if you can rock so fast on your back that it takes you up to your feet.

T Now see if you can keep rocking on your back without stopping, almost as if you can't stop. If it helps, use your hands and arms.

Rolling Sideways

Setting: A mat for every child or two or a large grassy space; children positioned so that they do not roll into each other

Tasks/Challenges:

T Now we are going to try something different: rolling sideways, like a log. Try to roll slow and fast.

T Can you find another way to roll sideways? Maybe like an egg?

The Ball

Setting: A mat for every child or two or a large grassy space; children positioned so that they do not roll into each other

Tasks/Challenges:

T Can you make your body like a ball? How many ways can your ball move around your space? Remember, only round balls roll.

Control Level: Learning Experiences Leading to Skill Development in Rolling

At the control level, children learn to roll in different directions and from different positions so they're able to perform other movements safely and to use rolling as a response to a fall. Children also practice rolling as a conclusion to jumping and landing.

A note about cues: Although several cues are listed for many of the learning experiences, it's important to focus on only one cue at a time. That way, the children can really concentrate on that cue. Once you provide feedback to the children and observe that most have learned a cue, then it's time to focus on another one.

Twin Rockers

Setting: Partners side by side on a mat or in a grassy area, with enough space between them so that they do not hit each other

> **Cue**
>
> **"C" Bodies** (Curve your body like the letter C to rock.)

Tasks/Challenges:

T To warm up a bit, practice rocking back and forth on your mat. See if you can make your rocks very smooth.

T This time you are going to play a game called Twin Rockers. You and your partner will be side by side. On the signal, you'll start to rock on your back. The challenge is to rock the same way and at the same time as your partner so that you look like twins.

T This time, rock on your stomach.

C Now see if you and your partner can develop two other Twin Rockers. Practice them until you can do them so that they match exactly.

Log Roll

Setting: A mat (no larger than 4 feet by 6 feet) for every child or two or a large grassy space; children positioned so that they do not roll into each other

> **Cues**
>
> **Stretch Arms** (Stretch your arms above your
>   head.)
> **Straight Body** (Straighten your body.)
> **Feet Together** (Bring your feet tight together.)

Tasks/Challenges:

T See if you can roll to the right and to the left with your log roll. Practice until you can go both ways just as smoothly.

T This time try to make your log roll go in a straight line. Try to go from one end of your mat to the other without rolling off.

T Try changing the speed of your log roll: Sometimes roll slowly as if you were rolling on flat land and sometimes move quickly as if rolling downhill.

T If you feel comfortable doing the log roll with your hands over your head, try to do it with your arms at your sides.

C Try to make a sequence of log rolls: for example, one slow to the right, two quickly to the left, one slow to the right, and then repeat the sequence. Be sure to stay in your space or on your mat.

✓ *Portfolio.* Children can write their sequences out, date them, and include them in their portfolios as an assessment task.

Egg Roll

Setting: A mat for every child or two or a large grassy space; children positioned so that they do not roll into each other

> **Cues**
>
> **"C" Bodies** (Curve your body like the letter C to
>   roll.)

Figure 23.6 Arm positions for keeping ankles and knees together during an egg roll.

> **Hold Knees** (Hold your knees together, either
>   from the outside or from the inside
>   out; *see Figure 23.6.*)

Tasks/Challenges:

T This time try to roll sideways like an egg in a curled position. Practice rolling this egg in different directions—sometimes left, sometimes right.

T Try rolling on different body parts—shoulder, back, even upper legs.

T In your space or on your mat, practice using the egg roll to travel. Can you roll around the whole space?

T Roll at different speeds around your space or mat.

Shoulders Sideways

Setting: A mat for every child or two or a large grassy space; children positioned so that they do not roll into each other

> **Cues**
>
> **Drop** (Drop one shoulder to the mat.)
> **Tuck** (Tuck the elbow and knee of the dropped
>   shoulder under.)
> **Roll** (Roll over.)

Tasks/Challenges:

T This time we are going to roll over a shoulder. To do that you need to start on your hands and knees, drop one shoulder to the mat, tuck your elbow and knee under your body, and roll over. Your roll should take you back up to your hands and knees. *(Demonstrate the roll.)* Let's all do it together this first time. Ready? Hands and knees, drop, tuck, roll. Good.

T Practice the roll on your own. **Say the cues out loud as you go, to help you remember the process.** Do one roll across your mat, get up, and try another one. You know you are really good when you can come up to your hands and knees each time.

T Once you feel comfortable rolling in one direction, try dropping the other shoulder and rolling that way.

C See if you can do three rolls in each direction that stay round throughout the whole roll.

T If you feel really good about rolling on your shoulder from your hands and knees, you may want to try it from a squatting position. The cues are the same; just the starting position changes.

✓ *Children's Drawing.* This would be a wonderful time to use children's drawings of rocking and rolling to assess their knowledge of the critical cues. *See Chapter 14 for the development of children's drawings as assessment items.*

Back Rocker

Setting: Each child with a space at a mat or in a large grassy area; children positioned so that they do not roll into one another; music conducive to rocking and a boom box

Cues	
"C" Back	(Round your back like the letter C.)
Tuck	(Tuck your chin to your chest.)
Knees to Chest	(Pull your knees to your chest and hold.)

Tasks/Challenges:

T Remember when we explored rocking horses and did Twin Rockers? This time we are going to try a back rocker. Start by squatting down with your back to the mat, place your fingers on the floor, slowly transfer your weight backwards to the mat, and as your back reaches the mat, tuck your chin in, bring your knees to your chest, wrap your arms around them, and rock backward until your head touches the mat. Rock forward to your starting position. Watch me as I show you. *(Demonstrate.)* Squat, lower, tuck, knees, rock.

T Practice the back rocker on your own. Don't ever go over your head. See how smoothly you can make the rock.

T As you rock, try to come back up to your feet at the end. What does it take to do this?

C See if you can keep your back rocker going for as long as I play the music. *(Play music in increasingly longer intervals, beginning with about 5 to 10 seconds.)*

✿ What does it look like when body parts are round? Show me.

Through the Legs

Setting: Each child with a space at a mat or in a large grassy area; children positioned so that they do not roll into one another

Cues	
Hands	(Your hands should be on the floor on the outside of your knees.)
Lean	(Lean forward.)
Hike	(Hike your bottom up high into the air.)
Look	(Look back through your legs.)
Tip	(Tip over; place the top of your shoulders on the mat.)

⚠ We do not force children to do a specific roll. Some may still prefer to roll over their shoulder at this point. If so, we place the emphasis on being round and staying in control. Gradually, we encourage children to move to positions higher than their hands and knees—for example, squatting—and to start the roll from there.

Tasks/Challenges:

T Now we are going to try rolling forward. This roll goes over your head. To do it, begin in a squat position, lean forward, hike your seat up in the air, look through your legs, and tip over. Everyone watch me do it once. *(Demonstrate.)* Now, let's do it together on the cues. Hands, lean, hike, look, tip.

T Now practice on your own. Practice once across your mat. **Say the cues as you roll so you don't forget them.** Get up and go again.

C See if you can do three rolls that stay round all the way.

T When you can stay round all the way through the roll, you may want to try and return to a standing position after the roll. The starting position is the same.

Rolling Forward

Setting: Each child with a space at a mat or in a large grassy area; children positioned so that they do not roll into one another

Figure 23.7 Hand positions on forward roll.

Cues	
"C" Back	(Round your back like the letter C.)
Tuck	(Tuck your chin to your chest.)
Hike	(Hike your bottom up high into the air.)
Push	(Push off with your legs and make sure your weight is on your arms so that your shoulders and back touch the mat in a very controlled way. The top of your head should not touch the mat. Imagine there is paint on the top of your head; try not to get any on the mat.)

🔆 Have children touch the back of their heads with their hand so that you know they can distinguish between the back and top of their heads.

⚠️ Children should not be forced to roll over their heads if they cannot support their body weight with their hands or are uncomfortable with the roll.

Tasks/Challenges:

T Now we are going to try a forward roll. Squat down at your mat and place your hands on the mat just to the outside of your knees. Make your back really round like the letter C. Tuck your chin all the way down to your chest. Hike your bottom way up in the air. Push with your arms and roll. Watch me while I show you how it will look. *(Demonstrate.)* Practice once with me all together as we say the steps: hands *(Figure 23.7),* C, tuck, hike, push, and roll.

⚠️ Some children may be more comfortable doing a shoulder roll. Encourage them to concentrate on

roundness and tucking, while gradually trying to get them to raise their starting position farther off the ground to kneeling or squatting.

Getting children to keep their heads down is often difficult when they are first learning to roll. One student teacher asked children to think of bubble gum connecting their chin and chest and others have actually had children hold a beanbag with their chin to their chest. Both ideas work.

There is some debate regarding the point of contact on the forward roll. Some prefer the shoulders and back; others indicate the back of the head. In our research we have found both. (We advocate the shoulders.) Regardless of which point of contact is used, several key points ensure the safety of the skill: (1) the weight is held by the arms, not the neck and head; (2) the body parts are in a round position; and (3) the transference of weight occurs under control so that there is no sudden crunching of weight onto any body part.

T Now practice on your own. Do one roll, get up, and start again. Roll straight across the mat. Say the cues aloud as you practice so you won't forget them.

C See if you can do three forward rolls that stay round from beginning to end.

T If you feel really good about your forward roll, try to come up to your feet at the end.

C See if you can do five forward rolls that the Olympic judges would give a "10."

🔆 What parts of your body have to be round to roll forward? Show me.

Smaller mats are adequate for introducing children to rolling; larger mats can be used for rolling in sequences and in relation to apparatus.

For many children it is easier to learn to roll forward on an inclined surface. To do this use a wedge mat approximately 10 inches high at the top tapering to 2 inches high at the bottom, and at least 30 inches long and 18 inches wide. You will need a box for children to stand on at the top of the mat. With this task be sure that children start their rolls from a squatting position. The cues remain the same.

Figure 23.8 Handclasp position for Back Touch.

Back Touch

Setting: Each child with a space at a mat or in a large grassy area; children positioned so that they do not roll into one another

Cues	
"C" Back	(Round your back like the letter C.)
Hands behind Head	(Clasp your hands behind your head with your elbows sticking out to the sides; *see Figure 23.8.*)

Tasks/Challenges:

T Start by squatting down with your back to the mat, clasp your hands behind your head with your elbows out as far as possible, slowly transfer your weight backward to the mat, and as your back slowly reaches the mat, tuck your chin in, bring your knees to your chest, and rock backward as far as possible until your weight is on your elbows. Rock forward to your starting position. Watch me as I show you. *(Demonstrate.)* Practice it once with me: squat, clasp, lower, tuck, knees, rock.

T When you feel comfortable bringing your weight back on your elbows, challenge yourself a little more—try to make your feet touch the mat over your head. Then rock back to the starting position.

C Try to do five rocks in which your feet touch the mat over your head.

Rolling from Different Positions

Setting: Each child with a space to roll on a mat or grassy area

Cues

Round Body	(Round your back and tuck your chin for a good roll.)
Strong Muscles	(Use strong arms and shoulders to slowly transfer weight to the roll.)

Tasks/Challenges:

T So far you have been starting your rolls from a low position, close to the mat. Now we are going to try starting your rolls from different positions. The first position we will try may be easier than the low position you have been using. It is called a straddle position. Watch me as I show you.

Stand behind your mat with your feet wide apart; stretch your hands to the ceiling. Now put your hands on the mat almost between your feet (don't reach forward), tuck your chin to your chest, and roll forward. You will land sitting down. As with all rolls, keep your back rounded. Let's practice one together as we say the steps out loud: feet apart, stretch arms, hands on mat, tuck chin, slowly roll.

T Practice the straddle roll on your own until you can do it slowly and smoothly.

T Now that you can roll from the squatting position and the straddle position, see if you can find other positions from which to roll. You may want to try your knees, standing, one leg, and one arm. **Each time, remember to use strong muscles to lower slowly to the mat.** Try to find four different starting positions.

C Choose the starting position you like most. See if you can do four rolls from that position that stay rounded and lower slowly to the mat. When you think you can, ask a friend to watch you and give "thumbs up" for each roll that you do correctly.

Rolling at Different Speeds

Setting: Each child with a space to roll on a mat or grassy area without rolling into each other

Cues

Round Body	(Round your back and tuck your chin and knees for a good roll.)
Arms	(Your arms are your brakes and accelerator for these rolls.)

Tasks/Challenges:

T Do you remember when you worked on traveling at different speeds? Now you are going to roll at different speeds: Sometimes you will roll fast,

sometimes you will roll slowly, and sometimes you will roll at a medium speed. Practice now doing rolls at different speeds. Your speed should be so clear that I can tell which speed it is just by watching. I shouldn't have to ask you.

C Now I am really going to give you a challenge. I'll call out a speed, and you roll at that speed. I'll be watching to see if you really roll at the speed I call out.

Back Shoulder

Setting: Each child with a space at a mat or in a large grassy area; children positioned so that they do not roll into one another

Cues

Round Body	(Round your back and tuck your chin and knees for a good roll.)
Arm to Side	(Keep the arm of the shoulder you are going to roll over out to the side of your body.)
Head to Side	(Tuck your head to one side as you go over.)

Tasks/Challenges:

T We are going to try rolling backward over a shoulder with our hands on the mat to push. Watch me as I show you what it looks like. *(Demonstrate.)* Squat with your back to the mat with your hands on the floor in front of you, push with your hands and rock backward to the mat, bring the arm of the shoulder you are going to roll over out to the side of your body and the other arm back over your head, tuck your head to one side, push with your arms, and roll over that shoulder. Let's practice one together as we say the steps: Squat, hands in front, push and rock back, arm to side, tuck head, roll *(Figure 23.9)*.

T Now practice the back shoulder roll on your own, **each time saying the steps so that you don't forget them.**

T When you feel good about going over one shoulder, try to tuck your head the other way and go over that shoulder.

C Try to do four backward rolls that stay round all the way through. When you think you can do it, raise your hand and ask me to come watch or have a friend watch.

🎞 What parts of your body have to be round to roll backward over your shoulder? Show me.

Figure 23.9 Hand and head positions for back shoulder roll.

Handclasp Backward

Setting: Each child with a space at a mat or in a large grassy area; children positioned so that they do not roll into one another

Tasks/Challenges:

🅣 Now we're going to practice rolling backward. It will be almost like when we did the rocking action with our hands behind our head, except this time we will try to roll over. Watch me as I show you what it looks like. *(Demonstrate.)* Squat with your back to the mat, clasp your hands behind the base of your head with your elbows sticking out to the sides, sit down quickly, tucking your knees and chin to your chest, and roll completely backward. Your weight should be on your elbows. Let's practice one together while I say the steps out loud: squat, clasp, sit, tuck, roll.

🅣 Practice the backward roll this way on your own. Remember, one roll at a time. **Stay round.**

⚠ If children cannot roll over backward, allow them to practice rocking back and forth with the elbows out. In no case should anyone apply force to a child's hips to attempt to help the child "get over."

Rolling Backward

⚠ Children should not attempt to roll backward with the "traditional" backward roll until they can support their bodies with their arms. Until then, have them practice with their hands clasped at the base of their heads or have them do a shoulder roll. Force should never be applied to the hips to help a child "get over."

Setting: Each child with a space at a mat or in a large grassy area; children positioned so that they do not roll into one another

Cues

Mickey Mouse Ears	(Hands back by shoulders, fingers pointing toward shoulders, thumbs near ears.)
Tight Ball	(Keep a tight, round shape all the way through the roll.)
Push	(Push with your arms all the way through the roll.)

Tasks/Challenges:

🅣 Now you are going to do a backward roll that goes over your head and uses your arms to push. This combines the two backward rolls you have done before. Watch me as I show you what this one looks like. *(Demonstrate.)* Start from a squatting position, place your hands on the floor in front of you, push and rock backward, tuck your knees and chin tight to your chest, bring your hands to your shoulders and make Mickey Mouse ears, *push* with both arms, and roll over your head. Let's do it together. Squat, hands in front, push, rock back, tuck, hands to shoulders, *push* and roll. Practice rolling backward *(Figure 23.10)*.

🅣 Practice on your own. **Remember to say the hints as you roll.**

When trying to roll backward, children often get stuck and roll no further, usually because they:

1. Make a flat rather than a round shape (knees move away from the chin), so they find it virtually impossible to roll
2. Fail to place their hands in the proper position and thus are unable to push with the force needed to complete the roll

Practicing to overcome these two critical errors will enable children to roll backward.

🅒 Do two backward rolls that stay tight and round. When you can do them, yell "yes!"

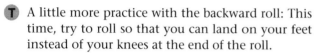

Figure 23.10 Hand positions for backward roll.

T A little more practice with the backward roll: This time, try to roll so that you can land on your feet instead of your knees at the end of the roll.

This is a good time to use teaching by invitation or intratask variation to let children practice the rolls they need to work on.

T This time, you are going to practice your backward rolls with a partner. Your partner will be your coach. He or she will watch and tell you if you have followed all the hints for the backward roll: tight ball, Mickey Mouse ears, push, and land on feet. After three tries, switch places.

✓ *Peer Observation.* This task works well as a peer observation opportunity, even with young children, provided the cues are simple and clear. It also gives children an opportunity to take responsibility for helping someone else learn.

Rolling in Different Directions

Setting: Each child with a space on a mat or grassy area to roll

Cues	
Round Body	(Round your back and tuck your chin and knees for a good roll.)
Three Directions	(Make sure you roll backward, sideways, and forward.)

Tasks/Challenges:

T You have practiced rolls that went sideways, forward, and backward. Now you are going to put all three together. Practice rolls from all three directions—one roll at a time. Remember as you work that only one of you rolls on the mat at a time; however, as soon as the person ahead of you finishes,

you can roll. I shouldn't see anyone standing in line, just rolling from all places around the mat.

T This time I am going to add one more thing to what I would like to see. Each time you roll, try to end up on your feet, not your knees or your seat.

T Decide which roll is the hardest for you to do. Practice that roll until you feel it is as good as your others.

Rolling from Different Directions and Positions

Setting: Each child with a space on a mat or grassy area to roll

Cues	
Round Body	(Round your back and tuck your chin and knees for a good roll.)
Strong Muscles	(Use strong arms and shoulders to slowly transfer weight to the roll.)

Tasks/Challenges:

T We are going to combine two things you have done: rolling in different directions and rolling from different positions. There are many combinations. Why not start by rolling forward from a standing position? You can use any version of forward, backward, and sideways rolls you want.

T Next roll backward from a sitting position.

T Now roll sideways from a squatting position.

T On your own, practice as many ways to roll as you can think of. You should always be able to tell me the direction of your roll and the position you are starting from.

C Now that you've practiced on your own, find three different direction/position combinations that you like, and practice them until they are very smooth and flowing. Be able to tell me what position and direction you are using, and then we will show them to the class.

✓ *Exit Slip.* This would be an appropriate time to use an exit slip *(see Chapter 14)* that asks the children to record the three combinations of rolls used and react to the difficulty they had in making the sequence flow together.

Linking Rolls

Setting: A large mat or a soft grassy space for each child to roll

Cues

Round Body	(Round your back and tuck your chin and knees for a good roll.)
Strong Muscles	(Use strong arms and shoulders to control your body from one roll to the next.)
Smooth Transfer	(Pause between rolls.)

⚠ *Having children do multiple (more than two) rolls in a row is not helpful—and can be dangerous. When more than two rolls are asked for in a sequence, some other movement or a balance should come between them.*

Tasks/Challenges:

T Now you get a chance to do what you have wanted to do for a long time: more than one roll at a time. First, practice by doing two forward rolls in a row. When you can do two smoothly, balance and try two more. To make the links look good, the transfer between rolls should be smooth. To make it smooth, pause for a second and then go into your next roll. Use only a pause, not a stop.

T When you feel comfortable doing forward rolls, try two backward rolls.

T Try sideways rolls: one, then a pause, then two.

T This time we are going to put together a sequence of three different rolls. For starters try forward, backward, forward. There should be one pause or balance in your sequence.

C Now make up your own sequence. It should have three or four rolls, pauses, and two directions. When you can do your sequence really well, ask a friend to watch. See if your partner can name

the sequence of rolls. Then watch your partner's sequence and name the rolls.

Rolling Using Different Directions and Speeds

Setting: Each child with a space on a mat or grassy area to roll; two bags: one containing index cards with a speed category on each card and the other containing index cards with a direction on each card; the number of cards in each bag should equal or exceed the number of children in the class; paper and pencil for each child

Cues

Round Body	(Round your back and tuck your chin and knees for a good roll.)
Arms	(Your arms are your brakes and accelerator.)

Tasks/Challenges:

T Here's another combination—directions and speeds. This means, for example, that sometimes you will roll backward at a fast speed and sometimes at a slow speed. Practice on your own using all three speeds—fast, medium, and slow—combined with all three directions—forward, backward, sideways. That makes nine different ways you can roll; practice all of them.

T Now you are going to draw your speeds and directions out of a bag. On the signal, one at a time come and draw one card from each bag. One card will have a direction on it, and the other card will have a speed on it. The two cards together will give you the direction and speed you are to practice.

T Now for the hardest rolling task yet. Imagine you are in the Olympics and you are going to do a rolling sequence that combines directions and speeds. Let's start with this sequence: forward, fast; pause, backward, slow; forward, fast. The sequence is written on the board in case you forget.

C Now make up your own combination. Practice it until it flows together well. When you finish, write it down. You can use the example on the board as a guide to tell you how to write it. Practice your combination three more times.

✓ *Portfolio.* The previous task can be used as an assessment task by having children record the sequence as an entry in their portfolios. This is also an opportune time to use a teacher or peer observation (check list, videotape) to assess the critical cues of rolling.

Jumping Off Equipment, Landing, and Rolling

Setting: A low box or milk crate placed against every mat the children are using for rolling (You can sometimes get milk crates from the local dairy. Low boxes can be made by filling soft-drink cases [24-can size] with flat newspapers and taping the outside of the boxes shut securely. Place crates or boxes against the mat so that they won't slide.)

Cues	
Jump, Land, Roll	(Jump; land on your feet; then roll.)
Strong Muscles	(Use strong muscles to lower slowly to the roll.)
Round Body	(Round your back and tuck your chin and knees for a good roll.)

The cues for the following tasks focus largely on rolling, not on jumping and landing. This assumes that children have already mastered jumping and landing. If they crash when they land or do not use soft landings, you will want to revisit jumping and landing (Chapter 21) before progressing.

⚠ The first observation you need to make after children begin this task is whether they are landing on their feet before they roll. Quite often, children begin dive-rolling here. If they do, stop the task immediately, and refocus or provide another demonstration that shows the correct way.

Tasks/Challenges:

ⓣ You're now going to jump off a box (crate), land, and then roll. There's a box (crate) at the end of your mat. One at a time, jump off the box (crate), land on your feet, and then roll. Go slowly at first until you get the hang of it. Always be sure to land on your feet. The next person can go as soon as the person in front gets off the mat. Don't rush, but go quickly.

⚠ Make sure children jump up, not out. When they jump out, they push against the box or crate, sending it sliding across the floor, which causes them to fall.

ⓣ It's getting harder. This time, change the direction of your jump. Sometimes jump backward, sometimes sideways, and sometimes forward; then roll in any direction you want. If you aren't sure about jumping backward, just try stepping off until you get used to it.

ⓣ We're going to change the activity again. This time, you'll still jump off in different directions, but you'll roll in the same direction as the jump.

So if you jump sideways, you roll sideways; if you jump backward, you roll backward.

✿ What does it mean to land before you roll?

Jumping for Height, Landing, and Rolling

Setting: A low box or milk crate placed against every mat the children are using for rolling

Cues	
Jump, Land, Roll	(Jump, land on feet, then roll.)
Strong Muscles	(Use strong muscles to lower slowly to the roll.)
Round Body	(Round your back and tuck your chin and knees for a good roll.)

Tasks/Challenges:

ⓣ This time, instead of changing directions, you're going to practice jumping higher off the boxes *(crates)*, still landing and rolling. Do you remember when we worked on jumping? What do you do to make your jump go higher? **Right—you bend your knees and throw your arms up as if you were reaching for the sky.** To warm up, just practice jumping high off the box *(crate)* and landing on your feet. If you fall on the landing, you know that you're jumping too high.

ⓣ Now add a roll after your jump and landing. Everything should be in control. If you're falling on your landing or crashing into your roll, you'll know that you're jumping too high. Try it: high jump, land, and roll.

ⓣ So far, most of what I've been seeing are jumps, lands, and rolls in forward directions. Go back and add different directions to your high jumps.

Jumping backward from the equipment is difficult for some children, as well as scary. Have the youngsters first step backward if they're hesitant or fearful.

⚠ Permit children to jump backward only to a height that they can control when they land. They should be able to land on their feet, on balance, absorbing their weight.

Jumping from Different Heights and Rolling

Setting: Boxes and benches of varying heights at stations around the room (Figure 23.11); arrows pointing from station to station on the floor; children in groups of four; mats at each station

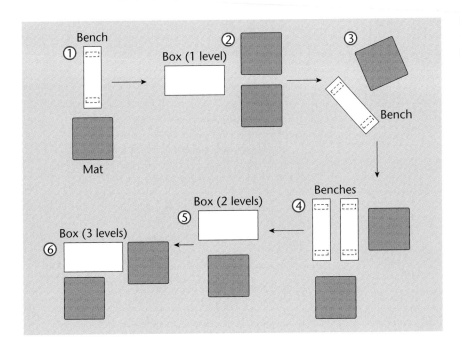

Figure 23.11 Stations to facilitate jumping from different heights, landing, and rolling.

Cues

Jump, Land, Roll (Jump, land on your feet, and then roll.)

Strong Muscles (Use strong muscles to lower slowly to the roll.)

Round Body (Round your back and tuck your chin and knees for a good roll.)

Tasks/Challenges:

(T) We're working at stations for this task, which will give you practice jumping from objects of different heights. This is how the activity works. There will be four of you at each station. On the signal, you'll begin to practice jumping, landing, and rolling from the equipment at your station. On the next signal, stop, rotate to the station the arrow on the floor points to, and then start all over again. Remember, you're practicing jumping, landing, and rolling from the equipment that's at your station.

Jumping Over Equipment, Landing, and Rolling

Setting: A hurdle set up at the end of each mat; see Chapter 18 (Figure 18.5) for hurdle construction details

Cues

Jump, Land, Roll (Jump, land on your feet, and then roll.)

Strong Muscles (Use strong muscles to lower slowly to the roll.)

Round Body (Round your back and tuck your chin and knees for a good roll.)

⚠ The hurdle should be only as high as children are able to jump over without difficulty and land in control (see Chapter 21). The hurdle should be an obstacle to cross, not a challenge to jump. Our hurdles are no higher than about 8 to 12 inches and may be as low as 3 to 4 inches.

Tasks/Challenges:

(T) Your task now is to jump over the hurdle, land, and roll. Remember, just as in jumping off objects, you must land on your feet before you roll.

(T) This time, change the direction of your jump. Sometimes try to jump sideways and backward as well as forward.

(T) Now change the direction of your roll after the jump to match the direction of the jump. So if you jump backward, roll backward. **Controlled jumps and round rolls are our goal.**

(T) You can also change the speed of the jump and of the roll. This time, practice mixing up the speeds of the jump and roll. In other words, you might mix a slow-motion jump with a fast roll or combine a fast jump and a fast roll. Make whatever speeds you use very clear.

Figure 23.12 Task sheet for rolling.

Name _____ Teacher _____

Rolling Task Sheet

Teacher Check	Challenge
	I can roll forward, coming up to my feet.
	I can roll sideways, coming up to my feet.
	I can roll backward, coming up to my feet.
	I can jump, land, and roll forward.
	I can jump, land, and roll sideways.
	I can jump, land, and roll backward.
	I can jump over an obstacle, land, and roll, coming back to my feet
	I can jump, land, change directions, and roll.
	I can jump, twist in the air, land, and roll without falling down.
	I can jump off a box, land, and roll without falling down.
	I can jump off a box in different directions, land, and roll.
	I can jump off a low box, make different body shapes in the air, land, and roll.
	I can jump off a box, twist in the air, land, and roll without falling down.
	I can

 What does it mean to have controlled jumps? What do they look like?

Rolling, Levels, Directions, and Jumping

Setting: A jumping and rolling space for each child; a task sheet (Figure 23.12) for each child

Cues	
Jump, Land, Roll	(Jump, land on your feet, and then roll.)
Strong Muscles	(Use strong muscles to lower slowly to the roll.)
Round Body	(Round your back and tuck your chin and knees for a good roll.)

Tasks/Challenges:

Today I'll give you the chance to test yourself and see how well you can do the rolls you've been practicing. I'll also give you time to practice the rolls that have been hardest for you. Each of you has a task sheet. Your challenge is to do all the tasks on the sheet. When you think you can do something well, have a friend watch you; if the friend thinks you did the challenge correctly, the friend puts his or her initials on the sheet. The area has been set up so that there's space to practice each challenge.

✓ *Self-assessment.* This task can serve as a self- and/or peer assessment. When completed, it can be included in the child's portfolio. See Chapter 13 for information on developing task sheets.

Traveling, Jumping, Landing, and Rolling

Setting: Mats spread throughout general space with sufficient space between for travel

Cues	
Jump, Land, Roll	(Jump, land on your feet, and then roll.)
Strong Muscles	(Use strong muscles to lower slowly to the roll.)
Round Body	(Round your back and tuck your chin and knees for a good roll.)

Tasks/Challenges:

Ⓣ Now you're going to use only the mats, but you're going to jump, land, and roll at your mats all on your own. Practice jumping, landing, and rolling in different directions at your mat. Remember, you can start or end at any place around the mat, so there should be no lines.

Ⓣ This time, begin to travel around the outside of the mat. When the mat is empty, take a little jump, land, and roll. You'll almost be jumping from a moving position, but not quite. You'll travel, jump, pause, and roll, so you really come to a short stop before you roll. If you crash, you're going too fast. One person on the mat at a time.

Ⓣ Here's a new challenge. Instead of just jumping this time, try jumping over the corners of the mat; then land, and roll. Remember to practice all the different jumps you learned: one foot to the other, one to the same, two to one, one to two, and two to two.

Ⓣ Now I'll challenge you even further. As you jump the corners of the mat, add a twist or turn in the air before you land. You still have to land on your feet before you roll.

Utilization Level: Learning Experiences Leading to Skill Development in Rolling

At the utilization level, children no longer focus on rolling as an isolated skill but concentrate on using rolling for other purposes. Children develop the ability to combine rolling with other skills, such as catching and throwing. Much of their rolling at this level is directed toward its use as a form of weight transfer between balances. Additionally, rolling is used to transfer weight onto, from, and over large apparatus.

Because at this level rolling is most often used not as an isolated skill but as an act of weight transference, many tasks at the utilization level of rolling are included in the earlier weight transference section of this chapter. When that occurs, reference is provided.

A note about cues: Although several cues are listed for many of the learning experiences, it's important to focus on only one cue at a time. That way, the children can really concentrate on that cue. Once you provide feedback to the children and observe that most have learned a cue, then it's time to focus on another one.

Busy Mat

Setting: Three or four children at a mat

Cues	
Jump, Land, Roll	(Jump, land on your feet, and then roll.)
Strong Muscles	(Use strong muscles to lower slowly to the roll.)
Round Body	(Round your back and tuck your chin and knees for a good roll.)

Two tips:

1. If students are not able to safely decide who is to roll when, specify the order in which they'll roll before they begin.
2. This is an exhausting task; if children are really doing it well, they usually can't continue it for a long time.

Tasks/Challenges:

Ⓣ This is a game called Busy Mat. It'll really give you a workout, so get ready. The object of the game is to always have someone rolling on the mat while the others are traveling around the outside of the mat. As soon as one person finishes rolling, another person should start. The timing should be split-second. Everyone should always be moving, either on the outside by jumping and landing, or on the mat by rolling. Let's do a practice round.

Touch-and-Go Rolls

Setting: A place to roll for each child

Cues	
Off Balance	(Be slightly off balance toward the mat as you land.)
Strong Muscles	(Use strong arms and shoulders to smoothly lower to the roll.)
Round Body	(Round your back and tuck your chin and knees for a good roll.)

Tasks/Challenges:

T Now you're going to practice making your jumps, landings, and rolls more professional. You've been coming to a clear stop after landing and before rolling. Now you're going to roll with no hesitation. Your feet should barely touch the floor before you're into the roll. Your roll just flows, but your feet still have to hit the floor before you roll. **To do this, you'll really have to bend your knees on landing, let your arms absorb your weight, and make sure your shoulders are round.**

T Practice making your jumps so that you land **a little off balance right before you move into the roll.** You are trying to make it as smooth as possible, as if to save yourself from crashing. No stopping—touch and go.

T Make sure you sometimes change the direction of your land and roll, making it backward or sideways as well as forward and still keeping your touch-and-go actions.

Rolling Over Low Hurdles

Setting: A low hurdle at each mat

⚠ The height of the hurdle should be low enough so that children can put their hands on the ground on the other side with no effort. Hurdles may be as low as 3 to 4 inches and no higher than 10 to 12 inches. Hands must be on the floor before the feet leave the floor.

Cues	
Strong Muscles	(Use strong arms and shoulders to slowly lower into the roll.)

Round Body	(Round your back and tuck your chin and knees for a good roll.)
Hands on Floor	(Start with your hands on the floor on the other side of the hurdle.)

Tasks/Challenges:

T Place your hands on the mat on the other side of the hurdle and try to roll over the hurdle without touching it. **You really have to raise your bottom in the air and push off with your legs. Remember to tuck your head to keep your body round. As you do this, make sure that your arms really give when your feet leave the floor. Bending your arms a little as you push off helps you let yourself down softly.**

Rolling on Low Equipment

(See Transferring Weight by Rolling [Bench, Box, or Table] earlier in this chapter.)

⚠ Rolling on equipment should be introduced only after children have mastered rolling on the floor or mats.

Setting: Low, wide benches and tables around the room with mats under them

⚠ At this point, the equipment should be low and wide, not more than 18 inches off the floor.

Cues	
Round Back	(Round your back and tuck your chin and knees for a good roll.)
Control	(Tight muscles, slow-motion action for control throughout the roll.)

Tasks/Challenges:

T At your piece of equipment, get on it in any way you like, and practice rolling on the top of it, lengthwise; then get off in any way you like. **To do this place your thumbs and the sides of your palms on the top of the bench, with your hands and fingers on the side of the bench.** Although this position is very different from the one you use for rolling on mats, it provides a steady base on equipment. Tuck your head and slowly roll forward on the equipment. If you fall off a lot, you may want to go to a wider piece of equipment.

T As you practice now, try to make your rolls very smooth.

T Now try to roll backward by very slowly transferring your weight to a rounded back. **Extend your hands above your head to hold onto the sides of the equipment, place your head to one side, and roll slowly over your shoulder.**

C Now you're going to make up a sequence using all you've practiced. First figure out how you want to get on the equipment; you don't have to get on by rolling. When you're on the equipment, roll along the equipment, get off any way, and roll after your dismount. The sequence will go like this: Get on, roll along, get off, roll on the mat. Practice on your own until your sequence looks the same each time you do it.

Practice your sequence three more times, just to make sure that it's really in your memory. When you finish, write it down (*Figure 23.13*).

Rolling Off Low Equipment

Setting: Low boxes, benches, and tables scattered throughout the space; mats around and under each piece of equipment. Children *must* be able to reach the mat from the equipment.

Cues	
Round Body	(Keep your back round and tuck your chin and knees for a good roll.)
Strong Muscles	(Use strong arms and shoulders to lower slowly into the roll.)

Tasks/Challenges:

T Assume a kneeling position at the end of your piece of equipment, place your hands on the mat, slowly lower your weight to the mat, and roll forward.

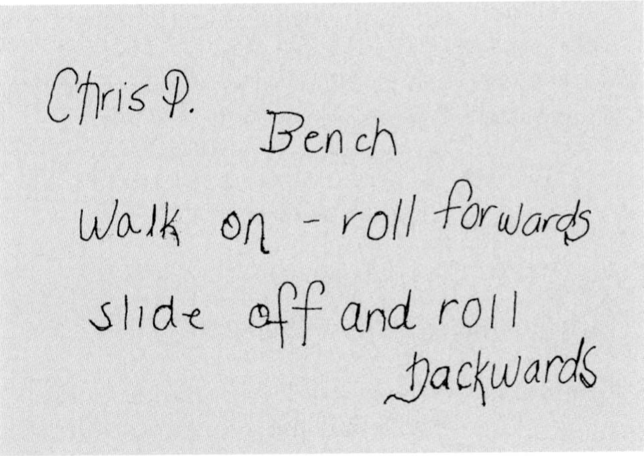

Chris P.
Bench
Walk on - roll forwards
slide off and roll
*   backwards*

Figure 23.13 Child's rolling sequence.

T Once you feel comfortable with one piece of equipment, try another one.

A This task should be preceded by the task of rolling over low hurdles. To do this activity safely, children must be able to absorb their body weight with their arms.

✿ What is the key to rolling off equipment safely?

Traveling and Rolling Between Pieces of Equipment

Setting: Two pieces of low, wide equipment placed about 2 to 3 feet apart at each station; mats under, around, and between all equipment.

Cues	
Round Body	(Keep your body round and tuck your chin and knees for a good roll.)
Control	(Use tight, strong muscles to roll slowly.)

Tasks/Challenges:

T This next activity is similar to others you have done. As you can see, there are two pieces of equipment at each station. Your task now is to get on the first piece of equipment, roll one way on it, travel to the second piece of equipment without touching the floor, roll a different way on the equipment, jump to get off, and roll on the mat. The sequence goes like this: Get on, roll, travel across, roll another way, jump off, roll. Practice these ideas.

C Now pick one sequence that you really like, and practice it until it's smooth and fluid. There should be no breaks, and you shouldn't have to stop and think about what comes next. Make sure you land on your feet after you jump off and before you roll.

✓ *Video/Digital Analysis.* As children develop sequences using selected skills, the videotaping of their sequences provides an excellent opportunity for videotaped assessment. As children watch the video for the first time, have them write down the moves they used to develop the sequence. When they watch for the second time, have them assess their execution of those skills in relation to the critical cues.

Rolling, Balancing, and Rolling

(See also Traveling Into and Out Of Balances by Rolling in Chapter 22, "Balancing.")

Setting: Mats around the room large enough for children to roll and balance

Cues

Round Body	(Keep your body round and tuck your chin and knees for a good roll.)
Control	(Tight, strong muscles to roll slowly.)

Tasks/Challenges:

Ⓣ You worked on balancing before; now you're going to combine balancing and rolling. At your mat, practice rolling forward into a symmetrical balance. Try to roll right into the balance so that there's no pause between the roll and the balance.

Ⓣ This time try to focus on the connection between the roll and the balance. **Instead of stopping after the roll and before the balance, see if you can roll right into the balance.**

Ⓣ Most of you are balancing on very stable body parts, such as knees and hands. This time, try some body parts that aren't quite so stable and see if you can still balance.

Ⓣ Now try rolls from different directions—backward and sideways—and still roll straight into the balance. Hold the balance still. **Shifting some of your weight backward, just as you balance, might make your balances a little easier.**

Rolling to Express an Idea

Setting: A soft, grassy area; children in pairs

Cues

Round Body	(Keep your back round and tuck your chin and knees for a good roll.)

Tasks/Challenges:

Ⓒ This time you're going to roll to express an idea. You're going to pretend and tell a story by rolling. The first thing you're going to tell is "being scared." Here's how it works. Your partner will come close to you and pretend to scare you, without using words. You're so scared that you fall down and roll backward trying to get away. Make sure that your roll really shows that you're afraid; it should be a very stiff roll. After two turns, switch places with your partner.

Ⓒ You're going to tell a desert story this time. Have any of you seen those old Westerns on television where tumbleweeds go blowing across the desert, with nothing stopping them? Well, you're going to be a tumbleweed, just blowing and rolling all over the desert. Remember, a tumbleweed is loose and bouncy as the wind just bumps it along.

Ⓣ Instead of being a loose piece of tumbleweed, this time you're going to be a seed. The wind is blowing you all over; you're bouncing all around. Suddenly, the wind stops and you sprout roots and start to grow. When you start to grow, remember the ideas we talked about earlier about rising and spreading. Your sequence goes like this: The wind blows you around, the wind stops, you send out roots and grow into a big tree or flower.

Throwing, Catching, and Rolling

Setting: A soft grassy area (or if done inside, a very large mat [like a wrestling mat] or a space completely covered with smaller mats); children in pairs; a variety of objects (beanbags, Frisbees, balls) for each set of partners to throw and catch

Aerial Rolls

Because of safety considerations, the student-teacher ratio, the varied student skill level, and the high skill level required to teach and spot aerial rolls, we feel that they are best left to the private setting. To explain this to the students who are capable of such tasks, we simply say that we don't have the facilities to practice the rolls and don't want to encourage the children who aren't ready to try them. The more skilled students can instead use physical education class for refining their skill or helping others. We do not advocate teaching aerial or dive rolls in physical education classes.

Cues

Tuck Shoulder	(Tuck your shoulder so that it is round.)
Round Body	(Round your back and tuck your chin and knees for a good roll.)

Tasks/Challenges:

Ⓣ With your partner, throw and catch the beanbag. Throw so that your partner has to really stretch to catch the beanbag. **Remember to make your partner stretch: You have to throw at a point away from your partner.**

Ⓣ Now that you're stretching to catch, as soon as you catch the beanbag, roll in the direction you had to stretch to catch the beanbag. Keep the beanbag in your hand as you roll. Remember the whole sequence: Stretch to catch, catch, and then roll.

Ⓣ Now, for just a little while, practice throwing and catching the beanbag to yourself. Throw to yourself so that you have to jump to catch the beanbag in an off-balance position and then roll to break the fall from being off balance. The hardest part is throwing so that you force yourself to be in an off-balance position.

Ⓣ Now go back to working with your partner. Try the same task. Throw so that your partner has to first catch the beanbag in an off-balance position and then roll after catching it. Catchers, make sure you're really off balance and have to roll to recover your balance or so that you won't be hurt. Throwers, really force the catchers off balance when they catch.

Ⓣ Once you feel comfortable with a beanbag, try using another object, such as a Frisbee or football.

Successful throwing and catching with partners depends on throwers' ability to force the catchers to be off balance or to move to catch. Before exposing children to these ideas, make sure they're at the utilization level of throwing and catching.

Rolling onto Low Equipment

Setting: Benches or low boxes with mats surrounding them

Cues	
Round Body	(Round your back and tuck your chin and knees for a good roll.)
Control	(Tight muscles, slow-motion action for control throughout the roll.)

Tasks/Challenges:

Ⓣ Use a roll to get onto your piece of equipment. Stand at the end of the equipment. **Place your thumb and the sides of your palms on the top of the equipment and your hands and fingers on**

the sides of the equipment; then slowly lower into a forward roll to get on the equipment. Get off in any way you like.

Ⓣ Now I'm going to add to your task. Roll onto the equipment, travel any way that you want while on the equipment, jump to get off, land, and roll. Again, make sure that you're actually using a roll to get onto the equipment.

Balancing and Rolling on Equipment

Setting: Tables, benches, and beams spread throughout the room, with mats surrounding all the equipment

Spotting

The question of spotting—physically assisting a child with a skill—often arises with gymnastics programs. Spotting isn't used often in educational gymnastics programs as it often encourages or forces children to attempt a skill before they are ready. See Chapter 30 for a more complete discussion on the use of spotting.

Cues	
Round Body	(Round your back and tuck your chin and knees for a good roll.)
Control	(Tight muscles, slow-motion action for control throughout the roll.)
Stillness	(Keep balances motionless.)

Tasks/Challenges:

Ⓣ At your equipment, practice mounting the equipment, balancing on the equipment, rolling out of the balance, and dismounting. Make sure your rolls out of the balances are going in the direction that seems natural for the balance, not necessarily the easiest way for you.

Ⓣ Now, keep the same balances, but for each balance find at least one more roll, going in a different direction than the first roll. Thus, you should have two rolls out of each balance, each roll going in a different direction.

Ⓒ See if you can develop five balances and rolls that you can do so they are smooth and round.

☑ *Student Display.* A fun assessment project at the utilization level is for students to develop a poster or bulletin board that displays how rolling is used in sports other than gymnastics. *See Chapter 14 for the development of scoring rubrics to accompany such a project.*

Rolling to Meet and Part

Setting: Groups of five; a large grassy area or wrestling mats

Cues

Smoothness	(Make your rolls flow smoothly into and out of each other.)
Planned Pauses	(Be sure any stops in your routine are on purpose.)

Tasks/Challenges:

T You're going to work with the idea of meeting and parting. There will be five people in each group. Start by spreading apart from one another and coming together by traveling on your feet. When you get together, make any group shape that you want and hold it still for a few seconds. Next, each of you leaves your group by rolling away and freezing in a shape by yourself. You need to plan your rolls so that all of you come together at the same time to form the group shape, and you know exactly when to roll away.

C Practice your routine until you can repeat it three times in a row, always doing it the same way. When you've done that, we will show the routines to the rest of the class.

✓ *Video/Digital Analysis.* Videotaping routines provides an excellent assessment option for seeing if children can both use the rolling cues and incorporate them with smoothness to express an idea. Either teachers or peers could use a check list to assess the tape.

Striking and Rolling

Setting: A large grassy area; a plastic ball or training volleyball or the like for each person; children by themselves initially and then in pairs

Cues

Tuck Shoulder	(Tuck your shoulder so that it is rounded.)
Round Body	(Round your back and tuck your chin and knees for a good roll.)

Tasks/Challenges:

T In a space by yourself, strike a plastic ball with any body part so that you fall off balance when you strike and have to roll in the direction that you're

falling. Make sure that you really strike the ball before you roll and roll in the direction that you're falling, not some other direction.

T Try to strike the ball so that you have to roll in directions other than forward, such as backward and sideways.

T Now work with a partner. The partner throws the ball to you; you try to strike the ball back to your partner, roll, and be ready for the next throw. The thrower should always throw the ball so the striker really has to reach for it. After five strikes, change places.

Catching, Throwing, and Rolling

Setting: A large grassy area; partners; one ball or beanbag per pair

Cues

Tuck Shoulder	(Tuck your shoulder so that it is rounded.)
Round Body	(Round your back and tuck your chin and knees for a good roll.)

Tasks/Challenges:

T This is a really tough task. Your partner will throw you a ball so that you have to stretch and roll to catch it. Your job is to try to throw the ball back to your partner as you begin the roll. **The secret is to keep your eyes open and try to catch with your throwing hand.** Remember, you must throw as you begin the roll, not after you've rolled. After five times, switch places.

Proficiency Level: Learning Experiences Leading to Skill Development in Rolling

At the proficiency level children enjoy aerial rolls that defy gravity and intricate combinations of rolls with other movements. Due to time limitations, equipment requirements, safety aspects, and the normal student-teacher ratio, we do not teach skills at this level. However, if you have students who have progressed to this level and enjoy the sensation these types of movements produce, encourage them to pursue out-of-school gymnastics clubs. These organizations allow children to increase their skill level beyond what we can do in a class setting.

Reading Comprehension Questions

1. List several examples of weight transfer.
2. What is the most common example of weight transfer?
3. Children at the precontrol, control, utilization, and proficiency levels are ready for what types of weight-transfer experiences?
4. Which relationship concepts are typically used as a subfocus in the study of weight transfer?
5. What does the question "Do the feet come down with control?" mean?
6. What are weight-transfer tasks at the utilization level designed to do?
7. What is the difference between a spring takeoff and a step takeoff? What is the purpose of each in gymnastics?
8. Define *rolling* and *rocking*.
9. How is rolling used in dance and in games?
10. In what way is rolling a safety skill?
11. What are the characteristics of rolling for each of the four skill levels? For example, what does a control-level roll look like?
12. What is our position on spotting? Why?
13. What problems does a child usually encounter when rolling backward?
14. What are the safety issues of back rolls? When should children be allowed to practice back rolls?
15. Identify three key safety points you would observe when teaching rolling.
16. Why don't we advocate teaching aerial rolls in physical education class?

References

National Association for Sport and Physical Education. (1995). *Moving into the future: National standards for physical education.* St. Louis, MO: Mosby.

National Association for Sport and Physical Education (2004). *Moving into the future: National standards for physical education* (2nd ed.). Reston, VA: National Association for Sport and Physical Education.

Kicking and Punting

A young boy kicking a stone along the sidewalk as he walks home from school, a neighborhood game of kick the can, kick ball on the school playground at recess, an aspiring athlete practicing the soccer dribble, and the professional punter—all are executing a similar movement: the kick. This movement requires accuracy, body control, point of contact, force, and direction. Some children seem to perform the kick with intense concentration; others, effortlessly.

We try to give children a variety of opportunities to practice kicking so that they'll develop a foundation of kicking skills that they can use in different situations. We emphasize the development of mature kicking patterns by focusing on experiences designed to elicit such patterns. For example, kicking for distance leads to the development of a mature kicking pattern, but this isn't true of kicking for accuracy. See Box 24-1 for information from the *National Standards for Physical Education* on kicking and punting.

Levels of Skill Proficiency in Kicking

Children at the precontrol level of kicking are challenged by the task of simply making contact with a stationary ball. They explore kicking a variety of balls, kicking balls just for fun at large targets, and tapping a ball as in the beginning skills of soccer. Appropriate precontrol-level tasks include:

1. Kicking a ball from a stationary position
2. Running to kick a stationary ball
3. Tapping a ball along the ground while moving behind it

At the control level, children are introduced to contacting a ball with different parts of the foot—inside, outside, back, and front. They're also given challenges that involve dribbling with either foot, at various speeds, and in different directions. Appropriate control-level activities include:

1. Sending a ball along the ground or through the air to a partner
2. Kicking toward a target
3. Making quick kicks
4. Starting/stopping, changing directions with the soccer dribble

Children at the utilization level of kicking are able to kick for both distance and accuracy. They enjoy and learn from the challenge of one-on-one keep-away situations (trying to prevent another child from getting the ball), which combine the skills of tapping a ball along the ground with the skills needed to dodge an opponent. Dynamic game situations children at the utilization level enjoy can involve:

1. Kicking a ball to a target while on the run
2. Kicking for accuracy while trying to maneuver around an opponent
3. Differentiating high from low kicks

Children who've reached the proficiency level in kicking enjoy group participation with more players, more complex relationships, and the excitement of strategy development. Sample tasks include:

1. Kicking for a target against defense
2. Gamelike situations
3. Kicking at moving targets

The entire spectrum of kicking experiences, from precontrol through proficiency, is represented in our progression spiral on page 443. The tasks are stated in terms that imply a direct approach (see Chapter 13), but teachers are encouraged to vary the approach according to the purpose of the lesson and the characteristics of the class.

The key observation points in Boxes 24-2 and 24-3 illustrate correct and incorrect ways of kicking along the ground and in the air, respectively. Ask yourself the questions in the boxes as you observe the youngsters in action.

Box 24-1

The Skills of Kicking and Punting in the *National Standards for Physical Education*

The movement skills of kicking and punting are referenced in the *National Standards for Physical Education* (National Association for Sport and Physical Education, 2004) under Standard 1: Demonstrates competency in motor skills and movement patterns needed to perform a variety of physical activities. The standard speaks of younger children demonstrating progress toward achieving mature form in the more complex manipulative skills, such as the foot dribble, and achieving mature form in the less complex manipulative skills. Older children then use the skills in dynamic and complex environments, and in combinations.

A sample performance outcome from the *National Standards:*

- Taps the ball from foot to foot, shifting weight and balancing the body on the nondribbling foot, while in one location, i.e., not moving (K–2)*

*Grade-level guidelines for expected student learning.

Box 24-2

Key Observation Points: Kicking along the Ground

Soccer Dribble

Does the child contact the ball for the dribble behind the ball, rather than on top?

Dribble/Kick for Distance

1. Does the child make contact with the instep (shoelaces) of the foot, not with the toes?
2. Is the child's trunk inclined slightly backward for the kick?

Box 24-3

Key Observation Points: Kicking in the Air

1. Does the child make contact below the center of the ball, not on top?

2. Is the child's kicking foot extended for contact on the shoelaces, not on the toes?

3. Does the child's kicking leg bend in preparation for the kick and follow through after contact?

Box 24-3 (continued)

4. Does the child's trunk incline slightly backward for the kick?

NO   YES

Mature Stage

When children are at the mature stage of kicking, do their kicks look similar to the following sequence? The approach to the ball involves one or more steps, with the distance just before the kick covered with a leap. The kicker is airborne in the approach. The knee of the kicking leg is slightly flexed because of the leap just before kicking. The trunk is inclined backward before and during contact. The kicker disperses the momentum of the kick by hopping on the support leg and stepping in the direction of the object that was struck.

Sources: "Developmental Sequence of Kicking," mimeographed materials, by V. Seefeldt and J. Haubenstricker, presented at the University of Georgia, Athens, June 1978; *Fundamental Motor Patterns,* 2nd ed., by R. L. Wickstrom, 1977, Philadelphia: Lea & Febiger.

Precontrol Level: Activities for Exploration of Kicking

At the precontrol level, we want children to make contact with a stationary ball for kicking. When they are able to do this, we add an approach to a stationary ball and tapping a ball gently along the ground.

Kicking a Stationary Ball from a Stationary Position

Setting: A variety of plastic, foam, and rubber balls for kicking, placed around the gymnasium approximately 10 feet from the wall

Tasks/Challenges:

T Stand behind a kicking ball. Kick the ball really hard so it travels to the wall.

C Practice until you can kick the ball three times in a row to the wall.

T Practice kicking with one foot and then with the other foot.

T Practice kicking the ball, making it go sometimes along the ground, sometimes in the air.

※ What determines whether the ball travels along the ground or in the air?

T Move outdoors and practice your kicking in an open space for maximum distance.

Kicking at Large Targets

Setting: Large targets on the wall at low level; freestanding targets placed 4 to 5 feet from the wall (Figure 24.1); a variety of plastic, foam, and rubber balls for kicking

Tasks/Challenges:

T Stand behind your kicking ball. Kick the ball toward the target, trying to hit it.

T Try kicking at the different types of targets. Which is your favorite? Which is your best for accuracy?

T Choose your favorite target; stand 8 feet away from the target and kick. When you can hit the target two times in a row, take a giant step backward and try from that distance.

Approaching a Stationary Ball and Kicking

Setting: Balls for kicking, placed around the gymnasium approximately 10 feet from the wall (Figure 24.2)

Tasks/Challenges:

T Stand 3 to 4 feet behind the kicking ball. Approach the ball and kick it forward to the wall.

T Alternate kicking with your right foot and your left foot so you will be skilled at using either foot.

C Practice until you can successfully approach and kick to the wall three times. Success equals foot contacting the ball, and ball contacting the wall.

Tapping the Ball

Setting: Children scattered throughout general space, with foam balls at their feet

Tasks/Challenges:

T Gently tap the ball from one foot to the other, using the inside of your foot.

T On the signal, begin tapping the ball from foot to foot; continue until you hear the signal to stop.

C I will time you for 30 seconds. Try to continue tapping between your feet for the full amount of time.

T Walk through general space, tapping the ball from foot to foot—left, right, left, right—as you go. Keep the ball between your feet throughout the travel.

T Walk through general space, tapping the ball from foot to foot, avoiding collisions with others. This means you must control for the tap and control for no collisions.

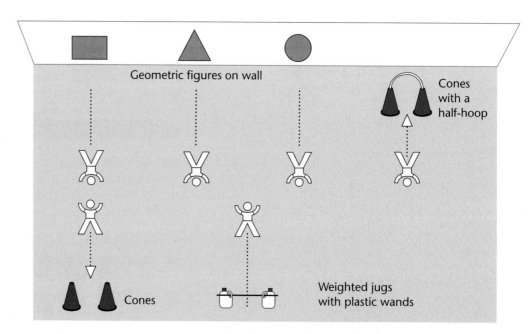

Figure 24.1 Target arrangement for kicking at large targets.

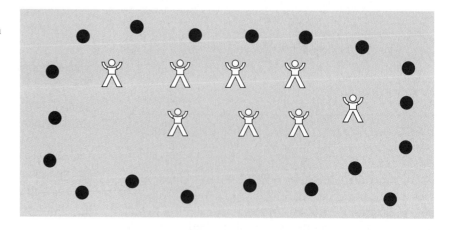

Figure 24.2 Arrangement for the approach and kick of a stationary ball.

After a couple of years, the 8½-inch inexpensive plastic balls become partially deflated. These half-life plastic balls are excellent for kicking, especially indoors. We mark them with a large K so children know which balls are for kicking, which ones for dribbling. Playground and kick balls can also be partially deflated for beginning practice and for use indoors.

Control Level: Learning Experiences Leading to Skill Development in Kicking

At the control level, we want children to make consistent contact with a ball. We provide a variety of kicking experiences that include kicking for accuracy, kicking in different directions, and partner relationships. We encourage use of different parts of each foot and greater control of speed and directions.

A note about cues: Although several cues are listed for many of the learning experiences, it's important to focus on only one cue at a time. That way, the children can really concentrate on that cue. Once you provide feedback to the children and observe that most have learned a cue, then it's time to focus on another one.

Kicking on the Ground

Setting: A variety of balls for kicking—foam, plastic, rubber—placed around the gymnasium approximately 10 feet from the wall (see Figure 24.2)

Cues	
Shoelaces	(Contact the ball with your instep—your shoelaces—not your toes.)
Behind the Ball	(Contact the ball directly *behind* center for travel forward at a low level.)
Beside the Ball	(Place your nonkicking foot *beside* the ball.)

Tasks/Challenges:

T When we were exploring kicking, you kicked balls that were positioned on the ground with you standing behind them. You also kicked balls placed on the ground with you running to the ball. Practice kicking the ball to the wall from both starting positions.

T Kick the ball hard so it hits the wall with enough force to rebound back to you.

Place a series of 2-inch tape markers on the walls of the gym, approximately 3 feet above the floor.

T Kick the ball so it hits the wall below the tape line. **Remember, contact the ball directly behind center so it will travel at a low level.**

T Practice your kicking with both your right and your left foot. In game situations, you need to be skilled with both feet.

C Practice kicking with each foot until you can kick three times in a row with each foot, the ball contacting the wall below the tape line.

T The balls for kicking are scattered around the edge of the gymnasium. Begin traveling in general space, avoiding collisions with others or the balls on the floor. On the signal, approach the ball nearest you and kick it toward the wall. Quickly retrieve the ball you kicked and place it 10 to 12 feet from the wall. You are now ready to move again. Ready? Travel in general space. Remember to listen for the signal to kick.

The skill of kicking improves with practice.

✓ ***Exit Slip.*** This would be an excellent time for an exit slip to assess student understanding of the critical cues for kicking. The exit slip might be a drawing of a shoe with directions for the child to circle the part of the foot that should be used for contact on the ball; a verbal statement, "shoelaces" versus "toes," to a partner or the teacher; or a whisper to the teacher as each child exits the gymnasium.

Kicking in the Air

Setting: A variety of balls for kicking—foam, plastic, rubber—placed around the gymnasium approximately 10 feet from the wall (see Figure 24.2)

Cues

Shoelaces   (Contact the ball with your instep—your shoelacess—not your toes.)

Under the Ball (Contact the ball *below* center for travel upward through the air.)

Step-Hop   (Step-hop on your nonkicking leg to complete a running approach.)

Tasks/Challenges:

🅣 When we were exploring kicking, you kicked balls that were positioned on the ground with you standing behind them and you kicked balls placed on the ground with you running to the ball. Practice kicking the ball to the wall from both starting positions.

🅣 Assume a starting position 5 to 6 feet behind the ball. Approach the ball for the kick; immediately after you kick the ball, take a small hop on your nonkicking leg, and then step forward in the direction of the kick. This step-hop checks your forward momentum.

🅣 Practice your kicking with the step-hop, sending the ball through the air so it contacts the wall above the tape line.

🅒 Practice kicking through the air until you can successfully complete the aerial kick five times.

Kicking for Distance

Setting: Balls for kicking placed in a large circle on the playground (Figure 24.3); children positioned inside the circle, facing outward

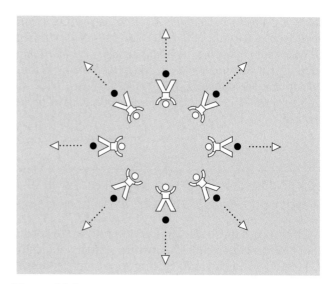

Figure 24.3 Circular pattern for distance kicking.

Cues

Shoelaces   (Contact the ball with your instep—your shoelaces—not your toes.)

Behind the Ball (Contact the ball directly *behind* center for travel at a low level, along the ground.)

Under the Ball   (Contact the ball *below* center for travel upward through the air.)

Step-Hop   (Step-hop on your nonkicking leg to complete the running approach.)

Tasks/Challenges:

🅣 Stand inside the circle, just behind a ball, facing away from the center of the circle. You are going to practice kicking along the ground and in the air. There's enough room for you to kick as hard as you wish. Practice your first series of kicks standing just behind the ball—no running approach. Kick the ball so it travels along the ground, at low level. After you kick, retrieve the ball and quickly bring it back to your starting place for the next kick.

🅣 Now kick the ball with your nonpreferred foot. Does the ball travel as far?

🅣 Kick the ball with your preferred foot, sending it through the air. Remember to stand just behind the ball for the kick.

🅟 What is the key for sending the ball along the ground? In the air? Where on the foot do you make contact for each kick?

🅣 Place the ball on the ground, and take three or four steps back from the ball. Approach the ball with three or four running steps, and then kick the ball

As they practice, children will discover that the force required to kick a ball for accuracy is initially different from that required to kick a ball for distance.

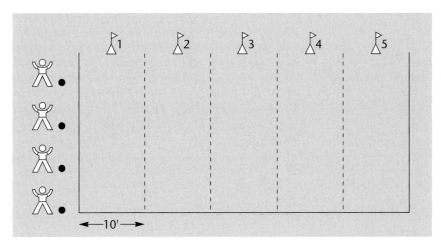

Figure 24.4 Numbered distance zones.

along the ground (*and in the air*). **Don't forget the step-hop on the nonkicking leg as you make contact.**

C Practice kicking both along the ground and through the air. Challenge yourself to kick farther each time. Can you attain that distance both along the ground and in the air?

Numbering the balls 1, 2, 3, 4, and so forth, eliminates confusion about which ball belongs to which child.

Kicking to a Distance Zone

Setting: Marker cones or plastic milk cartons placed at 10-foot intervals across the playground, numbered consecutively so the children can see the numbers from the kicking line (Figure 24.4)

Cues

Shoelaces	(Contact the ball with your instep—your shoelaces—not your toes.)
Under the Ball	(Contact the ball *below* center for travel upward through the air.)
Step-Hop	(Step-hop on your nonkicking leg to complete a running approach.)

Tasks/Challenges:

T Place the ball you are going to use at the kicking line. Approach the ball from about 5 to 6 feet. Kick the ball so it travels as far as possible through the air. Note the number of the zone in which the ball first contacts the ground. Kick five times, trying to improve your distance.

C Try to kick the ball so that it lands in the same zone three times in a row.

Kicking to Targets

Setting: A series of targets of different heights arranged throughout the gymnasium (Figure 24.5); a variety of balls for kicking

Cues	
Shoelaces	(Contact the ball with your instep—your shoelaces—not your toes.)
Under the Ball	(Contact the ball *below* the center for travel upward through the air.)
Behind the Ball	(Contact the ball directly *behind* center for travel at a low level, along the ground.)
Watch the Ball	(Focus on the ball, not the target, until the ball leaves your foot.)

Tasks/Challenges:

T Spaced around the gym are targets for kicking—suspended hoops, marker cones to kick between and to hit, ropes hung between chairs for kicking over, tape squares on the wall.

I'll assign you to a station; at that station practice kicking at the target. Place the ball at the kicking line. Approach the kicking line with two or three steps before you make contact. After your turn, retrieve the ball and return to your group to wait your next turn. Continue practicing at your station until the signal is given to change to another kicking station. You may need to adjust your force when you're kicking to hit a target.

Here's what you'll do at the different stations. At the hoops, kick the ball through the circle. At the large and small marker cones, kick the ball hard enough to make the cone fall over. At the rope between the chairs and the rope stretched between the standards, kick the ball so it travels over the rope. At the marker goals, kick the ball along the ground between the cones. At the tape square, kick the ball so it touches the wall inside the square.

Weighted jugs, cones, or tape marks on the wall can serve as goals. Vary the width of the goal according to individuals' abilities.

✓ ***Peer Observation.*** Station practice provides an opportune time for peer observation of critical cues. Designate one station, for example, marker cones, and have partners observe each other kicking for travel along the ground. When partners are observing for a critical cue, such as contact behind the ball or on shoelaces, remind the observers of what their focus is; accuracy of the kick is not what is being assessed. *See Chapter 14, "Assessing Student Learning," for development and recording of peer observation.*

Figure 24.5 Targets for kicking.

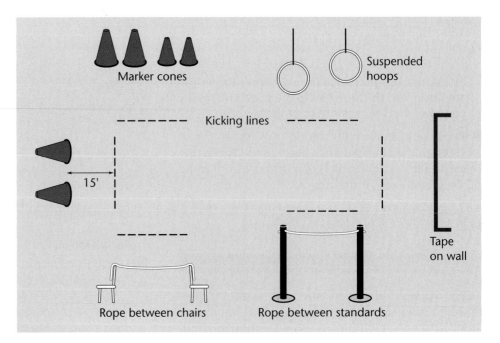

Kicking a Rolling Ball from a Stationary Position

Setting: Partners positioned 10 to 12 feet from each other, each pair with a ball for kicking

Cues

Shoelaces	(Contact the ball with your instep—your shoelaces —not your toes.)
Behind the Ball	(Contact the ball directly *behind* center for travel at a low level.)
Under the Ball	(Contact the ball *below* center for travel through the air.)
Watch the Ball	(Focus on the ball, not your partner, until the ball leaves your foot.)

Tasks/Challenges:

T Partner 1: Roll the ball along the ground to partner 2. Partner 2: Kick the ball so it travels back to partner 1. Kick only hard enough for the ball to travel to your partner.

T Practice the kick along the ground with both your right foot and your left foot.

T Practice the kick through the air to your partner. Sometimes in game situations you want to kick along the ground; sometimes you need to kick in the air.

C Practice until you can kick the ball along the ground five times to your partner so your partner does not have to move from self-space to retrieve the ball—five times with the left foot, five times with the right.

C Can you meet the challenge of kicking the ball through the air so your partner does not have to move to retrieve it? Give it a try!

Kicking to a Partner

Setting: Partners facing each other, 15 to 20 feet apart, each pair with a ball for kicking

Cues

Sender	Shoelaces (Contact the ball with your instep—your shoelaces—not your toes.)
	Behind the Ball (Contact the ball directly *behind* center for travel at low level, along the ground.)

	Watch the Ball (Focus on the ball, not your partner, as you kick and as you receive.)
Receiver	Trap (Stop the ball by placing your foot on top, slightly behind the ball.)

Tasks/Challenges:

T Kick the ball along the ground (or floor) to your partner so he or she can stop it with the foot without moving from self-space. This is called trapping the ball. To trap, place your foot slightly behind the ball, above the center back.

T Practice sending and receiving—kicking and trapping—with your partner. Always stop (trap) the ball before kicking it back to your partner.

C Practice until you can kick five times to your partner so he or she can trap without moving from self-space.

T When you are comfortable with your skill and can kick accurately five times, take a large step backward and repeat the task. Practice at different distances to determine your maximum distance for accuracy with your partner.

Tapping the Ball along the Ground (Soccer Dribble)

Setting: Children scattered throughout general space, with plastic (foam, rubber) balls for kicking; listening position is one foot resting on the ball

Cues

Tap, Tap	(Gently tap the ball so that it stays within 3 to 4 feet of you at all times.)
Inside of Foot	(Tap the ball with the inside of your foot—left and right.)
Open Spaces	(Look for open spaces as you travel.)

Tasks/Challenges:

T When we were exploring kicking, you practiced tapping the ball between your feet, inside to inside. Practice that skill of gently tapping back and forth.

T On the signal, begin traveling through general space, tapping the ball with the inside of your foot. When you hear the signal, quickly place one foot on top of the ball, slightly behind center, to stop the momentum—trap the ball.

T Alternate tapping on your right foot and then your left foot; turn your feet out like a duck.

C On the signal, begin traveling in general space, tapping the ball in the soccer dribble. Try to travel and tap with alternate feet and without letting the ball get away from you or colliding with another person. Ready? Tap, tap . . . open spaces.

C Now dribble in general space. See if you can keep it up for 30 seconds without colliding ball to ball or person to person.

As the children improve, you can increase the time to 45 seconds and then to one minute.

T Begin traveling in general space, dribbling the soccer ball as you go. Gradually increase your speed, keeping the ball within 3 to 4 feet of you at all times. Increase and decrease the speed of your travel, adjusting the force of your kick as you increase and decrease the speed.

C I will time you again for a 30-second dribble. Challenge yourself to dribble at your personal maximum speed—with soccer ball and using body control.

✓ *Teacher Observation.* Teacher observation of critical cues in a dynamic, noncompetitive setting is important at this point. *See Chapters 14 and 12 for teacher observation examples.*

Starting and Stopping

Setting: Children scattered throughout general space, each with a ball for kicking

Cues	
Tap, Tap	(Gently tap the ball so that it stays within 3 to 4 feet of you at all times.)
Inside of Foot	(Tap the ball with the inside of your foot—left and right.)
Trap	(Stop the ball by placing your foot on top, slightly behind the ball.)

Tasks/Challenges:

T Begin dribbling in general space. When you hear the signal, quickly trap the ball. **Maintain a balanced, ready position *(weight centered over support leg)*** so that you can move again quickly. Ready? Begin.

This activity provides practice in stopping the ball quickly. Frequent signals will be needed: 10 seconds of dribbling, stop; 30 seconds of dribbling, stop . . .

T Travel through general space, dribbling as you go. Each time you meet another person, trap the ball quickly with your foot, execute a quarter turn, and continue dribbling. The ability to stop and start quickly is an important offensive skill that helps you maintain control of the ball and avoid your opponents.

C Test your dribbling and trapping skills with this 2-minute activity: On the signal, begin dribbling in general space. Each time you hear the drum or meet another person, stop quickly, trapping the ball with one foot; execute a quarter turn; and continue dribbling. Your goal is to stop-start for 2 minutes without losing control of the ball or bumping another person or ball. The signal at the end of the 2 minutes will be a double drumbeat. **Look for the open spaces.**

Traveling in Pathways

Setting: Various pathways taped on the floor or spray-painted on the grass; children scattered throughout general space, each with a ball for kicking

Cues	
Tap, Tap	(Gently tap the ball so that it stays within 3 to 4 feet of you at all times.)
Inside/Outside	(Use both the inside of your foot and the outside of your foot—left and right—to tap the soccer ball.)

Tasks/Challenges:

T On the ground are straight, curved, and zigzag pathways. Travel through the formations using the soccer dribble, traveling at a speed you can control—no collisions, no loss of the ball. Be sure to travel all the pathways.

T As you tap/dribble the different pathways, you begin to discover that the inside of the foot is perhaps not always the best surface to use for the tap/dribble. Practice the tap/dribble with the outside of your foot as well as the inside. **Keep the tap gentle—with control.**

Dribbling Around Stationary Obstacles

Setting: Marker cones and/or milk jugs positioned throughout general space; a kicking ball for each child

Dribbling, kicking, and punting require visual focus and concentration.

Cues

Tap, Tap	(Gently tap the ball so that it stays within 3 to 4 feet of you at all times.)
Inside/ Outside	(Use both the inside of your foot and the outside of your foot—left and right—to tap the soccer ball.)
Heads Up	(Keep your head up to avoid collisions—people, obstacles, soccer balls.)

Tasks/Challenges:

T Tap/dribble the ball throughout general space, alternating contact with your right foot and your left foot. Avoid bumping into the cones (jugs) with either the ball or your body. Travel in zigzag and curved pathways to avoid the obstacles. Your visual range must now include the ball you're dribbling, other people, the balls they're using, and the obstacles.

T Tap/dribble in general space. Each time you approach an obstacle, trap the ball, execute a quarter turn to either the right or the left, and continue dribbling.

T Vary the speed of your travel—sometimes approach a cone (jug) very quickly, sometimes slowly.

T Tap/dribble in general space. As you near a cone (jug), tap the ball gently with the inside of your right foot, passing the ball to the left of the cone (jug). Quickly continue the dribble.

T Tap/dribble in general space. As you near a cone (jug), tap the ball gently with the inside of your left foot, passing the ball to the right of the cone (jug).

T Tap/dribble in general space. As you near the cone (jug), tap the ball gently with the outside of your right foot, passing the ball to the right of the cone (jug).

T Tap/dribble in general space. As you near a cone (jug), tap the ball gently with the outside of your left foot, passing the ball to the left of the cone (jug).

C This time as you practice dribbling, trapping, and turning, pretend you have 100 points. If the ball you are dribbling contacts a cone (jug), subtract 10 points from your score. If you have a collision with another person, subtract 25 points. Try to complete your practice with 100 points!

Keeping It Perfect: Zero, Zero

Setting: Marker cones and/or milk jugs positioned throughout general space; a kicking ball for each child

Cues

Tap, Tap	(Gently tap the ball so that it stays within 3 to 4 feet of you at all times.)
Inside/ Outside	(Use both the inside of your foot and the outside of your foot—left and right—to tap the soccer ball.)
Heads Up	(Keep your head up to avoid collisions—people, obstacles, soccer balls.)

Tasks/Challenges:

T Thus far in our tap/dribble study, you've practiced dribbling with control, trapping with one foot, avoiding obstacles, changing the speed of your travel, and tapping the ball to the right or the left, as in passing. The game of Keeping It Perfect: Zero, Zero will give you a chance to test these skills.

Each of you has a perfect score of zero. The object of the game is to still have the perfect score at the end of the 2 minutes of activity. On the signal, begin to tap/dribble in general space. You may travel at any speed you choose, increasing and decreasing your speed as you wish. When you hear the drum, trap the ball immediately; I'll give a verbal "go" for you to continue.

You earn negative points if you:

1. Don't trap the ball within 2 seconds of the drumbeat (−1)
2. Bump into another person or the ball they're dribbling (−1)
3. Bump into a marker cone (−1)

The key is control. Ready? Go.

You can use this activity to focus on specific skills. For example, in the first 2 minutes, children are to travel in general space (control); in the second 2 minutes, they are to travel in each area of the gymnasium (speed); in the third 2 minutes, they are to zigzag around as many cones as possible (passing, accuracy).

At the end of each 2 minutes, stop, rest, and calculate your scores. Remember, a perfect score is zero.

Utilization Level: Learning Experiences Leading to Skill Development in Kicking

At the utilization level, we focus on providing experiences for applying kicking skills in unpredictable situations of increasing complexity. Performing skills on the move and in relation to an opponent are important challenges. A great degree of accuracy and control is the goal at this level.

A note about cues: Although several cues are listed for many of the learning experiences, it's important to focus on only one cue at a time. That way, the children can really concentrate on that cue. Once you provide feedback to the children and observe that most have learned a cue, then it's time to focus on another one.

Changing Directions: Tap/Dribble

Setting: Children scattered throughout general space, each with a ball for kicking.

Cues	
Tap, Tap	(Gently tap the ball so that it is always within your control—no more than 3 to 4 feet from you—even with increased speed.)
Middle of Ball	(Contact directly behind the middle of the ball, using the insides, outsides, and heels of your feet for the dribble.)

Tasks/Challenges:

T Begin traveling in general space, tapping the ball 3 to 4 feet in front of you as you go. When you are comfortable with your control of the dribble, tap the ball ahead of you, run quickly beyond the ball, tap it gently with your heel, quickly turn, and continue the dribble. Be sure you run *beyond* the ball to tap the front of it; contact on top of the ball will cause you to fall.

Performing a Continuous Tap/Dribble and Change of Direction

Setting: Children scattered throughout general space

Cues	
Tap/Tap	(Tap the ball with control so that it stays within 3 to 4 feet of you at *all* times.)
Inside/Outside/ Heels of Feet	(Tap the ball with different parts of your feet as you dribble.)
Heads Up	(Keep your head up to avoid collisions—people, soccer balls.)

Tasks/Challenges:

T You learned to change the direction of the ball by tapping it to the right or left with the inside or outside of your foot. And you just learned one method of changing direction front to back. Travel within the boundaries of our work area using changes of direction to avoid contact with others and to avoid crossing the outside boundaries. Your task is continuous dribbling. Ready? Begin.

T Approach a boundary quickly; use the heel tap to change the direction of the dribble at the last moment, to prevent crossing the boundary.

T Purposely approach some other students; use a pass to the right or left to avoid contact with them.

C Challenge yourself by increasing your speed to the maximum rate you can travel with a controlled dribble and frequent changes of direction.

✔ *Videotape.* As children begin combining skills, the videotaping of their practice provides an excellent opportunity for self-assessment. Have them watch the video and code the number of skills they included in their practice, for example, inside of foot, outside of foot, trapping with heel. As they watch the video clip the second time, have them assess their execution of those skills relative to the critical cues.

Traveling and Kicking for a Goal

Setting: Hoops or milk jugs scattered throughout general space; marker cones for goals (Figure 24.6)

Cues	
Behind the Ball	(Contact the ball directly *behind* center for travel along the ground.)
Gentle Taps/ Hard Kicks	(Gently tap the ball for the dribble; kick hard for the goal.)

Tasks/Challenges:

T Travel at your own speed and tap the ball while avoiding obstacles and other people. On the signal, travel quickly to an open space, and kick for the goal. Retrieve the ball; begin dribbling again, listening for the signal to kick for the goal.

T Practice dribbling around obstacles and kicking for the goal on your own; I won't give the signal for the kick.

Playing One-on-One Soccer

Setting: Sets of partners in general space; kicking balls; marker cones (milk jugs) for goals

Cues	
Gentle Taps/ Hard Kicks	(Gently tap the ball for the dribble; kick hard for the goal.)
Heads Up	(Keep your head up to avoid collisions—people, soccer balls.)
Inside/Outside/ Heels of Feet	(Tap the ball with different parts of your feet as you travel.)
Offense	Open Spaces . . . Look for Them, Move to Them
Defense	Trap or Tap to Gain Possession

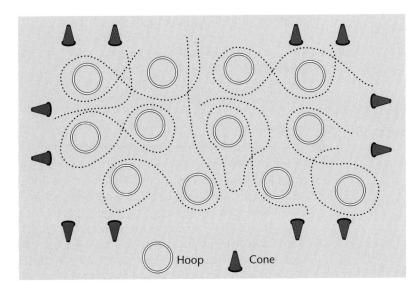

Figure 24.6 Setup for combination dribble and kick with varying degrees of force.

Hoop ⬤   Cone ▲

Dribbling in open space allows children to focus on kicking and their relationship to others.

Figure 24.7 Soccer Golf course arrangement.

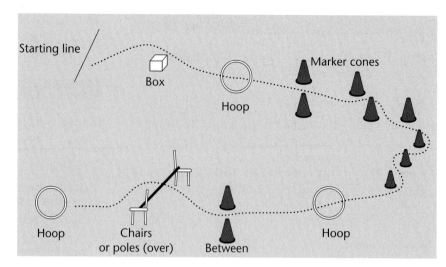

Tasks/Challenges:

T Select a partner whose tap/dribble skills are very similar to your skills. Cooperatively decide the boundaries for your area; a small area provides more practice. Partner 1 begins to travel and dribble the soccer ball within that area; partner 2 attempts to gain possession of the ball by using the feet to trap the ball or tap it away. Follow these rules:

1. Contact the ball, not the person.
2. Gain possession of the ball; don't kick it away.
3. If you gain possession of the ball, begin your dribble as the offensive player; your partner will be the defense.

If partners are unmatched in skill, give a signal for the change from offense to defense. That is, each time partner 2 gains possession of the ball, that person will give it back to partner 1, who continues to tap/dribble until the signal to switch positions is given.

T Within your area, set up two marker cones (milk jugs) as a goal. Partner 1 will tap/dribble until within scoring range (*10 to 12 feet of the goal*) and then kick for the goal. Partner 2 will attempt to gain possession of the ball, using the feet only. After each kick for the goal, switch positions.

C You may want to design a game using the skills of the soccer dribble and kicking for the goal. Work cooperatively with your partner to decide the rules of the game, scoring, boundaries. Can you think of a name for your game? (*See Chapter 31.*)

Playing Soccer Golf

Setting: Obstacle course arrangement (Figure 24.7); a kicking ball for each child

Cues

Behind the Ball	(Contact the ball directly *behind* center for travel along the ground.)
Under the Ball	(Contact the ball slightly *below* center for travel upward through the air.)
Gentle Taps/ Hard Kicks	(Gently tap the ball for the dribble; kick hard for the goal.)

Tasks/Challenges:

T The game of Soccer Golf involves the skills of dribbling in pathways, kicking for a goal, and kicking over a low height. The playground is arranged as a golf course. Your task is to complete the course with the fewest number of kicks. There are boxes to dribble around, zones to zigzag through, hoops to kick into, and poles to kick over. Count your kicks as you proceed through the course. When you finish the course, begin again, trying to lower your score.

To decrease waiting time, have the children begin at different holes on the course rather than having everyone start at the first hole.

Kicking to a Partner from Various Angles

Setting: Partners positioned 15 to 20 feet from each other, each pair with a kicking ball

Cues

Behind the Ball	(Contact the ball directly *behind* center for travel along the ground.)

Foot, Not Toes	(Kick the ball with the inside or the outside of your foot, not with your toes.)
Kick Hard	(Kick the ball with enough force to send it to your partner.)

Tasks/Challenges:

T Review the skill of kicking along the ground (the floor) so that your partner can trap the ball without moving. When you are comfortable with the kick, take three to four steps to the right so you are at an angle to your partner. Kick the ball from this position so it travels directly to your partner. Kick with the inside of your right foot and the outside of your left foot until you can kick four out of five times directly to your partner with each foot.

T Move to the left three to four steps from your original position. Kick the ball to your partner from this angle. Practice the kick with the inside of your left foot and the outside of your right foot. Then practice with the outside of your left foot and the inside of your right foot.

T Position yourself at different angles in relation to your partner, and practice kicking to your partner from these positions. The ability to kick at different angles is important in passing the ball to teammates and in kicking for a goal in games.

Kicking to a Traveling Partner

Setting: Sets of partners at one end of the playing field (gymnasium) approximately 15 feet from each other; one partner with the ball for kicking (Figure 24.8)

Cues	
Behind the Ball	(Contact the ball directly *behind* center for travel along the ground.)

Inside of Foot	(Kick the ball with the inside of your foot, not with your toes.)
Kick Hard	(Kick the ball with enough force to send it to your partner.)
Sender	Ahead of Partner (Kick beyond your partner.)
Receiver	On the Move (Don't stop and wait for the ball.)

Tasks/Challenges:

T Travel the length of the playing field (gymnasium) passing the ball to each other as you travel. Remember to pass to your partner while you are *on the move;* don't stop to execute the kick.

T Pass the ball *ahead* of your partner so he or she can continue traveling, rather than having to stop to receive the pass.

The second set of partners may begin their travel/pass when the partners in front of them are one-third the distance of the field (gymnasium) or you may signal when each set of partners is to begin traveling.

Passing to a Partner in General Space

Setting: Sets of partners in general space, each set with a ball for kicking

Cues	
Heads Up	(Keep your head up to avoid collisions—people, soccer balls.)
Pass at an Angle	(Use the inside/outside of your feet [right/left] to send the ball to your partner.)
Pass to the Open Space	(Kick the ball to the open space ahead of your partner.)

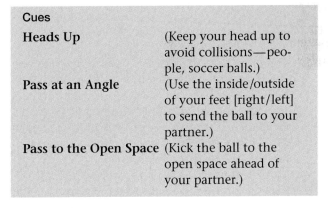

Figure 24.8 Kicking to a traveling partner.

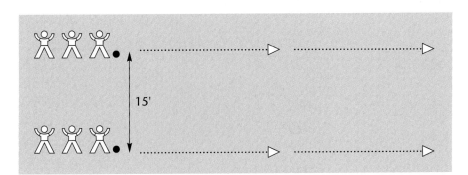

Tasks/Challenges:

T Travel in general space, dribbling and passing to your partner. All other players will be traveling and passing at the same time, so it is important that you be aware of others and of passing to open spaces. Ready? Begin.

T Challenge yourself always to pass the ball ahead of your partner—to the open space. If you are successful, your partner will never have to stop to receive the pass. Try for five successful completions: open space, partner on the move.

Playing Two-on-One Soccer

Setting: Groups of three in general space; marker cones for goals; balls for kicking

Cues	
Pass at an Angle	(Use the inside/outside of your feet [right/left] to send the ball to your partner.)
Pass to the Open Space	(Kick the ball to the open space ahead of your partner.)
Gentle Taps/Hard Kicks	(Gently tap the ball for the dribble; kick hard to pass and to make a goal.)

Tasks/Challenges:

T Form groups of three; two of you will be offensive players, and one of you will be a defensive player. The two offensive players will tap/dribble and pass to each other within the boundaries of your soccer area. The defensive player will attempt to gain possession of the ball by intercepting passes or tapping the ball away on the dribble.

Each team will have possession of the ball (*offense*) for 2 minutes. See how many goals you can score within that interval. The offensive team must execute at least two passes before attempting a kick for the goal.

Proficiency Level: Learning Experiences Leading to Skill Development in Kicking

At the proficiency level, we give children opportunities to use the skill of kicking in group games and for learning the strategy of offensive/defensive participation.

Kicking (passing) at angles and kicking (passing) to the open space are two of the most critical skills for game play. They provide the "bridge" between skill mastery in a static situation and successful skill execution in a dynamic environment.

Children play self-designed games, or the teacher chooses the games. These games involve relationships that are made increasingly complex by the number of players and types of strategies required.

A note about cues: At the proficiency level, tasks are more complex, typically requiring children to coordinate several movements simultaneously in a dynamic context. A list of cues is provided to assist the children in being more successful in the learning experience. The challenge for the teacher is in determining which cue will be most beneficial for each child . . . and when. Thus, careful observation and critical reflection become very important as you watch the children move and then decide which cue will be the most helpful to move each learner to a higher skill level.

Kicking at Small Stationary Targets

Setting: Sets of marker cones 6 feet apart to serve as targets; a line for kicking 15 to 20 feet from each target (Figure 24.9)

Cues	
Individual cues as needed	

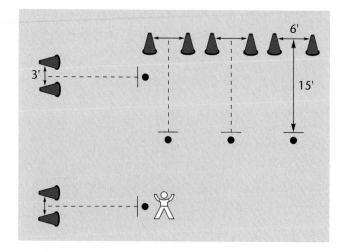

Figure 24.9 Kicking at small targets.

Tasks/Challenges:

Ⓣ Each person will have 10 kicks at the goal; mentally record your personal score. After each person has kicked 10 times, move the cones closer together until they are 3 feet apart. Now kick 10 times at this target. Compare this score with your score for the 6-foot target.

Ⓣ Position yourself at an angle facing the target. Repeat the tasks, kicking at an angle rather than in a direct line to the target. Compare your scores to your direct-line kicks.

Ⓒ Set a personal goal for successful kicks. Practice to meet that goal for both direct and angle kicks.

✓ *Teacher Observation.* At the utilization and proficiency levels, children's kicking should show mature patterns as well as accuracy. Check lists for recording accuracy scores can also include analysis of errors and correction cues. See Chapter 12 for the development of observation check lists.

Kicking at a Moving Target

Setting: Hoops suspended from a rope hanging from a frame, wall bars, or outdoor playground equipment (partners may also hold hoop for each other)

> **Cues**
>
> **Ahead of the Target** (Kick the ball to the open space just beyond the moving target.)

Tasks/Challenges:

Ⓣ Partner 1 starts the suspended hoop swinging or moves back and forth, holding the hoop in the hand. Partner 2, approximately 10 to 12 feet away, kicks the ball at the moving target, attempting to kick the ball through the hoop. After five trials, partners change places.

This learning experience reinforces "kicking to the open space" and "kicking at angles," which were introduced earlier. Remind children to kick the ball to the space where the hoop will swing, not to the space where the hoop is when they execute the kick, thus the concepts of angle and open-space target!

Playing Mini Soccer

Setting: Milk jugs and marker cones as boundaries; children in groups of four, six, or eight

> **Cues**
>
> *Offensive* Pass at an Angle to Teammates Pass to Open Space (Pass ahead of the receiver.)
> Body between Ball and Opponent (Keep your body between the ball and the defender at all times; quickly switch the tap/dribble to the outside foot.)
> *Defensive* Tap or Trap

Tasks/Challenges:

Ⓣ With your group, design a game of Mini Soccer, using the skills we have been practicing. Cooperatively decide the rules, scoring, and the boundaries. I will place only one limitation on the game: Each member of the offensive team must dribble the ball before making a kick for the goal.

✓ *Journal.* After children are involved in a dynamic kicking/dribbling situation involving combining of skills, have them reflect on their play with a journal entry. *See Chapter 14, "Assessing Student Learning," for journal entry guidelines.*

Playing Soccer Keep-Away

Setting: Children in teams of three to six; large open space

> **Cues**
>
> *Offensive* Pass at an Angle to Teammates Pass to Open Space (Pass ahead of the receiver.)
> Body between Ball and Opponent
> *Defensive* Close the Open Spaces (Move quickly to close the open spaces.)

Tasks/Challenges:

Ⓣ The object of Soccer Keep-Away is to keep the ball away from your opponents using the tap/dribble and passing skills you have been practicing. There is no kicking for the goal, only passing and dribbling, in the game. To begin the game, one person throws the ball (two hands, overhead) in from the sideline. Play continues with the ball being dribbled and passed as the other team attempts to gain possession by trapping, intercepting, or gaining control of the dribble. At the end of each 3 minutes of play, I will signal for the other team to execute the throw-in to begin a new game.

Alley Soccer and Cone Soccer (below) are proficiency-level games that demand combinations of skills. Because it is rare that all the students in a class will be ready for this type of game at the same time, some children will benefit from practicing different types of kicking while others are playing the game (see Chapter 31).

Playing Alley Soccer

Setting: A playing field divided into five equal alleys (Figure 24.10); marker-cone goals 6 feet apart at each end of the field; six-member teams

> **Cues**
>
> *Offensive* Pass at an Angle to Teammates Pass to Open Space
>   Body between Ball and Opponent
> *Defensive* Close the Open Spaces (Move quickly to close the open spaces.)

Tasks/Challenges:

T Alley Soccer is an activity that uses dribbling, passing, and kicking for a goal. Each team has six players—one player for each alley plus a goalie. Players may travel the length of their alley but can't cross into another alley. Your task is to dribble, avoid the opponent in your alley, pass to teammates, and kick for the goal. At regular intervals, I'll give the signal to rotate alleys; this rotation will allow each of you to play each position.

Playing Cone Soccer

Setting: A marker cone placed at either end of the playing area with a circle (spray paint or marking dust) 10 feet in diameter surrounding each cone (Figure 24.11); teams of two to six members

> **Cues**
>
> *Offensive* Kick at an Angle to Teammates
>   Pass to Open Space
>   Gentle Taps to Dribble/Hard Kicks to the Target
>   Body between Ball and Opponent
> *Defensive* Close the Open Spaces

Tasks/Challenges:

T Cone Soccer emphasizes dribbling, passing, and kicking for accuracy. The object of the game is to kick the ball, knock over the other team's cone, and protect your own cone. No one is allowed inside the circle to kick or to defend. If one team makes body contact, the other team gets a free kick on the spot; everyone must be 3 feet away for the free kick.

A good way to form teams for equal skill is to ask children to select a partner and then place the selected partners on opposite teams.

Figure 24.11 Cone Soccer. Dimensions of the playing area may be adjusted to the size of the available area and the number of players.

Figure 24.10 Alley Soccer.

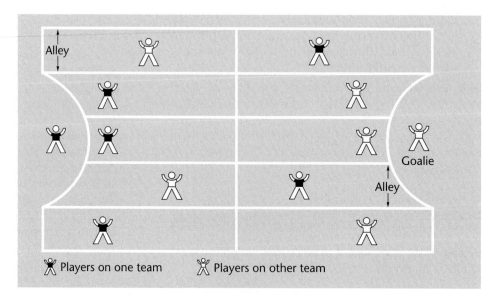

Players on one team   Players on other team

Levels of Skill Proficiency in Punting

Punting is a form of kicking: A ball is released from the hands and kicked while it is in the air. This is a difficult skill for children to master. Because the punt involves a complex coordination of body movements—moving the body forward, dropping the ball accurately, and kicking it before it reaches the ground—we have found it best to introduce the punt after children have practiced other types of kicking.

When children first try to punt, they toss the ball up and then "kick" it with a knee or leg rather than the foot. Often the novice punter will contact the ball after it bounces. We give children at the precontrol level round, lightweight balls and balloons, challenging them to contact the "ball" with the foot before it touches the ground.

Children at the control level are challenged to consistently contact the ball for the punt, to drop rather than toss the ball, and to move forward to make contact rather than standing in one place. When children can consistently contact the ball with the foot before the ball hits the ground, we begin to expand the basic skill with experiences that include:

1. Punting for distance
2. Punting for height
3. Punting different types of balls
4. Punting for accuracy

At the utilization level, experiences are designed to combine punting with other factors. Appropriate activities include:

This child practices punting, a difficult skill for youngsters to master.

1. Punting to a partner
2. Catching and punting within a limited time

At the proficiency level, children are able to punt in relation to unpredictable, dynamic situations, such as might occur in a football or a rugby game.

Ideas for varying the contexts in which punting skills can be practiced are presented in our progression spiral on page 462. As in previous chapters, we encourage you to alter the method of organization, as suggested in Chapter 13. Box 24-4 contains key observation points illustrating correct and incorrect punting. Ask yourself the questions in the box as you observe children punting.

Precontrol Level: Activities for Exploration of Punting

At the precontrol level, children explore punting different types of lightweight balls, sometimes with a bounce before contact, sometimes contacting the ball before it touches the ground. At this level we are not concerned with mastery, but with children enjoying a variety of experiences as an introduction to the skill of punting.

Dropping, Bouncing, and Kicking Lightweight Balls

Setting: Lightweight balls (plastic, foam) positioned around the perimeter of the gym, approximately 15 feet from the wall

Tasks/Challenges:

Ⓣ Drop the ball to the floor. After the first bounce, contact the ball with your shoelaces, sending it to the wall.

Ⓣ Try the kick with your right foot and with your left foot to determine which is your preferred foot.

Ⓒ With your preferred foot, drop and kick the ball after the bounce five times. Repeat several times to determine your personal best.

Dropping and Punting

Setting: Kicking balls (plastic, foam) positioned around the perimeter of the gym, approximately 15 feet from the wall

Tasks/Challenges:

Ⓣ Stand behind the kicking line, holding the ball in both hands. Drop the ball and kick it to the wall, making contact before the ball touches the floor. This drop-kick action is called a punt.

Box 24-4

Key Observation Points: Punting

1. Does the child drop the ball rather than toss it in the air for the punt?

2. Is the child's kicking foot extended for contact on the instep (shoelaces) rather than with the toes?

3. Does the child make contact at the right height for a 45-degree angle of flight rather than too soon or too late?

Box 24-4 (continued)

Mature Stage

When children are at the mature stage of punting, do their punts look similar to the following sequence? The child makes a rapid approach of one or more steps that culminates in a leap just before contact. If a leap does not precede contact, the child can enhance the forward momentum by taking a large step. The child makes contact with the ball at or below knee level as a result of having released the ball in a forward and downward direction. The momentum of the swinging leg carries the punter upward off the surface and forward after contact.

Sources: Adapted from "Developmental Sequence of Punting," mimeographed materials, by V. Seefeldt and J. Haubenstricker, presented at the University of Georgia, Athens, June 1978; *Fundamental Motor Patterns,* 2nd ed., by R. L. Wickstrom, 1977, Philadelphia: Lea & Febiger.

Skill Theme Development Sequence

Punting

Proficiency Level

Playing Punt-Over
Punting while traveling
Receiving and punting against opponents

Utilization Level

Playing Rush the Circle
Punting within a limited time
Receiving a pass, then punting
Punting to a partner
Punting at angles

Control Level

Punting for height
Punting for accuracy
Using punting zones
Punting for distance
Punting different types of balls
Punting with an approach
Punting over low ropes
Punting for consistency

Precontrol Level

Dropping and punting
Dropping, bouncing, and kicking lightweight balls

Children who are having difficulty with the drop-kick action can benefit from practicing punting with a balloon. This helps them understand the concept of dropping—rather than tossing—the object to be punted.

Control Level: Learning Experiences Leading to Skill Development in Punting

At the control level, children need experiences to develop consistency in contacting the ball for the punt. After they can consistently make contact, they are provided opportunities to punt different types of balls, to increase distance on the punt, and to improve accuracy.

A note about cues: Although several cues are listed for many of the learning experiences, it's important to focus on only one cue at a time. That way, the children can really concentrate on that cue. Once you provide feedback to the children and observe that most have learned a cue, then it's time to focus on another one.

Punting for Consistency

Setting: Lightweight balls for punting, placed around the perimeter of the gym, approximately 20 feet from the wall

Cues	
Shoelaces	(Contact the ball with your instep—your shoelaces—not your toes.)
Eyes on the Ball	(Watch the ball until it contacts your foot.)
Drop	(Drop the ball for the punt; don't toss it upward.)

Tasks/Challenges:

Ⓣ When we worked on punting earlier, you punted just for fun. Sometimes the ball went through the air, sometimes backward over your head, and sometimes nowhere! Today we will begin to practice punting so we can consistently kick the ball forward through the air. Stand behind the ball, holding it in both your hands at waist height. Take a small step on your nonkicking leg, then extend your kicking foot for contact on the shoelaces. Drop the ball as you swing your kicking leg forward; contact the ball just before it touches the floor (ground).

Ⓣ Punt the ball five times. How many times did you contact the ball before it touched the floor (ground)? Continue your practice until you make three or more contacts.

Ⓣ Good, you are now consistently contacting the ball before it touches the floor (ground). Now let's focus on the ball consistently traveling forward when you punt. Continue your practice with sets of five punts; mentally record how many times in each set you are successful at punting with your shoelaces and sending the ball forward to the wall.

Punting over Low Ropes

Setting: Ropes suspended between standards or across chairs at a height of 4 to 6 feet; lightweight balls for punting

Cues

Extend	(Extend your foot to contact the ball with your shoelaces, not your toes.)
Eyes on the Ball	(Watch the ball until it contacts your foot.)
Drop	(Drop the ball for the punt; don't toss it upward.)

Tasks/Challenges:

T Stand approximately 10 feet behind the rope. Punt the ball so it travels over the rope. Retrieve the ball and punt from the opposite side of the rope.

C Give yourself a point each time you are successful at punting the ball over the rope. How many points can you make out of 10 trials?

✓ *Teacher Observation.* Before children incorporate skills into dynamic situations, observation of critical cues is very important. A teacher observation check list is useful here.

Punting with an Approach

Setting: Lightweight balls for punting, placed around the perimeter of the gym, approximately 20 feet from the wall (*If indoor space is not sufficient for this task, move the class outside and punt away from the circle; see Figure 24.3.*)

Cues

Nonstop Approach	(Take a few running steps; then punt without stopping your forward momentum.)
Step-Hop	(Make your last step before contact a step-hop on your nonkicking leg, so that you'll be airborne for the punt.)

Tasks/Challenges:

T Take a series of quick steps forward. As your kicking leg moves back to front for the contact with the ball, hop slightly on your supporting leg so you are actually airborne for the contact. Quickly straighten your kicking leg at the moment of contact. (*Demonstrate or ask a child to demonstrate the step-hop action.*)

T Continue to practice the approach and punt. As you become more comfortable with the step-hop

action, you will probably want to lean slightly backward as you kick to counterbalance the forceful swing of your kicking leg.

C Practice until you can punt successfully three times in a row. When I watch your punting action, I should see the following:

1. A series of quick steps
2. Your body airborne for contact
3. The ball being dropped, not tossed
4. Your instep (your shoelaces) making contact with the ball

Punting Different Types of Balls

Setting: A variety of balls for punting—plastic, foam, deflated rubber, Nerf footballs—placed around an outdoor teaching area

Cues

Extend	(Extend your foot to contact the ball with your shoelaces, not your toes.)
Eyes on the Ball	(Watch the ball until it contacts your foot.)
Drop	(Drop the ball for the punt; don't toss it upward.)
Step-Hop	(Make your last step before contact a step-hop on your nonkicking leg, so that you'll be airborne for the punt.)

Tasks/Challenges:

T Scattered around the practice area are punting balls of different types and sizes. Practice punting with each type of ball, using your running approach and airborne action for the kick.

C Practice with each type of ball until you can punt successfully three out of five times.

T Select a football for punting. What is very different about this ball? Yes, all the others are round. Hold the football with one end facing the direction in which the ball is to travel; all your other actions are the same as for punting other types of balls. Compare how well you're able to punt the football with your success with the other types of balls.

When footballs are added to the selection, some children may want to practice punting only with the footballs; encourage the children to practice punting with each type of ball.

Punting for Distance

Setting: A variety of balls for punting; colored jugs for use as markers; children positioned at one end of an outdoor practice area

Cues

Extend (Extend your foot and your kicking leg for a really good punt.)

Step-Hop (Make your last step before contact a step-hop on your nonkicking leg, so that you'll be airborne for the punt.)

Kick Hard (Kick hard to send the ball really far.)

Tasks/Challenges:

Ⓣ Take a series of running steps, and punt the ball as far as possible. Place a colored jug at the spot where the ball first touches the ground, and then try to punt beyond that spot. Remember, making the ball travel at a 45-degree angle when you punt it gives you the best distance. **To achieve that angle, extend your foot and contact the ball just before it touches the ground.**

Continue to practice your punting, trying to extend your distance with each punt. Each time you better your distance, move your marker to that spot. **Straightening your kicking leg when you contact the ball will increase your power for distance.**

When a new factor (distance) is added, children may modify their kicking patterns. Some may need verbal cues as they practice.

Using Punting Zones

Setting: Colored tape, spray paint, marker cones, or colored streamers to mark a series of target zones, each approximately 15 feet in length (Figure 24.12); a variety of balls for punting (Target zones may be numbered, color-coded, or named for states, professional teams, etc.)

Cues

Extend (Extend your foot and your kicking leg for a really good punt.)

Step-Hop (Make your last step before contact a step-hop on your nonkicking leg, so that you'll be airborne for the punt.)

Nonstop Approach (Take a few running steps; then punt without stopping your forward momentum.)

Tasks/Challenges:

Ⓣ Approach the kicking line with a series of running steps; punt the ball for maximum distance. Mentally note the zone the ball first lands in. Retrieve the ball and be ready for another turn.

A key component in punting for distance is practice. Keeping the same distances and codes (colors, names) for zones permits children to check themselves against their best during previous lessons.

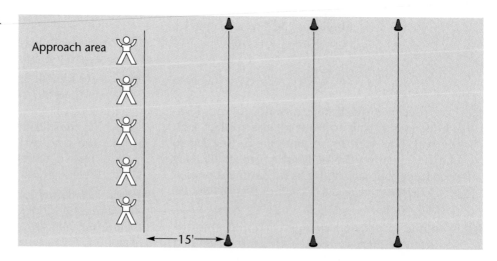

Figure 24.12 Punting zones.

Approach area

15'

Punting for Accuracy

Setting: Colored tape, spray paint, marker cones, or colored streamers to mark a series of target zones, each approximately 15 feet in length (see Figure 24.12); a variety of balls for punting

Cues	
Extend	(Extend your foot and your kicking leg for a really good punt.)
Step-Hop	(Make your last step before contact a step-hop, so that you'll be airborne for the punt.)
Hard Kick, Soft Kick	(Use a hard kick for maximum distance, a soft kick for shorter distances.)

Tasks/Challenges:

🅣 We previously used the target zones in punting for distance. Now we will use them to focus on accuracy—making the ball land within a particular area. Practice punting with a running approach to review the skill and to determine the zone that is your best distance. Try to punt the ball consistently to that zone.

🅒 Punt the ball five times, attempting to make it land within the same zone each time.

🅣 Punt the ball so it lands within the first target zone. To do that you must adjust the amount of force behind the kick.

🅣 Choose a zone midway between the first target zone and your best distance. Punt the ball so it lands within that target zone.

🅒 Select three zones as your targets. Practice until you can successfully punt three out of five balls into each of those zones.

🅣 Repeat the process for your three selected zones using each type of ball—foam, deflated rubber, soccer ball, football. Compare your accuracy with the different types of balls.

Being able to adjust force to kick a shorter distance is an important punting skill for playing games and one that does not come easily for children. Encourage them to select zones of varying distances, not just their maximum.

Punting for Height

Setting: Colored tape, spray paint, marker cones, or colored streamers to mark a series of target zones, each approximately 15 feet in length (see Figure 24.12); a variety of balls for punting.

Cues	
Under the Ball	(Contact the ball *below* center to send it upward and forward.)
Eyes on the Ball	(Watch the ball until it contacts your foot.)
Kick Hard	(Make a firm step-hop and swing of leg for good height.)

Tasks/Challenges:

🅣 Sometimes in a game you want the ball to travel in a high aerial path rather than at a 45-degree angle so that you can adjust the forward distance of the punt. What did we learn earlier about contacting a ball to send it upward rather than forward? Right, contact must be made directly underneath the ball for travel upward. You will also get more height on the punt if you contact the ball closer to waist height. Take a series of small steps, then punt the ball so it travels as high as possible.

🅣 Punt the ball high in the air; see if you can catch it before it touches the ground.

⚠ Because of the hazard of running to catch while looking up, this task must be done in a large outdoor field space. If such a space is not available, some children can practice punting for height while others practice punting for distance.

🅣 Select one of the first three target zones as your target area. Punt the ball so it travels in a high aerial path to that zone.

Children highly skilled in punting for accuracy will enjoy the challenge of smaller targets, such as hoops.

🌀 What makes the difference between the ball traveling in a very high aerial path versus a 45-degree angle for distance?

Utilization Level: Learning Experiences Leading to Skill Development in Punting

At the utilization level, we provide punting experiences in dynamic situations. This encourages children to use punting skills in combination with other factors, such as time and accuracy. To stress relationships

Figure 24.13 Punting at angles.

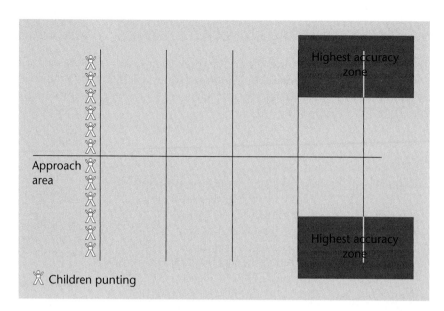

Approach area

⚥ Children punting

Highest accuracy zone

Highest accuracy zone

with a partner, focus on punting so that a partner can catch the ball on punting or shortly after receiving a throw from a partner.

A note about cues: Although several cues are listed for many of the learning experiences, it's important to focus on only one cue at a time. That way, the children can really concentrate on that cue. Once you provide feedback to the children and observe that most have learned a cue, then it's time to focus on another one.

Punting at Angles

Setting: Spray paint, marker dust, or milk jugs to mark target zones divided by width and length (Figure 24.13); lightweight balls for punting

Cues

Extend to Target (Extend your kicking foot and leg toward the target, to the right or left.)

Individuals and/or classes may need reminders of earlier cues (e.g., Eyes on the Ball, Drop, Step-Hop)

Tasks/Challenges:

T Practice punting into the different target zones—to the right and to the left of where you're standing.

T Select a target zone, and practice until you can consistently punt the ball into that zone. Then select a zone on the opposite side.

C Practice until you can select a target zone, tell a partner which one you've chosen, and then punt three out of five balls into that zone. How about five out of five?

Punting to a Partner

Setting: Colored tape, spray paint, marker cones, or streamers to mark target zones, each approximately 15 feet long; partners, each pair with a lightweight ball for punting (Figure 24.14)

Cues

Eyes on the Ball (Watch the ball—not your partner—until it contacts your foot.)

Step-Hop (Make your last step before contact a step-hop, so that you'll be airborne for the punt.)

Adjust (Adjust your power to match the distance your partner is from you.)

Tasks/Challenges:

T Using the target zones as a measure of distance, tell your partner where to stand for the two of you to punt to each other; choose a distance at which both of you have been successful. Punt the ball so your partner can catch it without moving more than a couple of steps.

T Punt so your partner can catch without moving from self-space.

T From behind the kicking line, practice punting to your partner in each of the target zones: near/far, right/left angles.

T Punt some balls high and lofty, others at a 45-degree angle.

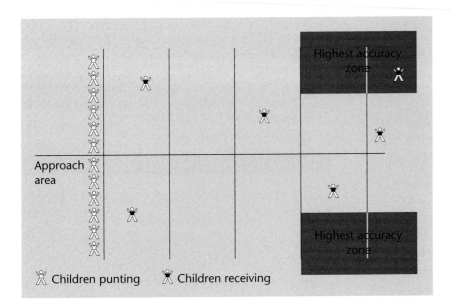

Figure 24.14 Punting to a partner.

Receiving a Pass, Then Punting

Setting: Partners scattered throughout general space in an outdoor area; a variety of balls for punting—playground, soccer balls, footballs

Cues

Eyes on the Ball (Watch the ball, not your partner.)

Step-Hop-Punt (Take a couple of steps only; then punt.)

Tasks/Challenges:

🅣 Select a partner with whom you can work well independently. Separate to a distance at which you can both throw and catch successfully. Partner 1 throws the ball to partner 2; partner 2 receives the ball and then quickly takes a couple of steps and punts the ball across the playing field. Your goal is to punt as quickly, yet correctly, as possible. Alternate positions as passer and punter.

⚠️ With children throwing, catching, and punting, space awareness can be a safety factor. Organize this activity with all passes and punts traveling in the same direction—across the playing area or end to end, not in multiple directions.

Punting within a Limited Time

Setting: Partners scattered throughout general space in an outdoor area; a variety of balls for punting—playground, soccer balls, footballs

Cues

Eyes on the Ball (Watch the ball, not your partner.)

Step-Hop-Punt (Take a couple of steps only; then punt.)

Tasks/Challenges:

🅣 Partner 2 throws the ball to partner 1. As soon as partner 1 receives the pass, partner 2 begins to count "one alligator, two alligators, three alligators." After receiving the pass, partner 1 punts it across the playing field as quickly as possible, trying to complete the punt before partner 2 counts "three alligators." Partner 1 retrieves the ball and switches positions with partner 2. Follow all the proper steps, even though you're punting quickly.

✓ *Videotape.* It would be beneficial to videotape a game situation containing a punt with added pressure. Use self-analysis or peer analysis or both of the execution of the punt. To structure the observation, provide the children with lead questions: Was the punt as well executed as it was when you were not rushed by a partner? What makes the difference? Should there be a difference in the execution? What cue do you consider most critical for success in this situation? Why?

Playing Rush the Circle

Setting: A spray-paint or marker-dust circle drawn on a field, with a diameter of 10 feet or larger, and a passing line approximately 15 feet from the edge of the circle

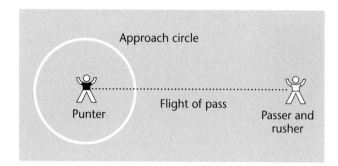

Figure 24.15 Partner pass-and-rush punting: Rush the Circle.

(Figure 24.15); children with partners; a variety of balls for punting—playground, soccer balls, footballs

Cues	
Eyes on the Ball	(Watch the ball, not your partner.)
Step-Hop-Punt	(Take a couple of steps only; then punt.)

Tasks/Challenges:

Ⓣ Select a partner whose throwing and catching skills are similar to yours. The punter will be positioned inside the circle; the passer will be approximately 20 feet away, behind the passing line. The passer throws the ball from behind the passing line. When the punter receives the catch, the passer runs toward the circle, trying to reach the circle before the punter can kick the ball. The punter punts the ball as quickly as possible when he or she receives the pass. In other words, the punter tries to punt the ball before the passer reaches the circle.

At this level of punting and kicking combined with throwing and catching, some children will enjoy developing point systems and minigames for each task. Others will continue to enjoy practicing the skill in the dynamic environment.

Proficiency Level: Learning Experiences Leading to Skill Development in Punting

Punting experiences at the proficiency level lead to the ability to punt accurately and for distance in dynamic and unpredictable situations. The relationships are more complex. Emphasis is on punting while traveling and on working with others in game situations.

A note about cues: At the proficiency level, tasks are more complex, typically requiring children to coordinate several movements simultaneously in a dynamic context. A list of cues is provided to assist the children

in being more successful in the learning experience. The challenge for the teacher is in determining which cue will be most beneficial for each child . . . and when. Thus, careful observation and critical reflection become very important as you watch the children move and then decide which cue will be the most helpful to move each learner to a higher skill level.

Receiving and Punting against Opponents

Setting: Groups of three, each group with a ball for punting

Cues
Focus on the ball, not your opponents. Drop—don't toss—the ball, even under pressure. Remember the approach, even with opponents. *Individual cues as needed*

Tasks/Challenges:

Ⓣ Working in groups of three, two partners will assume the offensive positions of passer and punter. The other player will be the defense, attempting to block the punt. Offense: Partner 1 (the passer) throws the ball to partner 2 (the punter) from a distance of about 20 feet. Partner 2 punts the ball down the playing field. Defense: Rush the punter, starting from the 20-foot distance at which the passer is standing, to tag the punter before the punter releases the kick. You can't begin the rush until the punter receives the pass.

Alternate positions until each person has been the punter, the passer, the defense.

Punting While Traveling

Setting: Spray paint, marker dust, or milk jugs to mark distance zones approximately 15 feet in length; a variety of balls for punting

Cues	
Nonstop Approach	(Take a few running steps; then punt without stopping your forward momentum.)
Step-Hop	(Make your last step before contact a step-hop on your nonkicking leg, so that you'll be airborne for the punt, even with a longer approach.)

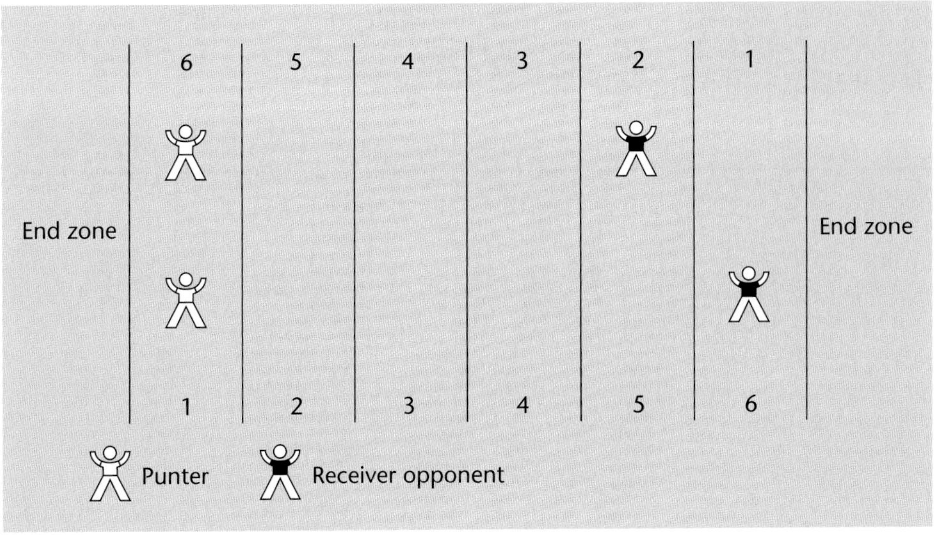

Figure 24.16 Punt-Over.

Tasks/Challenges:

- **T** Run with the ball the distance to two target zones, then quickly punt the ball. Focus on accuracy of contacting the ball for forward travel.

- **T** Focus on making the ball land accurately in a specific zone.

- **T** Focus on punting for maximum distance.

Playing Punt-Over

Setting: Spray paint to marker dust to mark target zones, approximately 10 feet in length; teams of four or six players; a choice of football or playground ball for each team

Cues

Individual cues as needed

Tasks/Challenges:

- **T** The object of the game Punt-Over is to punt the ball over your opponents so it lands in the end zone. You can play it in groups of four or six. Here are the basic rules:

1. Play begins with the punting team in their first zone; one person punts the ball toward the opposite end zone.
2. If the opponents catch the ball, they advance forward one zone before they punt.
3. If the opponents retrieve the ball short of the end zone, they punt from that spot.
4. The games consists of alternate punts; the number of points awarded for landing in the end zone corresponds to the zone from which the ball was punted *(Figure 24.16).*

The groups decide cooperatively:

1. If the defensive team catches the ball on the punt, can they run to the opposite end zone to score?
2. Can members of the opposite team rush the punter after the punter has received the pass?

Reading Comprehension Questions

1. What is the difference between a kick and a punt?
2. What is a mature kicking pattern? What is a mature punting pattern?
3. What kicking tasks lead to the development of a mature kicking pattern?
4. Describe appropriate kicking tasks for each of the four levels of skill proficiency.
5. At the precontrol level, why do you number the balls?
6. Where does a child's foot need to contact the ball so that it travels into the air? Along the ground?
7. What experiences do children have at each of the four skill levels when they're learning to punt a ball?

8. What is the outcome when a child makes contact with the ball too soon in a punt? What happens when the child makes contact too late?

9. How is the tap/dribble of soccer different from a regular kick?

10. List the kicking skills needed for success in soccer.

References

National Association for Sport and Physical Education. (1995). *Moving into the future: National standards for physical education.* St. Louis, MO: Mosby.

National Association for Sport and Physical Education. (2004). *Moving into the future: National standards for physical education.* (2nd ed.). Reston, VA: National Association for Sport and Physical Education.

Throwing and Catching

Throwing and catching go together just as nicely as soup and a sandwich. The two skills, however, are opposite in movement focus and unusually difficult for young children to master.

Although throwing and catching are complementary, we've learned that children have limited success in combining throwing and catching in game situations unless each skill has been given specific attention and developed in appropriate practice situations. It is important that the teacher be certain that children can throw *and* catch with relative success before progressing to the utilization and proficiency levels. Activities at those levels—throwing to a running partner or trying to prevent an opponent from catching a ball—require mature throwing *and* catching skills. Too often teachers neglect catching, feeling it isn't that important. But as anyone who has ever watched a professional baseball game knows, catching is a skill, a skill that often deter-

mines whether a game is won or lost. Box 25-1 contains information on throwing and catching from the *National Standards for Physical Education*.

Levels of Skill Proficiency in Throwing

Throwing is a basic movement pattern performed to propel an object away from the body. Although throwing style (overhand, underhand, sidearm) and purpose may vary, the basic pattern remains consistent:

1. An object to be sent away is grasped with one or both hands.
2. In a preparatory phase, momentum builds for the throw.
3. The actual propulsive phase—the release of the object—is performed.

Box 25-1

Throwing and Catching in the *National Standards for Physical Education*

The skill theme of throwing and catching is referenced in the *National Standards for Physical Education* (National Association for Physical Education, 2004) under Standard 1: Demonstrates competency in motor skills and movement patterns needed to perform a variety of physical activities. The standard speaks of the child's learning the skills as simple closed skills, developing a mature motor pattern, and increasing the variety and versatility of the action.

Sample performance outcomes for throwing and catching include:

- Drops a ball and catches it at the peak of the bounce (K–2)*
- Throws a ball underhand using mature form (e.g., places feet together and shoulders square to target, swings throwing arm straight back, shifts weight forward by stepping onto the opposite foot, rolls ball off fingers, and finishes with throwing arm outstretched toward target) (K–2)*
- Catches a fly ball using mature form (e.g., has eyes on ball, moves to position, reaches with hands, catches with hands only rather than trapping the ball, bends elbows to pull ball into chest to absorb force) (3–5)*
- Throws a ball overhand and hits a target on the wall (6-foot square centered 4 feet above the ground) from a distance of 40 feet (3–5)*
- Throws a ball overhand to a partner 15 yards away using mature form (e.g., turns side to target, uses T-position [ball held close to and behind ear], rotates hips and chest toward target, twists, releases, follows through across body) after fielding a ball (3–5)*

The skill theme of throwing and catching is also referenced under Standard 2: Demonstrates understanding of movement concepts, principles, strategies, and tactics as they apply to the learning and performance of physical activities. This standard speaks of the child's identifying the characteristics of a quality movement pattern and safety.

The sample performance outcomes state:

- Recognizes appropriate safety practices in general space by throwing balls only when others are not in the direct line of the throw (K–2)*
- Corrects movement errors in response to corrective feedback (e.g., remember to twist your tummy when throwing the ball) (K–2)*
- Accurately recognizes the critical elements of a catch made by a fellow student and provides feedback to that student (3–5)*

The skill theme of throwing and catching is further referenced under Standard 3: Participates regularly in physical activity. In this standard, throwing and catching are used in nonschool settings.

The sample performance outcome states:

- Participates in a variety of activities that involve the manipulation of objects in and outside of physical education class (e.g., tossing ball, juggling) (K–2)*

*Grade-level guidelines for expected student learning.

4. In a follow-through phase, the body maintains control and balance while using up the momentum of the throw.

In the elementary school setting a wide range of throwing abilities among a class will be observed. Initially, the teacher should focus on ascertaining each child's skill level. When the youngsters manipulate objects such as beanbags or yarn balls, the teacher can observe individual children for significant developmental characteristics. (As a guide, see Box 25-2 for the key observation points for throwing).

After making a gross assessment of each child's development in throwing, the teacher has a basis for structuring appropriate instructional tasks. (See our progression spiral for throwing and catching activities on page 475.)

For children at the precontrol level, the tasks are designed to provide exploration of a multitude of throwing experiences. Many of these experiences are designed to elicit distance throws, which force children to use a more mature throwing pattern. Tasks at this level are purely exploration and include such things as:

Catching while traveling demands movement behind and under the ball.

1. Throwing against a wall
2. Tossing to self and catching

We expose children at the control level to various contexts so that they use throwing actions in different but relatively static situations:

1. Throwing fast/throwing slow
2. Varying the distance of throws
3. Throwing under/throwing over (a net or other obstacle)
4. Tossing a beanbag at a target
5. Throwing a yarn ball through a hoop
6. Throwing a foam ball into a basket

When children begin to focus primarily on hitting a target, they appear to regress to inefficient throwing patterns. What they are actually doing is using a pattern that allows them to be accurate—a pattern in which they control as many segments as possible and thus use as few body parts as possible. They have adapted their skill level to the task. The normal characteristics of a mature throw are appropriate only for throwing for distance and speed. Asking children to use a mature throwing pattern when throwing at a close target is really an inappropriate request for the task. Generally, longer throws elicit mature throwing patterns. Therefore, it is a good idea to vary the distance of the throw, sometimes fostering success at hitting the target, other times enhancing the development of a mature throwing pattern.

Once the children are able to perform smooth throwing actions in a variety of static contexts, they're ready for utilization-level experiences. At this level, children are given tasks that encourage refinement of skills and an increase in the breadth of throwing abilities. Appropriate activities include:

1. Throwing accurately while running
2. Throwing to a moving target (for example, a partner)
3. Throwing at a goal while off the ground
4. Throwing a Frisbee accurately

Children are at the proficiency level of throwing when they are able to throw effectively in unpredictable, dynamic contexts and are ready to practice throwing as it's used in the relatively complex and changing environments characterized by gamelike situations. Appropriate tasks include:

1. Throwing a ball at a target (for example, as in team handball) as an opponent attempts to block and deflect the throw
2. Throwing a ball to a partner so it can be caught without being intercepted by an opposing player
3. Throwing a ball within a group of players to keep it away from another group of players

Box 25-2

Key Observation Points: Throwing

1. Does the child take a forward step on the foot opposite the throwing arm?

NO

YES

2. Do the child's hips and spine rotate so that they can uncoil in forceful derotation?

NO

YES

3. Is the child's elbow flexed and held away from the body and extended on the backswing?

NO

YES

Throwing and Catching

Proficiency Level

Throwing and catching while using simple offense and defense in a small sided invasion game
Throwing and catching with a team handball in a small sided invasion game
Throwing and catching with a football in a small sided invasion game
Throwing and catching with a Frisbee in a small sided invasion game
Throwing and catching in a small sided basketball-type game
Throwing at a stationary object while being defended
Throwing and catching in a small sided invasion game
Throwing to avoid a defender
Throwing and catching in a field, run, score gamelike situation
Throwing and catching a Frisbee in different places around the body with a partner

Utilization Level

Throwing while in the air
Catching to throw quickly to a target
Catching to throw quickly to a partner
Playing Frisbee Golf
Target backaway
Throwing for distance and accuracy
Throwing to a moving target
Throwing to make a partner move to catch
Throwing on the move
Throwing and catching while traveling
Moving to catch

Control Level

Bench Bounce Catch
Throwing and catching over a net with a partner
Throwing and catching with a partner
Throwing for distance
Throwing a ball against a wall and catching the rebound
Flying Beanbag Catch
Catching with a scoop
Throwing a Frisbee
Throwing backhand to a target
Throwing to high targets
Throwing underhand to hoops
Bowling for targets
Hit the Can
Throwing overhand at a stationary target
Catching in different places around the body
Throwing an object to different levels and catching it
Bouncing a ball to self and catching it
Overs, Unders, and Sides
Throwing sidearm
Throwing underhand
Throwing overhand

Precontrol Level

Tossing to self and catching
Drop—Catch
Catching from a skilled thrower
Catching a rolling ball
Throwing at a large target
Throwing a yarn ball against the wall

Box 25-3

Key Observation Points: Catching

1. Are the child's elbows flexed rather than extended in preparation for making the catch?

NO   YES

2. Does the child make the catch with the hands alone rather than by trapping the ball against the body?

NO   YES

Levels of Skill Proficiency in Catching

Catching is the receiving and controlling of an object by the body or its parts. Initially, a young child's reaction to an oncoming object is to fend it off, to protect self—often by using the whole body rather than the arms and hands. Typically, a ball bounces against the young child's chest as the remainder of the body scrambles to surround it and still maintain equilibrium.

Children's catching abilities, like their throwing skills, vary immensely. The teacher who plans learning sessions in which young children manipulate soft, textured objects (such as beanbags, foam balls, or yarn balls) can observe for the developmental characteristics of catching. (See the key observation points for catching in Box 25-3 as a guide.)

The progression spiral for throwing and catching (page 475) has activities the teacher can expand while leading children from the precontrol to the proficiency level. Initially, children need experiences that let them explore the whole action of catching—trying to accurately manipulate their arms and hands into a position to receive an object. When focusing on catching at the precontrol level, we simply let children explore catching in varying contexts—with different equipment, with the ball coming from different places. At this level, it is important to note that children are often also at the precontrol level of throwing and thus have

Box 25-3 (continued)

3. Are the child's elbows extended as the catch is made so the child can absorb the force of the ball?

4. Do the child's eyes track the ball into the hands?

difficulty throwing an object accurately to themselves or to a partner, and an inaccurate throw is difficult to catch. Consequently, we have found it helpful to find ways to minimize throwing inaccuracy. We often teach the skill of throwing before catching. More skilled throwers, such as older children or parents and grandparents serving as teacher aides, can gently and accurately throw a ball to children who are at the precontrol level. Additionally, children can work as partners. For example, one child stands on a chair with a ball held in an outstretched hand and drops the ball to the partner, who is positioned directly below, ready to catch. Children at the precontrol level generally have an easier time and experience more success when soft, textured, relatively large balls are used. The primary

task for precontrol-level children is to explore the act of catching a ball thrown directly to them.

Children at the control level need opportunities to develop the skills used when catching with the right and left hands, on either side of the body, and at various levels. Appropriate tasks for children at this level include:

1. Catching in different places around the body
2. Catching objects thrown to different levels
3. Moving one step in any direction to catch
4. Catching with the right hand and the left hand
5. Catching with an implement

When children are consistently able to catch a variety of objects with one or both hands, they're at the utilization level and can begin to use their catching skills in dynamic, unpredictable situations. Appropriate tasks include:

1. Catching a passed football while traveling
2. Catching a kicked soccer ball
3. Catching a rebounding ball

Children at the proficiency level are ready to learn to catch in changing environments. They are challenged by using catching skills in combination with other skills in gamelike situations. Appropriate activities include:

1. Losing a defender to catch a ball
2. Catching a rapidly thrown or hit ball that bounces against the ground
3. Catching a ball with one hand while off balance or in the air
4. Catching a ball that someone else is trying to catch

> *A student teacher once embellished Throwing at a Large Target (the second precontrol-level activity) with his own creativeness. It was Halloween, so on the target he painted the school, a full moon, corn stalks, and other autumn scenes. The children sure did throw hard to try and hit the target once there was a little colored paint and a semblance of a drawing to aim at! You don't have to be an artist—a little tempera paint, a little imagination, and a good story to tell the children are all that it takes.*

Precontrol Level: Activities for Exploration

Instructional tasks at the precontrol level give children opportunities to repeatedly explore the activities of throwing and catching. Emphasis is placed on catching throws made directly to the child and on throwing in static situations, to enable success.

Throwing a Yarn Ball Against the Wall

Setting: Carpet squares about 10 feet from the wall, one square for each child; one yarn ball per child (see Figure 25.1 for construction of a yarn ball)

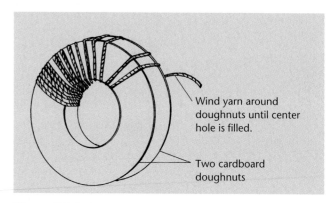

Wind yarn around doughnuts until center hole is filled.

Two cardboard doughnuts

Figure 25.1 Construction of a yarn ball.
1. Cut two "doughnuts"—rings made from cardboard—with a diameter 1 inch larger than you want the diameter of the yarn ball to be. The center hole of each doughnut should be about 1 inch in diameter.
2. Cut several 10-foot lengths of yarn. Rug yarn is excellent, but any heavy yarn will do. A 1-ounce skein will make two 3-inch balls.
3. Place one doughnut on top of the other. Wind yarn around each doughnut (through the hole and around the circle) until the cardboard is covered and each hole is full of yarn.
4. Slip scissors between the doughnuts at the outer edge, and cut the yarn all the way around.
5. Slip nylon string between the doughnuts, making a circle around the yarn in the middle. Pull tight, and then make a strong knot.
6. Pull the doughnuts off, and fluff the ball. You can trim any longer strands of yarn to make a smoother, rounder ball.

Catching is a skill that always seems to fascinate children.

Tasks/Challenges:

🅣 Throw the ball against the wall as hard as you can. Use the hand you hold your pencil with.

🅒 Practice until you can hit the wall three times in a row.

🅣 Practice throwing the ball with your other hand—the one you do not hold your pencil with.

🅣 This time move three steps farther away from the wall and try to hit the wall.

🅣 See how many different ways you can throw—sometimes overhand, sometimes underhand, and sometimes from the side of your body.

Throwing at a Large Target

Setting: Several large targets suspended in various places around the room; several balls or beanbags for each child; spaces marked on the floor about 10 feet from each target for four children to throw at each target (For the large targets, old sheets work well. Attach the top of the sheet to a broom or dowel stick, and weight the bottom with heavy washers. Attach a rope to both ends of the rod at the top of the sheet, and then hang the rope from basketball goals or rafters.)

Tasks/Challenges:

🅣 Now you have a target at which to aim. This kind of target will soak up your ball; your ball won't come bouncing back to you. Your job is to throw at the target as hard as you can and try to make the target move. Throw all the balls you have, then bring them back and start again. Remember not to get your balls until everyone at your target has thrown and not to throw until everyone is back to the throwing space.

🅣 When you can make the target move three times in a row, take one giant step backward and try again.

🅣 Move back to your starting position, and try to make the target move by throwing with your other hand.

🅣 When you can make the target move three times, take a giant step backward and try again.

🅣 Move back to your first spot and try to throw a different way than you threw the first time. Practice that throw about 15 times.

For children at the precontrol level, the emphasis is on providing many throwing experiences. Varying the context too

early (for example, placing children in gamelike situations) causes children to use immature throwing patterns in an attempt to achieve the results called for.

Catching a Rolling Ball

Setting: Partners about 5 feet apart; one large plastic or rubber ball per pair

Tasks/Challenges:

🅣 With your partner, you're going to practice catching the ball. You should be seated facing each other, with your legs like a V. One of you rolls the ball to the other, who catches it with the hands. The second partner then rolls the ball back to the first.

🅣 When the two of you can make five catches in a row, both of you should move backward a little and try again.

🅒 See if the two of you can make 10 catches without missing.

Catching from a Skilled Thrower

Setting: A skilled thrower (older students, classroom teacher, parents, or grandparents) partnered with each child; one light, medium- to large-sized ball per pair

This activity is a wonderful way to actively involve others in the physical education program. It serves as a great public relations activity.

Tasks/Challenges:

🅣 For this task you have a "big" partner. You and your partner will stand about 4 to 5 feet apart in your own space. Your big partner will throw the ball to you so you can practice catching. When you catch the ball, throw it back to your big partner so that he or she can throw it to you again.

🅣 After you can make five catches in a row from your partner, take one giant step backward. When you can make five more catches, take another giant step backward.

Drop—Catch

Setting: A stable chair (one that will not move or collapse) for every pair of partners; one light, medium to large-sized ball per pair

Tasks/Challenges:

T This is a fun task. One of you will stand on the chair and hold the ball in your hands with your arms straight out from your body. The other partner will stand close to the chair where your hands and arms can be under the ball. The partner on the chair drops the ball, and the other partner catches it. After five turns, switch places.

C Say one letter of your name every time you catch. See if you can spell your name before missing.

Tossing to Self and Catching

Setting: Self-space; a yarn ball, beanbag, or lightweight ball for every child

Tasks/Challenges:

T In a space by yourself, you're going to practice tossing and catching by yourself. Toss the ball (beanbag) very close to your body, close enough so the ball (beanbag) doesn't go very high over your head or very far out from your stomach. Catch it.

T When you can toss and catch the ball (beanbag) five times in a row, keeping it very close to your body, then toss it just a little farther away and see if you can still catch it.

C This is your challenge for the day. See if you can toss and catch the ball (beanbag) 10 times in a row without moving more than one step from your space.

Control Level: Learning Experiences Leading to Skill Development

Children at the control level still need practice developing mature throwing and catching patterns, yet they are also ready to focus on more complex learning experiences that still allow them to throw and catch in static situations. For example, they are challenged by catching at different levels, catching at different places around their bodies, and using either hand to catch. Throwing experiences are designed to help children learn to throw for accuracy and with varying degrees of force, and to throw a variety of objects.

A note about cues: Although several cues are listed for many of the learning experiences, it's important to focus on only one cue at a time. That way, the children can really concentrate on that cue. Once you provide feedback to the children and observe that most have learned a cue, then it's time to focus on another one.

At the control level, remind youngsters to concentrate on the catching cues: Eyes on the Ball, Reach, Pull It In.

Reed and Sophie, both 5 years old, were playing a game in which they threw a ball under their legs to knock over a pile of tin cans. Reed placed his head a bit too far under his legs and inadvertently fell into a forward roll as he released the ball. With an expression of sheer excitement, Reed announced that he'd discovered the "flip throw."

Throwing Overhand

Setting: Tape marks on the floor about 15 feet from the wall; one ball per child; children alone at first and later with a partner

Cues	
Side to Target	(Make sure the side of your body away from the hand you are throwing with is toward the wall; if you were to walk straight ahead, you would walk along the wall, not toward it.)
Arm Way Back	(Bring your throwing arm way back so that your elbow is

	almost above your ear and your hand is behind your head.)
Step with Opposite Foot	(Step forward on the foot opposite the hand you are using to throw.)
Follow Through	(After you throw, make your arm follow the ball. Your hand should end up almost at your knee.)

Tip: It is useful to demonstrate these cues. After the children understand them, it is easy to reduce them to one-word cues: Side, Arm, Step, Follow.

Some children have a hard time remembering which foot to step with to achieve opposition. To help these children, place an old wrist sweatband around the appropriate foot as a reminder to step with the opposite foot. You can also use a large loose-fitting rubber band for this purpose.

Tasks/Challenges:

T At your own mark, practice throwing at the wall. Throw the ball overhand as hard as you can. **Remember, in an overhand throw, your arm comes above your shoulder.**

T This time move three steps farther away from the wall, and practice overhand throwing.

T Move back to your first spot and try to throw with your other hand—the one you don't write with.

T This time you will have a partner, who is your coach. You throw three times, with your favorite hand, and your partner has to tell you if you used each of the *cues:* Side, Arm, Step, Follow. The partner gives you a thumbs-up if you did them all or a thumbs-down if you didn't. If you didn't use the cues, the partner tells you which part to practice, and you practice that two times. Then switch places.

Throwing Underhand

Setting: Tape marks on the floor about 15 feet from the wall; one ball per child

Cues	
Face Wall	(Your body should be looking at the wall.)
Arm Way Back	(Your throwing arm should come back behind your seat.)

Step with Opposite Foot	(Step forward on the foot opposite the hand you are using to throw.)
Follow Through	(Make your arm follow your throw straight to the wall.)

Make sure to demonstrate the throw.

Tasks/Challenges:

T This time, instead of throwing overhand, you are going to practice throwing almost as if you were bowling. You are going to throw to the wall, just like before. This is called an *underhand throw.*

T Move back three steps, and practice again.

T Move back to your first spot, and try to throw with the other hand.

T Again, move back, and try to throw with the hand you don't write with.

Throwing Sidearm

Setting: Tape marks on the floor about 15 feet from the wall; one ball per child

Cues	
Face Wall	(Your body should be looking straight at the wall.)
Arm Way Back	(Your throwing arm should come back sideways, behind your seat.)
Step with Opposite Foot	(Step forward on the foot opposite the hand you are using to throw.)
Follow Through	(Make your arm follow your throw across your body.)

Demonstrate the throw.

Tasks/Challenges:

T Now you are going to try another throw. Instead of throwing overhand or underhand, you are going to throw from the side. This is called a *sidearm* throw. To do this, you bring your arm around from the side of your body. You would use a throw like this to throw a Frisbee. Remember, it's not a fling. **Let loose of the ball just as your hand faces straight at the wall.**

T After you can hit the wall eight times in a row, move back one giant step. Try again.

👤 Which way should your body face when you are throwing overhand? Underhand? Sidearmed?

Overs, Unders, and Sides

Setting: Tape marks on the floor about 15 feet from the wall; one ball per child

Cues	
Face Wall/Side to Wall	(Remember, depending upon your throw, your body should be looking straight at the wall or be turned sideways to it.)
Arm Way Back	(Your throwing arm should come way back behind your back, head, or seat depending upon the throw.)
Step with Opposite Foot	(Step forward on the foot opposite the hand you are using to throw.)
Follow Through	(Follow your throw.)

Tasks/Challenges:

T Now that you know the names for the three different kinds of throws, you're going to practice the throws on your own. You can practice the throws in any order you want, but make sure that you practice each one at least 15 times.

C Here's some more practice. Pick out the throw you're having the most trouble with. Practice only that throw until you can hit the wall 10 times in a row. After you can hit the wall 10 times with the throw you found the most difficult, pick another throw you're having trouble with, and practice it until you can hit the wall 10 times in a row.

T When you can hit the wall 10 times in a row with all three throws, take three giant steps backward and try again.

✓ *Exit Slip.* This would be a good time to include a Helping Murgatroid (see Chapter 14) exit slip that has children explain to Murgatroid how to throw correctly.

Bouncing a Ball to Self and Catching It

Setting: Self-space; a playground ball (or tennis ball if you want to increase the complexity of the task) for each child

Cues	
Hands	(Always use your hands—not your arms or stomach—to catch.)
Watch the Ball	(Your eyes should be on the ball. You should see the ball as it comes into your hands.)

Tasks/Challenges:

T You're going to practice catching this time so you can get used to catching a ball that's coming down toward you. In your own space, bounce the playground ball (tennis ball) so that it barely goes over your head, and try to catch it as it comes down, before it hits the floor.

T If you can catch the ball six times in a row, bouncing it the way that you have been, try bouncing it a little higher and still catching it using only your hands. If you have to use your body to catch the ball, you know you're bouncing the ball too high.

Throwing an Object to Different Levels and Catching It

Setting: Self-space; a beanbag or yarn ball for each child

Cues	
Watch the Ball	(Keep your eyes on the ball; see it come into your hands.)
Reach	(Reach to meet the ball; don't wait for it to come to your hands.)
Pull It In	(Pull the ball toward you so your catches are soft and quiet; give with the ball.)

Tasks/Challenges:

T This task is to give you more practice catching. In your own space, throw the beanbag (yarn ball) up in the air and catch it. To warm up, throw the object at about head level.

T Now that you're warmed up, practice throwing the object about arm's length above your head and catching it. This makes catching a little more difficult because there's more force involved.

T Once you're able to catch the object 10 times in a row using soft, quiet catches, you're ready to throw it a little higher still, maybe 5 feet over your head. Always remember that you must still be able to catch quietly at each level you throw to. If you can't, then you know you're throwing too high and need to bring the throw down a little.

Catching in Different Places Around the Body

Setting: Self-space; a beanbag or yarn ball for each child

Cues

Watch the Ball (Keep your eyes on the ball; see it come into your hands.)

Reach (Reach to meet the ball; don't wait for it to come to your hands.)

Pull It In (Pull the ball toward you so your catches are soft and quiet; give with the ball.)

Tasks/Challenges:

T You practiced catching an object that goes to different heights; now you're going to practice catching an object that goes to different places around your body. Standing in your own space, throw the beanbag (yarn ball) so you have to reach in different places around your body to catch it. This may mean catching it to the sides sometimes, or behind your head. See how many different places you can find to catch the beanbag (ball) from without leaving your self-space.

C Most of us don't like to practice places that are really hard. This time as you practice, pick out two places that you tried to catch and had the hardest time with. Practice those two places until you can catch the beanbag (yarn ball) four out of five times.

T This time practice your same catches in new places around your body. **Always try to see that the catches are as quiet as possible.**

T I'm going to make this task a little harder still. It's easy to catch the beanbag (ball) when it's fairly close to your body, but now I want you to practice catching the beanbag (ball) so you have to reach to catch it. Really stretch so you feel you're almost going to fall over. It helps to think of keeping one foot glued in place all the time. You stretch from that glued foot—the foot that can't move.

T Don't forget, as you're stretching to catch, to keep trying to catch in different places. So the task should be like this: stretch and reach to catch in different places around your body.

The child's success with the previous tasks depends a great deal on the child's ability to throw so that she or he has to stretch. It helps to practice stretching without the throw or simply throwing away from the body. If the students aren't catching on as you think they should, look to see if the reason is the throw.

Throwing Overhand at a Stationary Target

Setting: Targets about 5 or 6 feet high on the wall, one for each student (paper plates with pictures on them make good targets), a carpet square for each child (to help maintain their spacing); a ball for each child.

When drawing targets for children to throw at, we do not draw faces on the targets. Putting faces on targets subtly reinforces the idea of throwing at people, a violent concept we do not support in physical education programs.

Two student teachers came up with a great target for Throwing Overhand at a Stationary Target. They partly filled self-tie plastic kitchen trash bags with old aluminum cans. On the outside of each bag they drew a target and then inserted a coat hanger in the top of each bag, closed it, taped it for reinforcement, and hung each one from various things in the gym. The children loved it—the targets were big and made noise when they were hit. The cleanup was much simpler than with plates, more than one child could work at a target, and the targets were reusable.

Cues

Eyes on Target (Your eyes should be on the target all the time.)

Side, Arm, Step, Follow (Don't forget the cues for throwing—always use them.)

Tasks/Challenges:

T This time you're going to throw at targets. **You'll have to keep your eyes on the target.** Each of you has a target in your own space. See how often you can hit it.

T When you can hit your target three times in a row, take a giant step backward and try from that distance.

This same task can be changed for underhand throwing by lowering the targets to 2 to 3 feet from the floor. The second cue would change from Side to Face, Arm, Step, Follow.

Assessment Example

From the *National Standards for Physical Education, 1st edition*

Peer Observation

Using an appropriate size ball, students practice throwing at a target on the wall, alternating with a partner in five-throw turns. The students should be instructed to concentrate on the critical elements of throwing as taught by the instructor (i.e., ready position, arm preparation, opposite side to the target, step with leg opposite the throwing arm, follow-through, accuracy of throw). After each bout of five throws the partner gives feedback on one of the critical elements by drawing a smiley face on a score sheet each time the element was employed as instructed. Note changes in performance with subsequent five-throw bouts.

Criteria for Assessment

a. Recognizes critical elements of basic movement pattern.
b. Adjusts conditions for success following feedback.

NASPE (1995, p. 20)

Hit the Can

Setting: Partners; one ball or beanbag per pair; institutional cans stacked on benches or other objects (or on the floor) to form a can target for each pair; carpet squares as starting points

Children love this activity because of the noise. Beware of the noise level of the cans, especially if you have a tile floor.

Cues	
Eyes on Target	(Your eyes should be on the target all the time.)
Side, Arm, Step, Follow	(Always use the throwing cues.)

Tasks/Challenges:

T With a partner, you're going to practice throwing at the tin cans stacked in front of you. Stand behind your carpet square as you throw. To start, one of you is the thrower, one of you the stacker. The stacker stands far enough behind the cans so as not to get hit if the thrower hits the cans but close enough to pick them up quickly if they topple. After six throws, trade places. The secret is in the stacking: The faster you stack, the faster the game goes.

T If you can knock the cans over two times in a row, move your carpet square back three giant steps and try throwing from the new distance.

When practicing throwing at targets, we always try to have a throwing area for each child or group or pair of partners to maximize the number of throwing opportunities.

Bowling for Targets

Setting: Partners, each with a target on the floor (such as several two-liter plastic bottles, weighted with sand or dirt) and a 4- to 6-inch playground ball

Cues	
Eyes on Target	(Your eyes should be on the target all the time.)
Face, Arm, Step, Follow	(Don't forget the cues for throwing—always use them.)

Tasks/Challenges:

T With a partner, you're going to practice throwing at targets on the ground by using an underhand throw that rolls along the floor. One of you is the setter; the other is the bowler. Using an underhand throw, roll the ball and try to knock the pins over. The setter will set the pins up again and roll the ball back to you. This is like bowling. After five turns trade places.

T If you knock the pins over twice in a row, move one giant step back and try again.

Throwing Underhand to Hoops

Setting: Partners with a hoop (on the floor between them) and a beanbag for each pair. Tape marks on the floor at various places around the hoop.

Cues	
Eyes on Target	(Your eyes should be on the target all the time.)
Face, Arm, Step, Follow	(Don't forget the cues for throwing—always use them.)

Tasks/Challenges:

T This time you're going to practice throwing so your beanbag lands in the hoop that's in the middle of your space on the floor. Throw the beanbag so it lands inside the hoop. Move one giant step back each time the beanbag lands in the hoop. Your partner will collect the beanbag and throw it back to you. After five throws, switch places. Remember: The best way to do this is to throw underhand.

C A game you can play is called Around the World. Start in one place and try to hit the hoop. If you hit the hoop from that place, move to the next spot, and try to hit the hoop from there. If you miss, your partner gets a chance to toss. Whenever you miss, trade places with your partner. You can keep adding new spots to throw from as you get better.

Assessment Example

From the *National Standards for Physical Education, 1st edition*

Peer Observation

Students are given a task of practicing the underhand throw at a target with a partner. Students may choose the type and size of ball, distance from the target (enough distance to produce a throw and not a toss), and the height of the target. Partners assist each other by marking a score sheet for accuracy for each of five throws. Partners change roles after five throws. Take as many turns as time allows.

Criteria for Assessment

a. Chooses appropriate ball and placement of target for personal competence.
b. Records partner's performance accurately and honestly.
c. Assists partner by speaking politely and taking turns.
d. Assumes personal responsibility for the results of the activity.

NASPE (1995, p. 27)

Throwing to High Targets

Setting: Partners, with a beanbag or ball for each pair; ropes with hoops attached strung across the space (Figure 25.2) at different heights as targets: some at chest height, others above the heads

Cues	
Eyes on Target	(Your eyes should be on the target all the time.)
Side, Arm, Step, Follow	(Don't forget the cues for throwing—always use them.)

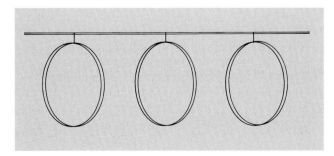

Figure 25.2 Hoops suspended from rope as targets.

Tasks/Challenges:

T You're going to be aiming at a high target or goal—the hoops. This task will give you good practice for basketball later. Decide how far away from your goal you want to stand. Use your overhand throw for this task.

C This time you're going to test yourself. Pick a place to stand, and see how many throws in a row you can put through the hoop. When you make 8 out of 10 goals, move to a new spot and try for 8 out of 10 goals again.

Throwing Backhand to a Target

Setting: Individuals or partners; sticks (similar to horseshoe stakes) in the ground and plastic deck rings for each child

Cues	
Eyes on Target	(Your eyes should be on the target all the time.)
Throwing Side to Target	(The side of the arm you throw with should be facing the target.)
Arm Way across Body	(Instead of bringing it to the back, bring the arm you throw with way across your body.)
Step with Same Foot	(This is one of the few times that you step toward the target with the foot on the same side as the arm you're throwing with.)
Follow Through	(Make your arm follow your throw toward the target.)

Tasks/Challenges:

T Try to throw the ring so it goes over your stick. This activity is a little different from anything you've done before, so start very close. The throwing action is also different; instead of throwing overhand or underhand, you're actually throwing sort of backward—sidearm using a flick of your wrist away from your body toward the stick. *(The teacher or a skilled child should demonstrate the throw.)*

T If you can ring the stick six times in a row from where you're standing, move back a couple of steps and try it again.

Throwing at a large target challenges youngsters at the control level.

Throwing a Frisbee

Setting: Partners; one Frisbee per pair

Cues	
Eyes on Target	(Your eyes should be on the target all the time.)
Throwing Side to Target	(The side of the arm you throw with should be facing the target.)
Arm Way across Body	(Instead of bringing it to the back, bring the arm you throw with way across your body.)
Step with Same Foot	(This is one of the few times that you step toward the target with the foot on the same side as the arm you're throwing with.)
Follow Through	(Make your arm follow your throw toward the target.)

Tasks/Challenges:

🅣 Now you get to practice throwing a Frisbee. The action involved is similar to the one you just did with the ring: a flick of the wrist to make the Frisbee fly. *(A demonstration is essential here.)* Practice throwing the Frisbee toward your partner, and have your partner throw it back to you. Don't worry about aiming—just try to throw to the general area where your partner is. You'll know you're

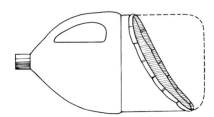

Figure 25.3 Plastic scoop. You can make scoops for throwing and catching by cutting the end and part of the side from large plastic jugs that have grip-type handles. For protection, place tape over the cut edges.

getting better when the Frisbee flies flat (not tilted) each time you throw it.

🅣 Now try to throw the Frisbee so it goes fairly close to your partner. Start off pretty close together, and slowly move farther apart as you improve.

Catching with a Scoop

Setting: Individuals alone at first, and then partners; a plastic scoop (Figure 25.3) and a beanbag for each child

Cues	
Watch the Bag	(Keep your eyes on the bag; see it come into your hands.)
Reach	(Reach to meet the bag; don't wait for it to come to your hands.)
Pull It In	(Pull the bag toward you so your catches are soft and quiet—give with the bag.)

Intratask variation can be used to adjust the catching task to the skill level of the children.

Tasks/Challenges:

T In your self-space, practice throwing the beanbag up with your hand and catching it in the scoop. To be a good catch, the beanbag must stay in the scoop and not bounce out.

T Now your partner will throw the beanbag to you, and you'll catch it with the scoop. The partner shouldn't be very far away to begin. After seven throws, trade places.

T The way you reach and pull in with the scoop as you catch the beanbag has changed a little now that a partner is throwing to you. **Instead of reaching up and pulling down, as you did when you caught from a throw you made yourself, you have to reach out and pull back.**

✓ Why is it so important to "watch, reach, and pull it in" when catching with a scoop?

Flying Beanbag Catch

Setting: Large space; groups of three or four; one playground ball and one beanbag per group (Humphries, Lovdahl, & Ashy, 2002)

Cues

Watch, Reach, Pull	(Watch the ball, reach for it, and pull it in.)
Get Behind	(As the beanbag comes toward you, position your body so that you are behind the beanbag, not to the side of it.)

Tasks/Challenges:

T We are going to work on catching a beanbag on a hop. This is like baseball players catching a baseball on a bounce. To do this, one person puts the beanbag on the ball and drops the ball. *(A demonstration would be good here.)* When the beanbag "flies" off the ball, the closest person to it catches it. Switch "droppers" after five turns.

C How many flying beanbags can you catch in a row?

Throwing a Ball against a Wall and Catching the Rebound

Setting: A wall with enough space so that the children can spread out and not be in each other's way as they throw; carpet squares as helpful reminders of self-space; one tennis ball per child; a line on the wall 3 feet above ground and one on the ground 10 feet from the wall

Cues

Throwing	Eyes on Target (Your eyes should be on the target all the time.)
	Side, Arm, Step, Follow (Don't forget the cues for throwing—always use them.)
Catching	Watch, Reach, Pull (Watch the ball, reach for it, and pull it in.)
	Get Behind (As the ball bounces off the wall, position your body so that you're behind the ball, not to the side of it.)

Tasks/Challenges:

T At your carpet square, throw the ball against the wall, let it bounce on the ground on the return, and catch it.

T **As you practice this time, try to catch the ball at stomach or chest level.**

T As you practice now, sometimes throw the ball hard and sometimes soft so that you have to move forward and backward to catch it.

T To make it a little harder, now try to catch the ball without letting it bounce.

T Now throw from behind the line on the ground so the ball hits the wall above the line on the wall. Catch the ball as it rebounds before it hits the ground. Give it a try.

C We'll make a game out of it this time. I'll time you for one minute. Count to yourself how many times you can hit the wall above the line and catch the ball in the air on the rebound. Remember the number, because we'll do it again so you can try to improve your score.

Assessment Example

From the *National Standards for Physical Education, 1st edition*

Peer Observation

Have partners observe the preparatory phase of a designated skill in an attempt to ascertain the correct use of critical elements. For example, student A will throw a ball toward a target five times using the overhand pattern while student B observes the performance, focusing on a single critical element during the preparatory phase (e.g., opposite foot forward, side to target, arm pulled way back). The observing student gives a "thumbs up" if the critical element is correct; if incorrect, the observing student tells what is needed to improve the movement.

Criteria for Assessment

a. Thrower displays the critical element that is the focus of the observation.
b. Observer makes an accurate judgment on the performance.

NASPE (1995, p. 33)

Throwing for Distance

Setting: Partners in a large outdoor field, each pair with a bucket of about 10 tennis balls; beanbags to mark where the balls land (often you can get old tennis balls from parents who play tennis. Send parents a note at the beginning of the year asking tennis players to save old tennis balls; collect them regularly. It doesn't take long to accumulate more balls than you need.)

Cues	
Side to Target	(Turn your hips and upper body toward your throwing hand when you pull it back in preparation to throw.)
Arm Way Back	(Pull your throwing arm way back before you begin the throw.)
Step	(Step forward on the foot opposite the hand that is throwing the ball.)
Follow Through	(Follow through toward the target, ending at your knees.)

Tasks/Challenges:

T You're going to practice throwing long distances—like playing the outfield in baseball. Throw each tennis ball as far as you can. With markers, your partner will mark your farthest throw and collect the balls. Each time, try to beat your last throw. After you've thrown all the balls you have, trade places with your partner.

A baseball glove is an implement that can be used to catch an object, but generally we prefer not to use gloves in our program. When children bring their own gloves to school, there are problems. Many children prefer to not share their gloves with children who don't have gloves. We also have a hard time justifying the expense of purchasing gloves for a physical education program. In the schools we've taught in, we've always wanted other equipment that needs to be purchased and is more important than baseball gloves.

Throwing and Catching with a Partner

Setting: Partners about 10 feet apart; one ball per pair

Cues	
Throwing	Eyes on Target (Your eyes should be on the target all the time.)
	Face, Arm, Step, Follow (Don't forget the cues for throwing—always use them.)
Catching	Watch, Reach, Pull (Watch the ball, reach for it, and pull it in.)
	Get Behind (As the ball comes toward you, position your body so that you're behind the ball, not to the side of it.)

Tasks/Challenges:

T Throw the ball so that your partner doesn't have to move to catch it. You'll probably want to start with an underhand throw.

T If you and your partner can make 10 throws and catches from the place where you are now without missing, then both of you move back two giant steps and practice from there. Do the same thing as before: Make good throws so your partner doesn't have to move more than a step in either direction to catch.

T Try to make sympathetic throws, which are throws that have enough force to get to your partner but are not so strong that your partner can't catch them.

C From wherever you are standing, see how many throws and catches you can make without a miss. To count, the ball must be caught, not just batted back to your partner.

C This time we'll play a game called One Step, which goes like this: Each time you and your partner make a catch, both of you move back one giant step; if you miss, you both move toward each other one giant step.

T Change and use an overhand throw. First, just practice back and forth. When you can make 10 in a row, move back two giant steps.

If children are relatively close to one another, don't expect mature throwing patterns. As the distance between the partners increases, you should start observing more mature patterns.

Assessment Example

From the *National Standards for Physical Education, 1st edition*

Event Task

Have the students pretend that Rapunzel recently enrolled in your school. She knows nothing about catching a ball. Students are asked to explain what Rapunzel needs to know to catch a ball thrown to her from the front at about chest height. Instruct the students to imagine themselves practicing with Rapunzel and providing feedback after each attempted catch. Have them imagine looking for critical elements (ready position, hand and arm position, eye contact, and absorption of force.)

Criteria for Assessment

a. Identifies critical elements of catching.
b. Uses appropriate feedback to improve performance.

NASPE (1995, p. 21)

Throwing and Catching over a Net with a Partner

Setting: Partners; nets or ropes between two chairs at various heights, enough for one per pair; beanbags and yarn balls

Cues

Throwing Eyes on Target (Your eyes should be on the target all the time.)
Face, Arm, Step, Follow (Don't forget the cues for throwing—always use them.)

Catching Watch, Reach, Pull (Watch the ball, reach for it, and pull it in.)
Get Behind (As the ball comes toward you, position your body so that you're behind the ball, not to the side of it.)
Thumbs/Little Fingers (When you catch over your head, make sure your thumbs are together; if the catch is low, make sure your little fingers are together.)

Tasks/Challenges:

T With your partner, choose a net (rope) that you want to practice throwing and catching over and a beanbag or a yarn ball. After you've chosen your net (rope), begin throwing underhand and catching. Try to throw so that the throw has an arch on it and your partner doesn't have to move more than one step in either direction to catch the beanbag or ball.

C See how many throws and catches you and your partner can make without missing. **Watch the object closely.** Use sympathetic throws.

T If you are really good with the underhand throws over the net, change to overhand throws.

C See if you and your partner can get 20 overhand throws and catches in a row without missing.

Teachers often ask, "How do I accommodate different skill levels in one class?" More specifically, "How do I do this with little equipment?" We've found that the best way is to vary the major task for individual children according to their needs (see Chapter 11). Often you can reduce or increase the complexity of the task without substantially changing the equipment used.

Consider the task of throwing a ball to a partner so that the partner is fully extended to catch. You can reduce the complexity of this task by changing the equipment from a ball to a beanbag or by having the partner use an outstretched arm as the target. Then, by changing the task so that the throw forces the partner to take a step to catch the ball, you increase the complexity of the same task.

You should make such changes by moving from group to group, observing, and modifying accordingly. In this way, the entire class is then practicing variations of the same task.

Bench Bounce Catch

Setting: Partners each pair with a playground ball and a bench or table

> **Cues**
>
> *Throwing*   Eyes on Target and Bench (Table) (Your eyes should see your partner and the bench (table) at the same time—they are both targets.)
>
> *Catching*   Watch, Reach, Pull (Watch the ball, reach for it, and pull it in.)
> Get Behind (As the ball comes toward you, position your body so that you're behind the ball, not to the side of it.)
> Thumbs/Little Fingers (When you catch over your head, make sure your thumbs are together; if the catch is low, make sure your little fingers are together.)

Tasks/Challenges:

🅣 Bounce the ball on your side of the bench (table) so that it travels over the bench (table) and your partner catches it. Your partner shouldn't have to move more than one step in either direction to catch the ball.

🅣 As you bounce the ball over the bench (table), sometimes bounce it with one hand and sometimes with two hands.

🅒 Try to keep the ball going back and forth as long as you can, using the bounce throw over the bench (table). **To do this you will have to remember your quick feet.** Remember, this is a throw and catch, not a volley across the bench.

Utilization Level: Learning Experiences Leading to Skill Development

Throwing tasks at the utilization level are designed to help children learn to throw while traveling, to throw accurately at moving targets, and to jump to throw. Catching experiences include catching while traveling, while in the air, and in gamelike activities that require the ability to catch while moving in relationship to various objects and/or people.

A note about cues: Although several cues are listed for many of the learning experiences, it's important to focus on only one cue at a time. That way, the children can really concentrate on that cue. Once you provide feedback to the children and observe that most have learned a cue, then it's time to focus on another one.

Moving to Catch

Setting: Individuals in self-space with a lot of extra space around each one; one ball per person

> **Cues**
>
> *Throwing*   Away, But Close (Throw away from your body so that you have to move, but don't throw so far that you can't catch the ball.)
>
> *Catching*   Under or Behind Ball (Move to a position that puts you under or behind the ball, not to the side.)
> Watch, Reach, Pull (As always, watch the ball, reach for it, and pull it in.)

Tasks/Challenges:

🅣 You're going to practice throwing so that you have to move to catch. Each of you has to be in your own self-space with much space around you so you don't run into others. To begin, toss the ball so you have to move just one step to catch it—put the ball just barely out of your reach. This is a skill often used in football and basketball.

🅣 Practice throwing and catching in all places around your body: forward, backward, and sideways.

🅣 I see some people catching at the same place; try to catch at different places, especially toward the back of your body.

Setting: A large area (a full-sized gymnasium or, preferably, outdoors in a large open space)

Tasks/Challenges:

🅣 This task will take a lot of concentration on your part, not only to catch the ball, but to make sure that you do not run into or hurt others. It's fun, but it must be done with a great deal of safety. You practiced moving one or two steps to catch the ball; now you are going to practice moving a long way to catch. Throw the ball away from you so that you have to move several steps to catch it. Make the catch; then throw again so you have to move to catch the ball. Your throws should always be catchable. In other words, don't throw so far that there is absolutely no way that you could possibly catch the ball. Start out with throws that make you move only a few steps and then try longer throws. **Remember, if at all possible you should be under and behind the ball when you catch it.**

🅣 After each successful catch, see if you can throw the ball a little farther the next time. In other words, see how far you can really move to make the catch.

✓ *Teacher Observation.* This would be an excellent time to use a teacher observation (videotape or checklist) of the critical catching cues developed at the control level. You know real learning has occurred if the children are able to catch in the dynamic situations of the utilization level using the cues.

Throwing and Catching While Traveling

Setting: Individuals in self-space with a lot of extra space around each one; one ball or beanbag per person

Cues	
No Stopping	(Both the throws and the catches should be on the move, with no stops.)
Throwing	Away, But Not Too Far (Throw away from your body so that you have to move, but not so far that you can't catch the ball.)
Catching	Under or Behind Ball (Move to a position that puts you under or behind the ball, not to the side.) Watch, Reach, Pull (As always, watch the ball, reach for it, and pull it in.)

At the control level throwing and catching different objects increases children's physical activity options.

Tasks/Challenges:

Ⓣ You practiced throwing that made you move to catch, but you were standing still when you threw. Now you are going to throw and catch while moving. To begin, toss the ball into the air and catch it while you walk around the space. You must be very careful while you do this and use two sets of eyes: one to watch the ball and one to watch out for other people so you don't run into them.

⚠ Mastery of space awareness—moving in relation to others—is a prerequisite to this activity.

Ⓣ If you can catch the ball almost all the time when you are walking and throwing and catching, try slowly jogging as you travel. Always watch closely so that you don't collide with others.

Throwing on the Move

Setting: A large space; partners; relatively large, stationary targets (a hoop hanging from a basket, a tire hanging from a tree, a target placed on a backstop) for each pair; one ball or beanbag per pair

Cues	
Straight Pathway	(The ball should travel in a straight pathway; not curved or arched.)
No Stopping	(The throws should be on the move, with no stops.)

Tasks/Challenges:

Ⓣ With a partner, you're going to practice throwing at a target while running. Run across in front of your target, and try to throw the ball through or into your target. Your partner will give the ball back to you so you can throw again. After four throws, trade places.

Ⓣ Sometimes when people perform this task, they tend to run, stop, and then throw. **What you really want to be doing is throwing as you run, so the throw just seems to flow out of the run and you keep running afterward.** This time, have your partner watch you closely as you run and throw. Your partner's task is to tell you whether you stop and throw or throw on the run. Sometimes it is hard to feel what we are actually doing; partners make good observers.

Throwing to Make a Partner Move to Catch

Setting: A large space; partners; one ball or beanbag per pair

Cues

Throwing Throw Beyond (Throw beyond your partner. Pick a spot just beyond your partner and aim for it.)

Catching React Quickly (As soon as the ball leaves the thrower's hand, move to the spot to catch.)
Watch, Reach, Pull (Watch the ball, reach for it, and pull it in.)

Tasks/Challenges:

🅣 With your partner, throw back and forth so that your partner has to stretch or move a few steps to catch. The idea is not to make your partner miss, but to force your partner to really stretch or move to catch so he or she can practice difficult catches.

Assessment Example

From the *National Standards for Physical Education, 1st edition*

Event Task

Students are requested to design a game of throwing and catching for one or two persons to play. The game must include the underhand throwing skill that has been taught in class. Students write a description of the game so students in another class could, after reading the information, play the game. They are also asked to describe how the critical elements of the skill might change when used in different conditions.

Criteria for Assessment

a. Game incorporates use of underhand throwing and catching skills.
b. Description of game adequately identifies needed skills and critical elements of each.
c. Description accurately describes how critical elements might change under varying conditions.

NASPE (1995, p. 35)

Throwing to a Moving Target

Setting: A large space; partners; one ball per pair

Cues

Throwing Lead the Receiver (Throw to an open space just in front of the catcher.)

Catching Know Where to Go (Know where the throw is supposed to go and run toward that spot.)
Watch Passer, Then Ball (Watch the passer as you start to run, and then after the ball is thrown, track it all the way into your hands.)

Tasks/Challenges:

🅣 We are going to practice throwing the ball to your partner, who is moving. Your ultimate goal is to throw so that your partner doesn't have to stop moving or turn around to catch the ball. The thrower should remain still; the catcher jogs away from the thrower. After six tries, trade places. *(Call the class together and ask where the ball should be so that the catcher can keep moving. There will be multiple responses that include: to them and in front of them.)*

🅣 Let's practice again. This time try to throw the ball to the receiver. Take five turns and trade places. *(Gather the class. How did that work? Could the catcher catch without having to stop? The answer is almost always no. What should we do? Throw the ball in front of the catcher.)*

🅣 This time try to throw the ball in front of the catcher. After five tries, switch places. *(Ask the class, Was the catcher able to catch without stopping? Usual answer: Sometimes. Why? Our timing was off. Sometimes it went in front and sometimes it didn't. How could we help that? Throw to a place in front of the catcher that both of us decide on.)*

🅣 This time practice throwing to a place that the two of you decide on. Seven times each and switch. How did that work?

🅣 Instead of your partner running away from you, change so your partner is running across in front of you. **As before, you still throw the ball to a space in front of the runner; the runner is simply coming from a different direction.** Decide ahead of time where you are going to try to give the runner the ball. *(A similar line of questioning can be used here, if needed.)*

🅣 There's one more way to practice this idea. This time the runner must be coming toward the thrower. **Again, target a space in front of the runner so that the runner doesn't have to stop and turn around to catch the ball.**

🅣 Until now each set of partners decided where the catch was to be made. Now practice without deciding ahead of time where you'll throw the ball. This means the thrower will have to be very accurate with the throws, and the catcher will have to be always on the alert to catch the ball whenever and wherever it goes.

Assessment Example

From the *National Standards for Physical Education, 1st edition*

Teacher Observation/Observational Record

Students are asked to receive and send a basketball pass to a partner on the move. The teacher observes the passing and uses a check list to annotate the performance.

At the utilization level, children profit from stretching and/or jumping to catch.

Criteria for Assessment

a. Receives the pass and sends it in one motion.
b. Passes ahead of the moving player (receiver does not have to stop).
c. Receiving student cuts into a space to receive the pass.

NASPE (1995, p. 32)

Throwing for Distance and Accuracy

Setting: A large space; partners; one ball per pair

Cues	
Watch the Target	(Look at your partner the whole time.)
Side, Arm, Step, Follow	(For long throws you really have to do all of these.)
Almost Straight	(The ball should travel in a pathway that is almost halfway between the ground and straight up in the air—at about a 45-degree angle.)

Tasks/Challenges:

T   The object of this task is to practice throwing and catching accurately to someone far away. You and your partner need to start throwing about 10 yards apart. Throw so your partner doesn't have to move to catch the ball. You want the ball to go straight to your partner.

T   If you can throw successfully 10 times to your partner 10 yards away, each of you back up two giant steps and try again. Each time you can successfully make 10 throws, back up another two giant steps. Try to find your maximum distance.

√   *Exit Slip.* This is a wonderful place to use an exit slip that asks each group of partners to evaluate the throwing and catching and plan an initial activity for the next class that will let students practice what they need to work on.

Target Backaway

Setting: A large space; stationary targets in various places (against baseball backstops, trees, or playground apparatus) around the space

Cues

Watch the Target	(Look at the target the whole time.)
Side, Arm, Step, Follow	(For long throws you really have to do all of these.)
Almost Straight	(The ball should travel in a pathway that is almost halfway between the ground and straight up in the air—at about a 45-degree angle.)

Tasks/Challenges:

T The task is now to try to hit the target from far away. Start close enough so you know you can hit the target. When you hit it three times, back up about five steps and throw again. After five successful throws, back up again.

C See how far you can get and still hit the target.

C See how many throws out of 10 you can make right to the target.

Playing Frisbee Golf

Setting: A Frisbee for each student; a Frisbee golf course: Use a hoop tied between two chairs or a hoop suspended from a tree as a target. The distance and angle of the target from the starting line can vary, depending on the amount of space available and the skill of the students. Trees, playground apparatus, fences, or backstops can be used as obstacles to throw over and around. (For a detailed analysis of Frisbee skills, write for *Frisbee: Flying Disc Manual for Students and Teachers*, International Frisbee Disc Association, P.O. Box 970, San Gabriel, CA 91776.)

Cues

Watch Target	(Always look at the target.)
Throwing Side to Target	(The side of the arm you throw with should be facing the target.)
Arm Way across Body	(Instead of bringing it to the back, bring the arm you throw with way across your body.)
Step with Same Foot	(This is one of the few times that you step toward the target with the foot on the same side as the arm you're throwing with.)
Follow Through	(Make your arm follow your throw toward the target.)

Tasks/Challenges:

T The name of this game is Frisbee Golf, a form of golf in which you use a Frisbee instead of a golf club and ball. The object is to throw the Frisbee for distance, and often around obstacles, eventually placing it through a target hoop. You want to use as few throws as possible. Here are the rules:

1. All players make their first throw from behind the starting line.
2. Players make the second throw and all throws after that from the landing spot of the previous throw. Players are allowed to take one step in throwing.
3. Players count how many throws were needed to place the Frisbee through the hoop.

Assessment Example

From the *National Standards for Physical Education, 1st edition*

Self-Assessment/Check List

Following a period of working on throwing different types of objects (Frisbees, footballs, deck tennis rings), students are asked to identify the number of different objects they have thrown and the types of throwing patterns they have used with these objects. They are also asked to do a self-assessment of their throwing performance using a check list provided by the teacher.

Criteria for Assessment

a. Recognizes difference in various types of throws.
b. Compares and contrasts throwing of different objects for different purposes.
c. Analyzes personal throwing skills accurately.

NASPE (1995, p. 47)

Catching to Throw Quickly to a Partner

Setting: Partners; one ball or beanbag per pair

Cues

Move and Face	(Move toward the approaching ball and begin to face the direction you are to throw.) *It is helpful to demonstrate this cue.*
Flow	(The catch and the throw should flow together; simply move directly into the throw.)

Tasks/Challenges:

T Sometimes it is necessary to throw very quickly after you catch the ball, much as baseball players do when they are trying to make a double play. With your partner you are going to practice throwing quickly after catching. Your partner will throw the ball to you; you throw it back as quickly as possible, like a hot potato. The throw to your partner needs to be accurate as well as quick. To begin, one of you practices quick throws; the other one simply makes the first throw and is a target. After seven throws, switch places.

T When most of the throws go directly to your partner, back up a few steps and try the task again.

T Now, to make the task even harder, try to catch the ball with one hand and throw it with the same hand. This is almost as if you don't really want to hold the ball—as if you need to get rid of the ball quickly. You may want to use a beanbag for this task.

Catching to Throw Quickly to a Target

Setting: Partners; fairly large (2-by-2-foot) targets spread around the area

Cues	
Move and Face	(Move toward the approaching ball and begin to face the direction you are to throw.) *It is helpful to demonstrate this cue.*
Flow	(The catch and the throw should flow together; simply move directly into the throw.)

Tasks/Challenges:

T With your partner, you're going to practice catching and throwing quickly to a target. This skill is used, for example, in the game of team handball. Your partner throws you the ball; you catch it and quickly throw it to the target. You're trying for a quick throw so no one can block your shot. After six times, switch places.

C See how many times out of 10 you can hit the target. Remember: Quick throws only; ones that stop don't count. Your partner is the judge.

Many of the throwing and catching skills at the utilization level can be transformed into gamelike situations for children. Some children at this level enjoy practicing in nongame contexts, whereas others are interested in practicing only if the skill is used in a gamelike situation. Generally, these are the children who continually want to know, "When do we get to play the game?"

Throwing While in the Air

Setting: A large grassy space; partners; one ball or beanbag per pair

Cues	
Face Target	(When you are in the air, your upper body should be facing the target.)
Follow	(Follow through to the target.)
Throw in Air	(Be in the air when you throw; don't jump, land, and then throw.)

Tasks/Challenges:

T Sometimes when you throw, you need to be in the air. This type of throwing is harder than throwing when you're on the ground. To start, run a few steps, jump in the air, and throw the ball to your partner while you're in the air. Make the throw as accurate as possible.

Often when people practice this task, they aren't in the air when they think they are. Sometimes people run, throw, and then jump; sometimes they run, jump, land, and then throw. It's hard to tell exactly what you're doing without some help, so your partner's job is to watch you very carefully to see if you're really in the air as you throw. For now, your partner takes the place of the teacher—your partner must tell you exactly what he or she saw.

Proficiency Level: Learning Experiences Leading to Skill Development

Experiences at the proficiency level include throwing and catching in relation to an opponent who attempts to prevent the throw or the catch. These tasks foster development of consistent degrees of accuracy and distance in throwing. Children learn to catch a variety of objects while traveling rapidly and suddenly changing direction and level.

Many of the activities at the proficiency level resemble traditional games. Yet, they are designed to enhance skill development. Thus, they are all designed to be played in small groups with multiple games being played at once. They are not designed to be played with large groups; for if we played with large groups many students would be waiting and not participating. Strategies for achieving maximum activity in game settings are included in Chapter 31.

A note about cues: At the proficiency level, tasks are more complex, typically requiring children to coordinate several movements simultaneously in a dynamic context. A list of cues is provided to assist the children in being more successful in the learning experiences. The challenge is in determining which cue will be most beneficial for each child . . . and when. Thus, careful observation and critical reflection become very important as you watch the children move and then decide which cue will be the most helpful to move each learner to a higher level.

Throwing and Catching a Frisbee in Different Places around the Body with a Partner

Setting: A large space; partners; one Frisbee per pair

Cues	
Catching	Behind and Under (Move so that you are behind and under the Frisbee when you catch it.)
	Watch, Reach, Pull (Watch the Frisbee, reach for it, and pull it in to your body.)
Throwing	Throw Away (Pick a spot just barely out of your partner's reach and aim for it.)

Tasks/Challenges:

Ⓒ The object of this activity is to throw the Frisbee so that your partner has to stretch to catch it. The scoring is this: If the Frisbee is caught, that counts as one point. If the body is stretched a long way while reaching to catch the Frisbee, that counts as three points. I'm going to throw a few to Mary. Let's watch to see how many points she'll get for each of her catches. *(Select a skilled catcher and throw, or have someone else throw the Frisbee so that the catcher has to stretch to make the catch.)*

Ⓒ You may want to change the way you score the game. You can work together to see how many points you can make; or you may want to play against your partner. Remember, though, that you'll have to make good throws if your partner is going to have a chance.

Throwing and Catching in a Field, Run, and Score Gamelike Situation

Setting: Two teams, four players each; four bases as in baseball; one ball

Cues	
Watch Target	(Your eyes should always watch the target. This time it is the chest of the catcher.)

Move and Face	(Move toward the approaching ball and begin to face the direction you are to throw.)
Flow	(The catch and the throw should flow together; simply move directly into the throw.)

Tasks/Challenges:

Ⓣ The object in this situation is to throw a ball around the bases twice before a runner can circle the bases once. Here are the rules:

1. The fielding team places a player at each base—first, second, third, and home plate.
2. The player at home plate (the catcher) begins with the ball. On the signal, two runners try to run the bases before the fielders throw the ball to each base twice.
3. If the runners travel the bases before the fielders throw and catch the ball twice, they score a run. If all the fielders throw and catch twice before the runners circle the bases, it's an out.
4. After three outs or when all runners have had a chance to run the bases twice, the teams switch roles.

Adjust the distance between the bases according to the throwers' ability and the runners' speed.

Throwing to Avoid a Defender

Setting: A 15-by-15-foot space; groups of three; one ball or beanbag per group

Cues	
Throwing	Lead the Receiver (Throw to an open space just in front of the catcher.)
	Quick (Make your throw quickly, as soon as you know the receiver is open.)
Catching	Move to Open Space (Move to a space that is at an angle from the thrower.)
	Watch Passer, Then Ball (Watch the passer as you start to run, and then after the ball is thrown, track it all the way into your hands.)
Intercepting	Hips (To tell where a person is going to move, watch the hips or the belly button.)
	Play the Ball (Always go after the person with the ball—to force the person to pass it.)

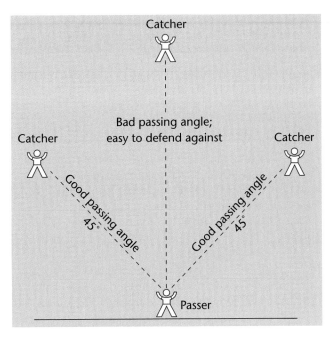

Figure 25.4 Passing angles for throwing against a defense.

It is very helpful to children to demonstrate the concept of moving away from the thrower at an angle of about 45 degrees (Figure 25.4).

Tip: When playing against a defense, the concept of catching changes to being able to catch while outmaneuvering the opponent. We assume that children at this point have mastered space awareness and dodging. The ability to move to an open space at an angle (approximately 45 degrees) away from the thrower is initially very difficult to understand. To get students to move away from the passer at an appropriate angle, a skilled soccer coach once provided these cues: **See the Passer, See the Ball, See as Much of the Field as Possible.** *You may want to try using them.*

Tasks/Challenges:

T In this task you'll practice throwing to someone against a defense. One of you is the thrower, one is the receiver, and the other one is the interceptor. Thrower, your job is to get the ball to the receiver. **Use quick moves, and get rid of the ball when you have a chance. Receiver, move to an open space to catch the ball. Interceptor, make them throw the ball, but don't forget that you are not allowed to touch the receiver or the thrower.** After five throws, change places.

🗝 What is one strategy that you can use to throw successfully when being defended? What can the catcher do to be successful in catching? What can you do to intercept the ball?

Throwing and Catching in a Small Sided Invasion Game

Setting: Self-determined space; cones for markers; groups of three; one ball

Cues	
Throwing	Lead the Receiver (Throw to an open space just in front of the catcher.) Quick (Make your throw quickly, as soon as you know the receiver is open.)
Catching	Move to Open Space (Move to a space that is at an angle from the thrower.) Watch Passer, Then Ball (Watch the passer as you start to run, and then after the ball is thrown, track it all the way into your hands.)
Intercepting	Hips (To tell where a person is going to move, watch the hips or the belly button.) Play the Ball (Always go after the person with the ball—to force the person to pass it.)

Tasks/Challenges:

T This is really a keep-away-like game. One of you will be trying to take the ball away from the other two. Here are the rules:

1. Decide your boundaries and mark them off with cones.
2. You can only catch the ball in the air.
3. If you get the ball, trade places with the person who threw it.
4. You may run with the ball, but you can't keep it for longer than 5 seconds.

Throwing at a Stationary Object While Being Defended

Setting: Groups of six; two pins and one ball (Figure 25.5)

Cues	
Throwing	Lead the Receiver (Throw to an open space just in front of the catcher.) Quick (Make your throw quickly, as soon as you know the receiver is open.)

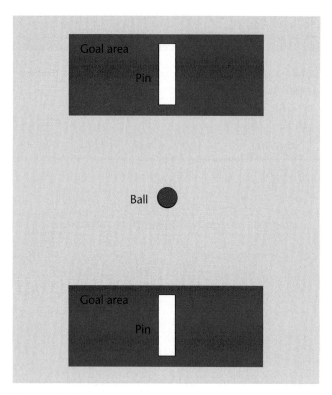

Figure 25.5 Setup for throwing at a stationary target while being defended.

Catching	Move to Open Space (Move to a space that is at an angle from the thrower.)
	Watch Passer, Then Ball (Watch the passer as you start to run, and then after the ball is thrown, track it all the way into your hands.)
Intercepting	Hips (To tell where a person is going to move, watch the hips or the belly button.)
	Play the Ball (Always go after the person with the ball—to force the person to pass it.)

Tasks/Challenges:

C This task could be called Hit the Pin; the object is to knock over the other team's pin. Here are the rules:

1. There are three players on each side.
2. Players can take only two steps when they have the ball; then they must pass the ball to a teammate or shoot (throw the ball) at the pin.
3. No players are allowed in the goal area.
4. If the ball touches the ground, the last player to touch the ball loses possession. The other team begins play at that location.

Throwing and Catching in a Small Sided Basketball-Type Game

Setting: Half a basketball court or comparable area around a basket; teams of three; one ball per court

Cues	
Throwing	Lead the Receiver (Throw to an open space just in front of the catcher.)
	Quick (Make your throw quickly, as soon as you know the receiver is open.)
Catching	Move to Open Space (Move to a space that is at an angle from the thrower.)
	Watch Passer, Then Ball (Watch the passer as you start to run, and then after the ball is thrown, track it all the way into your hands.)
Intercepting	Hips (To tell where a person is going to move, watch the hips or the belly button.)
	Play the Ball (Always go after the person with the ball—to force the person to pass it.)

Tasks/Challenges:

C This is a basketball game with one exception: It is all throwing and catching—no dribbling. Here are the rules:

1. When a player has the ball, the player must shoot it to the basket or pass it to a teammate. No dribbling or steps are allowed.
2. Every player must touch the ball before a shot.

Shooting Baskets

In addition to throwing and catching in relation to others, the game of basketball involves a specific type of throwing at a target—shooting a basket. When children are first learning the skill of shooting baskets, the following cues will be helpful:

Preparation
- Keep eyes focused on the goal.
- Bend the knees.
- Keep elbows close to the body, not extended outward from the body.
- Place hands behind the ball, fingers (not palms) touching the ball.

Release

- "Push" the ball upward from the chest toward the basket.
- Extend legs as arms extend toward the target.
- Arch the ball upward and over the front rim of the basket.

Have the children focus on traveling, with changes in direction, when they don't have the ball. When they receive the ball, have them focus on getting rid of it quickly—to a teammate or toward the goal.

Throwing and Catching with a Frisbee in a Small Sided Invasion Game

Setting: Playing field set up as in Figure 25.6; teams of two to four; one Frisbee (alternatives: a ball or a beanbag)

Cues

Throwing	Lead the Receiver (Throw to an open space just in front of the catcher.) Quick (Make your throw quickly, as soon as you know the receiver is open.)
Catching	Move to Open Space (Move to a space that is at an angle from the thrower.) Watch Passer, Then Ball (Watch the passer as you start to run, and then after the ball is thrown, track it all the way into your hands.)
Intercepting	Hips (To tell where a person is going to move, watch the hips or the belly button.) Play the Ball (Always go after the person with the ball—to force the person to pass it.)

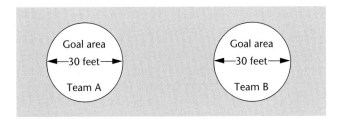

Figure 25.6 Setup for throwing and catching with a Frisbee in a small sided invasion game. There are no boundaries other than the two goal areas, each of which is 30 feet in diameter. Generally, the farther apart the goal areas can be placed, the more interesting the game is.

Tasks/Challenges:

C This task is like modified ultimate Frisbee. The object is to catch the Frisbee in the other team's goal area. Here are the rules:

1. When a player has the Frisbee, he or she can take no more than three steps before passing it to a teammate.
2. A point is scored when a player catches the Frisbee in the opposing team's goal area.
3. If the Frisbee touches the ground, the team that touched the Frisbee last loses possession. The opposing team puts the Frisbee in play from that location. There is no out-of-bounds.
4. The Frisbee can only be intercepted in the air. It can't be taken from someone's hands.

As you observe, you may see a need to stop the game and ask the children to practice throwing to a partner who's traveling or to reduce the difficulty by having the children practice two against two or two against one. The emphasis needs to be on leading the partner with the throw.

T To make the game a little harder, this time you always have to throw to a partner who is moving.

T To make the game a little easier, play two versus two or two against one.

Throwing and Catching with a Football in a Small Sided Invasion Game

Setting: A large space with goals on each end, about 20 yards from midfield (size of the field depends somewhat on the type of ball being used; children must be able to throw the football into the other team's goal area); teams of two; a foam football

Cues

Throwing	Lead the Receiver (Throw to an open space just in front of the catcher.) Quick (Make your throw quickly, as soon as you know the receiver is open.)
Catching	Move to Open Space (Move to a space that is at an angle from the thrower.) Watch Passer, Then Ball (Watch the passer as you start to run, and then after the ball is thrown, track it all the way into your hands.)
Intercepting	Hips (To tell where a person is going to move, watch the hips or the belly button.)

Play the Ball (Always go after the person with the ball—to force the person to pass it.)

Tasks/Challenges:

T This football game has just throwing and catching, no running with the foam football. You and your partner are a team. You try to throw the ball to your partner, who's being guarded by someone on the other team. Here are the rules:

1. Each team has four chances to throw and catch the ball in an attempt to move the ball from their goal line to the opposing team's goal area.
2. When on offense, one player is the thrower. He or she may not move forward. The thrower tries to accurately throw the ball downfield to her or his teammate, the receiver.
3. When on defense, one player tries to stay with the receiver to block or intercept the ball. The other player remains at the location where the play starts. That player counts aloud, "One alligator, two alligators," up to "five alligators," and then rushes the thrower, trying to touch the thrower or block the thrower's pass.
4. A play is over when the ball touches the ground or when a defensive player touches the offensive player who has possession of the ball.

Throwing and Catching with a Team Handball in a Small Sided Invasion Game

Setting: A large open space (see Figure 25.7 for setup); teams of three or four; a 5-inch playground ball or team handball

Cues	
Throwing	Lead the Receiver (Throw to an open space just in front of the catcher.) Quick (Make your throw quickly, as soon as you know the receiver is open.)
Catching	Move to Open Space (Move to a space that is at an angle from the thrower.) Watch Passer, Then Ball (Watch the passer as you start to run, and then after the ball is thrown, track it all the way into your hands.)
Intercepting	Hips (To tell where a person is going to move, watch the hips or the belly button.)

Figure 25.7 Setup for throwing and catching with a team handball in a small sided invasion game. Goals can be made of stacked tires; semicircles can be spray-painted on the ground.

Play the Ball (Always go after the person with the ball—to force the person to pass it.)

Tasks/Challenges:

T This game is a little like soccer because there's a goalie, but you throw the ball rather than kick it. The object is to throw the ball through the other team's goal. Here are the rules:

1. Players must stay out of the semicircle.
2. The goalie must stay in the semicircle. She or he tries to collect the ball, to prevent it from going through the goal.
3. A player who has the ball can bounce it, pass it to a teammate, or throw it toward the goal. Once a player stops bouncing the ball, he or she must pass or shoot it; she or he can no longer dribble it.

Throwing and Catching While Using Simple Offense and Defense in a Small Sided Invasion Game

Setting: A large open space (see Figure 25.8 for setup); teams of three; any type of ball or beanbag

Cues	
Throwing	Lead the Receiver (Throw to an open space just in front of the catcher.) Quick (Make your throw quickly as soon as you know the receiver is open.)
Catching	Move to Open Space (Move to a space that is at an angle from the thrower.)

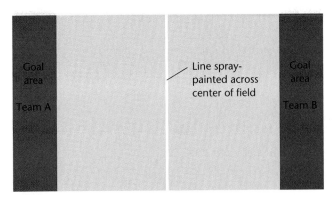

Figure 25.8 Setup for throwing and catching while using simple offense and defense in a small sided invasion game. Adjust the dimensions of the field according to the children's ability.

> Watch Passer, Then Ball (Watch the passer as you start to run, and then after the ball is thrown, track it all the way into your hands.)
>
> *Intercepting* Hips (To tell where a person is going to move, watch the hips or the belly button.)
>
> Play the Ball (Always go after the person with the ball—to force the person to pass it.)

Tasks/Challenges:

T This game is a little like football. The object is to pass a ball to someone on your team who's in the other team's goal area. It helps to decide the type of pathways the receivers will be running before each play: straight, curved, or zigzag. Here are the rules:

1. The quarterback must remain behind the line spray-painted across the middle of the field. No defensive player may cross the line.

2. The offensive team has three plays or attempts to have successful pass completions. Then the teams switch roles.

3. A point is scored each time a receiver catches the ball. Two points are scored when a receiver catches the ball in the end zone.

4. After each play, the ball is again placed at midfield.

5. No player may purposely bump or block another.

6. All players rotate to different positions after each play.

Assessment Example

From the *National Standards for Physical Education, 1st edition*

Journal

Students are asked to perform a self-assessment of their progress on throwing different types of objects (e.g., Frisbee, football, softball, deck tennis rings) and record this information in their journal. Moreover, they should describe the differences and similarities in throwing these objects and discuss which objects were easy/difficult to throw.

Criteria for Assessment

a. Correctly identifies personal status on the use of critical elements of throwing.

b. Identifies differences and similarities that occur when applying principles of throwing different objects.

c. Describes which objects they found easy/difficult to throw.

NASPE (1995, p. 49)

Reading Comprehension Questions

1. Name the three styles of throwing. What type of task encourages children to practice overhand throws?
2. What does the term *trunk rotation* mean when throwing a ball?
3. What does throwing in a static context mean? Describe an example of a task that includes throwing in a static context and an example of a task that includes throwing in a dynamic context.
4. Why do we focus on throwing before catching?
5. Name two characteristics of an individual at the utilization level in catching.
6. What does tracking a ball mean? How can a teacher tell if a child is tracking a ball appropriately?
7. Rank the following tasks by placing the number 1 in front of the easiest (most basic) task, the number 2 in front of the next more difficult task, and so on.
   ( ) Throw and catch while using simple offense and defense in a small sided invasion game.
   ( ) Toss up a beanbag and try to catch it with a plastic scoop.
   ( ) While running, throw a ball to a partner who's also running.

( ) Toss a yarn ball high in the air so you have to travel to catch it.

( ) Throw and catch with a partner.

8. What four cues do we use to remind children about the correct way of throwing a ball overhand? Explain the meaning of each cue.

9. What three cues do we use to remind children about the correct way of catching a ball? Explain the meaning of each cue.

References/Suggested Readings

Humphries, C., Lovdahl, P., & Ashy, M. (2002). Elementary physical education and the National Standards. *Journal of Physical Education, Recreation and Dance, 73* (5), 42–45.

National Association for Sport and Physical Education. (1995). *Moving into the future: National standards for physical education.* St. Louis, MO: Mosby.

National Association for Sport and Physical Education. (2004). *Moving into the future: National standards for physical education* (2nd ed.). Reston, VA: National Association for Sport and Physical Education.

Volleying and Dribbling

The word *volley* brings images of a high net, two teams, and the sport of volleyball, but the skill of volleying is much broader, as proven constantly by children's creative games. Games designed by youngsters, games of different cultures, and innovative equipment have opened our eyes as teachers to volleybirds, foot bags, bamboo balls, and balzacs, as well as to Don't Bounce Count, Power, and Hand Bumping. Volleying is no longer limited to volleyball; dribbling is no longer confined to basketball.

Volleying

For our purposes, we define *volleying* as striking or giving impetus to an object by using a variety of body parts—for example, hands, arms, head, or knees. Dribbling is a subdivision of volleying. Although our discussion here is divided into two separate sections—volleying and dribbling—when teaching, you may choose to develop dribbling and volleying together. Volleying and dribbling are almost exclusively game skills and are used in such sports as soccer, volleyball, handball, basketball, and speedball. See Box 26-1 for information on volleying from the *National Standards for Physical Education.*

Levels of Skill Proficiency in Volleying

Children at the precontrol level of volleying are still struggling to achieve the hand-eye coordination required to contact the ball. They are rarely able to intentionally direct the flight of a ball when contact is made. Therefore at the precontrol level we provide a variety of activities for the exploration of volleying. Appropriate activities at this level include:

1. Striking balloons in the air
2. Striking a variety of lightweight objects
3. Striking with different body parts

At the control level, children are able to strike a ball continuously (letting it bounce) in their own space. They're able to control the amount of force that they put into the volley so that they can control the ball in their own space. At the control level, children begin:

1. Volleying balls with different body parts
2. Striking a ball using the overhand and underhand patterns
3. Striking over low nets and lines on the floor with partners

At the utilization level, children can control the direction as well as the force of their strikes. They're

Box 26-1

The Skill of Volleying in the *National Standards for Physical Education*

The movement skill of volleying is referenced in the *National Standards for Physical Education* (National Association for Sport and Physical Education, 2004) under Standard 1: Demonstrates competency in motor skills and movement patterns needed to perform a variety of physical activities. The standard speaks of the child's showing progress toward achieving mature form in manipulative skills (grades K–2)* and using the skills in dynamic and complex environments (grades 3–5).

able, with a variety of body parts, to produce a level surface with which to strike the ball. The children can also combine several different concepts with the skill of striking. Children at the utilization level have mastered the basic skill patterns and can concentrate on:

1. Continuously volleying with body parts
2. Playing wall and corner handball games
3. Volleying over a high net

When children are able to strike an object and simultaneously focus on the activity around them, they're able to function at the proficiency level. Appropriate tasks include:

1. Volleying with different body parts while traveling
2. Striking to targets
3. Playing competitive games involving different striking patterns

We focus on volleying as a major skill in many of our game situations. Efficient striking patterns are generally the last of the fundamental manipulative patterns to develop because of the fine perceptual and motor adjustments that the child must make. Once the child does begin to strike an object, the range of possible activities is enormous. Our progression spiral for volleying (page 505) indicates activities and experiences at various levels. The text ideas include suggestions for children at the different levels, and a range of activities and experiences within each level, stated rather directly. Remember, though, that we encourage you to modify the suggested organizational structure to satisfy your objectives (see Chapter 13).

Skill Theme Development Sequence

Volleying

Proficiency Level

Playing modified volleyball
Volleying in a line formation
Spiking
Striking downward with force
Serving overhand over the net
Striking with different body parts while traveling

Utilization Level

Serving underhand over the net
Volleying three on three
Volleying continuously to a partner
Volleying over a net
Striking to the wall—varying levels, force, and body position
Volleying with a volleybird
Playing Aerial Soccer
Volleying with the foot
Striking a ball continuously with different body parts
Volleying game: Child-designed

Control Level

Obstacle-Course Volley
Playing One-Bounce Volleyball
Playing Keep It Up
Volleying to a partner (overhead pattern)
Volleying a ball upward (overhead pattern)
Volleying to the wall (overhead pattern)
Striking over a low net (underhand pattern)
Playing Four Square, Two Square (underhand pattern)
Playing Hoop Volley (underhand pattern)
Striking a ball over a line (underhand pattern)
Striking a ball to the wall (underhand pattern)
Striking a ball upward with the forearms (the bump)
Striking a ball upward (underhand pattern)
Striking a ball noncontinuously with different body parts

Precontrol Level

Striking lightweight objects
Striking with different body parts
Striking a balloon forward
Striking balloons in the air

Precontrol Level: Activities for Exploration

At the precontrol level, children need a variety of activities involving the skill of volleying. As with all skills involving sending and/or receiving an object, they will need to watch the object as it approaches (and contacts) the hand or body part used for the volley. At this exploration level, variety is the focus; contact is the measure of success.

Striking Balloons in the Air

Setting: Children scattered throughout general space, each with an inflated balloon and a carpet square (or poly-spot) to designate self-space

Tasks/Challenges:

T Strike the balloon upward with your open palm so it stays in the air. Try to keep the balloon from touching the floor.

T Strike the balloon high above your head. Practice striking with both your right and your left hand so you will be equally good with each hand.

C See if you can volley the balloon 10 times without letting it touch the floor.

T Volley the balloon in the air, staying close to your carpet square or spot.

C As you volley in the self-space of your carpet square or poly-spot, say one letter of the alphabet for each volley. Can you get to Z?

Striking a Balloon Forward

Setting: Children scattered throughout general space, each with an inflated balloon

Tasks/Challenges:

T Strike your balloon in the air so it travels forward as you walk through general space.

T Strike your balloon so it travels forward as you walk in curved pathways. Can you travel in zigzag pathways as you volley the balloon?

C Travel across the gymnasium (blacktop area) as you volley the balloon forward. Can you complete your volley/travel without letting the balloon touch the ground?

Where on the balloon is contact made for it to travel upward? Where is contact made for the balloon to travel forward?

Striking with Different Body Parts

Setting: Children scattered throughout general space, each with an inflated balloon

Tasks/Challenges:

T Keep the balloon in the air by striking it with different body parts. How many different body parts can you use to volley the balloon upward?

T Volley the balloon upward by striking it with your head, then your hand. Try a combination of hand, elbow, head. Try alternate volleys from foot to hand.

C Count how many times you can volley the balloon before it touches the floor. Don't use the same body part two times in a row.

T Let's try a combination of more than two body parts: volley the balloon with these body parts: hand, head, knee, elbow.

C Make your own combination of volleys using different body parts. You may choose a two-, three-, or four-body-part sequence.

Striking Lightweight Objects

Setting: Children scattered throughout general space; a variety of lightweight objects for exploration of the volley—beach balls, lightweight plastic balls, balloons, foam balls, newspaper balls, and so forth

Tasks/Challenges:

T You have been exploring volleying with balloons—striking them upward in self-space and forward while walking slowly through general space. Now we will try the volley with different types of lightweight balls. Select the ball (or balloon) of your choice and volley it upward in your self-space. On the signal, you will exchange that ball or balloon for a different type (rotate each 2 to 3 minutes until the children have volleyed with each type of ball or balloon).

T When you begin to volley with some of the balls, you may wish to let the ball bounce after each volley; the skill then becomes "volley, bounce, volley, bounce. . . ." Remember to strike the ball upward when you volley.

T Let's try one more exploration: This time the sequence will be "volley, bounce, catch; volley, bounce, catch. . . ." Are you discovering that some types of balls are better for the volley; that others require volley, bounce; and that some require volley, bounce, catch?

T Count the number of times you can volley the ball or balloon before it touches the ground. Repeat the task for a second trial; remember to count your score.

At the control level, children practice volleying an object upward.

At the precontrol and control levels, volleying activities are best done with larger, lightweight objects, such as beach balls, balloons, or inexpensive plastic balls. They float slowly, providing more time for visual tracking. This allows children time to move under the object and volley it without the fear that accompanies heavier objects. Most equipment companies have also developed a large lightweight volleyball that provides an excellent progression between the very lightweight objects and a regulation-weight ball. These "trainer" balls are lighter in weight and larger, yet their flight is true. None of these objects work well on windy days outside, however.

After two tries, switch to a different type of ball or a balloon. Which did you like best? Which one was easiest? Which gave you the highest score?

C Choose your favorite type of ball or balloon to volley. Choose your type of volley: continuous volley; volley, bounce, volley, bounce; or volley, bounce, catch. See how many times you can complete your volley sequence without a mistake.

Control Level: Learning Experiences Leading to Skill Development

At the control level, children learn an underhand and an overhead volley. They volley with different body parts, volley in relation to other people and with a variety of objects. Children at this level still find that it helps to let the ball bounce between volleys so they can gain control of the volley; they will eliminate the bounce when they are ready to do so.

This youngster experiments with using the flat surface of the thigh to volley.

A note about cues: Although several cues are listed for many of the learning experiences, it's important to focus on only one cue at a time. That way, the children can really concentrate on that cue. Once you provide feedback to the children and observe that most have learned a cue, then it's time to focus on another one.

Striking a Ball Noncontinuously with Different Body Parts

Setting: Children scattered throughout general space, each with a lightweight ball (beach ball, Nerf ball, plastic ball)

Cues	
Flat Surface	(Keep the striking surface—your leg, foot, hand—as flat as possible for contact.)
Extend to Target	(Extend upward as you contact the ball.)

Tasks/Challenges:

T Strike the ball upward with different body parts: foot, elbow, upper thigh, shoulder, head, hand. Catch the ball after each volley.

T Of the body parts you used for the volley, which parts can provide a flat surface for the volley? **This time as you volley the ball upward, contact the ball with the flattest surface possible—foot, upper thigh, hand.** Where is the contact surface for a head volley?

C Practice until you can do three single volleys, with a catch after each, without moving from your self-space. Practice with your foot, your thigh, your hand, your head.

T Try your body-part volleys with a beach ball, a Nerf ball, a plastic ball. When you are comfortable with the upward volley, you may wish to try the skill with a playground or soccer ball.

Striking a Ball Upward (Underhand Pattern)

Setting: Children scattered throughout general space, each with a beach ball, a Nerf ball, or an 8-inch plastic ball

Cues

Flat Surface	(Extend your hand with your palm flat, like a pancake.)
Extend to Target	(Extend your hand upward on contact.)
Quick Feet	(Move your feet quickly to always be in position to volley the ball upward.)

Tasks/Challenges:

T Strike the ball with your hand, palm flat, so it travels directly upward. **Where on the ball will you need to make contact if you want the ball to travel in a straight pathway upward?**

T Volley the ball directly upward so you can catch it without moving from your self-space.

T Volley the ball directly upward a distance of 4 to 5 feet above your head.

C Practice until you can do this underhand volley five times, never leaving your space.

T Volley the ball upward continuously. **Move your feet quickly to always be in position directly "under" the ball.**

C Record your personal best for today by counting the number of consecutive volleys you can complete without a mistake.

✓ *Peer Observation.* This is an excellent time for a peer observation of critical cues, for example, "flat surface for volley," "quick feet to be in position under the ball." Peer assessment can also include verbal recall of cues and peer feedback for improvement. *See Chapter 14, "Assessing Student Learning," for development of peer observations.*

Striking a Ball Upward with the Forearms (The Bump)

Setting: Children scattered throughout general space, each with a lightweight ball

Cues

Flat Surface	(Extend your arms forward, forearms together, to create a flat surface.)
Extend to Target	(Extend your arms upward on contact.)
Quick Feet	(Move your feet quickly to always be in position to volley the ball upward.)

Tasks/Challenges:

T Toss the ball slightly upward. Quickly extend your arms, bringing your forearms together to form a flat surface. Volley the ball upward above your head so it returns to you. Catch the ball after each volley.

T Toss the ball, and then volley (bump) it upward two times before you catch it again.

C How many volleys (bumps) can you do without a mistake?

Striking a Ball to the Wall (Underhand Pattern)

Setting: Children spaced around the perimeter of the gymnasium, facing the wall at a distance of about 6 feet; a lightweight plastic ball for each child

Cues

Flat Surface	(Keep your palm flat, like a pancake.)
Extend to Target	(Extend your legs, body, striking arm toward the wall.)
Quick Feet	(Move your feet quickly to always be in position behind the ball.)

Tasks/Challenges:

T Bounce the ball one time, then strike it with your open palm, underhand volley, so it travels to the wall. As the ball rebounds from the wall, let it bounce one time and then catch it *(Figure 26.1)*. **Where on the ball do you need to make contact for it to travel forward to the wall? Right, slightly below center and behind the ball.**

Select two children who are using the correct pattern to demonstrate for the class.

C Practice until you can execute the drop-hit-bounce pattern three times. Remember to catch after each sequence.

T Using the underhand action, strike the ball with your open palm so the ball contacts the wall 3 to 4 feet above the floor. Continue the volley after each bounce. The pattern will be this: volley, bounce; volley, bounce. . . . The ball will not always come back exactly to you; **move your feet quickly to be in position to extend toward the target as you volley.**

C Count the number of volleys you can make without a mistake. A mistake is two bounces on the rebound or a volley that hits the ceiling.

Figure 26.1 Underhand striking pattern.
1. Hold ball in one hand, with feet in front-back stance.
2. Let ball bounce once. Bring hitting arm back so it's ready to hit.
3. As ball bounces back, hit it from underneath with open palm and with body extending forward.

T Practice the volley with each hand. When the ball comes to your right side, contact it with your right hand; when it rebounds to your left side, use your left hand.

T You have been practicing volleying to the wall by yourself. Now you are going to add a partner. The rules are the same, except after you volley the ball, the next hit will be taken by your partner. You will be alternating volleys. **Now your quick feet will really be important!**

C See how many times you and your partner can volley without missing.

✓ *Peer Observation.* Partner work provides an opportune time for children to observe/assess the critical cues—for example, Flat Surface, Extend to Target. *See Chapter 14 for development of peer assessments.*

Striking a Ball over a Line (Underhand Pattern)

Setting: Sets of partners scattered throughout general space; tape line on floor between each set

Cues	
Flat Surface	(Keep your palm flat, like a pancake.)
Extend to Target	(Extend your legs, body, striking arm toward the wall.)
Quick Feet	(Move your feet quickly to always be in position behind the ball.)

Tasks/Challenges:

T You'll be practicing underhand hits with your partner. Stand approximately 3 feet from the tape line and face your partner across the line. Using the underhand action, strike the ball so it crosses the line and bounces on the other side. Your partner

Figure 26.2 Setup for Hoop Volley.

will then volley the ball back to you so it bounces on your side.

T Practice striking the ball with each hand so you will be skilled with your right and your left hand.

C Cooperate with your partner to see how many times you can strike the ball back and forth over the line. Set a personal goal for your volleys over the line.

Playing Hoop Volley (Underhand Pattern)

Setting: Children with partners/three hoops and one lightweight ball for each group; arrange two of the hoops across from each other/place the third hoop in the middle (Figure 26.2)

Cues	
Flat Surface	(Keep your palm flat, like a pancake.)
Extend to Target	(Extend your legs, body, striking arm toward the target.)
Control	(Adjust your force to control the volley.)

Tasks/Challenges:

T You have been practicing the underhand volley, striking the ball to the wall and over a line. Today you will practice striking the ball to send it to a partner; however, the ball must bounce inside the middle hoop on its way to the partner! Remember, we are practicing the underhand pattern; that is the skill you must use in your game.

Volley the ball through the center hoop. You need to stay in your hoop, and you can volley the ball only after it bounces in the center hoop coming from your partner.

C See how many times you can keep the ball going without missing.

Playing Four Square, Two Square (Underhand Pattern)

Setting: Children's choice: Some children in groups of four (Four Square); others in groups of two (Two Square); squares marked off on the floor for the games (Figure 26.3)

Cues	
Flat Surface	(Keep your palm flat, like a pancake.)
Extend to Target	(Extend your legs, body, striking arm toward the target.)
Quick Feet	(Move your feet quickly to always be in position behind the ball.)

Tasks/Challenges:

T Stand outside your assigned square. Serve the ball by dropping it and hitting it underhand after the bounce. The server can hit the ball to any of the other three courts (Four Square). The player receiving the ball must keep it in play by striking the ball with an underhand hit to any square. Play continues until one player fails to return the ball

or commits a fault. Faults include hitting the ball sidearm or overhand, stepping in another square to play the ball, catching the ball, and letting the ball touch any part of the body other than the hands. After each mistake, rotate positions and servers. (*Use two squares for a two-person game.*)

T Play your game cooperatively by counting the number of volleys made by your group before a mistake. Hit the ball so the person will be in the best position to contact the ball.

T Play the game competitively by changing force and angles of travel for the ball; however, the volley must be underhand—no sides, no overs. **The receiver will really need quick feet to move into position for the volley.**

✓ *Teacher Observation.* Game play provides an excellent setting for teacher observation of critical cues in dynamic situations, that is, alternative assessment. *See Chapter 14, "Assessing Student Learning," and Chapter 12, "Observing Student Responses," for examples.*

Striking Over a Low Net (Underhand Pattern)

Setting: Partners; nets at varying heights (lower standard nets or improvise nets from ropes: Figure 26.4) throughout the gym; one lightweight ball for each pair

Cues	
Flat Surface	(Keep your palm flat, like a pancake.)
Extend to Target	(Extend your legs, body, striking arm toward the target.)
Quick Feet	(Move your feet quickly to always be in position behind the ball.)

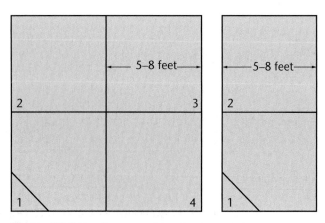

Figure 26.3 Four-Square and Two-Square courts.

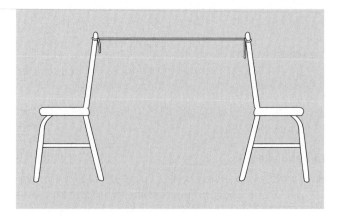

Figure 26.4 Construction of a net. Suspend a rope between two chairs.

Tasks/Challenges:

T You have practiced the underhand volley against the wall and over a line on the floor. Now you are ready to use the same skill to send the ball over a net to a partner. The server bounces the ball one time and then sends it over the net with the underhand volley. The partner returns the volley after the ball bounces one time.

C When you are ready, keep a collective score of how many volleys you and your partner can do before making a mistake.

T Slant your net from high to low, and repeat the skill, volleying the ball over the net at differing heights.

T Practice varying the force with which and the angles at which you volley the ball to your partner. Remember, the ball must bounce one time on each side before the contact.

C Based on your scores from the collective game, set a personal goal and see if you and your partner can attain that goal for the underhand volley over the net. Remember to volley the ball so your partner will always be in the best position for the return.

T Challenge your partner to a competitive game of volleys over the net. Add to the challenge with changes in force and angles; however, the hit must be the underhand volley you have practiced.

Volleying to the Wall (Overhead Pattern)

Setting: Lines taped on the wall, at heights of 5 to 7 feet; a lightweight ball or beach ball for each child

Cues	
Crab Fingers	(Curl your fingers for contact on the pads.)
Bend and Extend	(Bend your knees in preparation; extend your legs and arms upward on contact.)
Quick Feet	(Move your feet quickly to be in position behind and under the ball for contact.)

Tasks/Challenges:

T Stand approximately 4 feet from the wall at the tape height you choose. Toss the ball slightly in front and above your head, then volley it to the wall with both hands. Catch the ball after the volley and begin again.

Select two children who are contacting the ball with their fingerpads and using their legs for the force of the volley to

demonstrate the key concepts of the skill. Point out the critical cues to the children as they are demonstrated.

C Practice until you can execute three overhead volleys to the wall without catching the ball or letting it drop below the tape line.

C Count the number of volleys you can hit to the wall above the tape line. Remember, the volley must be with two hands; don't catch the ball.

✓ *Peer Observation.* As with all skills, the continued use of the critical cues is crucial to success in dynamic situations. A peer observation assessment of critical cues with appropriate feedback for improvement would be useful here.

Volleying a Ball Upward (Overhead Pattern)

Setting: Children scattered throughout general space, each with either a beach ball or a lightweight plastic ball

Cues	
Crab Fingers	(Curl your fingers for contact on the pads.)
Bend and Extend	(Bend your knees in preparation; extend your legs and arms upward on contact.)
Quick Feet	(Move your feet quickly to always be in position under the ball.)

Tasks/Challenges:

T Using your fingerpads, volley the ball upward above your head so the ball returns directly to you. Catch the ball after each volley.

T Toss the ball upward, and then volley it one time 2 to 3 feet above your head.

T Toss and then volley the ball upward two times before you catch it.

C How many times can you volley the ball before it touches the ground?

T Toss and then volley the ball from medium level: Let the ball drop until it's 3 to 4 feet from the floor; then volley. This really requires you to bend your knees!

C Now that you know how to volley the ball at a lower level, count the number of times you can volley before the ball touches the floor.

Volleying to a Partner (Overhead Pattern)

Setting: Sets of partners scattered throughout general space; one lightweight ball for each set of partners

Cues

Crab Fingers	(Curl your fingers for contact on the pads.)
Bend and Extend	(Bend the knees in preparation; extend the legs and arms upward on contact.)
Quick Feet	(Move your feet quickly to always be in position under the ball.)

Tasks/Challenges:

T Stand 3 to 4 feet from your partner. Using the overhead skill you just learned, volley the ball back and forth to your partner. Each of you gets two hits on your side: Volley the ball first to yourself for control and then to your partner.

T When you are comfortable with two volleys per side, try doing the task with only one hit per side.

C On the signal, begin your partner volleys. I will time you for 30 seconds. Try to continue without a mistake for the entire time . . . and beyond!

Playing Keep It Up

Setting: Groups of four or five children (the smaller the group, the more participation/practice of the skill each child gets); a lightweight ball (or a volleyball trainer—a larger, lightweight volleyball) for each group

Cues

Crab Fingers	(Curl your fingers for contact on the pads.)
Bend and Extend	(Bend the knees in preparation; extend the legs and arms upward on contact.)
Quick Feet	(Move your feet quickly to always be in position under the ball.)

Tasks/Challenges:

T The object of the game Keep It Up is to see how many times your team can volley the ball before it touches the ground. There are only two rules: A player cannot hit the ball twice in a row, and the hit must be the overhead volley. Practice several times; then count your team volleys.

T Continue your cooperative volleys with your team, this time calling out the volley number as you contact the ball.

T This time, as your group plays Keep It Up be sure each person in the group does a volley before anyone takes a second turn.

C As a group, set a goal for the number of volleys you wish to attain, then play the game to see if you can reach that number without a mistake.

Keep It Up can be played with the forehand volley (the bump) or with a combination of the bump and the overhead volley.

✓ **Teacher Observation.** Cooperative games provide an opportune time for teacher observation of critical cues. *See Chapters 12 and 14 for development of teacher observation assessments.*

Playing One-Bounce Volleyball

Setting: Children in teams of equal numbers (three or four per team) on either side of a low net; a lightweight ball that will bounce

Cues

Bend and Extend	(Bend the knees in preparation; extend the legs and arms upward on contact.)
Quick Feet	(Move your feet quickly to always be in position under the ball.)

Tasks/Challenges:

T A player begins the game by bouncing the ball one time and striking it over the net with an underhand serve (much like the underhand volley action). The receiving team may let the ball bounce one time before hitting it back (or may volley the ball with no bounce). Only one bounce is permitted before the ball is volleyed back over the net; however, any number of players may volley the ball before it crosses the net. You may use either the overhead volley (crab fingers) or the forearm volley (the bump). The serving team scores a point when the receiving team fails to return the ball over the net within bounds or when the ball bounces more than one time.

Obstacle-Course Volley

Setting: Prior setup: See Figure 26.5 for an example of a volley obstacle course. Once the course is ready, the class pretty much runs itself. Challenges in the obstacle course can require a student to use a number of different volleying skills. It may be helpful to provide

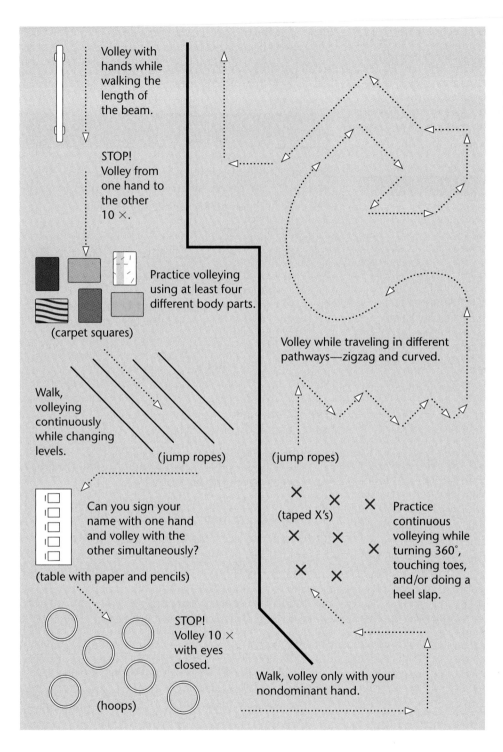

Figure 26.5 Setup for Obstacle-Course Volley.
Source: Adapted from *A Manual of Physical Education: Skill Theme Activities for Physical Education Specialists to Use in Collaboration with Classroom Teachers,* an unpublished master's project by Wendy Mustain, 1990, Blacksburg: Virginia Polytechnic Institute and State University. Used with permission.

a number of different objects to volley, to allow for differences in skill development.

Tasks/Challenges:

- **T** Work your way through the course, following the instructions at each station. *(This activity was adapted from Mustain, 1990.)*

Utilization Level: Learning Experiences Leading to Skill Development

For continuing skill development in volleying, children must develop consistency and accuracy. They should be able to use various body parts to volley and to move in relationship to other people and objects.

Strategic placement skills in a relatively stable situation are developed at the utilization level.

A note about cues: Although several cues are listed for many of the learning experiences, it's important to focus on only one cue at a time. That way, the children can really concentrate on that cue. Once you provide feedback to the children and observe that most have learned a cue, then it's time to focus on another one.

Volleying Game: Child-Designed

Setting: A variety of lightweight balls; paper and pencils for children to record their games

Cues	
Flat Surface	For underhand volley: (Keep your palms flat, like a pancake.)
Extend to Target	(Extend your legs, body, striking arm towards the target.)
Quick Feet	(Move your feet quickly to always be in position under the ball.)

Tasks/Challenges:

T Earlier in our work you practiced striking the ball against the wall and over a line using the underhand volley—striking with an open palm. You are very good at that volley. Today you will use that skill in a game situation. Your task is to design an original game for two partners or a small group to provide practice of the underhand volley in a dynamic, on-the-move situation. You can design your game so it can be played against the wall or over a line on the floor. Remember, the focus is the underhand volley; your game must use that skill. You will need to decide the following:

1. Will your game be against the wall or over a line?
2. Will the game be cooperative or competitive?
3. Will you keep score?
4. How does a player score a point?
5. Will the game be played with a partner or in a small group? *(Not more than three.)*
6. What are the boundaries?
7. What are the rules?

Record your game on a piece of paper so you can refer to it later and others in the class can learn how to play it. You may give your game a name if you want to *(Figure 26.6)*.

Children not experienced in designing games will need more direction from the teacher and fewer opportunities to

make decisions; for example, the teacher decides whether the game is against the wall or over a line and whether the game is cooperative or competitive. See Chapter 31 for more on child-designed games.

Striking a Ball Continuously with Different Body Parts

Setting: Children scattered throughout general space, each with an object suitable for the volley—plastic ball, soccer ball, playground ball, foot bags

Cues	
Flat Surface	(Keep the body part as flat as possible for contact.)
Bend and Extend	(Bend your knees to be in position for the head volley; extend upward on contact.)
Quick Feet	(Move your feet quickly to always be in position under the object.)

Tasks/Challenges:

T Volley the ball (foot bag) from your thigh to your foot by striking it with your upper thigh and then with the top of your foot. Catch the ball (foot bag) after the volley from your foot.

T Practice with your right leg and foot as well as with your left. You want to be equally skilled with both.

T When you are comfortable with the volley from your thigh to your foot (three times with no mistakes), add your head: In other words, volley the ball (foot bag) from your head—this is called heading in soccer—to your thigh to your foot or from your head to your foot to your thigh.

T Now choose any three body parts to keep the ball (foot bag) going. See if you can keep it going from part to part without letting it touch the ground.

C This time you are going to see how well you can use different body parts for consecutive volleys. Choose the three body parts with which you like to volley. Try to keep the ball (foot bag) going with your three parts. Can you keep it going for 15 seconds? 30 seconds? One minute?

Volleying with the Foot

Setting: Children scattered throughout general space, with access to beach balls, plastic balls, and/or playground balls

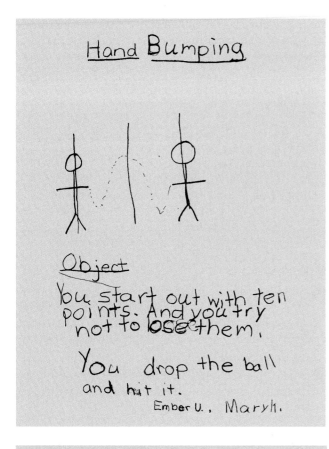

Hand Bumping

Object

You start out with ten points. And you try not to lose them.

You drop the ball and hit it.

Ember U., Marsh.

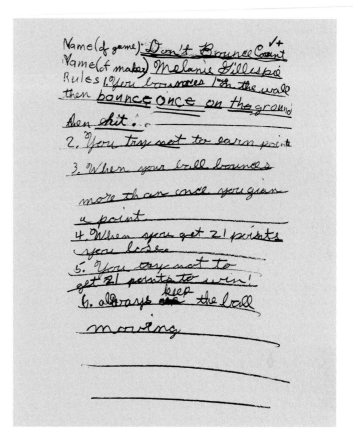

Name (of game): Don't Bounce Count ✓+

Name (of maker) Melanie Gillespie

Rules 1. You bounces 1 on the wall then **bounce once on the ground** then chit.

2. You try not to earn points

3. When your ball bounces more than once you gian a point

4. When you get 21 points you lose.

5. You try not to get 21 points to win!

6. always keep the ball moving

Figure 26.6 Child-designed games over a line (Hand Bumping) against the wall (Don't Bounce Count; Pomer).

Pomer

John Davis Peter Wiegand

We hit agensts the Wall. and let the Ball Bonch One nch, and the ather Parson hits it Agent the Wall

Cues

Flat Surface (Make the inside, outside, top of your foot as flat as possible for the contact.)

Tasks/Challenges:

T Volley the beach ball with your foot, keeping the ball in the air for several contacts. Use the inside, outside, and top of your foot and your heel to send the ball upward.

T If consecutive volleys with the beach ball are easy, try the plastic or the playground ball.

C On the signal, begin your foot volley. I'll give the count each 10 seconds; keep the ball in the air as long as possible.

Playing Aerial Soccer

Setting: Children scattered throughout general space, with 6-inch woven bamboo balls (or balls similar in texture, size, and weight)

Cues

Flat Surface	(Make the foot surface as flat as possible for the contact.)
Bend and Extend	(Bend the knees to be in position for the head volley; extend the legs and body upward on contact.)
Quick Feet	(Move your feet quickly to always be in position for a good volley—under and/or behind the ball.)

Tasks/Challenges:

T Practice your skills of heading, foot volleys, aerial kicks, and foot-to-head volleys with the bamboo ball. When you feel comfortable with the individual skills of Aerial Soccer and can keep the ball

---

What is a Foot Bag?

A very popular game that has made a resurgence in the past few years is foot bag. Foot bags are small leather-covered (or crocheted) beanbag-type balls. The game requires a great deal of skill but delights children and adults for hours. Children at the utilization and proficiency levels will enjoy using a foot bag at times instead of a ball. Foot bags are relatively inexpensive and are great on the playground or field trips.

---

aloft for at least 10 seconds, you can play a game of Aerial Soccer with a partner or in a small group. The ball must stay aloft at all times. You will need to decide the following:

1. Is the game to be cooperative or competitive?
2. How many will be in the group? *(Not more than six—three on three.)*
3. Will you play in self-space or travel in general space?
4. What boundaries do you need?

This game was observed at Regents Park in London, England. It's exciting for observers to watch and challenging for highly skilled soccer players.

Volleying with a Volleybird

Volleybirds are flat-bottomed shuttlecocks that have been used in Taiwan for centuries. The volleybirds are volleyed with different body parts, including hands, thighs, the instep of the foot, and the inside and outside of the foot. Because

the volleybirds are flat bottomed, they can also be caught on different body parts. Young children find these relatively slow moving and brightly colored "birds" very attractive.

Setting: Children scattered in general space, each with a volleybird

Cues

Flat Surface	(Make your hand, thigh, foot surface as flat as possible for the contact.)
Quick Feet	(Move your feet quickly to always be in position for the volley—under the volleybird.)

Tasks/Challenges:

T See how many times in a row you can strike the volleybird before it touches the ground. Start with one hand; then try your other hand. Other body parts you can use are your thigh, the instep of your foot, or the inside or outside of your foot.

C Make up a sequence that uses three different body parts. See if you can repeat the sequence without a miss.

Striking to the Wall—Varying Levels, Force, and Body Position

Setting: Lines marked on the wall at heights of 3 and 7 feet; a variety of balls for a combination of volleying and bouncing (plastic balls, playground balls)

Cues

Flat Surface	(Flat/open palm for contact.)
Extend to Target	(Extend your legs, striking arm, and body toward the target.)
Quick Feet	(Move your feet quickly into position for the volley.)

Tasks/Challenges:

T Strike the ball to the wall between the 3- and 7-foot tape marks so the ball contacts the wall at different levels. Strike the ball so it sometimes hits the wall at a high level, just below the 7-foot mark, and sometimes at a low level, just above the 3-foot mark.

T Vary your striking action; sometimes use an underhand strike, sometimes an overhead one.

T Vary the amount of force you hit the ball with. Sometimes hit the ball hard so it rebounds far from the wall; sometimes use just enough force to get the ball within the tape zones. How will the ball rebound this time? Right—close to the wall.

🅣 Strike the ball from different positions in relation to your body. Contact the ball while it's high over your head, close to the floor, on your right side, on your left side. Being able to contact the ball from different positions is important in game situations when you don't always have enough time to get in position.

🅣 With a partner play handball. Your target is the area between the 3- and 7-foot tape marks. Try to strike the plastic (playground) ball to the wall so your partner can't return the shot. Challenge your partner to a game of 15 points.

Each time you select a partner, both of you should agree on the rules, including the outside boundaries, type of hits, how to keep score, and number of bounces permitted on the rebound. Possible rules include alternating hits and hitting the ball to a certain space on the wall.

🅣 With a group of two or four, play Hand Corner Ball. *(See Figure 26.7 for court setup.)* The rules are these:

1. It can be a singles or a doubles game.
2. You serve by dropping the ball and underhand-volleying it against the wall.
3. The ball must contact the wall above the 18-inch line and rebound back into one of the three activity zones.
4. Volleying alternates between teams. In doubles play, it also alternates between players. So, if player 1 on team A serves and player 1 on team B returns it, player 2 on team A takes the next volley.

5. If a team is unable to return the ball, the other team earns the number of points of the zone in which the ball landed.
6. A game is 15 points.

✔ ***Videotape/Digital Analysis.*** Game play at the utilization and proficiency levels provides an excellent opportunity for videotaping or digital picture analysis of performance and student self-assessment. Students assess themselves in authentic settings in relation to the critical cues of skills performed in dynamic environments.

Volleying Over a Net

Setting: Nets at a 7-foot height; a variety of beach balls, 8-inch plastic balls, and volleyball trainers

Cues	
Crab Fingers	(Curl your fingers for contact on the pads.)
Bend and Extend	(Bend your knees in preparation; extend your legs and arms on contact.)
Quick Feet	(Move your feet quickly to be in position under and behind the ball.)

Tasks/Challenges:

🅣 Select a partner; stand on either side of the net, and face each other. Partner 1 tosses the ball over the net; partner 2 volleys the ball back over the net to partner 1 with the two-hand overhead hit. Partner 1 catches the ball and then tosses again. After 10 tries, partner 2 tosses, and partner 1 volleys.

🅣 Volley the ball so your partner can catch it without moving from self-space.

🅣 For this task, you will need four people, two on each side of the net. One of you will be on the court, and the other waits behind the end line. The activity is almost the same as the last one, with one exception: After you hit the ball, you run off the court, and the person behind comes up to return the shot. Then, that person runs off the court, and you come back on (*Figure 26.8*). The game goes very quickly, so you must be ready to move as soon as your partner hits the ball.

🅣 Now that you understand the basics of the activity, let's make one change: You may choose to let the ball bounce on your side and then use an underhand volley (the bump), or you may choose to take the volley before the bounce with an overhead

Cornerball

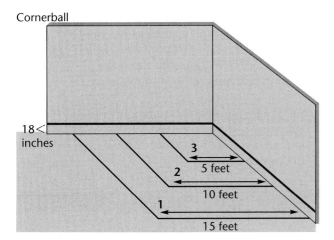

Figure 26.7 Setup for Hand Corner Ball.

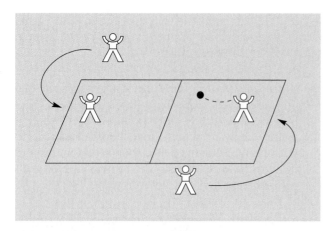

Figure 26.8 Two-person running volley.

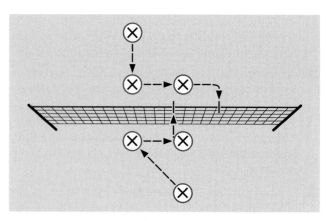

Figure 26.9 Three-on-three volleys: two patterns.

volley. **Remember the cue for the underhand volley—Flat Surface with Forearms.**

Volleying Continuously to a Partner

Setting: Nets at 7-foot height; a variety of beach balls, 8-inch plastic balls, and volleyball trainers

Cues	
Crab Fingers	(Curl your fingers for contact on the pads.)
Bend and Extend	(Bend your knees in preparation; extend your legs and arms on contact.)
Quick Feet	(Move your feet quickly to be in position under and behind the ball.)

Tasks/Challenges:

T Partner 1 tosses the ball slightly above the head, then volleys the ball over the net to partner 2. Partner 2 volleys the ball back over the net. Continue to volley, using the **overhead** volley for balls at both high and medium levels.

C Set a personal best goal with your partner. See if you can attain that goal. Give your partner your best volley each time.

The above tasks/challenges can be used for continuous volleys with the underhand volley (the bump) or a combination of overhead and underhand volleys. Review with the children the differences between the critical cues for the overhead and the underhand volleys.

Volleying Three on Three

Setting: Children in groups of six, with three on each side of the net (Figure 26.9)

Cues	
Crab Fingers	(Curl your fingers for contact on the pads.)
Bend and Extend	(Bend your knees in preparation; extend your legs and arms on contact.)
Quick Feet	(Move your feet quickly to be in ready position for the ball.)

Tasks/Challenges:

T Use only the overhand volley to hit the ball in the air three times on your side of the net. On the third contact, volley the ball over the net to the other team. Each team volleys the ball three times, sending it over the net on the third hit. A different player makes each one of the three hits.

T Rotate positions, so that you hit the ball from different places.

C Work cooperatively to keep the ball in the air as long as possible. Remember: three hits per side, one hit per person.

T Challenge the other team to a three-on-three game. Rather than cooperating to keep the ball in the air, use strategies to outscore the other team. Rather than just hitting the ball over the net, direct it to a certain location; vary the amount of force on the volley, sometimes sending it just over the net, sometimes sending it deep into the court. A point is scored when the ball hits the floor or lands out of bounds.

Serving Underhand Over the Net

Setting: Lines marked on the wall 7 feet from the floor; nets at a 7-foot height; plastic balls and volleyball trainers

Cues

Watch the Ball   (Watch the ball until the striking arm contacts it.)

Extend to Target (Extend the striking arm toward the target—over the net.)

Tasks/Challenges:

(T) You learned the underhand action of striking the ball with your open palm, swinging your arm forward/backward, stepping forward on your opposite foot, and contacting the ball slightly below center and back. Now you're going to modify that skill slightly for the underhand action of a volleyball serve. Stand 10 to 15 feet from the wall; serve the ball to the wall; your target is the area just above the 7-foot tape line.

(T) I'll walk around and observe the underhand action of your serve. When it's correct and you feel successful, select a partner for practice over the net. Partner 1 stands 10 to 15 feet from the net and serves the ball over the net. Partner 2 retrieves the ball and then serves it back over the net.

(T) After you feel successful serving over the net, your partner will select a position on the court and stand in that spot. Serve the ball away from your partner so your partner can't catch the ball without moving from self-space.

The last task may seem a bit backward from "what has always been done." It is. When children begin by "serving" to a partner, they tend to do the same thing in a game situation—the exact opposite response from the one required. This way, we get them to practice serving to an open space early on.

Proficiency Level: Learning Experiences Leading to Skill Development

Children at the proficiency level should be able to move consistently and accurately in relation to others and to react effectively to increasingly dynamic and unpredictable situations. They can simultaneously focus on volleying and on the game activity around them.

A note about cues: At the proficiency level, tasks are more complex, typically requiring children to coordinate several movements simultaneously in a dynamic context. A list of cues is provided to assist the children in being more successful in the learning experience. The challenge for the teacher is in determining which cue will be most beneficial for each child . . . and when. Thus, careful observation and critical reflection become very important as you watch the children move

Striking an object requires visual tracking.

and then decide which cue will be the most helpful to move each learner to a higher skill level.

Striking with Different Body Parts While Traveling

Setting: A variety of lightweight balls: 8-inch plastic, Nerf, volleyball trainers

Cue

Quick Feet (Move your feet quickly to always be in position to volley the ball.)

Tasks/Challenges:

(T) Travel the length of the gym, volleying the ball with different body parts as you go. Don't catch the ball at any time, and don't let it touch the floor.

(T) Select a partner. Travel throughout general space, volleying the ball back and forth with different body parts. Both of you should always be moving.

(T) This time as you travel and volley with your partner, vary the level of the volley—sometimes high, sometimes medium level. **Remember, flat surface, quick feet.**

Serving Overhand Over the Net

Setting: Nets at a 7-foot height; the court on one side of each net divided into four areas, using tape or chalk to mark divisions (Figure 26.10), and each of the target areas numbered; a variety of lightweight balls—plastic, Nerf, volleyball trainers—for partner practice

Cues

Good Toss   (Toss the ball slightly in front of and above your head.)

Watch the Ball (Watch the ball until your hand makes contact.)

Tasks/Challenges:

T Earlier you learned an underhand striking action that can be used as a serve in volleyball. However, when you watch a skilled volleyball team, you will notice they serve with an overhand striking action. The opponents have less time to get ready for this serve because it travels with less of an arch.

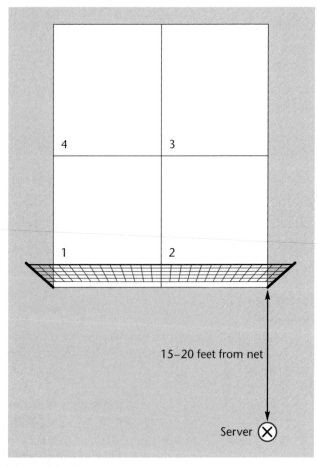

Figure 26.10 Target areas for serving.

Stand 15 to 20 feet from the net, and face a partner on the opposite side of the net. With your nonstriking hand, toss the ball slightly above your head. Contact the ball directly behind center with the heel or palm of your hand, so the ball travels just above the net to the opposite side. Your partner will retrieve the ball and then serve it back to you. (Demonstrate toss of ball, arm action, forward-backward stance.)

T Tell your partner where to stand in the opposite court. Serve the ball so your partner can catch it without moving from self-space.

T Now serve the ball so your partner must move from self-space to catch—serve not to the person, but to the open space.

T Stand 15 to 20 feet from the net and serve the ball into each target area.

C Practice serving to each target area until you can successfully serve four out of five tries to each area. Practice both your underhand and your overhead serve.

T Stand 15 to 20 feet from the net (behind the serving line). Verbally call the number of the zone to which you are going to serve. Strike the ball to that zone.

✓ ***Teacher Observation.*** As new skills are introduced, assessment of critical cues is needed. *See Chapter 14, "Assessing Student Learning," for the development of appropriate assessments.*

Striking Downward with Force

Setting: Tape lines on the wall at about 7 and 2 feet from the floor; a variety of lightweight balls for individual practice

Cues

Quick Feet   (Move your feet quickly to always be in position to volley the ball; transfer your weight forward as you volley.)

Up, Up, Up, Down: (Volley the ball up, up,
Soft, Soft, Soft, Hard! up, down; soft, soft, soft, hard.)

Tasks/Challenges:

T Standing 10 to 12 feet from the wall, begin volleying the ball between the tape lines, using the underhand pattern; you may or may not include a bounce with the volleys. After several volleys, strike the ball on top so it travels downward to the wall, contacting the wall just above the 2-foot tape line. Contact the ball with your hand slightly cupped. *(Demonstrate.)*

T Practice a pattern of three underhand volleys followed by a downward hit with force.

T Challenge a partner to a handball game against the wall. Throughout the game, use a combination of forceful downward hits and underhand volleys.

T Challenge the same partner to a competitive two-square game over a line. Use the forceful downward striking to create situations that move your partner/opponent out of position, making a good return more difficult.

Spiking

Setting: Sets of partners scattered throughout general space; slanted nets (Figure 26.11) with cones to mark target area; a variety of lightweight balls

Cues	
Step Jump	(Take one step and jump high with a 2-foot takeoff.)
Bend and Extend	(Bend the striking arm in preparation; extend toward the target on contact with the ball.)
Contact High, Hit Hard!	(Jump high in the air, striking the ball downward with force.)

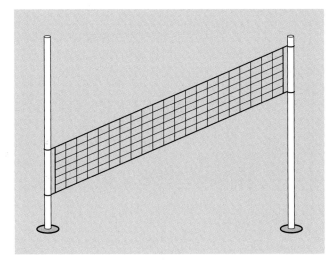

Figure 26.11 A slanted net for children who are learning to spike the ball.

Tasks/Challenges:

T Spiking is hitting the ball downward in volleyball. It takes a lot of practice to learn to spike effectively. We are going to begin our practice with a partner. Select a partner, and scatter throughout general space, away from the nets; we will use them later. Partner 1 tosses the ball upward. Partner 2 jumps into the air with a spring takeoff *("Jumping and Landing," Chapter 21),* and with an overhand hit tries to hit the ball toward the ground while it is still overhead. The secret to the spike is to contact the ball as high as possible. *(Select two children to demonstrate.)*

T When you and your partner can spike the ball consistently (four of five times), move to a net and continue your practice.

T Now try to spike over the net and into the target area marked by the cones.

Volleying in a Line Formation

Setting: Tape marks on the wall at a height of about 7 feet; groups of four, each in a line formation facing the wall and 3 to 4 feet from it; a variety of lightweight balls (8-inch plastic, Nerf, volleyball trainers)

Cues	
Crab Fingers	(Curl your fingers for contact on the pads.)
Quick Feet	(Always keep your feet on the move to be in position for the volley.)
Bend and Extend	(Bend the knees in preparation; extend the arms, legs, and body toward the target on contact.)

Tasks/Challenges:

T The first person in your line volleys the ball to the wall so it contacts the wall above the tape line; then that person moves quickly to the back of the line. The second person volleys the ball to the wall, moves quickly to the back, and so on. The objective is to keep the volley going. Don't let the ball touch the floor or touch the wall below the tape mark.

C Count the number of volleys your team can complete without a mistake.

T Continue the line volley, with each person calling "mine" just before he or she contacts the ball.

Remaining in your group of four, face another group, with approximately 10 feet between the two leaders. Team members should line up behind the leaders. One leader tosses the ball to the leader of the other team; that leader then volleys the ball back and quickly moves to the end of the line. This game is very similar to the volley against the wall: Each person volleys and then moves to the end of the line. The objective is to keep the volley going between the teams.

Playing Modified Volleyball

Setting: Teams of four or six, depending on space available *(Place an equal number of children with comparable skills on each team; the size of the court in relation to the number of players is the crucial element; don't expect children to cover the amount of space per person that adults do in volleyball);* a beach ball, plastic ball, or oversized volleyball

Cues	
Quick Feet	(Always keep "on the move" to be in position for the volley.)
Bend and Extend	(Bend the knees and arms in preparation; extend the arms, legs, and body toward the target on contact.)
Offense	Open Space (Hit to the open space.)
Defense	Ready (Bent knees, ready hands.)

Tasks/Challenges:

The game begins with a serve from the back boundary line; you will have two chances to serve the ball successfully over the net. In a regulation volleyball game, the ball may be hit only three times on a side; we'll decide as a class if we want three hits per side or unlimited. *(Discuss; vote.)* Here are the guidelines for play:

1. Remember, you score a point only if your team is serving.
2. A serve that touches the net is no good; a ball in play is good even though it touches the net.
3. Although this is not an official rule, try to use the skills you learned, such as the two-hand volley. Use one hand only for the spike and the serve.
4. A skilled volleyball game shows this pattern: set, set, over the net or bump, set, over the net—not

single hits back and forth. Try to use the three-part sequence for play on your side of the net.

Dribbling

Dribbling is striking or bouncing downward, generally with the hands. Basketball and team handball are the traditional sports in which dribbling is used. Dribbling a ball on the floor or ground, as in soccer, could have been included in this chapter, but because it's also a kicking skill, it's included in the kicking and punting discussion (Chapter 24). See Box 26-2 for information on dribbling from the *National Standards for Physical Education.*

Levels of Skill Proficiency in Dribbling

At the precontrol level of dribbling, children are satisfied with making contact with the ball so that the ball comes back to them, even if the return is somewhat sporadic. They explore dribbling from a stationary position with a ball that bounces back to them; they also explore walking and dribbling. Tasks that are appropriate at this level include:

Box 26-2

The Skill of Dribbling in the *National Standards for Physical Education*

The skill theme of dribbling is referenced in the *National Standards for Physical Education* (National Association for Physical Education, 2004) under Standard 1: Demonstrates competency in motor skills and movement patterns needed to perform a variety of physical activities. The standard speaks of the child's developing the mature motor skill in isolation and in combination with other actions and being able to use the skill in a dynamic situation.

Sample performance outcomes include:

- Drops a ball and catches it at the peak of the bounce (K–2)*
- Dribbles and passes a basketball to a moving receiver (3–5)*
- Dribbles a ball while preventing an opponent from stealing the ball (6–8)*

*Grade-level guidelines for expected student learning.

Skill Theme Development Sequence

Dribbling

Proficiency Level

Small-group basketball
Dribble/Pass Keep-Away
Dribbling and throwing at a target
Making up fancy dribbling/passing routines
Dribbling and passing in game situations
Dribbling while dodging
Dribble Tag
Now You've Got It, Now You Don't
Dribbling against opponents: Group situations

Utilization Level

Dribbling against an opponent: One on one
Dribbling and passing with a partner
Mirroring and matching while dribbling
Dribbling around stationary obstacles
Dribbling while stopping, starting, and turning (pivots and
  fakes)
Dribbling in different pathways
Dribbling while changing directions
Dribbling and changing speed of travel

Control Level

Moving switches
Dribbling and traveling
Dribbling in different places around the body while stationary
Dribbling with the body in different positions
Switches
Dribbling and looking
Dribbling at different heights
Dribble like a basketball player
All the time dribble

Precontrol Level

Dribbling and walking
Bouncing a ball down (dribbling) continuously
Bouncing a ball down and catching it

---

lenges that involve dribbling and traveling. Appropriate tasks include:

1. Dribbling at different heights and in different positions around the body
2. Dribbling continuously and switching hands
3. Dribbling while traveling and looking up

At the utilization level, children enjoy focusing on traveling while dribbling and on incorporating traveling into dynamic gamelike situations that allow them to combine the skills of throwing, catching, dodging, and dribbling. Appropriate tasks include:

1. Dribbling around obstacles
2. Dribbling in different pathways and while changing directions
3. Dribbling in one-on-one situations

When children reach the proficiency level, dribbling seems to be almost automatic. They enjoy dribbling in larger groups with more complex relationships and the excitement of strategy development. Appropriate tasks at this level include:

1. Starting and stopping, changing directions quickly while dribbling
2. Dribbling to keep the ball away from an opponent
3. Dribbling in gamelike situations.

Dribbling is a skill often associated with basketball or team handball. Yet, because its possible uses are endless, we focus on it as one aspect of striking rather than as a sport-specific skill. Children enjoy working with bouncing and dribbling skills and will spend many hours practicing the finest details of the skill. Remember, though, that dribbling—like striking upward—is one of the last fundamental skills to develop because it requires fine hand-eye coordination. Our progression spiral for dribbling appears on this page.

Precontrol Level: Activities for Exploration

At the precontrol level, we want children to strike a ball down repeatedly without losing the ball from self-space. When the children are able to do this, we add limited dribbling while walking. Relatively light balls—8-inch rubber playground balls or rubber basketballs—that bounce true (they aren't lopsided) are best for introducing children to dribbling. Be careful

---

1. Bouncing the ball and catching it
2. Bouncing the ball with both hands
3. Dribbling the ball in self-space with either hand
4. Dribbling with limited, slow travel

At the control level, children are introduced to varying their dribble while at the same time learning to use the nondominant hand. They are also given chal-

when inflating balls: Too much air equals too much bounce for control.

Bouncing a Ball Down and Catching It

Setting: Children scattered in general space, each with a ball

Tasks/Challenges:

Ⓣ Bounce the ball down in front of you so it comes straight back up to you. Catch it when it comes up.

Ⓣ Try bouncing the ball with two hands.

Ⓣ Now try bouncing with one hand.

Ⓣ Try bouncing with the other hand.

Bouncing a Ball Down (Dribbling) Continuously

Setting: Children scattered in general space, each with a ball

Tasks/Challenges:

Ⓣ Bounce the ball with both hands so that it keeps going. This bounce that keeps going is called a dribble.

Ⓣ Try dribbling the ball with one hand.

Ⓣ Now try the other hand.

Ⓒ Can you bounce three times in a row?

Ⓣ Try changing from one hand to the other.

Dribbling and Walking

Setting: Children scattered in general space, each with a ball

Tasks/Challenges:

Ⓣ Bounce the ball with two hands and catch as you walk forward slowly.

Ⓣ Try bouncing the ball with one hand while you walk forward slowly.

Ⓒ See if you can take three steps without losing the ball.

Control Level: Learning Experiences Leading to Skill Development

At the control level, children learn to dribble and travel at the same time. They'll also be able to dribble in different places around their bodies and vary both

direction and pathway. Some tasks very similar to those suggested for the precontrol level are repeated at the control level for continued practice and added skill development.

A note about cues: Although several cues are listed for many of the learning experiences, it's important to focus on only one cue at a time. That way, the children can really concentrate on that cue. Once you provide feedback to the children and observe that most have learned a cue, then it's time to focus on another one.

All the Time Dribble

Setting: Children scattered in general space, each with a ball (either a smaller basketball or a playground ball)

Cues	
Fingerpads	(Use the soft parts of your fingers near the end to dribble, not the very ends.) *Demonstrate.*
Knees Bent	(As you dribble, bend your knees a little, keeping your back straight, just like you are sitting down a little.)
Hand on Top of Ball	(Make sure your hand touches the ball almost on its top.)

Tasks/Challenges:

Ⓣ Remember when you bounced a ball down so it came back up to you and then pushed it down again so the bounce continued? This continuous bounce is called a dribble. Practice dribbling now.

Ⓒ Practice until you can dribble the ball five times without losing control of it.

Ⓒ Say one letter of the alphabet for each time you dribble. Can you get to z?

Tip: Children tend to dribble either with the whole palm or with the ends of the fingers. Besides using the term fingerpads, *we have also found it useful to put chalk or tape on the fingerpads to help children learn the correct part of their fingers to use.*

✷ Point to which parts of your fingers are used for dribbling.

Assessment Example

From the *National Standards for Physical Education, 1st edition*

Dribbling with control requires concentration.

Figure 26.12 Correct haand and body position for dribbling a ball.

Knees Bent	(As you dribble, bend your knees a little, keeping your back straight, just like you are sitting down a little.)
Hand on Top of Ball	(Make sure your hand touches the ball almost on its top.)
Forward Backward Stance	(The foot of the hand you are *not* dribbling with should be a little in front; *see Figure 26.12*.)

Student Drawing

Students are provided with a drawing of a handprint and are asked to color the portion of the hand that is used in mature dribbling. Students may also be asked to draw an entire person dribbling to show the overall critical elements of this movement task.

Criteria for Assessment

a. Correctly identifies position of hand used in mature dribbling.
b. Identifies the critical elements of dribbling.

Naspe (1995, pp. 20–21)

Dribble Like a Basketball Player

Setting: Children scattered throughout general space, each with a ball

Cues	
Fingerpads	(Remember to use the soft parts of your fingers.)

Tasks/Challenges:

- (T) Dribble the ball with one hand.
- (T) Dribble the ball with the other hand.
- (C) Count the number of times you can dribble without losing control.
- (T) On the signal, begin dribbling with one hand. Continue dribbling until the signal is given to stop.

Have children repeat each task with their nondominant hand throughout all levels of the skill. The proficient dribbler is equally skilled with each hand.

Dribbling at Different Heights

Setting: Children scattered throughout general space, each with a ball

Cues	
Knees Bent	(Make sure that your knees are bent just slightly.)

> **Firm, Flexible Wrists** (Make sure that your wrists are strong and bendable.)
> **Hand on Top of Ball** (Make sure your hand touches the ball almost on its top.)

Tip: The preceding cues focus on the skill of dribbling. At the same time it is good to check to see if children are also dribbling at the appropriate level. The cues would then change to high, medium, and low.

Tasks/Challenges:

Ⓣ Staying in self-space, dribble the ball with your preferred hand. Continue dribbling until you hear the signal to stop.

Ⓣ Dribble the ball at a low level so it bounces only to your knees. Keep your body in a standing position; don't kneel or squat to the floor.

Ⓣ Dribble the ball so it rebounds to a level between your waist and your knees. This medium-level dribble is the one most often used in games and the one we will concentrate on throughout our work.

Ⓣ On the signal, begin dribbling the ball at waist level. Continue dribbling until you hear the drumbeat. Stay in your self-space.

Dribbling and Looking

Setting: Children scattered in general space, alone at first and later with partners, each child with a ball for dribbling

> **Cue**
>
> **Look Up** (You may want to find a spot on the wall to look at to help you look up. Just sometimes glance down at the ball to check on it.)

Tasks/Challenges:

Ⓣ Begin dribbling the ball, then raise your head and continue dribbling without looking at the ball. Your peripheral vision enables you to look straight ahead and still see the ball. Your peripheral vision is your ability to see things at the edges of your field of vision and straight ahead at the same time. This is extremely important in a game involving dribbling.

Ⓣ For this task you will need a partner and each one of you will need a ball. Face your partner; decide which one of you will be the first leader. The leader

starts dribbling at any level he or she wants; the partner must follow by dribbling at any other level than the level at which the leader is dribbling. For example, if the leader is dribbling at a high level, the partner can dribble at a low or a medium level. The leader can change levels after three dribbles at the same level. Use quick changes of level to try to fake your partner. When you hear the signal *(about 30 seconds)*, change leaders. How many times before the signal can you catch your partner dribbling at the same level as you are?

 Peer Observation. Dribbling at the control level lends itself to partner assessment. Check cards (index cards with the critical cues listed) can be used. The observer calls out how the partner is to dribble (e.g., low and right-handed) and then checks off the critical cues that are used. Any combination of movement concepts can be combined with dribbling. *See Chapter 14 for examples of peer observation cards.*

Switches

Setting: Children scattered in general space, each with a ball for dribbling

> **Cue**
>
> **Hand to Side of Ball** (Keep your hand a little behind and to the outside of the ball.)

Tasks/Challenges:

Ⓣ Begin dribbling with your preferred hand. After several dribbles, switch to the other hand and continue dribbling. Don't catch the ball; simply switch from dribbling with one hand to dribbling with the other.

Ⓣ Begin dribbling with your preferred hand. Dribble five times, and then switch to your other hand. Continue to switch after five dribbles per hand. **One change here from the regular dribbling hints: Instead of having your hand directly on top of the ball, it is helpful to push the ball from the side when you want to change dribbling hands** *(Figure 26.13).*

Ⓒ On the signal, begin dribbling with your preferred hand. Each time you hear the drumbeat, switch hands. Continue to dribble and switch hands on each drumbeat until you hear the signal to stop.

Ⓟ When switching hands while dribbling, how does your hand position on the ball change?

Figure 26.13 Changing hands while dribbling.

Dribbling the ball in a variety of body positions challenges skill development in children.

Dribbling with the Body in Different Positions

Setting: Children scattered in general space, each with a ball

Cues	
Firm, Flexible Wrists	(Remember the strong, bendable wrists we used before—they are really important now.)
Ball to Side, A Little in Front	(Keep the ball a little in front of your body and out to the side.)

Tasks/Challenges:

🅣 Assume a kneeling position. Balance on one knee and one foot, with your body at a low level. Dribble with one hand while you maintain the balanced position.

🅣 Dribble while in a squat or tuck position, balanced on both feet at a low level.

🅒 Balance in different positions, dribbling with one hand. Create three different positions in which you can dribble with either your right or left hand.

🅣 Begin dribbling in a standing position. Continue to dribble as you change your position to a low level—a kneeling or squatting position. Continue changing body positions while maintaining the dribble.

Choose several children to demonstrate the combinations of body positions they assume while dribbling.

Dribbling in Different Places around the Body While Stationary

Setting: Children scattered in general space, each with a ball for dribbling

Cues	
Ball Close to Body	(Remember, the ball should be close to your body so you don't lose it.)
Firm, Flexible Wrists	(Your wrists have to be really strong and bendable for this dribbling—floppy will not work.)

Tasks/Challenges:

🅣 Standing in self-space, dribble the ball in different places around your body: on your right, on your left, behind your legs. **As you dribble, remember to keep the ball close to your body.**

🅣 Begin dribbling with your right hand; after several dribbles, bounce the ball under your right leg from back to front, and continue the dribble with your left hand. **The hand position will be like that for switching hands, a little to the side of the ball.**

🅣 Practice the skill from right to left and from left to right until you can execute it in both directions.

🅣 Dribble the ball directly in front of your body; bounce the ball between your legs from front to back. **You will need to twist your body to recover the dribble in the back.**

🅣 Can you dribble the ball from back to front?

🅒 Put together a dribbling sequence of all the ways you can dribble in self-space: in front, to the side, in back, around your body, between your legs. Remember to change levels as you go and to find different positions balanced on different parts.

✓ *Exit Slip.* This might be a good time to include an exit slip to assess students' knowledge of different positions, places around the body, and levels, as well as a self-assessment of skill. A possible exit slip could ask children to write out the dribbling sequence they performed, indicating which positions were easy and which they will want to practice in the future.

Dribbling and Traveling

Setting: Children scattered throughout general space, each with a ball

Cues	
Hand a Little behind the Ball	(For walking and dribbling, your hand position changes: Keep your hand just a little behind the ball.)

Tasks/Challenges:

🅣 This time start dribbling in self-space. After a few dribbles take two steps, then stop and dribble two times in self-space, then take two more steps, then stop and dribble twice. Keep traveling in general space like this until you hear the stop signal. **As you dribble, push the ball slightly forward.**

Tip: This task works well when children are first learning to travel and dribble because they are able to regain control of the ball if they are close to losing it. You can gradually increase the number of steps and decrease the stationary dribbles as the skill level increases.

🅣 Begin dribbling and walking in general space. When you hear the drumbeat, stop in self-space and continue dribbling. The second drumbeat is the signal to travel again. The pattern is this: drumbeat, travel with dribble, drumbeat, stop with continued dribble, ...

🅒 Each of you has 100 points. On the signal, begin traveling in general space. If you lose control of the ball, subtract 10 points; if you collide with another

person, subtract 25 points. I'll time you for 60 seconds; try to keep all 100 points. Ready? Begin.

✓ *Teacher Observation.* At this point, when children are beginning to combine skills and practice them in more dynamic situations, it is appropriate to use a teacher check list or observation to assess youngsters' continued use of the critical cues.

Moving Switches

Setting: Children scattered in general space, each with a ball

Cues	
Hand behind and to Side of Ball	(Your hand position changes again, just a little: Keep your hand a little behind and to the outside of the ball; *see Figure 26.13.*)
Look Up	(Remember to look at other peoples' faces as you dribble and just sneak glances at the ball.)

Tasks/Challenges:

🅣 Start dribbling with your favorite hand while walking. On the signal, without stopping, change the dribbling to the other hand and keep walking.

🅣 Begin dribbling in general space; each time you meet someone, switch hands, and continue to travel and dribble.

❋ We have now practiced three different hand positions on the ball. Where should your hand be for stationary dribbling? Where should it be for dribbling while traveling? Where should it be for switching from one hand to the other?

Utilization Level: Learning Experiences Leading to Skill Development

At the utilization level, we increase the complexity of the dribbling by providing children with situations in which they must dribble with either hand, without looking at the ball. We also provide beginning dynamic, gamelike situations in which youngsters combine skills.

A note about cues: Although several cues are listed for many of the learning experiences, it's important to focus on only one cue at a time. That way, the children can really concentrate on that cue. Once you provide feedback to the children and observe that most have learned a cue, then it's time to focus on another one.

Dribbling and Changing Speed of Travel

Setting: Children scattered in general space (alone at first and later with partners), each child with a ball

> **Cues**
>
> **Look Up** (Remember to look at faces.)
> **Ball Low** (Dribble the ball only as high as your waist.)

Tip: You may also need to refocus on speeds here. If so, the cues would be fast, medium, and slow. (See Chapter 17.)

Tasks/Challenges:

Ⓣ Travel throughout general space, maintaining a controlled dribble at all times. Travel sometimes very fast, sometimes slowly.

Ⓣ Begin moving through general space with a slow, steady walk. As you're dribbling, focus your eyes on a spot on the floor 15 to 20 feet away. Without stopping your dribble, move as quickly as possible to that spot. When you arrive, stop your travel but continue dribbling. Visually choose another spot, and repeat the sequence. The ability to change speeds and maintain a continuous dribble is a very important offensive skill in basketball.

Ⓣ This time as you travel, practice quickly changing the speed of your dribble as you travel to your chosen point. It will be as if you have almost invisible stops and starts along the way. Slow down and speed up, changing the speed of travel in mid-dribble.

Ⓣ Stand beside a partner whose dribbling skill is very similar to yours. Partner 1 begins the travel/dribble throughout space, changing from fast to slow speeds at will. Partner 2 attempts to stay beside partner 1 at all times. Both of you will dribble continuously. When the signal is given, rest for 10 seconds. Then partner 2 becomes the leader.

Dribbling While Changing Directions

Setting: Children arranged in a scattered formation, about 3 to 4 feet apart, all facing the same direction (Figure 26.14); teacher at the front of the group, facing the children

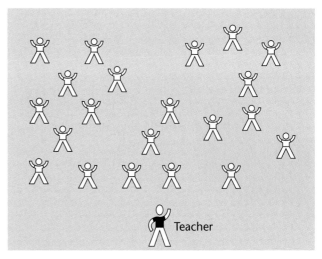

Figure 26.14 Formation for practicing dribbling and moving in directions the teacher suggests.

> **Cues**
>
> **Hand Position** (The hand positions we used before are important here. If you want to go to the side, your hand is on the side; to go forward, hand behind; to go backward, hand in front.)
> **Slide** (Especially when going sideways, be sure to slide your feet; don't cross them.)

Tasks/Challenges:

Ⓣ Begin dribbling in self-space, keeping your head up, eyes focused on me. On the first signal, I'll point to your left; dribble with your right hand as you sidestep to your left. When you hear the next signal, stop your travel but continue to dribble. I'll then point forward; travel backward as you dribble. Stop on the signal. Each time the signal is given, change the direction of your travel: right, left, forward, backward.

Children need both verbal and visual directional signs as well as audible signals (via drum or whistle) for change of directions. The children will mirror your visual cues.

Setting: Children scattered throughout general space, each with a ball for dribbling

Tasks/Challenges:

Ⓣ Dribble throughout general space, changing directions as you go: travel forward, backward, to the right, to the left. Travel slowly when you first begin the travel/dribble with a change of direction.

Figure 26.15 Dribbling in a curved or zigzag pathway.

Maintain the dribble during all your direction changes; don't stop and start again.

Traveling backward and dribbling isn't easy because the ball must move toward the body and often hits the feet. Children should develop this direction last and should be made aware of the difficulty of dribbling backward.

🅣 Begin dribbling in general space, traveling in a forward direction. Each time you hear the drumbeat, quickly change the direction of your travel and continue the travel/dribble.

Dribbling in Different Pathways

Setting: Children scattered in general space (alone at first, then with a partner), each with a ball

Cues	
Ball Close	(It is important to keep the ball close to your body, within half an arm's length.)
Ball on Outside	(In a curved or a zigzag pathway, keep the ball on the outside of the curve, the wide side.) *Demonstrate; see Figure 26.15.*

Tasks/Challenges:

🅣 Dribble throughout general space, traveling in straight, curved, and zigzag pathways.

🅣 Travel in a straight pathway as you dribble. Each time you meet another person or hear the drum,

turn quickly to your right or left and continue to travel/dribble in a straight pathway.

🅣 Follow the straight lines on the gym floor (or playground) as you travel/dribble.

🅣 Travel in a series of curved pathways as you dribble. **If you curve to the left, dribble with your right hand; if you curve to the right, dribble with your left hand. Always keep the ball on the outside of the curve.**

🅣 Travel/dribble throughout general space, quickly moving from side to side in a zigzag pathway. **Make sure the ball changes hands each time you move from side to side.**

🅣 Travel/dribble in a straight pathway. On the signal, quickly zigzag to miss an imaginary opponent and then continue dribbling in a straight pathway.

🅣 Stand approximately 3 feet behind a partner; each of you has a basketball (playground ball). Partner 1 (in front) travels/dribbles throughout general space, changing pathways. Partner 2 (in back) attempts to stay 3 feet behind the lead partner at all times. *(Give each partner several chances to be the leader.)*

🅒 Design a traveling/dribbling strategy to move from the center of the gym (or outside blacktop) to the end line. Design the strategy using combinations of pathways to outwit imaginary opponents. Practice the traveling/dribbling strategy until you can do it three times exactly the same way. After you are done, draw and write out your strategy *(Figure 26.16).*

🕸 If I were to place three opponents in your way, could you still execute your plan?

Dribbling While Stopping, Starting, and Turning (Pivots and Fakes)

Setting: Children scattered in general space, each with a ball

Tasks/Challenges:

🅣 Begin dribbling in general space. Travel slowly at first, and then gradually increase your speed until you are moving quickly while maintaining your dribble. On the signal, quickly stop both your travel and the dribble.

🅣 Begin dribbling throughout general space. On the signal, stop quickly in a forward-backward stance, maintaining the dribble. Pivot by reversing the way you are facing; turn on the balls of your feet. Continue your travel/dribble. **To pivot,**

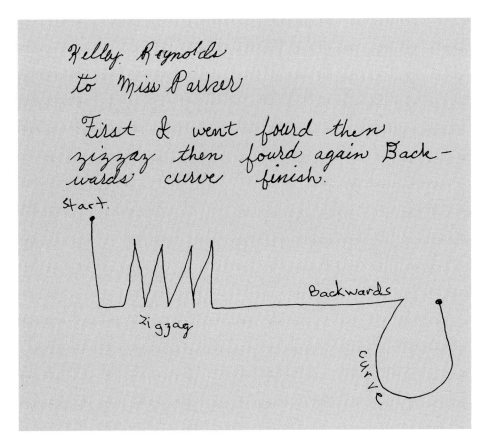

Figure 26.16 A child's dribbling pathway map.

(handwritten note in figure)
Kelly Reynolds
to Miss Parker

First I went foued then
zizzag then foued again Backwards curve finish.

Start.

Zigzag

Backwards

curve

turn backward on the foot toward the ball hand. Remember, the ball changes hands as you turn.

T Choose a point across the gym. Begin dribbling in general space, moving toward your point. Every time you come to a line on the floor, stop, fake as if you are going to change pathways, and keep going. **To use a fake, come to a stop, quickly take a step with one foot as if you are going to change pathways, and then keep going in the same pathway.** It may be easier if you pretend there is an imaginary defender in your way who you have to get around. When you reach your point, choose another one and keep going.

T This time, as you travel to your point, sometimes fake and sometimes change pathways. Remember, in a game you are trying to outsmart a defender.

Dribbling around Stationary Obstacles

Setting: Marker cones or milk jugs placed randomly (not in a line) throughout general space (spots do not work well because children can go over them) with varying space between the cones or jugs (place some 3 feet apart, others 5 to 6 feet apart)

Cue

Body, Ball, Cone (Remember, the cone [*jug*] is your opponent. Protect the ball by putting your body between the cone [*jug*] and the ball.)

Tasks/Challenges:

T Travel/dribble throughout general space, dribbling around the obstacles.

C See if you can dribble 60 seconds without bumping into an obstacle or another person—**Heads Up.**

Setting: The floor or blacktop divided into a series of alleys with colored tape; children in groups, one group per alley

Tasks/Challenges:

T One person in your group will be the dribbler; that person will stand at the end of the alley. The others in your group should arrange themselves in a zig-zag obstacle pattern in your alley *(Figure 26.17)*. The dribbler attempts to dribble the length of the alley, avoiding the obstacles and staying within the side boundaries. The obstacles try to gain possession of the ball. Obstacles can stretch and pivot, but one

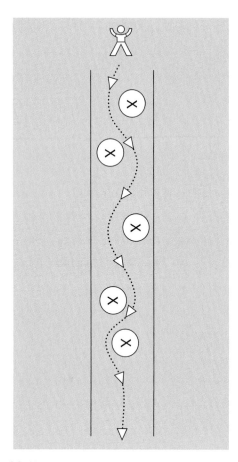

Figure 26.17 Dribbling around obstacles/persons.

foot must remain glued in place at all times. Obstacles can touch only the ball, not the dribbler.

The difficulty of this task can be increased or decreased by adjusting the width of the alley.

Setting: Children in groups of five or six, each child with a ball

Tasks/Challenges:

(T) Your group will again be the obstacles. You will need to spread out in a straight line about arm's distance apart. Everybody dribbles the ball while they are in line. The first person in line starts to dribble in a zigzag pathway into and out of the line, while all the others are dribbling. When the moving dribbler gets to the end of the line, the dribbler stops and begins to dribble in place, and the next person at the beginning of the line starts zigzagging through the line. This continues until all of you have had a chance to dribble through the line.

Mirroring and Matching While Dribbling

(See Chapter 18, "Relationships," for a discussion of mirroring and matching.)

Setting: Partners of approximately the same skill level facing each other about 3 to 4 feet apart

Cues	
Mirroring	(Remember, mirroring is like looking in a mirror. If your partner uses the left hand, you use your right hand.)
Matching	(Matching is harder than mirroring when you're facing your partner. If your partner uses the right hand, you use your right hand.)
Look Up	(For this activity it is really important to look at your partner.)

Tasks/Challenges:

(T) Face your partner. The partner whose name comes first in the alphabet is the first leader. The leader starts dribbling, and the follower has to mirror the actions of the leader. Remember, don't make it too hard on your partner. On the signal (*about 45 seconds*) change partners.

(T) Now that you have gotten to be so good, try matching your partner's actions. **Remember that if your partner works with the left hand, you will use your left hand.**

(T) This one is really hard. The leader can now travel in general space. The follower must try to copy exactly what the leader does. This is matching again.

Dribbling and Passing with a Partner

Setting: Partners, facing the same direction, about 10 feet apart at one side of the gymnasium or blacktop; one partner with a basketball for dribbling and passing

Cues	
Receiver Slightly ahead of Passer	(The receiver should be ahead of the passer by about four or five steps.)
Lead Receiver	(Pass the ball to the open space just in front of the receiver so he or she doesn't have to back up to catch it.)
No Stopping	(Both the passer and the receiver should always be moving to the other side; never stop moving forward.)

Dribbling at the precontrol and control levels requires an awareness of space.

Tasks/Challenges:

T The object of this task is to practice passing while moving forward. You and your partner are traveling in the same direction. Your job is to move across the space to the other line. Partner 1 will dribble three or four times and then pass to partner 2, who has been traveling forward. Partner 2 receives the pass, dribbles as he or she travels forward, and then passes back to partner 1. Partners continue to travel/dribble the length of the space.

Setting: Partners about 15 feet apart, scattered throughout general space, each pair with a ball

Tasks/Challenges:

T On the signal, begin traveling, dribbling, and passing to your partner. *(Allow about 2 minutes of activity, and then let the children rest for 10 seconds. Repeat.)*

Dribbling against an Opponent: One on One

Before beginning tasks that involve offense and defense, students should be skilled with the space awareness and dodging tasks that ask them to use the offensive and defensive skills of moving into open space; avoiding other persons; and using fakes, stops and starts, pivots, and other avoidance skills without manipulating equipment. (See Chapter 16, "Space Awareness," and Chapter 20, "Chasing, Fleeing, and Dodging.") Children need to have polished these skills before they are asked to use them while manipulating equipment.

One key to this task—and to other initial tasks involving offense and defense—is to clearly define the boundaries of the space the students are to use. A small space gives an advantage to the defense; a large space provides an offensive advantage. Similarly, a long, narrow space gives the advantage to the defense; a wider space helps the offense. Initial tasks should generally favor the offense.

Setting: Partners facing each other, scattered throughout general space, each pair with a ball

> **Cues**
>
> *Offense* Look Up (You have to be able to see your partner to avoid him or her.)
> Move to Goal (Always move to your end line.)
> Ball, Body, Defense (Keep your body between the ball and your defense.)
>
> *Defense* Body between Offense and Goal (Keep yourself between your partner and where he or she is trying to go. Your back should be to the partner's goal.)
> Watch Hips (Just like dodging, watch the hips or belly button if you want to know where your partner will move next.)
> Stay about Two or Three Feet Away (If you get too close, your partner can go right by you.)

Tasks/Challenges:

T Select a partner who dribbles while traveling as well as you do or slightly better. On the signal, partner 1 begins dribbling while traveling toward the end line; partner 2 (facing partner 1) attempts to gain possession of the ball by tapping it away. Neither partner should foul the other by bumping, pushing away, or reaching in. Partner 1 attempts to keep possession of the ball for 30 seconds; if partner 2 gets the ball, he or she gives it back. At the end of 30 seconds, partner 2 will dribble and partner 1 will try to take the ball away. Begin.

☑ *Videotape/Digital Analysis.* Videotaping or taking digital pictures and subsequent self-assessment of the use of the critical cues is essential when youngsters start to use skills in dynamic, changing situations. Students could be provided with a self-assessment check list and view the video or pictures with their partner to analyze "film" as coaches do.

Proficiency Level: Learning Experiences Leading to Skill Development

Children at the proficiency level seem to dribble without thinking about it. They're able to change direction, speed, and pathway at will. They're challenged by situations that involve other children as partners or as opponents who make the situation increasingly unpredictable.

Note about cues: At the proficiency level, tasks are more complex, typically requiring children to coordinate several movements simultaneously in a dynamic context. A list of cues is provided to assist the children in being more successful in the learning experiences. The challenge is in determining which cue will be most beneficial for each child . . . and when. Thus, careful observation and critical reflection become very important as you watch the children move and then decide which cue will be the most helpful to move each learner to a higher level.

Dribbling against Opponents: Group Situations

Setting: Children divided into two equal groups, one group with playground balls for dribbling; initially, a fairly open space; later, to increase the complexity of the task, a reduced amount of space

Cues

Offense Look Up (Remember to look up to see where your opponents are.)

Use Fakes (You'll need to use all the fakes we learned before—stopping and starting, changing speeds, changing directions—here.)

The cues at this level assume mastery of basic dribbling skills; hence, they are really strategy cues about how to use the dribble and how to stop the dribble. Many of the cues are taken from the concepts of space awareness and chasing, fleeing, and dodging. If needed, go back to and reinforce the dribbling cues and practice the basic offensive and defensive moves, but increasingly move toward children being able to use these skills in gamelike situations.

Tasks/Challenges:

Ⓣ Students without balls are the obstacles; you can spread out anywhere in the space. Your job is to try to steal the balls as the other group dribbles across the space. The only rules are you may not touch an offensive player, and one foot must always remain "glued" to your spot. In other words, you can step with one foot, but you cannot move from your spot. On the signal, the offense will begin dribbling from one end line and try to get to the other side without losing the ball. If the defense (the obstacles) gets a ball, just give it back. We'll trade places after three tries.

When the activity is a game situation with competing skills, it is best if you ask children to form groups with those "whose skill level is about the same as theirs" or you divide the children into groups, so that groups have relatively equal skill levels.

Now You've Got It, Now You Don't

Setting: Children divided into two groups on opposite sidelines of the gym or blacktop; one group with playground balls or basketballs

Cues

Defense Watch Hips and Ball (The best way to tell where the dribbler is going is to look at the hips or belly button and at the same time watch the ball.)

Slap Up (If you really want to knock the ball loose, slap from the bottom up.)

Offense Look Up (Remember to look up to see where your opponents are.)

Use Fakes (You'll need to use all the fakes we learned before—stopping and starting, changing speeds, changing directions.)

Tasks/Challenges:

T Each team stands on opposite sidelines of the gym (blacktop) and faces each other. Each member of team A has a playground ball for dribbling. On the signal, team A players begin dribbling toward the opposite sideline. Team B, without the playground balls, begins moving forward, trying to take away the balls. If a team B player gains possession of the ball, that player dribbles toward the opposite sideline. When the players from team A or team B make it over their goal line, they stay there until all the balls are behind one sideline. Team B is then given all the playground balls, and the game begins again.

Teacher Observation. As children begin to play in dynamic situations, it is critical that teachers continue to assess their use of the critical cues as they pertain to that situation. Any of the tasks at this level would allow for that. See Chapter 12 for the development of a teacher observation check list.

Dribble Tag

Setting: Each child with a playground ball for dribbling; two or three children designated "it" wearing identifying jerseys if possible

Cues

Look Up (Remember to look up to see where your opponents are.)

Use Fakes (You'll need to use all the fakes we learned before—stopping and starting, changing speeds, changing directions.)

Tasks/Challenges:

T On the signal, everyone with a ball will begin dribbling in general space. The players who are "it" will try to tag you as you're traveling and dribbling. You're caught if:

1. You're tagged by an "it."
2. You lose control of the ball.

If you're caught, stand and hold the ball above your head. You'll be free to travel if a player who is dribbling touches you. Each 2 minutes, we'll rest for 10 seconds while I choose new "its."

A way to make this activity more complex is to have the taggers not have to dribble. This small change calls for a significant increase in dribbling skills and more closely resembles basketball gamelike activities. Just remember the heightened level of dribbling skill that is needed.

Dribbling While Dodging

Setting: Children, each with a basketball or a playground ball and a flag tucked in the waist

Cues

Look Up (Remember to look up to see where your opponents are.)

Use Fakes (You'll need to use all the fakes we learned before— stopping and starting, changing speeds, changing directions.)

Ball, Body, Defense (Remember to protect the ball by keeping your body between the ball and the defense.)

Tasks/Challenges:

T You will need a partner of about your same ability level for this task. You will need to establish clear boundaries for your area, about 10 feet square. Start by facing each other and dribbling. The object is to keep dribbling and pull your partner's flag. See how many times you can pull your partner's flag in 2 minutes.

 What is one hint for not losing control of the ball in this activity?

Dribbling and Passing in Game Situations

Setting: A clearly defined space (the complexity of the task is increased or decreased depending upon the size of the space; initially, a larger space gives the advantage to the offense); groups of three

Cues

Offense Move to Open Space (When you don't have the ball, move to an open space at an angle to the passer; *see Chapter 25 for a detailed explanation of this idea.*)
Lead the Receiver (Throw to an open space in front of the receiver.)

Defense Go after the Ball (Go after the person with the ball; otherwise he or she doesn't have to throw it.)
Hustle (Move quickly when the ball changes players.)

Tasks/Challenges:

🅣 Working in your group of three, two of you will dribble and pass while the third player tries to steal the ball. We'll rotate the interceptor every 2 minutes.

Making Up Fancy Dribbling/Passing Routines

Setting: Groups of four to six; a space about 15 feet square; any number of basketballs; music and tape players (optional)

> **Cues**
>
> The cues for this task are dependent upon what you want students to include in the routine. Some possibilities:
>
> **Pathways** (In your routine be sure to include at least two different pathways: straight, curved, zigzag.)
> **Dribbling** (The dribbling part of your routine needs to include different levels of dribbling and dribbling in different places around the body.)
> **Passing** (Your routine might also include passing.)

Tasks/Challenges:

🅣 Put together a series of dribbling and passing skills in a fancy routine—kind of like a basketball warmup drill. Design the floor pattern, ways to travel, individual tricks, and partner or group skills. Practice your routine until you have it memorized and in time with the music.

☑️ *Videotape/Digital Analysis.* Routines such as this are good places to use videotape or digital pictures for observation and assessment. The videotaping or picture taking also adds incentive for students to perform well and do their best. Remember to design your scoring rubrics ahead of time so students know what is expected of their performance.

Dribbling and Throwing at a Target

Setting: Four-foot-square targets marked with colored tape on the wall at one end of or the sides of the gym, approximately 7 feet above the floor; each child with a ball at first, then later with partners and a shared ball

> **Cues**
>
> **No Stopping** (Pick up your dribble and throw to the target without coming to a complete stop.)
> **Watch the Target** (To increase your accuracy, watch the target.)

Tasks/Challenges:

🅣 Beginning at the center of the gymnasium, travel/dribble toward the wall with the target on it. When you're within 12 feet of the target, throw the ball, trying to hit the wall within the target square. Collect the ball, quickly move to the side, and return to midcourt.

🅣 Select a partner who will serve as defense. Partner 1 dribbles toward the wall and attempts to score by hitting the target; partner 2 tries to gain possession of the ball on the dribble or block the throw to the target. Change partner roles after each try.

🅣 Practice the dribble/target activity with an offensive partner. Combine dribbling and passing to a partner as you travel toward the target. Alternate the throw to the target between partners.

☑️ *Event Task.* By having partners join with another set of partners for a two-on-two game of dribbling, passing, and throwing at a target, you can create a self-designed game to be used as an event task. See Chapter 14 for how to design a scoring rubric to use with self-designed games.

Tip: Place targets around the walls as space allows. Place targets on both sides and on end walls to provide maximum activity.

Dribble/Pass Keep-Away

Setting: Groups of four in a space about one-quarter the size of a basketball court (or smaller)

> **Cues**
>
> **Defense** First Player Ball; Second Player Receiver (Play defense on the person with the ball first; then play defense on the receiver.) Don't Just Stand in the Middle (Make the passer throw the ball.)
> **Offense** Don't Pass until the Defense Commits (Until the defense plays defense on you, there is no need to pass. You might as well keep moving and dribbling the ball.)

Receiver Move to an Open Space (Move to an open space at an angle to the passer.)

Stay Away from the Passer (Wherever you go, your defense goes with you. If you stay close to the passer, everyone stays together and the passer has nowhere to throw.)

Tasks/Challenges:

T In your group, two of you will dribble and pass while the other two try to gain possession of the ball either by intercepting the pass or by stealing the ball on the dribble. Remember, on defense you cannot touch the other player. When you walk, you must dribble the basketball.

Small-Group Basketball

Setting: Groups of no more than three; half- or short basketball court with lowered baskets

Cues

Offense Don't Pass until the Defense Commits (Until the defense plays defense on you, there is no need to pass. You might as well keep moving and dribbling the ball.)

Receiver Move to an Open Space (Move to an open space at an angle to the passer.)

Stay Away from the Passer (Wherever you go, your defense goes with you. If you stay close to the passer, everyone stays together and the passer has nowhere to throw.)

Defense Go after Ball (Force the pass by pressuring the player with the ball.)

Ball, Body, Basket (Keep your body between the basket and the offensive player.)

Hustle Back (After a score, run back down the court.)

Tasks/Challenges:

C If you are comfortable with your skills of dribbling, passing, and throwing at a target, you may want to play a small-group basketball game. The maximum number of players on a team is three. The one rule I have is that every player must touch the ball before a shot is made. Match the skills on your team so the game will be a challenge for everyone; it's no fun if the score is a runaway.

J *Event Task.* At this point, it is helpful to have students think about their skill as well as doing it. Before beginning team play, have students think of all the skills needed for being successful in basketball: spatial awareness, throwing, catching, traveling, dodging, dribbling, shooting at a target. Within each group, discuss what a person needs to be able to do with each skill to be successful in basketball.

Reading Comprehension Questions

1. Discuss the difference between volleying and dribbling.
2. Name four body parts that can be used to volley a ball.
3. What is the primary focus of the tasks at the precontrol level of volleying? What is the teacher trying to accomplish before moving on to the control level?
4. List four different types of balls that can be used to practice volleying at the precontrol level.
5. What does the phrase "strike the ball with a level body part" mean? What does the phrase "meeting the ball" mean?
6. Rank the following tasks by placing the number 1 in front of the easiest (most basic) task, the number 2 in front of the next more difficult task, and so on.
   - (　) Striking a ball to different levels
   - (　) Striking a ball with two hands
   - (　) Striking a ball to outwit an opponent
   - (　) Striking a balloon
   - (　) Striking a ball to a partner
7. Explain the meaning of the phrase, "the location of the hit determines the direction of travel."
8. Give two examples of dynamic and unpredictable situations related to the skill of volleying.
9. What characterizes each of the four skill levels of dribbling?
10. What does it mean to keep one's hands firm and flexible as opposed to flat and stiff when dribbling?

11. How can you teach a child to use the fingerpads while dribbling?

12. How does the size of the space affect dribbling skills that are used in offensive and defensive situations?

13. How do the cues for dribbling and volleying change at the proficiency level?

References

Mustain, W. (1990). *A manual of elementary physical education skill theme activities for physical education specialists to use in collaboration with classroom teachers.* Unpublished master's project, Virginia Polytechnic Institute and State University, Blacksburg.

National Association for Sport and Physical Education. (1995). *Moving into the future: National standards for physical education.* St. Louis, MO: Mosby.

National Association for Sport and Physical Education. (2004). *Moving into the future: National standards for physical education* (2nd ed.). Reston, VA: National Association for Sport and Physical Education.

Striking with Rackets and Paddles

Striking with rackets and paddles, as well as striking with long-handled implements (Chapter 28), is one of the last skills that children develop. There are three basic reasons: (1) Children don't refine or develop visual tracking until the later elementary school years, (2) hand-eye coordination at greater distances from the body is more difficult, and (3) most often in striking situations with rackets and paddles there are two objects in motion at once—the paddle and the object being struck. Yet striking with these implements is a skill children enjoy and can be taught at younger ages with a few simple equipment modifications. Because of the complexities of striking, we teach the skill of striking with rackets and paddles after children have been introduced to the skill of striking with body parts, specifically the hand (see Chapter 26).

Children learning to strike with a racket or paddle must coordinate many familiar skills into one new one. They must learn to accurately toss or drop the object to be contacted, visually track the object while they're traveling to an appropriate location, and contact the object at exactly the right moment. And simultaneously they must adjust to the weight and length of the implement. A successful striker must coordinate *all* these variables. See Box 27-1 for information on striking with rackets and paddles from the *National Standards for Physical Education*.

Levels of Skill Proficiency

The difficulty of striking with an implement increases with the length of the implement. Children at the precontrol level struggle just to make contact between the implement and the object and are truly excited when they do—regardless of where the object goes. Children at this level benefit from exploring striking with short-handled, lightweight implements. Balloons, which travel slowly, expedite visual tracking and eye-hand coordination.

Appropriate tasks for children at the precontrol level include:

1. Striking a balloon with a lightweight paddle or hose racket
2. Striking a suspended ball
3. Tossing a ball or object upward and hitting it
4. Dropping an object and contacting it underhand
5. Dropping a ball and contacting it after a bounce

When children are able to strike a ball consistently in these contexts, they're ready for control-level expe-

Striking with Rackets and Paddles in the *National Standards for Physical Education*

The skill theme of striking with rackets and paddles is referenced in the *National Standards for Physical Education* (National Association for Sport and Physical Education, 2004) under Standard 2: Demonstrates understanding of movement concepts, principles, strategies, and tactics as they apply to the learning and performance of physical activities. This standard speaks of the child's recognizing and applying the concept of an appropriate grip to the striking action and the correct biomechanics of the striking action. The sample performance outcome states: Identifies and demonstrates key elements of a proper grip when holding a racket to perform a forehand strike (3–5)*.

*Grade-level guideline for expected student learning.

riences, which include contacting a rebounding ball a number of times in succession, sending the object in a desired direction, and varying the force of the contact. We also introduce the sidearm pattern at this level. Other appropriate control-level experiences include:

1. Striking a ball at a target
2. Sending a ball high enough to travel over a net

Children at the utilization level are able to contact a ball repeatedly without a miss (bouncing it up or down with a paddle or racket) and send a ball or other object various distances and in different directions. The youngsters are now ready to apply these skills in dynamic situations, such as moving into various positions to contact an object at different places around the body and returning shots to a partner. The skill of striking is now used in such learning experiences as:

1. Striking with a variety of rackets and objects
2. Continuously hitting to a rebound wall
3. Striking cooperatively with a partner for high scores
4. Striking with overhand, forearm, backhand, and underhand strokes

When the children have attained the proficiency level, they demonstrate a mature pattern of striking: the ability to control both body and implement while traveling and to select the most effective type of striking when responding to a partner. Experiences at the proficiency level center around gamelike situations. Fast-moving, quick-reacting patterns of striking are required in both cooperative and competitive games. Appropriate experiences include:

1. Playing cooperative or competitive games
2. Offensive-defensive movements involving others

Our progression spiral (this page) presents ideas for developing the skill of striking with rackets and paddles from the precontrol through the proficiency levels. The key observation points in Box 27-2 illustrate correct sidearm striking with rackets and paddles.

Precontrol Level: Activities for Exploration

At the precontrol level, we provide activities for the children to explore using lightweight paddles to contact balls, shuttlecocks, and other objects. These objects are often suspended from ropes at various heights to make the task easier.

We recommend balloons at the precontrol level because the flight of a balloon is longer and slower than that of a ball, and the child therefore has more time for visual tracking. Heavier balloons, although a bit more expensive, are more durable than inexpensive, lightweight balloons. They also tend to be less erratic during flight and consequently are easier for children to strike successfully.

 Striking is one skill theme in which safety plays an important role. Be sure to include wrist strings or guards on all rackets and paddles (and have children use them), and provide ample space for children to strike and move safely around one another.

Paddle Balance

Setting: A paddle and a balloon, beanbag, and ball for each child (Foam paddles are best because they are lightweight and easy to control.)

Tasks/Challenges:

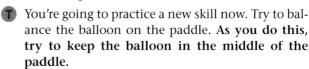 You're going to practice a new skill now. Try to balance the balloon on the paddle. **As you do this, try to keep the balloon in the middle of the paddle.**

If you are having a little trouble with the balloon on the paddle, you may want to try balancing a beanbag on the paddle.

Box 27-2

Key Observation Points: Striking with Rackets and Paddles

1. Does the child take a forward step on the foot opposite the striking arm?

2. Does the child's body coil and rotate forward as the child swings the racket?

3. Does the child draw the racket back and then swing it forward along a full arc?

Box 27-2 (continue

Mature Striking Patterns

When children are at the mature stage of striking with rackets and paddles, do their strikes look similar to the following sequence? In the preparatory phase, weight is shifted to the back foot, the trunk rotates 45 to 90 degrees, the hip and trunk are cocked, and the racket is drawn back. This is followed by movements that occur in such quick succession that they seem almost simultaneous: The weight shifts, the body rotates forward, and the racket is swung forward along a full arc (an arc around the body).

Source: Adapted from *Fundamental Motor Patterns*, 2nd ed., by R. L. Wickstrom, 1977, Philadelphia: Lea & Febiger.

T The balloon was fairly easy to balance, but this time we are going to make the task a little harder. Instead of a balloon, try to balance a ball on your paddle. Try to keep the ball on your paddle for as long as you can.

T If you are really good at keeping the ball on your paddle so that it doesn't fall off very often, try rolling the ball around on the paddle but still keeping it on the paddle. At times you will really have to do some fast work to keep the ball on the paddle.

C I will time you. See if you can keep your object on the paddle for 15 seconds. Ready? Go.

T This time we are going to try something even harder. Choose the object you like best. Try to walk around your self-space and balance the object on your paddle at the same time.

Volleybirds (badminton shuttlecocks with flat bottoms; see Chapter 26) also work well with children at the precontrol level. The youngsters learn to keep the paddle flat as they walk around carrying the volleybird on the paddle.

Balloon Strike (Lightweight Paddle)

Setting: A nylon-hose (Figure 27.1) or foam paddle and a balloon for each child; a carpet square or other way of defining self-space for each child (When children first begin striking balloons with paddles, tie the balloon with string to the paddle's handle. This saves much chasing time and makes it easier for the children to remain in their self-space.)

Tasks/Challenges:

T In your own space with your paddle and balloon, strike the balloon up in the air. Do one hit, then catch, and start again. Find out how to make the balloon go in the air.

T Now try to strike the balloon more than once— maybe twice—then catch.

C How many times can you strike the balloon, keeping it in the air without missing it or moving from your space? Five would be a really good number.

T So far, you've tried to stay still in your own space while you were striking the balloon. This time try and move around in your self-space.

T This time we are going to try to walk while striking the balloon. Go slowly and look where you are going so you don't hit others. To be safe, the balloon should be close to you.

This girl is seeing how many times she can strike her object before it touches the ground.

Figure 27.1 Construction of nylon-hose paddles. Lightweight paddles can be made from old coat hangers, nylon socks (or stockings), and tape.

At the park, I noticed a girl called Sarah. Her older brothers were busy playing street hockey and tennis (on the tennis courts). She was about 6, and, being ignored by her brothers, was in her own world. The boys had left a tennis racket and a ball lying aside. She picked them up, held the racket somewhere in the middle of the handle, and began to try to hit the ball. It took four tries before she even made contact, and the ball rolled away into the grass. It didn't matter; you could tell by the smile on her face that she was delighted. She ran after the ball, picked it up and (after a few attempts) hit it again, and was again off to chase it. Her game took her on a journey all over the park and continued for 20 minutes or so. Then she proudly walked over to her mother and declared, "I can play tennis!"

Striking a Suspended Ball

Setting: A ball suspended from a string (Figure 27.2) and a paddle for each child; for the first task suspend the balls above shoulder height; place carpet squares or other markings on the floor behind each ball

Tasks/Challenges:

T In your own space you have a ball that is hanging from a string. Try to strike the ball forward while standing on your carpet square. After each strike be sure to stop the ball before you try to hit it again.

Setting: Lower the balls to waist height; move the carpet squares to a position beside the suspended balls

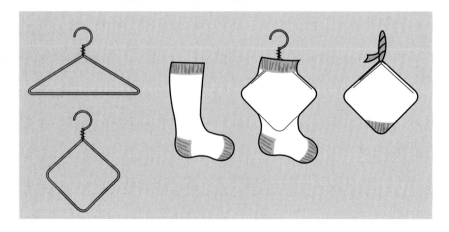

Tasks/Challenges:

T Things have changed a little this time. Now your carpet square is beside the ball. Again, try to strike the ball from your square so that it travels straight forward—like in baseball. Be sure to stop the ball after each hit.

C You have been striking the ball fairly well. This time, if you strike the ball well, yell "Whacko!" If you miss, just start again.

At this point, children should be striking on their preferred side. When the children begin to strike consistently, challenge them to strike on the opposite side of their bodies (for example, backhand).

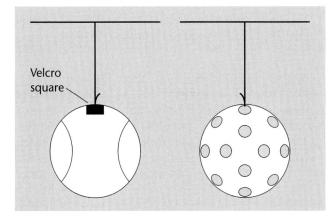

Figure 27.2 Suspending balls on strings. Glue a hook-and-loop tape square to a string and another to a tennis ball to enable the ball to drop from the string when the ball is struck, or knot string or elastic into the holes of a plastic whiffle ball. Balls can be hung from climbing apparatus, from traveling rings, and between vertical game standards, and they can be attached to walls in the corners of the gym.

Hit the Wall

Setting: A foam or wooden paddle and a foam ball, Nerf tennis ball, or volleybird for each child; spots on the floor or carpet squares about 5 feet away from the wall to identify self-space

Tasks/Challenges:

T At your spot, strike the ball so that it travels to the wall. Just try for one hit at a time. Remember, if the ball goes away from you, collect it and bring it back to your spot before striking again.

T Try hitting the ball on both sides of your body.

C Try for five single hits; if you can do five, try seven.

Paddles and Safety

Although wooden and Plexiglas paddles are very good for learning to strike, they do present a safety problem. Paddles made of foam—with both short and long handles—are available. We prefer foam paddles whenever the children are working in close spaces or in groups.

Recently equipment companies have developed a Nerf tennis ball. These balls come in variety of sizes—some slightly larger than a regular tennis ball—and have a density that facilitates striking. We have found that they are more effective for use with rackets and paddles than dead tennis balls.

By allowing children the choice of striking implement and type of object to strike, children are able to adapt the task to their ability.

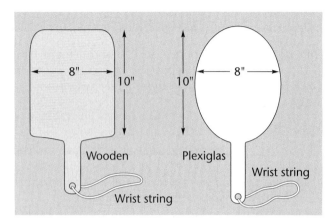

Figure 27.3 Construction of short-handled paddles. Short-handled paddles can be cut with a jigsaw from 1/2-inch finished plywood or from 1/4-inch Plexiglas. Sand plywood edges until they're smooth, and wrap the handles with fiberglass tape. *Each paddle should have a wrist string for safety.*

Upward Bound

Setting: A wooden, foam, or Plexiglas paddle (Figure 27.3); a shuttlecock or volleybird and a lightweight ball; a carpet square or some way to define self-space for each child

Tasks/Challenges:

🅣 This time try striking the shuttlecock *(volleybird)* upward. Drop the object, and try to strike it so it goes straight up.

🅣 Once you are comfortable with one hit, try to hit the shuttlecock *(volleybird)* more than once before catching it.

🅒 Try to hit the shuttlecock *(volleybird)* four times in a row.

🅣 Trade in your shuttlecock *(volleybird)* for a ball. Try to hit the ball up in the air. Remember, one hit and catch it; then hit again.

🅣 Try to strike the ball up more than once—maybe twice—and then catch it.

Control Level: Learning Experiences Leading to Skill Development

Experiences at the control level are designed to help children go beyond just contacting the ball. At this level, children learn to control the direction, force, and aerial pathway of an object. One of the first cues we give children when beginning striking activities is "watch the ball." This is hard for many youngsters because so

much else is going on around them. To help children focus on the ball, paint a bright dot or letter on it, and direct their concentration toward that mark.

Equipment Modifications

Visual tracking is a skill that is not refined until the later elementary grades; therefore, striking, unless modified, is a difficult skill theme for children. A few simple equipment modifications allow young children to experience success in tracking. The use of large, slow-moving, easy-to-see objects, such as balloons or beach balls, makes tracking easier. The use of lightweight, short-handled, easily maneuverable rackets compensates for the developing hand-eye coordination and limited arm strength and endurance. The basic guideline to follow is that the equipment should not hamper the movement pattern; if it does, modify the equipment.

At the control level we introduce children to a variety of striking implements and to objects with various surfaces, lengths, and types and degrees of bounce, including Ping-Pong paddles, racquetball paddles, paddleball paddles, badminton rackets, tennis rackets, paddleballs, Nerf tennis balls, tennis balls, racquetballs, rubber balls, shuttlecocks, Ping-Pong balls. This allows teachers to help children choose the equipment that best meets their needs. We also introduce children to the sidearm pattern. (At the utilization and proficiency levels, we continue to provide a variety of striking implements and objects.)

A note about cues: Although several cues are listed for many of the learning experiences, it's important to focus on only one cue at a time. That way, the children can really concentrate on that cue. Once you provide feedback to the children and observe that most have learned a cue, then it's time to focus on another one.

Downs

Setting: A wooden paddle, a dead tennis ball or a foam ball, and a carpet square or some way to define self-space for each child

Cues	
Flat Paddle	(Keep your paddle flat as a pancake.)
Watch the Ball	(Keep your eyes on the ball all the time.) *(It's helpful to paint a dot on the ball so children have something on which to focus.)*

Tasks/Challenges:

T In your own space strike the ball down with your paddle. See if you can keep it going without a miss.

T Once you can keep the ball going five times or more in a row without leaving your space, see if you can strike the ball so it stays below your waist.

C How many down strikes can you get in a row without having to leave your self-space? These strikes don't have to be below your waist. Ready? Go.

More Equipment Modifications

John Kessel of USA Volleyball recently introduced us to yet another ball modification that provides for a slow-moving, "real looking," cheap ball that is weighted a bit more and has a "true" flight. The trick is to sew a cover out of nylon fabric that is the size and shape of a ball you want (panels and all), leaving a buttonhole at the top. Buy heavyweight balloons. Insert the balloon through the buttonhole; inflate and tie off. The balloon ball lasts a long time and looks like the real thing. All you need is someone who can sew! These balls can be used for both striking with paddles and volleying.

Ups

Setting: A wooden paddle, a dead tennis ball or a foam ball, and a carpet square or some way to define self-space for each child

The difficulty of all striking tasks can be increased or decreased by changing the object being struck. We most often start with shuttlecocks or volleybirds and progress to foam balls and dead tennis balls or Nerf tennis balls. We tend to stay away from "live" tennis balls because they encourage children to "hit hard" rather than use the correct pattern and move to receive the ball. Adjust the equipment for each task as appropriate for your children.

Cues

Flat Paddle	(Keep your paddle flat as a pancake.)
Stiff Wrist	(Keep your wrist tight; don't let it flop around.)
Watch the Ball	(Keep your eyes on the ball all the time.) *(It's helpful to paint a dot on the ball so children have something on which to focus.)*

Even the youngest children are fascinated with striking.

Tasks/Challenges:

T Now let's see if you can stay in your self-space and keep the ball going, but hit it up so that it doesn't touch the floor.

T Can you hit the ball up so that it goes above your head every time and still stay in self-space?

C Every time the paddle hits the ball, say one letter of your name. Can you spell your first name? Your last name? Your best friend's name? Remember, each time you miss you have to start spelling the word over again.

Show me what a flat paddle looks like.

Ups and Downs

Setting: A foam or wooden paddle, a dead tennis ball or a foam ball, and a carpet square or some way to define self-space for each child

Cues

Flat Paddle	(Keep your paddle flat as a pancake.)
Stiff Wrist	(Keep your wrist tight; don't let it flop around.)

> **Watch the Ball** (Keep your eyes on the ball all the time.)

Tasks/Challenges:

T Now let's see if you can still stay in self-space and keep the ball going. One time bounce it off the floor, and the next time hit it into the air.

C Let's make up a sequence. For example, your sequence might be: up once, down once, up twice, down twice, up three times, down three times, and then start over. Practice until you can do your sequence two times in a row.

T Can you hit the ball up and down while walking around your self-space—without losing control of the ball?

C Try to do your sequence while you walk around in self-space.

T If that was easy, you might want to try skipping, or sliding, or galloping in self-space as you strike the ball.

T This time it becomes harder. We are going to walk in general space while striking the ball. Walk very slowly while you continue to strike the ball. For safety, be sure to look where you are going. If you think you are going to lose control of the ball, stand still for a second and catch the ball or let it bounce on the floor until you get control back; then keep going. If you do lose your ball, walk and pick it up, and start again.

⚠ When children begin moving and striking simultaneously, they tend to concentrate so much on the striking that they forget to watch out for others and for rolling balls. Besides reminding them to watch out, conduct these tasks in the largest possible space, preferably outdoors.

The skill of striking with rackets and paddles is complex and has a number of critical cues associated with it. These cues include, for the underarm striking pattern:

Slanted Paddle	Follow Through
Paddle Way Back	Watch the Ball
Opposite Foot	

For the sidearm pattern, cues include:

Paddle Way Back	Opposite Foot
Side to Target	Follow Through
Flat Paddle	Watch the Ball
Firm Wrist	

We have elected to highlight only some of these cues with various tasks throughout the remainder of the chapter. Feel free to interchange the cues that will best meet the needs of your students with those we have selected.

✓ Student Drawing. This would be a great time to have students draw a picture of themselves striking up and striking down to assess their knowledge of the critical cues of flat paddle and stiff wrist.

Up Against the Wall (Striking Forward)

Setting: A shuttlecock, a foam ball or a dead tennis ball, and a paddle for each child; children about 5 feet from the wall, with spots or carpet squares to remind them of their self-space

Cues	
Paddle Way Back	(Start the paddle back behind your hips.)
Opposite Foot	(Just as in throwing, step forward on the foot opposite the arm you are using to strike.)
Slanted Paddle	(For this hit, keep the paddle face flat, but slant it just slightly toward the ceiling so the ball will go to the wall.)

The slight angle (slant) of the paddle face is critical here. It is helpful to demonstrate the subtle difference between it and a flat paddle and what the skill looks like.

Tasks/Challenges:

T Facing the wall and at your own spot, drop the shuttlecock and try to strike it so it goes straight ahead—forward toward the wall. **This strike is a little like an underhand throw, you are actually striking the shuttlecock from slightly underneath, not from the side.**

T Now trade in your shuttlecock for a ball. This will be a little harder, but it's the same idea. Try to strike the ball with the paddle so it goes straight forward toward the wall. You may want to let the ball bounce first before you hit it. Remember, just one hit at a time. Drop, hit, catch—then go again.

C Practice until you can hit the ball so it travels to the wall five times.

C Ask the person beside you to watch you strike the ball. Your neighbor will give you a point if you step forward on the opposite foot as you hit. You'll get

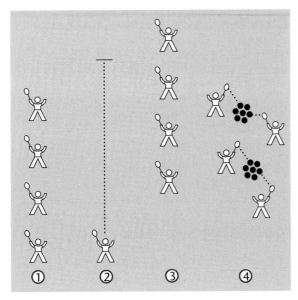

Figure 27.4 Station setup for ups, downs, and forwards.

a second point if you swing the paddle underhand, not sidearm or overhead. Practice with your neighbor watching for a few minutes; then watch your neighbor.

Ups, Downs, and Forwards

Setting: Four stations set up as in Figure 27.4, with children divided equally among the stations; at stations 1 and 3, foam balls or dead tennis balls and paddles for every child; at station 2, balloons and paddles for each child; at station 4, yarn balls and paddles for each child, as well as seven hoops in a cloverleaf pattern for each pair

Cues

Stations 1, 2, and 3

Flat Paddle	(Keep your paddle flat as a pancake.)
Stiff Wrist	(Keep your wrist tight; don't let it flop around.)
Watch the Ball	(Keep your eyes on the ball all the time.)

Station 4

Paddle Way Back	(Start the paddle back behind your hips.)
Opposite Foot	(Just as in throwing, step forward on the foot opposite the arm you are using to strike.)
Slanted Paddle	(For this hit, keep the paddle face flat, but slant it just slightly toward the ceiling so the ball will go to the hoops.)

Tasks/Challenges:

T The stations today provide a chance to practice all the striking activities we have been doing. Some are just practice; others are challenges. Do your best. Change on the signal.

Station 1: How many downward hits can you do with no mistakes? Count them.

Station 2: Travel across the gym, striking the balloon upward as you go.

Station 3: Can you do five single upward hits without moving from self-space? Try continuous hits.

Station 4: Strike the ball so that it travels forward and lands in a hoop. Each time you are successful, increase your distance by taking one giant step backward. One partner can strike and the other collect the balls. Switch every five strikes.

√ *Self-assessment.* The preceding task could easily be turned into a self-assessment by having children record on cards how they did at each station.

Both Sides (of the Paddle) Now

Setting: A wooden or foam paddle, a dead tennis ball or foam ball, and a carpet square or other way to define self-space for each child

Cues

Flat Paddle	(Keep your paddle flat as a pancake.)
Stiff Wrist	(Keep your wrist tight, don't let it flop around.)
Watch the Ball	(Keep your eyes on the ball at all times.)

Tasks/Challenges:

T In tennis, racquetball, or badminton, players use both sides of the paddle. Let's try this. Keep hitting the ball up. Try to hit the ball with one side of the paddle, then the other.

T If that is easy, see if you can use both sides of the paddle and both sides of the body. Try not always to strike the ball when it is right in front of you.

T Can you make a rainbow with the ball? Hit it on one side of your body and then the other so the ball travels in a rainbow shape. Remember, if you miss the ball and have to chase it, go back to your self-space before you start striking again.

C How many rainbows can you make? Each time the ball goes over your head, it counts as one. Five rainbows without a miss would be excellent!

Striking to Wall Targets

Setting: A wooden paddle and tennis ball for each student; 12- to 20-inch circles about 6 feet up on the wall in a scattered pattern

Cues

Paddle Way Back	(Start the paddle back behind your hips.)
Opposite Foot	(Just as in throwing, step forward on the foot opposite the arm you are using to strike.)
Slanted Paddle	(For this hit, keep the paddle face flat, but slant it just slightly toward the ceiling so the ball will go to the wall.)

Tasks/Challenges:

🅣 Find a spot about 10 feet from the wall in front of a circle. Strike the ball to the wall, trying to hit the circle. Remember, this is a back-to-front swing—like an underhand throw. **If you are doing it correctly, your arm will almost brush your hip on the way forward.**

🅣 For the next five hits, freeze your follow-through. **Check to see if you have the opposite foot forward and your arm extended, with the racket face slanted slightly toward the ceiling.**

🅒 When you think you can do five perfect hits with opposition and slanted racket facing the target, raise your hand and I will come to observe or a friend can observe for you.

🅣 Try to send the ball to the wall so that it touches within two to three inches of the target.

🅒 Can you come that close five times?

🅣 Take a giant step backward. Strike the ball so that it contacts the wall at the height of the target.

🅣 When you are successful in hitting the target six times, take another giant step backward.

🅣 Move back to your first space closest to the wall. See if you can use an underhand strike to make the ball drop just in front of the wall.

🅣 When you can successfully drop the shot just in front of the wall, take a giant step backward and try the drop shot from the longer distance.

🅒 Pick your favorite distance. Count how many times you can hit the target without a mistake. How many times can you drop the ball just in front of the wall?

👤 How does the paddle face differ when striking to the wall from when striking up or down?

Striking for Distance (Varying the Force)

Setting: Outdoors on a large field (so that children can work safely without hitting one another); children all facing the same way, either in a line or away from the center of a circle; a paddle and a variety of objects to strike for each child; objects (spots or cones) for use as markers

Cues

Opposite Foot	(Just as in throwing, step forward on the foot opposite the arm you are using to strike.)
Slanted Paddle	(For this hit, keep the paddle face flat, but slant it just slightly toward the ceiling so the ball will go to the target. Use less slant for longer hits.)
Follow Through	(Follow through with your racket so that it is aimed straight at the target.)

Tasks/Challenges:

🅣 Standing on the line, all facing the same direction so you won't hit anyone else, practice striking the objects, changing the amount of force that you use for hitting. Sometimes use a lot of force, sometimes not very much force. Each time, make sure that you use the proper underarm swing and that you follow through, no matter what amount of force you use. Use up all your objects and then go collect them.

🅒 This time you're going to play a game with yourself. First, strike an object as far as possible. Take a marker, and mark the place where your object fell. Be sure that you can see the mark from the striking line. Now try to hit an object to halfway between the striking line and your far object. Practice until you feel as if you've really figured out just exactly the right amount of force to use. Then see if you can hit the middle spot three times in a row.

🅣 After you're done this task three times in a row, hit another object as far as you can, mark it, and try the same thing all over again.

Striking for Hoops (Varying the Distance)

Setting: Partners; a wooden paddle and a variety of objects to hit for each child; a hoop to serve as a target for each pair

Opposite Foot (Just as in throwing, step forward on the foot opposite the arm you are using to strike.)

Slanted Paddle (For this hit, keep the paddle face flat, but slant it just slightly toward the ceiling so the ball will go to the target. Use less slant for longer hits.)

Follow Through (Follow through with your racket so that it is aimed straight at the target.)

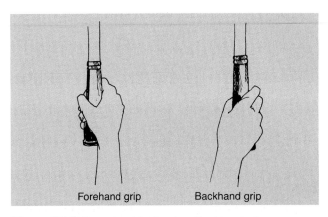

Forehand grip   Backhand grip

Figure 27.5 Examples of forehand and backhand grips.

ⓣ Place your hoop on the ground. One partner will be the hitter; the other, the catcher. The hitter strikes the object so that it lands in the hoop—hits the target. First, stay close, and then after you can hit the target three times, move back a few steps and try again. Your partner will keep the objects from going all over the place. After you take six hits, switch places with your partner for six hits and then switch back.

ⓒ Now you're going to make a game out of striking into hoops. Place three hoops on the floor, one about 3 feet away from you, one 6 feet away, and one 10 feet away. One partner will try to strike so that the object lands in each hoop; the other partner will collect the object after the hits. Then the partners switch places. You can make up any other rules that you wish, but you both need to practice striking into all three hoops.

✔ *Teacher or Student Observation.* This task lends itself well to a teacher or student observation checklist of the use of the critical cues for striking at various distances. *See Chapter 14 for the development of check lists.*

To the Wall—Sideways (Sidearm Forehand Pattern)

Setting: A paddle and ball for each child; marks or carpet squares to define self-space; large Xs placed about 3 feet high on the wall in front of each space

Cues

Flat Paddle (Keep your paddle flat as a pancake.)

Stiff Wrist (Keep your wrist tight; don't let it flop around.)

Side to Wall (Keep to the wall the side opposite the arm you're using to hit.)

Opposite Foot (Just as in throwing, step forward on the foot opposite the arm you are using to strike.)

An additional cue that is sometimes needed with the sidearm pattern is to keep the elbow away from the side. We use that cue as necessary with individuals or groups of children.

Tasks/Challenges:

ⓣ Until now you have used an underhand pattern to strike the ball. Now we are going to learn a new pattern: the sidearm pattern, like what is used in tennis and racquetball. **This time your side is to the wall and your paddle is flat.** This is called the *forehand,* and you will use the forehand grip *(Figure 27.5).* Practice striking the ball to the wall from a mark on the floor using the sidearm pattern. Remember, these are single hits—drop, hit, and catch, and go again.

ⓒ Practice until you can hit the ball so that it travels to the wall five times.

ⓣ After you can hit the wall five times, take one giant step backward and try from that distance. When you can hit the wall five times, move backward again.

ⓣ Return to your first spot, and try to hit the X on the wall in front of your space. When you can make five hits, move backward again.

ⓒ Pick your favorite distance. How many times can you hit the target without missing?

With the forehand and backhand grips, we demonstrate the grip before the task, observe the children's grips as they practice, and provide feedback as necessary. We do not spend a lot of time teaching the grip.

To the Wall Again—Sideways (Sidearm Backhand Pattern)

Setting: A paddle and a ball for each child; marks or carpet squares to define self-space; large Xs placed about 3 feet high on the wall in front of each space

Children at the control level benefit from repeatedly striking a ball against the wall.

Cues

Flat Paddle	(Keep your paddle flat toward the wall all the time.)
Stiff Wrist	(Keep your wrist tight; don't let it flop around.)
Watch the Ball	(Keep your eyes on the ball all the time. Watch it hit the paddle.)
Same Foot/ Same Shoulder	(Just as in throwing a Frisbee, step forward on the same foot. The shoulder of the arm you are using to strike should be toward the wall.)

Tasks/Challenges:

T This is also a sidearm pattern, but from the other side of your body. In tennis it is called the *backhand,* and you will use the backhand grip *(Figure 27.5).* It is the same as the forehand, except the side of your body with the striking arm is to the wall, and you step forward on the same foot

as your striking arm. You reach across your body to hit. Practice striking the ball to the wall from a mark on the floor using the backhand pattern. Remember, these are single hits—drop, hit, and catch, and go again.

C Practice until you can hit the ball so that it travels to the wall five times.

T After you can hit the wall five times, take one giant step backward and try from that distance. When you can hit the wall five times, move backward again.

T Return to your first spot, and try to hit the X on the wall in front of your space. When you can make five hits, move backward again.

C Pick your favorite distance. How many times can you hit the target without missing?

Striking at High and Low Targets

Setting: A paddle and a ball for each child; four stations set up as in Figure 27.6; at stations 1 and 2: spots marked on the floor about 6 and 10 feet from the wall; targets on the wall in front of each space about 3 feet high; at station 3: spots marked on the floor about 10 feet from the wall; targets on the wall about 6 feet high (see Figure 27.7); at station 4: hoops on the floor against the wall; spots marked in various places around the hoops about 3, 6, 10, and 15 feet away

Cues

Paddle Face	(Your paddle will be slightly slanted or flat depending on which striking pattern you use.)
Stiff Wrist	(Keep your wrist tight; don't let it flop around.)
Watch the Ball	(Keep your eyes on the ball all the time. Watch it hit the paddle.)
Opposite Foot/ SameFoot	(Step forward on the opposite foot for the forehand; the same foot for the backhand.)

Place a metal gong, small bells, loose plastic jugs, or similar sound-producing objects on a wall as targets. Young children enjoy the auditory feedback when contact is made.

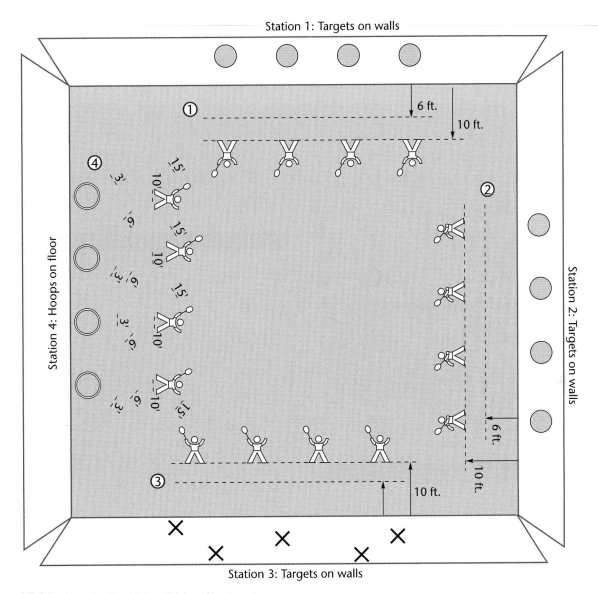

Figure 27.6 Station setup for striking at high and low targets.

Task/Challenges:

You have practiced both underhand and sidearm striking patterns. You can use them both, but one is better for some things, and the other is better for other things. The underhand pattern works best when you want to send the ball to high places or make it drop low. The sidearm pattern works when you want the ball to go in a more straightforward route. Now you will get a chance to mix them up. At each station you will have to decide which striking pattern is best to use. See if you can figure out each station. I will tell you that at station 2 you have to use the backhand.

Station 1: Try to hit the target as many times as you can. When you hit the target six times, move backward to the next mark.

Station 2: Try to hit the target with a backhand pattern. What is the highest number of times you can hit the wall from each spot?

Station 3: Pick out one X on the target and see if you can hit it five times; then choose another X, and another, and finally the last X. When you can hit all of them five times, move backward one step.

Station 4: From each of the marks on the floor see if you can drop the ball into the hoop.

Exit Slip. It would be appropriate here to use an exit slip to assess the children's understanding of the various striking patterns, their cues, and their uses. *See Chapter 14 for examples.*

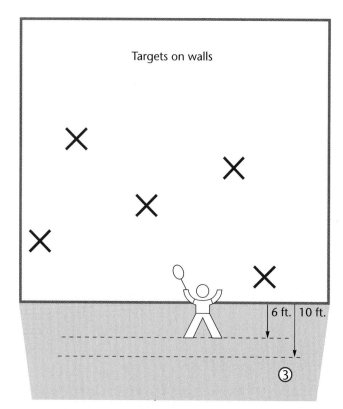

Figure 27.7 Target design for striking at high and low targets, station 3. *The Xs on the wall should be large enough to be hit easily.*

Striking to Different Places

Setting: A paddle and a ball for each child; marks or carpet squares to define self-space; large Xs about 3 feet high on the wall in front of each space

Cues	
Paddle Face	(Your paddle will be slightly slanted or flat depending on which striking pattern you use.)
Follow Through	(Follow through with the paddle straight toward your target.)
Watch the Ball	(Keep your eyes on the ball all the time. Watch it hit the paddle.)
Opposite Foot	(Just as in throwing, step forward on the foot opposite the arm you are using to strike.)

Tasks/Challenges:

T This time instead of trying to hit the X, pretend that the target is your opponent. Try to hit a space about 2 feet to the right of the X. Practice until you can hit your space six times. You can use an underhand or a sidearm pattern.

T Now practice trying to hit a space to the left of the X. Again, practice until you can hit the space six times.

T This time practice doing one hit to the right and the next hit to the left and the next hit to the X. See if you can repeat your pattern five times.

C Ask the person next to you to be your partner. You will call out where you are going to hit before the strike. Your partner gives a thumbs-up if you hit where you called out or a thumbs-down if you didn't. After eight hits, trade places.

Striking through a Target

Setting: A hoop suspended at about shoulder height for each group of two; a paddle for each child; one ball per group

Cues	
Paddle Face	(Your paddle will be flat or slightly slanted depending on which striking pattern you use.)
Watch Ball/ Watch Target	(Keep your eyes on the ball all the time: See it hit the paddle; see it go to the target. Watch the target out of the corner of your eye.)
Opposite Foot/ Same Foot	(Step forward on the opposite foot for the forehand; the same foot for the backhand.)

Tasks/Challenges:

T At your hoop, one of you will bounce the ball on the floor and then try to strike it through the hoop. The partner will catch the ball and return it to the striker. After 10 strikes, change places.

T Now that you've practiced by first letting the ball bounce, try it without letting the ball bounce. In other words, just drop the ball, hit it before it hits the ground, and try to make it go through the hoop.

C Since you are so good at this, why don't we make it a game? How many hits in a row can you and your partner combined get?

Striking an Object to Send It Over a Net

Setting: A net (or a rope between two chairs) about 2 to 3 feet high for each group of partners; a paddle for each child; one ball per group

⚠ When striking with a partner, children tend to forget their own space and often unknowingly encroach on the space of other groups, risking collisions. Therefore, for this task and all tasks that involve striking to a partner, have children clearly define their space with lines or poly-spots.

Cues

Paddle Face	(Your paddle will be flat or slightly slanted depending on which pattern you use.)
Watch Ball/ Watch Target	(Keep your eyes on the ball all the time: See it hit the paddle; see it go to the target. Watch the target out of the corner of your eye.)
Opposite Foot/ Same Foot	(Step forward on the opposite foot for the forehand; the same foot for the backhand.)

Tasks/Challenges:

Ⓣ With one partner on either side of the net, partner 1 strikes the ball across the net. Partner 2, instead of hitting the ball back, will catch it and throw it back to partner 1. After 10 hits, change roles. It helps to bounce the ball on the floor once before you hit it across the net.

Ⓣ This time, use three different striking patterns to hit the ball across the net: forehand swing, backhand swing, and underhand swing. Take 10 practices with one swing, and then switch; take 10 practices with another swing, and then switch; take 10 practices with the third swing, and then switch. Ready? Three different ways of striking, 10 practices each.

Ⓣ You can practice any way of striking you want this time, but try to pick a spot on the opposite side of the net and hit the ball to that spot, as if you were aiming for a target. Ten practices each, then switch.

So that children in every group have their own net to work over, simply suspend a rope between two chairs. This way you can set up nets of different heights and lengths at various places around the space.

Striking a Ball Rebounding from a Wall

Setting: Wall space, with a line marked about 3 feet up the wall and a line marked on the ground 6 to 8 feet from the wall; a paddle and a ball for each child

To be accomplished both safely and effectively, striking activities require a great deal of space. Unfortunately, many indoor facilities in elementary schools don't have such spaces available. If this is true at your school and there aren't any outdoor alternatives, you can have two activities going simultaneously in the space available. Some children can carry out striking activities against the walls while other children carry out activities that require less space, such as balancing or weight transference, in the center of the space or on a stage area.

Cues

Quick Feet	(As the ball returns, you want to be behind it and a little to the side. You will have to move quickly to get there.)
Watch the Ball	(Keep your eyes on the ball all the time. See it hit the paddle; see it go to the wall.)
Bend Knees	(You want to contact the ball at about your waist. You'll have to bend your knees to do this.)

Tasks/Challenges:

Ⓣ Now you're going to have a chance to strike the ball against a wall. In your space, about 6 feet from the wall, practice striking the ball against the wall with a forehand strike and the forehand grip *(Figure 27.5)*. **When you hit the ball, you should be slightly behind and about an arm's length to the side of the ball.**

Ⓒ Here comes the challenge. See how many times you can strike the ball against the wall and let the ball bounce only once before hitting it again. If you miss, just start counting over.

Ⓣ Now I'm going to make the activity a little harder for you. Hit the ball to different places on the wall, always trying to be ready to hit it when it comes back to you. **In other words, you'll have to figure out where the ball is coming when it bounces off the wall and be behind it so you can hit it again.** Remember, hit different places on the wall.

Ⓒ This time, the challenge is really hard. You need to see how many times in a row you can hit the ball above the line on the wall. The ball can bounce only once on the ground between hits. Ready? Go.

Ⓣ This time, you can do what you've wanted to do for a long time: Hit the ball as hard as you can. But

I have some rules. First, the ball must land behind the line marked on the ground; second, you're allowed only one bounce to hit the ball back. This prevents you from hitting the ball so hard that you can't get to it.

⚠ When allowing children to strike the ball as hard as they can, make sure they are spread far apart and clearly understand the rules for retrieving a ball that has gone into another person's space.

✸ When do you use a forehand grip and swing? A backhand grip and swing?

Striking Continuously Over and Through a Target

Setting: A hoop, hoop stand, two paddles, and a ball for each set of partners

Cues	
Quick Feet	(As the ball returns, you want to be behind it and a little to the side. You will have to move quickly to get there.)
Watch the Ball	(Keep your eyes on the ball all the time. See it hit the paddle; see it go over the hoop.)
Bend Knees	(You want to contact the ball at about your waist. You'll have to bend your knees to do this.)

Tasks/Challenges:

Ⓒ Now you'll play a game with your partner using all that you have learned. Set up the hoop on the hoop stand on the center line of your area. Hit the ball back and forth over the hoop, letting the ball bounce on your side before hitting it back. After five hits over the hoop, the receiver must hit the ball through the hoop so that it goes to the partner's side. If the hit through the hoop is good, play continues for another five "overs" and one "through." If the "through" is not good, the five "overs" start over again.

Utilization Level: Learning Experiences Leading to Skill Development

Experiences at the utilization level enable children to strike with an implement, not as an invariant skill, but in dynamic environments that involve partners and striking from different positions in relation to the body.

A note about cues: Although several cues are listed for many of the learning experiences, it's important to focus on only one cue at a time. That way, the children can really concentrate on that cue. Once you provide feedback to the children and observe that most have learned a cue, then it's time to focus on another one.

Hitting from Different Places

Setting: A space about 10 feet by 10 feet; partners, each with a paddle; one ball per group

Cues	
Watch the Ball	(Keep your eyes on the ball all the time. See it hit the paddle; see your partner hit it.)
Bend Knees	(You want to contact the ball at about your waist. You'll have to bend your knees to do this.)
Side to Target	(Whether you strike forehand or backhand, your side should face your partner.)
Get Home	(Return to a position in the center and near the back of your space after each hit. This is called home. It will take quick feet to get there.)

Tasks/Challenges:

Ⓣ This time, your partner is going to throw rather than hit to you. Partner 1 will throw the ball to partner 2 so that it bounces once before it reaches partner 2. Partner 2—the hitting partner—then tries to hit the ball straight back to partner 1—the thrower—regardless of where the ball has been sent. Partner 1 then catches the ball and throws to a new place. After 10 throws, switch places. The first time, always throw the ball to your partner's right side. The next time, always throw it to your partner's left side.

Ⓣ This time, don't let your partner know to which side you're going to throw the ball. **Hitters, as soon as you see the ball leave the thrower's hand, adjust your position so that you can return the ball.** Throw 10 times, and change.

In the beginning stages of striking a ball sent by a partner, children benefit from having the ball tossed consistently to their preferred or nonpreferred side. This way they can progress to adjusting the preparatory stage according to the direction of the oncoming ball.

✔ *Peer Observation.* This is an excellent time for a student observation of the critical cues practiced at the control level. True learning occurs when children can use the cues correctly in dynamic, unpredictable situations. *See Chapter 14 for assessment examples.*

Striking activities require well-defined spaces.

Hitting Cooperatively and Continuously with a Partner

Setting: A space about 10 feet by 10 feet; partners, each with a paddle and one ball

Cues	
Get Home	(Return to a position in the center and near the back of your space after each hit. This is called home. It will take quick feet to get there.)
Watch the Ball	(Keep your eyes on the ball all the time. See it hit the paddle; see your partner hit it.)
Bend Knees	(You want to contact the ball at about your waist. You'll have to bend your knees to do this.)

Tasks/Challenges:

Ⓣ With your partner, in a space by yourselves, see if you can strike the ball back and forth to each other. The ball should bounce in the middle, but remember to get ready to hit the ball again after each hit.

Ⓒ Set a personal-best goal with your partner for the number of hits you can get without missing. See if you can attain your goal. Give your partner your best hit each time.

Ⓣ Make sure that you and your partner practice hitting on both sides of your body.

Tip: The preceding task can be used with any of the striking patterns or a combination of patterns. You may need to remind children about the cue differences for sidearm and underhand striking.

🗝 Where is home position when hitting with a partner?

Striking to Different Places Around a Partner

Setting: A space about 10 feet by 20 feet for each set of partners; two paddles and a ball

Cues	
Get Home	(Return to a position in the center and near the back of your space after each hit. It will take quick feet to get there.)
Watch the Ball	(Keep your eyes on the ball all the time. See it hit the paddle; see your partner hit it.)
Follow Through	(Follow through with your paddle in the direction in which you want the ball to go.)

Tasks/Challenges:

Ⓣ With your partner, strike the ball back and forth, each time hitting to the alternate side of your partner's body. In other words, once you will hit to your partner's left and the next time to your partner's right. Try to keep the ball going for as long as possible. *(Have skilled students demonstrate what it looks like to hit to alternate sides.)*

Ⓒ As you practice now, see how long you can keep the ball going, but almost try to make your partner miss.

Striking Overhead

Setting: A wall space, with a line marked on the wall about 3 feet from the floor, a spot marked on the ground about 10 feet from the wall, and a paddle and a ball for each child

Cues	
Toss	(Toss the ball just barely above the top of the paddle.)
Reach and Stretch	(When you hit the ball, reach and stretch as high as possible.)
Flat and Down	(Your paddle should be flat and facing slightly downward and forward as you strike the ball.)

Demonstrate the skill of striking overhead.

Tasks/Challenges:

🅣 Stand on your spot, about 10 feet from the wall. Toss the ball higher than your racket can reach in the air and then stretch to hit the ball when it's at its highest point. In other words, throw the ball up, and when it reaches the very top of the throw—the point where it won't go up any farther and hasn't started to come down—hit it so it goes against the wall. Don't try to hit the ball back when it bounces off the wall; just catch it and start over.

🅣 Now that you've caught on to this idea, try to make the ball go down so that it hits the wall near the line, about 3 feet above the floor. **To make it go down like that, the face of your racket must point slightly down as you hit the ball. Give it a try. Remember to watch the ball contact the racket so that you can see what you're doing.**

🅣 This time, try to strike overhead again, but have the ball strike the wall just above the line. **Watch your racket contact the ball so that you can tell which direction your racket face is pointed.**

✔️ *Exit Slip or Self-Assessment.* After this task an exit slip or self-assessment would be an appropriate way to see how students feel about their ability to strike in overhead fashion. Questions on an exit slip might include a recall of the cues or a Helping Murgatroid question. A self-assessment might ask how well they did with each of the cues. *See Chapter 14 for further information on both of these techniques.*

Striking Overhead Over a Net

Setting: Balls, a paddle, and a net 2 to 3 feet high for each set of partners

Cues	
Toss	(Toss the ball just barely above the top of the paddle.)
Reach and Stretch	(When you hit the ball, reach and stretch as high as possible.)
Flat and Down	(Your paddle should be flat and facing slightly down and forward as you strike the ball.)

Tasks/Challenges:

🅣 You're going to practice hitting overhead again. Stand at the back of your court area, with your partner on the other side of the net. The partner with a paddle and some balls throws a ball in the air just above her or his reach, including the reach of the paddle, and then hits the ball down and over the net. This is like a tennis serve, only everything is smaller. The nonhitting partner should collect all the balls as they're hit. After 10 times, switch places.

🅣 As you begin to hit more balls over the net and in the court, start to try to hit the ball a little harder. But don't attempt this until you can get 10 hits in a row over the net and into the court.

⚠️ Whenever children are striking over a net, always have them clearly define the boundaries of their striking area so that they don't interfere with others.

Striking Continuously Upward with a Group

Setting: Groups of three; a paddle for each player; one ball for each group

Cues	
Flat Paddle	(Keep your paddle flat as a pancake.)
Watch Ball/ Watch Players	(Always watch the ball. Watch the other players and the space out of the corner of your eye.)
Quick Feet	(It will take quick feet to get behind and under the ball.)

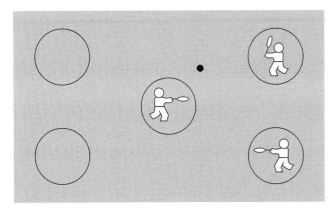

Figure 27.8 Setup for striking continuously upward with a group.

Tasks/Challenges:

T You need to clearly define the boundaries of your space; they should be approximately 8 to 10 feet apart. Your task is to keep the ball moving by striking it to each player without losing control. Bounces are allowed if you want them, but you do not have to use them. There is no set order in which you have to hit. See how long you can keep the ball going without losing control.

Setting: Groups of three, each group with one ball, three paddles, and five hoops; a space set up as in Figure 27.8

Tasks/Challenges:

C This is a game that will let you practice striking in the air. The person in the center hoop begins by striking the ball in the air to a person in one of the other hoops. That person receives the ball, strikes it twice to himself or herself and sends it back to the middle person, who also has to strike it twice before sending it to the other outside person. That outside person has to strike three times to himself before sending it back to the middle, where it is struck three times. This continues until the middle person has to strike seven times to himself or herself. Just to make it harder, the outside people, after striking the ball, have to move to one of the empty hoops. If anyone misses, the whole group starts over again. We will change middle hitters after seven hits or 3 minutes.

Striking in Various Aerial Pathways in Dynamic Situations

Setting: Different-colored pieces of yarn suspended one above the other—at 3 feet, 6 feet, and 10 feet—for use as nets (Figure 27.9); partners, each with a paddle; one shuttlecock or volleybird per group

Cues

Slanted Paddle	(Your paddle needs to have a flat face that is slanted upward.)
Follow Through	(Follow through toward the string you are trying to go over.)
Get Home	(After each hit, move back to your center back position to get ready to hit again.)

Tasks/Challenges:

T Using a shuttlecock (volleybird) and an underarm swing, try to make the object go over the lowest piece of yarn. After five tries, switch with your partner.

T Now try the middle piece of yarn. Do this five times each, then switch.

T Now the highest piece. For this one, you're really going to have to use a big underarm swing to get the object over the net.

C This task will be difficult. Try to keep the shuttlecock (volleybird) going with your partner, but this time, on the first hit, make it go over the low piece of yarn; on the next hit, make it go over the middle piece; on the third hit, make it go over the top piece. Then start over and reverse the order. Practice until you can do the sequence one time all the way through.

Striking Upward in a Dynamic Situation

Setting: Group of up to five people, each with a paddle; one ball per group

Cues

Flat Paddle	(Keep your paddle flat as a pancake.)
Watch Ball/ Watch Players	(Always watch the ball; watch the other players and the space out of the corner of your eye.)
Quick Feet	(It will take quick feet to get behind and under the ball.)

Tasks/Challenges:

C You are going to strike in a gamelike situation. Here are the rules:

1. One person stands in the middle of a circle.
2. The person in the middle hits the ball with a paddle straight up in the air and calls out the name of another person in the group.
3. The person whose name is called out must run to the middle of the circle, hit the ball up in

Figure 27.9 Setup for aerial pathways.

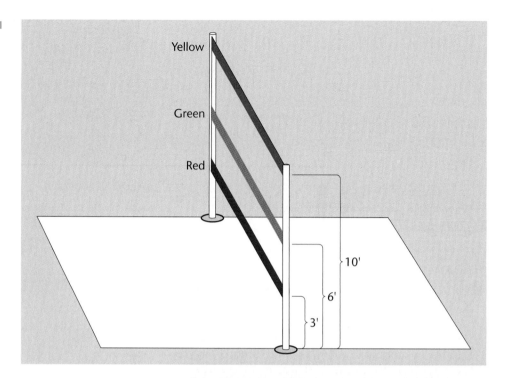

the air before it bounces, and call out another student's name.
4. The caller takes the place of the person whose name was called out.

The type of racket used can increase the complexity of any striking situation. A light, short-handled racket is the easiest for a child to master, a heavy, long-handled racket is the most difficult. As children begin to master the skills of striking with rackets, we gradually change the type of racket used, to make the task more difficult.

Proficiency Level: Learning Experiences Leading to Skill Development

Experiences at the proficiency level encourage children to enjoy the challenge of striking with short-handled implements in gamelike situations. These experiences involve partner or opponent relationships, spatial strategy, and the varied use of effort qualities.

Because of the gamelike nature of the tasks, it can be quite tricky to keep these activities developmentally appropriate, especially in terms of active participation for all children. There are several solutions here. Set up multiple courts around the gym. The courts may be odd sizes, but they should allow for maximum participation. Another option is to have stations where several offer gamelike activities and several have practice opportunities that require less setup and space. Finally, you could have peer assessment opportunities where half the members of a small group will play and half will observe; then switch. Regardless of the solution,

Striking using various aerial pathways provides challenges for utilization-level children.

please remember that gamelike activities should be appropriate for all children. See Chapter 31 for more information on game options in physical education.

A note about cues: At the proficiency level, tasks are more complex, typically requiring children to coordinate several movements simultaneously in a dynamic

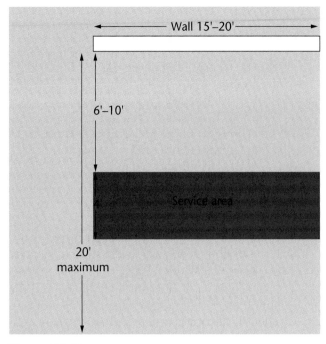

Figure 27.10 Setup for striking to one wall with a partner.

Figure 27.11 Setup for striking at angles to two walls with a partner.

context. A list of cues is provided to assist the children in being more successful in the learning experiences. The challenge is in determining which cue will be most beneficial for each child . . . and when. Thus, careful observation and critical reflection become very important as you watch the children move and then decide which cue will be the most helpful to move each learner to a higher level.

Striking to One Wall with a Partner

Setting: Two children per group, each with a paddle; one ball per group; court set up as in Figure 27.10

Cues	
Get Home	(Return to a position in the center and near the back of your space after each hit.)
Watch the Ball	(Keep your eyes on the ball all the time. See it hit the paddle; see it hit the wall; see your partner hit it.)
Mix 'Em up	(It's time to use all your different strikes: to different spots on the wall and soft and hard strikes.)

Tasks/Challenges:

We will call this task Wall Ball. The objective is to hit the ball against a wall so your opponent is unable to return it. Here are the rules:

1. You may score only when you serve.
2. The ball may be returned either after one bounce or before the bounce.
3. To make your partner miss, you must use placement, not force. All shots should be of a force that is playable.

The courts are marked on the floor. To start play, partner 1 serves the ball against the wall, and partner 2 tries to return it. Each time partner 1 hits the ball, partner 2 tries to return it. You get points only when you serve and your partner fails to return the ball; if the server misses the ball at any time during a rally, the partner gains the serve.

Striking at Angles to Two Walls with a Partner

Setting: Two people per group, each with a paddle; one ball per court; court set up as in Figure 27.11

Cues	
Get Home	(Return to a position in the center and near the back of your space after each hit.)
Watch the Ball	(Keep your eyes on the ball all the time. See it hit the paddle; see it hit the wall; see your partner hit it.)
Mix 'Em Up	(It's time to use all your different strikes: to different spots on the wall and soft and hard strikes.)

Tasks/Challenges:

Ⓒ This activity is very much like the last one you played, except that it's played in a corner instead of just flat against the wall. You might want to call it Racket Corner Ball. All the same rules apply as for Wall Ball: There are two players; points are won only when you serve; and the ball is hit either after one bounce or before it bounces. And ball placement should cause someone to miss, not force. Go ahead and get used to playing in the corner.

This and the preceding activity can be played cooperatively instead of competitively. That is, children may prefer to see how many hits they can make without a miss.

For a more advanced game of striking at angles to two walls with a partner, see Striking to the Wall—Varying Levels, Force, and Body Position in Chapter 26.

Striking To and From Different Places

Setting: Four square courts, each about 15 by 15 feet, labeled A, B, C, and D; groups of four students, with paddles and a ball

Cues	
Ready Position	(Keep your weight on the balls of your feet, with your knees slightly bent.)
Paddle in Front	(To be ready, hold your paddle in front of your body about waist high.)
Back of Square	(Stay near the back of the square so you can move forward.)

Tasks/Challenges:

Ⓒ This task you could call Racket Four Square. Here are the rules:

1. Square A starts the game.
2. You must hit the ball to another square.
3. The ball can't be hit to the person who hit it to you.
4. You must hit the ball after its first bounce.
5. The person who misses the ball goes to square D, and everyone else moves up a square.
6. All strikes must be underhand.

Partner Striking Across a Net

Setting: Partners; a low net on a surface that allows the ball to bounce, with a marked-off court at each net area for each pair

Cues	
Get Home	(Return to a position in the center and near the back of your space after each hit.)
Watch the Ball	(Keep your eyes on the ball all the time. See it hit the paddle; see your partner hit it.)
Mix 'Em Up	(It's time to use all your different strikes: to different spots on the court and soft and hard strikes.)

Tasks/Challenges:

Ⓒ The objective of this game is to send the ball over the net so that it bounces within the court, and the opponent hits the ball before it bounces twice. Here are the rules:

1. Play begins with an overhead strike behind the end line.
2. The ball can bounce no more than once on each side of the net.
3. You may hit the ball before it bounces.
4. The ball cannot be hit so hard that it is unreturnable.

You may or may not keep score; the choice is yours. If you decide to keep score, decide before you start to play how you'll do so.

Aerial Striking Over a Net

Setting: Solid rackets, paddles, or badminton rackets; shuttlecocks, tennis balls, or volleybirds; one net (between children's shoulder and head height) for each set of partners; a marked-off court at each net with a serving line (Figure 27.12)

Cues	
Get Home	(Return to a position in the center and near the back of your space after each hit.)
Watch the Ball	(Keep your eyes on the ball all the time. See it hit the paddle; see your partner hit it.)
Mix 'Em Up	(It's time to use all your different strikes: to different spots on the court and soft and hard strikes.)

Tasks/Challenges:

Ⓒ The objective of this aerial net game is to send the object over the net so that the opponent can return it before it touches the floor. Here are the rules:

1. Play begins with an underhand strike behind the serve line.

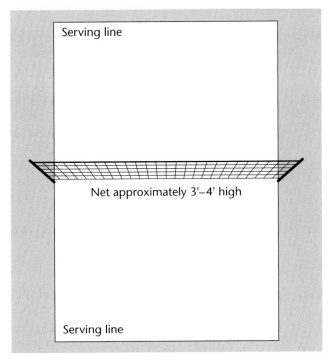

Figure 27.12 Court setup for aerial net games.

2. Aerial strikes continue until the object touches the floor or goes out of bounds.
3. If you like, you can make up your own way of changing serves and keeping points.

Aerial net games using a shuttlecock can be played with regular tambourines, with old ones that are discarded from rhythm bands because the jingles have been lost, or with tambourines with rubberized heads. Children enjoy the sound made when the shuttlecock strikes the tambourine.

Team Striking Across a Net

Setting: Groups of four with Nerf tennis balls, wooden paddles, and a net; a court of four equal squares, with a net running down the center

Cues	
Get Home	(Return to a position in the center and near the back of your space after each hit.)
Watch the Ball	(Keep your eyes on the ball all the time. See it hit the paddle; see your opponents hit it.)
Mix 'Em Up	(It's time to use all your different strikes: to different spots on the court and soft and hard strikes.)

Cover Space	(You want to block all the space on the court. One player usually plays near the net, and one back. When one moves, the other must adjust.)

Tasks/Challenges:

 This task is like tennis or pickleball doubles, only the mini version. Here are the rules:

1. There are two people on each team.
2. Team A serves underhand and diagonally to team B.
3. The two teams hit the ball back and forth across the net until one team misses.
4. When the team serving misses, the other team takes over serving.
5. When the receiving team misses, the serving team keeps serving.
6. The serve always begins in the back right-hand corner behind the line, alternates to the back left-hand corner on every consecutive serve, and then back to the right.
7. The ball may be hit before it bounces or after one bounce.
8. The ball cannot be hit so hard that it is unreturnable.

Homework. At this point in learning to strike, you might give children a homework assignment to observe a tennis match in person or on television and analyze how one player uses the strategies of getting home, watching the ball, mixing up shots, and covering space.

Group Striking Across a Net

Setting: Groups of six, with badminton rackets or paddles, shuttlecocks, and a net

Cues	
Quick Feet	(Move quickly to get behind and under the shuttlecock.)
Close to Net	(One player should be close to the net for the last hit.)
Get Home	(After each hit, move back to your position on the court so the space is covered.)

Tasks/Challenges:

 You're going to strike across a net with a team. Here are the rules:

1. There are three players on each side.

2. A player near the back of the court serves underhand to the other side of the net. The opponents hit the shuttlecock twice on their side of the net and then return it over the net.
3. The shuttlecock must be hit twice by two different players on each side of the net before it's returned.
4. The shuttlecock must be hit before it touches the ground.
5. When the serving team misses, the other team scores.
6. Keep score any way you want or not at all.

⚠ The preceding activity is an enjoyable game, but the use of long-handled rackets requires enough room to allow children to strike without hitting each other. Play the game in a space at least the size of a regulation volleyball court.

Self-Designed Racket Games

Setting: Depends on the game; groups of six or fewer, each child with a foam racket

Cues
Appropriate to the game

Tasks/Challenges:

Ⓒ Today you're going to combine all that you've practiced into a game. You'll make up your games yourselves. In your groups, make up a game that involves striking with a foam racket. You can have whatever rules you want as long as you include these two: (1) The game must involve striking with foam rackets, and (2) everyone in your group must be playing at the same time. In other words, nobody sits out and waits for a turn. Remember, groups of no more than six, striking with foam rackets, and everybody plays. Go.

After you've made up your rules and started to play your game, make sure you know your rules so that you can tell somebody else how to play your game. At the end of class, I'll ask you to write down your game.

✓ *Event Task.* An appropriate assessment task at this point would be to have children write down how to play their games and then share the games with others. *See Chapter 14 for more assessment examples.*

Reading Comprehension Questions

1. Students at the precontrol level benefit from striking an object suspended from a string. Describe three different ways to suspend objects.
2. What types of striking implements and objects are recommended for students at the precontrol level?
3. How does a teacher know when a child is ready to be challenged to strike the ball on the opposite side of the body (i.e., backhand)?
4. Describe the position of a child's arms and feet when the child is striking with a racket or paddle.
5. What characterizes each of the four generic levels of skill proficiency of striking with rackets and paddles?
6. What does a flat paddle look like? What does a slanted paddle face look like? What happens when an object is struck with a paddle held in each position?
7. What does it look like when children run around the ball instead of striking the ball on the opposite side of the body? Describe a task that would help them learn to not run around the ball.
8. A child swings a racket so that it remains at waist level throughout the swing. What direction does the ball travel if the child strikes the ball too early in the swing? Too late in the swing?
9. Design six tasks related to striking with rackets or paddles. Rank them in order from the easiest to the hardest. Be certain to include at least one task from each skill level. Use a different striking implement or object for each task.
10. Name the major safety cue regarding striking.

Reference

National Association for Sport and Physical Education. (2004). *Moving into the future: National standards for physical education.* (2nd ed.). Reston, VA: National Association for Sport and Physical Education.

Striking with Long-Handled Implements

The skill of striking is used in many games. We have divided striking into various categories: kicking and punting, volleying and dribbling, striking with rackets, and striking with long-handled implements. This division allows us to cover in some detail the gamut of striking activities. The basic action in all striking is the same—giving impetus to an object with a hit, punch, or tap—although often the purpose and the equipment differ.

As we subdivided striking activities in a variety of chapters, we also subdivide each proficiency level in this chapter into three parts to more fully cover the striking activities that use long-handled implements. This chapter focuses on striking using swings in horizontal (batting) and vertical (hockey and golf-type actions) planes. The implements used to accomplish these swings vary from bats to hockey sticks to golf clubs to polo sticks—yet all issue the underlying challenge of coordinating hands and eyes when striking with a long implement. Because vertical and horizontal swings have distinctive characteristics, key observation points for each are presented separately. Both swings involve striking away from the body, but the motor skills differ in relation to the purpose of the task.

Generally, striking is the last fundamental motor pattern learned because of the complexity of the hand-eye coordination involved. Within this skill theme there are also multiple levels of complexity. Actions that require striking a stationary ball (as in golf) are easier than actions that require the striking of a moving object as in hockey. Both of these actions are less complex than striking a pitched ball with a bat. In the latter action, both objects are moving and never come to rest. In all cases, children may possess a mature striking pattern before they're able to consistently make contact with the ball.

A sidearm pattern is used when striking a ball with a bat, to keep the bat at the same distance from the ground and in a horizontal plane throughout the swing. (See Box 28-1 for observation points for striking sidearm.) In contrast, a swing with a hockey stick or a golf club uses a more vertical arc—referred to as an underhand swinging pattern because in many ways it resembles the movement used to throw a ball underhand. (The key observation points for striking using an underhand pattern appear in Box 28-2.) Additionally, dribbling (stick handling) is also included as an underhand pattern.

We don't introduce children to striking with long-handled implements so that they'll become experts at golf, tennis, or hockey. We provide children opportunities to practice striking patterns they're likely to use in a variety of contexts throughout their lives. This rationale can be fully appreciated when watching an adult trying to strike with a long-handled implement. If that individual has had no previous experience with a particular striking pattern, the results can be disastrous. Frustration will result, and ultimately the person may abandon the sport. Our emphasis is on giving children a variety of movement opportunities rather than on perfecting the technical aspects of a particular swing. Specific opportunities to refine and perfect different swings are provided at the secondary level or in private instruction.

Most long-handled implements are designed for adults. Because children aren't "regulation size," they find it difficult to manipulate implements of official size, length, and weight, so we use lightweight, plastic implements in our programs, or we make implements that match the sizes of the children. This prevents the children from learning poor habits when they try to use equipment that is too heavy or too long. The equipment should never inhibit the mature striking pattern.

Levels of Skill Proficiency

Activities at the precontrol level ask children to explore all varieties of striking with long-handled implements. Due to the difficulty of the skill, tasks are developed using large and stationary objects to be struck. Initial striking tasks at this level explore:

1. Striking a large stationary object with a hockey stick
2. Traveling slowly while striking an object with a hockey stick
3. Striking a large ball off a batting tee with a plastic bat

When children are able to make contact with an object, they can be challenged with tasks that require them to include one or two other variables besides striking. Appropriate experiences at the control level include:

1. Striking on the ground to a stationary partner
2. Traveling, stopping, and controlling the ball or puck
3. Striking a ball while traveling in different pathways
4. Striking a ball various distances on the ground and in the air
5. Tossing a ball to oneself and striking it

At the utilization level, children are able to control a ball in the space around them and strike consistently with the appropriate striking pattern. We challenge them to use their striking skills in more dynamic

Box 28-1

Key Observation Points: Sidearm Striking

1. Does the child swing the bat in a horizontal plane?

NO   YES

2. Does the child take a forward step and follow it quickly with hip, trunk, and arm rotation?

NO   YES

3. Do the child's wrists uncock after contact?

NO   YES

Box 28-1 *(continued)*

Mature Stage

When children are at the mature stage of sidearm striking, do their strikes look similar to the following sequence? The child steps forward and then quickly rotates the hips, trunk, and arms. The forward movement of the trunk stops before contact, but the whipping rotation from the shoulders and arms continues. The pushing motion of the right arm (left arm, if the child is left-handed) and uncocking of the wrists are the final significant forces.

Source: Fundamental Motor Patterns, 2nd ed., by R. L. Wickstrom, 1977, Philadelphia: Lea & Febiger.

Box 28-2

Key Observation Points: Underhand Striking

1. Is the child's left arm (for right-handed children) kept firm at the top of the backswing?

NO   YES

2. Is the child's weight shifted to the back foot at the top of the backswing, with both knees remaining bent?

NO   YES

3. Is the child's weight shifted to the forward foot as the swing begins?

NO   YES

Box 28-2 (continued)

Mature Pattern

When children are at the mature stage of underhand striking, do their swings look similar to the following sequence? The joints are cocked—weight is shifted to the back foot, the hips and trunk rotate away from the ball, the implement is raised up and behind the back shoulder, and the wrists are cocked. The body weight is then shifted to the forward foot. The hips and spine rotate forward, the forearm swings downward, and the back arm and wrist uncock. The forward arm stays straight throughout the swing.

Source: Fundamental Motor Patterns, 2nd ed., by R. L. Wickstrom, 1977, Philadelphia: Lea & Febiger.

and unpredictable situations. Appropriate experiences might include:

1. Propelling an object while traveling, using changes of direction and speed to dodge an opponent
2. Striking an object on the ground against an opponent
3. Striking to open spaces, both in the air and on the ground
4. Passing to a traveling partner

When children reach the proficiency level, many possess mature striking patterns, and striking becomes a skill that can be used in complex, unpredictable, gamelike situations. At this point, children are able to incorporate previous experiences into situations that involve strategic and split-second decisions. Appropriate tasks include:

1. Striking with a golf club to targets in a strategic situation
2. Positioning the body to strike an oncoming object to an open space while traveling and while stationary
3. Passing and receiving an object while moving and dodging other children
4. Striking a pitched ball

Striking skills may be the last to develop. But once children have developed the ability to consistently strike objects with long-handled implements, they can participate in fascinating activities. The tasks in this chapter are organized according to the striking pattern used and to their relative difficulty within the patterns. (Our progression spiral for developing the skill themes of striking with long-handled implements, which is grouped by striking pattern within each proficiency level, appears on page 572.) We have developed tasks for all striking patterns. Each task is labeled with the equipment commonly used for the pattern. Tasks in which a sidearm pattern is called for are identified as "bats," though you could easily substitute a tennis racket or a badminton racket. Tasks that utilize an underhand pattern are largely identified as "hockey" and occasionally "golf." The major difference between a golf and a hockey swing is the length of the backswing, grip, and follow-through, so tasks at early stages of development could again be interchanged. We have developed most of the tasks that utilize an underhand striking pattern around the shortened hockey-type swing because that is the action most often developed in elementary physical education, in our experience. Numerous implements can be substituted for hockey sticks (see the "Implements for Underhand Striking" box). We have separated the different types of striking patterns throughout the chapter. However, although we like to initially mass

practice for children, each idea should be revisited thus providing them with distributed practice throughout their development. When practice is distributed over time, the learner is more apt to retain the skill.

Implements for Underhand Striking

Although we have associated hockey with tasks that use an underhand striking action, other sports also use the underhand swing pattern. Several striking implements may be substituted for hockey sticks or golf clubs; many times these alternatives may be more appropriate. Pilo Polo sticks are lighter and softer than hockey sticks. Short-handled broomball sticks provide a wider striking surface but unfortunately are available only in certain areas of the country. Substitution of either of these implements not only may reduce the complexity of the task, but also can take the focus away from a single sport.

Precontrol Level: Activities for Exploration

At the precontrol level, a chopping, downward swing is typical for any striking pattern. Children struggle just to make contact between the ball and the striking instrument. Therefore, we give children activities that let them explore striking with the added length that comes with bats and hockey sticks—and the greater demands that length places on their hand-eye coordination. Children explore striking stationary objects with bats, golf clubs, and hockey sticks, and they begin to develop the ability to control a ball with a hockey stick while traveling.

All activities at this level need to be done with balls of various sizes. For beginners, yarn balls or large plastic balls are easier because they're larger and/or don't roll as fast as other balls. For tasks that involve traveling, plastic pucks are easier to control initially if the lesson is being taught on a smooth wood or tile floor. Until children become skilled and responsible, we recommend using plastic balls. The flight of the balls won't be as true, but safety is an important consideration.

⚠ Working with long-handled implements involves some unique safety aspects. Ample space should be provided so that children can swing implements freely and with room to move around. Children should also learn to carry implements safely to their working space, and not to swing them around their bodies while walking. When moving around the space, children should walk well behind others so that they will not be hit by an implement or a struck ball.

Striking with Long-Handled Implements

Proficiency Level

Half Ball—bats
One-Base Baseball—bats
Six-player striking and fielding in a gamelike situation—bats
Directing the pathway, distance, and speed of an object—bats
Small-sided hockey invasion game—hockey
Keep Away—hockey
Striking to dodge an opponent—hockey
Whiffle Ball Golf—golf
Directing the pathway, distance, and speed of an object—golf

Utilization Level

Batting, combining distance and placement—bats
Striking a pitched object varying the distance—bats
Hitting to open spaces—bats
Directing the placement of an object—bats
Grounders and flies—bats
Two-on-one hockey—hockey
Keeping It Moving—hockey
Passing and receiving on the move—hockey
Striking from a stationary position to a moving target—hockey
One-on-one hockey—hockey
Traveling and striking for a goal—hockey
Pathways, speeds, and directions—hockey
Performing a continuous dribble and change of direction—hockey
Dribbling and changing directions backward—hockey
Playing Hockey Bowl (small targets)—hockey
Directing the air pathway of the struck object—golf
Playing Hoop Golf—golf
Striking to targets at various distances—golf

Control Level

Striking a pitched ball—bats
Striking a self-tossed ball to different distances—bats
Throwing a ball in the air and striking it—bats
Hit and Run—bats
Hitting a stationary ball from different places—bats
Striking suspended objects—bats
Striking a stationary ball for distance—bats
Level swings—bats
Striking a stationary ball—bats
Striking while dodging stationary obstacles—hockey
Striking to different places—hockey
Traveling and striking while changing pathways—hockey
Traveling and changing speeds—hockey
Traveling, stopping, and controlling the ball—hockey
Traveling slowly while striking a ball—hockey
Striking to a stationary partner—hockey
Striking to a target (Around the World)—hockey
Striking to targets—hockey
Striking to varying distances—golf
Striking in the air—golf
Striking for distance—golf and hockey
Striking a stationary ball on the ground—golf and hockey

Precontrol Level

Traveling slowly while striking a ball—hockey
Striking (dribbling) a ball in self-space—hockey
Striking to large targets—golf or hockey
Striking a stationary ball—golf or hockey

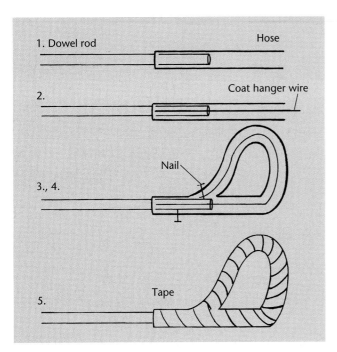

Figure 28.1 Construction of a golf club or a hockey stick (design by Tom Trimble, University of Georgia).

Materials
Hardwood dowel rod, 5/8″ by 3′
Garden hose or rubber tubing,
5/8″ (inside diameter)
Roll of electrical or adhesive tape (one roll is enough for at least 12 sticks)
Two flat-headed nails, 5/8″
Coat hanger

Directions
1. Cut an 18-inch-long piece of the garden hose and slip it approximately $3\frac{1}{2}$ onto the dowel.
2. Insert a piece of coat hanger wire into the hose so that it butts up against the bottom of the dowel and extends almost to the end of the hose.
3. Bend the hose so that the ends meet on the dowel rod. Form the hose at whatever angle you desire.
4. Use two nails to secure the hose to the dowel. One of the two nails can be used to attach the bottom portion of the hose, bent in half, to the top portion.
5. Use tape to further support the hose or the dowel.

Striking a Stationary Ball—Golf or Hockey

Setting: Preferably a large outdoor space (but can be adapted for an indoor space); golf club (Figure 28.1) or plastic field hockey stick (short-handled and long-handled street hockey sticks aren't appropriate) for each child; a variety of foam and plastic balls and pucks; each child in self-space, facing a wall or an object that will block the ball

Tasks/Challenges:

🅣 Stand beside your ball and strike it so it travels to the wall. Hit it hard so it goes all the way to the wall. Make sure to stop the ball when it comes back before you hit it again.

🅒 Practice until you can hit the wall three times in a row.

🅣 Practice hitting from both sides of your body. Each time try to make the ball go to the wall.

🅣 Try striking the ball so it sometimes goes along the floor and sometimes in the air. What makes it go in the air? On the ground?

🅣 Trade in the ball for another kind of ball or a puck. Try all the different things with your new piece of equipment.

🅣 Now move behind your ball. Try striking it to the wall from that position.

🅒 Practice until you can get the ball or puck to the wall three times.

🅣 If you are outside, practice striking the ball as far as you can. Practice strikes from the back and from the side. Which position do you like best?

Striking to Large Targets—Golf or Hockey

Setting: A plastic hockey stick and a foam or plastic ball or puck for each child; a large target marked on the wall within 6 inches of the floor for each child; children about 6 feet from the target and at least 5 feet apart

Tasks/Challenges:

🅣 Stand to the side of the ball. Strike the ball toward the target, trying to hit the target.

🅒 Your challenge is to see how many times in a row you can hit the target in front of you. Remember to stop the ball each time it comes back to you before hitting it again.

🅣 When you can hit the target three times in a row, move back one giant step and try again.

Striking (Dribbling) a Ball in Self-Space—Hockey

Setting: Children in self-space, each with a hoop, a hockey stick, and a foam or plastic ball or puck

Tasks/Challenges:

🅣 In your own space inside the hoop, use the hockey stick to gently move the ball around in as many ways as possible. Don't leave your self-space.

🅣 On the signal, begin striking the ball in your own space, and keep striking until you hear the signal

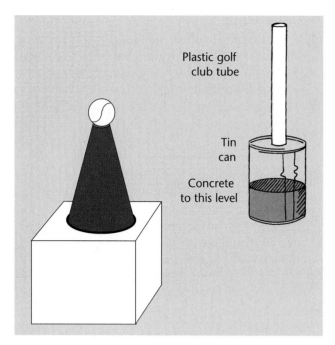

Figure 28.2 Construction of a batting tee. The easiest way to make a batting tee is to use a large (36-inch) traffic cone, which is high enough for young children. Increase the height by placing the traffic cone on a cardboard box. A batting tee can also be made out of a tin can and a plastic tube.

Materials
   Large tin can (available from the school cafeteria)
   Plastic golf club tube (obtained from a sporting goods store)
   Sack of ready-mixed concrete (1/10 to 1/8)

Directions
1. Place the golf club tube into the tin can.
2. Add water to the concrete mix, and fill the tin can approximately half full.
3. After a few minutes, when the concrete begins to harden, make sure that the golf club tube is not leaning to the side. Once the concrete dries, the batting tee is ready to use.

You can vary the heights of the batting tees by shortening the plastic golf club tubes before inserting them into the cans. We try to have batting tees of three different heights.

to stop. Remember to stay in your own space. Do not travel.

C I will time you for 15 seconds. Try to keep your strikes going for the whole time.

Traveling Slowly While Striking a Ball—Hockey

Setting: A hockey stick and a foam or plastic ball or puck for each child

Tasks/Challenges:

T This time instead of staying in your own space, you are going to travel using all the space. Begin

Batting tees let children at precontrol and control skill levels practice independently.

by walking throughout general space tapping the ball like you did in self-space. The ball must always be very close to your stick.

T This time as you are walking try to avoid running into others. This means you will have to keep the ball very close.

Striking Off a Batting Tee—Bats

Setting: Preferably outside in a large open space; for at least every two children (but preferably for every child) a box containing five plastic balls or beach balls, a bat, and a batting tee (Figure 28.2)

Tasks/Challenges:

T This time, you're going to hit a big ball off a tee with a plastic bat. Stand to the side of the tee so you are batting to the field. Now, line up facing the same way, so you won't hit one another. Hit all the balls in your box, and then wait until I give the signal before collecting them. Remember: Hit hard.

C Practice hitting until you can hit the ball three times in a row.

T Now see how far you can hit the ball.

Batting tees are helpful for children at the precontrol level who are unable to strike a moving ball and for children at the control level who are practicing ball placement.

Control Level: Learning Experiences Leading to Skill Development

At the control level, children begin to develop mature striking patterns that are used in increasingly complex contexts. Traveling while striking or tapping an object along the ground is combined with one or two variables, such as changing direction and/or speed. The children also practice striking a pitched ball and striking a golf ball for distance.

A note about cues: Although several cues are listed for many of the learning experiences, it's important to focus on only one cue at a time. That way, the children can really concentrate on that cue. Once you provide feedback to the children and observe that most have learned a cue, then it's time to focus on another one.

Striking a Stationary Ball on the Ground—Golf and Hockey

Setting: Preferably a large outdoor space (but can be adapted for an indoor space); a golf club or plastic field hockey stick (short-handled or long-handled street hockey sticks aren't appropriate) and a plastic or foam ball for each child; each child in self-space, facing a wall or an object that will block the ball; at least 5 feet between children

Cues	
Arms Way Back	(With both hands on the stick, bring your arms way back as you swing.)
Watch the Ball	(Keep your eyes on the ball all the time.)
Opposite Foot	(Step forward on your opposite foot as you hit.)

Tasks/Challenges:

🅣 When we explored striking with hockey sticks, you practiced hitting the ball to the wall by standing beside it and behind it and having it travel on the ground. Using a golf grip *(Figure 28.3)*, practice striking the ball, standing beside it, so that it travels to the wall.

🅣 As you practice, bring your backswing way back over your shoulders like a golfer. Follow through so that your arms end above your other shoulder—a full swing.

🅣 Practice the same swing, but use a hockey grip *(Figure 28.4)* and start the backswing below your waist and end below your waist. **An easy way to help it**

end below your waist is to turn your wrists over on the follow-through.

🅣 Using both swings—full and short—strike the ball to the wall with enough force so that it comes back to you. Which swing sends the ball harder?

🅣 Practice standing behind the ball and hitting.

Modified equipment allows for golf swings to be practiced indoors.

Figure 28.3 Golf club grip.

Figure 28.4 Hockey stick grip.

🅣 From that position try to strike the ball with enough force so that it rebounds back to you off the wall.

🅒 Practice striking the ball against the wall until you can hit the wall three times in a row from each starting position.

🅣 Stand behind the ball. In this position, most of you have been hitting the ball from the preferred side of your body. That is called your *forehand*. This time we are going to practice hitting the ball from the non-preferred side of your body. You don't change your hands; instead you use the back side of the stick to do it. Try to hit the ball to the wall this way.

🅣 Practice hitting the ball hard enough so that it rebounds back to you.

🅒 Again try for three hits in a row that are hard enough so that the ball comes back to you.

Which Swing?

The underhand swings that are used in hockey and golf situations can be confusing. There is the side-to-the-target swing characteristic of golf strokes and hockey passes that are intended to make the struck object travel a long distance. This is the swing illustrated in Box 28-2. The only real difference in this swing between hockey-type situations and golf is the length of the backswing and the follow-through. (In interactive settings—games like hockey, broomball, and Pilo Polo—it is unsafe for the swing to come above the waist on either the backswing or the follow-through.) Also, to complicate matters, in hockey-type situations there is also an underhand striking pattern that requires the passer to face the target. This striking action is used for most short (10 yards or less) passing situations using both a forehand and a backhand action.

Given the space restrictions of physical education classes, especially when they are taught inside, it is this underhand

swing that is most frequently used. Thus, at the precontrol and control levels, we have children practice swings from both the side and the back. Other than the starting position in relation to the ball, the swings have the same critical cues. As children learn to use each swing, they will naturally select the one that fits the situation.

Striking for Distance—Golf and Hockey

Setting: Markers of various colors (to be used for measuring) or zones at various distances from where the children are hitting; a plastic striking implement and five or six foam, plastic, or whiffle balls for each child; children positioned in a circle in the center of a field or playground, facing out

Cues	
Arms Way Back	(Bring your arms way back as you swing.)
Watch the Ball	(Keep your eyes on the ball all the time.)
Behind the Ball	(Contact directly behind the ball to make it travel on the ground or low.)
Under the Ball	(Contact the ball below its center so it will travel upward through the air.)

Tasks/Challenges:

🅣 Stand facing the outside of the circle, making sure there is enough space between you and the people next to you so that you can all swing your sticks without hitting one another. First, we are going to practice striking along the ground and in the air. There's enough room to strike as hard as you like. Practice your first strikes from behind the ball so the ball travels along the ground. Use your forehand strike and hockey grip. After you hit all the balls, wait for the signal, then go get yours and quickly bring them back to your starting place for the next hits.

🅣 This time try your backhand strike—along the ground. Does the ball travel as far with your backhand?

🅣 Move beside the ball. Hit the ball as far as you can with a golf grip.

🔑 Which starting position sends the ball farther? In "face-the-target" position, which sends it farther—forehand or backhand?

T This time we are going to stand beside the ball. Practice hitting the ball so that it travels through the air.

C Practice striking both on the ground and through the air. Before each strike call out loud "air" or "ground." Challenge yourself to be able to do the strike you called out.

✿ What is the key for sending the ball through the air? On the ground?

T Now see with each of your strikes if you can hit the ball farther each time. The markers on the field will help you remember how far you hit the ball each time. Each time, see if you can hit the ball a little farther than the last time. Practice air and ground strikes—all from the side.

C Can you hit the ball so that it lands in the same zone three times?

Striking in the Air—Golf

Setting: A striking implement (plastic golf club, broomball stick) and foam balls for striking placed about 10 feet from the wall; marks on the wall about 3 feet off the floor

Cues	
Arms Way Back	(Bring your arms way back as you swing.)
Watch the Ball	(Keep your eyes on the ball all the time.)
Under the Ball	(Contact the ball below its center so it will travel upward through the air.)

Tasks/Challenges:

T When we explored different ways to strike, you tried to make the ball go in the air. From a position beside the ball, with your shoulder to the wall, try to do that now. Practice striking the ball so that it travels in the air to the wall.

T Practice striking the ball so that it travels through the air and hits the wall above the mark.

C Try to send the ball in the air so that it hits above the mark three times in a row.

Striking to Varying Distances—Golf

Setting: Preferably a large outdoor space; a golf club and a bucket of plastic balls for each child; all children facing the same direction, with at least 6 feet between them; the field marked at various intervals

Children are challenged to see how far they can hit the ball.

Cues	
Full Swing	(Use a full swing—big backswing, follow-through above shoulders.)
Bend Knees	(Bend your knees throughout the whole swing.)
Watch the Ball	(Keep your eyes on the ball.)

Tasks/Challenges:

T Use the golf grip *(Figure 28.3)*. You're going to be practicing a golf swing—or a full swing—by yourself in a place that is facing away from everyone else. This is like the shortened swings that you have been using with the hockey sticks, except now you'll have a full backswing and follow-through. Let's practice first without the ball. **Stand to the side of the make-believe ball, side to the target (field), and take a full backswing, bend your knees, swing, and follow through.** Practice five times on your own.

T With your golf club, practice hitting the ball on your own.

T Practice hitting the ball as far as you can.

T There are markers on the field to help you judge the length of your hits. Hit on ball, and then try to hit the next ball farther. Try to find your maximum distance.

Striking to Targets—Hockey

Setting: Plastic hockey stick or other implement and a foam or plastic ball for each child; in front of each child, a target on the floor next to the wall marked with cones or spots about 4 feet apart and tape marks on the floor in front of each target at about 6 feet, 10 feet, and 12 feet

Cues	
Step	(Step forward on the opposite [front] foot.)
Watch the Ball	(Keep your eyes on the ball until it leaves your stick.)
Follow Through	(Follow through toward the target with your stick.)

There is much concern over the use of hockey sticks and the teaching of related skills in the elementary school. With the increased popularity of street and ice hockey, hockey sticks are being raised above the shoulders on both the backswing and the follow-through. Because elementary school physical education classes are usually crowded, raised hockey sticks can cause injuries. We've successfully reduced the chance of such injuries by not letting youngsters raise their hockey sticks higher than their waists on *any* stroke. This restriction doesn't significantly alter the striking action; in fact, it encourages the correct field hockey striking action while providing a much safer environment for learning skills involving striking with hockey sticks.

Tasks/Challenges:

🅣 Starting from behind the ball at the closest mark, try to strike the ball so it goes between the two cones.

🅣 Practice sending the ball between the cones from your forehand and backhand sides.

🅒 Practice striking until you can hit the ball between the cones five times from each side. Remember to stop the ball each time it comes back to you before hitting it again.

🅣 When you can hit the target five times in a row without missing from the closest mark, move back to the next mark. When you can hit the target from that spot five times without missing, move back again. If you hit the target four times and then miss, start your counting over. Practice from both the forehand and backhand sides.

🅣 Now start back at your closest spot and strike to the target from a starting position standing beside your ball.

🅐 With this task, make sure that students are spread well apart, that they stop the ball completely on its return, and that they move in front of others only when no one is striking.

Striking to a Target (Around the World)—Hockey

Setting: Targets, with five tape marks in a semicircle on the floor in front of each; three or fewer students per target; a hockey stick or other striking implement and ball or puck for each child (*Note:* This task is also appropriate as one of a series of stations.)

Cues	
Watch the Ball	(Keep your eyes on the ball until it leaves your stick.)
Step	(Step forward on the opposite [front] foot.)
Follow Through	(Follow through toward the target with your stick.)

Tasks/Challenges:

🅣 This time the striking is going to be a game. Have you ever played Around the World in basketball? This game is going to be Around the World in striking. As you see, there are five tape marks on the floor in front of you. You must hit the ball to the target from each tape mark. Strike from behind the ball. You can start on either side.

🅣 When you make it through once, go back and hit from each mark using the backhand strike.

🅣 Start over, striking from beside the ball.

✔️ *Teacher Observation.* This task lends itself easily to a teacher observation of the critical cues of striking with hockey sticks: Watch the Ball, Step, and Follow Through. *See Chapter 14 for the development of a teacher observation checklist.*

Striking to a Stationary Partner—Hockey

Setting: Partners about 6 to 7 feet apart, each with a hockey stick; one ball or puck per group

Cues	
Sending	Watch the Ball (Keep your eyes on the ball at all times.)
	Step (Step forward on the opposite foot.)

Follow Through (Follow through toward your partner with your stick.)

Receiving Give (Relax your grip and move your stick back a little just as the ball hits your stick, to absorb the force.)

Watch the Ball (Keep your eyes on the ball all the time.)

Tasks/Challenges:

T Strike the ball (puck) back and forth to your partner. Hit straight to your partner so that she or he doesn't have to move. You hit the ball to your partner; your partner stops the ball completely still and then hits it back. Remember to strike easily so that your partner is able to stop the ball.

T Before you worked with a partner, you practiced hitting the ball (puck) to different places. Now you're going to do that with your partner, and your partner is going to be a target for you to aim at. The partner who is to receive the ball will put his or her hockey stick out in one place and hold it still; the partner hitting the ball will use the stick as a target and try to hit it without the receiving partner's having to move the stick. Change roles each time.

C With your partner, see how many times you can hit the ball (puck) back and forth without a miss. Remember, you must stop the ball before you return it to your partner. If you miss, just start counting all over. If you get to 10, let me know.

T After you hit the ball (puck) successfully to your partner 10 times and your partner is able to stop the ball, move back two steps each and start again. When you're successful 10 times in a row, move back again.

T This will make it a little harder: Move back to your close position. After you pass the ball this time, move to a new space and stand still. The receiver must control the ball (puck), look to see where you are, and then pass. Each time after someone passes, move to a new space, stop, and then receive the ball.

C Now see how many times you can keep this up without missing.

In my career I must have seen at least 26 ways children can curve the blades of hockey sticks. Having the children keep the blade straight ensures two things: (1) The puck (ball) has a greater chance of staying on the floor, and (2) your hockey sticks last a lot longer.

Traveling Slowly While Striking a Ball—Hockey

Setting: A hockey stick and a tennis ball or puck for each child

For children at the control level, traveling while manipulating a ball with a long-handled implement takes practice.

Cues

Light Taps	(Use light taps to keep the ball close to your stick.)
Hands Apart	(Move your hands 8 to 10 inches apart to control the ball better.)
Ball in Front	(Keep the ball slightly in front of your body on the same side on which you are dribbling.)

Tasks/Challenges:

T Before, we practiced moving around the entire space while striking a ball with the hockey stick. Let's practice again—this is called dribbling or stick-handling. To begin, go slowly. Your task is to travel around the entire space while striking the ball and not touching anyone else.

T This time as you move around the room, I'm going to hold up different numbers of fingers. Tell me how many fingers I'm holding up. You'll have to look often, because I'll change the number of fingers often and try to trick you.

© You have 50 points. Your task is to keep all your points. Move around the room dribbling the ball. Every time you lose the ball, subtract 5 points. See how many points you have at the stop signal.

Traveling, Stopping, and Controlling the Ball—Hockey

Setting: A plastic hockey stick and a ball for each child

Cues	
Give	(Relax your grip and bring your stick back a little to absorb the force when trying to stop the ball.) *A demonstration is helpful here.*
Light Taps	(Use light taps to keep the ball close to your stick.)
Hands Apart	(Move your hands 8 to 10 inches apart to control the ball better.)

Tasks/Challenges:

T Before, you practiced traveling around the room keeping the ball close to you. This time you're going to do the same thing, but with something added. Whenever you hear the signal, stop the ball, using only your stick, and wait for the signal to go again.

Traveling, stopping, and controlling an object with a hockey stick takes an acute awareness of others.

T This time try going a little faster and doing the same thing. Move around the space, striking the ball with your hockey stick. On the signal, stop the ball and wait for the "go" signal. I'll know you can really do this if I always see the ball close to the stick and all the balls stopped on the signal, without your having to chase them all over the room.

T Now I am going to change the task a little. Again, you should move around the entire space striking the ball. But this time on the signal, instead of stopping the ball, stand still and keep moving the ball in your self-space until you hear the signal to travel again. This is called controlling the ball. You'll know you're really good at this when, as soon as you hear the whistle, you can stop and start moving the ball in your self-space without first having to chase the ball across the room.

© This time, the stopping will be like a game. When I say "stop," I'll start counting backward from 10. When all the balls have stopped, I'll stop counting. Your goal is to get me to stop counting before I get to zero.

T You're going to play a little game with the stopping this time. Every time you come near another person, stop or control the ball and then start again. It's as if you don't want anyone to come near your ball, so you are going to protect it—and the only way you can protect it is by controlling it in your self-space or stopping it.

✸ Why should you control the ball or puck before you send it back? What do you have to do to control it?

Traveling and Changing Speeds—Hockey

Setting: A striking implement and a ball or puck for each child

Cues	
Light Taps	(Use light taps to keep the ball close to your stick.)
Hands Apart	(Move your hands 8 to 10 inches apart to control the ball better.)
Ball in Front	(Keep the ball slightly in front of your body on the same side on which you are dribbling.)

Tasks/Challenges:

T One of the important things in games that use dribbling or stick-handling is the ability to change the speed at which you are traveling while you dribble. Travel in general space, and change your speed as you go. It should be easy for me to tell which speed you are using.

🅣 This time I will call out speeds as you travel. See if you can match every speed I call out.

🅣 Now you will practice using different speeds with a partner. It is like follow the leader. You will follow a partner, dribbling in general space. The first partner starts and travels, changing the speed of the travel often. The second partner follows, always trying to travel at the same speed as the first partner. On the signal, switch places.

Traveling and Striking While Changing Pathways—Hockey

Setting: A hockey stick and ball or puck for each child; various pathways (the more, the better) taped or marked on the floor

Cues	
Light Taps	(Use light taps to keep the ball close to your stick.)
Hands Apart	(Move your hands 8 to 10 inches apart to control the ball better.)
Ball in Front	(Keep the ball slightly in front of your body on the same side on which you are dribbling.)

Tasks/Challenges:

🅣 You're going to practice something new this time: changes in pathways. Do you remember pathways: straight, curved, and zigzag? Again, you're going to move around the entire space, but whenever you come to a pathway on the floor, try to follow it exactly. Once you finish one pathway, travel to another and follow it. As you follow the pathways, be sure you're striking the ball, not pushing it along.

🅣 Something very different happens when you follow a zigzag pathway. What is it? That's right— you have to move your stick from one side of the ball to the other, like moving the ball in self-space to keep control of it. Practice zigzag pathways on your own. **Remember, every time you come to a zig or a zag, you have to move your stick to the other side of the ball.**

🅣 This time we are going to practice striking while traveling in different pathways with a partner. You're going to play follow the leader. The leader travels in different pathways—curved, straight, and zigzag—as the follower tries to stay close behind,

copying the exact pathways the leader makes. Leaders: As you begin, make easy pathways. The object is not to lose your partner but to practice striking while traveling in different pathways. On the signal, change positions as leaders and followers.

🅣 This time, the following is going to be a little harder. Instead of staying right behind the leader, the follower is going to watch while the leader moves in a short pathway sequence. When the leader stops and freezes, the follower moves, copying the pathway of the leader until she or he catches up with the leader. When the follower catches up, the leader takes off again. This is a bit like a game of cat and mouse: Just as soon as you think you've caught someone, the person slips away again. As you move, remember that the purpose of this task is to practice different pathways, so include them in your movements. After five turns as a leader, switch places.

🅒 This is the real pathway test. By yourself, make up a sequence of traveling and striking that involves four changes of pathways. Practice your sequence until you can do it from memory three times without stopping. Each time the sequence should look the same. Then we'll all share the sequences.

Striking to Different Places—Hockey

Setting: A hockey stick, a ball, and three targets (plastic milk bottles, two-liter soda bottles, or tennis ball cans) placed against a wall or fence for each child

Cues	
Face Target	(Always face your upper body to the target.)
Step	(Step forward on the opposite foot toward the target.)
Follow Through	(Follow through with your stick toward the target.)

Tasks/Challenges:

🅣 This time you'll practice striking from the same place each time, but trying to hit one of three different targets. Take a minute and practice striking at the three targets in front of you.

🅒 This time, you're going to see how many points you can score in 2 minutes. You get one point if you hit a target and three points if you hit the particular target you call out ahead of time.

✓ *Student Display.* Have students either draw or collect pictures of people striking to different targets that indicate the use of the cues of facing the target, stepping into the hit, and following through. The pictures could then be displayed on a bulletin board to indicate the diverse targets that exist and how the cues are the same.

Striking While Dodging Stationary Obstacles—Hockey

Setting: An obstacle course of cones and hoops or other equipment; a hockey stick and a ball for each child

Cues	
Light Taps	(Use light taps to keep the ball close to your stick.)
Both Sides of Stick	(Use both sides of the stick to dribble around the obstacle.)
Look Up	(Look up as you travel so you can see the obstacles.)

Tasks/Challenges:

T You've traveled while dodging objects. This time, you're going to travel and dodge objects while striking a ball with a hockey stick. Your task is to travel throughout the space, striking the ball with the hockey stick. Try not to let the ball get away from you. Don't touch any of the obstacles or other people. Freeze on the signal, and have the ball with you.

T As practice for looking up, we're going to play the counting game again. I'll keep holding up a different number of fingers, and you tell me how many I'm holding up while you're striking the ball around the space.

T Dribble or stick-handle in general space. Each time you come to an obstacle, control the ball, execute a quarter turn to the right or left, and continue dribbling.

T You've all been going at fairly slow speeds. This isn't always good in game situations, so you're going to practice going at different speeds. Sometimes approach an obstacle very quickly, sometimes slowly. Make the change clear. The rules are still the same: No touching, and you must be able to stop on the signal and have the ball with you.

T Dribble in general space. As you near an obstacle, use both sides of your stick to dribble past the obstacle, then quickly continue regular dribbling. Sometimes go to the right and sometimes to the left.

C What you have just learned are called dodges. This time as you practice dodging, pretend you have

100 points. If the ball you are dribbling touches a cone, subtract 10 points from your score. If you have a collision with another person, subtract 25 points. Try to complete your practice with 100 points!

Striking a Stationary Ball—Bats

Setting: Preferably a large, open, outdoor space, one big enough for every child to hit against a backstop or a wall; children about 15 feet from the backstop or wall with sufficient space to swing freely without hitting others (or place a line on the ground about 15 feet from the batting positions for children to hit over); a box of about five balls (large, light plastic or beach balls, and whiffle balls), bats, and batting tees for each child or pair of children

Cues	
Side to the Field	(Turn your side to the target or field.)
Bat Back	(Bring the bat way back over your shoulder so that it sticks up like a toothpick.)
Watch the Ball	(Keep your eyes on the ball all the time.)
Level	(Extend your arms to swing flat as a pancake.)
Rotate and Shift	(Roll over the shoelaces of your back foot.)

A New Cue

The idea of shifting weight forward on a batting swing has long been accepted. Recently an accomplished softball coach told us a new (and probably more effective) cue for this. Instead of telling children to step forward or shift their weight, tell them, "Picture a shoe with the laces tied, facing upward as usual. As the hips rotate and the weight shifts during the swing, the back foot should roll so that the laces almost face the ground." This not only forces the rotation of the hips, but automatically causes the weight shift.

Tasks/Challenges:

T When we explored striking, you practiced hitting a ball off a tee. We're going to practice that again. Stand about a bat's length away and to the side of your batting tee. **Take a batting grip** *(Figure 28.5);* **bring your bat back over your shoulder so that it sticks up like a toothpick, extend your arms all the way so you have a level swing, shift your**

weight forward and rotate your hips and hit. Let's practice five times without hitting the ball. Just swing and say the cues out loud.

T Now practice striking off the tee. Use a plastic ball or a beach ball. **If you are batting the ball correctly, your swing will follow through over your other shoulder.**

T Practice until you can hit the plastic ball 10 times in a row off the tee.

T When you can hit the plastic ball 10 times in a row, trade it in for a whiffle ball. Now practice with that ball.

T Hit the ball so hard that it goes in the air to the wall *(over the line)*.

C Practice hitting with the bat until you can hit five times in a row so the ball hits the wall *(lands over the line)*.

Increasing the size of the ball reduces the complexity of the task. Increasing the size of the bat does the same thing. Some teachers also use soap bubbles for children to practice

striking. One partner blows bubbles; the other gets to swing away trying to pop them as they fall. It works!

 What is the most important cue for making contact with the ball? What is one hint that will help you do this?

Level Swings—Bats

Setting: Ropes suspended from the ceiling or a line hung across the room to about children's shoulder height (Figure 28.6); batting tees and bats for each child

Cues	
Side to the Field	(Turn your side to the target or field.)
Bat Back	(Bring the bat way back over your shoulder so your back elbow is level with your shoulder.)
Watch the Ball	(Keep your eyes on the ball all the time.)
Level	(Extend your arms to swing flat as a pancake.)
Rotate and Shift	(Roll over the shoelaces of your back foot.)

Tasks/Challenges:

T Place your batting tee directly under your rope. The tee should come up to your knees. The area between the end of the rope and the top of your tee is your strike zone. Step up to the tee and swing. There is no ball for this task. Your swing should go through the strike zone without touching the rope or the tee.

T Practice until you can get three strikes in a row through the strike zone without touching the rope or the tee.

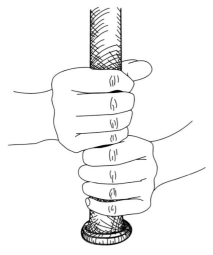

Figure 28.5 Batting grip.

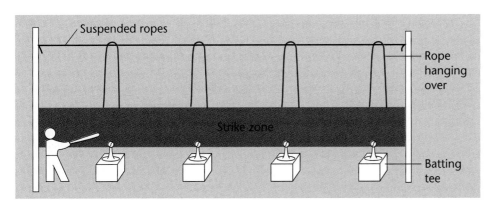

Figure 28.6 Setup for level swings.

T Now both raise the tee and lower the rope 1 inch. Take swings through this strike zone. Again, practice until you can get three. Then make the strike zone smaller again.

√ *Teacher Observation.* At this point it is appropriate to conduct a teacher observation of the use of the critical cues for batting before proceeding to a more complex use of the skill.

Striking a Stationary Ball for Distance—Bats

Setting: Partners, each pair with a batting tee, three whiffle balls, and a bat; batters in a circle in the middle of the playground facing out (Figure 28.7); fielders about 30 feet (or whatever is appropriate) in front of their partner; marker cones or zones at 10-foot intervals around the center circle

Cues	
Watch the Ball	(Keep your eyes on the ball all the time.)
Bat Back	(Bring the bat way back over your shoulder so your back elbow is level with your shoulder.)

Side to the Field	(Turn your side to the target or field.)
Level	(Extend your arms to swing flat as a pancake.)
Rotate and Shift	(Roll over the shoelaces of your back foot.)

Tasks/Challenges:

T Stand inside the circle about a bat's length away from your tee with your side to the field. You are going to practice batting the ball in the air. There's enough room to hit as hard as you like. Your partner will collect the balls. After three hits, trade places. Remember to watch the ball.

T This time have your partner stand where your ball landed. Try to hit the next ball farther. The partner moves to that spot. Try again to hit farther than the previous hit. After three hits, trade places with your partner.

T Bat the ball as far as possible. Take note of the zone in which the ball first lands. Bat three times, each time trying to improve your distance. Trade places.

C Try to bat the ball so that it lands in the same zone three times.

Figure 28.7 Setup for striking a stationary ball for distance.

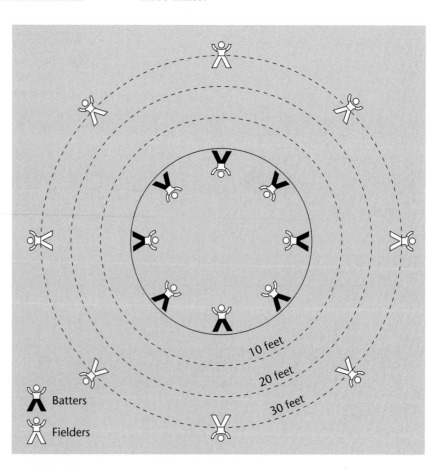

10 feet

20 feet

30 feet

∧ Batters

∧ Fielders

Striking Suspended Objects—Bats

Setting: Whiffle balls suspended about waist height from strings (see Figure 27.2) around the practice area; a bat for each child

Cues	
Side to the Field	(Turn your side to the target or field.)
Bat Back	(Bring the bat way back over your shoulder so that it sticks up like a toothpick.)
Watch the Ball	(Keep your eyes on the ball all the time.)
Level	(Extend your arms to swing flat as a pancake.)
Rotate and Shift	(Roll over the shoelaces of your back foot.)

How does rolling over your shoelaces help you bat?

Tasks/Challenges:

This task is a little harder than the last one. Instead of hitting balls that don't move from batting tees, you're going to hit balls that are hanging from

Balls suspended on strings give youngsters the opportunity to practice swinging level.

strings. Stand to the side of the ball about a bat's length away. Practice hitting the ball. Remember to stop the ball still before you hit it again.

Practice batting until you can hit five balls in a row without missing.

Now the game changes a little. See how many times you can strike the ball in a row without missing.

Hitting a Stationary Ball from Different Places—Bats

Setting: A batting tee, ball, and bat for each child or pair of children; place the tee so that the balls are batted into a fence or wall, or have the partner field balls; mark a home plate in the batting area

Cues	
Bat Back	(Bring the bat way back over your shoulder so that it sticks up like a toothpick.)
Watch the Ball	(Keep your eyes on the ball all the time.)
Side to the Field	(Turn your side to the target or field.)
Level	(Extend your arms to swing flat as a pancake.)
Rotate and Shift	(Roll over the shoelaces of your back foot.)

Tasks/Challenges:

Place the batting tee so the ball is on the inside corner of home plate at your knees. Hit five balls as hard as you can from this position. Switch places.

Move the tee to the inside corner with the ball chest high. Make five hits as hard as you can. Switch.

Move the tee to the outside corner, knee high. Go again.

Now try the outside corner, chest high. Five and switch.

Hit and Run—Bats

Setting: Partners; ball, bat, batting tee, and carpet square set up as in Figure 28.8

Cues	
Bat Back	(Bring the bat way back over your shoulder so that it sticks up like a toothpick.)

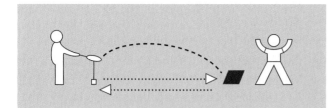

Figure 28.8 Setup for Hit and Run.
Source: On the Move, by S. Holt/Hale, 2003, New York: McGraw-Hill.

Watch the Ball	(Keep your eyes on the ball all the time.)
Side to the Field	(Turn your side to the target or field.)
Level	(Extend your arms to swing flat as a pancake.)
Rotate and Shift	(Roll over the shoelaces of your back foot.)

Tasks/Challenges:

T Partner A stands at the batting tee; partner B, on the carpet square about 15 feet away. Partner A strikes the ball off the tee, hitting it as far as possible. Then partner A runs to the carpet square and back to the batting tee. Partner B collects the ball and runs and replaces it on the tee. Switch places after each hit. Be careful: Both of you are running.

Throwing a Ball in the Air and Striking It—Bats

Setting: Preferably a large outdoor space, where children can bat against a wall or fence; large round targets on the wall; a plastic bat and a ball for each child

For this task and beginning tasks that involve hitting a pitched ball, sock balls work quite well. They won't travel too far, allowing children to focus on the swing. To make a sock ball, stuff an old sock with other socks and tie off. Cut off the tail.

Cues	
Bat Back	(Bring the bat way back over your shoulder so that it sticks up like a toothpick.)
Watch the Ball	(Keep your eyes on the ball all the time.)
Side to the Field	(Turn your side to the target or field.)

Level	(Extend your arms to swing flat as a pancake.)
Rotate and Shift	(Roll over the shoelaces of your back foot.)

Tasks/Challenges:

T You're going to practice hitting a ball you throw into the air yourself. In your own space facing the wall (fence) and about 10 feet from it, toss a ball up into the air and then hit it with the bat. You must have both your hands on the bat when you hit the ball, so you'll have to work quickly. *(Demonstrate.)*

T Practice now, trying to hit the large circle on the wall.

C Score five points for every ball that hits the target; three points for every ball that hits the wall, but misses the target; and one point for every ball you hit that doesn't hit the wall. Try to get to 21 points.

Striking a Self-Tossed Ball to Different Distances—Bats

Setting: Lines marked on a field for distance measurement; a number of whiffle (or tennis) balls and a plastic bat for each child

Cues	
Bat Back	(Bring the bat way back over your shoulder so that it sticks up like a toothpick.)
Watch the Ball	(Keep your eyes on the ball all the time.)
Side to the Field	(Turn your side to the target or field.)
Level	(Extend your arms to swing flat as a pancake.)
Rotate and Shift	(Roll over the shoelaces of your back foot.)

Tasks/Challenges:

T Now we're going to add something that you worked on before: striking to different distances. This involves using different amounts of force to hit the ball. There are a lot of lines on the field; you can use them to judge how far you hit the ball. Each time you hit a ball, see how far you can make it go. If you hit it over one line one time, try to hit it over the next line the next time you hit.

C Pick out a line you know you can hit the ball past. Try to hit the ball past that line five times in a row. After you've practiced at one line, pick another line and try again.

Striking a Pitched Ball—Bats

Setting: A large outdoor space, marked as follows: a pitcher's square and a batting box for each group of two, each batter's box marked with "neat feet" in the correct batting position (Figure 28.9); a skilled thrower (older student, classroom teacher, parent, or grandparent) as a partner for each child; one plastic or sock ball and a bat for each pair

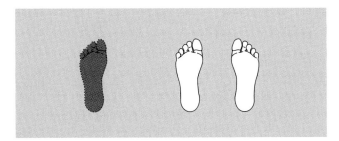

Figure 28.9 "Neat feet" for a right-handed striking action. You can easily make "neat feet" by painting them in the correct position on a rubber mat. Challenge the children to move the left foot to the position of the dotted foot as they swing.

This youngster has clearly rotated his hips forward by "rolling over his back shoelaces."

Cues	
Bat Back	(Bring the bat way back over your shoulder so that it sticks up like a toothpick.)
Watch the Ball	(Keep your eyes on the ball all the time.)
Side to the Field	(Turn your side to the target or field.)
Level	(Extend your arms to swing flat as a pancake.)
Rotate and Shift	(Roll over the shoelaces of your back foot.)

Tasks/Challenges:

T Before, you hit a ball off a batting tee or from a self-toss. This time you're going to practice batting a ball that's pitched by a "big" partner. Your big partner will be the pitcher, and you will get to bat all the time. Your partner stands on the pitcher's square and pitches the ball to you. You stand on the batter's square and try to hit the ball. The batter's square has a secret help in it: pictures of feet that show you exactly where to stand so you have the best chance of hitting the ball. Just try to hit the ball; it doesn't have to go far.

T Each time you bat, your big partner will give you a thumbs-up if you do everything correctly. If you miss a cue, he or she will tell you so you can use it for the next swing. *Note to teachers: Pitches from skilled throwers enhance the learning of batting skills.*

C Try to hit five balls in a row.

√ ***Homework.*** The same task of striking pitched balls could be done as a homework assignment. The assignment could be in the form of a task card that includes the cues and asks a parent, grandparent, or older brother or sister to pitch 20 balls to the child. The parent would check on every fifth throw whether the cues were used.

Utilization Level: Learning Experiences Leading to Skill Development

At the utilization level, we give the children situations in which they learn to consistently strike objects with long-handled implements. Many contexts involve more than one variable in an unpredictable or changing environment.

A note about cues: Although several cues are listed for many of the learning experiences, it's important to focus on only one cue at a time. That way, the children can really concentrate on that cue. Once you provide feedback to the children and observe that most have learned a cue, then it's time to focus on another one.

Striking to Targets at Various Distances—Golf

Setting: Targets of various sizes at different distances apart; a plastic golf club and a bucket of balls for each child

Unless "regular" golf clubs are available, children will need to use the following cues to vary the distance the ball travels. With regular clubs, they would change clubs, and the Under the Ball cue would not be applicable.

Cues	
Under the Ball	(Hit under the ball to make it travel a short distance.)
Behind the Ball	(Hit behind the ball to make it travel a long distance.)
Full Swing	(Use a swing with a big backswing and follow-through.)

Tasks/Challenges:

T This task is like target practice. There are a lot of targets set up on the field, and you have a number of balls. See if you can hit the targets from where you're standing. After you hit all the balls, wait until the signal before collecting them.

C Now see how many times in a row you can hit the target for which you are trying.

Playing Hoop Golf—Golf

Setting: Hoops and other targets of various sizes placed around a field at various distances apart; a plastic golf club and a ball for each child

Cues	
Under the Ball	(Hit under the ball to make it travel a short distance.)
Behind the Ball	(Hit behind the ball to make it travel a long distance.)
Full Swing	(Use a swing with a big backswing and follow-through.)

Tasks/Challenges:

T This is like a golf course, but there's no order to it. Strike the ball from hoop to hoop, using as few strokes as possible. You may want to go back and

do the same hoop over again, to see if you can make it in fewer strokes. Be careful not to get in anyone's way.

Directing the Air Pathway of the Struck Object—Golf

Setting: A plastic golf club and ball for each child; a space with obstacles (blocks and canes, cones, boxes, cones on top of boxes) of varying heights; carpet squares mark the starting point

Cues	
Under the Ball	(Hit under the ball to make it travel over the obstacle.)
Short Swing	(Use a swing with a short backswing and follow-through.)

Tasks/Challenges:

T When I say "Go," find an obstacle at which to practice. Two of you may be at one obstacle. Your task at the obstacle is to see if you can gently lift the ball off the ground with the golf club so it travels in the air over the obstacle. You may want to start at some of the lower obstacles and then move on to the higher ones. You can change obstacles whenever you like, but there can never be more than two people at an obstacle.

Playing Hockey Bowl (Small Targets)—Hockey

Setting: Pins (two-liter soft drink bottles or lightweight plastic bowling pins), a ball, and a hockey stick for every two children; a marked lane leading away from the pins, as for a bowling alley

Cues	
Eyes on Target	(Watch the target at all times.)
Step	(Step forward on the opposite foot.)
Follow Through	(Follow through toward the target with your stick.)

Tasks/Challenges:

C This game is called Hockey Bowl. Your task is to strike the ball from behind the line and see how many pins you can knock down. After three hits, or when all the pins have been knocked down (whichever happens first), trade places.

T The first time you can knock down all the pins three times in a row, move back three steps and try it again. If you still want to make the task harder, take away some of the pins so you have a smaller target.

Dribbling and Changing Directions Backward—Hockey

Setting: Children scattered throughout general space, each with a hockey stick and ball

Cues	
Light Taps	(Use light taps to keep the ball close to your stick.)
Back of Stick	(Use the back side of the stick to bring the ball backward.)
Pull Back	(Quickly pull the ball toward you.)

Tasks/Challenges:

T Travel in general space, dribbling the ball 2 to 3 feet in front of you as you go. **When you are comfortable with your control of the dribble, dribble the ball ahead of you; quickly put your stick in front of the ball; tap the ball lightly with the back of your stick, pulling it toward you; quickly turn; and continue the dribble.**

⚠ As hard as we try, somehow, at some time, hockey sticks and balls/pucks seem to get raised higher than they should, especially in dynamic situations. In fact, the most serious accident I've ever had while teaching involved a hockey stick and an eye. Therefore, we advocate the wearing of eye guards, especially in dynamic hockey situations.

Performing a Continuous Dribble and Change of Direction—Hockey

Setting: Children scattered throughout general space, each with a hockey stick and ball

Cues	
Light Taps	(Use light taps to keep the ball close to your stick.)
Both Sides of Stick	(Use both sides of the stick to dribble when you go around an obstacle.)
Heads Up	(Look up to avoid collisions.)

Tasks/Challenges:

T You learned to change the direction of the ball by dribbling it to your right and left with both sides of the stick. You have just learned one method

of changing direction from front to back. Travel within the space, using changes of direction to avoid collisions with others. Your task is continuous dribbling.

T Approach a line quickly; use the "pull back" with the stick to change the direction of the dribble at the last moment, to keep from crossing the line.

T Purposely approach others in the class; use a move to the right or left to avoid contact with each person.

T Gradually increase the speed of your travel to determine the maximum rate you can travel with a controlled dribble and frequent changes of direction.

Pathways, Speeds, and Directions—Hockey

Setting: A hockey stick and ball for each child

A while ago I was at a party where the hosts set up a croquet game. Adults and children alike were intrigued, and bingo, I realized: This is a striking game. Do you remember it? Croquet is a fun activity to add to physical education class as a special treat and ties together the ideas of striking at targets and varying force and distance really well. No croquet sets, you say? You'll be amazed how many families have croquet sets at home that they're willing to let you use (or sometimes even give to you). I just acquired an antique croquet set that was on its way to Goodwill. Give croquet a try sometime!

Cues	
Light Taps	(Use light taps to keep the ball close to your stick.)
Both Sides of Stick	(Use both sides of the stick to dribble when you go around an obstacle.)
Heads Up	(Look up to avoid collisions.)

Tasks/Challenges:

C This is a self-testing task. The task sheet *(Figure 28.10)* lets you assess your traveling and striking in different directions, pathways, and speeds. Practice the tasks one by one. When you think you can do a task well, have a partner watch you. If your partner thinks you did the task successfully, the partner signs the sheet. I'll check to see how you're progressing.

✓ *Peer Observation.* The preceding challenge is a wonderful peer-observation assessment. With the

Figure 28.10 Task sheet for striking.

Name _____ Class _____

Task Sheet for Striking

Verification	Task
	I can strike a ball with a hockey stick in a straight pathway, keeping the ball close to the stick.
	I can strike a ball with a hockey stick in a curved pathway, keeping the ball close to the stick.
	I can strike a ball with a hockey stick in a zigzag pathway, keeping the ball close to the stick.
	I can strike a ball with a hockey stick around four cones set up about four feet apart, keeping the ball close to the stick.
	I can strike a ball with a hockey stick through the cones while running, keeping the ball close to the stick.
	I can strike a ball with a hockey stick while traveling sideways.
	I can make up a sequence including two pathways, two changes in speed, and two different directions. I have written my sequence below.
	Sequence:

date recorded, it provides an indication of when students accomplished the skill.

Traveling and Striking for a Goal—Hockey

Setting: Cones scattered throughout general space; markers for goals around the outside boundary; a hockey stick and ball for each child

Cues	
Face Goal	(Your upper body must face the goal as you hit to it.)
Light Taps/	(Light taps to dribble the ball;
Hard Strikes	strike hard at the goal.)
Follow Through	(Follow through toward the goal with your stick.)

Tasks/Challenges:

Ⓣ Travel at your own speed and dribble or stick-handle the ball while avoiding the obstacles and other people. On the signal, travel quickly toward an open space, and strike for the goal. Retrieve your ball; begin dribbling again, listening for the signal to strike for the goal.

It's a challenge to try to keep the puck away from a partner while dribbling it.

🅣 Practice dribbling around the obstacles and striking for the goal on your own; I won't give the signal.

One-on-One Hockey—Hockey

Setting: Partners in general space, each with hockey sticks, a ball, and markers for a goal

Cues	
Light Taps/	(Light taps to dribble the ball; strike
Hard Strikes	hard at the goal.)
Heads Up	(Look up to avoid collisions.)
Dodges	(Use stopping/starting, both sides of the stick, and turns to avoid your partner.)

Tasks/Challenges:

🅣 Select a partner whose dribbling or stick-handling skills are about the same as yours. Cooperatively decide the boundaries for your area; a small area provides more practice. One of you begins to dribble the ball within the area; the other one tries to gain possession by using the stick to steal the ball. Follow these rules:

1. Contact the ball, not the person.
2. Gain possession; don't slap it away.
3. If you gain possession, begin dribbling as the offensive player; your partner is now defense.

If partners are unmatched in skill, provide a signal to change from offense to defense. Players stay on offense or defense until they hear the signal.

🅣 Within your area, set up two markers as a goal. The first partner will dribble until within scoring range (10 to 12 feet) and then shoot for a goal. The second partner will attempt to gain possession of the ball, using only the stick. After each strike for goal, switch positions.

🅒 Design your own game using the skills of stick-handling and shooting for the goal. Work with your partner to decide the rules of the game, scoring, and boundaries. Can you think of a name for your game?

✅ *Peer Observation.* After students have a chance to play their one-on-one games for a while, a peer observation would be appropriate. Have another pair of partners observe for the use of the cues of Light Taps/Hard Strikes, Heads Up, and Dodges. After a designated time, the observers and players switch roles.

 When playing one-on-one hockey, how can you steal the ball and not hit the other player's legs with the hockey stick?

Striking from a Stationary Position to a Moving Target—Hockey

Setting: Partners, each pair with two hockey sticks and a ball; a large enough space (about 10 feet by 10 yards) to send and receive the ball on the run

Cues	
Lead Receiver	(Pass the ball to an open space in front of the receiver.)
Angles	(Your receiver should always be to the side and in front of you.)
Heads Up	(Always look up so you can see where your receiver is.)

Tasks/Challenges:

🅣 You practiced striking the ball to a partner before, but then you were always standing still. When you're in a real game, how often are you able to pass to a partner who is standing still? Not very often. You're going to practice striking to a partner who is moving. One of you will be the passer, and the other the receiver. **The passer stands still and the receiver starts to run downfield, away from the passer at an angle. When the receiver is about 5 yards away, the passer sends the ball. The receiver should collect the ball on the run and then keep going for a few more steps.** Take five turns, and then switch positions.

🅣 You've been passing to the same side so far. Now try passing to the other side so the receiver has to receive with the backhand. This will seem awkward at first, but stick with it. Pass 10 times, and then switch.

Passing and Receiving on the Move—Hockey

Setting: A large, grassy outdoor area; children in pairs, with one ball for each pair and a hockey stick for each child

Cues	
Lead Receiver	(Pass the ball to an open space in front of the receiver.)
Angles	(Your receiver should always be to the side and in front of you.)
Heads Up	(Always look up so you can see where your receiver is.)

Tasks/Challenges:

🅣 Travel in the same direction as your partner, side by side, about 20 feet apart. As you're traveling, pass the ball back and forth using the hockey stick. The key is that you both must always be moving forward. When you get to the end of your area, turn around and come back.

🅣 Now travel with your partner in general space, dribbling and passing. All the other players will be doing the same thing, so it's important that you are aware of others and of passing to open spaces. Go.

🅒 Challenge yourself to always pass the ball ahead of your partner—to the open space. If you are successful, your partner will never have to stop to receive the pass. Try for five successful completions: open space, no stopping.

Keeping It Moving—Hockey

Setting: Four cones marking a space 5 yards by 5 yards; four children per group, each group with four hockey sticks and a ball or puck

Cues	
Lead Receiver	(Pass the ball to an open space in front of the receiver.)
Angles	(Your receiver should always be to the side of and in front of you.)
Heads Up	(Always look up so you can see where your receiver is.)

Tasks/Challenges:

🅒 This time you're going to play a game called Keeping It Moving. One person begins by passing the ball to another player. That player passes it to someone else, and so on. The object is to never let the ball stop moving and never let it go out of bounds.

Two-on-One Hockey—Hockey

Setting: Children in groups of three, each group with sticks, a ball, and cones to use as goals

Cues

Offense Lead Receiver (Strike the ball to an open space ahead of your receiver.)

Light Taps/Hard Strikes (Light taps to dribble the ball; strike hard at the goal.)

Angles (The receiver should be in an open space at an angle to and in front of the passer.)

Defense Play the Ball (Make your first move to the player with the ball.)

Tasks/Challenges:

C In your group, two of you will be the offensive players, and one will be the defensive player. The two offensive players will pass and dribble to each other within the boundaries of your area. The defensive player will attempt to gain possession of the ball by intercepting passes or tapping the ball away on the dribble.

Each team will have possession of the ball for 2 minutes. See how many goals you can score in that time. The offensive team must execute at least two passes before attempting a goal.

Grounders and Flies—Bats

Setting: Groups of three or four: one batter and one pitcher per group, the rest are fielders; a space large enough for all groups to bat without interfering with the others

Cues

Under the Ball	(Hit the ball slightly below its center for a fly ball.)
Behind the Ball	(Hit directly behind the ball for a line drive.)
Over the Ball	(Hit near the top of the ball for a grounder.)

Tasks/Challenges:

T So far you have practiced hitting from behind the ball. This usually makes the ball travel in a straight aerial pathway—a line drive. Yet, there are times when you will need to hit balls high, and other times when you will need to hit grounders. That is what we will practice first—grounders. Hit the pitches so they hit the ground about 6 to 10 yards away. After five hits, switch places.

T The next practice will be for fly balls. Practice hitting these pitches so they don't hit the ground until past the baseline. They should go higher in the air than a line drive.

T Do you remember the game where the pitcher told the batter which field the batter was to hit the ball to? This game is similar, but here the pitcher calls out line drive, pop fly, or grounder, and the batter has to hit that kind of ball. After five hits, switch places.

C This time the batter calls out the type of hit before the ball is pitched. The batter gets one point for each hit that goes the way it was called. Try for four points—out of five pitches.

Assessment Example

From the *National Standards for Physical Education, 1st edition*

Event Task

Students are placed in groups of five or six members and are asked to role-play the following scenario: The city Little League coach has asked your group to serve as assistant coaches this season. Specifically, the coach wants you to do a presentation of either (a) throwing and catching or (b) striking with a bat for a bunt versus a home run. Within each group, students should prepare a demonstration to include an oral presentation of the various skills, explaining the variation of each and demonstrate the skills. Each person within the group must be part of the presentation. Each group will present their minidemonstrations to the class.

Criteria for Assessment

a. Demonstrates the skill correctly.
b. Compares and/or contrasts variations within the skills.
c. Presentation is organized and interesting.

NASPE (1995, p. 47)

Directing the Placement of an Object—Bats

Setting: Partners, each pair with a batting tee, a bat, a cone, a hoop, and a ball; each pair with enough space to bat for distance. See Figure 28.11 for setup.

Cues

Front foot to Target (Change your stance so your front foot points toward your target.)

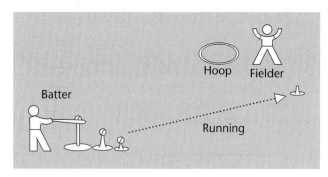

Figure 28.11 Setup for directing the placement of an object.

Tasks/Challenges:

🅣 Before, you practiced hitting the ball different distances; this time, you're going to practice hitting the ball to different places. To start, one person will be at bat, and the partner will be in left field. The batter first tries to hit five balls to left field, aiming for her or his partner. If everything works correctly, the partner shouldn't have to move very far to catch the balls. After the first five hits, the partner moves to center field, and the batter tries to hit the next five balls to right field. Then switch places. You'll know you're really good when your partner doesn't have to move to catch the balls.

🅣 This time, the fielder is going to make it harder. After every hit, the fielder moves to a new position, and the batter tries to hit the ball exactly to the fielder. The fielder can choose any place to go. After 10 hits, trade places.

🅣 Now that you've gotten the hang of placing the ball, you're going to try to hit where the fielder isn't. In softball, you want to be able to hit to open spaces, so you can get on base. Hit three balls off the tee, trying to send them to different places in the field. The fielder will collect them. After three hits, trade places.

🅒 As you hit the three balls this time, call out where the hit will go. You get one point for every hit that goes where you indicated. Try for a perfect three.

🅣 Now, you get to run as well. Bat the ball. As soon as you bat the ball, run around the cone and try to get home before the fielder has the ball in the hoop. After three hits, trade places.

Hitting to Open Spaces—Bats

Setting: A large outdoor area; children in groups of three or four, each group with a bat and a ball

Cues

Front Foot to Target (Change your stance so your front foot points toward your target.)

Tasks/Challenges:

🅣 You're going to practice hitting a pitched ball and try to make it go to open spaces. One of the fielders will become the pitcher. All pitches must be easy so they can be hit. The batter will try to hit the outfield and have the ball hit the ground before the fielder can touch it. After 10 hits, switch places.

🅒 You get one point for every ball that hits the ground untouched. Try for six points. Every 10 hits, trade places.

Striking a Pitched Object Varying the Distance—Bats

Setting: A large outdoor space; partners with a bat and ball

Cues

Full Swing (Swing quickly all the way through to send the ball a long way.)

Medium Swing (Swing at a medium speed all the way through to send the ball a shorter distance.)

Tasks/Challenges:

🅣 This time, you're going to practice hitting a pitched ball different distances. To begin, one of you will pitch, and the other will hit. Batter, your task is sometimes to hit the ball short so it lands near the pitcher and at other times to hit it long so it goes to the outfield. Try to decide ahead of time where you want the ball to go, and then hit it there.

🅒 Now, to show how good you are, call out where the ball is going—a short or a long distance—before you hit it. Do this 10 times, and then switch places.

🅣 This task is a little different from the last one. Instead of the batter calling out where the ball is to go, the pitcher calls out where the ball is to be hit. The batter changes places with the pitcher after five hits.

Batting, Combining Distance and Placement—Bats

Setting: A large open space where children can bat balls safely; bases marked in a diamond pattern; children in groups of four or five

Cues

Front Foot to Target	(Your front foot should be pointed to your target.)
Full Swing	(Swing quickly all the way through for hits that go a long way.)
Medium Swing	(Swing at a medium speed for shorter hits.)

Tasks/Challenges:

Ⓣ In your group, one of you will be the pitcher, one of you the batter, and the rest fielders. You're now going to combine hitting for distances and hitting to open spaces. The pitcher will pitch 10 balls to the batter, who tries to hit the balls to where no one is standing. Some hits need to be short and others long, but all hits should be to empty spaces.

Ⓣ This is a pretend baseball game. You are at bat; you get five swings. You will try to place each of the hits to advance the make-believe base runners. Your first two hits should be short, near the pitcher or third base. Your third swing is for a hit and run—try to place a ground ball between second and third so a runner could advance to second. Your fourth hit should move the runner to third—so hit a grounder between first and second. Your last swing is to score the run—hit a long fly ball to the outfield.

☑ *Homework.* Students at this point can profit from watching skilled players. An appropriate homework assignment would be to watch a baseball game (live or on television) and record all the places to which two selected players hit the ball (e.g., left field, bunt down third-base line).

Proficiency Level: Learning Experiences Leading to Skill Development

At the proficiency level, children are given situations that facilitate development of the ability to strike with implements while focusing on the strategy and outcome of the action and on their skill. The focus at this level is the attainment of consistency and accuracy while standing still or moving. Cues are focused on the *use* of the skill rather than on the skill itself.

As with other skill themes, at the proficiency level many appropriate activities call for the use of striking skills in a gamelike situation. It can be quite tricky to keep these activities developmentally appropriate, especially in terms of active participation for all children. There are several solutions here. One is to set up multiple playing areas around the space. Another option is to have stations where several offer gamelike activities and several have practice opportunities that require less space and setup. Finally, you could have peer assessment opportunities; within small groups, half will play and half observe and then they switch. Regardless of the solution, all game-type activities should be appropriate for all children. See Chapter 31 for more information on game options in physical education.

Note about cues: At the proficiency level, tasks are more complex, typically requiring children to coordinate several movements simultaneously in a dynamic context. A list of cues is provided to assist the children in being more successful in the learning experiences. The challenge is in determining which cue will be most beneficial for each child . . . and when. Thus, careful observation and critical reflection become very important as you watch the children move and then decide which cue will be the most helpful to move each learner to a higher level.

Directing the Pathway, Distance, and Speed of an Object—Golf

Setting: Boxes of various heights set up throughout the entire space; a hoop on the floor on the back side of each box; a golf club and a ball for each child; an appropriate station task (see Chapter 13)

Cues

Under the Ball	(Hit under the ball to make it travel a short distance.)
Short Swing	(Use a swing with a short backswing and follow-through.)

Tasks/Challenges:

Ⓣ The task is to hit the ball with the golf club so that the ball travels over the box and into the hoop. Once you're able to do this five times in a row standing close to the box, back up three steps and try it again.

Ⓣ When you succeed, move to a new place and try again.

C Design your own golf game. You may have up to three players in a group. When you are finished, write down the rules for the game. Include in your write-up what skills you need to master to be able to play your game successfully. *(See Chapter 31 for details about how to help children design their own games.)*

✓ *Event Task.* The written self-designed game is an appropriate assessment task to be included in a child's portfolio.

Whiffle Ball Golf—Golf

Setting: A Whiffle Ball Golf course (Figure 28.12); a golf club and whiffle ball for each child

Cues	
Under the Ball/Behind the Ball	(Under the ball = short distances; behind the ball = long distances.)
Short Swing/Full Swing	(Short swing = short distances; full swing = long distances.)

Tasks/Challenges:

C The game you're going to play is called Whiffle Ball Golf. It's played just as regular golf is played. The objective of the game is to get the ball to land in the hoop with as few strokes as possible. Each of you will start at the hole I assign you and then go to the next higher numbered hole. Each hole has

a tee area from which to start: This area is marked with big rubber balls, to guarantee that everyone starts from the same place. When you get to hole 9, go to hole 1. Keep score by counting the shots it takes you to go around the entire course.

One of our students made the sensible suggestion that we use old tires for the holes of the golf course, so the ball wouldn't roll out so easily. Old tires are easy to obtain.

Important points for the following activities: *Before beginning tasks that involve offense and defense, students should be skilled with the space awareness and dodging tasks that ask them to master the offensive and defensive skills of moving into open space; avoiding other persons; and using fakes, stops and starts, pivots, and other avoidance skills without manipulating equipment. (See Chapter 16, "Space Awareness," and Chapter 20, "Chasing, Fleeing, and Dodging.") Children need to have mastered these skills before they are asked to use them while manipulating equipment.*

One key to these tasks—and to other initial tasks involving offense and defense—is to clearly define the boundaries of the space the students are to use. A small space gives an advantage to the defense; a large space provides an offensive advantage. Similarly, a long, narrow space gives the advantage to the defense; a wider space helps the offense. Initial tasks generally favor the offense.

Striking to Dodge an Opponent—Hockey

Setting: A group of 10 or fewer children, several with hockey sticks and balls; the others positioned as obstacles, holding hockey sticks in their hands and wearing

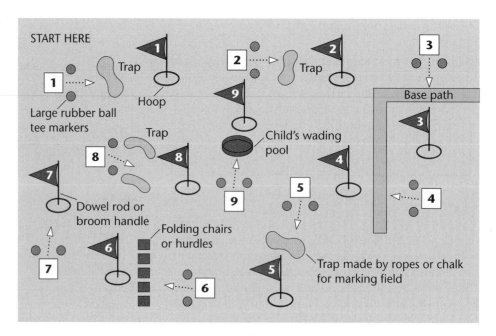

Figure 28.12 Whiffle Ball Golf course.

blue armbands or other identifying clothing (Figure 28.13)

Tasks/Challenges:

T This is a dodging game. We've played games like this before, but without equipment. To begin, those of you wearing blue will be the obstacles; the rest of you will be dodgers. Obstacles, find a self-space and stand there. Dodgers, try to cross the room without coming near an obstacle. The obstacles have the right to steal the ball if it comes within their area. Their area is that space they can reach while keeping one foot glued to the floor. The goal of the dodgers is to get to the other end of the space without having the ball stolen. The group gets five tries and then switches places.

C We're going to change the game a little this time. Instead of all the dodgers having their own balls, they're going to have only one ball. Their job is then to get the ball to the other end, as a team. The obstacles still have the same rule: They can take the ball only when it comes into their area. After four tries, switch places.

T Now that you have the idea, let's form groups of six. Two people are dodgers; four are obstacles. Switch every time so you all get a turn.

✓ *Teacher Observation.* At this point children should be demonstrating their ability to use skills and strategies to avoid other players. A teacher observation of the use of the cues of Heads Up, Dodges, Lead Receiver, and Angles would be appropriate before advancing to more complex tasks.

Keep-Away—Hockey

Setting: Groups of four: three players on the outside standing about 20 feet apart and one in the middle; each player with a hockey stick; one ball or puck per group

Tasks/Challenges:

C This is like keep-away, except that it's played with hockey sticks. There will be four in a group: three on the outside standing about 20 feet apart, and

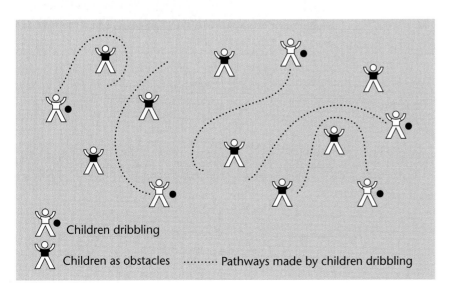

Figure 28.13 Arrangement for dribbling and dodging activity.

Children dribbling

Children as obstacles   ·········· Pathways made by children dribbling

one in the middle. The three on the outside pass the ball back and forth; the one in the middle tries to intercept the pass. After eight successful passes or four interceptions, trade places. You must stay in the boundaries of your space. There is no contact.

✓ *Video/Digital Analysis.* As children learn to play in dynamic situations, it helps them immensely to watch their own performance and analyze the use of the offensive and defensive cues.

Small Sided Hockey Invasion Game—Hockey

Setting: Groups of four or six, two or three players on each team; hockey sticks for every player; one ball or puck per group; milk crates, cones, or boxes for goals; a space at least 20 feet by 15 feet

Cues	
Offense	Don't Pass until the Defense Commits (Hold onto the ball until the defense makes you pass by coming close to you.)
	Receivers to Open Space (Receivers should move to an open space at an angle from the passer.)
	Stay Away from Passer (Receivers shouldn't go close to the passer.)
Defense	Ball First; Player Second (First play defense on the person with the ball; then cover the receivers.)
Hustle Back	(When you lose the ball to the offense, hurry back on defense.)

Tasks/Challenges:

Ⓒ This game is called Mini Hockey. The objective is to strike the ball into the opponent's goal. Here are the rules:

1. The players on the teams decide the boundaries and width of the goal. There should be one goal on each end of the space. Use milk crates, cones, or boxes for the goals.
2. One team gets the ball first.
3. The ball can be stolen only on the pass.
4. No contact.
5. Everyone must be playing—no standing around.
6. Make up your own form of scoring (if you want to keep score).
7. Make up any more rules you need.

Ⓣ We're going to change the game a little this time. Instead of one goal on each end of the field, there will be two.

Directing the Pathway, Distance, and Speed of an Object—Bats

Setting: Groups of five: one batter, one pitcher, and three fielders; one plastic bat and ball per group; a space large enough for groups to bat without interfering with other groups

Cues	
Quick Swing/Medium Swing	(Quick swing = long hit; medium swing = shorter hit.)
Below, over, behind the Ball	(Below = fly ball; over = ground ball; behind = line drive.)

Tasks/Challenges:

Ⓒ For this task you will use a plastic bat and ball. Here are the rules:

1. There are five people in a group: one batter, one pitcher, and three fielders.
2. Before the pitcher pitches the ball, she calls out the type of hit and the placement. The batter has to hit the ball the way the pitcher calls it.
3. Change batters after five hits.
4. Each player keeps his or her own score—one point for every ball that was hit as the pitcher called it.

Six-Player Striking and Fielding in a Gamelike Situation—Bats

Setting: Groups of six players, three-person teams; bases as in softball, but with the distance between each reduced to make the game challenging for the group; one bat, ball, and tee per group; sufficient space so that children can bat without interfering with one another

Cues	
Batters	Hit to Open Spaces (Always hit to open spaces.)
Fielders	Throw Quickly (Throw the ball as soon as you get it.)
	Have a Plan (Know where the runners are; plan where to throw the ball.)

Tasks/Challenges:

C This game involves the skills of striking, throwing, and catching. The objective is to place a batted ball, catch and throw, and run bases. Here are the rules:

1. There are three players on each team.
2. The batter strikes the ball from the tee and tries to run the bases.
3. The fielders try to catch or collect the ball and throw it to one another so that all three players catch the ball before the batter finishes running the bases.
4. Each player on a team bats, and then the teams switch places.

During the class, we focus on each child's individual improvements rather than on class or individual competition. Many children (and faculty!) enjoy voluntary tournaments, after school or at lunch.

Assessment Example

From the *National Standards for Physical Education, 1st edition*

Student Report

Partners videotape each other while striking a ball resting on a batting tee (five times) and while striking a ball thrown by a pitcher (five times). They review the tape with their partner and self-assess according to criteria presented to them in class. Based on this information they write a description of one or more of the following: the critical elements of batting; the consistency of their movement patterns; the differences in cues available when striking from a tee (closed skill) versus striking a pitched ball (open skill); and practice suggestions for improvement in each skill.

Criteria for Assessment

a. Accurately describes the criteria for good batting.
b. Accurately assesses their own consistency of performance.
c. Accurately identifies cues available in open or closed skills.
d. Selects appropriate practice options based on the difference between the two skills.

NASPE (1995, pp. 48–49)

One-Base Baseball—Bats

Setting: Groups of six or eight, three- or four-person teams; one base, one bat, and one ball per group; a field set up as in Figure 28.14

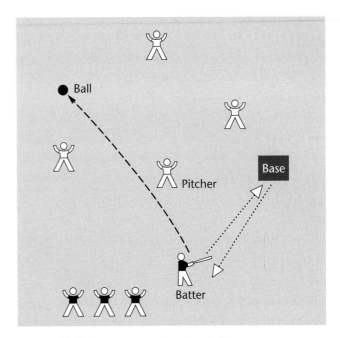

Figure 28.14 Setup for One-Base Baseball.

Cues

Batters Hit to Open Spaces (Always hit to open spaces.)
Fielders Throw Quickly (Throw the ball as soon as you get it.)
Have a Plan (Know where the runners are; plan where to throw the ball.)

Tasks/Challenges:

T You're going to play One-Base Baseball. The objective is to get to the base and back before the pitcher gets the ball. Here are the rules:

1. Each team has three or four people.
2. The batter bats and then tries to run to the base and back to home plate before the pitcher gets the ball again.
3. Each person on a team bats, and then the teams trade places.

Half Ball—Bats

Setting: Groups of six or eight; three- or four-person teams; a three- or four-inch solid rubber ball cut in half, as a ball, and a broom handle as a bat

Cues

Watch the Ball (Keep your eyes on the ball all the time.)

Tasks/Challenges:

T This game, called Half Ball, is really just for fun. It's basically played like baseball. Here are the rules that exist:

1. There are three or four players on each side.
2. Use a 3- or 4-inch solid rubber ball, cut in half, as a ball and a broom handle as a bat.
3. The rest is up to you.

This activity is great fun, although extremely difficult. For years, we played it on the beach at camp. It's a challenge to master, but it can be done! Kids love to try it!

Reading Comprehension Questions

1. What basic action is used in striking with any long-handled implement?
2. What is a sidearm pattern? What is an underhand swinging pattern? Which swings are used with which implements?
3. What is the purpose of introducing children to striking with long-handled implements?
4. What can be the long-term result when children try to swing implements that are too heavy or too long?
5. What are the observable characteristics of individuals at each level of skill proficiency in striking with long-handled implements?
6. Describe a mature striking pattern for striking a ball with a bat and with a golf club or a hockey stick.
7. How does the idea of "Roll over shoelaces" to enhance the cue of "rotate and shift" promote a mature striking pattern?
8. Why do we recommend that children initially practice striking using yarn or plastic balls?
9. What does a level swing look like when the player is attempting to strike a ball with a bat?
10. Describe two examples, one for bats and one for hockey sticks, of contexts that are unpredictable or changing.
11. In using a hockey stick to handle a ball, what do the terms *give* and *control* mean?
12. List three safety cues for striking with long-handled implements.

Reference

National Association for Sport and Physical Education. (1995). *Moving into the future: National standards for physical education.* St. Louis, MO: Mosby.

Movement Concepts and Skill Themes in Content Areas

The four chapters in this section depict how skill themes are integrated into the content areas of physical education and the larger elementary classroom. Chapters 29, 30, and 31 are discussions of how dance, gymnastics, and games are incorporated into the skill theme approach. However, you will not find a series of rules for games, steps for dance, or specific gymnastics stunts in these chapters. To do so would violate the very premise on which *Children Moving* is based—children have different needs and interests! If we were to provide a series of games organized by grade level, for example, we would be assuming that all children had the ability to play those games successfully. And we know that is not true.

Thus the three chapters on dance, games, and gymnastics are designed so that the skill themes and movement concepts most associated with games, dance, and gymnastics content are combined and developed within a context that typically uses those movement forms. For example, "Gymnastics" (Chapter 30) links the skill themes of jumping and landing, balancing, and transferring weight and such movement concepts as bending, stretching, and twisting into gymnastics-type situations. This, we hope, will enable you to see how skill themes are taught in gymnastics-type lessons. In fact, children often refer to lessons that involve rolling and transferring weight as gymnastics. That is fine with us as long as they are learning the skills that will eventually lead to success and participation not only in gymnastics but also in games and dance.

The final chapter in this section, "Integrating the Skill Theme Approach across the Curriculum," offers valuable insights into the reasons that classroom teachers and physical education teachers are encouraged to work together to develop integrated, or interdisciplinary, learning experiences for children. The chapter also provides a number of practical examples of integration and helpful references.

Skill Themes in Dance

One of the great values in the education of children comes from the experience of making their own forms to express, to communicate, to enjoy. Each child is unique in his individualism and in his environment. He needs a chance to say what he is, how he feels, what his world means to him.

—RUTH L. MURRAY

Key Concepts

- Dance experiences should give children freedom in movement, confidence in their movement, and most importantly, an enjoyment of dance.

- Dance experiences for children include rhythmic experiences; folk/cultural, ethnic, and square dances; and creative dance.

- Rhythmic experiences for children are designed to assist them in becoming competent and confident in recognizing and moving to internal and external rhythms.

- Folk, ethnic, and square dances can be studied in their authentic form as the cultural dances of a society, or they can be studied for their composition/component parts leading to children's creation of new dances.

- The focus of creative/expressive dance is performing movements to communicate a message, to express feelings and emotions through movement.

- Props and imagery can be helpful to the youngster insecure in dance, redirecting the child's attention and reducing self-consciousness; however, the focus of the dance should progress quickly to the child and his or her movement.

Movement skills and concepts form the curricular base for elementary physical education. Dance, educational gymnastics, and games/sports skills are the content areas through which these skills and concepts are explored, mastered, and applied. The development of the curricular content for the movement skills and concepts—that is, the skill themes—is found in Part 4, Chapters 19–28 of this text. Guidance on teaching these skill themes within the content areas of dance, gymnastics, and games/sports is found in Chapters 29–31.

Movement skills and concepts would be of little value to the mover without the applications that challenge the learner. Skill themes would lose their richness without their infusion into games, gymnastics, and dance. We have chosen to place the three chapters addressing skill themes in dance, gymnastics, and games/sports following the concept chapters and the chapters containing the tasks and challenges of the skill themes. Chapters with direct linkage to dance include the concept chapters of "Space Awareness," "Effort," and "Relationships" (Chapters 16–18) and the skill theme chapters of "Traveling," "Chasing, Fleeing, and Dodging," and "Jumping and Landing" (Chapters 19, 20, 21).

Skill theme chapters with less direct linkages to dance include "Balancing" and "Transferring Weight and Rolling" (Chapters 22–23).

Dance is probably the most difficult teaching area, for the same reason that games teaching is the easiest. Most teachers have an extensive background in games playing, but few teachers have experience as dancers. And most of us do teach best what we know best. Many teachers, because of their limited background in dance, omit dance or have only a few dance experiences in their programs. Others shy away from teaching dance, unsure of children's reactions and fearing a negative response from the class. Yet one need only teach Theresa Cone's "Spaghetti Dance" (2005, pp. 103–106) to realize that the dance is as much fun for the teacher as for the children actively involved in spaghetti that "moves in a box, jumps in boiling water, and slithers down a wall."

None of the authors of this book is a dancer, yet each of us has learned to give children exciting, interesting, and educational dance experiences. In fact, dance has become one of the most enjoyable areas for most of us to teach because of the children's enthusiasm and excitement about dance. We're convinced that individuals who've had a minimum of formal training in dance can learn to teach it successfully.

The Purpose of Dance in Elementary School

One key to providing children with successful dance experiences is to develop an understanding of dance and its purpose in an educational program. When we teach games, our purpose isn't to produce varsity athletes. Similarly, when we teach dance, our purpose isn't to train children to become professional dancers. Few, if any, physical education teachers have the expertise to train professional dancers, and not all children want to dance professionally. Dance experiences in physical education classes should give children:

1. The ability to use their bodies to express feelings and attitudes about themselves and others
2. A sense of self-satisfaction that can be derived from effectively using one's body as an instrument of expression
3. Enjoyment and appreciation of dance as a worthwhile experience for all, not for just a few
4. An appreciation of dance as an art medium that can have value for both the participant and the spectator
5. The ability to interpret and move to different rhythms

The Movement Movement

When we are children most of us can run and tumble and roll in the grass. We can yell and laugh and cry. We can sing our inner songs and dance our personal dances. Our feelings are visible in our actions. When we're unhappy, we stomp and mope. When we're happy we turn cartwheels and splash in puddles. Our imaginations have a direct line to our arms and legs. We can take giant steps and be giants. We can flap our arms and they will fly us away over houses and mountains. We can do all of this and more, for a while.

And then, somewhere between 5 and 20, we stop.

We stop running just for the fun of it. We stop letting out the shouts and belly laughs. We stop looking at the treetops and start walking the city sidewalks staring at the pavement. We begin, somewhere along the line, to "keep a stiff upper lip," to put "starch" in our spines, to speak softly and when spoken to. Our behavior becomes "acceptable" and, in the process, we are cut off bit by bit from ourselves and therefore from each other. If my impulses can't get through to me, how can I possibly share them with you? As we lose touch with our bodies, our heads take over and begin to monitor our actions, to restrict our responses until the simple interaction of children becomes an elaborate and inaccurate communication system between Brain A and Brain B.

Jules Feiffer pictures one of these disconnected, clever heads floating around complaining about its headless, funny-looking, malfunctioning body. "It's lucky," Feiffer's head says, "that I need my body to carry my head around . . . otherwise . . . out it would go."

Too drastic.

We can fit our heads back onto our bodies. We can rediscover the links between the headbone and the toebones. We can regain the freedom to spread our arms out wide; to run and shout without feeling awkward or embarrassed. We can learn to fall down, jump up, and bend over without breaking. We can unlock the sounds of our sadness and our joy. We can tune in to the beat of our pulse and stamp our feet to our inborn sense of rhythm. We can explore the sounds and the gestures of our feelings and our dreams. We can reclaim our bodies and our voices; free them to rediscover our inherent sense of balance and design, and use them to show each other who we are and what we hope to be.

Source: "The Movement Movement," by Ken Jenkins, in *California Living: The Magazine of the San Francisco Sunday Examiner and Chronicle,* Jan. 25, 1976, p. 19. Used with permission.

When children begin school, many are still in tune with their bodies as instruments of expression (Box 29-1). The task of the teacher of young children is not so much to teach them how to use their bodies as instruments of expression as to enhance the expressive abilities that the bodies of young children already possess. Sue Stinson (1988) refers to it as rediscovering the magic deep inside and using the magic to transform movement into dance. By helping children at an early age to become aware of how they use their bodies for expressive purposes, we can help each child avoid a mind-body dichotomy. We're able to help children develop an increasing awareness of their bodies as instruments for the expression of feelings and ideas. See Box 29-2 for information on dance in the *National Standards for Physical Education.*

The teacher challenges a class to rhythmic movement at a high level.

Dance Experiences

Dance experiences for children can be classified into three types: rhythmic experiences; folk/cultural, ethnic, or square dances; and creative dance. In rhythmic experiences, children learn about different rhythms; they develop an awareness of rhythm and the ability to move in relation to various beats. In folk/cultural dances, children are taught dances that are part of a society's heritage. The teaching of these dances is often

Dance and the *National Standards for Physical Education*

The *National Standards for Physical Education* (National Association for Sport and Physical Education, 2004) links to dance in the content statement, ". . .physical activity for health, enjoyment, challenge, self-expression, and/or social interaction," as well as with ". . .competency in motor skills and movement patterns" and the "understanding of movement concepts as they apply to the learning and performance of physical activities."

Sample performance outcomes from the *National Standards* include:

- Performs a simple dance step in keeping with a specific tempo (K–2)*
- Demonstrates clear contrasts between slow and fast movement when skipping, hopping, galloping, sliding, etc. (K–2)*

- Demonstrates a smooth transition between locomotor skills in time to music. (K–2)*
- Performs a basic tinikling step to 3/4 time (3–5)*
- Develops and refines a creative dance sequence demonstrating smooth transitions (3–5)*
- Demonstrates correct pattern for the polka step (3–5)*
- Performs a variety of simple folk and square dances (6–8)*
- Designs and performs gymnastics (or dance) sequences that combine traveling, rolling, balancing, and weight transfer into smooth, flowing sequences with intentional changes in direction, speed, and flow (6–8)*

*Grade-level guidelines for expected student learning.

coordinated with classroom studies, for example, the culture of Greece or the pioneer period of American history. In creative/expressive dance, children express feelings and ideas through movement. Whereas traditional folk dance and group rhythmic experiences often call for a correct response, there are no right or wrong answers in creative dance. Children are asked to provide interpretations or responses to a particular problem or situation. Individual responses are encouraged; diversity is valued.

Before learning structured dance forms, children need experiences in locomotor movements and response to rhythm. They need to move about in free space before they are asked to move within the set formations of circles, squares, and such. They need to move freely in response to their own internal rhythm before moving to music. For these reasons, our focus in dance for young children is on rhythmic experiences and creative dance.

Rapping

One of the earliest forms of rhythmic accompaniment for young children is their own voices. Observe preschoolers at play, and you will hear them talking and singing as they move. The popular teenage pastime of "rapping" is a rhythmic expression of voice and actions. Children should be encouraged to use the human voice to accompany their rhythmic and creative dance experiences as appropriate.

These youngsters enjoy matching rhythms.

Rhythmic Experiences

Rhythmic experiences for children are designed to assist them in becoming competent and confident in recognizing and moving to rhythm. Children respond to the beat and the tempo of an external rhythm; they

Figure 29.1 Easy-to-make rhythm instruments.

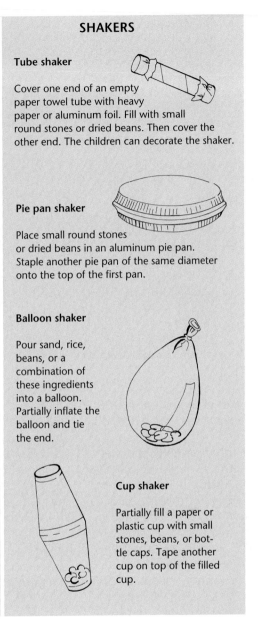

DRUMS

Tin can drum

Remove the top and bottom on any size tin can. Cut two circles, about an inch larger in diameter than the tin can, from an inner tube. Punch about six small holes around the edge of each rubber circle. Place one circle over each end of the can. Tighten by lacing strong string or nylon cord through the holes. Bells or bottle caps may be added for additional sound.

Bleach (or milk) jug drum

Screw top of jug and secure with tape or glue. Hit with dowel rod. The children can decorate the jug with paint or colored tape.

CLACKER

Cut two pieces of board to the same size. Drill holes in one end of each board and join the boards with nylon cord or wire. The children can decorate the boards.

SHAKERS

Tube shaker

Cover one end of an empty paper towel tube with heavy paper or aluminum foil. Fill with small round stones or dried beans. Then cover the other end. The children can decorate the shaker.

Pie pan shaker

Place small round stones or dried beans in an aluminum pie pan. Staple another pie pan of the same diameter onto the top of the first pan.

Balloon shaker

Pour sand, rice, beans, or a combination of these ingredients into a balloon. Partially inflate the balloon and tie the end.

Cup shaker

Partially fill a paper or plastic cup with small stones, beans, or bottle caps. Tape another cup on top of the filled cup.

---

walk, skip, and gallop to their internal rhythm and to external rhythms. At the precontrol level, the rhythmic experiences are chosen to reinforce the movement concepts and themes the children are already studying. They may move body parts (head, feet, knees) to a simple beat played on a drum, tambourine, or wood block. After experiencing the locomotor movements freely at their own tempo, children may be asked to walk three beats in one direction and change directions on the fourth beat. In this combination of skill (walking) and movement concept (direction), children are now matching the tempo of their movements to that imposed by the external beat. Figure 29.1 illustrates several rhythmic instruments that can be used

to provide the beat. Children may echo the beat by moving body parts or swinging the total body at fast or slow tempo to match a verbal rhythm. Moving body parts in self-space in accompaniment to a beat enhances children's body awareness.

Once the children are able to move (1) to their internal tempo and (2) to an external beat imposed by the teacher's voice or a simple instrument (e.g., a drum, shaker, clacker), music is introduced. The music should have a steady beat; although it provides the beat for the movements, it should accompany, not dominate, the children's movements.

Once children have grasped the basic concepts of rhythm and are able to respond correctly to different

For these partners, jumping rope becomes a rhythmic dance experience.

beats, they enjoy the addition of a manipulative to the rhythmic experiences. Streamers, scarves, cardboard pizza circles, lummi sticks, and playground balls are examples of equipment that enhances rhythmic experiences for children. Initial activities focus on individual responses to rhythm. Following this exploration phase, teacher-designed routines are used to elicit a group response to a given rhythm. These control-level experiences are designed to involve the children in working together as a group, responding correctly to the rhythm, and remembering a sequence of movements and/or actions to be performed. Appendix 29A at the end of this chapter includes group routines for lummi sticks, Chinese ribbons, jump ropes, and parachutes. Most of the ideas for our teacher-designed routines come from observing children during their exploration of the manipulative, listening to the music, and matching action to tempo and beat. Rhythmic group routines are excellent for promoting physical education at assemblies, PTA/PTO programs, and community functions (see Chapter 33).

The amount of time a teacher can spend on rhythmic group routines depends to a great extent on how often physical education is scheduled. When physical education classes meet only twice a week, for example, more time is spent on mastery of the basic skills involved in the rhythmic experiences—rope jumping, ball handling, and such.

Children at the utilization and proficiency levels focus on creating new lummi stick routines, designing

individual and partner jump rope routines, and using ball-handling skills in routines to music, like the activity Making Up Fancy Dribbling/Passing Routines in Chapter 26. Children at these levels of rhythmic experiences combine various movement qualities and patterns with their manipulative skills, for example, floor patterns, directions, levels, phrases, and variations in rhythm: double time, half time, and so on.

It isn't sufficient for the teacher to say, "Today we're going to design a jump rope routine. Find a partner and get started." As teachers, we provide guidelines for the routine. We tell the children the limitations we're imposing, such as the number of persons in a group, the length of the routine, the minimum number of skills to be included, and the music to be used (if this is a teacher decision). Children also need to know the necessary inclusions in the routine that are to be group decisions, for example, directions, pathways, floor patterns, and levels, as well as basic skills to be performed. If the teacher selects the music, there is maximum participation by the children during class, because all can practice to the same music. If each group of children selects the music, the variety of music is greater, but practice time is limited.

One of the most difficult parts of child-designed rhythmic or folk dance experiences is the time factor, that is, the matching of the length of the routine to the length of the music. Children often need guidance in choosing whether to add skills, repeat phrases, or repeat the entire routine.

Folk/Cultural and Ethnic Dances

Folk/cultural, ethnic, and square dances (line and country) are the cultural dances of a society, the cultural heritage of a people. Cultural dances range from simple to very complex; some are designed for partner and group formation, others have a focus on individual creativity. Folk and square dances involve a series of actions with one or more of the following: a stated progression, verses and a chorus, locomotor and non-locomotor actions, formations, changes in directions, right and left discrimination, and designated music. Ethnic dances have a combination of locomotor and nonlocomotor actions, often with a focus on individual creativity and a range of rhythmic and musical selection.

When children are first introduced to dance, it is important that they feel free to move, confident in their movement and, most important, that they enjoy the dance. This is especially true with folk/cultural dance, with definite formations and progressions. With these goals in mind, the following guidelines will be beneficial when introducing children to structured dance forms (Weikart, 1989, 1997):

- Start with free-space movement; allow students to move about the room with no set formation. Then proceed to simple circle and line dances with no changes in direction.
- Provide multiple opportunities for students to practice locomotor and nonlocomotor sequences in different combinations to a variety of music.
- Begin with dances that require neither partners nor holding hands.
- Choose dances that do not specify the use of the right or left foot.
- Choose dances that do not require complex footwork, rhythms, or changes in direction.
- Select music with a strong underlying beat; the musical phrases should be distinct and in groupings of 8 or 16 beats, with no resting beats.
- Select dances with a repetition of sequences; sequences should be short and uncomplicated.
- Choose dances that can be easily modified for beginners. For example, Kinderpolka and Jump Jim Joe (Box 29-3) are dances with partners that can easily be modified for introduction with no partners.

When children participate in the folk/cultural, ethnic, and square dance as an integrated study of a culture, the dances are performed in their traditional form with attention to maintaining the authenticity of the dance. This is also true when cultural dances are performed for a PTA/PTO program or school assembly for parents and community. The dance is representative of the culture,

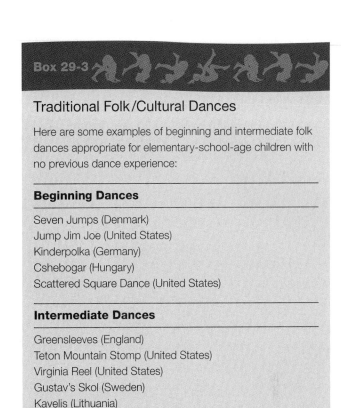

Box 29-3

Traditional Folk/Cultural Dances

Here are some examples of beginning and intermediate folk dances appropriate for elementary-school-age children with no previous dance experience:

Beginning Dances

Seven Jumps (Denmark)
Jump Jim Joe (United States)
Kinderpolka (Germany)
Cshebogar (Hungary)
Scattered Square Dance (United States)

Intermediate Dances

Greensleeves (England)
Teton Mountain Stomp (United States)
Virginia Reel (United States)
Gustav's Skol (Sweden)
Kavelis (Lithuania)
LaRaspa (Mexico)
Troika (Russia)
Mayim! Mayim! (Israel)

and as such is often demonstrated with children in the costumes of that culture. The focus is a demonstration of the enjoyment of dance from different cultures and dance as part of the heritage of the people.

When we have children participate in folk/cultural or ethnic dances as a study in dance, we often approach them differently. We may change the formation of the dance from circle to line or scattered. We may change the way partners are selected or do the dance without partners. We may change the travel patterns or actions of the dance. We may combine components of different dances or combine types of dances. These dances, usually teacher designed, still have set travel patterns and actions, repetition of sequences, and correct responses to rhythm. The focus is the study of dance, the enjoyment of participation in dance, and the freedom of movement and confidence in that movement.

When older children, who have acquired competence in rhythm and movement, study dances from different countries, they carry out a variety of locomotor and nonlocomotor actions to music. They learn formations for dances, moving to musical phrases, repetition of pattern, and so on. They're able to analyze the dances according to spatial awareness, effort qualities, and relationships. Based on the patterns of movement,

Box 29-4

Folk Dance Information Sources

Additional information on folk/cultural dances can be obtained from the following sources:

Bennett, J. P., & Riemer, P. C. (1995). *Rhythmic activities and dance,* Champaign, IL: Human Kinetics.

The Carper, Bailey, Steele Travelers. *Appalachian clogging and hoedown.* (Available from Bill Carper, 1537 4th Ave., Charleston, WV 25312.)

Czarnowski, L. K. (1963) *Folk dance teaching cues,* Palo Alto, CA: National Press.

Harris, J. A., Pittman, A. M., & Waller, M. S. (1988). *Dance awhile: Handbook of folk, square, contra and social dance,* New York: Macmillan.

Napier, E. P. *Kentucky mountain square dancing.* (Available from Christmas Dance School, Berea College, CPO 287, Berea, KY 40404.)

Powell, S. (1983). *The clogger's book of Appalachian square dance figures,* Huron, OH: Burdick Enterprises.

Hipps, R. H., & Chappell, W. E. (1970). *World of fun folk dances.* (Available from United Methodist Church, P.O. Box 871, Nashville, TN 37202, or Melody House, 819 NW 92nd, Oklahoma City, OK 73114.)

Weikart, P. S. (1997). *Teaching folk dance: Successful steps. Rhythmically moving,* Ypsilanti, MI: High Scope Press.

Dance experiences provide movement and joy for children.

formations, and specific steps they have learned, upper elementary and middle school students use the dance skills and concepts to create new dances.

With the richness of diversity increasing in our schools, it is important that we as teachers recognize the diversity within our classes, the wealth of ethnic and cultural dances that the children bring to us, and the appreciation for dance and cultures that can be gained by learning from each other.

Box 29-4 provides additional information about folk/cultural dances.

Creative Experiences

Creative and rhythmic experiences in dance aren't separated in our programs; many of the creative experiences are performed to rhythm. In fact, it isn't uncommon for us to switch the focus several times during a lesson, sometimes focusing on the rhythm of the movement, other times focusing on the expressive qualities of the movement. When concentrating on rhythmic experiences, the primary focus is on the children's ability to move to the rhythm. In contrast, creative experiences are intended to provoke creativity and expression. Creative experiences for children are designed to evoke the expressiveness and lack of body inhibition so characteristic of the young child.

At the precontrol level, experiences are designed to help children develop sensitivity and awareness to movement by focusing on fundamental body actions and travel skills. Stretching, curling, bending and skipping, galloping, and leaping are movements frequently used with precontrol children. Initially it's a good idea to focus on giving children opportunities to explore a wide range of movement possibilities. Once this has been accomplished, shift the emphasis to the spatial quality of the movements. For example, have the children do a complete, full stretch or a very tight curl, and use the movement concepts to enhance the children's sensitivity to the potential of movement. The primary emphasis, however, is still on the movement rather than the body's expressive or communicative possibilities.

At the control level, we begin to clarify for children the expressive and communicative aspects of movement. The focus now centers more on the effort and relationship concepts (Chapter 3). Box 29-5 describes the effort and relationship concepts used for expressive dance. Through these concepts, movement is explored

Box 29-5

Expressive and Communicative Activities

Time

Travel or gesture in slow motion.
Travel to an externally imposed beat or rhythmic pattern, such as a handclap or drumbeat.
Rise and sink suddenly or slowly.

A child freezes in a strong pose.

Flow

Combine two travel skills, such as running and leaping, always moving smoothly.

Display hesitant, jerky, mechanical flow to create the illusion of being a robot.
Feel and observe the differences in combining a step with a turn, first with smooth, continuous flow, then with pauses (stillnesses) interspersed between each step and turn.

Force

Travel or perform nonlocomotor actions to a strong beat.
Travel or perform nonlocomotor actions to light, gentle, delicate music.
Freeze in a strong, dramatic pose.

Youngsters explore the expressive possibilities of partner formation.

Relationships

Experience the sensation of matching, mirroring, or shadowing the movements of a partner.
Explore the expressive possibilities of group formations—for example, sculpture for the city park, or a mountain range.
Experience the feeling of contrasting the movements of a partner—for example, as one partner rises the other sinks, or one partner travels in a geometric path (square) while the other travels in a random path.

as a tool for expressing an idea, attitude, or feeling. Movement is no longer studied primarily as an entity in and of itself; it's viewed as a medium of expression. Challenge the children to structure their movements to an imposed beat or rhythmic pattern, or have them verbalize how their movements feel and describe their emotional reactions to classmates' expressive movements.

Children at the utilization level have learned to efficiently perform the movements studied at the precontrol level and to modify the movements intentionally by focusing on different movement concepts. At this level, children can begin to structure their communicative movements into organized forms. This structuring is often termed *sequencing* or *phrasing*.

It's usually a good idea to narrow the focus of a sequence or phrase to one, two, or at most three skills and concepts. When youngsters at this level are given too many possibilities, they're often unable to decide where to begin. The ability to move, however, combined with a working knowledge of movement concepts, enables pupils to elicit varying and qualitative responses to a single challenge.

Dance making—structuring several sequences or phrases into a whole—is the focus at the proficiency level. The idea behind a dance can be stimulated by an infinite variety of sources, such as machines, natural phenomena (flowers, snow flakes), sculpture, music, poetry, or painting. Dance making involves both design and evaluation.

Design of Dance

We've found it valuable to have upper elementary children view the dance-making process as composed of the following procedures:

1. Selection of the purpose, idea, or theme of a dance
2. Identification of appropriate movements and movement concepts to express the intended idea, attitude, feeling, or theme
3. Design of a powerful opening statement for the dance
4. Design of a series of actions rising to a climax
5. Design of the portion of the dance that is to be the climax or peak of the action
6. Design of the resolution or concluding statement of the dance

The possibilities for dance making are infinite. Dances can center around contrasting movement concepts, telling a story, interpreting a theme, or portraying emotions and ideas. Two examples illustrate how

dances can be designed to portray different emotions or thoughts. The first is an abstract dance contrasting tradition with the forces of change (Chapter 19). One group arranges itself as a solid square facing in one direction. Symmetrical movements prevail. Actions are firm, sustained. The other group is scattered widely, facing in random directions. Nonsymmetrical movements, free use of space, and variety are used.

The second dance is based on the theme of freedom and the journey of a people to freedom. Free use of space, meeting, and parting are appropriate. Displays of strength, courage, or pride are also suitable. See Box 29-6 for insight into children's design of this dance and working with children in the process of dance making.

Evaluation of Dance Making

The process of dance making, from simple sequences to complex choreography, is one of exploration and refinement. The evaluation of dance making is a continual process. Children need to be satisfied with the process and the product. Evaluation examines all movement skills and concepts the teacher and children have incorporated into the dance. Considerations include the following:

- Beginning location and pathway of each youngster—how the children choose to locate themselves at the beginning of the dance and the pathway they choose to express various feelings
- Selection of travel skills (leaping, skipping) and the quality with which they're performed—whether the children are using a variety of travel skills and executing them clearly and precisely as intended, with the desired impact
- Flow of the dance—how the parts of the dance are connected to give a unity of expression
- Relationship of the children to one another—whether the children are reacting to one another with sensitivity and whether the timing, strength, and speed of their responses are appropriate

Dance and rhythmic activities provide a rich environment for the fostering of positive social interaction and respect for differences among people. As youngsters actively participate in dances from different cultures, they expand their understanding of others and broaden their cultural world. As they cooperate in dance making and the creation of rhythmic routines, they develop cooperative skills and respect for others. Responsible social behavior, understanding and respect for others, and positive social interaction are important for all children (NASPE, 2004).

Box 29-6

Children Designing Their Own Dance: A Description of a Process

One goal in teaching dance is to work with children so that they learn to design dances to express feelings or thoughts that are important to them. This description of the process of creating a dance tells how one teacher worked with a group of upper-grade children, assisting them to create their own dance. The description is intended to reveal the process of creating dances; it isn't presented as a predesigned dance to be taught to other children.

Background

The population of the community in which the children in this class lived was predominantly black. The eight children in this group wished to create a dance that expressed pride and respect for their African American heritage.

We began by using several methods to develop an outline for the dance:

1. One student wrote a short paper describing what he considered the most important events in the movie *Roots*.
2. The school librarian provided several sources of information. Individual students read and outlined these sources for the remainder of the group.
3. Several students interviewed teachers and classmates about their family backgrounds. They also asked people to describe what emotions they had about their heritage.

Without question, the movie *Roots* had the biggest influence in determining the students' conception of black history. The pride and courage of Kunta Kinte and his descendants were the qualities the children wanted most to exhibit in their dance.

An Outline of the Dance

After gathering and reviewing this information, we discussed a sequential outline for the dance. It was agreed that:

1. We'd begin by depicting, in some way, the period of slavery.
2. The arrival of freedom would be expressed. Interestingly, the children didn't want this portion of the dance to be happy or exhilarating, for several reasons. They felt that blacks were always free, despite slavery, that many freedoms were long in coming, and that the struggle for equality continues today.
3. Upon arrival of freedom, it was important to display the pride and courage of African Americans in overcoming many injustices, both as individuals and as a people.
4. The conclusion of the dance would be spiritual, exhibiting respect and thankfulness to God for blessing a cherished people.

Creation of the Dance

Children focused on each section of the dance before putting it all together. For each portion the youngsters needed to decide upon and write down the following:

1. Beginning location of each dancer
2. Sequential travel pathway of each dancer or of the entire group

Travel Pattern for "Freedom"

Travel pathways
  Random: dancers weaving in, out, and around one another
Qualities
  Smooth, wavy, uncertain, looking to others for help
Actions
  Wavy gesturing of arms, held upward for protection or reaching out
  Slow stepping, with changes in direction and levels

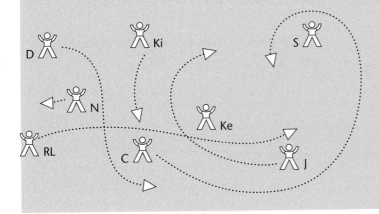

Box 29-6 *(continued)*

3. Expressive qualities they intended to exhibit in their movements
4. Sequence of specific gestures and travel skills incorporated to express desired qualities

Once the group could perform one section to the teacher's and their own satisfaction, work began on the next phase of the dance.

Slavery

After discussing the accumulated information, the children agreed to begin the dance by exhibiting the qualities and actions of field slaves laboring under a hot sun.

Freedom

This phase of the dance was the most difficult for the children. After experimenting with several ideas, the youngsters asked if they could select music to serve as background for the dance. They thought that if they had appropriate music as a stimulus, they'd be able to solve their dilemmas. After listening to several cuts from the *Roots* soundtrack album, the children unanimously agreed that the words and slow pulse of the song "Many Rains Ago (Oluwa)" was perfect for their purposes. They decided to express freedom by simply putting down their tools and slowly and smoothly beginning to interweave with one another, making eye contact with others for the first time. This was intended to express changed circumstances, in which they were free and proud but still struggling. During this phase, the youngsters' facial features exhibited fear and uncertainty about the future. The travel pattern was random.

Gathering Together: Strength As a People

To express their solidarity and pride as a people, the children's random travel began to be directed toward the center of the room where they gathered one by one, grasped one another's hands tightly, and formed a strong, unified statue.

From this point the youngsters were able to complete their dance with little teacher suggestion or intervention.

Dispersing: Strength As Individuals

Youngsters dispersed from center stage with new vigor and traveled along definite travel patterns.

Gathering Again: Strength, Pride, Confidence

Children leaped to the center of the room, where suddenly and simultaneously they clasped hands with one another overhead and formed a statue.

Respect and Thankfulness to God

From the statue position, youngsters slowly bowed and traveled to semicircle formation. Slowly they dropped to their knees, and then slowly they raised their hands and heads upward.

Conclusion: We Are Strong and Proud

Youngsters slowly bent to curled position. . . . Suddenly and simultaneously they rose on knees to grasp one another's hands to form a statue as a final statement of strength and pride.

Travel Pattern for "Gathering Again: Strength, Pride, Confidence"

Travel pathways
    All dancers suddenly and simultaneously gather in
    the middle with a run, leap, and turn
Qualities
    Strong, confident, proud, smooth, and fluent
Actions
    Smooth, fluent leap and landing, when dancers
    grasp each other's hands overhead and freeze into
    a stillness

Table 29.1 Overview of the Content and Rationale of Teaching Expressive Dance to Children

We Want Children to Acquire:	By Learning a Movement Vocabulary of:	That Can Be Used to Express Emotions and Thoughts Such As:	Stimulated by Catalysts Such As:
An ability to use their bodies as a means of expression	Movement concepts	Friendship	Sounds
	Space awareness	Warmth	Music
The sense of self-satisfaction that can be derived through expressive movement	Effort	Anger	Poetry
	Relationships	Unhappiness	Art
	Skill themes	Peace	History
An enjoyment and appreciation of dance	Locomotor	Hostility	Motion pictures
	Nonmanipulative	Joy	Personal experiences
An ability to interpret and move to different rhythms		Satisfaction	
		Harmony	

Source: Adapted from "Educational Dance," by K. R. Barrett, in B. Logsdon, K. Barrett, M. Ammons, M. Broer, L. Halverson, R. McGee, and M. Roberton (1984), *Physical Education for Children: A Focus on the Teaching Process.* Philadelphia: Lea & Febiger.

The Content of Expressive Dance

The movement framework, depicting the interaction of skill themes and movement concepts (Chapter 3), is used as the foundation for expressive dance experiences for children. The majority of skill themes categorized under locomotor skills (walking, running, hopping, skipping, and galloping) and nonmanipulative skills (turning, twisting, rolling, balancing, transferring weight, jumping and landing, and stretching and curling) are used in expressive dance. Virtually all the movement concepts (Chapter 3) are used to heighten and expand the child's ability to express feeling and emotion through movement (see Table 29.1).

The focus in expressive dance is not simply on executing a particular movement—a turn or a balance—but on performing the movement so that it communicates the message the child intends it to. Once children are able to perform turns efficiently, they can begin to experiment with different qualities of turning. Slow, hesitant turns or fast, sudden turns are two possibilities. Eventually these qualities of turning can be used to express inner feelings or attitudes. For example, slow, hesitant turns might be used to depict sadness or uncertainty; sudden, quick turns could be used to express anger, frustration, or perhaps joy. Turning, by itself, communicates little. It's the quality of the turn that communicates a message, just as it's the quality of any movement that is expressive. This is the reason it's so important to give children a movement vocabulary if they're to become expressive movers.

The Process of Teaching Dance

Teaching creative dance is different from teaching functional movements. A functional movement is performed correctly or incorrectly, and the teacher's task is to guide the child toward an appropriate execution. Dance movements, performed to express an idea or emotion, are more difficult to define clearly, and so the teacher's task is different.

Because the child is trying to express a feeling or an idea, observation and feedback are also more complex. In games and gymnastics, the purpose of a movement is obvious; this isn't true in creative dance. When teaching dance, the teacher initially encourages, expands, and embellishes rather than correcting or refining. As the teacher comes to know the children and understand them as individuals, and as the children begin to trust the teacher, the children will seek sensitive and supportive feedback from the teacher. Remember, though, that human expression is very fragile and easily misinterpreted. Nothing stifles expression more quickly than insensitivity or lack of understanding. The teacher of creative dance needs to be constantly aware of how easily creativity is threatened. The incident described in Box 29-7 illustrates how fragile a child's creativity is.

You don't have to be a dancer to be a successful teacher of children's dance. The following ideas may be helpful for those teachers unsure of their ability to teach dance, unsure of their students' reactions, yet searching for ways to develop effective programs of creative dance.

Don't Call It Dance!

Children who've had little exposure to creative dance experiences often react negatively to the prospect of studying dance. Children in the upper grades have been known to express their hostility to the idea with groans, frowns, sighs, and even emphatic refusals to participate. This resistance can be understood when you realize that too often children in the upper elementary grades have had few opportunities to move

Box 29-7

The Awful Beginning: A True Story, Unfortunately

I looked across the desk at my big girl. She'd come for help in planning her semester schedule.

"Look," I said, "you have some electives. Why don't you take a course or two for fun? You've worked hard and really should take something outside your major that will be pleasurable."

"Like what?" she asked.

My eyes scanned the college schedule of courses. "Like Dr. Mann's Creative Writing or Dr. Camp's Painting for Beginners or something like that."

She threw back her head and laughed. "Who me? Paint or write? Good grief, Dad, you ought to know better than that!"

"And this," I thought, "is the awful ending."

It was not always like this. I remembered an early golden September day when I went to my garage studio and gathered together my easel, paintbrushes, and watercolors. I sensed someone was watching me and looked up from my activity to see her framed in silhouette in the doorway. The breeze and the sun tiptoed in the gold of her curls. Her wide blue eyes asked the question, "Whatcha doin'?"

"I'm going to the meadow to paint," I said. "Want to come along?"

"Oh, yes." She bounced on her toes in anticipation.

"Well, go tell Mommy and get your paints." She was off but returned in no time carrying the caddy I had made to hold her jars of paint and her assortment of brushes.

"Paper?" she asked.

"Yes, I have plenty of paper. Let's go."

She ran down the hill before me, pushing aside the long soft grasses of the meadow. I watched closely for fear of losing her golden top in the tops of the goldenrod. She found a deserted meadowlark's nest and we stopped to wonder at it. A rabbit scurried from under our feet. Around us yellow daisies and goldenrod nodded in friendly greeting. Above, the sky was in infinite blue. Beyond the meadow, the lake slapped itself to match the blue of the sky.

On the lake, a single white sailboat tipped joyously in the breeze. My daughter looked up and saw it. "Here!" she said.

Trusting her wisdom as I always did, I set up our easels. While I deliberated over choice of subject and color, she had

no such problem. She painted with abandonment and concentration and I left her alone, asking no questions, making no suggestions, simply recognizing uncontaminated creative drive at work.

Before I had really begun, she pulled a painting off her easel.

"There!" she said. "Want to see?" I nodded.

I cannot describe the sense of wonder that flooded over me as I viewed her work. It was all there—that golden September day. She had captured the sunlight in her spilled yellows, the lake in her choppy, uneven strokes of blue, the trees in her long, fresh strokes of green. And through it all, there was a sense of scudding ships and the joyousness of wind that I experience when I sail, the tilting and swaying of the deck, the pitching of the mast. It was a beautiful and wondrous thing and I envied her ability to interpret so honestly, so uninhibitedly, so freshly.

"Are you going to give it a name?" I suggested.

"Yep! Sailboats!" she responded, as she taped another sheet of paper to the easel.

There wasn't a single sailboat in the picture.

She began school the following week. One dreary November day she came into my study with a sheet of paper in her hand.

"Daddy," she asked, "will you help me draw a sailboat?"

"Me? Help you draw a sailboat?"

My eyes turned to the wall where her golden September painting hung in a frame I had made for it.

"Me? Help you draw a picture of a sailboat? Why, sweetheart, I could never paint a picture like the one over there. Why don't you paint one of your own?"

Her blue eyes looked troubled.

"But, Daddy, Miss Ellis doesn't like my kind of painting."

She held up her sheet of paper in the middle of which was a dittoed triangle.

"Miss Ellis wants us to make a sailboat out of this."

And that was the awful beginning!

James A. Smith

Source: James A. Smith, "The Awful Beginning," *Today's Education,* April 1972. Used with permission.

creatively. Too often even those few opportunities have been poorly presented. Children have been forced, for example, to participate in uninteresting, unstructured forms of dance that had no purpose or reason for involvement that was apparent to the children.

When that happens, children turn away from the joy of dance instead of becoming excited about creative movement. For this reason, we recommend that you involve the children in enjoyable, challenging movement experiences without labeling the lesson as *dance*. People in Motion, an integrated project of art, music, and physical education with a focus on sport and physical activity, is one example of this type of movement experience/dance. (See Holt/Hale, 2006, for details.) As the youngsters become comfortable with dance and their awareness of dance as exciting and stimulating grows, the stigma attached to the word *dance* will disappear.

Begin Gradually

The class's first experiences with creative dance need not last for an entire class session. A few minutes at the beginning or end of a class are often sufficient to introduce creative movement concepts—and simultaneously build your confidence as a teacher of creative dance. A short creative dance activity at the beginning of class can serve as a review of a concept related to the skill theme for the day, for example, twisting and turning actions in Shadow Boxing (dance) before their use in the skill theme of balance (gymnastics). A short creative dance activity at the conclusion of an active lesson can also be effective. While the children lie on the floor, eyes closed, ask them to move only their fingers (or toes, arms, legs, elbows) to the music. Short segments of lively music are most effective. The children, whose eyes are closed, are less inhibited; the teacher, whose eyes are open, sees the creative dance potential that seems to be an inborn characteristic of the young child. At Linden Elementary School in Oak Ridge, Tennessee, almost all lessons designed for primary children include "A Moment of Dance,"—a few minutes, usually at the beginning of the lesson, for self- and/or general space dance activity.

Start with a Cooperative Class

Some classes are more agreeable to work with than others. Select a class that is generally cooperative as the first one to which you'll teach creative dance. You don't need to start dance programs with all your classes at the same time. Instead, pick one class that you feel comfortable with. As your confidence builds, start dance programs in other classes. Use the first class as a testing ground for your ideas.

Use Props

Creative dancers derive great pleasure and satisfaction from focusing on how they can move their bodies. In contrast, immature dancers often feel insecure when asked to focus on how they're moving. Props can serve as catalysts, redirecting the child's attention and so reducing self-consciousness. The use of such props as scarves, newspapers, balloons, dowel rods, stretch nylon, and even shadows can effectively divert the attention of uncertain children from their bodies. For example, when attempting to duplicate the light, airy movements made by a floating sheet of newspaper, the child focuses attention on moving as the newspaper does, rather than on trying to travel lightly. As confidence builds, the children gradually focus their attention on their own movements.

Imagery

Imagery is the use of a creative stimulus as a catalyst for movement. Many people believe, inaccurately, that imagery provides the content of dance. The content of expressive dance is movement; imagery is a helper. Asking children to use imagery as the content of expressive dance is similar to asking children to write a story when they have a vocabulary of only 50 words. One or two extraordinarily intelligent pupils might do well. Most, however, would fail miserably because they hadn't yet acquired the tools needed for successful story writing.

The same principle can be applied to expressive dance. Children must be provided with the tools of dance, the ability to use a variety of movements effectively. Only when children have developed these skills can they successfully combine the movements into dances that express what they want to communicate. Movement vocabularies, however, aren't acquired through imagery, as the following example illustrates.

A teacher focusing on the concept of slow, heavy movement may ask children to travel as if the floor were coated with 6 inches of peanut butter. But using the peanut butter image without first teaching the concept of slow and heavy travel is of little value. Children who are adept at such movements at the beginning of the class will remain adept. Those individuals who were unable to travel slowly and heavily might move in the desired manner when stimulated by the image of a peanut butter floor, but they won't have acquired a functional understanding of slow, heavy movement as a concept that can be transferred to other movement situations. In short, imagery can be useful as a reinforcer for certain movements, but imagery by itself doesn't enhance the quality of children's expressive movement.

Start with Exciting Movement Experiences

Fast, vigorous, large movements are attractive and appealing to young children. A lesson that focuses on running, leaping into the air, landing, and rolling evokes the exuberance associated with speed and flight. Gradually the teacher can begin to focus on the quality of the leaps, the effectiveness of the landings, and the use of gestures while in flight.

Dance to the Music

One of the most devastating experiences for poorly skilled or less confident children occurs when a teacher plays some music and simply says, "Today is a dance lesson. Go ahead and dance to the music." This can be a terrifying task for youngsters with no background or confidence in creative movement and no vocabulary of functional movements. The challenge "Move to the music" may be appropriate later, when children put together the movements they have acquired, but it is not appropriate in the early stages of teaching creative dance to children.

A Final Thought

One instructor's initial attempts at teaching creative dance are still vivid. She recalled teaching to a second-grade class an entire lesson that focused on running, jumping, and turning to different rhythms. Afterward she remarked to a friend that it was the best workout the children had experienced the entire year and added that she was going to teach another lesson because of the physical fitness benefits. After another lesson was received as enthusiastically as the first, she was struck with the realization that the reason the children had been so actively involved was that they were totally immersed in the exciting atmosphere that was generated by exploring fast and slow turns, acceleration and deceleration leading into jumps. The children loved creative dance.

The physical education instructor who doesn't offer creative movement experiences is being professionally irresponsible. You may be more qualified to teach gymnastics or games, but you'll always be teaching some children who might eventually choose creative dance as their primary form of participation in the motor domain. Depriving children of opportunities to experience creative movement is no more acceptable than eliminating all opportunities to practice throwing and catching. You may have to devote much time and work to developing a successful program. But any teacher, even one who has little background in creative dance, can provide children with effective creative movement experiences. Dance ideas within themes are found throughout the skill theme chapters, with a concentration in the locomotors of Chapter 19, "Traveling."

Summary

Teachers who lack experience and educational background in dance find it difficult to teach dance to children. But any teacher who's willing to try new and possibly unfamiliar ideas can learn to successfully teach children's dance. Children look forward to and enjoy dance experiences that are presented appropriately.

Because of the ages and abilities of children in elementary schools, we've found creative or expressive dance to be the most successful. Creative dance is also consistent with the nature and characteristics of young children, who are already adept at fantasizing and expressing their thoughts and feelings through movement.

The content of expressive dance is derived from the movement concepts and the majority of locomotor and nonmanipulative skill themes. The initial emphasis is on executing particular movements. As children learn to perform these skills efficiently, the emphasis shifts to varying the quality with which the movement is executed.

Children should have both rhythmic and expressive dance experiences. In rhythmic experiences, the focus is on moving in relation to different rhythmic beats. In contrast, creative dance experiences focus on expressive interpretation by children as they expand their movement vocabulary for communicating feelings and moods.

Through a process of trial and error, we've discovered numerous techniques that help make dance lessons for children both interesting and educational. For example, we suggest that teachers initially avoid the word *dance* because it has negative connotations for some children. Inexperienced dance teachers may find it helps to begin by teaching dance to one cooperative class. Using props and designing lessons that are vigorous and action-packed are also strategies that help excite children about dance.

Reading Comprehension Questions

1. What should dance in the elementary school provide for children?
2. Identify three dance forms. Where does each form fit into a curriculum, and why?
3. What skill themes and movement concepts generally appear in dance content?
4. Name three settings for cultural dance in the elementary school. Choose a folk, ethnic, square, or country dance and describe its development in each of the three settings.
5. What is the focus of expressive dance?
6. What is the role of imagery in dance? What must children possess before they can effectively use imagery?
7. Expressive dance can be classified into what two types of experiences? What is the primary focus of each experience, and how does the purpose differ at each proficiency level?
8. What is sequencing?
9. What is dance making? What procedures must be included in dance making?
10. How can you evaluate dance making?
11. Choose a theme for a creative dance for children. Outline the dance to show beginning and ending shapes, locomotor movements, travel pathways, and concepts that express the theme.
12. What cues do the authors give for starting to teach creative dance?

References/Suggested Readings

Austin, G., & Lipscomb, B. (1989). *Movement and dance.* London: Cassell Publishers. Teaching cards, booklet, and audiocassette.

Barlin, A. L. (1979). *Teaching your wings to fly.* Santa Monica, CA: Goodyear.

Bennett, J. P., & Riemer, P. C. (1995). *Rhythmic activities and dance.* Champaign, IL: Human Kinetics.

Benzwie, T. (1988). *A moving experience.* Tucson, AZ: Zephyr Press.

Boorman, J. (1969). *Creative dance in the first three grades.* New York: McKay.

Buchoff, R., & Mitchell, D. (1996). Poetry workouts. *Strategies, 10*(1), 18–21.

Carroll, J., & Lofthouse, P. (1969). *Creative dance for boys.* London: MacDonald & Evans.

Cone, T., & Cone, S. (2005). *Teaching children dance* (2nd ed.). Champaign, IL: Human Kinetics.

Davis, J. (1995). Laban movement analysis: A key to individualizing children's dance. *Journal of Physical Education, Recreation and Dance, 66*(2), 31–33.

Docherty, D. (1977). *Education through the dance experience.* Bellingham, WA: Educational Designs and Consultants.

Fleming, G. A. (1976). *Creative rhythmic movement.* Englewood Cliffs, NJ: Prentice Hall.

Fleming, G. A. (ed.). (1981). *Children's dance.* Reston, VA: American Alliance for Health, Physical Education, Recreation and Dance.

Holt/Hale, S. (2006). *On the move: Lesson plans to accompany Children Moving.* New York: McGraw-Hill.

Joyce, M. (1993). *Dance technique for children.* New York: McGraw-Hill.

Joyce, M. (1993). *First steps in teaching creative dance* (3rd ed.). New York: McGraw-Hill.

McGreevy-Nichols, S., & Scheff, H. (1995). *Building dances: A guide to putting movements together.* Champaign, IL: Human Kinetics.

Mehrhof, J. H., Ermler, K., & Kovar, S. (1993). Set the stage for dance. *Strategies, 6*(7), 5–7.

Murray, R. L. (1975). *Dance in elementary education* (3rd ed.). New York: Harper & Row.

National Association for Sport and Physical Education. (1992). *Outcomes of quality physical education programs.* Reston, VA: National Association for Sport and Physical Education.

National Association for Sport and Physical Education. (2004). *Moving into the future: National standards for physical education* (2nd ed.). Reston, VA: National Association for Sport and Physical Education.

Russell, J. (1975). *Creative movement and dance for children.* Boston: Plays.

Slater, W. (1974). *Teaching modern educational dance.* London: MacDonald & Evans.

Smith, J. A. (1972, April). The awful beginning. *Today's Education, 61*(4), 56.

Stinson, S. (1988). *Dance for young children: Finding the magic in movement.* Reston, VA: American Alliance for Health, Physical Education, Recreation and Dance.

Stinson, S. W. (1993). Voices from schools—The significance of relationship to public school dance students. *Journal of Physical Education, Recreation and Dance, 64*(5), 52–56.

Weikart, P. S. (1989). *Teaching movement and dance* (3rd ed.). Ypsilanti, MI: High Scope Press.

Weikart, P. S. (1997). *Teaching folk dance: Successful steps.* Ypsilanti, MI: High Scope Press.

Willis, C. M. (1995a). Creative dance education: Establishing a positive learning environment. *Journal of Physical Education, Recreation and Dance, 66*(4), 16–20.

Willis, C. M. (1995b). Creative dance: How to increase parent and teacher awareness. *Journal of Physical Education, Recreation and Dance, 66*(5), 48–53.

Appendix 29A Teacher-Designed Group Routines

Lummi Sticks

Lummi sticks for elementary-age children are usually 12 inches long and 1 inch in diameter. They may be made from rolled newspaper sealed with tape or cut from broom and mop handles or dowel rods. We have found it best to have children practice with the paper sticks until they master the basic patterns. Each child needs two sticks. The routine that follows is designed in two parts. First, children learn the basic patterns without tossing the sticks; then they work with a partner to add tossing and catching the sticks in the rhythm of the pattern.

Basic Patterns

Pattern 1: Hold sticks together vertically, one in each hand. Tap sticks down, tap sticks together, extend right hand forward. Tap down, tap sticks together, extend left hand forward. Repeat entire pattern two times.

Pattern 2: Hold sticks vertically, one in each hand. Tap both sticks down, tap them together, extend right hand, extend left hand. Repeat pattern four times.

Pattern 3: Hold sticks horizontally, with front tips extending toward the floor. Touch the edge of the sticks to the floor, and then half-flip the sticks, catching the sticks in your hands. Hold sticks vertically for one count. Repeat pattern 2. Touch edge of sticks to floor; half-flip the sticks, hold sticks one count. Then repeat pattern 2: Tap down, tap sticks together, extend right hand, extend left hand. Repeat entire pattern four times.

Pattern 4: Hold sticks horizontally on each side of your body. Touch the edge of each stick on the floor, and then half-flip the sticks. Bring sticks in front of you and perform pattern 3: Side touch, flip; front touch, flip; tap down, tap together, extend right hand, extend left hand. Repeat entire pattern four times.

Pattern 5: Hold sticks horizontally on each side of your body. Touch side front, side back, side front. Bring the sticks in front of your body; touch front, cross your arms over, touch on opposite side, uncross arms and touch. Repeat pattern 2: Side, touch front, back, front; front, side, cross, side. Tap down, tap together, extend right hand, extend left hand. Repeat entire pattern four times.

Tossing to a Partner
Children sit facing a partner, approximately 3 feet from the partner. Patterns are the same basic patterns, except that instead of an extension

Student-designed Lummi stick routine, to be performed with a partner.

of the arm, the stick is tossed to the partner, who catches it.

Chinese Ribbons

Chinese ribbons or streamers for elementary school students are 8 to 12 feet long and made of plastic. Crepe paper can be used, but it doesn't withstand children's practice or rough handling. Streamers can be made by attaching the plastic to a 12-inch dowel rod with either an eyelet and screw or a swivel hook and nylon fishing line.

In time with the music, the streamers are twirled in front of the body, to the side, or over the head. The following patterns represent a combination of skills suited for control level. Routines become more advanced as locomotor skills are added.

Pattern 1: Side circles—right side, left side

Pattern 2: Front circles

Pattern 3: Figure 8s—in front of the body

Pattern 4: Helicopter—circles overhead

Pattern 5: Lasso—front circles near the floor

Chinese ribbon patterns.

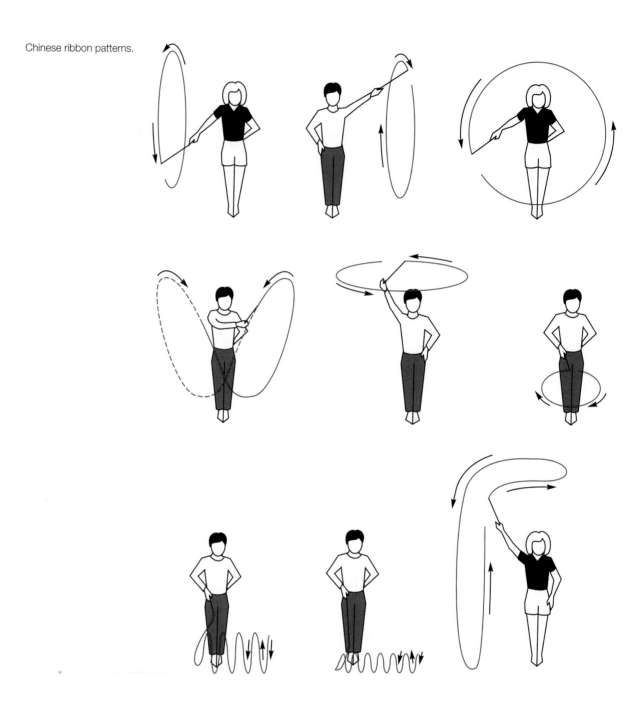

Pattern 6: Walk the Dog—waist-high vertical movements in front, to the sides

Pattern 7: Snake—forward, backward movements near the floor, in front, to the sides

Pattern 8: Mountain Peaks—slow vertical movements, high to low levels

The ribbon routines of rhythmic gymnastics in the Olympics are examples of this skill at the proficiency level. Videotapes of rhythmic gymnastics are available for educational use from the U.S. Olympic Committee, One Olympic Plaza, Colorado Springs, CO 80909.

Musical Parachute

Parachute routines are combinations of locomotor and nonlocomotor actions. Sample skills include:

Waves: Shaking the parachute up and down

Umbrella: Raising the parachute high overhead

Mountain: Bringing the umbrella down to touch the edges on the floor

Merry-go-round: Locomotor actions moving the parachute clockwise and counterclockwise

Floating cloud: Umbrella with release of the parachute

Mushroom: Inflating the umbrella and moving forward to a mushroom shape

Music that is flowing, smooth, and expressive with a strong underlying beat is good for parachute routines. The best music is a song with meaningful lyrics and expressive movements in the format of the music. Routines should be easy to understand and to perform, with creative movements and shapes that flow and change with the music. We have found it best to begin with instrumental music; words can be a distraction to the routine directions. After the students have mastered the routine, the music can be either instrumental or vocal.

The following routine is designed for students whose skills are at the control level and is done to the music "Pop Goes the Weasel":

Children sit around the parachute and face clockwise. They hold the parachute in their right hands. The children are numbered 1 and 2, with 2 being behind 1, who is the partner.

Start the introductory music ("Pop Goes the Weasel"). The children stand up on the first "pop," still holding the parachute with their right hands only.

The children march clockwise in time with the music until they hear "*Pop* goes the weasel," at which point the 1s let go of the parachute and walk under the chute and behind their partners. Now the 2s are in front.

Students march clockwise. On the next "pop," the 2s let go of the chute and go under the chute and behind their partners. Now the 1s are in front again.

Children now skip clockwise. On the "pop," the 1s go under the chute and behind their partners.

The children continue skipping. On the "pop," the 2s go under the chute and behind their partners.

Students now face the center of the circle, holding the parachute with both their hands. Using the slidestep, they travel clockwise. On the "pop," children stop, then repeat the slidestep counterclockwise. They stop again, raise the parachute high in the air, and bring it back to the tuck position; they don't let go of the chute.

Youngsters wait for the next "pop," at which point they raise the parachute high in the air, walk forward three steps, and then pull the parachute down behind them so they're "in the cave."

Students wait quietly in the cave. When they hear the final "pop," they come out of the cave.

Jump Rope

Jump-rope routines at the control level should be relatively short and include only the basic jumps that everyone in class can do. As a rhythmic experience, a group jump-rope routine involves executing the jump-rope skills correctly, staying in rhythm with the music, and staying in time with others in the group.

Music that has a strong beat and generates energy is best for jump-rope routines. The following is an example of a group jump-rope routine for children at the control level; it is designed for 4/4 rhythm.

The children place their ropes in a V shape on the floor, so they can stand inside the V and jump outside the V.

Start with a six-count introductory phrase. Then have the children execute six double jumping jacks. Starting inside the V, they clap thighs twice and clap hands above head twice. They jump outside the V as they clap overhead, inside the V as they clap thighs: out, out, in, in.

The children then pick up their ropes and step over the rope so it is behind them, ready for the first skill (four counts).

They jump the rope using two-foot jumps eight times.

Next, they hold both handles of the rope in their right hands and execute eight double side swings. They turn the ropes in a forward circle on each side of their bodies.

Then they open the ropes and jump 12 times, using the step-jump skill.

Children again hold handles in their right hands. This time, they twirl the rope overhead like a helicopter (16 counts).

Finally, they quickly place the ropes in a V on the floor and stand inside (four counts). Then they execute six double jumping jacks.

Skill Themes in Gymnastics

If gymnastics is to be for everyone, including the handicapped child, then all children cannot be asked to do the same gymnastic movement at the same time, in exactly the same way, for clearly some children are going to be underchallenged and some are going to be overchallenged.

—ANDREA BOUCHER

Key Concepts

- Educational gymnastics focuses on children challenging themselves to maneuver their bodies effectively against the force of gravity, with challenges appropriate for each child and his or her skill level.

- Olympic-style gymnastics centers on specialized skills, performed the same way by all children with a goal of formal competition.

- The content of educational gymnastics derives from the skill themes of balance, transferring weight, and rolling in combination with jumping/landing, traveling, and movement concepts.

- Educational gymnastics includes floor experiences and apparatus experiences.

- Educational gymnastics apparatus includes tables, benches, beams, bars, vaulting boxes, and playground apparatus.

- Children should never be forced into attempting a gymnastics skill or activity; the teacher's knowledge of individual students and selection of developmentally appropriate activities are critical for positive learning experiences and safety.

The skill themes of balancing and transferring weight, coupled with jumping and landing and traveling, form the foundation of educational gymnastics. As stated earlier in the text, movement skills and concepts form the curricular base for elementary physical education, with dance, educational gymnastics, and games/sports skills as the content areas through which these skills and concepts are explored, mastered, and applied. The development and mastery of skills would be of little value if left in isolation, without infusion into games, gymnastics, and dance. This chapter integrates the skills of traveling, jumping and landing, balancing, and transferring weight, as well as the concepts of space awareness, effort, and relationships, into the content area of educational gymnastics.

The Nature of Gymnastics

The self-testing nature of gymnastics is challenging to children. They constantly ask themselves, "Can I balance in this position without falling? Can I walk this curb? Can I stand on my head? Can I climb this tree and hang by my arms?" These self-testing challenges meet the criteria of effective teaching/learning in several ways.

First, children receive immediate feedback regarding the skill: "Yes, I can do a headstand, " or "No, I am still losing my balance." Second, the feedback is personal and not dependent on others; children do not have to rely on others to determine whether they are successful at the task. Third, the self-challenging tasks of gymnastics are a natural part of children's world; their environment, coupled with their curiosity and love of movement, creates multiple opportunities for climbing, hanging, supporting weight on different body parts, balancing, rolling, and so on. Finally, the self-testing nature of gymnastics permits younger children who are still in the egocentric stage of development to participate fully and successfully in a personal challenge without the necessity of team play or cooperative work with other children.

Children are exposed to advanced, competitive gymnastics through television coverage of the Olympics, as well as by watching local club gymnasts on the playgrounds and in their neighborhoods. Children without a background of gymnastics experiences often enter our gymnasiums saying, "I can't do those things" or asking "Will we do back handsprings today?" Our task is to present gymnastics for children in a way that is both challenging and appropriate for all students in our classes. The skills covered in the earlier chapters on balancing and transferring weight and rolling, along with those of jumping, landing, and locomotion, are the skills in educational gymnastics that are appropriate for elementary physical education.

To children, the self-testing, risk-taking nature of gymnastics brings excitement; to the teacher, it brings the challenge of creating a safe environment. We as teachers must always be sure the equipment arrangement, class organization, and selection of tasks maximize safety for our students. There must be a match between student and task, with intratask variation to allow for individual differences. The skills must progress from simple to complex, and the students must master each task before moving to the more complex. The teacher must never require that all students perform the same task. Performance of a certain skill must never be linked to a "grade" in physical education. The gymnastics tasks presented must be challenging to the less skilled, yet not boring to the highly skilled; tasks that are too easy or too difficult can lead to boredom and frustration. As a result, children may create their own agenda and an unsafe environment for learning in gymnastics. Finally, the mastery of gymnastics skills is a slow process and must not be rushed by us as teachers or by our students. *These considerations are critically important to creating a safe learning environment for all children.*

The Purpose of Gymnastics

Educational gymnastics as taught in physical education is not the same as Olympic gymnastics; the two have related but different purposes. Olympic-style gymnastics centers on specialized skills, with all students performing the same way, and on training for formal gymnastics competition. In educational gymnastics, we don't train children to become competitive gymnasts; rather, we provide experiences to teach children to maneuver their bodies effectively against the force of gravity with balance and transferring weight challenges in appropriate environments on both the floor and apparatus. We attempt to provide our students with a foundation of gymnastics experiences that increase their skills and introduce them to the types of activities characteristic of gymnastics.

The *National Standards for Physical Education* (NASPE, 2004) supports the inclusion of educational gymnastics in elementary physical education. See Box 30-1 for the sample benchmarks specific to gymnastics in the elementary school curriculum contained in the *National Standards.*

The specialization of skills for competitive, Olympic-style gymnastics is reserved for club gymnastics and after-school programs with trained gymnastics specialists and coaches. These programs provide the training needed for specialization in specific stunts, required routines, and advanced aerial skills. Children interested in Olympic-style gymnastics or advanced work beyond the level of educational gymnastics can

Children challenge themselves on the floor or mats before attempting balances on apparatus.

Moving in relation to apparatus is part of educational gymnastics.

Box 30-1

Educational Gymnastics and the *National Standards for Physical Education*

The *National Standards for Physical Education* (National Association for Sport and Physical Education, 2004) cites the following performance outcomes for educational gymnastics in elementary physical education:

- Discovers how to balance on different body parts, at different levels, becoming "like" a statue while making symmetrical and nonsymmetrical shapes (K–2)*
- Balances with control on a variety of objects, such as large apparatus (3–5)*
- Develops and refines a gymnastics sequence demonstrating smooth transitions (3–5)*
- Designs and performs gymnastics sequences that combine traveling, rolling, balancing, and weight transfer into smooth, flowing sequences with intentional changes in direction, speed, and flow (6–8)*

*Grade-level guidelines for expected student learning.

enroll in programs sponsored by youth agencies or private clubs. Some schools offer after-school programs for students who want additional practice in gymnastics.

Specializing in and teaching Olympic-style gymnastics in physical education class can educate a few students, but the majority will be left behind and the risk of injury for the less skilled students will increase. Educational gymnastics programs are designed to assist all children, regardless of ability, to improve their gymnastics skills—to become better able to control their bodies in the variety of planned and unplanned encounters they will have, as children and as adults, with the force of gravity (Box 30-2).

Do we exclude Olympic stunts from our curriculum? Not at all. Children at the utilization and proficiency levels who have a background in gymnastics experiences and the proper body control often use Olympic stunts as a response to a gymnastics task. When children use a handstand, walkover, or cartwheel, for example, the maneuver should be identified as such. With children who do have a background in gymnastics, we discuss the stunts they have chosen in response to the task given. We decide whether the response is appropriate for physical education class or best reserved for club gymnastics; for example, we consider whether the stunt requires a spotter and whether the other children will be tempted to imitate a stunt beyond their capabilities that could result in injury.

Other children in class may ask for help in learning a specific stunt or in perfecting one they've seen and are practicing on their own. The teacher's guidance is very important in these instances. As teachers, we can assess the child's skill level and the difficulty of the stunt. If these match, we can give the verbal cues and/or assistance to enable the child to learn the skill correctly and safely.

The Content of Educational Gymnastics

The content of educational gymnastics derives from the skill themes of balance, weight transference, and rolling in combination with jumping, landing, and traveling. The specifics of these themes, as well as appropriate challenges for children, are found in Chapters 19, 21, 22, and 23. The content also includes such concepts as directions, levels, pathways, time, shapes, and the actions of stretching, curling, and twisting (Chapters 16, 17, 18). These concepts and actions are incorporated into the gymnastics themes only after children have experienced them in isolation and/or in games and dance. For example, children do not study twisting into and out of balances before they have an understanding of the action of twisting.

Before studying a skill theme in educational gymnastics, children need an understanding of the concept of balance in gymnastics—maintaining stillness in a position and holding that position for 3 to 5 seconds. Many children can take weight on their hands momentarily or balance in a headstand for 1 to 2 seconds but cannot hold the position stationary for 5 seconds. Children need early experiences in aligning body parts for balance and in tightening the muscles to maintain balance as prerequisites to skill themes in educational gymnastics. Children often fall out of inverted balances because the body parts are not properly aligned over the base of support and muscular tension is not sufficient to hold the proper alignment. Introductory and review lessons focusing on these fundamental skills will contribute to a safer environment in which students experience balance and weight transference activities and will also enhance mastery in gymnastics learning experiences.

Box 30-2

Appropriate and Inappropriate Physical Education Practices

Educational Gymnastics

Appropriate Practice

Teachers facilitate children's development through lessons designed to sequentially develop skills appropriate to their ability and confidence level in gymnastics situations centered around the themes of balancing, rolling, jumping, landing, and transferring weight.

Children practice on apparatus designed for their levels of skill and confidence and design sequences which support and challenge their personal skill levels.

Inappropriate Practice

Teachers require all students to perform the same predetermined stunts and routines on and off apparatus, regardless of their skill level, body composition, and level of confidence.

Teachers have students perform solo while the remainder of the class sits and watches and compares performances to other students.

Activities require extensive teacher direction and spotting.

Source: Appropriate Practices for Elementary School Physical Education: A Position Statement of the National Association for Sport and Physical Education, 2000, Reston, VA: National Association for Sport and Physical Education. Reprinted with permission.

Educational gymnastics is divided into floor experiences and apparatus experiences. Floor experiences are movements executed on grass, mats, or carpeting that don't require equipment to enhance the challenge. Apparatus experiences involve moving in relation to one or several pieces of equipment (tables, benches, beam, bars, vaulting boxes, and playground apparatus). Although apparatus adds excitement to gymnastics, children can experience challenging, rewarding work in educational gymnastics with floor experiences only.

Even in a program rich in gymnastics apparatus, children should spend a large amount of time on floor/mat experiences before they begin work on apparatus. Balance, weight transference, and rolling activities should be mastered on mats and carpet squares before they are attempted on low or high gymnastics apparatus. Many of the movements performed on the floor will be replicated on apparatus, but the height and narrowness of the surfaces will increase the difficulty of the task. Students begin apparatus work on low, larger surfaces—that is, crates/boxes, low beams, and benches—before they work on higher, more narrow pieces of apparatus.

Floor Experiences

Children at the precontrol level in educational gymnastics explore balancing on different body parts as bases of support, balancing on wide bases, and balancing in different shapes. They learn to curve their bodies into rounded shapes and to maintain the rounded shape for rocking/rolling. They also learn to transfer weight safely on and off equipment and apparatus.

Control-level experiences include rolling from different positions and in different directions. Inverted balances are introduced, with a strong emphasis on alignment of body parts and muscular tension to maintain balance. The concept of stillness is studied in combination with weight-transfer actions and as a contrast to rolling. Beginning at the control level, children are challenged with combinations of skills and the combination of skills and concepts—for example, moving from a two-part balance into a three-part balance on new bases of support or balancing in a wide body shape at different levels.

Floor experiences for children are designed to lead children from exploration of balances and transferring weight to control of their bodies in these self-imposed challenges to application of the skills in gymnastics sequences. Children are introduced to sequences at the control level. Beginning-level sequences may be as simple as a beginning shape, followed by three balances on different bases of support and an ending

Exploring basic shapes on apparatus follows balances on the floor/mats.

shape. As children become more competent in gymnastics and more confident in the process, sequences become increasingly complex, with combinations of transfer actions and stillness, movement concepts, and transitions. These sequences still include a beginning and an ending shape.

More advanced and increasingly complex sequences of movements are enjoyable and challenging to children at the utilization level, who have developed control over movements executed singularly. Gymnastics sequences for these children include stretching, curling, twisting, and/or rolling actions as transitions between balances, as well as combinations of balances, weight-transfer actions, and traveling. Movement concepts and variations of a concept (e.g., changes in levels, variations in speed) are incorporated in the sequences.

Maintaining weight on hands, exploring the state of being "almost off" balance, and taking part or all of a partner's weight are appropriate proficiency-level tasks for children in educational gymnastics. Students at this level enjoy focusing on the quality of movement execution in gymnastics. The concepts of acceleration and deceleration, strong and light, bound and free are added to sequences. Matching or mirroring the

Children skilled on the floor move on to apparatus.

movements of a partner, repeating sequences of several gymnastics movements, and experiences that involve several students supporting one another's weight are all proficiency-level gymnastics floor experiences.

Apparatus Experiences

Once children demonstrate control of their bodies in educational gymnastics floor experiences, have an understanding of safety in gymnastics, and understand the concept of sequences, we introduce them to experiences on apparatus. Balance beams, parallel bars, side horses, vaulting boxes, and still rings are Olympic gymnastics equipment. Some elementary schools have this official gymnastics apparatus, but many elementary school programs use benches, tables, chairs, hoops, the edge of a stage, climbing ropes, and climbing frames to provide gymnastics experiences on apparatus. Unofficial equipment is often more compatible with the children's abilities, and children have fewer preconceived notions about what is expected when they practice movements on an unfamiliar or nontraditional piece of equipment.

You can introduce the children to a piece of apparatus by encouraging them to explore the equipment and to discover safe ways to get on and off it. Children at the precontrol level can start by walking along a low beam or bench, jumping from a chair or low table, hanging from a climbing rope at a low height, or traveling along a climbing frame. Obstacle courses designed from available equipment—tables, benches, chairs, hoops, ropes—are also challenging to children at this level as they learn the concepts of under, over, along, and through. Some children will begin immediately to explore the apparatus; other children will be more cautious. Never force any child onto a piece of apparatus.

Children at the control level, while continuing to explore apparatus, can begin to focus on different ways to move in relation to the equipment. They can try different ways of traveling along a beam, hanging from a bar or rope, jumping from a table or chair, or traveling from side to side on a climbing frame. They can balance on different bases of support and combine traveling with stationary balances on apparatus. Sequence work at the control level might include transferring weight onto the apparatus, balancing and traveling on the apparatus, and traveling off the apparatus. Skills that were mastered during the floor experiences present a new challenge to children as they attempt them on various pieces of gymnastics apparatus.

Children at the utilization level can try different ways to get onto equipment, vaulting over equipment, and forming shapes in flight while moving from apparatus to the floor. Apparatus experiences that involve supporting weight on different body parts, transferring weight on equipment, nonsymmetrical balances, and inverted balances are also appropriate for children at this level.

When children reach the proficiency level, they should continue to focus on increasingly demanding balances, shapes, ways of traveling, and ways of supporting body weight. As with gymnastics experiences on the floor that lead from exploration to mastery to application, children on gymnastics apparatus progress from exploration and safety on apparatus to control of their bodies and mastery of skills to application in sequences. Educational gymnastics sequences at the utilization and proficiency levels demonstrate mastery of advanced skills, complex combinations of skills and concepts, and individual and/or partner creativity.

From the beginning children should be encouraged to focus on the quality of their movements and to be creative and versatile in their sequence composition. The education gymnastic sequences is the child's expression of self—a portrayal of self in gymnastics showing skills and concepts that flow together smoothly and fluently.

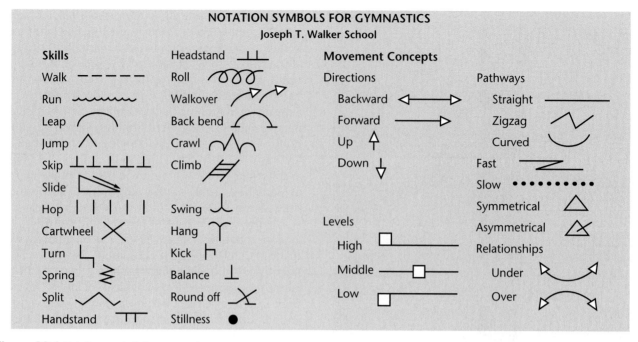

Figure 30.1 Notation symbols for gymnastics.
Source: Steve Sanders, Joseph T. Walker School, Marietta, GA. Used with permission.

Recording Sequences

A sequence in gymnastics can be compared to a recital piece in music. Once the children have learned the skills, they are to memorize and then repeat them in exactly the same order with exactly the same balances and actions. This is one of the most difficult parts of sequencing for children. They enjoy creating, but not memorizing for repetition. Recording the sequences with paper and pencil helps children retain them. They may record their gymnastics sequences with drawings and stick figures, and the class may devise a system of notation for balances and actions. You as a teacher may develop a method of recording sequences that will be used in all your gymnastics classes. Figure 30.1 shows a gymnastics notation system developed by Steve Sanders while working with students at the Walker School in Marietta, Georgia.

The notation system, which was inspired by Rudolf Laban's notation in dance, uses a symbol for each framework element most frequently used in gymnastics. For example, low level is represented by □——, movement in a backward direction is represented by ◁——▷, a roll is represented by ⌀⌀⌀, and a movement performed at a slow speed is represented by ●●●●●. In a written description of a gymnastics movement, the skill is listed first, and the movement concepts are written underneath the skill.

Sanders viewed the system as a way of enhancing the children's movement vocabulary so that they would better understand the meanings of the terms in the movement analysis framework. He also wanted to increase the amount of thought and creativity that the students put into building their gymnastics sequences. You may choose to have children create their own notation systems, or you may create one with the children to use throughout your program.

Outdoor Play Equipment As Gymnastics Apparatus

Outdoor playground equipment can serve as gymnastics apparatus in schools that have no indoor equipment or indoor physical education facility and as an additional avenue of exploration for children who've experienced indoor gymnastics. Children at the precontrol and control levels can focus on body control on various pieces of equipment. Children at the utilization and proficiency levels will be challenged by the complexity of structure, the number of bars, the distance between bars, and the variety of levels on playground equipment. Horizontal ladders, parallel bars, jungle gyms, monkey bars, and telephone pole balance beams can be used for rolling, balancing, and transferring weight on apparatus. (See Chapters 22 and 23 for these activities.)

Very often the key to successfully teaching gymnastics on the playground is the positioning of the playground equipment: grouping versus isolated pieces of

Rolling on a bench is a challenge for this utilization-level student.

These youngsters enjoy creating matching balances.

equipment. If the playground equipment is grouped, several pieces can easily accommodate a class of 25 to 30 children. But if the playground arrangement is such that instruction of the group on various apparatus as well as of individuals isn't possible, cable spools and milk crates can be added to supplement large apparatus.

Children's work on playground apparatus should begin with a study of the proper use of the equipment—the acceptable and unacceptable activities on the apparatus—and correct ways of getting on and off the apparatus. Early in the school year, let the children explore the various pieces of apparatus; this will lead to questions from the children and class discussions about what is permitted during both physical education

class and recess. Any safety rules needed should be developed cooperatively by teacher and students; the rules may vary for younger and older children.

The use of playground equipment in physical education class will lead to increased use of that equipment during recess, which may make classroom teachers uncomfortable with children on the equipment. However, a booklet of the rules established for physical education class and for recess will help the classroom teacher be more at ease. The use of apparatus during physical education can be very different from the use of apparatus during recess; it's our responsibility to be sure children understand the difference.

The Process of Teaching Educational Gymnastics

Teaching gymnastics is different from teaching either dance or games because of the self-testing nature of gymnastics and because apparatus is used. Successful educational gymnastics teachers are able to match interesting and challenging tasks to the children's ability levels. This is a teaching skill learned only with time and practice.

Some teachers avoid gymnastics because they are concerned about the safety of the children and are afraid that children might be injured; some administrators are hesitant to include gymnastics in the curriculum for the same reasons. Injury is always a possibility in physical education classes. When the focus is on educational gymnastics (as opposed to Olympic-style stunts) and when the experiences are presented sequentially and in an appropriate environment, gymnastics is no more dangerous than other physical education activities. The following ideas relating to the learning environment and the teaching of educational gymnastics help create successful and safe experiences for children. Taken together, these suggestions, along with the safety emphasis icon (⚠), will help establish a safe learning environment for the teaching of educational gymnastics.

The Learning Environment

From the initial lessons, children learn spatial awareness of their movements and the movements of others. They are taught not to interfere with others attempting their gymnastics work, either by touching or talking to them. Concentration on the task is essential in gymnastics.

An appropriate learning environment in gymnastics emphasizes safety throughout. Encourage the children

Children are encouraged to be responsible for themselves and their own safety.

to be responsible for their own safety. Stress that if they don't think they can do something, they should either not do it or ask you for help. Games of I Dare You and Follow the Leader are inappropriate in gymnastics classes. Remember, following the progression outlined in the spirals for gymnastics skills and mastering a skill before attempting the next is critical for safety. Gymnastics classes are not the place for off-task behavior; being off-task in games and/or dance may result in behavior that is inappropriate, but off-task behavior in gymnastics can lead to injury. When we encourage children to be responsible for themselves, they will rely less on us and more on themselves to determine what is appropriate. Acceptance of responsibility and self-reliance are goals of physical education; they are major goals in teaching gymnastics.

Gymnastics Equipment

Gymnastics apparatus is heavy, cumbersome, and difficult for one person to move. In some situations, gymnastics would never be taught if the teacher had to move the gymnastics equipment alone. Children can be taught to move gymnastics equipment correctly during the first few lessons in which the apparatus is used. Once they learn to maneuver the apparatus safely and efficiently, the children can set up or take down a gymnastics environment in a short time. The following guidelines should be followed when children move gymnastics apparatus:

1. An adequate number of children (as determined by the teacher) must be present before equipment can be moved.
2. Children are to lift the equipment together and lower it together, being careful of toes and fingers.
3. Each piece of apparatus has its own storage space to which it is to be returned.

Moving gymnastics apparatus correctly is as important a part of the children's learning in educational gymnastics as working safely on the apparatus. Taking the time during the initial lessons to teach them the proper procedure will help create a safe environment for gymnastics and increase valuable instructional time in subsequent lessons.

Stations

Initial gymnastics lessons for children at the precontrol level focus on floor experiences with large-group instruction. During this time, the children learn how to control their bodies when balancing, transferring weight, and rolling; they also learn about safety in gymnastics and working independently. After children demonstrate the ability to work safely and independently, allowing the class to work at stations (learning centers) can be a most efficient method of providing maximum participation on gymnastics apparatus. The stations are set up in different parts of the teaching area (see Chapter 13), with groups working on the same or different skills on the various pieces of equipment. Sample tasks include jumping from a low table or chair onto a mat, landing, and rolling; traveling different ways along a bench or beam; climbing a rope; practicing taking weight on hands; and traveling onto and off a table.

This method of organization allows the use of various pieces of equipment and eliminates long lines. Tasks for the stations can be written on poster boards and taped to the wall near each station. This increases practice time: The children can read the directions and begin work immediately. The number of stations and complexity of the setup are guided by the following considerations:

1. How many stations will the total available space accommodate?

Transferring weight from feet to hands is a control level activity that can later be used in gymnastics routines.

2. Are there enough mats to place under and around each piece of equipment?
3. Is the space surrounding the station adequate for the children to practice getting off the equipment—for example, jumping, landing, and rolling—safely?
4. Is the space between the stations sufficient to allow the children to work without interfering with those at the adjoining station?
5. Does the setup provide the teacher the freedom to move throughout the learning environment, giving individual assistance as needed?

Teach children very early in gymnastics to do a "Safety Check" before they begin work at any station: mats correctly placed under equipment, adequate space surrounding the equipment. In the beginning, stop the class frequently and ask the children to do a "Safety Check," visually scanning the working area for space and equipment safety.

Varying the Task

When all the children in a class are expected to perform the same skill the same way, two things are likely to happen. Many of the children in the class will be bored because they can already perform the task successfully. Some of the children will be frightened because the task is too difficult for them, and they know it. When you offer children some choices about how they'll perform a task, each child can select an appropriate level of activity. For example, it's unlikely that all the children in a particular class will be able to do a handstand. Some children may not be strong enough to support all their body weight on their hands; some won't be able to land safely if they lose their balance.

Instead of telling the entire class to do a handstand, you could tell the children to find a way to place some or all of their weight on their hands. An instruction that allows for individual differences in ability affords all children an opportunity for success.

Safety Rules

Rules for working safely on mats and apparatus should be explained, demonstrated, and enforced very carefully. We suggest posting the rules where the children can see them as they work. (See Chapter 9, "Establishing an Environment for Learning," for additional suggestions.)

Club Gymnasts

Some of the children in your classes may be studying gymnastics independently, perhaps in a club or recreation program. Most of the club gymnasts are more skilled than the other children—many are at the proficiency level in many skills. Their skills in gymnastics may exceed your teaching knowledge and ability in this area. Because you're responsible for the safety of all the children, the activities of these club gymnasts may cause you some uneasiness.

If you explain your concern to these children, you'll find that they appreciate your candor. Tell these young gymnasts that you're working to learn about the movements they're practicing. Assure them that once you're skilled enough to help them practice appropriately and safely, you'll be delighted to have them resume practice in class.

This approach makes it clear that you aren't criticizing but instead are respecting their proficiency. Students will, in turn, respect you for acknowledging your limitations and seeking their cooperation, and teacher-student rapport will be enhanced.

The other children will look to the club gymnasts as models and sources for new ideas. The presence of club gymnasts in a gymnastics class results in an interesting blend of child-created gymnastics skills and Olympic gymnastics skills, providing an interesting dimension to gymnastics lessons.

Demonstrating

Some teachers feel that because they aren't skilled gymnasts themselves, they won't be able to teach gymnastics effectively. Certainly a thorough background in a teaching area is an asset in teaching. But even teachers who aren't skilled gymnasts can provide children with appropriate gymnastics experiences. In educational gymnastics, the instructor doesn't need to be able to demonstrate a skill correctly, because the children are never expected to perform the same skill the same way. If you want to give children additional ideas or to emphasize a particular movement quality or concept, you can invite some of the more proficient children to demonstrate for the rest of the class. This technique has the added advantage of reinforcing those children who are working especially well.

Spotting

Spotting—the practice of physically assisting children as they perform a movement—isn't commonly used in educational gymnastics classes. Children who depend on such help are likely to be unsure and even afraid unless a teacher is nearby. And, conversely, spotting encourages children to attempt movements they may not be ready for. We've observed a number of programs, including our own, in which children have progressed to a relatively high level of skill proficiency without any spotting. To say we do not "spot" children when they are performing skills in educational gymnastics is not to say we do not strongly believe in safety for all children in the gymnastics setting. Throughout the skill themes for gymnastics (Chapters 19, 21–23) you will have noted the safety icon (⚠️) emphasizing safety tips for the teacher.

The Little Gymnast

Come with us, now, to a very nice place where little children swing on rings.

Where laughter is king—and happiness queen—and everyone likes who they are.

On a little green island called Mercer, in a big blue Washington lake surrounded by trees, is a wonderful building assembled by people who think it's important for children to play. And learn. And find out what they can do.

The building is called the Jewish Community Center, and children come from miles around to follow a Pied Piper of a man named Robin West.

Robin grew up in South Africa and then went to college at the University of Saskatchewan in Canada. Now he teaches movement, tumbling, and gymnastics to hundreds of boys and girls in the United States. One of his favorite classes is "kiddie gymnastics," for little gymnasts, four to six.

Most four-year-olds already know how to run, jump, and play when they come to their very first day of kiddie gymnastics. But in no time at all, Robin can open their eyes to hundreds of new ways to move, swing, roll, bend, and balance their bodies with success.

"Success for everyone" is the motto in kiddie gymnastics. It's such a simple motto—so easy to follow—that sometimes even Robin and the children's parents must stop to remind themselves of its magic.

A child is a butterfly in the wind. Some can fly higher than others; but each one flies the best way it can. Why compare one against the other? Each one is different. Each one is special. Each one is beautiful.

In kiddie gymnastics, everyone flies and nobody fails. There's plenty of praise for the attempt well-tried. To balance on a beam for the very first time is discovery. To be praised and applauded for the very same motion is joy.

In just a few short weeks the children in Robin's class have learned to move with a confidence, poise, and imagination that surprises and pleases both themselves and their parents.

But they've also learned something else along the way. You can see it in their eyes when they tug so gently on Robin's bushy black beard. You can see it in the way they lie on their backsides and stare at the ceiling and giggle. It's as if they've learned something deep and exciting about themselves.

"I'm me . . . I'm special . . . I can try."

"If I make a mistake, it's all right. I'll start over . . . I'll learn . . . I'll get better."

"Look at my friend. I'm helping him stand on his head. He's special, too."

"We're good. We're children. We're okay."

Dan Zadra

Source: "The Little Gymnast," by Dan Zadra, 1976, *Young Athlete Magazine*, June, p. 8. Reprinted with permission.

A Final Thought

Teaching educational gymnastics is, in the beginning, perhaps more difficult than teaching Olympic-style gymnastics. In Olympic gymnastics, the desired outcomes are clear—the teacher wants the children to learn to execute predetermined skills in specific ways. In educational gymnastics the skills to be learned aren't predetermined, nor are they to be executed in one correct way. Instead, the teacher helps the children to improve their abilities to move in relation to the force of gravity, to learn self-confidence and self-reliance in interpreting tasks and determining the best ways to execute skills. Often it's more difficult for a teacher to share decisions with children than it is for the teacher to make the decisions. You'll find, however, that the process of sharing decisions in educational gymnastics can be exciting for you the teacher and rewarding for the children, regardless of their gymnastics abilities.

Summary

Because of the self-testing nature of gymnastics, most children are fascinated by the challenge of attempting to defy the force of gravity. It's important to distinguish educational gymnastics from Olympic gymnastics. Educational gymnastics focuses on enhancing each child's ability to maneuver the body more effectively against the force of gravity. Olympic gymnastics emphasizes the learning of specific gymnastics stunts, usually for the purpose of entering individual or team competition.

Many gymnastics movements are learned on the floor (mats) first and then practiced on apparatus. Gymnastics apparatus can be purchased, or equipment available in schools—such as tables, chairs, and benches—can be adapted to serve the same purposes.

Because of the increased likelihood of injury in gymnastics, it's important to establish an appropriate learning environment so that children avoid games like Follow the Leader or I Dare You. Gymnastics tasks can be presented in ways that allow for individual differences, and this should be done so that children aren't tempted to try movements they aren't ready for.

Reading Comprehension Questions

1. Why do children find balancing, transferring weight, and supporting weight on different body parts fascinating skills?
2. What are the purposes of Olympic gymnastics and educational gymnastics?
3. What are the two types of experiences in educational gymnastics? Describe each type.
4. What activities are taught at the different levels of skill proficiency for both types of educational gymnastics experiences?
5. How are children introduced to equipment?
6. Why are equipment arrangement, class organization, and selection of tasks extremely important in the teaching of educational gymnastics? Explain the significance of each in establishing the learning environment.
7. Why is it important to vary the task in gymnastics?
8. Why is teaching Olympic gymnastics somewhat easier than teaching educational gymnastics?

References/Suggested Readings

Boucher, A. (1978). Educational gymnastics is for everyone. *Journal of Physical Education and Recreation, 49*(7), 48–50.

Cameron, W. McD., & Pleasance, P. (1971). *Education in movement—gymnastics.* Oxford, England: Basil Blackwell.

Carroll, M. E., & Garner, D. R. (1984). *Gymnastics 7–11: A lesson-by-lesson approach.* London: Falmer Press.

Council on Physical Education for Children. (2000). *Appropriate practices for elementary school physical education: A position statement of the National Association for Sport and Physical Education.* Reston, VA: National Association for Sport and Physical Education.

Holbrook, J. (1974). *Movement activity in gymnastics.* Boston: Plays, Inc.

Kirchner, G., Cunningham, J., & Warrell, E. (1970). *Introduction to movement education.* Dubuque, IA: Brown.

Mauldon, E., & Layson, J. (1965). *Teaching gymnastics.* London: MacDonald & Evans.

Morison, R. (1969). *A movement approach to educational gymnastics*. London: Dent.

National Association for Sport and Physical Education. (2004). *Moving in the future: National standards for physical education* (2nd ed.). Reston, VA: National Association for Sport and Physical Education.

Nilges, L. M. (1997). Stages of content development in educational gymnastics. *Journal of Physical Education, Recreation and Dance, 68*(3), 50–55.

Nilges, L. M. (1999). Refining skill in educational gymnastics: Seeing quality through variety. *Journal of Physical Education, Recreation and Dance, 70*(3), 43–48.

O'Quinn, G. (1978). *Developmental gymnastics*. Austin: University of Texas Press.

Parent, S. (ed.). (1978, September). Educational gymnastics. *Journal of Physical Education and Recreation, 31*–50.

Teaching children gymnastics [videotape]. (1994). Champaign, IL: Human Kinetics.

Trevor, M. D. (1985). *The development of gymnastics skills.* Oxford, England: Basil Blackwell.

Werner, P. H. (2004). *Teaching children gymnastics: A developmentally appropriate approach.* (2nd ed.). Champaign, IL: Human Kinetics.

Williams, J. (1974). *Themes for educational gymnastics.* London: Lepus Books.

Zadra, D. (1976, June). The little gymnast. *Young Athlete Magazine, 8.*

Note: Although several of the references for educational gymnastics are older books, the reader is encouraged to try to locate them for reading and possible purchase; they are excellent resources in the teaching and content of educational gymnastics.

Skill Themes in Games

The game is not sacred; children are.

—JIM STIEHL

Key Concepts

- The purpose of games in the elementary curriculum is to provide experiences that allow all children to develop into competent games players.

- Games and sports are different; sports (in their institutionalized form) are inappropriate for children in physical education classes—games are appropriate.

- The content of games is largely based on the manipulative skills themes.

- There are three types of games experiences in the elementary school: invariant game skill experiences, dynamic gamelike experiences, and games-playing experiences.

- Invariant experiences focus on self-testing or challenge activities as the "game."

- Dynamic gamelike experiences include using skills in a changing (open) environment, combining skills, and developing tactics and strategy.

- Games-playing experiences involve playing games that conform to all that is known about appropriate practices in physical education.

- In teaching games, there are five types of game designs to choose from: predesigned games, modified predesigned games, teacher-designed games, teacher/child-designed games, and child-designed games.

- Other factors to be considered when teaching games include whether the teacher should officiate or not, what to call the game, whether the game should be cooperative or competitive, what size and variety of equipment should be used, and what size the groups should be.

As content is developed, the manipulative skill themes coupled with traveling, chasing, fleeing, and dodging are largely applied in the context of games. As such, it is not the game that is important, but the use of skills in game settings. The "game" allows children to apply the skills they have learned in a dynamic environment. Thus, our task is to provide games experiences for children in a way that is both challenging and appropriate for all students in our classes.

You might ask at this point, why include this chapter here, since game and gamelike experiences are included in the skill theme chapters? Yes, games and gamelike experiences appear in skill theme activities as the challenges that allow children to use the skills they have learned. The notion that children must do boring "practice" tasks before "playing the game" is exactly what skill themes is not about. Our contention is that children should apply their newly acquired skills

in developmentally appropriate gamelike activities throughout their learning. This chapter is designed to let you see how those game and gamelike experiences are developed and the richness of game possibilities.

The Nature of Games

Games always seem to take us back. They take us back to our own childhood, when we played for hours on the school playground, in the streets, and in the backyards of our neighborhoods. We played our made-up games, we played games that had names like Red Rover and dodgeball that we had learned somewhere, and we played games that were called by "real" names such as baseball and football. Our games playing is steeped in tradition. And tradition can be good or bad. It is good when it enables us to pass on the best of what games have to offer—friendship, skill practice, teamwork, camaraderie, and the sheer excitement of playing.

Yet, all too often, games playing seems to be the content area that traps us in the negative aspects of our tradition. We are trapped by the same tradition that brought us joy, trapped into thinking that what gave us excitement and satisfaction will also bring excitement and satisfaction to all of today's children. That entrapment lets us forget how we were usually the highly skilled players and how even we changed those games. We become so ingrained in the tradition that we forget how we adjusted all those games to make them our own and to meet our needs.

We made the games fit us, rather than fitting ourselves to the games. Rarely if ever did we play on regulation fields with regulation equipment with the "right" number of players or by any rules other than our own. We had bricks for bases, four players on a baseball team, imaginary runners, and no gloves, and we played with whatever bat and ball we could find. We didn't have people sit out, as they were all our friends. Yet somehow when we teach games to children we tend to get caught in the rules that we learned later in life, rules that we played by as teenagers and adults. Our challenge is to help all children enjoy playing games that are theirs, not ours, and to help prepare them to want to play games forever—whatever those games may be. Our challenge is to make the games playing experience fit the child. Thus, you will not find "games" in this chapter or in the skill theme chapters, but you will find experiences that allow children to apply their skills in a variety of developmentally appropriate games playing situations.

The concept of a game holds a very different connotation for children than it does for adults. Children tend to view games as activities that use skills (most often manipulative) in a challenging, self-testing, or applied fashion. These activities may or may not look like adult versions of sports. Sports are designed primarily for adults, have standardized rules and procedures, and require a level of technical expertise to which children will never aspire. Games use the same basic skills as many sports but lack the standardized rules and procedures. Quite often, children call their game activities by names similar to those of standardized sports, and their games may use equipment similar to that of standardized sports; however, the "game" is quite different.

Games content occupies a large percentage of what is taught in many elementary physical education programs. Sport content should not. Sports happen after school. Games happen in school. Games may look like sports at times, but they are not. At no point in the elementary school curriculum should we see games being played with full-fledged sports rules. Never should there be full sided teams, regulation rules, regulation fields, and children waiting their turns. We should see small sided teams, modified fields, rules that don't stop the flow of the activity, and all children playing all the time. Never should the teacher be the pitcher. Understanding the difference between games and sports is critical to the reflective elementary school teacher: Games are appropriate elementary school content; sports in their common form are not. So what purpose should games serve?

The Purpose of Games in the Elementary School

The purpose of games in the elementary school is to help children apply the cognitive, affective, and psychomotor skills they have acquired to become competent and knowledgeable games players. *Our task is to provide experiences that allow this to happen and that are appropriate for all children.* As a result of participating in physical education games experiences, children should be excited

So What's Wrong with Playing the Game?

This question invariably arises. And yes, there are multiple answers. Here are just a few:

- The actual time a child is involved in activity is minimal.
- The game is not appropriate for all children in the class—in terms of physical, psychological, or skill readiness.
- The equipment is inappropriate for all children.
- Children are eliminated from play (and these are the children who need to play the most).
- Children are spotlighted for their lack of skill (or their skillfulness).
- Winners and losers rate one child or group of children better than the others.
- When teams are chosen some children are publicly humiliated.
- The game is often just played to play a game; it is not linked to skill development.

The list can go on. For a more extensive discussion of the inappropriateness of playing "*the game*" see Neil Williams's Hall of Shame articles in *Journal of Physical Education, Recreation and Dance* (1992; 1994; 1996).

about participating in games-playing activities on their own. Our purpose is not to develop elite athletes.

The *National Standards for Physical Education* (National Association for Sport and Physical Education [NASPE], 2004) support the inclusion of games in elementary physical education. Box 31-1 lists the sample performance indicators specific to games in the elementary school curriculum. Additionally, *Appropriate Practices for Elementary School Physical Education* (Council on Physical Education for Children, 2000) provides a useful analysis of the appropriateness of games in different situations. It is our responsibility as physical educators to teach developmentally appropriate games (Box 31-2).

So how do we teach games appropriate to the elementary school child? Essentially, there are two pieces to the elementary games puzzle: what is taught (the content) and how it is taught (the process). The two are inextricably linked, but for clarity they are developed separately here.

The Content of Elementary School Games

The primary content of elementary school games is derived largely from the manipulative skill themes, combined with traveling, chasing, fleeing, and dodging. The content is integrated with almost every possible movement concept. For example, a player is asked to run while dribbling a ball, using changes in speed and direction to dodge an opponent, all the while being aware of where two other teammates and opponents are. Dance takes isolated movement skills and concepts and reconfigures them into expressive movements; gymnastics uses skills to defy gravity; but games situations require players both to combine skills and to use those skills strategically to outsmart and outplay an opponent. This requirement assumes ongoing strategical

Box 31-1

Games and the *National Standards for Physical Education*

Games and game skills are referenced in the *National Standards for Physical Education* (National Association for Sport and Physical Education, 2004) as sample performance outcomes under Standards 1, 2, 3, 4, and 6.

The performance outcomes for Standard 1: Demonstrates competency in motor skills and movement patterns needed to perform a variety of physical activities, state:

- Drops a ball and catches it at the peak of the bounce (K–2)*
- Demonstrates skills of chasing, fleeing, and dodging to avoid others (2)*
- Receives and sends an object in a continuous motion (2)*
- Strikes a ball repeatedly with a paddle (2)*
- Throws a ball underhand using mature form (e.g., places feet together and shoulders square to target, swings throwing arm straight back, shifts weight forward by stepping onto opposite foot, rolls ball off fingers, and finishes with throwing arm outstretched toward target) (K–2)*
- Travels forward and sideways, changing directions quickly in response to a signal or obstacle using a variety of locomotor skills (K–2)*
- Taps a ball from foot to foot, shifting weight and balancing the body on the nondribbling foot, while in one location (i.e., not moving) (K–2)*
- Dribbles then passes a basketball to a moving receiver (3–5)*
- Catches a fly ball using mature form (e.g., has eyes on ball, moves to position, reaches with hands, catches with hands only rather than trapping the ball, bends elbows to pull ball into chest to absorb force) (3–5)*
- Throws a ball overhand and hits a target on the wall (6-foot square centered 4 feet above the ground) from a distance of 40 feet) (3–5)*
- Throws a ball overhand to a partner 15 yards away using mature form (e.g., turns side to target, uses T-position [ball held close to and behind ear], rotates hips and chest toward target, twists, releases, follows through across body) after fielding a ball (3–5)*

The performance outcomes for Standard 2: Demonstrates understanding of movement concepts, principles, strategies, and tactics as they apply to the learning and performance of physical activities, state:

- Recognizes appropriate safety practices in general space by throwing balls only when others are not in the direct line of the throw (K–2)*
- Identifies and demonstrates key elements of a proper grip when holding a racket to perform the forearm strike (3–5)*

- Explains the necessity of transferring weight from the back leg to the front leg during an action that propels an object forward (3–5)*
- Accurately recognizes the critical elements of a catch made by a fellow student and provides feedback to that student (3–5)*
- Describes the difference in foot placement when kicking a stationary ball, a ball moving away, and a ball moving forward (3–5)*
- Designs a new game incorporating at least two motor skills, rules, and strategies (3–5)*

The performance outcomes for Standard 3: Participates regularly in physical activity, state:

- Engages in a variety of activities that involve the manipulation of objects in and outside of physical education class (K–2)*
- Participates regularly in a variety of nonstructured and minimally organized physical activities outside of physical education class (K–2)*
- Participates in organized sport activities provided through local community programs (3–5)*
- Participates in an intramural sports program provided by the school (3–5)*

The performance outcome for Standard 4: Achieves and maintains a health-enhancing level of physical fitness, states:

- Participates in a variety of games that increase breathing and heart rate (K–2)*

The performance outcomes for Standard 5: Exhibits responsible personal and social behavior that respects self and others in physical activity settings, states:

- Uses equipment and space safely and properly (K–2)*
- Works in a diverse group setting without interfering with others (K–2)*
- Accepts all playmates without regard to differences (e.g., ethnicity, gender, disability) (K–2)*
- Demonstrates the elements of socially acceptable conflict resolution during class activity (K–2)*
- Takes seriously the role of teaching an activity or skill to his or her team (3–5)*

The performance outcome for Standard 6: Values physical activity for health, enjoyment, challenge, self-expression, and/or social interaction, states:

- Develops a dance (or game) that is personally interesting (3–5)*

*Grade-level guidelines for expected student learning.

Box 31-2

Appropriate Practices for Elementary School Physical Education

Component: Using Games and Setting Rules for Games Play

Appropriate Practice

Teachers select, design, sequence, and modify games to maximize the attainment of specific learning, skill enhancement, and enjoyment. Games should reinforce a "lesson theme."

Teachers modify the rules, regulations, equipment, and playing space to facilitate learning by children of varying abilities or to focus learning on particular games or skills components.

Inappropriate Practice

Teachers use games with no obvious learning purpose or goal other than to keep children "busy, happy and good."

Official, adult rules of sports govern the activities in physical education classes, resulting in low rates of success and/or lack of enjoyment and participation for many children.

Regulation equipment (adult size) is used regardless of the developmental or skill level of children.

Component: Forming Groups or Partners

Appropriate Practice

Groups or partners are formed in ways that preserve the dignity and self-respect of every child. For example, a teacher privately forms groups or teams by using knowledge of children's skill abilities in ways that will facilitate learning. Groups or teams may also be formed by grouping clothing colors, birthdays, and favorite activities.

Inappropriate Practice

Groups or teams are formed by student "captains" publicly selecting one child at a time, sometimes with a system of alternating gender, and always exposing the low-skilled children to peer ridicule or embarrassment.

Groups or teams are formed by pitting "boys against girls," emphasizing gender differences rather than cooperation and working together.

Component: Facilitating Maximum Participation

Appropriate Practice

Teachers organize small games, for example, two or three children per team, that allow numerous practice opportunities for children while allowing them to learn the various aspects of the game being taught.

Equipment is provided to permit active participation and practice for every child. A variety of equipment is selected to accommodate the size, confidence, and skill levels of the children.

Inappropriate Practice

Teachers organize full sided or large sided games (e.g., the class of 30 is split into two groups of 15 that play against each other), thereby limiting practice opportunities for individual students.

An insufficient amount of equipment is available to maximize practice repetitions. "Adult size" equipment is used that may inhibit skill development, injure, and/or intimidate the children.

Component: Competition

Appropriate Practice

Teachers plan activities that emphasize self-improvement, participation, fair play (shaking hands, positive comments, etc.), and cooperation. Teachers are aware of the nature of competition and incorporate appropriate levels and kinds of competition for children. For example, children may be allowed to choose between keeping score and skill practice in selected situations.

Teachers provide choices in levels of competition and teach participants how to compete positively and constructively at each level.

Inappropriate Practice

Teachers require children to participate in activities that designate children as "winners and losers."

Teachers use strategies that compare one child's or one team's performance with others.

Teachers use rewards and punishments for winning and losing in class games.

Component: Active Participation for Every Child

Appropriate Practice

Teachers involve *all* children in activities that allow them to participate actively, both physically and mentally. Classes are designed to meet every child's need for active participation in all learning experiences.

Inappropriate Practice

Teachers form large groups in which student participation is based on individual competitiveness or aggressive behavior, use rules permitting elimination with no reentry or alternative activity, or allow students to remain inactive for long periods of time. Activities such as relay races, dodgeball, and elimination tag provide limited opportunities for everyone in the class, especially the slower, less agile students, who need the activity the most.

Teachers provide activities that are physically and/or psychologically unsafe for many children (e.g., dodgeball, in any form, promotes the use of fellow students as targets, and Red Rover calls inappropriate attention to the less skilled student, as well as increasing risk of injury).

Source: Council on Elementary Physical Education. (2000). *Appropriate Practices for Elementary School Physical Education: A Position Statement of the National Association for Sport and Physical Education.* Reston, VA: National Association for Sport and Physical Education.

decision making. Additionally, games playing is the content area in which responsible personal and social behavior is most visible (and teachable). It is precisely these constructs that make it the most difficult to teach well. Thus, although many of us are most comfortable and familiar with games content, and although a game tends to be self-propelling once students grasp the basic concepts, games content is complex and takes the same care in planning as gymnastics and dance.

Historically, our teaching has largely been limited to the first aspect—the teaching of skills. The second and third pieces (strategies and social skills) have been assumed as by-products. We have done little to help children learn how to combine skills or learn tactics, let alone helped them learn how to make decisions or engage in responsible behavior. (Just as we have done little to teach the expressive skills necessary to make motor skills become dance, or to make gymnastics-oriented motor skills anything other than isolated skills.) The bottom line is that, just because a skill is linked to a content area (games, dance, or gymnastics), that doesn't mean that by acquiring the skill one can use it appropriately in games, dance, or gymnastics settings. Teaching throwing and catching is one thing; teaching how to throw and catch in a game situation is another. And although we talk about strategy and appropriate behavior, we haven't taught them. We have now realized that we need to teach all three as an integrated whole (Griffin et al., 1997; Rink, 2006). But first things first—children need to acquire some basic skills before moving to skills in changing environments and to using combinations of skill and strategy. This does not mean, however, that all basic skills are taught before any combinations and strategy are used.

The instructor who teaches children to play games successfully and effectively creates a variety of learning opportunities and situations in which children combine skills into gamelike situations, as well as situations in which children play games and in which they practice skills.

The children in such programs acquire a foundation of movement skills that enables them to participate successfully in a broad variety of games and sports. Once children have acquired the prerequisite game skills, sport becomes an attractive leisure-time alternative for them throughout their lives.

Games Experiences

We have divided games content into three types of games experiences: invariant game skill experiences, dynamic gamelike skill experiences, and games-playing experiences. Invariant experiences essentially involve the practice of the isolated skills used in games in closed or unchanging situations. Dynamic gamelike experiences involve the use of skills in a changing environment, the use of combinations of skills in progressively more complex, open environments similar to those found in traditional sport activities, and the development of tactics and strategy. Games-playing experiences allow children to focus on gaining knowledge and enthusiasm for playing a developmentally appropriate game while using the skills and strategies previously learned.

Unlike dance, in which the types of experiences are unrelated, and gymnastics, in which the experiences are hierarchical, games-playing experiences are developmental but not static. Children should have games-playing experiences on a continuous basis, and instruction in skill and strategy should grow out of that play (Griffin et al., 1977; Rink, 2006). Isolating skill development and keeping children in invariant games-playing experiences over a long period of time is just as inappropriate as teaching games playing before children possess the skills that are prerequisite. There is no clear line of demarcation for moving from one type of experience to the other—it depends on the level of development of the students. Players cannot reach high levels of skill (utilization or proficiency) without also being able to use that skill strategically. Similarly, players can only advance so far in the use of strategy before their skill level limits what they can choose to do (Rink, 2006). Thus, the type of games-playing experience offered is constantly changing, depending on what is to be taught and the level of the students. A broad rule might be that children at the precontrol and early control levels of development should be involved in invariant games-playing experiences because they are trying to master a skill. Players at control and utilization levels would be involved in dynamic gamelike activities. Utilization- and proficiency-level players will find games-playing experiences challenging. This does *not* mean that you never return to invariant game skill experiences (think of how many Olympic-caliber athletes practice basic skills for hours daily); it means that you can gradually make the invariant skills more complex so that they approach an increasingly open situation. As with the dynamic gamelike experiences, as students become more proficient players, you gradually extend the games-playing experience to make it more complex while ensuring that it remains developmentally appropriate.

Invariant Game Skill Experiences

The first experiences we give children involve basic skills in a closed or unchanging situation. Invariant game skill experiences really don't look like games at all to adults—they look like skill development, which is what they are. The "games" focus is the potential use of the skill in games-playing environments that will emerge later. The "game" experience here is that of a self-testing or challenge activity.

Such experiences allow the students to gain control of an object using a specific motor pattern (Rink, 2006). The experience is structured so that the task is as identical as possible each time—the experience is invariant in that the child isn't required to predict the flight of a ball or the movement of an opponent, for example. At this point, refinement is the major emphasis (Belka, 2000).

Competition/Cooperation

Some children love to compete; others prefer (and seem to learn better in) games that encourage cooperation. We attempt to respect each child's preference by giving choices, trying never to place an entire class in a competitive situation. Instead, we let children choose between two or more games or ask them to make up their own games. The teachers heighten or lessen the degree of competition. Teachers who constantly shout out the score, post team win-and-loss records, and reward the winners (thereby punishing the losers) place an emphasis on competition for which some children aren't ready. If you don't believe us, talk to the thousands of adults who were unskilled as children and yet were placed in highly competitive situations. They can describe, in vivid detail, the feelings of being picked last, shouted at for dropping a ball, and ridiculed for "letting the team down." Such distasteful experiences usually have lasting and negative influences on the individual's willingness to participate in sports.

Such experiences are appropriate for a child who is at the precontrol or control level of skill proficiency and who would have difficulty executing a skill in a dynamic or open situation. As a child's proficiency in a skill increases, you can increase the difficulty of the tasks while retaining the relative predictability of the skill. For example, when a child is learning to throw a ball to hit a stationary target, you can increase the distance to the target. If the child is learning to run and leap over a low obstacle, increase the height of the obstacle.

When a child who isn't able to perform a basic skill consistently (precontrol level) is placed in a game that requires that skill and the ability to perform it in a dynamic or changing situation, the results are often counterproductive. A child in that situation often fails and becomes frustrated because of continuing inability to

Young children's games rarely have game-playing qualities.

execute the prerequisite movements of the game. The child may then become a self-proclaimed, permanently terminated games player or a teenager or adult who vows to never again play in a game situation. And the other children are frustrated when an unskilled player interrupts the flow and their enjoyment of the game.

Dynamic Gamelike Skill Experiences

Games in dynamic gamelike experiences may look and feel like games to children, but they are designed to teach the use of basic skills in a changing environment, combinations of skills, and simple offensive and defensive strategies. During these experiences "games" are almost always small sided with restricted rules (two passes before a shot; no more than three dribbles before a pass) and limited space. They have clear learning goals and are permeated by stops and starts to refine skill and provide cues. In the beginning they are often cooperative; they develop into competitive games when children no longer find cooperative experiences challenging.

Trying to roll a ball through a target is an example of invariant game experience.

For example, within dynamic gamelike skill experiences, a child first practices dribbling and shooting a basketball along with passing off to a partner. Then the child practices the same skill with one person acting as a defensive player. The implication of this progression is that as the child slowly becomes more adept at using a motor skill or combination of motor skills, the child is simultaneously learning games-playing strategies to accompany the skill.

These three different and equally important aspects—the use of skills in a changing environment, the use of combinations of skills, and the development of game strategies and tactics—like games experiences themselves, are developmental but not hierarchical. In actual practice they intermingle greatly. Teaching skills in an open environment and teaching combinations of skills, as well as strategy, are critical to children learning to be competent games players. Yet it is precisely these experiences that are usually omitted.

Skills in an Open Environment

Research suggests that a child has little chance of actually being able to use basic skills in a changing or dynamic (game) environment unless he or she has first practiced them in an open, changing, and dynamic situation (Rovegno et al., 1995; Schmidt, 1977). The skill acquired by a child who throws and catches a yarn ball may transfer minimally to the skill of throwing and catching used in, for example, baseball or basketball. For this reason, as soon as a child displays a minimum level of mastery in an invariant situation, it is necessary to create open situations that are progressively and increasingly complex and in which skills are used in combination as they occur in games-playing situations. For example, shooting a basket with no opposition is a skill different from shooting a basket after stopping a dribble or while being guarded by an opponent.

Combinations of Skills

At this point children need to be exposed to many experiences that relate to a variety of sports. The infinite combinations of and linkages between skills has to be taught (Belka, 2004a). Skill combinations might include dribbling and passing, shooting off a pass, receiving a pass and dribbling, receiving a pass and passing, and the like. Practicing skills in combinations is a critical and often neglected aspect of learning how to play games. It is critical because it is the transition between the two skills that makes the combination skillful and effective. To make the transition well, preparation for performing the second skill must occur while the first skill is being performed. For example, when young players are learning receiving and passing with the feet, commonly they receive the ball, stop, move into position to pass, and then pass. The skilled player moves the ball into position to pass as he or she is receiving it and passes without stopping. The difference is the transition. For players to be successful in games situations, they have to learn the transitions after they learn the skills. The focus at this point is on the transition, not on the two isolated skills. Tasks and cues can be developed that focus on the transition. For example, in the above dribbling and passing scenario, the task might be to pass in a moving triangle. Cues might be step into the pass as the ball is received and not to stop.

Tactics/Strategy

The third critical and often neglected aspect that occurs in dynamic games skill experiences is learning offensive and defensive strategies that allow players to use the skills they have learned. At this point, children shouldn't have to devote their attention to controlling objects. They should already know to *how* to do a skill; their focus is now on *when* to use that skill. Thus, it is wise to teach strategies when children's skills are at the utilization level. Strategies,

Dribbling a ball past a defender into a goal is a dynamic gamelike skill experience.

like basic skills, can be taught and cued. One example might be learning to create space in soccer-type activities. In a two-on-two situation students can play a gamelike activity that asks them to provide a 45-degree passing angle for their partner. The focus is on the angle for passing rather than the pass itself. As with skills, it is best to learn these activities in less complex situations first, then gradually increase the complexity. For example, the idea of passing angles can first be learned with no defense, then with a passive defense or in a two-on-one situation, and then with an aggressive defense. Complexity can be increased by adding players, boundaries, or scoring. The key aspect here is to add complexity *very* gradually. The utilization- and proficiency-level activities described in the manipulative skill theme chapters contain cues for simple offensive and defensive strategies.

During these experiences, many teachers use inquiry teaching to teach strategies (Doolittle & Girard, 1991; Griffin et al., 1997). For example, in a one-on-one situation of striking over a net, you are trying to teach the idea of hitting to open spaces and covering space. Children already can keep the ball going back and forth to each other. A teacher may stop the lesson and ask, "Where do you have to hit to make your opponent miss?" Answer: "open space" (most often phrased as "where they are not"). "Where do you have to be to prevent your partner from having a lot of open space to which to hit?" Answer: "home" (middle of court just behind center). Then the teacher sends them back to practice doing those things, even giving them points for doing those things. Strategy can also

be taught through direct instruction, but it lends itself well to the inquiry approach, as it is a cognitive concept as well as a physical ability.

Games-Playing Experiences

Unlike the two previous experiences, in which games were characterized by starts and stops, games-playing experiences are somewhat different. The enjoyment and satisfaction derived from playing games frequently are products of playing a game without interruption. Yet, in the limited time most of us have to teach our classes, there's hardly enough time for skill practice and game playing in a single lesson.

This does not mean that the teacher does nothing during games-playing experiences. Observe the types of skill work that children need as they're playing games, and focus on those needs during later classes. Remember, games-playing experiences don't occur in every lesson; they are only a part of the total physical education program.

Take your cue from the children in determining when to provide feedback. A lull in the game, a water break, the end of class, or other natural interruption provides an opportunity to check with the children and offer guidance if needed. Try not to stop or interfere in the children's games to teach skills, unless the game has become unsatisfying and boring because of lack of ability. Adults prefer not to be interrupted during a game, even by someone who wants to provide feedback. Children share this feeling, and teachers must respect it if they want to create positive attitudes toward games.

Some skill development results from playing games, but game playing isn't the most efficient way for all children to improve the motor skills used in games. Thus, it's useful to distinguish lessons in which the primary purpose is to improve skills (invariant and dynamic gamelike skill experiences) from lessons in which the primary purpose is to develop enthusiasm for and a playing knowledge of a variety of games (games-playing experiences).

One implication teachers often draw from the progression of invariant, dynamic, gamelike, and games-playing experiences is that until children become exceedingly proficient with dynamic gamelike skills and approach the proficiency level of skill development, they shouldn't play games. This contention is only partially true. Although we don't advocate that children at the precontrol and control levels be involved in games-playing experiences, we encourage challenges, self-testing, and dynamic gamelike skill experiences. Children conceive of many of these types of experiences

Children enjoy playing a self-designed game.

as games. In other words, children are playing games in their own minds; what is different is our adult conception of what a game is. Thus, all children can play "games," depending on who is calling the activity a game. We try to acquaint children with many different types of games-playing experiences. These activities can help children experience the enjoyment, satisfaction, excitement, and sense of accomplishment that a developmentally appropriate game can bring about.

I would like to contrast the richness of children's natural play with the stultifying rigidity of play that is organized by adults. No better example can be found than that of the Little League, for what boys, left to their own devices, would ever invent such a thing? How could they make such a boneheaded error as to equate competition with play? Think of the ordinary games of boys—in sandlots, fields, parks, even stickball in the street. They are expansive and diverse, alternately intense and gay, and are filled with events of all kinds.

Between innings the boys throw themselves on the grass. They'll wrestle, do handstands, turn somersaults. They hurl twigs and stones at nearby trees, and yell at the birds that sail by. A confident player will make up dance steps as he stops a slow grounder. If an outfielder is bored, he does not stand there pulling up his pants and thumping his glove, but plays with the bugs in the grass, looks at the clouds. . . . There is almost always a dog on the field, and no part of the competition is gayer or more intense than that between the boys and the dog, who when he succeeds in snapping up their ball, leads them off in a serpentine line that is all laughter and shouts, the dog looking back over his shoulder and trotting with stiff legs, until

finally he is captured and flattens his ears as they take back their ball. No one has forgotten the score or who was at bat. The game goes on. The game goes on until darkness ends it, and the winners can hardly be distinguished from the losers, for by then everyone is fumbling the ball and giggling and flopping on the grass.

—George Dennison, *The Lives of Children*

The Process of Teaching Games

It is hard to modify the content without modifying the instruction, yet we have seen it done. It is our thought that for the content to be effective, instruction has to be modified as well. Teaching games to meet the developmental needs of children is not as simple as it initially appears. For many of us, it is intertwined with deeply imbedded sport experiences that make it difficult to "see differently." To see differently we must focus on the type of games-playing experience we choose, the equipment used, what we call the game, the number of players involved, our role as an official or teacher, and the learning environment. It is only then that we truly start to look at the child first and the game second.

Selecting a Games-Playing Experience

There are at least five types of game designs a teacher can use to structure games-playing experiences for the children's variety of skill levels: predesigned, modified predesigned, teacher-designed, teacher/child-designed, and child-designed. Each has its own inherent strengths and weaknesses.

Predesigned Games Predesigned games are those described in textbooks or learned in methods classes and taught to children without modification. The textbooks imply that such games will be appropriate, as well as interesting, for children. Brownies and Fairies; Duck, Duck, Goose; Red Rover; Four Square; and Steal the Bacon are well-known predesigned games.

Predesigned games are easy to teach because they require little preparation or teaching skill. The teacher selects a game and explains it to the children. When the children understand the game, they start to play, and the game continues until the lesson ends or the teacher changes the activity.

It has been our experience that *few* predesigned games are appropriate for all the children in a class. A few skilled children often dominate such games, whereas others are minimally involved, both physically and emotionally. Some (Belka, 2004b) say that these games should be discarded. However, you may occasionally encounter a situation in which a particular predesigned game is appropriate for a class or group of children. Usually, though, you'll find that although many of the ideas in a predesigned game are worthwhile, you have to extensively modify the structure of the game to the abilities and interests of different children (Belka, 2004b).

Nettie Wilson (1976) conducted a study to determine the number of throwing, catching, and kicking opportunities in the game of kick ball as played by third- and fourth-grade children under the direction of a classroom teacher. Her findings include the following:

- Less than half of the game was actually spent using the criterion skills.
- The average number of catches attempted in the kick ball games was slightly more than two—35 percent of the children never caught the ball. Of the children who didn't catch the ball, 83 percent were girls.
- The average number of throws made in the kick ball games, excluding those made by the pitcher and catcher, was slightly more than one—52 percent of the children never threw the ball at all during the entire game, and 67 percent of those who never threw the ball were girls.

Modified Predesigned Games Modifying predesigned games requires greater planning and organizing ability. Yet by modifying a predesigned game, you can do much to make the game more appropriate for a particular class.

Both Rink (2006) and Morris and Stiehl (1999) provide useful ideas for modifying predesigned games. The teacher can change the rules (e.g., allow two tries instead of only one), the equipment used (e.g., larger and lighter), the number of players involved (generally, it's best to decrease the number), the playing area (e.g., larger or smaller), or the skills involved (e.g., throwing instead of striking). Many teachers modify one aspect of the game at a time until it provides an experience appropriate for the skill level of the children (see Table 31.1). A good rule to follow is to change or eliminate anything that impedes or slows the flow of a game.

During the lesson, you may use the same teaching skills required to teach a predesigned game—explaining the game and intervening only when that's necessary to keep the game going. Evaluating the game is more complex. You'll have to decide, after observing the children, whether the game should be modified further or is satisfactory as currently structured.

Teacher-Designed Games Sometimes a teacher can't find a game appropriate for a particular class, and modifications of predesigned games don't seem effective. In such a situation, the teacher may design a game that satisfies a specific goal. Designing a game places a greater demand on a teacher's creative abilities than do either of the game lesson structures already discussed.

The teacher needs to understand the children's skill abilities and interests and be able to use this knowledge to design a game form that the children will find interesting and enjoyable. For example, a teacher could design a game to focus on striking a ball with a bat. The object would be to strike a pitched ball and then run around a cone and back before the other players catch or collect the ball and touch the home base with the ball. If the children used rather narrow boundaries and played in small groups, they would get more striking, throwing, and catching opportunities than the standardized nine-per-side version of softball provides. The teacher could design the game to be played by two teams or design it so that each child goes back "to the field" once she or he hits the ball and runs around the cone. Once you've created the game, the teaching skills used are virtually identical to the skills needed to teach a modification of a predesigned game.

Each of these three game lesson structures places the responsibility for selecting or designing a game on the teacher. One advantage of these games structures is that the children spend most of the time—once the game has been explained and organized—playing the game. But the children don't contribute to the design of the game, nor do they have anything to say about whether they would like to continue playing the game

Table 31.1 Game Aspects That Can Be Modified

Aspect	Possible Changes				
Players	Reduce the number of players	Increase the number of players	Mix skill levels	Combine like skill levels	
Purpose	To practice skill	To practice combined skills	To practice strategy	To play games	
Player Movement	Restrict the movement of some players	Allow some players to move			
Equipment	Use smaller equipment	Use larger equipment	Use lighter equipment	Use heavier equipment	Use more (or less) equipment
Organization	Define the organization—circle, etc.	Let the organization be random			
Space	Increase the space	Decrease the space	Make the space long and narrow	Make the space short and wide	
Rules	Omit rules that restrict the flow	Add rules to enhance opportunities			
Skills	Reduce the number of skills involved				

as is or change the game to make it better. The previous three game designs are direct instructional approaches; the following two game structures, by contrast, involve the children in the design of the game. They would be classified as inquiry or child-designed approaches and require more advanced teaching skills. (See Chapter 13 for a discussion of instructional approaches and the skills necessary to use each.)

Teacher/Child-Designed Games When the children and the teacher design a game together, the teacher presents the purpose of the game and the restrictions. The children and the teacher then work cooperatively to decide the rules, scoring, and equipment to be used. The whole class plays in small groups.

You'll find that it's wise to stipulate that once the game has begun, only the team with the ball (or the advantage) can stop play to suggest a change. (Unless the children are restrained by this rule, they're likely to stop the game and suggest a change every time the other team gains an advantage.) After a brief discussion of the proposed change, the class votes, with the majority decision prevailing. If a rule needs to be made to ensure safety, offer solutions to be voted on or ask the children to propose a solution.

One example of a teacher/child-designed game is Magladry Ball, which the children named after their school. The teacher was concerned about the children's inability to travel and pass a ball or other object to a teammate who was also traveling, particularly when an opponent attempted to intercept or prevent the pass from being made. After describing the purpose of the game, the teacher imposed two restrictions: Children

couldn't touch each other, and once the ball (object) touched the ground, it was automatically in the possession of the team that didn't touch it immediately before the object hit the ground. The object of the game was to throw the ball (beanbag, Frisbee) through a hoop suspended from a goal post by a rope at either end of a field. Once the game began, children made decisions about how long one child could remain in possession of the ball (object); what type of ball (object) to play the game with; boundaries, violations, and penalties; and scoring.

Teacher/child-designed games evolve slowly, and you may spend several lessons creating games that children are excited about and enjoy playing. Once the time and effort to create a game have been spent, the children will want to have opportunities to play it.

The instructor in a teacher/child-designed game serves as a facilitator, enhancing and expanding ideas rather than imposing personal ideas on the children. The teacher helps the children modify the games, offers suggestions, and manages a group of charged-up children who are eager to get the game going again. This isn't an easy task, and it often takes some time to master this approach.

Child-Designed Games The underlying assumption of the first four game structures is that the entire class is playing the same game, either as a whole group or in small groups. With child-designed games, however, we assume that many games are being played simultaneously and that few, if any, are identical. Such an environment is a far more complex one in which to teach (Rovegno et al., 1995). The teacher is assisting groups of children to develop different games and is also responsible for observing a number of different games and assisting or staying away when appropriate.

When I first started teaching, I was looking for games that were recommended for first-grade children and did not require a great deal of game skill. Brownies and Fairies, a simple running and chasing game, was prescribed in one text as appropriate for 6-year-olds. The first time the game was played, two children fell down and bloodied their knees when they tried to run in a crowd of children. They could run by themselves without falling. But when they were placed in a dynamic situation that involved both running and dodging, they were unsuccessful. They probably forgot that experience many years ago—once their knees healed. I haven't.

Child-designed games have some definite advantages. Children in groups of similar skill ability (given a choice, children typically choose to be with others of similar ability) are allowed to design games that are interesting and exciting to them. These may be cooperative or competitive, active or passive, depending on the children's intent.

Initially, children need help in designing their own games. Teachers who've met with success in using child-designed games have found that in the beginning it's helpful to suggest a structure for the game—that is, the purposes, boundaries, and rules (Rovegno & Bandhauer, 1994). For example, the teacher may say, "Make up your own striking game. There may be up to four people in the group. All of you must play at once; there's to be no waiting in line. And the space can be no larger than 15 feet by 15 feet." The teacher can also help the children organize the game by asking them to identify their rules, either verbally or in writing (Figure 31.1).

As children learn to make decisions about their games, you can decrease the amount of imposed structure. If children are to make significant and worthwhile decisions about their game, you must stay out of as many decisions as possible; this is just as important as providing proper initial guidance. Even if you're certain some idea won't work, it's no longer your role to tell them so (except in the case of safety). They'll find out soon enough.

You may consider it a disadvantage that some children take a great deal of time to design games. Children who've had little experience in designing their own games may spend as much as half of a lesson seriously working out the way they want a game to be played, perhaps without ever actually playing the game. But you'll

Figure 31.1 Example of a child-designed game—sixth grade.

find that as students gradually become more adept at designing games, playing time increases substantially.

Most children enjoy participating in the design of their own games. But the children must be ready—they must be able to function successfully in a small group (two or three is an appropriate number) when playing a game they know before they can begin to design games (see Chapter 13 for more detail on the skills a teacher and the children need in order to implement child-designed activities). Some teachers, even of younger children, can use child-designed games from the time they begin teaching and have exciting, successful lessons. But when a teacher—even one who believes in the philosophy represented by child-designed games—tries to have children design their own games before the children (and the teacher) are ready, the outcome can be a disaster. Start with the design that you think is most appropriate to a class and situation, and proceed from there. See Box 31-3 for suggestions on helping children create their own games.

The ecology of the particular teaching situation determines which game design is best. When selecting a games-playing lesson design for a class, consider the purpose for playing the game, the skills required, the children's interests and abilities, the playing area and equipment available, and your skills as a teacher.

We try very carefully to match the skills required in games-playing experiences to the children's skills. Nothing is so counterproductive as having children participate in games for which they don't possess the prerequisite skills. The teacher who has closely assessed the children's skill level can discover and/or design well-matched games-playing situations to ensure the children's success and pleasure.

Other Considerations

The type of game selected for a class is the first critical aspect with respect to the process of teaching games. However, the fundamental instructional pieces discussed in the following paragraphs are paramount to making the type of game selected "work" for a group. If your choice of game is perfect for a class and then the instructional aspects contradict your game choice, the class climate negates the content.

Games Equipment   The equipment used to play games most certainly affects the quality and difficulty of the game (Graham, 2001). Large, regulation-size sport equipment slows the play and promotes the use of incorrect skills. In recent years equipment manufacturers have begun to design equipment for children: Foam

paddles, balls, and hockey sticks are three examples. Smaller, lighter, more colorful balls that don't hurt reduce the fear of catching. Basketball goals that can be adjusted to multiple heights (not just one or two) allow all children to be able to shoot at an appropriate basket. The bottom line is this: Adult equipment is almost always inappropriate for elementary school children. Make sure the equipment matches the child.

> *A true game is one that frees the spirit—the true game is the one that arises from the players themselves.*
>
> —PETER OPIE AND IONA OPIE, *Children's Games in Street and Playground*

The Name of the Game   By calling a game by the name of the sport its skills are usually associated with, we effectively limit children's options. The skilled children think they have to play by the rules of the sport, and the unskilled unconsciously evaluate themselves against some external standard, whether they really know much about the sport or not. As a result, some children are disenfranchised and others are frustrated. We have found that children are much more creative and open in their games playing if we refer to the experience by a new name or by the name of the skill. This is why in the index you will find games linked to

---

Box 31-3

Helping Children Create Their Own Games

1. Limit group size to six or less.
2. Provide structure:

   - Identify the equipment that can be used.
   - Identify the skills and movements to be included.
   - Identify the space each group may use and having them mark the space.

3. Allow adequate time:

   - Provide time for thinking and creativity, but then indicate a time needed to start play.
   - Provide time for "sorting out" the game as they play.
   - Provide time for playing.

4. Create accountability:

   - Have children name their game.
   - Have children identify the rules.
   - Have children teach others.
   - See if children are able to and want to play the game another day.
   - Have children write their game down.

THE FAMILY CIRCUS   **By Bil Keane**

6-28
Copyright 1978.
The Register and Tribune
Syndicate, Inc.

"We made it up ourselves. You don't need nine guys on a team, or grownups, or uniforms. . . . It's like baseball, only better!"

the skill theme they are used to develop, but not listed separately by their name.

Group Size   To many there is a "right" number of players for a game. Because of our conscious or unconscious sport orientation, the "right" number of players is often the number of players associated with the sport in which the skill is most commonly used. And because predesigned games are usually designed for entire classes, they often call for 15, 20, or more players. Rarely does either of the preceding scenarios contain the "right" number of players for games appropriate to the elementary school setting. Games experiences should never involve more players than can be active at any one time or so many that the flow of the game is slowed. We have found this usually means four to six (and maybe eight) players as a maximum in any games experience. Choose the "right" number of players for the children's experience.

To Ref or Not to Ref?   We do not believe in officiating children's games. Officiating does several things that detract from the ultimate value of the games-playing experience. First, officiating places the responsibility for coming to decisions about the process of the game on the teacher, taking away all responsibility and decision making from the children. The end result is that they can "blame the teacher" for what happened and avoid learning to cooperate and decide for themselves. Second, officiating takes the teacher out of the teaching role and limits the teacher's ability to provide feedback and instruction—our primary goal. Third, a teacher can only be in one place. If we officiate, only one game can be occurring; this means that all the

children aren't active and that more than likely we have created an inappropriate games environment.

We have been very successful in letting children "call" their own games. They not only adapt the rules to fit their situation but also develop decision-making and cooperation skills. The flow of the game is also generally more continuous; they stop only when they need to.

Cooperative or Competitive?   Much has been written about cooperative games versus competitive games. Competition is not inherently bad for children; inappropriate competition is. Children should never be forced to compete against another child until they are ready, and all children are not ready at the same time. Therefore, to have an entire class playing by the same rules of competition disenfranchises many children. We have found two guidelines that work for us. First, let children choose if they want to be in a competitive situation or not. If there are multiple small sided games occurring simultaneously, then some could be competitive and some cooperative. Second, cooperative experiences always precede competitive experiences. It is only when cooperative experiences are no longer challenging that competitive experiences are appropriate (Rink, 2006). Children, when left to their own devices, almost always follow this maxim.

The Learning Environment

The small group size we recommend implies that more than one game will be played simultaneously. Having several games going on at one time, however, can be uncomfortable for many of us. If this is true for you, we suggest you begin slowly. Start with a class you are

confident with, and have only two games play concurrently. As you feel more confident, gradually add more games. Amazingly, more games actually decreases many potential management problems. Because more children are actively and appropriately involved in playing and are spending less time waiting or otherwise unengaged, the amount of off-task behavior is substantially reduced. Judy Rink (2006) suggests four criteria for a physical education experience designed for learning outcomes: (1) The experience has the potential to improve motor skills; (2) there is maximum participation for all children, (3) the experience is at the appropriate experiential level of all children, and (4) there is the possibility of integrating cognitive, psychomotor, and affective learning. We suggest that these criteria are good ones to use in assessing the games-playing experiences designed and implemented in our programs. If our games-playing experiences do not meet these criteria they should probably be modified.

After-School Sport Programs

Many children in your classes may be participating in various sport programs. Often these children are very skilled—many are at the proficiency level of the skills involved in their sport—and so provide an interesting dimension to games lessons. We have found that by using small groups for games experiences and varying the task, these students can be challenged in our classes just as any other student can be.

Child Development and Games

The research on child development (Piaget, 1962) and the development of reasoning (Kohlberg & Mayer, 1972) further supports placing children in game situations designed to accommodate their skills, interests, and abilities. In order for moral and social development and growth to occur, a motivation to change must exist. This motivation requires both developmental readiness and opportunity (Brustad & Parker, 2005). Game situations provide an attractive opportunity for children to develop their social skills and reasoning when the situations are developmentally appropriate. Before the age of 8, children are in the egocentric stage. They have a personal conception of reality; the world centers around self. There's no sense of obligation to rules, no desire to check for accuracy. "I" am right at all times. Whatever meets the needs at the present time is what is true. Following rules is fine if it serves the purpose at the time. The concept of cheating doesn't exist, because rules constantly change to fit the child's needs. At this stage the child feels that everyone completely understands

him or her and is in agreement with what the child wants. Imagine placing 25 youngsters in a traditional group game when each child thinks he or she is completely understood and in agreement with all!

Piaget (1962) described the game play of the young child (from the child's viewpoint) as a situation in which everyone plays the game as each understands it, with no concern for "checking" on others. Nobody loses and everybody wins at the same time, because the purpose is to have fun (Piaget & Inhelder, 1969).

Children between 8 and 11 have a strong social need. To be a part of the group, to belong, is extremely important to children in the upper elementary years. In the early phases of this stage, however, children still have strong egocentric tendencies. Group interaction is desired, but they also desire to cling to the comfortable self-centered view. The earlier "absolute" view is now confronted with the viewpoints of others, viewpoints perhaps not in agreement with one's own. How many children do we see get upset and leave the game when things don't go their way or they're asked to sacrifice themselves for the good of the team? Cooperative game situations with small groups of children can facilitate establishing the child as a member of the group and foster acceptance of differing points of view.

Students entering the higher level of cognitive development, ages 11 and above, begin to create strategies and mentally test their abilities. They enjoy group activity and respect the physical and mental skills of others in the game situation. The game no longer rules the group; the game is made for the use of the group—to be adapted as needed.

A Final Thought

Much has been written about the inappropriateness of adult versions of sports for children (Orlick & Zitzelsberger, 1996; Smoll & Smith, 1996). The child who seeks sport experiences can find them outside the school. Most communities in the United States offer adequate sports at the middle and high school levels, in after-school programs, and in programs sponsored by youth agencies.

Tyson-Martin (1999) has challenged us to refocus, recycle, reorganize, and restructure games for children. It seems an appropriate challenge to take. Physical educators have a responsibility to provide instruction for all children, to help them become skillful games players who enjoy participating in games and are eager to play games on their own time. We must do more than produce a few good athletes. In a successful physical education program, all the children improve their games-playing skills and are eager and excited about playing games.

Summary

Because games playing is the content area we are comfortable with, we find games easier to teach than dance or gymnastics. This deceptive ease, however, is an educationally unacceptable rationale for curricular decision making. Games in the elementary school allow children to apply the psychomotor, cognitive, and affective skills acquired in a dynamic, challenging situation. Thus teachers need to provide children with developmentally appropriate experiences that lead to the acquisition of games-playing skills. We give children experiences that involve invariant games skills, dynamic gamelike skills, and games-playing skills.

Invariant games experiences focus on skill acquisition in a predictable, closed environment in which the movement is essentially the same each time. Dynamic gamelike experiences require children to use skills in a changing environment and to use combinations of skills and strategies in situations that resemble those found in games-playing experiences. Games-playing experiences are designed to expose children to the joy and satisfaction that can be found in games. In these experiences children use skill and strategy in an attempt to outwit an opponent.

Several variables affect the process of teaching games to children. The type of game selected can influence the success of the experience. Other factors to be considered when teaching games to children are the equipment used, the number of children in the game, the role of the teacher as an official, the learning environment, and what the game is called.

The role of games in elementary physical education is to provide all children the chance to be successful in playing in dynamic, unpredictable situations that challenge them to outwit their opponents. It is the teacher's responsibility to design game experiences that meet the needs of all students.

Reading Comprehension Questions

1. What is meant by the statement: It is not the game that is important, but the use of skills in game settings?
2. How does the discussion of games in this chapter relate to the skill theme chapters? What is the difference between games and sports?
3. What are the characteristics of developmentally appropriate and inappropriate games for children? Identify one activity that you know is appropriate and one that is inappropriate.
4. Games are organized into what three types of experiences? Define the purpose of each experience.
5. What happens when we place children in dynamic situations before they're ready?
6. When is it appropriate to move children from an invariant to a dynamic gamelike situation? Why is such movement necessary?
7. How are situations that require children to use games skills different from actual games?
8. What is one difference between a games-playing lesson and a skill-development lesson? What role should a teacher take in each lesson?
9. What factors should be taken into account when teaching games?
10. What are the differences between the five game designs presented? What is the ultimate criterion for using any game in physical education?
11. Why do we recommend small group sizes and multiple games in physical education class?

References/Suggested Readings

Belka, D. (1994). *Teaching games: Becoming a master teacher.* Champaign, IL: Human Kinetics.

Belka, D. (2000). Developing competent games players. *Teaching Elementary Physical Education, 11*(3), 6–7.

Belka, D. (2004a). Combining and sequencing games skills. *Journal of Physical Education, Recreation and Dance. 75*(4), 23–27.

Belka, D. (2004b). Substituting developmental for traditional games in elementary physical education. *Teaching Elementary Physical Education. 15*(4), 21–24.

Brustad, R., & Parker, M. (2005). Enhancing positive youth development through sport and physical activity. *Psychologia 39*, 75–93.

Council on Physical Education for Children. (2000). *Appropriate practices for elementary physical education: A position of the National Association for Sport and Physical Education.* Reston, VA: National Association for Sport and Physical Education.

Dennison, G. (1969). *The lives of children.* New York: Random House.

Doolittle, S., & Girard, K. (1991). A dynamic approach to teaching games in elementary physical education. *Journal of Physical Education, Recreation and Dance, 62*(4), 57–62.

Graham, G. (2001). *Teaching children physical education: Becoming a master teacher.* (2nd ed.). Champaign, IL: Human Kinetics.

Griffin, L., Mitchell, S., & Oslin, J. (1997). *Teaching sports concepts and skills: A tactical games approach.* Champaign, IL: Human Kinetics.

Kolhberg, L., & Mayer, R. (1972). Development as the aim of education. *Harvard Educational Review, 42*(4), 449–496.

Morris, G. S., & Stiehl, J. (1999). *Changing kids' games* (2nd ed.). Champaign, IL: Human Kinetics.

National Association for Sport and Physical Education. (2004). *Moving into the future: National standards for physical education* (2nd ed.). Reston, VA: National Association for Sport and Physical Education.

Opie, P., & Opie, I. (1969). *Children's games in street and playground.* New York: Oxford University Press.

Orlick, T. D., & Zitzelsberger, L. (1996). Enhancing children's sport experiences. In R. E. Smith & F. L. Smoll (eds.), *Children and youth in sport: A biopsychosocial perspective* (pp. 330–337). New York: McGraw Hill.

Piaget, J. (1962). *Play, dreams, and imitation in childhood.* New York: Norton.

Piaget, J., & Inhelder, B. (1969). *The psychology of the child.* New York: Basic Books.

Rink, J. (2006). *Teaching physical education for learning* (5th ed.). St. Louis, MO: Mosby.

Rovegno, I., & Bandhauer, D. (1994). Child-designed games—Experience changes teachers' conceptions. *Journal of Physical Education, Recreation and Dance, 65*(6), 60–63.

Rovegno, I., Skonie, R., Charpenel, T., & Sieving, J. (1995). Learning to teach critical thinking through child-designed games. *Teaching Elementary Physical Education, 6*(1), 6–7, 15.

Schmidt, R. (1977). Schema theory: Implications for movement education. *Motor Skills: Theory into Practice, 2,* 36–48.

Smoll, F. L., & Smith, R. E. (1996). Competitive anxiety: Sources, consequences, and intervention strategies. In R. E. Smith & F. L. Smoll (eds.), *Children and youth in sport: A biopsychosocial perspective* (pp. 359–380). New York: McGraw Hill.

Tyson-Martin, L. (1999). The four "Rs" of enhancing elementary games instruction. *Journal of Physical Education, Recreation and Dance, 70*(7), 36–40.

Williams, N. (1992). The physical education hall of shame. *Journal of Physical Education, Recreation and Dance, 63*(6), 57–60.

Williams, N. (1994). The physical education hall of shame: Part II. *Journal of Physical Education, Recreation, and Dance, 65*(2), 17–20.

Williams, N. (1996). The physical education hall of shame: Part III: Inappropriate teaching practices. *Journal of Physical Education, Recreation and Dance, 67*(8), 45–48.

Wilson, N. (1976). *The frequency and patterns of selected motor skills by third- and fourth-grade girls and boys in the game of kickball.* Unpublished master's project, University of Georgia, Athens.

Integrating the Skill Theme Approach across the Curriculum

When asked what I teach, I like to respond "children."

—JOHN HICHWA

By now you have a thorough understanding of the skill theme approach, why it is important, and how teachers are implementing it in their programs. One advantage of the skill theme approach is that it provides numerous worthwhile experiences for teachers to focus on concepts being taught in the classroom while students also work to improve their motor skills and physical fitness. This concept of inte-grated learning experiences, or *interdisciplinary learn-ing,* has gained impetus in the past few years, and we believe it will continue to be recognized as a powerful way to help children make connections and learn.

This chapter will help you better understand how to integrate physical education concepts and skills with those from other subject areas throughout the elementary curriculum. Three approaches to integrat-ing skills and concepts are discussed—the content linkage approach, the shared integration approach, and the thematic unit approach. Examples from dif-ferent content areas are used to illustrate how these approaches work.

The chapter ends with a review of recent literature that makes the connection between physical activity and successful performance in the classroom, includ-ing research suggesting an important link between movement and brain function. Both the connection between physical education and other areas of school curriculum and the connection between physical ac-tivity and learning reinforce the importance of an ef-fective physical education program in all elementary schools.

Connecting Physical Education and the Classroom Curriculum through Interdisciplinary Learning

Any time we can make learning more relevant and per-sonally meaningful to the child's life, it has a more pro-found effect and will be remembered longer (Roberts & Kellough, 2000). For some children, especially those that are "kinesthetic" learners (Gardner, 1993), the connec-tions are best made through movement.

Defining Interdisciplinary Learning

A major thrust in curriculum development in schools today is the integration of subject content across the curriculum (Wood, 2001). "Interdisciplinary learning is an educational process in which two or more subject areas are integrated with the goal of fostering en-hanced learning in each subject area" (Cone et al., 1998). Integration helps kids make sense of what they know as it pertains to them and their world. The terms *interdisciplinary* and *integration* are usually considered synonymous and will be used interchangeably in this chapter.

Integration enhances learning by:

1. Reinforcing curriculum content in a variety of edu-cational settings
2. Encouraging children to transfer what is learned in one setting or situation to new settings and situa-tions, adding meaning to what is being learned
3. Providing children with multiple opportunities to practice particular skills and concepts
4. Encouraging children to better understand and to see the connectedness of what they are learning and how it relates to their own world

Interdisciplinary Learning and Quality Physical Education

The National Association for Sport and Physical Edu-cation (NASPE) and the Council of Physical Education for Children (COPEC) have developed a document outlining criteria for schools to follow to ensure a quality learning environment for students in physical education. This document, entitled *Opportunity to Learn: Standards for Elementary Physical Education,* was written to complement the content-focused *National Standards in Physical Education,* and it directly addresses the importance of interdisciplinary learning experiences. The criteria for providing an adequate learning environment for children related to physical education are listed in Box 32-1. The criteria clearly focus on a combined effort by both the physical education teacher and the classroom teacher to provide physical activity opportunities throughout the school day and to foster cognitive development through movement experiences.

Box 32-1

Opportunity to Learn: *Standards for Elementary Physical Education*

- The efforts of the physical education teacher are complemented by those of classroom teachers who have the unique opportunity to make physical activity a part of the daily life of the student. (p. 7)
- Because it is crucial to interdisciplinary work and program development, planning time is provided by physical education teachers to meet with other classroom teachers or specialists in other disciplines. (p. 9)
- The curriculum integrates kinesthetic experiences that reinforce math concepts, language arts, social studies, science, and health. (p. 12)
- The students have opportunities to develop critical thinking skills. (p. 12)

Source: Council on Physical Education for Children. (2000). Opportunities to Learn: Standards for Elementary Physical Education. *A position statement of the National Association for Sport and Physical Education.* Reston, VA: National Association for Sport and Physical Education.

Integrating Physical Education

Integrating physical education in the elementary school curriculum works in two directions—integrating other subject-matter content into the physical education curriculum and integrating physical education concepts and skills into the other curriculum areas. (See Table 32.1.) Any type of integrative curriculum most likely will encourage a new sense of respect and increased interest between teachers and about their subject areas. One physical education (PE) teacher who integrated an orienteering unit into the math and science core curriculum in an elementary classroom said that he felt rewarded by gaining respect from the other teachers in the school who then saw him as a more significant contributor to the overall school curriculum (Placek, 1992).

As a result of the connections among learning domains and between subject-specific information sets that integration allows, children often see the knowledge gained as having more importance in the real-life context. For example, students who are normally unenthusiastic about physical education may be motivated by the integrative activities that allow them success in both the cognitive and psychomotor domains, such as learning to swim while studying water in science. By the same token, students who excel in physical activities but are less interested in other subject areas may find an interesting connection that motivates them to learn other subject-specific content. One example might be the student who is struggling with reading but is excited to complete a reading assignment about a famous hockey player while learning the skill of striking with a hockey stick in physical education class. In either case, the integrative approach increases the potential for motivating children to learn.

Benefits of Integration

It is important to understand why integrating subject areas is worthwhile and to reflect on the benefits of integration for both physical education and other

Table 32.1 Example of Two-Directional Integration between Physical Education and Science

Physical Education	integrated ➡ into	Science	Plan a hike through a nearby park to identify trees, flowers, and other plants
Science	integrated ➡ into	Physical Education	Children use different locomotor movements to travel through a large replica of the heart on the gym floor to show the pathway of blood flow

Students are participating in a science lesson about the function of the heart before beginning lessons on rope jumping in physical education.

subject content areas. Following are some of the most notable benefits—from both the PE class and the classroom perspectives.

Benefits of Integrating Other Subject Skills/Concepts into the PE Class

1. Children learn best by seeing connections in what they are learning. PE for most children is fun! A quality physical education program helps them to become proficient in many skills and most elementary children are innately inclined to be physically active at every given opportunity. Kinesthetic learning of other subject content often helps children grasp concepts in language arts, science, and math that they might otherwise struggle with in a more inert classroom environment.

2. Some children who are not as proficient in motor skills and movement but who excel academically will find the connection between the cognitive and psychomotor domains and between the two content areas to be motivating and enjoyable.

3. When the physical education environment is used to reinforce other academic skills and concepts, physical education has a newfound importance to other teachers and administrators in the school. Even though the importance of the physical education program goals should be recognized foremost by the school, when teachers work together to help students succeed on standardized tests their efforts are applauded.

Benefits of Integrating Physical Education Skills/Concepts in the Regular Classroom

1. It is recommended that children be physically active at least 60 minutes a day (Institute of Medicine, 2002). Some of this recommendation can be met during the school day. In additional to physical education time, classroom teachers can provide multiple opportunities for physical activity for children throughout the day. By integrating physical education skills and concepts with other subject areas, children are able to simultaneously practice motor, language arts, and math skills, for example, while also gaining the benefits of being physically active. Additionally, short activity breaks every 20 to 30 minutes help children to concentrate more and be ready to learn.

2. Children love to move! For children, movement is a critical means of communication, expression, and learning. The "active" rather than "passive" involvement in learning that movement allows often makes children more excited and motivated to learn. (See Box 32-2.)

Important Considerations

Before deciding to use the interdisciplinary approach in your program, there are some important considerations to ponder. For successful integration, you should have a knowledge of and an appreciation for

Box 32-2

Gardner's Theory of Multiple Intelligences

According to Howard Gardner's Theory of Multiple Intelligences, we have seven types of intelligences—linguistic, logical-mathematical, spatial, bodily-kinesthetic, musical, interpersonal, and intrapersonal. His premise is that humans possess all of these intelligences to some degree, but we are gifted more in some than others. We learn best when given opportunities for them to interact and work to solve problems in a naturalistic setting.

Gardner's view of intelligence supports the interdisciplinary approach to learning. He encourages educators to look at different learning styles of children, and to help connect learning while focusing on the particular intelligences that individuals possess. Many children are kinesthetic learners—they learn best through movement—however, they all too often are expected to sit passively for hours in desks in classrooms. Classroom teachers should strive to focus on all of the seven intelligences, including bodily-kinesthetic, while physical education teachers can take the opportunity to help children expand as many intelligences as possible through integrated learning experiences in the physical education setting.

Source: Howard Gardner, *Frames of Mind, The Theory of Multiple Intelligence,* New York: Basic Books, 1983; and T. Armstrong, *Multiple Intelligences in the Classroom,* Alexandria, VA: Association for Supervision and Curriculum Development, 1994.

other subject area content, be prepared to put forth more effort, and always keep our goals in mind.

Reciprocal Respect for Subject Content Integrating physical education and other subject content is not always easy. Physical educators will have to alter the way they think about physical education. They will have to become familiar with developmentally appropriate content in other subject areas in order to promote real learning. The classroom teachers and administrators will have to see physical activity and physical education skills as important components of a child's education, and see physical educators as viable contributors to the overall education of the child.

Extra Effort Developing effective interdisciplinary learning experiences, as with any curricular innovation, requires effort and time. You may have to rearrange the order of your teaching to coincide with the lesson concept or theme that the classroom teacher is teaching, and vice versa. Some will be successful;

others may not. Be prepared to reflect on the learning experience, make changes, and try again.

Your Goals One challenge of interdisciplinary teaching is not to lose sight of the educational goals and objectives you want to accomplish as you plan integration activities with other subject areas. Always assess the potential benefits of the proposed integrative activity or unit, and if educational goals and objectives are not met, then it should not be considered a worthwhile endeavor. Remember, it is through the physical education program that children learn to perform locomotor, nonmanipulative, and manipulative movements proficiently, which will enhance their interdisciplinary learning.

The Process of Teaching Using Interdisciplinary Learning

A variety of interdisciplinary models have been introduced over the years. As we gain experience in integrating lessons, we typically develop and name our own "models" that guide us. We have chosen three approaches to discuss in this book that we hope will give you a general understanding of subject integration from simple to more complex. Other models and a more detailed breakdown of the approaches we are discussing here can be found in the related literature recommendations.

The three approaches—content linkage, shared integration, and thematic unit—all combine the teaching of skills and concepts from at least two subject areas. The content linkage approach can be used by one teacher independently, while the shared integration approach and the thematic unit approach both require a collaborative effort between at least two teachers from different subject areas in the school curriculum.

Content Linkage Approach

The *content linkage approach* is used by one teacher to connect content from at least two subject areas. One content area may be the primary focus of the lesson, but skills/concepts from another subject area enhance the learning experience and provide practice opportunities for learning the skills/concepts in the other subject area. Physical education teachers can find ways to reinforce classroom content without jeopardizing their primary focus of teaching skill themes, movement concepts, and fitness concepts using the content linkage approach. For example, the physical education teacher teaching a kindergarten class might reinforce the math concept of counting from 1 to 30 while focusing

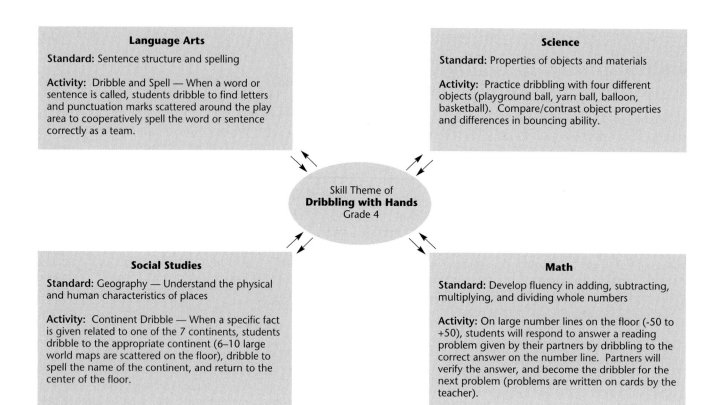

Language Arts

Standard: Sentence structure and spelling

Activity: Dribble and Spell — When a word or sentence is called, students dribble to find letters and punctuation marks scattered around the play area to cooperatively spell the word or sentence correctly as a team.

Science

Standard: Properties of objects and materials

Activity: Practice dribbling with four different objects (playground ball, yarn ball, balloon, basketball). Compare/contrast object properties and differences in bouncing ability.

Skill Theme of
Dribbling with Hands
Grade 4

Social Studies

Standard: Geography — Understand the physical and human characteristics of places

Activity: Continent Dribble — When a specific fact is given related to one of the 7 continents, students dribble to the appropriate continent (6–10 large world maps are scattered on the floor), dribble to spell the name of the continent, and return to the center of the floor.

Math

Standard: Develop fluency in adding, subtracting, multiplying, and dividing whole numbers

Activity: On large number lines on the floor (-50 to +50), students will respond to answer a reading problem given by their partners by dribbling to the correct answer on the number line. Partners will verify the answer, and become the dribbler for the next problem (problems are written on cards by the teacher).

Figure 32.1 Example of other subject content integrated with the skill theme of dribbling.

on traveling to pick up beanbags to transport across the gym.

Other examples are depicted in Figure 32.1, which shows how content-specific skills for fourth graders might be integrated in the physical education curriculum while focusing on practicing the skill theme of dribbling with hands.

Likewise, classroom teachers can use movement to teach specific concepts in subject areas throughout the curriculum. For example, a classroom teacher who is teaching a language arts spelling lesson might have her fourth graders throwing and catching a ball with a partner while spelling a specific word or group of words. A more detailed example is shown in Figure 32.2, illustrating how math content for second graders might be taught through movement and the reinforcement of physical education concepts.

Shared Integration Approach

Another strategy for connecting more than one subject-specific content area is the *shared integration model*. In this approach, two teachers work together to provide a lesson or multiple lessons that focus on shared concepts from the two distinct disciplines. (For a comparison between this approach and the content linkage approach, see Table 32.2.) This type of lesson integration can be used readily in both the

classroom and the physical education setting to reinforce skills and concepts. When teachers work together to teach and reinforce related skills from two or more subject areas, it helps integrate the cognitive, affective, and psychomotor domains of learning.

An example of shared integration is a lesson activity in Box 32-3 called "Stepping across the U.S." for fourth through sixth grades. This activity reinforces three physical education goals of teaching children about (1) the importance of physical activity, (2) what activities promote more movement and therefore more pedometer steps, and (3) the amount of physical activity needed to reach a set goal during each day. In addition, the learning experiences reinforce the social studies concepts of geography—location, distance, and facts about the states across the country. It could also be used to practice the math skills of estimation and comparison. This lesson would require both the physical education teacher and the classroom teacher to work together to equally reinforce these concepts.

Developing an Integrated Learning Experience

Once you have chosen a class or grade level with which you wish to teach an integrated lesson(s) using the content linkage approach, you will first need to review the grade-specific content scope and sequence and the state standards for the integrated subject and compare

Skill Theme: Jumping and landing

Activity: Students jump rope while counting the number that answers the specific math problem (addition, subtraction) given by the teacher.

Movement Concept: Relationship with objects

Activity: Hoop Fractions — Tape masking tape twice across hoops to form four equal sections. Each child will perform various movements with the hoop while using $1/4$, $1/2$, $3/4$, and the whole (i.e., jump in $1/2$ of your hoop, put body parts in $3/4$ of your hoop, etc.).

Math
Grade 2

Skill Themes: Traveling, chasing, fleeing, and dodging

Activity: Number Line Tag — All students are assigned a number 1–20 (# of students) and given a card with that number. One-fourth of students are taggers. If tagged, student holds his number card over his head and repeatedly says his number – must be untagged by someone with the number immediately above or below.

Fitness Concept: Muscular strength

Movement Concept: Relationship with others

Activity: High 5 Push Ups — Facing a partner, both in push up position, partners alternate High 5's while counting. Goals should be set, such as counting to 100 by 10's, 5's, and 1's.

Figure 32.2 Examples of reinforcing math concepts through skill themes and movement concepts.

Pedometers can be used to teach important concepts in mathematics.

those with your own. Then choose the concepts/ skills for each subject you wish to integrate, and you are ready to design an appropriate learning experience that focuses on the chosen concepts. (Use the format applied to the "Stepping across the U.S." lesson as a guide.) Before implementing your lesson, share it with a teacher(s) of the other content area for awareness and feedback. After teaching the lesson, assess the success of the learning experience.

For the shared integration approach, both teachers should share program scope and sequence and standards, discuss possible integration experiences, and decide which skills/concepts will be targeted. Together, write an appropriate lesson experience(s) that equally focuses on at least one skill/concept from each of the subject areas being integrated. Decide on the implementation date so that lessons can be adjusted, if necessary.

Criteria for Integrated Lesson Development

When preparing and implementing learning experiences using either the content linkage approach or the shared integration approach, ask yourself the following questions. Does the integrated lesson:

- Provide developmentally and instructionally appropriate tasks (for grade, for individual children)?
- Focus on a skill theme, movement concept, and/or fitness concept that is consistent with the program scope and sequence?
- Reinforce specific content standard(s) in one or more other subject area(s) for, and is consistent with, the specific program scope and sequence for that grade?
- Include assessment strategies for assessing effectiveness in both subject areas?

Table 32.2 Comparing Integrated Approaches

Comparison of Content Linkage and Shared Integration				
Approach	Number of Subject Areas	Number of Teachers Needed	Time	Focus
Content linkage	2 or more	1	Usually during 1 lesson	Primary focus on 1 content area, with another subject area used to enhance
Shared integration	2 or more	2 or more	Could be for 1 lesson, but often extends over a longer period	Equal focus on shared concepts from two distinct disciplines

Box 32-3

Example of a Shared Integration Learning Experience

Stepping across the U.S.

Grade level: 4–5
PE skill/concept focus: Fitness and wellness concepts
PE content standard: Exhibits a physically active lifestyle
Social studies skill/concept focus: Geography—U.S. states
Social studies content standard: Understands the physical and human characteristics of places
Math skill/concept focus: Convert steps to miles, estimate, compare stats, add class miles/steps
Math content standard: Computes fluently and makes reasonable estimates
Materials needed: Pedometers for each child, paper logs or daily access to the Web site peclogit.org, maps for classroom and gym to track class progress, state facts, flags, etc.
Description of activity: Children are given a pedometer by the physical education teacher at the beginning of each class, which are collected at the end by the classroom teacher after returning to their classroom. The classroom teacher has the students log their steps each day on paper logs, or at the Web site Log It. Students convert steps to miles using the conversion of 2,000 steps = 1 mile. Total class miles are calculated each day, and the class moves across the U.S. map according to the miles accumulated. When a new state capital is reached, both the classroom teacher and the physical education teacher will reinforce state facts such as the state seal, flag, bird, flower, animal, and the location, area, and population of the state, etc. Daily or weekly goals can be set, and estimation and comparisons can be taught.
Variation 1: Using PE Central Log It (peclogit.org) to record pedometer steps allows students to record their steps daily, compare their stats with others, and to take a "virtual hike" around the U.S. When a new state is reached, students are able to see state information online, as well as see how many miles their class must log to travel to the next state. Individual goal setting is built into the Web site, and students earn certificates for reaching daily goals. Teachers must register their classes online.
Variation 2: Students can wear pedometers for the entire school day.

Note: The physical education teacher should instruct students to set daily goals, to identify activities that promote the most physical movement by monitoring steps after specific activities, and to participate in physical activity outside of school.

Thematic Unit Approach

In the third approach to content integration, *the thematic unit approach,* teachers overlap the content across the curriculum over a set period, while focusing on one theme. Many educators believe that integrating subjects such as physical education, art, and music with the core subject areas of math, science, social studies, and language arts using a thematic approach should be considered in school curriculums (Roberts & Kellough, 2000; Wood, 2001).

The thematic approach in physical education was recommended by Evaul (1980) and others years ago

Table 32.3 Thematic Unit: Recreation in (Your State) (Grade 6)

Overview: This thematic unit focuses on the study of recreational areas in your state. Learning activities include students working in groups to study and report on a specific recreational area, preparing a budget associated with participating in the recreational opportunity, and practicing motor and fitness skills necessary for successful participation in the physical activity.

Social Studies	Math	Science	Language Arts	Physical Education	Health
Locate recreation opportunities throughout the state on the map; research each park or recreational area; determine distance from home area to each recreational area; study economy of the area; in a group, prepare a PSA or commercial to promote the area and its recreational opportunities.	Choose a recreational area that the class will visit; prepare a budget for a trip to the area, including cost of the trip (transportation, lodging, meals, fees), equipment, clothing, and any other costs associated with participating in the physical activity.	Decide what muscles need to be developed to prepare to participate in the physical activity.	Prepare a group report and poster about one recreational area in the state; use the Internet to read specific information about the recreational area you will visit.	Choose one recreational sport (e.g., snow skiing) and discuss and practice the motor skills and fitness levels necessary to enjoy participating in the sport.	Determine benefits of the physical activity; determine preferences; set personal goals—proper diet and activity; learn and practice basic first aid.

Culminating event: Plan a field trip to one of the recreational areas in the state, and participate in recreational opportunities in that area; utilize prepared budget, and apply the knowledge of the area and the physical activity.

Parental and community involvement: Parents join in on the trip, help organize and make arrangements for the trip; community resources that will be utilized are local recreation agencies, which will provide informational pamphlets, and clothing/equipment catalogs or retailers.

Source: B. McCracken, *It's Not Just Gym Anymore,* Champaign, Il: Human Kinetics, 2001.

by suggesting that developmental themes such as co-operation, courage, independence, and responsibility be used as themes for organizing the physical education curriculum. Now, the interdisciplinary thematic unit approach is being incorporated in many elementary school curricula to help connect student learning across a number of subject areas, including physical education. Thematic units can be planned and implemented by one teacher with his or her students, but to include subject areas across the curriculum, most teachers work together as a team to plan and implement learning experiences centered around a theme or topic over a specific period. A thematic unit of instruction might be a one-week study or it might focus on a theme on an ongoing basis over many weeks. An example of a theme that might be used to connect different subject content in a kindergarten class is "The Jungle." Young children are interested in and intrigued by animals. This theme could easily incorporate lessons related to jungle animals including characteristics of different types of animals, the jungle habitat, math concepts such as measuring and comparing (i.e., elephant foot to human foot), and many of the movement concepts (space awareness, relationships, and effort).

Included in this chapter are two examples of how thematic units can be developed to include a variety of subject areas, including physical education, connected through a theme. The thematic unit "Recreation in (Your State)" in Table 32.3 focuses on the study of recreational areas in a state and incorporates six subject areas that revolve around the theme. The "Wild

Physical Education and Social Studies: Integrated Activity Example for Grades 3–4

Have a large map of the United States painted on the play area, or use four to six large maps taped to the floor. Activities that incorporate traveling, space awareness, and/or other manipulative skills can be used to identify states by names, facts, relationships, etc.

Task Example: On each state, place tokens with the state names. Students on teams of three will answer questions posed by the teacher by sending a team member to the correct state to get a token (i.e., state bordering West Virginia that begins with a "P"). After 10 questions, check for correct number of tokens for each group.

Table 32.4 Thematic Unit: The Wild Wild West (Grade 4)

Overview: This thematic unit focuses on the westward expansion of America during the 19th century. The unit connects content in social studies, language arts, fine arts, and physical education.

Social Studies	Language Arts	Physical Education	Fine Arts
Map making of the U.S., locating landmarks and cities that travelers would see traveling west	"Wild West" theme folders to include a word web, vocabulary list, daily journal entries as a frontiersperson, and other related activities	Introduction to orienteering— map reading, compass reading	Art: Begin to create a quilt and discuss the history of quilt making
Identify famous people involved in the settlement of the Old West; hardships of the early settlers	"How the Settlers Lived" by George and Ellen Laycock	Complete an orienteering activity, using landmarks that represent the Old West	Art: Incorporate "The Quilt Story" by Tony Johnston
The Oregon Trail computer software (The Learning Co. Inc.) takes you on an educational adventure	Prepare and rehearse oral presentations on various aspects of the Wild West	Participate in simple folk and square dances representative of that period	Music: Video musical "Oklahoma"— socializing aspects and time period comparisons

Culminating event: The Wild Wild West Celebration will conclude the thematic unit, with demonstrations of quilting, square dancing, story-telling, and oral presentations by the students. Displays of student work will be shown. Parents will be invited and all will be invited to wear period clothes and bring period items to share, such as old hats, pictures, lanterns, and other unique items.

Parental and community involvement: Parents are invited to be guest storytellers, observers, and participants in the final celebration. They are asked to help with their child's period costume. Local media are invited to attend the culminating event.

Source: Developed by Brenda Cannon, Kevin Hutchinson, Rick Spreeder, and Shannon Owen, Concord College, Athens, WV.

Wild West" thematic unit in Table 32.4 is based on the westward expansion of America and incorporates four content areas. These examples illustrate only an overview of the partial unit, but will help you see how learning across subject areas can be interconnected and how children might better "connect" their learning in ways that are more meaningful to their everyday experiences.

Tips for Developing an Interdisciplinary Thematic Unit

1. Choose a theme, together with your students, that is motivating to them and that can incorporate skills/concepts from a variety of subject areas. If you are working with another teacher, include him or her in the theme selection process.

2. Inform school administrators and other teachers of your intent, and ask for their support and assistance. (Team teaching may require special planning time; outside speakers may be asked to come into the classroom; field trips may be planned, etc.)

3. Form a teaching team of interested teachers from other content areas. The team will:

- Share content materials and brainstorm ideas for the unit.
- Develop an overview of the unit, goals, and instructional objectives.
- Develop the theme-based learning experiences that meet subject areas content standards and those of the thematic unit, including a culminating event, assessment strategies, and timelines.

4. Inform parents and seek parental involvement. For example, parents may be asked to assist their children with special projects, bring expertise on a particular topic to the class, join the students for a special presentation, etc.

5. Locate instructional resources for the unit, including community resources. For example, if you are planning a unit around the theme of "Heart Health," you might have a pediatric cardiologist speak to the class, take children to a local park to explore physical activity possibilities, organize a field trip to the grocery store to analyze food selections, and have local "athletes" come to talk with the children about tobacco avoidance.

6. Implement the interdisciplinary thematic unit and assess the success of the unit (student learning).

Physical Education and Language: Integrated Activity Example for Grades K–2

Read the story "The Silly Tail Book" by Marc Brown and discuss the different kinds of tails that jungle animals have. As the teacher pulls different tails from a bag, the children identify the animal to which it belongs, and then move through the jungle (cones on the gym floor) as that animal would move (e.g., elephant, giraffe, snake, panther, monkey, etc.).

Source: Created by Debra Williamson, Concord College, Athens, WV.

Understanding the Scope and Sequence of Subject Area Content

For teachers to effectively integrate subject area content, they must be knowledgeable in the scope and sequence of the subjects being integrated. Cone et al. (1998) in their text *Interdisciplinary Teaching through Physical Education* have reviewed textbooks and projects in the content areas of math, language arts, social studies, science, and the arts and have compiled a scope and sequence for each area in grades kindergarten through six. They have given us permission to reprint their work in Tables 32.5 and 32.6 to help you better understand the skills/concepts taught at each grade level in two subject areas, math and social studies. *Interdisciplinary Teaching through Physical Education* also offers many suggestions in each subject area for active learning experiences that would be helpful to any physical education teacher planning interdisciplinary learning experiences.

Integrating physical education concepts with learning in other subjects in the school curriculum can be considered a viable approach to help physical education teachers enhance what is being learned in other subject areas and to help classroom teachers promote healthy lifestyles and physical activity. But clearly, it is the teachers that make integration work. If teachers recognize the contributions each field of study can make to the others, and strive to make connections

Table 32.5 Scope and Sequence of Mathematical Concepts Taught in Elementary Schools

Concept	K	1	2	3	4	5	6
Numbers	x	x	x	x	x	x	x
Meaning of numbers 1–12	x						
Meaning of numbers through 99		x					
Meaning of numbers through 999			x				
Meaning of addition and subtraction		x					
Addition and subtraction computation			x				
Meaning of numbers through 100,000				x			
Meaning of multiplication and division				x			
Meaning of numbers through 1,000,000					x		
Multiplication and division computation					x		
Meaning of decimals through hundredths					x		
Meaning of decimals through thousandths						x	
Meaning of addition and subtraction of fractions and decimals						x	
Number theory						x	
Meaning of multiplication and division of fractions and decimals							x
Integers and ratios							x
Percents							x
Measuring and graphing	x	x	x	x	x	x	x
Geometry	x	x	x	x	x	x	x
Patterns and functions	x	x	x	x	x	x	x
Probability and statistics	x	x	x	x	x	x	x
Logic		x	x	x	x	x	x
Algebra			x	x	x	x	x

Source: Reprinted, by permission, from T. P. Cone, P. Werner, S. L. Cone, and A. M. Woods, 1998, *Interdisciplinary teaching through physical education* (Champaign, IL: Human Kinetics), [p. 70].

Table 32.6 Scope and Sequence of Social Studies Concepts Taught in Elementary Schools

Concept	K	1	2	3	4	5	6
Family	x	x					
Home		x					
Neighborhoods	x	x	x				
Communities	x	x	x	x			
School	x	x					
Travel	x						
Necessity of rules	x						
Urban, suburban, and rural life		x					
Family life, past and present		x					
Citizenship		x	x	x	x		x
United States				x	x	x	
Famous people			x				
How people live and work				x	x		
First Americans					x		
Settling the land					x		
Own state					x		
How people change				x			
Geography of the United States						x	
History of the United States						x	
Economics of the United States						x	
Political system of the United States						x	
History of Western Hemisphere						x	
Geography of Western Hemisphere							x
The world, past and present							x
The world, regions							x

Source: Reprinted, by permission, from T. P. Cone, P. Werner, S. L. Cone, and A. M. Woods, 1998, *Interdisciplinary teaching through physical education* (Champaign, IL: Human Kinetics), [p. 172].

between the subject areas, then student learning can be enhanced in new ways. Children benefit from seeing teachers working together to focus different subject areas on a common theme and reinforce what they are learning across the curriculum.

The Connection between Physical Activity and Academic Performance

Current education reform movements, such as the No Child Left Behind (NCLB) Act of 2001, placed increased emphasis on math and reading for all grades, and schools and teachers are being held more accountable for adequate student progress toward achievement of state standards in the core subjects (NCLB, 2003). With high-stakes testing programs taking precedence across the nation, some administrators are tempted to reduce, or even eliminate, physical education as a solution to improve test scores. Recent evidence suggests this is ill-advised. Students who have regular physical education, are more physically fit, and have more opportunities to

be physically active may do better in school than those who are deprived of these valuable experiences.

What the Research Suggests: Physical Activity, Fitness, and Physical Education

In recent studies, researchers have focused on the connection between physical activity, physical fitness, and/or physical education and academic performance. One of the most compelling new studies conducted by the California Department of Education (CDE) matched scores on the Fitnessgram physical fitness test with reading and math scores on the Stanford Achievement Test (SAT-9) of 353,000 students in fifth grade. Results showed that higher achievement was associated with higher fitness levels. This evidence provides support for the assumption, held by many, that students learn better when they are physically fit. Physical education programs bear the primary responsibility for promoting physical fitness in school-age children (CDE, 2002).

What Is a Culminating Event?

An effective thematic unit includes a culminating event or finale that will bring closure to the unit. The culminating event should provide an opportunity for students to demonstrate their "connected" knowledge, through written, oral, and/or movement presentations. It allows students to share what they have learned in different and individual ways. Examples are individual/class presentations to parents or other students in the school, field trips, and class projects.

Other researchers are also finding compelling evidence that supports the relationship between physical activity and enhanced learning in the classroom, including:

- Increased physical activity time during the school day led to higher test scores in math (Shephard, 1997).
- Allocating less time for physical education, art, and music did not relate to higher standardized test scores (Graham et al., 2002).
- An intense school physical activity program had a positive effect on math, reading, and writing test scores (Symons et al., 1997).
- Children who participated in four times as much physical activity per day as previously reported, through exposure to a designated 14-week physical education program, showed improvements in fitness, classroom behavior, and academic performance (Institute of Medicine, 2005).
- Canadian children who spend an extra hour a day in physical education class performed higher on exams than their less active counterparts (Hannaford, 1995).

The obesity epidemic currently plaguing our nation focuses increased interest on the physical activity levels of children. As school administrators begin to be held accountable for the amount of physical activity time provided for children during the school day, this body of research will become increasingly important to support daily physical education.

Another compelling body of evidence is being compiled by neuroscientists and brain researchers related to the importance of movement and optimal brain function.

What the Research Suggests: Brain-Based Learning

Brain researchers have provided evidence that physical activity contributes to optimal brain functioning and optimal learning. In her book *Smart Moves* (1995),

Carla Hannaford cites a metanalysis of 13 studies that found exercise to be a stimulant for brain development. Jensen, in his book *Learning with the Body in Mind* (2000), reports:

- Vigorous daily physical exercise can promote new brain cell growth.
- Exercise and aerobic conditioning may help improve memory and strengthen other areas of the brain.
- Downtime, such as recess, is necessary for children to learn. It allows for the "strengthening of synaptic connections in the brain that solidify prior learning" (p. 66).
- Exercise of longer durations creates more cognitive boosts.

Both Hannaford and Jensen support the need for quality physical education programs in all schools, and additional physical activity time throughout the day for all children, to promote learning and, therefore, increase student achievement. Integrating physical activities with the core subjects helps the students engage both their bodies and brains in learning, as suggested in the brain research. The skill theme approach readily lends itself to "brain activities" and to promoting both cognitive and psychomotor learning.

The skill theme approach emphasizes many of the concepts that brain researchers say are so important to brain development and learning. Skills such as balancing, tracking, moving cross-laterally, and moving rhythmically are all included within the movement

Finding State and National Content Standards

An excellent source for locating national and state content standards in all subject areas is http://www.education-world.com/standards/.

concepts and skill themes. (Some examples of brain-enhancing activities are included in Box 32-4.) In addition, Prigge (2002) suggests other ways that we can increase "brain power" through physical education programs. These ideas include:

- Using music. Research on music and learning has shown that music improves learning and memory and increases optimum functioning.
- Teaching personal goal setting. Goal-setting skills help students to "think smart."
- Reinforcing good eating habits. To "eat smart," students should always eat breakfast, consume sugar

Box 32-4

Examples of Brain-Enhancing Activities

Tracking activities help prepare the eye muscles for reading. An example is following the flow of a scarf, a bubble, or a feather, as it falls to the ground, or tracking a balloon as it is struck with a racket from one side of the body to the other.

Cross-lateral movements enable the brain to cross the midsection from the right side across the center to the left side, which is important for allowing the brain to be ready to read and write. Examples of cross-lateral activities include basic scarf juggling, elephant walks, windmills, and rhythm ribbons.

Rhythmic movements such as tapping rhythms, moving body parts to the beat, moving equipment to the beat, and marching are all ways to stimulate the frontal lobes and can potentially enrich language development.

and carbohydrates in moderation, and increase fruit and vegetable intake.

- Reinforcing water consumption. Children should drink plenty of water throughout the day to avoid dehydration and less-than-optimal learning.
- Remembering the importance of first and last. We remember most what is presented first and last.

Have powerful beginnings, present new information early, and always review during lesson closure.
- Having fun. Laughter lowers stress and contributes to a relaxed learning environment.

A Final Thought

In concluding this chapter it is important to reemphasize that the goals of physical education, as expressed in national and state standards, must take top priority because they make such an important contribution to the overall health and well-being of youngsters. It is possible, however, to accomplish these goals and simultaneously reinforce the concepts that are being taught in the classroom and included on the high-stakes tests that have become so important in recent years. It also makes sense for us to ensure that we include "brain activities" that neuroscientists are telling us help with learning.

Striving to meet the *National Standards for Physical Education* that focuses on physical activity and the development of a healthy lifestyle is certainly a responsibility that should be considered by all those involved in educating children in the school setting, not only the physical education teachers. Because most children love to move and often learn best through kinesthetic experiences, physical education readily lends itself to interdisciplinary learning.

Summary

Interdisciplinary, or integrated, teaching are terms used to describe teaching subject matter from two different disciplines within the same lesson, thereby promoting learning in both subjects simultaneously and, when physical education is involved, making connections between the psychomotor and cognitive domains. Three approaches to interdisciplinary learning are described in the chapter—content linkage, shared integration, and thematic units. It is important that the teacher have a mastery of the subjects to be taught if the lessons (units) are going to be effective and maximize learning. The chapter also includes overviews of research related to the relationships among academic performance, optimal brain functioning, and human movement and physical fitness.

Reading Comprehension Questions

1. Define interdisciplinary learning. What are some advantages of using this approach to teaching/learning?
2. How does integration enhance learning?
3. How does the skill theme approach support interdisciplinary learning?

4. Describe and discuss three unique benefits for both classroom teachers and physical educators for integrating physical education with other subject areas.
5. Identify three approaches to integration discussed in this chapter. What are the characteristics of each? How are they alike/different?

6. What are some examples of two-directional integration between physical education and math? Language arts? Social studies? Science?
7. Briefly describe an integrated learning experience using both the content linkage approach and the shared integration approach.
8. Briefly describe a thematic unit overview that includes at least three subject areas for a primary or intermediate grade.
9. Briefly summarize key points made in the recent literature about the connection between physical education and academic performance.

References/Suggested Readings

Armstrong, T. (1994). *Multiple intelligences in the classroom.* Alexandria, VA: Association for Supervision and Curriculum Development.

Blaydes, J. (2002). Advocacy: A case for daily quality physical education. www.actionbasedlearning.com.

California Department of Education (CDE) News Release (Dec. 10, 2002). www.cahperd.org/images/pdf_docs/CDE_News_Release.pdf.

Cone, T., Werner, P., Cone, S., & Woods, A. (1998). *Interdisciplinary teaching through physical education.* Champaign, IL: Human Kinetics Publishing.

Elliott, E., & Sanders, S. (2002). Keeping children moving: Promoting physical activity throughout the curriculum. Teacher Source, PBS. www.pbs.org/teachersource/prek2/issues/202issue.shtm.

Evaul, T. (1980). Organizing centers for the 1980s. *Journal of Physical Education, Recreation and Dance, 51*(7), 51–54.

Fogarty, R. (1991). Ten ways to integrate curriculum. *Educational Leadership, 49*(2), 61–65.

Gardner, H. (1983). *Frames of mind, the theory of multiple intelligence.* New York: Basic Books.

Garrahy, D. (2001). To integrate or not to integrate? That is the question. *Strategies,* March/April, 23–25.

Graham, G., Wilkins, J. M., Westfall, S., Parker, S., Fraser, R., & Tembo, M. (2002). The effects of high-stakes testing on elementary school art, music and physical education. *Journal of Health, Physical Education, Recreation and Dance, 73*(8), 51–54.

Hannaford, C. (1995). *Smart moves.* Alexander, NC: Great Ocean Publishers.

Hichwa, J. (1998). *Right fielders are people too.* Champaign, IL: Human Kinetics.

Institute of Medicine (IOM), Dietary reference intakes for energy, carbohydrate, fiber, fat, fatty acids, cholesterol, protein, and amino acids, Report. (September 2002). Institute of Medicine, National Academies. www.iom.edu.

Institute of Medicine (IOM). 2005. *Preventing childhood obesity: Health in the balance.* Washington, DC: National Academies Press.

Jensen, E. (2000). *Teaching with the body in mind.* San Diego, CA: The Brain Store.

McCracken, B. (2001). *It's not just gym anymore.* Champaign, IL: Human Kinetics.

No Child Left Behind (NCLB). (2002). U.S. Department of Education. www.nclb.gov.

Placek, J. (1992). Rethinking middle school physical education curriculum: An integrated, thematic approach. *Quest, 44,* 330–341.

Prigge, D. (2002). 20 ways to promote brain-based teaching and learning. *Intervention in School and Clinic, 37*(4), 237–241.

Rauschenbach, J. (1996). Tying it all together: Integrating physical education and other subject areas. *Journal of Physical Education, Recreation and Dance, 67*(2), 49–51.

Roberts, P., & Kellough, R. (2000). *A guide for developing interdisciplinary thematic units.* Upper Saddle River, NJ: Prentice Hall.

Shephard, R. (1997). Curricular physical activity and academic performance. *Pediatric Exercise Science, 9,* 113–126.

Symons, C., Cinelli, B., James, T., & Groff, P. (1997). Bridging student health risks and academic achievement through comprehensive school health programs. *Journal of School Health, 67*(6), 220–227.

Wood, K. E. (2001). *Interdisciplinary instruction: A practical guide for elementary and middle school teacher.* Upper Saddle River, NJ: Merrill Prentice Hall.

Internet Sites

PEC Classroom Teacher/Integrated Lesson Ideas. PE Central. pecentral.org/lessonideas/classroom/classroom.asp.

Healthy Hearts: An e-learning module for 5th/6th grade children about physical activity, nutrition, and tobacco use. www.healthyhearts4kids.org.

The Future

Our last two chapters emphasize future directions in physical education. Chapter 33, "Building Support for Your Program," describes how teachers can work with seven different populations to gain support for their physical education programs. We offer practical ideas for working with other teachers in the school, the principal, parents, the school board, legislators, the children themselves, and the community at large.

Chapter 34, "Physical Education for Tomorrow's Children," is in many ways our favorite. We end the book by focusing on the future, presenting some of our thoughts. We hope our ideas will encourage you to dream too.

Building Support for Your Program

Many parents, students, teachers, and administrators do not know how physical education contributes to an individual's growth. The lack of a public relations plan can result in an absence of communication between the physical educator and the public, thereby hampering the growth of the physical education program.

—MICHAEL TENOSCHOK AND STEVE SANDERS

Key Concepts

- Successful teachers, in addition to everything else they are asked to do, must also successfully market or build support for their programs.
- Physical education programs need to be marketed to several populations—school and district administrators, other teachers in a school, parents, the school board, the community at large, and legislators.
- Teachers who create positive, enjoyable, and productive programs are building support with their most important population—the children they teach.

One of the undisputed facts about teaching in schools is that teachers need support from a variety of sources to develop the type of programs they want for their children. This is especially true in physical education, for two reasons. First, many people regard physical education as less important than other subjects, such as reading and math. Second, physical education is a relatively expensive program to conduct because of the necessary equipment involved. (It's important, however, that we continually remind others that physical education is for *every* child in the school—for the entire five or six years.) Thus, it's necessary to cultivate support from the various segments of a school community who have the potential to be allies in our quest for improved programs. We've identified seven related populations who need to be aware of and supportive of our program: the school administration, especially the principal; other teachers in the school; parents; the school board; the community at large; legislators, in some instances; and the children.

This chapter discusses ideas for building support within each of these seven populations. However, note that it's important that a teacher first build as good a physical education program as possible with the support available. Even with limited resources, it's possible to begin a good program, and this is a necessary first step because much of the work that will go toward building more support involves opening the program to administrators, parents, and the community in general. Obviously, if the program doesn't get off to a good start, you don't want visitors.

Once the program is off to a reasonable start, however, the teacher can invite observers to visit the classes. It may take months before the teacher is ready, but the learning environment has to be established, with the children and teacher working together comfortably, before visitors are welcome. Once the teacher

is ready, the principal and other teachers in the school will probably be the first visitors. You might want to consider your answers to the questions in Box 33-1 as you begin to build support for your program.

The Principal

Many principals, through no fault of their own, know very little about physical education—especially the approach we're advocating in *Children Moving*. Thus, it's important to not take for granted that the principal knows and understands the program you're trying to develop (Schneider, 1992). We believe part of our job is to educate our principal and administrators about our physical education programs. This is probably our most important task for gaining support for our programs. Principals are extremely important. In fact, if a principal is not "on our side," the opportunity to develop our desired program is reduced considerably (Giles-Brown, 1993). We suggest the following ideas for working with your principal. The ideas aren't arranged in order of implementation, and we don't suggest that they all need to be done. We've simply listed ideas you may find helpful in your particular situation.

Box 33-1

Why Should My Child Take Physical Education?

As you consider ways to build support for your program, it helps to formulate answers to the questions that a parent (administrator, board member) might ask:

- Why should my children take physical education?
- What benefits is he or she gaining from participating in your program?

Think about how other teachers might respond if they were asked the same questions about math or reading or social studies. Try to be as specific as possible. Provide evidence of what your students are actually learning (not just doing) in your program by sharing some of the assessments they have completed as suggested in Chapter 14. Be sure to show how your program reflects and puts into practice the recommendations in the Surgeon General's report (U.S. Department of Health and Human Services [USDHHS], 1996) and the *National Standards for Physical Education* (National Association for Sport and Physical Education [NASPE], 2004) so that it is clear your program is contemporary and on the cutting edge.

- Invite the principal of your school to observe the skill theme approach at a nearby school with you. Sit with your principal, and be certain that he or she focuses on the aspects of the program that are critical to the growth of your own program. Be certain to schedule a visit with the principal at the school you're observing so that the two administrators can discuss their programs and your principal can ask questions.

- Invite your principal to your classes that are beginning to work the way you intend. Be certain to follow up this visit so that you can answer any questions that may have arisen. Some administrators, for example, are unaccustomed to seeing every child with a ball and may be concerned about the "chaotic" appearance of a class that differs from their experiences in which there was only one ball for an entire class.

- If you're able to obtain videotapes of other teachers, invite your principal to view one of the tapes with you. Be sure to comment on the critical aspects of the program and relate them to your needs. Remember that the principal is busy, so you may want him or her to watch only certain key features, not the entire videotape.

- Occasionally give your principal a copy of an article or book you think is particularly well done and relevant to your program. Be certain to discuss the document after your principal has had a chance to read it. This is especially important if, for example, you're teaching 12 classes a day and you're able to locate a publication that recommends 9 classes a day as a complete load for a physical education specialist. We recommend the publication by the Council on Physical Education for Children (COPEC), *Appropriate Practices for Elementary Physical Education* (2000). It provides important guidelines written in an easy-to-understand format. It can be obtained from the Web site for the National Association for Sport and Physical Education (www.aahperd.org/naspe/). Also be sure to share overviews of the 1996 Surgeon General's report (USDHHS), and the *National Standards for Physical Education* (NASPE, 2004), and your state standards (www.pecentral.org/professional/statestandards.html) with your principal.

- Be on the lookout for research that you can use to support the importance of physical education, especially if your principal is feeling pressure to increase test scores in reading, math, and science. For example, one study that surveyed Virginia elementary school principals found that allocating less time for art, music, and physical education did not correlate with higher reading and math scores in elementary schools (Graham et al., 2002). Another study of 353,000 fifth graders discovered a positive relationship between physical fitness and reading and math scores (www.cahperd.org) (Figure 33.1).

Try to avoid falling into the trap of thinking that your principal really doesn't like your program, or physical education in general, if she isn't initially enthusiastic. It takes some principals several years to become active supporters of this program. In fact, we've worked with principals who took several months to find time to come view our programs. Eventually, however, they did support our program and came to view it as an asset to the school.

Teachers in the School

As you build your program, it's important that other teachers in the school understand and support your efforts. You'll certainly want to invite these teachers to observe your classes. Some of the ideas you use with your principal can also be used with your colleagues. Physical education specialists also find the following ideas helpful:

- Develop a thematic approach (Ward, 1999) to an integrated curriculum in which the entire school or a certain grade level focuses on an idea or theme. With this approach, content in all disciplines is centered around the same selected theme. This is quite a natural fit for music, art, and physical education, but it can also be used in a total-school or grade-level approach. (See Holt/Hale, 2003, and Cone et al., 1998, for more information on integrated curriculum.) Remember, when developing an integrated

The principal is an important component of a physical education program.

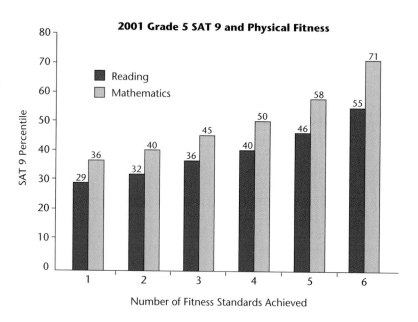

Figure 33.1 Fitnessgram scores and SAT-9 reading and math scores for 353,000 fifth-grade California children. *Source:* California Department of Education, 2002.

curriculum, that content should be integrated in a manner that does not compromise physical education content, force integration, or sacrifice the existing curriculum. Chapter 32 provides helpful suggestions for integrating curriculum.

- On a smaller scale, work in conjunction with a classroom teacher on certain projects (Chapter 32). Child-designed games, for example, provide marvelous opportunities for writing, math, and art projects. Expressive dance is an excellent catalyst for creative writing.

- If you require your students to keep student logs or do written assignments (Chapter 14), some classroom teachers will provide class time for students to do the writing immediately after physical education class (Stevens, 1994).

- Arrange for several of the primary grades to view the last 10 minutes of an intermediate grade's lesson, to show the younger children the progress that the older children have made. This motivates the younger children, encourages the older children, and also provides some extra physical education the younger children who attend the minishow.

- When a class has done a particularly good job on a physical education project, it's a treat for the classroom teacher to share in the children's efforts. Invite her to observe the last 10 minutes of a class while the children demonstrate their progress, for example, in child-designed games or gymnastics sequences. This also has the added incentive of encouraging the classroom teacher to observe your physical education program.

- When feasible, try to eat with other teachers in the lunchroom. This not only helps to fight isolation,

but also develops rapport and helps them see you as a caring person and professional.

The classroom teacher's support of the physical education specialist is important. Classroom teachers who understand that physical education is educational, not simply recess, will be less likely to keep children "in" to complete math or reading assignments. They also respect the fact that the physical education program has certain time limits and so make sure that their children arrive on time and are ready to return to the classroom on schedule. This may seem to be a minor point, but it can be a source of considerable friction when all the teachers in a school aren't working together to provide the best possible program for children. When teachers understand the value and quality of a physical education program, their support is easier to obtain.

Parents

The physical education teacher must be sure to establish administrator and colleague support before beginning a major program to cultivate enthusiasm among parents. Parent support is important, but it's not enough without the assistance of the principal and the other teachers. If "internal" support doesn't exist, a principal might feel that you're going "over her head" by appealing to parents, which can be disastrous for a new program. Once the administration understands your program and its needs, in many instances the principal will encourage you to generate parent support. And parent support can be especially helpful in obtaining funds that aren't available in the school's budget. There are many ideas for generating support among parents. Try a few of the following one year, a few the next year. Be sure to adapt the ideas to match the needs and interests of parents in your community.

- Attend PTA (PTO) meetings regularly, even if you aren't required to. Try not to sit in the back corner with the other teachers; take the time to meet some of the parents—introduce yourself, tell them what you teach, and invite them to observe your classes. This isn't necessarily the most enjoyable part of building a program, but it certainly can be a major factor in creating support.
- If you're invited to do a presentation for the parents' group, try to involve as many children as possible, to ensure a large turnout for your program. Be certain to include children at all skill levels, not only the utilization- and proficiency-level youngsters—and if possible, relate your program to the 1996 Surgeon General's report (USDHHS) and your state standards. (Most state physical education standards can be located at the following Web site: www.pecentral.org/professional/statestandards.html.)
- Send a letter home at the beginning of the year. Tell parents about your program and the general rules the children will be expected to follow (for example, shoes for physical education class). Invite parents to visit. Include an e-mail address so that parents can contact you if they have questions about the program or your policies.
- A one-page monthly or quarterly newsletter is very helpful for informing parents and creating enthusiasm (Figure 33.2). Include items such as community programs of interest, books and articles to read, special accomplishments of the children, upcoming television programs of interest, and future programs that you've scheduled. Also include a brief sketch of what you've been working on in physical education and suggest activities for the parents and the children to do together; for example, include the directions from this text for making a nylon-hose racket or golf club, and suggest several activities for the parents to do with their children. Be sure to have the newsletter proofread so there aren't any spelling or grammatical errors.
- Bulletin boards are a great way to let parents know about your program. If you don't have the skills to make attractive bulletin boards, try trading with another teacher, for example, one week of bus duty for one bulletin board. In many communities there are retail stores for teachers that have very attractive bulletin board letters, pictures, backgrounds, and so on, that even the least skilled person can use to make

an appealing bulletin board. Written student assessments, illustrated with their drawings, make appealing bulletin boards. PE Central features ideas for bulletin boards and links to other Web sites that contain tips for creating interesting and appealing bulletin boards. The Web address for these ideas is www.pcentral.org/websites/bulletinboardsites.html.
- Send home with the children a "good news" note, which informs the parents of their children's accomplishments in physical education class. Design and print a supply of notes at the beginning of the year, so it won't take long to send several every week (Figure 33.3). These notes are particularly effective for the children who work hard but rarely get noticed.
- Some teachers use positive phone calls to communicate with parents about the program. A positive phone call is just a brief phone call to tell a parent how pleased the teacher is about the child's progress (attitude, effort) in physical education. It doesn't take long, but the fact that the teacher takes the time to make the call means much to the parent. In many instances it's also unexpected because most phone calls from the school tend to be negative. Challenge yourself to make two good phone calls a week.
- Pete Tamm, a physical education teacher at Michael McCoy Elementary School in Orlando, Florida, writes letters to his students (Tamm, 1993). During a three-year period he has averaged more than 1,000 letters a year to his children. Figure 33.4 contains several examples of his letters.
- Several nights a year hold an open house for parents and the children. The children must have adults with them to gain admittance. At the open house, equipment is available, and the children show the adults what they've been practicing in physical education. Other ideas include mother-daughter, father-son, mother-son, and so forth, open houses. Some teachers hold these open houses on Saturday mornings because many of the parents work nights. If you schedule the open houses informally, parents are free to spend a few minutes or an hour, depending upon their schedule.
- Once a year schedule a parent work night, which is an evening in which parents can help build, repair, and paint equipment for the physical education program. The advantage of such an evening is that it gives parents an understanding of the need for physical education equipment. Make sure the evening is well organized; two hours is adequate.
- Walking is so popular today that parents may enjoy a family walk once the children have built up their ability to walk (or run) a limited distance. It's important to explain that it isn't a race but just a chance to get

Figure 33.2 Example of a physical education newsletter.

The Physical Education Quarterly Report

While some schools view physical education merely as a good break time for teachers or a time for students to blow off a little steam, this is not true for us at Davis. Physical Education is a necessary and integral part of the total curriculum and is viewed with the same seriousness as any other subject matter. One of my primary goals is to provide each student with specific instruction to enable them to become more skillful movers. As students become more proficient in the various motor skills taught in class, I hope that they will enjoy using these skills on a regular basis. Medical and exercise science research indicates that regular physical activity contributes to a healthier and more enjoyable lifestyle while decreasing the incidence and seriousness of various illnesses and diseases. This report will help you know more about the activities in which your child has been instructed this last quarter of the school year.

Space
The second grade students began the school year by reviewing the spatial awareness concepts related to safe, efficient movement. Some of these concepts included moving in personal and general space where students attempt to move either alone or among others without interfering with the others' movements. Additional space concepts included movement at different levels (low, medium, and high), in different directions (forward, backward, sideways, up, and down), and in pathways (straight, curved, and zigzag). A proper understanding and use of these movement concepts permit children to move more safely and effectively in all settings. Games like "Bridges & Boulders," "High-Five Freeze Tag," and "Octopus" made this learning a lot of fun for everyone. Ask your second grader how to play these games and which one they enjoyed the most.

Throwing and Catching
The students also worked on tossing, the underhand throw, the overhand throw, and catching. To help students learn these skills, we use learning cues, key words that help students remember how to perform a skill. Learning cues can also be used to prompt students when they are practicing these skills. The learning cues for the underhand throw are:
* arm back
* step (on opposite foot)
* swing, and
* throw (the ball toward target)

The cues for the overhand throw are:
* cock (arm back in ready position, elbow out)
* step (on opposite foot)
* twist (upper body in direction of throw), and
* throw (the ball toward target)

To put these steps together into a smooth progressive action was not easy, but a lot of practice helped!

The learning cues for catching are:
* watch (the ball)
* reach (for the ball)
* grab, and
* give (with the ball to absorb the ball's force and slow it down)

Students participated in various activities to further develop throwing and catching for accuracy, distance, and with partners. "Throw and Go" and "Bombs Away" were two of the most popular games. Play these games with your students; you will have fun.

Jump Rope & Kicking
We are currently refining and extending jump rope skills during the warm-up portion of class. We work on kicking skills for the remainder of the lesson. The kicking skills students are learning are most related to soccer, such as dribbling (with the feet) trapping, juggling (thigh and foot), and kicking with various amounts of force using the instep.

The Best
As teachers and parents, we want the very best for our students. One thing we desire most is for our students to be healthy, to enjoy the benefits of good health throughout their entire lives. You can help them establish healthy levels of physical activity and support the physical education program by encouraging your children to view physical education as a place to learn, to have a serious learning aptitude, to always try their best, and to practice at home to facilitate the learning process and insure success.

Our own example is one of the most important influencing factors in the lifestyle habits passed on to our children. We must take care of ourselves. Take time to go outside and play with your children—play ball or tag, jump rope, go roller skating. These are all fun ways to stay fit and show your children that good health is in many ways a matter of what you do, as well as what you do not do.

Feel free to contact me if you would like to know more about our program. Thanks for your support!

Scott Diller, Physical Educator
Davis Elementary School

together and run. A local celebrity walker makes an appropriate guest for such an event.
* Schedule a speaker for parents only. For example, you might invite a child psychologist, a medical doctor, a former athlete. Be certain that you've heard the speaker personally—don't trust someone else's opinion. The speaker has to be worthwhile if the parents are going to enjoy and benefit from the talk. The entire program should run a maximum of 60 minutes.
* Invite parents with special skills for example, a mountain climber, self-defense expert, or triathlete, to visit your physical education classes and discuss the skill.

The School Board

Another obviously important factor in building support for your program is the school board. Although the board may seem far removed, the members play an extremely important role in physical education. In fact, they're the ones who ultimately determine whether a school district will employ physical education specialists for their elementary schools. The time to gain the board's support is *not* when it's considering eliminating the physical education program at the elementary schools—that's often too late. Get to know the members, and let them get to know you and your program long before then.

Figure 33.3 Examples of "good news" notes. Reprinted with permission.

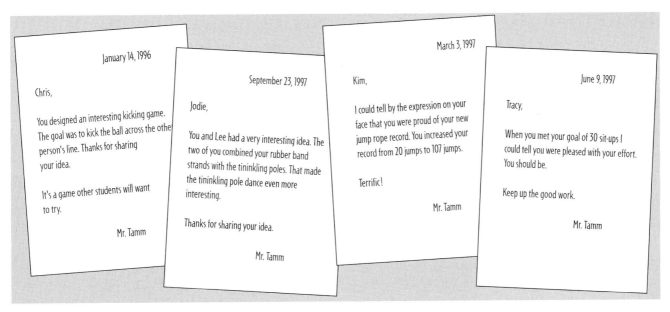

Figure 33.4 Letters to students.
Source: "Dear Physical Educator: Writing Letters Makes a Difference" by P. Tamm, 1993, *Strategies,* 6(8).

- Attend several school board meetings each year. They won't be your most entertaining evenings, but you'll learn much about how decisions are made in school districts. If there's an opportunity, try to speak to one or more of the board members so that you get to know them. Don't ask for anything; just introduce yourself and talk about the current business before the board. If you ever have an occasion to speak to the board, the fact that you understand how the meetings are conducted and know a few members of the board will make things substantially easier for you.

- Whenever you're offering a special program at your school, send the board a written invitation. Be sure you've attended enough board meetings so you can recognize the members and call them by name if they come to your program. If you know in advance that the members will attend, try to have someone, such as the principal or another teacher, available to serve as a host.

- If you come across an article you think the school board members should read, send them a copy with a brief note. The article should be short, well written, and important to the board members.
- NASPE's Web site contains "statistics for advocacy" if you need facts and figures for a presentation to the school board or a legislative group (www.aahperd.org/naspe).

Your relationship with the school board will be somewhat distant. It's important, however, to cultivate a relationship if your program of physical education is going to thrive within a school district.

The Community at Large

Realistically, the community at large is less important than the populations discussed so far. You can potentially enhance your program, however, by conducting a program with community appeal. Typically, these are major undertakings that require substantial time and effort. The workload can be lightened by conducting programs with other schools in the community.

- If your community has a shopping mall, check with the managers; the managers of malls are often looking for demonstrations. Such a presentation will give your program a great deal of public visibility. It's a good idea to have handouts available so that people who stop by for a few minutes to watch the program know exactly what they're watching. These leaflets can be distributed by the children who aren't currently in action.
- The halftime of basketball games is a good opportunity for displaying some of the highlights of your program. For the program to be effective, the announcer's script needs to be well done and rehearsed. Many children from different grades will make the program more appealing for the spectators. Contemporary, loud music is also stimulating. Be sure to include the younger children because they have enormous crowd appeal to help get your message across. Also, the children really enjoy performing, and their parents, grandparents, friends, and neighbors enjoy watching them.

Legislators

One of the eternal truths about teaching physical education is the seemingly endless need to convince others that physical education is important in the lives of children. There are times when, in addition to parents,

administrators, and school boards, it is important to contact a legislator about an impending bill that will have an impact on physical education programming. In recent years, for example, some states have considered legislation to substitute activities such as marching band, athletics, and/or ROTC for physical education. If this happens in your state, you will want to contact your legislator(s) to explain why you do not support a particular piece of legislation. When you do, there are several guidelines to follow.

- Mention the legislation specifically by its title, for example, House Bill 402.
- Be certain that the letter or e-mail is well written. Be especially careful that all words are correctly spelled and that the grammar and format follow recommended guidelines.
- Be concise and straightforward. Legislators may receive hundreds of letters about a piece of legislation, and long rambling letters are not as effective as ones that stick to the facts.
- Often a form letter is circulated by a professional association to be sent to legislators. Although it is acceptable to use the form letter, it is probably less effective than modifying the letter to make it more personal and unique.
- A handwritten letter may attract more attention than a typed letter. It will stand out from the computer-generated letters.
- Finally, if it can be arranged, a personal visit is also an effective way to advocate for legislation. Again, it is best to be concise and straightforward, as the visit will be limited in length and you will need to know your facts.

In 2004, 32 states proposed legislation to increase the amount of physical education or physical activity during the school day. Is your state one of them? Did the legislation pass?

Children as Advocates

We've saved the most important component until the end: the children. Obviously, if you hope to build support from the six populations just described, the children will have to benefit from and enjoy the program. If the children aren't avid supporters of your program, you'll have difficulty gaining support from others in the immediate community.

Children become advocates and talk positively about teachers who help them learn and improve in any subject, not only physical education. In any school, the best teachers are both known and respected by the children, other teachers, and the principal. The word gets out when a teacher and a program are good.

Unfortunately, building a quality program of physical education requires more than being a successful teacher. To cultivate all the other populations that contribute to the success of a program, a teacher also needs to be part politician, part public relations director, and part fund-raiser. Some teachers find that part of the job distasteful, but it is necessary, especially when one is beginning a program of physical education.

Summary

One role that teachers of successful physical education programs play is that of generating support. Seven different populations need to be aware and supportive of physical education if the programs are to be successful: school administration, other teachers in the school, parents, the school board, the community at large, legislators, and the children. Children are the most important advocates of a program, so a program must be of high quality if support from the other six groups is to be developed.

Reading Comprehension Questions

1. Why are seven different populations identified for building support for a program? Can't the same ideas be used for all seven groups?
2. What's the first step a teacher must take to develop a program with widespread support?
3. What does the phrase "principal education" mean?
4. Which of the suggestions for parents do you think you would use most frequently? Why?
5. Why is the school board so important to the success of a physical education program?
6. Why are the children the most important factor in developing support for a program?

References/Suggested Readings

California Department of Education. (2002). The relationship of reading, math and physical fitness scores in 5th, 7th, and 9th grade children. Available at: www.cahperd.org.

Cone, T. P., Werner, P., Cone, S. L., & Woods, A. M. (1998). *Interdisciplinary teaching through physical education*. Champaign, IL: Human Kinetics.

Council on Physical Education for Children. (1992). *Developmentally appropriate physical education practices for children*. Reston, VA: National Association for Sport and Physical Education.

Council on Physical Education for Children. (2000). *Appropriate practices for elementary physical education: A position statement of the National Association for Sport and Physical Education*. Reston, VA: National Association for Sport and Physical Education.

Diller, S. (1994). Newsletters make parents and professionals take note. *Strategies, 8*(1), 18–20.

Giles-Brown, E. (1993). Teach administrators why physical education is important. *Strategies, 6*(8), 23–25.

Graham, G., Wilkins, J. M., Westfall, S., Parker, S., Fraser, R., & Tembo, M. (2002). The effects of high-stakes testing on elementary school art, music and physical education. *Journal of Physical Education, Recreation and Dance, 73*(8), 51–54.

Holt/Hale, S. (2003). *On the move: Lesson plans to accompany* Children Moving. New York: McGraw-Hill.

National Association for Sport and Physical Education (2004). *Moving into the future: National standards for physical education* (2nd ed.). Reston, VA: National Association for Sport and Physical Education.

Schneider, R. E. (1992). Don't just promote your profession—market it. *Journal of Physical Education, Recreation and Dance, 63*(5), 70–71.

Stevens, D. (1994). Movement concepts: Stimulating cognitive development in elementary students. *Journal of Physical Education, Recreation and Dance, 65*(8), 16–23.

Tamm, P. (1993). Dear physical educator: Writing letters makes a difference. *Strategies, 6*(8), 13–15.

Tenoschok, M., & Sanders, S. (1984). Planning an effective public relations program. *Journal of Physical Education, Recreation and Dance, 55*, 48–49.

U.S. Department of Health and Human Services. (1996). *Physical activity and health: A report of the Surgeon General*. Atlanta, GA: Centers for Disease Control and Prevention, National Center for Chronic Disease Prevention and Health Promotion.

Ward, P. (1999). The saber-tooth project [monograph]. *Journal of Teaching Physical Education, 18*(4).

Physical Education for Tomorrow's Children

Some men see things as they are and say why. I dream things that never were and say why not.
—ROBERT F. KENNEDY

Key Concepts

- Successful children's teachers are by nature optimists and innovative thinkers who dream about the future.

- This chapter provides a series of dreams with the hope that it will stimulate readers to develop their own dreams about the future of physical education for children.

- Since the first edition of *Children Moving* was published in 1980 some of these dreams have become realities for some teachers and children.

All teachers have ideas about "the way things might be," and so do we. Since 1980, when the first edition of *Children Moving* was published, some of our dreams have become reality—in some schools, for some teachers, for some children. Some of our dreams may never become reality.

We believe, however, that it is as important to continue to dream as it is to see our dreams realized. Perhaps our hopes for the future will stimulate you to think and dream about the way things could be. The following discussion describes the world of children's physical education as it would be if we had our way.

- Every physical education program would be designed to lead children to develop the knowledge, skills, and attitudes that would allow them to become physically active for a lifetime.

- Physical education would be for all children, not only the athletes and physically fit youngsters.

- The public would continue to understand and value the important role regular physical activity can play in the prevention of cardiovascular disease, diabetes, certain types of cancer, alcohol and drug addiction, and obesity.

- K–12 physical education would be designed to assist children to discover their personal tendencies and interests related to physical activity and then guide them to develop the competence that leads to confidence and regular participation in a sport or physical activity.

- Parents would limit "screen time" (television viewing and computer usage) to a maximum of two hours a day, thereby encouraging youngsters to increase their physical activity at home.

- Negative physical education programs that discourage and humiliate youngsters would be banned from schools, along with their teachers.

- Every child would have positive instruction in physical education every day.

- All physical education programs, recreation programs, and youth-serving agencies would cooperate to enhance the lives of children. No longer would they exist as independent agencies that serve the same children but rarely communicate or coordinate their efforts.

- Parents would become involved in their children's education. The concepts and skills introduced at school would be enhanced and embellished at home, through parent-child activity nights, after-school programs for parents, and parent volunteer programs.

- Teachers, children, and parents would use their computers to communicate whenever they needed about programs, ideas, student progress, and other topics of interest.

- Children could be grouped—by interest in a specific activity, by ability, by experience—to accomplish the specific goals of a series of lessons, then regrouped when the teacher decides to move to a new skill theme. For example, some upper-grade children might be interested in putting on a dance performance for lower-grade children. Those upper-grade children could be grouped to meet together for two weeks to prepare their dance and perform it. When they accomplish that goal, they could be regrouped as appropriate for another activity.

- There would be time during the day for teachers to sit down with individual children and cooperatively plan a personalized curriculum for each child. This would help children learn to make significant decisions about what they want to learn and how they want to learn it.

- Physically challenged children would benefit from programs designed specifically for them to help them lead fuller lives. This implies that programs that attempt to force children to play (and enjoy) sports they'll never be able to play (or choose to play) on their own be eliminated from physical education.

- Assistance would be readily available for those children who require special remedial attention. This program would include instruction for parents so they could help their children at home.

- There would be times during each school day, beyond scheduled physical education classes, when children could choose to come to the gymnasium to practice something in which they were interested.

- Classes would be scheduled to facilitate cross-age teaching—fifth graders working with first graders, or children at the proficiency level working with those at the precontrol level, for example.

- Classes would be scheduled so that beginnings and endings were determined by the children's interest and involvement in a lesson rather than by an impersonal and insensitive time schedule.

- Teachers would have adequate time between lessons to jot down a few notes about the progress the last class made, rearrange equipment, review lesson plans, and shift their thoughts to the next class.
- Administrators and others who schedule classes would understand that physical education is intended to be an instructional experience, not a loosely organized recess. This understanding would be reflected by scheduling only one class rather than two or three classes with 60 or even 90 children at a time.
- Teachers would be able to arrange frequent visits to other schools and teachers easily.
- Teachers would be able to make arrangements to switch teaching assignments with other teachers for a day or a week. Then all teachers would have more experiences working in different environments and with children from various backgrounds.
- Teachers would collaborate and organize curriculum into organic, natural contexts (consistent with the way children view the world), rather than artificially separating learning into compartmentalized subjects like reading, mathematics, art, and physical education. For example, building a house involves reading, mathematics, climbing, balancing, and cooperating with others.
- All classroom teachers would understand that a quality program of physical education can significantly contribute to children's total development. No one would prevent children from going to physical education class because they hadn't finished their work or because they had misbehaved.
- All colleagues, parents, and administrators would be vitally interested in our teaching and physical education programs. They would demonstrate this interest by visiting our classes regularly, not only at the first PTA meeting of the year or during school lunch week.
- It would be common practice for individuals from the community to share their expertise and experiences with children. Children would learn about mountain climbing, hang gliding, hiking, human spatial ecology, and weightless gymnastics, for example.
- Schools would become community centers that could involve parents and children in educational projects of mutual interest and benefit. These would include child/parent-designed and -constructed playscapes, child/parent-designed and -implemented field days for preschool children or underserved children, and child-parent programs designed for senior citizens.

- Physical education, in both elementary and secondary schools, would receive as much emphasis as high school athletics. Communities would understand that an appropriate program of physical education for every child is at least as important as athletic programs for the gifted. And so all schools would have appropriate equipment, facilities, and budgets for physical education programs.
- All school districts would understand the differences between teaching children and teaching adolescents and would refuse to hire individuals whose primary interest and expertise is in coaching or teaching at a high school. Instead, school districts would hire, as elementary instructors, only teachers who are professionally qualified and dedicated to a career of teaching physical education to children.
- Pre-service teachers would work in elementary schools for several years before going to college so that they could learn the right questions to ask about children and teaching. Then as students they would ask the kinds of questions that experienced teachers ask.
- Teacher-education institutions would offer professional preparation programs for elementary school physical education specialists; these programs would be different from those for secondary school physical education teachers.
- College teachers would regularly trade teaching assignments with elementary school teachers, allowing the teachers to study current theories and practices at a college and giving the college teachers realistic opportunities to translate their theories into practice.
- Teachers and professors would collaborate to discover better ways to enhance the learning experiences of children, pre-service teachers, and in-service teachers.
- Teachers would be involved in conceptualizing and conducting action research. The resulting studies would have the potential for finding answers to the questions that teachers want answered.
- Research results would be disseminated in forms that teachers of children would find useful, practical, and interesting, for example, in weekly pamphlets or newsletters or monthly television programs that would use the language of the layperson, not professional jargon or advanced concepts related to experimental design or statistics.
- Every school would have a gymnasium designed specifically for children's physical education that would not have to be vacated for lunch, school assemblies, or plays.
- Every school would have the quantity and variety of equipment that would allow every child maxi-

mum practice at his or her level of physical development.

- Portable environments would be made available to schools throughout the year. Children would have opportunities to use portable swimming pools for swimming lessons, portable ski slopes for skiing lessons, and portable antigravity chambers to experience moving in a weightless atmosphere.
- A national association designed specifically for teachers of children's physical education would be started. The meetings, newsletter, research, and other functions would be designed to specifically address and answer the questions teachers in the schools are asking.
- Mentors would be available to teachers who want to improve their teaching effectiveness and be supported in their early years of teaching.
- Adequate funds would be made available for resource centers operated by teachers for teachers. Such centers would offer assistance in making materials or equipment, opportunities to hear visiting lecturers, in-service courses, discussion and sharing sessions, and up-to-date professional libraries.
- Computers would be readily available in gyms for children to keep track of their own progress and for teachers to design better programs and report the children's progress to the parents.
- All gyms would be equipped with the latest technology, such as digital video and still cameras, permanently mounted television monitors, pedometers, heart-rate monitors, and wireless handheld and laptop computers linked to the Internet.

We continue to dream about and search for better ways of teaching children. And we'd like to hear your dreams and ideas about children, teaching, and physical education. If you'd like to communicate with us, please write to us in care of the publisher.

One other dream emerged as we were writing this book. Wouldn't it be great if the ideas from our book help you become a more effective teacher of children! We've done our part—now it's up to you.

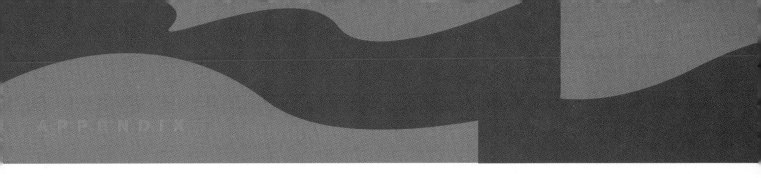

Sample School-Year Overviews

In this appendix we present four sample yearly overviews based on the material in *Children Moving*. The overviews are (1) a two-day-a-week program for an inexperienced class, (2) a five-day-a-week program for an inexperienced class, (3) a two-day-a-week program for an experienced class, and (4) a five-day-a-week program for an experienced class. As you study the programs, keep these important points in mind:

1. The content outlines show how we organize a year using the material in *Children Moving*. They are intended, not to be strictly followed, but rather to be used as starting points for developing your own yearly plans.
2. In this context, *inexperienced* generally refers to K–2 classes, *experienced* to grades 3–6. In your specific situation, *inexperienced* may refer to K–3 and *experienced* to grades 4–6. That's why the outlines should be used only as guides or examples and should not be taken literally.
3. The content listed for each day is intended to be the major focus of that day's lesson, but in many instances other content will be taught as well—for example, a review of a skill theme or concept from the previous day, or responsibility concepts (see Chapters 9 and 10) or a skill that needs to be worked on frequently but for short periods of time, such as jumping rope and transferring weight from feet to hands.
4. In both programs, the first few days are devoted to establishing a learning environment (see Chapter 9). Several other days are devoted to "reviewing" the learning environment. The period after winter or spring break, for instance, is often a good time to review the learning environment. Review days give you a chance to check the environment to determine if some areas, such as immediately stopping at the stop signal and paying careful attention when the teacher is talking, need additional work.
5. The sequencing of the skill themes and movement concepts takes typical weather patterns into account. Outdoor activities are grouped at the beginning and end of the school year, indoor activities toward the middle of the year. For the most part, the movement concepts are introduced early in the year and are revisited throughout the year when time permits.
6. Fitness concepts (see Chapter 4) are taught throughout the year on Wednesdays in the five-day-a-week schedules and every other week in the two-day-a-week schedules. Obviously they could be grouped differently, but this placement allows you to teach a concept or two and set aside time for the children to incorporate the concept into their lifestyle before you introduce another fitness concept. It also allows you to review and reinforce concepts throughout the year, instead of lumping them into a block of lessons.
7. In our program, time is allowed throughout the year for special events that take time away from teaching. (In most of the elementary schools in which we have taught, there are days when physical education must be missed because of field trips, holiday shows or assemblies, voting, or picture days.)
8. Notice that skill themes tend to be massed at the beginning (several days combined) and then distributed throughout the remainder of the year. Notice too that in the programs for the experienced classes, several days in a row are sometimes spent on a single skill theme. As children improve in skill proficiency, they tend to want to spend more days on the same skill because their success rate is much higher. When success rates are low, children seem to concentrate better when the skill themes are changed frequently and reviewed regularly.

Two-Day-a-Week Program for an Inexperienced Class
Content Outline for an Inexperienced Class That Meets Two Days a Week

Topic of Lesson/Activity	Percentage of School Year[a]	Number of Days
Establishing a Learning Environment	4	3
Space Awareness	9	6
Effort	5	4
Relationships	5	4
Traveling	7	5
Chasing/Fleeing/Dodging	4	3
Jumping and Landing	5	4
Rolling	7	5
Balancing	5	4
Transferring Weight	5	4
Kicking and Punting	7	5
Throwing and Catching	7	5
Volleying	3	2
Dribbling	3	2
Striking with Rackets	4	3
Striking with Hockey Sticks	2	1
Striking with Golf Clubs	2	1
Striking with Bats	3	2
Fitness and Wellness	8	6
Field Day and Other Events	5	3
	100	72

[a]Percentages are approximate

Two-Day-a-Week Program for an Inexperienced Class (72 Days a Year)

Week	Chapter	Day	
1	9	1	Establishing an Environment for Learning (p. 129)
	9	2	Establishing an Environment for Learning (cont.) (p. 129)
2	16	1	Exploring Self-Space (p. 254)
	16	2	Exploring General Space (p. 256)
3	16	1	Traveling in Different Directions (p. 258)
	16	2	Traveling and Freezing at Different Levels (p. 260)
4	4	1	Physical Fitness and Wellness for Children (p. 39)
	25	2	Throwing at a Large Target (p. 479)
5	25	1	Catching a Rolling Ball; Catching from a Skilled Thrower (p. 479)
	19	2	Traveling in General Space: Sliding; Galloping; Hopping; Skipping (pp. 316, 317)
6	19	1	Performing Locomotor Sequences (p. 319)
	20	2	Traveling to Flee; Fleeing from a Partner (pp. 338, 339)
7	20	1	Traveling to Dodge; Dodging the Obstacles (pp. 338, 339)
	24	2	Kicking a Stationary Ball from a Stationary Position (p. 443)
8	24	1	Approaching a Stationary Ball and Kicking; Kicking in the Air (pp. 443, 446)
	24	2	Dropping, Bouncing, and Kicking Lightweight Balls; Dropping and Punting (p. 459)
9	21	1	Jumping and Landing: Basic Patterns (p. 358)
	4	2	Physical Fitness and Wellness for Children (p. 39)
10	26	1	Striking Balloons in the Air (p. 505)
	26	2	Striking a Ball Upward (Underhand Pattern) (p. 507)
11	26	1	Bouncing a Ball Down (Dribbling) Continuously (p. 524)
	26	2	Dribbling and Walking (p. 524)
12	17	1	Exploring Time (p. 271)
	17	2	Exploring Force (p. 276)
13	17	1	Traveling and Changing Force Qualities (p. 276)
	9	2	Establishing an Environment for Learning (p. 129)
14	16	1	Exploring Pathways (p. 261)
	16	2	Exploring Extensions (p. 265)
15	19	1	Moving to Rhythms (p. 319)
	4	2	Physical Fitness and Wellness for Children (p. 39)
16	27	1	Downs; Ups (pp. 546, 547)
	27	2	Ups and Downs (p. 547)
17	21	1	Jumping over Low Obstacles: Hoops; Jumping over Low Obstacles: Hurdles (p. 360)
	21	2	Jumping a Turned Rope; Jumping a Self-Turned Rope (p. 362)
18	18	1	Identifying Body Parts; Balancing on Matching and Nonmatching Parts (pp. 285, 287)
	18	2	Traveling and Freezing in Different Body Shapes (p. 290)
19	4	1	Physical Fitness and Wellness for Children (p. 39)
	19	2	Leaping (p. 317)
20	18	1	Over, Under, Around, In Front Of, and Behind Concepts (p. 294)
	19	2	The Follow-Me Dance (p. 322)
21	23	1	The Rocking Horse; Twin Rockers (p. 419)
	23	2	Rolling Sideways; Rolling Forward (pp. 419, 421)
22		1	Special Event
	18	2	Matching; Mirroring; Matching and Mirroring (p. 299)
23	22	1	Balancing on Different Bases of Support (p. 376)
	22	2	Balancing in Different Body Shapes (p. 377)
24	23	1	Log Roll (p. 420)
	23	2	Back Rocker; Back Touch (pp. 421, 423)
25	23	1	Transferring Weight from Feet to Back (pp. 401–402)
	23	2	Transferring Weight from Feet to Hands (pp. 401, 407, 413)
26	25	1	Throwing Overhand; Throwing Underhand; Throwing Sidearm (pp. 480, 481)
	25	2	Throwing a Ball against a Wall and Catching the Rebound (p. 487)
27	22	1	Traveling on Low Gymnastics Equipment; Stationary Balances on Equipment (pp. 378, 385)
	22	2	Balancing Sequence (p. 388)

(continued)

Two-Day-a-Week Program for an Inexperienced Class (72 Days a Year)
(continued)

Week	Chapter	Day	
28	17	1	Traveling and Flow (p. 279)
	23	2	Jumping off Equipment, Landing, and Rolling (p. 428)
29	23	1	Transferring Weight to Hands across Mats (p. 402)
	23	2	Transferring off Low Apparatus (Bench, Crate, or Low Table) (p. 405)
30	24	1	Kicking a Rolling Ball from a Stationary Position; Kicking to a Partner (p. 449)
	24	2	Punting Different Types of Balls (p. 463)
31	4	1	Physical Fitness and Wellness for Children (p. 39)
	20	2	Dodging the Obstacles (p. 339)
32	25	1	Throwing and Catching with a Partner (p. 488)
	27	2	Striking a Ball Rebounding from a Wall (p. 555)
33	21	1	Jumping for Distance; Jumping for Height (p. 357)
	28	2	Striking a Stationary Ball—Golf or Hockey (p. 573)
34	28	1	Striking for Distance—Golf or Hockey (p. 576)
	28	2	Striking a Stationary Ball—Bats (p. 582)
35	4	1	Physical Fitness and Wellness for Children (p. 39)
	28	2	Striking a Pitched Ball—Bats (p. 587)
36		1	Field Day
		2	Field Day

**Two-Day-a-Week Program
for an Experienced Class**
Content Outline for an Experienced Class That Meets Two Days a Week

Topic of Lesson/Activity	Percentage of School Year[a]	Number of Days
Establishing a Learning Environment	3	2
Space Awareness	3	2
Effort	5	4
Relationships	4	3
Traveling	4	3
Chasing/Fleeing/Dodging	4	3
Jumping and Landing	5	4
Rolling	7	5
Balancing	4	3
Transferring Weight	7	5
Kicking and Punting	7	5
Throwing and Catching	8	6
Volleying	5	4
Dribbling	4	3
Striking with Rackets	7	5
Striking with Hockey Sticks	3	2
Striking with Golf Clubs	3	2
Striking with Bats	3	2
Fitness and Wellness	8	6
Field Day and Other Events	4	3
	98	72

[a]Percentages are approximate.

Two-Day-a-Week Program for an Experienced Class (72 Days a Year)

Week	Chapter	Day	
1	9	1	Establishing an Environment for Learning (p. 129)
	9	2	Establishing an Environment for Learning (p. 129)
2	16	1	Dodging in General Space (p. 257)
	16	2	Combining Pathways, Levels, and Directions (p. 264)
3	23	1	Transferring Weight from Feet to Hands (pp. 401, 407, 413)
	23	2	Transferring Weight to Hands: Walking (p. 408)
4	24	1	Kicking to a Partner (p. 449)
	24	2	Keeping It Perfect: Zero, Zero (p. 451)
5	25	1	Throwing Overhand; Throwing Underhand; Throwing Sidearm (pp. 480, 481)
	25	2	Throwing for Distance (p. 488)
6	20	1	Dodging Stationary Obstacles; Dodging and Faking Moves to Avoid a Chaser (p. 341)
	20	2	Faking Moves to Avoid a Chaser (p. 341)
7	24	1	Punting for Distance (p. 464)
	4	2	Physical Fitness and Wellness for Children (p. 39)
8	17	1	Combining Sport Skills and Time (p. 274)
	17	2	Using Imagery and Force (p. 276)
9	18	1	Creating Postcard Sculptures (p. 290)
	18	2	Creating Body Shapes in the Air (p. 291)
10	19	1	Performing Locomotor Sequences (p. 319)
	19	2	Slow Motion Replay: The Sports Dance (p. 324)
11	21	1	Jumping a Self-Turned Rope (p. 362)
	21	2	Jumping and Landing Task Sheet (p. 366)
12	23	1	Jumping off Equipment, Landing, and Rolling (p. 428)
	23	2	Busy Mat (p. 431)
13	26	1	Volleying a Ball Upward (Overhead Pattern) (p. 511)
	26	2	Volleying to a Partner (Overhead Pattern) (p. 511)
14	22	1	Performing Inverted Balances on Equipment (p. 393)
	22	2	Balancing Symmetrically and Nonsymmetrically (p. 380)
15	18	1	Meeting and Parting in a Cooperative Group (p. 302)
	4	2	Physical Fitness and Wellness for Children (p. 39)
16	17	1	Following Flow Sentences (p. 279)
	17	2	Combining Time, Force, and Flow (p. 280)
17	23	1	Rolling over Low Hurdles; Rolling on Low Equipment (p. 432)
	23	2	Rolling, Balancing, and Rolling (p. 433)
18	26	1	Dribbling and Traveling (p. 528)
	26	2	Dribbling Against an Opponent: One on One (p. 533)

Week	Chapter	Day	
19	27	1	To the Wall Again—Sideways (Sidearm Backhand Pattern) (p. 551)
	27	2	Striking a Ball Rebounding from a Wall (p. 555)
20	19	1	Shadowing (p. 327)
	4	2	Fitness Concepts (p. 46)
21	21	1	Jumping to an Accented Beat (p. 370)
	23	2	Transferring Weight to Hands and Forming a Bridge (p. 409)
22	22	1	Traveling into and out of Balances by Rolling; Moving out of and into Balances by Stretching, Curling, Twisting and Rolling (pp. 393, 392)
	23	2	Rolling to Express an Idea (p. 434)
23	23	1	Transferring Weight onto Large Apparatus (p. 409)
	23	2	Combining Weight Transfer and Balances in to Sequences on Mats and Apparatus (p. 414)
24	26	1	Volleying Game: Child-Designed (p. 514)
	26	2	Playing One Bounce Volleyball (p. 512)
25		1	Special Event
	4	2	Fitness Concepts (p. 46)
26	26	1	Playing Dribble Tag (p. 535)
	27	2	Hitting Cooperatively and Continuously with a Partner (p. 557)
27	27	1	Striking Upward in a Dynamic Situation (p. 559)
	27	2	Team Striking across a Net (p. 563)
28	25	1	Throwing and Catching with a Partner (p. 488)
	25	2	Throwing and Catching while Traveling (p. 491)
29	28	1	Striking to Targets at Various Distances—Golf (p. 588)
	28	2	Playing Hoop Golf (p. 588)
30	20	1	Dodging Semistationary Objects (p. 342)
	4	2	Fitness Concepts (p. 46)
31	24	1	Playing Soccer Golf (p. 454)
	24	2	Punting to a Partner (p. 466)
32	28	1	Traveling, and Striking While Changing Pathways—Hockey (p. 581)
	28	2	Striking to a Stationary Partner—Hockey (p. 578)
33	25	1	Throwing for Distance and Accuracy (p. 493)
	4	2	Fitness Concepts (p. 46)
34	25	1	Throwing and Catching in a Small Sided Invasion Game (p. 497)
	21	2	Jumping to Catch; Jumping to Throw (pp. 367, 368)
35	28	1	Striking a Pitched Ball—Bats (p. 587)
	28	2	One-Base Baseball (p. 599)
36		1	Field Day
		2	Field Day

Five-Day-a-Week Program for an Inexperienced Class

Content Outline for an Inexperienced Class That Meets Five Days a Week

Topic of Lesson/Activity	Percentage of School Year[a]	Number of Days
Establishing a Learning Environment	4	7
Space Awareness	9	16
Effort	5	9
Relationships	5	9
Traveling	7	12
Chasing/Fleeing/Dodging	4	7
Jumping and Landing	5	9
Rolling	7	12
Balancing	5	9
Transferring Weight	5	9
Kicking and Punting	7	12
Throwing and Catching	7	12
Volleying	3	6
Dribbling	3	6
Striking with Rackets	4	7
Striking with Hockey Sticks	2	4
Striking with Golf Clubs	2	4
Striking with Bats	3	6
Fitness and Wellness	9	16
Field Day and Other Events	4	8
	100	180

[a]Percentages are approximate.

Five-Day-a-Week Program for an Inexperienced Class (180 Days a Year)

Week	Chapter	Day	
1	9	1	Establishing an Environment for Learning (p. 129)
	9	2	Establishing an Environment for Learning (p. 129)
	9	3	Establishing an Environment for Learning (p. 129)
	9	4	Establishing an Environment for Learning (p. 129)
	16, 18	5	Exploring Self-Space; Identifying Body Parts (pp. 254, 285)
2	16	1	Curling, Stretching, and Twisting in Self-Space (p. 255)
	16	2	Moving the Whole Body in Self-Space (p. 255)
	16, 19	3	Exploring General Space; Traveling in General Space (pp. 256, 313)
	16	4	Reducing the Size of the General Space (p. 257)
	16	5	Traveling Over, Under, and Around Obstacles in General Space (p. 257)
3	16, 19	1	Traveling in Different Directions; Hopping; Skipping; Sliding; Galloping (pp. 258, 316, 317)
	16	2	Turning while Moving in Different Directions (p. 259)
	16	3	Traveling and Freezing at Different Levels (p. 260)
	16	4	Rising and Sinking to Create Different Levels (p. 261)
	16	5	Exploring Pathways (p. 261)
4	16	1	Exploring Extensions (p. 265)
	24	2	Kicking a Stationary Ball from a Stationary Position (p. 443)
	4	3	Physical Fitness and Wellness for Children (p. 39)
	24	4	Dropping, Bouncing, and Kicking Lightweight Balls (p. 459)
	17	5	Exploring Time (p. 271)
5	17, 19	1	Moving at Different Speeds; Traveling at Different Speeds (pp. 272, 323)
	17	2	Exploring Force (p. 276)
	17	3	Traveling and Changing Force Qualities (p. 276)
	17	4	Traveling and Flow (p. 279)
	17	5	Eliciting Flow Qualities (p. 279)
6	18	1	Round, Narrow, Wide, and Twisted Body Shapes; Traveling and Freezing in Different Body Shapes (pp. 288, 290)
	18	2	Balancing on Matching and Nonmatching Parts (p. 287)
	4	3	Physical Fitness and Wellness for Children (p. 39)
	18	4	Traveling Over, Close To, Far Away, Inside (p. 292)
	18	5	Over, Under, Around, In Front Of, and Behind Concepts (p. 294)
7	18	1	Matching; Mirroring; Matching and Mirroring (p. 299)
	18	2	Traveling Alongside/Following (p. 300)
	19	3	Running (p. 317)
	19	4	Performing Locomotor Sequences (p. 319)
	19	5	Moving to Rhythms (p. 319)
8	25	1	Throwing a Yarn Ball against the Wall (p. 478)
	19	2	Moving to Rhythms (cont.) (p. 319)
	4	3	Physical Fitness and Wellness for Children (p. 39)
	20	4	Traveling to Flee; Fleeing from a Partner (pp. 338, 339)
	20	5	Traveling to Dodge; Dodging in Response to a Signal (p. 338)
9	20	1	Dodging with Quick Changes of Direction (p. 339)
	21	2	Jumping and Landing: Basic Patterns (p. 358)
	21	3	Jumping for Distance; Jumping for Height (p. 357)
	24	4	Approaching a Stationary Ball and Kicking (p. 443)
	24	5	Dropping and Punting (p. 459)
10	23	1	Log Roll; Rolling Forward (pp. 420, 421)
	23	2	Rounds; Twin Rockers (p. 419)
	4	3	Physical Fitness and Wellness for Children (p. 39)
	20	4	Moving Obstacles (p. 337)
	21	5	Jumping and Landing: Basic Patterns (p. 358)

(continued)

Five-Day-a-Week Program for an Inexperienced Class (180 Days a Year) (continued)

Week	Chapter	Day	
11	21	1	Jumping over a Swinging Rope (p. 357)
	9	2	Review of Establishing an Environment for Learning (p. 129)
	4	3	Physical Fitness and Wellness for Children (p. 39)
	19	4	Traveling in Confined Spaces (p. 319)
	23	5	Rolling Sideways (p. 419)
12	23	1	Rolling Backward (p. 425)
	16	2	Creating Follow-the-Leader Pathways (p. 262)
	16	3	Using Extensions and Imagery (p. 265)
	20	4	Overtaking a Fleeing Person (p. 339)
	21	5	Jumping over Low Obstacles: Hoops; Jumping over Low Obstacles: Hurdles (p. 360)
13	21	1	Jumping Rhythmically (p. 361)
	17	2	Combining Imagery and Time (p. 273)
	4	3	Physical Fitness and Wellness for Children (p. 39)
	24	4	Kicking a Rolling Ball from a Stationary Position (p. 449)
	24	5	Tapping the Ball along the Ground (Soccer Dribble) (p. 449)
14	19	1	Traveling through Rope Pathways (p. 315)
	17	2	Using Imagery and Force (p. 276)
	25	3	Throwing at a Large Target (p. 479)
	23	4	Rolling in Different Directions (p. 426)
	23	5	Rolling from Different Positions (p. 423)
15	22	1	Balancing on Different Bases of Support (p. 376)
	17	2	Practicing Flow Sequences (p. 280)
	4	3	Physical Fitness and Wellness for Children (p. 39)
	25	4	Catching a Rolling Ball; Catching from a Skilled Thrower (p. 479)
	22	5	Traveling and Stopping in Balanced Positions; Balancing on a Wide Base of Support (pp. 378, 377)
16	22	1	Tightening the Gymnastics Muscles (p. 379)
	9	2	Review of Establishing an Environment for Learning (p. 129)
	18	3	Making Symmetrical and Nonsymmetrical Shapes (p. 290)
	20	4	Fleeing a Chaser (p. 340)
	23	5	Rolling from Different Directions and Positions (p. 426)
17	23	1	Rolling at Different Speeds (p. 424)
	18	2	Going Over and Under the Obstacle Course (p. 295)
	4	3	Physical Fitness and Wellness for Children (p. 39)
		4	Special Event
	22	5	Balancing in Different Body Shapes (p. 381)
18	22	1	Traveling on Low Gymnastics Equipment; Stationary Balances on Equipment (pp. 378, 385)
	23	2	Locomotor Actions; Transferring Weight from Feet to Combinations of Body Parts (pp. 401, 403)
	19	3	Leaping (p. 317)
	18	4	Meeting/Parting (p. 301)
	21	5	Jumping a Turned Rope (p. 362)
19	21	1	Jumping a Self-Turned Rope (p. 362)
	22	2	Balancing on Boards (p. 378)
	4	3	Physical Fitness and Wellness for Children (p. 39)
	22	4	Counterbalance (p. 380)
	23	5	Rolling Using Different Directions and Speeds (p. 427)
20	23	1	Jumping off Equipment, Landing, and Rolling (p. 428)
	23	2	Transferring Weight from Feet to Back, Transferring Weight from Feet to Hands (pp. 401–402, 407, 413)
	23	3	Transferring Weight onto and off Equipment (p. 402)
	23	4	Transferring Weight to Hands across Mats (p. 402)
		5	Special Event

Week	Chapter	Day	
21		1	Special Event
	20	2	Dodging with Quick Changes of Direction (p. 339)
	4	3	Physical Fitness and Wellness for Children (p. 39)
	21	4	Jumping Using Buoyant and Yielding Landings (p. 362)
	23	5	Jumping off Equipment, Landing, and Rolling (cont.) (p. 428)
22	25	1	Tossing to Self and Catching (p. 480)
	9	2	Review of Establishing an Environment for Learning (p. 129)
	24	3	Kicking to a Distance Zone (p. 447)
	24	4	Kicking to Targets (p. 448)
	23	5	Jumping for Height, Landing, and Rolling (p. 428)
23	23	1	Jumping from Different Heights and Rolling (p. 428)
	22	2	Traveling on Large Apparatus (p. 387)
	4	3	Physical Fitness and Wellness for Children (p. 39)
	22	4	Balancing Sequence (p. 388)
	23	5	Transferring Weight from Feet to Back (pp. 401–402)
24	23	1	Stretching, Curling, and Twisting into Transfers (p. 403)
	26	2	Striking Balloons in the Air; Striking with Different Body Parts (p. 505)
	26	3	Striking a Ball to the Wall (Underhand Pattern) (p. 508)
	27	4	Paddle Balance; Balloon Strike (Lightweight Paddle) (pp. 541, 543)
	27	5	Upward Bound (p. 546)
25	27	1	Downs; Ups; Ups and Downs (pp. 546, 547)
	24	2	Kicking to a Partner (p. 449)
	4	3	Physical Fitness and Wellness for Children (p. 39)
	24	4	Tapping the Ball along the Ground (Soccer Dribble) (p. 449)
	19	5	Traveling an Obstacle Course (p. 320)
26	28	1	Striking a Stationary Ball—Golf or Hockey (p. 573)
	16	2	Traveling Pathways and Obstacles (p. 263)
	16	3	Combining Pathways, Levels, and Directions (p. 264)
	19	4	The Follow-Me Dance (p. 322)
	23	5	Performing Spring/Step Takeoffs; Performing Spring/Step Takeoffs onto Crates and/or Benches (pp. 404, 405)
27	23	1	Transferring off Low Apparatus (Bench, Crate, or Low Table) (p. 405)
	25	2	Throwing Overhand; Throwing Underhand; Throwing Sidearm (pp. 480, 481)
	4	3	Physical Fitness and Wellness for Children (p. 39)
	26	4	Bouncing a Ball Down and Catching It (p. 524)
	26	5	Bouncing Down (Dribbling) Continuously (p. 524)
28	26	1	Dribble Like a Basketball Player (p. 525)
	19	2	Traveling Using Different Directions, Levels, Pathways, and Locations (p. 323)
	24	3	Starting and Stopping; Traveling in Pathways (p. 450)
	24	4	Punting Different Types of Balls (p. 463)
	25	5	Throwing an Object to Different Levels and Catching It (p. 482)
29	25	1	Catching in Different Places around the Body (p. 482)
	16	2	Review of Space Awareness Key Ideas (p. 250)
	4	3	Physical Fitness and Wellness for Children (p. 39)
	23	4	Traveling over Low Apparatus; Transferring onto Low Apparatus (p. 406)
	27	5	Ups and Downs (p. 547)
30		1	Special Event
	26	2	Striking Lightweight Objects (p. 506)
	26	3	Striking a Ball Upward (Underhand Pattern) (p. 507)
	27	4	Striking to Different Places (p. 554)
	27	5	Striking for Distance (Varying the Force) (p. 550)

(continued)

Five-Day-a-Week Program for an Inexperienced Class (180 Days a Year) (continued)

Week	Chapter	Day	
31	27	1	Striking through a Target (p. 554)
	26	2	Dribbling at Different Heights (p. 525)
	4	3	Physical Fitness and Wellness for Children (p. 39)
	26	4	Switches (p. 526)
	28	5	Striking off a Batting Tee—Bats (p. 574)
32	28	1	Striking Suspended Objects—Bats (p. 585)
	28	2	Striking for Distance—Golf and Hockey (p. 576)
	28	3	Striking to Targets—Hockey (p. 578)
	28	4	Striking a Pitched Ball—Bats (p. 587)
	28	5	Striking to Varying Distances—Golf (p. 577)
33	28	1	Striking for Distance—Golf and Hockey (p. 576)
	26	2	Volleying to a Partner (Overhead Pattern) (p. 511)
	4	3	Physical Fitness and Wellness for Children (p. 39)
	26	4	Playing Keep It Up (p. 512)
	28	5	Striking a Pitched Ball—Bats (cont.) (p. 587)
34	28	1	Striking a Pitched Ball—Bats (cont.) (p. 587)
	25	2	Throwing Overhand at a Stationary Target; Hit the Can (pp. 483, 484)
	25	3	Catching with a Scoop (p. 486)
	28	4	Striking to Targets—Hockey (p. 578)
	28	5	Traveling, Stopping, and Controlling the Ball—Hockey (p. 580)
35	28	1	Throwing a Ball in the Air and Striking It—Bats (p. 586)
	25	2	Throwing a Ball against a Wall and Catching the Rebound (p. 487)
	25	3	Throwing for Distance (p. 488)
	25	4	Throwing and Catching with a Partner (p. 488)
	26	5	Dribbling with the Body in Different Positions (p. 527)
36	26	1	Dribbling and Traveling (p. 528)
		2	Field Days and Special Events
		3	Field Days and Special Events
		4	Field Days and Special Events
		5	Field Days and Special Events

**Five-Day-a-Week Program
for an Experienced Class**

Content Outline for an Experienced Class That Meets Five Days a Week

Topic of Lesson/Activity	Percentage of School Year[a]	Number of Days
Establishing a Learning Environment	3	6
Space Awareness	3	6
Effort	5	9
Relationships	4	7
Traveling	4	7
Chasing/Fleeing/Dodging	4	7
Jumping and Landing	5	9
Rolling	7	12
Balancing	5	9
Transferring Weight	7	12
Kicking and Punting	7	12
Throwing and Catching	8	15
Volleying	5	9
Dribbling	4	7
Striking with Rackets	7	12
Striking with Hockey Sticks	3	6
Striking with Golf Clubs	3	6
Striking with Bats	4	7
Fitness and Wellness	9	16
Field Day and Other Events	3	6
	100	180

[a]Percentages are approximate.

Five-Day-a-Week Program for an Experienced Class (180 Days a Year)

Week	Chapter	Day	
1	9	1	Establishing an Environment for Learning (p. 129)
	9	2	Establishing an Environment for Learning (p. 129)
	9	3	Establishing an Environment for Learning (p. 129)
	16	4	Traveling over, under, and around Obstacles in General Space (p. 257)
	16	5	Turning While Moving in Different Directions (p. 259)
2	16	1	Traveling While Rising and Sinking (p. 261)
	16	2	Traveling Pathways and Obstacles (p. 263)
	17	3	Combining Imagery and Time (p. 273)
	17	4	Differentiating among Time Words (p. 274)
	17	5	Combining Sport Skills and Time (p. 274)
3	20	1	Dodging Stationary Obstacles (p. 341)
	20	2	Dodging and Faking Moves to Avoid a Chaser (p. 341)
	22	3	Performing Inverted Balances (p. 383)
	22	4	Performing Inverted Balances (cont.) (p. 383)
	21	5	Jumping a Self-Turned Rope (p. 362)
4	24	1	Kicking to a Partner (p. 449)
	24	2	Traveling in Pathways (p. 450)
	26	3	Dribbling and Traveling (p. 528)
	23	4	Transferring Weight from Feet to Hands (pp. 401, 407, 413)
	23	5	Transferring Weight to Hands: Walking (p. 408)
5	25	1	Throwing Overhand; Throwing Underhand; Throwing Sidearm (pp. 480, 481)
	25	2	Throwing a Ball against a Wall and Catching the Rebound (p. 487)
	4	3	Physical Fitness and Wellness for Children (p. 39)
	25	4	Throwing for Distance (p. 488)
	24	5	Punting with an Approach; Punting for Distance (pp. 463, 464)
6	24	1	Punting for Accuracy; Punting for Height (p. 465)
	20	2	Dodging While Manipulating an Object (p. 343)
	20	3	Dodging While Manipulating an Object (cont.) (p. 343)
	25	4	Throwing and Catching over a Net with a Partner (p. 489)
	25	5	Throwing and Catching While Traveling (p. 491)
7	25	1	Throwing to Make a Partner Move to Catch (p. 491)
	16	2	Combining Pathways, Levels, and Directions (p. 264)
	4	3	Physical Fitness and Wellness for Children (p. 39)
	16	4	Traveling and Extensions (p. 265)
	24	5	Keeping It Perfect: Zero, Zero (p. 451)
8	24	1	Traveling and Kicking for a Goal (p. 453)
	27	2	Ups, Downs, and Forwards (p. 549)
	27	3	Striking to Different Places (p. 554)
	27	4	Striking an Object to Send It over a Net (p. 554)
	27	5	Striking a Ball Rebounding from a Wall (p. 555)
9	27	1	Hitting Cooperatively and Continuously with a Partner (p. 557)
	28	2	Striking a Pitched Ball—Bats (p. 587)
	4	3	Physical Fitness and Wellness for Children (p. 39)
	28	4	Striking a Pitched Ball—Bats (cont.) (p. 587)
	26	5	Moving Switches (p. 528)
10	26	1	Dribbling around Stationary Obstacles (p. 531)
	26	2	Volleying to a Partner (Overhead Pattern); Playing Keep It Up (pp. 511, 512)
	26	3	Obstacle-Course Volley (p. 512)
	26	4	Playing Four Square, Two Square (Underhand Pattern) (p. 510)
	26	5	Playing One-Bounce Volleyball (p. 512)
11	26	1	Striking a Ball Continuously with Different Body Parts (p. 514)
	22	2	Balancing Symmetrically and Nonsymmetrically (p. 380)
	4	3	Physical Fitness and Wellness for Children (p. 39)

Week	Chapter	Day	
	22	4	Balancing on Crates (p. 391)
	22	5	Traveling into and out of Balances by Rolling (p. 393)
12	21	1	Jumping a Self-Turned Rope (p. 362)
	9	2	Establishing an Environment for Learning (p. 129)
	28	3	Striking for Distance—Golf and Hockey (p. 576)
	28	4	Striking for Distance—Golf and Hockey (cont.) (p. 576)
	17	5	Showing Contrasts of Force; Using Imagery and Force (pp. 277, 276)
13	19	1	Changing Speeds to Music (p. 323)
	19	2	A Dance of Water, Steam, and Ice (p. 323)
	4	3	Physical Fitness and Wellness for Children (p. 39)
	19	4	Slow Motion Replay: The Sports Dance (p. 324)
	21	5	Jumping Using Buoyant and Yielding Landings; Jumping on and off Equipment Using Buoyant and Yielding Landings (pp. 362, 365)
14	21	1	Jumping and Landing Task Sheet (p. 366)
	21	2	Jumping and Landing Task Sheet (cont.) (p. 366)
	22	3	Performing Inverted Balances on Equipment (p. 393)
	22	4	Performing Sequences That Combine Stationary Balances and Traveling on Mats (p. 394)
	22	5	Balancing While Supporting the Weight of a Partner (p. 394)
15	22	1	Balancing on Hanging Ropes (p. 395)
	23	2	Transferring Weight to Hands and Forming a Bridge (p. 409)
	4	3	Physical Fitness and Wellness for Children (p. 39)
	23	4	Transferring Weight onto Large Apparatus (p. 409)
	28	5	Pathways, Speeds, and Directions—Hockey (p. 589)
16		1	Special Event
	23	2	Jumping over Equipment, Landing, and Rolling (p. 429)
	23	3	Rolling, Levels, Directions, and Jumping (p. 430)
	23	4	Traveling, Jumping, Landing, and Rolling (p. 431)
	23	5	Jumping from Different Heights and Rolling (p. 428)
17	23	1	Busy Mat (p. 431)
	9	2	Establishing an Environment for Learning (p. 129)
	4	3	Physical Fitness and Wellness for Children (p. 39)
	19	4	Traveling with a Partner: Matching Pathways (p. 325)
	23	5	Transferring Weight to Head and Hands on Apparatus (Box, Beam, Table) (p. 410)
18	28	1	Striking to Different Places—Hockey (p. 581)
	17	2	Following Flow Sentences; Practicing Flow Sequences (pp. 279, 280)
	17	3	Using Flow Conversations (p. 280)
	17	4	Combining Time, Force, and Flow (p. 280)
	26	5	Dribbling While Changing Directions (p. 529)
19	26	1	Dribbling While Stopping, Starting, and Turning (Pivots and Fakes) (p. 530)
	23	2	Touch-and-Go Rolls (p. 432)
	4	3	Physical Fitness and Wellness for Children (p. 39)
	23	4	Rolling on Low Equipment; Rolling over Low Hurdles (p. 432)
	19	5	Shadowing (p. 327)
20	19	1	Performing Rhythmical Patterns (p. 328)
	18	2	Creating Postcard Sculptures (p. 290)
	18	3	Creating Body Shapes in the Air (p. 291)
	23	4	Traveling and Rolling between Pieces of Equipment (p. 433)
	23	5	Rolling, Balancing, and Rolling (p. 433)
21	18	1	Creating Postcard Sculptures (cont.) (p. 290)
	23	2	Rolling to Express an Idea (p. 434)
	4	3	Physical Fitness and Wellness for Children (p. 39)
	23	4	Rolling to Express an Idea (cont.) (p. 434)

(continued)

Five-Day-a-Week Program for an Experienced Class (180 Days a Year) (continued)

Week	Chapter	Day	
	26	5	Dribbling against an Opponent: One on One (p. 533)
22	26	1	Now You've Got It, Now You Don't (p. 534)
	19	2	Traveling to Express Age: The Fountain of Youth Dance (p. 328)
	23	3	Transferring Weight on Bars (p. 413)
	23	4	Transferring Weight over an Apparatus (Vaulting Box) (p. 411)
	23	5	Transferring Weight along Apparatus (p. 412)
23		1	Special Event
	26	2	Dribble Tag (p. 535)
	4	3	Physical Fitness and Wellness for Children (p. 39)
	28	4	Striking to a Stationary Partner—Hockey (p. 578)
	21	5	Jumping to an Accented Beat (p. 370)
24	21	1	Jumping with a Partner to Mirror Actions; Jumping with a Partner to Match Actions (pp. 370, 371)
	28	2	Traveling and Striking While Changing Pathways—Hockey (p. 581)
	18	3	Traveling along Equipment (p. 295)
	18	4	Forming Cooperative and Collaborative Relationships (p. 301)
	18	5	Forming Cooperative and Collaborative Relationships (cont.) (p. 301)
25	18	1	Meeting and Parting in a Cooperative Group (p. 302)
	9	2	Establishing an Environment for Learning (p. 129)
	4	3	Physical Fitness and Wellness for Children (p. 39)
	23	4	Rolling on Low Equipment; Rolling off Low Equipment (pp. 432, 433)
	25	5	Throwing to a Moving Target (p. 492)
26	25	1	Throwing for Distance and Accuracy (p. 493)
		2	Special Event
	23	3	Transferring Weight on Bars (p. 413)
	23	4	Combining Skills on Mats (p. 413)
	23	5	Combining Weight Transfer and Balances into Sequences on Mats and Apparatus (p. 414)
27	23	1	Combining Weight Transfer and Balances into Sequences on Mats and Apparatus (cont.) (p. 414)
	21	2	Jumping to Catch; Jumping to Throw (pp. 367, 368)
	4	3	Physical Fitness and Wellness for Children (p. 39)
	21	4	Throwing and Catching while Jumping (p. 369)
	24	5	Playing Soccer Golf (p. 454)
28	20	1	Dodging Semistationary Obstacles (p. 342)
	26	2	Volleying with a Volleybird (p. 516)
	26	3	Striking to the Wall—Varying Levels, Force, and Body Position (p. 516)
	26	4	Volleying Continuously to a Partner (p. 518)
	26	5	Volleying Three on Three (p. 518)
29	24	1	Playing One-on-One Soccer (p. 453)
	28	2	Striking While Dodging Stationary Obstacles—Hockey (p. 582)
	4	3	Physical Fitness and Wellness for Children (p. 39)
	28	4	Playing Hockey Bowl (Small Targets) (p. 588)
	28	5	Striking to Targets at Various Distances—Golf (p. 588)
30	20	1	Dodging and Chasing One Person in a Mass (p. 342)
	25	2	Catching to Throw Quickly to a Partner (p. 494)
	25	3	Throwing and Catching in a Field, Run, and Score Gamelike Situation (p. 496)
	25	4	Throwing to Avoid a Defender (p. 496)
	25	5	Throwing and Catching in a Small Sided Invasion Game (p. 497)
31	25	1	Throwing at a Stationary Object While Being Defended (p. 497)
	27	2	Striking to Different Places around a Partner (p. 557)
	4	3	Physical Fitness and Wellness for Children (p. 39)
	27	4	Striking Upward in a Dynamic Situation (p. 559)
	27	5	Striking to One Wall with a Partner (p. 561)
32	20	1	Dodging in a Dynamic Situation (p. 343)
	27	2	Striking at Angles to Two Walls with a Partner (p. 561)

Week	Chapter	Day	
	27	3	Partner Striking across a Net (p. 562)
	27	4	Partner Striking across a Net (cont.) (p. 562)
	27	5	Self-Designed Racket Games (p. 564)
33	27	1	Self-Designed Racket Games (cont.) (p. 564)
	24	2	Punting within a Limited Time (p. 467)
	4	3	Physical Fitness and Wellness for Children (p. 39)
	24	4	Playing Rush the Circle (p. 467)
	24	5	Playing Two-on-One Soccer (p. 456)
34	28	1	Directing the Air Pathway of the Struck Object—Golf (p. 588)
	28	2	Directing the Air Pathway of the Struck Object—Golf (cont.) (p. 588)
	28	3	Playing Hoop Golf (p. 588)
	28	4	Hitting to Open Spaces—Bats (p. 594)
	28	5	Striking a Pitched Object Varying the Distance—Bats (p. 594)
35	28	1	Directing the Pathway, Distance, and Speed of an Object (Call Your Hit)—Bats (p. 598)
	25	2	Playing Frisbee Golf (p. 494)
	25	3	Throwing and Catching a Frisbee in Different Places around the Body with a Partner (p. 496)
	4	4	Physical Fitness and Wellness for Children (p. 39)
	28	5	Six-Player Striking and Fielding in a Gamelike Situation (p. 598)
36	28	1	One-Base Baseball (p. 599)
		2	Special Event
		3	Special Event
		4	Special Event
		5	Field Day

dk online

space travel

previously published as *e.guides Space Travel*

LONDON, NEW YORK, MELBOURNE,
MUNICH, and DELHI

Author Ian Graham

Senior Editor Jayne Miller
Project Editor Robert Dinwiddie
Weblink Editors Clare Lister, Mariza O'Keeffe,
Roger Brownlie, John Bennett

Managing Editor Camilla Hallinan

Digital Development Manager Fergus Day
DTP Co-ordinator Sarah Pfitzner
Production Erica Rosen

Category Publisher Sue Grabham

Consultant Peter Bond

Senior Designers Owen Peyton Jones, Smiljka Surla, Yumiko Tahata
Illustrators Mark Longworth, Darren Poore
Cartography Simon Mumford

Managing Art Editor Sophia M Tampakopoulos Turner

Picture Researcher Fran Vargo
Picture Librarians Sarah Mills, Karl Strange, Kate Ledwith
Jacket Neal Cobourne

Art Director Simon Webb

First American hardback edition 2004
This edition first published in 2006.

Published in the United States by DK Publishing, Inc.
375 Hudson Street, New York, New York 10014

04 05 06 07 08 09 10 9 8 7 6 5 4 3 2 1

A Cataloging-in-Publication record for this book
is available from the Library of Congress.

ISBN-13: 978-0-75662-227-5
ISBN-10: 0-7566-2227-1

Color reproduction by Colourscan, Singapore
Printed in China by Toppan Printing Co. (Shenzen) Ltd.

Discover more at
www.dk.com

dk online

space travel

Written by **Ian Graham**

Google

How to use the Web site

DK Online Space Travel has its own Web site, created by DK and Google™. When you look up a subject in the book, the article gives you key facts and displays a keyword that links you to extra information online. Just follow these easy steps.

http://www.spacetravel.dkonline.com

Enter this Web site address...

Address : http://www.spacetravel.dkonline.com

Find the keyword in the book...

Shuttle

Enter the keyword...

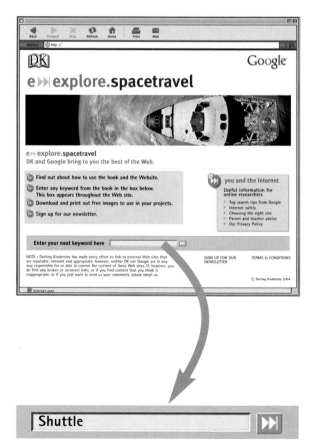

Shuttle

You can only use the keywords from the book to search on our Web site for the specially selected DK/Google links.

Be safe while you are online:

- Always get permission from an adult before connecting to the Internet.

- Never give out personal information about yourself.

- Never arrange to meet someone you have talked to online.

- If a site asks you to log in with your name or email address, ask permission from an adult first.

- Do not reply to emails from strangers—tell an adult.

Parents: Dorling Kindersley actively and regularly reviews and updates the links. However, content may change. Dorling Kindersley is not responsible for any site but its own. We recommend that children are supervised while online, that they do not use Chat Rooms, and that filtering software is used to block unsuitable material.

 Click on your chosen link...

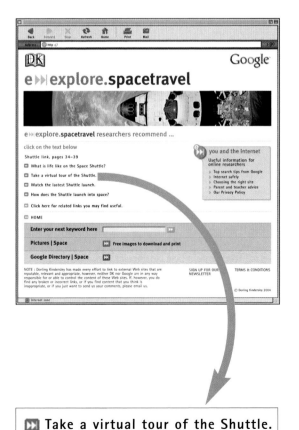

 Take a virtual tour of the Shuttle.

Links include animations, videos, sound buttons, virtual tours, interactive quizzes, databases, timelines, and real-time reports.

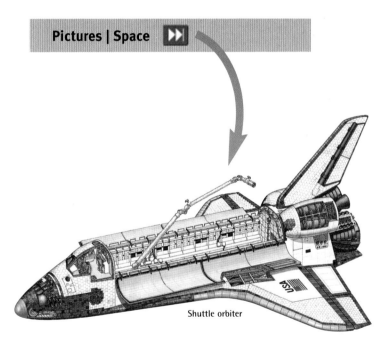

Shuttle orbiter

5 Download fantastic pictures...

Pictures | Space

The pictures are free of charge, but can be used for personal, noncommercial use only.

Go back to the book for your next subject...

WHY EXPLORE SPACE?

People have gazed up at the night sky for thousands of years and wondered what the countless wandering points of light were. Improved technology means we can observe and explore further into the Universe. Just as ancient explorers traveled across uncharted lands and oceans to see what was there, modern explorers venture into space. By studying space, scientists can discover what is out there, find out how the Universe began, and learn more about Earth.

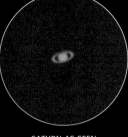

SATURN AS SEEN THROUGH A TELESCOPE

Eyepiece–observer looks through the eyepiece lens, which magnifies the image

Telescope tube moves in and out to bring the image into sharp focus

Main mirror captures light from objects and reflects it onto the side of the tube

astronomy

◄ NEWTON'S REFLECTOR TELESCOPE

English scientist Sir Isaac Newton invented a new type of telescope in 1668. Telescopes had been used to see further into the Universe since Italian astronomer Galileo turned one to the sky in 1609. The first telescopes used glass lenses to gather light from the sky and bend it to a focus. They bent different colors of light unequally, so the image was distorted. Newton's telescope used mirrors to capture the light and reflect it, without bending it. This produced clearer images. The giant telescopes used today can trace their ancestry back to Newton's reflector.

THE MILKY WAY ►

Our Sun is just one of more than 100 billion stars that travel through space together in a swirling flattened spiral called the Milky Way galaxy. If the sky is clear and dark enough, you might be able to see a bright band stretching across it. You are looking sideways through the galaxy. The Milky Way is so big that if you could travel at the speed of light, 186,411 miles per second (300,000 km per second), it would take 100,000 years to cross it.

▲ LOOKING DEEPER INTO SPACE

When astronomers look into space with powerful modern telescopes, they see fuzzy regions called nebulae. Many are vast clouds of gas and dust where new stars form. The Eskimo Nebula is made from gas thrown out into space by a dying star. It is about 2,930 light years from Earth. One light year is about 5.9 million million miles (9.5 million million km).

◄ GIANT TELESCOPES

Observatories, such as the Keck Observatory in Hawaii, help astronomers to explore beyond the atmosphere and into space. Each of the twin Keck telescopes uses a mirror 30 ft (10 m) across to collect starlight. Earth's atmosphere distorts the light from stars, so most telescopes are built on mountains above the thickest part of the atmosphere. Keck is 14,700 ft (4,205 m) above sea level on top of Mauna Kea.

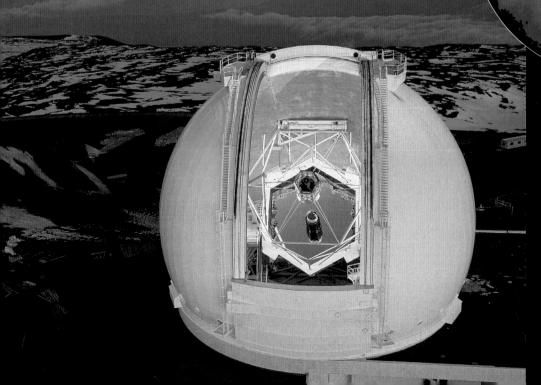

▲ EYES IN SPACE

Some objects in the Universe give off X-rays. These are invisible beams of radiation from areas far hotter than the Sun, such as clusters of galaxies or the remains of stars that have exploded. Telescopes designed to receive X-rays have to be sent into space to work, as X-rays from space do not reach Earth. The Chandra X-ray telescope (above) is a space telescope. Chandra is powerful enough to see something as small as a period at a distance of nearly 12 miles (20 km).

◄ PICTURING X-RAYS

When the Chandra X-ray telescope observed a distant galaxy called NGC 4631, its images showed a cloud of hot gas all around it. The galaxy is about 25 light years away, but it is similar to our own Milky Way. Scientists have wondered for nearly 50 years whether the Milky Way was surrounded by a cloud of hot gas. Chandra's observations may help scientists to find out.

CAMERAS IN SPACE ►

Space probes sent out from Earth to explore the planets and their moons carry cameras to take close-up pictures. Compare this image of the ringed planet Saturn, to the view seen through an ordinary telescope at the top of page 8. Probes have shown us craters on Mercury, the poisonous atmosphere around Venus, huge canyons on Mars, and volcanoes erupting on one of Jupiter's moons. Each photograph contains valuable information for scientists to study.

ROBOTIC SPACE EXPLORERS ▲

We cannot yet travel to all of the planets that circle the Sun in our solar system. Instead, we send spacecraft to do it for us. Space probes spend years crossing oceans of space to distant worlds. The Cassini spacecraft took seven years to reach Saturn. Nearly everything we know about the planets and their moons has been discovered by unmanned space probes. These robots are the explorers of the 21st century.

VENUS   MARS

MERCURY   EARTH

SUN

JUPITER   SATURN

URANUS   NEPTUNE

PLUTO

◄ PLANETARY FORCES

All the planets and their moons exert a gravitational pull on spacecraft, although this pull is quite weak until a craft gets fairly close to the planet. For craft flying through the outer solar system, the gravity of the largest planet, Jupiter, has the biggest effect. Gravity can help an interplanetary spacecraft to reach its destination. Some probes save fuel by using one planet's gravity to accelerate them toward the next planet.

◄ SUN'S EFFECTS

The Sun affects spacecraft in many ways. First, its enormous gravity pulls them toward it. Second, it heats a spacecraft and bathes it in potentially harmful radiation. Third, sunlight striking a spacecraft exerts a tiny push on the craft. Big spacecraft are affected the most, because the sunlight acts over a larger area. The effect tends to make a spacecraft drift off-course. From time to time, the craft's engines may have to be fired to bring it back onto the correct flight path.

FLYING IN SPACE

The laws of nature that govern spaceflight were written down by the scientist Sir Isaac Newton (1642-1727) 300 years ago. Scientists who plan spaceflights today use his law of gravitation and his laws of motion to plot a spacecraft's course through space. These laws are simple, but calculating a spacecraft's flight path is difficult. The planets and spacecraft are all moving in different directions at different speeds, so the sizes and directions of the many forces acting on a spacecraft are constantly changing.

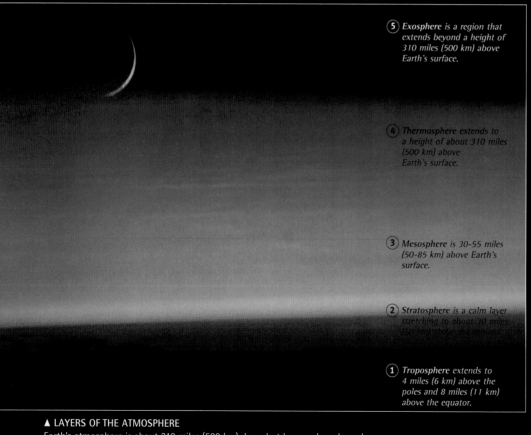

⑤ *Exosphere is a region that extends beyond a height of 310 miles (500 km) above Earth's surface.*

④ *Thermosphere extends to a height of about 310 miles (500 km) above Earth's surface.*

③ *Mesosphere is 30-55 miles (50-85 km) above Earth's surface.*

② *Stratosphere is a calm layer stretching to about 30 miles (50 km) above the equator.*

① *Troposphere extends to 4 miles (6 km) above the poles and 8 miles (11 km) above the equator.*

LEAVING THE ATMOSPHERE ►

An Ariane rocket powers its way up through the atmosphere. Boosters give the maximum power necessary to lift the rocket off the ground. The vehicle accelerates slowly at the beginning of its flight, when it is at its heaviest. As the rocket rapidly burns fuel, it becomes lighter. The lighter it is, the faster it accelerates. It climbs vertically at first and then tilts over further and further until it is flying horizontally as it reaches its orbital height.

▲ LAYERS OF THE ATMOSPHERE

Earth's atmosphere is about 310 miles (500 km) deep, but has no sharp boundary, fading into space as it gets thinner in the layer called the exosphere. Spacecraft have to pass through the atmosphere to get to space. While satellites and space probes are boosted through the lowest part of the atmosphere, where the air is densest, they are enclosed in a protective aerodynamic casing, called a fairing. The fairing protects the spacecraft from the air and weather outside. It also gives them a smooth, streamlined shape that allows them to slip easily through the air.

GOING INTO ORBIT

When a rocket is used to blast an object into space, the result depends on how much horizontal speed the object is given. If the speed is relatively small (for example, 5,000 mph or 8,000 kph), Earth's gravity will soon pull the object back to the ground. Such a flight is called suborbital. The greater the speed the object is given, the further it will go before it reaches the ground. If it is given a speed of about 17,400 mph (28,000 kph), the object never reaches the ground but goes right around Earth—in other words, into orbit.

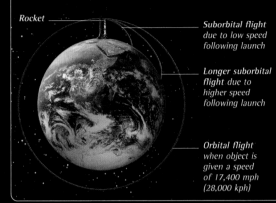

Rocket

Suborbital flight due to low speed following launch

Longer suborbital flight due to higher speed following launch

Orbital flight when object is given a speed of 17,400 mph (28,000 kph)

THRUST AND ACCELERATION ▶

A rocket burns fuel to produce a jet of hot, expanding gas. The action of the gas being blasted downward causes a reaction force, or thrust, that pushes the rocket upward. This provides a classic example of Newton's third law of motion, which states that every action has an equal and opposite reaction. The upward thrust on the rocket exceeds the force of gravity pulling the rocket toward the ground. There is therefore an overall upward force on the rocket that causes it to accelerate up through the atmosphere.

Thrust acts on a rocket to accelerate it upward

Rocket propelled upward, in reaction to explosive downward flow of its exhaust gases

Gravity acts downward, toward Earth's center

rockets

Solid-fuel boosters deliver more than 90 per cent of the total launch thrust

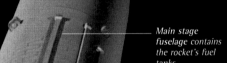

Main stage fuselage contains the rocket's fuel tanks

GRAVITY IN SPACE ▶

When astronauts float through space, it seems that gravity is no longer affecting them. In fact, the force of gravity on the astronaut is almost the same as the gravity acting on someone on Earth. The difference is that the astronaut is in a state called free fall—falling without ever reaching the ground. An astronaut in free fall is weightless. If he or she were to stand on some scales, they would show no weight, because the scales would be falling, too.

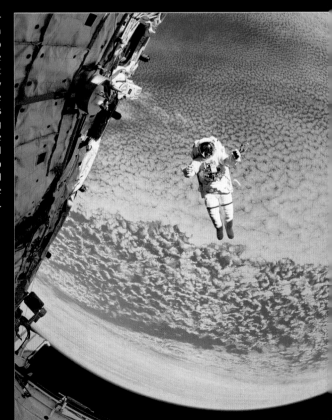

Main engine burns for about 10 minutes on launch, varying slightly according to the mission

Fiery hot exhaust gases propel the rocket upward

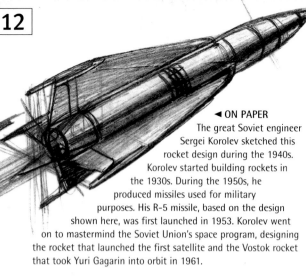

◄ ON PAPER
The great Soviet engineer Sergei Korolev sketched this rocket design during the 1940s. Korolev started building rockets in the 1930s. During the 1950s, he produced missiles used for military purposes. His R-5 missile, based on the design shown here, was first launched in 1953. Korolev went on to mastermind the Soviet Union's space program, designing the rocket that launched the first satellite and the Vostok rocket that took Yuri Gagarin into orbit in 1961.

ROCKET HISTORY

The rockets that launch spacecraft today can trace their history back to Germany in the 1930s. People in other countries had been building small rockets and thinking about space travel for many years, but it was a team of scientists and engineers in Germany that led the world in rocket design. They eventually went on to build the most advanced rockets of the day, such as the V-2. Many of these scientists and engineers later developed rockets for the US and the Soviet Union, including the rockets that took astronauts to the Moon.

Igniter system at top of rocket contained match heads and black gunpowder

Rocket's combustion chamber where gasoline was burned in oxygen

Liquid oxygen line

Gasoline line

◄ AN EARLY START
The first liquid-fueled rocket was launched in 1926 by the American Robert Goddard. During launch and flight, oxygen gas was produced at high pressure and used to force gasoline and liquid oxygen along separate lines to the combustion chamber. Goddard's rocket climbed to a height of 41 ft (12.5 m) during a flight that lasted 2.5 seconds. Later liquid-fueled rockets had the great advantage over solid-fueled rockets that they could be turned on and off.

rockets

Frame that held rocket prior to launch

Liquid oxygen tank

Alcohol burner vaporized liquid oxygen, producing gaseous oxygen at high pressure

Gasoline tank

Pressure line held the pressurized oxygen gas

Base of rocket

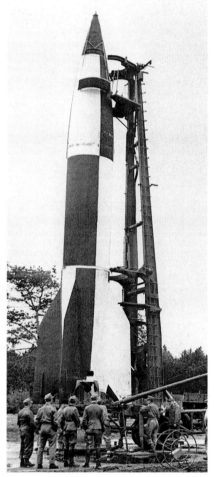

WAR ROCKET ▲
During World War II (1939-1945), Germany produced a series of new weapons. The most important was the V-2 rocket. It was developed by a team led by Wernher von Braun. The V-2 stood 50 ft (14 m) high and weighed more than 12 tons. It was fueled by alcohol and liquid oxygen and its engine burned for about 60 seconds. In that short time, it boosted the V-2 to a speed of about 3,500 mph (5,600 kph) and to a height of nearly 62 miles (100 km).

◄ MONUMENT TO TSIOLKOVSKY
This monument in Kaluga, Russia, honors
Konstantin Tsiolkovsky, a Russian school-
teacher who figured out many of the
principles of rocketry more than 50 years
before the Space Age began. Tsiolkovsky
had been fascinated by the idea of space
travel since his childhood and started
writing about space flight in 1898. He
could not afford to build and test his
own rockets, so most of his work was
in the form of theories and calculations
on paper.

Escape system
propelled the
command module
to safety in the
event of a
launch failure

Command module
housed the three
astronauts for most
of their trip

Service module
contained fuel,
a rocket motor,
and oxygen for
the astronauts

Housing for the
lunar module,
which took two
astronauts to the
Moon's surface

Third stage fired
to place Apollo
in Earth orbit,
then reignited
to send it to
the Moon

▲ LAUNCHING A SATELLITE
The Jupiter C rocket launched
the first US satellite in 1958.
When used to launch satellites,
the rocket was known as Juno I.
It was developed by Wernher
von Braun and members of his
V-2 rocket team, who had
moved to the US at the end of
World War II. The Jupiter C was
developed from designs for the
Redstone rocket, which went on
to launch the first two American
astronauts in 1961.

ROCKET TO THE MOON ►
Saturn V, the giant rocket that sent US
astronauts to the Moon, was developed at
NASA's Marshall Space Flight Center under
the leadership of Wernher von Braun. With
an Apollo spacecraft on top of its three
stages, it stood 363 ft (111 m) high and
weighed 3,000 tons. It could launch a
spacecraft weighing 152 tons into Earth
orbit or send a 53-ton spacecraft to the
Moon. After the Apollo missions ended, a
two-stage version of Saturn V launched
the Skylab space station in 1973.

ROCKET POWER

It takes an enormous amount of energy to boost a spacecraft into orbit. Rockets powered by explosive chemical reactions are still the only vehicles capable of getting to space. A rocket is propelled by a jet of gas produced by burning fuel. Oxygen is needed to burn the fuel. Since there is no oxygen in space, rockets carry their own supply. The largest launchers are actually two or more rockets, called stages, on top of each other. As each stage uses up its fuel, it falls away to save weight.

FOUR STEPS TO ORBIT

LIFTOFF
During liftoff, Ariane 5's main engine fires first, followed 7 seconds later by its solid fuel boosters. Two minutes later, the boosters separate. In that short time, each has burned 238 tons of fuel. The boosters fall away when the rocket has reached a height of about 40 miles (65 km) and a speed of about 4,620 mph (7,450 kph).

FAIRING JETTISONED
Just over 3 minutes after liftoff, the rocket is more than 62 miles (100 km) above the ground. It has passed through the thickest part of the atmosphere, so the streamlined fairing around the payload is no longer needed. It splits in two and falls away. Different fairings are used depending on the size and shape of the payload that has to fit inside.

STAGE SEPARATION
Ariane 5's first or main stage engine is shut down about 9 minutes 42 seconds after liftoff. The rocket is now at a height of 93 miles (150 km) and traveling at 17,400 mph (28,000 kph). A few seconds later, the first stage separates from the rest of the rocket. As it falls back through the atmosphere, it breaks up and falls into the Pacific Ocean.

SECOND STAGE IGNITES
Finally, Ariane 5's second or upper stage engine fires to boost the payload into the correct orbit. The second stage engine can burn for up to about 18 minutes. The precise burn time depends on the type and height of orbit into which the payload is to be placed. Once the payload has been released, Ariane 5 has completed its work.

ARIANE 5 ▶
An Ariane 5 rocket blasts off from the European Space Agency's spaceport in French Guiana, South America. The 750-ton rocket's first flight was in June 1996 and it first successfully launched a commercial satellite into space in December 1999. It can launch satellites weighing up to 17,600 lb (8,000 kg).

release payload

Payload can include two large satellites and several small microsatellites

Second stage engine boosts the payload into its final orbit

Solid fuel booster supplies extra power for takeoff

Hydrogen tank contains 25 tons of liquid hydrogen; at the top is the liquid oxygen tank

Solid rocket boosters hold 238 tons of solid propellant and burn for 130 seconds

Exhaust nozzle of first, main stage engine can be swiveled to steer the rocket

Exhaust flame of solid-fuel booster rocket

SPACECRAFT MANEUVERING

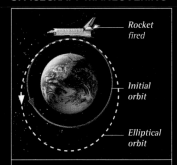

FORWARD THRUST

Firing a rocket to speed up a spacecraft in the direction it is already moving pushes it further away from Earth into an elliptical orbit. In this orbit, the spacecraft speeds up as it comes closer to Earth and slows down as it travels further away. If the rocket is fired when the craft is at its furthest point from Earth, the orbit will become circular.

Rocket fired
Initial orbit
Elliptical orbit

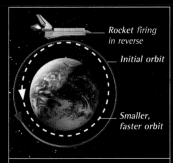

REVERSE THRUST

Turning around and firing a rocket in the direction a spacecraft is moving slows the craft down. Gravity then pulls it down into a lower orbit. As it falls, it speeds up. The closer to Earth it gets, the faster the craft must go to resist gravity and stay in orbit. If reverse thrust is used for long enough, gravity wins and the craft returns to Earth.

Rocket firing in reverse
Initial orbit
Smaller, faster orbit

CHANGING THE ORBITAL PLANE

To change the plane of its orbit, a spacecraft must fire a rocket at an angle to its direction of motion. This may sound simple, but figuring out exactly how long to fire the rocket for and in which direction is quite complicated. Spacecraft rarely change their orbital plane, because it uses up large amounts of fuel.

Rocket fired at an angle
Plane of orbit changes

RADIAL THRUST

Firing a rocket straight away from Earth usually has a similar result to a forward thrust. Unless the rocket burns long and powerfully enough to cause the spacecraft to completely escape Earth's gravity, the spacecraft eventually falls back toward Earth again. As it does so, the spacecraft speeds up and its circular orbit becomes elliptical.

Spacecraft boosted straight upward
Orbit stretched into an ellipse

STEERING ROCKETS ▶

As a rocket soars away from the launchpad, control systems on board monitor its direction of motion and make many tiny adjustments to keep it on a stable flight path. They steer the rocket in the right direction by swiveling its engine nozzle. Swiveling the nozzle like this is called gimbaling. A gimbaled nozzle doesn't have to move much. A rocket travels so fast and so far that it can be kept on course by very small adjustments to its direction of motion.

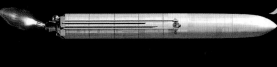

Rocket swings in opposite direction to nozzle orientation

rockets

Gimbaled nozzle swivels to change direction

Rocket swings round and flies in a new direction

Fiery jet is sent along the ground as the rocket is test-fired sideways

Instruments measure the rocket's exhaust

TESTING ROCKETS ▲

New rocket engines are test-fired on the ground to make sure that they work and to measure precisely how powerful they are. They have to be held down securely in test-stands to stop them from moving. Successful rockets are continually improved and tested again and again. The Vulcan engine that powers the first stage of the Ariane 5 rocket was test-fired about 300 times during its development.

Exhaust nozzle of engine being tested

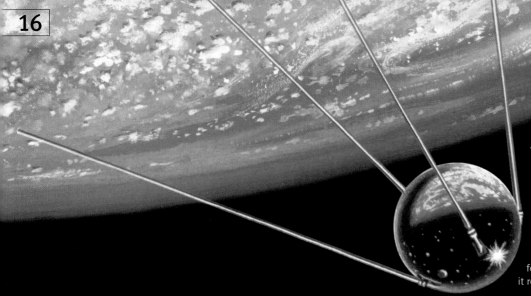

◄ SPUTNIK 1
Sputnik's full name was Iskustvennyi Sputnik Zemli, ("Fellow Traveler of Earth"). Sputnik 1 was a metal ball with four radio antennae sticking out of it, each about 10 ft (3 m) long. It was launched by a modified R-7 military rocket. When it passed overhead, every 96 minutes, its bleep radio signal could be picked up on the ground below. After three weeks, its batteries were exhausted and it fell silent. On January 4, 1958, after 1,400 orbits, it re-entered Earth's atmosphere and burned up.

FIRST SATELLITES

The Space Age began on October 4, 1957, when the Soviet Union launched Sputnik 1, the first artificial satellite. Early satellites were small, simple, and powered by batteries, which lasted for only a few weeks. At first, just getting a satellite into orbit was an achievement, because rockets were so unreliable. If they didn't go off course or explode, upper stages sometimes failed to fire. Many early satellites were blown to bits or crashed back to Earth a few minutes after liftoff.

"The assault on space has begun"

Sergei Korolev, Russian rocket scientist

Thin outer shell was highly polished to reflect heat radiation

Inner shell was filled with nitrogen gas

Two small radio transmitters fitted under the inner shell

BUILDING SPUTNIK ►
Sputnik 1 was made from an alloy of aluminum, the same material used to make aircraft. Aluminum was chosen because it is lightweight, inexpensive, and easily shaped. The Soviet space program's chief designer, Sergei Korolev, stood at the shoulders of the metalworkers and engineers while they made and attached each part. Sputnik 1 was built from standard parts inside a simple casing.

◄ EARLY SPACE STUDIES
The first US satellite, Explorer 1, was launched on January 31, 1958. It carried instruments to study cosmic rays (tiny particles whizzing through space) and discovered the Van Allen radiation belts—a doughnut-shaped region around Earth filled with charged particles trapped by Earth's magnetic field. Its radio transmissions stopped in May 1958, but it stayed in space for another 12 years and made 58,000 orbits before burning up in the atmosphere.

Zinc batteries provided power to the two radio transmitters

Thermometer monitored temperature as Sputnik reached altitudes as high as 588 miles (946 km)

U.S. 'MOON' DUD
RUSS CHARGE YANKS HOLD FALLEN SPUTNIK ROCKET

IKE'S SPUTNIK IS DUDNIK

◄ BAD NEWS
America's first attempt to put a satellite in orbit had been a failure. The Vanguard satellite was due to launch on December 6, 1957, two months after Sputnik 1. When the countdown reached zero, the rocket fired. It rose just 3 ft (1 m) off the launchpad, then fell back and exploded. Some newspapers nicknamed the satellite Dudnik or Kaputnik. Within two months, the US successfully launched Explorer 1.

satellites

SATELLITE DATA

Sputnik 1 (USSR)
Diameter: 23 in (58 cm)   Mass: 185 lb (84 kg)
Orbit: 141 x 587 miles (227 x 945 km)

Explorer 1 (US)
Length: 80 in (203 cm)   Mass: 31 lb (14 kg)
Orbit: 220 x 1,563 miles (354 x 2,515 km)

Vanguard 1 (US)
Diameter: 6 in (15 cm)   Mass: 4.4 lb (2 kg)
Orbit: 406 x 2,404 miles (654 x 3,868 km)

Explorer 6 (US)
Diameter: 26 in (66 cm)   Mass: 141 lb (64 kg)
Orbit: 152 x 26,350 miles (245 x 42,400 km)

TIROS 1 (US)
Diameter: 42 in (107 cm)   Mass: 264 lb (120 kg)
Orbit: 408 x 432 miles (656 x 696 km)

Telstar (US)
Diameter: 35 in (88 cm)   Mass: 170 lb (77 kg)
Orbit: 587 x 3,507 miles (945 x 5,643 km)

DECADES IN SPACE ▶

The first Vanguard satellite went into space on March 17, 1958, and is still orbiting Earth. It is a small sphere with two radio transmitters inside, though these no longer work. One was powered by a battery and the other by six solar cells stuck on the satellite's body. The radios transmitted by using six antennae. It also contains two sensors, called thermistors, which measured the temperature inside the satellite.

Radio antennae were 12 in (30 cm) long

Satellite body was made in two halves, joined by a ring around the middle

SCIENTIFIC SUCCESS ▲

Explorer 6 was a small scientific research satellite launched on August 7, 1959, to study radiation, cosmic rays, Earth's magnetism, and micrometeorites. It was also equipped with a TV camera. Electric power was supplied by four solar panels sticking out from the satellite like waterwheel paddles. Although one of these failed to unfold properly, the others supplied enough power to operate the camera. It sent back the first pictures of Earth from space.

SATELLITE TELEVISION ▶

Telstar was the first of a new type of communications satellite. Satellites had relayed radio signals before, but the signals bounced off them like light off a mirror. Telstar received signals and then re-transmitted them. It could relay signals across the Atlantic Ocean for 20 minutes per orbit. It relayed the first live transatlantic television pictures and the first telephone call to travel through space on July 23, 1962. Telstar caught the public's imagination—a British pop group (the Tornadoes) even had a hit with a tune called *Telstar*.

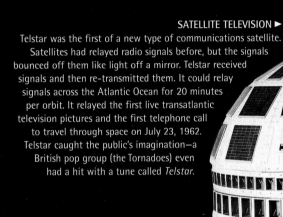

Live TV pictures were first relayed across the Atlantic by Telstar

Receiving antenna received radio signals from Earth

Solar cells generated electricity from sunlight

WATCHING THE WEATHER ▶

TIROS 1 was the first weather satellite. TIROS stood for Television and Infra-Red Observation Satellite. It was launched on April 1, 1960. Each of its two television cameras could take 16 pictures on each Earth orbit. Two tape recorders stored up to 48 pictures until the satellite passed over a ground station that could receive them. By the time its batteries ran out, after 78 days, it had transmitted 22,952 pictures of Earth's weather.

Transmitting antennae sent weather pictures to Earth

Shuttle's robot arm
pushes the satellite away
from the Shuttle

◄ PUTTING A SATELLITE IN ORBIT
This satellite, called a Spartan 201, is designed to study the Sun's corona (outer layer). Here it has just been lifted out of the Space Shuttle's payload bay. When the arm lets go, the satellite doesn't fall back to Earth, but stays close by. That is because the Shuttle has already boosted it to orbital speed. Most satellites orbit further from Earth than the Space Shuttle does, so satellites launched by the Shuttle have a small rocket attached to them to boost them to a higher orbit.

Instrument carrier
contains equipment to
study the Sun's corona

Service module
contains data recorders,
an altitude control
system, and electronics

VARIOUS EARTH ORBITS ►
Satellites and other spacecraft can orbit around Earth's equator or from pole to pole, or at any angle in between. They can orbit close to Earth or further away. The orbit may be circular or stretched into an ellipse. A spacecraft's orbit is chosen according to what it has been put in space to do. For example, some satellites are put into a special orbit at a fixed height above the equator, called a geostationary orbit. A satellite in a geostationary orbit goes around Earth in exactly the same time it takes Earth to spin once on its own axis, which means the satellite always sits above a particular point on the equator. This can be a very useful orbit for communications satellites.

ORBITS

When a spacecraft's speed is boosted to about 17,400 mph (28,000 kph), Earth's gravity can no longer pull it back down to the ground. Instead, gravity combines with the spacecraft's speed to cause the craft to follow a curved path around the planet. The endless path of a spacecraft or moon around a planet is called an orbit and can be shaped either like a circle or an ellipse (a stretched circle). The speed of an orbiting craft depends on how far it is from the planet. The closer it is, the faster it has to fly to balance the pull of gravity.

Geostationary orbit is a
circular orbit at a height of
22,250 miles (35,800 km)
above the equator and in
the same direction as Earth
spins on its own axis

Antenna dish is kept
facing in one direction
while other parts of
the satellite spin

THE PHYSICS OF ORBITS

If you are whirled around by a fairground ride, your body tries to fly outward, but the seat or outside wall of the ride holds you in place by exerting a force toward the ride's center. Similarly, a ball whirled in a circle on a piece of string is constantly pulled toward the center by tension in the string.

A spacecraft orbiting a planet behaves in a similar way. The planet's gravity stops the craft from flying away by pulling it toward the center of the planet and curling its path into a curve.

If the force is removed,
the ball carries on in the
same direction

String under
tension pulls
ball toward
center

Force toward
center pulls ball
around in a circle

orbits

Solar panel generates
electricity as sunlight
falls on it

Equipment is designed
to fit into the satellite's
cylindrical shape

Wheel riders are
moved in a circle
by a constant
force directed
toward the
center of the
wheel as it spins

◄ SPIN-STABILIZED SATELLITE
Satellites must be kept steady in space so that their antennae, cameras, or other instruments are kept pointing in the right direction.
One way of stabilizing a satellite is to make use of a basic principle of physics called the gyroscopic principle. This states that if an object is made to spin, it resists any change to the direction in which it is pointing.
A spin-stabilized satellite, like this HS 376 communications satellite, is kept pointing in one direction by making the main part of the satellite spin. Only its antennae and equipment like cameras are not made to spin.

Thruster
corrects spin if
sensors in the
satellite detect
a wobble

Cylindrical shape
is typical for a
spin-stabilized
satellite

THREE-AXIS STABILIZED SATELLITE ►
Some satellites, such as this advanced communications satellite called Artemis, are kept steady in space by a method called three-axis stabilization. Small thrusters turn the satellite until it points in the right direction. These thrusters can rotate the satellite around any of three directions, or axes, at right angles to one another. If the satellite starts turning out of position, the thrusters automatically fire and bring it back again.

Ion thruster nozzles fire to adjust the satellite's orbit

Solar panels extend like wings and always face the Sun

Thermal blanket keeps sensitive components from becoming too hot or cold

Antenna dish sends and receives signals

Satellite footprint is the region of Earth that an orbiting satellite can communicate with

Communications satellites like this are often placed in a geostationary orbit

Low-Earth orbit (LEO), 100-600 miles (150-1,000 km) above Earth's surface, is used for the Hubble Space Telescope, the International Space Station, and navigation satellites

Polar orbit goes over Earth's poles, usually at a height of about 500 miles (800 km), and is often used for Earth-monitoring satellites

Elliptical orbit varies from hundreds to many thousands of miles in height and is used for some scientific and communications satellites

FORMATION FLYING ►
Most satellites spend their whole working lives orbiting Earth on their own, but the Cluster II project is different. Four identical satellites were launched in 2000 and orbit together in close formation. Their elliptical orbit varies from 11,200 to 74,000 miles (19,000 km to 119,000 km) above Earth's surface. The instruments on board take simultaneous measurements and so give a three-dimensional picture of the changes that are happening in the space around Earth.

FIRST SPACE PROBES

The first space probes to visit other worlds were aimed at our closest neighbor in space, the Moon. To break away from Earth orbit and head into space, they had to be boosted to a speed of 24,850 mph (40,000 kph). Once the race to land the first astronauts on the Moon was under way, the US and Soviet Union sent dozens of probes to study and photograph the Moon in great detail. Space probes flew past the Moon, crashed into it, orbited it, and made controlled landings on its surface.

Hinged panel was one of four that opened up like flower petals

Television camera took the first photographs on the Moon's surface

Rod antenna was one of four that transmitted pictures to Earth

Radio antenna transmitted data from onboard instruments

Metal sphere contained scientific instruments and a radio transmitter

▲ LUNA 1

The Soviet probe Luna 1 was the first spacecraft to escape from Earth and go into space. The spherical craft, launched on January 2, 1959, was meant to hit the Moon but missed and became the first spacecraft to go into orbit around the Sun. Luna 3, launched on October 7, 1959, took the first photographs of the far side of the Moon.

probes

▲ LUNA 9 CAPSULE

Luna 9 was the first spacecraft to make a controlled or "soft" landing on the Moon. It landed in a region of the Moon called the Ocean of Storms, on February 3, 1966. As it touched the surface, it ejected an egg-shaped capsule, 24 in (60 cm) long and weighing 220 lb (100 kg). When the capsule came to rest, it opened to reveal a camera and radio antennae. They enabled Luna 9 to send the first pictures from the Moon's surface.

Spacecraft stood 10 ft (3.1 m) high and weighed 807 lb (366 kg)

TV cameras gave two wide-angle and four narrow-angle views

Television system and omnidirectional radio antennae

RANGER 9 COLLISION COURSE

TARGET MOON
Ranger 9 was the last Ranger craft. It was launched on March 21, 1965. Just over 64 hours later, at a distance of 1,404 miles (2,261 km) from the Moon, its cameras were switched on and it began transmitting pictures.

CLOSING IN
Ranger 9's pictures showed it had drifted 3 miles (4.8 km) off course after a flight of 259,000 miles (417,054 km). It was heading into the middle of a crater called Alphonsus, not far from the center of the Moon's near side.

CRASH!
Ranger 9's cameras took 5,814 photographs in the last 14 minutes of its flight. The final frames showed rocks and craters as small as 1 ft (30 cm) across. Then the probe crashed into the surface at 5,975 mph (9,617 kph).

RANGER 9 MOON-PROBE ▲

The US Ranger probes were designed to take close-up photographs of the Moon. The photographs were needed to find suitable landing sites for later, manned missions. The probes were deliberately crashed into the Moon, sending back pictures all the way. The pictures showed 1,000 times more detail than could be seen by telescopes on Earth. Rangers 1-6 failed, but Rangers 7-9 were successful and sent back more than 17,000 photographs.

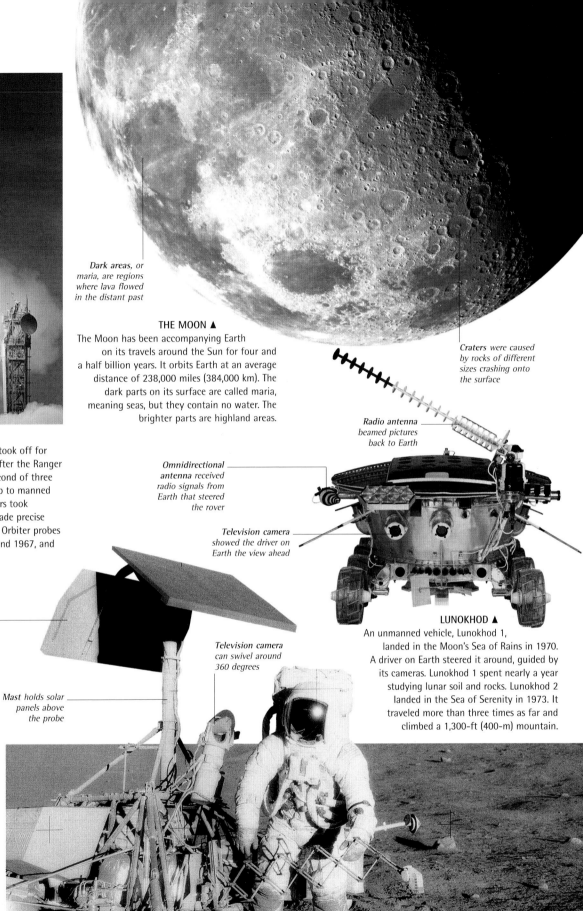

▲ LUNAR ORBITER BLAST OFF
The first US Lunar Orbiter probe took off for the Moon on August 10, 1966. After the Ranger probes, Lunar Orbiter was the second of three US unmanned projects leading up to manned Moon-landings. The Lunar Orbiters took photographs of the Moon and made precise measurements of its gravity. Five Orbiter probes were sent to the Moon in 1966 and 1967, and all five were successful.

Dark areas, or maria, are regions where lava flowed in the distant past

THE MOON ▲
The Moon has been accompanying Earth on its travels around the Sun for four and a half billion years. It orbits Earth at an average distance of 238,000 miles (384,000 km). The dark parts on its surface are called maria, meaning seas, but they contain no water. The brighter parts are highland areas.

Craters were caused by rocks of different sizes crashing onto the surface

Radio antenna beamed pictures back to Earth

Omnidirectional antenna received radio signals from Earth that steered the rover

Television camera showed the driver on Earth the view ahead

Solar panels produce electricity from sunlight

Television camera can swivel around 360 degrees

Mast holds solar panels above the probe

LUNOKHOD ▲
An unmanned vehicle, Lunokhod 1, landed in the Moon's Sea of Rains in 1970. A driver on Earth steered it around, guided by its cameras. Lunokhod 1 spent nearly a year studying lunar soil and rocks. Lunokhod 2 landed in the Sea of Serenity in 1973. It traveled more than three times as far and climbed a 1,300-ft (400-m) mountain.

SURVEYOR 3 ▶
Surveyor 3 landed in the Moon's Ocean of Storms on April 20, 1967. It took 6,317 photographs and dug a trench in the surface. Surveyor was the third US unmanned Moon project. Each Surveyor spacecraft was designed to make a controlled landing on the Moon and test the firmness of its surface. In November 1969, Apollo 12's lunar module landed close to Surveyor 3. The Apollo astronauts returned parts of the probe to Earth, where scientists studied how its stay on the Moon had affected them.

EARLY MANNED CRAFT

The first manned spacecraft were also called capsules: they were small and extremely cramped. Each type was built to achieve a specific objective. The US Mercury and Soviet Vostok capsules were designed to get one person into space and back to Earth again. They could keep an astronaut or cosmonaut alive in space for about a day. The next generation of Soviet spacecraft, called Voskhod, could carry more than one person, while the US Gemini spacecraft were designed to carry two astronauts on longer spaceflights, lasting up to about two weeks.

Storage compartment contained parachutes for landing

Corrugations strengthened the capsule

Astronaut entered through a hatch in the wall

MERCURY SPECIFICATIONS

Height: 9.6 ft (2.92 m)	
Base diameter: 6.2 ft (1.89 m)	
Mass: 4,265 lb (1,935 kg)	
Crew: One	
Launch rocket: Redstone (suborbital flights) Atlas (orbital flights)	
Manned missions: Two suborbital missions Four orbital missions	
Longest mission: 1 day 10 hours 20 minutes by Mercury 9 (22 Earth orbits)	
Landing method: After re-entry, the capsule parachuted into the ocean with the astronaut on board	

Heat shield protected capsule on re-entry

◄ **MERCURY CAPSULE**
The Mercury capsule was made from titanium, a strong but light metal. It contained an atmosphere of pure oxygen, sealed inside an inner hull. In space, the astronaut could turn the capsule around by firing small thrusters. Three solid-fuel rockets were fired to slow the capsule down and begin re-entry. A heat shield covered the broad end of the capsule to protect it during re-entry.

Radio antenna for communications with Earth

Re-entry capsule was the part that detached and returned to Earth

Spherical tanks held oxygen and nitrogen for life support

Instrument module contained instruments for controlling orbital flight

◄ **VOSTOK SPACECRAFT**
Vostok's re-entry capsule, where the cosmonaut sat, was a steel sphere covered with heat shield material. It contained life support equipment, TV and film cameras, a radio system, control panels, food, and water. Four metal straps attached it to an instrument module. The re-entry capsule separated from the instrument module just before it re-entered Earth's atmosphere.

first astronauts

VOSTOK SPECIFICATIONS

Height: 24.2 ft (7.35 m)	
Diameter: 8.2 ft (2.50 m)	
Mass: 10,416 lb (4,725 kg)	
Crew: One	
Launch rocket: Vostok 8K72K (also called A-1)	
Manned missions: Six orbital missions	
Longest mission: 4 days 23 hours 6 minutes by Vostok 5 (81 Earth orbits)	
Landing method: Soon after re-entry, an ejection seat in the capsule fired, and the cosmonaut parachuted to the ground	

INSIDE VOSKHOD ▲

To fit three people inside the Voskhod capsule, the ejection seat and other gear that had been fitted to Vostok were removed. It was still very cramped, so the crew did not wear space suits for the launch and landing. Voskhod 2 also carried a device called an airlock, which allowed one of its crew to make the first space walk.

VOSKHOD SPECIFICATIONS

Height: 16.45 ft (5 m)	
Diameter: 8 ft (2.43 m)	
Mass: Up to 12,526 lb (5,682 kg)	
Crew: Two or three	
Launch rocket: Voskhod 11A57 (also called A-2)	
Manned missions: Two orbital missions	
Longest mission: 1 day 2 hours 2 minutes by Voskhod 2 (17 orbits)	
Landing method: Capsule parachuted to the ground with the crew on board	

▲ VOSKHOD CAPSULE

The Soviet Union launched two manned missions between the last Vostok mission and the start of the Soyuz program. They used a modified Vostok capsule, called Voskhod. The Voskhod spacecraft were the first to carry more than one person. Unlike Vostok, the Voskhod capsules landed by parachute with the crew still inside. When probes dangling from the parachute lines touched the ground, rockets fired to soften the landing.

GEMINI SPECIFICATIONS

Height: 18.5 ft (5.61 m)	
Base diameter: 10 ft (3.05 m)	
Mass: 8,290 lb (3,760 kg)	
Crew: Two	
Launch rocket: Titan	
Manned missions: Ten orbital missions	
Longest mission: 13 days 18 hours 35 minutes by Gemini 7 (206 Earth orbits)	
Landing method: Re-entry module parachuted into ocean with crew on board	

Window in cockpit cover

Heat shield covered rear end of module

Swimmers from helicopters attached flotation collar to re-entry module

Life raft for astronauts while they waited to be picked up

Ejection seat could be fired out in an emergency

GEMINI RE-ENTRY MODULE ▶

At the end of a Gemini mission, swimmers would be dropped from a helicopter into the water near the re-entry module. They would attach a flotation device and then help the astronauts into a raft. The Gemini spacecraft had two parts, or modules. The re-entry module, shown here, carried the two astronauts. Attached to its base was a larger part, the adapter module, which contained life support and electrical equipment.

Green dye made the module easier to spot from the air

HUMANS IN SPACE

When the Soviet Union started launching animals into space in 1957, it was clear that a manned spaceflight was in preparation. Less than four years later, Yuri Gagarin became the first human in space. More soon followed—over the next 26 months, there were 12 US and Soviet manned flights. Soviet missions were shrouded in secrecy, but the US flights attracted huge attention. Two suborbital flights (ones not encircling Earth) by Alan Shepard and Gus Grissom were followed by four orbital flights by John Glenn, Scott Carpenter, Wally Schirra, and Gordon Cooper.

▲ GAGARIN
At 9:06 a.m. Moscow time on April 12, 1961, Yuri Gagarin heard the rocket beneath his Vostok 1 capsule rumble as it rose into the air. Nine minutes later, he was in orbit. As the capsule gently rotated, the blackness outside gave way to the brilliant blue Earth, then the Sun's blinding glare. He made one orbit of the Earth and then re-entered the atmosphere.

SOVIET SUCCESS ▶
The trio of cosmonauts shown here sharing a joke with Soviet Premier Nikita Khrushchev all flew in space. Andrian Nikolayev was the third cosmonaut (after Gagarin and Gherman Titov) to go into orbit, aboard Vostok 3 on August 11, 1962. He made 64 orbits in a flight that lasted nearly four days. Valentina Tereshkova became the first woman in space, on June 6, 1963.

FRONT PAGE NEWS ▶
As a result of his historic flight, Gagarin was transformed overnight from being an unknown Soviet Air Force officer into the most famous person in the world. His face looked out from newspapers and everyone wanted to meet him. Wherever he went, crowds lined the roads to see him. In Britain, he was invited to lunch with the Queen.

Nikita Khruschev   Valentina Tereshkova   Andrian Nikolayev

Yuri Gagarin

◀ MERCURY 3 LAUNCH
On May 5, 1961, a Redstone rocket carried Alan Shepard into space on the first US manned space mission, Mercury 3. The rocket was not powerful enough to put Shepard's capsule, which was given the call sign Freedom 7, into orbit. It reached a height of 116 miles (187 km), then fell back to Earth, splashing down in the Atlantic 15 minutes after liftoff and 303 miles (488 km) from the launch site in Florida.

FIRST AMERICAN IN SPACE ▶
Alan Shepard was a navy test-pilot before joining NASA. After his successful Mercury flight, he was scheduled to fly in the first Gemini mission, but was grounded because of a problem with his inner ear. After surgery in 1969, he returned to flight. Less than 10 years after his Mercury mission, he stood on the Moon as commander of Apollo 14.

Capsule on Glenn's flight was given the call sign Friendship 7

Window replaced two small portholes of earlier capsules

Hatch sealed by a cover held in place by 70 bolts

Glenn's flight capsule, Friendship 7

President Kennedy presents Glenn with his medal

▲ FIRST AMERICAN INTO ORBIT

On February 20, 1962, American astronaut John Glenn squeezed into his capsule for the Mercury 6 mission. At 9:47 a.m., flames erupted from its Atlas booster and Glenn soared into space. During the flight, an indicator showed that the capsule had a loose heat shield and might burn up during re-entry. Glenn was told not to jettison his retro-rockets, because their straps might hold the heat shield on. He landed safely—the heat shield was not loose after all.

◄ CELEBRATED AS A HERO

Three days after Glenn's flight, President John F. Kennedy presented him with a Distinguished Service Medal to recognize his achievement. The ceremony took place at the Cape Canaveral launch site in Florida. A week later, on March 1, 1962, four million people turned out in New York City when Glenn arrived for celebrations and to address the United Nations.

e first astronauts

ANIMALS IN SPACE

The first space travelers were animals, not humans. Animals were sent first to see if it was possible to survive a spaceflight and to test the craft carrying them. The Soviet Union used mainly dogs, and the US used chimpanzees.

DOGS

The first living creature to orbit Earth was a dog called Laika, traveling aboard the Sputnik 2 satellite on November 3, 1957. Several more test-flights were made with dogs to test the Vostok capsule.

CHIMPANZEE

Ham, a chimpanzee, was one of the most famous animals to travel into space aboard an early US space mission.

He was launched in a Mercury capsule on a suborbital flight on January 31, 1961.

MICE

Living creatures are still carried into space as the subjects of scientific experiments. The Space Shuttle carried some mice in 2001, to test a protein that may one day help astronauts resist bone loss during long missions.

SPIDERS

Skylab 3 carried two spiders, called Anita and Arabella. Scientists wanted to see if they could spin webs while weightless—they could. Spiders were carried again in the ill-fated last flight of the Space Shuttle Columbia.

> *"I believe this nation should commit itself to achieving the goal, before this decade is out, of landing a man on the Moon...."*
>
> President John F. Kennedy

SPACE RACE

The Soviet Union's early successes in space took the US by surprise. In 1961, the newly elected American President, John F. Kennedy, considered what to do. Some advisers urged him to cancel the space program, because the Soviets were already so far ahead. But Kennedy argued that American technology and industry should be able to match or overtake the Soviet Union. He challenged the Soviet Union to a head-on contest in space. Success was no longer a mere technical challenge, it was a matter of national pride. The Space Race was on, with both sides desperate to be the first to put a person on the Moon.

> *"Let the capitalist countries try to overtake us"*
>
> Premier Nikita Khrushchev

▲ KHRUSHCHEV IN CONTROL
Premier Nikita Khrushchev held power in the Soviet Union when the Space Age began. He was immensely proud that Soviet technology had beaten the US, and that the world could see it. First, a Soviet satellite flew unchallenged over American territory. Then, in April 1961, Gagarin made his epic trip to space. Soviet firsts kept coming.

KENNEDY COMMITS TO SPACE ▲
On May 25, 1961, President John F. Kennedy made an historic speech to the US Congress. It committed the US to a manned Moon landing by the end of the 1960s. It was an amazingly bold announcement, because at that time, the US had not even put an astronaut into Earth orbit. In his speech Kennedy said, "No single space project in this period will be more impressive to mankind, or more important for the long-range exploration of space."

Space Race

SOYUZ TAKES OFF ►
After Vostok and Voskhod, the Soviet Union's next spacecraft was Soyuz. With Soyuz, the Soviet Union would make longer spaceflights, learn to maneuver in orbit, and dock with other craft. Meanwhile, Moon-landing spacecraft and a giant rocket to launch it were being built in great secrecy. When the US won the race to the Moon in 1969, Soviet Moon-landing plans were scrapped, and Soyuz became a ferry craft to transport cosmonauts to and from a series of space stations.

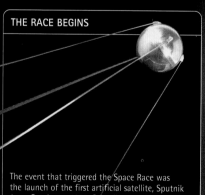

THE RACE BEGINS

The event that triggered the Space Race was the launch of the first artificial satellite, Sputnik 1, on October 4, 1957. Sputnik 1 was just a small, harmless metal ball that bleeped as it passed overhead, but it worried Americans for two reasons. It showed that the Soviet Union was more advanced technologically than had previously been thought. It also showed that the Soviet Union had long-range rockets powerful enough to fly over US territory, spy on it, and possibly even attack it with nuclear missiles.

GEMINI 7 IN ORBIT ▶

This photograph of Gemini 7 was taken from Gemini 6 when the two spacecraft met up in Earth orbit. The Space Race really heated up with the Gemini missions. Over the course of just 21 months in 1965-1966, the US launched 10 two-man missions. Their aim was to learn how to do everything that would be necessary for a Moon-landing mission. Astronauts practiced maneuvering spacecraft, changing orbit, docking one craft with another, and walking in space. The Gemini 7 mission lasted 14 days—a record at that time.

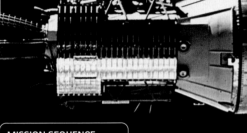

Aft section contained a restartable rocket engine with a thrust of 16,000 lbf (71 kN)

Mid section contained propellant tanks

Radio antenna allowed the Agena to be controlled by Gemini craft

Exhaust nozzle of main engine

Forward section contained guidance systems and control electronics

Docking cone designed for Gemini craft to dock with

MISSION SEQUENCE

USSR	US
1961	
Vostok 1	
	Mercury 3
	Mercury 4
Vostok 2	
1962	
	Mercury 6
	Mercury 7
Vostok 3 + 4	
	Mercury 8
1963	
	Mercury 9
Vostok 5 + 6	
1964	
Voskhod 1	
1965	
Voskhod 2	
	Gemini 3
	Gemini 4
	Gemini 5
	Gemini 6 + 7
1966	
	Gemini 8
	Gemini 9
	Gemini 10
	Gemini 11
	Gemini 12
1967	
Soyuz 1	

▲ TARGET FOR GEMINI 8

US astronaut David Scott took this photograph of an Agena rocket hanging in space during the Gemini 8 mission. As he did so, his pilot Neil Armstrong inched the spacecraft toward the rocket and then docked with it. This was the first space docking. Their triumph nearly ended in disaster when a thruster (a small rocket engine) jammed on. It fired continuously and sent the two spacecraft into a dangerously fast spin. Armstrong undocked, turned off Gemini 8's main thrusters, and switched to a back-up system to stop the spacecraft from spinning.

COOPERATION AT LAST ▶

American astronaut Donald (Deke) Slayton and Soviet cosmonaut Alexei Leonov posed for photographs during the Apollo-Soyuz Project in 1975. After the Moon landings, which marked the end of the Space Race, the US and Soviet Union began cooperating in space. During this joint US-Soviet mission, an Apollo spacecraft docked with a Soyuz spacecraft. The crews visited each other's craft and carried out joint experiments. Slayton had been one of the first seven Americans selected for astronaut training in 1959, but this was his first trip into space.

APOLLO PROGRAM

The final US-manned space project in the race to the Moon was Apollo. The Apollo spacecraft was composed of three parts, or modules, launched by the giant Saturn V rocket. The tiny command module provided living quarters for the three-man crew. For most of the mission, it was attached to the service module, containing propulsion, electrical power, and life support systems. On Moon-landing missions, two astronauts would descend to the Moon's surface in the spiderlike lunar module, while the third orbited the Moon in the command module.

Command module would contain three astronauts on manned flights

Adapter was designed to contain a lunar module

Third stage put spacecraft in orbit and sent it to the Moon on lunar missions

Second stage boosted vehicle to a height of 115 miles (185 km)

◄ APOLLO 4 LIFTOFF

A Saturn V rocket rose from the launchpad for the first time at the start of the unmanned Apollo 4 mission on November 9, 1967. At 8.9 seconds before launch, the rocket's first stage engines started. Six seconds later, a deafening roar reached the spectators. As the countdown reached zero, computers released the rocket and it slowly climbed away into orbit 115 miles (185 km) above Earth. There, the third stage fired and pushed the Apollo spacecraft even higher. The flight was a great success.

First stage separated from rest of rocket about 150 seconds after liftoff

First stage engines, fueled by kerosene and liquid oxygen, boosted vehicle to a height of 37 miles (60 km)

Apollo

Adapter doors opened to release lunar module

Adapter could split in four to open

▲ APOLLO 7

The third stage of the Saturn V rocket used in the Apollo 7 mission is seen here with its attached adapter doors open. At the start of a Moon-landing mission, the adapter would house a lunar module. Apollo 7's adapter was empty. Even so, the crew put the spacecraft through all maneuvers necessary to extract a lunar module from it. The Apollo 7 mission lasted nearly 11 days and was a success, although the three crew members developed severe colds in space.

APOLLO–SATURN V SPECIFICATIONS
APOLLO SPACECRAFT
Command module (CM) Length: 11 ft (3.5 m) Mass: 5.8 tons
Service module (SM) Length: 25 ft (7.6 m) Mass: 24.5 tons
Lunar module (LM) Length: 21 ft (6.4 m) Mass: 15 tons
SATURN V ROCKET
First stage (S-IC) Height: 138 ft (42 m) Mass: 2,287 tons
Second stage (S-II) Height: 82 ft (25 m) Mass: 488 tons
Third stage (S-IVB) Height: 59 ft (18 m) Mass: 119 tons
Apollo-Saturn V Height: 365 ft (111m) Mass: 3,000 tons

HEADING FOR THE MOON

A series of unmanned and manned Apollo missions led up to the first Moon-landing.

APOLLO 1

During a ground test of the new Apollo spacecraft on January 27, 1967, a fire broke out, killing the crew of Virgil (Gus) Grissom, Ed White, and Roger Chaffee. The spacecraft was later named Apollo 1.

APOLLO 2, 3

After the Apollo 1 fire, project plans changed. No missions were called Apollo 2 or 3.

APOLLO 4

On November 9, 1967, the Saturn V rocket made its first successful test-flight with an unmanned Apollo spacecraft.

APOLLO 5

On January 22, 1968, an Apollo lunar module was given its first unmanned test-flight in space.

APOLLO 6

On April 4, 1968, a Saturn V launched an Apollo spacecraft for a final unmanned test.

APOLLO 7

Launched on October 11, 1968, the manned Apollo 7 mission tested Apollo in Earth orbit.

APOLLO 8

Launched on December 21, 1968, Apollo 8 was the first manned flight to the Moon, which it orbited 10 times.

APOLLO 9

Launched on March 3, 1969, the manned Apollo 9 mission tested the lunar module in Earth orbit.

APOLLO 10

Launched on May 18, 1969, Apollo 10 was a dress rehearsal for the first Moon-landing. The lunar module was taken down almost to the Moon's surface.

EARTH RISE FROM APOLLO 8 ▲

This stunning view of Earth rising above the Moon's horizon was photographed by Frank Borman from the command module of Apollo 8, the first manned spacecraft to orbit the Moon. Borman, James Lovell, and Bill Anders made 10 Moon orbits on December 24 and 25, 1968, and transmitted the first live television pictures of the surface. After that, the only piece of Apollo hardware to test was the lunar module.

◄ DRESS REHEARSAL

This photograph of Apollo 10's command and service module (CSM) was taken by a crew member in the lunar module (LM). The Apollo 10 mission rehearsed everything for a Moon landing except the landing itself. Once the craft was in lunar orbit, two astronauts took the LM to within 9 miles (14.5 km) of the Moon's surface. The LM's top, ascent stage then separated from the descent stage and climbed to meet the CSM for the return flight to Earth.

Discarded third stage

Lunar module

Command and service module

(1) After orbiting Earth, the third stage engine fires the spacecraft toward the Moon.

(2) The command and service module (CSM) separates from the third stage and turns around.

(3) Facing in the opposite direction, the CSM docks with the lunar module, which is housed in the third stage.

(4) The CSM and attached lunar module turn around. The third stage is discarded.

(5) The spacecraft maneuvers into lunar orbit.

(6) The lunar module separates from the CSM and lands on the Moon.

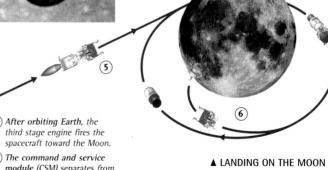

▲ LANDING ON THE MOON

The Apollo spacecraft had to perform a complex series of maneuvers to achieve a Moon landing. It had to be turned and steered with great precision. Fine control of position and speed was essential for docking the command and service module (CSM) with the lunar module. The crew controlled the spacecraft by firing small thrusters arranged around the service module and lunar module. The service module's main engine was used for maneuvers that needed more power, such as entering and leaving lunar orbit.

APOLLO 11 – MOONWALK

On the morning of July 16, 1969, nearly a million people gathered around the Kennedy Space Center to see history being made. Hundreds of millions more people all over the world, one fifth of Earth's population, watched the events unfold live on television. At 9:32 a.m. local time, a deafening roar erupted from launchpad 39A and Apollo 11 climbed into a clear blue sky, carrying the first explorers in history to travel to another world. Four days later, first Neil Armstrong and then Edwin (Buzz) Aldrin stepped onto the surface of the Moon.

Aldrin, suit, and backpack weigh 60 lb (27 kg) on the Moon, one sixth of their weight on Earth

Neil Armstrong and the lunar module are reflected in Aldrin's gold-coated visor

Control unit allows Aldrin to adjust his life support and communications systems

Multilayered suit composed mainly of tough artificial fibers

◄ NEIL ARMSTRONG'S FOOTPRINT
Neil Armstrong made the first human footprint on the Moon as he stepped off the lunar module's footpad onto the surface. The fine gray dust recorded his footprint perfectly. Without wind or rain to wear it away, it could still be there 10 million years from now. Eventually it will disappear, leveled by moonquakes or covered with dust thrown out by meteorites hitting the surface.

"one small step for man; one giant leap for mankind"
Neil Armstrong

BRINGING BACK MOON ROCK ►
Armstrong and Aldrin laid out several scientific experiments on the Moon's surface and collected 48 lb (21.7 kg) of lunar rocks and soil. After the astronauts left, the experiments continued working and sending their measurements to Earth by radio. Solar panels supplied electricity to the experiments, which included a seismometer to detect moonquakes.

Overhead hatch for transfer to the command module

Casing for the ascent propulsion fuel tank

◄ THE EAGLE HAS LANDED
Once both astronauts were on the Moon, Aldrin began unloading equipment from Eagle, the lunar module. Eagle's landing, about six hours earlier, almost didn't happen. As the spacecraft approached its landing site, Armstrong noticed boulders and flew for some distance above the surface looking for a level spot to land on. He finally touched down with only about 20 seconds flying time remaining before the landing would have been called off.

ALDRIN ON THE MOON ►
Aldrin and Armstrong spent more than 21 hours on the Moon, including a moonwalk lasting two and a half hours. Everything was new to them. They kicked the soil to see how deep and dusty it was, tested different ways of moving around in the Moon's weak gravitational field, took photographs, and planted an American flag.

Overboot with ribbed silicone-rubber sole, worn over smaller inner boot

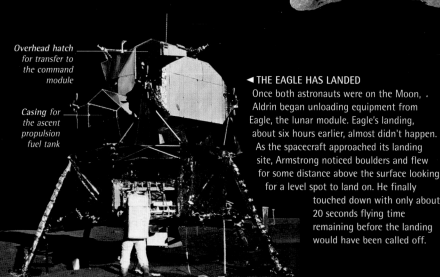

Backpack contains oxygen for Aldrin to breathe and water to keep him cool in his suit

Outer glove fits over an inner glove molded to Aldrin's hand

Thigh pocket carries tools for experiments and a bag to fill with moondust for analysis

(1) *Eagle's lower half remains on the Moon and acts as a launch pad for the top half, which blasts off to join the CSM.*

(2) *After the astronauts transfer to the CSM, Eagle is cast off. CSM fires its engine to return to Earth.*

(3) *The CSM approaches Earth, and the service module (SM) is jettisoned, leaving the CM with three astronauts inside.*

(4) *Heat shield protects the CM as it descends through Earth's atmosphere.*

(5) *Parachutes open and the CM splashes down in the Pacific Ocean.*

RETURNING TO EARTH ▲

The journey home began with Eagle's ascent stage blasting off from the Moon. The command and service module (CSM), piloted by Michael Collins, had stayed orbiting the Moon. Three hours after Eagle's ascent stage took off, Collins saw the craft approaching, steered toward it, and docked. Eagle was cut adrift and the CSM engine was fired to set a course back to Earth.

▲ SPACE TRAVELERS IN QUARANTINE

President Richard Nixon welcomes the crew back to Earth. The astronauts were quarantined (kept apart from other people) inside a sealed, mobile box as soon as they landed in case they had brought any dangerous microbes back with them. They spent the next few weeks in a laboratory where they underwent medical tests and debriefing. Soon after their eventual release, the three heroes were honored with a huge ticker tape parade in New York City.

SUBSEQUENT MISSIONS

After Apollo 11, six more Apollo missions were launched. All except Apollo 13 landed successfully on different parts of the Moon.

APOLLO 12

Struck by lightning as it took off, but undamaged. Two of the Apollo 12 astronauts landed in the Ocean of Storms in November 1969.

Alan Bean, Apollo 12's lunar, module pilot

APOLLO 13

Abandoned its mission to land on the Moon in April 1970 after an explosion in the spacecraft. The crew returned to Earth safely.

APOLLO 14

Landed in Fra Mauro region in February 1971. Apollo 14 was commanded by Alan Shepard, the first US astronaut.

Command module after splashdown

APOLLO 15

Landed in the Hadley-Apennine mountain region of the Moon in July 1971. Apollo 15 was the first of three science missions and the first to take a lunar rover.

APOLLO 16

Landed in the Descartes highlands in April 1972. Apollo 16 was commanded by John Young, the first astronaut to orbit the Moon on two missions (Apollo 10 and Apollo 16).

APOLLO 17

Landed between the Taurus mountains and Littrow crater in December 1972. Apollo 17 was the last manned Moon landing.

Astronaut Cernan and lunar rover

SOYUZ PROGRAM

The Soyuz spacecraft was introduced in 1967. Since then, it has been modified and updated several times. An improved version, called Soyuz TM, was developed in 1986 to transport crews to the Mir space station. Soyuz TMA services the needs of the International Space Station. Most Soyuz spacecraft carry a crew of two or three cosmonauts. An unmanned version, called Progress, is used as a cargo craft to deliver supplies of food, water, and fuel to space stations.

Launch escape system blasts spacecraft clear in an emergency

Fairing protects spacecraft during launch

Soyuz spacecraft carries up to three cosmonauts

LAUNCHING SOYUZ ►
Moments after liftoff, a Soyuz spacecraft heads for orbit. Soyuz craft are launched by a three-stage rocket. The boosters strapped around the outside form the first stage. The central core is the second stage. The first and second stages are fired together to launch the rocket. Almost five minutes after liftoff, the third stage fires to place the craft in orbit. The rocket can be fitted with a fourth, Fregat, stage to launch satellites and interplanetary probes.

Third stage burns for about 4 minutes

Second/core stage burns for 290 seconds

First stage boosters burn for 118 seconds and then fall away

Descent module contains control systems

Orbital module is the largest module and provides living space

Instrumentation/ propulsion module with attached solar arrays

SOYUZ SPACECRAFT ►
A Soyuz spacecraft is composed of three modules. While the craft is in space, the crew works and sleeps in the orbital module. At one end, this has a mechanism to dock with space stations. At the other end, a hatch gives access to the bell-shaped descent module. The descent module is the only part of a Soyuz craft that returns to Earth. Finally, the instrumentation/ propulsion module contains the spacecraft's main engines.

INSIDE SOYUZ ▲
A cosmonaut settles into his seat inside a Soyuz descent module. This module has a habitable volume of 142 cu ft (4 m³), or about two-thirds the size of an Apollo command module. Each crew member lies on a seat molded to the shape of his or her body. A good fit is essential to hold the cosmonaut securely for launch and landing. The controls and instruments in the latest Soyuz have been updated to include full-color computer screens.

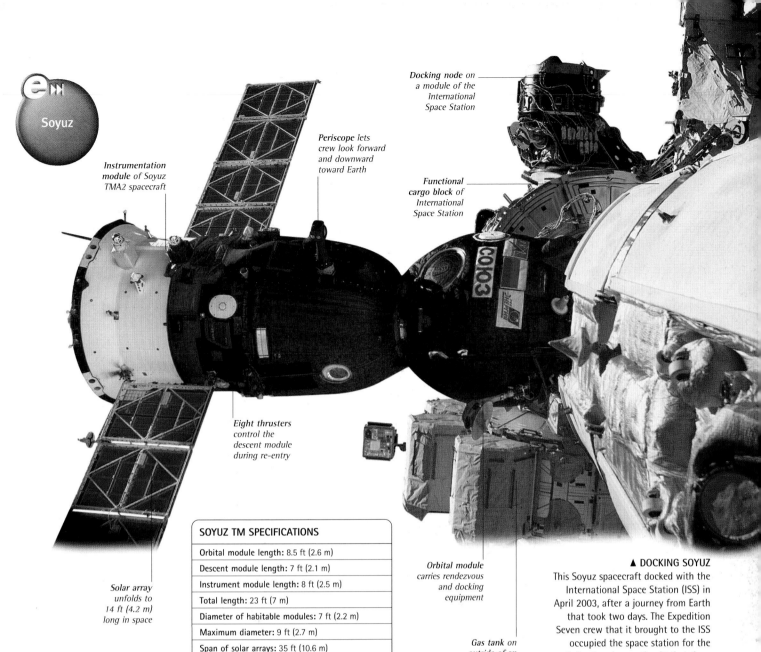

Soyuz

Docking node on a module of the International Space Station

Periscope lets crew look forward and downward toward Earth

Functional cargo block of International Space Station

Instrumentation module of Soyuz TMA2 spacecraft

Eight thrusters control the descent module during re-entry

Solar array unfolds to 14 ft (4.2 m) long in space

Orbital module carries rendezvous and docking equipment

Gas tank on outside of an airlock

SOYUZ TM SPECIFICATIONS

Orbital module length: 8.5 ft (2.6 m)	
Descent module length: 7 ft (2.1 m)	
Instrument module length: 8 ft (2.5 m)	
Total length: 23 ft (7 m)	
Diameter of habitable modules: 7 ft (2.2 m)	
Maximum diameter: 9 ft (2.7 m)	
Span of solar arrays: 35 ft (10.6 m)	
Habitable volume: 355 cu ft (10 m³)	
Crew: Two or three	
Mass: 15,586 lb (7,070 kg)	

▲ DOCKING SOYUZ

This Soyuz spacecraft docked with the International Space Station (ISS) in April 2003, after a journey from Earth that took two days. The Expedition Seven crew that it brought to the ISS occupied the space station for the following six months. At that time, Soyuz spacecraft provided the only means of ferrying crews to and from the ISS while NASA's Space Shuttle was grounded after the Columbia accident.

SOYUZ LANDING

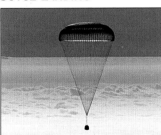

PARACHUTES DEPLOYED
After re-entry, a Soyuz descent module releases a series of parachutes to slow its descent in stages. Two pilot parachutes emerge first. The second of these pulls out a drogue chute, which slows the module to less than 185 mph (300 kph). Then the 11,000 sq ft (1,000 m²) main parachute slows it to 15 mph (25 kph).

ROCKET BRAKING
The parachute holds the descent module at an angle of 30°, to present the maximum surface area to air-flow and so cool it down. Later, the module is moved into a fully upright position. Just before landing, with the module about 3 ft (1 m) above the ground, six rockets fire to slow its descent to 3 mph (5 kph).

TOUCHDOWN
More than 3 hours after undocking from the rest of the spacecraft, the Soyuz descent module reaches the ground. Shock absorbers built into the crew members' seats cushion the final bump on landing. Cosmonauts and astronauts have described their landing in the latest type of Soyuz craft as "soft."

RECOVERY
Soyuz descent modules land in the flat steppes of Kazakhstan, northeast of the Baikonur Cosmodrome where Soyuz craft are launched. As soon as a descent module lands, helicopters carrying medical experts arrive. The crew is taken out and helped into reclining chairs before having medical examinations.

SPACE SHUTTLE

The Space Shuttle is the world's first spaceplane. It takes off like a rocket, spends up to a month in orbit, and then lands like an airliner. Travelling at speeds of 18,000 mph (28,800 kph), the Orbiter vehicle can carry a crew of seven astronauts. Its large payload bay carries science experiments and other equipment. A remote arm can be deployed from the bay to launch satellites. Four Orbiters were built, called Columbia, Challenger, Discovery, and Atlantis. Columbia made the first flight on April 12, 1981 from the Kennedy Space Center, Florida. A fifth, Endeavour, was built in 1992.

e▶▶
Shuttle

SHUTTLE SPECIFICATIONS

Orbiter wingspan: 78 ft (23.8 m)	
Orbiter length: 122 ft (37.2 m)	
Orbiter height: 56 ft (17.3 m)	
Main engines: weigh 7,480 lb (3,393 kg each)	
Maximum speed: 18,000 mph (28,800 kph)	
Weight: 165,000 lb (75,000 kg)	
Payload bay: 160 ft (18.3 m) long by 15 ft (4.6 m) wide	
Crew compartment: 2,525 cubic feet (71.5 m³) habitable volume	
External Tank: contains 526,000 gallons (2 million litres) of fuel	
Boosters: provide a thrust of 3.3 million 1b (1.5 million kg) at take-off	
Total take-off weight: 4.4 million lb (2 million kg)	

SHUTTLE IN ORBIT ▶

In space, the Orbiter opens its payload bay doors. The doors are lined with large panels that work as space radiators. A liquid coolant absorbs heat from equipment inside the Orbiter and then flows through more than I mile (1.5 km) of tubing in the radiators. Heat radiates away into space and stops the Orbiter from overheating. Mission specialists can see into the payload bay through windows at the back of the crew compartment.

Launch tower stands 348 ft (106 m) tall, from the ground to the tip of its lightning mast

◄ ON THE LAUNCHPAD
A Space Shuttle on the launchpad is prepared for takeoff. It is launched with the help of two Solid Rocket Boosters (SRBs) and a giant External Tank of fuel. When the three main engines in the Orbiter's tail fire, fuel and oxygen pour into them at the rate of 1,040 gallons (4,000 litres) every second. The boosters supply most of the power needed for takeoff.

External Tank covered with orange insulating foam

Solid Rocket Boosters provide 71 per cent of the thrust needed to lift the Shuttle

Orbiter is the only part of the Space Shuttle to travel into orbit

Payload bay carries cargo into orbit

USA   NASA Discovery

FROM EARTH TO SPACE

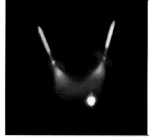

SRB SEPARATION
Two minutes after liftoff, when the Space Shuttle is about 27 miles (45 km) high, its two Solid Rocket Boosters separate and fall away. Rockets in their nose fire to push them away from the Orbiter. They parachute into the Atlantic Ocean 140 miles (225 km) from the shore.

EXTERNAL TANK SEPARATION
Just over eight minutes after liftoff, the Orbiter's main engines shut down and, a few seconds later, the External Tank separates. The tank tumbles back through the atmosphere and breaks up. Any pieces that do not burn up come down in a remote part of the Indian Ocean.

SRBS COLLECTED
When the Shuttle's Solid Rocket Boosters come down in the ocean, they float ready to be collected by ships sent out to retrieve them. The empty rocket casings are returned to their manufacturer and filled with fuel again. They are then sent back to the Kennedy Space Center to be reused.

ORBITAL INSERTION
The Orbiter is now in an elliptical orbit 40 miles (65 km) to 184 miles (296 km) above Earth. At the highest point, the Orbiter fires its engines to make the orbit circular. Without the External Tank, it cannot use its main engines. Instead it uses two engines in pods either side of its tail.

Elevon swivels for steering in Earth's atmosphere

Payload bay can carry satellites, equipment and a laboratory

Orbital engines are used to change orbit

Tail fin with a rudder that doubles as an air brake

Payload bay doors stay open in orbit to cool the Orbiter

INSIDE THE ORBITER ▲
On the flight deck, the mission commander sits in the left seat and the pilot sits in the right seat. The commander is in overall control of the spacecraft and its mission, like an airliner's captain. The pilot assists the commander. The instrument panel in front of them uses similar multi-function display screens to those in the latest airliners. There are two seats for other crew members behind the commander and pilot. Below them, on the mid-deck, there are another three seats.

Wings are short and stubby to withstand reentry

Flight deck where the commander and pilot fly the Orbiter

Mid-deck work, storage, eating and sleeping area

Radiators inside the doors dump excess heat overboard into space

Thrusters in the nose and tail control the Orbiter's position

Nose cone houses the front landing wheels

▲ CREW EXPLORATION VEHICLE
Scientists and engineers are planning a new orbiter to ferry astronauts and scientists to the Space Station and beyond. Designs include the Crew Exploration Vehicle (CEV) above. This is a capsule similar to that used by the Apollo craft. It is launched by a single-use rocket, rather than a reusable spaceplane. The new CEV will replace the Space Shuttle fleet which is nearing the end of its days. Two Orbiters, Challenger and Columbia, have been lost in accidents, along with their crews.

COUNTDOWN

Preparations for launching a Space Shuttle begin up to three months before liftoff and follow a carefully planned sequence of events. The Orbiter is completely overhauled, and its main engines are removed, serviced, and rebuilt, and then rolled out to the launchpad at Kennedy Space Center, Florida. The countdown clock is started 43 hours before takeoff. "Holds," when the clock stops for up to four hours, allow time to deal with problems without delaying the launch.

▲ ENGINES ATTACHED TO ORBITER
The serviced and cleaned main engines are delivered to the Orbiter Processing Facility and refitted in the craft's tail.

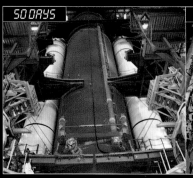

50 DAYS

▲ EXTERNAL TANK ARRIVES
The huge External Tank arrives by barge from New Orleans. It is hoisted between the boosters on a mobile launch platform.

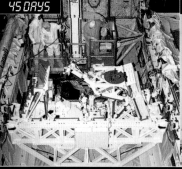

45 DAYS

▲ PAYLOAD INSTALLED
Some of the payload for the mission is installed in the Orbiter's payload bay. This is a robotic arm destined for the ISS.

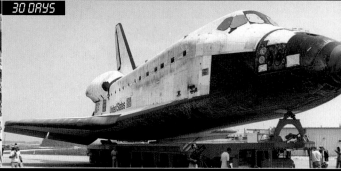

30 DAYS

▲ ORBITER DELIVERED
The Orbiter is ready for its next mission. Its engines, heat-resistant tiles, computers, instruments, and electrical systems have been checked. The Orbiter is now towed to the Vehicle Assembly Building where the engines and fuel tanks are added.

28 DAYS

▲ MAKING CONNECTIONS
The Orbiter is bolted to the External Tank at three points. The fuel and electricity supplies are connected between them.

21 DAYS

▲ STACK COMPLETED
A crawler transporter moves the completed stack to the launchpad, two or three weeks before launch.

T-43 HOURS

▲ AT THE LAUNCHPAD
With three days to go before launch, the countdown clock is started at T-43 hours (Takeoff minus 43 hours).

T-2 HOURS 25 MINS

▲ CREW ENTERS ORBITER
The crew ride an elevator up the launch tower, walk across the crew access arm, and take their seats.

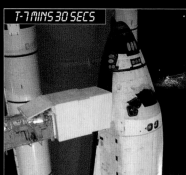

T-7 MINS 30 SECS

▲ CREW ACCESS ARM RETRACTS
The crew access arm pulls back from the Orbiter. Computers monitor the system thousands of times every second.

T-50 SECS

▲ SWITCH TO INTERNAL POWER
With 50 seconds left, the Orbiter cuts off electrical power from the outside and switches to its own onboard fuel cells.

T-6.6 SECS

▲ MAIN ENGINES FIRE
If the Orbiter's computers detect a problem as the main engines fire, they shut down the engines and halt liftoff.

T-0 SECS

▲ SOLID BOOSTERS FIRE
Once the two Solid Boosters fire, it is impossible to switch them off. No one can stop the Shuttle taking off now.

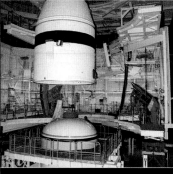

▲ SOLID ROCKET BOOSTERS BUILT
A pair of Solid Rocket Boosters arrive in sections by rail from Utah. They are built in the Vehicle Assembly Building.

▲ ORBITER HOISTED
A giant crane hoists the 68-ton Orbiter off the ground and inches it toward the External Tank and Solid Rocket Boosters.

▲ GO/NO-GO FOR LAUNCH
Mission controllers check all data to make a final decision to launch. The clock is restarted at T-9 minutes.

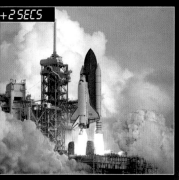

▲ LIFTOFF
As the Solid Rocket Boosters fire, bolts holding the Shuttle down on the launch platform are cut by explosive charges.

▲ "WE HAVE A LIFT-OFF"
Mission time is started at 000:00:00.00 (zero hours, zero minutes, zero seconds). Steam and smoke engulfs the launch pad, as the Shuttle soars away. The mission has begun. As soon as the Shuttle clears the top of the launch tower, about seven seconds after lift-off, control is handed over from the Kennedy Space Center to Mission Control at the Johnson Space Center in Houston,Texas. Here, teams work around the clock on shifts to monitor the Orbiter's systems.

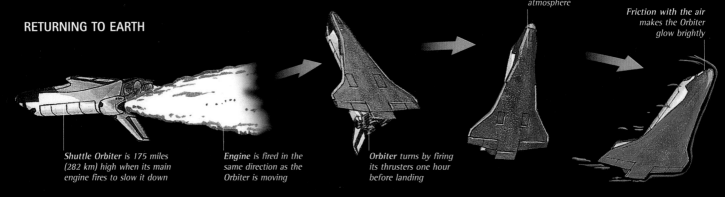

atmosphere

Friction with the air makes the Orbiter glow brightly

Shuttle Orbiter is 175 miles (282 km) high when its main engine fires to slow it down

Engine is fired in the same direction as the Orbiter is moving

Orbiter turns by firing its thrusters one hour before landing

COMING HOME

Every spacecraft returning to Earth has to re-enter the atmosphere. Re-entry begins with an engine burn to slow the craft down, and gravity then takes over. The Space Shuttle Orbiter dives into the air at 15,500 mph (25,000 kph), and other craft, past and present, have had to re-enter at similar speeds. Without protection, spacecraft would burn up at these speeds. Early manned craft were protected by heat shields that slowly charred. Soyuz spacecraft still use them today, but they can be used only once. In contrast, the Shuttle is protected by a variety of reusable, heat-resistant materials.

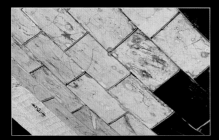

▲ HEAT-RESISTANT TILES

Almost 25,000 heat-resistant tiles and other materials cover the Shuttle Orbiter to protect it from the high temperatures it encounters during re-entry. The main body of the Orbiter is made from aluminum, which must be kept below 350°F (175°C). During re-entry, parts of the spacecraft's surface reach 2,300°F (1,260°C). The tiles radiate this heat outward, keeping the rest of the Orbiter cool.

PROTECTION FROM SCORCHING TEMPERATURES

The Orbiter is covered with materials that can withstand re-entry many times over. These materials vary depending on the temperatures experienced. The nose, the front edges of the wings, the front edge of the tail fin, and the underside of the Orbiter are heated the most. The black ceramic tiles used to cover these areas provide extra protection. Thousands of tiles that originally covered the top and some side areas of the Orbiter have now been replaced by lighter sheets of heat-resistant fabric. The weight saved enables the Orbiter to carry heavier payloads.

Reinforced carbon-carbon gives protection against temperatures of more than 2,300°F (1,260°C).

High-temperature black insulation tiles protect areas exposed to temperatures up to 2,300°F (1,260°C).

Low-temperature white insulation tiles or insulation blankets give protection up to 1,200°F (650°C).

Flexible, reusable surface insulation blankets protect areas where temperatures never rise above 700°F (370°C).

Glass, metal alloys with high melting points, and other materials are used in other areas of the Orbiter's surface.

◄ RIDING THE FLAMES
As the Orbiter plunges into the atmosphere, the crew sees flames flashing across the windows. Thrusters fire to keep the spacecraft at the right angle. Re-entering belly-first increases drag and helps to slow the Orbiter down. Sixteen minutes from touchdown, the Orbiter starts making a series of four S-shaped turns that slow it down even more. Four minutes before touchdown, the commander takes over from the autopilot for the final approach to the runway.

Shuttle

TOUCHDOWN

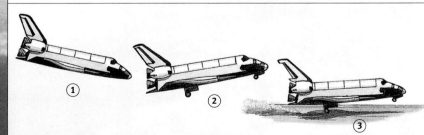

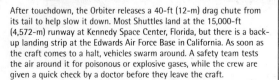

① **The Orbiter glides** down through the atmosphere, descending 20 times faster than an airliner.

② **The pilot raises the nose** 35 seconds before touchdown and, 20 seconds later, lowers the landing gear.

③ **The Orbiter touches down** at a speed of about 220 mph (350 kph), twice as fast as a commercial airliner.

After touchdown, the Orbiter releases a 40-ft (12-m) drag chute from its tail to help slow it down. Most Shuttles land at the 15,000-ft (4,572-m) runway at Kennedy Space Center, Florida, but there is a back-up landing strip at the Edwards Air Force Base in California. As soon as the craft comes to a halt, vehicles swarm around. A safety team tests the air around it for poisonous or explosive gases, while the crew are given a quick check by a doctor before they leave the craft.

SPACE STATIONS

When the US won the race to the Moon, the Soviet Union switched its attention to building space stations. Between 1971 and 1982, it launched seven successful Salyut space stations. In 1973, the US launched its first space station, Skylab. Although damaged during launch, it operated successfully for six years. Then in 1986, the Soviet Union launched the Mir space station. It was constructed in orbit by connecting up a series of modules. During 15 years in space, some of its occupants stayed for more than a year at a time.

Soyuz space ferry carried crews to Salyut 7

Propulsion module contained main engines

Main control console was located here

SALYUT 7 ▲

Salyut 7 was the last Salyut space station. During 50 months in operation, it was visited by 10 different crews and a total of 22 cosmonauts, including French and Indian cosmonauts. In 1986, it was moved to a higher orbit, and some of its equipment was moved to Mir. However, it began to spiral in toward Earth and re-entered the atmosphere earlier than originally expected.

SPECIFICATIONS: SALYUT 7

Length: 47 ft (14.4 m)

Diameter: 14 ft (4.15 m)

Mass: 19 tons

Launched: April 19, 1982

Orbit: 173 x 176 miles (279 x 284 km)

Time in orbit: 8 years 10 months

Re-entry: February 7, 1991

Re-entry fate: Burned and broke up over South America, producing an impressive light show; some pieces fell to the ground in Argentina

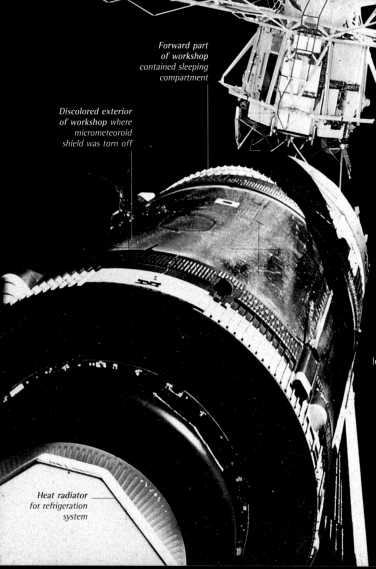

Solar arrays for Skylab's solar observatory

Solar observatory studied the Sun

Forward part of workshop contained sleeping compartment

Discolored exterior of workshop where micrometeoroid shield was torn off

Heat radiator for refrigeration system

◄ INSIDE SKYLAB

Living conditions inside Skylab were better than in any previous US spacecraft. There was much more room—enough for acrobatics. The crew quarters contained sleep compartments and a ward room where meals were prepared. Skylab's astronauts also had the luxury of a shower, although they rationed its use to once a week, to save water. They used an exercise bike to help counter the effects of weightlessness on their bodies.

◄ SKYLAB

Skylab was made mainly from leftover Apollo hardware. The largest part, the orbital workshop, was the empty third stage of a Saturn V rocket. On launch, one of Skylab's solar panels and a combined micrometeoroid/heat shield were torn off. Astronauts had to make a sunshield to stop the spacecraft from overheating. Despite this perilous beginning and the fact that Skylab was only operational for 9 months, its crews took 40,000 pictures of Earth.

SPECIFICATIONS: SKYLAB

Length: 119 ft (36.12 m) when docked with Apollo spacecraft

Diameter: 22 ft (6.58 m)

Mass: 76.3 tons

Launched: May 14, 1973

Orbit: 265 x 273 miles (427 x 439 km)

Time in orbit: 6 years 2 months

Re-entry: July 11, 1979

Re-entry fate: Partially burned up in atmosphere, but some parts came down in the Indian Ocean and western Australia

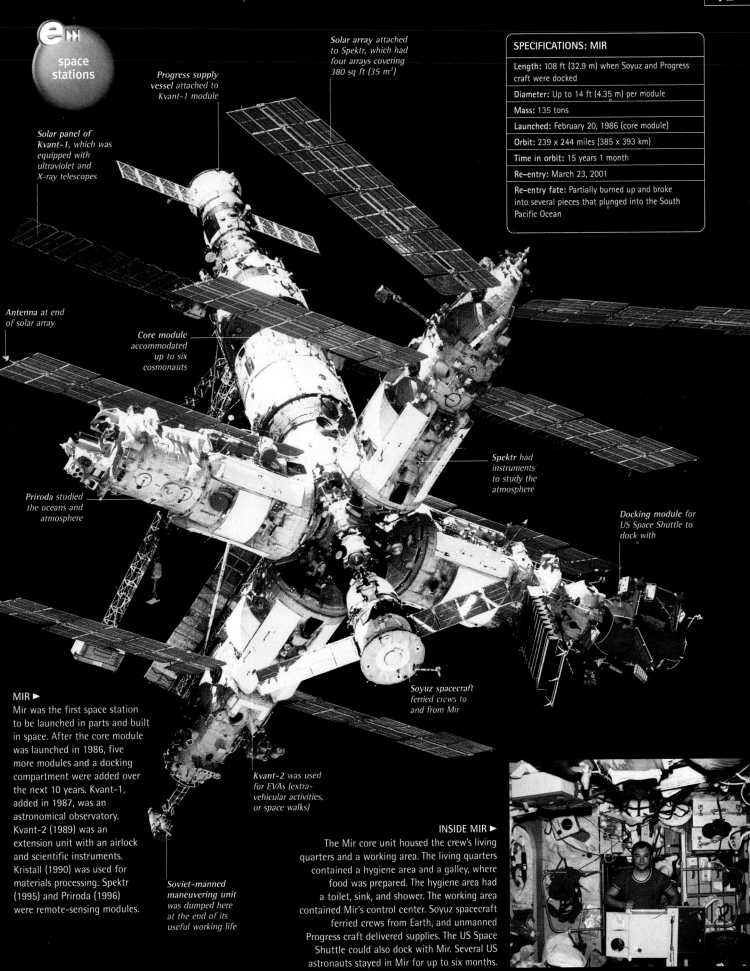

e ▶▶
space
stations

Solar panel of Kvant-1, which was equipped with ultraviolet and X-ray telescopes

Progress supply vessel attached to Kvant-1 module

Solar array attached to Spektr, which had four arrays covering 380 sq ft (35 m²)

SPECIFICATIONS: MIR

Length: 108 ft (32.9 m) when Soyuz and Progress craft were docked

Diameter: Up to 14 ft (4.35 m) per module

Mass: 135 tons

Launched: February 20, 1986 (core module)

Orbit: 239 x 244 miles (385 x 393 km)

Time in orbit: 15 years 1 month

Re-entry: March 23, 2001

Re-entry fate: Partially burned up and broke into several pieces that plunged into the South Pacific Ocean

Antenna at end of solar array

Core module accommodated up to six cosmonauts

Priroda studied the oceans and atmosphere

Spektr had instruments to study the atmosphere

Docking module for US Space Shuttle to dock with

Soyuz spacecraft ferried crews to and from Mir

Kvant-2 was used for EVAs (extra-vehicular activities, or space walks)

Soviet-manned maneuvering unit was dumped here at the end of its useful working life

MIR ▶

Mir was the first space station to be launched in parts and built in space. After the core module was launched in 1986, five more modules and a docking compartment were added over the next 10 years. Kvant-1, added in 1987, was an astronomical observatory. Kvant-2 (1989) was an extension unit with an airlock and scientific instruments. Kristall (1990) was used for materials processing. Spektr (1995) and Priroda (1996) were remote-sensing modules.

INSIDE MIR ▶

The Mir core unit housed the crew's living quarters and a working area. The living quarters contained a hygiene area and a galley, where food was prepared. The hygiene area had a toilet, sink, and shower. The working area contained Mir's control center. Soyuz spacecraft ferried crews from Earth, and unmanned Progress craft delivered supplies. The US Space Shuttle could also dock with Mir. Several US astronauts stayed in Mir for up to six months.

INTERNATIONAL SPACE STATION

The International Space Station (ISS) is taking shape in Earth orbit and is expected to be finished by around the year 2008. The size of the spacecraft, and the fact that 16 nations are involved in building it, make this the most complex space project ever. The station's main purpose is science. Its internal volume, about the same as that of a Jumbo Jet passenger cabin, will include six laboratories. Crews of up to seven scientists and astronauts will live on the station for up to six months at a time.

▲ CONSTRUCTION TAKES OFF
In November 1998, a Russian Proton rocket carried the Zarya module, the first part of the ISS, into space. In December of the same year, the Space Shuttle Endeavour delivered the Unity module. In July 2000, the Zvezda service module was added. The first crew to live on-board, Expedition One, arrived in November 2000. In February 2001, the Destiny module was delivered by the Space Shuttle Atlantis, and two months later, the station's remote manipulator system, a robot arm, arrived.

Solar panels generate 110 kw of power

Thermal control panels regulate temperature inside the ISS

BUILDING THE SPACE STATION ▲
The ISS is being constructed from pressurized cylindrical sections, called modules, connected together by a framework of beams and towers, called trusses. Parts called nodes have up to six docking ports where several modules can connect together. Spacecraft can dock with vacant ports on the nodes and modules. The US, Russia, Europe, and Japan are all contributing modules.

Space tugs deliver supplies of food, water, gases, and fuel

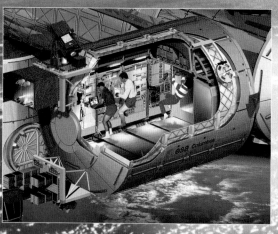

◄ SCIENCE LABORATORY
Astronauts work in shirt-sleeve comfort inside the ISS's laboratories, including the Columbus Laboratory provided by the European Space Agency (ESA). Columbus is a general-purpose science laboratory. Scientists will use it for research in materials, fluids, life sciences, and technology. It can house 10 payload racks, each a complete miniature laboratory. Some experiments will be remotely controlled by scientists working on Earth.

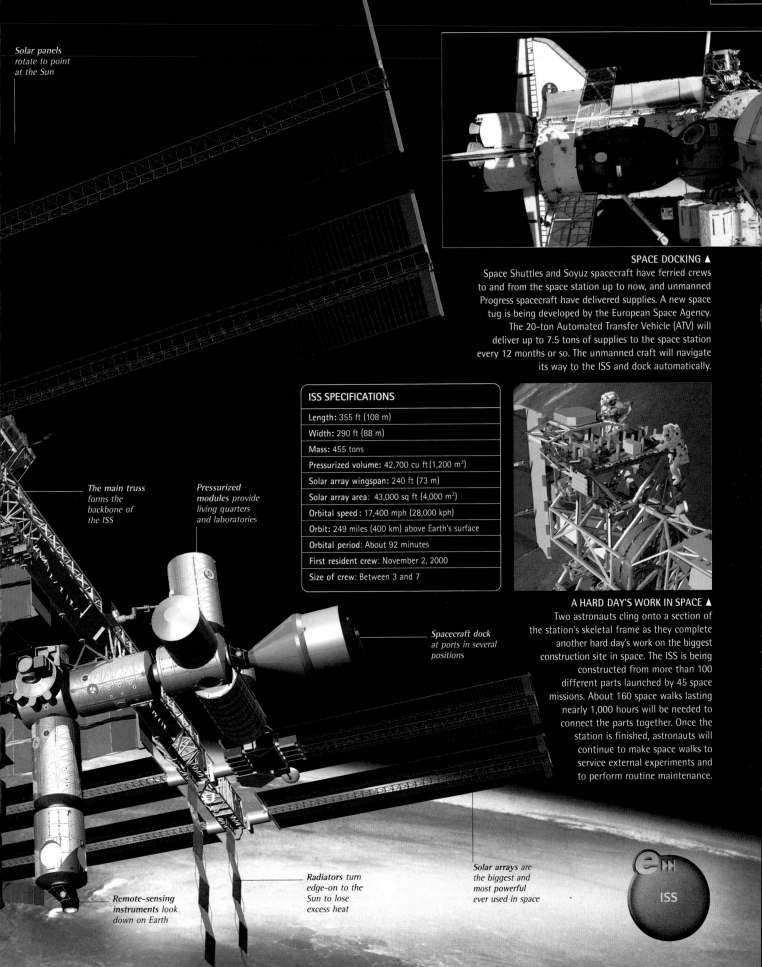

Solar panels rotate to point at the Sun

SPACE DOCKING ▲

Space Shuttles and Soyuz spacecraft have ferried crews to and from the space station up to now, and unmanned Progress spacecraft have delivered supplies. A new space tug is being developed by the European Space Agency. The 20-ton Automated Transfer Vehicle (ATV) will deliver up to 7.5 tons of supplies to the space station every 12 months or so. The unmanned craft will navigate its way to the ISS and dock automatically.

ISS SPECIFICATIONS

Length: 355 ft (108 m)	
Width: 290 ft (88 m)	
Mass: 455 tons	
Pressurized volume: 42,700 cu ft (1,200 m³)	
Solar array wingspan: 240 ft (73 m)	
Solar array area: 43,000 sq ft (4,000 m²)	
Orbital speed: 17,400 mph (28,000 kph)	
Orbit: 249 miles (400 km) above Earth's surface	
Orbital period: About 92 minutes	
First resident crew: November 2, 2000	
Size of crew: Between 3 and 7	

The main truss forms the backbone of the ISS

Pressurized modules provide living quarters and laboratories

Spacecraft dock at ports in several positions

A HARD DAY'S WORK IN SPACE ▲

Two astronauts cling onto a section of the station's skeletal frame as they complete another hard day's work on the biggest construction site in space. The ISS is being constructed from more than 100 different parts launched by 45 space missions. About 160 space walks lasting nearly 1,000 hours will be needed to connect the parts together. Once the station is finished, astronauts will continue to make space walks to service external experiments and to perform routine maintenance.

Radiators turn edge-on to the Sun to lose excess heat

Remote-sensing instruments look down on Earth

Solar arrays are the biggest and most powerful ever used in space

ISS

THE BODY IN SPACE

Humans have evolved to work best in the atmosphere and gravity that exist on the Earth's surface. To survive in space, astronauts have to take an Earthlike environment with them. Fresh oxygen is circulated around the craft for them to breathe. The main difference in space, is the weightlessness causing astronauts to float around. As soon as astronauts go into space, their bodies start adapting to this weightlessness. Muscles, bones, heart, and blood all undergo changes. At the end of a lengthy spaceflight, astronauts have to adapt to living with weight again.

e ▸▸
life in space

FEELING WEIGHTLESS ▶

Floating around inside a spacecraft looks fun, but at least half of all astronauts suffer an unpleasant reaction to weightlessness. On Earth, gravity exerts a force on our bodies, which gives us weight and keeps us rooted to the ground. It also pulls body fluid downward. In space, astronauts lose their sense of balance. They can also feel sick, and lose their appetites. It can take two weeks for the digestive system to fully adjust. NASA plans no space walks during the first three days of a mission, because an astronaut who vomits inside a spacesuit risks suffocation.

INSIDE AN ASTRONAUT'S BODY

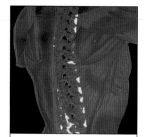

STRETCHING SPINES
Astronauts are taller in space than they are on Earth. Gravity normally pulls the vertebrae, the bones of the spine, close together. In space, vertebrae can spread out a little more, lengthening the spine. This makes the astronaut around 2 in (30-60 mm) taller, and slimmer-looking. It is not a lasting effect. An astronaut's height returns to normal when he or she comes back to Earth.

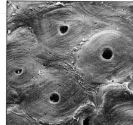

WEAKENED BONE
Bones become weaker because they no longer need to support the body weight. This bone cross section shows minerals densely packed in rings to give them strength. Blood vessels run through the center. In space, calcium dissolves out of the bones into the blood. This makes bones more brittle. Astronauts returning to Earth after a long mission are more likely to suffer a bone fracture.

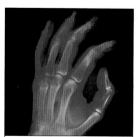

SPACE AGEING
In the 1980s, scientists realized that weightlessness affects the body in a similar way to ageing. Bones lose their mass in space over long periods, just as ageing bones become thinner. Loss of bone calcium is similar to a condition called osteoporosis that affects some older people, usually women. By studying the effects of weightlessness, scientists can understand the ageing process.

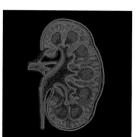

WASTING MUSCLES
Without the full force of gravity to work against, an astronaut's muscles quickly begin to atrophy (waste). They become smaller and weaker. The large weight-bearing muscles in the legs are affected the most, because they are used the least in space. Fortunately, most of the muscle lost during a spaceflight is rebuilt within a month of returning to Earth.

INTERNAL ORGANS
Some of the body's internal organs change or feel different in weightlessness. Astronauts often say their stomach feels fuller, possibly because their digestive system is breaking down food more slowly. The kidneys have to work harder. They remove waste materials from the blood, including calcium lost from the bones. Extra calcium can form painful lumps called kidney stones.

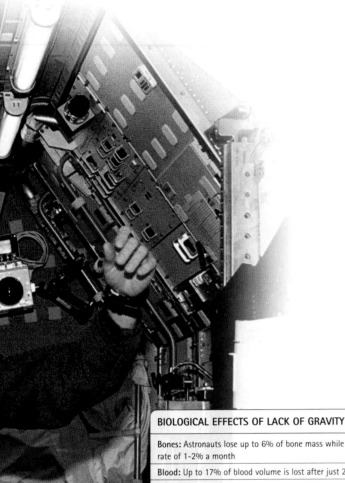

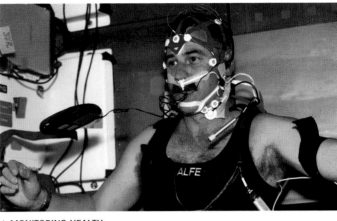

▲ MONITORING HEALTH

Many astronauts report problems sleeping for long periods in space, perhaps because of the excitement and pressures of the the mission, or the constant noise inside the craft. This Shuttle astronaut is taking part in a sleep experiment. He is fitted with a set of sensors to monitor his brainwave activity, and a sensor suit to study his breathing as he sleeps. Sensors stuck to the skin pick up the body's electrical activity, which is transmitted to Earth and monitored by doctors at mission control.

BIOLOGICAL EFFECTS OF LACK OF GRAVITY

Bones: Astronauts lose up to 6% of bone mass while in space, at the rate of 1–2% a month

Blood: Up to 17% of blood volume is lost after just 2-3 days

Muscles: Up to 20% of muscle mass is lost, at the rate of 5% a week

Teeth: Less saliva is produced in space, causing plaque build-up – astronauts chew gum to help them produce saliva

Nose and eyes: Astronauts sneeze a lot—as much as 30 times an hour—and suffer eye irritations. This is because of the dust and shed human skin cells floating around the craft

Head: About two pints of extra fluid moves up to the head, so astronauts feel as though they have a head cold

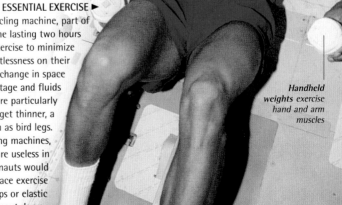

ESSENTIAL EXERCISE ▶

This astronaut uses a cycling machine, part of the daily exercise routine lasting two hours or more. Astronauts exercise to minimize the effects of weightlessness on their body. Their figures change in space because of muscle wastage and fluids moving upward. Legs are particularly affected—they get thinner, a condition known as bird legs. Normal treadmills, rowing machines, and exercise bikes are useless in space, because astronauts would just float off them. Space exercise machines have straps or elastic ropes to hold the astronaut down and give their muscles something to work against.

Handheld weights exercise hand and arm muscles

Cycling prevents bones and muscles from wasting

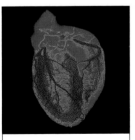

SHRINKING HEART

The heart is a muscle, so in space it wastes just like the leg muscles. It normally pumps blood against gravity. In space, it has less work to do. As a result, it shrinks in size. It also slows down and pumps less blood each time it beats. Although astronauts feel normal in space, these changes reduce their ability to do hard physical work for long periods when they return to Earth.

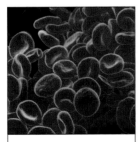

LOSING BLOOD CELLS

Gravity normally pulls blood down toward the feet. In space, it spreads out evenly throughout the body. There is more blood than usual from the waist up. The body tries to reduce the amount of blood in the head by slowing down the heart. Astronauts also lose about 20% of red blood cells, which causes anaemia and tiredness. This can last for two or more years after the trip.

24 HOURS IN SPACE

Each day of a space mission is planned in meticulous detail. Space Shuttle trips are planned to the last second, long before the crew leaves Earth. Crews on longer missions to the International Space Station have a basic plan, which is modified during daily conferences between the crew and ground controllers. Plans have to be adaptable to allow for problems with equipment or jobs taking longer in space. Essential exercise is written into the daily mission plan, along with a little time for play.

▲ 05:30—WAKE UP, SLEEPY HEAD!
International Space Station astronauts are woken up by an alarm buzzer, but music plays to wake up Shuttle crews.

▲ 06:10—IN THE GALLEY
The first meal of the day might be fruit and cereal followed by coffee or tea and a roll—all eaten straight from the pack.

▲ 07:00—WORK PREPARATION
Each morning, a detailed, timed plan of the day's work is drawn up in conjunction with ground controllers.

▲ 07:45—ALL SYSTEMS GO
First work sessions include monitoring vital spacecraft systems and performing routine maintenance jobs.

▲ 07:55—EXERCISE
Daily exercise sessions, lasting up to an hour, work muscles that otherwise do not get used in microgravity.

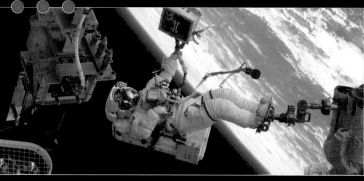

▲ 12:00—WORKING ABOVE THE EARTH
Extra Vehicular Activity (EVA) involves going outside the spacecraft to carry out repairs or to assemble parts of the ISS. Some EVAs last two to three hours. Many spacewalkers can spend their entire working day outside on a tiring seven-hour shift.

▲ 13:35—A WORKING LUNCH
The crew gather in the galley for lunch, although busy Shuttle schedules mean astronauts often snack while working.

▲ 14:50—INTERVIEWS
TV and radio shows, or webcasts, are part of the job. Astronauts give interviews from space to journalists on Earth.

▲ 18:10—BACK TO WORK
The spacecraft serves as a workshop and a science laboratory. Each crew takes its own set of tools for their mission.

▲ 18:15—CONFERENCE
The crew get together to discuss how the day's work has progressed and make any necessary changes to the schedule.

▲ 19:00—DINNER IS SERVED
Two astronauts eat rice with chopsticks on mid-deck. They choose their meals months in advance, before leaving Earth.

▲ 20:00—LEISURE
It's finally time to relax. Astronauts take their own books and CDs, watch DVDs, and sometimes play instruments.

05:40—WASH AND GO
Water is limited in space, so astronauts stay clean by using washcloths and rinseless soap and shampoo.

09:25—PREPARING FOR AN EVA
Two astronauts don their space suits in preparation for a spacewalk, helped and closely monitored by crew members.

17:10—MORE EXERCISE
Back to the exercise bike or treadmill for the second workout, to tone up the muscles and protect against weak bones.

21:00—SLEEP
After a demanding day's work, the astronauts strap themselves into sleeping bags for an eight hour sleep.

HERE COMES THE SUN ... AGAIN!

Our lives on Earth are regulated by the 24-hour day and night cycle. Sunrises mark the start of each day and darkness signals night's arrival. In space, astronauts see the Sun rise and set far more often. The number of sunrises depends on the spacecraft's speed and that depends on its height. A spacecraft 310 miles (500 km) above the Earth is traveling at 18,000 mph (28,800 kph). This means it orbits roughly once every 90 minutes, so astronauts see 16 sunrises every 24 hours.

e ▸▸
life in space

THE NIGHT SHIFT ▶
Astronauts work on the Hubble Space Telescope, bathed in the rosy glow of the Shuttle's lights as the last rays of sunshine retreat behind the Earth. With a sunrise every 90 minutes, astronauts spend many periods in darkness with just the lights of the craft to illuminate their work. But they also see several sunrises during a long space walk. Astronauts describe a sunrise in space as a rainbow of light bursting from the horizon like an erupting volcano.

LIVING IN SPACE

Living in space is a bit like living with several other people in a cramped trailer. Astronauts work hard, but they don't have to do some of the daily chores that have to be done on Earth. One-use food containers means there is no dish washing to do. Clothes don't have to be cleaned either, because astronauts wear disposable clothes. Garbage is disposed of in an unusual way. Space Station astronauts load their garbage into empty supply ships. These unmanned craft are then steered into the atmosphere and burn up.

Satellite's antenna
used to send and
receive data

Antenna dish
opens once the
satellite is in place

LONGLIFE CANNED FOOD

DRIED FOOD WITH TUBE
FOR WATER

VACUUM-PACKED FRESH FOOD

▲ EATING IN SPACE

Astronauts on early missions ate unappetizing meals of paste-like food squeezed from tubes, or dried meat cubes coated with gelatine to trap crumbs. Choices on the space menu today range from breakfast cereals and fresh fruit to steak. Astronauts have a poor sense of taste in space, so they prefer highly flavored and spiced foods. Ketchup or spicy sauce are often added to meals, which are heated in an onboard oven.

◄ PACKAGING FOOD FOR SPACE

Space food is packaged in airtight containers to keep it fresh until needed. Foods sterilized by heat are supplied in metal tins or pouches. Irradiated and low-moisture foods, such as dried apricots, are sealed in foil. Foods that have to be rehydrated have plastic containers with tubes to inject water. Fresh foods, such as nuts and crackers, are packed in plastic pouches. Drinks come in squeeze bottles, or as powders to be mixed with water.

Astronaut can
easily move a
satellite weighing
several tons

Foot restraint
secured to the
payload bay holds
astronaut firmly

SPACE MENU	
Breakfast	Cereal with raisins (rehydratable with water)
	Breakfast roll (fresh food)
	Pears (thermostabilized—heat treated to preserve)
	Vanilla breakfast drink (beverage)
	Tea or coffee (beverage)
Lunch	Chicken strips in salsa (thermostabilized)
	Macaroni and cheese (rehydratable)
	Rice with butter (thermostabilized)
	Macadamia nuts (fresh)
	Apple cider (beverage)
Dinner	Shrimp cocktail (rehydratable)
	Beef steak (irradiated, treated with radiation to preserve)
	Macaroni and cheese (rehydratable)
	Fruit cocktail (thermostabilized)
	Strawberry drink (beverage)

▲ LIVING IN MICROGRAVITY

Working astronauts have to anchor themselves behind rails so they don't float away from their workstation. Weightlessness makes it easy to move around, but it also presents problems. Nothing stays where an astronaut puts it. The tiniest movement can send something floating across the spacecraft. Everything has to be held down by hook-and-loop pads or straps, or be put away. There is no defined floor or ceiling in the Shuttle—equipment is arranged over all surfaces, so crew have to orientate themselves.

▲ KEEPING CLEAN

Early astronauts didn't bathe at all. Space missions last much longer today, so hygiene is important. The Skylab space station had a shower, but showers are not effective in space. As water doesn't fall in orbit, a fan has to blow the water at the bather, and users have to be careful not to let droplets escape to float around. Usually, astronauts use wet cloths and rinseless cleansing liquids to keep clean and brush their teeth as they would on Earth.

GROWING PLANTS IN SPACE ▶

Future space missions may depend on plants to provide food and recycle water and air. Normally, gravity makes plant roots grow downward and shoots grow upward. Without gravity, plants can't sense which way to grow, so the plants and their roots grow in all directions. They have to be watered in a different way too, because weightless water doesn't sink into soil or plant. It rests on the plant or soil in bubbles.

Remote Manipulator System arm provides a mobile platform

e ▶▶ life in space

◀ WORKING IN SPACE

Launching and servicing satellites is part of an astronaut's job. While working outside, the crew are always clipped to a foot restraint or safety line to stop them from floating away. Once secure, they can do things in space that are impossible on Earth. Weightlessness means that an astronaut can move a huge object by hand, such as this 1,760-lb (800-kg) satellite. However, when a massive object starts moving, a lot of force is needed to stop it.

▲ SLEEPING ARRANGEMENTS

Astronauts are allocated eight hours of sleep in every 24 hours. Usually, crew work in shifts, so some sleep while others work during their day. Eye and ear plugs are essential. They stick their sleeping bags to a wall to stop them from floating off and banging into things. Despite the lack of a bed, astronauts report that they still turn over in their sleep. The Shuttle commander often sleeps on the flight deck in case a problem arises.

SPACE WALKS

Astronauts routinely go on space walks, or EVAs (Extra-Vehicular Activities), to work outside. Leaving the safety of the spacecraft to walk outside, 245 miles (400 km) or so above Earth, is dangerous. It takes 15 minutes to put on a space suit, but it takes much longer to prepare to leave the craft. A space suit supplies pure oxygen at less than one third the air pressure inside the spacecraft. A sudden drop in pressure, from the cabin to the space suit, could cause a condition called decompression sickness, which can be fatal. The pressure inside the craft has to be lowered gradually, over several hours, before it is safe for an astronaut to go outside.

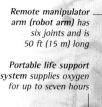

Remote manipulator arm (robot arm) has six joints and is 50 ft (15 m) long

Portable life support system supplies oxygen for up to seven hours

▲ THE FIRST SPACE WALK
On March 18, 1965, Alexei Leonov became the first person to walk in space. During Voskhod 2's second orbit, Leonov crawled through an inflatable airlock and floated into space 310 miles (500 km) above Earth, at the end of a 16-foot (5-m) safety line. Ten minutes later, he tried to go back inside, but couldn't squeeze into the airlock as his suit had ballooned in the vacuum. He eventually let air out of his suit and squeezed in head-first.

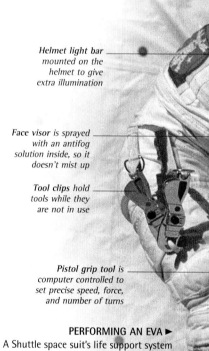

Helmet light bar mounted on the helmet to give extra illumination

Face visor is sprayed with an antifog solution inside, so it doesn't mist up

Tool clips hold tools while they are not in use

Pistol grip tool is computer controlled to set precise speed, force, and number of turns

PERFORMING AN EVA ▶
A Shuttle space suit's life support system supplies enough oxygen to last seven hours, but space walks can be even longer. In 2001, two astronauts made a space walk lasting almost nine hours by plugging into the Space Shuttle's main life support system for two hours. Astronauts performing EVAs are constantly monitored by cameras, other astronauts, and ground controllers. It can be tricky to tell which astronaut is which, so their space suits have colored stripes on the legs to help identify them.

◀ ED WHITE
Less than three months after Leonov's historic space walk, Ed White became the first US spacewalker. On June 3, 1965, he opened his Gemini 4 hatch and pulled himself out. He spent about 20 minutes outside, filmed by fellow crewman James McDivitt. White experimented with moving himself around by using jets of gas from a handheld gas-gun. When he got back inside, he had trouble with the hatch. McDivitt had to hold onto White's legs while he closed and locked it!

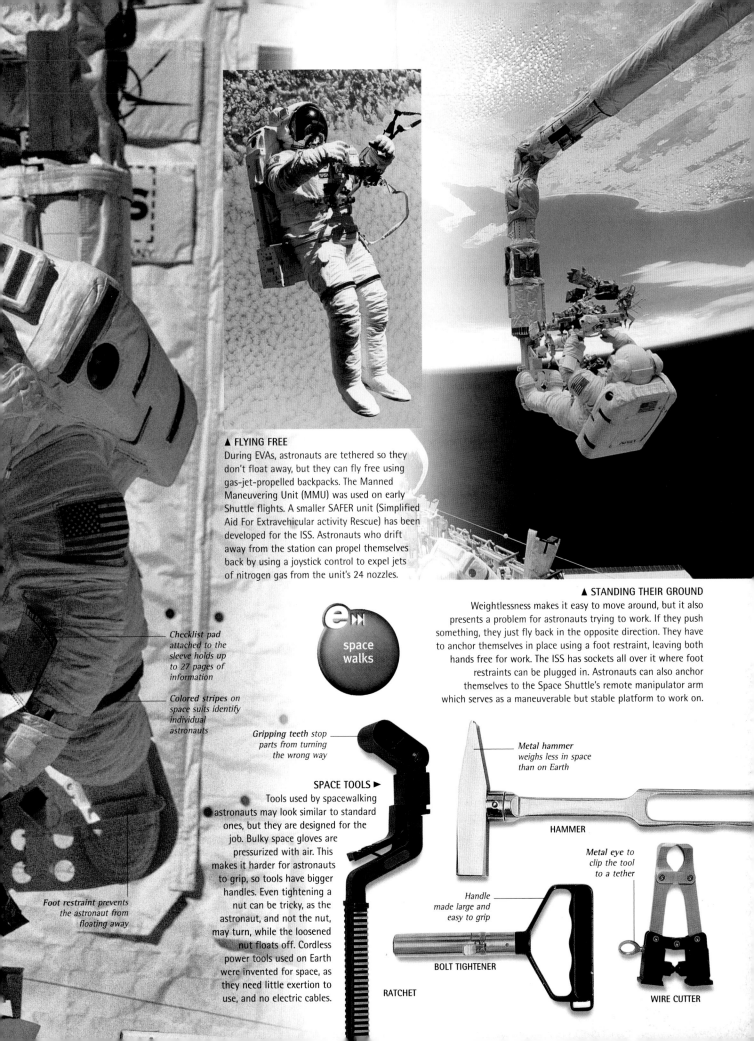

▲ FLYING FREE
During EVAs, astronauts are tethered so they don't float away, but they can fly free using gas-jet-propelled backpacks. The Manned Maneuvering Unit (MMU) was used on early Shuttle flights. A smaller SAFER unit (Simplified Aid For Extravehicular activity Rescue) has been developed for the ISS. Astronauts who drift away from the station can propel themselves back by using a joystick control to expel jets of nitrogen gas from the unit's 24 nozzles.

e►►
space walks

Checklist pad attached to the sleeve holds up to 27 pages of information

Colored stripes on space suits identify individual astronauts

Foot restraint prevents the astronaut from floating away

▲ STANDING THEIR GROUND
Weightlessness makes it easy to move around, but it also presents a problem for astronauts trying to work. If they push something, they just fly back in the opposite direction. They have to anchor themselves in place using a foot restraint, leaving both hands free for work. The ISS has sockets all over it where foot restraints can be plugged in. Astronauts can also anchor themselves to the Space Shuttle's remote manipulator arm which serves as a maneuverable but stable platform to work on.

Gripping teeth stop parts from turning the wrong way

SPACE TOOLS ►
Tools used by spacewalking astronauts may look similar to standard ones, but they are designed for the job. Bulky space gloves are pressurized with air. This makes it harder for astronauts to grip, so tools have bigger handles. Even tightening a nut can be tricky, as the astronaut, and not the nut, may turn, while the loosened nut floats off. Cordless power tools used on Earth were invented for space, as they need little exertion to use, and no electric cables.

Metal hammer weighs less in space than on Earth

HAMMER

Metal eye to clip the tool to a tether

Handle made large and easy to grip

BOLT TIGHTENER

RATCHET

WIRE CUTTER

SPACE SUITS

A space suit is more than a set of work clothes, it's a survival system. If astronauts stepped out into space without any protection, they would be unconscious within 15 seconds and all their body fluids would bubble and freeze. A space suit not only supplies oxygen to breathe, it also protects the astronaut from the vacuum of space, from temperature extremes of 250°F (121°C) to -250°F (-156°C), and from meteorite particles. There are two types of space suit. One is worn during takeoff and re-entry, the other for spacewalks.

▲ THE MERCURY SPACE SUIT
Space suits worn by Mercury astronauts in the early 1960s were developed from pressure suits designed for Navy pilots in the 1950s. The suit, worn over longjohn underwear, was made from three layers of nylon. The outer layer was impregnated with aluminum to give better flame resistance. It was worn with gloves, helmet, and lace-up flying boots, and oxygen was supplied for the astronaut to breathe. The suit was not pressurized unless the Mercury capsule lost cabin pressure.

Boots are made as part of the suit to stop air leaking out

▲ RECORD-BREAKING SUIT
The first pressurized suit worn by a pilot was made for the record-breaking American aviator, Wiley Post, in 1934. He found he could go faster by flying higher, so he had a pressure suit made to let him fly in thin air for longer. It was made of rubber covered by cotton, with a metal helmet and an oxygen supply. The suit was produced by B. F. Goodrich, which later made space suits for the Mercury astronauts.

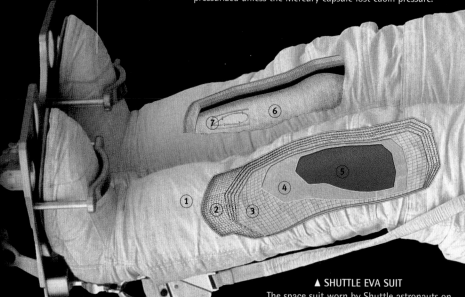

▲ SHUTTLE EVA SUIT
The space suit worn by Shuttle astronauts on space walks is called the EMU (Extravehicular Mobility Unit). Most of the suit is made from 11 layers of different coated, noncoated, and aluminized materials, many of them invented for use in space. It houses a water cooling system, drink bag, and urine collection device. On Earth, the suit weighs up to 104 lb (47 kg) and the life support system another 148 lb (67 kg). With the camera, it weighs a total of 260 lb (117.6 kg).

(1) *Tough outer layer is a mixture of three fire-retardant fibers, Gore-Tex, Kevlar, and Nomex, to protect against heat and puncture.*

(2) *The five-layer Thermal Micrometeoroid Garment Liner (TMG), made from aluminum-coated fabric, deflects the Sun's heat.*

(3) *The TMG is lined with a layer of material made from neoprene-coated (rubberized) nylon to prevent damage from micrometeoroids.*

(4) *The restraint layer, made from Dacron, stops the pressure bladder inside it from blowing up like a balloon. Its pattern aids bending.*

(5) *The innermost layer of the space suit is known as the bladder. It is pressurized and airtight, as seams are heat-sealed and overtaped.*

(6) *The Liquid Cooling and Ventilation Garment is a two-layer suit made from nylon. It stretches by 300% to fit snugly to the body.*

(7) *Cool water flows through 300 ft (91.44 m) of plastic tubing laced between the layers of the Cooling and Ventilation Garment.*

DRESSING FOR A SPACE WALK

 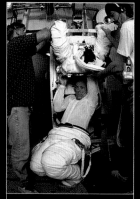 

LEGS FIRST
A Space Shuttle astronaut wearing a Liquid Cooling and Ventilation Garment steps into the space suit's Lower Torso Assembly (LTA).

SLIDING INTO THE TOP
Next, the astronaut rises into the suit's Hard Upper Torso (HUT), which normally hangs on the wall of the Space Shuttle's airlock.

LOCKING UP
The two halves of the suit are locked together. Helmet and gloves are added and locked in place. Then the pressure inside the suit is adjusted.

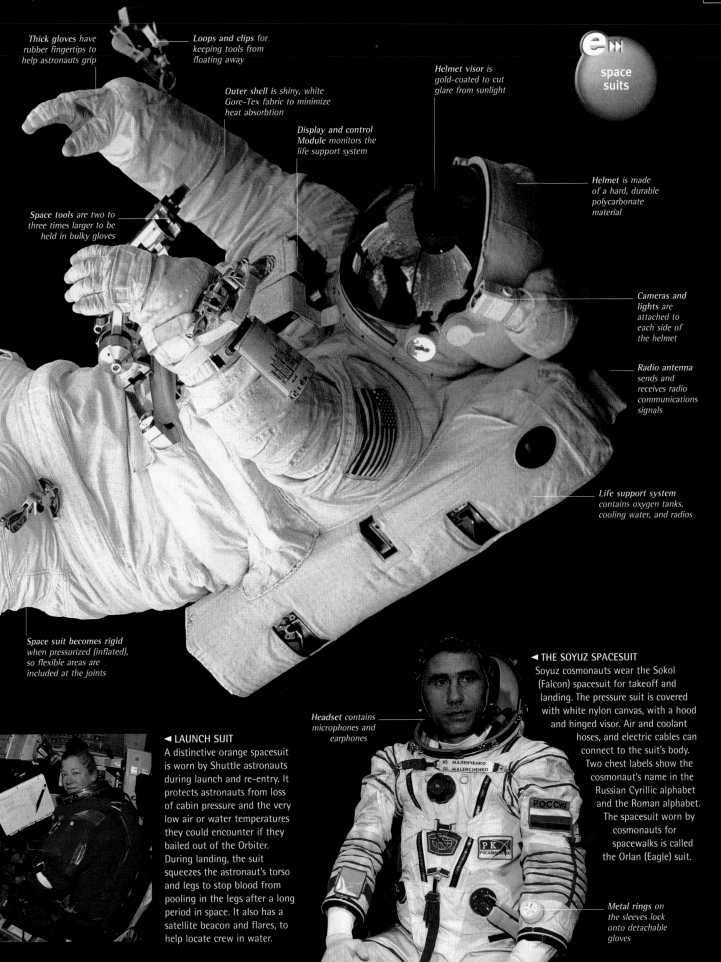

space suits

Thick gloves have rubber fingertips to help astronauts grip

Loops and clips for keeping tools from floating away

Outer shell is shiny, white Gore-Tex fabric to minimize heat absorbtion

Display and control Module monitors the life support system

Helmet visor is gold-coated to cut glare from sunlight

Space tools are two to three times larger to be held in bulky gloves

Helmet is made of a hard, durable polycarbonate material

Cameras and lights are attached to each side of the helmet

Radio antenna sends and receives radio communications signals

Life support system contains oxygen tanks, cooling water, and radios

Space suit becomes rigid when pressurized (inflated), so flexible areas are included at the joints

Headset contains microphones and earphones

◄ LAUNCH SUIT

A distinctive orange spacesuit is worn by Shuttle astronauts during launch and re-entry. It protects astronauts from loss of cabin pressure and the very low air or water temperatures they could encounter if they bailed out of the Orbiter. During landing, the suit squeezes the astronaut's torso and legs to stop blood from pooling in the legs after a long period in space. It also has a satellite beacon and flares, to help locate crew in water.

◄ THE SOYUZ SPACESUIT

Soyuz cosmonauts wear the Sokol (Falcon) spacesuit for takeoff and landing. The pressure suit is covered with white nylon canvas, with a hood and hinged visor. Air and coolant hoses, and electric cables can connect to the suit's body. Two chest labels show the cosmonaut's name in the Russian Cyrillic alphabet and the Roman alphabet. The spacesuit worn by cosmonauts for spacewalks is called the Orlan (Eagle) suit.

Metal rings on the sleeves lock onto detachable gloves

TRAINING FOR SPACE

When a space agency invites applications from people who want to be astronauts, thousands of people reply. Only one in 200 is accepted. After an initial year's basic training, the successful candidates become astronauts, but they may have to wait several years before going into space. During that time, they continue taking training courses. When they are allocated a mission, they begin intensive training for that specific mission, often using simulators—mock-ups of the craft or equipment they will have to use in space. Crews often say a real mission is easy compared to their training sessions in simulators.

training

Astronaut floats as if weightless

◄ **FLIGHT TRAINING**
Pilot astronauts keep their flying skills up to scratch by flying NASA's T-38 jets regularly during training. The T-38 is a two-seat training jet. Mission and payload specialists fly in the back seat to get experience of using navigation and communications systems. The Shuttle lands without engine power, so the pilot has only one chance to land it. Pilot astronauts practice landing in simulators and in the Shuttle Training Aircraft, a converted Gulfstream business jet.

Eyepieces display a computer-generated view of inside a craft

Gloves sense hand positions

VOMIT COMET ►
An astronaut can experience weightlessness without having to go into space, by using an aircraft known as the Vomit Comet! The KC-135 climbs steeply upward and then dives, over and over again. As it tips over the top of each climb, the plane and everything inside is in free fall (moving around without restraint), so everyone inside becomes weightless for up to 25 seconds. It can also simulate lunar and Martian gravity.

◄ **VIRTUAL SPACE**
This astronaut is using a Virtual Reality (VR) training system. VR is used to train astronauts without having to use a simulator. The astronaut sees a computer-generated version of equipment displayed on screens in front of his eyes. He might see part of the ISS or the Shuttle payload bay. He can move around in the virtual space and pick up virtual objects and move them around, because his gloves have sensors linked to the screens.

◄ UNDERWATER TRAINING

NASA's Neutral Buoyancy Laboratory is one of the world's largest swimming pools. It's 202 ft (31 m) long, 102 ft (31 m) wide, and 40 ft (12.5 m) deep, and contains 6 million gallons (20 million liters) of water. It's big enough to hold a full-size mock-up of the Shuttle payload bay. Astronauts use the tank to train for EVAs (spacewalks). The buoyancy of the water lets them float as if they were in space.

Full-size equipment is used in the training tank

Air bags make equipment float as if weightless

Video cameras record progress in the tank

Divers prepare equipment and act as lifeguards

ASTRONAUT SELECTION AND TRAINING DATA

Career backgrounds: Three types of astronauts take part in space missions—pilots, mission specialists, and payload specialists

Pilot astronauts: The commander and pilot—the astronauts who fly the craft. They must have at least 1,000 hours' experience of flying jet aircraft.

Mission specialists: Coordinate all onboard operations, perform spacewalks, and handle the payload.

Payload specialists: Chosen from scientists or engineers outside NASA to carry out particular experiments or operate specific payloads.

Numbers: NASA takes 20-30 new candidates every two years.

Selection: The process takes about eight months and includes interviews, medical examinations, and orientation tests.

Training: There is a minimum of two years' training before they are assigned a flight. Then, they train for up to a year for that mission.

Height: Candidates are usually between 64 and 76 in (160 cm and 185 cm) tall.

Education: Most astronauts have an advanced (Master's) degree.

▲ SCIENTIST ASTRONAUTS

Until 1972, all astronauts were pilots. They were trained to carry out specific scientific experiments for their missions. In 1972, the Apollo 17 lunar module pilot was Dr Harrison Schmitt (above), a trained geologist. Schmitt conducted tests to find out if the Moon was volcanically active. Since then, astronauts have come from a variety of backgrounds, among them many highly trained scientists who are assigned missions because of the experiments that will be taking place on board.

FLIGHT SIMULATORS ▼

Soyuz crews train for missions in the Soyuz cockpit simulator in Star City—the Russian space training center, near Moscow. Pilot astronauts practice their missions hundreds of times in simulators, which have identical controls and displays to those in the spacecraft. US Space Shuttle crews train in the Shuttle Mission Simulator in Houston, where they can practice launch, ascent, and docking. A straight up 90° tilt simulates acceleration and takeoff.

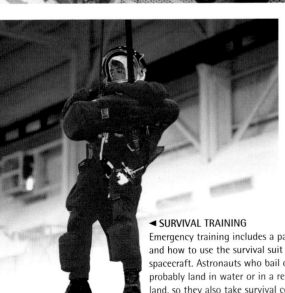

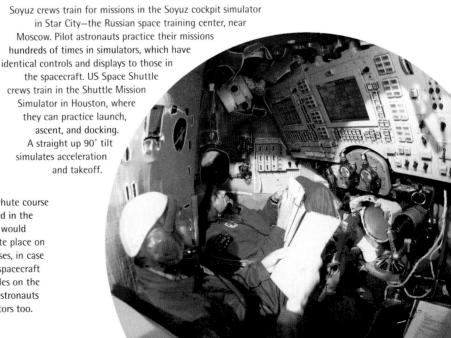

◄ SURVIVAL TRAINING

Emergency training includes a parachute course and how to use the survival suit used in the spacecraft. Astronauts who bail out would probably land in water or in a remote place on land, so they also take survival courses, in case they are marooned for days. Soyuz spacecraft are used as emergency escape vehicles on the International Space Station, so US astronauts visit Russia to train in Soyuz simulators too.

SPACE RESCUE

Spacecraft designers and mission planners work hard to make space missions as safe as possible. However, rockets are so powerful, fuel is so explosive, and spacecraft are such complex machines that accidents still happen. Apollo 13 was launched at 13:13 Houston time on April 11, 1970. On April 13, 205,000 miles (330,000 km) from Earth, the crew heard a bang. An oxygen tank had exploded. The spacecraft quickly lost power and oxygen. Engineers, scientists, and astronauts fought for four days to bring the spacecraft home.

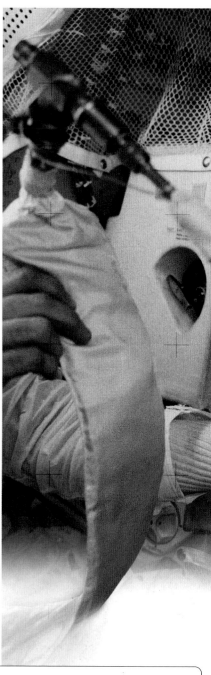

A SOLUTION FROM HOUSTON ▶
Mission control instructed the Apollo 13 crew to power down the command module, to save it for re-entry, and move into the lunar module (LM). With three astronauts instead of the two it was designed for, the LM's chemical air scrubber could not cope. Spare filter cartridges from the command module would not fit the LM's air filters. Engineers on Earth had to design something to take carbon dioxide out of the air using only items the astronauts had with them.

"Houston, we've had a problem"

Jack Swigert, command module pilot

A MAKESHIFT REPAIR ▶
Conditions in the lunar module were cramped, cold, and uncomfortable. It was equipped to support two men for less than 50 hours. The three Apollo 13 astronauts would be inside for at least 84 hours. The amount of carbon dioxide in the air, from the crew breathing out, started rising. Following step-by-step instructions from ground control, John Swigert (far right) and James Lovell had to make an air filter using spare cartridges, a plastic bag, an air hose from a spacesuit, and tape. It worked.

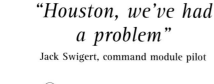

THE ROUTE HOME

Mission controllers debated whether to turn Apollo 13 around and bring it home or let it continue around the Moon. They decided that firing the service module's engine to come home was too risky. Sending the spacecraft around the Moon was also risky as it had only half the electrical power it needed for the return journey. The craft continued to the Moon, using the lunar module's engine to put the craft back on course for Earth. This shows Apollo 13's route from takeoff at 000:00:00.

Apollo 13's flight path

(1) 004:01:00 (hours, mins, secs)
Command and service module docks with the lunar module on the way to the Moon.

(2) 030:40:49
A midcourse correction puts Apollo 13 on course for its Moon landing.

(3) 055:54:53
The crew hears a loud bang as an oxygen tank explodes. Two hours later, they enter the lunar module.

(4) 077:33:10
The spacecraft reappears from behind the Moon, 25 minutes after disappearing behind it.

(5) 105:18:28
The lunar module engine is fired for 14 seconds to fine-tune the spacecraft's course.

(6) 138:01:48
The wrecked service module is jettisoned. The crew see, and photograph, the damage for the first time.

(7) 140:10:00
The command module is powered up for re-entry into the Earth's atmosphere.

(8) 141:30:00
The lunar module is discarded and the command module begins its journey through the atmosphere.

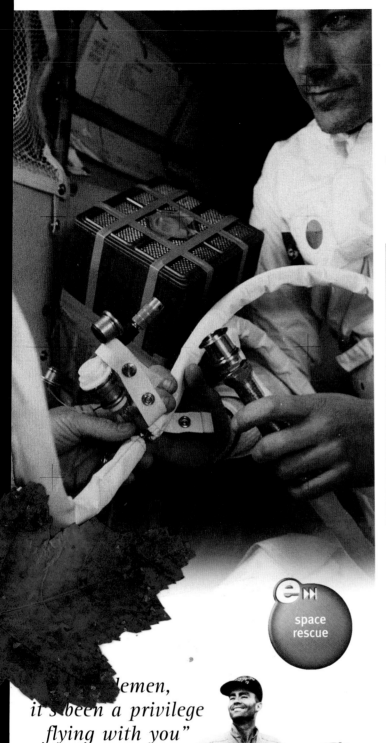

DAMAGE REPORT ▶
About five hours before splashdown, Jack Swigert threw the SM JETT switch to jettison the service module. As it floated away, the crew peered through the command module windows to watch it go. They could hardly believe their eyes when they spotted the damage. One whole equipment bay, from the engine bell at the bottom all the way to the top, had been blasted out by the explosion. Shreds of insulation material and tangled wiring trailed from the mangled metalwork.

▲ SPLASHDOWN
As the command module re-entered Earth's atmosphere, the usual four-minute radio blackout began. Controllers hoped the command module was undamaged or the crew would not survive. After four minutes, they called the crew. After 33 tense seconds, they answered. Minutes later, the command module landed. The crew was flown to safety and the command module was hoisted out of the sea.

space rescue

> *lemen,*
> *it's been a privilege*
> *flying with you"*
> James Lovell

RETURN TO EARTH ▶
Lovell, Swigert, and Fred Haise were cheered by sailors as they stepped from the recovery helicopter onto the *USS Iwo Jima*'s deck. Below decks they were given medical examinations. Haise was suffering from a kidney infection and a high fever caused by the freezing conditions and shortage of water in the spacecraft. All three astronauts were dehydrated, tired, and they had lost weight. Lovell lost more than 13.2 lb (6 kg) in six days.

INVESTIGATION TECHNIQUES

If a spacecraft fails in space, investigators may never know the cause. If it fails in the atmosphere, the wreckage is studied closely for clues.

The Space Shuttle Orbiter Columbia broke up while re-entering the atmosphere on February 1, 2003. Wreckage fell over 27,800 sq miles (72,000 km^2) of the US. Every piece found was gathered and brought to the Kennedy Space Center, where it was laid out on a hangar floor. Investigators also studied data received from the Orbiter, a film of the launch, and images from space. They concluded that insulation falling from the external tank had damaged Columbia's left wing, causing the Orbiter to break up during re-entry. Discovering the cause means that a similar accident can be prevented in the future.

Hexagonal body
with two solar
panels attached

Ground link dish used
for communications
with ground station

Radio dish is 16 ft
(4.9 m) wide and can
be steered to track
other spacecraft

◀ **RELAY SATELLITE**
A network of Tracking and Data Relay Satellites (TDRS)
circles Earth, providing radio communication
between ground stations and spacecraft in
Earth orbit. The Space Shuttle, International
Space Station, military satellites, and science
satellites communicate through the TDRS
system. Each satellite measures up to 57 ft
(17.4 m) across and bristles with radio antennae.

SPACE COMMUNICATION

Reliable radio communication is vital for spaceflight.
Ground controllers need to monitor a spacecraft's
operation and transmit commands to it. They need to talk
to astronauts in manned craft and during space walks. In
the early days of spaceflight, ground controllers could
communicate with a spacecraft in Earth orbit only when
it was in sight of a ground station. When it disappeared
below the horizon, contact was lost. Now, a network of
satellites around the world keeps ground controllers in
constant communication with orbiting craft.

A 3-ft (90-cm)
parabolic antenna
dish operates
using microwaves

Radio
communications
system is housed in
front part of Orbiter

Communications
system is attached
to the backpack

Microphones and
earphones in
headset

Helmet contains air,
allowing astronaut to
speak into microphone
as well as breathe

◀ **SPACE WALKING AND TALKING**
During a space walk outside the Space
Shuttle Orbiter, astronauts keep in
touch by radio. The headset inside
the helmet has two microphones
and earphones. Cables from
these and from biomedical
sensors pass through the
suit to a communications
system attached to the
backpack (biomedical sensors
are small devices that monitor
the astronaut's heartbeat and
other body processes). The astronaut
controls the system using switches on
the control box on the space suit's chest.

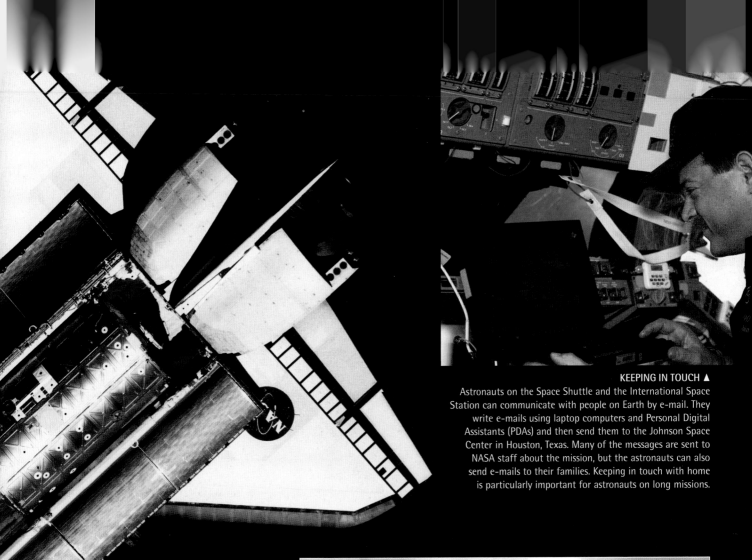

KEEPING IN TOUCH ▲

Astronauts on the Space Shuttle and the International Space Station can communicate with people on Earth by e-mail. They write e-mails using laptop computers and Personal Digital Assistants (PDAs) and then send them to the Johnson Space Center in Houston, Texas. Many of the messages are sent to NASA staff about the mission, but the astronauts can also send e-mails to their families. Keeping in touch with home is particularly important for astronauts on long missions.

◄ ORBITER COMMUNICATIONS

The Space Shuttle Orbiter has four separate radio communications systems. Three of them carry voice, engineering data, and science data. One of these also handles communications with astronauts outside the Orbiter. The fourth communications system is a high-bandwidth one that carries television pictures. Inside the Orbiter, astronauts connect to the communications system by plugging their headset into one of the audio terminals dotted around the crew compartment.

TWIN COMMUNICATORS ►

A ground station at White Sands, near Las Cruces, New Mexico, handles radio traffic to and from spacecraft orbiting Earth. The traffic passes to and from the spacecraft via Tracking and Data Relay satellites. The White Sands ground station houses two almost identical terminals. The system was developed because one ground station and a network of satellites provides a better service, and also costs less, than a worldwide network of ground stations.

space talk

SCIENCE IN SPACE

Scientific research has been carried out in space since the very first spaceflight. Radio signals from Sputnik 1 were used to study how the atmosphere affects radio waves. Modern scientific satellites study the Earth from space and the Universe beyond. Science experiments are also carried out on manned space missions. Scientists use space experiments to remove the effect of gravity and learn more about materials, to understand living organisms better, and to study the effects of weightlessness on the human body.

Head houses a skull with a plastic brain

Radiation monitors attached to head and torso

Skin made from fireproof material

▲ CRYSTALS GROWN IN SPACE

Crystals are used in computers, cameras, DVD players, and a variety of scientific instruments, as well as in medical research. Crystals grown on Earth are distorted by gravity—the growing crystals are pulled against the walls of their container. Crystals grown in space tend to be larger and better quality because they can spread out freely. Studying crystal growth in space is leading to ways of growing better-quality crystals on Earth.

science in space

FLAMES IN SPACE ▶

Flames look very different in space. Without gravity, the hot gases do not rise to form the familiar teardrop shape of a flame on Earth. In space, a flame spreads out in all directions. As it burns more slowly and evenly, there are no color variations. Flames have been studied in experiments carried out in the Space Shuttle. The research helps engine manufacturers who want to develop new, cleaner-burning engines. Understanding how flames behave is also important in developing ways of fighting fires in spacecraft.

FLAME ON EARTH IS ELONGATED WITH A YELLOW TIP

SPACE FLAME IS SPHERICAL AND BLUE

▲ PHANTOM TORSO

The Phantom Torso is a model of a human body used in radiation research in the International Space Station. The Earth's atmosphere blocks some of the Sun's radiation. When astronauts go into space, they lose the atmosphere's protection. Scientists are concerned about the radiation hazard. The Phantom Torso contains real bones and plastic organs packed with hundreds of sensors to measure radiation. The data produced will help scientists to predict the radiation doses humans would receive on long spaceflights.

◀ MICROGRAVITY GLOVEBOX

The International Space Station is equipped with a workstation for scientists called the Microgravity Science Glovebox. It is a sealed 56-gallon (255-liter) box where astronauts can do experiments without any risk of gases or liquids escaping into the rest of the spacecraft. Two glove-ports let astronauts reach inside and handle things without breaking the seal. Video cameras are linked to Earth so scientists here can monitor activities inside the box. The box is also equipped with its own laptop computer to control experiments and record results.

SPACELAB MISSIONS

Spacelab was an orbiting laboratory carried in the Shuttle's payload bay. There were 25 Spacelab missions, including:

Spacelab–1, 1983: 73 experiments included astronomy, life sciences, and material research.

Spacelab D1, 1985: Funded by Germany, tests included botany, biology, and crystal growing.

Astro 1, 1990: Ultra-violet and X-ray telescopes were used to observe the Universe.

SLS 1, 1991: First Spacelab mission dedicated solely to life sciences.

Spacelab J, 1992: Crew brought back the first animal embryos fertilized and developed in space.

Neurolab, 1998: Last mission, it studied the effects of microgravity on the nervous system.

Blacked-out goggles minimize distractions

Cable carries data on the astronaut's head position to a computer

Tape recorder records astronaut's comments

Headphones block distracting noises

▲ EXPERIMENTING ON ASTRONAUTS

Space Shuttle payload specialist Martin Fettman was spun on a rotating chair by mission specialist Rhea Seddon to study the effect on his balance. His headset sensed his head movements, so they could be compared to similar experiments on Earth. They worked inside Spacelab SLS-2, a laboratory carried in the Shuttle's payload bay in 1993. It was one of many experiments carried out to study the effects of weightlessness on the human body. The whole mission was dedicated to life sciences research.

TETHERED SATELLITES ▶

Satellites tethered to the Shuttle have been used to try to generate electricity. The satellite collects data for science experiments and houses thrusters that keep the tether tight. The action of the tether cutting through the Earth's magnetic field produces an electric current. This may lead to a new way of generating electricity for space stations. On the first experiment, the tether jammed after only 840 feet (256 m) of the 12 miles (20 km) had been unreeled. On the second, it broke and the satellite flew away!

▲ EXPERIMENTS ON THE MOON

All the Apollo missions took experiments to the Moon. They collected data about moonquakes, magnetism, heat flow through the surface, and the solar wind. Instruments left behind continued to send back data for decades. Three reflectors left were hit by laser beams fired from Earth—this helped scientists to discover that the average distance between the centers of the Earth and the Moon is 239,000 miles (385,000 km), and that the Moon is receding from Earth at about 1.5 in (3.8 cm) a year.

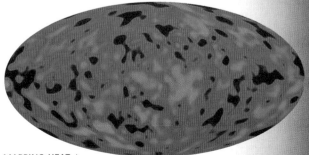

MAPPING HEAT ▲

The Cosmic Background Explorer (COBE) satellite was launched in 1990 to map the heat given out soon after the Universe began. This cosmic background radiation had first been detected in 1965, but COBE made a very accurate map of it. COBE's instruments were sensitive enough to detect changes of only a few millionths of a degree. The different colors in the map are tiny variations in energy intensity. Scientists think these ripples became the matter that formed the stars and galaxies.

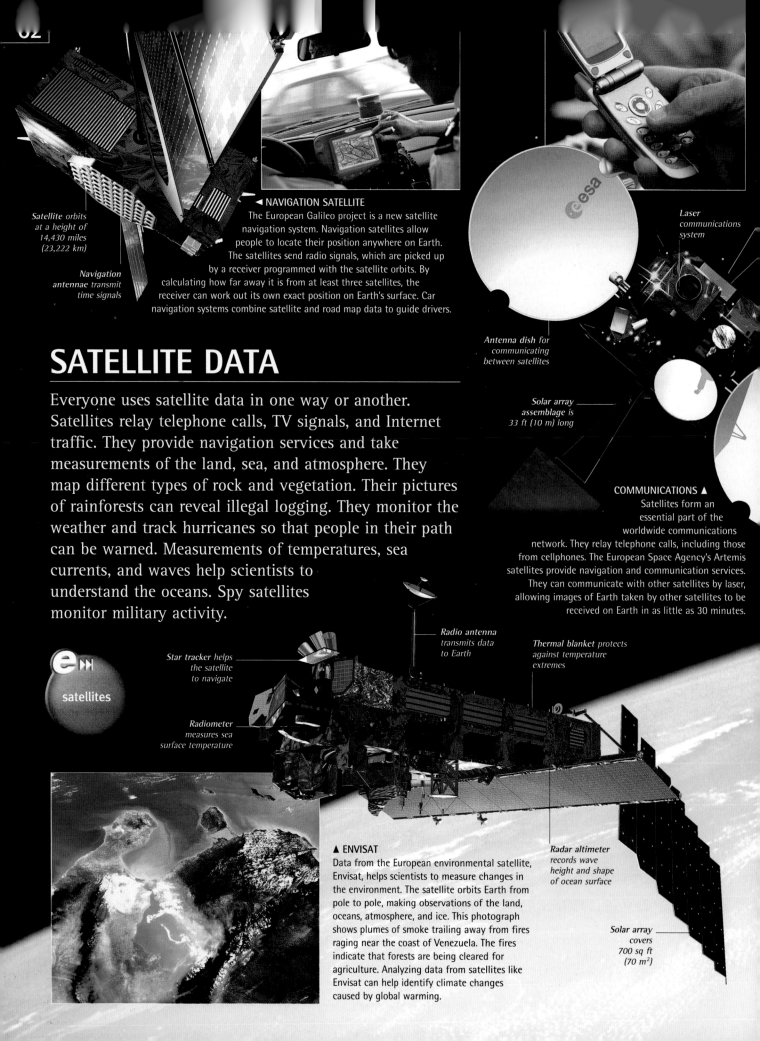

Satellite orbits at a height of 14,430 miles (23,222 km)

Navigation antennae transmit time signals

◄ **NAVIGATION SATELLITE**
The European Galileo project is a new satellite navigation system. Navigation satellites allow people to locate their position anywhere on Earth. The satellites send radio signals, which are picked up by a receiver programmed with the satellite orbits. By calculating how far away it is from at least three satellites, the receiver can work out its own exact position on Earth's surface. Car navigation systems combine satellite and road map data to guide drivers.

Laser communications system

Antenna dish for communicating between satellites

Solar array assemblage is 33 ft (10 m) long

SATELLITE DATA

Everyone uses satellite data in one way or another. Satellites relay telephone calls, TV signals, and Internet traffic. They provide navigation services and take measurements of the land, sea, and atmosphere. They map different types of rock and vegetation. Their pictures of rainforests can reveal illegal logging. They monitor the weather and track hurricanes so that people in their path can be warned. Measurements of temperatures, sea currents, and waves help scientists to understand the oceans. Spy satellites monitor military activity.

COMMUNICATIONS ▲
Satellites form an essential part of the worldwide communications network. They relay telephone calls, including those from cellphones. The European Space Agency's Artemis satellites provide navigation and communication services. They can communicate with other satellites by laser, allowing images of Earth taken by other satellites to be received on Earth in as little as 30 minutes.

satellites

Star tracker helps the satellite to navigate

Radiometer measures sea surface temperature

Radio antenna transmits data to Earth

Thermal blanket protects against temperature extremes

Radar altimeter records wave height and shape of ocean surface

▲ **ENVISAT**
Data from the European environmental satellite, Envisat, helps scientists to measure changes in the environment. The satellite orbits Earth from pole to pole, making observations of the land, oceans, atmosphere, and ice. This photograph shows plumes of smoke trailing away from fires raging near the coast of Venezuela. The fires indicate that forests are being cleared for agriculture. Analyzing data from satellites like Envisat can help identify climate changes caused by global warming.

Solar array covers 700 sq ft (70 m²)

Radio antennae
can transmit to the
whole Earth or to
small areas

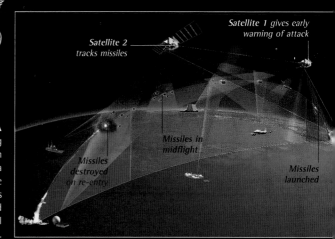

Satellite 2
tracks missiles

Satellite 1 gives early
warning of attack

Missiles in
midflight

Missiles
destroyed
on re-entry

Missiles
launched

MILITARY SATELLITES ▲

Some countries use satellites for spying
and defense. Satellites like the one shown
above are used by US military forces for secret data
communications. The US Space Tracking and Surveillance
System (right) is due to start working in 2006-2007. It includes
satellites that will spot missiles on launch, track their flights, and
relay information to ground-based defense systems. These will
destroy the missiles when they re-enter the atmosphere.

Solar panel
supplies electricity

Payload includes
cameras and
infrared sensors

Solar sail balances
the spacecraft

Infrared sensors
create images by
detecting heat

PHOTOGRAPHING THE PLANET ▶

Earth resources satellites take photographs for all
sorts of purposes, from making maps to monitoring
land usage. Landsat 7 takes detailed pictures of
strips of ground 115 mile (183 km) wide. Its
cameras can detect both visible and infrared
light. The photograph shows the Capitol
building in Washington D.C. It was
made by using a computer to
combine photographic data from
several different satellites.

Solar array provides
1.5 kw of electrical
power for the
satellite

WEATHER SATELLITE ▶

The Geostationary Operational Environmental Satellite (GOES),
like many other weather and environmental satellites, is in a
geostationary orbit, which means it always looks down on the
same part of Earth. The false-color infrared image above, taken by
GOES, shows a hurricane over the Caribbean. An infrared camera
detects heat rather than light so the image shows information about
temperature variation that is not visible in normal photographs.

Solar array rotates
to track the Sun

HUBBLE SPACE TELESCOPE

In April 1990, a telescope the size of a large bus was launched into Earth orbit. It was named the Hubble Space Telescope (HST), after the American astronomer Edwin Hubble. Soon after it was launched, astronomers found that it would not produce a sharp image. An error of just one-fiftieth the width of a human hair had been made in the manufacture of the telescope's main mirror. In 1993, the Space Shuttle returned to the telescope and astronauts fixed the problem. Since then, the telescope has taken thousands of spectacular photographs of the Universe.

HUBBLE DATA
Length: 44 ft (13.2 m)
Diameter: 14 ft (4.2 m) (without solar arrays) 40 ft (12.0 m) (with solar arrays)
Solar arrays: 40 x 9 ft (12.0 x 2.8 m)
Mass: 11.1 tons
Orbit: 355 miles (569 km) above Earth
Speed: 17,500 mph (28,000 kph)

▼ HUBBLE IN OPERATION
Light enters the narrow end of the telescope and travels down to the primary mirror. It then bounces back up to a small secondary mirror and finally passes through a hole in the primary mirror to arrive at an instrument package. This contains cameras that can photograph stars, objects in our solar system, and galaxies. One camera, the Faint Object Camera, can detect objects five times fainter than the dimmest object visible with a telescope on Earth.

▲ COMMANDING HUBBLE
The telescope is controlled from the Space Science Institute in Baltimore, Maryland. Its flight operations team sends commands that turn it to point in the right direction. To make sharp images, it must stay pointed in one direction with extreme accuracy, equivalent to focusing on a dot the width of a human hair at a distance of 1 mile (1.6 km). Hubble operates all day, every day. It transmits enough data to fill a dozen DVDs every week.

Hubble

High-gain antenna receives commands from Earth

Secondary mirror has a diameter of 12 in (30 cm)

Primary (main) mirror is 8 ft (2.4 m) in diameter

Solar array unfurls during deployment

Instrument module contains cameras and other instruments

◄ LAUNCHING HUBBLE
The Hubble Telescope was launched onboard the Space Shuttle Discovery on April 24, 1990. The Orbiter's robot arm gently lifted it out of the payload bay. The solar arrays were designed to unfurl automatically. The first one deployed successfully, but the second one stuck. Astronauts suited up in case they would have to fix the problem, but a second attempt to deploy the array succeeded.

Remote manipulator arm deploys Hubble

CHANDRA X-RAY IMAGE

HUBBLE OPTICAL IMAGE

VLA RADIO IMAGE

KPNO OPTICAL IMAGE

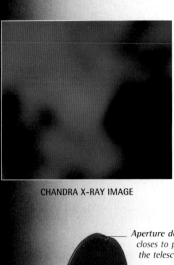

Aperture door closes to protect the telescope

Handrail for astronauts to hold while servicing the telescope

Magnetometer senses telescope's movement through Earth's magnetic field

Solar array contains 25,000 solar cells

High-gain antenna sends images and data to Earth

WORKING TOGETHER ▶
Images of one object made by different types of telescope, showing different features, can be combined to form a single image. This picture was created using optical images from the Hubble Telescope and the Kitt Peak National Observatory (KPNO), an image from the group of radio telescopes called the Very Large Array (VLA), and an image from the Chandra X-ray Observatory. It shows a galaxy, called C153, being ripped apart as it races through a cluster of other galaxies at 4.4 million mph (7 million kph).

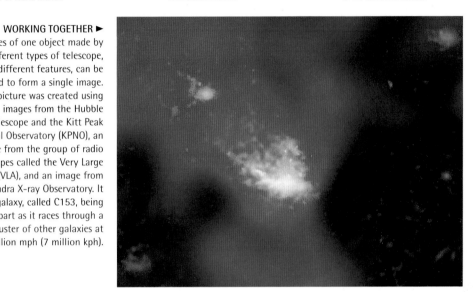

◀ SPITZER SPACE TELESCOPE
The Spitzer Space Telescope, formerly known as the Space Infrared Telescope Facility (SIRTF), was launched on August 25, 2003. It makes images from the heat given out by objects. It has to be in space to work, because most infrared heat rays are blocked by Earth's atmosphere. The telescope, which is 34 in (85 cm) wide, can see through clouds of dust and gas, and can reveal objects that are normally hidden from optical telescopes. It can also detect cool stars and planets orbiting other stars.

Sunshield keeps telescope cool

Optical telescope with 21-ft (6.5-m) diameter main mirror

JAMES WEBB TELESCOPE ▶
The James Webb Space Telescope (JWST) will continue Hubble's work from about the year 2011. Its mirror is more than twice the diameter of Hubble's. Large mirrors are hard to make, so the James Webb telescope's mirror is made from 18 smaller segments. It will be placed about 1 million miles (1.5 million km) from Earth. A sunshield will stop solar radiation from overheating the telescope, which will operate at a temperature of about -400°F (-240°C).

HUBBLE GALLERY

The Hubble Space Telescope has given astronomers an unimaginable view of the Universe. Some of the most beautiful images captured by the telescope show objects called planetary nebulae. These are vast clouds of gas and dust thrown off by dying stars. Hubble has also pictured colliding galaxies, jets of matter speeding through space, and some of the most distant galaxies ever seen.

Hubble

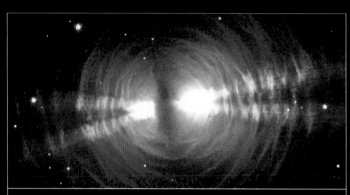

EGG NEBULA
Dust ripples outward from an ageing star 3,000 light years away. One light year equals 5.9 million million miles (9.5 million million km), the distance light travels in a year. False colors have been added to show how light is reflected by the smoke-sized bits of dust.

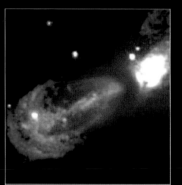

ROTTEN EGG NEBULA
The Calabash Nebula is also called the Rotten Egg, because it contains sulfur, which smells like rotten eggs!

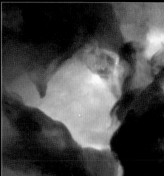

TORNADOES IN THE LAGOON NEBULA
This funnel-like structure is a pair of gas clouds spiraling around a central hot star, 5,000 light-years away.

TWIN JET NEBULA
Hubble captures twin jets made from gas streaming away from a central star at 186 miles (300 km) per second.

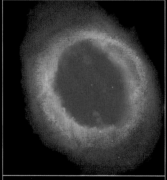

RING NEBULA
In one of the most famous planetary nebulae, the Ring Nebula, a dying star floats in a blue haze of hot gas.

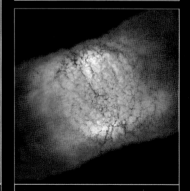

CAT'S EYE NEBULA
This 1,000-year-old planetary nebula features shells, jets, and knots of gas surrounding one or two dying stars.

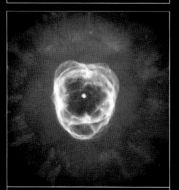

ESKIMO NEBULA
This dying, sunlike star is known as the Eskimo Nebula, because it resembles a face surrounded by a fur hood.

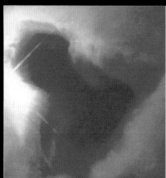

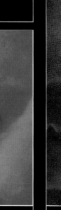

THE REFLECTION NEBULA
NGC 1999 is also called the Reflection Nebula, because dust around it reflects starlight, like fog around a street lamp.

EAGLE NEBULA
Hubble found these columns of cool hydrogen gas and dust where new stars are forming in the Eagle Nebula.

RETINA NEBULA
This rainbow of colors is a side view of a doughnut-shape of dust and gas thrown out by a dying star.

CYGNUS LOOP SUPERNOVA
Gas flies out from the explosion of a star, a supernova, 15,000 years ago. A supernova is brighter than a galaxy.

A SWARM OF ANCIENT STARS
This swarm of stars, known as NGC 6093, or M80, is one of the densest clusters in our galaxy, the Milky Way.

THE QUINTUPLET CLUSTER
Hubble zoomed in on this cluster of young stars, close to the center of our galaxy, but hidden from Earth by dust.

X MARKS THE BLACK HOLE
An "X" visible at the center of nearby spiral galaxy M51 marks a black hole with a mass equal to a million Suns.

EXPANDING HALO
This shell-like shape is an expanding ball of gas and dust illuminated by a red supergiant star, V838 Monocerotis.

THE LIFE CYCLE OF STARS
The giant nebula, NGC 3603, includes stars of all ages, from newly formed stars at the center to old supergiants.

LOOKING INTO THE PAST
These are among the oldest galaxies seen by Hubble, forming a few hundred million years after the Big Bang.

JUPITER
Hubble has taken beautiful images of the planets in our solar system. This one focuses on Jupiter's atmosphere.

STAR FORMATION
Long streaks of gas whirling around the galaxy NGC 3079 were probably caused by a burst of star formation.

STAR NURSERY
Hubble pinpointed an area of activity in one arm of the spiral galaxy M33, a region where new stars are forming.

BIRTH OF A STAR
The dwarf galaxy, NGC 1569, is a hotbed of star formation, producing clusters of brilliant blue young stars.

SPINNING TADPOLE
The blue stars in this spiral galaxy are massive stars, 10 times hotter and a million times brighter than our Sun.

A MEETING OF GALAXIES
These two galaxies, NGC 2207 (left) and IC 2163, are spinning into each other. The stronger gravitational pull of the larger galaxy has distorted its smaller partner, sending stars and gas flying out into streamers 100,000 light years long.

A DUSTY SPIRAL
The arms of this majestic spiral galaxy are rich in clouds of dust and glowing hydrogen gas emitted by young stars.

SPACE JUNK

Wherever rockets and spacecraft go, they leave pieces of debris, or junk, behind. This space junk ranges from microscopic specks of paint and metal to whole spacecraft. Space debris is a problem, because it can collide with working satellites and manned spacecraft. Traveling at speeds of 17,500 mph (28,000 kph), even pea-sized pieces can cause serious damage. The first known collision happened in July 1996 when the French Cerise satellite collided with debris and tumbled off course. Most of the debris orbiting Earth came from exploding rockets.

space junk

▲ A NEEDLE IN THE HAYSTACK

Space junk is tracked by radar. NASA's main source of data on pieces of ½-12 in (1-30 cm) across is the Haystack X-Band radar operated by the Massachusetts Institute of Technology. It can spot an object the size of a pea over 373 miles (600 km) away, so craft in the area can be alerted. Scanners like Haystack have shown that most debris orbits within 1,242 miles (2,000 km) of Earth, with thick bands at 497 miles (800 km), 621 miles (1,000 km), and 932 miles (1,500 km).

Each dot is a piece of space junk orbiting the Earth

Moon-buggy's metal parts will not rust in space

Soft fabrics in the seats are most likely to perish

Titanium wheel treads will not corrode

▲ MOON SCRAP

The Moon is littered with junk from Earth. There are space probes that crashed or landed there before the manned landings. The descent stages of six Apollo lunar modules still stand on the surface. Three of them have had lunar rovers parked beside them since they were abandoned in the 1970s. Without air or moisture, they will not rust or rot. The only thing stopping the lunar rovers from being driven away, now or in a thousand years, is a dead battery!

Debris travels at speeds of about 18,000 mph (29,000 kph)

More than 100,000 pieces of debris are ½-12 in (1-30 cm) across

JUNK IN ORBIT ▶

Earth is surrounded by space debris. Pieces in the lowest orbits, below 373 miles (600 km), spiral back into the atmosphere within a few years. At a height of about 497 miles (800 km), debris can stay in orbit for decades. Debris more than 621 miles (1,000 km) above Earth may stay in orbit for a century or more. Nothing can be done about debris in orbit, but space-faring nations have introduced guidelines to minimize orbital debris in the future.

SKYLAB FALLS TO EARTH ▶

The largest pieces of junk are old space stations. When they have ended their working life, they re-enter the atmosphere. The last of three crews left the US space station Skylab on February 8, 1974. Its orbit gradually decayed (lowered) until it re-entered the atmosphere on July 11, 1979. Skylab was too big to burn up. Pieces as big as 1,000 lb (373 kg) landed in the Indian Ocean and Australia. In 2001, Russia's Mir space station shattered into 1,500 pieces 45 miles (72 km) above Earth before landing in the Pacific Ocean.

More than 11,000 pieces of debris are 4 in (10 cm) across or larger

BEYOND THE EARTH ▶

Apollo 17's lunar module travels to the Moon, visible inside the S-IVB rocket (top). The particles surrounding it are paint and insulation flakes shed when the S-IVB, the third stage, separated from the Saturn V rocket. Once it had delivered the astronauts into orbit, the useless S-IVB was put on course to hit the Moon to test the seisometers (shock wave detectors) left there. Debris from earlier discarded spacecraft that traveled to the Moon now orbits the Sun.

◀ MICRO-TROUBLE

Microscopic particles of debris cause damage because of their high speed. This ⅙ in (4 mm) pit was made in a Space Shuttle window by a flake of paint measuring less than ¹⁄₅₅ in (0.5 mm)! After 15 years in space, the Mir space station was covered with dents and pits. The International Space Station is more heavily shielded than any other spacecraft, to protect it from dust and debris.

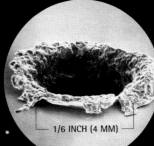

1/6 INCH (4 MM)

Energy flash on the target inside a NASA test chamber

Tens of millions of junk particles are smaller than ½ in (1 cm) across

IMPACT STUDIES ▶

This flash was produced by an object hitting a solid surface at 17,500 mph (28,000 kph). Experiments like this, at NASA's Hypervelocity Ballistics Range in California, simulate what happens to a spacecraft hit by a piece of debris. In 1985, a satellite was deliberately smashed to pieces in orbit to see what would happen to the debris. The impact produced 285 pieces, which were each tracked. By January 1998, all but eight had re-entered the atmosphere.

GOING TO THE PLANETS

Space probes have been exploring the solar system since the early 1960s. They have flown past, orbited, crashed into, landed on, or driven across every planet except Pluto. They bristle with instruments to learn as much as possible about our planetary neighbors. Probes sent to the outer planets are also equipped with nuclear power generators, because there is too little sunlight to use solar panels. These robotic explorers have sent back thousands of stunning images and revealed many secrets.

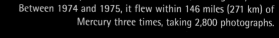

Mariner 10 revealed Mercury's crater-scarred surface

▲ MARINER REACHES MERCURY

Mariner 10 gave scientists their first close-up view of Mercury. Launched in 1973, it was the first probe to visit two planets. The gravitational pull of Venus was used to swing the 1,109 lb (503 kg) probe around and propel it toward Mercury. Mariner 10 was the first probe to use this maneuver, called gravity assist. Between 1974 and 1975, it flew within 146 miles (271 km) of Mercury three times, taking 2,800 photographs.

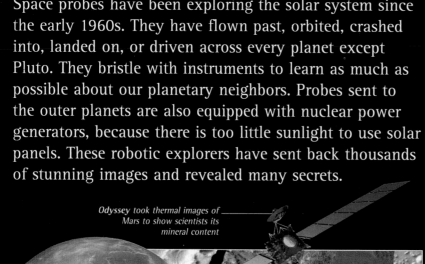

Odyssey took thermal images of Mars to show scientists its mineral content

◄ MARS

Mars has fascinated people for generations. In 1965, Mariner 4 took photographs looking for signs of life, but found none. Two Viking probes landed in 1976 and tested soil, but the results weren't clear. A tiny rover called Sojourner landed in 1997, sending back 550 images. In 2001, Odyssey entered Mars' orbit to study climate and geology. In 2004, two larger rovers, Spirit and Opportunity landed. Other probes have mapped its surface, still searching for life-forms.

Galileo photographed Jupiter and its moons, including Europa

◄ JUPITER

Jupiter is the solar system's biggest planet. More than 1,300 Earths would fit inside it. A vast storm, called the Great Red Spot, has been raging there for the past 300 years. Pioneer 10 took the first close-up pictures of Jupiter in 1973. Pioneer 11 and two Voyager probes followed. In 1995, after a six-year flight, Galileo went into orbit around Jupiter and dropped a mini-probe into its atmosphere. It found that the gas giant is mostly hydrogen.

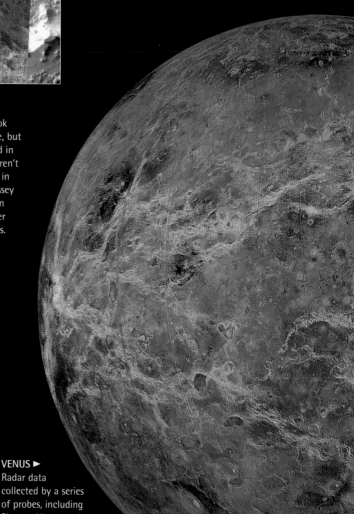

VENUS ►

Radar data collected by a series of probes, including Pioneer, Venus, and Magellan, was used to make this false-color image of Venus. The planet is hidden beneath a thick, poisonous atmosphere, but radar can see through it and map the surface. Computers use the data to create 3-D views (far right). The Soviet Venera 3 probe was the first to land on Venus in 1965.

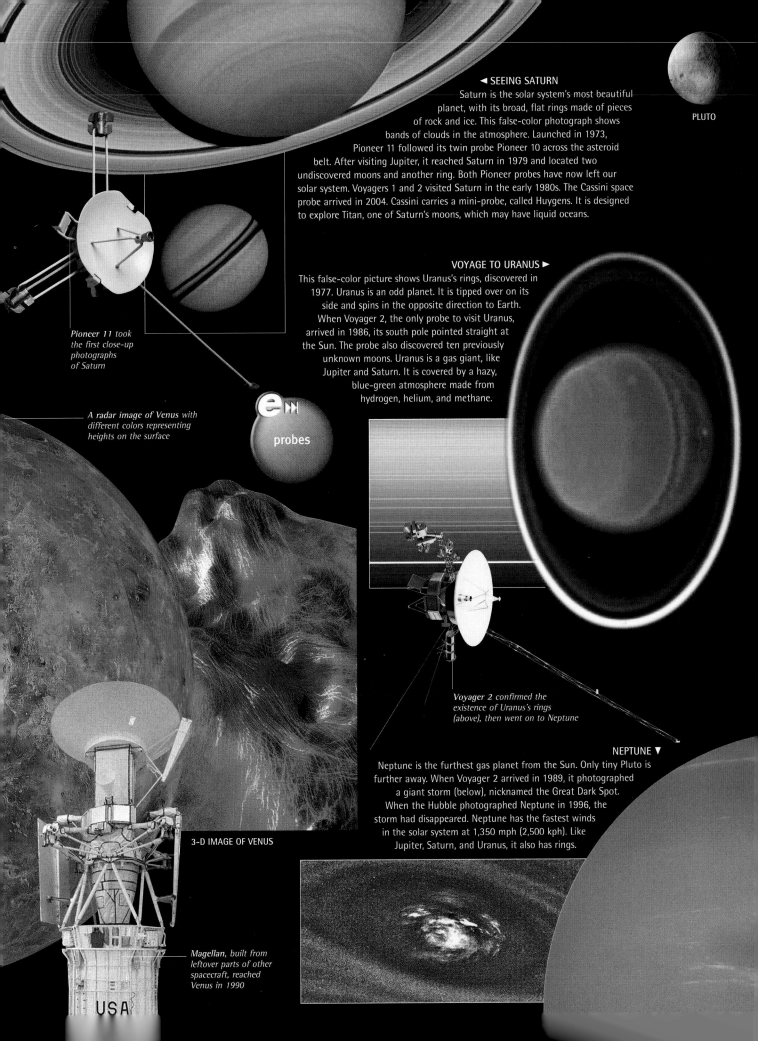

PLUTO

◄ SEEING SATURN

Saturn is the solar system's most beautiful planet, with its broad, flat rings made of pieces of rock and ice. This false-color photograph shows bands of clouds in the atmosphere. Launched in 1973, Pioneer 11 followed its twin probe Pioneer 10 across the asteroid belt. After visiting Jupiter, it reached Saturn in 1979 and located two undiscovered moons and another ring. Both Pioneer probes have now left our solar system. Voyagers 1 and 2 visited Saturn in the early 1980s. The Cassini space probe arrived in 2004. Cassini carries a mini-probe, called Huygens. It is designed to explore Titan, one of Saturn's moons, which may have liquid oceans.

Pioneer 11 took the first close-up photographs of Saturn

A radar image of Venus with different colors representing heights on the surface

e ▶▶

probes

VOYAGE TO URANUS ►

This false-color picture shows Uranus's rings, discovered in 1977. Uranus is an odd planet. It is tipped over on its side and spins in the opposite direction to Earth. When Voyager 2, the only probe to visit Uranus, arrived in 1986, its south pole pointed straight at the Sun. The probe also discovered ten previously unknown moons. Uranus is a gas giant, like Jupiter and Saturn. It is covered by a hazy, blue-green atmosphere made from hydrogen, helium, and methane.

Voyager 2 confirmed the existence of Uranus's rings (above), then went on to Neptune

3-D IMAGE OF VENUS

NEPTUNE ▼

Neptune is the furthest gas planet from the Sun. Only tiny Pluto is further away. When Voyager 2 arrived in 1989, it photographed a giant storm (below), nicknamed the Great Dark Spot. When the Hubble photographed Neptune in 1996, the storm had disappeared. Neptune has the fastest winds in the solar system at 1,350 mph (2,500 kph). Like Jupiter, Saturn, and Uranus, it also has rings.

Magellan, built from leftover parts of other spacecraft, reached Venus in 1990

USA

MISSION MARS

Two Mars Exploration Rovers (MER), called Spirit and Opportunity, landed on opposite sides of Mars in January 2004. As part of NASA's long-term Mars Exploration Program, their main aim was to seek evidence for the existence of water on Mars in the past. Spirit touched down in Gusev Crater and Opportunity landed in the Meridiani Planum. The landing sites were chosen because Gusev Crater may once have been a lake and Meridiani Planum has minerals that are normally associated with water.

ACIDALIA PLANITIA

METEORITE IMPACT CRATERS

LUNAE PLANUM   GANGES CHASMA

VALLES MARINERIS GIANT CANYON SYSTEM

SOLIS PLANUM

SWIRLING DUST STORM

RADIATION LEVELS ON MARS

These maps show radiation levels all over Mars. They are hundreds of times higher than on Earth. Astronauts should be able to survive a mission to Mars, but for now it is safer to send robots to explore.

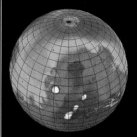
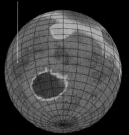

False-color map highlights radiation levels

In the US, the annual radiation dose is 1.5 millisievert (150 millirem) at sea level. Millirems and millisieverts are units of radiation dose.

KEY: annual radiation dose on Mars

| 20 rem/year | 22 | 24 | 26 | 28 | 30 |

◄ **HOSTILE ENVIRONMENT**
Mars is the most Earthlike of all the planets. It has polar ice caps, an atmosphere, weather and seasons, but it is still a very hostile environment compared to Earth. The Martian atmosphere is 100 times thinner than Earth's and made mainly from carbon dioxide. The Viking spacecraft that landed there in 1976 recorded night temperatures as low as -148°F (-100°C). The surface is dry and dusty. Winds sometimes whip up the fine dust into sand-storms that can rage at 249 mph (400 kph).

◄ **EVIDENCE OF WATER?**
Opportunity took this false-color photograph of a rock outcrop on Mars in an area called Shoemaker's Patio. It shows finely layered sediments, giving the rocks a striped appearance. Tiny round grains, nicknamed blueberries, are spread all over the rocks. These features, or concretions, are known to form in wet conditions. They may be strong evidence pointing to the existence of water in the past.

MARS DATA

Diameter at equator:	4,222 miles (6,794 km)
Average distance from Sun:	141.6 million miles (227.9 million km)
Year (time to orbit Sun):	687 days
Day (time to spin once):	24.62 hours
Mass:	0.11 x Earth's
Gravity:	0.38 x Earth's
Average temperature:	-81°F (-63°C)
Moons:	2 (Phobos and Deimos)

▲ **RUSTY RED PLANET**
This panoramic picture shows the part of the planet where the Spirit rover landed. Mars' dusty surface is red because it contains a lot of iron chemically combined with oxygen—rust! The shallow depression on the left of the rock-strewn area is a 656-foot (200-m) crater called Bonneville. The crater was probably caused by a massive meteorite slamming into the Martian surface. Mars has been repeatedly hit by meteorites, leaving a layer of debris over it.

LANDING ROVERS ON MARS

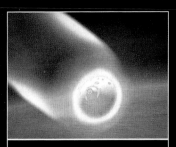

PLUNGING TO THE PLANET
The lander enters the atmosphere at nearly 12,428 mph (20,000 kph). Friction between the craft and the atmosphere heats it to 2,642°F (1,450°C). The atmosphere acts like a brake and slows the craft down.

RETRO-FIRE
About 29,526 ft (9,000 m) above Mars, a parachute is deployed. Twenty seconds later, the heat shield falls away. Air bags inflate to protect the lander. Then rockets fire and bring it to a halt 33 ft (10 m) above the surface.

TOUCHDOWN
The lander is released from the parachute and falls to the surface. It bounces and rolls for nearly a mile before it comes to a halt. Then it transmits its first radio signal to Earth to announce its arrival.

DRIVING AWAY
The air bags are deflated and the lander opens up to form a platform and ramps. The lander unfolds its solar panels to generate electricity. Then it is carefully steered down one of the ramps and onto the Martian surface.

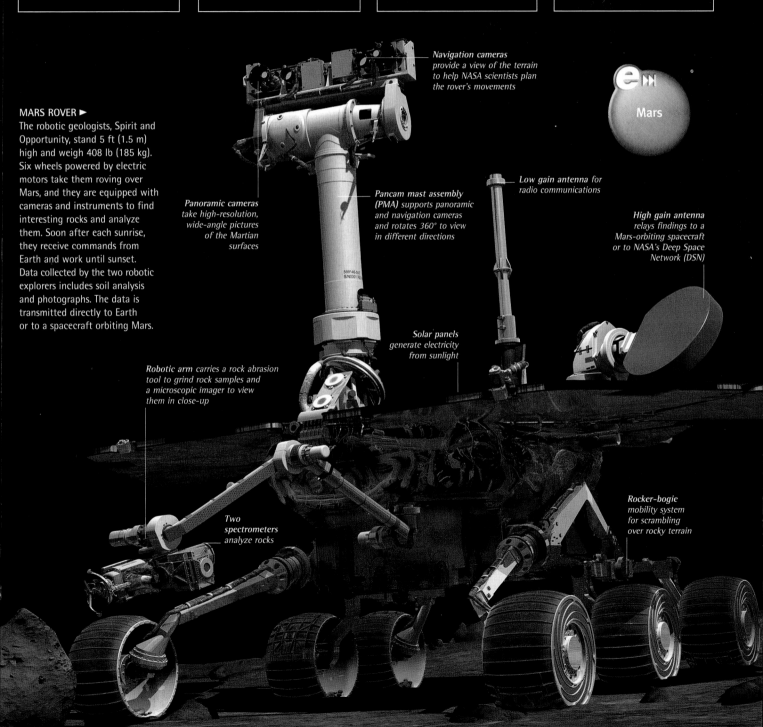

Navigation cameras provide a view of the terrain to help NASA scientists plan the rover's movements

MARS ROVER ►
The robotic geologists, Spirit and Opportunity, stand 5 ft (1.5 m) high and weigh 408 lb (185 kg). Six wheels powered by electric motors take them roving over Mars, and they are equipped with cameras and instruments to find interesting rocks and analyze them. Soon after each sunrise, they receive commands from Earth and work until sunset. Data collected by the two robotic explorers includes soil analysis and photographs. The data is transmitted directly to Earth or to a spacecraft orbiting Mars.

Panoramic cameras take high-resolution, wide-angle pictures of the Martian surfaces

Pancam mast assembly (PMA) supports panoramic and navigation cameras and rotates 360° to view in different directions

Low gain antenna for radio communications

High gain antenna relays findings to a Mars-orbiting spacecraft or to NASA's Deep Space Network (DSN)

Mars

Solar panels generate electricity from sunlight

Robotic arm carries a rock abrasion tool to grind rock samples and a microscopic imager to view them in close-up

Two spectrometers analyze rocks

Rocker-bogie mobility system for scrambling over rocky terrain

ASTEROID ALERT

The solar system formed from a cloud of gas and dust that collapsed in on itself about 4.5 billion years ago. Clumps of matter in the cloud attracted more matter onto them. The clumps collided and joined together, making bigger objects and eventually forming the planets. Asteroids are chunks of rock that did not form into planets and have survived to the present day. Most orbit the Sun between Mars and Jupiter, but collisions occasionally send one into a new orbit that may bring it closer to Earth, posing the risk of a disastrous impact.

DACTYL

IDA

◄ ASTEROID AND MOON
Asteroids are smaller than planets and exert a much weaker gravitational pull. Even so, asteroids can attract small objects toward them. In 1993, as the Galileo space probe made its way to Jupiter, it passed an asteroid called Ida. Ida is about 36 miles (58 km) long, and its cratered surface suggests that it is about one billion years old. Galileo's photographs revealed that Ida has a companion. It is being orbited by its own tiny moon, called Dactyl.

Communication antenna is 6 ft (1.5 m) in diameter

Solar arrays generate 1.8 kW of electrical power

NEAR SHOEMAKER PROBE

LANDING ON AN ASTEROID ►
The Near Earth Asteroid Rendezvous (NEAR) was the first space mission designed solely to study an asteroid. In February 2000, the NEAR Shoemaker probe approached an asteroid called 433 Eros. Ground controllers maneuvered the spacecraft into orbit around the asteroid. After a year in orbit, photographing Eros from as little as 3 miles (5 km) away, the spacecraft was commanded to land on the asteroid in February 2001.

Thruster used to steer probe

3 MILES (5 KM)

METEORITES ►
Billions of pieces of rock, most as small as grains of sand, enter Earth's atmosphere from space every day. Most burn up in a streak of light called a meteor, or shooting star. Meteorites are larger rocks that reach the ground. Most meteorites are made of rock. A few are made of iron or a mixture of rock and iron. Some meteorites originated from the Moon or Mars, but (like asteroids) most consist of material from the early solar system.

EFFECTS OF ASTEROIDS HITTING EARTH

SIZE OF ASTEROID	POSSIBLE DAMAGE
165 ft (50 m)	Most of the asteroid would burn up or explode in the atmosphere. The remainder would be slowed down so much that it could do little damage outside the impact site.
165–330 ft (50–100 m)	Cities the size of London, Tokyo, or New York could be destroyed. Hundreds of square miles of land would be devastated and forests flattened.
3,300 ft (1 km)	Enough dust would be thrown up into the atmosphere to reduce temperatures and dim sunlight around the world, causing environmental damage in most countries. Up to 1.5 billion people could be killed.
6 miles (10 km)	The impact would cause earthquakes worldwide. Red-hot ash thrown up into the atmosphere would cause widespread fires as it rained down. Chemicals released by the impact would destroy the ozone layer and cause acid rain. So much dust would be thrown up that temperatures would fall and sunlight would be dimmed enough to kill crops all over the world. Most of the human race would die.

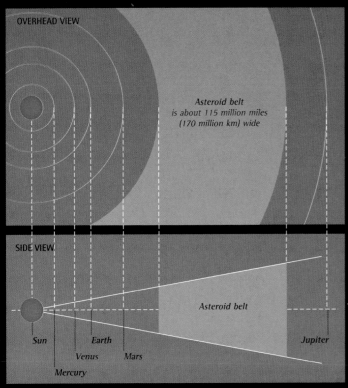

OVERHEAD VIEW

Asteroid belt
is about 115 million miles
(170 million km) wide

SIDE VIEW

Sun
Mercury
Venus
Earth
Mars
Asteroid belt
Jupiter

▲ THE ASTEROID BELT

Most asteroids orbit the Sun in a broad band called the asteroid belt, which is located between the orbits of Mars and Jupiter. The belt extends from about 185 to 300 million miles (330 million km to almost 500 million km) from the Sun. There are also two groups of asteroids in the same orbit as Jupiter. Known as the Trojans, one group orbits the Sun ahead of Jupiter and another group follows the giant planet.

asteroids

ROCKS IN SPACE ▶

Asteroids range in size from large boulders to rocks hundreds of miles across. Most are lumpy, not spherical like planets, because their gravity is too weak to pull them into a round shape. The largest, Ceres, was the first to be discovered, in 1801. Ceres is 584 miles (940 km) wide and orbits at an average of 258 million miles (415 million km) from the Sun. It contains one-third of the total mass of all asteroids in the solar system.

RIDING A COMET

Comets have fascinated people since ancient times. They are chunks of dust and ice that originate in the outer reaches of the solar system. Occasionally, a collision or a tug of gravity from a star or planet changes a comet's orbit and sends it closer to the Sun. As it approaches the Sun, ice and frozen chemicals in the comet melt and evaporate. They form tails of gas and dust that stream away from the comet. Now spacecraft are being sent to study comets close-up, and even land on them.

Tails always point away from the Sun

Dust tail can be over 6 million miles long

Head *is a solid nucleus surrounded by a coma of gas and dust*

Gas tail can be hundreds of miles long

ORBITING A COMET ▶
The Rosetta spacecraft will orbit Comet 67P/Churyumov-Gerasimenko after a ten-year journey through space. The comet was discovered in 1969. The 2.5-mile (4-km) wide ball of ice and dust is traveling at 85,000 mph (136,000 kph). Maneuvering the spacecraft into orbit around the comet is very tricky, because the spacecraft's flight path is affected by dust and jets of gas coming from the comet, and also by its weak and irregular gravity.

◀ INSIDE A COMET
Hale-Bopp was the brightest comet for over 20 years when it passed the Sun in 1997. Millions of people on Earth saw it. Most comets are less than 10 miles (15 km) across. Hale-Bopp's nucleus, the solid part in the middle, is 25 miles (40 km) across. As it neared the Sun, it developed two tails—a yellow dust tail and a blue gas tail. It passed within 86 million miles (138 million km) of the Sun on April 1, 1997. Hale-Bopp will return in 2,392 years.

GIOTTO

In 1986, a European spacecraft called Giotto met up with the most famous comet of all, Halley's Comet, and took close-up photographs of it. The comet is named after English astronomer Edmond Halley (1656-1742). He realized that comets seen in 1531, 1607, and 1682 were the same comet returning every 76 years. He predicted it would return in 1758. He was right.

▲ HALLEY'S COMET IN 1066...
Halley's Comet appears on the Bayeux Tapestry. This medieval embroidery shows the story of the Norman Conquest of England in 1066. One of the scenes on the 229-ft (70-m) long tapestry depicts a bright star with a long, fiery tail. Calculations have shown that this is actually Halley's Comet. The comet is also portrayed in a fresco on the birth of Christ by Italian artist Giotto di Bondone, painted in 1304. In fact, appearances of Halley's Comet have been recorded all the way back to 240 B.C.

▲ ...AND TODAY
Halley's Comet is still making its regular appearances today. The 10½-mile (16-km) long chunk of rock and ice made its latest appearance in 1986. It passed within about 55 million miles (88 million km) of the Sun. It is expected to return in the year 2061. Some comets have much shorter or longer orbits than Halley. Comet Encke returns every 3.3 years, while Comet Hyakutake, last seen in 1996, will probably not return for another 14,000 years.

ROSETTA'S COMET ENCOUNTER

ORBITER
Rosetta will be the first craft to orbit a comet, one of the most difficult maneuvers ever attempted. It will be the first to accompany a comet as it travels toward the Sun. It will study the comet for nearly two years, and carries a craft that will land on the surface of the comet's nucleus.

LANDER
The orbiter has to be guided with precision to ensure that the lander is ejected in the right direction to land on the comet's nucleus. As the lander touches down, it anchors itself on the surface by firing two harpoons into the nucleus. Its legs automatically adjust themselves to keep upright.

EXPERIMENTS
The lander will analyze the chemical composition of the comet's surface and drill into the nucleus to analyze material from below the surface. It will also test the strength of the surface, its texture, ice content, and how porous it is. Data will be transmitted to Rosetta to relay back to Earth.

Navigation cameras help to keep the craft on course

Cameras take high-resolution images of the comet's nucleus

Radio antenna uses radio waves to study the comet's orbit

The CONSERT experiment will probe the comet with radio signals

Solar panels, 45 ft (14 m) long, rotate to face the Sun

Philae, the 220-lb (100-kg) lander, will land on the nucleus

comets

ROSETTA MISSION SCHEDULE

PLANNED PHASE	PREDICTED DATE
Rosetta launched by Ariane 5	March 2004
First Earth gravity assist	March 2005
Mars gravity assist	March 2007
Second Earth gravity assist	November 2007
Third Earth gravity assist	November 2009
Rosetta enters hibernation	July 2011
End of hibernation	January 2014
Rendezvous with comet	May 2014
Global mapping	August 2014
Lander delivery	November 2014
Perihelion (closest to Sun)	August 2015
End of mission	December 2015

Steerable high gain radio dish, 7 ft (2.2 m) wide, is used for communication with Earth

▲ ROSETTA SPACECRAFT
Rosetta's flight path to Comet Churyumov-Gerasimenko takes it around Earth three times and Mars once, using the planets' gravity to swing it around onto the right course. The spacecraft has a cube-shaped body measuring 10 ft by 7 ft by 6 ft 6 in (2.8 m by 2.1 m by 2.0 m), and weighs 6,614 lbs (3,000 kg). More than half of this is propellant. The scientific package, carrying 20 scientific instruments, weighs only 363 lb (165 kg).

SATURN'S RINGS

Saturn is the sixth planet from the Sun. It is encircled by a broad band of rings. These were a mystery when astronomers saw them for the first time in the early 1600s. They are still not fully understood, even though they have now been studied by telescopes and space probes. In 2004, the Cassini space probe arrived at Saturn to study the giant gas planet and its rings and moons. It carried a miniprobe, called Huygens, to investigate Saturn's largest moon, Titan. Scientists think that the air in Titan's atmosphere is similar to the air that existed on Earth billions of years ago.

Five instruments analyze Titan's atmosphere

Gold foil insulates and protects instruments

▲ HUYGENS

The 700-lb (318-kg) Huygens probe enters Titan's atmosphere at 13,500 mph (21,600 kph). The atmosphere slows it to 900 mph (1,440 kph), then it descends to the surface by parachute. In the two hours it takes to reach the surface, its camera takes more than 1,100 images. Onboard instruments sample the atmosphere and radio their results to the Cassini spacecraft. The probe is named after Dutch astronomer Christiaan Huygens (1629-1695), who discovered Titan.

CASSINI-HUYGENS ▶

Cassini-Huygens is a joint NASA-ESA mission. ESA's contribution is the Huygens probe. The Cassini spacecraft, named after the Italian astronomer Giovanni Cassini who first spotted and charted Saturn's moons, is touring the Saturn system for four years. The tour includes 74 orbits of Saturn, 44 flybys of its largest moon, Titan, and numerous flybys of Saturn's other moons. The spacecraft is powered by three nuclear electricity generators. Its science package includes instruments designed to study Saturn's gravity and its magnetic field. It also carries a digital imaging system to photograph Saturn and its moons.

Boom carries instruments to measure Saturn's magnetic field

High-gain radio dish is 13 ft (4 m) in diameter

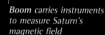

Saturn

PLANETS WITH RINGS

JUPITER
Saturn is not the only planet with rings. All the giant gas planets (Jupiter, Saturn, Uranus, and Neptune) have rings, although none is as visible or complex as Saturn's. Voyager 2 photographed this faint ring system around Jupiter in 1999.

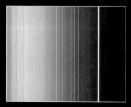

URANUS
Voyager 2 photographed rings around Uranus in 1986. This false-color image was taken from 2.6 million miles (4.2 million km) away. Astronomers discovered them in 1977 when they noticed that a star dimmed as it passed behind each ring.

NEPTUNE
Neptune's rings, photographed by Voyager 2 in 1979, are so faint that they are invisible from Earth. The darkest parts of the rings dimmed starlight passing through them, but astronomers were not sure if they were rings until Voyager visited Neptune.

SATURN'S RINGS ▶

Saturn's rings are made from billions of chunks of ice and rock of all sizes. The rings are very broad, but also extremely thin. As seen from Earth, they are about 168,000 miles (275,000 km) across, but their overall diameter is around 258,000 miles (415,000 km). They are possibly only about 328 ft (100 m) thick. No one knows where the rings came from. They may be the remains of comets, asteroids, or moons that were smashed apart by collisions.

Pan   Atlas   Prometheus Janus   Telesto   Helene   Titan   Hyperion   Phoebe
Pandora Epimetheus   Calypso
Mimas Enceladus Tethys   Dione   Rhea   Iapetus

SATURN'S MOONS ▲
Until 1977, astronomers had spotted nine moons orbiting Saturn.
Since then, the Hubble Space Telescope and space probes have found
more. Pioneer 11, Voyager 1, and Voyager 2 flew past Saturn between 1979
and 1981. By the time the Cassini space probe approached Saturn in 2004, the
number of discovered moons had risen to 31. Saturn's largest moon,
Titan, is bigger than the planets Mercury and Pluto. As a moon,
it is second in size only to Jupiter's moon, Ganymede.

SATURN ▶
Saturn is the solar system's second biggest planet.
About 746 Earths would fit inside it. For such a big
planet, it spins remarkably quickly. It rotates about
once every 10 hours – more than twice as fast as
tiny Earth. It orbits the Sun nearly 10 times
further out than the Earth and takes 29.5 years
to circle it. Saturn is the only planet that is
less dense than water. If you could find a big
enough pool, Saturn would float in it.

*Two identical engines
are fitted—one is used,
the other is a back-up*

*Rings are composed of
about 1,000 ringlets*

*Huygens probe
travels inside this
dish-shaped aeroshell*

LOOKING CLOSER AT THE RINGS

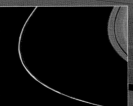

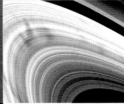
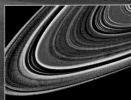

BRAIDING
The Voyager 2 probe took pictures of a ring (called the F ring) twisting around itself. Scientists call it braiding. They think the braiding is caused by the gravity of two tiny moons, Pandora and Prometheus.

MOON EFFECTS
Saturn's many moons exert an influence on the rings. The gravitational pull of each moon attracts billions of ring particles. This may be the reason for some of the gaps and fine details in the rings.

SPOKES
Scientists are puzzled by dark lines on the rings, like spokes on a wheel. They are thought to be fine dust raised above the rings by an electrostatic effect (electrically charged particles being forced apart).

COLOR
Photographing the rings through colored filters shows extra detail. This Voyager 2 image is composed of frames taken through clear, orange, and ultraviolet filters from 5.5 million miles (8.9 million km).

DEEP SPACE NETWORK

NASA's Deep Space Network is responsible for tracking, commanding, and receiving data from space probes throughout the solar system. Some of the spacecraft are so far away and they use such small transmitters, that radio signals received from them are about 20 million times weaker than a watch battery. To receive such weak signals, the Deep Space Network uses huge dish-shaped antennae up to 230 ft (70 m) across. To dispatch commands to the most remote spacecraft, the same giant dishes are used to send radio signals from immensely powerful, 400-kilowatt transmitters.

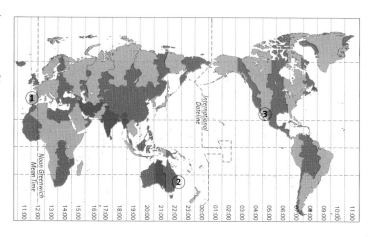

▼ DISHES IN THE DESERT

The American part of the Deep Space Network is the Goldstone Complex, 45 miles (72 km) northeast of Barstow, in the Mojave Desert in California. Goldstone is the center of the Deep Space Network and it has the most dishes. In addition to the big 230-ft (70-m) dish, it also has six 112-ft (34-m) dishes and one 85-ft (26-m) dish. The first spacecraft it communicated with were the interplanetary space probes Pioneer 3 in 1958 and Pioneer 4 in 1959.

Deep Space Network

▲ DISH LOCATIONS

The Deep Space Network's antennae are located at three sites: **1** Madrid, Spain, **2** Canberra, Australia, and **3** California. The sites were chosen because they are spaced out at roughly 120 degrees, or one third of the way around the world, from each other. As the Earth turns, at least one of the receiving stations is always in contact with a space probe. This ensures a 24-hour observation, with overlapping time to transfer the radio link to the next station. The locations are also surrounded by mountains that shield them from radio interference. The map shows the time differences between the three countries.

FROM SPACE TO SPAIN ▶

The Spanish Deep Space Network complex is located near the village of Robledo de Chavela, 35 miles (56 km) west of Madrid. It became operational in 1965, replacing an earlier ground station near Johannesburg, South Africa. A new 112-ft (34-m) dish was built at the Madrid complex at the end of 2003 to add another 70 hours of tracking time per week. The increase in capacity was necessary because of the large number of space probes exploring the solar system.

AUSTRALIAN ARRAYS ▶

The Australian complex was first used in 1964 and participated in the Mariner 4 mission to Mars. It is located in the Tidbinbilla Valley, 22 miles (35 km) southwest of Canberra. The 98-ft (64-m) Parkes radio dish, named after the nearby town of Parkes, also handles Deep Space Network communications. It was linked to the Canberra and Goldstone dishes to receive signals from the Galileo spacecraft, a technique called arraying.

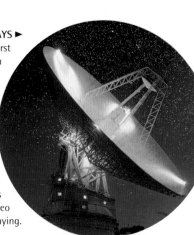

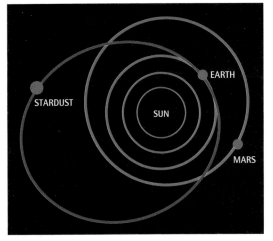

▲ TRACKING STARDUST

One of the missions being tracked by the Deep Space Network is the Stardust mission to collect particles of dust from a comet and return them to Earth. The Stardust spacecraft was launched on February 7, 1999, and it will return to Earth with its precious samples in 2006. The Deep Space Network will track Stardust during its journey to Comet Wild-2 and back, send the command signals to keep it on course, and receive the data it sends back.

Gas and dust trail from Comet Wild-2

High-gain antenna sends data to Earth

DATA ON THE DEEP SPACE NETWORK

Tracking distance: A 230-ft (70-m) dish is capable of tracking a spacecraft more than 10 million miles (16 billion km) from Earth.

Tracking time: The radio signal from Voyager 1 takes 12 hours and 39 minutes to reach Earth.

DSN power: Transmitter power needed to command a distant probe is 400,000 watts.

Probe power: Typical space probe transmitter power is 20 watts.

Power from probe: Power recieved on Earth from distant space probe is one billionth of one trillionth of one watt.

Most distant probe: Voyager 1 is 8.5 billion miles (13.6 billion km) from the Sun.

STARDUST'S DISCOVERIES ►

On January 2, 2004, after a journey of 2 billion miles (3.2 billion km), the Stardust probe successfully flew through the gas and dust coma around the nucleus of Comet Wild-2 and collected dust samples. It came within 150 miles (240 km) of the icy nucleus and took the most detailed close-up pictures of a comet ever captured by a spacecraft. The images received by the Deep Space Network show what looks like a pock-marked rock 3 miles (5 km) across, with dust and gas jets streaming out of its surface.

LONG-DISTANCE PHOTOGRAPHY

RAW DATA FROM THE PROBE

When a spacecraft camera takes a picture, light from the object strikes a microchip called a CCD (Charge-Coupled Device). The chip's surface is divided into a grid of hundreds of thousands of light-sensitive picture elements, or pixels. The brightness of each pixel is changed into a number, from 0 (black) to 255 (white). The same view is also photographed through color filters. Then all the numbers are converted to digital code and transmitted to Earth.

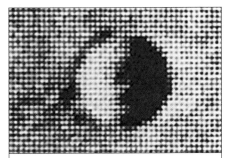

FORMING AN IMAGE

The stream of digital data from a spacecraft is received by the Deep Space Network and relayed to the Jet Propulsion Laboratory (JPL) in Pasadena, California. JPL's computers form the data into a series of lines. They change the digital code back into numbers, and the numbers into spots of light of the right level of brightness. The black-and-white pictures taken through colored filters are also combined to form false-color images.

PROCESSING PICTURES

The first pictures created often have faults where data had become corrupted or is missing. The pictures are processed by computer to improve their quality by removing faults and unwanted noise, (background data). Ultraviolet, infra-red, and radar data from space probes are processed to make pictures too, by giving false colors to the different numbers in the data. False-color images show information that is normally invisible, such as heat, speed, or height.

SEARCHING FOR LIFE

The Universe is so vast that many astronomers think it is unlikely that Earth is the only planet hosting life. The outer planets were thought to be too cold and dark. Then the discovery of creatures in the cold, dark world at the bottom of Earth's oceans showed that life could exist in such conditions. Scientists look for signs of life in the solar system by analyzing images and soil samples sent back by probes. They also look for life in the Universe by searching for radio signals that intelligent beings might have sent. The work is called SETI, the Search for Extraterrestrial Intelligence.

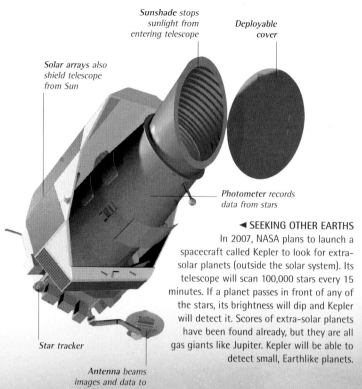

Sunshade stops sunlight from entering telescope

Deployable cover

Solar arrays also shield telescope from Sun

Photometer records data from stars

Star tracker

Antenna beams images and data to Earth once a week

◄ **SEEKING OTHER EARTHS**
In 2007, NASA plans to launch a spacecraft called Kepler to look for extra-solar planets (outside the solar system). Its telescope will scan 100,000 stars every 15 minutes. If a planet passes in front of any of the stars, its brightness will dip and Kepler will detect it. Scores of extra-solar planets have been found already, but they are all gas giants like Jupiter. Kepler will be able to detect small, Earthlike planets.

Three towers and 18 cables support the 900-ton platform

Arecibo's dish reflects radio waves to and from space

ARECIBO RADIO TELESCOPE ►
Arecibo is the world's most sensitive radio telescope. Astronomers use it to study radio signals from distant stars and galaxies. SETI scientists scan about 1,000 stars for any radio signals that might be artificial, as these may come from extraterrestrial beings. The 1,000-ft (305-m) dish lies in a natural hollow on the Caribbean island of Puerto Rico. The reflector's surface is made of 40,000 aluminum panels.

◄ EUROPA

Jupiter's moon Europa is about the same size as Earth's Moon, but Europa is covered with ice. Lines as long as 1,850 miles (3,000 km) on its surface look like cracks in the ice. Scientists think there may be a liquid ocean underneath. If it contains water, there may be life there too. In 2012, NASA is planning to send the Jupiter Icy Moons Orbiter to scan Europa and two other moons, Granymede and Callisto, which may have oceans beneath ice.

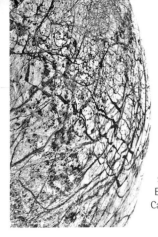

SENDING MESSAGES ►

In 1974, the Arecibo radio telescope transmitted a coded message toward the M13 star cluster. M13 contains 300,000 stars and lies near the edge of our galaxy, 21,000 light years away. The message consisted of 1,679 bits of information. If intelligent beings receive the code, they should be able to rearrange it into 73 lines of 23 bits. In this form, it shows a series of shapes, including the Arecibo dish, our solar system, and a human. If life forms do work it out, a return message would take about 48,000 years to get here from M13.

Binary code gives the numbers one to ten

Symbols represent the chemicals hydrogen, carbon, oxygen, nitrogen, and phosphorus

Twisted lines stand for DNA, the molecule that passes on the blueprint of life

Human figure and Earth's population

Solar system, with Earth out of line to highlight it

Arecibo radio telescope with radio waves

PAST LIFE ►

Photographs of Mars taken by orbiting spacecraft show features that look very similar to riverbeds and flood plains on Earth that were formed by flowing water. The Mars Exploration Rovers have found layered rocks that look like seabed sediments. These features suggest that water did flow on Mars long ago. This means that even if Mars is a dead planet today, scientists may be able to find evidence of past life in its rocks, or even microorganisms living below the dead surface.

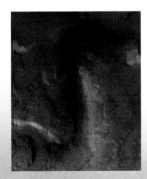

ET life

Dome contains reflectors that focus radio waves onto antennae

SETI AT HOME

Millions of home computer users all over the world have joined the search for extraterrestrial intelligence. Data from the Arecibo telescope is divided up into smaller units and sent to home computer users running software called SETI@Home. Their screensavers analyze data received from the telescope and send it back to the SETI headquarters. The software looks for very narrow-band radio signals, which are most unlikely to come from natural sources. These would show up as spikes flickering on the screen.

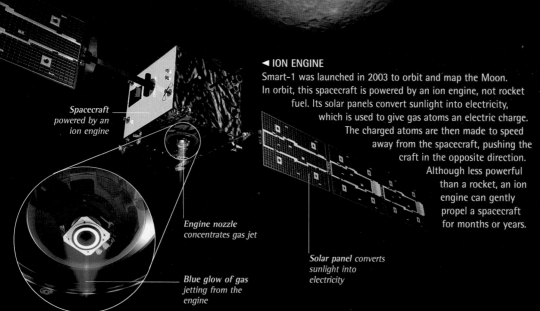

◄ ION ENGINE

Smart-1 was launched in 2003 to orbit and map the Moon. In orbit, this spacecraft is powered by an ion engine, not rocket fuel. Its solar panels convert sunlight into electricity, which is used to give gas atoms an electric charge. The charged atoms are then made to speed away from the spacecraft, pushing the craft in the opposite direction. Although less powerful than a rocket, an ion engine can gently propel a spacecraft for months or years.

Spacecraft powered by an ion engine

Engine nozzle concentrates gas jet

Blue glow of gas jetting from the engine

Solar panel converts sunlight into electricity

THE FUTURE IN SPACE

Scientists and engineers are planning new manned and unmanned space missions for the future. In 2004, President George W. Bush announced that the US intends to send astronauts back to the Moon by 2020 and to Mars after that. One of the most exciting unmanned missions will search for signs of life on Earthlike planets orbiting other stars. Looking further into the future, spacecraft will need new engines that improve on the fuels and rockets used today. One of these, the ion engine, has already been test-flown on several unmanned missions.

▲ MOON BASE

Robots such as the rovers that have been put on the Moon and Mars have been a great success, but some scientists think that human exploration is much more effective. It is likely that humans will return to the Moon in the 21st century. After that, the next stop is Mars. If astronauts do one day make the six-month flight to Mars, separate cargo craft will probably already have delivered supplies for them, along with a module to live in.

Heat radiator sheds excess heat into space

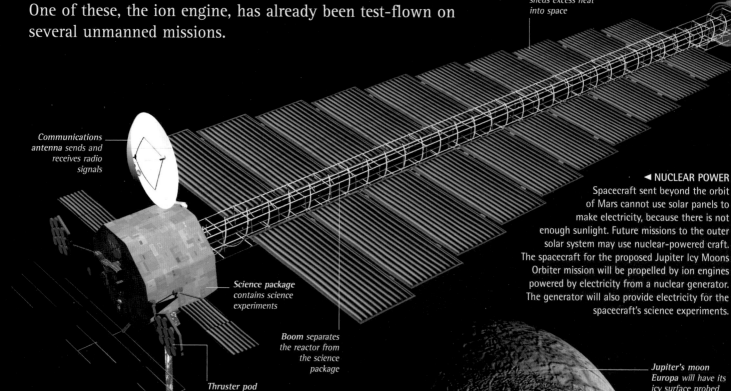

Communications antenna sends and receives radio signals

◄ NUCLEAR POWER

Spacecraft sent beyond the orbit of Mars cannot use solar panels to make electricity, because there is not enough sunlight. Future missions to the outer solar system may use nuclear-powered craft. The spacecraft for the proposed Jupiter Icy Moons Orbiter mission will be propelled by ion engines powered by electricity from a nuclear generator. The generator will also provide electricity for the spacecraft's science experiments.

Science package contains science experiments

Boom separates the reactor from the science package

Thruster pod houses an ion engine

Radar antenna probes below the surface of moons

Jupiter's moon Europa will have its icy surface probed

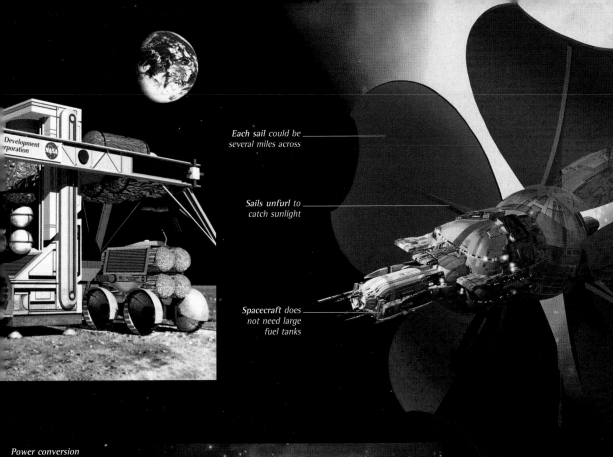

Each sail could be
several miles across

Sails unfurl to
catch sunlight

Spacecraft does
not need large
fuel tanks

Power conversion
system changes
nuclear energy into
electricity

Shielding
surrounds the
reactor's
radioactive
material

future

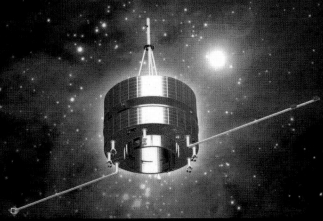

SOLAR SAILS ▲

Sunlight itself can propel a spacecraft. When sunlight strikes something, it gives a tiny push. The effect is so small that it is not noticed normally—but if the sunlight strikes a big enough surface, the tiny pushes all over it add up to something big enough to move a spacecraft. Spacecraft propelled by sunlight would have giant sails of a paper-thin material. The acceleration produced by the sunlight would be small—but it would be constant, so over time, the craft could be boosted to very high speeds.

▲ DOUBLE STAR

The Double Star mission is a joint project between the European Space Agency and the Chinese National Space Administration to study the Sun's effect on Earth. It is called Double Star because there are two spacecraft. One is orbiting close to Earth's equator and the other will orbit its poles. Some time after June 2004, they will start working together and also with four Cluster satellites already in orbit. Data from the satellites will be beamed down to ground stations in Spain and China.

Each telescope
will be 5 ft (1.5 m)
in diameter

Solar panels supply
power to operate
each telescope

DARWIN ▶

The Darwin mission will use a fleet of space telescopes to look for life on planets orbiting distant stars. This is a big challenge, because the light from a star swamps nearby planets and makes them hard to see. A telescope 100 ft (30 m) across is needed, but it is impossible to launch such a big telescope. Six smaller telescopes will work together as if they were one big telescope. They will look for telltale changes in each planet's atmosphere caused by life.

Telescope
is cooled to

SPACE TIMELINE

The Space Age began in 1957, although the rocket technology underlying space travel can be traced back to some key developments earlier in the 20th century. Since 1957, virtually every year has seen significant developments in space exploration.

timelines

1926 Robert H. Goddard launches the first liquid-fueled rocket.

1944 The V-2 rocket, from which all modern space rockets are derived, is developed by Germany as a weapon toward the end of World War II.

1957 Soviet Union launch Sputnik 1, the first artificial satellite.

Laika is the first dog in space, traveling aboard the Sputnik 2 satellite.

1958 First US artificial satellite, Explorer 1, is launched.

1959 The Soviet space probe Luna 1 is the first to leave Earth orbit.

Luna 2 is the first space probe to reach the surface of a celestial object—the Moon.

Luna 3 probe returns the first photographs of the far side of the Moon.

The first seven American astronauts, called the Mercury Seven, are selected.

1960 The first weather satellite, TIROS 1, is launched.

The Soviet Union puts two dogs, Strelka and Belka, into space and returns them safely.

1961 The first manned spaceflight by the Soviet cosmonaut Yuri Gagarin in the Vostok 1 spacecraft.

First US manned spaceflight by Alan Shepard in the Mercury 3 spacecraft.

President John F. Kennedy announces America's intention to land humans on the Moon by the end of the 1960s.

The Soviet space probe, Venera 1, is the first to fly by Venus, although contact with it is lost before it reaches Venus.

1962 The first US manned orbital spaceflight, Mercury 6, with John Glenn on board.

First successful communications satellite, Telstar 1, sends the first direct TV pictures from US to Europe.

The pop record *Telstar*, by the Tornadoes, climbs to number one in the singles charts in both the UK and US.

The US space probe Mariner 2 flies by Venus and sends back data about the planet.

1963 Valentina Tereshkova becomes the first woman to fly in space, aboard Vostok 6.

1964 First three-person spacecraft, Voskhod 1, is launched.

Ranger 7, a US space probe, crash-lands into the Moon, giving the first high-resolution images of the lunar surface.

1965 First space walk, by a crew member (Alexei Leonov) of the Soviet spacecraft, Voskhod 2.

The first US two-person spaceflight, Gemini 3.

The US space probe Mariner 4 flies by Mars, the first spacecraft ever successfully to do so.

1966 First soft-landing of a spacecraft on the Moon, the Soviet craft Luna 9.

NASA launches the first Earth observation satellite, ESSA-1.

Both the Soviet Union and the US put space probes, Luna 10 and Lunar Orbiter 1, into orbit around the Moon.

The first American soft-landing on the Moon, by the Surveyor 1 space probe.

1967 Fire during Apollo 1 ground test kills three astronauts.

First test-flight of the Saturn V rocket, launching the unmanned Apollo 4 spacecraft.

The Soviet space probe Venera 4 is the first to descend through the atmosphere of Venus and send back data.

Vladimir Komarov dies during re-entry of the Soyuz 1 spacecraft.

1968 The first US three-man spaceflight, Apollo 7.

First manned spacecraft to leave Earth and orbit the Moon, Apollo 8.

The film *2001: A Space Odyssey* is released; though many are baffled by the plot, it gives a scientifically accurate picture of various aspects of living and traveling in space.

1969 Two Apollo 11 astronauts are the first humans to walk on the surface of the Moon.

A second Moon landing is made by two Apollo 12 astronauts.

1970 An explosion occurs aboard the Apollo 13 spacecraft as it travels to the Moon, but the crew of three return safely to Earth.

The Soviet space probe Venera 7 is the first to make a controlled landing on Venus.

Luna 16 is the first robotic space probe to land on the Moon, take a sample, and send it back to Earth.

The Soviet robotic vehicle Lunokhod is landed on the Moon and begins to explore.

China and Japan launch their first artificial satellites.

1971 The first space station, Salyut 1, is launched by the Soviet Union.

Three cosmonauts die during re-entry of Soyuz 11 after becoming the first crew to live on a space station.

The US space probe Mariner 9 becomes the first human-built object to orbit Mars, where it detects huge volcanoes and deep canyons on the planet's surface.

1972 The Soviet probe Mars 2 is the first human-made object to reach the surface of Mars.

NASA launches Pioneer 10, the first space probe to travel to the outer planets.

Last Apollo moon-landing, Apollo 17.

First Earth Resources Technology Satellite, ERTS, is launched.

1973 First US space station, Skylab, is put in orbit.

Pioneer 10 is the first space probe to fly past Jupiter and take close-up pictures of the planet and some of its moons.

1974 The US probe Mariner 10 is the first space probe to fly past the planet Mercury.

1975 The Soviet space probe Venera 9 is the first to send pictures back from the surface of Venus.

The United States and the Soviet Union cooperate in space for the first time when an Apollo craft docks with a Soviet Soyuz craft.

1976 Two US space probes, Viking 1 and Viking 2, land on Mars, send back numerous pictures of the planet's surface, and look for life.

1977 Voyager 2, the only space probe to visit four planets (Jupiter, Saturn, Uranus, and Neptune), is launched, closely followed by Voyager 1.

1978 The first of 24 Global Positioning System navigation satellites is put in Earth orbit.

Czech Vladimir Remek becomes the first non-American, non-Soviet citizen to fly in space.

1979 Pioneer 11 is the first space probe to pass by Saturn and take close-up photographs of its rings.

First launch of Europe's Ariane rocket.

The Voyager 1 and Voyager 2 space probes fly by Jupiter and return dramatic pictures of the planet, its rings, and some of its larger moons.

1980 The Voyager 1 probe sends back pictures of Saturn, revealing it has thousands of ringlets.

The Pioneer Venus 1 probe discovers mountains higher than Mount Everest on Venus.

1981 The first US Space Shuttle mission, Columbia, STS-1.

1982 The last Russian Salyut space station, Salyut 7, is launched.

1983 The world's first infrared astronomical satellite, called IRAS, is launched.

Dr. Sally Ride becomes the first American woman in space on board the Space Shuttle Challenger.

First Spacelab flies on the Space Shuttle.

Pioneer 10 becomes the first object made by humans to leave the solar system.

President Ronald Reagan announces the Strategic Defense Initiative, a space-based system designed to defend the US from attack by nuclear missiles; it is dubbed Star Wars by opponents.

1984 The first untethered space walks are made by Space Shuttle astronauts, using manned maneuvering units.

1986 The first part of the Russian Mir space station is launched.

Space Shuttle Orbiter Challenger explodes just after launch, with loss of all seven of its crew members.

The Japanese space probes Suisei and Sakigake make successful flybys of Halley's comet.

European Space Agency Giotto probe makes a successful flyby of Halley's comet.

Voyager 2 space probe flies past Uranus, returning pictures of the planet, its numerous rings, and moons.

1989 Voyager 2 flies past Neptune, returning pictures of the planet, its rings, and moons.

1990 Magellan space probe begins to orbit the planet Venus and maps its surface.

Hubble Space Telescope is launched.

1991 European Remote Sensing satellite (ERS-1), Europe's first environmental satellite, goes into orbit.

The Soviet Union breaks up and is partially replaced by a Commonwealth of Independent States (CIS), consisting of Russia and ten smaller countries. The former Soviet Union's space program effectively becomes Russia's space program.

1992 The ESA/NASA space probe Ulysses swings by Jupiter and goes into an orbit that will take it over both of the Sun's poles.

The COBE satellite maps the cosmic microwave background radiation for the first time.

1994 Ulysses probe makes first flight over the Sun's south pole.

1995 Galileo space probe goes into orbit around Jupiter.

Russian cosmonaut Valeri Poliakov returns to Earth after spending a record 438 days in space, aboard the Mir space station.

The Solar and Heliospheric Observatory mission (SOHO) is launched into a solar orbit.

1996 NASA confirms that water has been detected on the Moon by the Lunar Prospector spacecraft.

The French satellite Cerise is the first to collide with a cataloged piece of space junk.

1997 NASA's Pathfinder space probe lands on Mars and releases the Sojourner rover onto the planet's surface.

1998 First part of the International Space Station is launched.

1999 The powerful Chandra X-ray Observatory is launched into Earth orbit by the Space Shuttle Columbia.

2000 Two Russian cosmonauts and an American astronomer become the first occupants of the International Space Station.

2001 NEAR Shoemaker is the first space probe to be landed on an asteroid, Eros.

The Mir space station burns up in Earth's atmosphere after 15 years in orbit.

NASA's Deep space 1 probe successfully flies by comet Borrelly.

2002 Mars Odyssey spacecraft starts mapping the planet Mars and looks for water.

2003 Space Shuttle Orbiter Columbia breaks up and is destroyed when re-entering Earth's atmosphere, with loss of all seven of its crew members.

2004 President George W. Bush announces America's intention to send more astronauts to the Moon by the year 2020 and to use Moon missions as a stepping stone for future space exploration.

Stardust spacecraft flies through the coma of Comet Wild-2 and captures thousands of fresh cometary dust particles.

Spirit and Opportunity rovers successfully land on the surface of Mars.

Cassini-Huygens space probe scheduled to go into orbit around Saturn.

2005 Deep Impact probe scheduled to encounter Comet 9P/Tempel 1.

2006 Mars Reconnaissance Orbiter mission is scheduled to reach the planet Mars.

2011 NASA's Messenger space probe is scheduled to start orbiting the planet Mercury.

2012 European Space agency's BepiColombo spacecraft, which includes two Mercury orbiters, is scheduled for launch.

2014 European Space Agency's Rosetta space probe is scheduled to encounter the comet 67P/Churyumov-Gerasimenko and put a small lander on its surface.

MOON LANDING SITES

More than 55 spacecraft have reached the Moon since 1959. Some flew by it, went into orbit around it, or orbited it and then returned to Earth. Below is a summary of 19 of the more important missions that have actually landed or crash-landed on the Moon up to 2004.

maps

① LUNA 2 (USSR)

Landing date: September 14, 1959
Location: Near Autolycus crater
Details: The first spacecraft to land on any object outside Earth, though it crash-landed.

② AND ③ RANGERS 7 AND 8 (US)

Landing dates: July 28, 1964 and February 20, 1965
Locations: Near Mare Nubium (Sea of Clouds) and Mare Tranquillitatis (Sea of Tranquillity)
Details: Each spacecraft transmitted a series of pictures as it crash-landed on to the Moon.

④ LUNA 9 (USSR)

Landing date: February 3, 1966
Location: Western side of Oceanus Procellarum (Ocean of Storms)
Details: The first craft to soft-land on any object outside Earth. Luna 9 sent photographs and TV pictures back to Earth for 3 days.

⑤ SURVEYOR 1 (US)

Landing date: June 2, 1966
Location: Near the center of Oceanus Procellarum (Ocean of Storms)
Details: The first successful soft-landing by a US spacecraft on any object outside Earth. The spacecraft found it had landed in a 1 inch- (2 cm-) thick layer of dust.

⑥ LUNA 13 (USSR)

Landing date: December 24, 1966
Location: Western side of Oceanus Procellarum (Ocean of Storms)
Details: As well as returning TV pictures and data, the probe tested the lunar soil's density and measured its radioactivity.

⑦ SURVEYOR 3 (US)

Landing date: April 20, 1967
Location: Eastern side of Oceanus Procellarum (Ocean of Storms)
Details: The probe was the first to carry a surface soil-sampling scoop. Samples were placed in front of the spacecraft's television cameras for image transmission back to Earth.

⑧ AND ⑨ SURVEYORS 5 AND 6 (US)

Landing dates: September 11 and November 10, 1967
Locations: Mare Tranquillitatis (Sea of Tranquillity) and Sinus Medii (Central Bay)
Details: Performed soil surveys and sent back large numbers of photographs to Earth.

⑩ APOLLO 11 (US)

Landing date: July 20, 1969
Location: Western side of Mare Tranquillitatis (Sea of Tranquillity)
Astronauts: Neil Armstrong and "Buzz" Aldrin
Details: The first mission in which humans walked on the lunar surface. During their 21.5-hour stay on the Moon, Armstrong and Aldrin walked a distance of about 800 ft (250 m), set up scientific experiments, took photographs, and collected lunar samples.

⑪ APOLLO 12 (US)

Landing date: November 19, 1969
Location: Eastern side of Oceanus Procellarum (Ocean of Storms)
Astronauts: "Pete" Conrad and Alan Bean
Details: Conrad and Bean set up scientific experiments, examined the nearby Surveyor 3 spacecraft, collected lunar samples, and took photographs during two moonwalks. Their stay on the Moon lasted 31.5 hours.

⑫ LUNA 16 (USSR)

Landing date: September 17, 1970
Location: Mare Fecunditatis (Sea of Fertility)
Details: This probe drilled into the Moon's surface, took a sample, and then successfully sent the sample back to Earth.

⑬ LUNA 17 (USSR)

Landing date: November 17, 1970
Location: Mare Imbrium (Sea of Rains)
Details: Delivered the first Lunokhod rover to the Moon's surface. Lunokhod journeyed over the Moon's surface for 10 months and returned over 20,000 photographs.

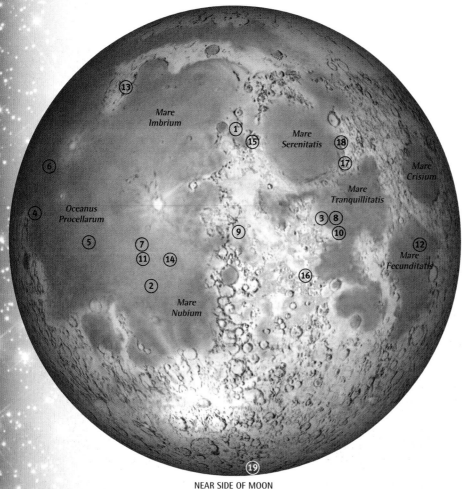

Mare Imbrium
Mare Serenitatis
Mare Crisium
Mare Tranquillitatis
Oceanus Procellarum
Mare Fecunditatis
Mare Nubium

NEAR SIDE OF MOON

maps

MARS LANDING SITES

The 10 spacecraft listed below are the only ones that have landed, or are thought to have landed, on Mars up to 2004. Others have flown by Mars or gone into orbit around it.

⑭ APOLLO 14 (US)

Landing date: February 5, 1971
Location: Fra Mauro region
Astronauts: Alan Shepard and Edgar Mitchell
Details: During their stay on the Moon, the two astronauts set up science experiments, collected Moon rocks, and took photographs. Shepard hit two golf balls. Their stay on the Moon lasted for 33.5 hours.

⑮ APOLLO 15 (US)

Landing date: July 30, 1971
Location: Hadley Rille highland region
Astronauts: David Scott and James Irwin
Details: During their 67-hour stay on the Moon, Scott and Irwin made three extra-vehicular activities (EVAs) or Moon explorations. This was the first mission to employ the Lunar Roving Vehicle, which was used to explore regions within 3 miles (5 km) of the landing site.

⑯ APOLLO 16 (US)

Landing date: April 20, 1972
Location: Descartes highland region
Astronauts: John Young and Charles Duke
Details: During their 3-day stay on the Moon, Young and Duke made three EVAs (Moon explorations). They drove 16 miles (27 km) using the Lunar Roving Vehicle, collected 210 lb (95 kg) of rock and soil samples, took photographs, and set up scientific experiments.

⑰ APOLLO 17 (US)

Landing date: December 11, 1972
Location: Taurus-Littrow region
Astronauts: Eugene Cernan and Harrison Schmitt
Details: Schmitt, the first scientist on the Moon, and Cernan made three EVAs (Moon explorations) totaling over 22 hours. During this time they covered 18 miles (30 km) in the Lunar Roving Vehicle, and collected 243 lb (110.5 kg) of rocks and dust. The total duration of their stay on the Moon was 75 hours.

⑱ LUNA 21 (USSR)

Landing date: January 15, 1973
Location: Mare Serenitatis (Sea of Serenity)
Details: Delivered the Lunokhod 2 lunar rover, which journeyed over the Moon's surface for a total of 4 months.

⑲ LUNAR PROSPECTOR (US)

Landing date: July 31, 1999
Location: A shadowed crater not far from the Moon's south pole
Details: It was hoped that the impact of the probe would liberate water vapor from suspected ice deposits in the crater and that the plume would be detectable from Earth. However, no plume was observed.

① MARS 2 (USSR)

Landing date: November 27, 1971
Location: Hellas Planitia
Details: Crash-landed while a dust storm was raging on the surface of Mars.

② MARS 3 (USSR)

Landing date: December 2, 1971
Location: Near Terra Sirenum
Details: Soft-landed and operated for 20 seconds before failing, possibly due to a dust storm on Mars. One dark, fuzzy image of the Martian surface was returned.

③ MARS 6 (USSR)

Landing date: March 12, 1974
Location: Margaritifer Sinus region
Details: Communication with lander craft was lost just before landing.

④ VIKING 1 (US)

Landing date: July 20, 1976
Location: Chryse Planitia
Details: Soft-landed and transmitted images of the Martian surface, took soil samples, and chemically analyzed them for composition and signs of life. Viking 1 studied Mars' atmosphere and weather, and deployed Marsquake-measuring devices. Communications ended on November 13, 1982.

⑤ VIKING 2 (US)

Landing date: September 3, 1976
Location: Near Utopia Planitia
Details: Very similar to the Viking 1 mission (above) except for the location and the fact that communications ended on April 11, 1980.

⑥ MARS PATHFINDER (US)

Landing date: July 4, 1997
Location: Chryse Planitia
Details: After a soft-landing, the Pathfinder lander deployed a small rover (Sojourner) and made measurements of conditions on Mars. The lander returned almost 10,000 images. The rover explored the Martian surface, analyzed rocks and soil, and returned a total of 550 images. Communications ended on September 27, 1997.

⑦ MARS POLAR LANDER (US)

Landing date: December 3, 1999
Location: Toward the south pole of Mars
Details: Contact with the lander was lost as it began the final stages of its descent.

⑧ BEAGLE 2 (EUROPEAN SPACE AGENCY)

Landing date: December 25, 2003
Location: Isidis Planitia
Details: Declared lost after no communications were received following the scheduled landing.

⑨ SPIRIT ROVER (US)

Landing date: January 4, 2004
Location: Gusev crater
Details: After a successful soft-landing, began exploring Mars. The mission's main goal was to search for and analyze rocks and soils that may hold clues to past water activity on Mars.

⑩ OPPORTUNITY ROVER (US)

Landing date: January 25, 2004
Location: Meridiani Planum
Details: Mission goal was the same as for Spirit rover; soon found direct evidence for the existence of past water on surface of Mars.

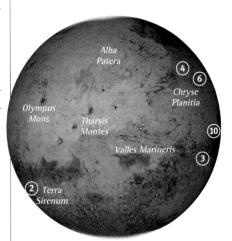

WESTERN HEMISPHERE OF MARS

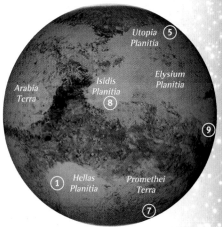

EASTERN HEMISPHERE OF MARS

SPACE TRAVEL BIOGRAPHIES

These biographies provide short descriptions of the lives of some notable people who have traveled in space (selected from a total of well over 400 who have been in space since 1961) or were important pioneers of spaceflight science and technology.

biographies

EDWIN "BUZZ" ALDRIN   born 1930

Known by the childhood nickname Buzz, Edwin Aldrin was the second person ever to walk on the Moon. As the pilot of Apollo 11's lunar module, he stepped onto the lunar surface 19 minutes after Neil Armstrong on July 21, 1969. Born in New Jersey, Aldrin received a degree in engineering and then became a pilot with the Air Force. After further studies in astronautics, Aldrin was selected for astronaut training in 1963. Before his trip to the Moon, he had made a record 2½-hour spacewalk during the Gemini 12 mission. Aldrin retired from NASA in 1971 and became one of the world's leading advocates of space exploration through writing and public speaking.

NEIL ARMSTRONG   born 1930

Neil Armstrong achieved worldwide fame for being the first person to step onto the Moon, as the commander of Apollo 11, at 2:56 a.m. Greenwich Mean Time on July 21, 1969. Born in Ohio, Armstrong had flying lessons as a teenager and gained his pilot's license before he was legally old enough to drive a car. He studied aeronautical engineering at college, became a Navy fighter pilot, and later a test-pilot for NASA. Armstrong made his first spaceflight as command pilot for the Gemini 8 mission in 1966, and three years later made his historic voyage to the Moon. A lunar crater close to the Apollo 11 landing site is named Armstrong in his honor. Armstrong left NASA in 1971 and became a university professor before going into business.

SERGEI AVDEYEV   born 1956

The Russian cosmonaut Sergei Avdeyev holds the record for the most time spent in space, with 748 days accumulated on three flights in the 1990s. Born in Chapayevsk in south central European Russia, Avdeyev graduated in 1979 from the Moscow Institute as an engineer-physicist. In 1987, he was selected for cosmonaut training. His three spaceflights were as a flight engineer aboard the Mir space station in 1992-1993, 1995-1996, and 1998-1999. His body has been examined and monitored many times over by doctors researching the consequences of space travel.

EUGENE CERNAN   born 1934

Eugene Cernan is best known for being the last person to have stood on the Moon, as commander of Apollo 17 in 1972. Born in Chicago, Cernan received a degree in engineering before becoming a US Navy pilot. NASA selected him as an astronaut in 1963. His first spaceflight, in 1966, was aboard Gemini 9. On this mission, Cernan became the second American to walk in space. In 1970, Cernan was lunar module pilot on Apollo 10, which traveled to the Moon but did not land. During the Apollo 17 mission, Cernan and his companion Harrison Schmitt set records for the longest time moving around on the lunar surface (over 22 hours) and largest return of lunar rocks (243 lb or 110.5 kg). Cernan left NASA in 1976 to go into business.

EILEEN COLLINS   born 1956

NASA astronaut Eileen Collins was the first woman to command a Space Shuttle mission. Born in New York State, Collins holds several degrees in science, mathematics, economics, and management, and worked as an Air Force pilot before selection for astronaut training in 1990. She has made three Space Shuttle flights, in 1995, 1997, and 1999, the last as Shuttle commander. A highlight of the 1999 mission (Shuttle mission STS-93) was the deployment of a special space telescope (the Chandra X-Ray Observatory), which is designed to help scientists study phenomena such as exploding stars and black holes.

MICHAEL COLLINS   born 1930

Michael Collins was one of the three astronauts on the Apollo 11 mission that put the first people on the Moon in 1969. Collins was in charge of the command module Columbia, which stayed in lunar orbit as his colleagues, Neil Armstrong and Edwin "Buzz" Aldrin, visited the Moon's surface. Born in Rome, Italy, Collins graduated from the US Military Academy in 1952 and then became an Air Force test pilot. In 1963, he was selected for astronaut training and in 1966 made his first spaceflight aboard Gemini 10. Collins resigned from NASA the year after his Apollo mission. He worked as a museum director at the Smithsonian Institution in Washington D.C. and later entered business.

CHARLES "PETE" CONRAD   1930-1999

Charles "Pete" Conrad was the third US astronaut to set foot on the Moon, as commander of the Apollo 12 mission in 1969. Born in Philadelphia, Conrad received a degree in aeronautical engineering before becoming a pilot with the US Navy. In 1962, he was selected for astronaut training. As well as his Apollo 12 journey to the Moon, Conrad flew on two Gemini missions (Gemini 5 and Gemini 11) and was commander of Skylab II, the first crew to man a US Space Station. In 1973, he left NASA to pursue a business career.

MICHAEL FOALE   born 1957

British-born Michael Foale holds the record for being the NASA astronaut who has spent longest in space. By the end of April 2004, he had spent a total of 374 days in space, including stints on six Space Shuttle missions, one stay on the Russian space station Mir, and as a commander of the International Space Station. Born in Lincolnshire, England, Foale completed a degree in physics in 1978 and a PhD in astrophysics in 1982. He then moved to Houston, Texas, to work for the US space program and was selected as an astronaut candidate in 1987. In 1997, he spent 145 days living and working on Mir and narrowly escaped death when an unmanned cargo craft accidentally collided with the space station during a docking test.

YURI GAGARIN   1934-1968

The Russian cosmonaut Yuri Gagarin was the first person ever to fly in space, aboard the Vostok 1 spacecraft in 1961. The 108-minute flight, during which he traveled 25,000 miles (40,000 km), was his only trip into space. Born in the village of Klushino in the Smolensk region, Gagarin studied at an industrial college in his teens while learning to fly airplanes. In 1957, he became a pilot in the Soviet Air Force, then joined the cosmonaut corps and four years later was chosen as the first person to journey into space. After his spaceflight, Gagarin became internationally famous and a world hero. He received many honors, including the renaming of his hometown as Gagarin. He was killed in an airplane crash in 1968 while training for another flight.

JOHN GLENN
born 1921

John Glenn was the first American to orbit Earth, aboard the Mercury 6 spacecraft. His flight took him on three orbits of Earth in less than 5 hours. Born in Ohio, Glenn served in the Marine Corps during World War II, and later in Korea. In 1954, he started work as a test pilot and in 1957 made the first nonstop supersonic flight from Los Angeles to New York. In 1959, he was selected for astronaut training, and was back-up pilot for the first two Mercury missions. During his Mercury 6 flight, he became the third American in space and the third person to orbit Earth. After retiring from the space program in 1964, Glenn took up politics, and in 1974 was elected Senator in Ohio. In 1998, he became the world's oldest astronaut at age 77 when he flew on a Space Shuttle mission.

ROBERT GODDARD
1882-1945

Robert Goddard was an American physicist and rocket engineer who, in 1926, launched the world's first liquid-fueled rocket. Born in Massachusetts, Goddard became fascinated by the idea of space travel from an early age and, after obtaining a degree in physics, put his mind to developing a space rocket. In 1919, he published his theory of rocketry, and in the 1930s he launched his first stabilized rocket. The US space program grew out of his pioneering efforts, although his work was largely ignored until after his death. NASA's Goddard Space Flight Center, Maryland, is named for him.

VIRGIL "GUS" GRISSOM
1926–1967

In July 1961, Virgil Grissom became the second American to go into space, aboard the Mercury 4 spacecraft. Four years later, his second space flight aboard Gemini 3 earned him the distinction of being the first person to fly in space twice. Grissom was born in Indiana, and after earning a degree in mechanical engineering, became a jet pilot who saw action in the Korean War. In 1959, he was selected for astronaut training. His successful flight on Mercury 4 lasted just over 15 minutes. After the capsule splashed down in the Atlantic it started sinking, and Grissom only just managed to swim clear. He died in 1967 as a result of a fire in the Apollo 1 spacecraft.

MAE JEMISON
born 1956

Mae Jemison was the first African-American woman in space, flying aboard the Space Shuttle Endeavour in 1992. Born in Alabama, she has degrees in both chemical engineering and medicine and was working as a doctor in Los Angeles when in 1987 she was selected for astronaut training. She resigned from NASA in 1993, not long after her Space Shuttle mission, and founded an organization committed to the advancement and beneficial uses of space technology and exploration.

SERGEI KOROLEV
1906-1966

Sergei Korolev was a Ukrainian-born designer and engineer who directed the Soviet Union's space program during its early years. His name is linked with many of the great achievements of the first decades of the space age. He was responsible for the Cosmos, Vostok, and Soyuz series of spacecraft. He also played a key role in the launch of Sputnik 1 (the first satellite in space), the first human spaceflight by Yuri Gagarin, and the first space walk, by Alexei Leonov.

ALEXEI LEONOV
born 1934

Alexei Leonov is famous for being the first person to walk in space. Born in Listvyanka, Siberia, Leonov is a former jet pilot and was selected for cosmonaut training in 1960. On March 18, 1965, he was launched into orbit aboard Voskhod 2 along with fellow Russian Pavel Belyayev. During the flight, Leonov spent over 20 minutes outside the capsule. This was longer than originally planned because excess pressure in his space suit meant that he had great difficulty re-entering the spacecraft's hatch. Leonov made a second flight 10 years later, making history when his Soyuz craft docked with an American Apollo craft, joining the two nations in space.

YANG LIWEI
born 1965

Yang Liwei was the first Chinese person to travel in space, in 2003 aboard the Shenzhou V spacecraft. Born in China's Liaoning Province, Yang Liwei became an Air Force pilot and was selected for cosmonaut training in 1998. The Shenzhou spacecraft that Yang traveled in, similar to a Soyuz spacecraft, was launched from Jiuquan Satellite Launching Center on October 15, 2003. The successful flight lasted over 21 hours and ended with the re-entry capsule landing the next day on the grasslands of the Gobi Desert, in central Inner Mongolia.

JIM LOVELL
born 1928

Jim Lovell is best known as the commander of the ill-fated Apollo 13 spacecraft, bringing it back to Earth after it had been crippled by an explosion on an oxygen tank on the way to the Moon. Lovell also flew on the Gemini 7 and Gemini 12 missions and the epic six-day journey of Apollo 8—humanity's maiden voyage to the Moon. Born in Ohio, Lovell spent four years as a test pilot for the US Navy before selection in 1962 for astronaut training. He retired from NASA and the Navy in 1973 and spent several years in business. Lovell was depicted by the actor Tom Hanks in the film *Apollo 13*, based on Lovell's book *Lost Moon: The Perilous Voyage of Apollo 13*. Lovell made a brief appearance at the end of the movie, playing the captain of the recovery ship *USS Iwo Jima*.

SHANNON LUCID
born 1943

American astronaut Shannon Lucid holds the record for the most time spent in space by a woman. In 1996, she spent 188 days in space, living and working aboard the Russian Mir space station. Lucid's total time in space is 223 days. This total includes her Mir mission as well as four Space Shuttle missions. Born in Shanghai, China, Shannon Lucid grew up in Oklahoma, earned several science degrees, and worked as a biologist before being selected for astronaut training in 1978.

HERMANN OBERTH
1894-1989

Hermann Oberth was a Romanian-born scientist who pioneered the development of space rocketry. His work on the theories of rocket propulsion and guidance systems in the 1930s resulted in the V-2 rocket. In the 1950s, he worked on the American space program. Oberth's understanding of the interconnections of fuel consumption, rocket speed, distance and duration of flight, and other factors, helped establish the laws that govern modern rocket flight.

VALERI POLIAKOV
born 1942

The Russian doctor and ex-cosmonaut Valeri Poliakov holds the record for the longest single stay in space, aboard the Mir station, 438 days from January 8, 1994 to March 22, 1995. He also stayed on Mir for 241 days in 1988-1989, and for several years held the record for the most time spent in space. Born in Tula, Russia, Poliakov graduated as a doctor in 1965 and was selected for astronaut training in 1972. In connection with his spaceflights, Poliakov took part in an unusual medical experiment. Before each mission, some of his bone marrow was removed so that it could be compared with another sample of bone marrow taken when he returned after months of weightlessness. Poliakov retired as an astronaut in 1995 and now works for a public health ministry in Moscow.

SALLY RIDE
born 1951

Sally Ride became the first American woman to travel into space in 1983, when she was launched aboard the Space Shuttle Challenger as a mission specialist. Ride's 6-day journey made her the third woman to travel into space (after Valentina Tereshkova in 1963 and Svetlana Savitskaya in 1982). Born in Los Angeles, Ride was a nationally ranked tennis player in her teenage years. A physicist by training, in 1977 she answered a NASA advertisement for Space Shuttle astronauts and was accepted. In addition to her 1983 flight, she made a second Shuttle flight in 1984. Ride helped the movement toward a more equal role for women in the American space program. In 1987, she left NASA and for many years was a Professor of Physics at the University of California.

HARRISON SCHMITT
born 1935

Harrison Schmitt is famous for being the only scientist to have visited the Moon, as lunar module pilot for the Apollo 17 mission. A geologist by training, Schmitt was born in New Mexico. He was selected by NASA as an astronaut-scientist in 1965. As well as training for space flight, he taught other Apollo crew members how to collect suitable rocks on the Moon and later took part in the analysis of those rocks. Schmitt left NASA in 1975 to enter politics and for six years was a Senator for New Mexico.

HELEN SHARMAN
born 1963

Helen Sharman was the first British person to travel into space, aboard the Soviet Soyuz TM-12 spacecraft in 1991. Sharman spent 8 days in space, 6 of them aboard the space station Mir. Born in Sheffield, England, she obtained a chemistry degree in 1984, and worked for five years as a research scientist. In 1989, she answered an advertisement: "Astronaut wanted—no experience necessary". Not long afterward, she found that she had been selected as a trainee cosmonaut for a Soviet space mission. One of the main aspects of her 18-month training program was to learn Russian. Since her return from space, Helen Sharman has continued to work as a scientist and broadcaster.

ALAN SHEPARD
1923-1998

Alan Shepard was the first American in space, as the occupant of the Mercury 3 spacecraft, which was blasted into space on May 5, 1961. The flight lasted just 15 minutes and did not orbit Earth. Instead, the Mercury capsule landed in the Atlantic Ocean 303 miles (488 km) down range from its launch pad at Cape Canaveral, Florida. Born in New Hampshire, Shepard obtained a degree in aeronautics in 1944 and later became a test pilot for the US Navy. In 1959, he was chosen among the first group of seven American astronauts. As well as his Mercury flight, Shepard was commander of the Apollo 14 mission that landed on the Moon in 1971. During one moonwalk, Shepard famously hit two golf balls for hundreds of yards over the Moon's surface. Shepard retired from NASA in 1974 and went into business.

VALENTINA TERESHKOVA
born 1937

Valentina Tereshkova was the first woman to fly in space. In June 1963, she made 48 Earth orbits aboard the Vostok 6 spacecraft. Born near Yaroslavl in western Russia, Tereshkova left school at 16 to work in a textile factory. She also became an amateur parachutist, and in 1962 was selected for space flight. After her 71-hour Vostok 6 flight, at the end of which Tereshkova parachuted to the ground, she was made a Hero of the Soviet Union. It was to be another 19 years before another woman traveled in space.

DENNIS TITO
born 1940

Dennis Tito is an American multimillionaire who in June 2001 became the world's first space tourist, traveling for 8 days on board the Soyuz TM-32 spacecraft and the International Space Station. During the trip, Tito spent hours gazing at Earth and taking photographs. He paid $20 million to go on the mission. Born in New York City, Tito earned degrees in astronautics and aeronautics and worked as a scientist at NASA's Jet Propulsion Laboratory before founding an investment management company. After his space journey, he described it as a "trip to paradise."

GHERMAN TITOV
1935-2000

Gherman Titov was the second person in space (after Yuri Gagarin), flying on board the Soviet spacecraft Vostok 2, which orbited Earth for 24 hours on August 6-7, 1961. Unlike Gagarin, Titov was briefly allowed to take manual control of his spacecraft during the flight. Born in the Altai region of Siberia, Titov graduated as a Soviet Air Force pilot and was selected for cosmonaut training in 1960. Just short of age 26 at the launch of Vostok 2, he is the youngest person ever to have flown in space. Following his flight, Titov worked in various senior positions in the Soviet Union's space program until his retirement in 1992. In 1995, he entered politics.

KONSTANTIN TSIOLKOVSKY
1857-1935

Konstantin Tsiolkovsky was a Russian pioneer of the theory of spaceflight. He produced theories of rocketry but did not have the resources to build a rocket. By 1898, he had produced a theory that showed how much fuel a rocket would use and how its velocity was related to the thrust of its engines. He was the first person to propose the use of liquid propellants for rockets. He also worked out that multistage rockets would be needed to leave Earth's gravity and showed how these could be stacked on top of one another.

WERNHER VON BRAUN
1912-1977

Wernher von Braun was a German-born rocket engineer responsible for the development of several important liquid-fueled rockets in Germany and the US. During World War II, he led the development of rockets for the German army, in particular the V-2 rocket. Because this was used as a weapon against cities in England, Belgium, France, and the Netherlands, and because thousands of people enslaved by the Nazis were killed while working on von Braun's missile projects, he is a controversial figure. At the end of the war, von Braun and his team surrendered to US forces. The team eventually joined NASA and was responsible for the launch of the first US satellite and for the Saturn V rocket, which was used to launch the Apollo missions to the Moon.

CARL WALZ
born 1955

Carl Walz is co-holder of the record for the longest single US spaceflight. During Expedition 4 of the International Space Station in 2001-2002, he and NASA astronaut Daniel Bursch spent nearly 196 days in space. A veteran of four spaceflights (the other three were Space Shuttle missions), Walz was born in Ohio and trained as a physicist. Selected as an astronaut in 1990, overall he has spent 231 days in space.

EDWARD WHITE
1930-1967

Ed White achieved fame in 1965, when he became the first American to go for a space walk, outside of the Gemini 4 spacecraft. White was outside Gemini 4 for 21 minutes, and became the first man to control himself during a space walk using a gun filled with compressed gas. When told to return to the spacecraft, White said, "It's the saddest moment of my life." Born in Texas, White earned a degree in aeronautical engineering in 1959 and then became an Air Force pilot. He was selected for astronaut training in 1962. White died in 1967, along with Gus Grissom and Roger Chaffee, as a result of a fire in the Apollo 1 spacecraft.

JOHN YOUNG
born 1930

American astronaut John Young was commander of the Apollo 16 mission to the Moon in 1972, the first Space Shuttle flight in 1981, and a second Space Shuttle flight in 1983. He also flew in two Gemini missions (Gemini 3 and 10) during the 1960s, and made 31 lunar orbits in Apollo 10, the dress rehearsal for the first Moon landing. Born in California, Young earned a degree in aeronautical engineering before becoming a test pilot in the US Navy. In 1962, he was selected as an astronaut. During the Apollo 16 mission in 1972, Young and Charlie Duke collected some 210 lb (95 kg) of moon rocks and drove over 16 miles (27 km) in a lunar rover on three separate explorations. John Young continues to work for NASA and, as an active astronaut, remains eligible to command future Space Shuttle missions. In preparation for prime and backup crew positions on 11 spaceflights, it is calculated that Young has spent more than 15,000 hours in astronaut training, mostly in simulators and simulations.

GLOSSARY

Terms in *italics* are other glossary entries.

Airlock A sealed chamber in which air pressure can be changed. Astronauts use an airlock to transfer between a pressurized spacecraft and the airless environment of space.

Antenna A device used to send and receive radio signals between a spacecraft and a ground station on Earth or another spacecraft.

Atmosphere A layer of gas held around a planet or moon by its *gravity*.

Celestial object Any object in space, such as a planet, asteroid, moon, *star*, or *galaxy*.

Communications satellite An artificial *satellite* that is used for transferring TV, radio, or telephone signals from one place to another.

Cosmonaut An astronaut from the former Soviet Union or present-day Russia.

Dock To link up one spacecraft with another.

Electromagnetic radiation A form of energy that can travel through the *vacuum* of space.

Electromagnetic spectrum A range of different types of *electromagnetic radiation*, including *radio waves*, *infrared radiation*, light, *ultraviolet radiation*, *X-rays*, and gamma rays.

Elliptical orbit An *orbit* in the shape of an ellipse (a stretched or squashed circle).

Environmental satellite A type of artificial *satellite* that monitors aspects of Earth's environment, such as weather patterns.

Extra-vehicular activity (EVA) Any activity in which an astronaut or *cosmonaut* goes outside the spacecraft. Also called a space walk.

Fairing The protective aerodynamic casing around a rocket's *payload* during launch.

Force A push or a pull that can change the velocity of an object.

Free fall A situation in which an object is traveling in space or orbiting a planet or moon and, in the case of a spacecraft and its occupants, the craft's engine is turned off.

Fuel cell A device that produces electrical energy by combining hydrogen and oxygen.

Flyby An encounter between a *space probe* and a planet, moon, comet, or asteroid in which the probe does not stop to orbit or land.

Galaxy A collection of millions or billions of *stars*, gas, and dust held together by *gravity*.

Gravitational assist A spacecraft's use of a planet or moon's *gravity* to change its speed or direction of travel.

Gravity A *force* that attracts objects together. The higher the *mass* of the objects, and the closer they are, the greater the gravitational attraction between them.

Heat shield A coating of heat-resistant material on the outer shell of a spacecraft.

Infrared radiation A form of invisible *electromagnetic radiation*. Radiant heat is a form of infrared radiation.

Ion An electrically charged atom or group of atoms.

Ion engine A means of propulsion in space that relies on shooting a fast-moving stream of *ions* out of the spacecraft; this moves the craft itself in the opposite direction.

JPL The Jet Propulsion Laboratory, a part of *NASA* that operates unmanned spacecraft.

Lander A part of a *space probe* designed to land on a planet, moon, asteroid, or comet.

Light year The distance traveled by light through a *vacuum* in a year, about 5.9 million million miles (9.5 million million km).

Lunar Related to the Moon. Being in lunar *orbit* means being in orbit around the Moon.

Magnetic field Magnetism generated by a planet, *star*, or *galaxy*, that extends into space.

Magnetometer A scientific instrument used to detect and study the *magnetic fields* of planets and other *celestial objects*.

Manned maneuvering unit A special jet backpack used by some astronauts to help them move around in space.

Mass The amount of matter an object contains, measured in pounds or kilograms.

Micrometeoroid shield A protective casing on the outside of a spacecraft, designed to reduce damage caused by the impact of small objects traveling at high speed through space.

Microgravity A state of almost total *weightlessness* experienced when in *free fall*.

NASA The National Aeronautics and Space Administration, an agency responsible for the American civilian space program.

Orbit The curved path of one object around another under the influence of *gravity*.

Orbiter A spacecraft designed to go into *orbit* around Earth or another *celestial object*.

Payload The cargo that a rocket or shuttle carries into *orbit*, such as an artificial *satellite* or a scientific instrument.

Radar A method of detecting the position and motion of a distant object by using a narrow beam (or pulses) of *radio waves*, which are transmitted to and reflected from the object.

Radio telescope A type of telescope that detects *radio waves* instead of light.

Radiothermal Describes a power source that uses some radioactive material to produce heat, which is then converted into electricity.

Radio wave A form of invisible *electromagnetic radiation*. As well as being used for space communications, radio waves are emitted by various types of *celestial object*.

Re-entry The return of a spacecraft into Earth's *atmosphere*.

Remote-sensing satellite An artificial *satellite* that gathers information about Earth by using a variety of sensors.

Retro-rocket A small rocket engine that is fired opposite to a spacecraft's direction of motion, to reduce the craft's speed.

Rover A type of *lander*, or part of a lander, that is designed to move around on the surface of a planet or moon.

Satellite An object in *orbit* around a more massive object. The planets of the *solar system* are natural satellites of the Sun. Artificial satellites are launched into orbit for purposes of research, observation, or communication.

Simulator A machine that recreates the conditions of spaceflight.

Soft-land A controlled landing of a spacecraft onto the surface of a planet or other solid *celestial object*.

Solar array See *Solar panel*.

Solar panel A surface covered in devices that convert light into electrical energy.

Solar system The Sun and all the objects that orbit the Sun, such as planets and asteroids.

Solar wind A continuous outflow of charged particles radiating from the Sun.

Space probe A spacecraft sent from Earth to explore other parts of the *solar system*.

Star A hot, massive, ball of gas whose energy output is produced by nuclear reactions.

Star tracker A camera system linked to a computer that can help a spacecraft navigate by reference to *star* positions.

Suborbital The path of an object that leaves and then re-enters the *atmosphere* without going into *orbit*.

Supernova The massive explosion of a giant *star* at the end of its life, with release of fantastic amounts of light and other energy.

Thrust A sustained *force* in a particular direction produced by a rocket.

Thruster A small rocket used by spacecraft for maneuvering.

Ultraviolet radiation A form of invisible *electromagnetic radiation*.

Vacuum A region containing no matter. Most of space is a vacuum or a near-vacuum.

Weightlessness A condition in which an astronaut or *cosmonaut* or the contents of a spacecraft seem no longer to be affected by *gravity*, because they are in *free fall*.

X-ray A form of invisible *electromagnetic radiation*. Certain types of high-energy, very hot *celestial objects* emit X-rays.

INDEX

A page number in **bold** refers to the main entry for that subject.

ACKNOWLEDGMENTS

Dorling Kindersley would like to thank Alyson Lacewing for proof-reading; Sue Lightfoot for the index; Jenny Siklós for Americanization; Tony Cutting for DTP support; and ILC Dover Inc. for information on space suits for the Space Shuttle..

Dorling Kindersley Ltd. is not responsible and does not accept liability for the availability or content of any web site other than its own, or for any exposure to offensive, harmful, or inaccurate material that may appear on the Internet. Dorling Kindersley ltd. will have no liability for any damage or loss caused by viruses that may be downloaded as a result of looking at and browsing the web sites that it recommends. Dorling Kindersley downloadable images are the sole copyright of Dorling Kindersley Ltd., and may not be reproduced, stored, or transmitted in any form or by any means for any commercial or profit-related purpose without prior written permission of the copyright owner.

Picture Credits

The publisher would like to thank the following for their kind permission to reproduce their photographs:

Abbreviations key:
t-top, b-bottom, r-right, l-left, c-center, a-above, f-far

1 NASA: c. **2** NASA: c. **3** NASA: c. **6–7** NASA. **7** NASA: cl. **8** Corbis: Roger Ressmeyer bc. DK Images: cl. Galaxy Picture Library: tl. **8** Science Photo Library: Californian Association for Research in Astronomy cr; **8–9** Science Photo Library: Detlev Van Ravanswaay c; Frank Zullo t. **9** NASA: cb, bc. Science Photo Library: Davis Ducros br. **10** NASA: tc, cbl, tcl, tcr. Science Photo Library: European Space Agency tl. **11** NASA: br. Science Photo Library: David Ducros bl. **12** Corbis: Hulton-Deutsch Collection cr. NASA: bl. Novosti (London): tl. **13** Corbis: Bettmann cl. NASA: r. Novosti (London): tl. **14** European Space Agency: cfr. **15** NASA: cb. **16** Corbis: Bettmann bcl. NASA: bl. Science Photo Library: David A. Hardy tl; Novosti cfr. **17** Corbis: Bettmann cb. DK Images: Science Museum cfr. Genesis Space Photo Library: cfl. NASA: tr. Science Photo Library: David A. Hardy br. **18** Alamy Images: Carol Dixon bl. NASA: tl. **19** European Space Agency: tr, br. **20** NASA: bl, bc, br, bcl. Science Photo Library: Novosti Press Agency cl. **21** NASA: tl, tr, br. **22** Science & Society Picture Library: bl. Smithsonian Institution: tr. **23** NASA: b. Science Photo Library: Novosti Photo Library tl, cb. **24** Corbis: bl. NASA: br. Novosti (London): tl. Science Photo Library: NASA cra; Novosti cr. **25** Corbis: Marc Garanger tr. Genesis Space Photo Library: NASA br. NASA: tl, cr, bl. **26** Corbis: cla; Bettmann tr. Novosti (London): clb. Science Photo Library: Starsem bc. **27** NASA: tr, cr. Science Photo Library: NASA br. **28** NASA: cr, l. **29** Corbis: Bettmann c. NASA: crb, bl, t. **30** NASA: cl, c, bl. **30–31** Corbis: NASA. **31** NASA: tc, tr, c, cr, bc, br. **32** Corbis: Bill Ingalls l. DK Images: NASA cr, br. **33** Genesis Space Photo Library: br. NASA: t. Reuters: bl, bcl, bcr. **34** NASA: crb, bra. Reuters: cr. Science Photo Library: David Campione l; NASA br. **35** Courtesy of Lockheed Martin Aeronautics Company, Palmdale: br. NASA: tr. **36–37** Corbis: pic 10; Bettmann pic 3; Roger Ressmeyer pic 9. NASA: pic 1, pic 11, pic 12, pic 13, pic 14, pic 15, Pic 16, pic 2, pic 4, pic 6, pic 7, pic 8, pic 5. **37** NASA: r. **38** NASA: cfl. **40** Corbis: Bettmann cb; Roger Ressmeyer tr. NASA: bl. **41** NASA: c. Novosti (London): br. **42** European Space Agency: bl. NASA: tl. **43** European Space Agency: cfr. NASA: tr, bc. **44** Science Photo Library: bc; Andrew Syred cbl; Eye of Science bcr; GJLP bl. **44–45** NASA: t. **45** NASA: tr, br. Science Photo Library: bl; Alfred Pasieka br; Susumu Nishinaga bc. **46** NASA: tr, cla, cla, cra, cr, bl, br, bcl, bcr, cal, car, cfl, cfr. **47** NASA: tl, bl, cfl, r. **48** NASA: cal, r. **49** NASA: tl, cra, crb, cfr. **50** Corbis: Bettmann cl. NASA: bl. **50–51** Corbis: NASA. **51** NASA: tc, tr. **52** Corbis: Roger Ressmeyer clb, cb, cbl. **52** NASA: tcr. Topfoto.co.uk: cfl. **52–53** NASA. **53** NASA: clb, bcr. **54** NASA: bl, br, cfl. **54–55** NASA. **55** European Space Agency: br. NASA: cra, bl. **56** NASA: ca, cl, br. **56–57** NASA: t **57** NASA: tr, cr, bc, br. **58** NASA: bl, bc, tcl. **58–59** NASA. **59** Associated Press: J R Hernandez cbr. NASA: tr, br. **62** Alamy Images: CoverSpot tcr. European Space Agency: tl, cb, bl, car. Nokia: tcl. **62–63** NASA. **63** Corbis: Reuters cr. Northrop Grumman Space Technology: tr. Science Photo Library: GE Astro Space tc, cfr; NASA cl, cbl. **64** Corbis: Bettmann br. **64** NASA: cla, bl. **64–65** Corbis: Bettmann **65** NASA: tl, tr, cra, cb, tcl, tcr. Science Photo Library: European Space Agency br. **66** NASA: tl, ca, cb, bl, br, bcl, cal, car, cbl, clb, cbr. **67** NASA: tl, tr, bl, bc, br, cal, call, car, car, cbl, clb, cbr, crb, tcl, tcr. **68** NASA: cla, clb. **68–69** Science Photo Library: Detlev Van Ravenswaay. **69** Corbis: NASA br. NASA: tc, tr, br. Science Photo Library: NASA cr. **70** NASA: cal, cal, cbl, cbl. Science Photo Library: US Geological Survey cfl, tcr. **70–71** NASA. **71** NASA: tl, cr, br, bcl, bcr, cal, cbl, cbr. Science Photo Library: Chris Butler tr; Space Telescope Science Institute/NASA cfr. **72** NASA: cra, cr, cb. Science Photo Library: US Geological Survey cfl. **73** NASA: cla, cra, b, cal, car. **74** DK Images: Natural History Museum cr. NASA: tc, cl, crb. Science Photo Library: David Nunuk br; Detlev Van Ravenswaay bl; Francois Gohier bl; John Hopkins University Applied Physics Laboratory ca; Novosti Press Agency br. **75** NASA: tr, clb, cb, crb. Science Photo Library: Roger Harris r. **76** Corbis: Gianni Dagli Orti cb. European Space Agency: clb, bcl. **76** Galaxy Picture Library: cbr, cfl. **76–77** European Space Agency. **77** European Space Agency: ca, cra, car, cbr. **78** NASA: clb, bl, bla. National Space Centre, Leicester: br. Science Photo Library: Detlev Van Ravenswaay tr. **78–79** NASA: bl, br, bcl, t. **82** NASA: car. Science Photo Library: David Parker b. **82–83** Science Photo Library: David Parker. European Space Agency: cal. Galaxy Picture Library: car. NASA: tl. Science Photo Library: David Parker br. **84** European Space Agency: cla, b, tcl. **84–85** NASA. **85** European Space Agency: cl, crb, bc. Science Photo Library: Victor Habbick Visions tr. **86** NASA: l. **87** NASA: r.

Jacket images
Front: NASA: (cfl, cfr, cr); Science Photo Library: NASA (cl). **Spine:** NASA. **Back:** Corbis: Bettmann (cfr); NASA: (cr). Science Photo Library: NASA (cfl, cl).

All other images © Dorling Kindersley.
For further information see:
www.dkimages.com